Selected Verb Forms

P9-AOK-779

Regular Verbs — Simple Tenses and Present Perfect (Indicative)

	PRESENT	PRETERITE	IMPERFECT	PRESENT PERFECT
hablar	hablo	hablé	hablaba	he hablado
comer	como	comí	comía	he comido
vivir	vivo	viví	vivía	he vivido

Common Irregular Verbs — Present and Preterite (Indicative)

caer	caigo	caí	**poner**	pongo	puse
dar	doy	di	**querer**	quiero	quise
decir	digo	dije	**saber**	sé	supe
estar	estoy	estuve	**ser**	soy	fui
hacer	hago	hice	**tener**	tengo	tuve
ir	voy	fui	**traer**	traigo	traje
oír	oigo	oí	**venir**	vengo	vine
poder	puedo	pude	**ver**	veo	vi

Irregular Verbs — Imperfect (Indicative)

ir	iba	**ser**	era	**ver**	veía

Regular Verbs — Simple Tenses and Present Perfect (Subjunctive)

	PRESENT	IMPERFECT	PRESENT PERFECT
hablar	hable	hablara	haya hablado
comer	coma	comiera	haya comido
vivir	viva	viviera	haya vivido

Regular and Irregular Verbs — Future and Conditional

hablar	hablaré	hablaría
comer	comeré	comería
vivir	viviré	viviría

decir	diré	diría	**querer**	querré	querría
hacer	haré	haría	**saber**	sabré	sabría
poder	podré	podría	**tener**	tendré	tendría
poner	pondré	pondría	**venir**	vendré	vendría

puntos
de partida

seventh edition

puntos
de partida

An Invitation to Spanish

Marty Knorre

Thalia Dorwick

Ana María Pérez-Gironés
Wesleyan University

William R. Glass

Hildebrando Villarreal
California State University, Los Angeles

INSTRUCTOR'S EDITION

Ana María Pérez-Gironés
Wesleyan University

A. Raymond Elliott
University of Texas, Arlington

McGraw Hill

Boston   Burr Ridge, IL   Dubuque, IA   Madison, WI   New York   San Francisco   St. Louis
Bangkok   Bogotá   Caracas   Kuala Lumpur   Lisbon   London   Madrid   Mexico City
Milan   Montreal   New Delhi   Santiago   Seoul   Singapore   Sydney   Taipei   Toronto

The McGraw·Hill Companies

This is an FBI book.

Puntos de partida
An Invitation to Spanish

Published by McGraw-Hill, an imprint of The McGraw-Hill Companies, Inc., 1221 Avenue of
the Americas, New York, NY 10020. Copyright © 2005, 2001, 1997, 1993, 1989, 1985, 1981 by
The McGraw-Hill Companies, Inc. All rights reserved. No part of this publication may be
reproduced or distributed in any form or by any means, or stored in a database or retrieval
system, without the prior written consent of The McGraw-Hill Companies, Inc., including,
but not limited to, in any network or other electronic storage or transmission, or broadcast
for distance learning.

This book is printed on acid-free paper.

1 2 3 4 5 6 7 8 9 0 VNH VNH 9 0 9 8 7 6 5 4

ISBN 0-07-287394-9 (Student's Edition)
ISBN 0-07-295130-3 (Instructor's Edition)

Vice president and Editor-in-chief: *Thalia Dorwick*
Publisher: *William R. Glass*
Senior sponsoring editor: *Christa Harris*
Developmental editor: *Pennie Nichols-Alem*
Director of development: *Scott Tinetti*
Executive marketing manager: *Nick Agnew*
Lead production editor: *David M. Staloch*
Lead production supervisor: *Randy Hurst*
Art director: *Jeanne M. Schreiber*
Art manager: *Robin Mouat*

Designer manager: *Violeta Díaz*
Interior designer: *Amanda Cavanaugh*
Cover designer: *Preston Thomas*
Cover illustrator: *Jill Arena*
Photo research coordinator: *Nora Agbayani*
Photo researcher: *Susan Friedman*
Senior supplements producer: *Louis Swaim*
Compositor: *The GTS Companies/York, PA Campus*
Typeface: *10/12 Palatino*
Printer and binder: *Von Hoffmann Press*

Because this page cannot legibly accommodate all the copyright notices, credits are listed
after the index and constitute an extension of the copyright page.

Library of Congress Cataloging-in-Publication Data

Puntos de partida: An invitation to Spanish / Marty Knorre ... [et al.]—7th ed.
    p. cm
    Includes index
    ISBN 0-07-287394-9
    1. Spanish language—Textbooks for foreign speakers—English. I. Knorre, Marty.

PC4129.E5P86 2004
468.2'421—dc21

2003055638

www.mhhe.com

brief table of contents

contents

preface

> " . . . to help students develop proficiency in the four language skills essential to truly communicative language teaching . . ."
>
> from the Preface to Puntos de partida, *first edition, 1981*

Market research. Reviewer feedback. Special consultants. Focus groups. Merely buzz words? On the contrary! When the authors and editors of *Puntos de partida* (or *Puntos*, as the series has come to be called) began preparing for this new edition, we once again turned to you—instructors and students—to help us formulate a plan that would respond to your needs. This has always been our approach. Over the years, more than 450 individuals have provided the necessary feedback to keep *Puntos* in step with changes in the classroom and in the profession. For this edition in particular we reached out to more than 160 students and instructors. The result is a thoroughly revised edition both in appearance and content. Be assured, however, that *Puntos* continues to provide the solid foundation in communicative language development that is its hallmark. At the same time, your feedback has guided us in ways that enrich and improve that foundation. Your feedback has also called our attention to the need for a number of other important changes to the text. Some of the changes that you will find include the following:

A DESIGN THAT PROMOTES LEARNING AND TEACHING

- More than 600 new color illustrations and photographs bring an exciting new visual appeal to the program and enhance the pedagogy of the text. Beautiful drawings illustrate vocabulary words in each chapter, allowing students to make important connections between the Spanish word and the conceptual meaning. Many activities are also enlivened through lively illustrations that review vocabulary and grammar and promote real communication.

- The flow of presentations and activities within the chapter has been carefully crafted to keep students on task and focused. Activities do not break over the front and back of pages, thus eliminating the need for students and instructors to "flip" pages while completing activities.

- Sentence-formation and cloze passage activities are now pedagogically improved through the use of special shading and color that highlight key elements of the activity and keep students focused on the tasks they are performing.

STUDENT-FRIENDLY GRAMMAR FEATURES

- Paradigms and charts within grammar presentations have been enhanced by the use of a colored font that directs students' attention to key aspects of the grammar point, such as spelling changes in stem-changing verbs and agreement of adjectives.

- New timelines place major grammar tenses on a continuum from Past ←→ Present ←→ Future and help students understand the "big picture" as they move through the sequence of tenses presented throughout the text.

- **Autoprueba** quizzes allow students to do quick self-assessments of their understanding of key grammar points in every chapter, before they begin the exercises and activities.

- New drawings illustrate many new verb infinitives, encouraging students to learn meaning through visual association.

- A grammar checklist in the new **En resumen** section at the end of every chapter offers a quick review of the major grammar topics in the chapter, helping to ensure that students have a comfortable understanding before moving on to the next chapter.

- Interactive **Flash Grammar** tutorials on the CD-ROM and the *Online Learning Center* Website allow students to "see" core grammar structures. The tutorials are enriched by interactive paradigms and sample sentences.

AN INTRODUCTION TO LITERARY MASTERPIECES

- Renowned authors from different countries are profiled in each chapter, accompanied by a brief extract from one of their works. These brief extracts—just a "taste" of some **obras maestras**—will enrich students' appreciation of the literary heritage of the Spanish-speaking world and hopefully motivate some students to continue reading when their Spanish language skills are better developed.

AN ALL-NEW VIDEO PROGRAM THAT BRINGS LANGUAGE AND HISPANIC CULTURES TO LIFE

- The **Entrevista cultural** segments introduce students to a Spanish-speaker from a different country in each chapter, providing a unique glimpse into their lives and their culture. Accompanying activities in the new **Perspectivas culturales** section of each chapter both prepare students for viewing and assess comprehension.

- The **Entre amigos** episodes present four students from different countries (Spain, Mexico, Venezuela, and Cuba) who tell entertaining stories as they meet and talk at a university in Mexico. These entertaining vignettes also review vocabulary themes and grammatical structures in each chapter, bringing the language to life. Taken together, both video segments provide an opportunity for students to hear authentic Spanish spoken by real Spanish speakers who interact with each other, rather than actors speaking for the camera.

- The popular video episodes from the previous edition of *Puntos de partida* continue to be available on the *Video Program,* and can still be used, chapter-by-chapter, with the seventh edition.

DIVERSE CULTURAL CONTENT

- Each chapter focuses on one area of the Spanish-speaking world. A large photo on the chapter opening pages introduces students to the chapter's themes as well as to the country of focus, and provides an engaging starting point for conversation.

- Special cultural features, including the **Nota cultural** and the **En los Estados Unidos y el Canadá** boxes, give quick and interesting glimpses into Hispanic cultures.

- The new **Perspectivas culturales** section in each chapter highlights the country of focus through video segments, texts, and photos.

While much is new to this edition of *Puntos*, you will continue to find the many hallmarks that make it the book of choice for hundreds of instructors across the country. These hallmark features include:

- an abundance of classroom-tested practice material, ranging from form-focused activities to communicative activities that promote real conversation

- vocabulary, grammar, and culture that work together as interactive units, unifying this important aspect of language learning

- an emphasis on the meaningful use of Spanish

- a positive portrayal of contemporary Hispanic cultures

- print and media supplementary materials that are carefully coordinated with the core text

The pages that follow provide a more detailed overview of changes to this edition in a section called "What's New in the Seventh Edition?" The next section, "A Guided Tour," explains and shows the organization and features of *Puntos* (useful to both instructors and students!). A comprehensive discussion of supplementary materials follows a brief explanation of how to use *Puntos de partida* in the classroom. The Preface closes with the acknowledgment of the many instructors and students who helped shape this new edition.

what's new to the seventh edition?

NEW DESIGN AND ART

Instructors will immediately notice the new look of *Puntos de partida.* While the design and art of previous editions have always been well received, we felt it was time for a change. The result is a new design: contemporary, beautiful, and most importantly, student- and instructor-friendly. Great care has been taken to ensure that activities and presentations flow smoothly from one page to the next and that the design itself enhances the teaching and learning experiences. The art program for this edition of *Puntos* is also entirely new. The artists were carefully guided so that the art would be both pedagogically sound and visually beautiful. The result of the new design and art is a visually enhanced seventh edition that satisfies the needs of today's sophisticated students and instructors, both pedagogically and visually.

CHAPTER THEMES

The positive response from instructors using earlier editions confirmed that the chapter themes found in *Puntos* provide engaging and relevant content for exploration and discussion. Theme vocabulary for all chapters has, of course, been updated to reflect changes in the areas of technology, recreational activities, and so forth. The vocabulary of **Capítulo 14** has been modified to focus more on the natural world, and the vocabulary of **Capítulo 18** now reflects travel vocabulary students are likely to use in today's traveling environment.

NEW CHAPTER-OPENING SPREAD

We have redesigned the chapter-opening spread. The result is an introduction to the chapter that is more engaging and more purposeful to the instructor and the student. Spending class time on the chapter opener will provide a useful introduction to the chapter for the student and set the stage for a more successful experience with the chapter content. (A visual presentation of the new Chapter Opener is provided in the Guided Tour presented in this Preface.)

CAPÍTULO PRELIMINAR: ANTE TODO

Responding to reviewer feedback, the authors have carefully recrafted and shortened the **Capítulo preliminar.** Its purpose remains the same: to introduce students to the sounds of Spanish and to a variety of high-frequency language that will ease their transition into the course. In addition, this special chapter continues to introduce students to the geographic and cultural diversity of the Spanish-speaking world. However, the amount of material has been considerably reduced, resulting in two sections rather than three. The material that has been eliminated from the preliminary chapter has been integrated into other chapters of *Puntos.*

USER-FRIENDLY ACTIVITIES

In addition to being carefully ordered from form-focused to more open-ended, communicative tasks, the activities are now also carefully placed on the pages so that students and instructors will not need to flip pages as they complete an activity. Additional models provide more support and materials, and elicit more student interaction. Many activities focus even more on reviewing and recycling vocabulary and structure from previous chapters.

NOTAS CULTURALES

More than half of the **Notas culturales** have been replaced with new **Notas** or have been revised considerably. Instructors will find that the **Notas culturales** consistently reflect some aspect of the chapter theme and focus on high-interest topics. In addition, the *Instructor's Edition* now features a series of follow-up questions for each **Nota,** providing instructors with ready-made activities to use in class.

PERSPECTIVAS CULTURALES

The new **Perspectivas culturales** spread now found in every chapter uniquely presents Hispanic cultures through a combination of video, readings, photos, and graphics. These two pages, as is evident in their title, provide students with a variety of cultural perspectives, related directly to the chapter theme and to the country or countries of focus. There are three separate sections within the **Perspectivas culturales** spread.

- **Entrevista cultural,** a video-based interview with a native speaker from the country of focus. When two countries are covered, there is a corresponding interview with a native speaker from each country. These interviews are directly related to the chapter theme as well: The native speakers' interests, professions, studies, or background are directly linked to that theme, and the topic of the interviews reflect this connection. Thus, students not only benefit from the country-specific cultural information in the interview but also from language that corresponds to the vocabulary and grammar covered in the chapter.

- **Entre amigos,** a video-based feature that follows the entertaining discussions of a group of four college students. These students reflect the geographic and cultural diversity of the Spanish-speaking world. Rubén is from Spain, Miguel from Mexico, Karina from Venezuela, and Tané from Cuba. In these segments, these four students informally discuss chapter-related topics that affect their daily lives. The language is natural and non-scripted, resulting in spontaneous discussions that reflect the interests and concerns of today's Spanish-speaking young adults, in an environment that encourages cross-cultural comparison.

- **Conozca... ,** based on readings, photographs, almanac information, and video footage. This section provides the opportunity for students to learn more about the chapter's country or countries of focus. After students have been exposed to a native speaker from that country in the **Entrevista cultural** section, they are then provided with the opportunity to expand their knowledge about the country in the **Conozca...** section. The variety of information provided is designed to give students a broad overview of the particular country or countries.

UN POCO DE TODO

The **Un poco de todo** review sections are now part of the **Gramática** section of the chapter, as the final step in the presentation and practice of the new grammatical structures. As in previous editions of *Puntos*, this section reviews the grammatical and lexical material from both the corresponding chapter and previous chapters. In addition, and new to this edition, each **Un poco de todo** section features a cloze paragraph with a cultural focus. This cultural focus is directly related to the theme of the chapter or the chapter's country of focus. Thus, culture and language are naturally integrated in the **Un poco de todo** sections of every chapter.

UN PASO MÁS: READING AND WRITING

- **Literatura de...** Instructors familiar with previous editions of *Puntos* will notice a new feature in the **Un paso más** section following each chapter: the **Literatura de...** section. This section, developed in response to instructor's requests for more country-specific literature and culture, features an important author from the chapter's country of focus and includes an excerpt from one of that author's works. A short biographical note provides information on the author's life. The intent of this section is to raise students' awareness of the amazingly rich literary tradition of the Spanish-speaking world, as well as give them a "taste" of some **obras maestras.**

  While these brief readings will be challenging for most students, some at least will profit from and be motivated by reading them . . . and perhaps a few will become Spanish majors in part because they were "touched" by one or more selections. While choosing these excerpts was not an easy task for the *Puntos* author team, all of us—whether we are linguists or literary specialists—remembered and reconnected with our early enthusiasm for Spanish literature as we tried to read the excerpts through the eyes of today's students.

- The **Lectura** section, which has traditionally provided optional content to develop learners' reading and writing skills, continues to serve this important function. Approximately one-third of the readings are new to the seventh edition (chapters 6, 8, 9, 11, and 15), and all of these are authentic readings chosen from sources written for native speakers of Spanish. We believe it is crucial that students be exposed to authentic written language not only for the development of reading skills but also for the acquisition of language. Students also feel a tremendous sense of accomplishment knowing that they have read (and understood!) a text written for native speakers.

  All readings are introduced by a specific reading strategy (**Estrategia**) that will help to make the reading more accessible and the reading task more enjoyable. These strategies, which are informed by second-language reading research, can be carried from one reading to the next, as well as to texts that students might read on their own outside of class.

- The **Escritura** activity provides the final task of this section. These activities serve to introduce students to the writing process and range from brief tasks such as filling out a form to longer tasks such as writing a letter, a descriptive paragraph, an essay, and so forth. The theme of the writing tasks is related to the theme of the reading passage, thereby integrating and uniting the two skills in a purposeful way.

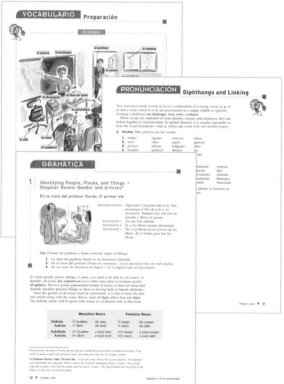

CHAPTER-OPENING SPREAD

Each chapter opens with an engaging two-page spread that provides a purposeful introduction to the chapter for both the instructor and the student. On the left-hand page of each spread a photo introduces students to both the chapter theme and the chapter's country of focus. In the *Instructor's Edition,* instructors will find theme-related questions that introduce students to the vocabulary and themes of the chapter.

The right-hand page of the spread provides a brief overview of the chapter objectives, including vocabulary, grammar, and cultural topics, as well as an introduction to the interviewee featured in the country-specific **Entrevista cultural** section of the Video Program. The map focuses student attention on the chapter's country of focus and on the interviewee's country of origin.

VOCABULARIO: PREPARACIÓN

This section presents and practices the chapter's thematic vocabulary. The vocabulary items in these sections, marked with a headphones icon, are available in audio format on the *Online Learning Center.* A special *Textbook Listening CD,* containing these audio files, is also included in the *Laboratory Audio Program.* Each new vocabulary presentation is followed by a **Conversación** section that practices the new vocabulary in context.

PRONUNCIACIÓN

This section, a feature of the first seven chapters, focuses on individual sounds that are particularly difficult for native speakers of English.

GRAMÁTICA

This section presents two to four grammar points. Each point is introduced by a minidialogue, a cartoon or drawing, realia, or a brief reading that presents the grammar topic in context. Grammar explanations, in English, appear in the left-hand column of the two-column design; paradigms and

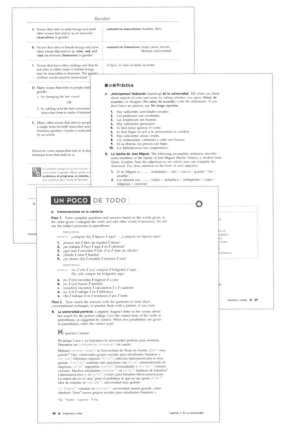

sample sentences appear in the right-hand column. Each grammar presentation is followed by a series of contextualized activities that progress from more controlled (**Práctica**) to open-ended (**Conversación**). Often, the first activity in the **Práctica** section is an **¡Anticipemos!** activity. These activities are specifically designed to introduce students to the use of the grammar point without requiring that they actively produce the new structure. Thus, these **¡Anticipemos!** activities focus on the recognition of the new grammar structure.

The **Conversación** sections contain many partner-pair activities, including many **Entrevista** activities, which require students to interview each other in order to accomplish the goal of the activity.

Gramática closes with the **Un poco de todo** section, which offers activities that combine and review grammar presented in the chapter as well as important grammar from previous chapters. Major topics that are continuously spiraled in this section include **ser** and **estar,** preterite and imperfect, gender and number agreement, and indicative and subjunctive. The cloze paragraph activity of this section actively integrates into the activity itself a cultural topic related to the chapter theme and/or target country.

PERSPECTIVAS CULTURALES

This new two-page spread has two sections: **Videoteca** on the left and **Conozca…** on the right

The **Videoteca** page presents activities related to the new *Puntos de partida Video Program:* **Entrevista cultural** and **Entre amigos.** The **Entrevista cultural** features an interview with a native speaker from the country of focus, on a topic directly related to the chapter theme. In the **Entre amigos** segment students follow the adventures of a group of four college students in Mexico. The four students are from different regions of the Spanish-speaking world: Rubén is from Spain, Miguel from Mexico, Karina from Venezuela, and Tané from Cuba. Thus, students are exposed to differing cultural perspectives within the Spanish-speaking world. In the **Perspectivas culturales** section of the textbook, students can read excerpts of the interviews they viewed, as well as answer questions about the interviews and do follow-up activities.

Conozca… is a cultural section that focuses on an individual country of the Spanish-speaking world (or in a few instances, two countries presented together). This in-depth look at the Hispanic world features information about prominent figures, the arts, cuisine, politics, history, and so forth. Additional country-specific video footage is available on the *Video Program* to further enhance students' understanding of each country and its culture; this footage is indicated in the **Conozca…** section with a video icon.

EN RESUMEN

This end-of-chapter grammar and vocabulary summary consists of two sections: **Gramática** and **Vocabulario.** The **Gramática** section provides students with a quick overview of the major grammar points within the chapter as well as a reminder of what they should know for assessment purposes. The **Vocabulario** section includes all important words and expressions from the chapter that are considered active.

UN PASO MÁS

Following every chapter, this optional supplementary section presents tasks and activities that further develop learners' reading and writing skills and complement the chapter theme and country of focus.

The **Literatura de…** section presents a brief biography of an important writer from the chapter's country of focus and includes a fragment of an important literary work by that writer.

Following **Literatura de…** is the **Lectura** or reading section. Each reading is accompanied by a reading strategy (**Estrategia**). Readings are author-written in the early chapters and realia-based or completely authentic in later chapters. Authentic readings have been chosen from Spanish-language magazines and journals and include literary selections in the final three chapters. Some readings have been edited for length but not for content or language.

Following the reading is **Escritura,** comprised of writing tasks that vary from writing simple sentences to extended narrations.

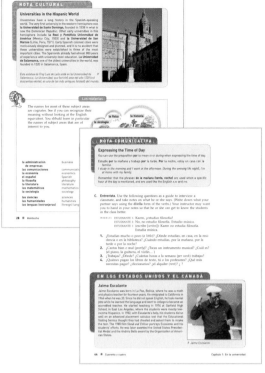

ADDITIONAL FEATURES

Other important features that appear throughout the text include:

- Theme-related **Nota cultural** features that highlight an aspect of Hispanic cultures throughout the world

- **Nota comunicativa** sections that provide additional information and strategies for communicating in Spanish

- **En los Estados Unidos y el Canadá** sections that focus on U.S. and Canadian Hispanics and Hispanic communities

- **Vocabulario útil** boxes that give additional vocabulary that may be helpful for completing specific activities

- **Autoprueba** boxes that follow grammar presentations and provide students with the opportunity to quickly check their understanding of a specific grammar point

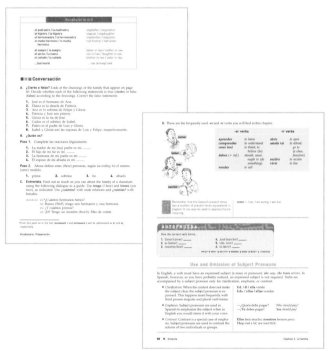

using *puntos de partida* in the classroom

DEVELOPING LANGUAGE PROFICIENCY

The authors believe that students' (and instructors') class time is best spent using Spanish: listening to and speaking with their instructor and classmates, listening and viewing audiovisual materials of many kinds, and reading in-text and supplementary materials. For that reason, grammar explanations have been written to be self-explanatory, and sample answers for many exercises are provided in the back of the book so that students can check their work before coming to class. Thus, instructors can spot-check exercises as needed in class but devote more time to the multitude of extensions, follow-up suggestions, and special activities offered in the *Instructor's Edition.* Consequently, class time can be focused on new material and novel language experiences that will maintain student interest and provide more exposure to spoken and written Spanish. Research in second-language acquisition has revealed that environments that offer learners opportunities to use the language in meaningful ways provide an optimal learning situation. Students make few gains in language learning when all of their class time is spent correcting exercises.

The preceding comments underscore the authors' conceptualization of *Puntos* throughout its many editions as a text that fosters students' proficiency in Spanish. The following features help realize this objective:

- a focus on the acquisition of vocabulary during the early stages of language learning (**Ante todo**) and then in each chapter throughout the text
- an emphasis on meaningful and creative use of language
- careful attention to skills development rather than grammatical knowledge alone
- a cyclical organization in which vocabulary, grammar, and language functions are consistently reviewed and reentered
- an integrated cultural component that embeds practice in a wide variety of culturally significant contexts
- content that aims to raise student awareness of the interaction of language, culture, and society

The overall text organization progresses from a focus on formulaic expressions, to vocabulary and structures relevant to the here and now (student life, family life), to survival situations (ordering a meal, travel-related activities), and to topics of broader interest (current events, social and environmental issues). This breadth of thematic diversity—coupled with the focus on vocabulary, grammatical structures, and language functions—helps develop students' language proficiency, thus preparing them to function in Spanish in situations that they are most likely to encounter outside the classroom.

PUNTOS DE PARTIDA AND THE NATIONAL STANDARDS

In response to the Goals 2000: Educate America Act, the American Council on the Teaching of Foreign Languages (ACTFL) received funding to develop K-12 content standards for foreign language education. Working in collaboration with professional organizations such as the American Association of Teachers of Spanish and Portuguese, among others,[1] ACTFL launched the National Standards in its 1996 volume *Standards for Foreign Language Learning: Preparing for the 21st Century.* The Standards and their challenging vision of educational reform have been embraced by government, business, and over fifty professional and state organizations.

The Standards are organized into five goal areas: Communication, Cultures, Connections, Comparisons, and Communities. These "five Cs" are symbolized by five interlocking circles, representing the close interrelationship among these goals. Each includes two or three content standards that describe what students should know and be able to use as a result of their language study. The Standards differ from a skill-based paradigm, where listening, speaking, reading, and writing are divorced from content and communication. Rather, the Standards emphasize these four skills as instruments for acquiring cross-disciplinary knowledge as well as developing critical thinking skills and communicative strategies. While the Standards do not prescribe curriculum, they necessarily influence pedagogical approaches and performance outcomes.

More specifically, the Standards ask us to reconceptualize our approach to culture. As Phillips notes:

> In spite of much lip service over the years, culture remained at the periphery of instruction, most frequently referred to as a fifth skill, a capsule, a cultural note at the bottom of a textbook page, or a Friday "fun" activity. . . . Teachers taught the culture as they knew it; students learned items randomly, not as connected threads or themes. In most courses, no systemic process was visible that enabled students to observe cultural manifestations; to analyze the patterns of behavior; to hypothesize about origins, usage, or context; and to understand the perspectives of the people in the target cultures. In sum, most cultural content learned was fact or act in isolation from how it related to the values and attitudes of a person or a people.[2]

With its integrated approach to culture, *Puntos* exemplifies the spirit of the Standards. Culture is organized thematically by chapter. Then, within each chapter of the text and via the various multimedia supplements (Video, CD-ROM, *Online Learning Center*), students are exposed to a multiplicity of *products, processes,* and *perspectives.* From interviews with native speakers, to in-depth cultural commentary on the countries of the Spanish-speaking world, to reflections on the Hispanic community in the United States and Canada, *Puntos* provides sustained opportunities for hypothesis and analysis, inviting students to make connections between beliefs, behaviors, and cultural artifacts.

---

[1] The other organizations included in this project were the American Association of Teachers of French, and the American Association of Teachers of German.
[2] June K. Phillips, ed., *Foreign Language Standards: Linking Research, Theories, and Practices* (Lincolnwood: NTC, 1999), p. 8.

In addition to **Culture,** *Puntos* integrates the four additional goal areas described in the National Standards. Through its presentation of functional language, role-play and interview activities, and personalized activities, *Puntos* emphasizes **Communication.** The readings and other exploratory activities help students make **Connections** among discipline areas. Ample opportunities are provided for cross-cultural **Comparisons** in the *Video Program* and on the *Puntos Online Learning Center* Website as well as in activities like those found in **Un poco de todo.** Finally, Internet-based and experiential activities allow students to explore **Communities.** Throughout the *Instructor's Edition,* a special recurring feature devoted to the National Standards indicates how and in what manner the Standards are represented in the content of the material.

supplementary materials

A variety of additional components are available to support *Puntos de partida*. Many are free to adopting institutions. Please contact your local McGraw-Hill representative for details on policies, prices, and availability.

FOR STUDENTS

- The *Workbook,* by Alice A. Arana (formerly of Fullerton College) and Oswaldo Arana (formerly of California State University, Fullerton), continues the successful format of previous editions by providing additional practice with vocabulary and structures through a variety of input-based, controlled, and open-ended activities and guided compositions. Special features include the **Prueba corta,** now preceded by a new grammar self-check feature called **A ver si sabe... ,** which allows students to quickly assess their knowledge of grammatical structures before completing the final quiz. The **Perspectivas culturales: Conozca...** section offers focused vocabulary and fact-based activities related to the same feature found in the student textbook.

- The *Laboratory Manual* and *Laboratory Audio Program,* by María Sabló-Yates (Delta College), continue to emphasize listening comprehension activities as well as cultural listening passages with listening strategies. Chapters offer form-focused speaking practice as well as interview and dialogue-based activities, including activities that correspond to the **Videoteca** section of the student textbook. The **Prueba corta** is a chapter-ending self-quiz that allows students to assess their language development before moving on to the next chapter. Audio CDs are free to adopting institutions and are also available for student purchase upon request. (An *Audioscript* is also available for instructors.)

- The *Online Workbook* and *Online Laboratory Manual,* developed in collaboration with Quia™, offer an online version of these printed supplements. Increasingly popular, these online versions of the printed materials offer such benefits for the student as an integrated *Laboratory Audio Program,* self-scoring activities, and instant feedback. Benefits for the instructor include a gradebook that automatically scores, tracks, and records student grades and provides the opportunity to review individual and class performance. Other benefits include customizable activities and features and instant access to grades and performance.

- The *Online Learning Center* Website provides students with a wealth of exercises and activities specially created for use with *Puntos de partida*. The *Online Learning Center* consists of two general areas: the free content and the **Premium Content.** Free content includes additional vocabulary and grammar practice quizzes, cultural activities, chapter overviews, and more. Packaged free with every new student text is an *Online Learning Center* passcode card that provides students purchasing a new text with access to the **Premium Content.** This **Premium Content** includes the *Laboratory Audio Program,* the **Conozca...** video footage, and the **Flash Grammar Tutorials.** Students that purchase a used text may purchase a passcode separately at a nominal price if they wish to access this **Premium Content.** The *Online Learning Center* can be accessed at **www.mhhe.com/puntos7.**

- The *Interactive CD-ROM* is an exciting, multimedia supplement that offers additional vocabulary and grammar practice activities, vocabulary games, review activities, interactive grammar tutorials, video-based activities, speaking activities that simulate conversations with native speakers, cultural activities, reading and writing activities, a "talking" dictionary, and much more. This highly popular interactive supplement has been revised and upgraded for the seventh edition and includes new activities and features not available on earlier versions.

- The *Video on CD* provides students with access to the entire *Puntos de partida Video Program.* Available for purchase, this set of two CD-ROMs includes every video segment from the *Video Program,* as well as follow-up activities for every segment. Instructors who find they do not have the time to show the *Video Program* in class will be pleased to know that it is available to students in this format, providing students with a wealth of authentic and natural linguistic and cultural input. For more information, see the *Video Program* below.

- The *Ultralingua en español Spanish-English Bilingual Dictionary on CD-ROM* (Guyer, Beliakov, Carpenter, Ondich, and Caudron) is also available for purchase. It is an ideal electronic Spanish-English dictionary for all levels. It includes 180,000 words and expressions, a special wild-card search function, and a hyperlinked grammar reference, among other things.

- A *Practical Guide to Language Learning,* by H. Douglas Brown (San Francisco State University), provides beginning foreign language students with a general introduction to the language-learning process. This guide is free to adopting institutions, and it can also be made available for student purchase.

FOR INSTRUCTORS

- The *Instructor's Edition,* which has always been regarded as a principal teaching resource for both novice and experienced instructors, provides an enlarged trim size with a wide variety of additional instructional ideas, suggestions, and activities. Revised by Ana María Pérez-Gironés (Wesleyan University) and A. Raymond Elliott (University of Texas, Arlington), this very useful supplement contains suggestions for implementing activities, supplementary exercises for developing listening and speaking skills, and abundant variations and follow-ups on student text materials. A special new feature of the *Instructor's Edition* are the **Bright Idea** suggestions, which were provided by instructors from across the country who use *Puntos de partida* on a daily basis. We are grateful for their wonderful ideas and suggestions. In addition, special features found in the wrap-around annotation space include a recurring **Resources** note at the beginning of each chapter identifying key supplements and resources for that chapter, notes and suggestions for adapting certain activities to accommodate **Heritage Speaker** students, and notes that identify activities that support the National Standards. There are also additional exercises for the **Vocabulario: Preparación and Gramática** sections, the **Videoteca,** and the **Lectura** and **Escritura** sections.

- The *Instructor's Manual and Resource Kit* offers an extensive introduction to teaching techniques, general guidelines for instructors, suggestions for lesson planning in semester and quarter schedules, and blackline master activities created for use with the various segments on the *Video Program,* thus making it easy for instructors to provide concrete tasks that accompany the video material. Also included are a wide variety of interactive and communicative games for practicing vocabulary and grammar, many of which are new to this edition of the *Instructor's Manual and Resource Kit.* We are very grateful to Linda H. Colville of Citrus College for creating these excellent games.

- The seventh edition of the printed *Testing Program* has been considerably revised based on extensive instructor feedback. All tests have been carefully reviewed and edited. In particular, the reading and listening sections have been revised to make their level and language more consistent. Five different tests are provided for each chapter, as well as sample mid-term and final exams.

- A new and exciting instructor supplement is the *Test Generator.* This brand-new supplement has been created in response to instructors' requests for a true test generator that allows them to easily and quickly create new, customized tests at the click of a mouse. This *Test Generator* provides a wealth of testing questions for every chapter, in a wide variety of formats. Testing categories include vocabulary, grammar, reading, writing, listening, and culture. Instructors can easily create a new test for every class, multiple tests for one class, save and store those tests, and add and save their own testing questions. We are delighted to offer this useful new supplement to instructors.

- The *Online Learning Center* Website to accompany *Puntos de partida* offers instructors a variety of additional resources. Instructors have password-protected access to all portions of the *Online Learning Center,* which includes such resources for instructors as electronic versions of the *Instructor's Manual and Resource Kit* and the *Audioscript,* as well as *Digital Transparencies* and links to **Professional Resources.** The *Online Learning Center* can be accessed at **www.mhhe.com/puntos7.** For password information, please contact your McGraw-Hill sales representative.

- A new *Video Program* accompanies the seventh edition of *Puntos.* It includes two new video segments for every chapter: The **Entrevista cultural** segment and the **Entre amigos** segment. In addition, the highly popular **Minidramas** vignettes, the **En contexto** functional segments, and the **Conozca...** cultural footage have been retained from the previous edition, resulting in a *Video Program* of approximately five hours in length. This rich resource offers instructors a wide variety of video material of differing types that correspond directly to every chapter of the textbook.

- The *Adopter's Audio CD Program,* provided free to adopting institutions, contains all of the audio CDs from the *Laboratory Audio Program* as well as the *Textbook Listening CD.* It also contains an *Audioscript.* Adopting institutions may use this *Adopter's Audio CD Program* in their Language Laboratory. In addition, institutions may make copies of these materials for students, provided that students are only charged for the cost of blank tapes or CDs.

- The *Institutional CD-ROM* package consists of twenty copies of the *Interactive CD-ROM.* This package is made available for purchase by departments and laboratories.

- A set of *Overhead Transparencies,* most in full color, contains drawings from the text and supplementary drawings for use with vocabulary and grammar presentations. An electronic online version of the *Transparencies* is available to instructors on the *Puntos Online Learning Center* Website.

- An *Instructor's Resource CD* is available to instructors, and contains Word files of the tests from the printed *Testing Program,* as well as the *Digital Transparencies* and an electronic version of the *Instructor's Manual and Resource Kit.*

- Also available are *Supplemental Materials to accompany Puntos de partida,* by Sharon Foerster and Jean Miller (University of Texas, Austin). Comprised of worksheets and a teacher's guide, these two supplements are a compilation of materials that include short pronunciation practice, listening exercises, grammar worksheets, integrative communication-building activities, comprehensive chapter reviews, and language games.

acknowledgments

The suggestions, advice, and work of the following friends and colleagues are gratefully acknowledged by the authors of the seventh edition.

- Dr. Bill VanPatten (University of Illinois, Chicago), whose creativity has been an inspiration to us for a number of editions and from whom we have learned so very much about language teaching and about how students learn

- Dr. A. Raymond Elliott (University of Texas, Arlington) and Ana María Pérez-Gironés (Wesleyan University), whose contributions to the *Instructor's Edition* have served to make that supplement an even more invaluable teaching resource

- Dr. Gail Fenderson (Brock University), whose work on the revised **En los Estados Unidos y el Canadá** sections has expanded our knowledge of the Hispanic community in Canada

- Dr. Lynne Lemley (University of Texas, Austin), who created the engaging new "cultural cloze passages" that appear in the **Un poco de todo** sections.

- Dr. Jane Johnson (University of Texas, Austin), who created the activities that accompany the new **Entrevista cultural** video segments.

- Katherine Lincoln (University of Texas, Arlington), who compiled and edited the material for the new *Test Generator.*

- Laura Chastain (El Salvador), whose invaluable contributions to the text range from language usage to suggestions for realia

In addition, the publisher wishes to acknowledge the suggestions received from the following instructors and professional friends across the country. The feedback we received through their formal reviews of the sixth edition and through their participation in focus groups was instrumental in shaping the revision of the seventh edition. The appearance of their names in this list does not necessarily constitute their endorsement of the text or its methodology.

INSTRUCTOR FOCUS GROUP PARTICIPANTS

We thank our instructor focus group participants, who graciously gave us their detailed feedback and suggestions for the *Puntos de partida* program. Their honesty and constructive criticism have greatly enhanced the seventh edition.

Juan Bernal, *San Diego City College*
Ezequiel Cárdenas, *Cuyamaca College*
Margaret Eomurian, *Houston Community College*
Raquel N. González, *University of Michigan, Ann Arbor*
María Grana, *Houston Community College*
Yolanda Guerrero, *Grossmont College*
Carmen M. Hernández, *Grossmont College*
Judy Hittle, *Indiana University Northwest*
Casilde Isabelli, *University of Nevada, Reno*
Joseph P. Kelliher, *Cuyamaca College*
Ruth Fátima Konopka, *Grossmont College*

José Manuel Lacorte, *University of Maryland*
Eva Mendieta, *Indiana University Northwest*
Judith Minarick, *Grossmont College*
Lizette Moon, *Houston Community College*
Nora Olmos, *Houston Community College*
Nancy Pinnick, *Indiana University Northwest*
Janet Sandarg, *Augusta State University*
Jacquelyn Sandone, *University of Missouri–Columbia*
Edda Temoche-Weldele, *Grossmont College*
Omaida Westlake, *Grossmont College*
Carlos H. Villacis, *Houston Community College*

STUDENT FOCUS GROUP PARTICIPANTS

We are grateful to the following Introductory Spanish students who commented in detail on all parts of the *Puntos de partida* program. Their unique and practical perspective has resulted in a particularly student-friendly, up-to-date seventh edition.

University of Colorado, Boulder
Nicole Bower
Robert Deland
Sam Frieseman
Lauren Haseman
Kristin Kauflin
Devon Kelleher
Eric Larson
Ryann MacDonald
Jessica Mallik
Joshua Martinsons
Elyza Pierce
Carlie Roberts
Noah Schum
Evan Sutton
Jennifer Troy
Jaclyn Welch
Kate White

Indiana University Northwest
Sheila Chandler
Aarica N. Correa
Stephanie Davis
Annette Gibson
Crystal Jelks
Kandis Knight
Annie Koehler
Larry Massey
Debbie Prieto
Linda Scheuer
Jennifer Schulte
Carrie Scott
Gabriela Tirado

SPECIAL CONSULTANTS

We are especially indebted to the many instructors who completed intense "how does this work in the classroom?" reviews of the text. Their comments and the comments of their students about every aspect of *Puntos,* especially the grammar explanations and activities, were truly the informing voice of this edition, helping us fine-tune every aspect of the text to ensure that, as has been said of *Puntos* since the first edition, everything "works." These consultants also provided the **Bright Idea** annotations for the *Instructor's Edition.*

Yvette Aparicio, *Grinnell College*
Ellen Brennan, *Indiana University–Purdue University Indianapolis*

Obdulia Castro, *University of Colorado, Boulder*
Arleen Chiclana, *University of North Florida*
Stephen Clark, *Northern Arizona University*
Elisabeth Combier, *North Georgia College and State University*
Kathy Dwyer Navajas, *University of Florida at Gainesville*
Delia Escalante, *Phoenix College*
Celia Esplugas, *West Chester University of Pennsylvania*
Charles Grove, *West Chester University of Pennsylvania*
Marilen Loyola, *University of Wisconsin, Madison*
April Marshall, *New York University*
Delia Montesinos, *University of Texas, Austin*
Sherrie Nunn, *University of Florida at Gainesville*
Lynne Overesch-Maister, *Johnson County Community College*
Tina Peña, *Tulsa Community College*
Marcia Picallo, *County College of Morris*
Stacy Powell, *Auburn University*
Silvia Ramírez, *University of Texas, Austin*
Jeffrey T. Reeder, *Sonoma State University*
Jaime Sánchez, *Volunteer State University*
Emily Scida, *University of Virginia, Charlottesville*
Louis Silvers, *Monroe Community College*
Bretton White, *University of Wisconsin, Madison*
María José Zubieta, *New York University*

REVIEWERS

We are grateful to the following reviewers, whose insight and suggestions have helped shape the seventh edition.

Esther Aguilar, *San Diego State University*
Serge Ainsa, *Yavapai College, Prescott*
Enrica J. Ardemagni, *Indiana University–Purdue University Indianapolis*
Bobbie L. Arndt, *Pennsylvania State University, Altoona*
Haydee Ayala-Richards, *Shippensburg University of Pennysylvania*
Angela Bagués, *Shippensburg University of Pennsylvania*
Nancy J. Barclay, *Lake Tahoe Community College*
Brenda Calderon, *Oral Roberts University*
Stephen Clark, *Northern Arizona University*
Daria Cohen, *Princeton University*
Linda H. Colville, *Citrus College*
Brian Cope, *University of California, Irvine*
Roselyn Costantino, *Pennsylvania State University, Altoona*
Kit Decker, *Piedmont Virginia Community College*
Danion L. Doman, *Truman State University*
Hector F. Espitia, *Grand Valley State University*
Rafael Falcón, *Goshen College*
Alla N. Fil, *New York University*
Laura A. Fox, *Grand Valley State University*
Khédija Gadhoum, *Grand Valley State University*

Martha Goldberg, *California Polytechnic State University*
Andrew Steven Gordon, *Mesa State College*
Antonio Gragera, *Southwest Texas State University*
Betty Gudz, *Sierra College*
Ellen Haynes, *University of Colorado, Boulder*
Candy Henry, *Westmoreland Community College, Youngwood*
Carmen M. Hernández, *Grossmont College*
Todd Anthony Hernández, *University of Kansas*
María Cecilia Herrera, *University of Wisconsin, Oshkosh*
Ann M. Hilberry, *University of Michigan*
Danielle Holden, *Oakton Community College*
Valerie Y. Job, *South Plains College, Levelland*
Hilda M. Kachmar, *Southern Methodist University*
Paula A. Kellar, *Pennsylvania State University, Altoona*
Marilyn Kiss, *Wagner College*
Sara Smith Laird, *Texas Lutheran University*
Paul Larson, *Baylor University*
Leticia P. López, *San Diego Mesa College*
María López Morgan, *Okaloosa-Walton Community College*
Monica Malamud, *Cañada College*
Jude Thomas Manzo, *San Antonio College*
Patricia A. Marshall, *Wesleyan University*
Lisa M. McCallum, *Auburn University*
Bette J. McLaud, *Onondaga Community College*
María-Teresa Moinette, *University of Central Oklahoma*
Kathryn A. Mussett, *Pennsylvania State University, Altoona*
Eunice D. Myers, *Wichita State University*
Duane C. Nelson, *Cloud County Community College*
Michelle Renee Orecchio, *University of Michigan*
Jorge Pérez, *University of California, Santa Barbara*
Oralia Preble-Niemi, *University of Tennessee, Chattanooga*
Jessica J. Ramírez, *Grand Valley State University*
Tracy Rasmussen, *Lake Tahoe Community College*
Kathleen Regan, *University of Portland*
Duane Rhoades, *University of Wyoming*
Zaira Rivera Casellas, *University of the Sacred Heart, San Juan*
Claudia Sahagún, *Broward Community College*
Maritza Salgueiro-Carlisle, *Bakersfield College*
Jaime Sánchez, *Volunteer State Community College*
Carmen Schlig, *Georgia State University*
Charles C. Schroeder, *North Iowa Area Community College–Mason City*
Georgia Seminet, *Texas A&M University, Commerce*
Philippe P. Seminet, *Texas A&M University, Commerce*
Mary-Lee Sullivan, *Binghamton University*
Fausto Vergara, *Houston Community College*
Deborah Walker, *Muscatine Community College*
Alex Whitman, *Lower Columbia College*
Gloria Williams, *Lincoln University*

Joy S. Woolf, *Westminster College*
Jiyoung Yoon, *University of North Texas*
Francisco Zabaleta, *San Diego State University*
Patricia Zuker, *University of California, San Diego*

Many other individuals deserve our thanks and appreciation for their help and support. Among them are the people who, in addition to the authors, read the seventh edition at various stages of development to ensure its linguistic and cultural authenticity and pedagogical accuracy: Alice A. Arana (United States), Oswaldo Arana (Peru), Laura Chastain (El Salvador), and María Sabló-Yates (Panama).

Special thanks are also due to Margaret Metz who arranged and conducted the instructor focus groups and coordinated the contributions of our Special Consultants. Margaret's participation made it possible for us to incorporate such a vast amount of feedback from instructors, and we are very grateful for her help.

Within the McGraw-Hill family, we would like to acknowledge the contributions of the following individuals: Linda Toy and the McGraw-Hill production group, especially Violeta Díaz for her inspired work on the design of the seventh edition, David Staloch for his invaluable assistance as Production Editor, and Randy Hurst and Louis Swaim for their work on various aspects of production. We would also like to thank Daniela Reissmann and Stacey Shearer for their helpful editorial assistance. Special thanks are due to Eirik Børve, who originally brought some of us together, and to Nick Agnew and the McGraw-Hill marketing and sales staff for their constant support and efforts. We especially thank Christa Harris, whose role as Sponsoring Editor went far beyond the call of duty and who helped us keep our sights and efforts focused on the main goals of this edition. We are especially appreciative of the work of Pennie Nichols-Alem, who adroitly wove together the feedback and contributions from many sources into a coherent whole.

The only reasons for publishing a new textbook or to revise an existing one are to help the profession evolve in meaningful ways and to make the task of daily classroom instruction easier and more enjoyable for experienced instructors and teaching assistants alike. Language teaching has changed in important ways since the publication of the first edition of *Puntos de partida*. We are delighted to have been—and to continue to be—agents of that evolution. And we are grateful to McGraw-Hill for its continuing support of our ideas.

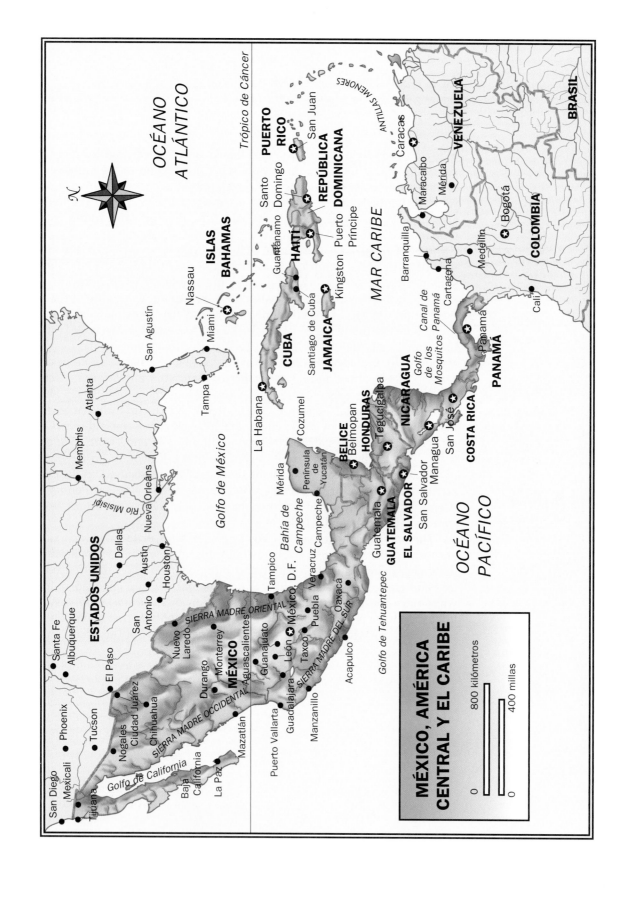

MÉXICO, AMÉRICA CENTRAL Y EL CARIBE

OCÉANO ATLÁNTICO

OCÉANO PACÍFICO

Trópico de Cáncer

Golfo de México

MAR CARIBE

ESTADOS UNIDOS

San Diego
Mexicali
Tijuana
Phoenix
Tucson
Nogales
Ciudad Juárez
Chihuahua
Santa Fe
Albuquerque
El Paso
Nuevo Laredo
San Antonio
Austin
Dallas
Houston
Memphis
Atlanta
Nueva Orleans
Tampa
San Agustín
Miami
Nassau

Baja California
La Paz
Mazatlán
Golfo de California
Durango
Monterrey
Aguascalientes
MÉXICO
Guanajuato
León
Taxco
SIERRA MADRE DEL SUR
Acapulco
Golfo de Tehuantepec
SIERRA MADRE OCCIDENTAL
SIERRA MADRE ORIENTAL
Puerto Vallarta
Guadalajara
Manzanillo
México, D.F.
Puebla
Veracruz
Oaxaca
Tampico
Bahía de Campeche
Campeche
Mérida
Península de Yucatán
Cozumel

Río Misisipí

ISLAS BAHAMAS

La Habana
CUBA
Santiago de Cuba
JAMAICA
Kingston

HAITÍ
Puerto Príncipe
REPÚBLICA DOMINICANA
Santo Domingo
Guantánamo
PUERTO RICO
San Juan
ANTILLAS MENORES

BELICE
Belmopan
GUATEMALA
Guatemala
EL SALVADOR
San Salvador
HONDURAS
Tegucigalpa
NICARAGUA
Managua
COSTA RICA
San José
PANAMÁ
Panamá
Canal de Panamá
Golfo de los Mosquitos

Barranquilla
Cartagena
Cali
Medellín
Bogotá
COLOMBIA
Maracaibo
Mérida
Caracas
VENEZUELA

BRASIL

800 kilómetros

400 millas

0

0

MAR CARIBE

OCÉANO ATLÁNTICO

Maracaibo
Barranquilla
Caracas
PANAMÁ
VENEZUELA
GUYANA
Georgetown
Paramaribo
Medellín
Panamá
Río Orinoco
Cayena
Bogotá
SURINAME
GUYANA FRANCESA
Cali
COLOMBIA
Quito
Ecuador
ECUADOR
Río Amazonas
Belém
Guayaquil
Manaus
PERÚ
BRASIL
Recife
CORDILLERA DE LOS ANDES
Lima
Cuzco
La Paz
Brasília
Arequipa
BOLIVIA
Sucre
PARAGUAY
Antofagasta
Río de Janeiro
CHILE
Trópico de Capricornio
Asunción
San Miguel
de Tucumán
São Paulo
OCÉANO PACÍFICO
La Serena
OCÉANO ATLÁNTICO
Córdoba
Rosario
URUGUAY
Valparaíso
ARGENTINA
Santiago
Buenos Aires
Montevideo
Concepción
Río de la Plata
N
Bahía Blanca
Puerto Montt
Bariloche
Chiloé

AMÉRICA DEL SUR

Islas Malvinas
0   1500 kilómetros
Estrecho de Magallanes
Punta Arenas
Tierra del Fuego
0   1000 millas
Cabo de Hornos

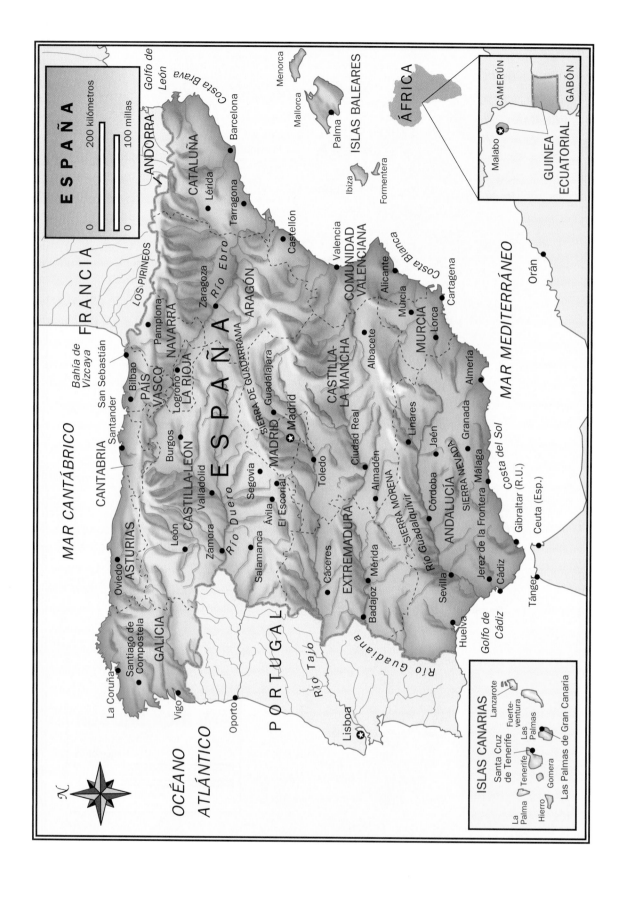

puntos
de partida

CHAPTER OPENER PHOTO

Note

Every chapter begins with a photo that introduces the theme of the chapter and places it within the context of the students' knowledge of their own culture *vis-à-vis* the Hispanic cultures.

Point out the chapter-opener photos, and have students talk about the ethnic makeup of their own campus. Encourage them to consider whether the proportion of students of diverse backgrounds is ideal. Ask what opportunities the campus offers for language learners to meet and talk to Heritage Speakers from this country and to native speakers from here and abroad. Request and offer information about available Spanish clubs and Spanish "houses" or "tables" where participants speak only Spanish.

CAPÍTULO preliminar

Ante **todo**°

▼ Santiago, Chile

▼ San Juan, Puerto Rico

▼ Lima, Perú

▼ Madrid, España

As you study Spanish in *Puntos de partida*, you will also learn about the ethnic, racial, and cultural diversity of the Spanish-speaking world.

°**Ante...** *First of all*

Resources

For Students

- Workbook
- Laboratory Manual and Laboratory Audio Program
- Quia™ Online Workbook and Online Laboratory Manual
- Video on CD
- Interactive CD-ROM
- *Puntos de partida* Online Learning Center (**www.mhhe.com/puntos7**)

For Instructors

- *Instructor's Manual and Resource Kit,* "Chapter-by-Chapter" Supplementary Materials
- Overhead Transparencies 1–6
- Testing Program
- Test Generator
- Video Program
- Audioscript
- *Puntos de partida* Online Learning Center (**www.mhhe.com/puntos7**)

Note
The table on this page of the chapter opener introduces the main cultural content, vocabulary themes, and grammar points of the chapter. This is intended to serve as an advance organizer for the chapter and, in later chapters, to help students recognize material they may have seen before.

Puntos de partida means *points of departure* in Spanish. This book will be your point of departure in Spanish language and culture. With *Puntos de partida* you will begin to learn Spanish and get ready to communicate with Spanish speakers in this country and elsewhere in the Spanish-speaking world.

To speak a language involves much more than just learning its grammar and vocabulary; to know a language is to know the people who speak it. For this reason *Puntos de partida* will provide you with cultural information to help you understand and appreciate the traditions and values of Spanish-speaking people all over the world.

Are you ready for the adventure of learning Spanish? **Pues, ¡adelante!** (*Well, let's go!*)

PRIMERA PARTE

- Saludos y expresiones de cortesía
- El alfabeto español
- ¿Cómo es usted?

SEGUNDA PARTE

- Los números 0–30; *hay*
- Gustos y preferencias
- ¿Qué hora es?

PRONUNCIACIÓN

- Las vocales: *a, e, i, o, u*

CULTURA

- **Nota cultural:** Spanish in the United States and in the World
- **Lectura:** La geografía del mundo hispánico
- **Videoteca**

    Entre amigos: ¡Encantada!

The Spanish-Speaking World

EL CANADÁ

LOS ESTADOS UNIDOS

ESPAÑA

MÉXICO

AMÉRICA CENTRAL

OCÉANO PACÍFICO

AMÉRICA DEL SUR

GUINEA ECUATORIAL

OCÉANO ATLÁNTICO

◀ ¡Buenos días! ¿Cómo te llamas?

MULTIMEDIA

- The multimedia materials that accompany this chapter are referenced in the Student and Instructor's Editions with icons to help you identify when and where to incorporate them.

- The *Instructor's Manual and Resource Kit* (IM/RK) provides suggestions for using the multimedia materials in the classroom.

Saludos° y expresiones de cortesía
Greetings

Here are some words, phrases, and expressions that will enable you to meet and greet others appropriately in Spanish.

1. Sevilla, España

1. MANOLO:	¡Hola, Maricarmen!
MARICARMEN:	¿Qué tal, Manolo? ¿Cómo estás?
MANOLO:	Muy bien. ¿Y tú?
MARICARMEN:	Regular. Nos vemos, ¿eh?
MANOLO:	Hasta mañana.

2. Quito, Ecuador

2. ELISA VELASCO:	Buenas tardes, señor Gómez.
MARTÍN GÓMEZ:	Muy buenas, señora Velasco. ¿Cómo está?
ELISA VELASCO:	Bien, gracias. ¿Y usted?
MARTÍN GÓMEZ:	Muy bien, gracias. Hasta luego.
ELISA VELASCO:	Adiós.

¿Qué tal?, ¿Cómo estás?, and **¿Y tú?** are expressions used in informal situations with people you know well, on a first-name basis.

¿Cómo está? and **¿Y usted?** are used to address someone with whom you have a formal relationship.

3. La Ciudad de México, México

3. LUPE:	Buenos días, profesor.
PROFESOR:	Buenos días. ¿Cómo te llamas?
LUPE:	Me llamo Lupe Carrasco.
PROFESOR:	Mucho gusto, Lupe.
LUPE:	Igualmente.

1. MANOLO: Hi, Maricarmen! MARICARMEN: How's it going, Manolo? How are you? MANOLO: Very well. And you? MARICARMEN: OK. See you around, OK? MANOLO: See you tomorrow.
2. ELISA VELASCO: Good afternoon, Mr. Gómez. MARTÍN GÓMEZ: Afternoon, Mrs. Velasco. How are you? ELISA VELASCO: Fine, thank you. And you? MARTÍN GÓMEZ: Very well, thanks. See you later. ELISA VELASCO: Bye.
3. LUPE: Good morning, professor. PROFESSOR: Good morning. What's your name? LUPE: My name is Lupe Carrasco. PROFESSOR: Nice to meet you, Lupe. LUPE: Likewise.

Saludos y expresiones de cortesía

Note

The word *usted* appears in its unabbreviated form in this chapter and at the beginning of *Capítulo 1*. After that, it will appear as *Ud.*

Suggestions

■ See the model for vocabulary presentation and other material in the *Ante todo* "Chapter-by-Chapter Supplementary Materials," in the IM.

■ Model pronunciation for each dialogue. Use multiple choral repetitions followed by individual repetitions. See "Teaching Techniques: *Minidiálogos,*" IM.

■ Act out dialogues with several students.

■ Have students use their own names in the exchanges. See "Teaching Techniques: Small Groups," IM.

■ Point out that English equivalents of *minidiálogos* will always appear at the foot of the page.

■ Offer this optional vocabulary for *Minidiálogo 1: así así, más o menos, hasta pronto.*

■ For *Minidiálogo 2,* discuss the use of courtesy titles and formal forms: first-name-basis vs. last-name-basis relationships.

■ Point out that *buenas* and *muy buenas* can be used at any time of the day, instead of *buenos días, buenas tardes,* or *buenas noches.*

■ For *Minidiálogo 3,* point out the formal *¿Cómo se llama usted?* vs. familiar *¿Cómo te llamas?* Have students use the familiar form with other students.

■ For *Minidiálogo 4,* have students practice the exchange using *usted.*

■ Have students practice questions with a chain drill.

Student 1 asks: *¿Cómo te llamas?* Student 2 answers and asks the same question of Student 3, and so on.

■ Point out that *encantado* is used by males and *encantada* is used by females.

■ Model *mucho gusto* and *encantado/a* in exchanges with several students, reversing roles. Have students practice the exchange.

Resources: Transparency 1–3

Note: Transparencies 1–3 are maps of the Spanish-speaking world. You may wish to use these now to identify the countries in which the video segments take

---

MULTIMEDIA: Video

■ These four dialogues appear at the beginning of the Video to accompany *Puntos de partida.*
■ See suggestions in the IM for using this chapter of *Puntos de partida* with video supplements.

MULTIMEDIA: Audio

Point out that the headphones Web icon indicates audio material included on the Online Learning Center that accompanies the text (**www.mhhe.com/puntos7**).

¿**Cómo se llama usted?** is used in formal situations. ¿**Cómo te llamas?** is used in informal situations—for example, with other students. The phrases **mucho gusto** and **igualmente** are used by both men and women when meeting for the first time. In response to **mucho gusto,** a woman can also say **encantada;** a man can say **encantado.**

4. La Ciudad de México, México

4. MIGUEL: Hola, me llamo Miguel René. ¿Y tú?
   ¿Cómo te llamas?
   KARINA: Me llamo Karina. Mucho gusto.
   MIGUEL: Mucho gusto, Karina. Y, ¿de dónde eres?
   KARINA: Yo soy de Venezuela. ¿Y tú?
   MIGUEL: Yo soy de México.

¿**De dónde eres?** is used in informal situations to ask where someone is from. In formal situations the expression used is ¿**De dónde es usted?** To reply to either question, the phrase **Soy de** _____ is used.

NOTA COMUNICATIVA

Otros saludos y expresiones de cortesía

buenos días	good morning (*used until the midday meal*)
buenas tardes	good afternoon (*used until the evening meal*)
buenas noches	good evening; good night (*used after the evening meal*)
señor (Sr.)	Mr., sir
señora (Sra.)	Mrs., ma'am
señorita (Srta.)	Miss (**¡OJO!*** *There is no Spanish equivalent for Ms. Use* **Sra.** *or* **Srta.** *as appropriate.*)
gracias	thanks, thank you
muchas gracias	thank you very much
de nada, no hay **de qué**	you're welcome
por favor	please (*also used to get someone's attention*)
perdón	pardon me, excuse me (*to ask forgiveness or to get someone's attention*)
con permiso	pardon me, excuse me (*to request permission to pass by or through a group of people*)

4. MIGUEL: *Hello, my name is Miguel René. And you? What's your name?* KARINA: *My name is Karina. Nice to meet you.* MIGUEL: *Nice to meet you, Karina. And, where are you from?* KARINA: *I'm from Venezuela. And you?* MIGUEL: *I'm from Mexico.*

Watch out!, Careful!* **¡OJO! *will be used throughout* Puntos de partida *to alert you to pay special attention to the information that follows.*

Follow-Up

- Help students compare the *minidiálogos* and find patterns of formal vs. informal exchanges. Write on the board two columns, one for formal, the other for informal; list students' responses (*tú* vs. *usted; te* vs. *se; estás* vs. *está; hola* vs. *muy buenas;* and so on).
- Have students work in pairs to practice the four dialogues using their own names. Use the phrase *trabajen en parejas* to cue students.

NOTA COMUNICATIVA

Suggestions

- Model phrases in brief exchanges with students, using *señor, señorita,* or *señora;* help students use the appropriate title for you.
- Model phrases of thanks, creating situations in which these expressions are appropriate. For example, give a student a book and elicit *gracias.* You respond *de nada,* and so on.
- Provide optional vocabulary: *permiso* (without *con*); model the use of *con permiso* to take leave of someone, *cómo no* (as a rejoinder), *perdone* (in addition to *perdón*), *perdón* (to request permission to pass by or through), *disculpe, oiga.*

CULTURE

- Lunchtime is often around 2 P.M.; the evening meal may be as late as 10 or 11 P.M. in Hispanic countries. For this reason, you may hear Spanish speakers say *Buenas tardes* as late as 9 or 9:30 P.M.
- Titles of respect are not capitalized when spelled out. When abbreviated, they are capitalized: *señor Sánchez; Sr. Sánchez.*
- *Don* and *doña* are titles of respect used only before the first name, as in *don José* or *doña Ana.* These terms are not capitalized nor do they have standard abbreviations.

☼ Heritage Speakers

Los títulos *don* y *doña* no tienen equivalente en inglés. Cuando se traduce, por ejemplo, *don Tomás,* se dice simplemente *Tomás* o *Mr. Tomás.* Pídales a los estudiantes hispanohablantes que le den ejemplos a la clase de algunas personas a las cuales ellos se refieren con estos títulos.

Con. A: Suggestion

Conduct a rapid response drill with students' books closed. See "Teaching Techniques," IM.

Con. B: Note

More than one answer is possible for some items.

Con. B: Extension

5. you and your Spanish professor, at 11 A.M.
6. you and your cousin, at 10 P.M.
7. you and the president of your university, at 4 P.M.

Con. D: Suggestion

■ Model an interview with two or three students before asking others to form pairs and follow your example.
■ Remind students to use informal expressions in student exchanges, but formal expressions when addressing you, the instructor.

■ ■ ■ Conversación

A. Cortesía. How many different ways can you respond to the following greetings and phrases?

1. Buenas tardes.
2. Adiós.
3. ¿Qué tal?
4. Hola.
5. ¿Cómo está?
6. Buenas noches.
7. Muchas gracias.
8. Hasta mañana.
9. ¿Cómo se llama usted?
10. Mucho gusto.
11. ¿De dónde eres?

B. Situaciones. If the following people met or passed each other at the times given, what might they say to each other? Role-play the situations with a classmate.

1. Mr. Santana and Miss Pérez, at 5:00 P.M.
2. Mrs. Ortega and Pablo, at 10:00 A.M.
3. Ms. Hernández and Olivia, at 11:00 P.M.
4. you and a classmate, just before your Spanish class

C. Más (More) situaciones. Are the people in these drawings saying **por favor, con permiso,** or **perdón?**

D. Entrevista (Interview). Turn to a person sitting next to you and do the following.

■ Greet him or her appropriately, that is, with informal forms.
■ Ask where he or she is from.
■ Find out his or her name.
■ Ask how he or she is.
■ Conclude the exchange.

Now have a similar conversation with your instructor, using the appropriate formal forms.

National Standards: Connections

Have students ask Spanish-speaking children in the community to recite the alphabet in Spanish. If students have a hand-held recording device, they can record the children's recitals and play them in class.

Resources: Transparency 4

El alfabeto español

There are twenty-nine letters in the Spanish alphabet (**el alfabeto** or **el abecedario**)—three more than in the English alphabet. The three additional letters are the **ch,** the **ll,** and the **ñ.** The letters **k** and **w** appear only in words borrowed from other languages.

In 1994, the **Real Academia Española** (*Royal Spanish Academy*), which establishes many of the guidelines for the use of Spanish throughout the world, decided to adopt the universal Latin order when alphabetizing. In that order, **ch** and **ll** are not considered separate letters. Thus, in dictionaries and other alphabetized materials published since 1994, you will not find separate listings for the letters **ch** and **ll.** They are, however, still considered separate letters by the **Real Academia** and are part of the Spanish alphabet.*

Letters	Names of Letters	Examples		
a	a	Antonio	Ana	(la) Argentina
b	be	Benito	Blanca	Bolivia
c	ce	Carlos	Cecilia	Cáceres
ch	che	Pancho	Chabela	La Mancha
d	de	Domingo	Dolores	Durango
e	e	Eduardo	Elena	(el) Ecuador
f	efe	Felipe	Francisca	Florida
g	ge	Gerardo	Gloria	Guatemala
h	hache	Héctor	Hortensia	Honduras
i	i	Ignacio	Inés	Ibiza
j	jota	José	Juana	Jalisco
k	ca (ka)	(Karl)	(Kati)	(Kansas)
l	ele	Luis	Lola	Lima
ll	elle	Guillermo	Estrella	Sevilla
m	eme	Manuel	María	México
n	ene	Nicolás	Nati	Nicaragua
ñ	eñe	Íñigo	Begoña	España
o	o	Octavio	Olivia	Oviedo
p	pe	Pablo	Pilar	Panamá
q	cu	Enrique	Raquel	Quito
r	ere	Álvaro	Rosa	(el) Perú
s	ese	Salvador	Sara	San Juan
t	te	Tomás	Teresa	Toledo
u	u	Agustín	Lucía	(el) Uruguay
v	ve *or* uve	Víctor	Victoria	Venezuela
w	doble ve, ve doble, *or* uve doble	Oswaldo	(Wilma)	(Washington)
x	equis	Xavier	Ximena	Extremadura
y	i griega	Pelayo	Yolanda	(el) Paraguay
z	ceta (zeta)	Gonzalo	Esperanza	Zaragoza

*The **ch** is pronounced with the same sound as in English cherry or chair, as in **nachos** or **muchacho.** The **ll** is pronounced as a type of y sound. Spanish examples of this sound that you may already know are **tortilla** and **Sevilla.** The grouping **rr** is not considered a separate letter by the **Real Academia.**

Heritage Speakers

■ Invite a sus estudiantes hispanohablantes a pronunciar estas palabras. Pregúnteles a los otros estudiantes si ellos oyen alguna diferencia entre el modo en que los hispanohablantes pronuncian los sonidos, especialmente la *j* y la *ll.*

■ Anime a los estudiantes hispanohablantes a que les pidan a varios parientes y conocidos que pronuncien estas palabras mientras ellos graban sus voces. Luego pueden tocar sus grabaciones en clase y comentar sobre las diferencias en la pronunciación de personas de varios países de habla hispana.

El alfabeto español

Notes

■ *El abecedario* (ABCs) is a synonym for *el alfabeto.*

■ *Ch* and *ll* do not appear as separate letters in vocabulary lists in the seventh edition of *Puntos de partida.*

■ The website of the *Real Academia Española* includes a clear explanation of the Spanish alphabet and its letters, as well as much other interesting information. It can be found at **www.rae.es.**

■ Common Hispanic first names and place names are used as examples of letters.

Suggestions

Point out that the **ch** and the **ll** represent sounds not represented by any other letter in Spanish. This is not the case with the two-letter grouping **rr,** whose sound is also represented by the single **r** when it appears at the beginning of a word or when preceded by the letters **n, l,** or **s.** This distinction explains why the **rr** is not considered a separate letter.

Suggestions

Point out that . . .

■ *ce, ci* produce an [s] sound; *ca, co, cu* produce a [k] sound.

■ *ga, go, gu* produce a [g] sound; *ge, gi* are pronounced like Spanish *j.*

■ *r* at the beginning of a word is pronounced like the trilled (double) *r.*

■ the letter *v* is pronounced like the Spanish *b;* to distinguish *b* and *v,* Spanish speakers sometimes call the letter *b be grande* or *be de burro,* and the letter *v ve chica* or *ve de vaca.* In Spain the *v* is called *uve.*

■ the letter *x* is sometimes pronounced like [ks], sometimes like [s], and sometimes like the Spanish *j* (*México, Texas*).

■ In Castilian Spanish *ce, ci,* and *z* produce an English *th* sound [Θ].

■ In most dialects of Spanish, there is no difference in the pronunciation of the letters *ll* and *y;* however, from one area to another the dialectal variation in *ll/y* is great. Teach the pronunciation of your own dialect and allow for variation. When possible, point out dialectal variation such as the lateral pronunciation of the *ll* in northern Peninsular Spanish or the strong palatal fricative from Argentina [zh].

Variation

Use common Hispanic last names: *Álvarez, Hernández, Fernández, Gómez, Pérez,* and so on.

Primera parte ■ **7**

8 ■ Capítulo preliminar: Ante todo

Prác. A: Note

See the Index for chapter references to pronunciation practice with specific sounds and letters. Vowel sounds are presented in *Ante todo: Segunda parte.* This activity is intended only for immediate practice with sounds and letters that may be strange to some students.

Prác. B: Notes

- For use of *Pasos* organization in this and subsequent activities, see "Using *Pasos* Activities," IM.
- The word *paso* in the headers *Paso 1* and *Paso 2* means "step."
- The word *paso* in the place name *El Paso* refers to a pass or a passageway.

Prác. B: Suggestions

- Introduce the phrase *¿Cómo se deletrea... ?*
- Explain that *acentuada* means "stressed" and that in Spanish the stressed vowel in some words must carry a written accent mark so that the word can be read correctly. Accent marks are presented in *Capítulos 2* and *3.*

Prác. B: Follow-Up

Have students think of other U.S. place names of Hispanic origin and spell them aloud in Spanish as other students pronounce them.

NOTA COMUNICATIVA

Note

This *Nota* offers opportunities for pronunciation practice as well as being a vehicle to make students comfortable with Spanish and to encourage self-expression.

Additional cognates and cognate practice are available in the Workbook and on the Quia™ Online Workbook.

Suggestions

- Interview students in the classroom, asking them to indicate whether the following statements are *cierto* (true) or *falso* (false).
    1. *Roseanne Barr es muy elegante.*
    2. *El presidente de los Estados Unidos no es muy importante.*

■ ■ ■ Práctica

A. ¡Pronuncie! The letters and combinations of letters listed below represent the Spanish sounds that are the most different from English. You will practice the pronunciation of some of these letters in upcoming chapters of *Puntos de partida.* For the moment pay particular attention to their pronunciation when you see them. Can you match the Spanish letters with their equivalent pronunciation?

EXAMPLES/SPELLING

1. mucho: **ch**
2. Geraldo: **ge** (also: **gi**) Jiménez: **j**
3. hola: **h**
4. gusto: **gu** (also: **ga, go**)
5. me llamo: **ll**
6. señor: **ñ**
7. profesora: **r**
8. Ramón: **r** (to start a word) Monterrey: **rr**
9. nos vemos: **v**

PRONUNCIATION

a. like the *g* in English *garden*
b. similar to *tt* of *butter* when pronounced very quickly
c. like *ch* in English *cheese*
d. like Spanish **b**
e. similar to a "strong" English *h*
f. like *y* in English *yes* or like the *li* sound in *million*
g. a trilled sound, several Spanish **r**'s in a row
h. similar to the *ny* sound in *canyon*
i. never pronounced

B. ¿Cómo se deletrea... ? [*How do you spell . . . ?*]

Paso [*Step*] **1.** Pronounce these U.S. place names in Spanish. Then spell the names aloud in Spanish. All of them are of Hispanic origin: **Toledo, Los Ángeles, Texas, Montana, Colorado, El Paso, Florida, Las Vegas, Amarillo, San Francisco.**

Paso 2. Spell your own name aloud in Spanish, and listen as your classmates spell their names. Try to remember as many of their names as you can.

MODELO: Me llamo María: **M** (eme) **a** (a) **r** (ere) **í** (i acentuada) **a** (a).

NOTA COMUNICATIVA

Los cognados

As you begin your study of Spanish, you will probably notice that many Spanish and English words are similar or identical in form and meaning. These related words are called *cognates* (**los cognados**). You will see them used in **Ante todo** and throughout *Puntos de partida.* At this early stage of language learning, it's useful to begin recognizing cognates and how they are pronounced in Spanish. Here are some examples of Spanish words that are cognates of English words. These cognates and others will help you enrich your Spanish vocabulary and develop your language proficiency!

SOME ADJECTIVES		SOME NOUNS	
cruel	optimista	banco	hotel
elegante	paciente	bar	museo
flexible	pesimista	café	oficina
importante	responsable	diccionario	parque
inteligente	sentimental	estudiante	teléfono
interesante	terrible	examen	televisión

CULTURE

- For additional pronunciation practice write the following *trabalenguas* (tongue twister) on the board. Have students practice it in groups, paying special attention to how they pronounce the *r* in Spanish.
    Tres tristes tigres comen trigo en un trigal.
- A palindrome is a word, phrase, or sentence such as "Madam I'm Adam" that reads the same backwards and forwards. Have students practice the following palindrome in Spanish, paying attention to their pronunciation: *Dábale arroz a la zorra el abad.*

Refrán

«Cuando los números hablan se acaban las discusiones.»

Write the *refrán* on the board. Help students with the meaning of *cuando* and *hablan,* then have them guess the meaning of *se acaban.* What does the saying mean? Is there an equivalent in English? [*Numbers talk.*]

¿Cómo es usted?°

You can use these forms of the verb **ser**
(*to be*) to describe yourself and others.

¿Cómo... What are you like?

(yo)	**soy**	I am
(tú)	**eres**	you (*familiar*) are
(usted)	**es**	you (*formal*) are
(él, ella)	**es**	he/she is

—¿Cómo es usted?
—Bueno...° Yo soy moderna, independiente,
sofisticada...

Well . . .

■■■ Conversación

Descripciones

Paso 1. Form complete sentences with the cognate nouns and adjectives
given. Use **no** when necessary.

1. Yo (no) soy...
   estudiante.
   cruel.
   responsable.
   optimista.
   paciente.
2. El presidente (no) es...
   importante.
   inteligente.
   pesimista.
   flexible.
   extrovertido.
3. Jennifer López (no) es...
   elegante.
   introvertida.
   romántica.
   sentimental.
   egoísta.

Paso 2. Now think of people you might describe with the following
additional cognates. Use **es** to express *is*.

MODELO: eficiente → La profesora es eficiente.

1. arrogante
2. egoísta
3. emocional
4. idealista
5. independiente
6. liberal
7. materialista
8. realista
9. rebelde
10. paciente

Primera parte

Nueve ■ 9

☼ Heritage Speakers

Pídales a los estudiantes hispanohablantes que
recopilen una lista de lugares latinoamericanos o
españoles que ellos conocen y que les lean sus listas a
sus compañeros monolingües.

National Standards: Community

Poll students to see who has heard of the following
famous U.S. Hispanics: Edward James Olmos,
Selena, Raúl Julia, Rosie Pérez, Celia Cruz, Gloria
Estefan, Andy García, Jimmy Smits, Jennifer López,
Carlos Santana, and Sammy Sosa. Invite students to
add other famous personalities to the list.

---

3. *Oprah Winfrey es muy
inteligente.*
4. *El programa de televisión
«Survivor» es muy
interesante.*

Have students provide corrections for the statements they feel
are false.

■ Point out that words in English
and in Spanish may look alike
but will not sound alike.
■ Tell students that they need not
try to memorize all words in
this *Nota.*
■ Model pronunciation of
adjectives in brief sentences
about yourself: *cruel... No soy
cruel* (pointing to yourself), and
so on.
■ Provide optional vocabulary for
pronunciation or listening practice, for example, adjectives:
*legal, superior, normal, diligente,
excelente, natural, horrible,
prudente, popular, inferior,
intelectual, indiferente, arrogante,
eficiente, egoísta, emocional,
idealista, independiente, liberal,
materialista, realista, rebelde,
valiente, vulnerable.* Some additional nouns: *restaurante, libertad, declaración, león, dólar,
hamburguesa, béisbol,
guitarra, piano.*
■ Although *simpático/a* is not a
cognate, students may
recognize it and be able to use
it in communicative activities.

¿Cómo es usted?

Suggestions

■ Introduce the forms of *ser* in brief
sentences using the adjectives just
presented in the *Nota.*
■ Make sure students connect the
eres/es forms with informal/formal
concepts already discussed for
greetings.

Con: Note

Students have not learned
adjective/noun agreement. If possible,
avoid having students produce
sentences that require gender agreement by using adjectives and nouns
that are the same for masculine and
feminine. Gender is taught in
Gramática 1 (*Capítulo 1*) and *Gramática
5* (*Capítulo 2*).

Notes

- *Islas Canarias* and *Islas Baleares* are shaded but not labeled because they are part of Spain. Belize and Andorra are *not* Spanish speaking. This is not obvious on this map.
- Top twelve world languages (source: World Almanac, 2000)

  Chinese (Mandarin) 1,075 million
  English 514 million
  Hindi 496 million
  Spanish 425 million
  Russian 275 million
  Arabic 256 million
  Bengali 215 million
  Portuguese 194 million
  Malay Indonesian 176 million
  French 129 million
  German 128 million
  Japanese 126 million

Suggestion

Have students give examples of uses of Spanish in the U.S.: place and street names, restaurants, advertising, music, friends of Hispanic descent, television programs about Hispanics or with Hispanic characters, and so on. Explain the derivations of these terms, if you know them.

Comprensión

1. How many native Spanish speakers are there in the world? In the United States?
2. Where are the larger Hispanic communities in the United States?

Follow-Up

- Use the place names on this map to continue pronunciation practice. Write the names of the countries on the board as students say them, then use the list as a basis for choral repetition drill.
- Have students research and make pie charts that illustrate the ethnic make-up of their community.

NOTA CULTURAL

Spanish in the United States and in the World

Although no one knows exactly how many languages are spoken around the world, linguists estimate that there are between 3,000 and 6,000. Spanish, with 425 million native speakers, is among the top five languages. It is the official language spoken in Spain, in Mexico, in all of South America (except Brazil and the Guianas), in most of Central America, in Cuba, in Puerto Rico, in the Dominican Republic, and in Ecuatorial Guinea (in Africa)—in approximately twenty-one countries in all. It is also spoken by a great number of people in the United States and Canada.

Like all languages spoken by large numbers of people, modern Spanish varies from region to region. The Spanish of Madrid is different from that spoken in Mexico City, Buenos Aires, or Los Angeles. Although these differences are most noticeable in pronunciation ("accent"), they are also found in vocabulary and special expressions used in different geographical areas. Despite these differences, misunderstandings among native speakers are rare, since the majority of structures and vocabulary are common to the many varieties of each language.

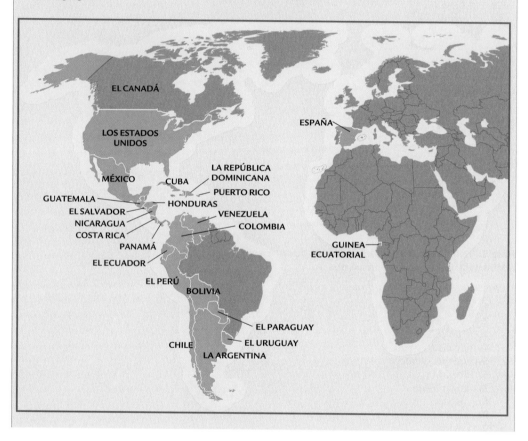

Capítulo preliminar: Ante todo

- Not all people of Hispanic origin have Spanish surnames. Many people with Spanish surnames do not consider themselves of Hispanic origin.
- *Chicano*, although not as popular today as it was in the 1970s and early 1980s, is another term still used by many Mexican-Americans to refer to themselves and the literature, art, and dialect of their community. Students should be aware of different terms and expect individual preferences from the Mexican-American community.

☼ Heritage Speakers

Los hispanohablantes de los Estados Unidos usan palabras adaptadas del inglés en el habla cotidiana. Muchas veces los hispanohablantes de países latinoamericanos o de España no conocen estas palabras, lo cual puede impedir la comprensión. Algunas de estas palabras son *elevador* en vez de *ascensor*, *aplicación* en vez de *solicitud*, *bonche* en vez de *montón*, *grados* en vez de *notas*, *lonche* en vez de *almuerzo*, entre otras.

Resources: Transparency 5

You don't need to go abroad to encounter people who speak Spanish on a daily basis. The Spanish language and people of Hispanic descent have been an integral part of United States and Canadian life for centuries. In fact, the United States has the fifth largest Spanish-speaking population in the world!

There is also great regional diversity among U.S. Hispanics. Many people of Mexican descent inhabit the southwestern part of the United States, including populations as far north as Colorado. Large groups of Puerto Ricans can be found in New York, while Florida is host to a large Cuban and Central American population. More recent immigrants include Nicaraguans and Salvadorans, who have established large communities in many U.S. cities, among them San Francisco and Los Angeles.

As you will discover in subsequent chapters of *Puntos de partida,* the Spanish language and people of Hispanic descent have been and will continue to be an integral part of the fabric of this country. Take special note of **En los Estados Unidos y el Canadá,** a routinely occurring section of *Puntos de partida* that profiles Hispanics in these two countries.

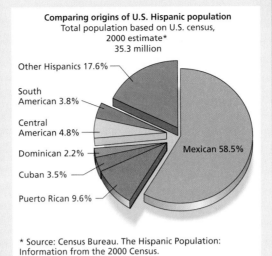

Comparing origins of U.S. Hispanic population
Total population based on U.S. census,
2000 estimate*
35.3 million

Other Hispanics 17.6%
South American 3.8%
Central American 4.8%
Dominican 2.2%
Cuban 3.5%
Puerto Rican 9.6%
Mexican 58.5%

* Source: Census Bureau. The Hispanic Population: Information from the 2000 Census.

▲ *Mural en la Pequeña Habana, el barrio cubano de Miami*

NOTA CULTURAL *(continued)*

Note
The following are the 10 states in the United States with the highest Hispanic population according to the U.S. Census Bureau.

STATE	TOTAL NUMBER OF HISPANICS	% OF STATE POPULATION
California	10,966,556	32.4
Texas	6,669,666	32.0
New York	2,867,583	15.1
Florida	2,682,715	16.8
Illinois	1,530,262	12.3
Arizona	1,295,617	25.3
New Jersey	1,117,191	13.3
New Mexico	765,386	42.1
Colorado	735,601	17.1
Nevada	393,970	19.7

Suggestions
■ Point out that mural art has been popularized by Hispanic artists. Mural projects were initiated in the U.S. by Mexican muralists and other artists.
■ Have students study the mural and tell what aspects are distinctly Hispanic.

MULTIMEDIA: Internet

Have students find information on the Internet about murals in the United States. They can also search for community programs that foster mural-making, for example, the Precita Eyes Mural Arts Center in San Francisco.

☼ **Heritage Speakers**

Anime a los estudiantes hispanohablantes a que les pregunten a sus parientes y conocidos de origen hispánico los nombres por los cuales se refieren a sí mismos, nombres tales como *nica* o *boricua*. Luego invítelos a compartir esta información con sus compañeros de clase.

Pronunciación

Note
Point out the different pronunciations of the English vowel *a: far, fat, fate, fail, sofa;* also point out the silent letter *e: make, mate, crate.*

Suggestion
Emphasize diphthongized pronunciation of the English *a* and *o* in *ate, make, same, oh, gold,* and *note.* Pronounce each word slowly, calling attention to the movement of your lips. Contrast with Spanish *me, te, de, lo, no.*

Las vocales: *a, e, i, o, u*

Preliminary Exercises

■ Pronounce these words in random order and have students tell whether each word is *español* or *inglés.* You may wish to translate unfamiliar words for the students.

Eng.	Sp.	Eng.	Sp.
me	*mi*	may	*me*
Fay	*fe*	no	*no*
ace	*es*	Sue	*su*
cone	*con*	lay	*le*
tea	*ti*	two	*tú*
low	*lo*	say	*se*
dose	*dos*	day	*de*
sea	*si*	Kay	*que*

■ Write the following two columns on the board. Read aloud one word at a time. Students will decide if the word you read was from column A or B. You may wish to translate unfamiliar words for the students.

A	B
1. *mesas*	*meses*
2. *señoras*	*señores*
3. *calor*	*color*
4. *emite*	*imite*
5. *pelar*	*polar*
6. *legar*	*lugar*

Note
The following lyrics are from a song Hispanic children are taught to learn the order of the vowels.

La marcha de las vocales

Que dejen toditos los libros abiertos,
ha sido la orden que dio el general.
Que todos los niños estén muy atentos,
las cinco vocales van a desfilar.

Primero verás
que pasa la A
con sus dos patitas
muy abiertas al marchar.

Ahí viene la E
alzando los pies,
el palo de en medio
es más chico como ves.

Pronunciación

You have probably already noted that there is a very close relationship between the way Spanish is written and the way it is pronounced. This makes it relatively easy to learn the basics of Spanish spelling and pronunciation.

Many Spanish sounds, however, do not have an exact equivalent in English, so you should not trust English to be your guide to Spanish pronunciation. Even words that are spelled the same in both languages are usually pronounced quite differently. It is important to become so familiar with Spanish sounds that you can pronounce them automatically, right from the beginning of your study of the language.

Las vocales (*Vowels*): *a, e, i, o, u*

Unlike English vowels, which can have many different pronunciations or may be silent, Spanish vowels are always pronounced, and they are almost always pronounced in the same way. Spanish vowels are always short and tense. They are never drawn out with a *u* or *i* glide as in English: **lo** ≠ *low;* **de** ≠ *day.*

a: pronounced like the *a* in *father,* but short and tense
e: pronounced like the *e* in *they,* but without the *i* glide
i: pronounced like the *i* in *machine,* but short and tense*
o: pronounced like the *o* in *home,* but without the *u* glide
u: pronounced like the *u* in *rule,* but short and tense

 The *uh* sound or schwa (which is how most unstressed vowels are pronounced in English: *canal, waited, atom*) does not exist in Spanish.

■ ■ ■ Práctica

A. Sílabas. Pronounce the following Spanish syllables, being careful to pronounce each vowel with a short, tense sound.

1. ma fa la ta pa
2. me fe le te pe
3. mi fi li ti pi
4. mo fo lo to po
5. mu fu lu tu pu
6. mi fe la tu do
7. su mi te so la
8. se tu no ya li

---

*The word **y** (and) is also pronounced like the letter **i**.*

CULTURE

■ When it appears in a Spanish text, "U.S.A." is pronounced as a single word.
■ Another abbreviation of "United States," preferred in some countries, is *EE.UU.* (The repeated letters stand for the plural noun *Estados Unidos.*)

B. Palabras (*Words*). Repeat the following words after your instructor.

1. hasta tal nada mañana natural normal fascinante
2. me qué Pérez Elena rebelde excelente elegante
3. sí señorita permiso terrible imposible tímido Ibiza
4. yo con como noches profesor señor generoso
5. uno usted tú mucho Perú Lupe Úrsula

C. Trabalenguas (*Tongue-twister*)

Paso 1. Here is a popular nonsense rhyme, the Spanish version of "Eeny, meeny, miney, moe." (*Note:* The person who corresponds to **fue** is "it.") Listen as your instructor pronounces it.

> Pin, marín
> de don Pingüe
> cúcara, mácara
> títere, fue.

Paso 2. Now pronounce the vowels clearly as you repeat the rhyme.

D. Naciones

Paso 1. Here is part of a rental car ad in Spanish. Say aloud the names of the countries where you can find this company's offices. Can you recognize all of the countries?

ai Ansa International
RENT A CAR

Si necesita un coche para su trabajo o placer, nosotros tenemos el adecuado para Vd.

Con una flota de 40.000 coches y 1.000 oficinas, estamos a su servicio en los siguientes países;

● ALEMANIA	● IRLANDA
● ARABIA SAUDITA	● ISLANDIA
● ARGENTINA	● ITALIA
● AUSTRIA	● JAMAICA
● BELGICA	● LUXEMBURGO
● BRASIL	● MALASIA
● CHIPRE	● MARRUECOS
● DINAMARCA	● MARTINICA
● ESPAÑA	● PARAGUAY
● FINLANDIA	● PORTUGAL
● FRANCIA	● SUECIA
● GRAN BRETAÑA	● SUIZA
● GRECIA	● URUGUAY
● HOLANDA	● U.S.A.

En la mayoría de los casos, podemos confirmar su reserva inmediatamente.

Cuando esto no sea posible, su reserva le será confirmada en un plazo máximo de 48 horas.

Paso 2. Find the following information in the ad.

1. How many cars does the agency have available?
2. How many offices does the agency have?
3. What Spanish word expresses the English word *immediately*?

Aquí está la I,
la sigue la O,
una es flaca y otra gorda
porque ya comió.

y luego hasta atrás
llegó la U
como la cuerda
con que saltas tú.

Prác. B: Extension

Present the last names in the following sentences; practice the phrases and then complete sentences. Emphasize clear diction and the use of mouth muscles.
a: *Hasta mañana, señora Santana.*
e: *De nada, señora Pérez.*
i: *¿Eres tímida, señorita Muñoz?*
o: *Con permiso, señor Ortega.*
u: *¿Y usted, señora Cruz?*

Prác. C: Variation

Use the following nursery rhyme to continue practice with vowel sounds. You may wish to translate the rhyme for the students.
A, a, a: mi gatita mala está.
E, e, e: a mí me gusta el café.
I, i, i: en un libro yo la vi.
O, o, o: mi madre me la bordó.
U, u, u: a mí no me pegas tú.

Prác. D: Note

Vd. is a less common abbreviation for *usted.* The more common abbreviation is *Ud.*, which students will learn in *Capítulo 1.*

Prác. D: Suggestions

- Model the names of the countries, followed by choral and individual repetitions.
- Have students identify other cognates in the ad.

Need more practice?
- Workbook and Laboratory Manual
- Interactive CD-ROM
- Online Learning Center (www.mhhe.com/puntos7)

CULTURE

Have students look for ads in Spanish magazines or newspapers either in their community or on the Internet and share them with their classmates. How are ads in Spanish similar or different from the ads they have seen in English?

Los números 0-30; *hay*

- Practice the *Canción infantil.*
- Practice the numbers 0–10: count forward; count by twos in evens and odds; count backwards from 10–0.
- Practice the numbers 11–20: evens 0–20.
- Practice the numbers 21–30: odds 0–30.
- Count from 0 to 30 by threes; by fives; by tens.
- Point out the written accents on 16, 21 (shortened masculine form), 22, 23, 26; final *-e* of *veinte* and final *-a* of *treinta.*
- Write numbers on the board and identify them (sometimes incorrectly). Students indicate their comprehension with *sí* or *no.* Encourage them to correct your "mistakes."
- Say these pairs of numbers; have students repeat the larger one: *dos / doce; once / uno; treinta / veinte; tres / trece; cuatro / catorce; quince / cinco; diez / once.*
- Point out that *hay* means both *there is* and *there are.*
- Model the question form. *¿Hay _____?* with rising intonation.

 Reciclado

Using magazine or newspaper ads or photos, ask *¿Hay _____?* questions with previous cognate vocabulary.

SEGUNDA PARTE

Los números 0-30; *hay*

Los números 0-30

Canción infantil

Dos y dos son cuatro,
cuatro y dos son seis,
seis y dos son ocho,
y ocho dieciséis.

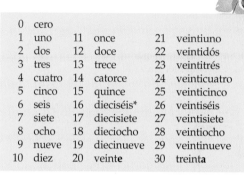

0	cero				
1	uno	11	once	21	veintiuno
2	dos	12	doce	22	veintidós
3	tres	13	trece	23	veintitrés
4	cuatro	14	catorce	24	veinticuatro
5	cinco	15	quince	25	veinticinco
6	seis	16	dieciséis*	26	veintiséis
7	siete	17	diecisiete	27	veintisiete
8	ocho	18	dieciocho	28	veintiocho
9	nueve	19	diecinueve	29	veintinueve
10	diez	20	veinte	30	treinta

The number *one* has several forms in Spanish. **Uno** is the form used in counting. The forms **un** and **una** are used before nouns. How will you know which one to use? It depends on the gender of the noun.

In **Capítulo 1,** you will learn that all Spanish nouns are either masculine or feminine in gender. For example, the noun **señor** is masculine (*m.*) in gender, and the noun **señora** is feminine (*f.*) in gender. (As you will learn, Spanish nouns that are not sex-linked also have gender.) Here is how *one* is expressed with these nouns: **un señor, una señora.** Also note that the number **veintiuno** becomes **veintiún** before masculine nouns and **veintiuna** before feminine nouns: **veintiún señores, veintiuna señoras.** Do learn how to use **un** and **uno** with nouns now, but don't worry about the concept of gender for the moment.

 noun = a word that denotes a person, place, or thing

 uno, dos, tres,... veinti**uno,** veintidós,...
but
un señor, veinti**ún** señores
una señora, veinti**una** señoras

A children's song Two and two are four, four and two are six, six and two are eight, and eight (makes) sixteen.

*The numbers 16 to 19 and 21 to 29 can be written as one word (**dieciséis... veintiuno...**) or as three (**diez y seis... veinte y uno...**).

☼ Heritage Speakers

Pregúnteles a los estudiantes hispanohablantes qué canciones infantiles aprendieron de niño y anímelos a cantar alguna.

Hay

Use the word **hay** to express both *there is* and *there are* in Spanish. **No hay** means *there is not* and *there are not*. **¿Hay… ?** asks *Is there . . . ?* or *Are there . . . ?*

hay = there is / there are

—¿Cuántos estudiantes **hay** en la clase?
—(**Hay**) Treinta.

How many students are there in the class?
(There are) Thirty.

—¿**Hay** pandas en el zoo?
—**Hay** veinte osos, pero **no hay** pandas.

Are there any pandas at the zoo?
There are twenty bears, but there aren't any pandas.

■■■ Práctica

A. Los números. Practique los números según (*according to*) el modelo.

MODELO: 1 señor → Hay un señor.

1. 4 señoras
2. 12 pianos
3. 1 café (*m.*)
4. 21 cafés (*m.*)
5. 14 días
6. 1 clase (*f.*)
7. 21 ideas (*f.*)
8. 11 personas
9. 15 estudiantes
10. 13 teléfonos
11. 28 naciones
12. 5 guitarras
13. 1 león (*m.*)
14. 30 señores
15. 20 oficinas

B. Problemas de matemáticas. Do the following simple mathematical equations in Spanish. *Note:* + (**y**), − (**menos**), = (**son**).

MODELOS: $2 + 2 = 4$ → Dos y dos son cuatro.
$4 - 2 = 2$ → Cuatro menos dos son dos.

1. $2 + 4 = ?$
2. $8 + 17 = ?$
3. $11 + 1 = ?$
4. $3 + 18 = ?$
5. $9 + 6 = ?$
6. $5 + 4 = ?$
7. $1 + 13 = ?$
8. $15 - 2 = ?$
9. $9 - 9 = ?$
10. $13 - 8 = ?$
11. $14 + 12 = ?$
12. $23 - 13 = ?$
13. $1 + 4 = ?$
14. $1 - 1 + 3 = ?$
15. $8 - 7 = ?$
16. $13 - 9 = ?$
17. $2 + 3 + 10 = ?$
18. $28 - 6 = ?$
19. $30 - 17 = ?$
20. $28 - 5 = ?$
21. $19 - 7 = ?$

■■■ Conversación

Preguntas (*Questions*)

1. ¿Cuántos (*How many*) estudiantes hay en la clase de español? ¿Cuántos estudiantes hay en clase hoy (*today*)? ¿Hay tres profesores o un profesor / una profesora?
2. ¿Cuántos días hay en una semana (*week*)? ¿Hay seis? (No, no hay…) ¿Cuántos días hay en un fin de semana (*weekend*)? ¿Cuántos días hay en el mes de febrero? ¿en el mes de junio? ¿Cuántos meses hay en un año?
3. Hay muchos edificios (*many buildings*) en una universidad. En esta (*this*) universidad, ¿hay una cafetería? (Sí, hay… / No, no hay…) ¿un teatro? ¿un laboratorio de lenguas (*languages*)? ¿un bar? ¿una clínica? ¿un hospital? ¿un museo? ¿muchos estudiantes? ¿muchos profesores?

Prác. A: Suggestion

Have students read aloud, practicing pronunciation.

Prác. A: Variation

Use this or a similar activity for in-class dictation. See "Teaching Techniques: Dictation," IM.

Prác. B: Variations

- Do as a pair activity in which one partner reads the equation and the other provides the answer.
- Write additional problems on large flash cards. Have students read the problems aloud and give answers.
- Teach ¿*Cuántos son?* Give additional problems orally.

Prác. B: Follow-Up

- *Un problema para Einstein:* $10 - 5 + 7 - 4 + 12 - 15 + 9 - 11 + 17 - 14 + 16 = ?$ (Answer: 22)
- Explain that $\times$ = *por.* Have students read and solve these equations orally.

1. $2 \times 2 = ?$
2. $2 \times 6 = ?$
3. $18 \times 1 = ?$
4. $3 \times 7 = ?$
5. $4 \times 4 = ?$
6. $11 \times 0 = ?$
7. $3 \times 8 = ?$
8. $2 \times 15 = ?$

Con: Notes

- Students may answer in complete sentences.
- A double no (*No, no…*) is used in complete sentences that express negative answers.

Con: Extension

3. Use the same items, but ask questions about your campus, using *muchos/as* plus plural forms of nouns.
4. *Hay muchos animales en un zoo. ¿Hay un zoo en* (your city) *o en una ciudad cercana? ¿Cuántos elefantes hay? ¿Cuántas jirafas? ¿Hay muchos animales exóticos?*

CULTURE

If you go to a restaurant or café in Latin America or Spain, your bill may look very different from those in this country. Handwritten numbers can be quite different. For example, the number 1 is usually written as an inverted check mark (), and can easily be mistaken for the number 7. The 7, however, is usually written with a slash across the middle (7). The number 8 is frequently written starting with the lower loop, and the number zero (0) is sometimes written with a diagonal slash through it (∅).

☼ Heritage Speakers

Recuérdeles a los estudiantes hispanohablantes que la forma *hay* es impersonal y que no cambia: *Hay un hombre; Hay dos libros.* Recuérdeles que lo mismo ocurre en los tiempos pasados: cuando expresan *there was/were,* había y hubo no cambian al aparecer ante un sustantivo plural: *Había muchos libros; Hubo varios problemas.*

Gustos y preferencias

Suggestions

- Encourage students to learn all of the *gustar* phrases as set expressions. There is no need to explain the *gustar* construction at this time; activities will not require students to produce *gustan* on their own.
- Students should relate *te/le gusta* to the informal/formal concept discussed in *Ante todo: Primera parte*.
- Contrast the indefinite articles practiced earlier and the definite articles practiced here, but do not require mastery of the concept at this time.

Note

Introduce *gustar* + infinitives to expand the communicative use of *gustar* phrases, as well as to introduce the concept of the infinitive.

Preliminary Exercise

Ask the following questions. *¿Qué te/le gusta más, el fútbol o el fútbol americano? ¿el tenis o el vólibol? ¿Qué le gusta a* (name of classmate)? Do not emphasize or expect students to produce the *a* (*al*).

Vocabulario útil

Notes

- The *Vocabulario útil* boxes and sections occur throughout *Puntos de partida* when additional vocabulary is needed to complete an activity. Similar boxes provide useful phrases, expressions, and verbs: *Frases útiles, Expresiones útiles, Verbos útiles*.
- Students need not memorize this vocabulary. It is provided to help them complete activities in the text.
- When *Vocabulario útil* features appear, model new vocabulary for students in the context of brief sentences, if possible, before letting them continue the activity.
- In Latin America, rap is sometimes called *el cotorreo* (*cotorrear* means to talk without saying anything interesting) or *la música rap*.

Con. A: Extension

Use other names of currently famous people and cognates for sports and games: *el béisbol, el vólibol, el basquetbol, hacer jogging, jugar al bingo, practicar deportes*, and so on.

Gustos° y preferencias

Likes

¿Te gusta el fútbol? → ■ Sí, me gusta mucho el fútbol.
■ No, no me gusta el fútbol.

To indicate you like something: **Me gusta ____.**
To indicate you don't like something: **No me gusta ____.**
To ask a classmate if he or she likes something: **¿Te gusta ____?**
To ask your instructor the same question: **¿Le gusta ____?**

In the following conversations, you will use the word **el** to mean *the* with masculine nouns and the word **la** with feminine nouns. Don't try to memorize which nouns are masculine and which are feminine. Just get used to using the words **el** and **la** before nouns.

You will also be using a number of Spanish verbs in the infinitive form, which always ends in **-r**. Here are some examples: **estudiar** = *to study;* **comer** = *to eat.* Try to guess the meanings of the infinitives used in these activities from context. If someone asks you, for instance, **¿Te gusta *beber* Coca-Cola?,** it is a safe guess that **beber** means *to drink.*

▲ *En español,* **fútbol** = soccer *y* **fútbol americano** = football

verb = a word that describes an action or a state of being

infinitive = a verb form without reference to person or tense

■ ■ ■ Conversación

A. Gustos y preferencias

Paso 1. Make a list of six things you like and six things you don't like, following the model. If you wish, you may choose items from the **Vocabulario útil** box. All words are provided with the appropriate definite article **el** or **la**, the Spanish equivalent of *the*, depending on the gender of the noun.

MODELO: Me gusta *la clase de español.* No me gusta *la clase de matemáticas.*

1. Me gusta ____. No me gusta ____.
2. Me gusta ____. No me gusta ____.
3. ____
4. ____
5. ____
6. ____

Paso 2. Now ask a classmate if he or she shares your likes and dislikes.

MODELO: ¿Te gusta la clase de español? ¿y la clase de matemáticas?

Vocabulario útil*

el café, el té, la limonada, la cerveza (beer)
la música moderna, la música clásica, el rap, la música country
la pizza, la pasta, la comida mexicana, la comida de la cafetería (cafeteria food)
el actor ____, la actriz ____
el/la cantante (singer) **____** (¡OJO! cantante is used for both men *and* women)
el cine (movies), **el teatro, la ópera, el arte abstracto, el fútbol**

Do you like soccer? → • Yes, I like soccer very much. • No, I don't like soccer.
*The material in **Vocabulario útil** lists is not active; that is, it is not part of what you need to focus on learning at this point. You may use these words and phrases to complete exercises or to help you converse in Spanish, if you need them.*

Capítulo preliminar: Ante todo

CULTURE

In *Capítulo 7* students will learn that in some dialects of Spanish, the verb *gustar* can have romantic connotations when used in the first and second person singular forms (*yo* and *tú*).

¿Te gusto? Do you like me? / Are you attracted to me?

Appropriate substitutes are *encantarle, agradarle,* or *caerle bien.*

B. Más gustos y preferencias

Paso 1. Here are some useful verbs and nouns to talk about what you like. For each item, combine a verb (shaded) with a noun to form a sentence that is true for you. Can you use context to guess the meaning of verbs you don't know?

MODELO: Me gusta _____. → Me gusta *estudiar inglés*.

1. **beber**   café   té   limonada   chocolate
2. **comer**   pizza   enchiladas   hamburguesas   pasta   ensalada
3. **estudiar**   español   matemáticas   historia
                computación   (*computer science*)
4. **hablar**   español   con mis amigos (*with my friends*)
                por teléfono (*on the phone*)
5. **jugar**   al tenis   al fútbol   al fútbol americano   al béisbol
                al basquetbol
6. **tocar**   la guitarra   el piano   el violín

Paso 2. Ask a classmate about his or her likes using your own preferences as a guide.

MODELO: ¿Te gusta *comer enchiladas*?

Paso 3. Now ask your professor if he or she likes certain things. ¡OJO! Remember to address your professor in a formal manner.

MODELO: ¿Le gusta *jugar al tenis*?

¿Qué hora es?

Es la una.   **Son** las dos.   **Son** las cinco.

¿Qué hora es? is used to ask *What time is it?* In telling time, one says **Es la una** but **Son las dos** (**las tres, las cuatro,** and so on).

Es la una y { cuarto. / quince. }   Son las dos y { media. / treinta. }

Son las cinco **y diez.**   Son las ocho **y veinticinco.**

Note that from the hour to the half-hour, Spanish, like English, expresses time by adding minutes or a portion of an hour to the hour.

Con. B: Follow-Up

Paso 1. Have students expand each interview to three sentences by adding rejoinders like *a mí* and *también: A mí me gusta tocar el violín también.*

¿Qué hora es?

Suggestions

- Use a clock made from a paper plate to introduce telling time, and follow the step-by-step progression of the explanation in the text.
- Remind students that *Es la una* but *Son las dos* (*las tres,* and so on).
- Point out that *son* is the plural form of *es.*
- In Mexico and some parts of Central America, one frequently hears *¿Qué horas son?*
- Practice telling time with the most basic forms before presenting the *Nota comunicativa.*

☼ Heritage Speakers

Pregúnteles a los hispanohablantes de la clase si ellos mismos dicen o si conocen a personas que dicen *¿Qué horas son?* en vez de *¿Qué hora es?* No critique, sino repita que esta forma se oye en muchas partes de Latinoamérica.

National Standards: Communication

Have students interview their classmates, asking them about their *gustos y preferencias.* Provide students with sample questions.

    ¿Te gusta estudiar español?
    ¿Te gusta la comida italiana?
    ¿Te gusta jugar al basquetbol?

Once students complete their interviews, follow up with questions that have students share information: *¿A quién le gusta la comida italiana?*

NOTA COMUNICATIVA

Suggestions

- Model expressions with various times shown on your clock.
- Point out that *de la mañana* is used until lunch and *de la tarde* until the evening meal. Make sure students associate this information with the greetings *buenos días* and *buenas tardes/noches*.
- Emphasize the difference between *Es/Son* vs. *A la(s)*.
- Ask *¿A qué hora es la clase de español?* After the students respond, repeat the answer, adding *en punto*. Repeat the question for a number of shared experiences: *la sesión de laboratorio, la clase de historia*, and so on.

Prác. A: Suggestion

You might present the items in this order: *Son las nueve y media de la mañana.* **(6)** *Son las dos de la tarde.* **(2)** *Son las seis y dieciséis de la tarde.* **(8)** *Son las doce menos veinte de la noche.* **(1)** *Son las cinco y cuarto de la noche* (*mañana*). **(5)** *Son las diez y veintidós de la noche.* **(3)** *Son las dos y diecinueve de la tarde.* **(4)** *Es la una y cinco de la noche* (*mañana*). **(7)**

Prác. A: Follow-Up

Have students respond *sí* or *no* to the following statements. Vary the time as needed for your students. This is an opportunity to review the infinitives from *Conversación B* (p. 17). Pantomime as needed to convey meanings.

1. *Son las once de la noche. Es hora de estudiar.*
2. *Son las siete de la mañana. Es hora de hablar español.*
3. *Son las ocho de la mañana. Es hora de beber café en la cafetería.*
4. *Son las seis y media de la tarde. Es hora de comer en un restaurante elegante.*

Son las dos **menos** { **cuarto.** / **quince.** }   Son las ocho **menos diez.**   Son las once **menos veinte.**

From the half-hour to the hour, Spanish usually expresses time by sub-tracting minutes or a part of an hour from the *next* hour.

NOTA COMUNICATIVA

Para expresar° la hora   *Para... To express*

de la mañana	A.M., in the morning
de la tarde	P.M., in the afternoon (and early evening)
de la noche	P.M., in the evening
en punto	exactly, on the dot, sharp
¿a qué hora...?	(at) what time . . . ?
a la una (las dos,...)	at 1:00 (2:00, . . .)

Son las cuatro de la tarde **en punto.**   *It's exactly 4:00 P.M.*

¿A qué hora es la clase de español?   *(At) What time is Spanish class?*

Hay una recepción **a las once** de la mañana.   *There is a reception at 11:00 A.M.*

Don't confuse **Es la... / Son las...** with **A la(s)...** The first two are used for telling time, the third for telling *at* what time something happens (at what time class starts, at what time one arrives, and so on).

■■■ **Práctica**

A. **¡Atención!** Listen as your instructor says a time of day. Find the clock or watch face that corresponds to the time you heard and say its number in Spanish. (Note the sun or the moon that accompanies each clock; they indicate whether the time shown is day or night.)

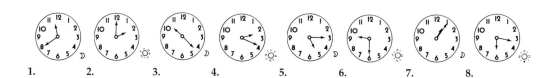

1.   2.   3.   4.   5.   6.   7.   8.

Capítulo preliminar: Ante todo

CULTURE

Time is often listed in military style for Spanish publications such as TV guides and transportation schedules.

12:01 A.M.	= 00:01	4:15 P.M.	= 16:15
8:00 A.M.	= 08:00	7:05 P.M.	= 19:05
12:00 Noon	= 12:00	10:20 P.M.	= 22:20
1:30 P.M.	= 13:30	11:10 P.M.	= 23:10

Resources: Transparency 6

B. **¿Qué hora es?** Express the time in full sentences in Spanish.

1. 1:00 P.M.
2. 6:00 P.M.
3. 11:00 A.M.
4. 1:30
5. 3:15
6. 6:45
7. 4:15
8. 11:45 exactly
9. 9:10 on the dot
10. 9:50 sharp

■ ■ ■ Conversación

A. Entrevista

Paso 1. Ask a classmate at what time the following events or activities take place. He or she will answer according to the cue or will provide the necessary information.

> MODELO: la clase de español (10:00 A.M.) →
> ESTUDIANTE 1: ¿A qué hora es la clase de español?
> ESTUDIANTE 2: A las diez de la mañana... ¡en punto!

1. la clase de francés (1:45 P.M.)
2. la sesión de laboratorio (3:10 P.M.)
3. la excursión (8:45 A.M.)
4. el concierto (7:30 P.M.)

Paso 2. Now ask at what time your partner likes to perform these activities. He or she should provide the necessary information.

> MODELO: cenar (to have dinner) →
> ESTUDIANTE 1: ¿A qué hora te gusta cenar?
> ESTUDIANTE 2: Me gusta cenar a las ocho de la noche.

1. almorzar (to have lunch)
2. mirar (to watch) la televisión
3. ir (to go) al laboratorio de lenguas
4. ir al cine

B. Situaciones. How might the following people greet each other if they met at the indicated time? With a classmate, create a brief dialogue for each situation.

> MODELO: Jorge y María, a las once de la noche →
> JORGE: Buenas noches, María.
> MARÍA: Hola, Jorge. ¿Cómo estás?
> JORGE: Bien, gracias. ¿Y tú?
> MARÍA: ¡Muy bien!

1. el profesor Martínez y Gloria, a las diez de la mañana
2. la Sra. López y la Srta. Luna, a las cuatro y media de la tarde
3. usted y su (your) profesor(a) de español, en la clase de español

Need more practice?

■ Workbook and Laboratory Manual
■ Interactive CD-ROM
■ Online Learning Center (www.mhhe.com/puntos7)

Prác. B: Suggestions

■ Ask students at what time they like to . . . tocar (un instrumento musical), comer, estudiar (español), practicar deportes, and so on.
■ Introduce the interrogative ¿cuándo?
■ Emphasize that students must include the phrase a la(s): Me gusta (comer) a las (doce en punto).

Prác. B: Note

This activity helps students prepare for Conversación A.

Con. A: Variation

Expand the exchange in Paso 2 with a mí and también: A mí me gusta estudiar español a las ocho de la noche también.

Con. A: Follow-Up

Put the following television schedule on the board. Read incomplete sentences and have students respond with a la(s)... : Hay un programa cómico (romántico, dramático, de animales, de música, para toda la familia, interesante) a _____.

7:00—Los Simpson
7:30—El Zoo de Barcelona
8:00—¡Festival de música!
8:30—Dibujos animados
9:00—E.R.
10:00—Cine Club: Historia de amor

You may want to challenge students more by using military times as is common in Latin American countries and in Spain. 7:00 = 19:00 hours; 7:30 = 19:30; 8:00 = 20:00, and so on.

Con. B: Suggestion

Have several pairs of students present brief dialogues to the class. Encourage the others to listen to the skits and ask brief comprehension questions based on them.

 Heritage Speakers

En algunos dialectos, almorzar significa comer a media mañana y corresponde a la expresión to have brunch en inglés.

Suggestions

- Before students begin the reading, review the definite and indefinite articles (for recognition) with them. Emphasize *un → el* and *una → la.* Present the plural definite articles (*los, las*).
- Point out that students should guess the underlined words from context, and discuss the first such word (*pampas*) with them.
- Have students point out or underline words in the text that they recognize as cognates. This practice will be useful in future *Lecturas,* where they will have to understand the meaning of a sentence by referring to the whole context.
- Point out other morphological endings that students can recognize very easily.

  -ción = -tion
    acción; legalización
  -gión = -gion
    religión; región
  -tad = -ty
    facultad
  -dad = -ty
    universidad; ciudad
  -tud = -tude
    multitud
  -mente = -ly
    rápidamente; constantemente
  -ista = -ist
    artista; dentista; oculista
  -able = -able/-ible
    responsable

Note

The underlining system for words to guess will continue in all *Lectura* sections.

LECTURA

ESTRATEGIA: Guessing Meaning from Context

You will recognize the meaning of a number of cognates in the following reading about the geography of the Hispanic world. In addition, you should be able to guess the meaning of the underlined words from the context (the words that surround them); they are the names of geographical features. The photo captions will also be helpful.

Note also that a series of headings divides the reading into brief parts. It is always a good idea to scan such headings before starting to read, in order to get a sense of a reading's overall content.

La geografía del mundo[a] hispánico

Introducción

La geografía del mundo hispánico es impresionante y muy variada. En algunas[b] regiones hay de todo.[c]

En las Américas

En la Argentina hay <u>pampas</u> extensas en el sur[d] y la <u>cordillera</u> de los Andes en el oeste. En partes de Venezuela, Colombia y el Ecuador, hay regiones tropicales de densa <u>selva</u>. En el Brasil está[e] el famoso <u>Río</u> Amazonas. En el centro de México y también en El Salvador, Nicaragua y Colombia, hay <u>volcanes</u> activos. A veces[f] producen erupciones catastróficas. El Perú y Bolivia comparten[g] el enorme <u>Lago</u> Titicaca, situado en una <u>meseta</u> entre los dos países.[h]

▲ La **cordillera** de los Andes, Chile

En las naciones del Caribe

Cuba, Puerto Rico y la República Dominicana son tres <u>islas</u> situadas en el <u>Mar</u> Caribe. Las bellas playas[i] del Mar Caribe y de la <u>península</u> de Yucatán son populares entre[j] los turistas de todo el mundo.

▲ La **isla** de Caja de Muertos, Puerto Rico

[a]*world* [b]*some* [c]*de... a bit of everything* [d]*south* [e]*is* [f]*A... Sometimes* [g]*share* [h]*naciones* [i]*bellas... beautiful beaches* [j]*among*

En la Península Ibérica

España comparte[k] la Península Ibérica con Portugal. También tiene[l] una geografía variada. En el norte están los Pirineos, la <u>cordillera</u> que separa a España del[m] resto de Europa. Madrid, la capital del país, está situada en la <u>meseta</u> central. En las <u>costas</u> del sur y del este hay playas tan bonitas como las de[n] Latinoamérica y del Caribe.

▲ Una **selva** tropical en Colombia

▲ La **ciudad** de Montevideo, Uruguay

▲ Una **meseta** de La Mancha, España

¿Y las <u>ciudades</u>?

Es importante mencionar también la gran[o] diversidad de las ciudades del mundo hispánico. En la Argentina está la gran ciudad de Buenos Aires. Muchos consideran a Buenos Aires «el París» o «la Nueva York» de Sudamérica. En Venezuela está Caracas, y en el Perú está Lima, la capital, y Cuzco, una ciudad antigua de origen indio.

Conclusión

En fin,[p] el mundo hispánico es diverso respecto a la geografía. ¿Y Norteamérica? ■

[k]shares [l]it has [m]from the [n]tan... as pretty as those of [o]great [p]En... In short

Suggestions

■ Have students bring images from magazines, books, and the Internet that illustrate different aspects of Hispanic geography. You might assign specific topics to students or groups, and have them give brief oral presentations based on their findings.

■ Ask students to give examples of geographical features from the Hispanic world that are not found in the reading. Accept answers in English, and give the Spanish equivalents if you know them.

■ Have students write short sentences with the following words, based on the information provided in the *Lectura* (*Parte 2*) or on their own knowledge of world geography. You can provide them with these examples:

ciudad → *Buenos Aires es una ciudad de la Argentina.*
lago → *En el Canadá hay lagos.*

1. *ciudad*
2. *capital*
3. *lago*
4. *volcán*
5. *playa*
6. *isla*
7. *nación*
8. *península*
9. *río*
10. *mar*

National Standards: Comparison

Have students compare the geographical diversity of the Spanish-speaking world with the geography of this country. How many features can they match? Which ones are related, for example, the Andes and the Rockies and the Pacific Ring of Fire?

Follow-Up

Remind students of the meanings of *¿Dónde?* and *¿Qué?* (*Where?* and *What?*), then ask questions to practice new vocabulary from this reading passage. For example:

¿Dónde hay pampas?
¿Dónde hay volcanes?
¿Qué forman España y Portugal?
¿Qué ciudad sudamericana es como París y Nueva York?
¿Qué son Cuba, Puerto Rico y la República Dominicana?
¿Dónde están?

VIDEOTECA

Entre amigos

Note

Entre amigos is a new feature of this edition of *Puntos*. Beginning in *Capítulo 1*, the *Videoteca* section will present two video activities: *Entrevista cultural* and *Entre amigos*. The follow-up questions for *Entre amigos* will appear in Spanish throughout. The questions practice vocabulary and structures that the students have learned.

Suggestions

■ Before viewing the video, review the questions with the students and ask them similar questions.

1. *¿De dónde es Ud.?*
2. *¿Cuántos años tiene* (How old are) *Ud.?*

Have students answer or work in small groups to ask and answer these questions.

■ After viewing the video, have volunteers read and answer the questions.

Comprensión

Demonstrate your understanding of the words underlined in the reading and other words from the reading by giving an example of a similar geographical feature found in this country or close to it. Then give an example from the Spanish-speaking world.

> MODELO: un río → *the Mississippi,* el Río Orinoco

1. un lago
2. una cordillera
3. un río
4. una isla
5. una playa
6. una costa
7. un mar
8. un volcán
9. una península

Videoteca

Entre amigos: ¡Encantada!

You will watch a video clip of four college students who meet each other for the first time. What questions do you think they will ask each other? Before watching the video, read the following questions. As you watch, don't worry if you don't understand every word. Try to get the gist of the conversation, listening carefully for names and where people are from. Watch the video a second time and listen for the answers to the questions.

1. ¿De dónde es Miguel?
2. ¿Cómo se llama la señorita de Venezuela?
3. ¿Cuántos años tiene (*How old is*) Tané, la señorita de Cuba?

EN RESUMEN

Vocabulario
Practice this vocabulary with digital flash cards on the Online Learning Center (www.mhhe.com/puntos7).

Although you have used and heard many words in this preliminary chapter of *Puntos de partida*, the following words are the ones considered to be active vocabulary. Be sure that you know all of them before beginning **Capítulo 1.**

Saludos y expresiones de cortesía

Buenos días. Buenas tardes. Buenas noches. Hola. (Muy) Buenas. ¿Qué tal? ¿Cómo está(s)? Regular. (Muy) Bien. ¿Y tú? ¿Y usted? Adiós. Hasta mañana. Hasta luego. Nos vemos.

**¿Cómo te llamas? ¿Cómo se llama usted?
  Me llamo _____.**

**¿De dónde eres? ¿De dónde es usted?
  Soy de _____.**

señor (Sr.), señora (Sra.), señorita (Srta.)

**(Muchas) Gracias.
De nada. No hay de qué.
Por favor. Perdón. Con permiso.
Mucho gusto. Igualmente. Encantado/a.**

¿Cómo es usted?

soy, eres, es

Los números 0–30

cero
uno
dos
tres
cuatro
cinco
seis
siete
ocho
nueve
diez
once
doce
trece
catorce
quince
dieciséis
diecisiete

dieciocho
diecinueve
veinte
treinta

Gustos y preferencias

¿Te gusta _____? ¿Le gusta _____?

Sí, me gusta _____. No, no me gusta _____.

¿Qué hora es?

**es la... , son las...
y/menos cuarto (quince)
y media (treinta)
en punto
de la mañana (tarde, noche)
¿a qué hora?, a la(s)...**

Palabras interrogativas

¿cómo?   how?; what?
¿dónde?   where?
¿qué?   what?

Palabras adicionales

sí	yes
no	no
hay	there is/are
no hay	there is not / are not
hoy	today
mañana	tomorrow
y	and
o	or
a	to; at (*with time*)
de	of; from
en	in; on; at
pero	but
también	also

EN RESUMEN
Vocabulario

Note
Students are *not* expected to know every word they have used in *Ante todo.* Only active vocabulary is listed here.

Suggestion
Use the material from the inside front cover to familiarize students with frequently used classroom commands and other useful phrases.

Bright Idea

Suggestion

Give students a phrase or question. They should respond with an appropriate rejoinder. For example:
  *¿Qué tal? → Muy bien.
  Gracias. → De nada.
  Hola. → Muy buenas.*
and so on.

Bright Idea annotations have been provided by users of *Puntos de partida.* Look for these wonderful ideas from your colleagues across the country in every chapter.

Refrán

«Antes hoy que mañana.»

Write the *refrán* on the board and help students with the meaning of *antes* (before). Then have them brainstorm possible English equivalents (*Don't put off until tomorrow what you can do today.*). Point out that there are many sayings in English and Spanish about today and tomorrow.

 ## Heritage Speakers

Anime a los hispanohablantes a presentar diálogos en clase usando los saludos y expresiones de cortesía.

CHAPTER OPENER PHOTO

Point out the chapter-opener photo and have students talk about their own experiences interacting with Hispanic students studying in this country or as exchange students. Encourage them to focus on the individual characteristics of the people they talk about, rather than any generic "national traits."

Suggestions

- You may wish to address the question of the existence of a *typical* student with the class: Is there a *typical student*?
- Ask students the following questions to introduce the chapter topic.

  1. Are you a full-time or part-time student?
  2. How old were you when you started your university studies?
  3. Is your campus large or small? Is it urban or set apart from the city?
  4. Do most students on your campus live in a dorm? off-campus?
  5. When will you select your major? If you've already selected one, what is it?

- Ask questions that use *cognados* and to which students can answer *sí* or *no*.
  - *¿Es usted un estudiante típico / una estudiante típica?*
  - *¿Usted tiene 15 años? ¿16 años? ¿20 años?* (Write *año = year* on the board, and point to each student to indicate that you are referring to him/her.)
  - _____ (Name of college or university), *¿es grande? ¿Es pequeño/a?* (Pantomime gestures for *grande* and *pequeño/a*.)
  - *¿Hay muchas residencias estudiantiles? ¿Los estudiantes prefieren apartamentos?*
  - *Su especialización/concentración,* (write the word on the board) *¿es matemáticas? ¿historia? ¿español? ¿biología? ¿arte?*

Note

The *Puntos de partida* Online Learning Center includes an interview with a Hispanic-American student, who answers questions similar to those in the preceding *Suggestions*.

◄ Unos estudiantes universitarios que hablan de (*who are talking about*) las clases

Resources

For Students

- Workbook
- Laboratory Manual and Laboratory Audio Program
- Quia™ Online Workbook and Online Laboratory Manual
- Video on CD
- Interactive CD-ROM
- *Puntos de partida* Online Learning Center (**www.mhhe.com/puntos7**)

For Instructors

- *Instructor's Manual and Resource Kit*, "Chapter-by-Chapter" Supplementary Materials
- Overhead Transparencies 7–13
- Testing Program
- Test Generator
- Video Program
- Audioscript
- *Puntos de partida* Online Learning Center (**www.mhhe.com/puntos7**)

En la **universidad**

CULTURA

- **Perspectivas culturales**

  Entrevista cultural: Los hispanos en los Estados Unidos

  Entre amigos: ¿Qué clases tomas?

  Conozca a... los hispanos en los Estados Unidos

- **Nota cultural:** Universities in the Hispanic World

- **En los Estados Unidos y el Canadá:** Jaime Escalante

- **Literatura de los Estados Unidos:** Sandra Cisneros

- **Lectura:** Las universidades hispánicas

VOCABULARIO

- En la clase
- Las materias

PRONUNCIACIÓN

- Diphthongs and Linking

GRAMÁTICA

1 Singular Nouns: Gender and Articles

2 Nouns and Articles: Plural Forms

3 Subject Pronouns: Present Tense of **-ar** Verbs; Negation

4 Asking *Yes/No* Questions

Entrevista cultural

Carlos Rivera
San Antonio, Texas ▶

♻ Reciclado

Encourage students to generate cognate adjectives by asking:

- *¿Cómo son los estudiantes en _____ (name of university)?*
- *¿Son inteligentes? ¿elegantes? ¿idealistas? ¿interesantes? ¿pesimistas? ¿responsables? ¿serios? ¿extrovertidos?*

You can also call on individual students to provide additional adjectives describing the students at your university.

Note

As you review the content with students, remind them about the *cognados* they studied in *Ante todo* and point out that the Spanish cognates for *articles* and *verbs*, respectively, are *artículos* and *verbos*.

Suggestion

Have students list their ideas about the Hispanic population in this country, including the areas where they live, the different groups, as well as food, music, and socio-political impact. When you finish the chapter, return to the lists and ask students what ideas they would change and/or add.

MULTIMEDIA

- The multimedia materials that accompany this chapter are referenced in the Student and Instructor's Editions with icons to help you identify when and where to incorporate them.

- The *Instructor's Manual and Resource Kit* (IM/RK) provides suggestions for using the multimedia materials in the classroom.

En la clase

Note

See the model for vocabulary presentation and other material in the *Capítulo 1 Vocabulario: Preparación* section of "Chapter-by-Chapter Supplementary Materials," in the IM.

Suggestions

- Hold up objects or photographs, or point to class members; model pronunciation while students listen. Use both definite and indefinite articles.
- Pronounce seven or eight vocabulary words from this chapter. Encourage students to identify the "class" of the word, that is, whether it responds to *¿Dónde?*, *¿Qué?*, or *¿Quién?*
- Identify and, at times, misidentify several objects or persons (point to them, show pictures, and so on). Have students respond *sí/no* or *correcto/incorrecto.*
- Indicate objects or persons and offer a choice: *¿Qué es esto, una mesa o una silla?* Have students answer in Spanish.
- Emphasize the difference between *librería* and *biblioteca.*
- Point out classroom objects, alternating the use of definite and indefinite articles. Students will learn the concept of gender later. For now, they should only listen to the words.
- Offer optional vocabulary: *el borrador, la carpeta, el estadio, el gimnasio, el laboratorio (de lenguas), el pupitre, el reloj, el sacapuntas, la tiza.*
- Check students' comprehension by asking the following *¿Cierto o falso?* questions.

1. *Una librería es un lugar. No es una persona.*
2. *La residencia es para los profesores.*
3. *Un consejero es una persona. No es un animal.*
4. *En clase, son necesarios un libro, unos escritorios, papel y un secretario.*
5. *En la clase de español, hay _____ estudiantes.*

VOCABULARIO Preparación

En la clase

¿Dónde? Lugares en la universidad

la biblioteca	the library
la cafetería	the cafeteria
la clase	the class
el edificio	the building
la librería	the bookstore
la oficina	the office
la residencia	the dormitory

¿Quién? Personas

el bibliotecario	the (male) librarian
la bibliotecaria	the (female) librarian

el compañero de clase	the (male) classmate
la compañera de clase	the (female) classmate
el compañero de cuarto	the (male) roommate
la compañera de cuarto	the (female) roommate
el consejero	the (male) advisor
la consejera	the (female) advisor
el hombre	the man
la mujer	the woman
el secretario	the (male) secretary
la secretaria	the (female) secretary

MULTIMEDIA: Audio

Students can listen to and practice this chapter's vocabulary on the Online Learning Center (**www.mhhe.com/puntos7**) as well as on the Textbook Listening CD, part of the Laboratory Audio Program.

Resources: Transparency 7

CULTURE

In most Hispanic countries, there is no equivalent of an academic or guidance counselor like those in this country.

■ ■ ■ Conversación

A. **¿Dónde están ahora** (*are they now*)**?** First, tell where these people are. Then identify the numbered people and things: 1 = **la consejera**, 2 = **la estudiante**, and so on. Refer to the drawing and lists on page 26 as much as you need to.

1. Están en _la clase_

2. Están en _la biblioteca_

3. Están en _La tienda_
   la cafetería

MATRÍCULA I TRIMESTRE

4. Están en _____ _la oficina_

B. **Identificaciones.** ¿Es hombre o mujer?

MODELO: ¿La consejera? → Es mujer.

1. ¿El profesor?
2. ¿La estudiante?
3. ¿El secretario?
4. ¿El estudiante?
5. ¿La bibliotecaria?
6. ¿El compañero de cuarto?

Vocabulario: Preparación

Con. A: Suggestions

- Point out the use of *están* for location.
- Give statements about the drawings. Have students tell whether your statements are true or false. For example: *Hay un consejero en la clase.* (falso)

Con. A: Variations

- Present *el → un, la → una* before doing this variation. Then have students identify persons and objects, using short complete sentences: *Hay un profesor / una profesora. Hay un(a)…*
- Have students tell where individual objects and persons are, using short complete sentences: *La estudiante está en la biblioteca.*

Con. A: Extension

Have students write short dialogues to present in front of the class. The only restriction is that they cannot say where the conversation is occurring. Students should guess where the speakers are based on the context clues they hear.

Con. B: Follow-Up

Have students give male counterparts of *la profesora, la secretaria, la estudiante, la consejera, la compañera de cuarto*. Then have them give the female counterparts of *el profesor, el consejero, el compañero de cuarto*.

☼ Heritage Speakers

- Anime a sus estudiantes hispanohablantes a nombrar otros objetos en el salón de clase, por ejemplo: *el reloj de pared, la luz,* etcétera.
- Pídales que expliquen en inglés la diferencia entre *dormitorio* (= *habitación*) y *residencia estudiantil* (= dorm).

- La palabra *bolígrafo* se usa mayormente en España. Anime a los estudiantes hispanohablantes a indicar cómo se dice *bolígrafo* en su casa o en el país de donde viene la familia (*la pluma, la lapicera, el rotulador*).

Resources: Transparency 8

Vocabulario: Preparación ■ 27

NOTA CULTURAL

Suggestion

Have students talk about the oldest universities in this country. Which ones are they? Where are they located? Compare the locations of these universities to the ones mentioned in the *Nota cultural*. What was important about the cities? What do they have in common? Are they still significant social and/or economic centers?

Note

These are some of the oldest universities of the United States and Canada.

United States

1636	Harvard University, Cambridge, Massachusetts
1693	College of William and Mary, Williamsburg, Virginia
1701	Yale University, New Haven, Connecticut
1746	Princeton University, Princeton, New Jersey
1754	Columbia University, New York City

Canada

1663	Université Laval, Quebec, Quebec
1785	University of New Brunswick, Fredericton, New Brunswick
1789	University of King's College, Halifax, Nova Scotia
1802	Saint Mary's University, Halifax, Nova Scotia
1818	Collége Universitaire de Saint-Boniface, Saint-Boniface, Manitoba; Dalhousie University, Halifax, Nova Scotia

Las materias

Suggestions

- Model the names of academic subjects. Have students stand each time they hear the name of a subject that they are taking.
- Point out the many cognates that end in *-ía* and *-ción*.
- Explain that another word for *la computación* is *la informática*.
- Have students generate as many words as possible that they associate with the following categories: *las ciencias, la sicología, la biblioteca, el diccionario, el lápiz, el libro, el comercio.*
- Offer the following optional vocabulary: *la antropología, la biografía, la contabilidad* (accounting), *la geografía, la geología, la ingeniería, el mercadeo, el periodismo.*

NOTA CULTURAL

Universities in the Hispanic World

Universities have a long history in the Spanish-speaking world. The very first university in the western hemisphere was **la Universidad de Santo Domingo,** founded in 1538 in what is now the Dominican Republic. Other early universities in this hemisphere include **la Real y Pontificia Universidad de América** (Mexico City, 1553) and **la Universidad de San Marcos** (Lima, Peru, 1571). Early Spanish colonial cities were meticulously designed and planned, and it is no accident that these universities were established in three of the most important cities. The Spaniards already had almost 800 years of experience with university-level education. **La Universidad de Salamanca,** one of the oldest universities in the world, was founded in 1220 in Salamanca, Spain.

Esta estatua de Fray Luis de León está en la Universidad de Salamanca. La Universidad, que (which) data del año 1220 (mil doscientos veinte), es una de las más antiguas (oldest) del mundo. ▶

Las materias

The names for most of these subject areas are cognates. See if you can recognize their meaning without looking at the English equivalent. You should learn in particular the names of subject areas that are of interest to you.

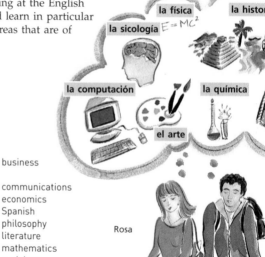

la física   la historia
la sicología $E = MC^2$
la computación   la química   el inglés
el arte

Rosa   Javier

la administración de empresas	business
las comunicaciones	communications
la economía	economics
el español	Spanish
la filosofía	philosophy
la literatura	literature
las matemáticas	mathematics
la sociología	sociology
las ciencias	sciences
las humanidades	humanities
las lenguas (extranjeras)	(foreign) languages

28 ■ Veintiocho

National Standards: Connections

Provide information students may need to complete *Conversación A* on p. 29.

1. Dr. Joyce Brothers (1928–): A famous psychologist who earned her Ph.D. from Columbia University in 1957. She was the second contestant to win the $64,000 Question television show.

Sigmund Freud (1856–1939): Austrian author and father of psychoanalysis.

2. Socrates (470 B.C.–399 B.C.): A celebrated Greek philosopher born in Athens, Greece. Nietzsche (1844–1900): A famous philologist and philosopher born in Rocken, Prussia.

■ ■ ■ Conversación

A. Asociaciones. ¿Con qué materia(s) asocia usted las siguientes (*following*) cosas y las siguientes personas?

1. el nitrógeno, el hidrógeno
2. la doctora Joyce Brothers, el doctor Sigmund Freud
3. NBC, CBS
4. Sócrates, Nietzsche
5. Mark Twain, Toni Morrison, J. K. Rowling
6. Frida Kahlo, Pablo Picasso
7. Microsoft, IBM
8. la civilización azteca, una guerra (*war*) civil

B. ¿Qué estudias? (*What are you studying?*) The right-hand column lists a number of university subjects. Tell about your academic interests by creating sentences using one word or phrase from each column. You can tell what you *are* studying (**Estudio…**), *want* to study (**Deseo estudiar…**), *need* to study (**Necesito estudiar…**), and *like* to study (**Me gusta estudiar…**). Using the word **no** makes the sentence negative.

(No) Estudio _____.
(No) Deseo estudiar _____.
(No) Necesito estudiar _____.
(No) Me gusta estudiar _____.

+

español, francés, inglés
arte, filosofía, literatura, música
ciencias políticas, historia
antropología, sicología, sociología
biología, física, química
matemáticas, computación
¿ ?

NOTA COMUNICATIVA

Palabras interrogativas

You have already used a number of interrogative words and phrases to get information. Those and some other useful ones are listed here. You will learn more in later chapters.

¿a qué hora?	¿A qué hora es la clase?	¿cuántos?, ¿cuántas?	¿Cuántos días hay en una semana?
¿cómo?	¿Cómo estás? ¿Cómo es Gloria Estefan? ¿Cómo te llamas?		¿Cuántas naciones hay en Sudamérica?
¿cuál?*	¿Cuál es la capital de Colombia?	¿dónde?	¿Dónde está España?
¿cuándo?	¿Cuándo es la fiesta?	¿qué?*	¿Qué es un hospital? ¿Qué es esto (*this*)?
¿cuánto?	¿Cuánto es?		¿Qué hora es?
		¿quién?	¿Quién es el presidente?

Note that in Spanish the voice falls at the end of questions that begin with interrogative words.

¿Qué es un tren?   ¿Cómo estás?

---

*Use **¿qué?** to mean *what?* when you are asking for a definition or an explanation. Use **¿cuál?** to mean *what?* in all other circumstances. See also **Gramática 29** in **Capítulo 9**.

Vocabulario: Preparación   Veintinueve ■ **29**

National Standards: Connections (*continued*)

3. Mark Twain (1835–1910): Famous American author born as Samuel Clemens in Hannibal, Missouri. He was the author of *The Adventures of Tom Sawyer* and *Huckleberry Finn*. Toni Morrison (1931–): Born in Lorain, Ohio, she was the first black woman to receive the Nobel Prize in literature. J. K. Rowling (1965–): Born in Chepstow,

Gwent, England. She is the author of the *Harry Potter* series.
4. Frida Kahlo (1907–1954): Mexican surrealist artist who was married to Diego Rivera. Pablo Picasso (1881–1973): Famous Spanish painter born in Malaga, Spain.

Con. A: Extension

Hold up various books that students have at their desks and have them identify by the titles the subjects for which they use the books. Then have students identify the classes for which they might need the following books: *Introducción a Pascal*, *La revolución de los zares*, *Mein Kampf*, *La familia*, *Cómo usar el telescopio*, *Los microbios*.

Con. B: Variation

Invite students to play the role of *consejero/a* and advise incoming freshman on what to study, depending on their majors. Follow these models: *Usted necesita estudiar _____. Usted necesita tomar _____ créditos de _____.* Sample majors: *un estudiante de inglés, un estudiante de biología, un estudiante de ciencias políticas, un estudiante de francés.* Other words students may need to know are: *campo* or *especialización*, to indicate student majors in an academic subject or discipline.

NOTA COMUNICATIVA

Suggestion

Have students tell what interrogative words they associate with the following information. Then have them ask the questions that would result in these answers.

1. *¡A las tres en punto!*
2. *En el centro de la península.*
3. *Soy profesor.*
4. *Muy bien, gracias.*
5. *¡Es muy arrogante!*
6. *Hay 5 millones (de habitantes).*
7. *Dos pesos.*
8. *(La capital) Es Caracas.*
9. *Es un instrumento musical.*
10. *Mañana, a las cinco.*
11. *Son las once.*
12. *Soy Roberto González.*

Notes

- This section is a review. Students have probably seen and heard all of these forms already.
- Plural forms of most interrogatives are not presented until *Capítulo 9*.

Model the names of the academic subjects before asking for student responses. Then encourage students to listen to their classmates. Check for comprehension: *Tim, ¿qué estudia Susie?* If students do not recall the names of the subjects spontaneously, give them clues: *¿Estudia física?*

Con. C: Suggestions

■ Use the drawings as a springboard for questions that reenter all of the *Ante todo* material. Encourage students to listen to questions for meaning only and to respond with one word or phrase. Top drawing: *¿Quién es el hombre? ¿Quién es la mujer? ¿Cuántos niños* (pantomime) *hay?*, and so on.

■ Have students form questions about the drawings. Then have them answer questions asked by others, inventing details. Coach them to keep the sequence of questions going.

Con. D: Extension

Make a handout that requires students to interview their class-mates. Examples may include:

¿Quién...
   estudia biología, alemán, ... ?
   no estudia los fines de semana?
   estudia solamente por la noche/ por la mañana?
   estudia en la biblioteca, en la cafetería, en la residencia estudiantil?

Have students report what they found out about their classmates to the entire class.

C. **Preguntas.** What questions are being asked by the indicated people? More than one answer is possible for some items. Select questions from the following list or create your own questions.

PREGUNTAS

¿A qué hora es el programa sobre (*about*) México?
¿Cómo estás?
¿Cuál es la capital de Colombia?
¿Cuándo es la fiesta?
¿Cuántas personas hay en la fiesta?

¿Dónde está Buenos Aires?
¿Dónde está el diccionario?
¿Qué es esto?
¿Qué hay en la televisión hoy?
¿Quién es?

D. **Entrevista.** Work with a classmate and use the following questions to interview each other. Find out as much as possible about each other's classes and schedules. Follow up your answers by returning the question or asking for more information.

MODELO: ESTUDIANTE 1: ¿Qué estudias este semestre/trimestre (*this term*)?
ESTUDIANTE 2: Estudio matemáticas, historia, literatura y español. Y tú, ¿qué estudias?

1. ¿Qué estudias este semestre/trimestre?
2. ¿Cuántas horas estudias por semana (*per week*)?
3. ¿Cuándo estudias, por la mañana, por la tarde o por la noche?
4. ¿Dónde te gusta estudiar?
5. ¿Quién es tu profesor favorito (profesora favorita)? (Mi profesor...)
6. ¿Cuál es tu clase favorita? (Mi clase...)

Need more practice?

■ Workbook and Laboratory Manual
■ Interactive CD-ROM
■ Online Learning Center (www.mhhe.com/ puntos7)

Capítulo 1: En la universidad

Resources: Transparency 9

Refrán

«Estudiante que no estudia, en nada bueno se ocupa.»

Write the *refrán* on the board. Have students guess the meaning of *nada* and *se ocupa*. What are some similar sayings in English? (*Idle hands, idle minds.*)

Two successive weak vowels (**i, u**) or a combination of a strong vowel (**a, e,** or **o**) and a weak vowel (**i** or **u**) are pronounced as a single syllable in Spanish, forming a *diphthong* (**un diptongo**): **L**u**is, s**ie**te, c**u**aderno.**

When words are combined to form phrases, clauses, and sentences, they are linked together in pronunciation. In spoken Spanish, it is usually impossible to hear the word boundaries—that is, where one word ends and another begins.

A. Vocales. Más práctica con las vocales.

1. hablar	regular	reservar	ahora
2. trece	clase	papel	general
3. pizarra	oficina	bolígrafo	libro
4. hombre	profesor	dólares	los
5. universidad	gusto	lugar	mujer

B. Diptongos. Practique las siguientes palabras.

1. historia	secretaria	gracias	estudiante	materia
2. bien	Oviedo	siete	ciencias	diez
3. secretario	biblioteca	adiós	diccionario	Antonio
4. cuaderno	Eduardo	el Ecuador	Guatemala	Managua
5. bueno	nueve	luego	pueblo	Venezuela

C. Frases y oraciones (*sentences*). Practice saying each phrase or sentence as if it were one long word, pronounced without a pause.

1. el papel y el lápiz
2. la profesora y la estudiante
3. las ciencias y las matemáticas
4. la historia y la sicología
5. la secretaria y el profesor
6. el inglés y el español
7. la clase en la biblioteca
8. el libro en la librería
9. Es la una y media.
10. Hay siete estudiantes en la oficina.
11. No estoy muy bien.
12. No hay un consejero aquí.

Pronunciación: Diphthongs and Linking

Notes
■ The letter *y* is pronounced like the vowel *i* when standing alone (*y* means *and*) or when ending a word (*¡ay!, hay*).
■ Hint for remembering weak vowels: *u* and *i* are weak.

Preliminary Exercise
Pronounce these English and Spanish words in random order. Have students identify each as *español* or *inglés.*

English	**Spanish**
Ray	*rey*
lay	*ley*
eye	*hay*
soy	*soy*

A: Suggestion
Review the pronunciation of single vowel sounds before beginning the activity.

A: Note
Hombre should not be pronounced as *hambre* (hunger); *dólares* should not sound like *dolores* (pains).

B: Follow-Up
Have students sound out the vowels and diphthongs first; then add consonant sounds:

1. *la civilización india*
2. *los negocios internacionales*
3. *una bibliotecaria italiana*
4. *una especialidad fascinante*
5. *los tiempos verbales*

C: Suggestion
Before students attempt to pronounce the phrases, do the activity as a dictation, and emphasize the linking effect.

C: Extension
9. *Hay siete edificios en la universidad.*
10. *Estudio historia y comercio.*
11. *Deseo estudiar computación y matemáticas.*
12. *Necesito un diccionario y una mochila.*

☼ Heritage Speakers

Escriba la siguiente canción en la pizarra para que los estudiantes la copien. Pídales que graben las voces de hispanohablantes a quienes conocen mientras leen la selección. Luego toque las grabaciones en clase para que los estudiantes oigan la variedad de acentos.

¡Al Uruguay, iguay!
Yo no voy, voy
porque temo naufragar.
Mándeme a París
si es que le da igual.

Notes

- The *minidiálogo* introduces material that appears in both *Gramática 1* and *2*. Continue to use the previous guidelines for the presentation of the *minidiálogos*.
- Remind students that the English equivalent for *minidiálogos* is always provided at the foot of the page.
- Spanish equivalents for English grammatical terms will be given throughout this text.
- Point out to students that the grammar explanations are presented in a two-column format, with the explanation on the left and examples with important material to be learned on the right.

Follow-Up

1. *¿Dónde están las personas del diálogo?*
2. *¿Quiénes son?*
3. *¿Hay profesor o profesora en esta clase?*
4. *¿Cuántos estudiantes hay en la clase?*

GRAMÁTICA

1 Identifying People, Places, and Things •
Singular Nouns: Gender and Articles*

En *la clase* del *profesor* Durán: *El primer día*

PROFESOR DURÁN: Aquí está *el programa* del *curso.* Son necesarios *el libro de texto* y *un diccionario.* También hay *una lista* de novelas y libros de poesía.

ESTUDIANTE 1: ¡Es *una lista* infinita!

ESTUDIANTE 2: Sí, y los libros cuestan demasiado.

ESTUDIANTE 1: No, *el problema* no es *el precio* de los libros. ¡Es *el tiempo* para leer los libros!

Elija (*Choose*) las palabras o frases correctas según el diálogo.

1. La clase del profesor Durán es de (literatura / filosofía).
2. En el curso del profesor Durán (es necesario / no es necesario) leer (*to read*) mucho.
3. En un curso de literatura (es lógico / no es lógico) usar un diccionario.

To name people, places, things, or ideas, you need to be able to use nouns. In Spanish, all *nouns* (**los sustantivos**) have either masculine or feminine *gender* (**el género**). This is a purely grammatical feature of nouns; it does not mean that Spanish speakers perceive things or ideas as having male or female attributes.

Since the gender of all nouns must be memorized, it is best to learn the definite article along with the noun; that is, learn **el lápiz** rather than just **lápiz**. The definite article will be given with nouns in vocabulary lists in this book.

	Masculine Nouns		**Feminine Nouns**	
Definite Articles	el hombre	*the man*	la mujer	*the woman*
	el libro	*the book*	la mesa	*the table*
Indefinite Articles	un hombre	*a (one) man*	una mujer	*a (one) woman*
	un libro	*a (one) book*	una mesa	*a (one) table*

---

*The grammar sections of Puntos de partida are numbered consecutively throughout the book. If you need to review a particular grammar point, the index will refer you to its page number.

In Professor Durán's class: The first day PROFESSOR DURÁN: Here's the course syllabus. The textbook and a dictionary are required. There is also a list of novels and poetry books. STUDENT 1: It's a really long list! STUDENT 2: Yes, and the books cost too much. STUDENT 1: No, the problem isn't the price of the books. It's the time to read the books!

National Standards: Comparisons

Like Spanish, many other languages have the concept of gender. For example, French, Italian, and Portuguese have both masculine and feminine nouns. In German, nouns can be masculine, feminine, and neuter. English has gender as well (masculine, feminine, and neuter), but it is not as obvious. Have students identify the gender of the subjects in the following sentences using the underlined possessive adjectives as a guide.

The boy has <u>his</u> book.
The girl has <u>her</u> homework.
The committee has <u>its</u> meeting in October.

Gender

A. Nouns that refer to male beings and most other nouns that end in **-o** are *masculine* (**masculino**) in gender.	**sustantivos masculinos:** hombre, libro
B. Nouns that refer to female beings and most other nouns that end in **-a, -ción, -tad,** and **-dad** are *feminine* (**femenino**) in gender.	**sustantivos femeninos:** mujer, mesa, nación, libertad, universidad
C. Nouns that have other endings and that do not refer to either male or female beings may be masculine or feminine. The gender of these words must be memorized.	el lápiz, la clase, la tarde, la noche
D. Many nouns that refer to people indicate gender . . . 1. by changing the last vowel OR	el compañero → la compañera el bibliotecario → la bibliotecaria
2. by adding **-a** to the last consonant of the masculine form to make it feminine	un profesor → una profesora
E. Many other nouns that refer to people have a single form for both masculine and feminine genders. Gender is indicated by an article.	**el** estudiante (*the male student*) → **la** estudiante (*the female student*) **el** cliente (*the male client*) → **la** cliente (*the female client*) **el** dentista (*the male dentist*) → **la** dentista (*the female dentist*)
However, a few nouns that end in **-e** also have a feminine form that ends in **-a.**	el presidente → la presidenta el dependiente (*the male clerk*) → la dependienta (*the female clerk*)

 A common exception to the normal rules of gender is the word **el día,** which is masculine in gender. Many words ending in **-ma** are also masculine: **el problema, el programa, el sistema,** and so on. Watch for these exceptions as you continue your study of Spanish.

Articles

A. In English, there is only one *definite article* (**el artículo definido**): *the.* In Spanish, the definite article for masculine singular nouns is **el;** for feminine singular nouns it is **la.**	definite article: *the* m. sing. → **el** f. sing. → **la**

Gender

Emphasis D: Suggestion
Emphasize that *la persona* is used whether the person talked about is male or female: *Ernesto es una buena persona.*

Emphasis E: Suggestions
- Point out that, like *estudiante,* some words refer to both men and women: *turista, artista, dentista.* The feminine of the word *poeta* is traditionally *poetisa,* but, is often replaced today by *la poeta.*
- Explain that the "matching" between the article and the noun is called *la concordancia* (agreement).

Emphasis E: Notes
- Many Spanish speakers use *cliente / clienta, presidente / presidenta, dependiente / dependienta.*
- Some *-pa* and *-ta* words are also masculine: *el mapa, el cometa, el planeta.* Like the *-ma* words, they are of Greek origin.

 Heritage Speakers

- Pídales a los estudiantes hispanohablantes que le den otros sustantivos que no cambian al referirse a hombres o mujeres, como *turista, artista* o *dentista.*

- Pregúnteles si usan *clienta, presidenta* o *dependienta.*

- Señáleles que en algunos países hispanohablantes se dice *la presidente* o *la jefe* en vez de *la presidenta* o *la jefa. La presidenta* también puede significar *la esposa del presidente.*

- Pídales a los estudiantes hispanohablantes que investiguen los géneros de los nuevos términos tecnológicos (por ejemplo, *el impresor* y *la impresora, el grabador* y *la grabadora, el Internet* y *la Internet*).

Articles

Emphasis B: Suggestions

- Point out the words *un/una* can mean *one*, *a*, or *an*.
- Remind students that in English, too, the context in which we find a word can determine our understanding of it. Have students consider how they know what the word *will* means in the examples *Will you do this?*, *Will and I went to the park*, and *The lawyer wrote the will*.

Emphasis B: Note

Plural forms of the definite and indefinite articles are presented in *Gramática 2* of this chapter.

Preliminary Exercises

- As a gender quiz, give students these words and have them tell whether each is *femenina* or *masculina*:

1. artista   6. hombre
2. mujer   7. estudiante
3. noche   8. día
4. programa   9. compañero
5. comedia   10. ciudad

- Have students try the *Autoprueba* before they begin the *Práctica* section.

Prác. A: Follow-Up

Have students give the feminine or masculine counterparts for the following words (ask for articles with answers).

1. el hombre
2. la compañera
3. el secretario
4. un cliente
5. una presidenta
6. un turista

Prác. A: Extension

13. fiesta   17. apartamento
14. clase   18. cuarto
15. puerta   19. cerveza
16. amigo   20. lápiz

Prác. B: Variation

Vary *Paso 1* of this activity by using the following model to form the sentences: *estudiante/librería → El estudiante está en la librería.*

Prác. B: Extension

Have students continue the activity with the words from *Práctica A*.

B. In English, the singular *indefinite article* (**el artículo indefinido**) is *a* or *an*. In Spanish, the indefinite article, like the definite article, must agree with the gender of the noun: **un** for masculine nouns, **una** for feminine nouns. **Un** and **una** can mean *one* as well as *a* or *an*. Context determines meaning.

> indefinite article: *a, an*
>
> m. sing. → **un**
> f. sing. → **una**

AUTOPRUEBA*

Give the correct definite article: **el** or **la**.

1. _el_ libro   3. _la_ oficina
2. _la_ mujer   4. _el_ escritorio

Answers: 1. el 2. la 3. la 4. el

■ ■ ■ Práctica

A. Artículos

Paso 1. Dé (*Give*) el artículo definido apropiado (**el, la**).

1. escritorio _el_   5. hombre _el_   9. mujer _la_
2. biblioteca _la_   6. diccionario _el_   10. nación _la_
3. bolígrafo _el_   7. universidad _la_   11. bibliotecario _el_
4. mochila _la_   8. dinero _el_   12. calculadora _la_

Paso 2. Ahora (*Now*) dé el artículo indefinido apropiado (**un, una**).

1. día _un_   4. lápiz _una_   7. papel _un_
2. mañana _una_   5. clase _una_   8. condición _una_
3. problema _un_   6. noche _una_   9. programa _un_

B. Escenas de la universidad

Paso 1. Haga una oración (*Form a sentence*) con las palabras (*words*) indicadas.

> MODELO: estudiante / librería → Hay un estudiante en la librería.

1. consejero / oficina   6. bolígrafo / silla
2. profesora / clase   7. palabra / papel
3. lápiz / mesa   8. oficina / residencia
4. cuaderno / escritorio   9. compañero / biblioteca
5. libro / mochila

Paso 2. Now create new sentences by changing one of the words in each item in **Paso 1.** If you do this with a partner, try to come up with as many variations as possible.

> MODELO: Hay un estudiante en *la residencia.* (Hay *una profesora* en la librería.)

Need more practice?

- Workbook and Laboratory Manual
- Interactive CD-ROM
- Online Learning Center (www.mhhe.com/puntos7)

Autoprueba means self-quiz. These self-quizzes appear at the end of **Gramática** sections and will help you determine if you understand the basics of the grammar point.

Capítulo 1: En la universidad

National Standards: Communication

Have students give the male or female counterparts, as needed:

1. *Pablo Ortiz es consejero. ¿Y Paula Delibes?*
2. *Camilo es estudiante. ¿Y Conchita?*
3. *Carmen Leal es profesora. ¿Y Carlos Ortega?*
4. *Juan Luis es dependiente. ¿Y Juanita?*
5. *Josefina es una amiga de Luz. ¿Y José?*

■ ■ ■ Conversación

A. **Definiciones.** Con un compañero / una compañera, definan estas palabras en español según el modelo.

> **MODELO:** biblioteca / edificio → ESTUDIANTE 1: ¿La biblioteca?
> ESTUDIANTE 2: Es un edificio.

Categorías: cosa, edificio, materia, persona

1. cliente / persona   **4.** dependiente / ¿ ?   **7.** computación / ¿ ?
2. bolígrafo / cosa   **5.** hotel (*m.*) / ¿ ?   **8.** inglés / ¿ ?
3. residencia / edificio   **6.** calculadora / ¿ ?   **9.** ¿ ?

B. **Asociaciones.** Identifique una cosa y una persona que usted asocia con los siguientes lugares.

> **MODELO:** la clase → una silla, un profesor

1. la biblioteca   **2.** la librería   **3.** una oficina   **4.** la residencia *mujer*

bibliotecara   *librero*   *secretaria*

---

2   Identifying People, Places, and Things • Nouns and Articles: Plural Forms

Cursos de Idiomas en el **Extranjero**

Financiación **SIN INTERESES** en 3, 6 ó 12 meses

- Cursos para jóvenes de 7 a 17 años
- Cursos para adultos a partir de 18 años
- Cursos en Universidades: Idioma general y/o técnico
- Minimasters en Universidades USA, Inglaterra e Irlanda
- Programa residencial en Sevilla y/o Madrid con inglés
- Preparación para TOEFL, GMAT, SAT, GRE, USMLE
- Cursos de idiomas en Madrid

Instituto ProLengua ofrece pagar su curso aplazado en 3, 6 ó 12 meses

🌐 **INSTITUTO PROLENGUA**

Infórmate **902-253 797**

- You can find many nouns in this ad. Can you guess the meaning of most of them?
- Some of the nouns in this ad are plural. Can you tell how to make nouns plural in Spanish, based on these nouns?
- Look for the Spanish equivalent of the following words.

  adult   preparation   program   course

- **Idioma** is another word for *language*, and it is a false cognate. It never means *idiom*.
- Using the vocabulary in the ad, guess what **en el extranjero** means.

	Singular	Plural	
Nouns Ending in a Vowel	el libro	los libros	*the books*
	la mesa	las mesas	*the tables*
	un libro	unos libros	*some books*
	una mesa	unas mesas	*some tables*
Nouns Ending in a Consonant	la universidad	las universidades	*the universities*
	un papel	unos papeles	*some papers*

Gramática   Treinta y cinco ■ 35

☀ **Heritage Speakers**

- Anime a los estudiantes a ayudar a sus compañeros monolingües a traducir el anuncio.
- Invite a un estudiante hispanohablante a leer el anuncio en voz alta para que la clase oiga la pronunciación de las vocales.

Con. A: Suggestion

Use place and person names from your campus and city as cues.

Con. A: Extension

10. *la librería*
11. *el profesor*
12. *la historia*
13. *el cuaderno*
14. *el libro*
15. *el dinero*
16. *la compañera de clase*
17. *la física*
18. *el manual de laboratorio*
19. *el laboratorio de lenguas*
20. *el profesor / la profesora* (name)

Con. B: Note

Clase means both *class* and *classroom*. The context of the sentence differentiates them.

Con. B: Extension

5. *el laboratorio de lenguas*
6. *la capital de los Estados Unidos (del Canadá)*
7. *la universidad*
8. *Puerto Rico*

Con. B: Follow-Up

Have students compare their lists. What items are similar? What items are different?

Gramática 2

Nouns and Articles: Plural Forms

Note

Review the *minidiálogo* that precedes *Gramática 1* before presenting the material in this section.

Suggestions

- Have students form small groups to translate the main points of the ad.
- Have students read the ad out loud to practice pronunciation of vowels.
- Point out that this advertisement did not actually appear in newspapers, but that it accurately reflects those that are seen on a regular basis in Spain and Latin America.
- Point out that *idioma* is another word for language, and it is a false cognate. It never means *idiom*.

Emphasis A: Suggestion

Point out that the stress does not shift when plurals are formed. Word stress and accentuation will not be formally presented until *Capítulo 3*, so you may prefer to discuss addition/deletion of accent marks in plurals now.

Emphasis C: Suggestion

Point out that even if a group includes only one male but many females, the masculine plural form is used. If the feminine plural is used, it excludes any male membership in the group: *los estudiantes* refers to males or females; *las estudiantes* includes only females.

Preliminary Exercises

■ Have students listen to the following words and tell whether they are singular or plural.

1. *el diccionario*
2. *la librería*
3. *los papeles*
4. *el lápiz*
5. *unos bolígrafos*
6. *las clases*
7. *una profesora*
8. *las universidades*

■ Remind students to try the *Autoprueba* before they begin the *Práctica* section.

Prác. A: Follow-Up

Have students give the plural of the following.

1. *Juana, una estudiante; Juana y Elena...*
2. *Ramón, un extranjero; Ramón y Ricardo...*
3. *Ramón, un extranjero; Ramón y Raquel...*
4. *David, un amigo; David y Cecilia...*
5. *David, un amigo; David y Roberto...*

Prác. B: Extension

Have students provide examples of certain nouns (some plural, some singular). Use names in the class or at the university (the name of the instructor, the names of two or three students together, the name of the president, the names of professors, and so on).

A. Spanish nouns that end in a vowel form plurals by adding **-s.** Nouns that end in a consonant add **-es.** Nouns that end in the consonant **-z** change the **-z** to **-c** before adding **-es: lápiz → lápices.**

Plurals in Spanish:

> vowel + **s**
> consonant + **es**
> **-z → -ces**

B. The definite and indefinite articles also have plural forms: **el → los, la → las, un → unos, una → unas. Unos** and **unas** mean *some, several,* or *a few.*

> **el → los**   **un → unos**
> **la → las**   **una → unas**

C. In Spanish, the masculine plural form of a noun is used to refer to a group that includes both males and females.

> **los** amig**os**
> *the friends* (both male and female)
>
> **unos** extranjer**os**
> *some foreigners* (both male and female)

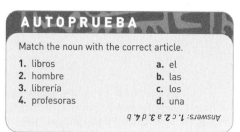

AUTOPRUEBA

Match the noun with the correct article.

1. libros   a. el
2. hombre   b. las
3. librería   c. los
4. profesoras   d. una

Answers: 1. c 2. a 3. d 4. b

■ ■ ■ Práctica

A. **Singular → plural.** Dé la forma plural.

1. la mesa
2. el papel
3. el amigo
4. la oficina
5. un cuaderno
6. un lápiz
7. una universidad
8. un bolígrafo
9. un edificio

B. **Plural → singular.** Dé la forma singular.

1. los profesores
2. las calculadoras
3. las bibliotecarias
4. los estudiantes
5. unos hombres
6. unas tardes
7. unas residencias
8. unas sillas
9. unos escritorios

36 ■ Treinta y seis

Need more practice?

■ Workbook and Laboratory Manual
■ Interactive CD-ROM
■ Online Learning Center (www.mhhe.com/puntos7)

Capítulo 1: En la universidad

National Standards: Comparison

Point out that Spanish, like English, has nouns that are used mainly or only in the plural. Many of these are the same in English and Spanish. Here are several examples:

> binoculars (*los prismáticos, los gemelos*)
> eyeglasses (*los anteojos, los lentes*)
> pants (*los pantalones*)
> scissors (*las tijeras*)

Ask students if they can think of additional English examples.

■ ■ ■ Conversación

A. Identificaciones. Identifique las personas, las cosas y los lugares.

> MODELO: Hay _____ en _____. → Hay *unos estudiantes* en *la clase.*

Palabras útiles

la computadora
el experimento
la planta
el teléfono

1.

2.

B. ¡Ojo alerta! (*Eagle eye!*)*

Paso 1. ¿Cuáles son las semejanzas (*similarities*) y las diferencias entre los dos cuartos? Hay por lo menos (*at least*) seis diferencias.

> MODELO: En el dibujo A, hay _____.
> En el dibujo B, hay sólo (*only*) _____.
> En el escritorio del dibujo A, hay _____.
> En el escritorio del dibujo B, hay _____.

Palabras útiles

la alfombra (rug)
la almohada (pillow)
la cama (bed)
el cuadro (picture)
el espejo (mirror)
la lámpara (lamp)
el monitor

Ⓐ

Ⓑ

Paso 2. Ahora indique qué hay en su propio (*your own*) cuarto. Use palabras del **Paso 1.**

> MODELO: En mi cuarto hay _____. En mi escritorio hay _____.

_____

*In Spanish, activities like this one are often called **¡Ojo alerta!**

Gramática

Con. A: Suggestions

■ Encourage students to speak further about people, places, and things by asking questions such as: *¿Quién es? (¿Quiénes son?) ¿Qué es? ¿Cuántos/as _____ hay? ¿Dónde está(n)?*

■ Introduce *muchos/as.*

♻ **Reciclado:** Combine your review of numbers and questions with the practice of singular and plural forms, by asking questions such as: *¿Cuántos/as estudiantes / mesas / sillas / libros hay en la clase?* Remind students to use *hay* in their answers.

Con. B: Extension

Ask questions and pantomime keywords to elicit chapter vocabulary, for example, *¿Qué hay en nuestra (pantomime) (sala de) clase?*

♻ **Reciclado:** Have students form pairs to review cognates presented in the explanations and activities in *Ante todo* and scan the realia and drawings in that chapter and in *Capítulo 1.* Then invite them to give as many nouns as they can that fit into the following categories:

1. *lugares de la universidad*
2. *cosas en una librería*
3. *personas en una librería*
4. *problemas de los estudiantes*

Con B: Follow-Up

As a whole-class activity, ask students what things they associate with certain places, for example: *¿Qué hay en una oficina típica de la universidad? ¿Qué hay en una clase que no hay en una oficina? ¿y en la biblioteca?*

**Resources:
Transparencies 10, 11**

National Standards: Comparisons

The formation of plural nouns in Spanish is quite easy and predictable in comparison to English. Note that some English nouns ending in *-f* or *-fe* change to *-ves* in the plural (*wife → wives; calf → calves*). Others undergo a vowel change such as *fireman → firemen, foot → feet; goose → geese.* Some nouns ending in *-o* take *-s* in the plural while others take *-es* (*memo → memos; potato → potatoes*). Still, there are other nouns that do not change at all in the plural: *deer, fish,* and *sheep.* Pluralization of nouns in English is further complicated by the sheer number of borrowings from other languages. Have students give the plural forms for the following nouns: *antenna, fungus, addendum, appendix, parenthesis,* and *phenomenon.*

Note

The *minidiálogo* between Diego and Lupe introduces material that will appear in *Gramática 3*. You may prefer to focus on subject pronouns alone before introducing the *minidiálogo*. Continue to use the previous guidelines for *minidiálogo* presentation.

Suggestion

Model Lupe's possible responses to Diego's questions; encourage student repetition and expansion. Translate unfamiliar vocabulary on the board as you proceed.

1. *No, no pago mucho en cuentas de teléfono. ¿Trabajas?*
2. *No, ahora* (translate on board) *no trabajo. ¿Qué te gusta hacer* (translate)*?*
3. *Yo también bailo los fines de semana. Pero no busco libros de antropología. Busco libros de arte moderno.*

Follow-Up

Ask students if these statements are true for them [¿*sí o no?*]:

1. *Yo hablo francés (inglés).*
2. *Nosotros hablamos español (francés) en esta clase.* [Suggestion: Introduce *un poco*]
3. *Nosotros bailamos en esta clase.*
4. *Yo bailo muy mal (muy bien).*

Notes

- The subject of a sentence is the word or group of words about which something is said or asserted. Usually the subject indicates who or what performs the action of the sentence: *The girl threw the ball.*
- A pronoun (*pronombre*) is a word used in place of a noun or to represent a person (I, you): *She (the girl) threw the ball.*

Suggestion

Have students indicate the subjects in the following sentences:

1. Olga is going to write a message.
2. The car ran off the road.
3. Have Jack and Joyce arrived yet?
4. Love conquers all.

Subject Pronouns

Emphasis A: Suggestion

Point out that there is no Spanish equivalent for *it* as a subject.

---

3 | Expressing Actions • Subject Pronouns; Present Tense of -ar Verbs; Negation

Diego *habla* de su vida con su amiga Lupe

Imagine que usted es Lupe y conteste las preguntas de Diego. Use **no** si es necesario.

DIEGO: *Yo hablo* con mi familia con frecuencia. Por eso *pago* mucho en cuentas de teléfono. ¿Y *tú*?

LUPE: [...]

DIEGO: *Necesito* dinero para comprar libros. Por eso *enseño* inglés a un estudiante de matemáticas. ¿Y *tú*?

LUPE: [...]

DIEGO: En mi tiempo libre *escucho* música. También *toco* la guitarra. En las fiestas *bailo* mucho y *tomo* cerveza con mis amigos. Los fines de semana, *busco* libros de antropología en las librerías. ¿Y *tú*?

LUPE: [...]

Comprensión: ¿Cierto o falso?

1. Diego no habla mucho con su familia.
2. Es estudiante de ciencias.
3. No le gusta la música.
4. Es una persona introvertida y solitaria.
5. Habla francés.

Subject Pronouns

Subject Pronouns			
Singular		**Plural**	
yo	I	**nosotros / nosotras**	we
tú	you (*fam.*)	**vosotros / vosotras**	you (*fam. Sp.*)
usted (Ud.)*	you (*form.*)	**ustedes (Uds.)***	you (*form.*)
él	he	**ellos / ellas**	they
ella	she		

subject = the person or thing that performs the action

pronoun = a word that takes the place of a noun

Diego talks about his life with his friend Lupe Imagine that you are Lupe and answer Diego's questions. Use **no** if necessary.

DIEGO: I speak often with my family. That's why I pay a lot in telephone bills. And you? LUPE: [. . .] DIEGO: I need money to buy books. That's why I teach English to a math student. And you? LUPE: [. . .] DIEGO: In my spare time I listen to music. I also play the guitar. At parties I dance a lot and drink beer with my friends. On weekends, I look for anthropology books in bookstores. And you? LUPE: [. . .]

*****Usted** and **ustedes** are frequently abbreviated in writing as **Ud.** or **Vd.**, and **Uds.** or **Vds.**, respectively.

Point out that students have learned that there are four different ways to say *you* in Spanish: *tú/vosotros* and *usted/ustedes*. Although in English there is only one gramatically acceptable way to convey the third person, several dialectal forms have evolved in order to differentiate between singular and plural *you*. In casual speech, it is not uncommon to hear expressions such as *you all, y'all, you(s) guys,* and *you 'ens*. Although these forms are not considered to be gramatically correct, one can often hear them in daily conversations.

A. *Subject pronouns* (**Los pronombres personales**) can represent the person or thing that performs the action in a sentence.

In Spanish, several subject pronouns have masculine and feminine forms. The masculine plural form is used to refer to a group of males as well as to a group of males and females.

Mark → *he*	Marcos → **él**
Martha → *she*	Marta → **ella**
Mark and Paul → *they*	Marcos y Pablo → **ellos** (*all male*)
Mark and Martha → *they*	Marcos y Marta → **ellos** (*male and female*)
Martha and Emily → *they*	Marta y Emilia → **ellas** (*all female*)

B. Spanish has different words for *you*. In general, **tú** is used to refer to a close friend or a member of your family, while **usted** is used with people with whom the speaker has a more formal or distant relationship. The situations in which **tú** and **usted** are used also vary among different countries and regions.

tú → close friend, family member
usted (Ud.) → formal or distant relationship

C. In Latin America and in the United States and Canada, the plural for both **usted** and **tú** is **ustedes**. In Spain, however, **vosotros/vosotras** is the plural of **tú**, while **ustedes** is used as the plural of **usted** exclusively.

Latin America, North America

tú
usted (Ud.) → ustedes (Uds.)

Spain

tú → vosotros/vosotras
usted (Ud.) → ustedes (Uds.)

D. Subject pronouns are not used as frequently in Spanish as they are in English and may usually be omitted. You will learn more about the uses of Spanish subject pronouns in **Capítulo 2.**

Present Tense of -*ar* Verbs

Past ---------------------**PRESENT**---------------- Future
present

A. The *infinitive* (**el infinitivo**) of a verb indicates the action or state of being, with no reference to who or what performs the action or when it is done (present, past, or future). In Spanish all infinitives end in **-ar, -er,** or **-ir.** Infinitives in English are indicated by *to:* *to* speak, *to* eat, *to* live.

-ar:	hablar	*to speak*
-er:	comer	*to eat*
-ir:	vivir	*to live*

Gramática

Emphasis B: Suggestion

As you introduce *tú* and *Ud.*, review what students already know about formal and informal usages by asking them to address these questions to you or to another student, as appropriate.

1. *¿Cómo está?*
2. *¿Le gusta la universidad?*
3. *¿Te gusta la clase de español?*
4. *¿Cómo se llama Ud.?*
5. *¿Cómo te llamas?*
6. *¿Cómo estás?*

Emphasis C: Note

Vosotros will not be actively practiced in the regular activities and exercises of *Puntos de partida.*

Preliminary Exercises

Have students answer the following questions.

■ What subject pronoun would you use in English to speak about the following persons?

1. yourself
2. two men
3. a female child
4. yourself (male) and your sister
5. yourself (female) and your mother
6. your uncle

■ What subject pronoun would you use in Spanish to speak to the following persons?

1. *una profesora*
2. *unos consejeros*
3. *un estudiante*
4. *unas amigas*
5. *tu mamá*
6. *un dependiente*

■ What subject pronoun would you substitute in Spanish for each of the following persons?

1. *tu amiga Eva*
2. *Luis*
3. *Fausto y yo* (male)
4. *tú* (female) *y Cecilia*
5. *tú* (male) *y Cecilia*
6. *Vicente y David*
7. *la señora Álvarez y tú*

Present Tense of -*ar* Verbs

Note

A new feature in this edition of *Puntos de partida* are the verb tense timelines. The timelines will appear with *Gramática* sections that cover verbs, especially when a new tense is introduced. The timelines will help students, particularly visual learners, understand the relationship between the tenses and get a "fix" on the specific tense they are learning in a given grammar section.

Gramática ■ **39**

CULTURE

■ Emphasize the difference between *tú* and *Ud.*, explaining that the nature of the relationship between two people determines the form they will use. Point out that the contexts for *tú* and *Ud.* are very different throughout the Spanish-speaking world, and they vary from country to country, and from one generation to another. In some countries (for example:

Spain, Puerto Rico, and Cuba) people are much more liberal in the use of *tú* than others (for example: Colombia, Honduras, or Costa Rica).

■ Remind students that people in some countries (among them, Argentina, Uruguay, and Costa Rica) use *vos* instead of *tú*. This form will not be presented formally in *Puntos de partida.*

Suggestions

- Model the pronunciation of each infinitive several times. Then use the *yo* form of each in a brief, simple sentence about yourself, repeating several times and pantomiming if necessary.
- Have students generate all forms of one verb, after you give the subject pronouns.
- Transform the base sentence into a simple *Ud.* question directed to a student, coaching him or her to answer using the *yo* form. Example: *bailar → Me gusta bailar. Bailo muy bien. Y Ud., ¿baila bien?*
- Have students generate all forms of one verb, after you give the subject pronouns.
- Ask students *¿Cómo se dice* I/we dance, I/we sing, I/we buy... ?
- Emphasize *tocar* (music), and those infinitives that include prepositions in their meaning.
- Offer the following optional verbs: *caminar, fumar, hablar por teléfono, mirar* (la televisión).

Note

Students are introduced to the verb *desear* in this chapter. *Querer,* which is introduced in *Capítulo 3,* is more common, but using *desear* (a regular *-ar* verb) now allows students to communicate their wants and desires.

Emphasis F: Suggestion

Explain the use of present tense questions to indicate near-future actions: *¿Hablas con Juan mañana?* (Will you speak to Juan tomorrow?)

Negation

Suggestion

Point out that the second *no* = the English *not.*

B. To *conjugate* (**conjugar**) a verb means to give the various forms of the verb with their corresponding subjects: *I speak, you speak, she speaks,* and so on. All regular Spanish verbs are conjugated by adding *personal endings* (**las terminaciones personales**) that reflect the subject doing the action. These are added to the *stem* (**la raíz** or **el radical**), which is the infinitive minus the infinitive ending.

Infinitive	Stem
hablar	→ habl-
comer	→ com-
vivir	→ viv-

C. The right-hand column shows the personal endings that are added to the stem of all regular **-ar** verbs to form the *present tense* (**el presente**).

Regular **-ar** verb endings in the present tense: **o, -as, -a, -amos, -áis, -an**

hablar (*to speak*): habl-					
Singular			**Plural**		
(yo)	hablo	*I speak*	(nosotros) (nosotras)	hablamos	*we speak*
(tú)	hablas	*you speak*	(vosotros) (vosotras)	habláis	*you speak*
(Ud.) (él) (ella)	habla	*you speak* *he speaks* *she speaks*	(Uds.) (ellos) (ellas)	hablan	*you speak* *they (m.) speak* *they (f.) speak*

D. Some important **-ar** verbs in this chapter include those in the drawings and list on the right.

Note that in Spanish the meaning of the English word *for* is included in the verbs **buscar** (*to look for*) and **pagar** (*to pay for*); *to* is included in **escuchar** (*to listen to*).

bailar
cantar
escuchar
tocar

buscar	*to look for*
comprar	*to buy*
desear	*to want*
enseñar	*to teach*
estudiar	*to study*
hablar	*to speak; to talk*
necesitar	*to need*
pagar	*to pay (for)*
practicar	*to practice*
regresar	*to return (to a place)*
tomar	*to take; to drink*
trabajar	*to work*

☀ Heritage Speakers

- Pídales a los estudiantes hispanohablantes que expliquen la diferencia entre *regresar, volver* y *devolver.* También explique que para expresar *to return a phone call* es preferible decir *devolver una llamada* o *volver a llamar,* no *llamar atrás.*
- Anime a los estudiantes hispanohablantes a formar parejas con estudiantes monolingües para que hagan y contesten preguntas con estos verbos. Por ejemplo: *¿Cuándo regresas de la universidad? → Regreso a las seis.*

E. As in English, when two Spanish verbs are used in sequence and there is no change of subject, the second verb is usually in the infinitive form.

Necesito llamar a mi familia.
I need to call my family.

Me gusta bailar.
I like to dance.

F. In both English and Spanish, conjugated verb forms also indicate the *time* or *tense* (**el tiempo**) of the action: *I speak* (present), *I spoke* (past).

Some English equivalents of the present tense forms of Spanish verbs are shown at the right.

hablo	*I speak*	Simple present tense
	I am speaking	Present progressive (indicates an action in progress)
	I will speak	Near future action

Negation

In Spanish the word **no** is placed before the conjugated verb to make a negative sentence.

El estudiante **no** habla español.
The student doesn't speak Spanish.

No, **no** necesito dinero.
No, I don't need money.

■ ■ ■ Práctica

A. Mis compañeros y yo

Paso 1. **¡Anticipemos!*** Read the following statements and tell whether they are true for you and your classmates and for your classroom environment. If any statement is not true for you or your class, make it negative or change it in another way to make it correct.

> **MODELO:** Toco el piano → Sí, toco el piano.
> (No, no toco el piano. Toco la guitarra.)

1. Necesito más (*more*) dinero.
2. Trabajo en la biblioteca.
3. Tomo ocho clases este semestre/trimestre.
4. En clase, cantamos en francés.
5. Deseamos practicar español.
6. Tomamos Coca-Cola en clase.
7. El profesor / La profesora enseña español.
8. El profesor / La profesora habla muy bien el alemán (*German*).

Paso 2. Now turn to the person next to you and restate each sentence as a question, using **tú** forms of the verbs in all cases. Your partner will indicate whether the sentences are true for him or her.

> **MODELO:** ¿Tocas el piano? → Sí, toco el piano. (No, no toco el piano.)

---

*¡Anticipemos! (*Lets look ahead!) *identifies activities or* **pasos** *that allow you to see words and structures in context before you begin to use them actively.*

AUTOPRUEBA

Give the present tense endings for **pagar.**

1. yo pag____
2. tú pag____
3. ella pag____
4. nosotros pag____
5. ellos pag____

Answers: 1. pago 2. pagas 3. paga 4. pagamos 5. pagan

Preliminary Exercises

■ Explain the purpose of a rapid response drill. Have students give the corresponding forms.
yo: *bailar, estudiar, tocar, escuchar*
tú: *buscar, hablar, pagar, tomar*
Ud./él/ella: *cantar, necesitar, regresar, enseñar*
nosotros: *comprar, pagar, estudiar, escuchar*
vosotros: *desear, regresar, cantar, bailar*
Uds./ellos/ellas: *practicar, tomar, desear, tocar*

■ Have students give the subject pronouns for *enseño, cantamos, estudian, paga, trabajan, desean, buscas, compra, habláis, regresas, bailan, tomo, escucha, necesitamos, toco.*

■ Explain the purpose of the pattern practice (see "Teaching Techniques: Drills" in the IM), and tell students how you want them to do it.

En la clase de español

1. *Ud. estudia mucho. (nosotros, yo, ellos, Juan, tú, vosotras)*
2. *Sara necesita un diccionario. (yo, Carlos y tú, tú, nosotras, Ada, vosotros)*

En una fiesta en la residencia

1. *Clara toma Coca-Cola. (tú, Ud., él, Uds., Elena y yo, vosotras)*
2. *Tú cantas y bailas. (nosotros, los amigos, Uds., Eva y Diego, yo, vosotros)*

Prác. A: Notes

■ See the IM for a discussion of input activities such as this one.
■ Generally, the subject pronoun is not used before the verb in a sentence except for clarity or emphasis. The conjugated verb informs the listener as to the identity of the subject.

Prác. A: Follow-Up

Paso 1. Convert students' statements into questions addressed to other students: *¿Necesita dinero (Jim)? ¿(Jim) cree que tomamos cerveza en la clase? ¿Bailas tú en las fiestas?*

Prác. A: Suggestions

■ **Paso 2.** Encourage students to create their own questions.
■ Encourage student partners to write a summary of their similarities and differences, using the *nosotros* forms: *(Nosotros) Necesitamos mucho dinero y no tomamos cerveza en las fiestas.*

Gramática ■ **41**

Prác. B: Suggestion

Have students explain their answers in simple sentences, for example,

1. *Falso. Marcos está en el apartamento con los estudiantes.* Students might disagree about and discuss items of this kind. For example, another student might say: *¡Sí! Hay profesores en las fiestas de los estudiantes,* and so on.

Prác. B: Follow-Up

Do orally or as dictation.

Cambie por el plural.

1. *Él no desea tomar una cerveza.*
2. *Ud. baila con un estudiante.*
3. *¿Compro el lápiz mañana?*
4. *Hablas con la dependienta.*
5. *¿Hay sólo una extranjera en la clase?*

Cambie por el singular.

6. *Ellas no buscan el dinero.*
7. *¿Enseñan Uds. sólo dos clases de español?*
8. *Necesitamos unos libros de texto.*
9. *Las mujeres estudian sicología.*
10. *¿Pagan Uds. sólo 30 pesos?*

Con. A: Note

This kind of activity is called a sentence builder. Each subject and verb can be used with more than one item from the right-hand column; many sentences are possible. The use of *no* is optional. (See the IM for more information.) Emphasize that forms of *desear* and *necesitar* must be followed by an infinitive. Also emphasize that verbs of motion, like *regresar*, are followed by *a*.

B. En una fiesta. The following paragraphs describe a party. First scan the paragraphs to get a general sense of their meaning. Then complete the paragraphs with the correct form of the numbered infinitives.

Esta noche[a] hay una fiesta en el apartamento de Marcos y Julio. Todos[b] los estudiantes (cantar[1]) y (bailar[2]). Una persona (tocar[3]) la guitarra y otras personas (escuchar[4]) la música.

Jaime (buscar[5]) una Coca-Cola. Marta (hablar[6]) con un amigo. María José (desear[7]) enseñarles a todos[c] un baile[d] de Colombia. Todas las estudiantes desean (bailar[8]) con el estudiante mexicano —¡él (bailar[9]) muy bien!

La fiesta es estupenda, pero todos (necesitar[10]) regresar a casa[e] o a su[f] cuarto temprano.[g] ¡Hay clases mañana!

[a]*Esta... Tonight* [b]*All* [c]*enseñarles... to teach everyone* [d]*dance* [e]*a... home* [f]*their* [g]*early*

Comprensión: ¿Cierto o falso?

1. Marcos es profesor de español.
2. A Jaime le gusta el café.
3. María José es de Colombia.
4. Los estudiantes desean bailar.

Need more practice?

■ Workbook and Laboratory Manual
■ Interactive CD-ROM
■ Online Learning Center (www.mhhe.com/puntos7)

■ ■ ■ Conversación

A. Oraciones lógicas. Form at least eight complete logical sentences by using one word or phrase from each column. The words and phrases may be used more than once, in many combinations. Be sure to use the correct form of the verbs. Make any of the sentences negative, if you wish.

MODELO: Yo no estudio francés.

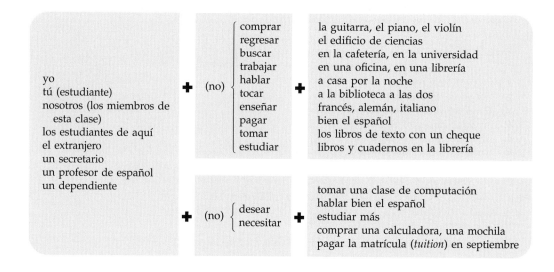

National Standards: Comparisons

In Latin America and Spain, parties and social gatherings are intended for all age groups, from the very young to the very old. Parents will bring their children, and often grandparents will attend and participate in the festivities as well. This intergenerational approach to partying is considered quite normal. Arriving on time to an informal social gathering in Hispanic countries is not an issue. If a party starts at 8:00 P.M., do not be surprised to have guests showing up at 11:00 at night. However, attendees will arrive on time for formal social events such as weddings or business-related events (meetings and conferences).

NOTA COMUNICATIVA

The Verb *estar*

Estar is another Spanish **-ar** verb. It means *to be*, and you have already used forms of it to ask how others are feeling or to tell where things are located. Here is the complete present tense conjugation of **estar**. Note that the **yo** form is irregular. The other forms take regular **-ar** endings, and some have a shift in the stress pattern (indicated by the accented **á**).

yo	**estoy**	nosotros/as	**estamos**
tú	**estás**	vosotros/as	**estáis**
Ud., él, ella	**está**	Uds., ellos, ellas	**están**

You will learn the uses of the verb **estar**, along with those of **ser** (the other Spanish verb that means *to be*) gradually, over the next several chapters. In the questions below, **estar** is used to inquire about location or feelings.

1. ¿Cómo está Ud. en este momento (*right now*)?
2. ¿Cómo están sus (*your*) compañeros? (Mis companeros...)
3. ¿Dónde está Ud. en este momento?

B. ¿Qué hacen? (*What are they doing?*) Tell where these people are and what they are doing. Note that the definite article is used with titles when you are talking about a person: **el señor, la señora, la señorita, el profesor, la profesora.**

MODELO: La Sra. Martínez _____. →
La Sra. Martínez está en la oficina. Busca un documento, trabaja…

Frases útiles: hablar por teléfono, preparar la lección, pronunciar las palabras, tomar apuntes (*to take notes*), trabajar en la caja (*at the register*), usar una computadora

 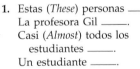  

1. Estas (*These*) personas _____.
La profesora Gil _____.
Casi (*Almost*) todos los estudiantes _____.
Un estudiante _____.

2. Estas personas están _____.
El Sr. Miranda _____.
La bibliotecaria _____.
El estudiante _____.

3. Estas personas _____.
El cliente _____.
La dependienta _____.

Gramática   Cuarenta y tres ■ **43**

Resources: Trahsparency 12

Preliminary Exercises

Have students use the cues to form sentences.

■ *¿Cómo están Uds.?*

1. *yo / muy bien*
2. *tú / bien / ¿no?*
3. *el profesor (la profesora) / muy bien*
4. *nosotros / no / enfermo* (pantomime)
5. *Julio / mal*
6. *Uds. / bien / también*

■ *¿Dónde están las siguientes ciudades?*

1. *Amarillo, Los Ángeles, San Agustín, Toledo, Santa Fe, Reno*
2. *Managua, Guadalajara, Buenos Aires, La Habana, Quito, La Paz, Bogotá*

NOTA COMUNICATIVA

Suggestions

■ Point out the irregular *yo* form and the accents on other forms.

■ Emphasize the use of *estar* for (1) condition or state of health, (2) location. Students have used *estar* to express both concepts since *Ante todo*.

■ At this time, avoid explaining differences between *ser* and *estar*. If students ask, just tell them more than one verb translates as *to be* in Spanish.

♻ **Reciclado:** Emphasize interrogative words, presented in *Ante todo*.

Con. B: Note

Emphasize the use of the definite article with titles when talking about persons, as in *El Sr. Ramírez habla español.* Contrast this with *Buenos días, Sr. Ramírez.* No article is used when speaking directly to a person.

Con. B: Variation

Bring illustrations to class. Using *¿quién(es)?*, ask questions based on them, for example, *¿Quién busca el libro?*, and so on. Students respond with the name of the person only.

NOTA COMUNICATIVA

Suggestion
Point out that the Spanish prepositions do not translate as exactly as they might expect: *at night = por la noche; de la noche.* In these phrases the preposition *a* is not used.

Con. C: Follow-Up

Ask a sample question of several individual students, then have them report answers to others, for example, *Juan, ¿Ana estudia mucho o poco? → Ana estudia mucho.*

Con. C: Variation

Say the following statements. If students believe you, they respond with *Es verdad.* If they think you are lying, they say *Es falso.*

1. *Hablo español, inglés y francés.*
2. *Bailo muy bien.*
3. *No regreso a casa hoy.*
4. *Por la noche, enseño a estudiantes extranjeros.*
5. *Toco la guitarra.*

Encourage students to make up original statements of their own to say to the class.

NOTA COMUNICATIVA

Expressing the Time of Day

You can use the preposition **por** to mean *in* or *during* when expressing the time of day.

Estudio **por** la mañana y trabajo **por** la tarde. **Por** la noche, estoy en casa con la familia.
I study in the morning and I work in the afternoon. During the evening (At night), I'm at home with my family.

Remember that the phrases **de la mañana (tarde, noche)** are used when a specific hour of the day is mentioned, and are used like the English *A.M.* and *P.M.*

C. **Entrevista.** Use the following questions as a guide to interview a classmate, and take notes on what he or she says. (Write down what your partner says using the **él/ella** form of the verbs.) Your instructor may want you to hand in your notes so that he or she can get to know the students in the class better.

MODELO: ESTUDIANTE 1: Karen, ¿estudias filosofía?
ESTUDIANTE 2: No, no estudio filosofía. Estudio música.
ESTUDIANTE 1: (escribe [*writes*]): Karen no estudia filosofía. Estudia música.

1. ¿Estudias mucho o poco (*a little*)? ¿Dónde estudias, en casa, en la residencia o en la biblioteca? ¿Cuándo estudias, por la mañana, por la tarde o por la noche?
2. ¿Cantas bien o mal (*poorly*)? ¿Tocas un instrumento musical? ¿Cuál es? (el piano, la guitarra, el violín...)
3. ¿Trabajas? ¿Dónde? ¿Cuántas horas a la semana (*per week*) trabajas?
4. ¿Quiénes pagan los libros de texto, tú o los profesores? ¿Qué más necesitas pagar? ¿diccionarios? ¿el alquiler (*rent*)? ¿ ?

EN LOS ESTADOS UNIDOS Y EL CANADÁ

Jaime Escalante

Jaime Escalante was born in La Paz, Bolivia, where he was a math and physics teacher for fourteen years. He emigrated to California in 1964 when he was 33. Since he did not speak English, he took menial jobs while he learned the language and went to college to become an accredited teacher. He started teaching in 1974 at Garfield High School, in East Los Angeles, where the students were mostly low-income Hispanics. In 1982, with Escalante's help, his students did so well on an advanced placement calculus test that the Educational Testing Service thought they had cheated and asked them to retake the test. The 1988 film *Stand and Deliver* portrays Escalante and his students' efforts. He was later awarded the United States Presidential Medal and the Andrés Bello award by the Organization of American States.

▲ *Jaime Escalante*

EN LOS ESTADOS UNIDOS Y EL CANADÁ

At the age of 33, Jamie Escalante took a job as a busboy at a restaurant to support his wife and daughter, but, understanding his need to learn English in order to have the kind of job he wanted, he also took classes at Pasadena City College. The movie *Stand and Deliver* is not the only tribute to his success. He was also awarded the United States Presidential Medal and the Andrés Bello award by the Organization of American States. He is also the subject of the book *Jaime Escalante: Sensational Teacher* by Ann Byers (1996), featured in the TV special *Math: Who Needs It?!* Encourage students to use the Internet to find current information about Jamie Escalante and the film *Stand and Deliver.* Have them write three sentences about their findings and then share what they wrote with their classmates.

Getting Information • Asking Yes/No Questions

En una universidad: La oficina de matrícula

ESTUDIANTE: Necesito una clase más por la mañana. *¿Hay sitio* en la clase de sicología 2?
CONSEJERO: Imposible, señorita. No hay.
ESTUDIANTE: *¿Hay un curso* de historia o de matemáticas?
CONSEJERO: Sólo por la noche. *¿Desea Ud. tomar* una clase por la noche?
ESTUDIANTE: Es imposible. Trabajo por la noche.
CONSEJERO: Pues... ¿qué tal el francés 3? Hay una clase a las diez de la mañana.
ESTUDIANTE: *¿El francés 3?* Perfecto. Pero, *¿no necesito tomar* primero el francés 1?

Comprensión

1. ¿Necesita la señorita dos clases más?
2. ¿Hay sitio en sicología 2?
3. ¿Hay cursos de historia o de matemáticas por la mañana?
4. ¿A qué hora es la clase de francés 3?
5. ¿Cuál es el problema con la clase de francés 3?

There are two kinds of questions: information questions and yes/no questions. Questions that ask for new information or facts that the speaker does not know often begin with *interrogative words* such as *who, what,* and so on. (You learned some interrogative words in **Ante todo.**) *Yes/no questions* permit a simple *yes* or *no* answer.

Information questions:
¿**Qué** lengua habla Ud.? →
Hablo español.

Yes/no questions:
¿Habla Ud. francés? →
No. (No, no hablo francés.)

Rising Intonation

A common way to form yes/no questions in Spanish is simply to make your voice rise at the end of the question.

 There is no Spanish equivalent of the English *do* or *does* in questions. Note also the use of an inverted question mark (¿) at the beginning of a question in Spanish.

STATEMENT: Ud. trabaja aquí todos los días.
You work here every day.

Arturo regresa a casa hoy.
Arturo is returning home today.

QUESTION: ¿Ud. trabaja aquí todos los días?
Do you work here every day?

¿Arturo regresa a casa hoy?
Is Arturo returning home today?

At a university: The registration office STUDENT: I need one more class in the morning. Is there space in Psychology 2? ADVISOR: Impossible, Miss. There isn't (space). STUDENT: Is there a history or math class? ADVISOR: Only at night. Do you want to take a night course? STUDENT: I work at night. That's why I need a class in the morning. ADVISOR: Well . . . what about French 3? There's a class at ten in the morning. STUDENT: French 3? Perfect. But don't I need to take French 1 first?

Gramática 4
Asking Yes/No Questions
Follow-Up
Encourage students to react (*sí* or *no*) to the desirability of taking the following courses at the following times: *el inglés por la mañana / por la noche; el cálculo por la mañana / por la tarde; la sicología por la tarde / por la mañana; las ciencias por la noche.*

Inversion

Suggestions

- Point out that English also puts a verb form in front of the subject when forming *yes/no* questions: *You work here? → Do you work here?*
- Explain that if the subject is long, an adverb, object, or prepositional phrase may come between the subject and verb: *¿Baila Ud. con Guillermo? ¿Baila con Guillermo la estudiante alemana?*

Preliminary Exercise

Have students listen to and identify the following as statements or questions.

1. *¿Regresa Ud. mañana?*
2. *Pepe necesita un bolígrafo.*
3. *¿Hablamos bien?*
4. *¿Bailas con Carmen?*
5. *Uds. estudian mucho.*
6. *¿Desean tocar el piano?*

Prác: Suggestion

Point out that the answer and the question do not need to contain identical information. For example: (Question) *¿Es Ud. turista?* (Answer) *Sí, soy de los Estados Unidos.* See how many different questions students can invent.

Prác: Extension

7. *Sí, regreso a casa a las diez.*
8. *No, no canto bien.*
9. *Sí, hablo mucho por teléfono.*
10. *Sí, bailo en las fiestas.*

Another way to form yes/no questions is to invert the order of the subject and verb, in addition to making your voice rise at the end of the question.

STATEMENT: **Ud.** trabaja aquí todos los días.

QUESTION: ¿Trabaja **Ud.** aquí todos los días?

STATEMENT: **Arturo** regresa a casa hoy.

QUESTION: ¿Regresa **Arturo** a casa hoy?

AUTOPRUEBA

Give the English equivalent for these yes/no questions.

1. ¿Habla Ud. inglés?
2. ¿Necesitan Uds. otra clase?
3. ¿Tomas biología?
4. ¿Trabajo mañana?

Answers: 1. Do you speak English? 2. Do you (pl.) need another class? 3. Are you taking a biology class? 4. Do (Will) I work tomorrow?

■■■ Práctica

A. ¿Pregunta o declaración (statement)**?** Listen as your instructor reads either a question or a statement from the list. Then tell if what you hear is a question or a statement.

MODELOS: ¿El consejero está en la oficina? → Es una pregunta.
La bibliotecaria habla con el estudiante. → Es una declaración.

1. ¿Alicia toca el violín? — Alicia toca el violín.
2. ¿Tomas una clase de comunicaciones? — Tomas una clase de comunicaciones.
3. ¿Uds. compran cuadernos en la librería? — Uds. compran cuadernos en la librería.
4. ¿El profesor sólo habla español en clase? — El profesor sólo habla español en clase.
5. ¿La profesora habla bien el francés? — La profesora habla bien el francés.

B. Una conversación entre (between) **Diego y Lupe.** Diego and Lupe recently met each other. While having coffee, Lupe asks Diego some questions to find out more about him. Ask Lupe's questions that led to Diego's answers.

MODELO: Sí, estudio antropología. → ¿Estudias antropología?

1. Sí, soy estadounidense (from the United States).
2. Sí, estudio con frecuencia.
3. No, no toco el piano. Toco la guitarra clásica.
4. No, no deseo trabajar más horas.
5. No, no hablo francés, pero hablo un poco de (a little bit of) italiano.
6. ¡No, no soy reservado! Soy muy extrovertido.

Need more practice?
- Workbook and Laboratory Manual
- Interactive CD-ROM
- Online Learning Center (www.mhhe.com/puntos7)

Capítulo 1: En la universidad

National Standards: Comparisons

Many people believe that intonation is a reflection of a speaker's emotions, but the use of intonation in languages is conventionalized. When a speaker uses the wrong intonation in a second language, the message may be unclear or distorted.

 Heritage Speakers

Anime a los hispanohablantes a leer algunas preguntas y repuestas y pídales a los angloparlantes a imitar la entonación.

■ ■ ■ Conversación

A. ¿Qué haces? (*What do you do?*)

Paso 1. Use the following cues as a guide to form questions to ask a classmate. Of course, you may ask other questions as well. Write the questions on a sheet of paper first, if you like. **¡OJO!** Use the **tú** form of the verbs with your partner.

> MODELO: escuchar música por la mañana →
> ¿Escuchas música por la mañana?

1. estudiar en la biblioteca por la noche
2. practicar español con un amigo/una amiga
3. tomar un poco de café por la mañana
4. bailar mucho en las fiestas
5. tocar un instrumento musical
6. regresar a casa muy tarde (*late*) a veces (*sometimes*)
7. comprar los libros en la librería de la universidad
8. hablar mucho por teléfono
9. trabajar en la universidad
10. usar (*to use*) un diccionario bilingüe

Paso 2. Now use the questions to get information from your partner. Jot down his or her answers for use in **Paso 3.**

> MODELO: ESTUDIANTE 1: ¿Escuchas música por la mañana?
> ESTUDIANTE 2: Sí, (No, no) escucho música por la mañana.

Paso 3. With the information you gathered in **Paso 2,** report your partner's answers to the class. (You will use the **él/ella** form of the verbs when reporting.)

> MODELO: Jenny no escucha música por la mañana.

B. ¿Qué clases tomas?

Paso 1. Make a list in Spanish of the classes you are taking. Ask your instructor or use a dictionary to find the names of classes you don't know in Spanish. If you ask your instructor, remember to ask in Spanish: **¿Cómo se dice _____ en español?**

Paso 2. Circulate to interview three to five classmates about classes they are taking by asking yes/no questions. Remember to use the correct intonation when asking questions. If you do not understand the name of a class that you hear, ask, **¿Qué significa _____?** (*What does _____ mean?*).

> MODELO: ESTUDIANTE 1: ¿Tomas una clase de matemáticas?
> ESTUDIANTE 2: Sí, tomo matemáticas. Tomo cálculo.
> ESTUDIANTE 1: ¿Cálculo? ¿Qué significa (*means*) cálculo?
> ESTUDIANTE 2: Significa *calculus.*

Con A: Variation

Paso 2. Invite students to interview you to practice *Ud.* forms.

Con A: Follow-Up

■ Have students use the cues in *Paso 1* to write a short paragraph in Spanish about themselves.

■ **Paso 3.** Ask students: *¿Cuántas personas en la clase... bailan mucho (poco) en las fiestas / practican español con un compañero (una compañera) / solo/a? ¿Quién baila mucho (poco) / fuma / bebe cerveza? ¿Quién no toma café? ¿Qué le gusta tomar por la mañana?* As much as possible, use words like *poco* vs. *mucho, pocos/as* vs. *muchos/as,* and *solo/a.*

Suggestion

Model and practice the comic strip with students. Have several pairs of students read it or act it out.

National Standards: Communication

In activities like the one included in the *Conversación* section, students are asking real questions about real information. Note the suggestion in this activity that students write the questions on a piece of paper. You may also provide the questions in the form of a handout.

UN POCO DE TODO

A: Suggestions

- Explain that this type of exercise is called a "dehydrated sentence." Explain its purpose (see the "Drills" section of the "Teaching Techniques" chapter in the IM).
- Have students describe the following persons by telling what they do and, if possible, where they do it.

1. *un secretario*
2. *una profesora*
3. *un estudiante*
4. *una dependienta*
5. *un bibliotecario*

A: Note

The subject pronouns in parentheses should not be used; they are cues only.

A: Variation

Have students work in pairs in which one student produces the question, the other, the answer. Emphasize that they should correct each other's mistakes. Finally, the whole class can go over all answers quickly.

A: Follow-Up

¿Qué busca en una librería? ¿Qué necesita para estudiar español? ¿Cuánto tiempo desea estudiar por la noche? ¿Trabaja? ¿Dónde? ¿Usa una mochila?

B: Follow-Up

Encourage students to form groups of three in which two students are journalists and one plays Ángela. The journalists interview Ángela for the school newspaper. They should ask all relevant and/or possible questions that can be answered using the letter's information.

B: Note

Chévere means *muy bien* (in Puerto Rican Spanish).

B: Suggestion

Using Ángela's letter as a springboard, have students guess when she does things: *¿A qué hora le gusta ir a la cafetería?, ¿A qué hora es la clase de español?*, and so on. Follow up with questions directed to students in class. *Susie, ¿te gusta ir a la cafetería por la mañana? ¿A qué hora?*

Bright Idea

B: Suggestion

Have students indicate what they felt was most important when they were looking for a university.

¿los profesores?
¿la fama de la universidad?
¿las «fraternidades»?
¿los grupos sociales?
¿Existe una universidad perfecta?

UN POCO DE TODO

A. Conversaciones en la cafetería

Paso 1. Form complete questions and answers based on the words given, in the order given. Conjugate the verbs and add other words if necessary. Do not use the subject pronouns in parentheses.

PREGUNTAS

MODELO: ¿comprar (tú) / lápices / aquí? → ¿Compras los lápices aquí?

1. ¿buscar (tú) / libro de español / ahora?
2. ¿no trabajar / Paco / aquí / en / cafetería?
3. ¿qué más / necesitar / Uds. / en / clase de cálculo?
4. ¿dónde / estar / Juanita?
5. ¿no desear (tú) / estudiar / minutos / más?

RESPUESTAS

MODELO: no, / sólo / (yo) comprar / bolígrafos / aquí →
No, sólo compro los bolígrafos aquí.

a. no, / (yo) necesitar / regresar / a casa
b. no, / (yo) buscar / mochila
c. (nosotros) necesitar / calculadora / y / cuaderno
d. no, / él / trabajar / en / biblioteca
e. ella / trabajar / en / residencia / por / tarde

Paso 2. Now match the answers with the questions to form short conversational exchanges, or practice them with a partner, if you wish.

B. La universidad perfecta.

Complete Ángela's letter to her cousin about her search for the perfect college. Give the correct form of the verbs in parentheses, as suggested by context. When two possibilities are given in parentheses, select the correct word.

Mi querida Carmen:

Mi amiga Luisa y yo buscamos la universidad perfecta para nosotras. Deseamos ser (compañeras/consejeras[1]) de cuarto.

Mañana (*nosotras:* visitar[2]) la Universidad de Texas en Austin. ¡(Ser[3]) muy grande[a]! Hay veinticuatro grupos sociales para estudiantes hispanos y (un/una[4]) biblioteca especial. (El/La[5]) colección latinoamericana es muy grande. (Los/Las[6]) materias más populares son (el/la[7]) administración de empresas, (el/la[8]) ingeniería, (los/las[9]) humanidades y (los/las[10]) comunicaciones. Muchos estudiantes (estudiar[11]) en (el/la[12]) Instituto de Estudios[b] Latinoamericanos y en (el/la[13]) Centro para Estudios Mexicoamericanos. La matrícula no es cara,[c] pero el problema es que no me gusta (el/la[14]) idea de estudiar en (un/una[15]) universidad muy grande.

(*Yo:* Desear[16]) estudiar en (un/una[17]) universidad menos grande, como Stanford. Tiene[d] nueve grupos sociales para estudiantes hispanos y

[a]*big* [b]*Studies* [c]*expensive* [d]*It has*

☀ Heritage Speakers

Pídales a los estudiantes hispanohablantes que mencionen otras palabras que tengan el mismo significado que *chévere*. Esta actividad puede ser el comienzo de una más extensa en la que estos estudiantes hacen una colección de variantes lingüísticas y entregan su lista al terminar el curso.

(un/una[18]) casa especial para estudiantes de español. Se llama la Casa Zapata y es (un/una[19]) residencia. (Los/Las[20]) estudiantes (practicar[21]) español y participan en celebraciones hispanas. Las (mochilas/materias[22]) más populares de Stanford (ser[23]) la biología, la economía, la sicología, (el/la[24]) inglés y (los/las[25]) ciencias políticas. Luisa y yo (visitar[26]) Stanford en dos semanas.[e] Pero la matrícula... ¡Los estudiantes (pagar[27]) mucho (dinero/papel[28]) para estudiar en Stanford!

Te hablo[f] por teléfono pronto.[g]
Con cariño,
Ángela

[e]weeks   [f]Te... I'll speak to you   [g]soon

Comprensión. Which of these statements do you agree with after reading Ángela's letter? Change incorrect statements to make them true.

1. Luisa y Ángela son amigas.
2. Ángela desea estudiar en una universidad muy grande.
3. En el Instituto de Estudios Latinoamericanos hay pocos (*few*) estudiantes.
4. La Casa Zapata es una biblioteca importante.

C. **¿Qué pasa** [*What's happening*] **en la fiesta?**

Paso 1. With a classmate, describe what's going on in the following scene.

MODELO: Pilar y Ana bailan en la fiesta.

Paso 2. Now compare the scene above with parties *you* go to. Use the **nosotros** form of verbs to describe what you and your friends do at these parties.

MODELO: Mis amigos y yo bailamos en las fiestas.

Vocabulario útil
descansar (to rest)
escuchar
fumar (to smoke)
mirar (to watch)
una película (a movie)
la tele (TV)
tocar
la guitarra
el piano
tomar
cerveza
refrescos (soft drinks)
vino

Resources for Review and Testing Preparation

- Workbook and Laboratory Manual
- Interactive CD-ROM
- Online Learning Center (www.mhhe.com/puntos7)

Reciclado
Remind students that some subject pronouns reflect gender. For example, *él/ella, nosotros/nosotras, vosotros/vosotras, ellos/ellas.* Gender, however, is not evident with *yo, tú, Ud.,* and *Uds.*

C: Preliminary Exercise
Have students respond *lógico* or *ilógico.*

1. Cuando estoy en el cine, fumo.
2. Descanso generalmente por la mañana.
3. Los estudiantes tocan la batería en mis clases.
4. Uds. escuchan música cuando estudian.
5. Uds. miran películas en el laboratorio de lenguas.

C: Note
Escuchar means *to listen to*: the Spanish verb does not need a preposition in front of the object. Note, however, that the personal *a* is used with animate nouns.
  I listen to my mother. → *Escucho a mi madre.*

C: Variations

■ Describe the scene shown in the illustration and have students draw what they hear in your description.
■ Have several students draw on board what other classmates describe for them.

Reciclado
Point out words learned in fixed expressions in *Ante todo* or used passively as cognates.

Resources: Transparency 13

Resources: Desenlace
In the *Capítulo 1* segment of "Chapter-by-Chapter Supplementary Materials" in the IM/RK, you will find a chapter-culminating activity. You can use this activity to consolidate and review the vocabulary and grammar skills the students have acquired.

The *Perspectivas culturales* spread is a new feature in this edition of *Puntos de partida*. The left page will feature the new *Entrevista cultural* and *Entre amigos* from the Video Program to accompany *Puntos de partida*.

Entrevista cultural

Note

The follow-up questions for the *Entrevista cultural* video segments are given in English through *Capítulo 5* because these video segments might require students to produce answers in Spanish for which they are not yet linguistically prepared. Students should be able to produce answers in Spanish for the *Entre amigos* segments. Spanish questions for *Entrevista cultural* are provided in the Instructor's Edition through *Capítulo 5* for instructors who prefer to check comprehension in Spanish.

Suggestions

- Before viewing the video, ask students questions about their instructors.

  ¿Cuántos profesores tiene Ud. (do you have)?
  ¿Cuántas clases enseñan los profesores en general?
  ¿Hay profesores hispanos en esta universidad?

  Have volunteers answer the questions.

- Have volunteers role-play Professor Rivera and his interviewer.
- Show the video and allow students one to two minutes to work on the questions. Encourage them to answer in Spanish if possible. You might want to ask questions in Spanish when you review the answers as a class.

  1. *¿Dónde enseña el profesor Rivera ahora?*
  2. *¿Qué materias enseña?*
  3. *¿Cuántas clases enseña el profesor este semestre?*
  4. *¿Tiene una clase favorita? ¿Cuál es?*
  5. *¿Por qué le gusta su trabajo al profesor Rivera?*

Entre amigos

Suggestions

- Before viewing the video, review the questions with the students and ask them similar questions.

  ¿Qué clases toma Ud.?
  ¿Toma muchas clases difíciles (difficult)?

PERSPECTIVAS culturales

●●●
Videoteca

Entrevista cultural: Los Estados Unidos

Carlos Rivera is from San Antonio, Texas. He is a university professor. In this interview, Professor Rivera talks about where he now lives and his experiences as a professor. Before watching the video clip, read the following excerpt from the interview.

INTERVIEWER: ¿Cuántas clases enseña Ud.?
PROF. RIVERA: Este semestre, enseño tres clases. Una clase de literatura contemporánea de los Estados Unidos, una clase de literatura chicana y una clase de composición.

Now watch the video clip and answer the following questions based on the interview.

1. Where does Professor Rivera live now?
2. What subject does Professor Rivera teach?
3. How many classes is Professor Rivera teaching this semester?
4. Does he have a favorite class? If so, what is it?
5. Why does Professor Rivera like his job?

Entre amigos: ¿Qué clases tomas?

Miguel, Tané, Rubén, and Karina are getting to know each other. What questions do you think they will ask each other? Before watching the video, read the following questions. As you watch, don't worry if you don't understand every word. Try to get the gist of the conversation, listening specifically for information about classes. Watch the video a second time and listen for the answers to the questions.

1. ¿De dónde es Rubén?
2. ¿Qué clases toma Rubén?
3. ¿Qué hace Miguel (*What does Miguel do*) los fines de semana?

Capítulo 1: En la universidad

National Standards: Comparisons

The requirements for degrees vary from country to country, and in most Hispanic countries, there is no exact equivalent to the standard university degrees one can earn in this country (Bachelor, Master, Doctorate). When professors immigrate from Hispanic countries to teach in this country, the program of studies they used to earn their degree is often reviewed by the university before they can be hired for certain positions.

Conozca a[a]... los hispanos en los Estados Unidos

Datos[b] esenciales

- La población hispánica total de los Estados Unidos: más de 35 (treinta y cinco) millones en el año 2000 (dos mil).
- Orígenes de la población hispánica en los Estados Unidos:
  México: 58% (cincuenta y ocho por ciento)
  Centroamérica, Sudamérica y otros países:[c] 28,4% (veintiocho coma cuatro por ciento)
  Puerto Rico: 9,6%
  Cuba: 3,5%

[a]Conozca a... *Meet, Get to know*   [b]*Facts*   [c]otros... *other countries*

¡Fíjese![a]

- En 2001 (dos mil uno) había[b] veintiún hispanos en el Congreso de los Estados Unidos. ¿Cuántos hay ahora? (www.house.gov)
- De los más de[c] 35 millones de hispanos en los Estados Unidos, la mayoría[d] habla español (mucho o poco).
- Las palabras **hispano** e[e] **hispánico** se refieren al[f] idioma y a la cultura, no a la raza[g] o grupo étnico.

[a]*Check it out!*   [b]*there were*   [c]De... *Of the more than*   [d]*majority*   [e]*y*   [f]se... *refer to the*   [g]*race*

Learn more about Hispanics in the United States with the Video, Interactive CD-ROM, and the Online Learning Center (www.mhhe.com/puntos7).

Personas famosas: César Chávez

La contribución de César Chávez (1927–1993 [mil novecientos veintisiete a mil novecientos noventa y tres]) al movimiento de los trabajadores agrícolas[a] es enorme. La educación de Chávez, hijo de campesinos migrantes,[b] sólo llega al séptimo grado.[c]

En 1962 (mil novecientos sesenta y dos), Chávez organiza a los campesinos que cosechan uvas.[d] Como resultado de las huelgas[e] y el boicoteo de las uvas de mesa,[f] los campesinos reciben contratos más favorables para ellos; el United Farm Workers se establece[g] como sindicato[h] oficial.

En 2003 (dos mil tres), el servicio postal de los Estados Unidos honra a Chávez con un sello[i] especial.

Hoy en día,[j] la vida,[k] los sacrificios y los ideales de Chávez sirven de[l] inspiración a muchas personas.

[a]trabajadores... *agricultural workers*   [b]campesinos... *migrant farm workers*   [c]llega... *reaches the seventh grade*   [d]que... *who harvest grapes*   [e]*strikes*   [f]uvas... *table grapes*   [g]se... *is established*   [h]*union*   [i]*stamp*   [j]Hoy... *Nowadays*   [k]*life*   [l]sirven... *serve as an*

El sello estadounidense (U.S.) con la imagen de César Chávez ▶

MULTIMEDIA: Internet

For more information on the United Farm Workers students can visit the organization's website.

CULTURE

- *Latinoamérica* means *Hispanoamérica* and *Iberoamérica*.
- Use *hispano/a* for people; *hispánico/a* as an adjective. This second word, in Spanish, refers to people from Spanish-speaking countries, and not to U.S. Hispanics. *Hispanic American* as a term for U.S. Hispanics cannot be translated as *hispanoamericano/a* or *latinoamericano/a*. The term *latino/a* is often used.

Have students answer or work in small groups to ask and answer these questions.

- After viewing the video, have volunteers read and answer the questions.

Conozca a... los hispanos en los Estados Unidos

Follow-Up

After students review the *Datos esenciales* section, ask: *¿Es grande la población hispana en _____ (name of your state)? La mayoría de los hispanos de _____ (name of your state), ¿son de origen mexicano (puertorriqueño/cubano and so on)?*

Follow-Up

After students read the *¡Fíjese!* section, ask: *¿Conocen a un político hispano en _____ (name of your state)?* Point out that recent estimates project that Hispanics will be the largest minority group in the U.S. by the year 2005.

Notes

- *El idioma* means *la lengua*.
- Students can read an excerpt of the novel *Caramelo* by the United States' writer Sandra Cisneros in *Un paso más 1*.

Suggestion

In order to engage students in a frank discussion of their own, possibly inaccurate, stereotypes, have them describe how they picture Hispanics physically (White, Indian, Mestizo, Black, and so on). Non-Hispanic (and even Hispanic) students from different regions of this country may have different images of Hispanics, according to the predominance of Hispanics of one origin or another in their area. Follow up by showing magazine (or family) pictures of very different-looking Hispanics.

☼ Heritage Speakers

- *Latino/a* e *hispano/a* en español no significan «U.S. Hispanic / Latino», sino una persona de un país donde se habla español. *Hispanoamericano/a* y *latinoamericano/a* sólo se usan para referirse a personas de Latinoamérica.
- Pídales a los estudiantes hispanohablantes que investiguen más a fondo la vida y labor de César Chávez. Luego pueden preparar y presentarle a la clase un informe oral.

Suggestions

- Have students create word puzzles that they can exchange and solve.
- Have students play charades, using nouns from the list, for example, *profesor* (the student stands and pantomimes teaching the class).

- Have students draw pictures on the board depicting the vocabulary and have their classmates describe what is happening in Spanish.
- Have students guess who is talking based on the following context clues:

  1. *Trabajo en la escuela. Hablo con muchos estudiantes sobre los cursos que toman y sobre sus planes para sus estudios en la universidad.* (consejero/a)
  2. *Soy de Colombia pero ahora vivo en los Estados Unidos.* (extranjero/a)
  3. *Enseño español y matemáticas y tengo muchos estudiantes en la universidad.* (profesor[a])
  4. *Trabajo en JCPenney y hablo con muchos clientes todos los días.* (dependiente/a)

- Encourage students to develop various strategies for learning vocabulary, such as flash cards or tri-fold lists. For flash cards, they write English on one side and Spanish on the reverse. For tri-fold lists, they write Spanish in one column (far left) and English in a column on the far right. They fold the sheet to see only English or only Spanish. Have students share other strategies they have used that work for them.

EN RESUMEN

Gramática

To review the grammar points presented in this chapter, refer to the indicated grammar presentations. You'll find further practice of these structures in the Workbook and Laboratory Manual, on the Interactive CD-ROM, and on the *Puntos de partida* Online Learning Center (www.mhhe.com/puntos7).

1. Identifying People, Places, and Things—Singular Nouns: Gender and Articles

   Do you understand the gender of nouns and how to use the articles **el, la, uno,** and **una**?

2. Identifying People, Places, and Things—Nouns and Articles: Plural Forms

   Do you know how to make nouns plural and use the articles **los, las, unos,** and **unas**?

3. Expressing Actions—Subject Pronouns: Present Tense of **-ar** Verbs; Negation

   You should be able to use subject pronouns, conjugate regular **-ar** verbs in the present tense, and form negative sentences.

4. Getting Information—Asking Yes/No Questions

   Do you know how to form questions? You should know how to make intonation rise at the end of a question.

Vocabulario

Practice this vocabulary with digital flash cards on the Online Learning Center (www.mhhe.com/puntos7).

Los verbos

bailar	to dance
buscar	to look for
cantar	to sing
comprar	to buy
desear	to want
enseñar	to teach
escuchar	to listen (to)
estar (*irreg.*)	to be
estudiar	to study
hablar	to speak; to talk
hablar por teléfono	to talk on the phone
necesitar	to need
pagar	to pay (for)
practicar	to practice
regresar	to return (*to a place*)
regresar a casa	to go home
tocar	to play (*a musical instrument*)
tomar	to take; to drink
trabajar	to work

Los lugares

el apartamento	apartment
la biblioteca	library
la cafetería	cafeteria
la clase	class
el cuarto	room
el edificio	building
la fiesta	party
la librería	bookstore
la oficina	office
la residencia	dormitory
la universidad	university

Las personas

el/la amigo/a	friend
el/la bibliotecario/a	librarian
el/la cliente	client
el/la compañero/a (de clase)	classmate
el/la compañero/a de cuarto	roommate
el/la consejero/a	advisor
el/la dependiente/a	clerk
el/la estudiante	student
el/la extranjero/a	foreigner
el hombre	man
la mujer	woman
el/la profesor(a)	professor
el/la secretario/a	secretary

Palabras interrogativas

¿cuál?	what?; which?
¿cuándo?	when?
¿cuánto?	how much?
¿cuántos/as?	how many?
¿quién?	who?; whom?

Repaso: ¿cómo?, ¿dónde?, ¿qué?

Las lenguas (extranjeras)

el alemán	German
el español	Spanish
el francés	French
el inglés	English
el italiano	Italian

Otras materias

la administración de empresas
el arte
las ciencias
la computación
las comunicaciones
la economía
la filosofía
la física
la historia
las humanidades
la literatura
las matemáticas
la química
la sicología
la sociología

Las cosas

el bolígrafo	pen
la calculadora	calculator
el cuaderno	notebook
el diccionario	dictionary
el dinero	money
el escritorio	desk

el lápiz (pl. lápices)	pencil
el libro (de texto)	(text)book
la mesa	table
la mochila	backpack
el papel	paper
la pizarra	chalkboard
la puerta	door
la silla	chair
la ventana	window

Otros sustantivos

el café	coffee
la cerveza	beer
el día	day
la matrícula	tuition

¿Cuándo?

ahora	now
con frecuencia	frequently
el fin de semana	weekend
por la mañana	in the morning
(tarde, noche)	(afternoon, evening)
tarde/temprano	late/early
todos los días	every day

Pronombres personales

yo, tú, usted (Ud.), él/ella, nosotros/nosotras,
vosotros/vosotras, ustedes (Uds.), ellos/ellas

Palabras adicionales

aquí	here
con	with
en casa	at home
mal	poorly
más	more
mucho	much; a lot
muy	very
poco	little
un poco (de)	a little bit (of)
por eso	therefore
sólo	only

Suggestions

- Have students use the adverbs from *¿Cuándo?* and the verbs from *Los verbos* to make a chart that plots when and how often they do some things.
- Have students indicate whether or not they have the following things.

cuaderno	*mochila*
lápiz	*papel*
calculadora	*bolígrafo*
diccionario	*dinero*

Un paso más 1

Note

The *Un paso más* section is optional.

Literatura de los **Estados Unidos**

Notes

- Sandra Cisneros is the daughter of a Mexican father and a Chicana mother. She is the only daughter of seven children.
- Cisneros' writing often reflects the years of growing up with six brothers who protected her, attempted to control her, and wanted her to be a traditional Hispanic woman. Growing up, her family often moved back and forth between Mexico and the United States because her father missed his homeland and was very devoted to his mother, who lived there. This gave Cisneros a sense of displacement.
- Cisneros' poetry and prose bridge the gap between Anglo and Hispanic cultures.
- *Caramelo* is a multigenerational story of a Mexican-American family. The novel is textured with humor and passion. The protagonist, Lala Reyes is the granddaughter of a woman from a family of famous shawl makers. Lala becomes the inheritor of one of the most beautiful *rebozos* or shawls, the striped *caramelo* one.

LECTURA

Suggestion

Do the *Estrategia* section in class the day before you intend to cover the reading. Remind students to continue to practice this strategy actively as they read, as part of their homework assignment. Remember to follow up on the underlined words the next day.

Un paso más 1

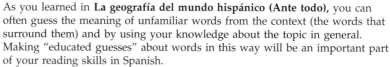

Literatura de los **Estados Unidos**

Sobre la autora: *Sandra Cisneros was born in Chicago. She is one of the most prominent Hispanic female writers in the United States. She writes in English, but her prose and poetry are infused with the Hispanic-American experience. She now lives and writes in San Antonio, Texas. The following is from the novel* Caramelo *(2002).*

Outside, roaring like the ocean, Chicago traffic from the Northwest and Congress Expressways. Inside, another roar; in Spanish from the kitchen radio, in English from TV cartoons, and in a mix of the two from her boys begging for, —*Un nikle* for Italian lemonade. But Aunty Licha doesn't hear anything. Under her breath Aunty is bargaining,

—*Virgen Purísima*, if we even make it to Laredo, even that, I'll say three rosaries . . .

▲ Sandra Cisneros (1954–)

L E C T U R A

ESTRATEGIA: More on Guessing Meaning from Context

As you learned in **La geografía del mundo hispánico (Ante todo),** you can often guess the meaning of unfamiliar words from the context (the words that surround them) and by using your knowledge about the topic in general. Making "educated guesses" about words in this way will be an important part of your reading skills in Spanish.

What is the meaning of the underlined words in these sentences?

1. En una lista alfabetizada, la palabra **grande** aparece <u>antes de</u> **grotesco.**
2. El edificio no es moderno; es <u>viejo</u>.
3. Me gusta estudiar español, pero detesto la biología. En general, <u>odio</u> las ciencias como materia.

Some words are underlined in the following reading (and in the readings in subsequent chapters). Try to guess their meaning from context.

Like the passages in **Ante todo** and some others in subsequent chapters, this reading contains section subheadings. Scanning these subheadings in advance will help you make predictions about the reading's content, which will also help to facilitate your overall comprehension. Another useful way to manage longer passages is to read section by section. At this point, don't try to understand every word. Your main objective should be to understand the general content of the passage.

■ **Sobre la lectura...** This reading was written by the authors of *Puntos de partida* for students of Spanish like you. Later on in this text, you will have the chance to read more "authentic" selections.

Las universidades hispánicas

Introducción
En el mundo hispánico —y en los Estados Unidos y el Canadá— hay universidades grandes[a] y <u>pequeñas</u>; públicas, religiosas y privadas; modernas y antiguas. Pero el concepto de «vida[b] universitaria» es diferente.

El *campus*
Por ejemplo, en los países[c] hispánicos la universidad no es un centro de actividad social. No hay muchas residencias estudiantiles. En general, los estudiantes <u>viven</u> en pensiones[d] o en casas particulares[e] y <u>llegan</u> a la universidad en coche o en autobús. En algunas[f] universidades hay un *campus* similar a los de[g] las universidades de los Estados Unidos y el Canadá. En estos casos se habla[h] de la «ciudad[i] universitaria». Otras universidades ocupan sólo un edificio grande, o posible-

mente varios edificios, pero no hay zonas verdes.[j]

Los deportes
Otra diferencia es que en la mayoría de las universidades hispánicas los <u>deportes</u> no son muy importantes. Si los estudiantes desean practicar un deporte —el tenis, el fútbol o el béisbol— hay clubes deportivos, pero estos[k] no forman parte de la universidad.

Las diversiones[l]
Como se puede ver,[m] la forma y la organización de la universidad son diferentes en las dos culturas. Pero los estudiantes estudian y se divierten[n] en todas partes.[o] A los estudiantes hispanos, así como[p] a los estadounidenses* y canadienses,[q] les gusta mucho toda clase de música: la música clásica, la música con raíces[r] tradicionales y la música moderna —la nacional[s] y la <u>importada</u>. Y hay para todos: Madonna, N Sync, R.E.M., ... Otras diversiones preferidas por los estudiantes son las discotecas y los cafés. Hay cafés ideales para hablar con los amigos. También hay exposiciones de arte, <u>obras</u> de teatro y películas[t] interesantes.

Conclusión
Los días favoritos de muchos jóvenes[u] hispánicos son los fines de semana. ¿Realmente son muy distintos los estudiantes hispanos? ■

▲ *Estudiantes de medicina en Caracas, Venezuela*

[a]*large* [b]*life* [c]*naciones* [d]*boardinghouses* [e]*private* [f]*some* [g]*los... those of* [h]*se... one speaks* [i]*city* [j]*green* [k]*they (lit. these)* [l]*Las... Entertainment* [m]*Como... As you can see* [n]*se... have a good time* [o]*en... everywhere* [p]*así... like* [q]*estadounidenses... people from the U.S. and Canadians* [r]*roots* [s]*la... (music) from their own country* [t]*movies* [u]*young people*

*Although, technically, **norteamericano** refers to all North Americans, the term is sometimes used to refer solely to people from the United States of America. In this book, **estadounidenses** will refer to people of the United States and **norteamericanos** to North Americans.*

- After students have completed the *Lectura*, check their comprehension by writing key words on the board. Then ask students to use the words to create factual sentences based on the reading.

  1. *residencias*
  2. *casas particulares*
  3. *autobús*
  4. *zonas verdes*
  5. *deportes*
  6. *la música*
  7. *otras diversiones*

- Have students give two reasons why the Hispanic university campus is not *un centro de actividad social*.
- Encourage students to describe their own university by using adjectives taken from the text. They can also refer to some of the cognates presented in *Ante todo*. Ask: *¿Cómo es esta* (this) *universidad? ¿Es liberal? ¿grande? ¿privada?* and so on.
- Ask students what aspects of campus life are important to them. *¿Son importantes las actividades sociales en la universidad? ¿Y los deportes? ¿Qué más es importante?*
- Have students describe the photo, using as many words from the *Vocabulario* list as possible. Elicit some sentences using questions.

National Standards: Comparison

In the Hispanic world most students live with their families throughout their education. The students who live in dormitories, pensions, and private homes are from out of town. However, an increasing number of these students rent and share their apartments with other students, like many students in this country.

Old universities are typically in the downtown area of large, important cities. Therefore, they are surrounded by the downtown life, with lots of bars and cafés. Many university buildings have their own *bar-cafetería*. Such bars and cafés are the equivalent of U.S. cafeterias and dining facilities in that they bring students together outside the classroom. It is normal for students to meet with each other and even with their professors after classes and chat over a beer or coffee.

Comprensión

A: Suggestion

For items 1–3, have students substitute *los Estados Unidos* (*el Canadá*) and *de/en los Estados Unidos* (*del/en el Canadá*), for *hispánico/a(s)*, and respond *cierto* or *falso* to the new statement. Then, have them restate each sentence with themselves (*yo*) as the subject (*Yo vivo en una residencia*) and also respond *cierto* or *falso*.

Comprensión

A. ¿Cierto o falso? Indique si las siguientes oraciones son ciertas o falsas.

1. En los países hispánicos, la mayoría de los estudiantes vive en residencias.
2. En las universidades hispánicas, los deportes ocupan un lugar esencial en el programa de estudios del estudiante.
3. En una universidad hispánica, no hay mucho tiempo para asistir a (*time for attending*) conciertos y exposiciones de arte.
4. No hay mucha diferencia entre (*between*) una universidad hispánica y una universidad norteamericana con respecto al *campus*.
5. La música es una diversión para los estudiantes en todas partes.
6. Hay grandes jardines (*gardens*) y zonas verdes en las universidades hispánicas.

B. ¿Qué universidad? Indique si las siguientes oraciones son de un estudiante de la Universidad de Sevilla o de un estudiante de la Universidad de Michigan… ¡o de los dos!

	SEVILLA	MICHIGAN	LOS DOS
1. «Me gusta jugar al Frisbee en el *campus*.»	☐	☐	☐
2. «La casa es muy cómoda (*comfortable*) y tengo derecho a usar la cocina (*I have kitchen privileges*).»	☐	☐	☐
3. «Después de mi clase, ¿qué tal si tomamos un café?»	☐	☐	☐
4. «El sábado (*Saturday*) hay un partido de basquetbol. ¿Deseas ir (*to go*)?»	☐	☐	☐
5. «Me gusta hablar con mis amigos entre clases en los jardines de la universidad.»	☐	☐	☐

☀ Heritage Speakers

Pídales a los estudiantes hispanoamericanos que hagan una lista de las actividades extra-académicas que se realizan en la típica universidad iberoamericana: actividades deportivas, publicaciones, derechos humanos, etcétera. Puede pedirles que preparen y presenten un informe oral acerca de estas actividades.

ESCRITURA

A. Una comparación. Compare su propia (*your own*) universidad con una universidad hispánica, completando (*by completing*) la siguiente tabla con información de la lectura.

	La universidad hispánica	Mi universidad
Alojamiento (*Housing*)	pensiones, casas particulares	
El *campus*		
Deportes		
Diversiones	música, discotecas, cafés, películas, exposiciones de arte	

B. Mi universidad

Paso 1. In light of what you now know about some differences and similarities between universities in this country and in Hispanic countries, what information do you think would be important to share with a Hispanic student planning on studying at *your* university?

First, use the following questions to organize your ideas.

1. ¿Es grande o pequeña la universidad? (Mi universidad...)
2. ¿Es pública o privada?
3. ¿Cuántas residencias hay en el *campus*?
4. ¿Cuántas cafeterías hay? ¿En qué edificios están las cafeterías?
5. En general, ¿viven los estudiantes en residencias, en apartamentos o con su (*their*) familia?
6. ¿Cuántas bibliotecas hay? ¿Hay bibliotecas especializadas? ¿Hay computadoras para los estudiantes en las bibliotecas?
7. ¿Dónde vive Ud.? (Yo vivo...)
8. ¿Cómo llega Ud. al *campus*? ¿en coche o en autobús? ¿O camina Ud.? (*Or do you walk?*)
9. ¿En que edificios del *campus* estudia Ud.?
10. ¿Qué materia le gusta más?

Paso 2. Now use your answers to form two paragraphs: 1–6 for the first paragraph and 7–10 for the second paragraph. Remember that you are describing your university and your university life to a student from a Spanish-speaking country.

Mi universidad...

MULTIMEDIA: Internet

After students have finished the *Escritura* section, have them visit the website for *la Universidad Iberoamericana* in Mexico City. Then have students write a brief description of the *Universidad Iberoamericana* campus, based on the interactive map (*mapa del plantel*).

ESCRITURA

A: Suggestions

■ Go over the assignment orally in class to be sure that students understand the meaning of all suggested words and phrases. Assign the preparation of answers in writing as homework. The following day, use one student's answers as a model to form two coherent paragraphs, writing the sentences on the board. Then have students write paragraphs for the next day.
■ Have students make similar tables to compare individuals in the class, using *alojamiento, diversiones, comidas* (¿*cafetería?*), and so on, as the headings.

B: Suggestions

■ If students created charts comparing individuals, collate and analyze the results on the board. Ask: Can you account for any differences based on age? gender? national origin? and so on. After discussing the comments as a class, have students write a brief report on the findings.
■ If you prefer that your students do a journal activity, see *Mi diario* in this chapter of the Workbook.

CHAPTER OPENER PHOTO

Point out the chapter-opener photo and have students talk about their own family experiences and activities. What are their ideas about Hispanic families? Ask questions to encourage students to describe the people in the photo. Pantomime descriptive adjectives.

- *¿Cómo es La mujer, ¿es la madre o la abuela? ¿Es inteligente? ¿elegante? ¿alta? ¿baja? ¿delgada?*
- *Y el hombre, ¿es el padre o el abuelo? ¿Cómo es? ¿Es elegante? ¿inteligente? ¿bajo? ¿gordo?*
- *Y los niños, ¿cómo son? ¿pequeños? ¿extrovertidos?*

Suggestions

- Ask students the following questions to introduce the chapter topic.

  1. Do you live near other members of your family?
  2. When did you leave home? Do you expect to leave home in the future? If so, when?
  3. What expectations does/did your family have in regard to marriage and a family? Do you share those opinions?
  4. Where do/did your grandparents live?

- Ask yes/no and short-answer questions in Spanish using cognates. Write the new vocabulary necessary for these questions on the board: *tener → tienes/tiene/ tienen; vivir → vive/viven; padres = padre y madre; hermanos; abuelos; hijos, mi/mis.*

  1. *¿Su familia vive en (name of the state)? ¿Dónde viven sus padres? ¿Dónde viven sus abuelos? (¿Dónde viven sus hijos?)*
  2. *¿Cuántos hermanos tiene Ud.? ¿Cuántos hermanos tiene su padre/madre?*
  3. *¿Tiene Ud. hijos? ¿Desea tener hijos? ¿Cuántos hijos desea tener?*
  4. *¿Trabaja su padre? ¿Y su madre?*

♻ Reciclado

Encourage students to describe some of their family members using cognates by asking questions.

¿Cómo es su abuelo/tía/madre? ¿Es/Son inteligente(s)? ¿interesante(s)? ¿responsable(s)?

Note

The *Puntos de partida* Online Learning Center includes an interview with a native speaker from Mexico who answers questions similar to those in the preceding *Suggestions.*

CAPÍTULO 2

◀ Una familia mexicana en el Parque Ecológico de Xochimilco, en la Ciudad de México

Resources

For Students

- Workbook
- Laboratory Manual and Laboratory Audio Program
- Quia™ Online Workbook and Online Laboratory Manual
- Video on CD
- Interactive CD-ROM
- *Puntos de partida* Online Learning Center (**www.mhhe.com/puntos7**)

For Instructors

- *Instructor's Manual and Resource Kit,* "Chapter-by-Chapter" Supplementary Materials
- Overhead Transparencies 14–20
- Testing Program
- Test Generator
- Video Program
- Audioscript
- *Puntos de partida* Online Learning Center (**www.mhhe.com/puntos7**)

La familia

CULTURA

- **Perspectivas culturales**

  Entrevista cultural: México

  Entre amigos: ¿Cuántos hermanos tienes?

  Conozca... México

- **Nota cultural:** Hispanic Last Names

- **En los Estados Unidos y el Canadá:** Los Sheen, una familia de actores

- **Literatura de México:** Rosario Castellanos

- **Lectura:** La unidad familiar: ¿Perspectivas culturales válidas o estereotipadas?

VOCABULARIO

- La familia y los parientes
- Los números 31–100
- Adjetivos

PRONUNCIACIÓN

- Stress and Written Accent Marks (Part 1)

GRAMÁTICA

5 Adjectives: Gender, Number, and Position

6 Present Tense of **ser;** Summary of Uses

7 Possessive Adjectives (Unstressed)

8 Present Tense of **-er** and **-ir** Verbs; More About Subject Pronouns

Entrevista cultural

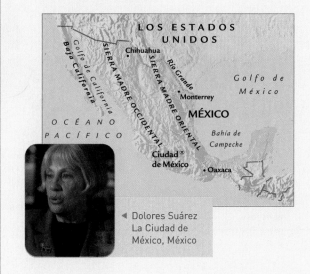

◄ Dolores Suárez
La Ciudad de México, México

Suggestions

- Point out that *esposo* is a cognate, but that *prima* is a false cognate, a word that, although it sounds much like the word in English, does not have a similar meaning. Then, offer the following cognates: *vocabulario, gramática, familia, adjetivo, posesivo, descriptivo.*
- Have students provide examples in English of possessive and descriptive adjectives.
- Have students list their ideas about Mexico, including information on geography, politics, economy, culture, music, and cuisine. When you finish the chapter, return to the lists and ask students what ideas they would change and/or add.

☀ Heritage Speakers

Según proyecciones del censo más reciente, hay más de 35 millones de hispanos en los Estados Unidos. El 58,5 por ciento de estos hispanos tienen sus raíces en México.

MULTIMEDIA

- The multimedia materials that accompany this chapter are referenced in the Student and Instructor's Editions with icons to help you identify when and where to incorporate them.

- The *Instructor's Manual and Resource Kit* (IM/RK) provides suggestions for using the multimedia materials in the classroom.

La familia y los parientes

Notes

- See the model for vocabulary presentation and other material in the *Capítulo 2 Vocabulario: Preparación* section of "Chapter-by-Chapter Supplementary Materials" in the IM.
- Point out that *parientes* is a false cognate.
- Point out the use of the masculine plural form—*el abuelo y la abuela* becomes *los abuelos*, and so on.

Suggestions

- Have students give feminine equivalents of *el padre, el abuelo*, and so on; then give the masculine equivalents of *la tía, la esposa*, and so on.
- Have students identify relationships.

  1. *Es el hijo de mis tíos.*
  2. *Es la esposa de mi hermano.*
  3. *Es la madre de mi padre.*
  4. *Es el hijo de mi madrastra.*
  5. *Es la hija de mi hermana.*

- Point out that many terms of endearment (*términos de cariño/afecto*) are used among Hispanic family members. *Los padres a los hijos: mi hijo (m'ijo), mi hija (m'ijo); nene/a; cielo* (lit. heaven); *corazón* (lit. heart); *mi vida* (lit. my life); *mi amor* (lit. my love). *Los hijos a los padres: papá, papi, papito, papaíto; mamá, mami, mamita, mamaíta.*
- Point out that diminutives are commonly used as terms of endearment: *abuelo → abuelito; hija → hijita; Juan → Juanito; Elena → Elenita.* Use diminutives freely, as appropriate, as you speak Spanish in class.

♺ Reciclado

Have your students describe what particular family members like or do not like.

¿A su padre le gusta comer enchiladas?
¿A su madre le gusta bailar?

VOCABULARIO Preparación

La familia y los parientes°   *relatives*

La familia de Patricia*

los abuelos de Patricia

el abuelo   **la abuela**

Pedro Vargas Núñez ——   —— Eliana Gómez Vargas

los padres de Patricia

la madre   **el padre**

Felipe Castro Ruiz

Gloria Vargas Castro

los tíos de Patricia

el tío   **la tía**

Luis Vargas Gómez

Isabel López de Vargas

los hermanos de Patricia

la hermana   **el hermano**

José Castro Vargas

Rita Castro Vargas

*Patricia Castro Vargas

los primos de Patricia

el primo   **la prima**

Carlos Gómez López

Ana Gómez López

Pícaro, el perro de Carlos

la madre (mamá)	mother (mom)	**la nieta**	granddaughter
el padre (papá)	father (dad)	**el nieto**	grandson
la hija	daughter	**la sobrina**	niece
el hijo	son	**el sobrino**	nephew
los hijos	children		
la esposa	wife	**Las mascotas°**	*Las... Pets*
el esposo	husband		
		el gato	cat
		el pájaro	bird
		el perro	dog

Students can listen to and practice this chapter's vocabulary on the Online Learning Center (**www.mhhe.com/puntos7**), as well as on the Textbook Audio CD, part of the Laboratory Audio Program.

Resources: Transparencies 14–16

☼ Heritage Speakers

- El concepto de la familia para los hispanos no solamente incluye a la familia nuclear sino también a la familia extendida. Cuando llega un nuevo miembro a la familia, como el marido de una hermana, el concepto de la familia crece para incluir a consuegros, cuñados, los concuños o concuñados, etcétera.
- Pregúnteles a los hispanohablantes de la clase qué términos de cariño se usan en sus familias.

Vocabulario útil

el padrastro / la madrastra	stepfather / stepmother
el hijastro / la hijastra	stepson / stepdaughter
el hermanastro / la hermanastra	stepbrother / stepsister
el medio hermano / la media hermana	half-brother / half-sister
el suegro / la suegra	father-in-law / mother-in-law
el yerno / la nuera	son-in-law / daughter-in-law
el cuñado / la cuñada	brother-in-law / sister-in-law
...(ya) murió	. . . has (already) died

■ ■ ■ Conversación

A. ¿Cierto o falso? Look at the drawings of the family that appear on page 60. Decide whether each of the following statements is true (**cierto**) or false (**falso**) according to the drawings. Correct the false statements.

1. José es el hermano de Ana.
2. Eliana es la abuela de Patricia.
3. Ana es la sobrina de Felipe y Gloria.
4. Patricia y José son primos.
5. Gloria es la tía de José.
6. Carlos es el sobrino de Isabel.
7. Pedro es el padre de Luis y Gloria.
8. Isabel y Gloria son las esposas de Luis y Felipe, respectivamente.

B. ¿Quién es?

Paso 1. Complete las oraciones lógicamente.

1. La madre de mi (*my*) padre es mi _____.
2. El hijo de mi tío es mi _____.
3. La hermana de mi padre es mi _____.
4. El esposo de mi abuela es mi _____.

Paso 2. Ahora defina estas (*these*) personas, según (*according to*) el mismo (*same*) modelo.

1. prima   2. sobrino   3. tío   4. abuelo

C. Entrevista. Find out as much as you can about the family of a classmate using the following dialogue as a guide. Use **tengo** (*I have*) and **tienes** (*you have*), as indicated. Use **¿cuántos?** with male relations and **¿cuántas?** with females.

> MODELO: E1:*¿Cuántos hermanos tienes?
> E2: Bueno (*Well*), tengo seis hermanos y una hermana.
> E1: ¿Y cuántos primos?
> E2: ¡Uf! Tengo un montón (*bunch*). Más de veinte.

---

*From this point on in the text, ESTUDIANTE 1 and ESTUDIANTE 2 will be abbreviated as E1 and E2, respectively.

Con. A: Suggestions

- Introduce your own or a fictitious family with a family tree on the board or on an overhead transparency. Start with recognizable cognates *padre* (*papá*) and *madre* (*mamá*); do two family members at a time, assigning names and defining relationships as you go along; students just listen during this phase. Use family photographs to personalize this activity even more.
- After several generations are on the board, go back to check comprehension, asking questions with alternatives: *¿Quién es él, mi abuelo o mi padre?*
- Model the names or integrate them in the tree on the board. Ask students if they have a brother, grandmother, and so on. You may also introduce related vocabulary such as: *soltero/a, casado/a, la familia nuclear*, and *la familia extendida*.
- To follow up, have students use your presentation as a guide when presenting their own family members to the class.

Con. B: Suggestions

- Do as listening comprehension activity, with students providing completion.
- Have students identify the members of each group: *los hijos → el hijo y la hija.*

1. *los abuelos*
2. *los padres*
3. *los hermanos*
4. *los nietos*
5. *los tíos*
6. *los sobrinos*

Con. C: Suggestion

Model dialogue with several students before allowing class to work in pairs. Model options for a small family.

Refrán

«Hijo fuiste, padre serás, como lo hiciste, así te harán.»

Write the *refrán* on the board. For the verbs, write the infinitives.

fuiste = ser	hiciste = hacer
serás = ser	harán = hacer

Give students the meaning of *hacer* (to do) and the two tenses used (past and future). Have students give the meaning of the saying and try to think of similar sayings in English. (*Like father, like son.* OR *The apple doesn't fall far from the tree.*)

Los números 31–100

Reciclado ♻

- Review numbers 1–30 with counting drills and math games.
- Remind students of the -e ending in *veinte* vs. the -a in *treinta*, *cuarenta*, *cincuenta*, and so on.

Suggestions

- Ask ¿*Cómo se dice* thirty-one? ¿thirty-two? Students produce numbers 31–39.
- Model 40, 50, . . . 100.
- Have class count in unison (40–49, 50–59). Then have students count in round robin (60–69, 70–79). Finally, have volunteers count (80–100). Count from 1 to 100 by 10s and 5s. Have volunteers count in reverse.
- Set up a bingo (*lotería*) game in which students fill out cards with numbers from 1–100 using digits and without repeating numbers. Call out numbers in Spanish. The winner (across, down, or diagonal) declares ¡*Lotería*! and must read back winning numbers in Spanish.
- Remind students that, from 31 on, numbers must be written as three words (except the 10s).
- Write on the board: *un coche, cuarenta y un coches; una mesa, sesenta y una mesas.* Point out similarities and emphasize ending of *un* and *una* for plural.
- Remind students that *ciento* is used for numbers greater than 100: *ciento uno, ciento dos,* and so on.
- Dictate cognate nouns and numbers with several students working at the board: *100 estéreos, 76 trombones, 65 saxofones, 92 guitarras, 56 pianos,* and so on.
- Write the following series on the board and have volunteers read and complete them aloud.

1. *1, 4, 7, 10, ¿ ... ?*
2. *0, 1, 10, 2, 3, 32, ¿ ... ?*
3. *10, 15, 13, 18, 16, 21, ¿ ... ?*
4. *2, 4, 3, 9, 4, 16, 5, 25, 6, ¿ ... ?*

NOTA CULTURAL

Follow-Up

Have students say what their full names would be if they were Latin American or Spanish.

Suggestions

- Point out that this is a very traditional wedding invitation in which the groom's and bride's parents appear as the announcers of their children's wedding.
- Have students name the bride's and groom's *apellidos.*

62 ■ Capítulo 2: La familia

Continúe la secuencia:

treinta y uno, treinta y dos...
ochenta y cuatro, ochenta y cinco...

31	treinta y uno	**40**	cuarenta
32	treinta y dos	**50**	cincuenta
33	treinta y tres	**60**	sesenta
34	treinta y cuatro	**70**	setenta
35	treinta y cinco	**80**	ochenta
36	treinta y seis	**90**	noventa
37	treinta y siete	**100**	cien, ciento
38	treinta y ocho		
39	treinta y nueve		

El abuelito Pedro tiene 85 años.
La abuelita Eliana tiene 78 años.

cincuenta y cinco
setenta y ocho
treinta y nueve
cuarenta y cinco
cuarenta y siete
ochenta y cinco

Beginning with 31, Spanish numbers are *not* written in a combined form; **treinta y uno,*** **cuarenta y dos, sesenta y tres,** and so on, must be three separate words.

Cien is used before nouns and in counting.

cien casas	*a (one) hundred houses*
noventa y ocho, noventa y nueve, **cien**	*ninety-eight, ninety-nine, one hundred*

■ ■ ■ Conversación

A. Más problemas de matemáticas. Recuerde: **+ y, − menos, = son.**

1. $30 + 50 = ?$
2. $45 + 45 = ?$
3. $32 + 58 = ?$
4. $77 + 23 = ?$

NOTA CULTURAL

Hispanic Last Names

In most Hispanic countries, people are given two last names (**apellidos**). The custom is demonstrated in this wedding invitation. The names of the bride's parents are in the top left corner: Ramón Ochoa Benítez and Ana Márquez Blanco de Ochoa. Their daughter's name, before her marriage, is Ana Luisa Ochoa Márquez. Her first last name (Ochoa) is her father's first last name, and her second last name (Márquez) is her mother's first last name. The groom's parents are in the top right corner. What do you think his full name (with both last names) is? If you said Antonio Lázaro Pérez, you are correct. Some Spanish-speaking women take their husband's first last name as their new second last name, dropping the second last name they had before marriage. Ana Luisa Ochoa Márquez's name will change to Ana Luisa Ochoa de Lázaro.

> Ramón Ochoa Benítez
> Ana Márquez Blanco de Ochoa
>
> Antonio Lázaro Aguirre
> Susana Pérez de Lázaro
>
> *tienen el gusto de anunciar la boda de sus hijos*
>
> ## Ana Luisa y Antonio
>
> *La ceremonia tendrá lugar*
> *el 2 de julio, a las 12 del mediodía*
> *en la Iglesia de la Candelaria*
>
> *Almuerzo en Restaurante Don Paco*
> *Avda. de la Constitución, 7*
>
> *Lista de bodas: El Corte Inglés*

---

*Remember that when **uno** is part of a compound number (**treinta y uno,** and so on), it becomes **un** before a masculine noun and **una** before a feminine noun: **cincuenta y una mesas; setenta y un coches.***

Refrán

«Más vale pájaro en mano que cien volando.»

Write the *refrán* on the board. Have students guess the meaning of *mano* and *volando*. What is a similar saying in English? (*A bird in the hand is worth two in the bush.*)

National Standards: Comparisons

Have students look up telephone books for different Spanish-speaking cities online. Some phone books allow you to look at multiple listings, and others will search specific names and last names. In some cases, searches of last names require the two last names.

B. Los números de teléfono

Paso 1. Here is part of a page from an Hispanic telephone book. What can you tell about the names? (See the **Nota cultural** on page 62.)

Paso 2. With a classmate, practice giving telephone numbers at random from the list. Your partner will listen and identify the person. **¡OJO!** In many Hispanic countries phone numbers are said differently than in this country. Follow the model.

MODELO: 4–15–00–46 →
    E1: Es el *cuatro-quince-cero cero-cuarenta y seis.*
    E2: Es el número de *A. Lázaro Aguirre.*

Paso 3. Now give your classmate your phone number and get his or hers.

MODELO: Mi número es el…

LAZARO AGUIRRE, A. –Schez Pacheco, 17	415 0046
LAZCANO DEL MORAL, A. –E. Larreta, 14	215 8194
LAZCANO DEL MORAL, A. –Ibiza, 8	274 6868
LEAL ANTON, J. –Pozo, 8	222 3894
LIEBANA RODRIGUEZ, A.	
Guadarrama, 10	463 2593
LOPEZ BARTOLOME, J. –Palma, 69	232 2027
LOPEZ CABRA, J. –E. Solana, 118	407 5086
LOPEZ CABRA, J. –L. Van, 5	776 4602
LOPEZ GONZALEZ, J. A. –Ibiza, 27	409 2552
LOPEZ GUTIERREZ, G. –S. Cameros, 7	478 8494
LOPEZ LOPEZ, J. –Alamedilla, 21	227 3570
LOPEZ MARIN, V. –N. Rey, 7	218 6630
LOPEZ MARIN, V. –N. Rey, 7	463 6873
LOPEZ MARIN, V. –Valmojado, 289	717 2823
LOPEZ NUÑEZ, J. –Pl. Pinazo, sñ	796 0035
LOPEZ NUÑEZ, J. –Rocafort, Bl. 321	796 5387
LOPEZ RODRIGUEZ, C. –Pl. Jesús, 7	429 3278
LOPEZ RODRIGUEZ, J. –Pl. Angel, 15	239 4323
LOPEZ RODRIGUEZ, M. E.	
B. Murillo, 104	233 4239
LOPEZ TRAPERO, A. –Cam. Ingenieros, 1	462 5392
LOPEZ VAZQUEZ, J. –A. Torrejón, 17	433 4646
LOPEZ VEGA, J. –M. Santa Ana, 5	231 2131
LORENTE VILLARREAL, G. –Gandia, 7	252 2758
LORENZO MARTINEZ, A. –Moscareta, 5	479 6282
LORENZO MARTINEZ, A. –P. Laborde, 21	778 2800
LORENZO MARTINEZ, A.	
Av. S. Diego, 116	477 1040
LOSADA MIRON, M. –Padilla, 31	276 9373
LOSADA MIRON, M. –Padilla, 31	431 7461
LOZANO GUILLEN, E.	
Juan H. Mendoza, 5	250 3884
LOZANO PIERA, F. J. –Pinguino, 8	466 3205
LUDEÑA FLORES, G. –Lope Rueda, 56	273 3735
LUENGO CHAMORRO, J.	
Gral Ricardos, 99	471 4906
LUQUE CASTILLO, J. –Pío Arlaban, 121	478 5253
LUQUE CASTILLO, L. –Cardeñosa, 15	477 6644

Con. B: Note

Point out that two last names are used in the Mexican phone book.

Con. B: Variation

Do as a dictation, with several students working at the board.

NOTA COMUNICATIVA

Suggestions

- Introduce singular forms of *tener.* (Review them if you introduced them in the context of the family tree.)
- Model age dialogue with several students, asking about the ages of some of their relatives.

NOTA COMUNICATIVA

Expressing Age

NORA: ¿Cuántos años tienes, abuela?
ABUELA: Setenta y tres, Nora.
NORA: ¿Y cuántos años tiene el abuelo?
ABUELA: Setenta y cinco, mi amor (*love*). Y ahora, dime (*tell me*), ¿cuántos años tienes tú?
NORA: Tengo cuatro.

In Spanish, age is expressed with the phrase **tener** _____ **años** (literally, *to have. . . years*). You have now seen all the singular forms of **tener** (*to have*): **tengo, tienes, tiene.**

C. ¡Seamos (*Let's be*) lógicos! Complete las oraciones lógicamente.

1. Un hombre que (*who*) tiene _____ años es muy viejo (*old*).
2. Un niño (*small child*) que tiene sólo _____ año es muy joven (*young*).
3. La persona más vieja (*oldest*) de mi familia es mi _____.
   Tiene _____ años.
4. La persona más joven (*youngest*) de mi familia es mi _____.
   Tiene _____ años.
5. En mi opinión, es ideal tener _____ años.
6. Si (*If*) una persona tiene _____ años, ya (*already*) es adulta.
7. Para (*In order to*) tomar cerveza en este estado, es necesario tener _____ años.
8. Para mí (*For me*), ¡la idea de tener _____ años es inconcebible (*inconceivable*)!

Need more practice?

- Workbook and Laboratory Manual
- Interactive CD-ROM
- Online Learning Center (www.mhhe.com/puntos7)

Vocabulario: Preparación

National Standards: Communication

Have students ask six classmates how old they are and how old their grandparents are. Students share information by answering questions that you ask to determine the following information:

1. *la persona más vieja* (oldest)
2. *la persona que tiene el abuelo más viejo*
3. *la persona que tiene la abuela más vieja*

 Heritage Speakers

Pregúnteles a los hispanohablantes qué apellidos tienen. Si son estudiantes de la segunda o tercera generación, ¿siguen usando este sistema?

Adjetivos

Suggestions

- Present adjectives in pairs or semantic groups (as organized in the box), using magazine images, names of famous people, and people in class.
- Suggestions for negative adjectives: *feo* (Frankenstein, *un gorila*); *gordo* (Pavarotti, Dom DeLuise), *malo* (Dennis the Menace, Darth Vader), *tonto* (Jim Carrey, Steve Martin).
- Do several pairs; then check comprehension, offering students alternatives: *¿Es guapo o feo Enrique Iglesias?*
- Point out that *bajo/a* refers to height and *corto/a* to length. Also, explain that *joven* is used with people, *nuevo/a* with things, and that *guapo/a* refers to males and females whereas *bonito/a* usually only refers to females and things.
- Have students provide antonyms. *¿Cuál es el antónimo de rico?* → *pobre; ¿bajo?* → *alto;* and so on.
- Describe famous people or people in class using adjectives, sometimes incorrectly. Students respond *sí* or *no*.

Con. A: Suggestion

Have students make similar comparisons of classmates and people they know.

♲ Con. B: Reciclado

Have students review cognates from *Ante todo* before beginning the activity.

guapo	handsome; good-looking
bonito	pretty
feo	ugly
grande	large, big
pequeño	small
casado	married
soltero	single
simpático	nice, likeable
antipático	unpleasant
corto	short (*in length*)
largo	long
bueno	good
malo	bad
listo	smart; clever
tonto	silly, foolish
trabajador	hardworking
perezoso	lazy
rico	rich
pobre	poor
delgado	thin, slender
gordo	fat

Pepe   Juan

Luisito   Esteban

don Paco   Jaime

nuevo   viejo

To describe a masculine singular noun, use **alt*o*, baj*o*,** and so on; use **alt*a*, baj*a*,** and so on for feminine singular nouns.

■ ■■ Conversación

A. Preguntas. Conteste según los dibujos.

1. Einstein es listo. ¿Y el chimpancé?

José   Roberto

2. Roberto es trabajador. ¿Y José?

Pablo   Pepe

3. Pepe es bajo. ¿Y Pablo?

Jaime   Memo

4. Jaime es bueno y simpático. También es guapo. ¿Y Memo?

Paco   Ramón

5. Ramón Ramírez es casado. ¿Y Paco Pereda?

6. El libro es viejo. ¿Y el lápiz?

Capítulo 2: La familia

Resources: Transparencies 17, 18

National Standards: Comparisons

In the U.S. and Canada, to indicate height using a hand gesture, we extend our arm with the palm of the hand facing the floor. In several Latin American countries, this same gesture is used to indicate the height of animals. To indicate the height of humans, Latin Americans generally extend the arm out, turning the hand horizontally, with the palm facing outward.

B. **¿Cómo es?** Describe a famous personality, using as many adjectives as possible so that your classmates can guess who the person is. Don't forget to use cognate adjectives that you have seen in **Ante todo** and **Capítulo 1.**

MODELO: Es un hombre importante; controla una gran compañía de *software.* Es muy trabajador y muy rico. (Bill Gates)

PRONUNCIACIÓN
Stress and Written Accent Marks (Part 1)

Some Spanish words have *written accent marks* over one of the vowels. That mark is called **el acento (ortográfico).** It means that the syllable containing the accented vowel is stressed when the word is pronounced, as in the word **bolígrafo (bo-LI-gra-fo),** for example.

Although all Spanish words of more than one syllable have a stressed vowel, most words do not have a written accent mark. Most words have the spoken stress exactly where native speakers of Spanish would predict it. These two simple rules tell you which syllable is accented when a word does not have a written accent.

> In this chapter you will learn predictable patterns of stress. In the next chapter, you will learn when the written accent mark is needed.

■ Words that end in a vowel, or **-n,** or **-s** are stressed on the next-to-last syllable.

co-sa	e-**xa**-men	i-ta-**lia**-no
gra-cias	**e**-res	**len**-guas

■ Words that end in any other consonant are stressed on the last syllable.

us-**ted**	es-pa-**ñol**	doc-**tor**
na-tu-**ral**	pro-fe-**sor**	es-**tar**

A. **Sílabas.** The following words have been separated into syllables for you. Read them aloud, paying careful attention to where the spoken stress should fall.

1. Stress on the next-to-last syllable

chi-no	si-lla	li-te-ra-tu-ra
ar-te	Car-men	cien-cias
cla-se	li-bro	o-ri-gen
me-sa	con-se-je-ra	com-pu-ta-do-ra

2. Stress on the last syllable

se-ñor	co-lor	sen-ti-men-tal
mu-jer	po-pu-lar	lu-gar
fa-vor	li-ber-tad	u-ni-ver-si-dad
ac-tor	ge-ne-ral	con-trol

B. **Vocales.** Indicate the stressed vowel in each of the following words.

1. mo-chi-la
2. me-nos
3. re-gu-lar
4. i-gual-men-te
5. E-cua-dor
6. e-le-gan-te
7. li-be-ral
8. hu-ma-ni-dad

☼ Heritage Speakers

Anime a los estudiantes hispanohablantes a leer una serie de palabras, modelando la pronunciación para los estudiantes angloparlantes. Déles palabras agudas (*papel, popular, regatear*), llanas (*biblioteca, consejero, profesora*) y esdrújulas (*música, América, bolígrafo*). Después, pídales a los otros estudiantes que imiten la pronunciación de las palabras.

Notes

■ Stress and accent marks are presented in this chapter and in *Capítulo 3.*

■ If you emphasize correct spelling and pronunciation on graded material, cover these sections on written accents carefully. Once you have introduced "Stress and Written Accent Marks (Part 2)," you can practice using accents through short dictations.

Preliminary Exercises

■ Read these words and ask whether the stress is on the last syllable or on the next-to-last syllable. Ask students to raise their hands when the stress is on the last syllable:

hable, hablé	*espere, esperé*
doblo, dobló	*pasó, paso*
bajé, baje	*pasé, pase*

■ Ask whether stress is on the next-to-last or the third-from-last (antepenultimate) syllable. Have students raise their hands if the stress is on the penultimate syllable.

como, cómico	*político, polo*
pero, período	*cinco, simpático*

Suggestions

■ You may wish to point out that a diphthong constitutes one syllable and follows the normal rules of accentuation. Emphasize that *a, e, o* in combination with each other cannot form a diphthong in Spanish. Any such combination remains as two different syllables.

■ Dictate the following words, then have students decide: *¿Diptongo o no? Mao, Luis, Hawai, Leo, Bea, sierra, caos, poeta, ciencias, lengua.*

■ Teach students to divide words into syllables to practice syllable structure in Spanish. This will help them recognize patterned prefixes and suffixes as well as write stress marks accurately.

■ Point out that there are no short (schwa) syllables in Spanish; all syllables with their vowels must be fully pronounced. At this point it is better for students to overpronounce slowly and carefully rather than rush through the words.

A, B: Variation

Ask students to listen to the following familiar words and indicate where the spoken stress falls: *universidad, compañero, consejero, biblioteca, profesora, estudiante, extranjero, comedia, programa.* Ask them which of the two rules explains the placement of the stress.

Suggestion

Read both versions of the poem. Point out that there is only one English equivalent given. Have the students note the differences between the two versions and who is described in each.

Follow-Up

- Have the students tell which adjectives could be used to describe themselves.
- Ask questions about the couple in the photo.

  ¿Quiénes son?
  ¿Dónde están?
  ¿De dónde son?
  ¿Son hermanos (amigos, estudiantes, and so on)?
  ¿Qué hacen?
  ¿Cómo son?
  ¿Son _____ (cue students with adjectives)?
  ¿Les gusta hablar (bailar, estudiar, and so on)?

Bright Idea

Suggestion

Have students write their own *poemas sencillos* in class, using the one presented as a model. Suggest possible topics: *mi perro / madre / compañero/a de cuarto / novio/a*, and so on.

Adjectives with *ser*

Suggestion

Bring or have students bring magazine clippings of famous people. Have students identify and describe them.

---

5 **Describing • Adjectives: Gender, Number, and Position**

Un poema sencillo

Amigo
Fiel
Amable
Simpático
¡Lo admiro!

Amiga
Fiel
Amable
Simpática
¡La admiro!

According to their form, which of the adjectives below can be used to describe each person? Which can refer to you?

Marta: ⎰
Mario: ⎱ fiel   amable   simpática   simpático

Adjectives (**Los adjetivos**) are words used to talk about nouns or pronouns. Adjectives may describe or tell how many there are.

You have been using adjectives to describe people since **Ante todo.** In this section, you will learn more about describing the people and things around you.

> **adjective** = a word used to describe a noun or pronoun

large desk
tall woman

few desks
several women

Adjectives with *ser*

In Spanish, forms of **ser** are used with adjectives that describe basic, inherent qualities or characteristics of the nouns or pronouns they modify. **Ser** establishes the "norm," that is, what is considered basic reality: *snow is cold, water is wet.*

Tú **eres amable.**
You're nice. (You're a nice person.)

El diccionario **es barato.**
The dictionary is inexpensive.

A simple poem   Friend Loyal Kind Nice I admire him/her!

National Standards: Comparisons

In this chapter students will learn that the majority of adjectives in Spanish are placed after the noun. In English, however, descriptive adjectives precede the noun. When using more than one adjective, English has strict rules with regard to adjective placement in pre-noun position. Placement of these adjectives depends on the type of information that is communicated. For example, adjectives of opinion are placed before those of size, followed by age, shape, color, origin, and then material. English speakers will naturally say, "The big old red brick house." Usually, however, no more than three adjectives are used before a noun.

Forms of Adjectives

Spanish adjectives agree in gender and number with the noun or pronoun they modify. Each adjective has more than one form.

A. Adjectives that end in **-o (alto)** have four forms, showing gender and number.*

	Masculine	Feminine
Singular	amigo alto	amiga alta
Plural	amigos altos	amigas altas

B. Adjectives that end in **-e (amable)** or in most consonants (**fiel**) have only two forms, a singular and a plural form. The plural of adjectives is formed in the same way as that of nouns.

[Práctica A–D]

	Masculine	Feminine
Singular	amigo amable	amiga amable
	amigo fiel	amiga fiel
Plural	amigos amables	amigas amables
	amigos fieles	amigas fieles

Notes in brackets, like [**Práctica A–D**] here, let you know that you are now ready to do all of the indicated activities, in this case, **Práctica A–D** (pages 69–70). Then, after you read grammar point C (the next one in this section), you will be prepared to do Práctica E on page 70, as the bracketed reference in C indicates.

C. Most adjectives of nationality have four forms.

The names of many languages—which are masculine in gender—are the same as the masculine singular form of the corresponding adjective of nationality: **el español, el inglés, el alemán, el francés,** and so on.

[Práctica E]

Note that in Spanish the names of languages and adjectives of nationality are not capitalized, but the names of countries are: **español, española,** but **España.**

	Masculine	Feminine
Singular	el doctor	la doctora
	mexicano	mexicana
	español	española
	alemán	alemana
	inglés	inglesa
Plural	los doctores	las doctoras
	mexicanos	mexicanas
	españoles	españolas
	alemanes	alemanas
	ingleses	inglesas

Placement of Adjectives

As you have probably noticed, adjectives do not always precede the noun in Spanish as they do in English. Note the following rules for adjective placement.

A. Adjectives of quantity, like numbers, *precede* the noun, as do the interrogatives **¿cuánto/a?** and **¿cuántos/as?**

Hay **muchas** sillas y **dos** escritorios.
There are many chairs and two desks.

¿Cuánto dinero necesitas?
How much money do you need?

---

*Adjectives that end in **-dor, -ón, -án,** and **-in** also have four forms: **trabajador, trabajadora, trabajadores, trabajadoras.**

Gramática

Forms of Adjectives

Note
Gender agreement with adjectives has been used by students since *Ante todo.* Handling of this grammar section will depend on how much you have stressed agreement.

Suggestions
- Emphasize the concept of agreement.
- Point out that adjectives must agree with the gender of the noun they modify grammatically: *Pepe es una persona muy simpática.*
- Remind students that adjectives must also agree with the noun they modify in number.
  Mi profesor es inteligente. / Mis profesores son inteligentes.
- Point out that adjectives of nationality can also be used as nouns: *el español* = the Spaniard, *los ingleses* = the English people, and so on.

Placement of Adjectives

Emphasis D: Suggestions
Ask students the following questions:

- *¿Cómo se dice en inglés... una ciudad grande / una gran ciudad; un estado grande / un gran estado?*
- *¿Cómo se dice en español... a large university / a great university; a large book / a great book?*

National Standards: Comparisons

Explain to students that the concept of gender is marked in many languages in adjective and noun forms, and, in some languages such as Arabic, even in verb forms. In English the gender of people and some animals is distinguished lexically (boy/girl, bull/cow, waiter/waitress), but descriptive adjectives do not vary (tall boy, tall girl; brown bull, brown cow; nice waiter, nice waitress). And although English does not assign grammatical gender to objects or concepts, some traditionally have gender associations: Mother Earth, Mother Nature, Father Time, Father Sun. Ask students if they can think of additional items or concepts that they consider masculine or feminine (cars, ships, countries, cities, death).

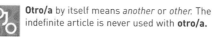

Otro/a by itself means *another* or *other.* The indefinite article is never used with **otro/a.**

Busco **otro** coche.
I'm looking for another car.

B. Adjectives that describe the qualities of a noun and distinguish it from others generally *follow* the noun. Adjectives of nationality are included in this category.

un perro **bueno**
un dependiente **trabajador**
una joven **delgada** y **morena**
un joven **español**

C. The adjectives **bueno** and **malo** may precede or follow the noun they modify. When they precede a masculine singular noun, they shorten to **buen** and **mal,** respectively.

[Conversación]

un **buen** perro / un perro **bueno**
una **buena** perra / una perra **buena**
un **mal** día / un día **malo**
una **mala** noche / una noche **mala**

D. The adjective **grande** may also precede or follow the noun. When it precedes a singular noun—masculine or feminine—it shortens to **gran** and means *great* or *impressive.* When it follows the noun, it means *large* or *big.*

[Conversación]

Nueva York es una ciudad **grande.**
New York is a large city.

Nueva York es una **gran** ciudad.
New York is a great (impressive) city.

Forms of *this/these*

A. The demonstrative adjective *this/these* has four forms in Spanish.* Learn to recognize them when you see them.

este	hijo	*this son*
esta	hija	*this daughter*
estos	hijos	*these sons*
estas	hijas	*these daughters*

B. You have already seen the neuter demonstrative **esto.** It refers to something that is as yet unidentified.

¿Qué es esto?
What is this?

AUTOPRUEBA

Give the correct adjective endings.

1. una casa viej_____
2. los tíos español_____
3. un primo alt_____
4. est_____ sobrino
5. las hermanas rubi_____
6. est_____ amigos

Answers: 1. vieja 2. españoles 3. alto 4. este 5. rubias 6. estos

---

*You will learn all forms of the Spanish demonstrative adjectives (this, that, these, those) in **Gramática 9.**

Note

In *Puntos de partida*, students will learn that some adjectives (*buen/bueno, mal/malo,* and demonstrative adjectives) appear in the pre-noun position. They do not learn, however, that adjectives may come before the noun when they provide gratuitous or subjective information: *la elegante princesa, la blanca nieve, la sangrienta guerra.* All of the forms for the demonstrative adjectives will be taught in *Gramática 9.*

Forms of *this/these*

Note

Forms of *este* are not actively practiced in this section, but are included for recognition only, so that they may be used freely in direction lines and in reading passages. The complete set of demonstratives is introduced in *Capítulo 4.*

Suggestion

Remind students to try the *Autoprueba.*

National Standards: Communication

Note that in some Hispanic countries, the word *perrita* is preferred when speaking about female dogs. For some native speakers, the term *perra* has negative connotations.

■ ■ ■ Práctica

A. ¡Anticipemos! Hablando (*Speaking*) **de la universidad.** Tell what you think about aspects of your university by telling whether you agree (**Estoy de acuerdo.**) or disagree (**No estoy de acuerdo.**) with the statements. If you don't have an opinion, say **No tengo opinión.**

1. Hay suficientes actividades sociales.
2. Los profesores son excelentes.
3. Las residencias son buenas.
4. Hay suficientes gimnasios.
5. Es fácil (*easy*) aparcar el coche.
6. Es fácil llegar (*to get*) a la universidad en autobús.
7. Hay suficientes zonas verdes.
8. Los restaurantes, cafeterías y cafés son buenos.
9. En la librería, los precios son bajos.
10. Los bibliotecarios son cooperativos.

B. La familia de José Miguel. The following incomplete sentences describe some members of the family of José Miguel Martín Velasco, a student from Quito, Ecuador. Scan the adjectives to see which ones can complete the statement. Pay close attention to the form of each adjective.

1. El tío Miguel es _____. (trabajador / alto / nueva / grande / fea / amable)
2. Los abuelos son _____. (rubio / antipático / inteligentes / viejos / religiosos / sinceras)
3. La madre de José Miguel es _____. (rubio / elegante / sentimental / buenas / casadas / simpática)
4. Las primas son _____. (solteras / morenas / lógica / bajos / mala)

Vocabulario útil			

Here are some additional adjectives to use in this section. You should be able to guess the meaning of some of them.

agresivo/a	¿ ?	**difícil**	difficult
amistoso/a	friendly	**encantador(a)**	delightful
animado/a	lively	**fácil**	easy
atrevido/a	daring	**sensible**	sensitive
cariñoso/a	affectionate	**suficiente**	¿ ?
chistoso/a	amusing	**tolerante**	¿ ?
comprensivo/a	understanding	**travieso/a**	mischievous

C. ¡Dolores es igual! Cambie (*Change*) Diego → Dolores.

Diego es un buen estudiante. Es listo y trabajador y estudia mucho. Es estadounidense de origen mexicano, y por eso habla español. Desea ser profesor de antropología. Diego es moreno, guapo y atlético. Le gustan las fiestas grandes y tiene buenos amigos en la universidad. Tiene parientes estadounidenses y mexicanos.

Gramática   Sesenta y nueve ■ 69

Prác. A: Preliminary Exercise

Ask students specific questions about their university.

> *¿Cómo son los profesores de su universidad?*
> *¿Son buenas las residencias?*
> *¿Es deliciosa la comida de la cafetería?*
> *¿Son baratos los libros de la librería?*
> *¿Hay muchas actividades sociales?*

Prác. A: Suggestion

Have students correct statements given or provide their own.

Prác. B: Preliminary Exercise

Have students describe the following things. Cue students with questions and adjectives.

1. *¿Su famila?* → (*No*) *Es una familia grande.* (*interesante, importante, amable, intelectual*)
2. *¿Los perros?* → (*No*) *Son valientes.* (*fiel, impaciente, inteligente, importante*)
3. *¿Su universidad?* → (*No*) *Es nueva.* (*viejo, grande, pequeño, bueno, famoso, malo*)

Prác. B: Suggestion

Have students correct the form of the adjectives when inappropriate forms are provided.

♺ Reciclado

Remind students that the indefinite article (*un, una*) is not used after *ser* before unmodified nouns of profession.

> *Ella es profesora.*
> *Ella es una buena profesora.*

Prác. C: Follow-Up

■ Have students respond *cierto* or *falso*.

1. *A Diego no le gusta estudiar.*
2. *Diego es de Sudamérica.*
3. *Le gustan los deportes.*
4. *No habla español porque es norteamericano.*

■ Have students change *Diego* to *Dolores* and change the text when possible to describe her as being the opposite of Diego. Then, change the subject of the paragraph to *Diego y Dolores.* **¡OJO!** Help students make changes they do not yet know how to make, for example, *le gustan* → *les gustan* and *tiene* → *tienen.*

Gramática ■ **69**

Name famous people (imagine that they are all alive). Have students tell what language they speak and what their nationality is or where they are from. Examples: *Pablo Picasso, Napoleón, Antonio Banderas, Beethoven, Enrique Iglesias, Marc Anthony, María Callas y Renata Tebaldi, Pancho Villa, Juan y Eva Perón.*

Con: Suggestions

- Encourage students to give simple explanations using *porque* and *por eso.*
- Reenter or introduce expressions such as *¿Ah, sí?, ¿De veras?, No, hombre,* and so on, and encourage students to use them in their reactions.

D. Descripciones. Describa a su familia, haciendo oraciones completas con estas palabras.

MODELO: Mi familia no es grande. Es pequeña. Mi padre tiene 50 años.

| Mi familia
Mi padre/madre
Mi ¿ ? (otro pariente)
Mi perro/gato | **+** | (no) es | **+** | interesante
amable
grande
intelectual
nuevo | bueno
famoso
importante
(im)paciente
pequeño | fiel
viejo
malo
¿ ? |

+ tiene...años

NOTA COMUNICATIVA

Más nacionalidades de Latinoamérica

Centroamérica		**Sudamérica**	
costarricense	nicaragüense	argentino/a	ecuatoriano/a
guatemalteco/a	panameño/a	boliviano/a	paraguayo/a
hondureño/a	salvadoreño/a	brasileño/a	peruano/a
		chileno/a	uruguayo/a
		colombiano/a	venezolano/a

E. Nacionalidades. Tell what nationality the following persons could be and where they might live: **el Brasil, Alemania** (*Germany*), **China, Inglaterra** (*England*), **un país de Centroamérica, Francia, Italia.** The answer for number 2 can vary.

1. Monique habla francés; es _____ y vive (*she lives*) en _____.
2. José habla español; es _____ y vive en _____.
3. Greta y Hans hablan alemán; son _____ y viven en _____.
4. Gilberto habla portugués; es _____ y vive en _____.
5. Gina y Sofía hablan italiano; son _____ y viven en _____.
6. Winston habla inglés; es _____ y vive en _____.
7. Hai (*m.*) y Han (*m.*) hablan chino; son _____ y viven en _____.

■ ■ ■ Conversación

Asociaciones. With several classmates, talk about people you associate with the following phrases. Use the model as a guide. To express agreement or disagreement, use **(No) Estoy de acuerdo.**

MODELO: un gran hombre →
E1: Creo que (*I believe that*) el presidente es un gran hombre.
E2: No estoy de acuerdo.

1. un mal restaurante
2. un buen programa de televisión
3. una gran mujer, un gran hombre
4. un buen libro (¿una novela?), un libro horrible

Need more practice?

- Workbook and Laboratory Manual
- Interactive CD-ROM
- Online Learning Center (www.mhhe.com/puntos7)

National Standards: Communication

Have students interview each other to determine at least three adjectives that best describe the interviewees. Have them report their findings about their classmates.

¿Recuerda Ud.?

Before beginning **Gramática 6,** review the forms and uses of **ser** that you have already learned by answering these questions.

1. ¿Es Ud. estudiante o profesor(a)?
2. ¿Cómo es Ud.? ¿Es una persona sentimental? ¿inteligente? ¿paciente? ¿elegante?
3. ¿Qué hora es? ¿A qué hora es la clase de español?
4. ¿Qué es un hospital? ¿Es una persona? ¿una cosa? ¿un edificio?

6   Expressing *to be* • Present Tense of *ser*; Summary of Uses

Presentaciones

Manolo Durán y Lola Benítez *son* esposos. Manolo habla de quiénes *son.*

—Hola. Me llamo Manolo Durán.

- *Soy* profesor en la universidad.
- *Soy* alto y moreno.
- *Soy* de Sevilla, España.

—¿Y Lola Benítez, mi esposa? Complete la descripción de ella.

Es _____ (profesión).
Es _____ y _____ (descripción).
Es de _____ (origen).

Málaga, España
bonita
profesora
delgada

ser (*to be*)			
yo	soy	nosotros/as	somos
tú	eres	vosotros/as	sois
Ud. él ella	es	Uds. ellos ellas	son

As you know, there are two Spanish verbs that mean *to be:* **ser** and **estar.** They are not interchangeable; the meaning that the speaker wishes to convey determines their use. In this chapter, you will review the uses of **ser** that you already know and learn some new ones. Remember to use **estar** to express location and to ask how someone is feeling. You will learn more about the uses of **estar** in **Capítulo 5.**

Some basic language functions of **ser** are presented here. You have used or seen all of them already in this and previous chapters.

Gramática 6

Present Tense of *ser*; Summary of Uses

🔁 **Reciclado**

Before teaching the conjugations of *ser*, review subject pronouns. Review the differences between *tú* and *Ud.* Have students tell you the difference between *nosotros/as* and *vosotros/as.* Ask where *vosotros* is used most.

Notes

■ Students have already used forms of *estar* in ¿*Cómo está(s)?* and for telling location. There is no need to go into more detail about *estar* at this time.
■ Explain that *Manolo* is a nickname for *Manuel.*

Suggestion

Ask the following questions about the *minidiálogo.*

¿*Qué es Manolo?*
¿*Es estudiante o profesor?*
¿*De dónde es?*
¿*Quién es Lola?*
¿*Cómo es Lola?*
¿*Y Manolo?*

Variation

Have students practice the *minidiálogo* in small groups, using information about themselves (Manolo's introduction) and about an important person in their lives (Lola's introduction).

🔁 **Reciclado**

Review *ser* for telling time (from *Ante todo*). Telling time is not explicitly listed or reviewed in this section. You may wish to add it to your presentation or discussion.

National Standards: Comparisons

Explain to students that in many languages, the most commonly used verbs such as *to be, to have,* and *to go* are often irregular. English and Spanish are no exception. Point out to students that *ser* will be irregular in many verb tenses, and ask students to name the forms of *to be* (I am, you are, he is, . . . ; I was, you were, he was, . . .). They will note that *to be* is also irregular in many tenses in English.

72 ■ Capítulo 2: La familia

- Most uses of *ser* in this section are a review of material formally presented or used in *Ante todo*. Other uses of *ser* will appear in the later chapters: in *Capítulo 3*, to tell what something is made of; in *Capítulo 5*, in contrast with *estar*; in *Capítulo 8*, to mean *to take place*.
- Point out that the indefinite article is not used after *ser* before unmodified (undescribed) nouns of profession. *Ella es profesora.*

Possession

Suggestions

- Practice possessive phrases to emphasize that there is no *'s* in Spanish: *Es el libro de Anita. Son los lápices de la profesora.*
- Point out the difference between *el* (article) and *él* (subject pronoun). Emphasize that *de* does not contract with *él*.

Suggestion

Remind students to try the *Autoprueba*.

♻ Prác. A: Reciclado

Review classroom vocabulary and practice *ser* + noun. Hold up or point to classroom objects, asking *¿Qué es esto?* Elicit plural forms by holding up two books, pencils, and so on.

Prác. A: Preliminary Exercise

Do a chain drill: *Ana es estudiante. yo → Yo soy estudiante.* (*Mario y Juan, Uds., Lilia y yo, tú, vosotros, Teresa*)

To Identify

To *identify* people and things [Práctica A]	Yo soy **estudiante.** **Alicia y yo** somos **amigas.** La doctora Ramos es **profesora.** **Esto** es **un libro.**
Remember that the notes in brackets refer you to activities that practice the grammar point.	

To Describe

To *describe* people and things*	Soy **sentimental.** *I'm sentimental (a sentimental person).* El coche es **muy viejo.** *The car is very old.*

Origin

With **de,** to express *origin* [Práctica B–C]	Somos **de los Estados Unidos,** pero nuestros padres son **de la Argentina.** ¿**De dónde** es Ud.? *We're from the United States, but our parents are from Argentina. Where are you from?*

Generalization

To express *generalizations* (only **es**) [Conversación B]	Es **importante** estudiar, pero no es **necesario** estudiar todos los días. *It's important to study, but it's not necessary to study every day.*

Here are two basic language functions of **ser** that you have not yet practiced.

Possession

With **de,** to express *possession* [Práctica D]	Es el perro **de Carla.** *It's Carla's dog.* Son las gatas **de Jorge.** *They're Jorge's (female) cats.*
Note that there is no **'s** in Spanish.	
The masculine singular article **el** contracts with the preposition **de** to form **del.** No other article contracts with **de.**	de + el → del Es la casa **del** profesor. *It's the (male) professor's house.* Es la casa **de la** profesora. *It's the (female) professor's house.*

---

*You practiced this language function of **ser** in **Gramática 5** in this chapter.

National Standards: Communication

Point out different things you can express with the verb *ser:* who someone/something is, whom something is for, and so on.

| With **para**, to tell for whom or what something *is intended* | ¿*Romeo y Julieta*? Es **para** la clase de inglés. *Romeo and Juliet? It's for English class.* |
| [Conversación A] | —¿**Para** quién son los regalos?
 —(Son) **Para** mi nieto.
 Who are the presents for?
 (They're) For my grandson. |

■■■ Práctica

A. ¡Anticipemos! Los parientes de Gloria. Look back at the family drawings on page 60. Then tell whether the following statements are true (**cierto**) or false (**falso**) from Gloria's standpoint. Correct the false statements.

1. Felipe y yo somos hermanos.
2. Pedro es mi esposo.
3. Pedro y Eliana son mis (*my*) padres.
4. Carlos es mi sobrino.
5. Mi hermano es el esposo de Isabel.
6. El padre de Felipe no es abuelo todavía (*yet*).
7. Mi familia no es muy grande.

AUTOPRUEBA

Give the correct forms of **ser**.

1. yo _____
2. Ud. _____
3. tú _____
4. Pedro _____
5. Inés y yo _____
6. ellos _____

Answers: 1. *soy* 2. *es* 3. *eres* 4. *es* 5. *somos* 6. *son*

B. Nacionalidades

Paso 1. ¿De dónde son, según los nombres, apellidos y ciudades (*cities*)?

MODELO: João Gonçalves, Lisboa → João Gonçalves es de Portugal.

1. John Doe, Nueva York
2. Karl Lotze, Berlín
3. Graziana Lazzarino, Roma
4. María Gómez, Ciudad Juárez
5. Claudette Moreau, París
6. Timothy Windsor, Londres

Paso 2. Ahora, ¿de dónde es Ud.? ¿De este estado? ¿de una metrópoli? ¿de un área rural? ¿Es Ud. de una ciudad que tiene un nombre hispano? ¿Es de otro país (*country*)?

Naciones

Alemania
los Estados Unidos
Francia
Inglaterra
Italia
México
Portugal

C. Personas extranjeras

Paso 1. ¿Quiénes son, de dónde son y dónde trabajan ahora?

MODELO: Teresa: actriz / de Madrid / en Cleveland → Teresa es actriz. Es de Madrid. Ahora trabaja en Cleveland.

1. Carlos Miguel: médico (*doctor*) / de Cuba / en Milwaukee
2. Maripili: profesora / de Burgos / en Miami
3. Mariela: dependienta / de Buenos Aires / en Nueva York
4. Juan: dentista* / de Lima / en Los Ángeles

Paso 2. Ahora hable sobre un amigo o pariente según el **Paso 1.**

---

*A number of professions end in **-ista** in both masculine and feminine forms. The article indicates gender: **el/la dentista, el/la artista,** and so on.

Prác. A: Suggestions

■ Do as listening activity. Have students assume that you are Gloria or Felipe. Adjust items 1, 2, and 6 as needed.

■ Ask personalized questions based on statements:

> ¿Tiene Ud. un esposo (una esposa)?
> ¿Tiene abuelos/as?
> ¿Cuántos?
> ¿Tiene primos?
> ¿De quién es sobrino?
> ¿Es tío/a?

and so on.

Prác. B: Suggestion

Model the pronunciation of names and countries.

Prác. B: Extension

■ Review names of languages (*francés, español, italiano, inglés, alemán*). Have students expand by telling where people are from and what language they speak.

■ Name real or fictitious people from countries listed, asking ¿*De dónde es* _____?

■ Imagine that you are a friend of persons listed in *Práctica B*. Tell where both of you are from: *John y yo somos de* _____. *Hablamos* _____.

Prác. B: Follow-Up

¿*Es Ud. del norte de los Estados Unidos / del Canadá? ¿del oeste? ¿del este? ¿del sur?*

Prác. C: Follow-Up

Have students create sentences about famous Hispanics. Put information on the board in columns to help students form sentences or ask cue questions:

> ¿De dónde es _____?
> Personas: Laura Esquivel, Alex Rodríguez, Lee Treviño, Salvador Dalí, Julio Iglesias, Edward James Olmos, José Lima, Antonio Banderas
> Categorías: atleta, pintor, cantante, escritor (writer), actor
> Naciones: la Argentina, España, los Estados Unidos, México, la República Dominicana

Prác. D: Suggestion

Have students give simple explanations using *porque, por eso.*

Prác. D: Follow-Up

Have students answer based on what they consider to be a typical family. *¿De quién es el coche (son los coches)? ¿A quién escucha más el hijo / la hija, al padre o a la madre? ¿De quién son los discos compactos? ¿De quién son las herramientas (tools)? ¿De quién es la cocina (kitchen)?*

Prác. E: Suggestion

Have students write/narrate brief descriptions about themselves based on this paragraph.

NOTA COMUNICATIVA

🔄 **Reciclado**
Por eso (expression with *por*) was presented in *Capítulo 1.*

D. **¡Seamos lógicos!** ¿De quién son estas cosas? Con un compañero/una compañera, haga y conteste preguntas (*ask and answer questions*) según el modelo. Las respuestas pueden variar (*can vary*).

> MODELO: E1: ¿De quién es el perro?
> E2: Es de…

¿De quién es/son… ?

1. la casa en Beverly Hills
2. la casa en Viena
3. la camioneta (*station wagon*)
4. el perro
5. las fotos de la Argentina
6. las mochilas con todos los libros

Personas
las estudiantes
la actriz
el niño
la familia con diez hijos
el estudiante extranjero
los Sres. Schmidt

E. **¡Somos familia!** Complete el párrafo con la forma correcta de **ser.**

Me llamo Antonia y _soy_ [1] de Chicago. (Yo) _soy_ [2] estudiante de ingeniería en la Universidad de Illinois, y tengo muchos amigos en Chicago. Mis amigos _son_ [3] de muchas partes[a] y muchos _son_ [4] hispanos. Mi familia _es_ [5] de origen mexicano y aunque nunca he vivido[b] en México, hablo bastante bien[c] el español. Me gusta practicar español con mi amigo Javier. Javier _es_ [6] de Costa Rica y estudia ingeniería también. Javier y yo _somos_ [7] los asistentes del profesor Thomas; por eso pasamos mucho tiempo juntos.[d] Javier _es_ [8] muy guapo y simpático, pero nosotros sólo _somos_ [9] buenos amigos. Javier _es_ [10] el novio de mi mejor[e] amiga.

[a]*places* [b]*aunque… although I have never lived* [c]*bastante… rather well* [d]*pasamos… we spend a lot of time together* [e]*best*

Need more practice?

- Workbook and Laboratory Manual
- Interactive CD-ROM
- Online Learning Center (www.mhhe.com/puntos7)

■ ■ ■ **Conversación**

NOTA COMUNICATIVA

Explaining Your Reasons

In conversation, it is often necessary to explain a decision, tell why someone did something, and so on. Here are some simple words and phrases that speakers use to offer explanations.

porque because	**para** in order to
— ¿Por qué necesitamos un televisor nuevo?	*Why do we need a new TV set?*
— Pues… **para** mirar el partido de fútbol… ¡Es el campeonato!	*Well . . . (in order) to watch the soccer game . . . It's the championship!*
— ¿Por qué trabajas tanto?	*Why do you work so much?*
— **¡Porque** necesitamos el dinero!	*Because we need the money!*

Note the differences between **porque** (one word, no accent) and the interrogative **¿por qué?** (two words, accent on **qué**), which means *why?*.

National Standards: Communication

Students will learn the word *la camioneta* (*Práctica D*, item 3) as active vocabulary in *Capítulo 7*. They have already learned the word *el coche* (*Capítulo 2*). You might point out that words for vehicles vary from country to country. *El coche* is the most common term for car in Spain, while *el carro* is more common in most of Latin America. For some Spanish speakers, *la camioneta* means a van or pickup truck. *El camión* for some speakers refers to a large, commercial truck, but for others it is a pickup truck. In the Caribbean, a truck is often called *un guagua*. Interestingly, in Andean regions, *el guagua* means baby.

A. El regalo ideal. Look at Diego's list of gifts and what his family members like. With a partner, decide who receives each gift and why. The first one is done for you.

MODELO: **1.** una novela de Stephen King →
E1: ¿Para quién es la novela de Stephen King?
E2: Es para la prima.
E1: ¿Por qué?
E2: Porque le gustan las novelas de horror.

REGALOS

2. la calculadora
3. los libros de literatura clásica
4. los discos compactos de Andrés Segovia
5. el televisor
6. el radio
7. el dinero

MIEMBROS DE LA FAMILIA

a. el padre: Le gusta escuchar las noticias (*news*).
b. los abuelos: Les gusta mucho la música de guitarra clásica.
c. la madre: Le gusta mirar programas cómicos.
d. el hermano: Le gustan mucho las historias viejas.
e. la hermana: Desea estudiar en otro estado.
f. el primo: Le gustan las matemáticas.
g. la prima: Le gustan las novelas de horror.

B. ¿Qué opinas? Exprese opiniones originales, afirmativas o negativas, con estas palabras.

MODELO: Es importante hablar español en la clase de español.

(No) Es importante
(No) Es muy práctico
(No) Es necesario
(No) Es tonto (*foolish*)
(No) Es fascinante
(No) Es una lata (*pain, drag*)
(No) Es posible

+

mirar la televisión todos los días
hablar español en la clase
tener muchas mascotas
llegar a clase puntualmente
tomar cerveza en clase
hablar con los animales / las plantas
tomar mucho café y fumar cigarrillos
trabajar dieciocho horas al día
tener muchos hermanos
ser amable con todos los miembros de la familia
estar en las fiestas familiares
pasar mucho tiempo con la familia

Con. A: Suggestions

- Provide several additional models with simple explanations, using *porque, para,* and *por eso.*
- Have students interview each other to find out what some of their classmates would like to receive for their next birthday, anniversary, or Christmas. After students have completed the interviews, have them report their findings back to the class. As a group, you might want to review numbers by discussing how much each gift might cost. Introduce words such as *caro/a* and *barato/a.*

 Bright Idea

Suggestion

Ask the class as a whole questions like the following. Have them explain why using *porque.*

¿Quién necesita un nuevo televisor / un carro nuevo / más dinero? ¿Por qué?

Con. A: Follow-Up

¿Qué son buenos/malos regalos para las madres? ¿Y para los padres? ¿Qué les regala Ud. a sus hermanos?

Con. B: Suggestions

- Have students guess the meaning of *fumar cigarrillos* from context.
- Present phrases such as *¿Ah, sí? No me digas. ¿De veras? No, hombre,* and so on, for students to use to respond to answers given by others.
- Have students imagine that they are at a family party in their parents' house. Have them answer these questions:

¿A qué hora llegan todos?
¿Quién(es) llega(n) tarde? ¿Quién(es) no llega(n)?
¿Qué toman Uds.?
¿Es posible bailar? ¿cantar? ¿hablar con muchos parientes?
¿Es necesario ser amable con todos? ¿A qué hora termina la fiesta?

Con. B: Follow-Up

- Have students present information about themselves, their families, and where they are from. Remind them not to overuse *yo: Yo soy Phillip. Soy de Garfield Heights. Tengo tres hermanos y una hermana. Mis abuelos son de Rusia.*
- Have students present the information about themselves in a brief composition, which you correct before they present it to the class.

Gramática ■ **75**

Suggestions

- Present *mi(s)*, *tu(s)*, *su(s)*. Students have seen *mi(s)* since the beginning of the chapter, and they may have been exposed to *tu(s)* and *su(s)* if you have used it in your teacher talk.
- Point out the formal vs. informal in *su* and *tu*.
- Remind students that *'s* does not exist in Spanish. To express possession, the preposition *de* is used.

  el libro de Juan   la chaqueta de Susana

- Have students identify the possessive forms that are the same for two different grammatical persons (*Ud.* and *él/ella*). Point out that the ambiguity of *su(s)* (*su hijo* = your/his/her/their son) can be clarified using *el hijo de él / de ella*, and so on.
- Remind students that *nuestro* and *vuestro*, like most *-o* adjectives, have four forms: *nuestro, nuestra, nuestros, nuestras; vuestro, vuestra, vuestros, vuestras.*
- Emphasize that possessive adjectives must agree with the noun they modify, that the choice between *mi/mis, tu/tus, su/sus,* and so on, depends on the number of the following noun, not on the number of possessors.
- Remind students to try the *Autoprueba*.
- Point out that centuries in Spanish are written with Roman numerals and are pronounced as ordinal numbers through ten.

  el siglo VIII (octavo) = the 8th century
  el siglo XIII (trece) = the 13th century

♻ Reciclado

Have students describe people they know using adjectives from this chapter and *Ante todo* (*Mis tíos son ricos.*).

---

7 · Expressing Possession • Possessive Adjectives (Unstressed)*

La familia de Carlos IV (cuarto)

Aquí está la familia de Carlos IV, un rey español del siglo XVIII. En el cuadro están *su* esposa, *sus* hijos… ¿y *sus* padres y *sus* abuelos? ¿Quiénes son las personas a la izquierda del rey?

¿Tiene Ud. una foto reciente de su familia? ¿Quiénes están en la foto?

▶ *La familia de Carlos IV, por el pintor español Francisco Goya y Lucientes*

Possessive adjectives are words that tell to whom or to what something belongs: *my* (book), *his* (sweater). You have already seen and used several possessive adjectives in Spanish. Here is the complete set.

Possessive Adjectives					
my	mi hijo/hija mis hijos/hijas		*our*	nuestro hijo nuestros hijos	nuestra hija nuestras hijas
your	tu hijo/hija tus hijos/hijas		*your*	vuestro hijo vuestros hijos	vuestra hija vuestras hijas
your, his, her, its	su hijo/hija sus hijos/hijas		*your, their*	su hijo/hija sus hijos/hijas	

In Spanish, the ending of a possessive adjective agrees in form with the person or thing possessed, not with the owner or possessor. Note that these possessive adjectives are placed before the noun.

The possessive adjectives **mi(s), tu(s),** and **su(s)** show agreement in number only. **Nuestro/a/os/as** and **vuestro/a/os/as,** like all adjectives that end in **-o,** show agreement in both number and gender.

Son { mis / tus / sus } hermanos.

Es { nuestra / vuestra / su } familia.

possessive adjective = adjective that shows who owns or has something

---

*Another kind of possessive is called the stressed possessive adjective. *It can be used as a noun. You will learn more about using stressed possessive adjectives in* **Gramática 49.**

Carlos IV's family *Here is the family of Carlos IV, an 18th-century Spanish king. In the painting are his wife, his children . . . and his parents and grandparents? Who are the people to the left of the king?*

CULTURE

This collective portrait of the family of Carlos IV was painted in 1800–1801 by Francisco de Goya y Lucientes (1746–1828), who was named Court Painter by that Spanish king in 1800. This was the last royal portrait done by Goya. While other artists painted the royal families as they wanted to appear, Goya rendered them as they really were. In this large portrait, he appears to express his disdain for Carlos IV. Here the *reina* María Luisa seems to preside over the *familia real*, as was in fact the case. Reminiscent of the style of one of Goya's mentors, Diego Velázquez (1599–1660), this painting includes a self-portrait of Goya (painting in the shadows on the left side of the canvas). Have students try to find it.

The forms **vuestro/a/os/as** are used extensively in Spain, but are not common in Latin America.

 Su(s) can have several different equivalents in English: *your* (*sing.*), *his, her, its, your* (*pl.*), and *their*. Usually its meaning will be clear in context. When the meaning of **su(s)** is not clear, **de** and a pronoun are used instead, to indicate the possessor.

el padre
la madre   } de él (de ella, de Ud., de
los abuelos   ellos, de ellas, de Uds.)
las tías

¿Son jóvenes los hijos **de él**?
Are his children young?

¿Dónde vive el abuelo **de ellas**?
Where does their grandfather live?

■ ■ ■ Práctica

A. Posesiones. Which nouns can these possessive adjectives modify without changing form?

1. su: problema primos dinero tías escritorios familia
2. tus: perro idea hijos profesoras abuelo examen
3. mi: ventana médicos cuarto coche abuela gatos
4. sus: animales oficina nietas padre hermana abuelo
5. nuestras: guitarra libro materias lápiz sobrinas tía
6. nuestros: gustos consejeros parientes puerta clase residencia

B. ¿Cómo es la familia de David?

Paso 1. Mire la familia de David en el dibujo (*drawing*). Complete las oraciones según el modelo.

> MODELO: familia / pequeño →
> Su familia es pequeña.

1. hijo pequeño / guapo
2. perro / feo
3. padre / viejo
4. hija / rubio
5. esposa / bonito

Paso 2. Imagine que Ud. es David y cambie las respuestas (*answers*).

> MODELO: familia / pequeño →
> Mi familia es pequeña.

Paso 3. Imagine que Ud. es la esposa de David y hable por (*for*) Ud. y por su esposo. Cambie sólo las respuestas del 1 al 4.

> MODELO: familia / pequeño →
> Nuestra familia es pequeña.

David

AUTOPRUEBA

Give the correct possessive adjective.

1. la casa de nosotros = _____ casa
2. los perros de Juan = _____ perros
3. la clase de Luisa = _____ clase

Answers: *1.* nuestra *2.* sus *3.* su

Need more practice?

■ Workbook and Laboratory Manual
■ Interactive CD-ROM
■ Online Learning Center (www.mhhe.com/puntos7)

Prác. A: Preliminary Exercises

■ Have students give the forms orally:

1. *Dé la forma singular: nuestras abuelas, sus universidades, tus amigos, vuestros consejeros.*
2. *Dé la forma plural: nuestro profesor, nuestra clase, vuestro compañero, vuestra actividad, tu familia, su perro.*

■ Have students relate possessives to their respective subject pronouns: *mi → yo* (*sus, tus, mi, nuestras, vuestros, su, tu*)

Prác. B: Variation

Have students work in pairs to think of famous families, like presidents' families or those from TV programs, and to describe each member to the rest of the class until their classmates guess them correctly.

Resources: Transparency 19

Con. A: Suggestion

Remind students to use *tu* forms with classmates. Students will need to use *su* forms, however, to report information to the class about someone else (his/her/their).

Con. B: Follow-Up

Ask students what they associate with the following phrases: *su perro/gato, sus padres, la casa del presidente de los Estados Unidos / del primer ministro del Canadá, la casa del profesor / de la profesora.*

Con. B: Extension

1. *nuestra cafetería*
2. *nuestro libro de español*
3. *nuestro presidente*
4. *nuestros estudiantes*
5. *nuestros profesores*
6. *nuestro equipo de fútbol*

■ ■ ■ Conversación

A. Entrevista. Take turns asking and answering questions about your families. Talk about what family members are like, their ages, some things they do, and so on. Use the model as a guide. Take notes on what your partner says. Then report the information to the class.

> MODELO: tu abuela →
> E1: Mi abuela es alta. ¿Y tu abuela? ¿Es alta?
> E2: Pues, no. Mi abuela es baja.
> E1: ¿Cuántos años tiene?…

1. tu familia en general
2. tus padres
3. tus abuelos
4. tus hermanos / hijos
5. tu esposo/a / compañero/a de cuarto

B. Asociaciones. Working with several classmates, see how many words you can associate with the following phrases. Everyone in the group must agree with the associations decided on. Remember to use the words and phrases you know to agree or disagree with the suggestions of others.

> MODELO: nuestro país →
> Nuestro país es _____. (En nuestro país hay _____. En nuestro país uno puede [*can*] _____.)

1. nuestro país
2. nuestra clase de español
3. nuestra universidad (librería)
4. nuestra ciudad (nuestro estado)
5. el centro de nuestra ciudad

EN LOS ESTADOS UNIDOS Y EL CANADÁ

Los Sheen, una familia de actores

Two generations of Sheens have made names for themselves in film and television. Martin Sheen, the father, was born Ramón Estévez in Dayton, Ohio (1940–), to a Spanish father and an Irish mother. Martin explains that he felt he needed to change his Hispanic name in order to successfully pursue an acting career in the 1950s. In his heart, however, he says he is still Ramón. Martin's acting career spans several decades and includes important movies such as *Apocalypse Now.*

▲ *Charlie Sheen, Martin Sheen y Emilio Estévez*

Most recently, he stars in the television series "The West Wing," which won several 2002 Emmy awards, including Best Drama Series.

Martin and his wife of more than 40 years, Janet Sheen, have four children—Emilio (1962–), Ramón (1963–), Carlos (1965–), and Renée (1967–)—all of whom have pursued acting careers. Emilio, who uses his father's original last name, Estévez, and Carlos, who is known as Charlie Sheen, are the most famous actors of the Sheen children.

EN LOS ESTADOS UNIDOS Y EL CANADÁ

- Have students search the Sheen family on the Internet and write a description of each family member in Spanish, using adjectives in this chapter and cognates in *Ante todo.*
- Before reading the passage, ask students the following: *¿Quién es Martin Sheen? ¿Es guapo/feo? ¿Es rica la familia Sheen? ¿Quién es más guapo? ¿Cuáles son las películas más famosas de ellos?*

☼ Heritage Speakers

Pídales a los hispanohablantes de la clase que nombren a los actores y directores hispanos que más admiran. ¿Por qué los admiran? ¿Qué películas o programas han hecho?

¿Recuerda Ud.?

The personal endings used with **-ar** verbs share some characteristics of those used with **-er** and **-ir** verbs, which you will learn in the next section. Review the present tense endings of **-ar** verbs by telling which subject pronoun(s) you associate with each of these endings.

1. -amos   2. -as   3. -áis   4. -an   5. -o   6. -a

8 Expressing Actions • Present Tense of *-er*; and *-ir* Verbs; More About Subject Pronouns

Diego se presenta

Hola. Me llamo Diego González. Soy estudiante de UCLA, pero este año *asisto* a la Universidad Nacional Autónoma de México. *Vivo* con mi tía Matilde en la Ciudad de México. *Como* pizza con frecuencia y *bebo* cerveza en las fiestas. Me gusta la ropa de moda; por eso *recibo* varios catálogos. *Leo* muchos libros de antropología para mi especialización. También *escribo* muchas cartas a mi familia. *Creo* que una educación universitaria es muy importante. Por eso estudio y *aprendo* mucho. ¡Pero *comprendo* también que es muy importante estar con los amigos y con la familia!

¿Es Diego un estudiante típico? ¿Cómo es Ud.? Adapte las oraciones de Diego a su conveniencia.

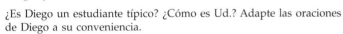

Past ----------------- **PRESENT** ----------------- Future
present

Verbs That End in *-er* and *-ir*

A. The present tense of **-er** and **-ir** verbs is formed by adding personal endings to the stem of the verb (the infinitive minus its **-er/-ir** ending). The personal endings for **-er** and **-ir** verbs are the same except for the first and second person plural.

comer (*to eat*)		vivir (*to live*)	
como	comemos	vivo	vivimos
comes	coméis	vives	vivís
come	comen	vive	viven

Diego introduces himself   *Hello. My name is Diego González. I'm a student at UCLA, but this year I attend the* **Universidad Nacional Autónoma de México.** *I live with my aunt Matilde in Mexico City. I eat pizza frequently and I drink beer at parties. I like fashionable clothes; that's why I receive various catalogues. I read lots of anthropology books for my major. I also write a lot of letters to my family. I think that a university education is very important. That's why I study and learn a lot. But I also understand that it's very important to be with friends and family!*

Gramática

Gramática 8

Present Tense of *-er* and *-ir* Verbs; More About Subject Pronouns

¿Recuerda Ud.?: Suggestion
Have students conjugate the following verbs chorally.

bailar	desear
buscar	enseñar
cantar	pagar

Suggestion
Read Diego's speech sentence by sentence. Ask students whether each sentence is true or false for them. Students correct each false sentence to make it true for them.

Note
Gustar appears in this narration. Students will learn more about the verb *gustar* and other verbs like *gustar* in *Capítulo 7.*

Verbs That End in *-er* and *-ir*

Suggestions

■ Introduce *comer* as a model *-er* verb. Talk through the conjugation, using forms in complete sentences and questions, but writing only the verb forms on the board.

■ Emphasize that the only two endings that differ between *-er* and *-ir* verbs are *nosotros* (*comemos* / *vivimos*) and *vosotros* (*coméis* / *vivís*). All other endings are exactly alike.

■ Point out that only the *vosotros* forms have an accent mark.

♻ Reciclado

■ Review subject pronouns and have students indicate the difference between *tú/vosotros* and *Ud./Uds.*

■ Have students recite chorally regular *-ar* verb endings.

MULTIMEDIA: Internet

Have students look up the website for *la Universidad Nacional Autónoma de México.* You might assign specific topics to different students or groups, for example, campus information, classes offered. Then have a class discussion comparing *UNAM* to your university or other universities in the United States and Canada.

Suggestions

- Introduce meaning of *leer* and use forms in questions to students, writing only the verb forms on the board.
- Follow the same procedure with *escribir* and *vivir*.
- You may want to point out the emphatic phrases: *I do eat . . .* → *yo sí como...*

Use and Omission of Subject Pronouns

Note

Emphasize that the omission of the subject pronouns is the norm in Spanish: *Bebemos café por la mañana.*

Preliminary Exercises

- Have students give the corresponding forms.

  yo: *aprender, vender, comprender, escribir*

  tú: *comer, leer, beber, vivir*

  Ud./él/ella: *beber, creer, abrir, recibir*

  nosotros: *comprender, deber, asistir, vivir*

  vosotros: *deber, vender, aprender, abrir*

  Uds./ellos/ellas: *creer, leer, comer, escribir*

- Do a transformation activity:

  Ud./tú → yo.
  ¿Come Ud.? → Sí, como.
  ¿Comen Uds.? → Sí, comemos.

- Have students give new sentences based on cues.

En la sala de clase

1. *Yo asisto a clase todos los días.* (*tú, nosotros, Ud., todos los estudiantes, Carlos, vosotros*)
2. *Aprendes español en clase, ¿verdad?* (*nosotros, yo, Ud., la estudiante francesa, Uds., vosotros*)

En una fiesta de Navidad (Christmas)

1. *Todos comen y beben.* (*yo, los tíos, tú, Uds., la prima y yo, Ud., vosotras*)
2. *Los niños reciben regalos.* (*papá, tú, nosotras, los hijos de Juan, Alicia, los nietos, vosotros*)

B. These are the frequently used **-er** and **-ir** verbs you will find in this chapter.

-er verbs		-ir verbs	
aprender	*to learn*	**abrir**	*to open*
comprender	*to understand*	**asistir (a)**	*to attend, go to (a class, function)*
creer (en)	*to think; to believe (in)*		
deber (+ inf.)	*should, must, ought to (do something)*	**recibir**	*to receive*
		vivir	*to live*
vender	*to sell*		

Remember that the Spanish present tense has a number of present tense equivalents in English. It can also be used to express future meaning.

como = *I eat, I am eating, I will eat*

AUTOPRUEBA

Give the correct verb forms.

1. Elena (comer) _____
2. yo (beber) _____
3. nosotros (leer) _____
4. José (escribir) _____
5. Uds. (vivir) _____
6. tú (abrir) _____

Answers: 1. come 2. bebo 3. leemos 4. escribe 5. viven 6. abres

---

Use and Omission of Subject Pronouns

In English, a verb must have an expressed subject (a noun or pronoun): *she says*, *the train arrives*. In Spanish, however, as you have probably noticed, an expressed subject is not required. Verbs are accompanied by a subject pronoun only for clarification, emphasis, or contrast.

- *Clarification:* When the context does not make the subject clear, the subject pronoun is expressed. This happens most frequently with third person singular and plural verb forms.

  Ud. / él / ella vende
  Uds. / ellos / ellas venden

- *Emphasis:* Subject pronouns are used in Spanish to emphasize the subject when in English you would stress it with your voice.

  —¿Quién debe pagar? *Who should pay?*
  —¡**Tú** debes pagar! *You should pay!*

- *Contrast:* Contrast is a special case of emphasis. Subject pronouns are used to contrast the actions of two individuals or groups.

  Ellos leen mucho; **nosotros** leemos poco.
  They read a lot; we read little.

Capítulo 2: La familia

National Standards: Communication

Generally, *tú* is used as the familiar form and *Ud.* is used to show respect. As mentioned previously, the form *vos* is similar to *tú* and is used mainly in Argentina and Uruguay. The use of *tú*, *vos*, or *Ud.* depends on a variety of factors: age, social status, or socioeconomic status. For example, professors, teachers, and parents use *tú* with young adults and children. Nevertheless, an abrupt change from *tú* or *vos* to *Ud.* can indicate a change of tone in a conversation. In Bogota, Colombia, the use of *tú* is very limited. It is used mainly by parents, grandparents, and couples.

■ ■ ■ Práctica

A. En la clase de español

Paso 1. ¡Anticipemos! Read the following statements and tell whether they are true for your classroom environment. If any statement is not true for you or your class, make it negative or change it in another way to make it correct.

> MODELO: Bebo café en clase. →
> Sí, bebo café en clase.
> (No, no bebo café en clase. Bebo café en casa.)

1. Debo estudiar más para esta clase.
2. Leo todas (*all*) las partes de las lecciones.
3. Comprendo bien cuando mi profesor(a) habla español.
4. Asisto al laboratorio con frecuencia.
5. Debemos abrir más los libros en clase.
6. Escribimos mucho en esta clase.
7. Aprendemos a hablar español en esta clase.*
8. Vendemos nuestros libros al final del año.

Paso 2. Entrevista. Now turn to the person next to you and rephrase each sentence, using **tú** forms of the verbs. Your partner will indicate whether the sentences are true for him or her.

> MODELO: Debes estudiar más para esta clase, ¿verdad (*right*)? →
> Sí, debo estudiar más.
> (No, no debo estudiar más.)
> (No. Debo estudiar más para la clase de matemáticas.)

B. Diego habla de su padre.
Complete este párrafo con la forma correcta de los verbos entre paréntesis.

Mi padre (vender[1]) coches y trabaja mucho. Mis hermanos y yo (aprender[2]) mucho de papá. Según[a] mi padre, los jóvenes (deber[3]) (asistir[4]) a clase todos los días, porque es su obligación. Papá también (creer[5]) que no es necesario mirar la televisión por la noche. Es más interesante (leer[6]) el periódico[b] o un buen libro. Por eso nosotros (leer[7]) o (escribir[8]) por la noche y no miramos la televisión mucho. Yo admiro mucho a[†] mi papá y (creer[9]) que él (comprender[10]) la importancia de la educación.

[a]*According to* [b]*newspaper*

---

*Note: **aprender** + **a** + *infinitive* = *to learn how to* (do something)

[†]*Note the use of **a** here. In this context, the word **a** has no equivalent in English. It is used in Spanish before a direct object that is a specific person. You will learn more about this use of **a** in **Capítulo 6.** Until then, the exercises and activities in* Puntos de partida *will indicate when to use it.*

Gramática   Ochenta y uno ■ **81**

⚙ Reciclado
Remind students that the verb *asistir* is a false cognate.

☼ Heritage Speakers

Anime a los estudiantes hispanohablantes a hablar de uno de sus parientes que más admira (padre, madre, tío, abuela). Pídales que expliquen a qué se dedica esa persona, cuáles son sus pasatiempos y por qué lo/la admira.

Prác. A: Preliminary Exercises

Paso 2. Have students respond *sí* or *no* to the following sentences.

- *Los estudiantes de esta clase deben...*

  comer durante la clase.
  asisitir a clase todos los días.
  ir al laboratorio de lenguas con frecuencia.
  aprender muchas cosas nuevas todos los días.

- *El professor (La profesora) de español cree en...*

  hablar español en clase.
  explicar toda la gramática.
  dar exámenes con frecuencia.
  llevar sombrero para enseñar.

- *¡Estos estudiantes son fantásticos!*

  Have students give sentences starting with *Debemos...* to show how good they are.

Prác. A: Extension

Paso 1.

9. *Recibo muchos paquetes de mi familia.*
10. *Como en casa / _____ (dining facility) por la noche.*
11. *Vivo con mi familia este semestre/trimestre.*
12. *Mi profesor(a) cree que yo debo estar en clase con más frecuencia.*
13. *Debo aprender a leer más rápido.*

Prác. A: Follow-Up

Paso 2. Ask students about their partner's answers; they will use third person singular verbs.

Prác. B: Suggestions

- Model the pronunciation of each infinitive in the paragraph. Use the *yo* form of each in a brief simple sentence about yourself; then in *Ud.* and *Uds.* questions to students.
- Have students scan the paragraph for meaning before attempting to do the items. After the individual items are done, have a volunteer read the entire paragraph.

Gramática ■ **81**

Prác. C: Follow-Up

¿Quién lee el periódico?
¿Quién mira la televisión?
¿Quién abre y lee cartas?
¿Por qué reciben cartas del tío Ricardo?
¿De dónde es el tío Ricardo?
¿A qué hora come la familia de Manolo?

NOTA COMUNICATIVA

Note
Use *casi nunca* and *nunca* at the beginning of a sentence only, to avoid the double negative. Students will learn the double negative in *Gramática 19*.

Reciclado
Todos los días and *con frecuencia* were presented in *Capítulo 1*.

C. **Un sábado** [*Saturday*] **en Sevilla.** In this activity you will take the part of Manolo, who lives with his family in Sevilla. Using all the cues given, form complete sentences about a Saturday at home with your family. Make any changes and add words when necessary. When the subject pronoun is in parentheses, do not use it in the sentence.

MODELO: (nosotros) beber / café / por / mañana →
Bebemos café por la mañana.

1. yo / leer / periódico
2. mi hija, Marta / mirar / televisión
3. también / (ella) escribir / composición / en inglés
4. no / (ella) comprender / todo / instrucciones
5. (ella) deber / usar / diccionario
6. mi esposa, Lola / abrir / y / leer / cartas (*letters*)
7. ¡hoy / (nosotros) recibir / carta / de / tío Ricardo!
8. (él) ser de / España / pero / ahora / vivir / en México
9. ¡ay! / ser / dos / de / tarde
10. ¡(nosotros) deber / comer / ahora!
11. (nosotros) comer / a / dos / todo / días
12. hoy / un / amigos / comer / con / nosotros

■■■ Conversación

NOTA COMUNICATIVA

Telling How Frequently You Do Things

Use the following words and phrases to tell how often you perform an activity. Some of them will already be familiar to you.

todos los días, siempre	every day, always
con frecuencia	frequently
a veces	at times
una vez a la semana	once a week
casi nunca	almost never
nunca	never

Hablo con mis amigos **todos los días.** Hablo con mis padres **una vez a la semana. Casi nunca** hablo con mis abuelos. Y **nunca** hablo con mis tíos que viven en Italia.

For now, use the expressions **casi nunca** and **nunca** only at the beginning of a sentence. You will learn more about how to use them in **Gramática 19.**

Need more practice?

- Workbook and Laboratory Manual
- Interactive CD-ROM
- Online Learning Center (www.mhhe.com/puntos7)

CULTURE

Many Hispanic families spend Saturdays and/or Sundays together as a family, often for an outing similar to the family taking a boat ride in Xochimilco in the chapter opener photo (p. 58). Families also gather frequently in homes of extended family members, in restaurants, and in parks. The day may simply be spent at home together, as in *Práctica C*. Ask students what some of the weekend routines and traditions of their families are. Do they spend the time together as a family?

A. ¿Con qué frecuencia?

Paso 1. How frequently do you do the following things?

	CON FRECUENCIA	A VECES	CASI NUNCA	NUNCA
1. Asisto al laboratorio de lenguas (o uso las cintas [*tapes*]).	☐	☐	☐	☐
2. Recibo cartas.	☐	☐	☐	☐
3. Escribo poemas.	☐	☐	☐	☐
4. Leo novelas románticas.	☐	☐	☐	☐
5. Como en una pizzería.	☐	☐	☐	☐
6. Recibo y leo catálogos.	☐	☐	☐	☐
7. Aprendo palabras nuevas en español.	☐	☐	☐	☐
8. Asisto a todas las clases.	☐	☐	☐	☐
9. Compro regalos para los amigos.	☐	☐	☐	☐
10. Vendo los libros al final del semestre/trimestre.	☐	☐	☐	☐

Paso 2. Now compare your answers with those of a classmate. Then answer the following questions. (*Note:* **los/las dos** = *both* [*of us*]; **ninguno/a** = *neither*)

	YO	MI COMPAÑERO/A	LOS/LAS DOS	NINGUNO/A
1. ¿Quién es muy estudioso/a?	☐	☐	☐	☐
2. ¿Quién come mucha pizza?	☐	☐	☐	☐
3. ¿Quién compra muchas cosas?	☐	☐	☐	☐
4. ¿Quién es muy romántico/a?	☐	☐	☐	☐
5. ¿Quién recibe mucho por correo (*by mail*)?	☐	☐	☐	☐

B. ¿Qué hacen? [*What do they do?*] Form complete sentences using one word or phrase from each column. Be sure to use the correct form of the verbs. Make any of the sentences negative if you wish. Add a reaction or a second logical sentence if you can.

MODELO: Tú lees novelas de horror. No me gusta leer novelas de horror.

yo tú, estudiante Ud., profesor(a) los estudiantes de aquí los hombres / las mujeres un consejero mis padres / hijos me gusta	**+**	abrir leer escribir beber vender comprender recibir vivir deber ¿ ?	**+**	mucho / poco la situación / los problemas de los estudiantes Coca-Cola / café / cerveza antes de (*before*) la clase mi ropa (*clothing*), un estéreo viejo la puerta para las mujeres / los hombres novelas de ciencia ficción / de horror el periódico / una revista (*magazine*) todos los días muchas / pocas cartas, novelas, revistas muchos / pocos ejercicios, libros, regalos en una casa / un apartamento / una residencia en otra ciudad / en otro estado/país en un cuaderno / con un bolígrafo / con un lápiz mirar mucho la televisión llegar a casa temprano

Con. A: Extension

Have students add three original items before doing *Paso 2*.

Con. A: Follow-Up

■ Have students interview their partner to obtain more specific information about the items in *Paso 2*. Examples: *¿Cuál es tu pizzería favorita? ¿Qué recibes por correo, cartas o revistas?* and so on. Remind students to use *tu*(*s*) in this activity.

■ Have students prepare a brief *informe oral* about their partner or about the similarities and differences between themselves and their partner, using all the information they have learned about him/her.

UN POCO DE TODO

A: Suggestion

Have students give invented last names to all the members of the family tree to practice last-name assignment in Spanish-speaking countries. Have the whole class make a list of Hispanic last names before starting the activity.

UN POCO DE TODO

A. La familia del nuevo nieto

Paso 1. The following sentences will form a description of a family in which there is a new grandchild. The name of the person described is given in parentheses after each description when necessary. Form complete sentences based on the words given, in the order given. Conjugate the verbs and add other words if necessary. Be sure to pay close attention to adjective endings.

As you create the sentences, complete the family tree given below with the names of the family members. The first one is done for you. *Note:* Hispanic families pass on first and middle names just as families in this country do.

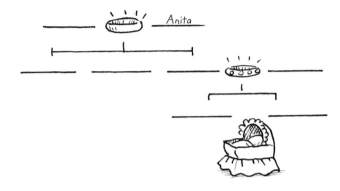

MODELO: **1.** yo **/** ser **/** abuela **/** panameño (Anita) →
Yo soy la abuela panameña.

2. nuevo **/** nieto **/** ser **/** de **/** Estados Unidos (Juan José)
3. Juan José **/** ser **/** padre **/** nieto
4. Juan José **/** también **/** ser **/** hijo **/** abuelo **/** panameño
5. uno **/** de **/** tías **/** de **/** nieto **/** ser **/** médico (Pilar)
6. otro **/** tía **/** ser **/** profesor **/** famoso (Julia)
7. madre **/** niño **/** ser **/** norteamericano (Paula)
8. hermana **/** niño **/** se llama **/** Concepción

Paso 2. Ahora conteste estas preguntas según la descripción de la familia.

1. ¿De dónde son los abuelos y tíos?
2. ¿De dónde es la madre del niño?
3. ¿Cómo se llama el abuelo de la familia?

Resources: Transparency 20

 Heritage Speakers

Anime a los estudiantes hispanohablantes a crear un árbol genealógico parecido al que aparece en esta página. Invítelos a dar una breve descripción de los miembros de su familia.

B. ¿Existe la familia hispánica típica? Complete the following paragraphs about families. Give the correct form of the words in parentheses, as suggested by the context.

Muchas personas (creer[1]) que (todo[2]) las familias (hispánico[3]) son (grande[4]). Pero el concepto de la familia (ser[5]) diferente ahora, sobre todo[a] en las ciudades (grande[6]).

(Ser[7]) cierto que la familia rural (típico[8]) es grande, pero es así[b] en casi[c] (todo[9]) las sociedades rurales del mundo.[d] Muchos hijos (trabajar[10]) la tierra[e] con sus padres. Por eso es bueno y (necesario[11]) tener muchos niños.

Pero en los grandes centros (urbano[12]) las familias con sólo dos o tres hijos (ser[13]) más comunes. Es difícil[f] tener (mucho[14]) hijos en una sociedad (industrializado[15]). Y cuando los padres (trabajar[16]) fuera de[g] casa, ellos (pagar[17]) mucho para cuidar a[h] los niños. Esto pasa especialmente en las familias de la clase media.[i]

Pero es realmente difícil (hablar[18]) de una familia (hispánico[19]) típica. ¿Hay una familia (norteamericano[20]) típica?

[a]sobre... *especially*   [b]es... *that's the way it is*   [c]*almost*   [d]*world*   [e]*land*   [f]*difficult*   [g]fuera... *outside of the*   [h]cuidar... *care for*   [i]*middle*

Comprensión: ¿Cierto o falso? Corrija las oraciones falsas.

1. Todas las familias hispánicas son iguales.
2. Las familias rurales son grandes en casi todas partes del mundo.
3. Las familias rurales necesitan muchos niños.
4. Por lo general (*Generally*), las familias urbanas son más pequeñas.
5. Las madres urbanas típicamente cuidan a los hijos durante el día.

▲ La familia, *por Fernando Botero, de Colombia*

Resources for Review and Testing Preparation

- Workbook and Laboratory Manual
- Interactive CD-ROM
- Online Learning Center (www.mhhe.com/puntos7)

Un poco de todo   Ochenta y cinco ■ **85**

CULTURE

Fernando Botero (1932–) was born in Medellín, Colombia. He studied fresco technique and art history in Italy, and although he was not there long (1953–1955), the experience had a profound influence on his art. His round figures may seem humorous, but they are always informed by socio-political commentary and criticism.

Resources: Desenlace

In the *Capítulo 2* segment of "Chapter-by-Chapter Supplementary Materials" in the IM, you will find a chapter-culminating activity. You can use this activity to consolidate and review the vocabulary and grammar skills students have acquired.

- Before showing the video, have students role-play the part of grandparents. What kinds of things they would say about their grand-children? For students who are grandparents, have them tell how many grandchildren they have, their ages, and what they are like. Use questions to elicit and/or extend descriptions.

    ¿Cuántos nietos tiene Ud.?
    ¿Cómo se llama(n)?
    ¿Cuántos años tiene(n)?
    ¿Cómo es/son?

- Show the video and allow students one to two minutes to work on the questions. Encourage them to answer in Spanish if possible. You might want to ask the questions in Spanish when you review the answers as a class.

    1. *¿De qué ciudad es Dolores?*
    2. *¿Cómo describe a su familia?*
    3. *¿Cuántos nietos tiene Dolores?*
    4. *¿Cómo son sus nietos en general?*
    5. *¿Cuáles son algunos de los intereses particulares de sus nietos?*

    Have volunteers answer the questions.

- Have volunteers role-play Dolores and the interviewer

Entre amigos

Suggestions

- Before viewing the video, review the questions with the students and ask them similar questions.

    ¿Cuántos hermanos tiene Ud.?
    ¿Cómo son sus hermanos?
    ¿Vive Ud. con su familia o vive solo/a?

    Have students answer or work in small groups to ask and answer these questions.

- After viewing the video, have volunteers read and answer the questions.

Videoteca

Entrevista cultural: México

Dolores Suárez is from Mexico. In this interview, she talks about her family. Like many grandparents, she is proud of her grandchildren. Before watching the video clip, read the following excerpt from the interview.

INTERVIEWER: ¿Cómo se llama Ud. y de dónde es?
DOLORES: Me llamo Dolores Suárez. Soy de aquí, del Distrito Federal.[a]
INTERVIEWER: ¿Cómo es su familia, Sra. Dolores?
DOLORES: Pues es una familia muy bonita porque es una familia muy numerosa. Tengo seis hijos y tengo ocho nietos. Entonces eh,[b] somos muy unidos y por eso es muy bonito.

[a]Distrito... *What Mexicans call Mexico City*   [b]Entonces... *Well then*

Now watch the video clip and answer the following questions based on the interview.

1. What city is Dolores from?
2. How does she describe her family?
3. How many grandchildren does Dolores have?
4. How does she describe her grandchildren in general?
5. What are some of the specific interests of her grandchildren?

Entre amigos: ¿Cuántos hermanos tienes?

Miguel, Tané, Karina, and Rubén are talking about their families. What questions do you think they will ask each other? Before watching the video, read the following questions. As you watch, don't worry if you don't under-stand every word. Try to get the gist of the conversation, listening specifically for information about their family members. Watch the video a second time and listen for the answers to the questions.

1. ¿Cuántas hermanas tiene Karina?
2. ¿Cuántos hermanos tiene Rubén?
3. ¿Cómo son los hermanos de Rubén?
4. ¿Vive Karina con sus padres, o vive sola (*alone*)?

Capítulo 2: La familia

Conozca... México

Datos esenciales

- Nombre oficial: Estados Unidos Mexicanos
- Capital: la Ciudad de México, o México, Distrito Federal (el D.F.)
- Población: 105.000.000 (ciento cinco millones) de habitantes
- Moneda:[a] el nuevo peso
- Idiomas:[b] el español (oficial), el zapoteca, el mixteca, el náhuatl, varios dialectos mayas

[a]*Currency* [b]*Languages*

¡Fíjese!

- México tiene 31 estados y el Distrito Federal.
- La población de México es aproximadamente: 30% (por ciento) indígena, 9% blanca,[a] 60% mestiza (que se refiere a las personas de padres de razas indígena y blanca) y 1% de otros orígenes.
- Los indígenas mexicanos pertenecen a[b] grupos diversos: aztecas, mayas, zapotecas, mixtecas, olmecas y otros. La influencia de estas culturas indígenas contribuye a la diversidad y la riqueza de la cultura mexicana actual.[c]
- La ciudad de México ocupa el lugar del antiguo[d] Lago Texcoco. En el centro del lago estaba[e] Tenochtitlán, la capital del imperio azteca. Tenochtitlán era[f] una de las ciudades más grandes del mundo en el siglo XVI.[g]
- La Universidad Nacional Autónoma de México es una de las universidades más antiguas[h] de las Américas: es del año[i] 1551 (mil quinientos cincuenta y uno).

[a]*white* [b]*pertenecen... belong to* [c]*current* [d]*old, ancient* [e]*was* [f]*was* [g]*siglo... 16th century* [h]*más... oldest* [i]*es... it dates from the year*

Learn more about Mexico with the Video, Interactive CD-ROM, and the Online Learning Center (www.mhhe.com/puntos7).

Personas famosas: Los grandes muralistas mexicanos

El muralismo es el estilo de pintura[a] que decora las paredes[b] de edificios públicos. Con su obra,[c] los muralistas desean enseñar la historia y la cultura de su país, y con frecuencia sus murales representan sus ideales políticos también.

Los tres grandes muralistas mexicanos son Diego Rivera (1886–1957 [mil ochocientos ochenta y seis a mil novecientos cincuenta y siete]), José Clemente Orozco (1883–1949 [mil ochocientos ochenta y tres a mil novecientos cuarenta y nueve]) y David Alfaro Siqueiros (1898–1974 [mil ochocientos noventa y ocho a mil setecientos setenta y cuatro]). Hay muchos murales de estos tres grandes muralistas por todo México.

[a]*painting* [b]*walls* [c]*work*

▲ *El mural* The Epic of American Civilization *de Orozco, en Dartmouth College*

Conozca... México

Suggestions

- Bring or have students bring images of some of the murals by these artists to class. Have students compare the three artists.
- Point out that Rivera and Orozco created murals with social and political commentary. Siqueiros did not. What can they say about Rivera and Orozco's personal opinions by studying the murals? Have students compare the social commentary of the two artists.
- Bring in images of the work of muralist Susan Cervantes (available on the Internet). Explain that many U.S. muralists have been influenced by their Mexican counterparts. Ask students whether they can see Rivera's influence in Cervantes' work.
- Point out that Diego Rivera's wife was Frida Kahlo.

Note

Students can read an excerpt of the poem *"Economía doméstica"* by Mexico's Rosario Castellanos in *Un paso más 2.*

MULTIMEDIA: Internet

Have students search the Internet for more information and images of the ancient city of Tenochtitlán as well as of the Mexican muralists.

☀ Heritage Speakers

Pregúnteles a los hispanohablantes de la clase si conocen el Distrito Federal, Tenochtitlán o Teotihuacán, o si han oído hablar de la Universidad Autónoma de México. Si alguien contesta que sí, pídale que dé una breve descripción del lugar.

Suggestions

- Have students list adjectives that they associate with different nationalities. Encourage them to discuss whether or not these associations are stereotypical.
- To practice possessive adjectives, ask students questions about their family and possessions: *Su padre, ¿tiene coche? ¿Cuántos años tiene su coche? ¿Cuántos teléfonos hay en su casa? ¿en la casa de sus padres?,* and so on.
- Practice verb conjugations chorally with students using the verbs from the vocabulary list. Have them give you some infinitives of other verbs they have learned this semester and have them conjugate those verbs as well.
- **La familia y los parientes: ¿Quién es?** Have students identify the family member based on the following definitions.

  1. *Es el hermano de mi madre.* (mi tío)
  2. *Son los hijos de mi tío.* (mis primos)
  3. *Es la hija de mi hermana.* (mi sobrina)
  4. *Es el papá de mi mama.* (mi abuelo)

EN RESUMEN

Gramática

To review the grammar points presented in this chapter, refer to the indicated grammar presentations. You'll find further practice of these structures in the Workbook and Laboratory Manual, on the Interactive CD-ROM, and on the *Puntos de partida* Online Learning Center (www.mhhe.com/puntos7).

5. Describing—Adjectives: Gender, Number, and Position

You should know how to place adjectives as well as how to make adjectives like **alto, inteligente, español,** and **inglés** agree with the nouns they describe.

6. Expressing *to be*—Present Tense of **ser;** Summary of Uses

Can you conjugate and use the irregular verb **ser** in the present tense?

7. Expressing Possession—Possessive Adjectives (Unstressed)

You should be able to recognize and use the possessive adjectives **mi, tu, su, nuestro,** and **vuestro.**

8. Expressing Actions—Present Tense of **-er** and **-ir** Verbs; More About Subject Pronouns

Can you conjugate verbs like **comer** and **escribir** in the present tense? Do you know how to use subject pronouns and when to omit them?

Vocabulario

Practice this vocabulary with digital flash cards on the Online Learning Center (www.mhhe.com/puntos7).

Los verbos

abrir	to open
aprender	to learn
asistir (a)	to attend, go to (a class, function)
beber	to drink
comer	to eat
comprender	to understand
creer (en)	to think; to believe (in)
deber (+inf.)	should, must, ought to (do something)
escribir	to write
leer	to read
llegar	to arrive
mirar	to look at, watch
mirar la televisión	to watch television
recibir	to receive
ser (irreg.)	to be
vender	to sell
vivir	to live

La familia y los parientes

el/la abuelo/a	grandfather/grandmother
los abuelos	grandparents
el/la esposo/a	husband/wife
el/la hermano/a	brother/sister
el/la hijo/a	son/daughter
los hijos	children
la madre (mamá)	mother (mom)
el/la nieto/a	grandson/granddaughter
el/la niño/a	small child; boy/girl
el padre (papá)	father (dad)
los padres	parents
el/la primo/a	cousin
el/la sobrino/a	niece/nephew
el/la tío/a	uncle/aunt

Las mascotas

el gato	cat
el pájaro	bird
el perro	dog

Otros sustantivos

la carta	letter
la casa	house, home
la ciudad	city
el coche	car
el estado	state
el/la médico/a	(medical) doctor
el país	country
el periódico	newspaper
el regalo	present, gift
la revista	magazine

Los adjetivos

alto/a	tall
amable	kind; nice
antipático/a	unpleasant
bajo/a	short (*in height*)
bonito/a	pretty
buen, bueno/a	good
casado/a	married
corto/a	short (*in length*)
delgado/a	thin, slender
este/a	this
estos/as	these
feo/a	ugly
fiel	faithful
gordo/a	fat
gran, grande	large, big; great
guapo/a	handsome; good-looking
inteligente	intelligent
joven	young
largo/a	long
listo/a	smart; clever
mal, malo/a	bad
moreno/a	brunet(te)
mucho/a	a lot (of)
muchos/as	many
necesario/a	necessary
nuevo/a	new
otro/a	other, another
pequeño/a	small
perezoso/a	lazy
pobre	poor
posible	possible
rico/a	rich
rubio/a	blond(e)
simpático/a	nice, likeable
soltero/a	single (*not married*)
todo/a	all; every
tonto/a	silly, foolish
trabajador(a)	hardworking
viejo/a	old

Los adjetivos de nacionalidad

alemán/alemana
español(a)
estadounidense
francés/francesa
inglés/inglesa
mexicano/a
norteamericano/a

Los adjetivos posesivos

mi(s)	my
tu(s)	your (*fam. sing.*)
nuestro/a(s)	our
vuestro/a(s)	your (*fam. pl. Sp.*)
su(s)	his, hers, its, your (*form. sing.*); their, your (*form. pl.*)

Los números 31–100

treinta
cuarenta
cincuenta
sesenta
setenta
ochenta
noventa
cien (ciento)

¿Con qué frecuencia... ?

a veces	sometimes, at times
casi nunca	almost never
nunca	never
siempre	always
una vez a la semana	once a week

Repaso: con frecuencia, todos los días

Palabras adicionales

bueno...	well . . .
¿de quién?	whose?
del	of the, from the
esto	this
(no) estoy de acuerdo	I (don't) agree
para	(intended) for; in order to
¿por qué?	why?
porque	because
que	that; who
según	according to
si	if
tener (*irreg.*)... años	to be . . . years old

Repaso: ¿de dónde es Ud.?

Suggestions

- Have students make and exchange word puzzles.
- Play *hangman*, using family words and adjectives.
- Have students group the adjectives in different ways (opposites, negative/positive).

♻ Reciclado

Remind students that *asistir* is a false cognate. *To assist* in Spanish is *atender*, *ayudar*, or *servir*.

☼ Heritage Speakers

En México, la palabra *huevón* se usa como sinónimo de *perezoso* aunque se considera una grosería en muchos países latinoamericanos. Aunque se oye la palabra *huevón* en la conversación común y corriente, se recomienda el uso de *perezoso*.

Un paso más 2

Literatura de **México**

Notes

- Rosario Castellanos was named Ambassador of Mexico in Israel from 1971 to 1974. While in Tel Aviv, Israel, Castellanos died in a freak household accident. As a writer who often addressed the inequity women suffered and her own problems as a woman and a Mexican, she may have found irony in her place of burial: the rotunda of Illustrious Men, in Mexico City.
- Prizes that Castellanos received include *Premio Chiapas* 1958 for *Balún Canán*, *Premio Xavier Villaurrutia* 1961 for *Ciudad real*, *Premio Sor Juana Inés de la Cruz* 1962 for *Oficio de tinieblas*, *Premio Carlos Trouyet de Letras* 1967, *Premio Elías Sourasky de Letras* 1972.

LECTURA

Suggestions

- Do the *Estrategia* as an in-class activity the day before you assign the reading as homework. Remind students to look for words of this kind in the reading, and also remind them about the function of the underlined words (contextual guessing).
- Introduce or review the connecting words (*por otra parte, también, en cambio,...*) students have learned in this chapter, and encourage them to use as many as possible of these when they respond to the *Sobre la lectura...* question.
- Encourage students to give their opinions on family-related values, such as: *¿Es importante para Ud. la unidad familiar? ¿y la independencia personal?*

Literatura de **México**

Sobre la autora: *Rosario Castellanos was born in Mexico City in 1925 but spent much of her childhood in Chiapas, a region in the south of Mexico with a large indigenous population. She returned to the province of Chiapas as an adult to work with Indian theater groups and the Indigenous Institute of San Cristóbal. Castellanos wrote in many forms, from poetry to journalism. The following lines are from "Economía doméstica," a poem in her most famous collection of poetry,* Poesía no eres tú *(1972).*

> He aquí la regla de oro,[a] el secreto del orden:
>
> tener un sitio[b] para cada[c] cosa
> y tener
> cada cosa en su sitio. Así arreglé[d] mi casa.

[a]*He... Here is the golden rule* [b]*place* [c]*each* [d]*Así... That's how I organized*

▲ Rosario Castellanos (1925–1974)

LECTURA

ESTRATEGIA: Connecting Words; A Reminder About Cognates

Some words or phrases indicate what kind of information they introduce. For example, as you know, **por eso** (*for that reason, that's why*) is a signal that the information following it is a justification or a reason for the information that came before.

> Necesito dinero. **Por eso** trabajo en la librería.

What kinds of clues do these words give you about the information that follows?

1. Por otra parte,... (*On the other hand, . . .*)
2. También...
3. En cambio,... (*On the other hand, . . .*)
4. ...porque...
5. Por ejemplo,...
6. Por lo general,...
7. ¡Hasta... ! (*Even . . . !*)

Scan the following reading to see if you can find any of the preceding connectors. You may wish to circle them in the reading so that you pay particular attention to them when you get to them.

Note: The following reading contains a number of cognates whose meanings you should be able to guess from the context, including some verb forms with endings different from those you have learned about. You will recognize the meaning of most of those verbs easily, however.

☼ Heritage Speakers

Pídales a los hispanohablantes que ofrezcan su opinión a la clase con respecto a las diferencias entre las familias norteamericanas y las hispánicas. Pídales también que indiquen, según su opinión, qué afirmaciones hechas en la *Lectura* son estereotipos y cuáles son realidades.

MULTIMEDIA: Internet

Have students search the Internet for more information about Carmen Lomas Garza.

Sobre la lectura... The following reading was written by the authors of *Puntos de partida* for language learners like you. Do you think that the authors were being completely serious when they presented this contrast between families in this country and in Spanish-speaking countries?

La unidad familiar: ¿Perspectivas culturales válidas o estereotipadas?

▲ Tamalada (Making Tamales), *por Carmen Lomas Garza (estadounidense)*

La familia estadounidense y canadiense

Cuando un hispano observa la estructura de la familia estadounidense o canadiense, puede[a] llegar muy pronto a esta conclusión: La familia ya no[b] existe en estos países. ¿Por qué podría creer[c] esto?

Los padres e hijos estadounidenses o canadienses no se quieren.[d] Cuando los hijos tienen unos 18 años, sus padres los mandan[e] a vivir a otra parte. A veces los hijos trabajan en otras ciudades y a veces abandonan la casa familiar sólo porque sí.[f] Los padres ancianos viven <u>solos</u> porque cuando sus hijos ya tienen otra familia los padres son para ellos una gran <u>molestia.</u> ¡Hasta hay <u>hospicios</u> para los viejos!

No están en casa, que es donde deberían[g] estar.

La familia hispánica

Por otra parte, un estadounidense o un canadiense que mira la estructura de la familia hispánica puede <u>concluir</u> lo siguiente: La influencia de la familia es demasiado fuerte.[h] ¿Por qué podría creer esto?

Los padres no confían[i] en sus hijos, y no los[j] preparan para la vida. Por ejemplo, hay hijos ya <u>mayores</u> —de 30 años o más— que todavía viven en la casa de sus padres. Estos hijos tienen buenos trabajos y suficiente dinero para vivir aparte. Obviamente los

[a]*he can* [b]*ya... no longer* [c]*podría... might he think* [d]*no... don't love each other* [e]*los... send them off* [f]*sólo... just because they want to* [g]*they should* [h]*demasiado... too strong* [i]*trust* [j]*them*

Un paso más 2

Noventa y uno ■ **91**

CULTURE

Carmen Lomas Garza is a Chicana artist who was born in Kingsville, Texas, near Corpus Christi. She started painting when she was 13 years old. She currently lives in San Francisco, California, where she continues to paint today. Her paintings depict fond memories of her childhood, and her daily life with family and the community, as well as memorable joyous events.

You may wish to bring a copy of Carmen Lomas Garzas' book *Family Pictures* (*Cuadros de familia*) (Children's Book Press, 1999) and have students describe the activities of family members.

A: Suggestions

- Emphasize that these are generalizations and that there is individual
  variation in each culture, as well
  as among individual families and
  social groups.
- If students are comfortable with
  the topic, discuss stereotypes
  about different family structures
  and style among ethnic groups in
  the United States and Canada.

A, B: Suggestion
Have students write three to four
sentences that describe typical
circumstances or situations in their
families. Invite them to share their
sentences. Take a poll to find out
which sentences are true for the
majority of the students and which
are unique to a given family.

padres no desarrollan[k] en ellos la capacidad de vivir independientemente y por eso los hijos no dejan el nido.[l]

Culturas diferentes

¿Son válidas estas conclusiones? El concepto de la unidad familiar existe en las dos culturas. En los Estados Unidos y el Canadá, la independencia personal tiene gran importancia social. Es una gran responsabilidad de los padres el hacer[m] independientes a sus hijos. La integridad de la familia depende menos de la cercanía[n] física y geográfica.

En cambio, en la cultura hispánica es muy importante <u>mantener</u> intacto el grupo familiar. En muchos casos, los hijos dejan la casa cuando <u>contraen</u> matrimonio y no cuando terminan sus estudios o <u>comienzan</u> a trabajar. Las dos sociedades tienen perspectivas diferentes; es imposible evaluar una cultura según las normas de otra. ■

[k]*develop* [l]*dejan... leave the nest* [m]*el... to make* [n]*closeness*

Comprensión

A. **¿Opinión o hecho** (*fact*)**?** Indique si las siguientes oraciones representan una opinión o un hecho.

	OPINIÓN	HECHO
1. A veces los hijos estadounidenses y canadienses trabajan en otras ciudades porque sus padres no los quieren (*don't love them*).	☐	☐
2. En muchos casos, los hijos hispanos viven con su familia aun (*even*) cuando tienen buenos trabajos.	☐	☐
3. La proximidad geográfica de los parientes es muy importante para la familia hispana.	☐	☐
4. Los padres ancianos representan una molestia para los hijos estadounidenses y canadienses.	☐	☐

B. **¿Quién habla?** Indique quién habla en las siguientes oraciones. **¡OJO!** Hay diferentes normas culturales.

	UN HISPANO / UNA HISPANA	UN(A) ESTADOUNIDENSE O CANADIENSE
1. «Tengo 28 años. Soy soltero y vivo con mis padres.»	☐	☐
2. «Necesito visitar a mi madre. Tiene 79 años y vive sola (*alone*).»	☐	☐
3. «La independencia es muy importante en mi vida. No deseo depender de mis padres el resto de mi vida (*life*).»	☐	☐
4. «Mi hija tiene un buen trabajo en una gran compañía. Vive con una amiga en la ciudad y yo vivo aquí, en el pueblo.»	☐	☐

CULTURE

Offer students statements about typical families in this country; they agree or disagree: (*No*) *Estoy de acuerdo.* When they disagree they should correct the statement and elaborate their disagreement (ask questions to elicit more details and opinions):

1. *La familia típica norteamericana es grande.*
2. *La familia típica es igual en todos los lugares y en todas las clases sociales.*
3. *En este país el divorcio no es normal.*
4. *Pocos hijos viven sólo con el padre o con la madre.*
5. *Los abuelos son muy importantes en la familia norteamericana.*
6. *Sólo los padres (no las madres) trabajan.*

ESCRITURA

A. Ud. y su familia. ¿Cómo son sus relaciones con su familia? ¿Es Ud. como el típico hijo estadounidense o canadiense de la lectura? ¿Es Ud. independiente o todavía vive con sus padres? ¿Por qué? ¿Tiene relaciones estrechas (*close*) con su familia? ¿O son un poco distantes? Conteste en un breve párrafo (*paragraph*). Trate de (*Try to*) usar palabras y frases de la **Estrategia** (página 90).

B. ¿Quién es Ud.? You have already learned enough Spanish to be able to say a lot about yourself and your family. Answer the following questions. Then rewrite them in the form of one or two brief paragraphs that tell as much about you as possible.

1. ¿Cómo se llama Ud.?
2. ¿Cuántos años tiene Ud.?
3. ¿Qué profesión tiene? (¿Es estudiante?)
4. ¿Dónde estudia Ud.? ¿Qué estudia?
5. ¿Vive Ud. solo/a, con amigos o con la familia? ¿En qué ciudad vive?
6. Económicamente, ¿es Ud. completamente independiente de sus padres? ¿O depende en parte o mucho de ellos?

ESCRITURA

Suggestions

■ Before assigning as homework, review connecting words from the section indicated in the text. The following day, before class, scan several students' paragraphs and have one of the most coherent put on the board. Go over the paragraph with students, emphasizing the use of connecting words.

■ If you prefer that your students do a journal activity, see *Mi diario* in this chapter of the Workbook.

B: Follow-Up

Encourage students from different ethnic backgrounds to read their paragraphs to the whole class. Together with the students, make a list of differences and similarities among their answers to questions 5 and 6.

◀ De compras en Plaza Inter, un centro comercial en Managua, Nicaragua

CHAPTER OPENER PHOTO

Point out the chapter-opener photo and have students talk about their own shopping experiences and ideas about shopping in Hispanic countries. Encourage them to describe the woman in the photo. Where is she? Does the place remind them of places where they shop?

Suggestion

Ask students the following questions to introduce the chapter topic.

1. How often do you shop at a mall?
2. What shopping do you do in your neighborhood? For example, do you shop for clothing there?
3. How do you generally get to the place where you shop?
4. Have you ever done any shopping on the Internet?
5. With the exception of food and entertainment, how do you spend most of your money?

Notes

- It is not uncommon for shopping centers to be spread throughout the city in many Latin American countries, instead of being located in one specific area, as is common in the United States.
- The *Puntos de partida* Online Learning Center includes an interview with a native speaker from Nicaragua who answers questions similar to those in the preceding *Suggestion.*

Reciclado

Use the questions to poll students and have one student tally the survey on the board. Have volunteers explain the numbers in Spanish: *Once estudiantes de la clase compran en un centro comercial* (mall).

☼ Heritage Speakers

Pregúnteles a sus estudiantes hispanohablantes si usan el Internet para comprar cosas de países hispánicos. ¿Cuál es su sitio Web hispánico favorito?

Resources

For Students

- Workbook
- Laboratory Manual and Laboratory Audio Program
- Quia™ Online Workbook and Online Laboratory Manual
- Video on CD
- Interactive CD-ROM
- *Puntos de partida* Online Learning Center (**www.mhhe.com/puntos7**)

For Instructors

- *Instructor's Manual and Resource Kit,* "Chapter-by-Chapter" Supplementary Materials
- Overhead Transparencies 21–29
- Test generator
- Electronic Testing Program
- Video Program
- Audioscript
- *Puntos de partida* Online Learning Center (**www.mhhe.com/puntos7**)

De compras°

Suggestions

- Students from large urban centers may be familiar with the word *mercado*. Have students describe *mercados* they have seen or tell what they think a *mercado* would be like. Ask them where a *mercado* might be located, how it would be set up, what products vendors might sell, and so on.
- If students are not familiar with *mercado*, define the word. Also ask them to guess the meaning of *centro comercial*. You might have someone take notes of students' ideas and revisit them after completing this chapter.
- Have students list their ideas about Nicaragua, including information on geography, politics, economy, culture, music, and cuisine. When you finish the chapter, return to the lists and ask students what ideas they would change and/or add.

CULTURA

- **Perspectivas culturales**

  Entrevista cultural: Nicaragua

  Entre amigos: ¡Está súper fuera de moda!

  Conozca... Nicaragua

- **Nota cultural:** Clothing in the Hispanic World

- **En los Estados Unidos y el Canadá:** Los hispanos en el mundo de la moda

- **Literatura de Nicaragua:** Rubén Darío

- **Lectura:** La psicología de los colores

VOCABULARIO

- De compras: La ropa
- ¿De qué color es?
- Más allá del número 100

PRONUNCIACIÓN

- Stress and Written Accent Marks (Part 2)

GRAMÁTICA

9 Demonstrative Adjectives and Pronouns

10 **Tener, venir, preferir, querer,** and **poder;** Some Idioms with **tener**

11 **Ir; ir** + **a** + Infinitive; The Contraction **al**

Entrevista cultural

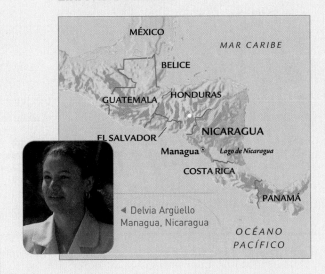

◄ Delvia Argüello
Managua, Nicaragua

°**De...** *Shopping*

MULTIMEDIA

- The multimedia materials that accompany this chapter are referenced in the Student and Instructor's Editions with icons to help you identify when and where to incorporate them.

- The *Instructor's Manual and Resource Kit* (IM/RK) provides suggestions for using the multimedia materials in the classroom.

De compras: La ropa

Notes

- See the model for vocabulary presentation and other material in the *Capítulo 3 Vocabulario: Preparación* section of "Chapter-by-Chapter Supplementary Materials," in the IM.
- In many Hispanic countries, store hours in the morning are similar to those in the United States and Canada; however, some shops close in the early afternoon until 4 P.M. and generally reopen until 9 or 10 P.M. All stores are generally closed on Sundays and holidays.
- Some Spanish speakers use the singular *el pantalón* to talk about pants.

Suggestions

- Model the pronunciation of clothing, pointing out items in the classroom or in photos. Stop after every three or four items to go back and review, indicating the item and asking students: *¿Es una blusa o una camisa?, ¿Es una camisa o un suéter?*, and so on.
- Offer additional vocabulary: *los pantalones cortos, el anillo, los pendientes / los aretes, el collar, de cuero, a la medida.*
- Make statements about what students are wearing and have them respond *sí* or *no.*

    Roberto lleva un abrigo. → *No, Roberto lleva una chaqueta.*

  To follow up, have students invent similar sentences about classmates.
- Discuss the concept of *mercado* vs. *tienda.* Point out the existence of large department stores and malls as well as small shops and open-air markets.
- To avoid stereotypes about bargaining (*regatear*) in Hispanic countries; point out situations in which one bargains in the U.S. and Canada: car sales, flea markets, and so on.
- Have students give words that they associate with *comprar, el almacén, el precio, la librería, pagar, el centro comercial, las rebajas.*

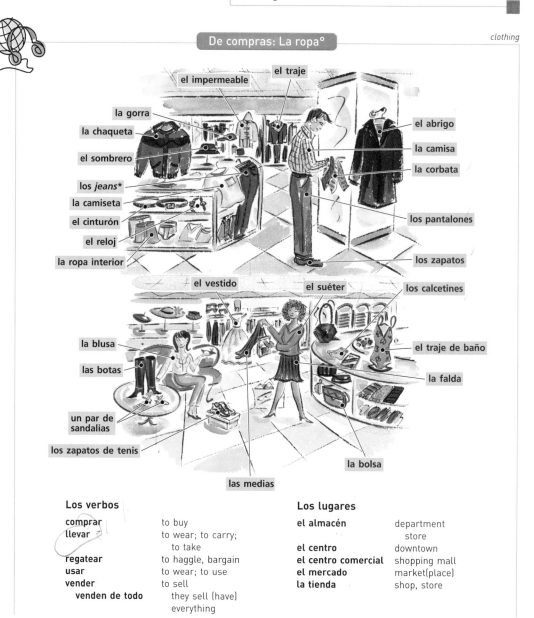

De compras: La ropa°   *clothing*

Los verbos			Los lugares	
comprar	to buy		**el almacén**	department store
llevar	to wear; to carry; to take		**el centro**	downtown
regatear	to haggle, bargain		**el centro comercial**	shopping mall
usar	to wear; to use		**el mercado**	market(place)
vender	to sell		**la tienda**	shop, store
venden de todo	they sell (have) everything			

---

*The influx of U.S. goods to Latin America and Spain has affected common language. Jeans is one example of an English word that is commonly used in Spanish-speaking countries.

CULTURE

In some Spanish-speaking countries, *vaqueros* is used for *jeans.* In Mexico, jeans are often called *pantalones de mezclilla. Billetera* is used for a man's wallet. *Cartera*, on the other hand, is often used for a woman's purse.

Resources: Transparencies 21–23

MULTIMEDIA: Audio

Students can listen to and practice this chapter's vocabulary on the Online Learning Center (**www.mhhe.com/puntos7**), as well as on the Textbook Audio CD, part of the Laboratory Audio Program.

¿Cuánto cuesta?

la ganga	bargain
el precio	price
el precio fijo	fixed (set) price
las rebajas	sales
barato/a	inexpensive
caro/a	expensive

Otras palabras y expresiones útiles

la cartera	wallet
es de (algodón, lana, seda)*	it is made of (cotton, wool, silk)
¡Es de última moda!	It's the latest style!

■ ■ ■ Conversación

A. La ropa

Paso 1. ¿Qué ropa llevan estas personas?

1. El Sr. Rivera lleva _____.

2. La Srta. Alonso lleva _____. El perro lleva _____.

3. Sara lleva _____.

4. Alfredo lleva _____. Necesita comprar _____.

Paso 2. De estas personas, ¿quién trabaja hoy? ¿Quién va a (*is going to*) una fiesta? ¿Quién no trabaja en este momento?

B. Asociaciones. Complete las oraciones lógicamente con palabras de **De compras: La ropa.**

1. Un ~~almacén~~ _____ es una tienda grande.
2. No es posible ~~regatear~~ _____ cuando hay precios fijos.
3. En la librería, ~~hay~~ _____ de todo: textos y otros libros, cuadernos, lápices, discos compactos. Hay grandes ~~rebajas~~ _____ al final del semestre/trimestre, en los cuales (*in which*) todo es muy barato.
4. Siempre hay *boutiques* en los ~~centros~~ _____.
5. El ~~centro~~ _____ de una ciudad es la parte céntrica.
6. Estos artículos de ropa no son para hombres: _____. *en cambio son para mujeres*
7. Estos artículos de ropa son para hombres y mujeres: _____.
8. La ropa de ~~lana~~ _____ (*material*) es muy elegante.
9. La ropa de ~~seda~~ _____ es muy práctica.

---

*Note another use of **ser** + **de**: to tell what material something is made of.

Refrán

«Bueno y barato no caben en un zapato.»

Write the *refrán* on the board and have students guess the meaning of the word *caber* (to fit). Then ask what they think the saying means. Are there similar sayings in English? (*You get what you pay for.*)

☼ Heritage Speakers

Pídales a sus estudiantes hispanohablantes que describan la ropa que llevan hoy mismo.

Resources: Transparency 24

Preliminary Exercises

■ Have students give the words defined:

1. *el antónimo de vender*
2. *una tienda grande*
3. *la cantidad de dinero que es necesario pagar*
4. *un sinónimo de llevar*
5. *la parte céntrica de una ciudad*
6. *el antónimo de tienda pequeña*
7. *el antónimo de vender muy poco*
8. *el antónimo de pagar el precio indicado*
9. *el antónimo de caro*
10. *el antónimo de estilos de los años setenta.*

■ Point out a new use of *ser: ser + de* (to be made of). Write the following phrases on the board: *de metal, de papel, de plástico, de madera.* Point to objects and have students tell what they are made of. ¿*De qué es esto* (point to a chair or another wooden object)? → *De madera.*

1. *el dinero*	5. *el bolígrafo*
2. *el lápiz*	6. *la mesa*
3. *el libro*	7. *la foto*
4. *el cuaderno*	

Con. A: Extension

Have students give the appropriate clothing (*ropa apropiada*) for the following:

¿*para los yuppies?*
¿*los cantantes* country-western?
¿*los líderes militares?*
¿*los detectives?*
¿*los personajes* (characters) *bíblicos?*

Con. B: Follow-Up

Have students answer the following questions:

1. ¿*Dónde compra Ud. la ropa generalmente, en una tienda o en un almacén?*
2. *En esta ciudad,* ¿*hay tiendas o mercados donde regateen los clientes?* ¿*donde haya buenas rebajas?*
3. ¿*Lleva Ud.* _____ *hoy?*
4. ¿*Necesita Ud. comprar ropa nueva?* ¿*Qué necesita comprar?* ¿*Qué tipo de ropa compra con más frecuencia?*
5. *Imagine que Ud. es un profesor conservador / un estudiante típico / el presidente / un famoso artista de Hollywood.* ¿*Qué lleva hoy?*
6. *Por lo general,* ¿*le gusta llevar ropa elegante o ropa vieja?*

NOTA COMUNICATIVA

Note

Point out that there are many tag questions in English, e.g., *won't you?*, *doesn't he?*, *will they?*, and so on. Spanish tag questions are invariable, i.e., they don't change regardless of the number or gender of the subject.

Con. D: Preliminary Exercise

Have students respond *sí* or *no.*

1. *Ud. trabaja en la biblioteca, ¿no?*
2. *Ud. siempre llega tarde a clase, ¿verdad?*
3. *Ud. lleva jeans hoy, ¿no?*
4. *Ud. toma café por la mañana, ¿verdad?*
5. *Uds. llegan a la universidad a las seis de la mañana, ¿no?*

C. ¿Qué lleva Ud.? Para hablar de Ud. y de la ropa, complete estas oraciones lógicamente.

> ### Vocabulario útil
>
> The preposition **para** can be used to express *in order to*, followed by an infinitive.
>
> **Para ir** al centro, me gusta llevar pantalones, una camiseta y sandalias.
> (*In order*) *To go downtown, I like to wear pants, a T-shirt, and sandals.*

1. Para ir a la universidad, me gusta llevar _____.
2. Para ir a las fiestas con los amigos, me gusta usar _____.
3. Para pasar un día en la playa (*beach*), me gusta llevar _____.
4. Cuando estoy en casa todo el día, llevo _____.
5. Nunca uso _____.
6. _____ es un artículo / son artículos de ropa absolutamente necesario(s) para mí.

NOTA COMUNICATIVA

More About Getting Information

Tag phrases can change statements into questions.

Venden de todo aquí,	{ **¿no?** **¿verdad?**	*They sell everything here, right?* *(don't they?)*
No necesito impermeable hoy, **¿verdad?**		*I don't need a raincoat today, do I?*

¿Verdad? is found after affirmative or negative statements; **¿no?** is usually found after affirmative statements only. Note that the inverted question mark comes immediately before the tag question, not at the beginning of the statement.

D. Entrevista. Using tag questions, ask a classmate questions based on the following statements. He or she will answer based on general information—or as truthfully as possible—if the question is about aspects of his or her life.

> MODELO: E1: Estudias en la biblioteca por la noche, ¿verdad?
> E2: No. Estudio en la biblioteca por la mañana. (No, no estudio en la biblioteca. Me gusta estudiar en casa.)

1. En un almacén hay precios fijos.
2. Regateamos mucho en este país.
3. No hay muchos mercados en esta ciudad.
4. Los *jeans* Gap son muy baratos.
5. Es necesario llevar traje y corbata a clase.
6. Eres una persona muy independiente.
7. Tienes una familia muy grande.
8. No hay examen (*test*) mañana.

National Standards: Comparisons

Have students search the Internet for department stores in Latin America and Spain and write one or two paragraphs describing the clothes and fashions these sites advertise, including the predominant colors, styles, and fabrics. Have them convert prices in the local currency into dollars. Some department stores with online sites are: *Eclipse* (Nicaragua), *El Palacio de Hierro* (Mexico), *El Corte Inglés* (Spain), *Almacenes París* (Chile), *Beco* (Venezuela). There are also many exclusively online stores.

Here are colors you can use to describe clothing and other objects.

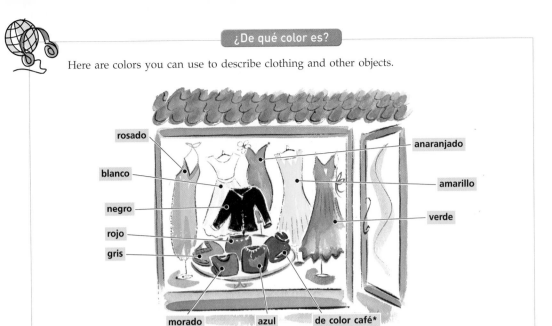

rosado
blanco
negro
rojo
gris
morado
azul
de color café*
anaranjado
amarillo
verde

 Remember that colors, like all adjectives, must agree in gender and number with the nouns they modify. Note that some colors only have one form for masculine and feminine nouns.

el traje **azul,** la camisa **azul**

■■■ Conversación

A. Muchos colores. ¿Cuántos colores hay en este cuadro (*painting*) de Gonzalo Endara Crow? ¿Cuáles son?

◄ Después de (*After*) la noche, *por Gonzalo Endara Crow*

---

*The expression (**de**) **color café** is invariable: **el sombrero (de) color café, la falda (de) color café, los pantalones (de) color café.**

Vocabulario: Preparación

Suggestions

■ Model words and phrases using clothing students are wearing. Verify student comprehension periodically with *¿sí o no?* questions.

■ Emphasize gender and number agreement for colors. Remind students that gender is invariable for *azul, verde,* and *gris.*

■ Offer these optional colors: *pardo* is a type of brown; *beige* (pronounced with English sound *j* at the end); *purpúreo* or *púrpura* = *morado.*

■ Use nominalized forms as you review colors, for example, *La camisa de Janet es roja. ¿Y la de Susie?*

■ Have students tell what colors they associate with the following: *¿Qué color asocia con... ?* el mar Caribe, una cebra, un limón, el dinero, el café, una rosa, un gato, esta universidad, los Estados Unidos / el Canadá, una jirafa, un pingüino, un elefante, un teléfono.

■ Offer the following phrases.

de cuadros	plaid
de lunares	polka-dotted
de rayas	striped

Con. A: Note

Gonzalo Endara Crow is a *naif* artist. His paintings are also described as part of a style called magical realism. Ask students what *naif* (primitivistic) and magical realism elements they can see in this painting. (This is probably best discussed in English.)

National Standards: Connections

Gonzalo Endara Crow was born in Bucay, Ecuador, in 1936 and died in 1996. He was interested in popular art and was inspired by the artisans of his native country. In his work, one can see the bright colors and *naif* approach present in Ecuador's pottery and textiles. Have students search for more information and images about Endara Crow on the Internet. Ask them to write sentences about the colors and designs in his works.

Resources: Transparency 25

NOTA CULTURAL

Suggestions

- Poll students to find out what they typically wear to classes. Then ask those who work in office environments how they are expected to dress there. What are the tendencies of those in the class, to dress more formally or more casually?
- Ask students follow-up questions for comprehension.

1. *En general, ¿quiénes son más formales, los hispanos o los estadounidenses/ canadienses?*

2. *¿Qué llevan los estudiantes hispanos a clase, una camiseta y jeans o una camisa y pantalones?*

3. *¿Qué llevan los estudiantes de ESAN para ir a clase?*

Con. B: Note

Point out that the adjective *alerta* is used to modify both masculine and feminine nouns.

Con. B: Expansion

Have students describe the differences between these department stores: J.C. Penney's, Saks Fifth Avenue, Macy's, and WalMart.

Con. B: Follow-Up

Dictate the following items for students to write down.

1. *una camisa negra*
2. *un impermeable viejo*
3. *medias blancas*
4. *una falda de cuadros*
5. *una camisa de rayas*
6. *(colors of your university)*
7. *una camisa o chaqueta verde militar*

After the dictation, ask students which items from the dictation they associate with the following.

1. *un detective famoso de la televisión*
2. *una persona que se llama Scottie McTavish*
3. *un cantante (country-western)*
4. *un estudiante de (university)*
5. *un grupo de beisbolistas*
6. *un prisionero*
7. *Fidel Castro*

NOTA CULTURAL

Clothing in the Hispanic World

In Hispanic countries, people tend to dress more formally than do people in this country. As a rule, Hispanics consider neatness and care for one's appearance to be very important.

In the business world, women wear dressy pants, skirts, or dresses, and many wear high-heeled shoes. Men generally dress in trousers, shirts, and ties. Jeans, T-shirts, and tennis shoes are considered inappropriate in traditional business environments. Students at some business schools, like ESAN (**Escuela de Administración de Negocios**) in Peru, are even required to wear formal business attire to attend classes as if they were already working at a company. Shorts and sweatpants are considered very casual and are reserved almost exclusively for use at home, for a day at the beach, or for sports.

Young adults generally dress casually in social situations, and as in other countries, are often concerned with dressing according to current styles. As a rule, what is considered stylish in this country is also in style in Europe and Latin America.

▲ *Ropa diseñada por (designed by) la famosa venezolana Carolina Herrera*

B. **¡Ojo alerta! ¿Escaparates (*Window displays*) idénticos?** These window displays are almost alike . . . but not quite! Can you find at least eight differences between them?

MODELO: En el dibujo A hay _____, pero en el dibujo B hay _____.

Palabras útiles
de rayas (striped) **multicolor**

A.

B.

C. **Asociaciones.** ¿Qué colores asocia Ud. con... ?

1. el dinero
2. la una de la mañana
3. una mañana bonita
4. una mañana fea
5. el demonio
6. los Estados Unidos
7. una jirafa
8. un pingüino
9. un limón
10. una naranja
11. un elefante
12. las flores (*flowers*)

National Standards: Connections

Have students research clothing associated with different areas of the Hispanic world (for example, *sarapes* in Mexico, bowlers and other kinds of hats in Bolivia). Remind them to note the materials used and suggest reasons for using these particular ones (for example, wool in the Andes for warmth and because it is an available resource).

CULTURE

In the Caribbean and other warm parts of Latin America, it is common for men to wear an article of clothing called *una guayabera*. It's an elegant short-sleeved shirt, often embroidered or with pleats, which is worn outside the pants (not tucked in). It is ideal for warm, humid climates and can be worn in formal or informal situations.

Resources: **Transparency 26**

D. ¿De qué color es?

Paso 1. Tell the color of things in your classroom, especially the clothing your classmates are wearing.

MODELO: El bolígrafo de Anita es amarillo. Roberto lleva calcetines azules, una camisa de cuadros (*plaid*) morados y azules, *jeans*…

Paso 2. Now describe what someone in the class is wearing, without revealing his or her name. Can your classmates guess whom you are describing?

MODELO: E1: Lleva botas negras, una camiseta blanca y *jeans*.
E2: Es Anne.

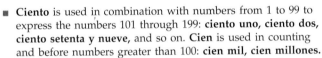
Más allá del° número 100

Más… Beyond the

Continúe la secuencia:

noventa y nueve, cien, ciento uno…
mil, dos mil…
un millón, dos millones…

100	cien, ciento	**700**	setecientos/as
101	ciento uno/una	**800**	ochocientos/as
200	doscientos/as	**900**	novecientos/as
300	trescientos/as	**1.000***	mil
400	cuatrocientos/as	**2.000**	dos mil
500	quinientos/as	**1.000.000**	un millón
600	seiscientos/as	**2.000.000**	dos millones

- **Ciento** is used in combination with numbers from 1 to 99 to express the numbers 101 through 199: **ciento uno, ciento dos, ciento setenta y nueve,** and so on. **Cien** is used in counting and before numbers greater than 100: **cien mil, cien millones.**
- When the numbers 200 through 900 modify a noun, they must agree in gender: **cuatrocientas niñas, doscientas dos casas.**
- **Mil** means *one thousand* or *a thousand*. It does not have a plural form in counting, but **millón** does. When used with a noun, **millón** (**dos millones,** and so on) must be followed by **de.**

3.000 habitantes — tres mil habitantes
14.000.000 **de** habitantes — catorce millones **de** habitantes

- Note how years are expressed in Spanish.

1899 — mil ochocientos noventa y nueve
2005 — dos mil cinco

In many parts of the Spanish-speaking world, a period in numerals is used where English uses a comma, and a comma is used to indicate the decimal where English uses a period:* **$1.500; $1.000.000; $10,45; 65,9%.

National Standards: Comparisons

In this chapter, students learn that numbers are written differently in Latin America and Spain. The decimal point is used for a comma and vice-versa. If you are working on a computer spreadsheet in a Spanish-speaking country, you will quickly notice that the default setting for numbers is the opposite. This can be remedied easily by changing the default settings on the computer to the decimal point/comma protocol of your choice.

Refrán

«Amor y dolor son del mismo color.»

After writing the *refrán* on the board, have students guess the meaning of the words *amor* and *dolor*. Ask students if they think *color* refers to an actual color or something else, and if there are any similar sayings in English. (*There's a fine line between love and hate.*)

Con. C: Suggestion

Have students bring a copy of their favorite painting (or choose one in *Puntos de partida*) and explain the colors and clothing (if any) they see in it. Have them explain why they like the painting.

Más allá del número 100
Suggestions

- Model pronunciation of hundreds forms. Give addition and subtraction problems using hundreds (some incorrect) and have students respond *sí* or *no*. When a problem is incorrect, have them give the correct answer.
- Point out the following number facts.
  1. 500, 700, 900 have irregular forms.
  2. *Un* is not used with *mil* (1000).
  3. The hundreds must agree in gender; use *-cientas* before feminine nouns.
  4. There is no *y* in *ciento uno*, and so on.
  5. A period marks the thousands in Spanish, instead of a comma as in English.
- Write complex numbers on the board for students to read aloud, for example, 154, 672.
- Have students count by thousands (*mil, dos mil,…*) and then by millions (*un millón, dos millones,…*) to emphasize the singular *mil* and plural *millones.*
- Have students say the following in Spanish.
  1. 500 men, 500 women, 700 male professors
  2. 1,000 books, 2,000 friends, 3,000 universities
  3. a million dollars; 3 million Americans; 7 million euros
- Students will get further practice in saying the years in *Capítulo 5.* Introduce this skill here by saying the current year in Spanish, and writing it on the board as you speak. Say a few more years, writing at the same time. Then begin to make mistakes as you write, asking students to verify the numbers as you write.

Con. A: Preliminary Exercises

- Dictate the following numbers in Spanish as students write them in digit form.

  1. *100, 50, 60*
  2. *400, 600, 800*
  3. *2.000, 1.000.000, 50.000*
  4. *150, 500, 1.500*
  5. *660, 960, 760*

- Write these numbers on the board and model them. Then have students say them.

  1. *2, 12, 20, 200*
  2. *3, 13, 30, 300*
  3. *4, 14, 40, 400*

and so on.

Con. A: Suggestions

- Ask students the following questions.

  1. *Las palabras* peso, pesado *y* pesar *están relacionadas. ¿Qué significan?*
  2. *¿Qué animal del gráfico es el más pesado? ¿el menos pesado? ¿Cuánto pesa cada uno?*
  3. *Busque las palabras en español para* terrestrial *y* mammal.
  4. *¿Cuánto pesan los animales en libras (pounds)?*

- For *Paso 2*, model the question: *¿Cuánto pesa tu gato/perro?*

Note

To convert kilograms to pounds, use the following formula: *kilogram × 2.2 = lbs.*

Con. B: Variation

Play a *¿más o menos?* guessing game. Think or have students think of a number for others to guess. After each guess, the leader tells whether the number is *más* or *menos*. 650: *¿500?* → *más, ¿700?* → *menos, ¿600?* → *más, ¿650?* → *¡Eso es!* (That's right!)

Bright Idea

Con. C: Follow-Up

Tell students they have a budget of $500 or $1,000 (or ?). Have them tell what they would buy.

■■■ Conversación

A. ¿Cuánto pesan? (*How much do they weigh?*)

Paso 1. Estos son los animales terrestres más grandes. ¿Cuánto pesan en kilos? **¡OJO!** Use el artículo masculino para todos los nombres, menos para (*except for*) los nombres que terminan (*that end*) en **-a.**

> **MODELO:** El elefante pesa cinco mil kilos.

Paso 2. Pregúntele (*Ask*) a un compañero / una compañera aproximadamente cuánto pesan en libras las siguientes cosas.

1. su perro/gato
2. su mochila con los libros para hoy
3. su coche
4. su libro de español
5. el animal más grande del mundo (*world*)

B. ¿Cuánto es? Diga los precios.

el dólar (los Estados Unidos, el Canadá, Puerto Rico)
el nuevo peso (México)
el bolívar (Venezuela)
el euro (España)
el quetzal (Guatemala)

1. 7.345 euros
2. $100
3. 5.710 quetzales
4. 670 bolívares
5. $1.000.000
6. 528 nuevos pesos
7. 836 bolívares
8. 101 euros
9. $4.000.000,00
10. 6.000.000 quetzales

C. Compras personales

Paso 1. With a classmate, determine how much the following items probably cost, using **¿Cuánto cuesta(n)... ?** (*How much does . . . cost?*). Keep track of the prices that you decide on. Follow the model.

> **MODELO:** una chaqueta de cuero (*leather*) →
> E1: ¿Cuánto cuesta una chaqueta de cuero?
> E2: Cuesta dos cientos dólares.

1. una calculadora pequeña
2. un coche nuevo/usado
3. una computadora Mac o IBM
4. un reloj Timex / de oro (*gold*)
5. unos zapatos de tenis
6. una casa en esta ciudad

Paso 2. Now compare the prices you selected with those of others in the class. What is the most expensive thing on the list? (**¿Cuál es la cosa más cara?**) What is the least expensive? (**¿Cuál es la cosa más barata?**)

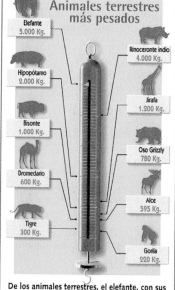

Animales terrestres más pesados

Elefante
5.000 Kg.

Rinoceronte indio
4.000 Kg.

Hipopótamo
2.000 Kg.

Jirafa
1.200 Kg.

Bisonte
1.000 Kg.

Oso Grizzly
780 Kg.

Dromedario
600 Kg.

Alce
595 Kg.

Tigre
300 Kg.

Gorila
220 Kg.

De los animales terrestres, el elefante, con sus 5.000 kilos de peso medio entre todas sus especies, es sin duda el mamífero más pesado. El hipopótamo y el rinoceronte son los siguientes en la lista, y el hombre, ni aparece.

Need more practice?

- Workbook and Laboratory Manual
- Interactive CD-ROM
- Online Learning Center (www.mhhe.com/puntos7)

MULTIMEDIA: Internet

Have students look up currency conversion websites to convert from one currency to another.

☼ Heritage Speakers

Invite a sus estudiantes hispanohablantes a que lean en voz alta los nombres de los animales del anuncio y que la clase los repita.

Stress and Written Accent Marks (Part 2)

¿Recuerda Ud.?

Most Spanish words do not need a written accent mark because their pronunciation is completely predictable by native speakers. Here are the two basic rules.

- A word that ends in a vowel, **-n,** or **-s** is stressed on the next-to-last syllable.
- A word that ends in any other consonant is stressed on the last syllable.

The written accent mark is used in the following situations.

- A written accent mark is needed when a word does not follow the two basic rules presented. Look at the words in this group.

ta-bú	a-le-mán	in-glés
ca-fé	na-ción	es-tás

These words end in a vowel, **-n,** or **-s,** so one would predict that they would be stressed on the next-to-last syllable. But the written accent mark shows that they are in fact accented on the last syllable. Now look at the words in this group.

lá-piz	dó-lar	ál-bum	á-gil	dó-cil

These words end in a consonant (other than **-n** or **-s**), so one would predict that they would be stressed on the last syllable. But the written accent mark shows that they are in fact accented on the next-to-last syllable.

- All words that are stressed on the third-to-last syllable must have a written accent mark.

bo-lí-gra-fo	ma-trí-cu-la	ma-te-má-ti-cas

- When two consecutive vowels do not form a diphthong (see **Capítulo 1**), the vowel that receives the spoken stress will have a written accent mark. This pattern is very frequent in words that end in **-ía.**

Ma-rí-a	po-li-cí-a	as-tro-no-mí-a
dí-a	bio-lo-gí-a	

- Contrast the pronunciation of those words with the following words in which the vowels **i** and **a** *do* form a diphthong.

  Patricia   Francia   infancia   distancia

Reciclado

Review information from *Capítulo 2.* Write *bailar* and its present tense paradigm on the board. Use it for the following.

- Have students separate the forms into syllables.
- Encourage them to read syllables out loud slowly.
- Ask them whether *-ai-* is a diphthong or not.
- Have them identify the stressed syllables.
- Ask why words do or do not require accent marks.

Note

Students are not accustomed to separating syllables in English. Syllable division in English is not as necessary as it is in Spanish. Also, English syllables are not as obvious as Spanish syllables.

Suggestion

Point out that accent marks are added or deleted to preserve the original stress pattern when words are made plural.

Accent deleted: *nación → naciones; francés → franceses.*
Accent added: *joven → jóvenes; examen → exámenes.*

 Heritage Speakers

Anime a los hispanohablantes a modelar la pronunciación de las palabras que se usan en esta sección para la colocación de los acentos escritos. Invite a los angloparlantes a imitar la pronunciación repitiendo las palabras que oyen.

Preliminary Exercises

■ Write pairs of words on the board that vary only in stress. Read one word of each pair of words aloud at random. Students decide which word you said.

hable	hablé	espere	esperé
doblo	dobló	paso	pasó
baje	bajé	pase	pasé
bajo	bajó	papa	papá

■ Have students identify the stressed syllable.

¿Última o penúltima?

esta	español	inglés
está	Pérez	chimpancé

¿Penúltima o antepenúltima?

política	Italia	teléfono
delgado	estados	Toledo
simpático		

¿Última, penúltima o antepenúltima?

busco	clásico	clasifico
buscó	lógico	clasificó
típico		

■ ¿Diptongo o no?

María	estudia	geo (¡OJO!)
baila	patio	geografía
día	tío	

A: Follow-Up

■ Give students a *Dictado* that includes sentences such as:

1. *José es rico.*
2. *Ramón es romántico.*
3. *El Sr. Gómez es simpático.*
4. *David es perezoso y antipático.*
5. *Joaquín es alto y guapo.*
6. *El Sr. Pérez es bajo y viejo.*

■ Have several students write the dictation on the board while the rest of the class works at their seats. Correct errors on the board, paying special attention to accents and why they are needed or not needed.

■ Some one-syllable words have accents to distinguish them from other words that sound like them. For example:

él (*he*)/el (*the*)
sí (*yes*)/si (*if*)
tú (*you*)/tu (*your*)
mí (*me*)/mi (*my*)

■ Interrogative and exclamatory words have a written accent on the stressed vowel. For example:

¿quién?
¿dónde?
¡Qué ganga! (*What a bargain!*)

A. Sílabas. The following words have been separated into syllables for you. Read them aloud, paying careful attention to where the spoken stress should fall. Don't worry about the meaning of words you haven't heard before. The rules you have learned will help you pronounce them correctly.

1.	a-quí	pa-pá	a-diós	bus-qué
2.	prác-ti-co	mur-cié-la-go	te-lé-fo-no	ar-chi-pié-la-go
3.	Ji-mé-nez	Ro-drí-guez	Pé-rez	Gó-mez
4.	si-co-lo-gí-a	so-cio-lo-gí-a	sa-bi-du-rí-a	e-ner-gí-a
5.	his-to-ria	te-ra-pia	Pre-to-ria	me-mo-ria

B. Reglas (*Rules*). Indicate the stressed vowel of each word in the following list. Give the rule that determines the stress of each word.

1. exámenes
2. lápiz
3. necesitar
4. perezoso
5. actitud
6. acciones
7. dólares
8. francés
9. están
10. hombre
11. peso
12. mujer
13. plástico
14. María
15. Rodríguez
16. Patricia

National Standards: Comparisons

Like Spanish, other Romance languages have written accent marks or diacriticals. French, for example, has five different accent marks: an acute accent (´), a grave accent (`), the circumflex (^), the cedilla (ç), and the trema or dieresis (¨). In addition to the acute, grave, and circumflex diacriticals, Portuguese has a tilde (~), which nasalizes the vowels.

GRAMÁTICA

Gramática 9
Demonstrative Adjectives and Pronouns

¿Recuerda Ud.?

You have already used the forms of **este** (*this*), one of the Spanish demonstrative adjectives. Review them by describing objects near you and the clothes you are wearing.

> **MODELO:** Esta camisa es de rayas. Estos lápices son amarillos.

9 Pointing Out People and Things • Demonstrative Adjectives and Pronouns

Suéteres a buenos precios

Susana necesita comprar un suéter en el mercado.

VENDEDOR: *Estos* suéteres de aquí cuestan 150 pesos y *ese* suéter en su mano cuesta 250 pesos.

SUSANA: ¿Por qué es más caro *este*?

VENDEDOR: Porque *esos* son de pura lana virgen, de excelente calidad.

SUSANA: ¿Y *aquellos* suéteres de rayas?

VENDEDOR: *Aquellos* cuestan cien pesos solamente; son acrílicos.

¿Quién habla, Susana, Jorge o el vendedor?

1. Me gustan estos suéteres de rayas, y sólo cuestan cien pesos.
2. Señores, miren (*look at*) estos suéteres en mi mesa. Cuestan 150 pesos.
3. Voy a (*I am going to*) comprar este suéter. Me gusta la ropa de lana.
4. Este suéter acrílico es más barato que aquel suéter de lana.

Sweaters at good prices Susana needs to buy a sweater in the market. SALESMAN: *These sweaters here cost 150 pesos and that sweater in your hand costs 250 pesos.* SUSANA: *Why is this one more expensive?* SALESMAN: *Because those are of pure virgin wool, of excellent quality.* SUSANA: *What about those striped sweaters over there?* SALESMAN: *Those cost only one hundred pesos; they are acrylic.*

Gramática

Ciento cinco ■ **105**

Resources: Transparency 27

Gramática 9
Demonstrative Adjectives and Pronouns

Suggestions

■ Have students act out the *minidiálogo* and try to define the italicized words before checking the translation below.

■ Ask students to explain the difference between a demonstrative adjective and demonstrative pronoun. Ask them to provide examples in English.

> *This* car is John's. vs. *This* (*one*) is John's.
> *That* cat is white. vs. *That* (*one*) is white.

Bright Idea

Suggestion

Have three students stand in three distinct areas of the room, perhaps placing one student just outside the classroom door. Stand at one end with one student. Then as you indicate the student closest to you, say, "*Este/a estudiante se llama* [name of student]." Then point to the student who is farther away, but not farthest away, from you and say, "*Ese/a estudiante se llama* [name of student]." Finally point to the student who is farthest away and say "*Aquel* (*Aquella*) *estudiante se llama* [name of student]."

Follow-Up
Give students the following information:

> *En los países hispánicos no es extraño ver vendedores en la calle. Algunos vendedores están siempre en el mismo lugar. Otros son ambulantes. ¿Es esto normal en su país? ¿En qué contextos?* (large cities, university centers, Girl Scouts, and so on)

Note
Although bartering is normally limited to flea markets (*rastros* or *pulguerías*) in this country, it is not uncommon to hear people bartering in most open-air markets of Latin America. Prices in Latin American malls or other commercial shopping centers, however, are not usually negotiable.

Note

Some Spanish speakers prefer to use accents on these forms: *este coche y ése, aquella casa y ésta.* However, it is acceptable in modern Spanish, per the *Real Academia Española* in Madrid, to omit the accent on these forms when context makes the meaning clear and no ambiguity is possible. Students will not be exposed to these accented forms in *Puntos de partida*, unless these appear in a piece of realia that is reproduced as originally published. You may wish to make students aware of these accented forms.

Suggestions

- Hold up a book and say *este libro.* Place the book near a student and say *ese libro.* Place the book far from both yourself and the student and say *aquel libro.*
- Emphasize that the masculine singular forms do not end in *-o.*
- Point out that distance may be physical (*aquella casa que está lejos*) or temporal (*en aquella época*). Also remind students that distance is relative to the speaker and also depends on the context.
- In order to practice demonstrative adjectives, use real objects in the classroom: *este pupitre, esa pizarra, estos cuadernos.* You may also bring or have students bring in photographs or magazine clippings of buildings, houses, or city scenes to use in small group activities or to display in the classroom. Students can then describe the scenes.

Esta casa es bonita.
Esta ciudad es moderna.
Estos edificios son enormes.

Demonstrative Adjectives

	Demonstrative Adjectives					
	Singular			**Plural**		
this	este abrigo	esta gorra		*these*	estos abrigos	estas gorras
that	ese abrigo / aquel abrigo (allí)	esa gorra / aquella gorra (allí)		*those*	esos abrigos / aquellos abrigos (allí)	esas gorras / aquellas gorras (allí)

 Note that **este** becomes **estos** and **ese** becomes **esos** in the plural (no **o** in the masculine singular forms).

Demonstrative adjectives (**Los adjetivos demostrativos**) are used to indicate a specific noun or nouns. In Spanish, demonstrative adjectives precede the nouns they modify. They also agree in number and gender with the nouns.

In the chart above, **allí** is provided as a clue that **aquel, aquella, aquellos,** and **aquellas** refer to a more remote location. However, it is not obligatory to use the word **allí** when using forms of **aquel.**

demonstrative adjective = adjective used in place of a definite article to indicate a particular person, object, or concept

There are two ways to say *that/those* in Spanish. Forms of **ese** refer to nouns that are not close to the speaker in space or in time. Forms of **aquel** refer to nouns that are even farther away.

Este niño es mi hijo. **Ese** joven es mi hijo también. Y **aquel** señor allí es mi esposo.
This boy is my son. That young man is also my son. And that man over there is my husband.

Demonstrative Pronouns*

- *Demonstrative pronouns* (**Los pronombres demostrativos**) are used to point out or indicate people, places, or things when omitting the noun they refer to (remember that pronouns replace nouns). *Demonstrative pronouns* are the same as *demonstrative adjectives,* except that the noun is not used. In English, the demonstrative pronouns are *this one, that one, these,* and *those.*

—¿Te gusta aquella casa?
Do you like that house?

—¿Cuál?
Which one?

—**Aquella,** con las ventanas grandes.
***That one,** with the big windows.*

—¡Ah, **aquella** me gusta mucho!
*Oh, I like **that one** a lot!*

---

*Some Spanish speakers prefer to use accents on these forms: **este coche y ése, aquella casa y ésta.** However, it is acceptable in modern Spanish, per the **Real Academia Española** in Madrid, to omit the accent on these forms when context makes the meaning clear and no ambiguity is possible. To learn more about these forms, consult Appendix 2, Using Adjectives As Nouns.*

- In Spanish, demonstrative pronouns agree in gender and number with the noun they are replacing.

- Use the neuter demonstratives **esto, eso,** and **aquello** to refer to as yet unidentified objects or to a whole idea, concept, or situation.

¿Qué es **esto**?
What is this?

Eso es todo.
That's it. That's all.

¡**Aquello** es terrible!
That's terrible!

AUTOPRUEBA

Match each word with the corresponding meaning in English.

1. _____ estas
2. _____ aquellos
3. _____ ese
4. _____ esas
5. _____ este

a. that
b. those (over there)
c. these
d. this
e. those

Answers: 1. c 2. b 3. a 4. e 5. d

■■■ Práctica

A. Comparaciones

Paso 1. Restate the sentences, changing forms of **este** to **ese** and adding **también,** following the model.

MODELO: Este abrigo es muy grande. →
Ese abrigo también es muy grande.

1. Esta falda es muy pequeña.
2. Estos pantalones son muy largos.
3. Este libro es muy bueno.
4. Estas corbatas son muy feas.

Paso 2. Now change the forms of **este** to **aquel.**

MODELO: Este abrigo es muy grande. →
Aquel abrigo también es muy grande.

B. Situaciones. Find an appropriate response for each situation.

Posibilidades

¡Eso es un desastre!   ¡Eso es magnífico!
¿Qué es esto?   ¡Eso es terrible!

1. Aquí hay un regalo para Ud.
2. Ocurre un accidente en la cafetería: Ud. tiene tomate en su camisa favorita.
3. No hay clases mañana.
4. La matrícula cuesta más este semestre/trimestre.
5. Ud. tiene una A en su examen de español.

Need more practice?

- Workbook and Laboratory Manual
- Interactive CD-ROM
- Online Learning Center (www.mhhe.com/puntos7)

Prác. A: Preliminary Exercise

Have students respond to the following requests.

1. *Dé el plural de* (point to or hold up objects): *este lápiz, este libro, este bolígrafo, esta mesa, esta bolsa, esta carta.*
2. *Dé el singular de* (point to or hold up objects): *estos libros, estos bolígrafos,* and so on.
3. *Dé el plural de* (point to articles of clothing worn by students): *ese zapato, ese traje, ese abrigo, esa chaqueta, esa falda, esa camisa,* and so on.

Expand to practice with other objects and articles of clothing in the classroom.

Prác. A: Follow-Up

Have students point out things in class using the demonstratives. Students must repeat the appropriate form of demonstrative to double-check comprehension, for example, *Esa ventana es grande.* → *¿Esta/Esa Aquella ventana?* → *Sí, esa.*

↻ Prác. A: Reciclado

Ask personalized questions regarding items in the classroom. Use possessive pronouns as well as demonstrative. Have students respond with the correct statements: *¿Es ese mi lápiz, _____?* → *No, este es el lápiz de _____. ¿Son estos libros de los estudiantes de filosofía?* → *No, son nuestros libros.* Emphasize the *de* + noun in case of ambiguity.

Prác. B: Variation

Have students provide cues similar to those given in items 1–5 to other students, who then react appropriately.

National Standards: Communication

Point out to students that interjections are an integral part of everyday language. As in English, Spanish interjections evolve and go into and out of fashion with different generations. Students should already be familiar with the interjection *¡Ojo!* For *Práctica B*, students might enjoy using some interjections with the responses. List some of the following for them.

¡Ah! ¡Huy! ¡Oh! (pain)
¡Vaya! ¡Ajá! (admiration or approval)
¡Ay, no! (irritation)
¡Anda! ¡No me digas! ¡Vaya! (surprise)
¡Oiga! ¡Oigan! ¡Oye! (disapproval)
¡Ánimo! ¡Sus! ¡Ándale! (encouragement)
¡Hurra! ¡Viva! (enthusiasm)

Ask the following questions.

1. *¿Qué va a hacer Ud. esta noche?*
   ¿Y este fin de semana?
2. *¿Cómo es esta universidad?*
   ¿Cómo es esta clase? Y este libro,
   ¿cómo es?
3. *¿Cómo es esta ciudad? ¿Y este*
   estado?
4. *¿Cómo se llama el decano (dean)*
   de esta facultad? ¿el rector (presi-
   dent) de esta universidad? ¿el
   presidente / primer ministro de
   este país?
5. *¿Cuántos estados hay en este*
   país?
6. *¿Tiene Ud. muchos exámenes esta*
   semana? ¿Tiene que estudiar
   mucho esta noche?

Resources:
Transparency 28

EN LOS ESTADOS UNIDOS Y EL CANADÁ

Los hispanos en el mundo de la moda

Christy Turlington is one of many Hispanic celebrities in the U.S. world of fashion. Born in San Francisco, California (1969), to a Salvadoran mother, Turlington has been a household name since the 1990s. During her career as a supermodel, she became an activist for and benefactor of several causes, including breast cancer and animal rights. Furthermore, after being diagnosed with early-stage emphysema and subsequently quitting smoking, Christy became the spokesperson for a government antitobacco campaign.

▲ *Christy Turlington*

■ ■ ■ Conversación

Una tarde en un patio mexicano

Paso 1. Write brief descriptions of the following people and pets without identifying their location in the drawing.

> MODELO: Lleva una falda y zapatos azules…

Paso 2. Now take turns with a partner reading a description. Your partner will guess who you're talking about. You should use demonstratives (**este/ese/aquel**) to identify the person.

> MODELO: E1: Lleva una falda y zapatos azules…
> E2: Es esta mujer.

Paso 3. Now work with your partner to invent information about the people. Include names, where they're from, and their relationship to others in the drawing.

> MODELO: Esta mujer se llama María. Es de Cuernavaca. Es la hermana de aquel hombre…

EN LOS ESTADOS UNIDOS Y EL CANADÁ

Suggestions

■ Have students search the Internet for nonprofit organizations that target Hispanic causes. Ask them to identify prominent Hispanics in the world of film, TV, music, sports, and politics who donate time and money to these causes.

■ Have students imagine that they are fashion critics. Have them write a short paragraph describing the fashion for next season. Provide vocabulary on the board to facilitate the paragraph: *invierno* = winter; *verano* = summer. Students should include colors, fabrics, and styles. Suggest the following phrase to get started: *La moda para la próxima temporada* (season) *va a tener… / usar…*

10 Expressing Actions and States • *Tener, venir, preferir, querer, and poder*; Some Idioms with *tener*

Una gorra para José Miguel

Elisa acompaña a su hijo José Miguel para buscar una gorra.

ELISA:	¿Qué gorra *prefieres*, José Miguel?
JOSÉ MIGUEL:	*Prefiero* la gris.
ELISA:	¡Pero ya *tienes* una gris, y es casi idéntica!
JOSÉ MIGUEL:	Pues, no *quiero* esas otras gorras. ¿*Podemos* mirar en la tienda anterior otra vez?
ELISA:	¿Otra vez? Bueno, si realmente insistes…

Comprensión: ¿Sí o no?

1. José Miguel quiere comprar una corbata.
2. Él prefiere la gorra azul.
3. No puede decidir entre las gorras.
4. Parece que (*It seems that*) Elisa tiene mucha paciencia.

Tener, venir, preferir, querer, and *poder*

tener (*to have*)

tengo	tenemos
tienes	tenéis
tiene	tienen

venir (*to come*)

vengo	venimos
vienes	venís
viene	vienen

preferir (*to prefer*)

prefiero	preferimos
prefieres	preferís
prefiere	prefieren

querer (*to want*)

quiero	queremos
quieres	queréis
quiere	quieren

poder (*to be able, can*)

puedo	podemos
puedes	podéis
puede	pueden

- The **yo** forms of **tener** and **venir** are irregular.

- In other forms of **tener, venir, preferir,** and **querer,** when the stem vowel **e** is stressed, it becomes **ie.**

- Similarly, the stem vowel **o** in **poder** becomes **ue** when stressed. In vocabulary lists these changes are shown in parentheses after the infinitive: **poder (ue).** Verbs of this type are called *stem-changing verbs.* You will learn more verbs of this type in **Gramática 11.**

Irregularities:
tener: yo ten**go**, tú t**ie**nes (e → ie)…
venir: yo ven**go**, tú v**ie**nes (e → ie)…
preferir, querer: (e → ie)

poder: (o → ue)

 The **nosotros** and **vosotros** forms of these verbs do not have changes in the stem vowel because it is not stressed.

A cap for José Miguel *Elisa accompanies her son José Miguel to look for a cap.* ELISA: *Which cap do you prefer, José Miguel?* JOSÉ MIGUEL: *I prefer the gray one.* ELISA: *But you already have a gray one, and it's almost identical!* JOSÉ MIGUEL: *Well, I don't want those other caps. Can we look in the previous store again?* ELISA: *Again? Well, if you really insist . . .*

Follow-Up

Ask for quick answers to the following questions. Have students start their responses with *prefiero*: *Para la ropa, ¿prefiere el azul o el negro? ¿el verde o el amarillo? ¿el anaranjado o el morado? ¿el rosado o el rojo? Para un coche, ¿prefiere colores oscuros* (write on board) *o claros?*

Suggestions

- Model infinitives and talk through conjugations, using the forms in complete sentences and questions.
- Point out the similarities and differences among stem-changing verbs: some *yo* forms have a *-g-*, the *nosotros* and *vosotros* forms have the same stem as the infinitive; the stem becomes a diphthong (e → ie and o → ue) when stressed (with the exception of *tengo* and *vengo*).
- You might want to relate stem-changing verbs to stress. Note that stem-changing verbs are conditioned by stress. Whenever the vowel in question in the stem-changing verb appears in the stressed syllable, the vowel change occurs. Note that in *nosotros* and *vosotros* forms, stress falls on the vowel in the ending and not on the verb stem. *Quiero* vs. *Queremos; vienes* vs. *venís.*

 Bright Idea

Suggestion

Point out to students that a helpful way to remember which forms have a stem change is to remember the "boot" shape shown in the paradigms. Forms inside the boot show a stem change; those outside do not.

Some Idioms with *tener*

Suggestions

- Point out that there is generally no word-to-word correspondence of idioms between the two languages.
- Tell students some complete sentences about yourself that model the idioms.
- Give students these optional phrases: *mucha prisa, mucho miedo.*

Note

Students will learn *tener calor / frío* in *Capítulo 5* with weather and *tener hambre / sed* in *Capítulo 6* with foods.

A. Many ideas expressed in English with the verb *to be* are expressed in Spanish with idioms (**los modismos**) using **tener.** You have already used one **tener** idiom: **tener... años.** At the right are some additional ones. Note that they describe a condition or state that a person can experience.

 Idiomatic expressions are often different from one language to another. For example, in English, *to pull Mary's leg* usually means *to tease her*, not *to grab her leg and pull it*. In Spanish, *to pull Mary's leg* is **tomarle el pelo a Mary** (literally, *to take hold of Mary's hair*).

tener miedo de

tener prisa

tener razón

no tener razón

tener sueño

B. Other **tener** idioms include **tener ganas de** (*to feel like*) and **tener que** (*to have to*). The infinitive is always used after these two idiomatic expressions.

 Note that the English translation of one of these examples results in a verb ending in *-ing*, not the infinitive.

Tengo ganas de **comer.**
I feel like eating.

¿No tiene Ud. que **leer** este capítulo?
Don't you have to read this chapter?

 Heritage Speakers

Pregúnteles a sus estudiantes hispanohablantes si se les ocurren otras expresiones con *tener*, como *tener ánimo, tener ganas (de), tener fama* y *tener suerte.*

AUTOPRUEBA

Give the missing letters in each verb.

1. p___des
2. pr___fiere
3. ve___o

4. t___nemos
5. qu___ro
6. t___nen

Answers: 1. puedes 2. prefiere 3. vengo 4. tenemos 5. quiero 6. tienen

■■■ Práctica

A. ¡Sara tiene mucha tarea (homework)!

Paso 1. Haga oraciones con las palabras indicadas. Añada (Add) palabras si es necesario.

> **MODELO:** Sara / tener / que / estudiar / mucho / hoy →
> Sara tiene que estudiar mucho hoy.

1. Sara / tener / muchos exámenes
2. (ella) venir / a / universidad / todos los días
3. hoy / trabajar / hasta / nueve / de / noche
4. preferir / estudiar / en / biblioteca
5. querer / leer / más / pero / no poder
6. por eso / regresar / a / casa
7. tener / ganas de / leer / más
8. pero / unos amigos / venir a mirar / televisión
9. Sara / decidir / mirar / televisión / con ellos

Paso 2. Now retell the same sequence of events, first as if they had happened to you, using **yo** as the subject of all but sentence number 8, then as if they had happened to you and your roommate, using **nosotros/as.**

B. Situaciones. Expand the situations described in these sentences by using an appropriate idiom with **tener.** There is often more than one possible answer.

> **MODELO:** Tengo un examen mañana. Por eso… →
> Por eso tengo que estudiar mucho.

1. ¿Cuántos años? ¿Cuarenta? No, yo…
2. Un perro grande y feo vive en esa casa. Por eso yo…
3. ¿Ya son las tres de la mañana? Ah, por eso…
4. No, dos y dos no son cinco. Son cuatro. Tú…
5. Tengo que estar en el centro a las tres. Ya (Already) son las tres menos cuarto. Yo…
6. Cuando hay un terremoto (earthquake), todos…
7. ¿Los exámenes de la clase de español? ¡Esos son siempre muy fáciles (easy)! Yo no…
8. Sí, la capital de la Argentina es Buenos Aires. Tú…

Need more practice?

- Workbook and Laboratory Manual
- Interactive CD-ROM
- Online Learning Center (www.mhhe.com/puntos7)

- Have students imagine that it is exam week and the following situations take place. Have them give new sentences based on the cues.

  1. *Sara tiene muchos exámenes.* (Pepe, nosotros, Alicia y Carlos, yo, tú, vosotras)
  2. *Ramón viene a la biblioteca todas las noches. Prefiere estudiar aquí.* (yo, los estudiantes, tú, Uds., nosotras, vosotros)
  3. *Silvia quiere estudiar más, pero no puede.* (yo, ella, nosotros, todos, tú, vosotros)

- Have students answer these questions based on the cues:

  1. *¿Qué tiene Ud. que hacer* (to do) *esta noche? → Tengo que llegar a casa temprano.* (asistir a una clase a las siete, aprender una palabra en español, estudiar el Capítulo 3, leer toda la noche, hablar con un amigo, ¿ … ?)
  2. *Pero, ¿qué tiene ganas de hacer? → Tengo ganas de descansar.* (abrir una botella de vino, mirar la televisión, comer en un buen restaurante, ¡no estudiar más!, ¿ … ?)

Prác. B: Preliminary Exercises

- Dictate the following sentences.

  1. *Tienen prisa y miedo.*
  2. *Tiene toda la razón.*
  3. *Nunca tiene razón.*
  4. *No tienen ganas de estudiar.*
  5. *Tenemos que trabajar.*

- Have students give expressions they associate with the following.

  1. *el cliente*
  2. *los tres cochinitos* (draw a pig face or tail on the board)
  3. *el conejo blanco* (draw rabbit ears on the board)

Con. A: Suggestion

Coach students to help them invent a situation for or a story about the drawing. Caution them to stay within the limits of the language they know. Offer brief model sentences: *Isabel no estudia mucho.*

Con. A: Follow-Up

Ask the following questions

¿Es Ud. como Isabel?
¿Qué problemas tienen Isabel y Ud. en común?
¿Cómo es su cuarto?
¿Vive Ud. solo/a?

NOTA COMUNICATIVA

Follow-Up

- Ask: *¿Cuál es el antónimo de mucho/a(s)?*
- Have students give sentences using *poco/a(s)*.

■ ■■ **Conversación**

A. Estereotipos. Draw some conclusions about Isabel based on this scene. Think about things that she has, needs to or has to do or buy, likes, and so on. When you have finished, compare your predictions with those of others in the class. Did you all reach the same conclusions?

MODELO: Isabel tiene cuatro gatos. Tiene que…

Palabras útiles

los aretes (earrings)
el juguete (toy)
los muebles (furniture)
el sofá

hablar por teléfono
tener alergia a (to be allergic to)

NOTA COMUNICATIVA

Using *mucho* and *poco*

In the first chapters of *Puntos de partida*, you have used the words **mucho** and **poco** as both adjectives and adverbs. *Adverbs* (**Los adverbios**) are words that modify verbs, adjectives, or other adverbs: **quickly**, **very** *smart*, **very** *quickly*. In Spanish and in English, adverbs are invariable in form. However, in Spanish adjectives agree in number and gender with the word they modify.

ADVERB

Rosario estudia **mucho** hoy.
Julio come **poco**.

Rosario is studying a lot today.
Julio doesn't eat much.

ADJECTIVE

Rosario tiene **mucha** ropa.
  Sobre todo tiene **muchos** zapatos.
Julio come **poca** carne.
  Come **pocos** postres.

Rosario has a lot of clothes. She especially has a lot of shoes.
Julio doesn't eat much meat. He eats few desserts.

adverb = a word that modifies a verb, adjective, or another adverb

CULTURE

Remind students that a word they learned for pet is *mascota* (*Capítulo 2*). Point out that, as in this country, cats, dogs, and birds are popular pets in the Spanish-speaking world. A pet with ancient origins is the Chihuahua. There are many legends about the ancestors of the present-day Chihuahua, a breed of dog discovered in Mexico about 100 years ago. Its true origins are still a mystery, but we do know that it was a popular pet and a religious necessity among the ancient Toltec and Aztec tribes. Archaeologists have found remains of this breed in human graves in Mexico and in some parts of the United States. Mexicans favor the jet black Chihuahua with tan markings or the black and white spotted Chihuahua. In this country, people prefer the solid colors.

Resources: Transparency 29

B. Preferencias

Paso 1. Try to predict the choices your instructor will make in each of the following cases.

> MODELO: El profesor / La profesora tiene… muchos / pocos libros →
> muchos libros

1. El profesor / La profesora tiene…
   mucha ropa / poca ropa   sólo un coche / varios coches
2. Prefiere…
   los gatos / los perros   la ropa elegante / la ropa informal
3. Quiere comprar…
   un coche deportivo (*sports car*), por ejemplo, un Porsche / una
      camioneta (*station wagon*)
   un abrigo / un impermeable
4. Viene a la universidad…
   todos los días / sólo tres veces a la semana
   en coche / en autobús / en bicicleta / a pie (*on foot*)
5. Esta noche tiene muchas ganas de…
   mirar la televisión / leer   comer en un restaurante / comer en casa

Paso 2. Now, using tag questions, ask your instructor questions to find out if you are correct.

> MODELO: muchos libros →
> Ud. tiene muchos libros, ¿verdad?

C. Entrevista: Más preferencias

Paso 1. With a classmate, explore preferences in a number of areas by asking and answering questions based on the models. Use **No tengo preferencia** for answering that you have no preference.

> MODELOS: ¿Prefieres los gatos o los perros?
> ¿Te gusta más bailar o cantar?

1. Los animales: ¿los gatos siameses o los persas? ¿los perros pastores alemanes o los perros de lanas (*poodles*)?
2. El color de la ropa informal: ¿el color negro o el blanco? ¿el rojo o el azul?
3. La ropa informal: ¿las camisas de algodón o las de seda? ¿los *jeans* de algodón o los pantalones de lana?
4. La ropa de mujeres: ¿las faldas largas o las minifaldas? ¿los pantalones largos o los pantalones cortos?
5. La ropa de hombres: ¿las camisas de cuadros o las de rayas (*striped*)? ¿las camisas de un solo (*single*) color? ¿chaqueta y pantalón o un traje formal?
6. Las actividades en casa: ¿mirar la televisión o leer una novela? ¿escribir cartas o hablar con unos amigos?

Paso 2. Report some of your findings to the class.

> MODELOS: Preferimos… / No tenemos preferencia.
> Yo prefiero…, pero Cecilia prefiere…

Con. B: Suggestions

- Have students work in groups to compare notes. Then assign different areas of the board so that all groups make a short list of their conclusions. Compare all of the lists. Emphasize note taking.
- After students have used items to ask you questions, reverse the situation, using the same items or different ones.

Con. B: Extension

6. *Su color favorito es… verde / rojo / amarillo.*
7. *Prefiere usar… botas / zapatos / sandalias.*

Con. C: Suggestion

Have students add two or three options of their own invention.

Con. C: Follow-Up

Have selected students report back information they have learned. You may wish to help them organize their presentations.

☼ Heritage Speakers

En algunos dialectos del español del suroeste de los Estados Unidos, se oye decir *muncho* por *mucho*. Aunque *muncho* es parte del habla cotidiana, *mucho* es la forma preferida.

**Ir; ir + a + Infinitive;
The Contraction al**

Notes

■ *Ir* and *venir* are used somewhat differently than their English equivalents. *Venir* means *to come to where* (the speaker is). *Ir* refers to some place other than where the speaker is. The speaker of ¿*Vienes a mi casa?* is at his/her house when asking the question. Otherwise, he/she would ask ¿*Vas a mi casa?*

■ *¡Ya voy!* means *I'm coming*, not *I'm going.*

Follow-Up

Ask students:

¿Qué voy a hacer yo mañana / esta tarde / noche?

Then give them sentences about things you may or may not do.

Voy a bailar en una fiesta esta noche.

Students guess if your sentences are true (*Es verdad*) or false (*No es cierto*).

The Contraction al

Preliminary Exercise

Have students give the Spanish equivalents.

1. I'm going to the market.
2. He's going to class.
3. My mother is going to teach Spanish.
4. You are going to read.
5. We are going to be sleepy.
6. You and Mrs. Robinson are going to eat.

Suggestion

Point out the difference between *el* (article) and *él* (subject pronoun). Remind students that *de + él* and *a + él* do not contract.

---

11 Expressing Destination and Future Actions • *Ir; ir + a + Infinitive; The Contraction al*

¿Adónde vas?

Rosa y Casandra son compañeras de cuarto.

CASANDRA: ¿Adónde *vas*?
ROSA: *Voy al* centro.
CASANDRA: ¿Qué *vas a* hacer en el centro?
ROSA: *Voy a* comprar un vestido para la fiesta de Javier. ¿No *vas a ir* a su fiesta este fin de semana?
CASANDRA: ¡Claro que *voy*!

Comprensión: ¿Sí o no?

1. Rosa va a estudiar.
2. Rosa va a hacer (*give*) una fiesta.
3. Casandra va a asistir a la fiesta.

Ir is the irregular Spanish verb used to express *to go.*

ir (*to go*)	
voy	vamos
vas	vais
va	van

The first person plural of **ir, vamos** (*we go, are going, do go*), is also used to express *let's go.*

Vamos a clase ahora mismo.
Let's go to class right now.

Ir + a + Infinitive

Ir + a + infinitive is used to describe actions or events in the near future.

Van a venir a la fiesta esta noche.
They're going to come to the party tonight.

The Contraction al

In **Capítulo 2** you learned about the contraction **del (de + el → del).** The only other contraction in Spanish is **al (a + el → al). ¡OJO!** Both **del** and **al** are obligatory contractions.

a + el → al

Voy **al** centro comercial.
I'm going to the mall.

Vamos **a la** tienda.
I'm going to the store.

Where are you going? *Rosa and Casandra are roommates.* CASANDRA: *Where are you going?* ROSA: *I'm going downtown.* CASANDRA: *What are you going to do downtown?* ROSA: *I'm going to buy a dress for Javier's party. Aren't you going to go to his party this weekend?* CASANDRA: *Of course I'm going!*

☼ **Heritage Speakers**

Los hispanohablantes tienden a usar la expresión *ir a +* infinitivo en vez del futuro. Por ejemplo, es más común oír *va a llamar* en vez de *llamará.* Pregúnteles a los hispanohablantes de la clase en qué situaciones usan el futuro en vez de *ir a +* infinitivo.

■ ■ ■ Práctica

A. ¿Adónde van de compras? Haga oraciones completas usando **ir**. Recuerde: **a + el = al.**

MODELO: Marta / el centro → Marta *va al* centro.

1. nosotros / una *boutique*
2. Francisco / el almacén Goya
3. Juan, Raúl / el centro comercial
4. tú / un mercado
5. Ud. / una tienda pequeña
6. yo / ¿ ?

B. ¡Vamos de compras! Describa el día, desde el punto de vista (*from the point of view*) de Lola, la esposa de Manolo. Use **ir** + **a** + el infinitivo, según el modelo.

MODELO: Manolo compra un regalo para su madre. →
Manolo *va a comprar* un regalo para su madre.

1. Llegamos al centro a las diez de la mañana.
2. Mi hija Marta quiere comer algo (*something*).
3. Compro unos chocolates para Marta.
4. Manolo busca una blusa de seda.
5. No compras esta blusa azul, ¿verdad?
6. Buscamos algo más barato.
7. ¿Vas de compras mañana también?

■ ■ ■ Conversación

A. ¿Adónde vas si... ? ¿Cuántas oraciones puede hacer Ud.?

MODELO: Me gusta leer novelas. Por eso voy a una librería.

Me gusta **+**
leer novelas.
ir de compras —y ¡no regateo!
buscar gangas y regatear.
hablar con mis amigos.
comer en restaurantes elegantes.
mirar programas de detectives.
+ Por eso voy a _____.

B. Entrevista: El fin de semana

Paso 1. Interview a classmate about his or her plans for the weekend. "Personalize" the interview with additional questions. For example, if your partner is going to read a novel, ask **¿Qué novela?** or **¿Quién es el autor?**

¿Vas a... ?

1. ir de compras
2. leer una novela
3. asistir a un concierto
4. estudiar para un examen
5. ir a una fiesta
6. escribir una carta
7. ir a bailar
8. escribir los ejercicios para la clase de español
9. practicar un deporte (*sport*)
10. mirar mucho la televisión

Paso 2. En el **Paso 1**, los números pares (2, 4, 6,...) son actividades pasivas o tranquilas. Los números impares (1, 3, 5,...) son más activas. ¿Cómo es su compañero/a? ¿Es activo/a? ¿O prefiere la tranquilidad?

Gramática   Ciento quince ■ **115**

AUTOPRUEBA

Give the subject pronouns for these forms of **ir**.

1. va
2. vamos
3. voy
4. van
5. vas

Answers: 1. usted 2. nosotros 3. yo 4. ellos 5. tú

Need more practice?

- Workbook and Laboratory Manual
- Interactive CD-ROM
- Online Learning Center (www.mhhe.com/puntos7)

Prác. B: Note

Students may need extra help with item 7. *¿Vas a ir de... ?*

Prác. B: Variation

Personalize the sequence, having students do all items with *yo* forms; then change the details as necessary.

Prác. B: Follow-Up

Make statements that are true for students right now, varying the information according to individuals in your class. Using the follow-up question, students will tell what they will do in the future.

1. *Este semestre / trimestre Ud. toma clases muy fáciles. ¿Y el próximo semestre?*
2. *Ud. vive ahora en la residencia. ¿Y el próximo semestre?*
3. *Ahora _____ es el presidente / primer ministro. ¿Y en cuatro años?*
4. *Ud. lleva ropa muy vieja hoy. ¿Y mañana?*
5. *Ud. tiene problemas económicos ahora. ¿Y en cinco años?*
6. *Este año Ud. escucha música rap. ¿Y en diez años?*

Con. A: Suggestion

Do the activity as a conversational exchange between you and the students, or have students work in pairs to ask and answer questions. *¿Adónde vas si te gusta... ?* → *Voy a...*

Con. B: Suggestion

Have students add their own preference to the questions. The answers in *Paso 2* can be reported back, with students using the *nosotros* form whenever possible.

Con. B: Follow-Up

Ask the following questions
¿Cuál es su actividad favorita? ¿y su autor favorito (autora favorita)?
¿Cuántas horas mira la televisión por semana?
¿Con qué frecuencia les escribe a sus padres / a sus amigos / a otras personas?

National Standards: Communication

In English, when someone calls or summons you, it is not uncommon to answer by saying, "I'm coming." In Spanish, however, the verb of choice is *ir*. To say "I'm coming." in Spanish, speakers say *"Ya voy"* or *"Voy en seguida."* In Mexico, speakers might say *"¡Ahorita voy!"*

UN POCO DE TODO

A: Suggestion

Have each student make two or three statements about himself (herself), using verbs from the second column.

B: Follow-Up

■ Have students give the names of stores.

*La tienda donde se venden
zapatos se llama...* → *una
zapatería
fruta* → *frutería
carne* (meat) → *carnicería
papel* → *papelería
pan* (bread) → *panadería
perfume* → *perfumería
¿y animales? ¡OJO!* → *tienda de
animales*

■ Have students write similar paragraphs, comparing shopping experiences in different towns and cities, or in different kinds of stores and shopping areas.

♻ Reciclado

■ Do a quick review of verb endings for *-ar*, *-er*, and *-ir* regular verbs.
■ Review chorally the conjugations of irregular verbs such as *ir*, *poder*, and *tener*.
■ Review adjective-noun agreement rules and the four possible forms for adjectives ending in *-o*.

UN POCO DE TODO

A. ¿Qué prefieren? Haga oraciones completas usando una palabra o frase de cada (*each*) columna. Si quiere, las oraciones pueden ser negativas también.

yo mi mejor (*best*) amigo/a mis padres / hijos nuestro profesor / nuestra profesora mi familia tú y yo	**+** (no) { poder tener que tener ganas de querer preferir ir (a)	**+** estudiar en la biblioteca visitar mi universidad ir de compras en el centro comprar cuando hay rebajas escribir un informe (*report*) para la clase de ¿ ? ir al cine (*movies*) llevar ropa informal leer novelas de ciencia ficción / terror / ¿ ?

B. Pero, ¿no se puede (*can't one*) **regatear?** Complete the following paragraph with the correct form of the words in parentheses, as suggested by the context. When two possibilities are given in parentheses, select the correct word.

A Ud. le gusta ir de compras? ¿Le gusta regatear? En (los/las[1]) ciudades hispánicas, hay una (grande[2]) variedad de tiendas para (ir[3]) de compras. Hay almacenes, centros comerciales y *boutiques* (elegante[4]), como en (los/las[5]) Estados Unidos, donde los precios son siempre (fijo[6]).

También hay tiendas (pequeño[7]) que venden un solo[a] producto. Por ejemplo,[b] en una zapatería sólo hay zapatos. En español el sufijo **-ería** se usa[c] para (formar[8]) el nombre de la tienda. ¿Dónde (creer[9]) Ud. que venden papel y (otro[10]) artículos de escritorio? ¿A qué tienda (ir[11]) a ir Ud. a comprar fruta?

Si Ud. (poder[12]) pagar el precio que piden,[d] (deber[13]) comprar los recuerdos[e] en (los/las[14]) almacenes o *boutiques*. Pero si (tener[15]) ganas o necesidad de regatear, tiene (de/que[16]) ir a un mercado: un conjunto[f] de tiendas o locales[g] donde el ambiente[h] es más (informal[17]) que[i] en los (grande[18]) almacenes. Ud. no (deber[19]) pagar el primer[j] precio que menciona el vendedor.[k] ¡Casi siempre va (a/de[20]) ser muy alto!

[a]*single* [b]*Por... For example* [c]*se... is used* [d]*they ask* [e]*souvenirs* [f]*group* [g]*stalls* [h]*atmosphere* [i]*than* [j]*first* [k]*seller*

Comprensión: ¿Cierto o falso? Corrija las oraciones falsas.

1. En el mundo hispánico, todas las tiendas son similares.
2. Uno puede regatear en un almacén hispánico.
3. Es posible comprar limones en una papelería.
4. En un mercado, el vendedor siempre ofrece un precio bajo al principio (*beginning*).

C. ¿Somos tan diferentes?

Paso 1. Use the following information to survey your classmates about clothing. Tally the affirmative answers you receive. For item 3, tally both **cierto** and **falso** answers. Speak with as many classmates as possible.

1. De la siguiente lista, ¿qué cosa tienes ganas de tener? **¡OJO!** También es posible contestar: **No quiero tener ninguna.**
   _____ un abrigo de pieles (*fur*)
   _____ unas botas de cuero (*leather*)
   _____ unos aretes de oro (*gold*)
   _____ un reloj Rolex
   _____ Ninguna de estas cosas.

2. ¿Cuál de las siguientes cosas que dicta la moda es la más tonta, en tu opinión?
   _____ llevar aretes en la nariz (*nose*)
   _____ llevar las gorras de atrás para delante (*backward*)
   _____ los *jeans* de los grandes diseñadores como Calvin Klein y Guess
   _____ la ropa de estilo hip-hop

3. ¿Cierto o falso?
   _____ cierto _____ falso Las personas mayores (*older*) deben llevar siempre ropa de colores oscuros, como negro, gris, etcétera.
   _____ cierto _____ falso Una mujer que tiene más de 30 años nunca debe llevar minifalda.
   _____ cierto _____ falso Sólo las mujeres deben usar arete(s).
   _____ cierto _____ falso Cuando la moda cambia (*changes*), es necesario comprar mucha ropa nueva.

Paso 2. Use your tallies to have a class discussion about style and shopping tendencies in your class. Take turns summarizing and analyzing the results.

MODELO: Diez estudiantes quieren comprar botas de cuero pero nadie (*no one*) tiene ganas de comprar abrigos de pieles.
Pienso que nuestra clase no puede decidir si quiere usar productos de animales o no.

Resources for Review and Testing Preparation

- Workbook and Laboratory Manual
- Interactive CD-ROM
- Online Learning Center (www.mhhe.com/puntos7)

C: Suggestions

- Allow students five minutes to survey their classmates.
- Have students work in pairs to create their own options for item 1. Encourage them to be creative and funny! As a follow-up, have students share some of their options and answers: *¿Qué prefieres* (tener)? *Prefiero* (tener) _____ *a* _____. *No quiero tener ninguno/a.* Students then elaborate on their answers.

C: Extension

Paso 2. Have students discuss their opinions about the following.

1. *las personas que sólo llevan ropa oscura*
2. *las personas que llevan los jeans rotos en las rodillas* (torn at the knees)
3. *la ropa de los diseñadores famosos que vemos* (we see) *en las revistas como* Elle, Vogue, *etcétera.*
4. *las personas que siempre visten formalmente*
5. *la ropa que llevan los artistas que van a la ceremonia del Óscar*
6. *los padres que escogen la ropa de sus hijos*

To help students ask and answer questions, model the use of *¿Qué opinas de... ?, ¿Qué piensas de... ?, Creo que... ,* and *Pienso que...*

Resources: Desenlace

In the *Capítulo 3* segment of "Chapter-by-Chapter Supplementary Materials" in the *Instructor's Manual and Resource Kit*, you will find a chapter-culminating activity. You can use this activity to consolidate and review the vocabulary and grammar skills students have acquired.

Entrevista cultural

Suggestions

■ Before showing the video, have students play the role of a clothing store clerk. Ask them questions about their store and what they sell.

¿Dónde está la tienda?
¿Qué tipo de ropa venden?
¿Qué días y cuántas horas trabaja?

■ Show the video and allow students one to two minutes to work on the questions. Encourage them to answer in Spanish if possible. You might want to ask the questions in Spanish when you review the answers as a class.

1. *¿Cuántos años tiene Delvia?*
2. *¿De qué ciudad es?*
3. *¿Cuál es el negocio de su familia?*
4. *En el negocio de la familia, ¿quién maneja la tienda y quién viaja?*
5. *¿Qué le gustaría a Delvia hacer en el futuro?*

Have volunteers answer the questions.

■ Have volunteers role-play Delvia and the interviewer

Entre amigos

Suggestions

■ Before viewing the video, review the questions with the students and ask them similar questions.

En su opinión, ¿es importante o no la moda? ¿Por qué?
¿Qué tipo de ropa usa Ud. para ir a clase? ¿para asistir a una fiesta? ¿para trabajar?

Have students answer or work in small groups to ask and answer these questions.

■ After viewing the video, have volunteers read and answer the questions.

PERSPECTIVAS culturales

●●●
Videoteca

Entrevista cultural: Nicaragua

Delvia Argüello is a young woman from Nicaragua who works in her family's business. In this interview she talks about herself, her work, and her plans for the future. Among other things, she mentions how climate affects clothing styles in her country. Before watching the video clip, read the following excerpt from the interview.

INTERVIEWER: …¿Cómo se llama Ud. y de dónde es?
DELVIA: Me llamo Delvia Argüello y soy de Managua, Nicaragua. Tengo 24 años.
INTERVIEWER: ¿En dónde vive Ud.?
DELVIA: En Managua con mi familia. Mi familia tiene una tienda de ropa, eh, para mujeres. Ahí se vende ropa, de… pantalones, camisas, zapatos y accesorios.

Now watch the video clip and answer the following questions based on the interview.

1. How old is Delvia?
2. What city is she from?
3. What is her family's business?
4. In the family business, who takes care of the store, and who travels?
5. What would Delvia like to do in the future?

Entre amigos: ¡Está súper fuera de moda (*out of style*)!

Miguel, Tané, Karina, and Rubén are shopping in small flea market. What questions do you think they will ask each other? Before watching the video, read the following questions. As you watch, don't worry if you don't understand every word. Try to get the gist of the conversation, listening specifically for information about clothing. Watch the video a second time and listen for the answers to the questions.

1. ¿A Karina le gusta la chaqueta que escoge (*chooses*) Tané? ¿Por qué?
2. En la opinión de Karina, ¿es importante o no la moda? ¿Por qué?
3. ¿Qué tipo de ropa usa Rubén?
4. ¿Qué artículo de ropa compra Tané?

Conozca... Nicaragua

Datos esenciales

- Nombre oficial: República de Nicaragua
- Capital: Managua
- Población: Más de 5.000.000 de habitantes
- Moneda: el córdoba
- Idiomas: el español (oficial), el misquito, el sumo*

¡Fíjese!

- En 1856, un norteamericano, William Walker, se declaró[a] presidente de Nicaragua. Dos años después, fue derrotado por[b] los nicaragüenses, liberales y conservadores que se unieron[c] para expulsarlo[d] del país.
- El Lago de Nicaragua es el lago más grande de Centroamérica. También se llama Lago Cocibolca. Hay más de 300 islas en el lago. En estas «Isletas», hay pequeñas comunidades agrícolas[e] y, en algunas,[f] casas de personas ricas. En la isleta de San Pablo, hay una fortaleza[g] construida por los españoles para protegerse[h] de los piratas ingleses. Los nicaragüenses llaman el lago su «mar dulce»[i] porque es muy grande y porque tiene agua dulce.[j] Tiene los únicos tiburones[k] de agua dulce del mundo.[l]

[a]se... declared himself   [b]fue... he was defeated by   [c]se... joined together   [d]expel him   [e]agricultural   [f]some (of them)   [g]fort   [h]protect themselves   [i]mar... sweet (fresh water) sea   [j]agua... fresh water   [k]únicos... only sharks   [l]world

Learn more about Nicaragua with the Video, Interactive CD-ROM, and the Online Learning Center (www.mhhe.com/puntos7).

---

*En la costa oeste (west coast) de Nicaragua, también se habla un dialecto criollo (creole) que está basado en el inglés.

Nota histórica

Cristóbal Colón llegó[a] a las costas de Nicaragua en 1502, pero la región no fue colonizada[b] hasta[c] 1524.

Nicaragua tiene una historia turbulenta por las luchas[d] entre las fuerzas conservadoras y las fuerzas liberales. La lucha se complicó[e] por la intervención de los Estados Unidos en la política del país. En 1990 terminó[f] una época[g] difícil de dictadura y lucha: hubo[h] una revolución y un movimiento en contra de la revolución. Esta lucha fue entre los sandinistas (revolucionarios marxistas) y los «contras» (antirrevolucionarios).

[a]arrived   [b]no... was not colonized   [c]until   [d]struggles   [e]se... was complicated   [f]ended   [g]time   [h]there was

▲ Parte de las ruinas de la fortaleza en la isleta San Pablo en el Lago de Nicaragua

Conozca... Nicaragua

Note

Students can read part of an excerpt of the poem "Eheu" by Nicaragua's Rubén Darío in *Un paso más 3*.

Suggestions

Share some or all of the following pieces of information with students. Encourage students to research more detailed information and other information about Nicaragua.

- The Nicaraguan priest, poet, and author Ernesto Cardenal was born on the coast of *el Lago de Nicaragua* in the city of Granada in 1925. He is a major poet not only in Nicaragua but in the Spanish-speaking world. A Christian-Marxist, Cardenal is known as a spokesperson for justice and self-determination in Latin America. He has served as the Minister of Culture of Nicaragua, and currently codirects *la Casa de Los Tres Mundos*, a literary and cultural organization.
- Violeta Barrios de Chamorro was president of Nicaragua from 1990 to 1997. She was the first female president of that country.
- In 2001, Enrique Bolaños Geyer was elected president of Nicaragua.
- *El Lago de Nicaragua* has freshwater sharks and fish we associate with oceans and seas because, scientists believe, the lake was once part of the Pacific Ocean. The lake probably separated from the ocean after seismic or volcanic activity. The saltwater creatures that were trapped in the lake adapted as the water turned fresh to become freshwater creatures.
- Other topics of interest include the Nicaraguan sign language (developed almost entirely by children), the Nicaraguan civil war, and the history of the United Fruit Company in Nicaragua.

Perspectivas culturales ■ **Ciento diecinueve ■ 119**

MULTIMEDIA: Internet

Have students look up additional information about Nicaragua's history, government, people, culture, geography, tourism, and media on the Internet. You might assign specific topics and have students give brief oral reports about Nicaragua.

Perspectivas culturales   ■   **119**

EN RESUMEN

Gramática

To review the grammar points presented in this chapter, refer to the indicated grammar presentations. You'll find further practice of these structures in the Workbook and Laboratory Manual, on the Interactive CD-ROM, and on the *Puntos de partida* Online Learning Center (www.mhhe.com/puntos7).

9. Pointing Out People and Things—Demonstrative Adjectives and Pronouns.

Do you know the forms for **este, ese,** and **aquel?**

10. Expressing Actions and States—**Tener, venir, preferir, querer,** and **poder;** Some Idioms with **tener**

You should be able to conjugate the verbs **tener, venir, preferir, querer,** and **poder.** Do you know how to use expressions like **tengo ganas de, tenemos miedo,** and **tienes razón?**

11. Expressing Destination and Future Actions—**Ir; ir + a +** Infinitive; The Contraction **al**

You should know the forms of **ir** and how to express *going to do* (*something*). You should also know when to use the contraction **al.**

Vocabulario Practice this vocabulary with digital flash cards on the Online Learning Center (www.mhhe.com/puntos7).

Los verbos

ir (*irreg.*)	to go
ir a + *inf.*	to be going to (*do something*)
ir de compras	to go shopping
llevar	to wear; to carry; to take
poder (ue)	to be able, can
preferir (ie)	to prefer
querer (ie)	to want
regatear	to haggle, bargain
tener (*irreg.*)	to have
usar	to wear; to use
venir (*irreg.*)	to come

Repaso: comprar, vender

La ropa

el abrigo	coat
los aretes	earrings
la blusa	blouse
la bolsa	purse
la bota	boot
el calcetín	sock
los calcetines	socks
la camisa	shirt
la camiseta	T-shirt
la cartera	wallet
la chaqueta	jacket
el cinturón	belt
la corbata	tie
la falda	skirt
la gorra	cap
el impermeable	raincoat
los *jeans*	jeans
las medias	stockings
los pantalones	pants
el par	pair
el reloj	watch
la ropa interior	underwear
la sandalia	sandal
el sombrero	hat
el suéter	sweater
el traje	suit
el traje de baño	swimsuit
el vestido	dress
el zapato (de tenis)	(tennis) shoe

Los colores

amarillo/a	yellow
anaranjado/a	orange
azul	blue
blanco/a	white
(de) color café	brown
gris	gray
morado/a	purple
negro/a	black
rojo/a	red
rosado/a	pink
verde	green

☀ **Heritage Speakers**

Es muy probable que los hispanohablantes de su clase usen otras palabras para hablar de la ropa. Por ejemplo, en algunos países hispanohablantes se dice *calzoncillos* en vez de *ropa interior.* Pregúnteles a los hispanohablantes si han oído las siguientes palabras y pídales que den sinónimos de algunas palabras de la lista de vocabulario en esta página.

el chaleco = la chaqueta
los vaqueros = los jeans
la bañera = el traje de baño
la cartera = la bolsa
la correa = el cinturón
la billetera = cartera
los pendientes = los aretes = los aros
el púlover/pulóver = el suéter = el jersey

Suggestions

■ Bring or have students bring magazine clippings with images of people wearing a variety of clothes and colors. Hold up one image and allow students twenty seconds to look at it. Then put it away and have them jot down in Spanish as many things about the picture as they can remember. You might place a volunteer at the board to write his or her version, and use that as a starting point for students to recall what they saw.

■ Give students five minutes to write a short paragraph that uses as many words from the vocabulary as possible. Find out who used the most words. Have volunteers read their paragraphs.

De compras

de última moda	the latest style
la ganga	bargain
el precio (fijo)	(fixed, set) price
las rebajas	sales, reductions
¿cuánto cuesta?	how much does it cost?
¿cuánto es?	how much is it?

Los materiales

es de...	it is made of . . .
algodón (m.)	cotton
lana	wool
seda	silk

Los lugares

el almacén	department store
el centro	downtown
el centro comercial	shopping mall
el mercado	market(place)
la tienda	shop, store

Otros sustantivos

la cinta	tape
el ejercicio	exercise
el examen	exam, test

Los adjetivos

barato/a	inexpensive
caro/a	expensive
poco/a	little

Más allá del número 100

doscientos/as
trescientos/as
cuatrocientos/as
quinientos/as
seiscientos/as
setecientos/as
ochocientos/as
novecientos/as
mil
un millón (de)

Repaso: cien(to)

Formas demostrativas

aquel, aquella, aquellos/as	that, those (over there)
ese/a, esos/as	that, those
eso, aquello	that, that (over there)

Repaso: este/a, esto, estos/as

Palabras adicionales

¿adónde?	where (to)?
al	to the
algo	something
allí	(over) there
de todo	everything
tener (irreg.)...	
ganas de + inf.	to feel like (doing something)
miedo (de)	to be afraid (of)
prisa	to be in a hurry
que + inf.	to have to (do something)
razón	to be right
sueño	to be sleepy
no tener razón	to be wrong
¿no?, ¿verdad?	right?, don't they (you, and so on)?

Suggestions

- Have a "number bee" competition. Give the contestants increasingly complicated numbers in digit form, and have them say the number in Spanish. Continue until you have one number bee champion.
- Use the *tener* expressions to ask absurd questions. Have students respond with corrections.

—*¿Tienes miedo de los zapatos?*
—*No, pero tengo miedo de hablar en público.*

Un paso más 3

Note

The *Un paso más* section is optional.

Literatura de **Nicaragua**

Notes

- Rubén Darío was raised by an aunt. He began writing at a very young age, and by 11 years old he was known as the "boy poet." He chose the name Darío from a family name.
- Darío attributed the success of his poetic innovations to having learned to think in French and write in Spanish. For some, Darío's style was the result of a brilliant synthesis of the French, Spanish, and American spirits.
- Darío was a world traveler. He traveled extensively from 1882 on, primarily in South America and Europe.

Literatura de **Nicaragua**

Sobre el autor: *The Nicaraguan writer, journalist, and diplomat Rubén Darío was one of the most recognized poets of the movement known as* **modernismo.** *Darío was born Félix Rubén García Sarmiento, in Metapa, a city in Nicaragua now named Darío. He was a major influence on later writers in Latin America, Spain, and Europe. These lines are from the poem "¡Eheu!,"[a]* El canto errante *(1907).*

> Aquí, junto al[b] mar latino,
> digo[c] la verdad:
> siento[d] en roca, aceite[e] y vino,
> yo mi antigüedad.[f]
>
> ¡Oh, qué anciano soy, Dios santo,
> oh, qué anciano soy!...
> ¿De dónde viene mi canto?[g]
> Y yo, ¿adónde voy?

[a]*A Latin word that means "Alas!"* [b]*junto... next to the* [c]*I tell* [d]*I feel* [e]*oil* [f]*antiquity, age* [g]*song*

▲ Rubén Darío (1867–1916)

LECTURA

ESTRATEGIA: Using Visual Clues to Predict Content

In **Capítulo 1** you learned that you can use section subheadings to help you better understand a passage. Another useful strategy is to use photographs and other visual clues (charts, drawings, graphic images, and so on) that accompany the reading as tools to help you predict the content of the passage. A successful reader is able to make predictions about content in advance, and then confirms or rejects these predictions while reading.

Before reading the article that follows, look at the titles above each paragraph. What predictions can you make based on the visual presentation of these paragraph titles?

Capítulo 3: De compras

National Standards: Connections

Rubén Darío was a Modernist poet. The term Modernism refers to the wide range of experimental and avant-garde trends in the literature and the fine arts of the early 20th century. Modernist writers rejected literary conventions of the 19th century. Modernist poets experimented with free verse, and modernist novelists with stream of consciousness. Their works were typically cosmopolitan. European as well as American writers are included in what has become known as Modernism, some of whom include Gertrude Stein (1874–1946, U.S.), Ezra Pound (1885–1972, U.S.), T.S. Eliot (1888–1965, U.S.), James Joyce (1882–1941, Ireland), Virginia Woolf (1882–1941, England), Joseph Conrad (1857–1924, Poland), William Faulkner (1897–1962, U.S.), José Asunción Silva (1865–1896, Colombia), Leopoldo Lugones (1874–1938, Argentina), José Enrique Rodó (1872–1917, Uruguay).

- **Sobre la lectura...** This reading is adapted from an article that appeared in *Quo*, a magazine published in Spain that is comparable to *Vanity Fair, Details,* and other glossy general interest magazines. *Quo* publishes articles about topics ranging from diet and health to fashion to politics.

Suggestions

- Do the *Estrategia* in class before assigning the reading.
- Have students read the title of the article and jot down their ideas about the psychological effects of colors. In their opinion, are there any colors that make them feel relaxed, tense, aggressive, or uncomfortable?
- Have students brainstorm and list some images they think would help illustrate the article, based on their predictions. After reading, ask which images would work and which would not.

La psicología de los colores

«Está demostrado[a] que los colores percibidos[b] por la vista[c] <u>provocan</u> una reacción psicológica sobre nuestro estado de ánimo[d]», asegura Carlos Obelleiro, <u>experto</u> en la utilización de color. Y de un buen estado de ánimo depende mucho la salud física. Según expertos en psicología de los colores, cada uno indica una actitud en quien lo lleva puesto.[e]

Rojo
Es el color que produce mayor impacto visual. Actúa como un estimulante psíquico, pero activa la <u>agresividad</u> y si alguien lo lleva puede incomodar a los demás.[f]

Amarillo
Está íntimamente relacionado con la autoestima[g] y <u>estimula</u> la creatividad, pero puede resultar agresivo para gente emocionalmente <u>frágil</u>.

Azul
Favorece la calma y la concentración en trabajos que exigen[h] esfuerzo[i] mental. Tranquiliza, pero puede dar imagen de frialdad.[j] Cuanto más oscuro es,[k] más idea da[l] de eficiencia y autoridad.

Verde
Es el color más relajante y suele[m] provocar una sensación de <u>equilibrio</u> y de tranquilidad personal.

Blanco
Aunque[n] es muy higiénico, puede resultar muy severo y dar la impresión de que la persona que lo lleva quiere crear una barrera.[o]

Rosado
Es la más pura expresión de la <u>feminidad</u>. Utilizado en decoración actúa como relajante, pero en exceso causa debilitamiento.[p]

Negro
Es elegante, pero puede resultar amenazador[q] y, como el blanco, crear barreras entre la persona que lo lleva y el resto de la gente.

Violeta
Es el color de la introversión. Puede transmitir la sensación de que quien lo viste[r] quiere estar solo, sin intromisiones.[s]

Gris
Se trata del único color totalmente <u>neutro</u>, con lo que no tiene apenas[t] propiedades psicológicas. A veces puede indicar falta[u] de confianza en uno mismo.

[a]*Está... It has been shown* [b]*perceived* [c]*sight* [d]*estado... state of mind* [e]*quien... the person who wears it* [f]*incomodar... make others uncomfortable* [g]*self-esteem* [h]*demand* [i]*effort* [j]*coldness* [k]*Cuanto... The darker it is* [l]*it gives* [m]*it tends to* [n]*Although* [o]*crear... to create a barrier* [p]*debilitation, weakness* [q]*threatening* [r]*quien... the person who wears it* [s]*sin... without intrusions* [t]*hardly any* [u]*a lack*

Comprensión: Follow-Up

After students have completed both *Comprensión* activities, have them form small groups. Have them choose any color and write a list of words in Spanish that they associate with the chosen color. Encourage them to read the list to the class without naming the color, to see if the other students can guess it.

Comprensión

A. **¿Qué color?** Identify the color (or colors!) that corresponds to each psychological trait below, according to the reading.

1. Este color no se asocia con la extroversión, sino lo contrario (*but rather the opposite*).
2. A veces este color se asocia con la frigidez.
3. Estos dos colores dan la impresión de crear obstáculos.
4. Este color provoca reacciones muy agresivas.
5. Este color provoca la creatividad.
6. Este color es un estimulante psíquico.
7. Este color tiene muy poco estímulo psíquico.
8. Estos colores son relajantes.
9. Este color puede expresar eficiencia.

B. **¿Qué color recomienda Ud.** (*do you recommend*)**?** Which color do you recommend a person use in order to make the following impressions or provoke the following reactions?

1. Una persona desea dar una impresión de control y poder (*power*).
2. Una persona quiere expresar su confianza en sí misma (*confidence in him or herself*).
3. Una persona no quiere producir ningún (*any*) impacto.
4. Una persona quiere tener un lugar muy tranquilo y relajante en su casa.

National Standards: Comparisons

The customs and protocols of many countries are now published for the international business travelers. These publications can help the traveler be more at ease before meeting clients or company executives for the first time. Often included in these are descriptions of the kinds of clothes and colors that are worn to the office and different functions.

Additional information may include greetings, body language, gift giving, and table manners. Encourage students to choose a Spanish-speaking country and look up business protocol or etiquette. You might have students find information on different countries so they can compare the information.

ESCRITURA

A. Mi ropa favorita. In a brief paragraph, write a description of your favorite article of clothing. Use the questions that follow to organize your thoughts. Your instructor can help you with words or constructions that are unfamiliar to you.

¿De qué materia es?
¿Por qué le gusta?
¿De qué color es?
¿Cómo se siente (*do you feel*) cuando lleva este artículo de ropa? (Me siento... tranquilo/a, enérgico/a, etcétera.)
¿Provoca el color algunas (*any*) reacciones como las reacciones descritas (*described*) en la lectura? ¿Cuáles?

B. El inventario. Take an inventory of the clothing you have and express it in Spanish.

What items do you have?
How many of each?
What colors?
Do you have clothes that you wear almost every week?
What items are they?
Why do you wear them often?
How many things do you have in your closet and drawers that you no longer wear or do not need?
What are they?

You can describe your clothing inventory in paragraph form or create a table or list to show the things you have.

ESCRITURA

Suggestion
If you prefer that your students do a journal activity, see *Mi diario* in this chapter of the Workbook.

A: Suggestions

- Have students conduct a classroom poll in which they identify their favorite colors in clothing and surroundings. Then, have them write a short paragraph about one of the following topics.
  - the relationship between their choice of favorite color and their personality
  - the validity of the reading's premise: that there is a relationship between personality and color. Suggest the following phrase to get them started: *Estoy de acuerdo / No estoy de acuerdo* (I agree / I do not agree) *con el autor de la lectura porque...*

 Heritage Speakers

Invite a los estudiantes hispanohablantes a describir algunos artículos de ropa que se usan en Latinoamérica pero no en los Estados Unidos. Por ejemplo, pregúnteles qué son las guayaberas, los zarapes, las ruanas o los ponchos. ¿Todavía llevan esta ropa o conocen a alguien de su familia que siga usando la ropa típica latinoamericana?

◀ Una casa en el campo (*countryside*) de Costa Rica

CHAPTER OPENER PHOTO

Point out the chapter-opener photo. Have students talk about the places they and their families live and about their ideas about housing in Hispanic countries. Have them imagine and describe the home in the photo. Ask: *¿Cómo cree Ud. que es la casa?* Encourage students to give as many adjectives as they can. Help them along by using word pairs: *moderno/antiguo, bonito/feo, caro/barato, elegante/simple, de buen gusto / de mal gusto*, and so on.

Suggestion

Ask students the following questions to help introduce the topic of this chapter. The words in **boldface** are included in the active vocabulary of this chapter. Have students discuss the words and use context to understand their meaning. Model the words they cannot guess in new sentences and contexts.

1. *¿Vive Ud. en una casa, en una residencia o en un apartamento? ¿Cómo es?*
2. *¿Es grande? ¿Cuántos cuartos tiene? ¿Qué **muebles** tiene Ud. en su casa?*
3. *¿Tiene Ud. un cuarto favorito? ¿Qué **hace** Ud. en ese cuarto?*
4. *¿Qué parte de la casa es **la más** importante para Ud.?*
5. *¿Hay tiendas cerca de (near) su casa, residencia o apartamento? ¿Qué venden?*

Note

The *Puntos de partida* Online Learning Center includes an interview with a native speaker from Costa Rica who answers questions similar to those in the preceding *Suggestion*.

Resources

For Students

- Workbook
- Laboratory Manual and Laboratory Audio Program
- Quia™ Online Workbook and Online Laboratory Manual
- Video on CD
- Interactive CD-ROM
- *Puntos de partida* Online Learning Center (**www.mhhe.com/puntos7**)

For Instructors

- *Instructor's Manual and Resource Kit*, "Chapter-by-Chapter" Supplementary Materials
- Overhead Transparencies 30–36
- Testing Program
- Test Generator
- Video Program
- Audioscript
- *Puntos de partida* Online Learning Center (**www.mhhe.com/puntos7**)

En casa°

CULTURA

- **Perspectivas culturales**

  Entrevista cultural: Costa Rica

  Entre amigos: Quiero cambiar los muebles

  Conozca... Costa Rica
- **Nota cultural:** Houses in the Hispanic World
- **En los Estados Unidos y el Canadá:** The California Missions
- **Literatura de Costa Rica:** Carmen Naranjo
- **Lectura:** Anuncios puertorriqueños

VOCABULARIO

- ¿Qué día es hoy?
- Los muebles, los cuartos y otras partes de la casa
- ¿Cuándo? Preposiciones

PRONUNCIACIÓN

- **b** and **v**

GRAMÁTICA

12 **Hacer, oír, poner, salir, traer,** and **ver**

13 Present Tense of Stem-Changing Verbs

14 Reflexive Pronouns

Entrevista cultural

Alexander Burbón ▶
San José, Costa Rica

°**En...** *At home*

Suggestions

- Have students compare their living situations.

  ¿Cuántos viven en una residencia estudiantil?
  ¿Cuántos viven en un apartamento?
  ¿Cuántos viven en una casa?
  ¿Quiénes tienen compañero o compañera de cuarto?
  ¿uno? ¿dos?
  ¿Quiénes viven solos?
  ¿Quiénes viven con su familia?

- Have students list their ideas about Costa Rica, including information on geography, politics, economy, culture, music, and cuisine. When you finish the chapter, return to the lists and ask students what ideas they would change and/or add.

 Heritage Speakers

Pregúnteles a sus estudiantes hispanohablantes si viven en una casa de arquitectura mexicana o latinoamericana. Si alguien contesta que sí, pídale que describa su casa.

MULTIMEDIA

- The multimedia materials that accompany this chapter are referenced in the Student and Instructor's Editions with icons to help you identify when and where to incorporate them.

- *Instructor's Manual and Resource Kit* (IM/RK) provides suggestions for using the multimedia materials in the classroom.

¿Qué día es hoy?

Note

See the model for vocabulary presentation and other material in the *Capítulo 4 Vocabulario: Preparación* section of "Chapter-by-Chapter Supplementary Materials" in the IM.

Suggestions

■ Model the pronunciation of the words in the list.

■ Give the day of the week and have students say the next day.

■ Have students make associations: *¿Qué día de la semana asocia Ud. con... ?* (*las fiestas, la religión, el laboratorio de lenguas, la clase de español,* Friends [*el programa de la tele*]*, el fin de semana, las elecciones*).

■ Emphasize that *on Monday* is *el lunes;* and *on Mondays, los lunes.* Remind students that days of the week are not capitalized in Spanish and that *lunes* is the first day of the week on Hispanic calendars.

■ Point out that *a week from today* can be expressed *de hoy en ocho días.*

■ Have students respond *sí* or *no.*

1. *Hoy es _____.*
2. *Mañana es _____.*
3. *No tenemos clase el miércoles.*
4. *Los lunes siempre tenemos examen.*

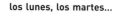

VOCABULARIO **Preparación**

¿Qué día es hoy?

lunes

Javier asiste a clase
a las ocho el lunes.

martes

Javier mira la televisión
el martes.

miércoles

jueves

Javier va al gimnasio
el miércoles.

Javier trabaja cuatro
horas el jueves.

viernes

El viernes va al mercado
con unos amigos.

sábado

El sábado Javier va a un
restaurante con Elena.

domingo

El domingo va a jugar al
basquetbol con sus amigos.

los lunes, los martes...	on Mondays, on Tuesdays . . .
Hoy (Mañana) es viernes.	Today (Tomorrow) is Friday.
Ayer fue miércoles.	Yesterday was Wednesday.
el fin de semana	(on) the weekend
pasado mañana	the day after tomorrow
el próximo (martes, miércoles,...)	next (Tuesday, Wednesday, . . .)
la semana que viene	next week

■ In Spanish-speaking countries, the week usually starts with **lunes.**

■ The days of the week are not capitalized in Spanish.

■ Except for **el sábado / los sábados** and **el domingo / los domingos,** all the days of the week use the same form for the plural as they do for the singular.

■ The definite articles are used to express *on* with the days of the week.

■ Use **el** before a day of the week to refer to a specific day (**el lunes** = *on Monday*), and **los** to refer to that day of the week in general (**los lunes** = *on Mondays*).

MULTIMEDIA: Audio

Students can listen to and practice this chapter's vocabulary on the Online Learning Center (**www.mhhe.com/puntos7**), as well as on the Textbook Audio CD, part of the Laboratory Audio Program.

National Standards: Communication

Have students work in pairs to describe and compare their weekly schedules with their partner's.

Resources: Transparency 30

■ ■ ■ Conversación

A. Entrevista. Con un compañero / una compañera, haga y conteste las siguientes (*following*) preguntas.

1. ¿Qué día es hoy? ¿Qué día es mañana? Si hoy es sábado, ¿qué día es mañana? Si hoy es jueves, ¿qué día es mañana? ¿Qué día fue ayer?
2. ¿Qué días de la semana tenemos clase? ¿Qué días no?
3. ¿Estudias mucho durante (*during*) el fin de semana? ¿y los domingos por la noche?
4. ¿Qué te gusta hacer (*to do*) los viernes por la tarde? ¿Te gusta salir (*to go out*) con los amigos los sábados por la noche?

B. Mi semana. Indique una cosa que Ud. quiere, puede o tiene que hacer cada (*each*) día de esta semana.

MODELO: El lunes tengo que (puedo, quiero) ir al laboratorio de lenguas.

Palabras útiles
dormir (to sleep) **hasta muy tarde** **ir al bar** (**al parque, al museo, a…**) **ir al cine** (movies) **jugar** (to play) **al tenis** (**al golf, al vólibol, al…**)

NOTA CULTURAL

Houses in the Hispanic World

There is no such thing as a typical Hispanic house. Often, the style of housing depends on geographic location. For example, in hot regions such as southern Spain, many houses are built around a central interior patio. These patios are filled with plants, and some even have a fountain.

The population in Hispanic countries tends to be centered in urban areas. Due to population density in cities, many people live in apartments, like people in larger cities in this country.

Here are some more details about Hispanic houses.

■ While the Spanish word **hogar** literally means *home*, the word **casa** is often used to mean *home*.

Voy a casa.   *I'm going home.*   Estoy en casa.   *I'm at home.*

■ In Spain, people use the word **piso** or **apartamento** to refer to an apartment; in some Hispanic countries, the word **departamento** is used.
■ In big Latin American cities and especially with reference to more modern homes, a small front yard with ornamental plants and/or small trees is called **un jardín.** Large backyards are uncommon (except in rural areas and small towns) because the lots where houses are built are rather small. If a house has a back area, it is generally referred to as **el patio.** This area, usually paved, adjoins the house and is commonly enclosed by the walls of neighboring buildings.

▲ *Un patio interior de una casa, en Sevilla, España*

Con. A: Note

Stress the use in item 1 of *ayer*, which students should understand in context. *Fue* and other forms of the preterite are introduced in *Capítulo 7*.

♻ Con. A: Reciclado

Remind students of the meaning of *de la mañana* (*tarde, noche*) and contrast it with *por la mañana* (*tarde, noche*).

Con. A: Follow-Up

Dictate the following sentences. Then have students respond *sí* or *no* to each.

1. *Los viernes por la tarde hay muy pocas personas en la biblioteca, ¿verdad?*
2. *Por lo general, los lunes son días fenomenales, ¿no?*
3. *Los días del fin de semana son martes y miércoles, ¿no?*
4. *Muchas personas no tienen que trabajar los sábados, ¿verdad?*

NOTA CULTURAL

Suggestions

■ Describe some Hispanic houses or house styles you know.
■ Ask some follow-up questions.

1. *¿Dónde hay casas con un patio central? ¿Qué hay en los patios?*
2. *¿Cuáles son otras palabras para* apartamento?

■ Point out that most Hispanic households reflect the cultural importance of socializing with family and friends. Especially in older homes, more attention and space are dedicated to interior, shared spaces and *patios* than to private areas such as bedrooms and bathrooms.

National Standards: Comparisons

■ Ask students whether features mentioned in the *Nota cultural* can also be found in the U.S. and Canada. Then ask what they consider typical of U.S. and Canadian housing.
■ Generalizations about housing in the Hispanic world are particularly difficult to make. Additional features of Hispanic housing in some parts of the world that seem different to some U.S. or Canadian residents include the presence of a room for a servant and the relatively plain exterior of many Hispanic homes, especially compared with their well-decorated interior. Some Hispanics note the following about the housing in this country: the reliance on air conditioning (compared with fresh air ventilation/cooling), and the lawn and extensive landscaping, especially in suburban areas.

Los muebles, los cuartos y otras partes de la casa

Suggestions

- Offer optional vocabulary, such as *el balcón, la cama de matrimonio / sencilla, la entrada, el inodoro, la terraza.*

- Point out that *habitación* is used for rooms in general. Some other synonyms for *alcoba* are *cuarto* and *dormitorio.*

- Read through the list once while students listen and look at their books; they need not repeat. Then, with books open, have students give the correct words for the following definitions.

   1. *Allí se duerme* (pantomime).
   2. *Allí se nada* (pantomime).
   3. *Los niños nadan allí.*
   4. *Da iluminación.*
   5. *Donde se prepara la comida.*
   6. *La parte de una casa donde se pone el coche.*
   7. *Allí se pone la ropa.*

- Have students tell what they associate with the following.

   ¿Qué palabras asocia Ud. con... ? el coche, los picnics o las barbacoas, la ropa, nadar (to swim), estudiar, una cena elegante, las mascotas, los libros

- Have students tell whether each of the following associations is *lógico* or *ilógico.*

   1. *los platos y la cocina*
   2. *el sofá y la piscina*
   3. *el garaje y el coche*
   4. *la alcoba y el armario*
   5. *la cama y el comedor*

- Have students draw a simple sketch of their bedroom, then describe it to a partner, who tries to draw it based on what he/she hears. Introduce the phrases: *a la derecha, a la izquierda.*

- Ask students the following questions: *En su casa o apartamento, ¿tiene Ud. un cuarto o mueble favorito? ¿Cuál es? ¿Por qué lo prefiere?*

Con. A: Suggestion

Have students draw a sketch of their home. Then have them describe their homes and indicate what they like to do in each room. If students live in a dorm, have them sketch their family's home.

Con. B: Suggestion

Do as a pair activity, then have partners report each other's answers to the class.

la alfombra	rug
la bañera	tub
el escritorio	desk
el estante	bookshelf
la lámpara	lamp
el lavabo	sink
la pared	wall
los platos	dishes; plates
el televisor	television set

Note: This is the first group of words you will learn for talking about where you live and the things found in your house or apartment. You will learn additional vocabulary for those topics in **Capítulos 9, 12,** and **14.**

■ ■ ■ Conversación

A. ¿Qué hay en esta casa? Con un compañero / una compañera, identifique las partes de esta casa y diga lo que (*what*) hay en cada cuarto.

MODELO: 7 →
   E1: El número 7 es un patio.
   E2: ¿Qué hay en el patio? ¿Hay una piscina?
   E1: No, sólo hay plantas.

B. Asociaciones

Paso 1. ¿Qué muebles o partes de la casa asocia Ud. con las siguientes actividades?

   1. estudiar para un examen
   2. dormir la siesta (*taking a nap*) por la tarde
   3. pasar una noche en casa con la familia
   4. celebrar con una comida (*meal*) especial
   5. tomar el sol (*sunbathing*)
   6. hablar de temas (*topics*) serios con los amigos (padres, hijos)

Paso 2. Ahora compare sus asociaciones con las (*those*) de otros estudiantes. ¿Tienen todos las mismas costumbres (*same customs*)?

---

*Other frequently used words for bedroom include **el dormitorio** and **la habitación.***

☀ Heritage Speakers

Explique a la clase que en algunos países hispanos se usa la palabra *tina* en vez de *baño.* Pregúnteles a los hispanohablantes de la clase cuál de las dos palabras usan, o si usan otra. ¿Qué otras variaciones saben o usan para las partes de la casa?

Resources: Transparencies 31–33
Transparency 33 includes additional vocabulary you may want to present to your students.

Refrán

«Mientras en casa estoy, rey me soy.»

Write the *refrán* on the board and have students guess the meaning. (*I'm the king of my castle.*) Ask how they feel about being at home.

Antes de la fiesta, Rosa prepara la comida.

Durante la fiesta, Rosa baila.

Después de la fiesta, Rosa limpia la sala.

Prepositions express relationships in time and space.

The book is *on* the table.   The homework is *for* tomorrow.

Some common prepositions you have already used include **a, con, de, en, para,** and **por.** Here are some prepositions that express time relationships.

antes de	*before*	**durante**	*during*
después de	*after*	**hasta**	*until*

The infinitive is the only verb form that can follow a preposition.

¿Adónde vas **después de estudiar**? *Where are you going after studying (after you study)?*

■■■ Conversación

A. ¿Antes o después? Complete las oraciones lógicamente, con **antes de** o **después de.** Luego, empareje (*match*) los dibujos (*drawings*) con las oraciones correspondientes.

1. Voy a la clase de español _____ preparar la lección.
2. Por lo general, prefiero estudiar _____ mirar un poco la televisión.
3. Los viernes siempre descanso (*I rest*) _____ salir para una fiesta.
4. Me gusta investigar un tema _____ escribir una composición.
5. Prefiero comer fuera (*to eat out*) _____ ir al cine.
6. Tengo que estudiar mucho _____ tomar un examen.

(A)
(B)

(C)
(D)

Vocabulario: Preparación

Resources: Transparency 34

¿Cuándo?: Preposiciones

Suggestions

- This is the first of two vocabulary sections on prepositions. The second, on spatial relationships, is in *Capítulo 5.*
- Model the pronunciation of the prepositions.
- Ask the following questions.

  1. *¿Qué día viene después del miércoles (jueves / domingo)? ¿Qué día viene antes del martes (miércoles / viernes)?*

  2. *¿Hasta qué hora mira Ud. la televisión los lunes? ¿y los viernes? ¿Hasta cuándo estudia cuando tiene un examen?*

- Point out the accent mark on the interrogative *¿cuándo?* and the lack of one in the noninterrogative *cuando.*

Note

The concept of the infinitive following prepositions was seen in *Capítulo 3: para* + infinitive.

♺ **Reciclado**

Review telling time. Write the following times on the board.

9:15 A.M.	7:45 P.M.
1:10 P.M.	3:30 A.M.

Then ask students: *¿Cómo se dice... ?* Encourage them to ask partners for specific times of day when they provide answers.

Con. B: Follow-Up

Use the information in this activity to create a descriptive table of students' habits. Have students try to characterize themselves as a class (*¿trabajadores? ¿estudiosos?*).

Suggestions

- Articulate an English *b*, showing how the lips are tightly closed and how the flow of air is stopped briefly before being released.
- Point out that the English *v* is a labiodental fricative, that is, it is produced by the friction of air passing between the lower lip and upper teeth. Spanish fricative *b* is bilabial; it is produced by the friction of air passing between the lips.

A: Follow-Up

1. *Viven bien en Venezuela.*
2. *Vicente viene a Venezuela el sábado.*
3. *Bárbara trabaja en la biblioteca.*
4. *Víctor es el abuelo de Vicente.*

B: Suggestions

- Point out that *la letra b* is the answer to the riddle.
- Point out that the letter *b* also appears twice in the *English* word *lightbulbs.*

B. Entrevista. Con un compañero / una compañera, haga y conteste las siguientes preguntas.

1. ¿Estudias durante tu programa favorito de televisión? ¿Qué más haces (*do you do*) cuando estudias?
2. ¿Hablas por teléfono antes o después de estudiar? ¿Dónde hablas por teléfono, en la sala o en tu cuarto?
3. ¿Hasta qué hora estudias, generalmente? ¿Estudias después de medianoche (*midnight*)?
4. ¿Lees durante las conferencias (*lectures*) en una clase? ¿Lees la lección antes o después de la explicación (*explanation*) del profesor / de la profesora?
5. ¿Trabajas durante las vacaciones? ¿Cuántas horas? ¿Trabajas por la noche hasta muy tarde?

Need more practice?

- Workbook and Laboratory Manual
- Interactive CD-ROM
- Online Learning Center (www.mhhe.com/puntos7)

PRONUNCIACIÓN *b and v*

In Spanish, the pronunciation of the letters **b** and **v** is identical. At the beginning of a phrase or sentence—that is, after a pause—or after **m** or **n**, the letters **b** and **v** are pronounced like the English stop [b], but without the puff of air. Everywhere else they are pronounced like the fricative [ƀ], produced by creating friction when pushing the air through the lips. This sound has no equivalent in English.

A. Práctica. Practique las siguientes palabras y frases.

1. [b]   bueno   viejo   verde   venir   barato   Vicente   viernes también   hombre   sombrero
2. [ƀ]   nueve   llevar   libro   pobre   abrir   abrigo   universidad abuelo
3. [b/ƀ]   bueno / es bueno   busca / Ud. busca   bien / muy bien en Venezuela / de Venezuela   vende / se vende en Bolivia / de Bolivia
4. [b/ƀ]   beber   bebida   vivir   biblioteca   Babel   vívido

B. Adivinanza (*Riddle*). Practice saying the following riddle aloud. Pay special attention to the pronunciation of the **b** sound.

Busca, busca, estoy abajo;
busca, busca, estoy arriba;
busca, busca, en la cabeza,
busca, busca, en la barriga.

¿No me encuentras? Busca, busca,
que me doblo en las bombillas.

Look, look, I'm below;
look, look, I'm above;
look, look, in your head,
look, look, in your belly.

You can't find me? Look, look,
because I appear twice in
lightbulbs.

 Heritage Speakers

- Explique que algunos hispanohablantes, especialmente los puertorriqueños, pronuncian la *v* en algunas palabras en español como la *v* del inglés. Se debe este fenómeno mayormente al deseo de diferenciar entre los grafemas *b* y *v*. Pídales a varios estudiantes hispanohablantes que pronuncien la *v* para que sus compañeros oigan cómo la pronuncian.
- Anime a los estudiantes hispanohablantes a leer en voz alta la adivinanza y luego pídales a los demás estudiantes que la repitan.

GRAMÁTICA

12 Expressing Actions • *Hacer, oír, poner, salir, traer,* **and** *ver*

Los jóvenes de hoy

«¡Estos muchachos sólo quieren *salir*! No *ponen* sus cosas en orden en sus cuartos... Los jóvenes de hoy día no *hacen* nada bien; no son responsables... ¡Hasta quieren *traer* muchachas a sus cuartos!»

¿Son estos comentarios típicos de las personas mayores (*older adults*) de su país?

¿Cree Ud. que tienen razón?

¿Tienen los jóvenes algunos (*any*) estereotipos sobre (*about*) las personas mayores?

hacer (*to do; to make*)		oír (*to hear*)		poner (*to put; to place*)		salir (*to leave; to go out*)		traer (*to bring*)		ver (*to see*)	
hago	hacemos	oigo	oímos	pongo	ponemos	salgo	salimos	traigo	traemos	veo	vemos
haces	hacéis	oyes	oís	pones	ponéis	sales	salís	traes	traéis	ves	veis
hace	hacen	oye	oyen	pone	ponen	sale	salen	trae	traen	ve	ven

- **hacer**

  Some common idioms with **hacer:**

  hacer ejercicio (*to exercise*)
  hacer un viaje (*to take a trip*)
  hacer una pregunta (*to ask a question*)

  ¿Por qué no **haces** la tarea?
  Why aren't you doing the homework?

  Quieren **hacer un viaje** al Perú.
  They want to take a trip to Peru.

  Los niños siempre **hacen muchas preguntas.**
  Children always ask a lot of questions.

- **oír**

  The command forms of **oír** are used to attract someone's attention in the same way that English uses *Listen!* or *Hey!*

  oye (tú) **oiga** (Ud.) **oigan** (Uds.)

  Oye, Juan, ¿vas a la fiesta?
  Hey, Juan, are you going to the party?

  ¡Oigan! ¡Silencio, por favor!
  Listen! Silence, please!

  No **oigo** bien por el ruido.

Today's young people These boys only want to go out! They don't put things in order in their rooms . . . Today's young people don't do anything right; they are not responsible people . . . They even want to bring girls to their rooms!

Gramática

Gramática 12

Hacer, oír, poner, salir, traer, and *ver*

Follow-Up
Ask students if they experience differences in opinion (conflicts) about how the rooms or house should be kept.

Suggestions

- Point out that *hacer, oír, poner, salir,* and *traer* have the irregular *yo* form with a *-g-.*
- You might point out that *hacer,* like *to do* in English, is a "busy" verb (has many meanings), but that it does not function as a helping verb in questions and negative expressions and for emphasis. Contrast the following sentences, in which the meaning of English *do* is contained in the verbs *oír* and *ver.*

¿Oyes eso?	Do you hear that?
No veo a Pablo.	I don't see Pablo.

☀ **Heritage Speakers**

Anime a los estudiantes hispanohablantes a hablar de las diferencias de generaciones en los países de habla hispana. ¿Son parecidas a las diferencias generacionales que existen en este país?

The expression *pensar de* is used in Spanish to indicates one's opinion of someone or something: *¿Qué piensas de esta situación?*

Suggestions

■ Emphasize the spelling change for the second and third person of *oír*: *i → y.*

■ Point out that *traer* is an antonym of *llevar*. As with *ir* vs. *venir* (see note in *Gramática 11*), *traer* implies that the speaker is in the place to which something would be brought.

■ Use the verbs in sentences about yourself, following up with questions about the students.

Veo las noticias en la televisión antes de clase. ¿Ud. ve la televisión en la mañana?

Bright Idea

Suggestion

Point out that after the verbs *ponerse* and *quitarse*, the singular form is used in Spanish, whereas English frequently uses the plural. Compare the following.

The children take off their hats.
Los niños se quitan el sombrero.

The children put on their coats.
Los niños se ponen el abrigo.

In some cases, where each individual has two of any given object, the plural form is used in Spanish.

Se ponen los zapatos / los guantes / los calcetines.

Prác: Preliminary Exercises

■ Have students give the corresponding *yo* form to the following *Ud.* forms.

hace	oye
trae	sale
pone	ve

■ Have students give the corresponding subject pronouns.

hago	sale
hacemos	sales
pongo	salgo
pone	traéis
pones	traemos
oye	traigo
oyes	traes

■ **poner**

Many Spanish speakers use **poner** with appliances to express *to turn on.*

Voy a **poner** el televisor.
I'm going to turn on the TV.

Siempre **pongo** leche y mucho azúcar en el café.

■ **salir**

Note that **salir** is always followed by **de** to express leaving a place.

Salir con can mean *to go out with, to date.*

Use **salir para** to indicate destination.

Salgo con el hermano de Cecilia.
I'm going out with Cecilia's brother.

Salimos para la sierra pasado mañana.
We're leaving for the mountains the day after tomorrow.

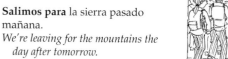

Salen de la clase ahora.

■ **traer**

¿Por qué no **traes** la radio a la cocina?
Why don't you bring the radio to the kitchen?

■ **ver**

No **veo** bien sin mis lentes de contacto.
I can't see well without my contact lenses.

■ ■ ■ Práctica

Cosas rutinarias

Paso 1. ¡Anticipemos! ¿Cierto o falso?

1. Hago ejercicio en el gimnasio con frecuencia.
2. Siempre veo la televisión por la noche.
3. Nunca salgo con mis primos por la noche.
4. Siempre hago los ejercicios para la clase de español.
5. Salgo para la universidad a las ocho de la mañana.
6. Nunca pongo la ropa en la cómoda o en el armario.
7. Siempre traigo todos los libros necesarios a clase.
8. Siempre oigo todo lo que dice (*says*) el profesor / la profesora de español.

Paso 2. Now rephrase each sentence in **Paso 1** as a question and interview a classmate. Use the **tú** form of the verb.

MODELO: Hago ejercicio en el gimnasio con frecuencia. →
¿Haces ejercicio en el gimnasio con frecuencia?

AUTOPRUEBA

Give the correct present tense **yo** forms for these verbs.

1. hacer	4. oír
2. ver	5. traer
3. poner	6. salir

Answers: 1. hago 2. veo 3. pongo 4. oigo 5. traigo 6. salgo

Need more practice?

■ Workbook and Laboratory Manual
■ Interactive CD-ROM
■ Online Learning Center (www.mhhe.com/puntos7)

Capítulo 4: En casa

☼ Heritage Speakers

Hay muchos hispanohablantes que usan *encender* o *prender* para expresar *to turn on*. Pregúnteles a sus estudiantes hispanohablantes cómo expresan las siguientes ideas en español.

to turn on . . .
. . . the lights   . . . the car
. . . the television   . . . the water
. . . the oven

■ ■ ■ Conversación

A. Consecuencias lógicas. Con un compañero / una compañera, indique una acción lógica para cada situación, usando (*using*) las **Frases útiles**.

MODELO: No tengo tarea. Por eso... → pongo el televisor.

Frases útiles
hacer un viaje / una pregunta
oír al profesor / a la profesora*
poner el televisor / el estéreo
salir con/de/para...
traer el libro a clase
ver mi programa favorito

1. Me gusta esquiar en las montañas. Por eso...
2. En la clase de español usamos este libro todos los días. Por eso...
3. Mis compañeros de cuarto hacen mucho ruido en la sala. Por eso...
4. El televisor no funciona. Por eso...
5. Hay mucho ruido en la clase. Por eso...
6. Estoy en la biblioteca y ¡no puedo estudiar más! Por eso...
7. Queremos bailar y necesitamos música. Por eso...
8. No comprendo la lección. Por eso...

EN LOS ESTADOS UNIDOS Y EL CANADÁ

The California Missions

The twenty-one **misiones** in California along what was called **el Camino Real** (the Royal Highway) were founded between 1769 and 1817 as outposts for bringing the Catholic religion to new lands. The indigenous people of California whose territories were colonized by these first Spanish settlements were deeply impacted. Some groups eventually became known by the name of a nearby **misión**—for example, the **diegueños (Misión de San Diego),** the **luiseños (Misión de San Luis Obispo),** and the **gabrielinos (Misión de San Gabriel).** Many of these missions later became important cities, including San Diego, San Francisco, and Santa Barbara.

The California Missions Study Association, a nonprofit public benefit corporation, is dedicated to "the Study and Preservation of the California Missions, Presidios, Pueblos, and Ranchos and their Native American, Hispanic, and Early American Past." The missions have now become popular tourist attractions and are visited by millions of tourists every year.

▲ *La Misión San Juan Capistrano en San Juan Capistrano, California*

---

*Remember that the word **a** is necessary in front of a human direct object. You will study this usage of **a** in **Capítulo 6.** For now, you can answer following the pattern of the **Frase útiles.**

Con. A: Follow-Up

Have students give the Spanish equivalents for the following sentences.

1. I'm going to turn on the TV. I want to turn on the radio.
2. She's going out with her boyfriend. He wants to go out with Margarita.
3. She's leaving for Rome tomorrow. I'm leaving for Bogotá on Friday.
4. We have to take a trip. They should ask a question.

♻ Con. A: Reciclado

Help students review clothing vocabulary. Write on the board:

La ropa. Voy a hacer un viaje y en mi maleta voy a poner...

Divide the class into small groups and have students take turns adding an item to the list of clothing they will pack. Each student must name all the items previously mentioned by others before adding his or her own.

EN LOS ESTADOS UNIDOS Y EL CANADÁ

Suggestions

■ Point out that *misión*, like all *–ión* words in Spanish, loses its written accent mark when it is plural: *misiones*.

■ Have students identify current Californian cities named after old missions.

■ Point out that Spaniards did not occupy what is today the state of California until the second half

of the 18th century. California was called *Alta California*; together with the peninsula of *Baja California*, it was part of *Nueva España*. After the independence of Mexico from Spain, California was Mexican territory. In fact, the last founded mission, *San Francisco de Padua*, was founded by Mexico as an independent nation (not by Spain).

NOTA COMUNICATIVA

Suggestion
Model phrases about yourself
using these verbs, then ask yes/no
questions.

NOTA COMUNICATIVA

Más sobre *hacer, oír, salir* y *ver*

The verbs in this **Nota comunicativa** are used in many different expressions. Below is an overview of some expressions that you have already used. Some will be new to you.

■ **Hacer** is used to express *to do* physical and academic exercises. To express *to do exercises* for a Spanish or math class, for example, the plural **ejercicios** is used. To express *to exercise* in a gym, the singular is used, except for aerobics.

Hacen los ejercicios en el cuaderno.	*They do the exercises in the notebook.*
Hace ejercicio en el gimnasio.	*He exercises in the gym.*
Inés **hace** ejercicios aeróbicos por la mañana.	*Inés does aerobics in the morning.*

■ **Oír** means *to hear*. In **Capítulo 1**, you learned the verb **escuchar**, which means *to listen* (*to*). Some speakers use **oír** for *to listen* when referring to things like music or the news. **Escuchar** never means *to hear*.

No **oigo** bien a la profesora.	*I can't hear the professor well.*
Escuchamos/Oímos música en clase.	*We listen to music in class.*

■ A useful expression with **salir** is **salir bien/mal**, which means *to turn/come out well/poorly, to do well/poorly*.

Todo va a **salir bien**.	*Everything will come out (turn out) well.*
Necesito **salir bien** en el examen.	*I need to do (come out) well on the exam.*
No quiero **salir mal** en esta clase.	*I don't want to do poorly in this class.*

■ **Ver** means *to see* or *to watch*. In **Capítulo 2**, you learned that **mirar** means *to look* (*at*) or *to watch* something. Some speakers use **ver** for *to watch*, but **mirar** can never mean *to see*. **Buscar** (from **Capítulo 1**) is used to express *to look for* something, but never *to look at* or *to watch*.

¿**Ven** Uds. las plantas en el patio?	*Do you see the plants on the patio?*
Luis **ve** mucho la televisión.	*Luis watches a lot of television.*
Los niños **ven/miran** los dibujos animados.	*The kids are watching / looking at cartoons.*
Busco los platos nuevos.	*I'm looking for the new plates.*

B. Entrevista. Con un compañero / una compañera, haga y conteste las siguientes preguntas.

En casa

1. ¿Qué pones en el armario? ¿en la cómoda? ¿Siempre pones todo en orden en tu alcoba antes de salir?
2. ¿Te gusta hacer ejercicio? ¿Haces ejercicios aeróbicos? ¿Dónde haces ejercicio? ¿En casa? ¿en el gimnasio? ¿en la piscina?
3. ¿Ves mucho la televisión? ¿Qué programas ves todas las semanas? ¿Pones el televisor en la mañana o en la noche? ¿o en las dos ocasiones?
4. ¿Cuándo pones la radio? ¿Qué música escuchas? ¿Oyes las noticias (*news*) todos los días? ¿Pones la radio o el televisor para oír las noticias?
5. ¿Sales con amigos los días de entresemana (*during the week*)? ¿Con quién sales los fines de semana? ¿Qué haces los fines de semana?

Para las clases

1. ¿Qué pones en tu mochila o bolsa todos los días para ir a clase? ¿Siempre traes los libros de texto a clase?
2. ¿A qué hora sales para las clases los lunes? ¿A qué hora sales de clase los viernes?
3. ¿Cuándo haces la tarea? ¿Por la mañana? ¿por la tarde? ¿por la noche? ¿Dónde haces la tarea? ¿En casa? ¿en la biblioteca? ¿Haces la tarea mientras (*while*) ves la televisión? ¿mientras escuchas música?
4. ¿Siempre sales bien en los exámenes? ¿En qué clase no sales bien? ¿Qué haces si sales mal en un examen? ¿Hablas con tu profesor(a)?

¿Recuerda Ud.?

The change in the stem vowels of **querer** and **poder** (**e** and **o,** respectively) follows the same pattern as that of the verbs presented in the next section. Review the forms of **querer** and **poder** before beginning that section.

querer: **e** → ¿ ?

qu__ro	queremos
qu__res	queréis
qu__re	qu__ren

poder: **o** → ¿ ?

p__do	podemos
p__des	podéis
p__de	p__den

13 Expressing Actions • Present Tense of Stem-Changing Verbs

Una fiesta para Marisa

Hoy es el cumpleaños de Marisa. Gracia y Catalina preparan una pequeña sorpresa para su compañera de cuarto.

GRACIA: ¿A qué hora *vuelve* Marisa?
CATALINA: No estoy segura pero *pienso* que *vuelve* a las cinco.
GRACIA: ¡No podemos estar listas a las cinco!
CATALINA: ¡Con calma! La sala está limpia ahora y los entremeses casi están listos. A las cinco, *vuelve* Marisa, *empezamos* a gritar «¡Sorpresa!» y *sirvo* el champán y los entremeses. Ya verás. Una sorpresa pequeña pero perfecta.

Comprensión: ¿Cierto o falso?

1. Gracia y Catalina empiezan a preparar una fiesta muy grande para Marisa.
2. Marisa vuelve a casa por la noche.
3. Marisa va a servir los entremeses.
4. Catalina piensa que necesitan más tiempo (*time*).

A party for Marisa   *Today is Marisa's birthday. Gracia and Catalina are preparing a small surprise for their roommate. GRACIA: When is Marisa getting back? CATALINA: I'm not sure but I think she returns at five. GRACIA: We can't be ready by five! CATALINA: Calm down! The living room is clean now and the hors d'oeuvres are almost ready. At five, Marisa returns, we begin to shout "Surprise!," and I serve champagne and hors d'oeuvres. You'll see. A small surprise, but perfect.*

Gramática

Follow-Up
Ask students the following questions after reading the *minidiálogo:*

¿Piensan preparar una fiesta de sorpresa esta semana?
¿A qué hora vuelven Uds. de clase?

CULTURE

In this *minidiálogo*, Gracia and Catalina are throwing a small surprise party for Marisa. Point out to students that throwing a surprise party in Spanish-speaking countries can be complicated, as people often do not come to a party at the given time. If you invite people to a party that begins at 7:00 P.M., many guests will begin arriving around 7:30, if not later. Additionally, invitations generally do not include a specified time for the end of the party. Many Spanish-speakers would consider it rude to ask guests to leave at a specific time.

Emphasis A: Suggestion
Write one of the verb paradigms on the board and draw a boot around the stem-changing verbs to help illustrate the pattern.

Emphasis B: Suggestions

■ Model infinitives you have not yet presented, creating a brief conversational exchange with each.
■ Emphasize the spelling differences between *perder* and *pedir*.
■ Model verbs with infinitives to emphasize the use of prepositions with some, and not with others: *empezar a* + infinitive; *volver a* + infinitive; *pensar* + infinitive.
■ Remind students that *volver* means *to return (to a place)* and *devolver* means *to return (something)*.

🔄 **Reciclado**
Review *querer* and *poder*, pointing out the diphthongization of the stem vowel in stressed positions, except for the *nosotros* and *vosotros* forms.

Past	---	**PRESENT**	---	Future
		present		

e → ie **pensar (ie)** (*to think*)	o (u) → ue **volver (ue)** (*to return*)	e → i **pedir (i)** (*to ask for; to order*)
pienso pensamos piensas pensáis piensa piensan	vuelvo volvemos vuelves volvéis vuelve vuelven	pido pedimos pides pedís pide piden

A. You have already learned five *stem-changing verbs* (**los verbos que cambian el radical**).

querer   preferir   tener   venir   poder

In these verbs the stem vowels **e** and **o** become **ie** and **ue,** respectively, in stressed syllables. The stem vowels are stressed in all present tense forms except **nosotros** and **vosotros.** All three classes of stem-changing verbs follow this regular "boot" pattern in the present tense.

In vocabulary lists, the stem change will always be shown in parentheses after the infinitive: **volver (ue).**

Stem vowel changes:

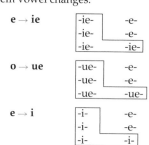

Nosotros and **vosotros** forms do not have a stem vowel change.

B. Some stem-changing verbs practiced in this chapter include the following.

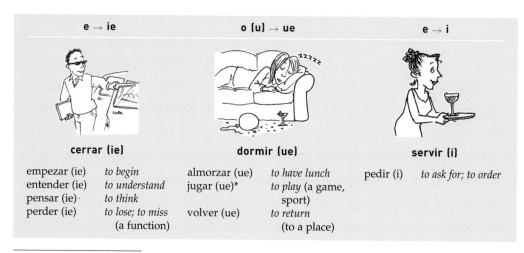

e → ie	o (u) → ue	e → i
cerrar (ie)	**dormir (ue)**	**servir (i)**
empezar (ie) *to begin*	almorzar (ue) *to have lunch*	pedir (i) *to ask for; to order*
entender (ie) *to understand*	jugar (ue)* *to play (a game, sport)*	
pensar (ie) *to think*		
perder (ie) *to lose; to miss (a function)*	volver (ue) *to return (to a place)*	

Jugar is the only **u → ue stem-changing verb in Spanish. **Jugar** is usually followed by **al** when used with the name of a sport: **Juego al tenis.** Some Spanish speakers, however, omit the **al**.*

138 ■ Ciento treinta y ocho

Capítulo 4: En casa

☀️ **Heritage Speakers**

■ En México y en algunos dialectos del español del suroeste de los Estados Unidos, el verbo *almorzar* significa *desayunar.* Pregúnteles a los hispanohablantes de su clase qué palabras usan para expresar los nombres de las comidas del día.
■ En algunos dialectos del español del suroeste de los Estados Unidos, se dice *volver (para) atrás* o *regresar* por *devolver.* Explique la diferencia entre *volver, devolver* y *regresar.*

■ When used with an infinitive, **empezar** is followed by **a**.	Uds. **empiezan a hablar** muy bien el español. *You're beginning to speak Spanish very well.*	

■ When used with an infinitive, **volver** is also followed by **a**. The phrase then means *to do (something) again.*	¿Cuándo **vuelves a jugar** al tenis? *When are you going to play tennis again?*

■ When followed directly by an infinitive, **pensar** means *to intend, plan to.* The phrase **pensar en** can be used to express *to think about.*	¿Cuándo **piensas** almorzar? *When do you plan to eat lunch?* —¿**En** qué **piensas**? *What are you thinking about?* —**Pienso en** las cosas que tengo que hacer el domingo. *I'm thinking about the things I have to do on Sunday.*

AUTOPRUEBA

Complete the verb forms with the correct letters.

1. ent___ndemos
2. d___rmo
3. c___rras
4. j___gan
5. s___rve
6. alm___rzo

Answers: 1. entendemos 2. duermo 3. cierras 4. juegan 5. sirve 6. almuerzo

■■■ Práctica

A. ¿Dónde están Jacobo y Margarita? Tell in what part of Jacobo and Margarita's house the following things are happening. More than one answer is possible in some cases.

MODELO: Jacobo y Margarita empiezan a preparar el desayuno (*breakfast*). →
Están en la cocina.

1. Jacobo sirve el desayuno.
2. Margarita cierra la revista y pone el televisor.
3. Los dos almuerzan con un amigo del barrio (*neighborhood*).
4. Los dos juegan al ajedrez (*chess*), y Jacobo pierde.
5. Margarita piensa en las cosas que tiene que hacer hoy.
6. Jacobo vuelve a casa después de ir al supermercado.
7. Margarita duerme la siesta.
8. Jacobo pide una pizza por teléfono.

Need more practice?

■ Workbook and Laboratory Manual
■ Interactive CD-ROM
■ Online Learning Center (www.mhhe.com/ puntos7)

■ Have students give the correct form of each verb for the subject given.

yo:	cerrar	almorzar
	empezar	pedir
	entender	
tú:	pensar	jugar
	preferir	dormir
Ud./él/ella:	perder	volver
	empezar	servir
nosotros:	empezar	jugar
	preferir	volver
vosotros:	pensar	dormir
	cerrar	servir
	entender	
Uds./ellos/ ellas:	preferir	jugar
	almorzar	pedir

■ Have students give new sentences based on the subject cues:

1. *Sara y Anita almuerzan en el patio.*

Ud.	tú
nuestros hijos	yo
nosotros	vosotros

2. *Felipe pide un refresco.*

yo	Lisa
nosotros	tú
ellos	vosotros

3. *Yo prefiero descansar en la playa (beach).*

Sergio	ellas
nosotros	tú
Ana	vosotras

4. *Yo pierdo muchas cosas.*

ellos	tú
yo	los niños
Fernando	vosotros

5. *Los González vuelven de su viaje el sábado.*

yo	Manuel
nosotras	tú
mis primas	vosotros

Con. B: Suggestion

Have students work in small groups
and use *tú* forms for items 2–3.

B. **Una tarde típica en casa.** ¿Cuáles son las actividades de todos? Haga oraciones completas con una palabra o frase de cada grupo. Use sólo los sujetos que son apropiados para Ud.

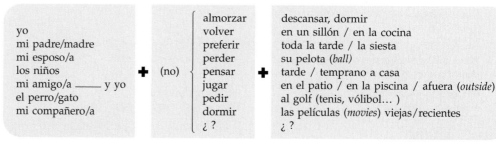

| yo
mi padre/madre
mi esposo/a
los niños
mi amigo/a _____ y yo
el perro/gato
mi compañero/a | **+** | (no) | almorzar
volver
preferir
perder
pensar
jugar
pedir
dormir
¿ ? | **+** | descansar, dormir
en un sillón / en la cocina
toda la tarde / la siesta
su pelota (*ball*)
tarde / temprano a casa
en el patio / en la piscina / afuera (*outside*)
al golf (tenis, vólibol...)
las películas (*movies*) viejas/recientes
¿ ? |

■ ■ ■ **Conversación**

A. **¿Qué piensas hacer esta semana?**

Paso 1.   Organice la semana que viene. Puede usar las **Frases útiles** a la derecha, pero invente por lo menos tres actividades que no están en la lista.

	por la mañana	**por la tarde**	**por la noche**
lunes			
martes			
miércoles			
jueves			
viernes			
sábado			
domingo			

Frases útiles

almorzar en un
  restaurante
  con _____
dormir una siesta
empezar un proyecto
  para _____
hacer ejercicio
hacer la tarea
  de _____
jugar al tenis/golf/
  basquetbol
  con _____
servir una comida
  (food) para mis
  amigos
ver televisión
volver a ver a _____

Paso 2.   Ahora, hable con un compañero / una compañera de sus horarios esta semana, basándose (*based on*) en la agenda del **Paso 1.**

MODELO: E1: ¿Qué piensas hacer el domingo por la tarde?
      E2: Pienso ver un poco la televisión y dormir una siesta. ¿Y tú, qué haces el domingo?
      E1: El domingo juego al tenis con mi amigo Alex.

B. **Preguntas**

1. ¿A qué hora cierran la biblioteca? ¿A qué hora cierran la cafetería? Y durante la época de los exámenes finales, ¿a qué hora cierran?
2. ¿A qué hora almuerza Ud., por lo general? ¿Dónde le gusta almorzar? ¿Con quién? ¿Dónde piensa Ud. almorzar hoy? ¿mañana?
3. ¿Es Ud. un poco olvidadizo/a? Es decir (*That is*), ¿pierde las cosas con frecuencia? ¿Qué cosa pierde Ud.? ¿El dinero? ¿su cuaderno? ¿su mochila? ¿sus llaves (*keys*)?

Expressing *-self/-selves* • Reflexive Pronouns

La rutina diaria de Andrés

La rutina de Andrés empieza a las siete y media.

1.

2.

3.

4.

5.

6.

7.

(1) *Me despierto* a las siete y media y *me levanto* en seguida. (2) Primero, *me ducho* y (3) luego *me cepillo* los dientes. (4) *Me peino*, (5) *me pongo* la bata y (6) voy al cuarto a *vestirme*. Por fin, (7) salgo para mis clases. No tomo nada antes de salir para la universidad porque, por lo general, ¡tengo prisa!

¿Cómo es la rutina diaria de Ud.?

1. Yo me levanto a las _____.
2. Me ducho por la (mañana/noche).
3. Me visto en (el baño/mi cuarto).
4. Me peino (antes de/después de) vestirme.
5. Antes de salir para las clases, (tomo/no tomo) el desayuno.

Andrés' daily routine *Andrés's routine begins at seven-thirty. I wake up at seven-thirty and I get up right away. First, I take a shower and then I brush my teeth. I comb my hair, I put on my robe, and I go to my room to get dressed. Finally, I leave for my classes. I don't eat or drink anything before leaving for the university because I'm generally in a hurry!*

Gramática   Ciento cuarenta y uno ■ **141**

Resources: Transparency 35

Gramática ■ **141**

Follow-Up

Have students respond *cierto* or *falso* based on their own situations.

1. *Me despierto temprano.*
2. *Me levanto a las seis.*
3. *El sábado me levanto a las siete.*
4. *Prefiero bañarme por la mañana.*
5. *Me gusta acostarme a las diez.*
6. *El sábado me acuesto a las doce.*

Uses of Reflexive Pronouns

Suggestion

Contrast *I bathe the kids* with *I bathe* (*myself*) (*I take a bath*). In the first sentence, the subject and object are different; in the second they are the same person (the object pronoun reflects the subject).

Emphasis A: Suggestion

Refer students to the vocabulary list to see the *-se* at the end of reflexive verbs.

bañarse (*to take a bath*)		
(yo)	me baño	*I take a bath*
(tú)	te bañas	*you take a bath*
(Ud.)		*you take a bath*
(él)	se baña	*he takes a bath*
(ella)		*she takes a bath*
(nosotros)	nos bañamos	*we take baths*
(vosotros)	os bañáis	*you take baths*
(Uds.)		*you take baths*
(ellos)	se bañan	*they take baths*
(ellas)		*they take baths*

A. The pronoun **se** at the end of an infinitive indicates that the verb is used reflexively. The reflexive pronoun in Spanish reflects the subject doing something to or for himself, herself, or itself. When the verb is conjugated, the reflexive pronoun that corresponds to the subject must be used.

bañarse = to take a bath (to bathe oneself)
me baño = I take a bath (bathe myself)

Reflexive Pronouns			
me	myself	**nos**	ourselves
te	yourself (*fam, sing.*)	**os**	yourselves (*fam. pl. Sp.*)
se	himself, herself, itself; yourself (*form. sing.*)	**se**	themselves; yourselves (*form. pl.*)

 Many English verbs that describe parts of one's daily routine—to get up, to take a bath, and so on—are expressed in Spanish with a reflexive construction.

B. Here and on the following page are some reflexive verbs you will find useful as you talk about daily routines. Note that some of these verbs are also stem-changing.

despertarse (ie)   **ducharse**   **afeitarse**   **vestirse (i, i)**   **sentarse (ie)**

Refrán

«Camarón que se duerme, se lo lleva el corriente.»

Write the *refrán* on the board. Give students the meaning of *camarón* (shrimp), and have them guess what *corriente* means (current). Have students guess the meaning of this saying, and ask them if they know similar or related sayings in English. (*You snooze, you lose. The early bird gets the worm.*)

acostarse (ue)	to go to bed	levantarse	to get up; to stand up
bañarse	to take a bath		
cepillarse los dientes	to brush one's teeth	peinarse	to brush one's hair
divertirse (ie)	to have a good time, enjoy oneself	ponerse	to put on (clothing)
dormirse (ue)	to fall asleep	quitarse	to take off (clothing)

Note also the verb **llamarse** (*to be called*), which you have been using since **Ante todo: Me llamo** _____. **¿Cómo se llama Ud.?**

All of these verbs can also be used nonreflexively, often with a different meaning. Some examples of this appear at the right:

 After **ponerse** and **quitarse,** the definite article, not the possessive as in English, is used with articles of clothing.

[Práctica A–B]

dormir = to sleep **dormirse** = to fall asleep
poner = to put, place **ponerse** = to put on

Se pone **el** abrigo.
He's putting on his coat.

Se quitan **el** sombrero.
They're taking off their hats.

Placement of Reflexive Pronouns

Reflexive pronouns are placed before a conjugated verb. In a negative sentence, they are placed after the word **no** and before the conjugated verb: **No se bañan.** When a conjugated verb is followed by an infinitive, they may either precede the conjugated verb or be attached to the infinitive.

[Práctica C]

Me tengo que levantar temprano.
Tengo que levantar**me** temprano.
I have to get up early.

AUTOPRUEBA

Match each reflexive pronoun with the correct verb form.

1. se _____
2. nos _____
3. te _____
4. me _____

a. bañas
b. afeitamos
c. acuesto
d. levanta

Answers: 1. d 2. b 3. a 4. c

- Emphasize the change in meaning of some verbs: *dormir* (to sleep) vs. *dormirse* (to fall asleep); *poner* (to put, place) vs. *ponerse* (to put on).
- Model verbs from the chart in a conversational setting, saying sentences about yourself and following up with questions to students.

   Generalmente me acuesto a las once. Y Ud., ¿a qué hora se acuesta?

- Rapid response drill. Ask student short, yes/no questions.

   ¿Se baña? → Sí, me baño.
   ¿Se bañan? → Sí, nos bañamos.

   Use all of the verbs in the chart.

- Point out that other verbs can change meaning in the reflexive. Write the following examples on the board:

nonreflexive	meaning
caer	to fall
comer	to eat
decidir	to decide
ir	to go

reflexive	meaning
caerse	to fall down
comerse	to eat (something) up
decidirse	to make up one's mind
irse	to go away

144 ■ Capítulo 4: En casa

Preliminary Exercises

■ Have students give the subject pronoun that corresponds to each reflexive pronoun.

   te me nos os

Ask what subject pronouns correspond to the reflexive pronoun *se*.

■ Have students give the *yo* form of the following verbs.

bañarse	*ponerse*
levantarse	*despertarse*
ducharse	*dormirse*
vestirse	*acostarse*

■ Read the following sentences and have students tell whether they are reflexive or not.

1. *María se despierta a las ocho de la mañana.*
2. *María acuesta a los niños a las nueve de la noche.*
3. *Se quita la ropa.*
4. *Baña a los niños.*
5. *María se sienta.*
6. *Sienta a los niños.*
7. *Levanta a los niños a las siete.*
8. *Todos se divierten.*

Prác. A: Variation

Have students correct the sentences to express what they actually do.

Prác. B: Follow-Up

Have students use the verbs and situations to describe a typical day in the life of their husband, wife, best friend, parents, children, and so on.

Prác. C: Note

Point out the use of the preposition + infinitive.

Prác. C: Suggestion

Have students make up routines for some typical characters: *los estudiantes típicos de esta universidad, su compañero/a de cuarto,* and so on.

■ ■ ■ Práctica

A. ¡Anticipemos! Su rutina diaria

Paso 1. ¿Hace Ud. lo mismo (*the same thing*) todos los días? Marque los días que hace las siguientes cosas.

	LOS LUNES	LOS SÁBADOS
1. Me levanto antes de las ocho.	☐	☐
2. Siempre me baño o me ducho.	☐	☐
3. Siempre me afeito.	☐	☐
4. Me pongo un traje / un vestido / una falda.	☐	☐
5. Me quito los zapatos después de llegar a casa.	☐	☐
6. Me acuesto antes de las once de la noche.	☐	☐

Paso 2. ¿Tiene Ud. una rutina diferente los sábados? ¿Qué día prefiere? ¿Por qué?

B. La rutina diaria de los Durán

Paso 1. ¿Qué acostumbran hacer los miembros de la familia Durán? Conteste, imaginando (*imagining*) que Ud. es Manolo Durán. Use el sujeto pronominal cuando sea (*whenever it is*) necesario.

> MODELO: yo **/** levantarse **/** a las siete → Me levanto a las siete.

1. mi esposa Lola **/** levantarse **/** más tarde
2. nosotros **/** ducharse **/** por la mañana
3. por costumbre **/** nuestro **/** hija Marta **/** bañarse **/** por la noche
4. yo **/** vestirse **/** antes de tomar el desayuno
5. Lola **/** vestirse **/** después de tomar un café
6. por la noche **/** Marta **/** acostarse **/** temprano
7. yo **/** acostarse **/** más tarde, a las once
8. por lo general **/** Lola **/** acostarse **/** más tarde que (*than*) yo

Paso 2. En la familia Durán, ¿quién... ?

1. se levanta primero
2. se acuesta primero
3. no se baña por la mañana
4. se viste antes de tomar el desayuno

C. Un día típico

Paso 1. Complete las siguientes oraciones lógicamente para describir su rutina diaria. Use el pronombre reflexivo cuando sea necesario. **¡OJO!** Use el infinitivo después de las preposiciones.

1. Me levanto después de _____.
2. Primero (yo) _____ y luego _____.
3. Me visto antes de / después de _____.
4. Luego me siento a la mesa para _____.
5. Me gusta estudiar antes de _____ o después de _____.
6. Por la noche me divierto un poco y luego _____.
7. Me acuesto antes de / después de _____ y finalmente _____.

Paso 2. Con las oraciones del **Paso 1,** describa los hábitos de su esposo/a, su compañero/a de cuarto / casa, sus hijos…

Need more practice?

■ Workbook and Laboratory Manual
■ Interactive CD-ROM
■ Online Learning Center (www.mhhe.com/puntos7)

☼ Heritage Speakers

Pídales a sus estudiantes hispanohablantes que escriban una breve composición en la que describan un día típico de su vida.

■ ■ ■ Conversación

A. Entrevista: ¿Cómo es tu rutina diaria?

Paso 1. Con un compañero / una compañera, haga y conteste preguntas sobre su rutina diaria. Anote (*Jot down*) las respuestas de su compañero/a.

1. Los días de la semana (*weekdays*), ¿te levantas temprano? ¿antes de las siete de la mañana? ¿A qué hora te levantas los sábados?
2. ¿Te bañas o te duchas? ¿Cuándo lo haces (*do you do it*), por la mañana o por la noche?
3. ¿Te afeitas todos los días? ¿Usas una afeitadora eléctrica? ¿Prefieres no afeitarte los fines de semana?
4. Por lo general, ¿te vistes con elegancia o informalmente? ¿Qué ropa te pones cuando quieres estar elegante? ¿cuando quieres estar muy cómodo/a (*comfortable*)? ¿Qué te pones para ir a la universidad?
5. ¿A qué hora vuelves a casa, generalmente? ¿Qué haces cuando regresas? ¿Te quitas los zapatos? ¿Te pones ropa más cómoda? ¿Estudias? ¿Miras la televisión? ¿Preparas la cena (*dinner*)?
6. ¿A qué hora te acuestas? ¿Cuál es la última (*last*) cosa que haces antes de acostarte? ¿Cuál es la última cosa o persona en que piensas antes de dormirte?

Paso 2. Ahora, describa la rutina de su compañero/a a la clase, usando las respuestas del **Paso 1.** ¿Cuántos estudiantes de la clase tienen rutinas parecidas (*similar*)?

B. Hábitos. ¿Dónde hace Ud. lo siguiente? Indique el cuarto o la parte de la casa donde Ud. hace cada actividad. Debe indicar también los muebles y otras cosas que usa.

> MODELO: estudiar →
> Cuando estudio, prefiero estar (por lo general estoy) en la alcoba. Uso el escritorio, una silla, los libros y la computadora.

1. estudiar
2. dormir la siesta
3. quitarse los zapatos
4. bañarse o ducharse
5. despertarse
6. tomar el desayuno
7. sentarse a almorzar
8. vestirse
9. divertirse
10. acostarse

Con. A: Suggestions

■ **Paso 1.** Have students add two questions of their own.
■ **Paso 2.** Have students compare a classmate's routine with their own: *Jim se levanta a las siete, pero yo me levanto a las ocho,* or *Jim y yo nos levantamos a las ocho,* and so on.

Con. B: Suggestions

■ Have students work in pairs or trios to elaborate on their answers and ask for extra information.
■ Remind students to use the appropriate reflexive pronouns with infinitives, for example: *Tengo que levantarme, Queremos divertirnos,* and so on.
■ Emphasize that when two verbs work together, the reflexive object pronouns can be placed before the conjugated verb or come after and be attached to the infinitive. Students will learn more about object pronoun placement in *Capítulos 6, 7,* and *8.*

UN POCO DE TODO

A: Note

Point out that *atender* means *to assist* or *to help out*. *Asistir* means *to attend* (*go to* [an event, a class]).

A: Extension

Have students retell the story in the third person singular (*ella*).

A. Un día normal. Ángela es dependienta en una tienda de ropa para jóvenes en El Paso. ¿Cómo es un día normal de trabajo para ella? Complete la narración con los verbos apropiados, según los dibujos. **¡OJO!** Algunos verbos se usan más de una vez (*more than once*).

1.   2.   3.

4.   5.   6.

Vocabulario útil
These adverbs will help you understand the sequence of events. **primero** (first) **entonces** (then, next) **luego** (then, afterward) **finalmente** (finally)

1. Llego a la tienda a las 9:50 de la mañana con mis compañeras de trabajo. Primero (yo) _____ a ordenar (*put in order*) la ropa. La ropa de la tienda _____ bonita.
2. A las 10:00 abren la tienda y entonces los clientes _____ a llegar.
3. Mis compañeras no _____ español. Por eso yo siempre atiendo a los clientes hispanos.
4. (Yo) _____ a las 12:30 con mi amiga Susie, que trabaja en una zapatería. Generalmente (nosotras) _____ en la pizzería San Marcos y casi siempre _____ pizza.
5. Luego, (yo) _____ a la tienda y _____ a trabajar. Nunca _____ la siesta.
6. Finalmente, la supervisora _____ la tienda a las 6:00 en punto. Entonces yo _____ a casa.

Verbos
almorzar
cerrar
comer
dormir
empezar
hablar
ir
pedir
ser
volver

B. ¡Qué diferencia! Complete the following letter with the correct forms of the words in parentheses, as suggested by the context. When two possibilities are given in parentheses, select the correct word. In addition to reviewing vocabulary from previous chapters, you will decide when to use **ser** or **estar** in situations that you have already learned. You will learn more about **ser** and **estar** in **Capítulo 5.**

 Heritage Speakers

Invite a sus estudiantes hispanohablantes a inventar diálogos basados en los dibujos para presentar a la clase. Luego, los otros estudiantes pueden hacerles preguntas sobre los diálogos.

Resources: Transparency 36

Melissa es una estudiante universitaria de los Estados Unidos que está en Costa Rica por seis semanas. Escribe su primera carta a dos amigas curiosas.

¡Hola, Sonia y Katie!

¿Qué tal? Pues[a], por fin (*yo: contestar*[1]) (*su/sus*[2]) carta para contarles[b] que (*ser/estar*[3]) en San José en la casa (*de/en*[4]) los Arriaga[c]. (*Yo: Divertirse*[5]) mucho con ellos (*todo*[6]) los días. La familia (*ser/estar*[7]) superamable, y los ticos[d] en general (*ser/estar*[8]) muy simpáticos también. Siempre me (*ellos: hacer*[9]) muchas preguntas cuando se dan cuenta de[e] que (*yo: ser/estar*[10]) de los Estados Unidos. A propósito[f], muchos estadounidenses que (*venir*[11]) a Costa Rica ¡no (*tener*[12]) ganas (*en/de*[13]) dejar[g] este país!

La casa de esta familia (*costarricense*[14]), como[h] muchas otras casas de San José, es más pequeña que[i] (*nuestro*[15]) casas en Chicago. Está pintada de un azul claro[j] muy bonito —por aquí hay muchas otras casas pintadas de (*unas/unos*[16]) colores pastel que yo no (*ver*[17]) mucho en los Estados Unidos. Los ticos (*tener*[18]) las casas abiertas al aire libre[k] todo el día, porque la temperatura casi nunca (*llegar*[19]) a los 80° (grados). Por (*eso/ese*[20]), casi no tienen aire acondicionado. ¡Es (*muy/mucho*[21]) agradable!

Costa Rica es famosa por (*su/sus*[22]) parques nacionales y por la ecología. Los parques incluyen un 25 por ciento del país y (*un/una*[23]) variedad de volcanes, selvas[l] (*tropical*[24]) y playas. (*Yo: Ir*[25]) a visitar varios parques durante mi visita. También la familia Arriaga me quiere llevar a Sarchí, (*un/una*[26]) pueblo cerca de[m] San José. En Sarchí, uno (*poder*[27]) comprar muchas artesanías de Costa Rica. El pueblo también es famoso por (*su/sus*[28]) carretas[n] de brillantes colores.

Bueno, con esto, voy a despedirme[o] porque tengo (*a/que*[29]) (*ducharse*[30]). Si yo no (*vestirse*[31]) pronto, voy a (*salir*[32]) tarde para las clases.

Un abrazo muy fuerte,
Melissa.

[a]*Well* [b]*tell you* [c]*los... the Arriaga family* [d]*a nickname commonly used to indicate Costa Ricans* [e]*se... they realize* [f]*A... by the way* [g]*leaving behind* [h]*like* [i]*than* [j]*light* [k]*abiertas... open to fresh air* [l]*jungles* [m]*cerca... close to* [n]*wooden carts* [o]*say good-bye*

Comprensión: ¿Hay evidencia o no? Decide whether there is evidence in Melissa's letter to support the following statements. For each statement, say **Sí, hay evidencia de esto** or **No, no hay evidencia de esto.** Change statements for which there is no evidence in the letter so that they will contain information that is included in the letter.

1. Melissa escribe muchas cartas a sus amigas en los Estados Unidos.
2. Melissa toma clases en la universidad.
3. A Melissa le gusta mucho estar en Costa Rica.
4. Los ticos tienen cierta curiosidad acerca de (*about*) los estadounidenses.
5. Melissa prefiere las casas de los Estados Unidos.
6. Los ticos no tienen mucha necesidad del aire acondicionado.

Resources for Review and Testing Preparation

- Workbook and Laboratory Manual
- Interactive CD-ROM
- Online Learning Center (www.mhhe.com/ puntos7)

B: Suggestion
Point out that Costa Ricans often use the diminutives -*ico/-tico* and the nickname for their nationality is *ticos*. Have students think of nicknames given to people of different areas in this country, for example, *Hoosiers*, which is used to refer to people from Indiana.

Resources: Desenlace
In the *Capítulo 4* section of "Chapter-by-Chapter Supplementary Materials" in the IM/RK, you will find a chapter-culminating activity. You can use this activity to consolidate and review the vocabulary and grammar skills students have acquired.

Entrevista cultural

Suggestions

■ Before showing the video, ask students questions about where they work. If they do not work during the school year, ask if they work during the summer.

> ¿Dónde trabaja Ud.?
> ¿Cuántas horas por semana trabaja?
> ¿Cuáles son sus responsabilidades en el trabajo?

■ Show the video and allow students one to two minutes to work on the questions. Encourage them to answer in Spanish if possible. You might want to ask the questions in Spanish when you review the answers as a class.

1. ¿En qué ciudad trabaja Alexander?
2. ¿Qué hace para sus clientes?
3. ¿Qué diferencias hay entre una casa «típica» en la ciudad y una fuera de la ciudad?
4. ¿Cómo describe la diferencia entre un apartamento amueblado y un apartamento sin muebles? ¿Qué muebles menciona?
5. ¿Alexander tiene su propia casa?

Have volunteers answer the questions.

■ Have volunteers role-play Alexander and the interviewer.

Entre amigos

Suggestions

■ Before viewing the video, review the questions with the students and ask them similar questions. Then have volunteers describe the furniture they have and tell what furniture they would like to buy.

■ After viewing the video, have volunteers read and answer the questions.

PERSPECTIVAS culturales

●●● Videoteca

Entrevista cultural: Costa Rica

Alexander Burbón is a Costa Rican who works in real estate. In this interview he talks about his country and his work. One topic he discusses is the "typical" Costa Rican home. Before watching the video clip, read the following excerpt from the interview.

INTERVIEWER: ¿Cómo te llamas tú y en dónde trabajas?
ALEXANDER: Mi nombre es Alexander Burbón y trabajo en Costa Rica en una compañía de bienes raíces[a] que queda[b] en San José, en la capital. Eh, los bienes raíces, básicamente lo que yo hago es ir y mostrarles casas a personas que las quieren comprar o alquilar.[c] Y entonces, luego, los ayudo con los trámites[d] para comprar o para alquilar.

[a]bienes... real estate [b]está [c]rent [d]details

Now watch the video clip and answer the following questions based on the interview.

1. In what city does Alexander work?
2. What does he do for his clients?
3. What differences are there between a "typical" home in the city and outside the city?
4. How does he describe the difference between a furnished and unfurnished apartment? What items does he mention?
5. Does Alexander own his home?

Entre amigos: Quiero cambiar los muebles

Rubén is waiting for Karina when Tané arrives. Tané is going shopping for furniture. What questions do you think they will ask each other? Before watching the video, read the following questions. As you watch, don't worry if you don't understand every word. Try to get the gist of the conversation, listening specifically for information about their plans for the day. Watch the video a second time and listen for the answers to the questions.

1. ¿Por qué espera Rubén a Karina?
2. ¿Trabaja Rubén mucho o poco? ¿Cuándo estudia?
3. ¿Por qué está cansada (tired) Karina?
4. ¿Adónde va Rubén?

Conozca... Costa Rica

Datos esenciales

- Nombre oficial: República de Costa Rica
- Capital: San José
- Población: 3.896.092 habitantes
- Moneda: el colón
- Idioma oficial: el español

¡Fíjese!

- El ecoturismo es importante para la economía de Costa Rica y para la preservación de la biodiversidad y la belleza[a] natural que existe en el país. El ecoturismo tiene como propósito[b] controlar la entrada[c] de turistas en regiones protegidas[d] y, a la vez,[e] obtener fondos[f] para continuar con la protección de las regiones naturales. Aproximadamente un treinta por ciento (%) del territorio costarricense está cubierto de selvas o bosques.[g] En total, más de un cuarto[h] del territorio del país ha sido destinado[i] para la preservación.

- Costa Rica es una de las primeras democracias de las Américas. En 1821, convocaron[j] las primeras elecciones. Costa Rica tiene tres ramas[k] gubernamentales: ejecutiva (un presidente y dos vicepresidentes), legislativa y judicial. Es notable que Costa Rica no tiene un esfuerzo militar[l] permanente. Muchos consideran que Costa Rica es «la Suiza[m] de las Américas» porque es un país «amistoso»[n] que se mantiene neutro durante conflictos entre naciones. A menudo[o] los líderes de Costa Rica intervienen para negociar la paz[p] durante un conflicto internacional.

[a]beauty [b]purpose [c]entrance [d]protected [e]a... at the same time [f]funds [g]está... is covered with jungles or forests [h]fourth [i]ha... has been set aside [j]they held [k]branches [l]esfuerzo... military force [m]Switzerland [n]friendly [o]A... Often [p]peace

Learn more about Costa Rica with the Video, the Interactive CD-ROM, and the Online Learning Center (www.mhhe.com/puntos7).

Personas famosas: Óscar Arias Sánchez

Óscar Arias Sánchez (1941–), presidente de Costa Rica de 1986 a 1990, asistió a[a] la Universidad de Costa Rica, a Boston University y a otras universidades en Inglaterra.[b] En 1987, Arias recibió[c] el Premio Nóbel de la Paz[d] por sus esfuerzos[e] por aliviar las tensiones entre el gobierno sandinista de Nicaragua y los Estados Unidos. El acuerdo de paz[f] de Arias se firmó[g] en 1986. Desde 1990, se encarga de[h] la Fundación Arias para la paz y el progreso humano.

[a]asistió... attended [b]England [c]received [d]Premio... Nobel Peace Prize [e]efforts [f]acuerdo... peace agreement [g]se... was signed [h]se... he has been running

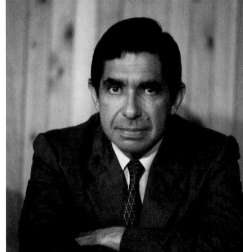

▲ Óscar Arias Sánchez

Notes

- Students can read "*XLVII*," a poem by Costa Rica's Carmen Naranjo in *Un paso más 4*.
- Costa Rica was not developed as a Spanish colony to the same extent that other Central American countries were. A number of factors caused this. Costa Rica was geographically distant from Guatemala, the seat of Spanish government, and it did not have extensive mineral resources, nor the abundant indigenous work force to develop those that did exist. As a result, the few settlers that arrived turned to agriculture.
- Coffee became a primary agricultural product in the nineteenth century.
- In 1871 U.S. engineers recruited Chinese and Italian workers to build a railroad. Later, Jamaican workers were used.
- The United Fruit Company, which developed with the coming of the railroad and which linked banana plantations to export centers, influenced national politics in Costa Rica for many years. Labor disputes against the company began early in the twentieth century and continued into the 1930s.
- Costa Rica currently has a parliamentary democracy and an advanced social welfare system.

MULTIMEDIA: Internet

Have students look up additional information about Costa Rica's history, government, people, culture, geography, tourism, and media on the Internet. You might assign specific topics and have students give brief oral reports about Costa Rica.

Suggestions

- Have students play hangman using different groups of words.
- Play password with the house vocabulary. The cues may not include the target word or any form of it. You can divide the class into two teams, and while one member takes a turn giving a cue the other team members try to guess the word.

EN RESUMEN

Gramática

To review the grammar points presented in this chapter, refer to the indicated grammar presentations. You'll find further practice of these structures in the Workbook and Laboratory Manual, on the Interactive CD-ROM, and on the *Puntos de pàrtida* Online Learning Center (www.mhhe.com/puntos7).

12. Expressing Actions—**Hacer, oír, poner, salir, traer,** and **ver**

Do you know the forms of **hacer, oír, poner, salir, traer,** and **ver** and how to use them?

13. Expressing Actions—Present Tense of Stem-Changing Verbs

Do you know the forms of verbs like **pensar (ie), volver (ue),** and **pedir (i)?**

14. Expressing -*self*/-*selves*—Reflexive Pronouns

You should be able to talk about your daily routine using reflexive verbs like **levantarse, bañarse,** and **afeitarse.**

Vocabulario

Practice this vocabulary with digital flash cards on the Online Learning Center (www.mhhe.com/puntos7).

Los verbos

almorzar (ue)	to have lunch
cerrar (ie)	to close
contestar	to answer
descansar	to rest
dormir (ue)	to sleep
dormir la siesta	to take a nap
empezar (ie)	to begin
empezar a + *inf.*	to begin to (*do something*)
entender (ie)	to understand
hacer (*irreg.*)	to do; to make
hacer ejercicio	to exercise
hacer un viaje	to take a trip
hacer una pregunta	to ask a question
jugar (ue) (al)	to play (*a game, sport*)
oír (*irreg.*)	to hear
pedir (i)	to ask for; to order
pensar (ie) (en)	to think (about); to intend
perder (ie)	to lose; to miss (*a function*)
poner (*irreg.*)	to put; to place
salir (*irreg.*) **(de)/(con)**	to leave (*a place*); to go out (with)
servir (i)	to serve
traer (*irreg.*)	to bring
ver (*irreg.*)	to see
volver (ue)	to return (*to a place*)
volver a + *inf.*	to (*do something*) again

Los verbos reflexivos

acostarse (ue)	to go to bed
afeitarse	to shave
bañarse	to take a bath
cepillarse los dientes	to brush one's teeth
despertarse (ie)	to wake up
divertirse (ie)	to have a good time, enjoy oneself
dormirse (ue)	to fall asleep
ducharse	to take a shower
levantarse	to get up; to stand up
llamarse	to be called
peinarse	to comb one's hair
ponerse (*irreg.*)	to put on (*clothing*)
quitarse	to take off (*clothing*)
sentarse (ie)	to sit down
vestirse (i)	to get dressed

Los cuartos y otras partes de una casa

la alcoba	bedroom
el baño	bathroom
la cocina	kitchen
el comedor	dining room
el garaje	garage
el jardín	yard
la pared	wall
el patio	patio; yard
la piscina	swimming pool
la sala	living room

Los muebles y otras cosas de una casa

la alfombra	rug
el armario	closet
la bañera	bathtub
la cama (de agua)	(water) bed
la cómoda	bureau; dresser
el estante	bookshelf
la lámpara	lamp
el lavabo	(bathroom) sink
la mesita	end table
los platos	dishes; plates
el sillón	armchair
el sofá	sofa
el televisor	television set

Repaso: el escritorio, la mesa, la silla

Otros sustantivos

el ajedrez	chess
el cine	movies; movie theater
el desayuno	breakfast
el/la muchacho/a	boy/girl
la película	movie
el ruido	noise
la rutina diaria	daily routine
la tarea	homework

Los adjetivos

cada (inv.)*	each, every
cómodo/a	comfortable
siguiente	following

Preposiciones

antes de	before
después de	after
durante	during
hasta	until
por	during; for
sin	without

¿Cuándo?

ayer fue (miércoles)	yesterday was (Wednesday)
pasado mañana	the day after tomorrow
el próximo (martes)	next (Tuesday)
la semana que viene	next week

Los días de la semana
- lunes
- martes
- miércoles
- jueves
- viernes
- sábado
- domingo

Repaso: el fin de semana, hoy, mañana

Palabras adicionales

por fin	finally
por lo general	generally
primero	first

*The abbreviation inv. means invariable (in form). The adjective **cada** is used with masculine and feminine nouns (**cada, libro, cada mesa**) and it is never used in the plural.

Suggestions

■ Write the following on the board.

> Ayer fue _____.
> Hoy es _____. _____ voy a _____.
> Pero antes, tengo que _____.
> Después voy a _____.
> Por lo general, _____ todos los _____.

Have students complete these sentences in writing, using vocabulary to fill the blanks. Then ask them to share and correct them with a partner. Have several students read their sentences aloud.

■ Have students write a paragraph about an activity that they perform routinely. Ask them to use as many of the new prepositions as possible and to:

1. tell when they perform this activity,
2. where they perform it, and
3. what steps they take and in what order.

Un paso más 4

Note

The *Un paso más* section is optional.

Literatura de Costa Rica

Notes

- Carmen Naranjo studied at the University of Costa Rica and did post-graduate studies at *la UNAM* in Mexico City and at Iowa City University.
- Naranjo, a member of the *Asociación Costarricense de Escritoras,* is considered one of the most important literary figures, a pioneer of internal discourse, in Costa Rica and Central America. She denounces and challenges social, political, religious, intellectual, and sexual order institutions. She has dedicated much time, energy, and ink to the fight for equality for women.
- She has served on international boards and organizations, including *la Asociación Mundial de Escritores y Periodistas, la Organización de Estados Americanos,* and UNICEF.
- She has received the *Aquileo J. Echeverría* prize two times: in 1966 for her novel *Los perros no ladraron* and in 1971 for her novel *Responso por el niño Juan Manuel.* In 1977 she received *el Orden Alfonso X el Sabio* from the Spanish government and in 1986 *el Premio Nacional de Cultura Magón.*

Literatura de **Costa Rica**

Sobre la autora: *Carmen Naranjo was born in Cartago, Costa Rica. She was a student of philology, and she has done graduate studies at the* **Universidad Nacional Autónoma de México** *as well as at the University of Iowa, Iowa City. She is a prolific writer of novels, stories, essays, and poetry. The following poem is from* En esta tierra redonda[a] y plana[b] *(XLVII) (2001).*

Ayer te busqué[c]
en ese asiento vacío[d]
del avión
en ese asiento vacío
del parque
en ese asiento vacío
del vestíbulo
en ese asiento vacío
del taxi
en ese asiento vacío
del comedor
en ese asiento vacío
de mi cuarto.
Hoy te seguiré buscando.[e]

[a]*round*   [b]*flat*   [c]*te... I looked for you*   [d]*asiento... empty seat*   [e]*te... I will continue to look for you*

▲ Carmen Naranjo (1929–)

L E C T U R A

ESTRATEGIA: Recognizing Cognate Patterns

Cognates are words that are similar in form and meaning from one language to another: for example, English *poet* and Spanish **poeta.** You learned many cognates in **Ante todo.** The more cognates you can recognize, the more easily you will read Spanish.

MULTIMEDIA: Internet

Have students look up the website for *la Asociación Costarricense de Escritoras.* The website states the mission of this association and has brief biographies of several Costa Rican women writers.

The endings of many Spanish words correspond to English word endings according to fixed patterns. Learning to recognize these patterns will increase the number of close and not-so-close cognates that you can recognize. Here are a few of the most common.

-dad / -tad → -ty
-mente → -ly
-ción → -tion
-sión → -sion
-ico → -ic, -ical
-oso → -ous

What are the English equivalents of these words?

1. unidad
2. reducción
3. explosión
4. idéntico
5. estudioso
6. frecuentemente
7. pomposo
8. libertad
9. fantástico
10. obviamente
11. desilusión
12. imperiosamente

Now try to deduce the meaning of the following words, which are taken from the reading in this section.

1. totalmente
2. transportación
3. espaciosa
4. información
5. conveniente
6. fabulosa

Try to spot additional cognates in the following reading, and remember that you should be able to guess the meaning of underlined words from context.

■ **Sobre la lectura...** The reading on the following page is adapted from real estate ads in a Puerto Rican newspaper. Since Puerto Rico is part of the United States, you will find examples of English or the influence of English scattered throughout the ads.

Suggestion

After students have completed the *Lectura*, encourage them to search the Internet or the local newspapers for real estate ads in English. Have them choose a house or apartment that they would want to buy or rent for themselves. Encourage them to describe in Spanish the house or apartment of their choice.

❶ Alto Apolo

Bonito «townhouse», área exclusiva. 3 dorms., 3 baños. Equipado. «Family», tres terrazas. Cerca centros comerciales, transportación. Bajos $80s. Hipoteca $57.250 al 8 1/2% Mens. $478. 790-6811, 789-9331.

❷ LOMAS DEL SOL

Hermosa res. 3 dorms., 2 baños. Fabulosa vista con lago en el patio. Gallinero, árboles frutales, marq. doble. 2.179 mts. de solar. Hip. $64.000 al 8%. Mens. $489. Pronto $36.000. Información 725-0773.

❸ Villa Ávila. Encantadora residencia totalmente redecorada. 3 dorms., 2 baños. Cocina y equipos nuevos. Toda empapelada y alfombrada. «Family». Preciosa piscina. Cable TV. Bajos $100s con términos. Conveniente mensualidad $509. 790-6811, 789-9331.

❹ Borinquen Gardens

Con un poquito de amor usted arregla esta amplia casa de 4 dorms., 2 baños. Su precio en los $60s.

❺ Torrimar I

Recién remodelada con buen gusto, casa de 5 dorms., 4 baños, en calle tranquila. Dueños bajan precio para venta rápida. Haga un cita exclusiva, hoy.

❻ Santa Paula

Amplísima residencia 4 dorms., 4 baños. Moderna fachada, espaciosa cocina. Inmenso cuarto de juego. Estudio, «family». Piscina. Solar sobre 1.000 metros. Medios $100s. Financiamiento especial. 790-6811, 789-9331.

❼ CAPARRA HILLS

Atractiva res. de 2 años construida, moderna, sencilla. Perfecta para familia pequeña. Con doble garaje, patio interior, terraza cubierta, en más de 650 m.s. Con hipoteca alta. En los medios $100s. Llama ahora. UNIVERSAL HOMES (Selected Homes Specialists) 781-7605.

❽ Sta. María

Preciosa residencia de ejecutivo con:
• 4 dorms
• 3 baños
• cuarto de servicio
• amplia terraza
• barra
• piscina
• y mucho más.
Haga su cita exclusiva, hoy.

Comprensión

A. El inglés en Puerto Rico. ¿Ve Ud. la influencia lingüística del inglés en el español en estos anuncios de Puerto Rico? A veces se «copian» algunas palabras directamente. Por ejemplo, la palabra *family* aparece en tres anuncios. ¿A qué tipo de cuarto se refiere? ¡Es muy fácil de deducir!

B. La casa perfecta. Vuelva a leer los anuncios rápidamente e indique cuáles de las siguientes casas serían (*would be*) apropiadas para los Juárez, una familia «extendida» que consiste en los padres, cuatro hijos y una abuela.

	SÍ	NO
Número 5, Torrimar I	☐	☐
Número 7, Caparra Hills	☐	☐
Número 3, Villa Ávila	☐	☐
Número 2, Lomas del Sol	☐	☐

ESCRITURA

A. Los clientes. Lea los anuncios en la lectura para encontrar la mejor casa para los siguientes clientes. Escriba por qué a estos clientes les gustaría (*would like*) esa casa.

1. Pedro Aquino, un carpintero a quien le gusta el trabajo manual.
2. Los Pino, un matrimonio mayor (*elderly couple*) que no tiene coche pero que le gusta ir de compras.
3. Óscar Sifuentes, un banquero por vocación pero mecánico por diversión. Los fines de semana repara su coche antiguo, llueva o no llueva (*rain or shine*).
4. Los Pérez, una familia con cuatro hijos muy activos. Desean una casa espaciosa donde los hijos puedan jugar sin molestar (*bothering*) a los adultos.

B. Mi anuncio. Imagine that you will rent or sell your house or apartment. Using the ads from the reading as models, write an ad describing your house or apartment. Include any amenities, special location, and so on. You might include a line about the kind of person that might find this house ideally suited for him or her.

Comprensión

B: Extension
Ask students the following questions.

¿Qué casas serían apropiadas para

1. *una madre soltera con tres hijos pequeños?*
2. *una familia que acaba de llegar al pueblo y necesita casa inmediatamente?*
3. *un matrimonio y sus hijos? El esposo es carpintero y la esposa es electricista. Los hijos adolescentes saben pintar.*

ESCRITURA

Suggestion
If you prefer that your students do a journal activity, see *Mi diario* in this chapter of the Workbook.

B: Suggestion
Encourage students to be very descriptive. Ask, for example, Is it furnished? How many rooms does it have? Is the kitchen large?

MULTIMEDIA: Internet

To follow up activity B, have students find similar Spanish language classified ads on the Internet, and determine the kind of individual or family that might live in each home. Ask them to print out several of these and hand them in along with a descriptive paragraph for each.

CHAPTER OPENER PHOTO

Point out the chapter-opener photo. Have students talk about the climate in their area and their ideas about climate in Spanish-speaking countries. Encourage them to describe the scene in the photo, and compare it to their own experience and/or ideas. Ask students: *¿Qué tiempo hace en el sitio que se ve en la foto? Hace sol, ¿verdad? Pero, ¿creen que hace frío?* (pantomime)

Suggestions

■ Ask the following questions to introduce this chapter's topic. Write the boldfaced words on the board and help students guess their meaning by context.

1. *¿Cómo es **el clima** en su país?*
2. *¿Son extremas **las estaciones** en su país? ¿Cuál es su estación favorita?*
3. *¿Cómo afecta su vida el clima de su país?*
4. *¿Qué tipo de clima prefiere para sus vacaciones? ¿Por qué?*
5. *¿Qué sabe Ud. del* (do you know about the) *clima de la Argentina? ¿de España?*

■ Introduce the names of the four seasons and *hace frío* and *hace calor,* for further discussion.

Note

The *Puntos de partida* Online Learning Center includes an interview with a native speaker from Guatemala who answers questions similar to those in the preceding *Suggestion.*

♻ Reciclado

Review clothing. Ask questions that relate weather to clothing.

¿Qué deben llevar las personas en este clima?
¿Qué llevan Uds. cuando hace calor?
¿Y cuando hace frío?

CAPÍTULO 5

104910

◀ Unos catamaranes en el lago Atitlán, en Guatemala

Resources

For Students

■ Workbook
■ Laboratory Manual and Laboratory Audio Program
■ Quia™ Online Workbook and Online Laboratory Manual
■ Video on CD
■ Interactive CD-ROM
■ *Puntos de partida* Online Learning Center (**www.mhhe.com/puntos7**)

For Instructors

■ *Instructor's Manual and Resource Kit,* "Chapter-by-Chapter" Supplementary Materials
■ Overhead Transparencies 37–45
■ Testing Program
■ Test Generator
■ Video Program
■ Audioscript
■ *Puntos de partida* Online Learning Center (**www.mhhe.com/puntos7**)

Las estaciones y el tiempo°

Entrevista cultural

MAR CARIBE

MÉXICO

BELICE

HONDURAS

GUATEMALA

Ciudad de Guatemala

NICARAGUA

EL SALVADOR

COSTA RICA

OCÉANO PACÍFICO

Débora David ▶ Ciudad de Guatemala, Guatemala

°**Las...** *The seasons and the weather*

Suggestion
Have students tell what they know about Guatemala. Have one student serve as recorder. After completing the chapter, review these initial ideas. Ask students how they would change them.

CULTURE

Although the weather can be hot around the equator and in many Latin American countries, not all Hispanic countries have tropical climates. Temperatures are closely related to altitude—the higher the altitude, the cooler the climate. The great mountain chains found in Latin America make for a varied climate throughout the continent. Both Argentina and Chile have territory in Antarctica (*la Antártida*).

MULTIMEDIA

- The multimedia materials that accompany this chapter are referenced in the Student and Instructor's Editions with icons to help you identify when and where to incorporate them.
- The *Instructor's Manual and Resource Kit* (IM/RK) provides suggestions for using the multimedia materials in the classroom.

¿Qué tiempo hace hoy?

Suggestions

- See the model for vocabulary presentation and other material in "Teaching Techniques" for the *Capítulo 5 Vocabulario: Preparación* section of "Chapter-by-Chapter Supplementary Materials," in the IM.
- Model weather expressions. As you present each, have students tell you what kind of clothing is worn for that weather condition.
- Point out the pronunciation of *llueve*. The pronunciation of *ll* and consonantal *y* is identical in most parts of the Spanish-speaking world. Therefore, the difference in spelling is not accompanied by a difference in pronunciation. In some areas of Spain, *ll* is a sound made with the tongue against the palate, resembling the sound in the English word *million*.
- Point out that *tiempo* means both weather and time. *Tiempo* should not be confused with *hora* as in ¿*Qué hora es?*
- Contrast *hacer, tener, estar*, and *ser*. Discuss the differences among the following expressions.

  hace frío/calor for weather
  tener frío/calor for people
  estar frío/caliente to indicate the condition of things

- Optional vocabulary: *Hay mucha humedad; está húmedo.*

Con. A: Suggestion

Have students work in groups to prepare descriptions of a particular city/state, identifying the weather there and the type of clothing that is appropriate. Have each group read its description to the class, which then guesses the city described. If students cannot guess immediately, allow them five *sí/no* questions.

Con. A: Follow-Up

Have students answer the following questions.

1. ¿*Dónde prefiere Ud. vivir, donde hace calor o donde hace fresco?*
2. ¿*Le gusta vivir donde llueve mucho? ¿donde nieva mucho?*
3. *Describa la diferencia entre el clima de Michigan y el de Texas.*
4. ¿*Prefiere Ud. vivir en un lugar con cuatro estaciones o con solamente una?*
5. ¿*En qué partes de este país hay solamente una estación?*

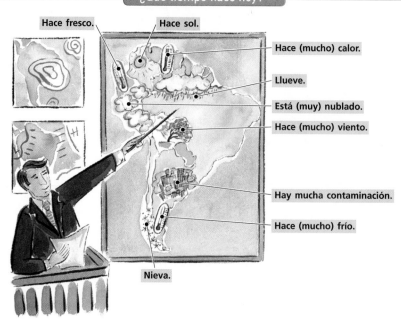

¿Qué tiempo hace hoy?°   ¿Qué... *What's the weather like today?*

- Hace fresco.
- Hace sol.
- Hace (mucho) calor.
- Llueve.
- Está (muy) nublado.
- Hace (mucho) viento.
- Hay mucha contaminación.
- Hace (mucho) frío.
- Nieva.

In Spanish, many weather conditions are expressed with **hace.** The adjective **mucho** is used with the nouns **frío, calor, viento,** and **sol** to express *very.*

Hace (muy) buen/mal tiempo.   It's (very) good/bad weather. The weather is (very) good/bad.

Pronunciation hint: Remember that, in most parts of the Spanish-speaking world, **ll** is pronounced exactly like **y: llueve.**

■ ■ ■ Conversación

A. **El tiempo y la ropa.** Diga qué tiempo hace, según la ropa de cada persona.

   MODELO: Miami: Todos llevan traje de baño y sandalias. →
            Hace calor. (Hace buen tiempo.)

   1. San Diego: María lleva pantalones cortos y una camiseta.
   2. Madison: Juan lleva suéter, pero no lleva chaqueta.
   3. Toronto: Roberto lleva suéter y chaqueta.
   4. San Miguel de Allende: Ramón lleva impermeable y botas y también tiene paraguas (*umbrella*).
   5. Buenos Aires: Todos llevan abrigo, botas y sombrero.

MULTIMEDIA: Internet

Have students search for a weather site in Spanish and bring a printout from it to class. Have students identify the weather expressions they are learning and others they may recognize, for example, *temperatura.*

Resources: Transparency 37

MULTIMEDIA: Audio

Students can listen to and practice this chapter's vocabulary on the Online Learning Center (**www.mhhe.com/puntos7**), as well as on the Textbook Audio CD, part of the Laboratory Audio Program.

B. Consejos (Advice) para Joaquín. Joaquín es de Valencia, España. El clima (*climate*) allí es mediterráneo: hace mucho sol y las temperaturas son moderadas. No hay mucha contaminación.

Paso 1. Joaquín tiene una lista de lugares que desea visitar en los Estados Unidos. Ayúdelo (*Help him*) con información sobre el clima. Como Joaquín no sabe (*As Joaquín doesn't know*) en qué estación va a viajar (*travel*), es bueno ofrecerle información sobre el clima de todo el año.

1. Seattle, Washington
2. Los Ángeles, California
3. Phoenix, Arizona
4. Buffalo, Nueva York
5. las islas (*islands*) hawaiianas

Paso 2. Es obvio que la lista de Joaquín no está completa. ¿Qué otros tres lugares cree Ud. que debe visitar? ¿Qué clima hace allí?

C. El tiempo y las actividades. Haga oraciones completas, indicando una actividad apropiada para cada situación.

> cuando llueve
> cuando hace buen tiempo
> cuando hace calor
> cuando hace frío
> cuando nieva
> cuando hay mucha contaminación
>
> **+**
>
> me quedo (*I stay*) en cama/casa
> juego al basquetbol/vólibol con mis amigos
> almuerzo afuera (*outside*) / en el parque
> me divierto en el parque / en la playa (*beach*) con mis amigos
> no salgo de casa
> vuelvo a casa y trabajo o estudio

NOTA COMUNICATIVA

More *tener* Idioms

Several other conditions expressed in Spanish with **tener** idioms—not with *to be*, as in English—include the following.

tener (mucho) calor	to be (very) warm, hot
tener (mucho) frío	to be (very) cold

These expressions are used to describe people or animals only. To be comfortable—neither hot nor cold—is expressed with **estar bien.**

D. ¿Tienen frío o calor? ¿Están bien? Describe the following weather conditions, and tell how the people pictured are feeling.

1.
2.
3.
4.
5.
6.
7.

Vocabulario: Preparación

Ciento cincuenta y nueve ■ **159**

Refrán

«Después de la tempestad viene la calma.»

Write the *refrán* on the board. Point out that *la tempestad* is a synonym. Can students guess what this word means? Describe in Spanish the weather conditions of a *tempestad* to help them guess. What does the *refrán* mean?

☼ Heritage Speakers

Aunque a veces se oye la palabra *polución* en algunos dialectos del español que se habla en este país, la palabra *contaminación* es la preferida.

> **Resources: Transparency 38**

Con. B: Follow-Up

Ask students the following questions.

> ¿Llueve mucho en Inglaterra? ¿en el desierto Sahara?
> ¿Nieva mucho en el Brasil? ¿en Minnesota?
> ¿Hace mucho frío en Siberia? ¿en el Ecuador?
> ¿Hace mucho sol en Florida? ¿en España?
> ¿Hace calor en Panamá? ¿en Alaska?

Con. C: Suggestions

- Ask students if the following activities are typical on their campus when it's bad weather.

  1. *Cuando hace frío, juegan al basquetbol en el gimnasio.*
  2. *Cuando nieva, pasan la tarde en la sala de la residencia estudiantil* (translate).
  3. *Cuando nieva, hacen muñecos de nieve (snowmen).*
  4. *Cuando llueve, no salen de la residencia.*
  5. *Cuando hace mucho calor, duermen todo el día.*

- Ask students if they do the following things when it is hot.

  Cuando hace calor...

  1. *¿bebe Ud. agua, refrescos o cerveza? ¿o jugo de fruta?*
  2. *¿prefiere estar en casa o afuera?*
  3. *¿prefiere estar en el parque o en la playa?*
  4. *¿juega al tenis (al golf, etcétera) o duerme?*

NOTA COMUNICATIVA

Suggestions

- With *tener* + noun expressions, *very* is expressed with *mucho/a*: *tener mucho frío/calor; tener muchas ganas.*
- Point out that *tener* means *to feel* in these idioms.
- Point out that *to have a cold* in Spanish is *tener catarro* or *tener gripe.*

Con. D: Preliminary Exercise

Ask students the following questions before beginning the activity:

1. *¿Qué tiempo hace hoy?*
2. *Imagine que hoy es un día fatal. ¿Qué tiempo hace hoy?*
3. *Hoy es un día estupendo. ¿Qué tiempo hace hoy?*

Los meses y las estaciones del año

Suggestions

- Model months of the year, linking them to seasons.

  Los meses de otoño son septiembre, octubre y noviembre, ¿verdad?
  Los meses de verano son mayo, junio y julio, ¿no?
  and so on.

  Then ask students what the weather is like in each season:

  En muchas partes de este país hace frío en enero, ¿cierto o falso?
  También nieva mucho en julio, ¿cierto o falso?

- Point out that September has two accepted spellings: *septiembre* and *setiembre.*
- Remind students that months are not capitalized in Spanish.
- Ask students what they prefer:

  ¿Prefiere Ud.... ?

  1. *¿los días cortos del invierno o los días largos del verano?*
  2. *¿el tiempo del otoño o el de la primavera?*
  3. *¿las actividades de verano o las de invierno?*

♲ **Reciclado:** Review numbers and years with the following questions.

¿En qué año estamos?
¿En qué año nació Ud.?
¿En qué año nació su padre (madre, abuela, etcétera)?
¿En qué año piensa graduarse?

Con. B: Note

- Point out that the Hispanic *Día de los Inocentes* (December 28) is a religious holiday (Catholic) commemorating the day King Herod had all babies slaughtered in Bethlehem.
- Friday the 13th is considered to be a day of bad luck in this country. In Spanish-speaking countries, however, it's *martes trece.*

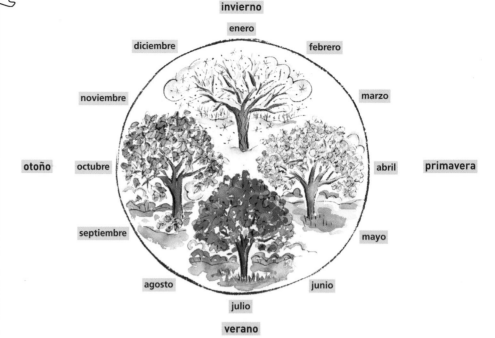

invierno
enero
diciembre · febrero
noviembre · marzo
otoño · octubre · abril · primavera
septiembre · mayo
agosto · junio
julio
verano

¿Cuál es la fecha de hoy?   What is today's date?
(Hoy) Es el primero de abril.   (Today) It's the first of April.
(Hoy) Es el cinco de febrero.   (Today) It's the fifth of February.

- The ordinal number **primero** is used to express the first day of the month. Cardinal numbers (**dos, tres,** and so on) are used for other days.
- The definite article **el** is used before the date. However, when the day of the week is expressed, **el** is omitted: **Hoy es jueves, tres de octubre.**
- As you know, **mil** is used to express the year after 999.

  1950   mil novecientos cincuenta   2004   dos mil cuatro

■ ■ ■ **Conversación**

A. El mes de noviembre. Mire este calendario para el mes de noviembre. ¿Qué día de la semana es el 12 (1, 20, 16, 11, 4, 29) de noviembre?

MODELO: ¿Qué día de la semana es el 5 de noviembre? → El 5 es viernes.

Capítulo 5: Las estaciones y el tiempo

☼ **Heritage Speakers**

Pregúnteles a los hispanohablantes de su clase qué días festivos celebran. Pídales que describan las celebraciones.

MULTIMEDIA: Internet

Have students who are interested look for the Colombian newspaper *El tiempo* on the Internet to find their horoscope in Spanish.

Refrán

«Febrerillo, mes loquillo.»

Write the *refrán* on the board. Point out that *-illo* is a Spanish diminutive. Ask students why they think the diminutive is used here.

Resources: Transparency 39

B. Fechas

Paso 1. Exprese estas fechas en español. ¿En qué estación caen (*do they fall*)?

1. March 7
2. August 24
3. December 1
4. June 5

5. September 19, 1997
6. May 30, 1842
7. January 31, 1660
8. July 4, 1776

Paso 2. ¿Cuándo se celebran?

1. el Día de la Raza (*Columbus Day*)
2. el Día del Año Nuevo
3. el Día de los Enamorados (de San Valentín)
4. el Día de la Independencia de los Estados Unidos

5. el Día de los Inocentes (*Fools*), en los Estados Unidos
6. la Navidad (*Christmas*)
7. su cumpleaños (*birthday*)

> Note that the word **se** before a verb changes the verb's meaning slightly. **¿Cuándo se celebran?** = *When are they celebrated?* You will see this construction throughout *Puntos de partida.* Learn to recognize it, for it is frequently used in Spanish.

NOTA CULTURAL

El Niño

Most people have heard of El Niño, a weather phenomenon that is often associated with devastating climatic events. But why is it called El Niño?

The name El Niño dates from the end of the nineteenth century, when Peruvian fishermen noticed the periodic appearance of an abnormally warm ocean current off the coast of Peru. This warm current made its appearance around Christmas time. The name El Niño is a reference to the Christ Child, or El Niño Jesús, who for Christians also arrived at Christmas. At the time the name only referred to the current. Nowadays, it is used to refer to the meteorological phenomenon as a whole. Torrential rains, flooding, and landslides can occur from the southwestern United States to Peru, whereas in Australia, Indonesia, and southeast Africa, the opposite may happen: severe droughts and the potential for destructive fires.

▲ *Destrucción en California causada por* (caused by) *El Niño*

C. Entrevista: ¡Feliz (*Happy*) **cumpleaños!**

Paso 1. Entreviste a un compañero / una compañera de clase acerca de (*about*) su cumpleaños. Use las siguientes preguntas.

1. ¿Cuál es la fecha de tu cumpleaños?
2. ¿En qué estación es?
3. Generalmente, ¿qué tiempo hace en tu ciudad el día de tu cumpleaños?
4. ¿Cómo celebras tu cumpleaños? (por lo menos tres actividades)
5. ¿Con quién(es) prefieres celebrar tu cumpleaños?

Paso 2. Su profesor(a) o un(a) estudiante va a escribir en la pizarra los nombres de los meses del año. Luego cada estudiante va a escribir la fecha de su cumpleaños en la columna apropiada. ¿En qué mes hay más cumpleaños de los estudiantes de esta clase? ¿Qué signo del horóscopo tienen?

Los signos del horóscopo	
Aries	Libra
Tauro	Escorpión
Géminis	Sagitario
Cáncer	Capricornio
Leo	Acuario
Virgo	Piscis

Vocabulario: Preparación   Ciento sesenta y uno ■ 161

Con. B: Extension

Ask students what holidays they associate with the following.

1. *desfiles* (parades)
2. *tomar/beber champán*
3. *mandar* (to send) *tarjetas, chocolates, flores*
4. *barbacoas y picnics en el parque, fuegos artificiales* (fireworks)
5. *bromas* (jokes)
6. *un árbol decorado, regalos*

Con. B: Extension

■ Write important years on the board and have students say them in Spanish. You might write the event of that year (out of order) to see if students can match the years and events.

1. 1492
2. 1776
3. 1945
4. 2001
5. 1963
6. 1984
7. ¿ ?

a. *la Declaración de la Independencia*
b. *el asesinato de John F. Kennedy*
c. *Cristóbal Colón llega a América*
d. *la bomba atómica*
e. *una película famosa*
f. *la novela de George Orwell*
g. *este año*

■ Give some additional important events in U.S. history and have students give the year.

1. *la llegada de los peregrinos* (pilgrims) *a Plymouth Rock* (1602)
2. *la llegada del primer hombre a la luna* (moon) (1969)
3. *el comienzo* (beginning) *de la Gran Depresión* (1929)
4. *el bombardeo de Pearl Harbor* (1941)
5. *el asesinato del presidente Lincoln* (1963)

NOTA CULTURAL

Suggestion

Ask the following questions to check comprehension.

1. *¿Con qué celebración o figura religiosa se asocia el nombre del fenómeno El Niño?*
2. *¿Qué condiciones climáticas se asocian con El Niño?*

Con. C: Note

Point out the difference between *la fecha de cumpleaños* and *la fecha de nacimiento*.

National Standards: Comparisons

Point out that the seasons in the southern hemisphere are the opposite of those in the U.S. and Canada. Have students associate seasons there, for example, *la primavera = agosto, septiembre, octubre*. Have students talk about how the difference in seasons in this country and South America may affect the dates that are important to them (holidays, birthdays, anniversaries). Would they, in this country, celebrate those dates differently if they fell in a different season? Also, have them calculate when the school year begins and ends in the southern hemisphere. Some schools list their calendars on the Internet.

¿Dónde está?: Las preposiciones

Suggestion

Have students locate their country, city, or university using these prepositions. Write model sentences on the board.

España está al lado de Portugal en la Península Ibérica. Está al sur de Francia y al norte de África.

Bright Idea

Suggestion

Teach students the following rhyme with hand signals.

Izquierda, derecha, delante, detrás, cerca, lejos y algo más, abajo, arriba, delante, encima, y ahora, señores, se acaba la rima.

> Nueva York está al norte de Miami. México está al sur de los Estados Unidos.

La silla está **a la derecha de** la puerta.

Teresa está **entre** Carmen y Pablito.

El libro está **encima de** la mesa.

La mochila está **debajo de** la mesa.

cerca de	close to	**delante de**	in front of
lejos de	far from	**detrás de**	behind
encima de	on top of	**a la izquierda de**	to the left of
debajo de	below	**a la derecha de**	to the right of
al lado de	alongside of	**al este / oeste /**	to the east / west /
entre	between, among	**norte / sur de**	north / south of

NOTA COMUNICATIVA

Los pronombres preposicionales

In Spanish, the pronouns that serve as objects of prepositions are identical in form to the subject pronouns, except for **mí** and **ti**.

Julio está delante de **mí**. *Julio is in front of me.*
María está detrás de **ti**. *María is behind you.*
Me siento a la izquierda de **ella**. *I sit on her left.*

Mí and **ti** combine with the preposition **con** to form **conmigo** (*with me*) and **contigo** (*with you*), respectively.

¿Vienes **conmigo**? *Are you coming with me?*
Sí, voy **contigo**. *Yes, I'll go with you.*

Note that **mí** has a written accent, but **ti** does not. This is to distinguish the object of a preposition (**mí**) from the possessive adjective (**mi**).

National Standards: Comparisons

The origin of the word *izquierda* has been the focus of much debate by linguists. The Latin word for left (*sinister, sinistra, sinistrum*) was not adopted in Spanish due to the negative context that was associated with *sinister*. Despite the existence of a Latinate word for *left*, the Basque word for *izquierda* was adopted instead.

 Heritage Speakers

Invite a los hispanohablantes a explicar la diferencia entre *delante de* y *enfrente de*. Pídales que den ejemplos de las dos expresiones.

Resources: Transparency 40

■ ■ ■ Conversación

A. Entrevista: ¿De dónde eres? Find out as much information as you can about the location of each others' hometown or state, or about the country you are from. You should also tell what the weather is like, and ask if the other person would like to go with you there.

> MODELO: E1: ¿De dónde eres?
> E2: Soy de Reserve.
> E1: ¿Dónde está Reserve?
> E2: Está cerca de…

B. ¿De qué país se habla?

Paso 1. Escuche la descripción que da (*gives*) su profesor(a) de un país de Sudamérica. ¿Puede Ud. identificar el país?

Paso 2. Ahora describa un país de Sudamérica. Sus compañeros de clase van a identificarlo. Siga el modelo, usando (*using*) todas las frases que sean (*are*) apropiadas.

> MODELO: Este país está al norte/sur/este/oeste de _____.
> También está cerca de _____.
> Pero está lejos de _____. Está entre _____ y _____. ¿Cómo se llama?

Paso 3. A la derecha hay una lista de los nombres de las capitales de varios países de Sudamérica. Sin mirar el mapa, empareje (*match*) los nombres con el país correspondiente.

> MODELO: _____ es la capital de _____.

Need more practice?

■ Workbook and Laboratory Manual
■ Interactive CD-ROM
■ Online Learning Center (www.mhhe.com/puntos7)

Capitales	
Asunción	La Paz
Brasilia	Lima
Bogotá	Montevideo
Buenos Aires	Quito
Caracas	Santiago

Vocabulario: Preparación

Con. B: Suggestion

Model a description: *Este país está al sur de los Estados Unidos. También está cerca de Panamá. Pero está lejos de la Argentina. ¿Cómo se llama?*

Con. B: Variations

■ Have students describe the location of someone or something in the classroom as accurately as they can, but without naming the person or object. The rest of the class must guess what or who is being described. For example: *Esta persona está al lado de _____. Está delante de _____ y está detrás de_____?*
Esta cosa (Este objeto) está encima de mi mesa, a la izquierda del libro de español…

■ Play Ten Questions. Think of a person or object in the classroom. Students are allowed ten yes/no questions to locate and identify the person or object, for example, *¿Está lejos de la puerta?* Follow up with students thinking of the object or person.

MULTIMEDIA: Internet

Have students search the Internet for more information about South America's geography, climate, people, economy, transportation, and military. You might assign different countries and have students give brief oral presentations about the geography and climate of their assigned country.

PRONUNCIACIÓN

Preliminary Exercise

Read the following words and have students respond *flap* or *trill*.

para	ahora	rico
parra	ahorra	coro
pero	carro	corro
perro	caro	Roberto

B: Follow-Up

Read and have students repeat the following sentences.

1. *Roberto quiere ir.*
2. *Ramón es rico.*
3. *Raquel Ramírez tiene un perro.*
4. *El perro es rebelde.*
5. *Roberto es el amigo de Ramón.*
6. *Raquel es de Puerto Rico.*

Bright Idea

E: Suggestion

Write the following variation to the tongue twister on the board for students to practice pronouncing the trilled *r*.

Erre con erre, cigarro.
Erre con erre, barril
Rápido ruedan los carros
llevando trigo para el ferrocarril.

E: Variation

Give students the following sentences to read aloud.

1. *El perro de Ramón Ramírez no tiene rabo porque Ramón Ramírez se lo ha cortado.*
2. *Un tigre, dos tigres, tres tristes tigres están comiendo trigo en un trigal.*

PRONUNCIACIÓN *r* and *rr*

Spanish has two **r** sounds, one of which is called a *flap*, the other a *trill*. The rapid pronunciation of *tt* and *dd* in the English words *Betty* and *ladder* produces a sound similar to the Spanish flap **r:** The tongue touches the alveolar ridge (behind the upper teeth) once. Although English has no trill, when English speakers imitate a motor they often produce the Spanish trill, which is a rapid series of flaps.

The trilled **r** is written **rr** between vowels (**carro, correcto**) and **r** at the beginning of a word (**rico, rosa**). Most other **r**'s are pronounced as a flap. Be careful to distinguish between the flap **r** and the trilled **r**. A mispronunciation will often change the meaning of a word—for example, **pero** (*but*) versus **perro** (*dog*).

A. Comparaciones

inglés:	*potter*	*ladder*	*cotter*	*meter*	*total*	*motor*
español:	para	Lara	cara	mire	toro	moro

B. Práctica

1.	rico	**5.**	Ramírez
2.	ropa	**6.**	rebelde
3.	roca	**7.**	reportero
4.	Roberto	**8.**	real

C. ¡Necesito compañero/a! With a classmate, pronounce one word from the following pairs of words, alternatively choosing one containing **r** or **rr**. Your partner will pronounce the one that you did not.

1.	coro/corro	**5.**	ahora/ahorra
2.	coral/corral	**6.**	caro/carro
3.	pero/perro	**7.**	cero/cerro
4.	vara/barra	**8.**	para/parra

D. Pronuncie

1.	el nombre correcto	**7.**	una mujer refinada
2.	un corral grande	**8.**	Enrique, Carlos y Rosita
3.	una norteamericana	**9.**	El perro está en el corral.
4.	Puerto Rico	**10.**	Estos errores son raros.
5.	rosas amarillas	**11.**	Busco un carro caro
6.	un libro negro y rojo	**12.**	Soy el primo de Roberto Ramírez.

E. Trabalenguas (*Tongue twister*)

Paso 1. Listen as your instructor says the following tongue twister.

Erre con erre, guitarra,
Erre con erre, barril;[a]
¡qué rápido corren[b] los carros
del ferrocarril[c]!

[a]*barrel* [b]*run* [c]*train*

Paso 2. Now repeat the tongue twister, paying special attention to the pronunciation of the trilled **r** sound.

 Heritage Speakers

Los puertorriqueños con frecuencia pronuncian la /rr/ como una [l] ante un consonante y como una [x] antes de una vocal: *Pue*[l]*to* [x]*ico.* Si hay estudiantes puertorriqueños en la clase, invítelos a pronunciar en voz alta *Puerto Rico* y otras frases y palabras parecidas.

GRAMÁTICA

15   ¿Qué están haciendo?   •   Present Progressive: *estar + -ndo*

¿Qué están haciendo en Quito, Ecuador?

Hoy es sábado y José Miguel y su madre Elisa no están en la universidad o en el trabajo. ¿Qué *están haciendo*?

José Miguel juega al tenis y levanta pesas con frecuencia. Ahora no *está jugando al tenis*. Tampoco *está levantando* pesas. ¿Qué *está haciendo*? Está _____.

Elisa es periodista. Por eso escribe mucho y habla mucho por teléfono. Pero ahora, no *está escribiendo*. Tampoco *está hablando* por teléfono. ¿Qué *está haciendo*? Está _____.

¿Y Ud.? ¿Qué está haciendo Ud. en este momento?

1. ¿Está estudiando en casa? ¿en clase? ¿en la cafetería?
2. ¿Está leyendo? ¿Está mirando la tele al mismo tiempo?
3. ¿Está escuchando al professor / a la profesora?

Past ----------------- **PRESENT** ----------------- Future
present
present progressive

Uses of the Progressive

In Spanish, you can use special verb forms to describe an action in progress—that is, something actually happening at the time it is being described. These Spanish forms, called **el progresivo,** correspond in form to the English *progressive: I am walking, we are driving, she is studying.* But their use is not identical. Compare the Spanish and English verb forms in the sentences on the next page.

What are they doing in Quito, Equador?   *Today is Saturday, and José Miguel and his mother Elisa aren't at the university or at work. What are they doing? José Miguel often plays tennis and lifts weights. Now he isn't playing tennis. He isn't lifting weights either. What's he doing? He's _____. Elisa is a journalist. Therefore she writes a great deal and she talks on the phone a lot. But now she isn't writing. She isn't talking on the phone either. What's she doing? She's _____.*

Gramática   Ciento sesenta y cinco   ■   **165**

Gramática 15

Present Progressive: *estar + -ndo*

Follow-Up

After covering the *minidiálogo*, ask students the following question.

> *¿Cuáles son algunas actividades que Ud. puede hacer pero que no está haciendo en este momento?*

Coach students, based on activities they mentioned in the previous class discussion.

> *Carlos, ¿estás mirando la televisión en este momento?*

Uses of the Progressive

Suggestions

■ Use visuals to teach the concept of the progressive; students should be able to produce progressive forms by following the models given.

■ Emphasize that the Spanish progressive is used only for describing actions actually in progress. Ask which of the following sentences would be expressed with progressive forms in Spanish.

1. They are reading the newspaper now.
2. Mary is typing all her homework this year.
3. I'm speaking English right now.
4. We're going to San Francisco next summer.

Preliminary Exercise
Have students give new sentences based on the cues.

1. *Todos los amigos de Ud. están en una fiesta. Ud. quiere asistir también. ¿Por qué?*
   Todos están bailando. (tomar, cantar, comer, abrir botellas de champán, hablar mucho)

   Point out that *todos* means *everyone* and is used with a plural verb.

2. *Pero Ud. no puede ir. ¿Por qué no?*
   Estoy estudiando. (trabajar, escribir los ejercicios, leer el periódico, mirar un programa muy interesante, aprender el vocabulario nuevo)

In Spanish, the present progressive is used primarily to describe an action that is actually *in progress*, as in the first example. The simple Spanish present is used in other cases where English would use the present progressive: to tell what is going to happen (the second sentence), and to tell what someone is doing over a period of time but not necessarily at this very moment (the third sentence).

1. Ramón **está comiendo** ahora mismo.
   Ramón is eating right now.

2. **Compramos** la casa mañana.
   We're buying the house tomorrow.

3. Adelaida **estudia** química este semestre.
   Adelaida is studying chemistry this semester.

Formation of the Present Progressive

A. The Spanish present progressive is formed with **estar** plus the *present participle* (**el gerundio**).

The present participle is formed by adding **-ando** to the stem of **-ar** verbs and **-iendo** to the stem of **-er** and **-ir** verbs.*

The present participle never varies; it always ends in **-o.**

estar + present participle

tomar → **tomando**   *taking; drinking*
comprender → **comprendiendo**   *understanding*
abrir → **abriendo**   *opening*

 Unaccented **i** represents the sound [y] in the participle ending **-iendo: comiendo, viviendo.** Unaccented **i** between two vowels becomes the letter **y:**
    leer: **le + iendo = leyendo**
    oír: **o + iendo = oyendo**

B. The stem vowel in the present participle of **-ir** stem-changing verbs also shows a change. From this point on in *Puntos de partida,* both stem changes for **-ir** verbs will be given with infinitives in vocabulary lists.

preferir (ie, i) → **prefiriendo**   *preferring*
pedir (i, i) → **pidiendo**   *asking*
dormir (ue, u) → **durmiendo**   *sleeping*

Using Pronouns with the Present Progressive

Reflexive pronouns may be attached to a present participle or precede the conjugated form of **estar.** Note the use of a written accent mark when pronouns are attached to the present participle.

Pablo **se** está bañando. }
Pablo está bañándo**se.** } *Pablo is taking a bath.*

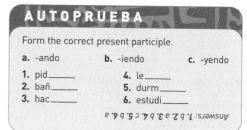

AUTOPRUEBA

Form the correct present participle.

a. -ando   b. -iendo   c. -yendo

1. pid_____   4. le_____
2. bañ_____   5. durm_____
3. hac_____   6. estudi_____

Answers: 1. b 2. a 3. b 4. c 5. b 6. a

*Ir, poder, and venir have irregular present participles: **yendo, pudiendo, viniendo.** These three verbs, however, are seldom used in the progressive.

 Heritage Speakers

Los tiempos progresivos también pueden formarse combinando el gerundio con los verbos *andar, continuar, ir, seguir* y *venir* (véase los ejemplos a la derecha). Invite a los estudiantes hispanohablantes a dar algunos ejemplos de estas construcciones. ¿Se puede usar el verbo *estar* en las mismas construcciones?

Carlos anda buscando su abrigo.
Estos días vamos entendiéndolo mejor.
Sigue lloviendo.
Lorena siempre viene quejándose de algo.

■■■ Práctica

A. ¡Anticipemos! Un sábado típico. Indique lo que Ud. está haciendo a las horas indicadas en un sábado típico. En algunos (*some*) casos hay más de una respuesta (*answer*) posible.

A las ocho de la mañana…   SÍ   NO

1. estoy durmiendo.   ☐   ☐
2. estoy tomando el desayuno.   ☐   ☐
3. estoy mirando los dibujos animados   ☐   ☐
   (*cartoons*) en la tele.
4. estoy duchándome.   ☐   ☐
5. estoy haciendo ejercicio.   ☐   ☐
6. estoy trabajando.   ☐   ☐
7. estoy _____.   ☐   ☐

A mediodía (*noon*)…   SÍ   NO

1. estoy durmiendo.   ☐   ☐
2. estoy almorzando.   ☐   ☐
3. estoy estudiando.   ☐   ☐
4. estoy practicando algún deporte.   ☐   ☐
5. estoy viendo una película.   ☐   ☐
6. estoy trabajando.   ☐   ☐
7. estoy _____.   ☐   ☐

A las diez de la noche…   SÍ   NO

1. estoy durmiendo.   ☐   ☐
2. estoy preparándome para salir.   ☐   ☐
3. estoy mirando un programa en la tele.   ☐   ☐
4. estoy bailando en una fiesta o en   ☐   ☐
   una discoteca.
5. estoy trabajando.   ☐   ☐
6. estoy hablando por teléfono con   ☐   ☐
   un amigo / una amiga.
7. estoy _____.   ☐   ☐

B. Un día especial. Ricardo Guzmán Rama, el tío de Lola Benítez, acaba de llegar (*has just arrived*) de México para visitar a su familia en Sevilla. Por eso, hoy es un día especial. Complete las siguientes oraciones para indicar lo que (*what*) está pasando en este momento en la familia de Lola.

> **MODELO:** Casi siempre, Lola *desayuna* con su hija por la mañana. Hoy Lola… (desayunar con su tío en un café) →
> *está desayunando* con su tío en un café.

1. Generalmente, Lola está en la universidad toda la mañana. Hoy Lola… (hablar con su tío Ricardo)
2. Casi siempre, Lola va a casa después de sus clases. Hoy Lola y su tío… (tomar un café en la universidad)
3. De lunes a viernes, la hija Marta va a la escuela (*school*) por la tarde. Ahora, a las dos de la tarde ella… (jugar con Ricardo)
4. Generalmente, la familia come a las dos. Hoy todos… (comer a las tres)

Gramática

Prác. A: Variation

Have students select someone to talk about (*amigo/a, compañero/a de cuarto, esposo/a*) and do the items in this activity using *nosotros.*

Prác. B: Follow-Up

Ask students the following personal questions.

1. *¿Está Ud. hablando español ahora? ¿cantando? ¿tomando Coca-Cola? ¿escribiendo?*
2. *¿Están Uds. bailando ahora? ¿regresando a casa? ¿regateando? ¿leyendo? ¿hablando con el profesor / la profesora?*

☀ Heritage Speakers

Los tiempos progresivos se usan para expresar acciones en curso, sean del presente o del pasado. El verbo *estar* puede conjugarse en cualquier tiempo verbal (*estoy / estaba / estuve / estaré / estaría comiendo*), pero el presente progresivo y el imperfecto progresivo ocurren con mayor frecuencia. Invite a los hispanohablantes a explicar la diferencia entre *Están viendo las noticias* y *Estarán viendo las noticias.*

MULTIMEDIA: Internet

Have students search the Internet for information and pictures of Seville. You might assign specific topics and have students give brief oral presentations based on their findings.

Generalmente, ¿qué está haciendo Ud. / su familia a las 6 de la mañana?
¿a las 8 de la mañana?
¿a las 7:30 de la tarde?
¿a las 9:30 de la noche?

♻ **Reciclado**

Remind students that with reflexive verbs, the article is used instead of the possessive adjective with body parts and personal possessions.

María se quita el sombrero / los zapatos / los guantes.

C. En casa con la familia Duarte

Paso 1. The Duarte family leads a busy life. Each set of drawings shows what the parents, the teen-age daughter, and the twins are doing at a particular time of their day. Read the following sentences and tell to which set each statement refers.

MODELO: Se está duchando. → por la mañana

1. Está levantándose.
2. Está haciendo la tarea.
3. Se está vistiendo.
4. Está preparando la cena (*dinner*).
5. Está leyendo el periódico.
6. Están durmiendo.
7. Está trabajando.
8. Están jugando con el perro.
9. Están comiendo.
10. Está quitándose la blusa.

Por la mañana

Más tarde

Por la tarde

Paso 2. Now tell what is happening at each time of day.

MODELO: Son las seis de la mañana. Los niños están...

Need more practice?
- Workbook and Laboratory Manual
- Interactive CD-ROM
- Online Learning Center (www.mhhe.com/ puntos7)

Resources: Transparency 41

NOTA COMUNICATIVA

El gerundio con otros verbos

As in English, the Spanish gerund can be used with verbs other than **estar**. The following verbs are commonly used with the gerund.

pasar tiempo + (gerund)	to spend time (doing something)
seguir (i) (g)/continuar + (gerund)	to continue (doing something)
¿**Pasas** mucho tiempo **viendo** la televisión?	Do you spend a lot of time watching television?
Sigue lloviendo en Nueva York.	It continues to rain in New York.

■ ■ ■ Conversación

Entrevista

1. ¿Pasas más tiempo leyendo o mirando la televisión? ¿tocando o escuchando música? ¿trabajando o estudiando? ¿estudiando o viajando?
2. ¿Cómo te diviertes más, mirando la tele o bailando en una fiesta? ¿practicando un deporte o leyendo una buena novela? ¿haciendo un *picnic* o preparando una cena (*dinner*) elegante en casa? ¿mirando una película en casa o en el cine?

EN LOS ESTADOS UNIDOS Y EL CANADÁ

Alfredo Jaar

Upon arriving in the United States, Chilean artist Alfredo Jaar was surprised to learn that English speakers generally don't think of Canadians, Mexicans, Colombians, and so forth as "Americans." It bothered him that he was perceived as "Hispanic" or "Latin" but not as "American." "This country has co-opted the word *America*," he claimed.

So, Jaar used his artistic talents in an effort to enlighten people in the United States about the true meaning of the word *America*. He created a computerized animation that appeared on a sign board above New York City's Times Square in April 1987. The computer animation depicted a lighted map of the United States with the statement "This is not America" written across it. Slowly the word *America* grew larger and larger until it filled the entire sign. At the same time, the letter *R* trans-

▲ *El arte electrónico de Alfredo Jaar*

formed itself into a map of North and South America. This use of *America* is the meaning used in Spanish, the meaning that Jaar had known.

The message that Jaar was trying to send was that *America* does not belong only to the United States. Another thirty-three nations say that they are a part of America and that their approximately 500 million inhabitants are also Americans.

Jaar was also trying to combat the stereotype that all Hispanics are alike and that all the inhabitants of South America are Hispanics. For one thing, many inhabitants of South America are Brazilians, and thus of Portuguese rather than of Spanish heritage. In addition, there are many indigenous peoples throughout the Americas that have traditions, cultures, and languages that precede Columbus's arrival in this hemisphere.

Con: Note

This activity shows how the present participle functions with other verbs, just as in the English sentence *Did you spend more time reading or watching TV?* Past participles can also function as nouns in English, but not in Spanish; only the infinitive functions as a noun in Spanish:

- subject: I like **reading.** = *Me gusta leer.*
- object of a preposition: I insist on **traveling** today. = *Insisto en viajar hoy.*

Students do not have to know these linguistic facts, yet they certainly can profit from knowing this information. For now, remind students that Spanish cannot use a present participle after a preposition, only an infinitive.

Con: Suggestion

Have students work in pairs and then report comparisons to the class.

Fred pasa más tiempo leyendo y yo paso más tiempo viendo la tele.
Fred y yo pasamos más tiempo leyendo.

EN LOS ESTADOS UNIDOS Y EL CANADÁ

Have students look up the following terms in a Spanish-Spanish dictionary: *americano, estadounidense, hispano, latino, latinoamericano, norteamericano.* Then, have them look up the English equivalents in an English-English dictionary (if there are such equivalents). Talk about the semantic and cultural differences between the same terms in both languages.

MULTIMEDIA: Internet

There are websites that display some of Jaar's other creations, for example, "The Eyes of Gutet Emerita." Have students search the Internet to find more images. Encourage them to describe the images they find.

Summary of the Uses of *ser* and *estar*

Follow-Up

Ask the following questions to check comprehension of the *minidiálogo*.

1. *¿Quiénes son las dos personas?*
2. *¿Dónde están?*
3. *¿Qué están haciendo en este momento?*
4. *¿Es una situación normal? ¿Es agradable para los esposos?*
5. *¿A la esposa le gusta viajar?*

Suggestions

- Review the uses of *ser* and *estar.*
- Have students give additional examples of each use listed, where possible.
- Have students explain why *ser* and *estar* are used each time in the *minidiálogo.*
- Point out that *ser* is used to tell where an event takes place, for example, *El baile (La fiesta, La reunión) es en la calle Goya.* This use is presented in *Capítulo 8.*
- Have students reenact the conversation as if they were talking on the phone. Have students sit back-to-back, if possible. Emphasize that they don't have to memorize the whole conversation on the phone between the two spouses.
- Assume the identity of a famous person (actor, artist, singer, athlete, and so on). Have students ask you yes/no questions in order to determine your identity. They may ask about your place of origin, your personality traits, your nationality, your profession, and so on. Model questions to get them started.

1. *¿Es Ud. hombre?* (mujer/niño/animal)
2. *¿Es Ud. viejo?* (joven/guapo/rubio/moreno)
3. *¿Es de los Estados Unidos?* (del Canadá / de México)
4. *¿Es casado?* (soltero/viudo)
5. *¿Está en* (lugar) *hoy?*
6. *¿Está muy ocupado con su vida estos días?* (contento)
7. *¿Está en* (programa de televisión / película)?

You have been using forms of **ser** and **estar** since **Ante todo,** the preliminary chapter of *Puntos de partida.* The following section will help you consolidate everything you know so far about these two verbs, both of which express *to be* in Spanish. You will learn a bit more about them as well.

Before you begin, think in particular about the following questions: **¿Cómo está Ud? ¿Cómo es Ud.?** What do these questions tell you about the difference between **ser** and **estar?**

16 ¿Ser o estar? • Summary of the Uses of *ser* and *estar*

Una conversación por larga distancia

Aquí hay un lado de la conversación entre una esposa que *está* en un viaje de negocios y su esposo, que *está* en casa. Habla el esposo. ¿Qué contesta la esposa?

Aló. [...¹] ¿Cómo *estás*, mi amor? [...²] ¿Dónde *estás* ahora? [...³] ¿Qué hora *es* allí? [...⁴] ¡Huy!, *es* muy tarde. Y el hotel, ¿cómo *es*? [...⁵] Oye, ¿qué *estás* haciendo ahora? [...⁶] Ay, pobrita, lo siento. *Estás* muy ocupada. ¿Con quién *estás* citada mañana? [...⁷] ¿Quién *es* el dueño de la compañía? [...⁸] Ah, él *es* de Cuba, ¿verdad? [...⁹] Bueno, ¿qué tiempo hace allí? [...¹⁰] Muy bien, mi vida. Hasta luego, ¿eh? [...¹¹] Adiós.

Comprensión

Aquí está el otro lado de la conversación... pero las respuestas no están en orden. Ponga las respuestas en el orden apropiado.

a. _____ Es muy moderno. Me gusta mucho.
b. _____ Sí, pero vive en Nueva York ahora.
c. _____ Son las once y media.
d. _____ Hola, querido (*dear*). ¿Qué tal?
e. _____ Es el Sr. Cortina.
f. _____ Pues, todavía (*still*) tengo que trabajar.
g. _____ Sí, hasta pronto.
h. _____ Estoy en Nueva York.
i. _____ Un poco cansada (*tired*), pero estoy bien.
j. _____ Pues, hace buen tiempo, pero está un poco nublado.
k. _____ Con un señor de Computec, una nueva compañía de computadoras.

A long-distance conversation Here is one side of a conversation between a wife who is on a business trip and her husband, who is at home. The husband is speaking. What does the wife answer? Hello . . . How are you, dear? . . . Where are you now? . . . What time is it there? . . . Boy, it's very late. And how's the hotel? . . . Hey, what are you doing now? . . . You poor thing, I'm sorry. You're very busy. Who are you meeting with tomorrow? . . . Who's the owner of the company? . . . Ah, he's from Cuba, isn't he? . . . Well, what's the weather like? Very well, sweetheart. See you later, OK? . . . Good-bye.

170 ■ Ciento setenta

Capítulo 5: Las estaciones y el tiempo

National Standards: Comparisons

Point out the use of different expressions to answer the telephone in Spanish: *aló* in many Latin American countries, *bueno* in Mexico, and *diga* or *dígame* in Spain. To ask who is calling in order to pass the message, Spanish speakers generally ask *¿De parte de quién?*

Summary of the Uses of *ser*

- To *identify* people and things

  Ella **es doctora.**
  Tikal **es una ciudad maya.**

- To express *nationality;* with **de** to express *origin*

  Son cubanos.
  Son de La Habana.

- With **de** to tell of what *material* something is made.

  Este bolígrafo **es de plástico.**

- With **de** to express *possession*

  Es de Carlota.

- With **para** to tell *for whom something is intended*

  El regalo **es para Sara.**

- To tell *time*

  Son las once.
  Es la una y media.

- With *adjectives* that describe *basic, inherent characteristics*

  Ramona **es inteligente.**

- To form many *generalizations*

  Es necesario llegar temprano.
  Es importante estudiar.

Summary of the Uses of *estar*

- To tell *location*

  El libro **está en la mesa.**

- To describe *health*

  Estoy muy **bien,** gracias.

- With *adjectives* that describe *conditions*

  Estoy muy **ocupada.**

- In a number of *fixed expressions*

  (No) Estoy de acuerdo.
  Está bien.

- With *present participles* to form the *progressive tense*

  Estoy estudiando ahora mismo.

Ser and *estar* with Adjectives

A. Ser is used with adjectives that describe the fundamental qualities of a person, place, or thing.

Esa mujer es muy **baja.**
That woman is very short.

Sus calcetines son **morados.**
His socks are purple.

Este sillón es **cómodo.**
This armchair is comfortable.

Sus padres son **cariñosos.**
Their parents are affectionate people.

Suggestion
Have students identify which verb would be used with the following.

  con la hora
  con participios presentes
  con generalizaciones
  para expresar posesión
  para expresar locación
  para expresar nacionalidad
  para indicar el material

Ser and *estar* with Adjectives

Emphasis A: Suggestion
Point out that *ser* + adjective represents the norm; *estar* + adjective represents a change from the norm.

♻ Reciclado
In *Ante todo* students learned that *ser* is also used to express time. Review the use of *ser* with time expressions.

Suggestions
- Review adjective-noun placement with students.
- Have students provide the four forms for adjectives ending in *-o.*
- Have students explain forms for adjectives of nationality such as *francés, inglés, portugués,* and *irlandés.*

Resources: Transparency 42

Emphasis B: Suggestion

Point out that *estar* is used to express an unexpected quality.

> *¡Qué fría está el agua!*

To express what is expected, *ser* is used.

> *El agua es fría.* (The speaker expects the water to be cold.)

Emphasis B: Suggestion

Offer the following additional vocabulary: *de buen humor, de mal humor, enojado/a, enfadado/a, roto/a.*

Emphasis C: Suggestion

Point out that to express how something looks, tastes, feels, or appears, *estar* is used. Contrast pairs of sentences and meanings found in this section.

Emphasis C: Note

Point out that *Daniel está muy guapo esta noche* does not imply that he is by nature ugly, but rather comments on his appearance at a given point in time (he is especially handsome) or expresses the surprise of the speaker at how handsome he is tonight.

Preliminary Exercises

■ Have students tell whether *ser* or *estar* is required for the following sentences.

1. She is a very pretty woman.
2. María is very pretty tonight.
3. I'm nervous because of the test.
4. We are in class now.
5. These students are from the U.S.
6. It's 2:00.
7. This is my mom.

■ Have students form sentences based on the cues, for example,

> *¿El vestido? (muy elegante) →*
> *El vestido es muy elegante.*

1. *¿John? (norteamericano)*
2. *¿Mi escritorio? (desordenado)*
3. *¿Los Hernández (The Hernández family)? (ocupados)*
4. *¿Yo? (muy bien)*
5. *¿Su abuelo? (muy viejo)*
6. *¿El problema? (difícil)*
7. *¿María? (de acuerdo con nosotros)*
8. *¿Mis hijos? (simpáticos y buenos)*
9. *¿La tienda? (abierta ahora)*

B. Estar is used with adjectives to express conditions or observations that are true at a given moment but that do not describe inherent qualities of the noun. The following adjectives are generally used with **estar.**

abierto/a	open	**limpio/a**	clean
aburrido/a	bored	**loco/a**	crazy
alegre	happy	**nervioso/a**	nervous
cansado/a	tired	**ocupado/a**	busy
cerrado/a	closed	**ordenado/a**	neat
congelado/a	frozen; very cold	**preocupado/a**	worried
contento/a	content, happy	**seguro/a**	sure, certain
desordenado/a	messy	**sucio/a**	dirty
enfermo/a	sick	**triste**	sad
furioso/a	furious, angry		

C. Many adjectives can be used with either **ser** or **estar,** depending on what the speaker intends to communicate. In general, when *to be* implies *looks, feels,* or *appears,* **estar** is used. Compare the following pairs of sentences.

Daniel **es** guapo.
Daniel is handsome. (He is a handsome person.)

Daniel **está** muy guapo esta noche.
Daniel looks very nice (handsome) tonight.

—¿Cómo **es** Amalia?
What is Amalia like (as a person)?
—**Es** simpática.
She's nice.

—¿Cómo **está** Amalia?
How is Amalia (feeling)?
—**Está** enferma todavía.
She's still sick.

AUTOPRUEBA

¿Ser o estar?

	SER	ESTAR
1. to describe a health condition	☐	☐
2. to tell time	☐	☐
3. to describe inherent qualities	☐	☐
4. to tell where a thing or person is located	☐	☐

Answers: 1. estar 2. ser 3. ser 4. estar

■■■ Práctica

A. Un regalo especial. Hay algo nuevo en el comedor. Es una computadora. ¿Qué puede Ud. decir de ella (*say about it*)? Haga oraciones completas con **es** o **está.**

La computadora es / está...

1. en la mesa del comedor.
2. un regalo de cumpleaños.
3. para mi compañero de cuarto.
4. de la tienda Computec.
5. en una caja (*box*) verde.
6. de los padres de mi compañero.
7. un regalo muy caro pero estupendo.
8. de metal y plástico gris.
9. una IBM, el último (*latest*) modelo.
10. muy fácil (*easy*) de usar.

Capítulo 5: Las estaciones y el tiempo

Por often expresses *because of* or *about*, especially with adjectives such as **preocupado, nervioso, contento,** and **furioso.**

Amalia está preocupada **por** los exámenes finales.
Amalia is worried about her final exams.

B. ¿Quiénes son? Ahora describa a los jóvenes que aparecen en esta foto, utilizando los verbos **son** y **están.**

Los jóvenes son/están…

1. mis primos argentinos.
2. de Buenos Aires.
3. aquí este mes para visitar a la familia.
4. al lado de los abuelos en la foto.
5. muy simpáticos.
6. muy contentos con el viaje en general.
7. un poco cansados por el viaje.

C. Actividades sociales. Complete the following description with the correct form of **ser** or **estar,** as suggested by the context.

as fiestas

Las fiestas (ser/estar[1]) populares entre los jóvenes de todas partes del mundo. Ofrecen una buena oportunidad para (ser/estar[2]) con los amigos y conocer[a] a nuevas personas. Imagine que Ud. (ser/estar[3]) en una fiesta con unos amigos hispanos en este momento: todos (ser/estar[4]) alegres, comiendo, hablando y bailando… ¡Y (ser/estar[5]) las dos de la mañana!

Los amigos
Ahora en el mundo hispánico no (ser/estar[6]) necesario tener chaperona. Muchas de las actividades sociales se dan[b] en grupos. Si Ud. (ser/estar[7]) parte de un grupo de amigos, sus amigos (ser/estar[8]) el centro de su vida social y Ud. y su novio[c] o novia salen frecuentemente con otras parejas[d] o personas del grupo.

¡Son!

[a]*meet* [b]*se… occur* [c]*boyfriend* [d]*couples*

Comprensión: ¿Sí o no? ¿Son estas las opiniones de un joven hispano?

1. Me gustan mucho las fiestas.
2. Nunca bailamos en las fiestas.
3. Es necesario salir con chaperona.
4. Mis amigos tienen poca importancia para mí.

Gramática   Ciento setenta y tres ■ **173**

☀ **Heritage Speakers**

Pregúnteles a los hispanohablantes de la clase cómo son sus amistades en este país. ¿Tienen un grupo grande de amigos? ¿Son todos sus amigos íntimos (*close*) hispanos? ¿Se reúnen regularmente?

Prác. A, B: Preliminary Exercise

Start both activities by asking for basic information.

¿Qué es?
¿Quién es?
¿Dónde está?
¿Cómo es?
¿Tiene una computadora?
¿Dónde está?
¿Le gusta?

Prác. A, B: Suggestion

Have students justify the use of *ser* or *estar* in each case.

Prác. B: Follow-Up

■ Think or have students think of an object or a person without saying who or what it is. Have students ask questions to guess.

¿Dónde está?
¿Cómo es?
¿De qué color es?
¿De dónde es?

■ Have students bring in magazine clippings and ask questions with *ser* and *estar* about the images.

Prác. B: Variation

Have students choose an object or person and create their own *ser/estar* sentences about it.

1. *la (sala de) clase*
2. *el profesor / la profesora*
3. *los estudiantes de la clase* (students use *nosotros*)

Prác. C: Suggestion

Follow the previous suggestions for handling contextual paragraph activities.

Prác. C: Follow-Up

Ask students the following questions to check comprehension and to personalize.

1. *¿Son populares las fiestas en esta universidad?*
2. *¿Cuándo hay fiestas aquí?*
3. *¿Tiene Ud. un grupo de amigos? ¿Cuántas personas hay en su grupo, más o menos?*

Prác. D: Note

The purpose of this activity is to give students practice with the "new" adjectives presented in the preceding section. No *ser* vs. *estar* decisions are called for.

Prác. D: Follow-Up

■ Have students talk about more permanent traits of the house and its inhabitants by making sentences with *ser: La casa es grande.*

■ Have students imagine what the following people are doing at 6:30 in the afternoon.

1. *Ud.*
2. *su profesor(a)*
3. *dos compañeros de clase*
4. *sus padres (hijos)*
5. *los españoles*

D. Una tarde terrible

Paso 1. Describa lo que (*what*) pasa hoy por la tarde en esta casa, cambiando por antónimos las palabras indicadas.

1. No hace *buen* tiempo; hace _____.
2. El bebé no está *bien*; está _____.
3. El gato no está *limpio*; está _____.
4. El esposo no está *tranquilo*; está _____ por el bebé.
5. El garaje no está *cerrado*; está _____.
6. Los niños no están *ocupados*; están _____.
7. La esposa no está *contenta*; está _____ por el tiempo.
8. El baño no está *ordenado*; está _____.

Paso 2. Ahora imagine que son las 6:30 de la tarde. Exprese lo que están haciendo los miembros de la familia en este momento. Use su imaginación y diga también lo que generalmente hacen estas personas a esa hora.

> MODELO: Hoy, a las seis y media, la madre está conduciendo su coche a casa. Generalmente prepara la comida a esa hora.

Palabras útiles	
cenar	to have dinner
conducir (conduzco)	to drive
ladrar	to bark
llorar	to cry

Need more practice?

■ Workbook and Laboratory Manual
■ Interactive CD-ROM
■ Online Learning Center (www.mhhe.com/puntos7)

 Heritage Speakers

En Latinoamérica, es más común usar el verbo *manejar* o *guiar* para expresar *to drive*, pero en España se dice *conducir*. Pregúnteles a los hispanohablantes de la clase qué término prefieren usar.

Resources: Transparency 43

■■■ Conversación

A. Ana y Estela. Describa este dibujo de un cuarto típico de la residencia. Conteste las preguntas e invente los detalles necesarios.

> **Palabras útiles**
>
> **el cajón** (drawer)
> **el cartel** (poster)
> **la foto**

1. ¿Quiénes son las dos compañeras de cuarto?
2. ¿De dónde son? ¿Cómo son?
3. ¿Dónde están en este momento?
4. ¿Qué hay en el cuarto?
5. ¿En qué condición está el cuarto?
6. ¿Son ordenadas o desordenadas las dos?

Ana   Estela

B. Sentimientos. Complete the following sentences by telling how you feel in the situations described. Then ask questions of other students in the class to find at least one person who completed a given sentence the way you did.

MODELO: Cuando saco (*I get*) una «A» en un examen, estoy _alegre._ →
¿Cómo te sientes (*do you feel*) cuando sacas una «A» en un examen?

1. Cuando el profesor / la profesora da una tarea difícil, estoy _____.
2. Cuando tengo mucho trabajo, estoy _____.
3. En otoño generalmente estoy _____ porque _____.
4. En verano estoy _____ porque _____.
5. Cuando llueve (nieva), estoy _____ porque _____.
6. Los lunes por la mañana estoy _____.
7. Los viernes por la noche estoy _____.
8. Cuando me acuesto muy tarde, estoy _____ al día siguiente (*the next day*).

Gramática   Ciento setenta y cinco ■ **175**

☀ Heritage Speakers

■ Pídales a los estudiantes hispanohablantes que hagan una lista de términos como *chicano, boricua* y *pachuco.* Pídales que le expliquen al resto de la clase el sentido de estos términos.

■ Invite a los estudiantes hispanohablantes a investigar entre sus familiares cuál es su opinión con respecto al término *americano* cuando sólo es empleado para referirse a los ciudadanos de los Estados Unidos. Pídales que compartan estas opiniones con el resto de la clase.

Resources: Transparency 44

Con. A: Suggestion

Have students prepare descriptions of famous people, using a minimum of five sentences. Then have volunteers present their descriptions to the class. For example:

> Elizabeth Taylor → *Es una actriz. Es muy guapa. Es muy rica. Tiene muchos diamantes. Tiene muchos ex esposos.*

Con. A: Extension

Bring or have students bring magazine ads and clippings to class. Have students describe what they see and invent background stories. Use questions similar to those in *Conversación A* to get students going.

Con. B: Extension

9. *Cuando otra persona habla y habla y habla, _____.*
10. *Cuando estoy con mi familia, _____.*
11. *Cuando estoy de vacaciones, _____.*
12. *Cuando tengo problemas con mi coche, _____.*
13. *Cuando voy al consultorio del dentista, _____.*

Con. B: Variation

Have students complete sentences, telling what they are usually doing if they are (adjective).

1. *Estoy preocupado/a cuando _____.*
2. *Estoy aburrido/a cuando _____.*
3. *Estoy furioso/a cuando _____.*
4. *Estoy de buen/mal humor cuando _____.*

Con. B: Suggestion

Read the following places aloud and have students tell where they are.

1. *Madrid, Barcelona, Toledo, Segovia*
2. *Bolivia, Colombia, el Paraguay, el Brasil*
3. *Acapulco, Cancún, Puerto Vallarta*
4. *Costa Rica, Guatemala, Nicaragua, Panamá*
5. *Amarillo, Toledo, Santa Cruz, San Agustín*

Follow-Up

Have students compare their university with another.

> ¿Cuál es más grande?
> ¿Es tan cara su universidad como _____ (la otra)?
> Los estudiantes de esta universidad, ¿estudian tanto como los estudiantes de la otra (universidad)?

Bright Idea

Follow-Up

Have students compare their city with New York, Chicago, Toronto, or Montreal.

> ¿Cuál es más grande/pequeña?
> ¿Cuál tiene edificios más altos?
> ¿Cuál es más bonita?
> ¿Cuál es más/menos cosmopolita?

17 Describing • Comparisons

Dos ciudades

▲ México, D.F. (Distrito Federal)

◀ El barrio de Santa Cruz, Sevilla, España

Ricardo, el tío de Lola Benítez, hace comparaciones entre la Ciudad de México, o el D.F. (Distrito Federal), y Sevilla.

«De verdad, me gustan las dos ciudades.

- La Ciudad de México es *más* grande *que* Sevilla.
- Tiene *más* edificios altos *que* Sevilla.
- En el D.F. no hace *tanto* calor *como* en Sevilla.

Pero…

- Sevilla es *tan* bonita *como* la Ciudad de México.
- No tiene *tantos* habitantes *como* el D.F.
- Sin embargo, los sevillanos son *tan* simpáticos *como* los mexicanos.

En total, ¡me gusta Sevilla *tanto como* la Ciudad de México!»

Ahora, hable Ud. de su ciudad o pueblo.

Mi ciudad/pueblo…

- (no) es tan grande como Chicago
- es más/menos cosmopolita que Quebec

Me gusta _____ (nombre de mi ciudad/pueblo)

- más que _____ (nombre de otra ciudad)
- menos que _____ (nombre de otra ciudad)
- tanto como _____ (nombre de otra ciudad)

Equal Comparisons		Unequal Comparisons
tan _____ como	**With Adjectives or Adverbs**	más/menos _____ que
tanto/a/os/as _____ como	**With Nouns**	
_____ tanto como	**With Verbs**	_____ más/menos que

Two cities *Ricardo, Lola Benítez's uncle, makes comparisons between Mexico City, or **el D.F.** (Federal District), and Seville. Really, I like both cities. ■ Mexico City is bigger than Seville. ■ It has more tall buildings than Seville. ■ It is not as hot in Mexico City as it is in Seville. But . . . ■ Seville is as beautiful as Mexico City. ■ It doesn't have as many inhabitants as Mexico City. ■ Nevertheless, the people from Seville are as nice as those from Mexico City. All told, I like Seville as much as Mexico City!*

176 ■ Capítulo 5: Las estaciones y el tiempo

MULTIMEDIA: Internet

Have students search the Internet for more information on attractions and tourism in Mexico City or Seville. You might assign specific topics and have students give brief oral presentations based on their findings.

☀ **Heritage Speakers**

Pídales a los estudiantes hispanohablantes que busquen información sobre la historia de la Ciudad de México o de Sevilla en la biblioteca y en el Internet. Anímelos a escribir varios párrafos acerca de la ciudad que escojan.

In English the *comparative* (**el comparativo**) is formed in a variety of ways. Equal comparisons are expressed with the word *as*. Unequal comparisons are expressed with the adverbs *more* or *less*, or by adding *-er* to the end of the adjective.

as cold *as*
as many *as*

more intelligent, **less** important
tall**er**, smart**er**

Comparison of Adjectives

EQUAL COMPARISONS	
tan + *adjective* + **como** (*as*) (*as*)	Enrique es **tan** trabajador **como** Amalia. *Enrique is as hardworking as Amalia.*

UNEQUAL COMPARISONS (REGULAR)	
más + *adjective* + **que** (*more*) (*than*)	Alicia es **más** perezosa **que** Marta. *Alicia is lazier than Marta.*
menos + *adjective* + **que** (*less*) (*than*)	Julio es **menos** listo **que** Jaime. *Julio is not as bright as Jaime.*

UNEQUAL COMPARATIVES WITH IRREGULAR FORMS	
bueno/a → mejor	Estos coches son **buenos,** pero esos son **mejores.** *These cars are good, but those are better.*
malo/a → peor	Mi lámpara es **peor que** esta. *My lamp is worse than this one.*
mayor (*older*)	Mi hermana es **mayor que** yo. *My sister is older than I (am).*
menor (*younger*)	Mis primos son **menores que** yo. *My cousins are younger than I (am).*

Comparison of Nouns

EQUAL COMPARISONS	
Tanto must agree in gender and number with the noun it modifies.	Alicia tiene **tantas** bolsas **como** Pati. *Alicia has as many purses as Pati* (*does*).
tanto/a/os/as + *noun* + **como** (*as much/many*) (*as*)	Pablo tiene **tanto** dinero **como** Sergio. *Pablo has as much money as Sergio* (*does*).

Comparison of Adjectives

Suggestions

- Point out the plural forms of irregular comparisons.
- Explain that *más grande* and *más pequeño* refer to size. *Mayor* and *menor* generally refer to age.
- Use model sentences to emphasize the exception, for example: *No tengo más que un hijo* (only one).

Comparison of Nouns

Suggestion

To practice comparisons, have students list the following information. Then have them ask each other questions about these topics and compare each others' information.

- how many classes they take and how many credits they have
- what time they generally get up and go to bed, and how many hours they sleep
- how old they are
- how many siblings or children they have
- how many hours per week they study

Preliminary Exercises

■ Have students name someone who meets the following criteria.

Dé el nombre de alguien...

1. *tan guapo como Enrique Iglesias.*
2. *tan bonita como Shakira.*
3. *tan rico como los Rockefeller.*
4. *tan inteligente como Einstein.*
5. *tan fiel como Romeo y Julieta.*

■ Have students tell if they have the following.

¿Tiene Ud.... ?

1. *¿tanto dinero como los Rockefeller?*
2. *¿tantos años como su profesor(a) de español?*
3. *¿tantas clases como su compañero/a de cuarto (esposo/a)?*
4. *¿tantos problemas como su mejor amigo/a?*
5. *¿tantos tíos como tías?*

UNEQUAL COMPARISONS

más/menos + *noun* + **que**
(more/less)   *(than)*

Alicia tiene **más/menos** bolsas **que** Susana.
Alicia has more/fewer purses than Susana (does).

The preposition **de** is used when the comparison is followed by a number.

más/menos de + *noun*
(more/less than)

Alicia tiene **más de** cinco bolsas.
Alicia has more than five purses.

[Práctica A–C]

Comparison of Verbs

EQUAL COMPARISONS

Note that **tanto** is invariable in this usage.

tanto como
(as much as)

Yo estudio **tanto como** mi hermano mayor.
I study as much as my older brother (does).

UNEQUAL COMPARISONS

más/menos que
(more/less than)

Yo duermo **más que** mi hermano menor.
I sleep more than my younger brother (does).

Comparison of Adverbs

EQUAL COMPARISONS

tan + *adverb* + **como**

Yo juego al tenis **tan** bien **como** mi hermano.
I play tennis as well as my brother (does).

UNEQUAL COMPARISONS

más/menos + *adverb* + **que**

Yo como **más** rápido **que** mi padre.
I eat faster than my father (does).

mejor/peor que

Yo juego al tenis **peor que** mi hermana.
I play tennis worse than my sister (does).

[Práctica D]

■ ■ ■ **Práctica**

A. ¿Es Ud. sincero/a? Conteste las preguntas lógicamente.

¿Es Ud… ?

1. tan guapo/a como Antonio Banderas / Jennifer López
2. tan rico como Bill Gates
3. tan fiel como su mejor amigo/a
4. tan inteligente como Einstein
5. tan honesto/a como su padre/madre (novio/a…)

¿Tiene Ud… ?

1. tantos tíos como tías
2. tantos amigos como amigas
3. tanto talento como Carlos Santana
4. tanta sabiduría (*knowledge*) como su profesor(a)

B. Alfredo y Gloria. Compare la casa y las posesiones de Alfredo y Gloria.

MODELOS: La casa de Alfredo tiene más cuartos que la casa de Gloria.
Gloria tiene tantas bicicletas como Alfredo.

	ALFREDO	GLORIA
cuartos en total	8	6
baños	2	1
alcobas	3	3
camas	3	5
coches	3	1
bicicletas	2	2
dinero en el banco	$500.000	$5.000

C. Opiniones. Cambie las siguientes oraciones para expresar su opinión personal. Si está de acuerdo con la oración, diga (*say*) **Estoy de acuerdo.**

MODELO: El invierno es *tan divertido* como el verano. →
El invierno es *más / menos divertido* que el verano.
Estoy de acuerdo.

1. Mi casa (apartamento / residencia) es tan grande como la casa del presidente de la universidad.
2. El fútbol (*soccer*) es tan popular como el fútbol americano.
3. Las artes son tan importantes como las ciencias.
4. Los estudios son menos importantes que los deportes.
5. La comida (*food*) de la cafetería es tan buena como la de mi mamá / papá (esposo/a, compañero/a…).

D. Cambie, indicando su opinión personal: **tanto como → más/menos que,** o vice versa. O, si es apropiado, diga **Estoy de acuerdo.**

1. Los profesores trabajan más que los estudiantes.
2. Me divierto tanto con mis amigos como con mis parientes.
3. Los niños duermen tanto como los adultos.
4. Aquí llueve más en primavera que en invierno.
5. Necesito más el dinero que la amistad.

Need more practice?

- Workbook and Laboratory Manual
- Interactive CD-ROM
- Online Learning Center (www.mhhe.com/puntos7)

Gramática

Ciento setenta y nueve ■ **179**

AUTOPRUEBA

Match each word with the corresponding conjunction.

a. como   **b.** que

1. más + _____
2. tantos + _____
3. peor + _____
4. tan + _____
5. menos + _____
6. tanta + _____

Answers: 1.b 2.a 3.b 4.a 5.b 6.a

Prác. A: Suggestion

Have students substitute other people to create sentences that are true.

No soy tan guapo como Antonio Banderas, pero soy tan guapo como mi hermano mayor.

Prác. C: Suggestions

- Have students create their own sentences about their university and have others tell whether they agree or not. Those that disagree should change the sentence so that it is true for them.

  Nuestra universidad es tan buena como la Universidad de Texas. →
  No, nuestra universidad es mejor que la Universidad de Texas.

- *¿Cómo se dice?* Ask students how the following are said in Spanish.

  1. I enjoy myself more/less than my roommate.
  2. I work as much as she does.
  3. She watches TV as much as all of us.
  4. We eat more/less than she does.

- Write the following funny comparisons on the board. These are actually idiomatic expressions.

  1. *Pesar (To weigh) menos que un mosquito.*
  2. *Ser más pesado que el matrimonio. (¡OJO! Ser pesado/a,* when used to refer to people, means *to be overbearing.*)
  3. *Ser más bueno que el pan.*
  4. *Estar más claro que el agua.* (for things and ideas)
  5. *Ser más alto que un pino.*
  6. *Ser más largo que un día sin pan.*

  Have students explain these sayings in their own words. Is *pan* a positive or a negative concept in Spanish? Have students think of some famous people or circumstances to whom/which these sayings are not necessarily insulting (except for 2).

Prác. C: Extension

6. *Los exámenes de matemáticas son más fáciles que los exámenes de español.*
7. *El dinero es tan importante como la salud (health).*
8. *Los amigos son tan importantes como la familia.*

National Standards: Community

- Antonio Banderas was introduced to U.S. audiences in the film *The Mambo Kings.* Banderas won two 2000 ALMA awards (American Latino Media Arts awards): one for directing *Crazy in Alabama* and another for his part in *13th Warrior.*
- Jennifer Lynn López's parents came to New York from Ponce, Puerto Rico. Jennifer was chosen to play Selena Quintanilla Pérez in the official biographical film of this popular Tejana singer, giving her a jumpstart in the film and music industries.

- Carlos Santana was born July 20, 1947, in Autlán, Mexico. His band, Santana, is one of the most influential bands in rock music. In 1969 Santana performed at Woodstock, reaching new audiences outside the Mission district of San Francisco. Santana's combination of rock and Latin music was completely new, powerful, and riveting. His comeback CD *Supernatural* won several Grammys.

Gramática ■ **179**

Con. A: Suggestion

Have students bring a picture of their family to class and introduce and compare members as in *Conversación A*.

Con. B: Follow-Up

■ Have students use the items as a guide to ask a partner about the same information. As follow-up homework, have students write a comparison of their activities with their partner's.

■ Have students report their findings to the class. Tally answers and end the activity with some generalizations provided by students, for example, *Por lo general, nos acostamos más tarde en el verano que en el invierno...*

■■■ **Conversación**

A. La familia de Lucía y Miguel

Paso 1. Mire el dibujo e identifique a los miembros de esta familia. Luego compárelos (*compare them*) con otro pariente. **¡OJO!** Lucía y Miguel tienen tres hijos: Amalia, Ramón y Sancho. Laura y Javier son los padres de Miguel.

Amalia (19)   Ramón (24)   Sancho (20)

Lucía (43)   Miguel (45)   Sarita (25)   Laura (75)   Javier (80)

Ramoncito (1)

> MODELO: Amalia es la hermana de Sancho. Ella es menor que Sancho, pero es más alta que él.

Paso 2. Su familia. Now compare the members of your own family, making ten comparative statements.

> MODELO: Mi hermana Mary es mayor que yo, pero yo soy más alto/a que ella.

Paso 3. Now read your sentences from **Paso 2** to a classmate. Then ask him or her questions about your comparisons and see if he or she remembers the details of your family.

> MODELO: ¿Qué miembro de mi familia es mayor que yo?

B. La rutina diaria... en invierno y en verano

Paso 1. ¿Es diferente nuestra rutina diaria en las diferentes estaciones? Complete las siguientes oraciones sobre su rutina.

EN INVIERNO...	EN VERANO...
1. me levanto a _____ (hora)	me levanto a _____
2. almuerzo en _____	almuerzo en _____
3. me divierto con mis amigos / mi familia en _____	me divierto con mis amigos / mi familia en _____
4. estudio _____ horas todos los días	(no) estudio _____ horas todos los días
5. estoy / me quedo en _____ (lugar) por la noche	estoy / me quedo en _____ por la noche
6. me acuesto a _____	me acuesto a _____

> **Palabras útiles**
>
> el gimnasio
> el parque
>
> afuera (outside)

Paso 2. Ahora compare sus actividades en invierno y en verano, según el modelo.

> MODELO: En invierno me levanto más temprano/tarde que en verano.
> (En invierno me levanto a la misma hora que en verano.)
> (En invierno me levanto tan temprano como en verano.)

Resources: Transparency 45

☀ **Heritage Speakers**

Invite a los estudiantes hispanohablantes que han vivido en un país latinoamericano a escribir unos párrafos comparando y contrastando su rutina diaria en este país con la que tenían en el país latinoamericano donde vivían. ¿Cómo es diferente su rutina diaria ahora?

UN POCO DE TODO

A. ¿Qué están haciendo? Diga qué están haciendo las siguientes personas, usando una palabra o frase de cada columna y la forma progresiva. Si Ud. no sabe (*know*) qué están haciendo esas personas, ¡use su imaginación!

MODELO: (Yo) Estoy escribiendo la tarea.

yo mi mejor amigo/a mis padres los Bills de Buffalo / los Bulls de Chicago el presidente / la presidenta de la universidad el presidente de los Estados Unidos el profesor / la profesora de español _____ (un compañero / una compañera de la clase de español que está ausente hoy) mi consejero/a	**+** jugar (al) dormir(se) leer descansar viajar (*to travel*) escuchar trabajar practicar hacer escribir ¿ ?	**+** fútbol / basquetbol un libro / una novela la radio a los estudiantes / a sus consejeros la tarea un informe ejercicio físico ¿ ?

B. Dos hemisferios. Complete the following paragraphs with the correct forms of the words in parentheses, as suggested by the context. When two possibilities are given in parentheses, select the correct word.

¿**S**abe Ud. algo de las diferencias entre los hemisferios del norte y del sur? Hay (mucho[1]) diferencias entre el clima del hemisferio norte y el del hemisferio sur. Cuando (ser/estar[2]) invierno en este país, por ejemplo, (ser/estar[3]) verano en la Argentina, en Bolivia, en Chile… Cuando yo (salir[4]) para la universidad en enero, con frecuencia tengo que (llevar[5]) abrigo y botas. En (los/las[6]) países del hemisferio sur, un estudiante (poder[7]) asistir (a/de[8]) clases en enero llevando sólo pantalones (corto[9]), camiseta y sandalias. En muchas partes de este país, (antes de / durante[10]) las vacaciones en diciembre, casi siempre (hacer[11]) frío y a veces (nevar[12]). En (grande[13]) parte de Sudamérica, al otro lado del ecuador, hace calor y (muy/mucho[14]) sol durante (ese[15]) mes. A veces en enero hay fotos, en los periódicos, de personas que (tomar[16]) el sol y nadan[a] en las playas sudamericanas.

Tengo un amigo que (ir[17]) a (hacer/tomar[18]) un viaje a Buenos Aires. Él me dice[b] que allí la Navidad[c] (ser/estar[19]) una fiesta de verano y que todos (llevar[20]) ropa como la que[d] llevamos nosotros en julio. Parece[e] increíble, ¿verdad?

[a]*are swimming*   [b]*Él… He tells me*   [c]*Christmas*   [d]*la… that which*   [e]*It seems*

Comprensión: ¿Probable o improbable?

1. Los estudiantes argentinos van a la playa en julio.
2. Muchas personas sudamericanas hacen viajes de vacaciones en enero.
3. Hace frío en Santiago (Chile) en diciembre.

Resources for Review and Testing Preparation

- Workbook and Laboratory Manual
- Interactive CD-ROM
- Online Learning Center (www.mhhe.com/puntos7)

UN POCO DE TODO

Preliminary Exercise
Describe the weather typical of three to four areas of this country, and have students guess which areas you are talking about. Ask them what role an area's climate plays in the image of that place.

Casi siempre hay mucha humedad (es muy húmedo) y llueve casi todas las tardes en el verano. También hay tormentas tropicales y huracanes. (Louisiana or Florida)

A: Suggestion
Encourage students to be creative and to use verbs and phrases other than those on the list.

B: Follow-Up
Ask students the following questions to personalize the information.

¿Le gustaría pasar la Navidad en Sudamérica? ¿Por qué?
¿Qué asocia Ud. con la Navidad?
¿Qué hizo el año pasado?

💡 **Bright Idea**

B. Comprensión: Extension

4. *Los estudiantes chilenos llevan abrigos en enero.*
5. *Los argentinos se ponen guantes en julio.*
6. *Muchos sudamericanos toman el sol en la playa en agosto.*

Extension
To review *ser, estar,* and *tener* phrases used in this chapter, have students ask and answer questions about the figures in Transparency 45.

Resources: Desenlace

In the *Capítulo 5* section of "Chapter-by-Chapter Supplementary Materials" in the IM/RK, you will find a chapter-culminating activity. You can use this activity to consolidate and review the vocabulary and grammar skills students have acquired.

Entrevista cultural

Suggestions

- Before showing the video, ask students questions about climate in your area and in other areas they are familiar with.

  ¿Cómo es el clima en esta región?
  ¿Qué tiempo hace típicamente en el verano? ¿en el invierno?

- Show the video and allow students one to two minutes to work on the questions. Encourage them to answer in Spanish if possible. You might want to ask the questions in Spanish when you review the answers as a class.

  1. *¿Dónde trabaja Débora?*
  2. *En general, ¿cómo es el clima en Guatemala?*
  2. *¿Cuál es el problema climático más severo en Guatemala?*
  2. *¿Qué tiempo hace cuando hace mal tiempo en Guatemala?*
  5. *¿Cuándo hace mal tiempo en Guatemala?*

  Have volunteers answer the questions.

- Have volunteers role-play Débora and the interviewer.

Entre amigos

Suggestions

- Before viewing the video, review the questions with students and ask them similar questions.

  ¿Cuándo es su cumpleaños?
  ¿Qué planes tiene Ud. para el verano?
  ¿Qué estación prefiere Ud.? ¿Por qué?

  Have students answer or work in small groups to ask and answer these questions.

- After viewing the video, have volunteers read and answer the questions.

Videoteca

Entrevista cultural: Guatemala

Débora David is a meteorologist from Guatemala. In this interview she describes the climate in her country. Before watching the interview, read the following excerpt.

INTERVIEWER: …Y ¿cómo es el clima en Guatemala?
DÉBORA: Bueno, este…[a] Guatemala está en la América Central y… y tiene un clima templado muy de grado[b], ni tanto frío ni tanto calor. Yo creo que por eso se le llama «el país de la eterna primavera».
INTERVIEWER: Y ¿hay temporadas[c] de mal tiempo en Guatemala?
DÉBORA: Sí sí sí, tenemos temporadas de mal tiempo, este…, cuando vienen las lluvias, eh, también a raíz de eso[d] los huracanes ¿no? que han pegado[e] lo que es las costas de Guatemala, eh, pero normalmente el clima en Guatemala es súper agradable así como también toda América Central.

[a]Este *is a filler word, like the English* uh *or* um.   [b]de… *mild*   [c]estaciones   [d]a… *por eso*
[e]han… *have hit*

Now watch the video and answer the following questions based on the interview.

1. Where does Débora work?
2. Basically, what is the climate like in Guatemala?
3. What is the most severe weather problem in Guatemala?
4. What is considered bad weather?
5. When does the bad weather come?

Entre amigos: ¡A mí me encanta (*I love*) el verano!

Tané, Karina, Miguel, and Rubén are talking about birthdays, seasons and different times of the year. What questions do you think they will ask each other? Before watching the video, read the following questions. As you watch, don't worry if you don't understand every word. Try to get the gist of the conversation, listening specifically for information about seasons and times of the year. Watch the video a second time and listen for the answers to the questions.

1. ¿Cuándo es el cumpleaños de Karina?
2. ¿Adónde va Tané este verano, y qué va a hacer allí?
3. ¿Qué planes tiene Rubén para el verano?
4. ¿Qué estación del año prefiere Miguel, y por qué?
5. ¿Por qué le gusta el verano a Karina?

CULTURE

Tornadoes turn counterclockwise in the northern hemisphere. Warm air sweeps up north, and the jet stream flows from the west, creating a situation in which storms rotate counterclockwise. In the southern hemisphere, it is the opposite.

Conozca... Guatemala

Datos esenciales

- Nombre oficial: República de Guatemala
- Capital: la Ciudad de Guatemala
- Población: 13.909.384 habitantes
- Moneda: el quetzal
- Idiomas: el español (oficial), 23 lenguas indígenas (que incluyen el quiché, el cakchiquel y el kekchi)

¡Fíjese!

Más del cincuenta por ciento de los habitantes de Guatemala son descendientes de los antiguos[a] mayas. Esta civilización antigua tenía[b] un sistema de escritura jeroglífica que usaban[c] para documentar su historia, sus costumbres[d] religiosas y su mitología. El calendario maya, base del famoso calendario azteca, era[e] el calendario más exacto de su época. Los mayas también tenían un sistema político y social muy desarrollado.[f] Tikal, en Guatemala, fue[g] una de las ciudades mayas más importantes y también una de las más grandes. Las ruinas de Tikal son muestra[h] de la grandeza de la civilización maya. Hoy día,[i] son un lugar turístico muy visitado.

[a]ancient [b]had [c]they used [d]customs [e]was [f]developed [g]was
[h]an example [i]Hoy... Nowadays

Learn more about Guatemala with the Video, Interactive CD-ROM, and the Online Learning Center (www.mhhe.com/puntos7).

Personas famosas: Rigoberta Menchú

Al período entre los años 1978 y 1985 en Guatemala se le llama[a] con frecuencia «La violencia». Durante este tiempo el ejército guatemalteco[b] empieza una campaña[c] violenta contra la población indígena[d] del norte del país.

Rigoberta Menchú, mujer de la región indígena y de lengua[e] quiché (un grupo étnico de la familia de los mayas) pierde a sus padres y dos hermanos, todos asesinados por el ejército. Menchú describe esta tragedia durante «La violencia» en su famosa autobiografía *Yo, Rigoberta Menchú*.

El trabajo de Menchú a favor de los derechos humanos[f] y del pluralismo étnico de Guatemala le otorgó[g] el Premio Nóbel de la Paz en 1992, exactamente quinientos años después de la llegada[h] de Cristóbal Colón a América.

[a]Al... *The period between 1978 and 1985 in Guatemala is called* [b]ejército... *Guatemalan army* [c]*campaign* [d]población... *indigenous population* [e]*language* [f]a... *on behalf of human rights* [g]le... *won her* [h]*arrival*

▲ *Tikal, Guatemala*

MULTIMEDIA: Internet

Have students search the Internet for information on the government, people, geography (and maps), economy, and transportation of Guatemala. You might assign specific topics and have students give brief oral presentations based on their findings.

National Standards: Communication

Rigoberta Menchú (1959–) was born near San Marcos and grew up in rural poverty. She had no formal education and worked as a domestic servant in Guatemala City. She fled to Mexico in 1981 after most of her family was killed by Guatemalan security forces. Questions have arisen about the accuracy of some of the details in her book. Still, the high esteem in which Menchú is held continues.

Conozca... Guatemala

Suggestion

Encourage students to research the following topics and report to the class.

- the colonial history of Guatemala, especially the figures of Pedro de Alvarado and his wife
- the twin volcanoes of the first Spanish capital, Antigua
- the U.S. involvement in Guatemala in the latter part of the twentieth century
- the controversies surrounding Rigoberta Menchú's book in the 1990s

Notes

- In the 17th century, Guatemala had the first female governor of the New World, Beatriz de la Cueva, widow of the famous conquistador, Pedro de Alvarado.
- Tikal, ruins of an important ancient Mayan city, is in the northern part of Guatemala.
- Students can read an excerpt from the poem *"Letanías del desterrado"* by Guatemala's Miguel Ángel Asturias in *Un paso más 5.*

Suggestions

- Divide the class into two teams. Call out the name of a month and have representatives from each team take turns mentioning a word or phrase related to that month. Other members of the team can offer suggestions if their representative falters. When all related terms have been suggested, call out another month.
- Play charades in Spanish, using nouns adjectives, and comparisons from the *Vocabulario* list.

EN RESUMEN

Gramática

To review the grammar points presented in this chapter, refer to the indicated grammar presentations. You'll find further practice of these structures in the Workbook and Laboratory Manual, on the Interactive CD-ROM, and on the *Puntos de partida* Online Learning Center (www.mhhe.com/puntos7).

15. ¿Qué están haciendo?—Present Progressive: **estar** + **-ndo**

Do you know how to form and when to use the present progressive in Spanish?

16. ¿**Ser o estar**?—Summary of the Uses of **ser** and **estar**

Should you use **ser** or **estar** to describe inherent qualities, to describe health and physical conditions, to express time, to form the present progressive?

17. Describing—Comparisons

Do you know how to compare things and people?

Vocabulario
Practice this vocabulary with digital flash cards on the Online Learning Center (www.mhhe.com/puntos7).

Los verbos

celebrar	to celebrate
pasar	to spend (*time*); to happen
quedarse	to stay, remain (*in a place*)

¿Qué tiempo hace?

está (muy) nublado	it's (very) cloudy, overcast
hace...	it's . . .
(muy) buen/mal tiempo	(very) good/bad weather
(mucho) calor	(very) hot
(mucho) fresco	(very) cool
(mucho) frío	(very) cold
(mucho) sol	(very) sunny
(mucho) viento	(very) windy
hay (mucha)	there's (lots of)
contaminación	pollution
llover (ue)	to rain
llueve	it's raining
nevar (ie)	to snow
nieva	it's snowing

Los meses del año

¿Cuál es la fecha de hoy?	What's today's date?
el primero de	the first of (*month*)

enero	julio
febrero	agosto
marzo	septiembre
abril	octubre
mayo	noviembre
junio	diciembre

Las estaciones del año

la primavera	spring
el verano	summer
el otoño	fall, autumn
el invierno	winter

Los lugares

la capital	capital city
la isla	island
el parque	park
la playa	beach

Otros sustantivos

el clima	climate
el cumpleaños	birthday
la fecha	date (*calendar*)
el/la novio/a	boyfriend/girlfriend
la respuesta	answer
el tiempo	weather

Los adjetivos

abierto/a	open
aburrido/a	bored
alegre	happy
cansado/a	tired
cariñoso/a	affectionate
cerrado/a	closed
congelado/a	frozen; very cold
contento/a	content, happy
desordenado/a	messy
difícil	hard, difficult
enfermo/a	sick
fácil	easy
furioso/a	furious, angry
limpio/a	clean
loco/a	crazy
nervioso/a	nervous
ocupado/a	busy
ordenado/a	neat
preocupado/a	worried
querido/a	dear
seguro/a	sure, certain
sucio/a	dirty
triste	sad

Las comparaciones

más/menos... que	more/less . . . than
tan... como	as . . . as
tanto como	as much as
tanto/a(s)... como	as much/many . . . as

mayor	older
mejor	better; best
menor	younger
peor	worse

Las preposiciones

a la derecha de	to the right of
a la izquierda de	to the left of
al lado de	alongside of
cerca de	close to
debajo de	below
delante de	in front of
detrás de	behind
encima de	on top of
entre	between, among
lejos de	far from

Los puntos cardinales

el norte, el sur, el este, el oeste

Palabras adicionales

afuera	outdoors
conmigo	with me
contigo	with you (*fam.*)
esta noche	tonight
estar (*irreg.*) bien	to be comfortable (*temperature*)
mí (*obj. of prep.*)	me
tener (*irreg.*) (mucho) calor	to be (very) warm, hot
tener (*irreg.*) (mucho) frío	to be (very) cold
ti (*obj. of prep.*)	you
todavía	still

Suggestions

■ Using a map or a globe, have students compare geographical locations. Prompt them with questions.

¿Qué ciudad está más al norte, Nueva York o Quito?

Have them answer in full sentences.

■ Place a common classroom item in different places in the classroom (behind the door, underneath a desk, and so on) and have students describe its location.

Un paso más 5

Note

The *Un paso más* section is optional.

Literatura de Guatemala

Notes

- Miguel Ángel Asturias spent much of his life in exile due to his outspoken opposition to the dictatorship in Guatemala. For many years his writing was not published or circulated in Guatemala. This poem, *"Letanías del desterrado,"* circulated orally for a long time before it was published and became important to many Guatemalan exiles.
- Asturias studied law at *la Universidad de San Carlos*. His thesis for that degree was "The Social Problem of the Indian."
- Asturias wrote his most famous novel, *El Señor Presidente,* during his stay in Paris (1923–1933). The novel criticized the social conditions to which an insensitive dictator condemns his people. This was a politically sensitive topic, especially in Guatemala, whose ruler was the dictator Jorge Ubico. Asturias could not bring his manuscript with him when he returned to Guatemala and didn't publish the original version for 13 years. In 1944, Ubico fell, and the new president, Professor Juan José Arévalo, appointed Asturias cultural attaché to the Guatemalan Embassy in Mexico, where *El Señor Presidente* was published for the first time.

Suggestion

Review possessive adjectives and point out the different forms of *nuestro* used in the poem.

LECTURA

Suggestion

Do the *Estrategia* in class the day you assign the reading as homework for the next class period. Note that the strategy is applied point by point to the reading.

Stress that this reading is authentic, with a few words changed to accommodate beginning students. If students can do the comprehension activities, they have understood enough. Emphasize the importance of this accomplishment at this stage of their language-learning.

Un paso más 5

Literatura de Guatemala

Sobre el autor: *Miguel Ángel Asturias was born near* La Ciudad de Guatemala. *One of the more important themes in his creative works is the indigenous peoples of Guatemala. In 1967, he was awarded the Nobel Prize for Literature. He spent many of his adult years in France, where he was buried in 1974. The following excerpt is from the poem* "Letanías del desterrado," *published in* Páginas de lumbre de Miguel Ángel Asturias (1999).

Y, tú, desterrado:[a]

Estar de paso,[b] siempre de paso,
tener la tierra como posada,[c]
contemplar cielos que no son nuestros,
vivir con gente[d] que no es la nuestra,
cantar canciones que no son nuestras,
reír con risa[e] que no es la nuestra,
estrechar manos[f] que no son nuestras,
llorar con llanto[g] que no es el nuestro,
tener amores que no son nuestros,
probar[h] comida que no es la nuestra,
rezar a dioses[i] que no son nuestros,
oír un nombre que no es el nuestro,
pensar en cosas que no son nuestras,
usar moneda[j] que no es la nuestra,
sentir caminos[k] que no son nuestros...

[a]*exiled* [b]*de... passing through* [c]*boarding house* [d]*people* [e]*reír... to laugh with laughter* [f]*estrechar... to shake hands* [g]*llorar... to cry with tears* [h]*to taste/try* [i]*rezar... to pray to gods* [j]*currency* [k]*roads*

▲ Miguel Ángel Asturias (1899–1974)

LECTURA

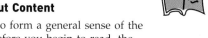

ESTRATEGIA: Forming a General Idea About Content

Before starting a reading, it is a good idea to try to form a general sense of the content. The more you know about the reading before you begin to read, the easier it will seem to you. Here are some things you can do to prepare yourself for reading. You have already applied some of these strategies to the readings thus far in *Puntos de partida*.

1. Make sure you understand the title. Think about what it suggests to you and what you already know about the topic. Do the same with any subtitles in the reading.
2. Look at the drawings, photos, or other visual clues that accompany the reading. What do they indicate about the content?
3. Read the comprehension questions before starting to read the selection. They will direct you to the kind of information you should be looking for.

You should be able to determine the general message of the reading if you apply the preceding strategies.

- **The title.** The reading, **"Todos juntos en los trópicos,"** contains a key word in the title: **trópicos.** It is a cognate. Can you guess what it means?
- **The art.** The reading is accompanied by a photograph and caption. What additional information do these tell you about the reading?
- **The comprehension questions.** Scan the questions in **Comprensión.** What additional clues do they give you about the content of the passage?

- **Sobre la lectura…** This reading is taken from the magazine *Muy interesante*, which generally contains articles about popular science and related topics. Remember that knowing the source of a passage can also help you formulate hypotheses about the reading before you begin to read.

Suggestion
Ask students questions about what they know about the tropics.

¿Conoce Ud. (Are you familiar with) *una región en los trópicos?*
¿Cómo es?
¿Qué tipos de flores se encuentran allí?
¿Qué animales están en las regiones tropicales?
¿Qué países tienen regiones tropicales?
¿Hay personas que vivan allí?

¿Hay regiones tropicales en este país?

Todos juntos en los trópicos

Los trópicos son las regiones biológicamente más diversas del planeta y cuentan con[a] el triple de <u>especies</u> que en cualquier otra zona. Pero, ¿por qué? Los biólogos no han sido capaces[b] de dar una respuesta unívoca.[c] Es más, las diferentes teorías que se han propuesto[d] tienen todos sus puntos débiles.[e]

En resumen, existen tres <u>razones</u> expuestas para esta riqueza.[f] La primera teoría fue diseñada[g] hace 20 años[h] por Michael Rosenzweigh, de Arizona. Según él, en los trópicos hay más especies, sencillamente[i] porque se cuenta con más espacio geográfico <u>habitable.</u>

<u>La segunda</u> es de los últimos años 80 y fue diseñada por George Stevens, de Nuevo México: las especies tropicales son esclavas[j] de sus condiciones térmicas;[k] por eso no pueden <u>colonizar</u> nuevos territorios menos cálidos[l] y se concentran como un gueto[m] en el trópico.

<u>La tercera</u> es una teoría histórica y explica que los trópicos fueron[n] las áreas de la Tierra

▲ *No hay una teoría única para explicar la exuberancia natural que se produce en los trópicos.*

que escaparon al efecto destructor del aumento[o] de las regiones heladas[p] durante las <u>glaciaciones.</u>

Ninguna de las tres ha sido confirmada.[q]

[a]cuentan… *tienen* [b]no… *have not been able* [c]respuesta… *unambiguous answer* [d]que… *that have been proposed* [e]puntos… *weak points* [f]expuestas… *given for this wealth* [g]fue… *was outlined* [h]hace… *20 years ago* [i]*simply* [j]*slaves* [k]*thermal* [l]*hot* [m]*ghetto* [n]*were* [o]*increase* [p]*frozen* [q]ha… *has been confirmed*

Comprensión

B: Extension

After students write summaries of the theories in the reading, have them work in small groups or as a class to brainstorm examples and additional information related to the reading.

Comprensión

A. **¿Se menciona o no?** ¿Cuáles de los siguientes temas se mencionan en la lectura?

	SÍ	NO
1. Información sobre la gente (*people*) indígena de los trópicos.	☐	☐
2. Teorías que explican (*explain*) la biodiversidad de los trópicos.	☐	☐
3. Información sobre la deforestación de los trópicos.	☐	☐
4. Teorías que explican la climatología de los trópicos.	☐	☐
5. La contaminación de algunas regiones de los trópicos.	☐	☐

B. **Resumen.** En inglés, escriba un breve resumen de las tres teorías presentadas en la lectura. Compare su resumen con el de otro estudiante. ¿Cuál de las teorías parece más factible (*feasible*)?

◄ *La biodiversidad de los trópicos se demuestra* (is demonstrated) *en la gran variedad de especies que viven en estas regiones. Las ranas* (frogs) *son parte de esta biodiversidad.*

◄ *Muchos loros* (parrots) *de colores brillantes viven en las regiones tropicales.*

MULTIMEDIA: Internet

After students have completed the *Lectura*, have them search the Internet for websites in Spanish about the Amazon and other rain forests (*selvas tropicales*) in Latin America. Encourage them to team up with a native speaker if there are any in the class. Then, have them write a list of new words that they recognize as cognates, using the reading strategies that they have learned so far. Encourage them to compare their lists with those of other classmates.

ESCRITURA

A. **La biodiversidad local.** La lectura comenta la gran biodiversidad de los trópicos, y propone teorías que explican este fenómeno. Escriba un breve ensayo (*essay*) que comente cómo es el clima donde Ud. vive y qué animales y plantas habitan la zona. Use las preguntas a continuación para empezar y consulte un diccionario bilingüe si es necesario.

¿Cómo es la biodiversidad en la región donde Ud. vive?
¿Hay muchos animales y plantas indígenas?
¿Cuál es la relación entre el clima de la región y la flora y la fauna?

B. **Las selvas latinoamericanas.** Busque información sobre las selvas en Latinoamérica. Use las siguientes preguntas como guía para empezar una introducción. Luego dé más detalles sobre la selva de un país específico.

¿Qué países tienen selvas tropicales?
¿Cómo se llaman las selvas?
¿Qué grupos indígenas viven en las selvas?
¿Qué tiempo hace en las selvas y cuáles son las estaciones?

Suggestions

■ If you prefer that your students do a journal activity, see *Mi diario* in this chapter of the Workbook.
■ Have several students read their essays. Ask the entire class two to three comprehension questions after each description, to encourage students to listen to one another.

A: Variation

Bring a weather map from a Hispanic country (you can obtain one from one of the many newspapers online). Have students study it and then prepare a short meteorological report (*Informe del tiempo*).

Point out the chapter-opener photo. Have students talk about where they buy their groceries, especially fruits and vegetables. Ask them if they like to shop at special fruit and vegetable markets.

Suggestion

Ask students the following questions to introduce the chapter topic.

1. *¿Qué **comidas** hispanas le gustan?*
2. *¿Cree que la comida hispana es más o menos picante (spicy) que la estadounidense o la canadiense?*
3. *¿Qué es una tortilla? (Puede contestar en inglés, si prefiere.) ¿**Conoce** otro tipo de tortilla? ¿Tiene equivalente la tortilla en la comida de este país?*
4. *Si en general come **carne,** ¿hay partes del animal que no coma nunca? ¿el cerebro (brain)? ¿la sangre (blood)? ¿los intestinos?*
5. *¿A qué hora **cena**? ¿Cuándo come la comida más **fuerte** del día?*

Note that the words in **boldface** are included in the active vocabulary of this chapter. Write them on the board and have students discuss them and use context to help them understand the meanings. Place the words they cannot guess in new sentences and contexts.

Note

The *Puntos de partida* Online Learning Center includes an interview with a native speaker from Panama who answers questions similar to those in the preceding *Suggestion*.

CAPÍTULO

6

◀ Un mercado en la Ciudad de Panamá

Resources

For Students

- Workbook
- Laboratory Manual and Laboratory Audio Program
- Quia™ Online Workbook and Online Laboratory Manual
- Video on CD
- Interactive CD-ROM
- *Puntos de partida* Online Learning Center (**www.mhhe.com/puntos7**)

For Instructors

- *Instructor's Manual and Resource Kit,* "Chapter-by-Chapter" Supplementary Materials
- Overhead Transparencies 46–50
- Testing Program
- Test Generator
- Video Program
- Audioscript
- *Puntos de partida* Online Learning Center (**www.mhhe.com/puntos7**)

¿Qué le gusta **comer**?

CULTURA

- **Perspectivas culturales**

    Entrevista cultural: Panamá

    Entre amigos: ¿Quién cocina en tu casa?

    Conozca... Panamá

- **Nota cultural:** Foods of the Spanish-Speaking World

- **En los Estados Unidos y el Canadá:** Goya Foods, Inc.

- **Literatura de Panamá:** Carlos Guillermo Wilson

- **Lectura:** La cocina de Palomino

VOCABULARIO

- La comida

- ¿Qué sabe Ud. y a quién conoce?

PRONUNCIACIÓN

- **d** and **t**

GRAMÁTICA

18 Direct Object Pronouns

19 Indefinite and Negative Words

20 Formal Commands

Entrevista cultural

Maír Citón Moreno ▶
David, Panamá

MULTIMEDIA

- The multimedia materials that accompany this chapter are referenced in the Student and Instructor's Editions with icons to help you identify when and where to incorporate them.

- The IM/RK provides suggestions for using the multimedia materials in the classroom.

La comida

Note

See the model for vocabulary presentation and other material in the *Capítulo 6 Vocabulario: Preparación* section of "Chapter-by-Chapter Supplementary Materials," in the IM.

Suggestions

- Use pictures of food items large enough to see easily. As you say each new target vocabulary item, write it on the board. As with family members, present foods a few at a time by food groups, check comprehension, present another group, check, and so forth.
- Work with half of the vocabulary one day (up to and including *Otras verduras*) and the other half on the second day.
- Use magazine clippings or other visuals to present words from the vocabulary. Model pronunciation and ask *sí/no* questions.
- Have students complete the following sentences.

  1. *Los niños beben _____.*
  2. *Se comen _____ y _____ en McDonald's.*
  3. *Con el desayuno se bebe _____.*
  4. *Los conejos (draw on the board) comen _____.*
  5. *Un almuerzo sencillo incluye sopa y _____.*
  6. *Generalmente se come _____ para el desayuno.*
  7. *Los Óreos son un tipo de _____.*

- Offer students the following optional vocabulary.

  los caramelos
  el cubierto (el tenedor, la cuchara, el cuchillo, la servilleta, el vaso, la copa, la taza)
  el helado de fresa (vainilla, chocolate)
  merendar (ie)/la merienda
  la toronja
  las uvas

La comida

Las comidas (meals)

el desayuno (breakfast)

el jugo (de fruta) — el cereal — la leche — la mantequilla — el té — el pan tostado — el huevo — el café

el almuerzo (lunch)

el sándwich — el queso — la manzana — el agua mineral* — la cerveza — la ensalada — el tomate — la lechuga — la hamburguesa — la sopa

la cena (dinner, supper)

el pastel — el vino blanco — el vino tinto — las zanahorias — el bistec — las arvejas — el pescado — el pan — la patata — el pollo (asado)

---

*The noun **agua** (water) is feminine, but the masculine articles are used with it in the singular: **el agua.** This occurs with all feminine nouns that begin with a stressed **a** sound, for example, **el (un) ama de casa** (homemaker).

192 ■ Ciento noventa y dos

Capítulo 6: ¿Qué le gusta comer?

☀ Heritage Speakers

- En muchos países latinoamericanos, se puede hacer las compras en supermercados modernos o en mercados al aire libre. Pídales a sus estudiantes hispanohablantes que comparen y contrasten los dos tipos de mercado.
- Recuerde que en algunos dialectos del español la palabra *almorzar* significa *comer a media mañana* y es parecida a la expresión en inglés *to have brunch*.

MULTIMEDIA: Audio

Students can listen to and practice this chapter's vocabulary on the Online Learning Center (**www.mhhe.com/puntos7**), as well as on the Textbook Audio CD, part of the Laboratory Audio Program.

Resources: Transparency 46–49

Otra bebida

el refresco	soft drink

Otras frutas

la banana	banana
la naranja	orange

Otras verduras

el champiñón	mushroom
los espárragos	asparagus
los frijoles	beans

Otras carnes

la chuleta (de cerdo)	(pork) chop
el jamón	ham
el pavo	turkey
la salchicha	sausage; hot dog

Otros pescados y mariscos

el atún	tuna
los camarones	shrimp

la langosta	lobster
el salmón	salmon

Otros postres

el flan	(baked) custard
la galleta	cookie
el helado	ice cream

Otras comidas

el arroz	rice
el yogur	yogurt

Otras expresiones

desayunar	to have (eat) breakfast
almorzar	to have (eat) lunch
cenar	to have (eat) dinner, supper
tener (irreg.) (mucha) hambre	to be (very) hungry
tener (irreg.) (mucha) sed	to be (very) thirsty

■■■ Conversación

A. **¿Qué quiere tomar?** Match the following descriptions of meals with a category.

1. una sopa fría, langosta, espárragos, una ensalada de lechuga y tomate, todo con vino blanco y, para terminar, un pastel
2. jugo de fruta, huevos con jamón, pan tostado y café
3. pollo asado, arroz, arvejas, agua mineral y, para terminar, una manzana
4. una hamburguesa con patatas fritas, un refresco y un helado

a. un menú ligero (*light*) para una dieta
b. una comida rápida
c. una cena elegante
d. un desayuno estilo norteamericano

B. **Definiciones.** ¿Qué es?

1. un plato (*dish*) de lechuga y tomate
2. una bebida alcohólica blanca o roja
3. un líquido caliente (*hot*) que se toma* con cuchara (*spoon*)
4. una verdura anaranjada
5. la carne típica para la barbacoa en este país
6. una comida muy común en la China y en el Japón

7. la comida favorita de los ratones (*mice*)
8. una verdura frita que se come con las hamburguesas
9. una fruta roja o verde
10. una fruta amarilla de las zonas tropicales

---

*Remember that placing **se** before a verb form can change its English equivalent slightly: **usa** (he/she/it uses) → **se usa** (is used).

Vocabulario: Preparación

♻ **Reciclado**

■ Review the names of the colors and have students tell what foods or drinks they associate with these colors. If you do this on the first day of vocabulary presentation, allow students to have their books open.

■ Recycle place names. Have students tell what foods or drinks they associate with the following places.

Francia	*Centroamérica*
Inglaterra	*Colombia*
México	*San Francisco*
China	

■ Have students give *tener* expressions for the following sentences.

1. *Si una persona quiere dormir,...*
2. *Tim tiene un examen a las nueve, pero ya son las nueve menos diez y todavía está en casa.*
3. *La temperatura está a 32 grados Fahrenheit y Ud. sólo lleva camiseta.*
4. *Es la una de la mañana y Ud. camina por un lugar peligroso de la ciudad.*
5. *Yo digo que 4 y 4 son 6.*

Con. A: Suggestion

Point out that *tomar* also means *to drink* and is synonymous with *beber*.

Con. A: Follow-Up

Have students give alternative menus for the types of meals listed.

Con. B: Variation

Do the activity once, according to the directions. Then, with books closed, give the names of food items and have students give the corresponding definitions, following the model of items in *Conversación B*.

Con. B: Note

The *se* + verb structure is not stressed for active use in *Puntos de partida*.

Refrán

«La manzana podrida, pierde a su compañía.»

Write the *refrán* on the board. Students may need help with the word *podrida* (rotten). Ask what rotten apple saying we have in English (*One rotten apple spoils the whole bushel.*), and have them brainstorm other apple sayings. (*You are the apple of my eye. Don't upset the apple cart. An apple a day keeps the doctor away. As American as apple pie. An apple doesn't fall far from the tree.*)

 Heritage Speakers

Algunos mexicanos y mexicoamericanos dicen *guajolote* en vez de *pavo*. Pregúnteles a los hispanohablantes de la clase qué otras variaciones usan para referirse a la comida.

Con. C: Follow-Up

Ask questions about foods.

1. *¿Cuál tiene más cafeína, el café o el té? ¿Cuál prefiere Ud.? ¿Cuándo lo toma, por la mañana o por la noche?*

2. *¿Bebe Ud. mucha cerveza? ¿mucho vino? ¿Qué tipo de vino prefiere, el vino tinto o el vino blanco?*

3. *¿Come Ud. carne? ¿Qué tipo de carne prefiere? ¿el bistec, la hamburguesa, el jamón o las chuletas de cerdo? ¿Le gusta comer sándwiches?*

4. *¿Come Ud. muchas ensaladas? ¿Come la ensalada antes o después del plato principal?*

5. *En su opinión, ¿cuál comida es más picante, la comida india o la comida mexicana? ¿la china? ¿la tailandesa? ¿Cuál es más popular en este país?*

NOTA CULTURAL

Suggestions

■ Ask questions in Spanish to check comprehension.

1. *¿Cuáles son algunas comidas originalmente de América?*

2. *¿De dónde son originalmente los siguientes ingredientes para un taco? ¿el tomate? (las Américas) ¿la carne de res (beef)? (Europa) ¿el queso? (Europa) ¿la tortilla? (las Américas)*

■ Have students plan which foods to prepare to celebrate international week. Have groups search the Internet or library for typical dishes from different Spanish-speaking countries. Then have them present their findings to the class. Invite them to describe in Spanish ingredients they will need. After presentations, discuss differences and similarities between foods from different places.

Note

The potato, first cultivated in the Andes mountains of Peru and Bolivia, was a staple in the Incan diet. Spanish conquistador Pedro Cieza de León wrote the first recorded information about potatoes in 1553 in his journal, *La crónica del Perú*. Imported to Europe, the potato from South America had a lasting effect on Irish history via the Irish Potato Famine.

C. Consejos (*Advice*) **a la hora de comer.** ¿Qué debe Ud. comer o beber en las siguientes situaciones?

1. Ud. quiere comer algo ligero porque no tiene hambre.
2. Ud. quiere comer algo fuerte (*heavy*) porque tiene mucha hambre.
3. Ud. tiene un poco de sed y quiere tomar algo antes de la comida.
4. Ud. quiere comer algo antes del plato principal (*main course*).
5. Ud. quiere comer algo después del plato principal.
6. Ud. está a dieta (*on a diet*).
7. Ud. está de vacaciones en Maine (o Boston).
8. Después de levantarse, Ud. no está completamente despierto/a (*awake*).

NOTA CULTURAL

Foods of the Spanish-Speaking World

Often when we think of dishes from the Spanish-speaking world, what comes to mind are rice, beans, spicy **chiles,** corn or flour **tortillas,** and **burritos.** That, however, is a misconception. Corn and flour tortillas and burritos are unknown in many Spanish-speaking countries. Many Hispanic cuisines are not spicy at all, and if you are in Spain and order **una tortilla,** you will be served a wedge of potato omelette!

The cuisines of Spanish-speaking countries are as diverse as their inhabitants. With the arrival of the Spaniards in the Americas, indigenous cuisines were influenced by European foods that did not exist there before, such as beef and chicken. Likewise, European cuisines were influenced by the introduction of foods from the Americas, such as the tomato, the potato, and chocolate. Later, immigration from countries such as Ireland, Germany, Italy, China, and Japan further influenced American cuisines.*

▲ *Una tortilla española*

▲ *Unas tortillas mexicanas*

*Remember that, in this context, American refers to all the countries in North, Central, and South America.

D. Preferencias gastronómicas

Paso 1. Haga una lista de sus tres platos favoritos y de sus tres lugares preferidos para comer en la ciudad donde Ud. vive.

Paso 2. Entreviste (*Interview*) a cinco compañeros de clase para averiguar (*find out*) cuáles son sus platos y lugares favoritos para comer.

MODELO: ¿Cuáles son tus tres lugares favoritos para comer?

Paso 3. Estudie los resultados de su encuesta (*survey*) para averiguar si hay gustos comunes entre todos los estudiantes de la clase. Después, comparta (*share*) con el resto de la clase sus observaciones.

National Standards: Comparisons

Have students imagine that they are going to plan which foods to prepare to celebrate international week. Have different pairs or groups research on the Internet or in the library typical dishes from different Spanish-speaking countries. Then have them present their findings to the rest of the class. Invite them to describe in Spanish some of the ingredients they will need. After the presentations, discuss the differences and similarities between foods from different places.

¡Gran apertura!ª
Restaurante panameño

Nuestro chef, Felipe Prado, los invita a disfrutar de nuestros platos típicos panameños.

El Restaurante Chiriquí está en la calle Remedios, esquina con la avenida Vizcaya.

—¿**Conoces** el restaurante Chiriquí?
—Sí, es muy bueno. Sirven platos panameños.
—¿**Sabes** la dirección[b]?
—Sí, **sé** la dirección. Está en la calle Remedios. ¡Y también **conozco al** chef! ¡Felipe **sabe preparar** mis platos panameños favoritos!
—¿Ah, sí? Pues... ¡quiero **conocer a** Felipe!

ª¡Gran... *Grand opening!*   [b]*address*

Saber and conocer

Two Spanish verbs express *to know:* **saber** and **conocer**.

saber (to know)		conocer (to know)	
sé	sabemos	conozco	conocemos
sabes	sabéis	conoces	conocéis
sabe	saben	conoce	conocen

Saber expresses *to know* facts or pieces of information. Followed by an infinitive, it means *to know how (to do something).*

¿**Sabes** la dirección?	*Do you know the address?*
¡Felipe **sabe** preparar mis platos panameños favoritos!	*Felipe knows how to prepare my favorite Panamanian dishes.*

Conocer is used to express *to know* or *be acquainted (familiar) with* a person, place, or thing. It can also mean *to meet.*

¿**Conoces** el restaurante Chiriquí?	*Do you know (Are you familiar with) the restaurant Chiriquí?*
Sí. ¡Y también **conozco** al chef!	*Yes. I also know the chef!*
¡Quiero **conocer** a Felipe!	*I want to meet Felipe!*

MULTIMEDIA: Internet

Have students imagine that they have won a cooking contest for the best homemade recipe. The prize is a trip for four to Spain to eat in the best restaurants, and the contest organizers have asked the winners to find five Spanish restaurants on the Internet. Have students work in small groups to search for restaurants in Spain on the Internet. You might assign a specific city to each group. Have the groups list the restaurants they find, the type of food served there (some menus are available online), price range, and so on, and present their findings to the class.

¿Qué sabe Ud. y a quién conoce?

Suggestions

- Model pronunciation and go over the statements in class.
- Ask the following questions to practice usage.

1. *¿Qué restaurantes conoce Ud. muy bien?*
2. *¿Es excelente la comida allí?*
3. *¿Come Ud. allí con frecuencia?*
4. *¿Cuántos platos sabe Ud. preparar?*
5. *¿Cuál es su favorito?*
6. *¿Conoce Ud. al dueño de un restaurante?*
7. *¿Conoce Ud. a un chef famoso?*

- Emphasize that the *yo* forms are irregular: *sé* and *conozco.*

Notes

- The uses of *saber* and *conocer* are not always exact. There are gray areas (knowing a language, history, or poetry, for example), where only context and the speaker's meaning determine whether *saber* or *conocer* is appropriate.
- Some native Spanish speakers will substitute the verb *poder* for *saber.*

  María sabe/puede esquiar bien.

Suggestions

- Illustrate the concept of direct objects by tapping someone on the shoulder, tossing an eraser to a student, breaking a piece of chalk. Ask: Who/What is first affected by the action? → person, eraser, chalk.
- Point out that the direct object answers the question *what?* or *whom?* after the verb.

Notes

- The personal *a* has been used passively in the text for some time.
- Pets are often treated like people and take a personal *a: Veo un perro allí* but *Veo a Bear, mi perro, allí.*

☀ Heritage Speakers

Note que la *a* personal no se usa con complementos directos cuando estos se refieren a personas indefinidas o cuya existencia se desconoce. Invite a los hispanohablantes a explicar la diferencia entre las siguientes oraciones.

Carlos busca un consejero que lo pueda ayudar.
Carlos conoce a un consejero que lo puede ayudar.

Sin embargo, los pronombres *alguien, nadie, alguno* y *ninguno* siempre requieren la *a* personal.

■ Use the following chain drill to practice the forms of *saber* and *conocer.*

1. *Conocemos muy bien a Julita.* (*yo, Uds., Juan y yo, Raúl y Mario, vosotros*)
2. *Sabemos que su familia es de Chile.* (*ellos, yo, Elvira, Uds., Ana y tú, vosotros*)

■ Use the following chain drill to practice the use of the *a personal.*

1. —¿*A quién o qué ve?*
   —*Veo el libro.* (*el profesor, la pizarra, los estudiantes, la mesa, mi amigo/a, la puerta*)
2. —¿*A quién o qué busca?*
   —*Busco a mi amigo José.* (*mi libro, Felipe, el amigo de Tomás, el profesor, un cuaderno*)

■ Have students state the following ideas in Spanish.

1. I know the truth.
2. She knows the vice president.
3. They know how to swim.
4. Do you know New York? (that is: Are you familiar with it?)
5. We don't know the answer.
6. Everyone wants to meet the new student in the class.

Con. A: Follow-Up

Have students say the following in Spanish.

1. I'm looking at the TV (at María).
2. We're listening to the radio (to the professor).
3. She's looking for her pen (for her brother).
4. They're waiting for the bus (for the doctor).

The Personal *a*

Note (on page 195) the use of the word **a** before the nouns **chef** and **Felipe** in the last two examples. In Spanish, the word **a** immediately precedes the direct object* of a sentence when the direct object refers to a specific person or persons. This **a,** called the **a personal,** has no equivalent in English.[†] Remember that **a** contracts with the article **el: a + el = al.**

 The personal **a** is used before the interrogative words **¿quién?** and **¿quiénes?** when they function as direct objects.

¿**A quién** llamas?
Who(m) are you calling?

 The verbs **buscar** (*to look for*), **escuchar** (*to listen to*), **esperar** (*to wait for; to expect*), and **mirar** (*to look at*) include the sense of the English prepositions *for, to,* and *at.* These verbs take direct objects in Spanish (not prepositional phrases, as in English).

Busco **mi abrigo.**
I'm looking for my overcoat.

Espero **a mi hijo.**
I'm waiting for my son.

■ ■ ■ Conversación

A. Personas famosas

Paso 1. ¿Qué saben hacer estas personas?

MODELO: Mikhail Baryshnikov sabe bailar.

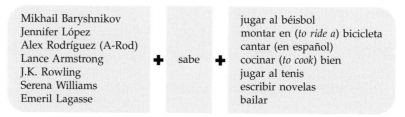

Mikhail Baryshnikov
Jennifer López
Alex Rodríguez (A-Rod)
Lance Armstrong
J.K. Rowling
Serena Williams
Emeril Lagasse

+ sabe **+**

jugar al béisbol
montar en (*to ride a*) bicicleta
cantar (en español)
cocinar (*to cook*) bien
jugar al tenis
escribir novelas
bailar

Paso 2. ¿Quién conoce a quién?

Adán
Napoleón
Romeo
Rhett Butler
Marco Antonio
George Washington

+ conoce a **+**

Martha
Cleopatra
Eva
Julieta
Scarlett O'Hara
Josefina

---

*The direct object (**el complemento directo**) is the part of the sentence that indicates to whom or to what the action of the verb is directed or upon whom or upon what it acts. In the sentence I saw John, the direct object is John. The direct object is explained in more detail in **Gramática 18** of this chapter.
[†]The personal **a** is not generally used with **tener: Tengo cuatro hijos.**

Capítulo 6: ¿Qué le gusta comer?

Refrán

«Unos saben lo que hacen, y otros hacen lo que saben.»

Ask students which phrase from this *refrán* describes them best, the first or the second.

☀ Heritage Speakers

Fíjese que en el habla cotidiano de algunos hispanohablantes no se usa la *a* personal. Su uso ocurre mayormente cuando hay confusión entre el complemento direct e indirecto. Compare las siguientes oraciones.

Le presento mi esposa al embajador.
Le presento el embajador a mi esposa.

Pregúnteles a sus estudiantes hispanohablantes si tienden a usarla o no, y en qué contextos.

B. ¿Dónde cenamos? En este diálogo, Lola y Manolo quieren cenar fuera. Pero, ¿dónde? Complete el diálogo con la forma correcta de **saber** o **conocer.**

LOLA: ¿(Sabes/Conoces[1]) adónde quieres ir a cenar?

MANOLO: No (sé/conozco[2]). ¿Y tú?

LOLA: No. Pero hay un restaurante nuevo en la calle Betis. Creo que se llama Guadalquivir. ¿(Sabes/Conoces[3]) el restaurante?

MANOLO: No, pero (sé/conozco[4]) que tiene mucha fama. Es el restaurante favorito de Virginia. Ella (sabe/conoce[5]) al dueño.[a]

LOLA: ¿(Sabes/Conoces[6]) qué tipo de comida tienen?

MANOLO: No (sé/conozco[7]). Pero podemos llamar a Virginia. ¿(Sabes/Conoces[8]) su teléfono?

LOLA: Está en mi guía telefónica. Y pregúntale[b] a Virginia si ella (sabe/conoce[9]) si aceptan reservas con anticipación[c] o no.

MANOLO: De acuerdo.

[a]owner   [b]ask   [c]con... in advance

C. ¡Qué talento!

Paso 1. Invente oraciones sobre tres cosas que Ud. sabe hacer.

MODELO: Sé tocar el acordeón.

Paso 2. Ahora, en grupos de tres estudiantes, pregúnteles a sus compañeros si saben hacer esas actividades. Escriba sí o no, según sus respuestas.

MODELO: ¿Sabes tocar el acordeón?

Paso 3. Ahora describa las habilidades de los estudiantes en su grupo.

MODELO: Marta y yo sabemos tocar el acordeón, pero Elena no. (En el grupo, sólo yo sé tocar el acordeón.)

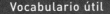

Vocabulario útil	

Cortes y preparaciones

These words are useful when talking about food.

Las carnes		**Huevos**	
las chuletas	rib steak	**los huevos cocidos/ duros**	boiled/hard-boiled eggs
las costillas	ribs	**los huevos fritos**	fried eggs
el filete	fillet	**los huevos revueltos**	scrambled eggs
la milanesa	cutlet	**los huevos tibios**	poached eggs
Las aves (fowl)		**Preparaciones**	
las alas	wings	**a la plancha**	grilled
el muslo	thigh	**empanado/a**	breaded
la pechuga	breast	**estofado/a**	stewed
Pescado		**molido/a, picado/a**	ground
el lenguado	flounder	**salteado/a**	sautéd
el róbalo	sea bass		
la trucha	trout		

Vocabulario: Preparación

Con. B: Follow-Up

Ask students the following questions to check comprehension.

¿Conocen Lola y Manolo el restaurante nuevo?
¿Saben qué tipo de comida se sirve allí?
¿Saben el número de teléfono de Virginia?

Con. C: Follow-Up

Discuss the results. *¿Qué sabe hacer más gente? ¿A cuántas personas conoce Ud. que (hacen...)?*

☼ **Heritage Speakers**

En algunos países latinoamericanos se dice *róbalo* en vez de *robalo*. Pregúnteles a sus estudiantes hispanohablantes cuál de las dos variantes prefieren. ¿Cuáles son otras variantes que usan para las palabras en la lista de la *Nota comunicativa*?

National Standards: Comparisons

Discuss the variety of words for names of food in the Spanish-speaking world. For example:

papas (L.A.) vs. *patatas* (Sp.)
banana (L.A.) vs. *plátano* (Sp.) or *guineo* (P. Rico)
frijoles (L.A.) vs. *judías* (Sp.)
camarones (L.A.) vs. *gambas* (Sp.)

arvejas (L.A.) vs. *guisantes* (Sp.)
tortilla (flat corn meal or flour pancake, L.A.) vs. *tortilla* (potato and onion omelet, Sp.)
sándwich (with *pan de molde*, like the U.S. loaf) vs. *bocadillo* (with *pan de barra*, like French bread)

Note

At the end of a word, the fricative [đ] is very weak, sometimes not even pronounced, for example, *usted* → *usté, verdad* → *verdá.*

Suggestion

Point out that *Capítulo 6* of the Laboratory Manual offers pronunciation practice for the letter *d.*

Preliminary Exercises

■ Have students pronounce the following English words, then repeat them without the initial *s.*

star	tar
stamp	tamp
station	tation
still	till
stop	top

■ Write the following columns on the board. Read the words aloud, switching columns at random, and have students tell which word was pronounced.

A	B
tono	dono
ti	di
te	de
toma	doma
tela	dela
tejas	dejas
tos	dos
tía	día

B: Extension

1. *el dos / un dos / los dos*
2. *un dedo / el dedo / diez dedos*
3. *Adela y Tomás*
4. *Trabalenguas: Magdalena trata de darle un dictado a David Treviño.*
5. *De tanto trabajo, Tristán tiene un dolor de cabeza.*

D. Entrevista

1. ¿Qué restaurantes conoces en esta ciudad? ¿Cuál es tu restaurante favorito? ¿Por qué es tu favorito? ¿Es buena la comida de allí? ¿Qué tipo de comida sirven? ¿Te gusta el ambiente (*atmosphere*)? ¿Comes allí con frecuencia? ¿Llamas primero para hacer reservaciones?
2. ¿Conoces a alguna persona famosa? ¿Quién es? ¿Cómo es? ¿Qué detalles sabes de la vida de esta persona?
3. ¿Qué platos sabes preparar? ¿Tacos? ¿enchiladas? ¿pollo frito? ¿hamburguesas? ¿Te gusta cocinar? ¿Cocinas con frecuencia?
4. ¿Esperas a tus amigos para ir a la universidad? ¿Esperas a tus amigos después de la clase? ¿A quién buscas cuando necesitas ayuda (*help*) con el español? ¿Dónde buscas a tus amigos por la noche? ¿Dónde buscas a tus hijos/amigos cuando es hora de comer?

Need more practice?

■ Workbook and Laboratory Manual
■ Interactive CD-ROM
■ Online Learning Center (www.mhhe.com/puntos7)

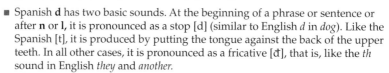

PRONUNCIACIÓN   *d* and *t*

Some sounds, such as English [b], are called *stops* because, as you pronounce them, you briefly stop the flow of air and then release it. *Fricatives*, such as English [f] and [v], are pronounced by pushing air out with a little friction.

■ Spanish **d** has two basic sounds. At the beginning of a phrase or sentence or after **n** or **l**, it is pronounced as a stop [d] (similar to English *d* in *dog*). Like the Spanish [t], it is produced by putting the tongue against the back of the upper teeth. In all other cases, it is pronounced as a fricative [đ], that is, like the *th* sound in English *they* and *another.*

■ The main difference in the pronunciation of Spanish **t** and English *t* is that in English the tip of the tongue is placed against the top of the mouth, while in Spanish it is placed against the upper teeth. In addition, Spanish **t** is not pronounced with as much aspiration (pushing air out of the mouth) as in English. Spanish **t** sounds more like the *t* in the English word *star.* When it appears between two vowels, Spanish **t** uses full dental pronunciation, not a short pronunciation as occurs in English *matter.*

A. Práctica. Practique las siguientes palabras y frases.

1. [d]	diez	dos	doscientos	doctor
	¿dónde?	el doctor	el dinero	venden
2. [đ]	mucho dinero	adiós	usted	seda
	ciudad	la doctora	cuadros	todo

B. Pronuncie

1. ¿Dónde está el dinero?
2. David Dávila es doctor.
3. ¿Qué estudia usted?
4. Venden de todo, ¿verdad?

C. Más práctica. Practique las siguientes palabras y frases.

1.	traje	patata	mantequilla
	trimestre	cartera	pastel
	zapatos	tomate	tinto

2. ¿Cómo te llamas?
3. ¿Cuánto cuesta?
4. Mi tío trabaja en una tienda.

 Heritage Speakers

Invite a sus estudiantes a pronunciar algunas palabras que contiene la *d* y la *t.*

18 **Expressing** *what* **or** *whom* • **Direct Object Pronouns**

De compras en el supermercado

LA MODERNA MARKET
930-932 State Street • New Haven, CT • (203) 776-2333

• **TODA CLASE DE CARNES FRESCAS**

• **VEGETALES FRESCOS**
• **GROCERY**

• **LÍNEA COMPLETA DE PRODUCTOS MEXICANOS**
La Moderna • La Morena
• La Costeña • Nestle

Solicite Nuestra Propia Longaniza y Cesina
ATENDEMOS PEDIDOS PARA NEGOCIOS

Indique cuáles de estas afirmaciones son verdaderas para Ud.

1. la carne
☐ *La* como todos los días. Por eso tengo que comprar*la* con frecuencia.
☐ *La* como de vez en cuando (*once in a while*). Por eso no *la* compro a menudo (*often*).
☐ Nunca *la* como. No necesito comprar*la*.

2. el café
☐ *Lo* bebo todos los días. Por eso tengo que comprar*lo* con frecuencia.
☐ *Lo* bebo de vez en cuando. Por eso no *lo* compro a menudo.
☐ Nunca *lo* bebo. No necesito comprar*lo*.

3. los huevos
☐ *Los* como todos los días. Por eso tengo que comprar*los* con frecuencia.
☐ *Los* como de vez en cuando. Por eso no *los* compro a menudo.
☐ Nunca *los* como. No necesito comprar*los*.

4. las bananas
☐ *Las* como todos los días. Por eso tengo que comprar*las* con frecuencia.
☐ *Las* como de vez en cuando. Por eso no *las* compro a menudo.
☐ Nunca *las* como. No necesito comprar*las*.

National Standards: Comparisons

In many Hispanic countries, families can purchase fresh (unpasteurized) milk on a daily basis from street vendors or from local shops. This milk has to be boiled in order to make it safe for consumption. During the boiling process, a thick cream separates from the milk and rises to the top. This cream, called *nata de leche*, is frequently used when making desserts. Are there any places where one can buy fresh milk in your area?

Extension
Give students additional sentences to answer.

5. *el agua: La tomo todos los días. La tomo de vez en cuando. Nunca la tomo.*
¡OJO! The direct object for *el agua* is *la* because it is a feminine noun.

6. *el pollo: Lo como todos los días...*

Suggestions

■ Introduce third person direct object pronouns first. Put a number of objects on the desk (*un libro, una flor, un coche* [toy car]) and model sentences with a noun-to-pronoun transformation: *Miro el libro.* → *Lo miro.*

■ Follow a similar sequence with feminine singular nouns, then plural masculine and feminine nouns.

■ After presenting third person object pronouns with visuals, expand their use to include the meaning of *you*. Have students stand up as appropriate.

Yo lo/la veo (a Ud., Roberto, and so on).
¿Ud. me ve (a mí)? → *Sí, profesor(a), lo/la veo.*

■ Point out that, like the subject pronoun *ellos*, the direct object pronoun *los* can refer to either a masculine group or a combination of masculine and feminine nouns.

■ Point out that like direct object nouns, direct object pronouns answer the question *what?* or *whom?* after the verb.

■ Point out that many verbs commonly used with reflexive pronouns can also be used with direct object nouns and pronouns when the action of the verb is directed at someone other than the subject of the sentence. The meaning of the verb will change slightly. Provide the following examples.

*Generalmente me despierto a las ocho. La radio **me** despierta.* (I generally wake up at eight. The radio wakes me.)
*En un restaurante, el camarero **nos** sienta.* (In a restaurant, the waiter seats us.)

Explicit practice with many verbs of this type is offered in *Práctica C*. Have students note these verbs as well: *afeitar, acostar,* and *bañar.*

Emphasis B: Suggestions

■ Stress the position of the object pronoun.

■ Use the following question to practice new words. Write a model answer on the board.

Ud. prepara un pastel. ¿Necesita las siguientes cosas? los huevos, *la* leche, el azúcar (sugar), *el chocolate, la vainilla, la sal, la harina* (flour)...

Students respond:
Claro que [no] lo necesito.

♻ Emphasis B: Reciclado

Review clothing vocabulary. Have students answer the following questions using direct object pronouns. Write a model answer on the board.

Claro que [no] lo necesito.
Ud. hace la maleta (You are packing) para un viaje a Acapulco. ¿Necesita las siguientes cosas?
　el traje de baño
　las sandalias
　las gafas de sol
　el libro de español
　el libro de sicología
　los pantalones cortos
　las camisetas
　la crema bronceadora
　el reloj

Preliminary Exercises

■ Personalize the use of the object pronouns by asking questions that involve the students.

　—*¿Quién me mira? ¿*[student] *me mira?* →
　—*Sí,* [student] *lo/la mira.*
　—*¿Quién nos mira* (the student stands with the instructor)? *¿*[student] *nos mira?* →
　—*Sí,* [student] *los/las mira.*

■ Ask the following questions to practice the use of *saber* and *conocer* with object pronouns.

1. *¿Sabe Ud. mi nombre?* → *Sí, lo sé.*
　¿los nombres de todos los estudiantes de la clase?
　¿la fecha de hoy?
　¿la fecha de mi cumpleaños?
　¿las formas del verbo saber?
　¿todo el nuevo vocabulario?

2. *¿Conoce Ud. a* [student in class]?
　¿Conoce Ud. personalmente a Demi Moore?
　¿a Antonio Banderas?
　¿a mis padres?
　¿al novio / a la novia de [student in class]?

Direct Object Pronouns

me	me	nos	us
te*	you (*fam. sing.*)	os	you (*fam. pl.*)
lo*	you (*form. sing.*), him, it (*m.*)	los	you (*form. pl.*), them (*m., m. + f.*)
la	you (*form. sing.*), her, it (*f.*)	las	you (*form. pl.*), them (*f.*)

A. Like direct object nouns, *direct object pronouns* (**los pronombres del complemento directo**) are the first recipient of the action of the verb. Direct object pronouns are placed before a conjugated verb and after the word **no** when it appears. Third person direct object pronouns are used only when the direct object noun has already been mentioned.

[Práctica A]

¿El menú? Diego no **lo** necesita.
The menu? Diego doesn't need it.

¿Dónde están el pastel y el helado? **Los** necesito ahora.
Where are the cake and the ice cream? I need them now.

Ellos **me** ayudan.
They're helping me.

> **direct object** = the noun or pronoun that receives the action of a verb

B. The direct object pronouns may be attached to an infinitive or a present participle.

[Práctica B–C]

Las tengo que leer. ⎫
Tengo que leer**las**. ⎭　*I have to read them.*

Lo estoy comiendo. ⎫
Estoy comiéndo**lo**. ⎭　*I am eating it.*

C. Note that the direct object pronoun **lo** can refer to actions, situations, or ideas in general. When used in this way, **lo** expresses English *it* or *that*.

Lo comprende muy bien.
He understands it (that) very well.

No **lo** creo.
I don't believe it (that).

Lo sé.
I know (it).

AUTOPRUEBA

Match the direct object pronouns with the nouns and subject pronouns.

1. _____ los　　a. Ana
2. _____ la　　 b. tú
3. _____ te　　 c. Pedro y Carolina
4. _____ lo　　 d. María y yo
5. _____ las　　e. Jorge
6. _____ nos　　f. Elena y Rosa

Answers: 1. c 2. a 3. b 4. e 5. f 6. d

---

*In Spain and in some other parts of the Spanish-speaking world, **le** is frequently used instead of **lo** for the direct object pronoun *him*. This usage, called **el leísmo,** will not be followed in *Puntos de partida.*

☀ Heritage Speakers

En España y en algunos países de Latinoamérica, a veces se usa *le* en vez de *lo*. Este fenómeno se llama *leísmo*. Por ejemplo, *Raquel lo/le conoció en Sevilla. Ella lo/le vio en el tren.* Aunque la mayoría de los españoles prefiere usar *le* en estos casos, la Real Academia Española y la mayoría de los latinoamericanos prefieren el uso de *lo*.

■ ■ ■ **Práctica**

A. **¿Qué comen los vegetarianos?**

Paso 1. Aquí hay una lista de diferentes comidas. ¿Van a formar parte de la dieta de un vegetariano? Conteste según los modelos.

> **MODELOS:** el bistec → No *lo* va a comer.
> la banana → *La* va a comer.

1. las patatas
2. el arroz
3. las chuletas de cerdo
4. los huevos
5. las zanahorias
6. las manzanas
7. los camarones
8. el pan
9. los champiñones
10. los frijoles
11. la ensalada

Paso 2. Si hay un estudiante vegetariano / una estudiante vegetariana en la clase, pídale que verifique (*ask him or her to verify*) las respuestas de Ud.

B. **La cena de Lola y Manolo.** La siguiente descripción de la cena de Lola y Manolo es muy repetitiva. Combine las oraciones, cambiando los nombres de complemento directo por pronombres cuando sea (*whenever it is*) necesario.

> **MODELO:** El camarero (*waiter*) trae un menú. Lola lee *el menú.* →
> El camarero trae un menú y Lola *lo* lee.

1. El camarero trae una botella de vino tinto. Pone *la botella* en la mesa.
2. El camarero trae las copas (*glasses*) de vino. Pone *las copas* delante de Lola y Manolo.
3. Lola quiere la especialidad de la casa. Va a pedir *la especialidad de la casa.*
4. Manolo prefiere el pescado fresco (*fresh*). Pide *el pescado fresco.*
5. Lola quiere una ensalada también. Por eso pide *una ensalada.*
6. El camerero trae la comida. Sirve *la comida.*
7. Manolo necesita otra servilleta (*napkin*). Pide *otra servilleta.*
8. «¿La cuenta (*bill*)? El dueño está preparando *la cuenta* para Uds.»
9. Manolo quiere pagar con tarjeta (*card*) de crédito. Pero no trae *su tarjeta.*
10. Por fin, Lola toma la cuenta. Paga *la cuenta.*

NOTA COMUNICATIVA

Talking About What You Have Just Done

To talk about what you have *just* done, use the phrase **acabar** + **de** with an infinitive.

Acabo de almorzar con Beto.	*I just had lunch with Beto.*
Acabas de celebrar tu cumpleaños, ¿verdad?	*You just celebrated your birthday, didn't you?*

Note that the infinitive follows **de.** As you already know, the infinitive is the only verb form that can follow a preposition in Spanish.

Prác. A: Variation

Have students answer the question: *¿Qué comen los niños pequeños?* Use the same list and add.

12. *la leche*
13. *los purés*
14. *el chocolate*
15. *el vino*

Prác A: Follow-Up

Follow up with these questions.

> *¿Qué come Ud. cuando está a dieta?*
> *¿el helado?* → *No, no lo como.*
> *¿la ensalada?*
> *¿los pasteles?*
> *¿las papas fritas?*
> *¿el pollo?*
> *¿la pizza?*
> *¿el queso?*
> *¿el pan?*

Prác. B: Follow-Up

Check comprehension with the following questions.

> *La ensalada, ¿la pide Lola?*
> *Y el pescado, ¿lo pide Lola también?*
> *¿Quién pide la especialidad de la casa?*

Prác. B: Variation

Ask students the following questions.

1. *¿Quién lo/la escucha a Ud. cuando tiene problemas?*
2. *¿Qué/Quién lo/la despierta?*
3. *¿Quién lo invita a cenar siempre?*
4. *¿Quién lo/la despierta a veces cuando quiere dormir?*

NOTA COMUNICATIVA

Suggestion

Do a series of actions, then state in Spanish what you have just done; for example, write your name on the board, then erase it, turn the lights off or on, open and close a book, sit down, stand up, and so on.

Note

Remind students that they have already learned the preposition + infinitive structure.

Have students answer questions
using *acabar de*.

¿Quiere comer? →
Acabo de comer.

1. *ver la televisión*
2. *leer*
3. *ir al centro*
4. *desayunar*
5. *almorzar*
6. *cenar*

Prác. C: Suggestion

Have students tell what they have
just done before leaving these places.

*¿Qué acaba de hacer Ud. cuando
sale de... ?*

1. *¿un mercado?*
2. *¿una discoteca?*
3. *¿un restaurante?*
4. *¿una librería?*
5. *¿el laboratorio de lenguas?*
6. *¿una clase de literatura inglesa?*
7. *¿un bar?*

Prác. C: Variation

Have students work in groups of two
or three to make suggestions to each
other. Students should respond to
suggestions by saying they have just
done it.

¿Quiere Ud. comer? →
No, acabo de comer.
¿Quiere Ud. mirar la televisión? →
No, acabo de mirarla.

C. ¡Acabo de hacerlo! Imagine that a friend is pressuring you to do the following things. With a classmate, tell him or her that you just did each one, using either of the forms in the model.

MODELO: E1: ¿Por qué no estudias la lección? →
E2: Acabo de estudiar*la*. (*La* acabo de estudiar.)

1. ¿Por qué no escribes las composiciones para tus clases?
2. ¿Vas a comprar el periódico hoy?
3. ¿Por qué no pagas los cafés?
4. ¿Vas a preparar la comida para la fiesta?
5. ¿Puedes pedir la cuenta?
6. ¿Tienes hambre? ¿Por qué no comes los tacos que preparé (*I made*)?

■ ■ ■ Conversación

A. ¿Quién ayuda? Todos necesitamos ayuda en diferentes circunstancias. ¿Quién los ayuda a Uds. con lo siguiente? Use **nos** en sus respuestas.

MODELO: con las cuentas → Nuestros padres *nos* ayudan con las cuentas.

Palabras útiles
nuestros padres (compañeros, consejeros, amigos...)

1. con las cuentas
2. con la tarea
3. con la matrícula
4. con el horario de clases
5. con los problemas personales

B. Una encuesta sobre la comida. Hágales (*Ask*) preguntas a sus compañeros de clase para saber si toman las comidas o bebidas indicadas y con qué frecuencia. Deben explicar por qué toman o *no* toman cierta cosa.

MODELO: la carne → E1: ¿Comes carne?
E2: No, no *la* como casi nunca porque tiene mucho colesterol.

Palabras y frases útiles	
la cafeína las calorías el colesterol la grasa (fat) estar a dieta ser alérgico/a a	ser bueno/a para la salud (health) me pone (it makes me) nervioso/a me da asco (it makes me sick) / me dan asco (they make me sick) lo/la/los/las detesto

1. la carne
2. los mariscos
3. el yogur
4. la pizza
5. las hamburguesas
6. el pollo
7. el café
8. los dulces (*sweets; candy*)
9. el alcohol
10. el atún
11. los espárragos
12. el hígado (*liver*)

Need more practice?

■ Workbook and
Laboratory Manual
■ Interactive CD-ROM
■ Online Learning
Center
(www.mhhe.com/
puntos7)

19 Expressing Negation • Indefinite and Negative Words

En la cocina de Diego y Antonio

Diego llega a casa y tiene hambre.

DIEGO: Quiero comer *algo,* pero *no* hay *nada* de comer en esta casa. Y *no* tengo ganas de ir de compras. Y además, ¡*no* tengo *ni* un centavo!

ANTONIO: ¡Ay! *Siempre* eres así. Tú *nunca* tienes ganas de ir de compras. Y lo del dinero… ¡esa ya es otra historia!

¿Quién… ?

1. tiene hambre
2. nunca tiene dinero
3. critica a su amigo
4. no quiere ir de compras

Here is a list of the most common indefinite and negative words in Spanish. You have been using many of them since the first chapters of *Puntos de partida.*

algo	something, anything	**nada**	nothing, not anything
alguien	someone, anyone	**nadie**	no one, nobody, not anybody
algún (alguno/a/os/as)	some, any	**ningún (ninguno/a)**	no, none, not any
siempre	always	**nunca, jamás**	never
también	also	**tampoco**	neither, not either

Pronunciation hint: Remember to pronounce the **d** in **nada** and **nadie** as a fricative, that is, like a *th* sound: **na đa, na đie.**

The Double Negative

When a negative word comes after the main verb, Spanish requires that another negative word—usually **no**—be placed before the verb. When a negative word precedes the verb, **no** is not used.

¿**No** estudia **nadie?**
¿**Nadie** estudia? } *Isn't anyone studying?*

No estás en clase **nunca.**
Nunca estás en clase. } *You're never in class.*

No quieren cenar aquí **tampoco.**
Tampoco quieren cenar aquí. } *They don't want to have dinner here, either.*

In Diego and Antonio's kitchen *Diego arrives home and he's hungry.* DIEGO: *I want to eat something, but there's nothing to eat in this house. And I don't feel like going shopping. And furthermore, I don't have a cent!* ANTONIO: *Ah! You're always like that. You never feel like going shopping. And that bit about the money . . . , that's another story!*

Gramática 19

Indefinite and Negative Words

Suggestions

■ Act out models for using indefinite and negative words. To show comprehension, have students produce sentences that describe the situations you are setting up. Hints: place one book on one desk, several on another, and none on a third to show some books vs. one book vs. no book (something vs. nothing) or point to a chair where no one is sitting, and so on.

■ Alternatively, use the drawing in *Práctica A* on page 209 as a vehicle for introducing these words.

Follow-Up
Ask the following questions to personalize information and to check comprehension of the *minidiálogo.*

1. *¿Tienen Uds. ganas de comer algo ahora mismo? ¿Qué?*
2. *¿Quién no tiene dinero nunca?*
3. *¿A alguien le gusta ir de compras para comprar comida?*
4. *¿A quién nunca le gusta ir de compras?*

♺ Reciclado
Remind students that the personal *a* is used before *alguien, nadie, alguno,* and *ninguno* when they refer to people and function as a direct object. Note that the personal *a* is omitted after *hay* and *tener.*

Emphasis B: Suggestion
Offer optional vocabulary: *o… o…* and *ni… ni…*

Emphasis B: Note
The plural forms *ningunos/as* are rarely used. As in the example, indefinite questions with plural *algunos/as* frequently require singular *ningún/ninguna* in the negative answers. The exceptions would be nouns usually used in plural in Spanish, for example, *pantalones, medias, vacaciones,* and so on.

☀ Heritage Speakers

En algunos dialectos del español del suroeste de los Estados Unidos, a veces se oye decir *nadien o naidien* por *nadie.* Estas formas se usan en el habla popular de algunos grupos, pero la forma *nadie* es la preferida. Pregúnteles a los estudiantes hispanohablantes si han oído este vocablo alguna vez o si ellos mismos lo usan entre amigos.

Bright Idea

Prác. A, B: Suggestion

Remind students that the personal *a* is omitted after *hay* and (in most cases) after forms of the verb *tener*.

Hay muchos estudiantes.
Tengo muchos estudiantes.
Veo a muchos estudiantes.

Prác. A: Suggestion

Use items from *Práctica A* as an inductive activity to present and practice the double negative.

Prác. A: Extension

Using several books, set up a similar pattern.

¿Hay algunos libros en el suelo (floor)? →
Sí, hay algunos. / No, no hay ninguno.

Expand the activity by using other classroom objects and student possessions at hand.

♻ Prác. A: Reciclado

Recycle words about houses and rooms. Ask students about things that they do or do not have in their rooms or houses.

¿Tiene un baño privado?

Also ask questions about their routines.

¿Come con frecuencia en la cocina?
¿Cocina todos los días?

Prác. B: Preliminary Exercise

Say the following words and have students respond with the corresponding opposite.

algo
alguien
alguno
siempre
también
nada
nadie
ninguno
nunca
tampoco

Prác. B: Note

Alert students that item 2 requires the singular form, *ninguno: No tienen ningún plato...*

Alguno and **ninguno** are adjectives. Unlike **nadie** and **nada** (nouns) or **nunca, jamás,** and **tampoco** (adverbs), **alguno** and **ninguno** must agree with the noun they modify.

Alguno and **ninguno** shorten to **algún** and **ningún,** respectively, before a masculine singular noun—just as **uno** shortens to **un, bueno** to **buen,** and **malo** to **mal.**

The plural forms **ningunos** and **ningunas** are rarely used.

—¿Hay **algunos** recados para mí hoy?
—Lo siento, pero hoy no hay **ningún** recado para Ud.
Are there any messages for me today?
I'm sorry, but there are no messages for you today.
(*There is not a single message for you today.*)

AUTOPRUEBA

Give the corresponding negative word.

1. siempre _____   4. alguna _____
2. también _____   5. algo _____
3. alguien _____

Answers: 1. nunca 2. tampoco 3. nadie 4. ninguna 5. nada

■ ■ ■ Práctica

A. ¡Anticipemos! ¿Qué pasa esta noche en casa? Tell whether the following statements about what is happening at this house are true (**cierto**) or false (**falso**). Then create as many additional sentences as you can about what is happening, following the model of the sentences.

1. No hay nadie en el baño.
2. En la cocina, alguien está preparando la cena.
3. No hay ninguna persona en el patio.
4. Hay algo en la mesa del comedor.
5. Algunos amigos se están divirtiendo en la sala.
6. Hay algunos platos en la mesa del comedor.
7. No hay ningún niño en la casa.

B. ¡Por eso no come nadie allí! Exprese negativamente, usando la negativa doble.

MODELO: Hay alguien en el restaurante. → *No hay nadie en el restaurante.*

1. Hay algo interesante en el menú.
2. Tienen algunos platos típicos.
3. El profesor cena allí también.
4. Mis amigos siempre almuerzan allí.
5. Preparan algo especial para grupos grandes.
6. Siempre hacen platos nuevos.
7. Y también sirven paella, mi plato favorito.

Resources: Transparency 50

C. Manolo está de mal humor (*in a bad mood*).

Paso 1. Lola y su esposo Manolo son profesores. Hoy Manolo está de mal humor y tiene una actitud muy negativa. ¿Qué opina Manolo de las afirmaciones de Lola sobre las clases y la vida universitaria en general?

> MODELO: LOLA: Tengo algunos estudiantes excelentes este año.
> MANOLO: Pues, yo *no* tengo *ningún* estudiante excelente este año.

LOLA:

1. Hay muchas clases interesantes en el departamento.
2. Me gusta tomar café con mis estudiantes con frecuencia.
3. Hay algunas personas buenas en la administración.
4. También hay un candidato bueno para el puesto (*position*) de rector de la facultad (*department*).
5. Hay muchas personas inteligentes en la universidad.
6. Me gustan algunas conferencias (*lectures*) que están planeadas para este mes.

Paso 2. Ahora imagine las preguntas que hace Lola, según las respuestas de Manolo.

> MODELO: MANOLO: No, no hay nada interesante en el periódico.
> LOLA: ¿Hay *algo* interesante en el periódico?

MANOLO:

1. No, no hay nada interesante en la tele esta noche.
2. No, no hay nadie cómico en el programa.
3. No, no hay ninguna película buena en el cine esta semana.
4. No, no como nunca en la facultad.
5. Tampoco almuerzo entre las clases.

Need more practice?
- Workbook and Laboratory Manual
- Interactive CD-ROM
- Online Learning Center (www.mhhe.com/puntos7)

 **Conversación**

Preguntas

1. ¿Vamos a vivir en la luna (*moon*) algún día? ¿Vamos a viajar (*travel*) a otros planetas? ¿Vamos a vivir allí algún día? ¿Vamos a establecer contacto con seres (*beings*) de otros planetas algún día?
2. ¿Algunos de los estudiantes de esta universidad son de países extranjeros? ¿De dónde son? ¿Algunos de sus amigos son de habla española (*Spanish-speaking*)? ¿De dónde son?
3. En esta clase, ¿quién...

   siempre tiene algunas buenas ideas?
   tiene algunos amigos españoles?
   siempre lo entiende todo?
   nunca contesta ninguna pregunta?
   va a ser muy rico algún día?
   nunca tiene tiempo para divertirse?
   nunca mira la televisión?
   no practica ningún deporte?
   siempre invita a los otros a comer?

Prác. C: Extension

Paso 1. *En casa...*

7. *Quiero escuchar algo en la radio.*
8. *Siempre me gusta escuchar música popular.*
9. *Hay algunas ideas fascinantes en este libro.*
10. *Tengo algunos libros muy interesantes.*

Con: Extension

4. *¿Hay algo más importante que el dinero? ¿que la amistad? ¿que el amor?*
5. *En la clase, ¿hay alguien más inteligente que el profesor / la profesora? ¿más estudioso/a que Ud.? ¿más rico/a que Ud.?*
6. *La perfección es una meta (*goal*) imposible, ¿verdad? ¿Hay alguna clase perfecta en esta universidad? ¿Hay alguna residencia perfecta? ¿una familia perfecta? ¿Tiene Ud. alguna idea de lo que es el compañero perfecto / la compañera perfecta? ¿un plan perfecto para esta noche?*

National Standards: Comparisons

In this country, people frequently refer to "the man in the moon." In Latin American countries, however, people see *el niño Jesús* (the Christ child). Argentine poet, Leopoldo Lugones (1874–1938), writes this in "*Lunario sentimental*" (1909):

> *y está todo; la Virgen con el niño, al flanco;*
> *San José (algunos tienen la buena fortuna*

> *de ver su vara); y el buen burrito blanco*
> *trota que trota los campos de la luna.*

(And everything is there: Virgin and child, by her side; / San José (some are lucky to see his staff); / and the good little white donkey that / trots and trots over the fields of the moon.)

Suggestion

Help students formulate recipes for simple foods, such as a salad or a sandwich.

Note

Commands are strong forms, even when they are formal. They show power or control on the part of the person who says them. Encourage students to use *por favor* whenever possible to soften their requests, particularly until they learn more polite forms. Also make them aware of the importance of tone: a command uttered with a soft tone will not sound like a command but rather communicate a request.

Formal Command Forms

Emphasis A: Suggestions

- Explain that formal command forms use the "opposite" vowel.

  -ar → -e; -er/-ir → -a

- Present the regular command forms.
- Use the following rapid response drill.

  ¿Cuál es el mandato formal (Ud.) de _____?
  cierro
  recomiendo
  vuelvo
  duermo
  prefiero
  sirvo
  pido

- Present commands with spelling changes, including these verbs.

  tocar
  llegar
  jugar
  almorzar

¿Recuerda Ud.?

In **Gramática 20,** you will learn to form one type of command. In Spanish, the formal commands are based on the first person singular of the present tense. Review what you already know about irregular first person present tense forms by giving the **yo** form of the following infinitives.

1. salir   3. conocer   5. hacer   7. sentir
2. tener   4. pedir   6. dormir   8. traer

20   Influencing Others • Formal Commands

Receta para guacamole

El guacamole

Ingredientes:
1 aguacate[a]
1 diente de ajo,[b] prensado[c]
1 tomate
jugo de un limón
sal
un poco de cilantro fresco[d]

Cómo se prepara
Corte el aguacate y el tomate en trozos[e] pequeños. *Añada* el jugo del limón, el ajo, el cilantro y la sal a su gusto. *Mezcle* bien todos los ingredientes y *sírvalo* con tortillas fritas de maíz.[f]

En español, los mandatos se usan con frecuencia en las recetas. Estos verbos se usan en forma de mandato en esta receta. ¿Puede encontrarlos?

añadir	to add
cortar	to cut
mezclar	to mix
servir (i, i)	to serve

[a]*avocado*   [b]*diente… clove of garlic*   [c]*crushed*   [d]*fresh*   [e]*pieces*   [f]*corn*

Past ------------------- **PRESENT** ------------------- Future

present
present progressive
formal commands

Formal Command Forms

In *Puntos de partida* you have seen formal commands in the direction lines of activities since the beginning of the text: **haga, complete, conteste,** and so on.

Commands (imperatives) are verb forms used to tell someone to do something. In Spanish, *formal commands* (**los mandatos formales**) are used with people whom you address as **Ud.** or **Uds.** Here are some of the basic forms.

	hablar	comer	escribir	volver	decir
Ud.	hable	coma	escriba	vuelva	diga
Uds.	hablen	coman	escriban	vuelvan	digan
English	*speak*	*eat*	*write*	*come back*	*tell*

> **command or imperative** = a verb form used to tell someone to do something

A. Most formal command forms can be derived from the **yo** form of the present tense.

-ar: -o → -e   -er/-ir: -o → -a
        -en   -an

hablo → hable
como → coma
escribo → escriba

B. Formal commands of stem-changing verbs will show the stem change.

piense Ud.
vuelva Ud.
pida Ud.

C. Verbs ending in **-car, -gar,** and **-zar** have a spelling change to preserve the **-c-, -g-,** and **-z-** sounds.

c → qu   buscar: busque Ud.
g → gu   pagar: pague Ud.
z → c   empezar: empiece Ud.

D. Verbs that have irregular **yo** forms in the present tense will reflect the irregularity in the **Ud./Uds.** commands.

conocer: conozco   → conozca Ud.
decir* (*to say, tell*): digo   → diga Ud.
hacer: hago   → haga Ud.
oír: oigo   → oiga Ud.
poner: pongo   → ponga Ud.
salir: salgo   → salga Ud.
tener: tengo   → tenga Ud.
traer: traigo   → traiga Ud.
venir: vengo   → venga Ud.
ver: veo   → vea Ud.

E. A few verbs have irregular **Ud./Uds.** command forms.

dar* (*to give*)   → **dé** Ud.
estar   → **esté** Ud.
ir   → **vaya** Ud.
saber   → **sepa** Ud.
ser   → **sea** Ud.

Position of Pronouns with Formal Commands

■ Direct object pronouns and reflexive pronouns must follow affirmative commands and be attached to them. In order to maintain the original stress of the verb form, an accent mark is added to the stressed vowel if the original command has two or more syllables.

Pídalo Ud.   *Order it.*
Siéntese, por favor.   *Sit down, please.*

■ Direct object and reflexive pronouns must precede negative commands.

No lo pida Ud.   *Don't order it.*
No se siente.   *Don't sit down.*

---

*Decir and **dar** are used primarily with indirect objects. Both of these verbs and indirect object pronouns will be formally introduced in **Capítulo 7**.*

☀ Heritage Speakers

En algunos dialectos del español que se hablan tanto en los países de habla hispana como en los Estados Unidos, a veces se oye decir *siéntensen, acuéstesen* o *vístasen* para la tercera persona plural (Uds.). Aunque haya personas que usen estas formas en el habla popular, las formas preferidas son *siéntense, acuéstense* y *vístanse*.

Emphasis D: Suggestion
Present irregular commands. Review irregular *yo* forms. Give students the *Ud.* command form and have students give the infinitive, then give students the infinitive and have them respond with the *Ud.* command form.

Emphasis E: Suggestion
Point out that there are only five irregular commands. The accent is needed on *dé* to distinguish it from the preposition *de,* but not on *den.* Remind students that *esté* and *estén* both require accents.

Position of Pronouns with Formal Commands

Suggestion
Stress the use of written accents in command forms with attached direct object and reflexive pronouns.

Preliminary Exercises

■ Have students give the singular formal command of the following verbs.

ir ~ vaya
comer — coma
bailar baile
estar este
ser sea
volver vuelva
levantarse se levante

■ Have students give the plural formal command of the following verbs.

saber sepan
conocer conozcan
tener tengan
esperar esperen
jugar juegen
dormir duerman
acostarse se acuestan

■ Ask students.
*¿Dónde se pone el pronombre de complemento directo **lo**, delante o detrás de estos verbos?*

no coma   no lo coma
mire   mírelo
estudie   estúdielo
no compren   no lo compren
no paguen   no lo paguen
haga   hágalo

Prác. A: Extension

Change the commands to plural forms.

Prác. A: Suggestion

Have students add more possible commands to the list and insert them in the proper order.

Prác. B: Suggestion

Have students offer commands about what you should or should not do in class. Remind them to add *por favor* for politeness, and perhaps a begging tone to convince you to be nice to them.

■ ■ ■ Práctica

A. ¡Anticipemos! Una cena en casa. Los siguientes mandatos describen las acciones posibles cuando se prepara una cena elegante en casa. Póngalos en orden cronológico, del 1 al 8.

- **a.** _____ Vaya a la tienda para comprar comida y bebidas. *Vayan*
- **b.** _____ Abra la puerta cuando lleguen los invitados. *Abran*
- **c.** _____ Prepare algunos platos especiales. *Preparen*
- **d.** _____ Haga una lista de invitados. *hagan*
- **e.** _____ Diviértase con sus amigos. *diviértanse*
- **f.** _____ Ponga (*Set*) la mesa. *Pongan*
- **g.** _____ Llame a los amigos para invitarlos. *llamen*
- **h.** _____ Póngase ropa elegante. *pónganse*

B. Profesor(a) por un día. Imagine que Ud. es el profesor / la profesora hoy. ¿Qué mandatos debe dar a la clase?

> **MODELOS:** hablar español → Hablen Uds. español.
> hablar inglés → No hablen Uds. inglés.

1. llegar a tiempo *lleguen*
2. leer la lección *lean*
3. escribir una composición *escriban*
4. abrir los libros *abran*
5. estar en clase mañana *estén*
6. traer los libros a clase *traigan*
7. estudiar los verbos nuevos *estudien*
8. ¿ ?

AUTOPRUEBA

Complete the **Ud.** commands with the correct endings.

1. sirv_____
2. com_____
3. estudi_____
4. duerm_____
5. le_____
6. prepar_____

Answers: 1. sirva 2. coma 3. estudie 4. duerma 5. lea 6. prepare

EN LOS ESTADOS UNIDOS Y EL CANADÁ*

Necesita Tenerlos

Goya Foods, Inc.

En Norteamérica muchos conocen la marca Goya: hay **frijoles, arroz, condimentos, bebidas, café, productos de coco,**[a] **jugos de frutas tropicales** y muchos productos más que son fundamentales para **las cocinas caribeña, mexicana, centroamericana y sudamericana.**

En los años 30 Prudencio Unanue, **un emigrante vasco** del norte de España, funda[b] la compañía Goya. Unanue y **su esposa puertorriqueña** llegan a Nueva York en 1916 y fundan Unanue Inc. en Manhattan en 1935, una compañía especializada en **importaciones de productos españoles** como **olivas, aceite de oliva**[c] **y sardinas enlatadas.**[d] En 1936 la compañía adopta el nombre de Goya. Desde 1974 la oficina principal está en Nueva Jersey. Hoy tiene **centros de procesamiento y distribución** en diversos estados, además de Puerto Rico, la República Dominicana y España.

La compañía Goya está todavía en manos de[e] la familia Unanue: los hijos de Prudencio y seis miembros de **la tercera**[f] **generación.** Goya es la primera compañía propiedad de hispanos representada en el Museo Nacional de Historia Americana del Instituto Smithsonian, en Washington, D.C., donde hay una colección de sus anuncios y envases.[g]

[a]*coconut* [b]*founds, starts* [c]*aceite... olive oil* [d]*canned* [e]*está... still belongs to* [f]*third* [g]*anuncios... ads and containers*

From this point on in* Puntos de partida, *the* **En los Estados Unidos y el Canadá *sections will be written in Spanish. Important words will be in boldface type. Scanning those words before you begin to read will help you get the gist of the passage.*

EN LOS ESTADOS UNIDOS Y EL CANADÁ

Suggestions

- Check comprehension with *¿cierto o falso?* statements: **1.** *La familia Unanue es originalmente de México.* **2.** *La compañía Goya siempre tuvo (had) el nombre «Goya».* **3.** *Los productos Goya sólo son productos de la cocina de España.* **4.** *Los propietarios de Goya en la actualidad no son hispanos.* Also ask: *¿Cuál es uno de los grandes honores de la compañía Goya?*

- Ask students which Latin American and Spanish dishes they have tried. Have them list ingredients they know are used in Spain and some Latin American countries. Supplement that list if necessary. Ask: *¿Qué ingredientes tiene la paella? ¿Qué ingredientes llevan las enchiladas? ¿Quién conoce el choclo (maíz) del Perú?*

- Ask students if they know or buy the Goya brand.

- Have students visit a grocery store that sells Hispanic food to find Goya products and learn what they are for. Have them find other brands of Hispanic foods. Students can also find the Goya website on the Internet.

C. ¡Pobre Sr. Casiano!

Paso 1. El Sr. Casiano no se siente (*feel*) bien. Lea la descripción que él da de algunas de sus actividades.

«Trabajo[1] muchísimo[a] —¡me gusta trabajar! En la oficina, soy[2] impaciente y critico[3b] bastante[c] a los otros. En mi vida personal, a veces soy[4] un poco impulsivo. Fumo[5] bastante y también bebo[6] cerveza y otras bebidas alcohólicas, a veces sin moderación… Almuerzo[7] y ceno[8] fuerte, y casi nunca desayuno[9]. Por la noche, con frecuencia salgo[10] con los amigos —me gusta ir a las discotecas— y vuelvo[11] tarde a casa.»

[a]*a great deal*   [b]critico → criticar   [c]*a good deal*

Paso 2. ¿Qué *no* debe hacer el Sr. Casiano para estar mejor? Aconséjele (*Advise him*) sobre lo que (*what*) no debe hacer. Use los verbos indicados en azul o cualquier (*any*) otro, según los modelos.

MODELOS: Trabajo → Sr. Casiano, no trabaje tanto.
soy → Sr. Casiano, no sea tan impaciente.

D. Situaciones.
El Sr. Casiano quiere adelgazar (*to lose weight*). ¿Debe o no debe comer o beber las siguientes cosas? Con otro/a estudiante, haga y conteste preguntas según los modelos:

MODELOS: ensalada → E1: ¿Ensalada?   postres → E1: ¿Postres?
E2: Cómala.   E2: No *los* coma.

1. alcohol (*m.*)   ~~No la beba~~ *No se beba*
2. verduras   *Cómalas*
3. pan   *No lo coma.*
4. dulces   *No los coma.*
5. leche   *Bébala.*
6. hamburguesas con queso   *Cómalas.*
7. frutas   *Cómalas*
8. refrescos dietéticos   *Cómalos*
9. pollo   *Cómalo*
10. carne   *No la coma mucho*
11. pizza   *No la coma mucho*
12. jugo de fruta   *No lo beba mucho*

E. ¡Estoy harto de Uds. dos!
(*I'm fed up with you two!*) Imagine que Ud. acaba de volver de clase y la casa es un desastre. Está enojado/a y empieza a gritarles (*yell*) mandatos a sus compañeros de casa sobre su apariencia física y sus hábitos.

MODELO: afeitarse → ¡Aféitense!

1. despertarse más temprano   *Despiértense*
2. levantarse más temprano   *Levántese*
3. bañarse más   *Báñense*
4. quitarse esa ropa sucia   *Quítense*
5. ponerse ropa limpia   *Pónganse*
6. vestirse mejor   *Vístanse*
7. estudiar más   *estudiense*
8. no divertirse todas las noches con los amigos
9. ir más a la biblioteca   *Váyanse*
10. no acostarse tan tarde   *No se acuesten*
11. ayudar con los quehaceres   *Ayúdense*
12. ¿ ?   *8 diviértense*

※ **Heritage Speakers**

Pídales a los hispanohablantes que le expliquen al resto de la clase las diferencias entre la comida auténtica de Latinoamérica y España, y la comida latinoamericana y española que se consume en este país.

Prác. C: Note
The verbs on which commands should be based are indicated in *italics*.

Prác. C: Variation
Have students give advice to *los Sres. Casiano*.

Prác. D: Preliminary Exercises
■ Have students give the negative command for each of these affirmative commands.

1. *Cómprelo.*   4. *Llámeme.*
2. *Estúdielas.*   5. *Apréndalo.*
3. *Mírelo.*   6. *Escríbame.*

■ Have students give the affirmative command for each of these negative commands.

1. *No lo coma.*   4. *No lo sirva.*
2. *No lo lea.*   5. *No lo traiga.*
3. *No lo haga.*

Prác. D: Follow-Up
Give students the following situation and have them provide appropriate commands.

Luisa y Carlos llegan a su primer día de escuela en la clase del primer año. La maestra les explica las reglas de conducta, especialmente la conducta prohibida. ¿Qué mandatos les da?

Offer students the following suggestions.

no comer en el salón de clase
no hablar cuando habla la maestra
no pegar (to hit) *a los amiguitos*
no traer animales a clase
no escribir en las paredes
no llegar tarde

¿Qué otros mandatos, afirmativos o negativos, recuerdan Uds. de la escuela primaria?

Prác. E: Preliminary Exercises
■ Have students give the negative command for each of the following affirmative commands.

1. *Acuéstese.*   3. *Lávese.*
2. *Aféitese.*   4. *Siéntese.*

■ Have students give the affirmative command for each of the following negative commands.

1. *No se bañe.*
2. *No se levante.*
3. *No se quite los zapatos.*
4. *No se ponga la chaqueta.*

Prác. E: Variation
Have students give advice (*Uds.* commands) to the roommates.

NOTA COMUNICATIVA

Note

This introduction to the subjunctive will familiarize students with its forms and uses. At this point, students will only be expected to passively recognize these forms and understand why/how they are used. More detailed explanations of and subsequent practice with the subjunctive are provided in *Capítulo 12*. From this point on, however, instructor's annotations may use the subjunctive so that students receive meaningful input.

Suggestion

Conjugate the present subjunctive of *bailar* and *comer* on the board. Start with *Quiero que* [*tú/él/ella...*]. Point out that if the subject of both clauses is the same, the second verb is often used in the infinitive.

Prác. F: Preliminary Exercises

■ Have students tell whether these verbs are *yo* subjunctive or *yo* indicative.

cene, cena   pido, pida
vaya, va   lleve, llevo
hago, haga   me visto, me vista

■ Have students complete the sentence with the correct *Uds.* forms of the subjunctive of the verbs that follow.

Yo deseo que Uds...
   estudiar
   bailar
   comprarme regalos
   hacerme feliz
   llegar a tiempo a clase
   divertirse

Prác. F: Note

This activity deals with recognition of forms and conceptualization of the subjunctive only.

Prác. F: Suggestion

Paso 1. Have students read for the general idea of the dialogues. They should pay close attention to the forms of the underlined verbs and begin thinking about why some are in the indicative and some in the subjunctive.

NOTA COMUNICATIVA

El subjuntivo

Except for the command form, all verb forms that you have learned thus far in *Puntos de partida* have been part of the *indicative mood* (**el modo indicativo**). In both English and Spanish, the indicative is used to state facts and to ask questions. It objectively expresses most real-world actions or states of being.

Both English and Spanish have another verb system called the *subjunctive mood* (**el modo subjuntivo**), which will be introduced in **Capítulo 12**. The Ud./Uds. command forms that you have just learned are part of the subjunctive system. From this point on in *Puntos de partida* you will see the subjunctive used where it is natural to use it. What follows is a brief introduction to the subjunctive that will make it easy for you to recognize it when you see it.

Here are some examples of the forms of the subjunctive. The **Ud./Uds.** forms (identical to the **Ud./Uds.** command forms) are highlighted.

hablar		comer		servir		salir	
hable	hablemos	coma	comamos	sirva	sirvamos	salga	salgamos
hables	habléis	comas	comáis	sirvas	sirváis	salgas	salgáis
hable	hablen	coma	coman	sirva	sirvan	salga	salgan

The subjunctive is used to express more subjective or conceptualized states, in contrast to the indicative, which reports facts, information that is objectively true. Here are just a few of the situations in which the subjunctive is used in Spanish.

■ to express what the speaker wants others to do (I want you to . . .)
■ to express emotional reactions (I'm glad that . . .)
■ to express probability or uncertainty (It's likely that . . .)

F. El cumpleaños de María. Fíjese en (*Notice*) los verbos subrayados (*underlined*) en los siguientes diálogos. Diga por qué razón están subrayados. (Use la lista de la **Nota comunicativa.**)

En el parque

RAÚL: Como hoy es tu cumpleaños, quiero invitarte a cenar. ¿En qué restaurante quieres que <u>cenemos</u>?

MARÍA: Prefiero que tú me[a] <u>prepares</u> una de tus espléndidas cenas.

RAÚL: ¡Con mucho gusto!

En casa de María

MADRE: (*Hablando por teléfono.*) No, lo siento,[b] pero María no está en casa.

LUISA: ¿Es posible que <u>esté</u> en la biblioteca?

MADRE: No. Sé que ella y Raúl están cenando en casa de él.

LUISA: Ah, sí. Bueno, ¿puede pedirle a ella que <u>llame</u> a Luisa cuando regrese?

MADRE: Sí, cómo no,[c] Luisa. Adiós.

LUISA: Hasta luego.

[a]*for me*   [b]*lo... I'm sorry*   [c]*cómo... of course*

Need more practice?

■ Workbook and Laboratory Manual
■ Interactive CD-ROM
■ Online Learning Center (www.mhhe.com/ puntos7)

National Standards: Comparisons

Students tend to be unfamiliar with the use of the subjunctive in English. The subjunctive is not used as often in English as in Spanish, but speakers and writers use it in phrases such as the following.

God bless you.
I wish I were rich.
We hope that he may be able to come.
If I were hungry, I would order the steak and lobster.
She demands that I be there at noon.

NOTA COMUNICATIVA

"Softening" Commands

In both English and Spanish, commands can be a very blunt way of requesting things. Here are some ways you can soften your requests.

■ using polite expressions

favor de + *inf.*	please (do something)
por favor	please
si me hace (Ud.) el favor	if you would do me the favor
si es (Ud.) tan amable	if you would be so kind

■ using a question in the present tense, as well as using an expression from the previous list

¿Me trae otra cerveza, **por favor**?   *Will you bring me another beer, please?*

■ using the verb **poder** to increase your politeness

Por favor, ¿**puede** traerme más pan?   *Could you please bring me more bread?*

Can you think of situations in which softer requests might be more appropriate than direct commands?

En la oficina del consejero. Imagine that you are a guidance counselor. Students consult you with all kinds of questions, some trivial and some important. Offer advice to them in the form of affirmative or negative commands, or softened requests. How many different commands can you invent for each situation?

MODELO: ¿Puede Ud. describir su horario, primero?
Y, por favor, incluya las comidas y…

1. EVELIA: No me gusta tomar clases por la mañana. Siempre estoy muy cansada durante esas clases y además a esa hora tengo hambre. Pienso constantemente en el almuerzo… y no puedo concentrarme en las explicaciones.

2. FABIÁN: En mi clase de cálculo, ¡no entiendo nada! No puedo hacer los ejercicios y durante la clase tengo miedo de hacer preguntas, porque no quiero parecer (*seem*) tonto.

3. FAUSTO: Fui (*I went*) a México el verano pasado y me gustó (*I liked it*) mucho. Quiero volver a México este verano. Ahora que lo conozco mejor, quiero ir en mi coche y no en autobús como el verano pasado. Desgraciadamente (*Unfortunately*) no tengo dinero para hacer el viaje.

Prác. F: Follow-Up

Ask students the following *sí/no* questions.

1. *¿María quiere ir a un restaurante? ¿Quiere cocinar?*
2. *Y Raúl, ¿quiere hacer algo por María? ¿Quiere María que Raúl haga algo por ella?*
3. *¿Quiere María que Raúl la invite a un restaurante? ¿Quiere que él cocine para ella?*
4. *La amiga de María, ¿quiere hablar con la madre de María? ¿Sabe la amiga dónde está María? Y la madre, ¿sabe dónde está María?*
5. *La amiga, ¿quiere ir a casa de Raúl para hablar con María? ¿Quiere que María la llame?*
6. *¿Quiere la amiga que María la llame durante la cena con Raúl? ¿cuando María vuelva a casa?*

NOTA COMUNICATIVA

Suggestion

Have students ask each other for classroom items. After one student makes a request, have others rephrase it.

Con: Follow-Up

■ Have students give affirmative and negative commands in response to the following statements.

1. *Estoy cansado.* Descanse
2. *Tengo sed.* Beba
3. *Tengo hambre.* Coma
4. *No puedo dormir.* Duerma
5. *No entiendo el ejercicio.* Estudié
6. *Necesito más dinero.* Gánelo
7. *Mis padres quieren saber cómo estoy.* Dígalos
8. *No puedo encontrar mi libro de español.* Encuéntrelo

■ Have students write commands that they would like to give to the following persons:

1. *el presidente / el primer ministro*
2. *los candidatos*
3. Jay Leno, David Letterman (or any other television personality)
4. *sus amigos*
5. *el profesor / la profesora*

Con: Extension

4. *RAMÓN: Siempre llego tarde a las clases. Como tengo tanta prisa, no traigo los libros ni los papeles que necesito. Hoy no desayuné pero, ¡ni eso (not even that) me ayudó!* (Note: Explain preterite forms.)

UN POCO DE TODO

A: Follow-Up
Have students narrate their routines on a given day of the week. This can be done in pairs or directed by questions.

A: Extension
Paso 2.
5. *Quiero que Samuel llegue ya. ¡Vamos a llegar tarde a clase!*
6. *¿Quieres ir a la conferencia de antropología esta tarde?*
7. *Yo sé que Uds. van a recibir una nota muy buena en este curso.*

B: Suggestion
Ask students the following questions:

1. *¿Prefiere Ud. cenar en casa o en la cafetería estudiantil?*
2. *¿Hay días que no almuerce/cene? ¿Por qué?*
3. *¿Prefiere Ud. una hamburguesa o un bistec?*
4. *¿Qué/Dónde come Ud. cuando tiene mucha prisa / mucho dinero / poco dinero?*
5. *¿Qué bebida prefiere por la mañana/noche?*
6. *¿Qué le gusta comer como merienda?*

UN POCO DE TODO

A. ¿Qué hace Roberto los martes?

Paso 1. Describa la rutina de Roberto, haciendo oraciones según las indicaciones.

> MODELO: martes / Roberto / nunca / salir / apartamento / antes de / doce →
> Los martes Roberto nunca sale de su apartamento antes de las doce.

1. esperar / su amigo Samuel / en / parada del autobús (*bus stop*)
2. (ellos) llegar / universidad / a / una
3. (ellos) buscar / su amiga Ceci / en / cafetería
4. ella / acabar / empezar / estudios / allí
5. (ella) no / conocer / mucha gente (*people*) / todavía
6. a veces / (ellos) ver / profesora de historia en / cafetería / y / hablar / un poco / con ella
7. (ella) ser / persona / muy interesante / que / saber / mucho / de / ese / materia
8. a / dos / todos / tener / clase / de / sicología
9. siempre / (ellos) oír / conferencias (*lectures*) / interesante / y / hacer / alguno / pregunta
10. a veces / tener / oportunidad de / conocer / conferenciante (*m., lecturer*)
11. a / cinco / Samuel y Roberto / volver / esperar / autobús
12. Roberto / preparar / cena / y / luego / mirar / televisión

Paso 2. ¿Quién habla? Base su respuesta en la información del **Paso 1.**

1. Quiero conocer a más gente. ¡Casi no conozco a nadie todavía!
2. Algunos estudiantes hacen buenas preguntas.
3. ¿Dónde está Roberto? Va a llegar tarde otra vez…
4. ¡Ay! ¡Ya son las doce! ¡Tengo que salir!

Paso 3. Ahora vuelva a contar la historia desde el punto de vista de Roberto, usando **yo** o **nosotros** como sujeto donde sea apropiado.

B. Educación culinaria. Complete the following passages with the correct forms of the words in parentheses, as suggested by the context. When two possibilities are given in parentheses, select the correct word. **¡OJO!** As you conjugate verbs in this activity, note that you will make formal commands with some infinitives.

> **U**nos estudiantes de la clase del Dr. Robles tienen que presentar hoy su informe oral[a] acerca de[b] varias comidas internacionales.
>
> TERRY: Este informe sobre la comida (japonés[1]) es interesante, pero yo no (saber/conocer[2]) si quiero comer tanto pescado crudo (que/como[3]) los japoneses… .
> MARTY: (*Yo:* Ser/Estar[4]) de acuerdo contigo. Pero sí me gusta la idea de comer mucho arroz.

[a]informe… *oral report* [b]*about*

National Standards: Comparisons

Use activity B as a springboard for a discussion about differences in cuisine among Spanish-speaking countries. Have students research different countries and areas, and have the class create a culinary map that shows traditional dishes from different countries. Remind students that some areas do have similar or the same dishes, for example, *moros y cristianos* (black beans and rice) is prepared in several Caribbean countries, including Puerto Rico, Cuba, and Colombia. Encourage them to find other similarities (*ceviche, sancocho,* and so on).

DR. ROBLES: ¡Clase, clase! ¡Silencio, por favor! Uds. están (hacer⁵) mucho ruido. Terry, Marty, no (hablar⁶), por favor, durante los informes. (*Uds.:* Escucharlos⁷) bien, porque mañana (ir⁸) a contestar unas preguntas sobre (este⁹) presentaciones. Ahora (venir¹⁰) el informe de Sonia sobre la comida de Panamá.

TERRY: Eh, Marty, te apuesto aᶜ que la comida (panameño¹¹) es igual a la comida mexicana: muchos tacos y tortillas, ¿no?

MARTY: Es probable.

SONIA: ¡Qué ignorantes (ser/estar¹²) Uds.! ¡No saben (algo/nada¹³) de la comida panameña!

Sonia empieza (a/de¹⁴) leer:

—Hoy en día, en gran parte debido aᵈ su famoso Canal, Panamá (ser/estar¹⁵) un país internacional que (mantener¹⁶)ᵉ relaciones (histórico¹⁷) y (amistoso¹⁸)ᶠ con varios países. Se nota mucho la influencia de los Estados Unidos. Muchos panameños (saber/conocer¹⁹) inglés, y (lo/la²⁰) hablan especialmente en las áreas metropolitanas. Se puede ver la influencia (extranjero²¹) en la comida cosmopolita de Panamá. Muchos restaurantes (especializarse²²) en comida internacional: italiana, francesa, estadounidense, del Oriente y del Medio Oriente. Pero los panameños no (perder²³) su identidad nacional, y frecuentemente (preferir²⁴) servir la comida tradicional. En la comida tradicional panameña hay muchos platos de mariscos y pescados, especialmente el ceviche. Las personas vegetarianas no (tener²⁵) problema con la comida tradicional porque hay una variedad de platos (preparado²⁶) con verduras y arroz. El arroz es un ingrediente importante en la comida de Panamá. Generalmente cuando los turistas (preguntar²⁷) «¿Cuál es el plato nacional de Panamá?», los panameños (contestar²⁸) «Es el arroz con pollo».

ᶜte... *I'll bet you*   ᵈdebido... *due to*   ᵉ*to maintain*   ᶠ*friendly*

Comprensión: ¿Qué pasa en clase hoy? Answer the following questions in Spanish.

1. ¿Qué están haciendo hoy en la clase del Dr. Robles?
2. ¿Qué piensan Terry y Marty de la comida japonesa?
3. Describe un poco la comida panameña. ¿Cómo es?
4. ¿Por qué no tienen problema los vegetarianos con la comida panameña?

Resources for Review and Testing Preparation

- Workbook and Laboratory Manual
- Interactive CD-ROM
- Online Learning Center (www.mhhe.com/puntos7)

B: Variation

Have students imagine that a foreigner in this country asks them about certain foods and where he/she can find them in your area. Have students give as much information as possible.

1. *una tortilla española*
2. *una langosta*
3. *una hamburguesa*
4. *unas chuletas*
5. *pizza*
6. *arándanos* (blueberries)

Resources: Desenlace

In the *Capítulo 6* segment of "Chapter-by-Chapter Supplementary Materials" in the IM, you will find a chapter-culminating activity. You can use this activity to consolidate and review the vocabulary and grammar skills students have acquired.

Entrevista cultural

Suggestions

- Before showing the video, ask students questions about restaurants.

    ¿Trabaja Ud. en un restaurante o conoce a alguien que trabaje en un restaurante? ¿Qué hace en el restaurante? ¿Le gusta su trabajo?

    ¿Cuáles son sus restaurantes favoritos? ¿Qué tipo de platos se sirven en esos restaurantes?

- Show the video and allow students one to two minutes to work on the questions.

    Have volunteers answer the questions. Encourage them to answer in Spanish if possible.

- Have volunteers role-play Maír and the interviewer.

Entre amigos

Suggestions

- Before viewing the video, review the questions with the students and ask them similar questions.

    ¿Quién cocina en su casa? ¿Sabe Ud. cocinar? ¿Qué platos sabe Ud. preparar?

    Have students answer or work in small groups to ask and answer these questions.

- After viewing the video, have volunteers read and answer the questions.

PERSPECTIVAS culturales

●●● Videoteca

Entrevista cultural: Panamá

Maír Citón Moreno es dueño de un restaurante en su país, Panamá. En esta entrevista habla de los platos que se sirven en su restaurante. También habla de los ingredientes más comunes y de su plato favorito. Antes de ver el vídeo, lea el siguiente fragmento de la entrevista.

ENTREVISTADORA: ¿Qué tipo de restaurante es, y qué tipo de comida se sirve?

MAÍR: Es un restaurante exclusivamente de comida típica panameña y en base al maíz[a] y el arroz.

ENTREVISTADORA: ¿Cuáles son los platillos más típicos de Panamá?

MAÍR: Los platillos más típicos de Panamá serían[b] el arroz de frijoles de palo,[c] el sancocho de gallina,[d] los tamales, las tortillas asadas, entre otros.

[a]*en... corn-based* [b]*would be* [c]*frijoles... palo beans* [d]*sancocho... dish with chicken, yucca, plantain, and other ingredients*

Ahora vea el vídeo y conteste las siguientes preguntas basándose en la entrevista.

1. ¿Dónde vive y trabaja Maír?
2. ¿Qué tipo de comida se sirve en el restaurante de Maír?
3. ¿Cuáles son los ingredientes básicos de la cocina panameña?
4. ¿Cuáles son unos ingredientes tropicales y unos tipos de carne que se mencionan en la entrevista?
5. ¿Cuál es el plato favorito de Maír?

Entre amigos: ¿Quién cocina en tu casa?

Tané prepara la comida para una fiesta. Karina, Rubén y Miguel van a ayudarla a cocinar. En su opinión, ¿qué preguntas van a hacerse? Antes de mirar el vídeo, lea las preguntas a continuación (*that follow*). Mientras mire el vídeo, trate de entender la conversación en general y fíjese en la información sobre la comida. Luego mire el vídeo una segunda vez, fijándose en la información que necesita para contestar las preguntas.

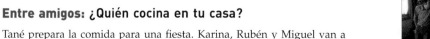

1. ¿Qué prepara Tané?
2. ¿Quién cocina en casa de Tané?
3. ¿Sabe cocinar Rubén? ¿Por qué sí o no?
4. Según Miguel, ¿cómo se prepara el posole, un plato mexicano muy conocido?

Conozca... Panamá

Datos esenciales

- Nombre oficial: República de Panamá
- Capital: Ciudad de Panamá
- Población: 2.960.784 habitantes
- Moneda: el balboa (también se usa el dólar estadounidense)
- Idioma oficial: el español

¡Fíjese!

- **Panamá** es una palabra indígena que significa «tierra de muchos peces[a]».
- La Carretera[b] Panamericana, el sistema de carreteras que va de Alaska a la Argentina, se interrumpe[c] en la densa e[d] impenetrable selva[e] panameña de Darién. Para llegar a Sudamérica es necesario tomar un barco[f] hasta Colombia, donde continúa la carretera.
- La Sra. Mireya Moscoso ganó[g] las elecciones presidenciales de 1998. La viuda[h] de otro presidente, doña Mireya es la primera mujer panameña en asumir el cargo.[i]

[a]fish [b]Highway [c]se... breaks off, is interrupted [d]y [e]jungle [f]boat [g]won [h]widow [i]post

▲ Una esclusa del Canal de Panamá

Learn more about Panama with the Video, the Interactive CD-ROM, and the Online Learning Center (www.mhhe.com/puntos7).

Lugares famosos: el Canal de Panamá

El Canal de Panamá, construido a través del[a] istmo entre los dos continentes americanos, comunica los océanos Atlántico y Pacífico. Mide[b] aproximadamente 80 kilómetros (50 millas) de largo, 12,5 metros (41 pies[c]) de ancho[d] y 200 metros (más de 63 pies) de profundidad. Su construcción facilita la comunicación marítima entre las costas este y oeste de los continentes. Antes de la existencia del canal, los barcos tenían que darle la vuelta a[e] América del Sur para ir de una costa a otra. Hoy, el viaje por el Canal de Panamá toma aproximadamente ocho horas, pues[f] es necesario pasar por un número de esclusas.[g]

La idea de construir un canal a través del istmo data de 1534, cuando el emperador español Carlos V (Quinto) la propone. Más tarde, en 1881, el ingeniero francés Fernando de Lesseps también sugiere un proyecto similar. Pero el canal no se construye hasta el siglo XX, por los Estados Unidos. Esto ocasiona[h] la presencia de los Estados Unidos en la vida de Panamá. Como resultado, hay un uso extendido del inglés en el país, se usa el dólar y ha habido[i] una gran intervención en la política del país.

El canal se inaugura en 1914 y es administrado por los Estados Unidos hasta 1999. Desde el primero de enero del año 2000, la República de Panamá está a cargo de[j] su gran canal.

[a]construido... built across the [b]It measures [c]feet [d]de... in width [e]tenían... had to go around [f]because [g]canal locks [h]brings about [i]ha... there has been [j]a... in control of

Notes

- Vasco Núñez de Balboa explored the Isthmus of Panama in 1513 and discovered that it was only a short distance from the Atlantic Ocean to the Pacific Ocean. He founded the first settlements on the north coast.
- Gold from Peru traveled across Panama during Spanish colonial times, as did prospectors headed for the California gold fields in 1849.
- General Manuel Noriega ousted the Panamanian president in 1985 and became acting head of government. After Noriega was indicted for drug activities and other illegal acts, the U.S. Army invaded Panama and brought Noriega to Miami for trial. He was convicted in 1992.
- Students can read *"Desarraigado"* by Panama's Carlos Guillermo Wilson in *Un paso más 6.*

MULTIMEDIA: Internet

Have students search the Internet for more information about traveling to Panama. Students will be able to find pages about Panamanian food, education, culture, newspapers, and more. Some pages are in both English and Spanish. Remind students to look for images of the Panama Canal as well.

Perspectivas culturales ■ 215

Suggestions

- Have students respond *cierto* or *falso*.

  1. *El bistec viene del cerdo.*
  2. *El bistec es más caro que la hamburguesa.*
  3. *Son populares los sándwiches de jamón.*

- Ask students: *¿Cuál es correcto?*

  1. *En Nebraska, ¿sirven mucho el bistec o muchos mariscos frescos?*
  2. *¿Cuál es más barata, la hamburguesa o la langosta?*
  3. *¿Se usa Shake 'n' Bake con los mariscos o con el pollo?*

- Have students work in small groups to write up a menu for tonight's meal. To compare the menus, have a member of each group read their menu. The class should vote on the most appealing menu.

- Remind students that *conocer* is irregular in the *yo* form: *conozco.*

EN RESUMEN

Gramática

To review the grammar points presented in this chapter, refer to the indicated grammar presentations. You'll find further practice of these structures in the Workbook and Laboratory Manual, on the Interactive CD-ROM, and on the *Puntos de partida* Online Learning Center (www.mhhe.com/puntos7).

18. Expressing *what* or *whom*—Direct Object Pronouns

Do you know how to avoid repetition by using direct object pronouns?

19. Expressing Negation—Indefinite and Negative Words

Do you know how to use the double negative in Spanish?

20. Influencing Others—Formal Commands

You should know how to use commands to order in restaurants and to have someone do something for you.

Vocabulario
Practice this vocabulary with digital flash cards on the Online Learning Center (www.mhhe.com/puntos7).

Los verbos

acabar de + *inf.*	to have just (*done something*)
ayudar	to help
cenar	to have (eat) dinner, supper
cocinar	to cook
conocer (zc)*	to know, be acquainted with
desayunar	to have (eat) breakfast
esperar	to wait (for); to expect
invitar	to invite
llamar	to call
preguntar	to ask (a question)
preparar	to prepare
saber (*irreg.*)	to know
saber + *inf.*	to know how to (*do something*)

Repaso: almorzar (ue) (c)*

La comida

el arroz	rice
las arvejas	peas
el atún	tuna
el bistec	steak
los camarones	shrimp
la carne	meat
el cereal	cereal
el champiñón	mushroom

la chuleta (de cerdo)	(pork) chop
los dulces	sweets; candy
los espárragos	asparagus
el flan	(baked) custard
los frijoles	beans
la galleta	cookie
el helado	ice cream
el huevo	egg
el jamón	ham
la langosta	lobster
la lechuga	lettuce
la mantequilla	butter
la manzana	apple
los mariscos	shellfish
la naranja	orange
el pan	bread
el pan tostado	toast
el pastel	cake; pie
la patata (frita)	(French fried) potato
el pavo	turkey
el pescado	fish
el pollo (asado)	(roast) chicken
el postre	dessert
el queso	cheese
la salchicha	sausage; hot dog
la sopa	soup
las verduras	vegetables
la zanahoria	carrot

---

*From this chapter on, the spelling changes for verbs in the subjunctive and formal commands such as **-c-** → **-qu-**, **-g-** → **-gu-**, **-z-** → **-c-**, as well as verbs with **-zc-** and **-g-** changes in the present tense **yo** form, will be indicated in parentheses in the vocabulary lists.*

Las bebidas

el agua (mineral)	(mineral) water
el jugo (de fruta)	(fruit) juice
la leche	milk
el refresco	soft drink
el té	tea
el vino (blanco, tinto)	(white, red) wine

Repaso: el café, la cerveza

Los cognados

la banana
la ensalada
la fruta
la hamburguesa
el salmón
el sándwich
el tomate
el yogur

Las comidas

el almuerzo	lunch
la cena	dinner, supper

Repaso: el desayuno

En un restaurante

el/la camarero/a	waiter/waitress
la cuenta	check, bill
el menú	menu
el plato	dish; course

Otros sustantivos

el consejo	(piece of) advice
el detalle	detail
el/la dueño/a	owner
la tarjeta de crédito	credit card

Los adjetivos

fresco/a	fresh
frito/a	fried
fuerte	heavy (*meal, food*); strong
ligero/a	light, not heavy
rápido/a	fast

Palabras indefinidas y negativas

alguien	someone, anyone
algún (alguno/a/os/as)	some, any
jamás	never
nada	nothing, not anything
nadie	no one, nobody, not anybody
ningún (ninguno/a)	no, none, not any
tampoco	neither, not either

Repaso: algo, nunca, siempre, también

Palabras adicionales

estar (*irreg.*) a dieta	to be on a diet
tener (*irreg.*) (mucha) hambre	to be (very) hungry
tener (*irreg.*) (mucha) sed	to be (very) thirsty

Suggestion
Have students write brief reviews of restaurants based on recent visits. Encourage them to use negative and indefinite words.

Un paso más 6

Literatura de Panamá

Notes

- Carlos Guillermo Wilson has published two novels, *Chombo* (1981) and *Los nietos de Felicidad Dolores* (1991), and several collections of short stories and poems.
- *Los nietos de Felicidad Dolores* is about the 500-year journey (1492–1992) through identity conflicts, racial discrimination, and injustice of the African slaves and their descendents in the Antilles and Latin America.
- Wilson himself is a descendent of French-speaking great-grandparents from the island of St. Lucia and English-speaking maternal grandparents from Barbados and Jamaica. The latter moved to Panama where they were contracted to work on the Panama Canal.
- Wilson studied in Panama and in the United States and holds a doctorate in Hispanic Language and Literature from UCLA. He writes extensively on African American issues in Latin America and the Caribbean.

LECTURA

Suggestion

Do the *Estrategia* in class on the day you assign the reading as homework. Have students come up with words in English that have multiple meanings. You can give *fly*, *can*, *trunk*, and *bill* as examples. Emphasize the importance of determining the appropriate translation when using a bilingual dictionary.

Literatura de Panamá

Sobre el autor: *Carlos Guillermo Wilson es originario de Panamá. Actualmente enseña literatura en San Diego State University en California. Su poesía y sus cuentos tratan con frecuencia los temas de la raza y el prejuicio racial. El siguiente poema es del cuento «Los mosquitos de orixá Changó[a]»[*]*

▲ Carlos Guillermo Wilson (1941–)

> Desarraigado[b]
>
> Abuelita africana,
> ¿no me reconoces?
>
> Mi lengua es cervantina
> Mi letanía[c] es cristiana
> Mi danza es flamenca
> Mi raza es mulata
>
> Abuelita africana,
> ¿por qué no me reconoces?

[a]*orixá... the ancient deity Changó, a god representing man's virility* [b]*Uprooted* [c]*litany (religious rite)*

LECTURA

ESTRATEGIA: Words with Multiple Meanings

It is easy to get off track while reading Spanish (or any language!) if you assign the wrong meaning to a word that has multiple English equivalents. For example, the word **como** in Spanish can cause confusion because it can mean *how, like, the way, as, since,* and *I eat,* depending on the context. Other common words with multiple meanings include **clase** (*class meeting, course, kind,* or *type*), and **esperar** (*to wait for, to hope, to expect*).

Often you must rely on the context to determine which meaning is appropriate. See if you can determine the correct meaning of **como** in the following sentences.

1. En España, como en Francia, se come mucho pescado.
2. Cuando voy a mi restaurante favorito, siempre como una ensalada.
3. Como tú no quieres estudiar, ¿por qué no tomamos un café?

Publication of the Afro-Latin/American Research Association (PALARA), #1, 1997: 138–142.

CULTURE

Traditional dishes throughout the Hispanic world use all parts of the pig and cow. This is not unlike other traditional cuisines, although it seems very removed from today's mainstream cuisine in the U.S. and Canada.

■ **Sobre la lectura...** The following reading was taken from *Américas* magazine, which is a publication of the Organization of American States. This bimonthly magazine publishes articles of interest about the Spanish-speaking countries of North, Central, and South America. Topics often include the environment, travel, cuisine, the arts, and politics. This excerpt profiles a Hispanic chef from New York and his outreach program to other Hispanic culinary professionals.

Suggestion
After students have completed the *Lectura*, have them make a list of all the ingredients mentioned in the article. Ask them which of these ingredients are commonly used in this country, in what kind of recipes, and if they differ from ingredients in Hispanic recipes.

La cocina de Palomino

Cualquiera pensaría[a] que <u>manejar</u> tres restaurantes, escribir libros de cocina y <u>supervisar</u> la fabricación y distribución de su propio[b] postre sería[c] trabajo suficiente para un solo hombre. Pero el chef Rafael Palomino tiene otro <u>proyecto</u>, que nació de la creencia[d] de que quizá los empleados de sus restaurantes, algunos muy <u>talentosos</u> y con gran potencial,[e] nunca cumplan[f] el sueño de abrir su propio negocio.

«Muchos de los que trabajaban para mí sentían[g] que lo más alto a que podían[h] llegar era[i] a sous chefs», dice Palomino. La mayoría eran <u>hablantes nativos</u> de español. Podrían estar cocinando[j] pasta primavera, pato[k] o costillas,[l] pero no importa cuán habilidosos sean, las <u>barreras</u> del idioma, la cultura y el entrenamiento hacen que encarar[m] un negocio tan complicado y riesgoso[n] como un restaurante parezca imposible.

Por eso, Palomino comenzó[o] la Asociación de Chefs Españoles de América. Es una organización <u>comunitaria</u> que procura servir de centro de información y asesoramiento[p] sobre:

- oportunidades de capacitación[q]
- información básica sobre el negocio
- experiencias de chefs y <u>empresarios</u> exitosos

Palomino, oriundo de Bogotá, Colombia, creció[r] en Queens, Nueva York y ahora dirige[s] «Vida», en Manhattan, y «Sonora», en Port Chester, Nueva York. El último libro de Palomino, *Viva la vida: Festive Recipes for Entertaining Latin-Style* (publicado por Arlen Gargagliano, Chronicle Books), se concentra en la cocina casera[t] latinoamericana, y pone al alcance del cocinero común[u] recetas no tan conocidas de ceviches, ensaladas y estofados.

A continuación hay una receta de su libro, para salsa de mango y lima.

[a]Cualquiera... *One would think* [b]*own* [c]*would be* [d]*que... which was born from the belief* [e]*con... full of potential* [f]*achieve* [g]*felt* [h]*they could* [i]*was* [j]Podrían... *They could be cooking* [k]*duck* [l]*ribs* [m]*facing, starting* [n]*risky* [o]*founded* [p]*counseling* [q]*training* [r]*grew up* [s]*he directs* [t]*home style* [u]pone... *makes available to the average cook*

© Arlen Gargagliano

▲ *Rafael Palomino*

National Standards: Comparisons

Have students research the names of famous chefs and cookbook writers from this country and from Spanish-speaking countries. Have students share information and compare the kinds of dishes the chefs prepare. Do Hispanic chefs have more of a tendency to prepare dishes that are culturally connected to a country, region, or ethnic group?

Comprensión: Suggestion
Suggest that students first read for general meaning, then do *Comprensión A*. Then read a second time and do *Comprensión B* and *C*.

Salsa de mango y lima (3 tazas)

1 mango, <u>pelado y cortado</u> en cubos de un cuarto de pulgada[v]

2 cucharadas[w] de tequila dorado

jugo de una naranja

jugo de dos limas

6 hojas de menta fresca, apiladas, enrolladas y cortadas en <u>tiras finas</u>

2 cucharadas de aceite de oliva

1 <u>cucharadita</u> de <u>mostaza</u> Pommery or Dijon

1 pepino,[x] sin semillas y cortado en cubitos de un cuarto de pulgada

Sal Kosher y pimienta recién molida, al gusto

En un recipiente mediano[y] de vidrio o cerámica, combine el mango, el tequila, el jugo de naranja y el jugo de lima. Mezcle revolviendo.[z] Agregue la menta, el aceite de oliva, la mostaza y el pepino. Añada la sal y la pimienta y revuelva. Sirva inmediatamente o <u>refrigere</u> hasta por tres días. ■

[v]*inch* [w]*tablespoons* [x]*cucumber* [y]*medium-sized*
[z]*Mezcle... Stir.*

▲ *El último libro de Palomino*

Comprensión

A. **¿Qué significa?** Las siguientes palabras <u>subrayadas</u> tienen doble significado. ¿Cuál es el significado correcto según el contexto?

1. «La <u>cocina</u> de Palomino»
El significado apropiado de **cocina** es:
☐ kitchen
☐ cuisine, cooking

2. «nunca cumplan el <u>sueño</u> de abrir su propio negocio»
El significado apropiado de **sueño** es:
☐ dream
☐ sleep

3. «pone al alcance del cocinero común <u>recetas</u> no tan conocidas»
El significado apropiado de **recetas** es:
☐ recipes
☐ prescriptions

4. «cortado en cubos de un <u>cuarto</u> de pulgada»
El significado apropiado de **cuarto** es:
☐ room
☐ one quarter, one fourth

B. ¿Cierto o falso? Conteste según la lectura y luego comente sus respuestas con otro estudiante.

	CIERTO	FALSO
1. El chef Palomino es muy ambicioso y tiene muchos proyectos.	☐	☐
2. El chef Palomino cree que sus empleados hispanos tienen poco talento.	☐	☐
3. La Asociación de Chefs Españoles de América es exclusivamente para los chefs de España.	☐	☐
4. La Asociación de Chefs Españoles de América ayuda a los hispanos que desean trabajar en la profesión culinaria.	☐	☐
5. El chef Palomino vive en Colombia.	☐	☐

ESCRITURA

A. Mi restaurante favorito. La cocina latina está de moda en este país, y es común ver restaurantes mexicanos, salvadoreños, argentinos, chilenos, etcétera, en muchas ciudades. ¿Cuál es su restaurante favorito? ¿y su plato favorito? ¿Es latina la comida? ¿china? ¿italiana? ¿japonesa? Prepare un breve informe de 100 palabras para presentar a la clase e incluya lo siguiente.

1. el nombre del restaurante
2. el tipo de comida que se sirve allí
3. su plato favorito (con detalles)
4. la bebida ideal para tomar con el plato
5. una descripción del ambiente del restaurante (formal, informal, para estudiantes, para familias, etcétera)

B. Entre familia. Write a brief paragraph about your eating preferences or those of your family. Use the following questions as a guide in developing your paragraph.

1. ¿Cuántas veces come(n) al día? ¿A qué hora?
2. ¿Comen juntos, a la misma (*same*) hora y en la misma mesa? ¿Come Ud. solo/a?
3. ¿Quién(es) prepara(n) la comida?
4. ¿Qué prepara(n) con frecuencia? ¿Es excelente la comida? ¿buena? ¿mala? ¿regular?
5. ¿Conversa(n) mientras (*while*) comen? ¿Quién habla más? ¿menos? ¿Mira(n) la televisión mientras comen?
6. ¿Qué comida prefiere(n) cuando va(n) a un restaurante? ¿Comida china? ¿mexicana? ¿italiana? ¿comida rápida? ¿En qué restaurantes comen?
7. ¿Come(n) allí con frecuencia? ¿Cuántas veces al año? ¿Cuándo va(n) a volver?

ESCRITURA

Suggestions

- If you prefer that your students do a journal activity, see *Mi diario* in this chapter of the Workbook.
- Have students write simple recipes, such as *un sándwich de jamón con queso, una hamburguesa, una ensalada mixta*, or *los huevos con salsa*. For this activity, students can use verbs in the infinitive for commands.

  cocinar la carne
  poner la cebolla y el tomate encima de la carne
  poner la carne entre las rebanadas (slices) *de pan*

  You can provide them with *vocabulario útil*.

  cortar
  freír
  mezclar
  agregar

A, B: Suggestion

Have several students read their descriptions. After each reading, ask the entire class two or three questions, to encourage students to listen to one another.

B: Suggestion

Before assigning this writing activity, ask students these questions in class. Offer information about yourself and encourage students to ask you these questions.

◀ Una estela (un monumento) en las ruinas mayas de Copán en Honduras

CHAPTER OPENER PHOTO

Point out the chapter-opener photo. Have students comment on ruins and statues that they have visited. Have them name places and artifacts that have become tourist attractions in this country. How important is the preservation of sites like these? Who is responsible for their preservation?

Suggestion

Write the following phrase and items on the board. The words in **boldface** are included in the active vocabulary of this chapter. Have students discuss the words and use context to help them understand the meanings. Place the words they cannot guess in new sentences and contexts.

Para mis vacaciones, **me gustaría...**

1. **viajar** *lejos de aquí.*
2. **hacer** **camping** *en* **las montañas.**
3. *ir a una ciudad histórica con muchos lugares de importancia cultural.*
4. *ir a una* **playa** *bonita.*
5. *viajar en* **autobús** *por todo el país.*

Follow-Up

Use these follow-up questions.

> *¿Adónde fue en sus vacaciones más recientes: a las montañas, a la playa, a otro país, a otro estado? ¿Fue en autobús/coche/tren/avión? ¿Por cuánto tiempo?*

Elicit *sí/no* answers, as students have not learned preterite forms. Pantomime and use drawings for unfamiliar vocabulary as necessary for communication.

Note

The *Puntos de partida* Online Learning Center includes an interview with a native speaker from Honduras who answers questions similar to those in the preceding *Suggestion.*

Resources

For Students

- Workbook
- Laboratory Manual and Laboratory Audio Program
- Quia™ Online Workbook and Online Laboratory Manual
- Video on CD
- Interactive CD-ROM
- *Puntos de partida* Online Learning Center (**www.mhhe.com/puntos7**)

For Instructors

- *Instructor's Manual and Resource Kit,* "Chapter-by-Chapter" Supplementary Materials
- Overhead Transparencies 51–56
- Testing Program
- Test Generator
- Video Program
- Audioscript
- *Puntos de partida* Online Learning Center (**www.mhhe.com/puntos7**)

De **vacaciones**

CULTURA

- **Perspectivas culturales**

  Entrevistas culturales: Honduras y El Salvador

  Entre amigos: El verano pasado me fui al Canadá

  Conozca... Honduras y El Salvador

- **Nota cultural:** Los nuevos turismos en el mundo hispano

- **En los Estados Unidos y el Canadá:** Ellen Ochoa

- **Literatura de Honduras:** Clementina Suárez

- **Lectura:** México es mucho más que playas

VOCABULARIO

- De viaje
- De vacaciones

PRONUNCIACIÓN

- **g, gu,** and **j**

GRAMÁTICA

21 Indirect Object Pronouns; **dar** and **decir**

22 Gustar

23 Preterite of Regular Verbs and of **dar, hacer, ir,** and **ser**

Entrevista cultural

MÉXICO

MAR CARIBE

BELICE

GUATEMALA

HONDURAS

Tegucigalpa

San Salvador

EL SALVADOR

NICARAGUA

COSTA RICA

PANAMÁ

OCÉANO PACÍFICO

▲ Rubén Alexis Guillén Irubasco, El Salvador

◄ Heidi Luna Tegucigalpa, Honduras

MULTIMEDIA

- The multimedia materials that accompany this chapter are referenced in the Student and Instructor's Editions with icons to help you identify when and where to incorporate them.

- The IM/RK provides suggestions for using the multimedia materials in the classroom.

De viaje

Note

See the model for vocabulary presentation and other material in the *Capítulo 7 Vocabulario: Preparación* section of "Chapter-by-Chapter Supplementary Materials," in the IM.

Suggestions

■ Model each word, then ask questions to contextualize it.

1. **El aeropuerto:** *¿Es una persona o un lugar? ¿Qué tipo de transporte hay allí, un tren o un avión?*

2. **La asistente de vuelo:** *¿Es una persona o un lugar? ¿Trabaja en el aeropuerto o en el avión?*

3. **El vuelo:** *¿Es una persona o una actividad? Generalmente, ¿tienen letras o números los vuelos? ¿Hay vuelos en tren?*

4. **El boleto:** *¿Es un lugar o un objeto? ¿Se necesitan los boletos sólo para los vuelos en avión?*

5. **La playa:** *¿Es una persona o un lugar? ¿Qué hacen las personas allí? ¿Toman el sol? ¿Nadan? ¿Qué más hacen?*

■ Point out that *vacaciones* is always plural. Also note the meanings of the verbs *bajar* and *subir: bajar* = to go down vs. *bajar de* = to get out of (a vehicle) and *subir* = to go up vs. *subir a* = to get in/on (a vehicle). Point out the spelling change for *sacar* in the formal command: *saque.* They will see this change for the preterite as well.

■ Have students name items and activities they associate with the following. *¿Qué asocia Ud. con... un avión, una asistente de vuelo, el equipaje, la sala de espera, la sección de fumar, las maletas, un boleto?*

■ Offer additional vocabulary for communication: *el/la viajero/a, el cheque de viajero, la cola* (line, queue)

■ Ask the following questions to personalize and contextualize vocabulary.

1. *Cuando Ud. viaja en avión, ¿es importante que haga buen tiempo? ¿Le molesta mucho cuando hay demora?*

2. *Cuando mi esposo/a (hijo/a) viaja solo/a, yo siempre le pido que me llame cuando llegue a su destino. ¿Llama Ud. siempre a sus padres (su esposo/a) cuando llega a su destino?*

De viaje

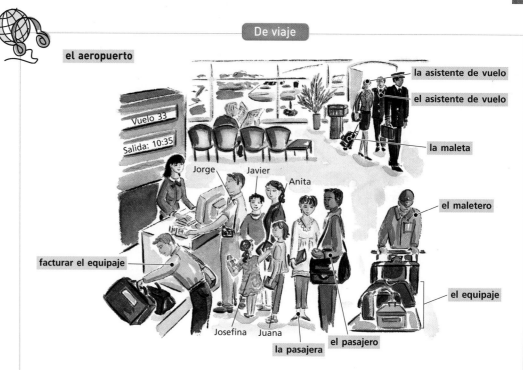

el aeropuerto

Vuelo 33
Salida: 10:35

la asistente de vuelo
el asistente de vuelo
la maleta
el maletero
el equipaje
el pasajero
la pasajera
facturar el equipaje

Jorge Javier Anita Josefina Juana

Modos de transporte

el barco	boat, ship
la cabina	cabin (*in a ship*)
la estación	station
de autobuses	bus
del tren	train
el puerto	port
la sala de espera	waiting room
la sección de (no)	(non)smoking
fumar	section
el vuelo	flight
ir (*irreg.*) en...	to go/travel by . . .
autobús	bus
avión	plane
barco	boat, ship
tren	train

El viaje

la agencia de viajes	travel agency
el/la agente de viajes	travel agent
el asiento	seat
el billete/el boleto/ el pasaje*	ticket
de ida	one way
de ida y vuelta	round-trip
la demora	delay
la llegada	arrival
la salida	departure

---

*Throughout Spanish America, **el boleto** is the word used for a ticket for travel. **El billete** is commonly used in Spain. **El pasaje** is used throughout the Spanish-speaking world. The words **la entrada** and **la localidad** are used to refer to tickets for movies, plays, or similar functions.

224 ■ Doscientos veinticuatro

Capítulo 7: De vacaciones

MULTIMEDIA: Audio

Students can listen to and practice this chapter's vocabulary on the Online Learning Center (**www.mhhe.com/puntos7**), as well as on the Textbook Audio CD, part of the Laboratory Audio Program.

Refrán

«Echar agua en el mar.»

Write the *refrán* on the board. Give students the meaning of *echar* (to throw), then have them guess the meaning of the saying. A similar saying in English is *To carry coals to Newcastle* (a needless task).

Resources: Transparency 51

bajar (de)	to get down (from); to get off (of)	**hacer** (*irreg.*) **la(s) maleta(s)**	to pack one's suitcase(s)
estar (*irreg.*) **atrasado/a**	to be late	**hacer** (*irreg.*) **un viaje**	to take a trip
guardar (un puesto)	to save (a place)	**pasar por el control de la seguridad**	to go/pass through security (check)
hacer (*irreg.*) **cola**	to stand in line	**subir (a)**	to go up; to get on (*a vehicle*)
hacer (*irreg.*) **escalas/paradas**	to make stops	**viajar**	to travel

■ ■ ■ Conversación

A. Un viaje en avión. Imagine que Ud. va a hacer un viaje en avión. El vuelo sale a las siete de la mañana. Usando los números del 1 al 9, indique en qué orden van a pasar las siguientes cosas.

a. _____ Subo al avión.

b. _____ Voy a la sala de espera.

c. _____ Hago cola para comprar el boleto de ida y vuelta y facturar el equipaje.

d. _____ Llego al aeropuerto a tiempo (*on time*) y bajo del taxi.

e. _____ Por fin se anuncia la salida del vuelo.

f. _____ Estoy atrasado/a. Salgo para el aeropuerto en taxi.

g. _____ La asistente me indica el asiento.

h. _____ Pido un asiento de ventanilla (*window seat*).

i. _____ Hay demora. Por eso todos tenemos que esperar el vuelo allí antes de subir al avión.

B. ¡Seamos (*Let's be*) **lógicos!** ¿Qué va a hacer Ud. en estas situaciones?

1. Ud. no tiene mucho dinero. Si tiene que viajar, ¿qué clase de pasaje va a comprar?
a. clase turística   **b.** primera clase   **c.** clase de negocios (*business*)

2. Ud. es una persona muy nerviosa y tiene miedo de viajar en avión. Necesita ir desde Nueva York a Madrid. ¿Qué pide Ud.?
a. una cabina en un barco
b. un vuelo sin escalas
c. un boleto de tren

3. Ud. viaja en tren y tiene muchas maletas. Pesan (*They weigh*) mucho y no puede cargarlas (*carry them*). ¿Qué hace Ud.?
a. Compro boletos.   **b.** Guardo un asiento.   **c.** Facturo el equipaje.

4. Su vuelo está atrasado, pero Ud. está tranquilo/a. ¿Qué dice Ud. (*do you say*)?
a. Señorita, insisto en hablar con el capitán.
b. Una demora más… no importa.
c. Si no salimos dentro de (*within*) diez minutos, bajo del avión.

5. Ud. quiere pedir dos asientos juntos, uno para Ud., el otro para su amigo/a. Él/Ella tiene la pierna rota (*broken leg*) y necesita estirarla (*to stretch it out*) durante el viaje. ¿Qué pide Ud. para él/ella?
a. un asiento de ventanilla
b. un pasaje sin escala
c. un asiento de pasillo (*aisle seat*)

Heritage Speakers

■ Anime a sus estudiantes hispanohablantes a hablar de sus vacaciones favoritas.
¿Adónde fue?
¿Cómo fue? ¿En avión, carro, tren?
¿Cuánto tiempo estuvo de vacaciones?

■ Pídales a sus estudiantes hispanohablantes que escriban una composición breve usando las oraciones de Conversación A. Pueden añadir otros detalles también.

■ Use the impersonal *se* in input or questions to prepare students for the *Nota comunicativa* of this section; for example: *¿Dónde se compran pasajes de avión?* or *En muchos casos se hace cola para facturar el equipaje.*

■ Read the following sentences as a *dictado* or as listening comprehension. In either case, have students correct false statements.

1. *Si hay una demora, el avión llega temprano.*
2. *Los pasajeros hacen las maletas después de hacer un viaje.*
3. *El avión está atrasado; no tenemos que esperarlo.*
4. *Hay mucha gente en la sala de espera; no hay ningún asiento desocupado.*
5. *El asistente de vuelo nos sirve la comida durante el vuelo.*
6. *Cuando se hace cola, generalmente es necesario esperar un poco.*
7. *No quiero subir las maletas al avión; voy a facturarlas.*
8. *El maletero es un objeto en que se pone la ropa.*
9. *Los billetes sólo pueden ser de ida y vuelta.*
10. *Al final de un vuelo, se baja del avión; no se sube.*

■ Read the following definitions and have students give the corresponding words:

1. *La persona que nos ayuda con el equipaje en la estación de trenes.*
2. *La cosa que se compra antes de hacer un viaje.*
3. *El antónimo de subir a.*
4. *Se va allí cuando se hace un viaje en avión.*
5. *Se va allí cuando se hace un viaje en tren.*
6. *La persona que nos ayuda durante un vuelo.*

Con. A: Follow-Up

Have students imagine they are traveling with children and need to give them commands for each circumstance represented in activity. MODELO: f: *Suban al taxi. Siéntense.*, and so on.

Con. B: Variation

The situations may be used as springboards for mini-role-playing.

Con. C: Preliminary Exercise

Read the following descriptions and have students identify the person described: *Gregorio, vicepresidente de la IBM,* or *Harry, típico estudiante universitario.*

1. *Siempre viaja en clase turística porque es más económico.*

2. *No le importan nada las demoras; no tiene prisa.*

3. *Nunca hace cola para comprar el boleto porque su secretaria le arregla todo el viaje.*

4. *Por lo general prefiere viajar en tren porque es más económico.*

5. *Muchas veces no lleva equipaje porque hace viajes de un solo día.*

6. *Siempre que viaja, lleva traje y corbata.*

Con. C: Suggestion

Do this as a whole-class activity or as a whole-class composition, with you or a student writing sentences on the board.

De vacaciones

Suggestions

■ Point out that *camioneta* can also mean *van* or *light truck.* Other words for *station wagon* are *la ranchera, la rubia, el coche rural,* and *el coche familiar.*

■ Model vocabulary in sentences about yourself and in communicative exchanges with the students.

  Mi familia va de vacaciones todos los años. Nos gusta hacer camping en la playa. And so on.
  ¿Le gusta a Ud. hacer camping? ¿Prefiere ir a la playa o a las montañas? ¿Sabe Ud. levantar una tienda de campaña? ¿Qué le gusta hacer cuando está de vacaciones? And so no.

■ Have volunteers compare this family's choices with a typical vacation they take with their family.

  Esta familia va de vacaciones en camioneta. Mi familia prefiere viajar en avión.

■ Offer additional vocabulary words to help students talk about their own vacations.

  el río   el lago
  esquiar   bucear
  hacer surf
  montar en tabla de vela

C. En el aeropuerto. ¿Cuántas cosas y acciones puede Ud. identificar o describir en este dibujo?

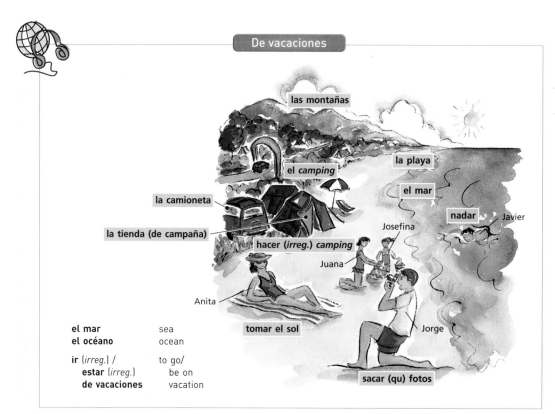

De vacaciones

el mar	sea	
el océano	ocean	
ir *(irreg.)* / estar *(irreg.)* de vacaciones	to go/ be on vacation	

Resources: Transparencies 52, 53

■ ■ ■ Conversación

A. ¿Qué hace Ud.? Lea las siguientes oraciones e indica si son ciertas o falsas para Ud.

	CIERTO	FALSO
1. Cuando estoy de vacaciones, tomo el sol.	☐	☐
2. Prefiero ir de vacaciones a las montañas.	☐	☐
3. Duermo muy bien en una tienda de campaña.	☐	☐
4. Saco muchas fotos cuando estoy de vacaciones.	☐	☐
5. Es fácil viajar a playas bonitas desde aquí.	☐	☐

NOTA CULTURAL

Los nuevos turismos en el mundo hispano

El turista de hoy ya no es el turista tradicional y fácil de complacer.[a] Por eso hay nuevas industrias para satisfacer su interés en **la ecología, la agricultura** o **la aventura:** el ecoturismo, el agroturismo y el aventurismo. Los países hispanos ofrecen ricas oportunidades para disfrutar de[b] estas nuevas formas de hacer turismo.

El ecoturismo consiste en viajar a **lugares no explotados por el ser humano.**[c] Los lugares del mundo hispano que ofrecen amplias oportunidades para el ecoturismo son **las selvas tropicales** de Centroamérica y la Amazonia, especialmente en Costa Rica y el Ecuador. Las Islas Galápagos y la Patagonia (en el sur de la Argentina y Chile) también son **destinos**[d] populares entre los ecoturistas.

El agroturismo indica **viajes a lugares rurales** donde el turista se queda[e] en casas rurales renovadas, a veces visitando más de una casa o un área durante su viaje. Algunas excursiones son informativas o educativas, con destinos a **granjas y campos de cultivo.**[f] Otras son simplemente parte de un programa para renovar casas y pueblos rurales. España ofrece varias oportunidades al agroturista por todo el país, especialmente en el País Vasco y en las Islas Baleares. La isla Chiloé de Chile también tiene una organización agroturística.

El aventurista, o sea[g] el turista que busca viajes emocionantes, a veces peligrosos,[h] también tiene amplias oportunidades en los países hispanos. En los Andes, la Patagonia y las montañas de España, puede hacer **el alpinismo, el montañismo en bicicleta, la navegación en rápidos, el esquí** y **el snowboard** extremos.

[a]*please* [b]*disfrutar... enjoying* [c]*por... by humans* [d]*destinations* [e]*se... stays* [f]*granjas... farms and croplands* [g]*o... or in other words* [h]*dangerous*

▲ *Un grupo de estudiantes que participan en un taller (workshop) ecoturístico en la Amazonia, en Perú*

B. Preguntas

1. Por lo general, ¿cuándo toma Ud. sus vacaciones? ¿En invierno? ¿en verano? En las vacaciones, ¿le gusta viajar o prefiere no salir de su ciudad? ¿Le gusta ir de vacaciones con su familia? ¿Prefiere ir solo/a (*alone*), con un amigo / una amiga o con un grupo de personas? ¿Prefiere viajar sólo a lugares en este país o le gustaría (*would you like*) viajar por otros países del mundo (*world*)?
2. De los medios de transporte mencionados en **De viaje** (página 224), ¿cuáles conoce Ud. por experiencia? ¿Cuál es el más rápido? ¿el más económico? ¿Cuáles hacen más escalas o hacen paradas con más frecuencia? ¿Cómo prefiere Ud. viajar? ¿Prefiere un asiento de ventanilla o un asiento de pasillo?

NOTA CULTURAL

Suggestions

■ Describe some of the places in the Hispanic world you have been to or know well. Then ask students the names of the places they have visited.

■ Ask students which places mentioned in the *Nota cultural* they would like to visit and why.

■ Have students discuss what are "alternative" vacations within the United States, in their opinion.

■ Ask students what type of vacation they would prefer to have in the Hispanic world. You might have students research their preferences on the Internet, making travel plans for a two- to three-week vacation. They should include itinerary and budget.

■ Ask the following questions to check comprehension.

1. *¿Qué es el ecoturismo? ¿En qué países hispanos hay mucho ecoturismo?*
2. *¿Cuál es la diferencia entre el agroturismo y el ecoturismo?*
3. *¿Cuáles son algunos de los deportes emocionantes que se mencionan?*
4. *¿Qué significan las siguientes palabras?*
   ■ *el alpinismo*
   ■ *el montañismo en bicicleta*
   ■ *la navegación en rápidos*

Con. B: Extension

3. *¿Cómo reacciona Ud. cuando hay una demora de 30 minutos? ¿Está furioso/a? ¿irritado/a? ¿indiferente? ¿Y cuando hay una demora de una hora?*

☼ **Heritage Speakers**

Invite a los estudiantes hispanohablantes a compartir unos comentarios sobre algún lugar hispánico interesante que conozcan.

National Standards: Culture

The Galapagos Islands are located some 650 miles off the western coast of South America. This remote group of volcanic islands remains much as it was a couple of million years ago. The archipelago was first discovered in 1535 by a Spanish bishop named Fray Tomás de Belanga. Over several centuries, animal and plant life from the Americas reached the islands and gradually evolved into new species, many of which are found nowhere else on the planet. Tourists visiting the Galapagos can go to the Charles Darwin Foundation.

Notes

- The passive *se* has been presented for passive recognition and used frequently in listening comprehension activities and reading passages.
- This *Nota* does not emphasize the difference between the personal *you / they* that refers to specific persons vs. the impersonal *you / they*, which is nonspecific. You may want to point out the difference.

Suggestions

- Have students state the following ideas in Spanish.

  1. You study a lot here.
  2. You don't talk in the library.
  3. You wear a suit in the office.
  4. You bargain at the market.

- Ask students the following questions to practice the impersonal *se*.

  1. *¿Qué lengua se habla en Francia? ¿en México? ¿en el Brasil? ¿en Alemania? ¿en Inglaterra? ¿en los Estados Unidos?*
  2. *¿Cuáles son las diferentes maneras de viajar?* (*Se viaja en... avión, coche, tren, autobús, bicicleta.*)

Con. C: Extension

9. *Se hacen las camas.*
10. *Se pide información sobre los viajes.*
11. *No se fuma.*
12. *Se hace cola.*

Con. D: Suggestions

- Have students make up similar items and present them to the class.
- Have students tell what is and is not done in certain places.

  ¿Qué se hace y no se hace en... la biblioteca? →
  En la biblioteca, se estudia, pero no se habla.

1. *¿en una clase de idiomas?*
2. *¿en un mercado al aire libre?*
3. *¿en un avión?*
4. *¿en una discoteca?*
5. *¿en una tienda de ropa?*
6. *¿en una fiesta?*
7. *¿en la cafetería?*

Other Uses of *se* (For Recognition)

It is likely that you have often seen and heard the phrase shown in the photo that accompanies this box: **Se habla español.** (*Spanish is spoken* [*here*]). Here are some additional examples of this use of **se** with Spanish verbs. Note how the meaning of the verb changes slightly.

Se venden billetes aquí.	*Tickets are sold here.*
Aquí no **se fuma.**	*You don't (One doesn't) smoke here.* *Smoking is forbidden here.*

Be alert to this use of **se** when you see it because it will occur with some frequency in readings and in direction lines in *Puntos de partida*. The activities in this text will not require you to use this grammar point on your own, however.

▲ *Nueva York*

C. **¿Dónde se hace esto?** Indique el lugar (o los lugares) donde se hacen las siguientes actividades.

Lugares
en el aeropuerto
en la agencia de viajes
en el avión
en casa
en la playa

1. Se factura el equipaje.
2. Se hacen las maletas.
3. Se compran los pasajes.
4. Se hace una reservación.
5. Se espera en la sala de espera.
6. Se pide un cóctel.
7. Se mira una película.
8. Se nada y se toma el sol.

D. **Prueba** (*Quiz*) **cultural.** ¿Cierto o falso? Corrija (*Correct*) las oraciones falsas.

1. Se habla español en el Brasil.
2. Se comen tacos en México.
3. Se puede esquiar en Chile en junio.
4. En España a veces se cena a las diez de la noche.
5. La paella se prepara con lechuga.
6. Se dice (*One says*) «chau» en la Argentina.
7. Se habla español en Miami.
8. En este país se puede votar a los dieciocho años.

Need more practice?

- Workbook and Laboratory Manual
- Interactive CD-ROM
- Online Learning Center (www.mhhe.com/puntos7)

Capítulo 7: De vacaciones

PRONUNCIACIÓN *g, gu,* and *j*

- In Spanish, the letter **g** followed by **e** or **i** has the same sound as the letter **j** followed by any vowel: [x]. It is similar to the English *h,* although in some dialects it is pronounced with a harder sound.

general	jamón, jota, jugo
gigante	jersey
	jirafa

- As you know, the letter **g** has another pronunciation, similar to *g* in the English word *go:* [g]. The Spanish letter **g** is pronounced [g] when it is followed directly by **a, o,** or **u** or by the combinations **ue** and **ui.**

  galante   gorila   gusto   guerrilla   siguiente

- The [g] pronunciation actually has two forms, a harder [g] and a fricative [g̶] that sounds softer. The [g] pronunciation is used at the beginning of a phrase (that is, after a pause) or after the letter **n.**

  mango   tango   ángulo

- In any other position, the softer, fricative [g̶] is used.

  el gato   el gorila   el gusto

Práctica. Practique la pronunciación de las siguientes palabras.

1. [x] jamón   gimnasio
       geranio   jipijapa
       Jijona   joya
       Juan   gitano
       genio   rojo
       Jorge   germinal
       Jesús

2. [g] gato   algodón
       tengo   gas
       galleta   ganga

3. [g/g̶] un gato / el gato
         un grupo / el grupo
         gracias / las gracias
         guapos niños / niños guapos

4. [x/g] gigante   juguete
         jugamos   jugar
         jugoso

PRONUNCIACIÓN

Note
This is the last *Pronunciación* section in the student text of *Puntos de partida. Pronunciación* sections continue in the *Laboratory Manual* and *Laboratory Audio Program.*

Suggestion
Model the examples.

Preliminary Exercise
Say the following words and have students raise their hands when they hear the soft [g].

gato	*un gato*	*los gatos*
guerrilla	*la guerrilla*	*tres*
		guerrillas
gigante	*gracias*	*jugar*

♻ **Reciclado**
Recycle syllables and written accents. Read the following sentences as a *dictado* and then have students divide each word into syllables and justify their use or nonuse of accent marks.

1. *Gema y Julio tienen un título en economía y japonés.*
2. *María y Mario no pueden viajar a Nepal sin un visado turístico.*

¿Recuerda Ud.?

Note

The direct object pronouns from the exchange are in **boldface.**

—Roberto, ¿tienes los boletos?
—No, todavía no **los** tengo, pero mi agente ya **los** tiene listos.
—Si quieres, **te** acompaño a la agencia.
—Sí, qué buena idea. Casi nunca **te** veo. Podemos pasar por la plaza a tomar un café también.
—Perfecto.

Gramática 21

Indirect Object Pronouns; *dar* and *decir*

Note

Direct object pronouns were presented in *Capítulo 6.*

Follow-Up

Ask the following question to introduce the concept of indirect objects.

¿Qué palabras en cada oración indican las personas afectadas por las acciones de los verbos?
Emphasize the meaning of the indirect object pronouns.

me = to me
le = to him/her/you (form. sing.)
les = to them/you (form. pl.)

¿Recuerda Ud.?

In **Gramática 18, Capítulo 6,** you learned how to use direct object pronouns to avoid repetition. Can you identify the direct object pronouns in the following exchange? To what or to whom do these pronouns refer?

—Roberto, ¿tienes los boletos?
—No, no los tengo, pero mi agente de viajes los tiene listos (*ready*).
—Si quieres, te acompaño a la agencia.
—Sí, qué buena idea. Casi nunca te veo. Podemos pasar por la plaza a tomar un café también.
—Perfecto.

21 Expressing *to whom* or *for whom* • Indirect Object Pronouns; *dar* and *decir*

Las vacaciones de primavera

Javier habla con sus padres de sus planes para las vacaciones de primavera. *Les* pide un poco de dinero para su pasaje de avión.

JAVIER: ... así que mis amigos y yo ya tenemos todas las reservaciones. Pero tengo muy poco dinero para el viaje. Nunca *les* pido dinero durante el semestre y trabajo mucho. ¿*Me* pueden dar un poco de dinero para el pasaje de avión?

MADRE: Siempre *le* digo a tu padre que eres muy trabajador y sé que nunca *nos* pides dinero.

PADRE: Es verdad. *Te* podemos dar un cheque para el pasaje y para la comida durante el viaje.

Comprensión

1. ¿Qué les pide Javier a sus padres?
2. ¿Qué le dice la madre al padre de Javier?
3. ¿Qué le dan los padres a Javier?

Spring vacation (break) *Javier talks to his parents about his plans for spring break. He asks them for a little money for his airplane ticket* JAVIER: *... so, my friends and I already have all of the reservations. But I don't have much money for the trip. I never ask you for money during the semester and I work very hard. Can you give me a little money for the airplane ticket?* MOTHER: *I always tell your father that you are very hard-working and I know you never ask us for money.* FATHER: *It's true. We can give you a check for the airplane ticket and for food during the trip.*

Indirect Object Pronouns

me	to/for me	nos	to/for us
te	to/for you (*fam. sing.*)	os	to/for you (*fam. pl.*)
le	to/for you (*form. sing.*), him, her, it	les	to/for you (*form. pl.*), them

 Note that indirect object pronouns have the same form as direct object pronouns, except in the third person: **le, les.**

A. Indirect object nouns and pronouns are the second recipient of the action of the verb. They usually answer the questions *to whom?* or *for whom?* in relation to the verb. The word *to* is frequently omitted in English.

Indicate the direct and indirect objects in the following sentences.

1. I'm giving her the present tomorrow.
2. Could you tell me the answer now?
3. El profesor nos va a hacer algunas preguntas.
4. ¿No me compras una revista ahora?

B. Like direct object pronouns, *indirect object pronouns* (**los pronombres del complemento indirecto**) are placed immediately before a conjugated verb. They may also be attached to an infinitive or a present participle.

No, no **te** presto el coche.
No, I won't lend you the car.

Voy a guardar**te** el asiento.
Te voy a guardar el asiento.
I'll save your seat for you.

Le estoy escribiendo una carta **a Marisol.**
Estoy escribiéndo**le** una carta **a Marisol.**
I'm writing Marisol a letter.

C. Since **le** and **les** have several different equivalents, their meaning is often clarified or emphasized with the preposition **a** followed by a pronoun (object of a preposition).

Voy a mandar**le** un telegrama **a Ud. (a él, a ella).**
I'm going to send you (him, her) a telegram.

Les hago una comida **a Uds. (a ellos, a ellas).**
I'm making you (them) a meal.

D. It is common for a Spanish sentence to contain both the indirect object noun and the indirect object pronoun, especially with third person forms.

Vamos a decir**le** la verdad **a Juan.**
Let's tell Juan the truth.

¿**Les** guardo los asientos **a Jorge y Marta?**
Shall I save the seats for Jorge and Marta?

E. As with direct object pronouns, indirect object pronouns are attached to the affirmative command form and precede the negative command form.

Sírva**nos** un café, por favor.
Serve us some coffee, please.

No **me** dé su número de teléfono ahora.
Don't give me your phone number now.

Gramática   Doscientos treinta y uno ■ **231**

Indirect Object Pronouns

Suggestion
Point out that indirect object pronouns have the same form as direct object pronouns except in the third person singular and plural: *le* and *les.* Gender is not reflected in third person indirect object pronouns.

Emphasis A: Suggestion
Illustrate the concept of the indirect object by suggesting that a student has asked you to get another student's attention for him/her. Tap the student: I tapped John for Tom. Ask: Who is directly affected? Students should answer: John, the direct object. Ask: Who was indirectly affected (second recipient of the action)? Students should answer: Tom, the indirect object.

 Bright Idea

Suggestion
Have students use these two questions to identify and distinguish direct and indirect objects.
To identify the direct object, they should ask:

   verb what/who?

To identify the indirect object they should ask:

   verb to/for what/whom?

   I bought them the cheapest tickets. →
   I bought what? (direct object = tickets)
   I bought for whom? (indirect object = them)

Emphasis A: Note
Direct and indirect object pronouns are not used together until *Gramática 26* in *Capítulo 8.*

Emphasis C: Suggestion
Point out that the use of the seemingly redundant *le(s)* with *a* + noun / pronoun is normal, not the exception. In general, the *le(s)* is obligatory and *a* + pronoun is optional, even if it conveys more information than *le(s).*

Refrán

«Quien algo quiere, algo le cuesta.»

Write the *refrán* on the board and point out that a similar saying in English is often used when talking about exercise (*No pain, no gain.*). Another similar saying is *There's no free lunch.* Ask if students recognize the indirect object pronoun in the Spanish saying.

 Heritage Speakers

Note que en español se usa la preposición *a* mientras que en inglés se usa *from.* Anime a sus estudiantes hispanohablantes a explicar la diferencia entre los siguientes pares de oraciones.

   Le robaron los dulces a Roberto.
   Le robaron los dulces de Roberto.

   Teresa le envió la carta a Fernando.
   Teresa le envió la carta de Fernando.

Gramática ■ **231**

Emphasis F: Suggestions

- Offer these additional verbs to practice indirect objects: *contar (ue), permitir*.
- Point out that the indirect object for verbs of separation, such as *comprar* and *quitar*, is also expressed with *a* in Spanish, whereas in English *from*, not *to* or *for*, is used.

  Le quito el bolígrafo al niño (from the child).
  Le compra un periódico al vendedor (from the salesperson).

  Native English speakers have a tendency to say *del niño* and *del vendedor* instead of the correct Spanish construction.

Dar and decir

Note

The introduction of *dar* and *decir* has been delayed so that they could be used naturally, with indirect object pronouns.

Suggestions

- Point out the irregular *yo* form of *dar*. Also, emphasize the forms of *decir*: the -*g*- in the first person singular (*yo*) and the *e → i* stem-changing pattern.
- Model the differences between *dar* vs. *regalar* and *decir* vs. *hablar* (*charlar*).

F. Here are some verbs frequently used with indirect objects.

escribir	*to write*	preguntar	*to ask (a question)*
explicar	*to explain*	prestar	*to lend*
hablar	*to speak*	prometer	*to promise*
mandar	*to send*	recomendar (ie)	*to recommend*
mostrar (ue)	*to show*	regalar	*to give (as a gift)*
ofrecer (zc)	*to offer*	servir (i, i)	*to serve*
pedir (i, i)	*to ask for*		

Dar and decir

Javier les dice a sus padres que necesita dinero.

dar (*to give*)		decir (*to say; to tell*)	
doy	damos	digo	decimos
das	dais	dices	decís
da	dan	dice	dicen

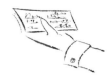

Su padre le da un cheque.

- **Dar** and **decir** are almost always used with indirect object pronouns in Spanish.

¿Cuándo **me das** el dinero?
When will you give me the money?

¿Por qué no **le dice** Ud. la verdad, señor?
Why don't you tell him/her the truth, sir?

 In Spanish there are two verbs for *to give*: **dar** (*to give in general*) and **regalar** (*to give as a gift*). Also, do not confuse **decir** (*to say or to tell*) with **hablar** (*to speak*).

- **Dar** and **decir** also have irregular formal command forms. There is a written accent on **dé** to distinguish it from the preposition **de**.

Formal commands of **dar** and **decir**:

  dar → **dé, den**
  decir → **diga, digan**

AUTOPRUEBA

Give the correct Spanish equivalent for the indirect object pronoun in each sentence.

a. me   **b.** te   **c.** le   **d.** nos   **e.** les

1. _____ John gave it to *you*, Carol.
2. _____ Mr. Hopkins, Mrs. Simmons sent *you* this message, sir.
3. _____ Bring *them* some cookies.
4. _____ Don't tell *me* anything more.
5. _____ He didn't give *us* much time.

Answers: 1. b 2. c 3. e 4. a 5. d

 Heritage Speakers

Pídale a un estudiante hispanohablante que explique la diferencia entre *pedir* y *preguntar*, y que dé ejemplos.

232 ■ Capítulo 7: De vacaciones

■ ■ ■ **Práctica**

A. ¡Anticipemos! ¿Qué va a pasar? Complete las respuestas con información lógica. Puede usar palabras de la lista.

1. Su amiga Elena está en el hospital con un ataque de apendicitis.
   Todos le mandan…
   Las enfermeras (*nurses*) le dan…
   Le escriben…
   De comer, le sirven…

2. Es Navidad.
   Los niños (*children*) les prometen a sus padres…
   Les piden…
   También le escriben…
   Le piden…
   Los padres les mandan… a sus amigos.
   Les regalan…

3. Hay una demora y el avión no despega (*takes off*) a tiempo.
   Un asistente de vuelo nos sirve…
   Otra asistente de vuelo nos ofrece…
   El piloto nos dice…

4. Mi coche no funciona hoy.
   Mi amigo me presta…
   Mis padres me preguntan…
   Luego me dan…
   Le muestro al mecánico (*mechanic*)…

5. Es la última (*last*) semana de clases y hay exámenes finales la próxima semana.
   En la clase de computación, todos le preguntan al profesor…
   El profesor les explica a los estudiantes…
   El profesor les muestra…

B. De vuelta a Honduras. Your friends the Padillas, from Honduras, need help arranging for and getting on their flight back home. Explain how you will help them, using the cues as a guide.

MODELO: confirmar el vuelo → *Les* confirmo el vuelo.

1. llamar un taxi
2. bajar (*to carry down*) las maletas
3. guardar el equipaje
4. facturar el equipaje
5. guardar el puesto en la cola
6. guardar el asiento en la sala de espera
7. comprar una revista
8. por fin decir adiós

Palabras útiles

las flores (flowers)
los juguetes (toys)
las medicinas
el motor (engine)
Santa Claus
**las tarjetas
navideñas**
(Christmas cards)

Preliminary Exercises

■ Use the following chain drill to practice indirect object pronouns.

1. *Les escribo tarjetas postales a mis padres. (a ti, a Ud., a Andrés, a Uds., a Alicia, a vosotros)*

2. *Ahora le compro un regalo a Jorge. (a Sergio, a ti, a Eva, a Uds., a Martín y Rosa, a vosotros)*

3. *El conductor le dice la hora de la llegada. (yo, ellos, tú, nosotros, Uds.)*

4. *Juan le da el billete, ¿verdad? (tú, nosotros, yo, Uds., ellas)*

■ Act out the following question/ answer series with students.

¿Ud. me da el libro?
¿Ud. nos da el dinero (student standing with you)?
¿Uds. me dicen siempre la verdad? ¿la hora? ¿las respuestas correctas?
¿Yo les digo siempre la fecha de los exámenes? ¿la tarea (homework) para mañana? ¿cosas interesantes sobre la cultura hispánica?

■ Have students answer the following questions.

En la clase de español, ¿quién le… a Ud.?
explicar la gramática
hacer preguntas
dar exámenes
prestar un papel
dar las respuestas durante un examen

Encourage students to answer in complete sentences. Model the first answer.

La profesora me explica la gramática.

As students answer, avoid overt correction; instead, repeat all answers, including corrections when necessary.

Prác. C: Follow-Up

Follow up the activity with these questions.

1. ¿A quién le manda Ud. flores?
   ¿Quién le manda flores a Ud.?
2. ¿A quién le escribe Ud. cartas?
   ¿Qué tipo de cartas escribe Ud.?
   ¿cartas políticas? ¿amistosas?
   ¿románticas? ¿Quién le escribe
   cartas a Ud.?
3. ¿Les va a comprar algo a sus
   padres/hijos este año? ¿a su mejor
   amigo/a? ¿a su profesor(a)?

Prác. D: Follow-Up

Ask questions about the story and have students answer as if they were Benjamín.

Con: Suggestions

- Ask some questions based on the cues before assigning the activity to pairs.

  ¿A quién le da consejos?
  ¿De quién acepta consejos?
  ¿A quién le pide ayuda con el español?
  ¿A quién le da ayuda?, and so on.

- Have students report to the class at least two interesting things they learned about their partner.
- Have students pass around a small object (ball, toy, book, pen). As they do it, have them provide a sentence about what they did or about what they are about to do. Their sentences should include both direct and indirect objects.

  Voy a darle la pelota a Jim. / Le doy la pelota a Jim.

Other useful verbs that you might write on the board are *tirar, pasar, llevar.*

Bright Idea
Con: Suggestion

If you have any heritage speakers in class, have them read the dialogue aloud.

C. **¿Qué hacen estas personas?** Complete las siguientes oraciones con un verbo lógico y un pronombre de complemento indirecto.

MODELO: El vicepresidente *le ofrece* consejos al presidente.

1. Romeo ———— flores a Julieta.
2. Snoopy ———— besos (*kisses*) a Lucy... ¡Y a ella no le gusta!
3. Eva ———— una manzana a Adán.
4. La Dra. Laura Schlessinger ———— consejos a sus radioyentes (*listeners*).
5. Los bancos ———— dinero a las personas que quieren comprar una casa.
6. Los asistentes de vuelo ———— bebidas a los pasajeros.
7. George Washington ———— a su padre decir la verdad.

D. **En un restaurante.** Imagine that your four-year-old cousin Benjamín has never eaten in a restaurant before. Explain to him what will happen, filling in the blanks with the appropriate indirect object pronoun.

Primero el camarero ___*to*___¹ indica una mesa desocupada.ª Luego tú ___*le*___² pides el menú al camarero. También ___*le*___³ haces preguntas sobre los platos y las especialidades de la casa y ___*le*___⁴ dices tus preferencias. El camarero ___*le*___⁵ trae la comida. Por fin tu papá ___*le*___⁶ pide la cuenta al camarero. Si tú quieres pagar, ___*le*___⁷ pides dinero a tu papá y ___*le*___⁸ das el dinero al camarero.

ªvacant

■ ■ ■ Conversación

Entrevista: ¿Quién... ? Read through the following items and think about people whom you associate with the indicated action. Then, working with a partner, ask and answer questions to find out information about each topic.

MODELO: darle consejos →
  E1: ¿A quién le das consejos?
  E2: Con frecuencia le doy consejos a mi compañero de cuarto. ¡Él los necesita!
  E1: ¿Quién te da consejos a ti?
  E2: Mis abuelos me dan muchos consejos.

1. darle consejos
2. pedirle ayuda con los estudios
3. prestarle la ropa
4. mandarle flores
5. decirle secretos
6. hacerle favores
7. escribirle tarjetas postales (*postcards*)
8. ofrecerle bebidas
9. mostrarle fotos de las vacaciones
10. servirle la comida

Need more practice?

- Workbook and Laboratory Manual
- Interactive CD-ROM
- Online Learning Center (www.mhhe.com/puntos7)

Verbos útiles

dar
ofrecer
prestar
prometer
servir

In **Ante todo** you started to use forms of **gustar** to express your likes and dislikes. Review what you know by answering the following questions. Then, changing their form as needed, use the forms of **gustar** to interview your instructor.

1. ¿Te gusta el café (el vino, el té...)?
2. ¿Te gusta jugar al béisbol (al golf, al vólibol, al...)?
3. ¿Te gusta viajar en avión (fumar, viajar en tren...)?
4. ¿Qué te gusta más, estudiar o ir a fiestas (trabajar o descansar, cocinar o comer)?

22 Expressing Likes and Dislikes • *Gustar*

Los chilenos viajeros

Según el anuncio, a muchos chilenos les gusta viajar a otros países. Lea el anuncio y luego indique si las oraciones son ciertas o falsas.

1. A los chilenos les gusta viajar sólo en este hemisferio.
2. A los chilenos les gustan mucho las playas.
3. Sólo les gusta viajar en países de habla española.
4. No les gustaría el precio del viaje.

MEDIO MILLON DE CHILENOS
DE VACACIONES 2003 AL EXTRANJERO
Y USTED... NO SE QUEDE SIN VIAJAR
¡ RESERVE AHORA MISMO !

El próximo verano '03, con el bajo valor del dólar, muchas personas desearán viajar, los cupos disponibles se agotarán rapidamente. ¡Asegure sus vacaciones! Elija ahora cualquiera de nuestros fantásticos programas.

MIAMI - ORLANDO - BAHAMAS - MÉXICO - CANCÚN
ACAPULCO - IXTAPA - COSTA RICA - RIO - SALVADOR
PLAYA TAMBOR - PUNTA CANA - LA HABANA
VARADERO - GUATEMALA - SUDÁFRICA

Infórmese sobre nuestro
SUPER CRÉDITO
PREFERENCIAL

Economy Tour

Santa Magdalena 94, Providencia
☎2334429 - 2331774 - 2314252
2328294 - 2318608 - 2334862
Fax: 2334428

Y a Ud. ¿le gusta viajar? ¿Le gustan los viajes en avión? ¿Cuál de estos lugares le gustaría visitar?

Constructions with *gustar*

Spanish	Literal Equivalent	English Phrasing
Me gusta la playa.	The beach is pleasing to me.	*I like the beach.*
No le gustan sus cursos.	His courses are not pleasing to him.	*He doesn't like his courses.*
Nos gusta leer.	Reading is pleasing to us.	*We like to read.*

You have been using the verb **gustar** since the beginning of *Puntos de partida* to express likes and dislikes. However, **gustar** does not literally mean *to like,* but rather *to be pleasing.*	Me gusta viajar. *Traveling is pleasing to me. (I like traveling.)*

Gramática

☼ Heritage Speakers

En algunos dialectos del español, el verbo *gustar* puede tener connotaciones románticas cuando se usa en la primera y segunda personas del singular (*yo y tú*).

¿Te gusto? (Do you like me? / Are you attracted to me?)

Sí, me gustas mucho. (Yes, I like you. / Yes, I am attracted to you.)

Gramática 22

Gustar

Note
Students have been using the *gustar* construction since *Ante todo.*

Follow-Up
After discussing the ad, ask the following questions.

1. *A las personas de los Estados Unidos / del Canadá, ¿les gusta ir a la playa? ¿Qué playas les gusta visitar? ¿Les gusta viajar en avión?*
2. *Y a Ud., ¿le gustan más las playas o las montañas? ¿Adónde le gustaría viajar este verano?*

Constructions with *gustar*

Note
Spanish constructions with *gustar* are similar to some English ones.

The very idea disgusts me.
Snakes frighten me.

Emphasis A: Suggestions

- Remind students to use the definite article when referring to something in general.

  *I like tacos. = Me gustan **los** tacos.*

- Point out that in Spanish there is no need to use equivalents of the English pronouns *it* or *them* to identify the thing or things liked.

  I like it. = Me gusta.
  I don't like them. = No me gustan.

Would Like / Wouldn't Like

Note
Gustaría will be used only with infinitives until all forms of the conditional are presented (*Capítulo 18*).

Suggestion
Introduce verbs that are similar to *gustar*.

encantar	interesar
faltar	parecer
importar	quedar

Preliminary Exercises

- To make sure the *gustar* construction is clearly understood, have students give the Spanish for the following sentences, then have them give literal equivalents in English of the Spanish construction, for example:

  I like the car. → Me gusta el coche. → The car is pleasing to me.

  1. We/He/You/I like(s) the car.
  2. I/We/She/They like(s) to read.
  3. She likes the soup/chicken/coffee.
  4. He likes tomatoes/tacos/movies/to go to the movies. (¡OJO! Use the definite articles.)

- Have students give the Spanish equivalents of these sentences to stress the redundancy of the indirect object pronoun and noun.

  1. My father likes to travel.
  2. My mother likes trains.
  3. The boys like the beach.
  4. María likes to ski.

A. **Gustar** is always used with an indirect object pronoun: Someone or something is pleasing *to* someone else. The verb must agree with the subject of the sentence—that is, the person or thing that is pleasing.

Me **gusta** la comida mexicana.
Mexican food is pleasing to me. (I like Mexican food.)

Me **gustan** los viajes aventureros.
Adventurous trips are pleasing to me. (I like adventurous trips.)

B. When the person pleased is a noun, a phrase with **a** + a *noun* must be used in addition to the indirect object pronoun. The prepositional phrase usually appears before the indirect object pronoun, but it can also appear after the verb.

A David no le gustan los aviones.
No le gustan los aviones a **David**.
David doesn't like airplanes.

C. A phrase with **a** + a *pronoun* is often used for clarification or emphasis. The prepositional phrase can appear before the indirect object pronoun or after the verb.

 Note that an infinitive is viewed as a singular subject in Spanish.

The indirect object pronoun *must* be used with **gustar** even when the prepositional phrase **a** + *noun* or *pronoun* is used.

CLARIFICATION
¿Le gusta **a Ud.** viajar?
Do you like to travel?

EMPHASIS
A mí me gusta viajar en avión, pero **a mi esposo** le gusta viajar en coche.
I like to travel by plane, but my husband likes to travel by car.

Would Like / Wouldn't Like

What one *would* or *would not* like to do is expressed with the form **gustaría*** + *infinitive* and the appropriate indirect objects.

A mí me gustaría viajar a Colombia.
I would like to travel to Colombia.

Nos gustaría hacer *camping* este verano.
We would like to go camping this summer.

AUTOPRUEBA

Complete each verb with **-a** or **-an**.

1. Me gust_____ las playas de México.
2. Les gust_____ esquiar en las montañas.
3. No nos gust_____ viajar con mi padre.
4. ¿Te gust_____ este restaurante?
5. A Julio le gust_____ mucho las fotos de mi viaje.

Answers: 1. gustan 2. gustan 3. gusta 4. gusta 5. gustan

---

*This is one of the forms of the conditional of **gustar**. You will study all of the forms of the conditional in **Gramática 50**.

■ ■ ■ Práctica

A. Gustos y preferencias

Paso 1. Using the models as a guide, tell whether or not you like the following.

MODELOS: ¿el café? → (No) Me gusta el café.
¿los pasteles? → (No) Me gustan los pasteles.

1. ¿el vino?
2. ¿los niños pequeños?
3. ¿la música clásica?
4. ¿Ricky Martin?
5. ¿el invierno?
6. ¿hacer cola?
7. ¿el chocolate?
8. ¿las películas de terror?
9. ¿las clases que empiezan a las ocho de la mañana?
10. ¿cocinar?
11. ¿la gramática?
12. ¿las clases de este semestre/trimestre?
13. ¿los vuelos con muchas escalas?
14. ¿bailar en las discotecas?

Paso 2. Now share your reactions with a classmate. He or she will respond with one of the following reactions. How do your likes and dislikes compare?

REACCIONES

A mí también.   *So do I.*
A mí tampoco.   *I don't either. (Neither do I.)*
Pues a mí, sí.   *Well, I do.*
Pues a mí, no.   *Well, I don't.*

B. ¿Adónde vamos este verano?

Paso 1. The members of the Soto family all prefer different vacation activities and, of course, would like to go to different places this summer. Imagine that you are one of the Sotos and describe the family's various preferences, following the model.

MODELO: padre/nadar: ir a la playa →
A mi padre *le gusta* nadar. *Le gustaría* ir a la playa.

1. padre / el océano: ir a la playa
2. hermanos pequeños / nadar: también ir a la playa
3. hermano Ernesto / hacer *camping*: ir a las montañas
4. abuelos / descansar: quedarse en casa
5. madre / la tranquilidad: visitar un pueblecito (*small town*) en la costa
6. hermana Elena / discotecas: pasar las vacaciones en una ciudad grande
7. mí/¿ ?

Paso 2. Now, remembering what you have learned about the vacation preferences of your imaginary family, answer the following questions.

1. ¿A quién le gustaría ir a Nueva York?
2. ¿A quién le gustaría viajar a Acapulco?
3. ¿Quién no quiere salir de casa?
4. ¿A quién le gustaría ir a Cabo San Lucas?
5. ¿Quién quiere ir a Colorado?

Need more practice?

- Workbook and Laboratory Manual
- Interactive CD-ROM
- Online Learning Center (www.mhhe.com/puntos7)

Prác. A: Suggestion

Paso 2. Model exchanges of several kinds for students.

—*Me gusta el café.*
—*A mí también.*
—*Pues a mí, no.*

—*No me gusta el café.*
—*A mí tampoco.*
—*Pues a mí, sí.*

Prác. A: Extension

Paso 1.

15. *¿el béisbol?*
16. *¿el fútbol?*

Paso 2. Have students add two or three things that they like or dislike to the list in *Paso 1*. Then the partners can respond in a similar manner as before.

Prác. B: Note

These sentences require the redundant use of the indirect object pronoun and noun.

Prác. B: Extension

Paso 1.

8. *ti / (no) / los sitios que prefiere la familia Soto: visitar a la familia*
9. *el perro / (no) / quedarse en casa: ir con la familia*
10. *la tía Ramona / las visitas de la familia: recibirlos en su casa*

Paso 2.

6. *¿Quién quiere recibir a la familia en su casa?*

National Standards: Comparison

Expand on *Práctica A*, item 4. Have students brainstorm the names of at least 30 top pop music artists and list them on the board. How many of the artists are Hispanic? (Some Hispanic pop stars include Marc Anthony, Jennifer López, Christina Aguilera, Gloria Estefan, Shakira, Santana.) Have a volunteer stand at the board and tally how many students like each artist (*¿A quién le gusta la música de… ?*), then compare how well the Hispanic artists fare against the other artists. Have students consider how U.S. and Canadian pop music has influenced Hispanic pop stars and how Hispanic music has influenced U.S. and Canadian pop stars.

Bright Idea

Con. A: Follow-Up

Now have students interview their classmates using the same questions. Once they have finished their interviews, have them report their findings.

Con. B: Suggestion

Do the activity as a whole-class discussion or whole-class composition, with you or a student writing sentences on the board. Use the activity as a vehicle for review of major structures presented so far: verbs of all classes, possessives, pronouns, and so on.

■ ■ ■ Conversación

A. ¿Conoce bien a su profesor(a)?

Paso 1. Piense en su profesor(a) de español. En su opinión, ¿le gustan o no las siguientes cosas?

	SÍ, LE GUSTA(N).	NO, NO LE GUSTA(N).
1. la música clásica	☐	☐
2. el color negro	☐	☐
3. las canciones (*songs*) de los años 70	☐	☐
4. viajar en coche	☐	☐
5. la comida mexicana	☐	☐
6. tener clases por la mañana	☐	☐
7. estudiar otras lenguas	☐	☐
8. el arte surrealista	☐	☐
9. las películas trágicas	☐	☐
10. las casas viejas	☐	☐

Paso 2. Entrevista. Ahora entreviste a un compañero / una compañera para saber si le gustan o no las cosas del **Paso 1.**

> MODELO: E1: ¿Te gusta la música clásica?
> E2: Sí, a mí me gusta. ¿Y a ti?

B. ¿Qué les gusta hacer? ¿Qué les gusta hacer a las siguientes personas? Conteste según los dibujos y trate de usar las Frases útiles. ¿Puede Ud. inventar otros detalles sobre su vida? Por ejemplo, ¿cuántos años tienen? ¿Tienen niños? ¿Dónde viven? ¿Qué cosas *no* les gusta hacer?

Frases útiles
bailar
cantar
escuchar (música *hip hop*)
ir de compras, de vacaciones
jugar a los vídeojuegos
pasar tiempo con (los hijos, los amigos, la familia)
patinar en un monopatín (to skateboard)
viajar (en coche, en avión, a las montañas)

1. Toño

2. los Sres. Sánchez

3. Memo

Resources: Transparency 54

This transparency can also be used as a springboard for talking about what someone else likes.

More About Expressing Likes and Dislikes

Here are some ways to express intense likes and dislikes.

■ Use the phrases **mucho/muchísimo** or **(para) nada.**

Me gusta mucho/muchísimo.	*I like it a lot / a whole lot.*
No me gusta (para) nada.	*I don't like it at all.*

■ To express *love* and *hate* in reference to likes and dislikes, you can use **encantar** and **odiar.**

Encantar is used just like **gustar.**

Me encanta el chocolate.	*I love chocolate.*
Les encanta viajar, ¿verdad?	*You love traveling, right?*

Odiar, on the other hand, functions like a transitive verb (one that can take a direct object).

Odio el apio.	*I hate celery.*
Mi madre **odia** viajar sola.	*My mother hates traveling alone.*

■ To express interest in something, use **interesar.** This verb is also used like **gustar** and **encantar.**

Me interesa la comida salvadoreña.	*I'm interested in Salvadoran food.*

C. **¿Qué te gusta? ¿Qué odias?** Almost every situation has aspects that one likes or dislikes, even hates. Pick at least two of the following situations and tell what you like or don't like about them. Add as many details as you can, using **me gustaría** when possible.

MODELO: en la playa →
Me gusta mucho el agua, pero no me gusta el sol. Por eso no me gusta pasar todo el día en la playa. Me encanta nadar pero odio la arena (*sand*). Por eso me gustaría más ir a nadar en una piscina.

Situaciones	
en un almacén grande	en clase
en un autobús	en el coche
en un avión	en una discoteca
en la biblioteca	en una fiesta
en una cafetería	en un parque
en casa con mis amigos	en la playa
en casa con mis padres/hijos	en un tren

Note
Odiar is not like *gustar:* (*Yo*) *Odio el café* / (*A mí*) *Me gusta el café.*

Suggestion
Ask students to make lists of their favorite and least favorite things and categorize them as:

*Cosas que odio, cosas que no me gustan
Cosas que me interesan
Cosas que me gustan mucho
Cosas que me encantan*

Then ask them to compare their lists with those of a partner.

A mí me encanta la música rock, pero Juan la odia.

Con. C: Suggestion

Use *me molesta(n)* instead of *odio.*

Con. C: Follow-Up

Have students describe the likes and dislikes of various family members on different topics. In addition to *gustar,* encourage students to use *encantar, interesar, molestar, odiar,* and *preferir.*

Follow-Up

Follow up the narration by having students respond to the following questions, using direct object pronouns.

Elisa Velasco, ¿visitó lugares intere-santes en Puerto Rico?
¿Entrevistó (write on board) *a muchas personas?*
¿Comió comida típica?
¿Visitó las playas puertorriqueñas?
¿Hizo el viaje en avión?
¿Pasó la semana en Puerto Rico?
¿Tomó el sol en las playas?

Preterite of Regular Verbs

Note

There will be opportunities to practice the preterite and the imperfect in *Capítulos 7–10*, and throughout the rest of the text.

---

23 Talking About the Past (1) • Preterite of Regular Verbs and of *dar*, *hacer*, *ir*, and *ser*

Elisa habla de su viaje a Puerto Rico

Elisa es reportera. Recientemente *fue* a Puerto Rico para escribir un artículo.

«Recientemente *fui* a Puerto Rico para escribir un artículo sobre esa isla. *Hice* el viaje en avión. El vuelo *fue* largo, pues el avión *hizo* escala en Miami. *Pasé* una semana entera en la isla. *Hablé* con muchas personas de la industria turística y *visité* los lugares más interesantes de Puerto Rico. También *comí* mucha comida típica de la isla. Además, *tomé* el sol en las preciosas playas puertorriqueñas y *nadé* en el mar Caribe. Me *divertí* mucho. ¡Mi viaje *fue* casi como unas vacaciones!»

Comprensión: ¿Cierto o falso?

1. Elisa fue a Puerto Rico para pasar sus vacaciones.
2. El avión hizo escala en los Estados Unidos.
3. Elisa no visitó ningún lugar importante de Puerto Rico.
4. Elisa también pasó tiempo cerca del océano.

In previous chapters of *Puntos de partida*, you have talked about a number of your activities, but always in the present tense. In this section, you will begin to work with the forms of the preterite, one of the tenses that will allow you to talk about the past. To talk about all aspects of the past in Spanish, you need to know how to use two *simple tenses* (tenses formed without an auxiliary or "helping" verb): the preterite and the imperfect. In this chapter, you will learn the regular forms of the preterite and those of four irregular verbs: **dar, hacer, ir,** and **ser.** In this chapter and in **Capítulos 8, 9, 10,** and **11,** you will learn more about preterite forms and their uses as well as about the imperfect and the ways in which it is used alone and with the preterite.

The *preterite* (**el pretérito**) has several equivalents in English. For example, **hablé** can mean *I spoke* or *I did speak.* The preterite is used to report finished, completed actions or states of being in the past. If the action or state of being is viewed as completed—no matter how long it lasted or took to complete—it will be expressed with the preterite.

PAST	Present	Future
preterite	present	
	present progressive	
	formal commands	

Elisa talks about her trip to Puerto Rico *Elisa is a reporter. She recently went to Puerto Rico to write an article. "Recently I went to Puerto Rico to write an article about that island. I made the trip by plane. The flight was long because the plane made a stop in Miami. I spent a whole week on the island. I spoke with many people in the tourist industry and I visited the most interesting places in Puerto Rico. I also ate lots of typical food from the island. Furthermore, I sunbathed on the beautiful Puerto Rican beaches and swam in the Caribbean Sea. I had lots of fun. My trip was almost like a vacation!"*

 Heritage Speakers

Anime a un(a) estudiante hispanohablante a leer en voz alta la narración de Elisa.

Preterite of Regular Verbs

hablar		comer		vivir	
hablé	*I spoke (did speak)*	comí	*I ate (did eat)*	viví	*I lived (did live)*
hablaste	*you spoke*	comiste	*you ate*	viviste	*you lived*
habló	*you/he/she spoke*	comió	*you/he/she ate*	vivió	*you/he/she lived*
hablamos	*we spoke*	comimos	*we ate*	vivimos	*we lived*
hablasteis	*you spoke*	comisteis	*you ate*	vivisteis	*you lived*
hablaron	*you/they spoke*	comieron	*you/they ate*	vivieron	*you/they lived*

■ Note that the **nosotros** forms of regular preterites are the same as the present tense forms for **-ar** and **-ir** verbs. Context usually helps determine meaning.

Hoy **hablamos** con la profesora Benítez.
Today we're speaking with Professor Benítez.

Ayer **hablamos** con el director de la facultad.
Yesterday we spoke with the head of the department.

■ Note the accent marks on the first and third person singular of the preterite tense. These accent marks are dropped in the conjugation of **ver: vi, vio.**

ver:	vi	vimos
	viste	visteis
	vio	vieron

■ Verbs that end in **-car, -gar,** and **-zar** show a spelling change in the first person singular (**yo**) of the preterite. (This is the same change you have already learned to make in present subjunctive forms.)

-car → **qu**	**buscar**	
	busqué	buscamos
	buscaste	buscasteis
	buscó	buscaron
-gar → **gu**	**pagar**	
	pagué	pagamos
	pagaste	pagasteis
	pagó	pagaron
-zar → **c**	**empezar**	
	empecé	empezaron
	empezaste	empezasteis
	empezó	empezaron

■ **-Ar** and **-er** stem-changing verbs show no stem change in the preterite.
-Ir stem-changing verbs do show a change.*

despertar (ie): **desperté, despertaste,...**
volver (ue): **volví, volviste,...**

■ An unstressed **-i-** between two vowels becomes **-y-**. Also, note the accent on the **í** in the **tú, nosotros,** and **vosotros** forms.

creer		leer	
creí	creímos	leí	leímos
creíste	creísteis	leíste	leísteis
creyó	creyeron	leyó	leyeron

*You will learn more about and practice the preterite of most stem-changing verbs in **Capítulo 8.**

Gramática · Doscientos cuarenta y uno ■ **241**

Suggestions

■ Model the pronunciation of regular forms, emphasizing the stress on *yo* and *Ud.* forms.

■ Point out that the *nosotros* preterite forms of *-ar* and *-ir* verbs are identical to present tense forms. Context will clarify the meaning.

■ Use *llamar, aprender,* and *recibir* in brief conversational exchanges with students, first in a sentence about yourself, then asking *Ud./Uds.* questions of the students.

■ Point out the importance of word stress to distinguish some verbal forms, such as *hablo* (I speak) vs. *habló* (he/she/you spoke); *hable* (speak, *Ud.* command) vs. *hablé* (I spoke).

■ Say the following word pairs and have students identify the preterite form: *hable, hablé; hablo, habló; bailé, baile; busqué, busque; estudio, estudió; tomó, tomo.*

■ Say the following verbs and have students give the corresponding subject pronoun.

Singular forms:

pregunté	*bajó*	*ayudaste*
fumé	*llamé*	*anunció*
mandaste	*bebió*	*aprendí*
comiste	*contesté*	*ayudó*

Plural forms:

escuchamos	*terminaron*	*mirasteis*
estudiamos	*bailaron*	*regresaron*
pagamos	*bebieron*	*comimos*
aprendisteis		

■ Say the following verbs and have students tell whether each could be present, past, or both.

miró	*mandé*	*escuché*
escucha	*escribimos*	*fumaste*
bebió	*ayudamos*	*vive*
volvió	*creo*	*empiezan*
leyó	*pagáis*	*buscaste*

■ Say the following verbs and have students tell whether each is a command or a form of the preterite.

estudie	*estudié*	*fumé*
fumen	*ayudé*	*busque*
leyó	*hablé*	*pagué*
lleve	*decidí*	

■ Point out that no written accent is needed for the *yo* and *Ud.* forms of *ver* because they are single syllables: *vi, vio.* Other single-syllable forms also will not require an accent (*dar, ir, ser*).

■ Write some formal commands using *-gar, -car,* and *-zar* verbs on the board (*toque, llegue, empiece*) to emphasize that these are the same spelling changes they use in the preterite.

Heritage Speakers

■ En algunos dialectos del español, hay una tendencia a añadirle una *-s* al final de la segunda persona del singular (*tú*) del pretérito, por ejemplo, *hablaste → hablastes, comiste → comistes, viviste → vivistes.* Aunque se oyen estas formas, es preferido no añadir la *-s* al final.

■ En algunos dialectos del español, a veces se oye *vide, vidiste, vido, ...,* en vez de *vi, viste, vio...* Aunque se oyen estas formas, las que se presentan aquí son las preferidas.

Resources: Transparency 55

This transparency includes additional practice items you may wish to present to your students.

Irregular Preterite Forms

Suggestions

- Present some sentences using the preterite of *ser* and *ir* to show that context clarifies the meaning.
- Remind students that single-syllable forms such as the *yo* and *Ud.* forms of *dar* and *ver* do not require an accent: *di, dio; vi, vio.*

Preliminary Exercises

- Use the following rapid-response drill before beginning the activities.

  Ud. → yo
  Uds. → nosotros.
  MODELO: *¿Llamó? → Sí, llamé,*

¿Estudió?	*¿Trabajó?*
¿Habló?	*¿Escuchó?*
¿Terminó?	*¿Mandó?*
¿Bajó?	*¿Cantó?*
¿Bailó?	*¿Comió?*
¿Bebió?	*¿Abrió?*
¿Asistió?	*¿Escribió?*

¿Preguntaron?	*¿Contestaron?*
¿Bajaron?	*¿Mandaron?*
¿Escucharon?	*¿Miraron?*
¿Bebieron?	*¿Comieron?*
¿Comprendieron?	*¿Vivieron?*
¿Recibieron?	

- Use the following chain drill before beginning the activities.

  1. *Pepe estudió hasta muy tarde. (yo, Uds. tú, Graciela, nosotros, vosotros)*
  2. *Tú escribiste todos los ejercicios. (Rodrigo, yo, nosotras, ellas, Uds., vosotros)*
  3. *Julio fue al laboratorio. (yo, Paula, tú, nosotros, Estela y Clara, vosotras)*
  4. *Ana hizo los experimentos. (yo, nosotros, Uds., tú, Adolfo)*

Prác. A: Variation

Have students work in pairs and report each other's actions to the class.

---

dar		hacer		ir/ser	
di	dimos	hice	hicimos	fui	fuimos
diste	disteis	hiciste	hicisteis	fuiste	fuisteis
dio	dieron	hizo	hicieron	fue	fueron

- The preterite endings for **dar** are the same as those used for regular **-er/-ir** verbs in the preterite, except that the accent marks are dropped.

- **Hizo** is spelled with a **z** to keep the [s] sound of the infinitive.

  $$\text{hic- + -o} \rightarrow \textbf{hizo}$$

- **Ir** and **ser** have identical forms in the preterite. Context will make the meaning clear.

  Fui a la playa el verano pasado.
  I went to the beach last summer.

  Fui agente de viajes.
  I was a travel agent.

AUTOPRUEBA

Give the correct preterite forms.

1. (nosotros) buscar
2. (mi papá) volver
3. (yo) despertarme
4. (Ud.) ver
5. (ellas) leer
6. (tú) ser

Answers: 1. buscamos 2. volvió 3. me desperté 4. vio 5. leyeron 6. fuiste

■ ■ ■ Práctica

A. ¡Anticipemos! ¿Qué hizo Ud. el verano pasado? Indique las oraciones que son ciertas para Ud., contestando con **sí** o **no.**

El verano pasado...

1. tomé una clase en la universidad.
2. asistí a un concierto.
3. trabajé mucho.
4. hice *camping* con algunos amigos / mi familia.
5. viví con mis padres / mis hijos.
6. me quedé en este pueblo / esta ciudad.
7. fui a una playa.
8. hice una excursión a otro país.
9. fui a muchas fiestas.
10. no hice nada especial.

B. El día de tres compañeras

Paso 1. Teresa, Evangelina y Liliana comparten (*share*) un apartamento en un edificio viejo. Ayer Teresa y Evangelina fueron a la universidad mientras Liliana se quedó en casa. Describa lo que (*what*) hicieron, según la perspectiva de cada una.

> **MODELO:** (nosotras) levantarse / a / siete y media →
> Nos levantamos a las siete y media.

TERESA Y EVANGELINA

1. (nosotras) salir / de / apartamento / a / nueve
2. llegar / biblioteca / a / diez
3. estudiar / toda la mañana / para / examen
4. escribir / muchos ejercicios
5. almorzar / con / amigos / en / cafetería
6. ir / a / laboratorio / a / una
7. hacer / todos los experimentos / de / manual (*m.*)
8. tomar / examen / a / cuatro
9. ¡examen / ser / horrible!
10. regresar / a casa / después de / examen
11. ayudar / Liliana / a / preparar / cena
12. cenar / todas juntas / a / siete

LILIANA

1. (yo) quedarse / en casa / todo el día
2. ver / televisión / por / mañana
3. llamar / mi / padres / a / once
4. tomar / café / con / vecinos (*neighbors*)
5. estudiar / para / examen / de / historia / y / escribir / composición / para / clase / sociología
6. ir / a / garaje / para / dejar / allí / muebles / viejo
7. ir / a / supermercado / y / comprar / comida
8. empezar / a / preparar / cena / a / cinco

Paso 2. ¿Quién lo dijo (*said*), Evangelina o Liliana?

1. Mis compañeras no pasaron mucho tiempo en casa hoy.
2. ¡El examen fue desastroso!
3. Estudié mucho hoy.
4. Me gustó mucho el programa de «Oprah» hoy.
5. ¿Saben? Hablé con mis padres hoy y…

Paso 3. Ahora vuelva a contar (*tell*) cómo fue el día de Liliana, pero desde el punto de vista de sus compañeras de cuarto. Luego diga cómo fue el día de Teresa y Evangelina según Liliana.

Prác. B: Suggestion

Reenter items using *tú* as the subject when appropriate.

Prác. B: Follow-Up

Ask the following question: *¿Cómo fue su día ayer?* Then have students work in pairs to describe what they did yesterday.

Gramática   Doscientos cuarenta y tres ■ **243**

National Standards: Communication

Have students work in small groups to invent stories of an imaginary vacation they took last summer. First, have them research Hispanic travel agencies or travel agencies that publish their information in Spanish on the Internet. Then, have them choose a destination in the Spanish-speaking world. Then, have them narrate the trip they took there. Remind them to use the *nosotros* form of the preterite and to address the following questions.

> *¿Adónde viajaron?*
> *¿Dónde se quedaron?* (Where did you stay?)
> *¿Qué atracciones turísticas visitaron?*

Prác. C: Suggestions

- Vary the subject of items as appropriate.
- Have students read through the list before starting the activity.
- Read the sentences using the present tense, and have students write them as dictation, changing all the verbs to the preterite.

C. Un semestre en México. Cuente la siguiente historia desde el punto de vista de la persona indicada, usando el pretérito de los verbos.

MODELO: (yo) viajar a México el año pasado →
Viajé a México el año pasado.

1. (yo) pasar todo el semestre en la ciudad de Guanajuato
2. mis padres: pagarme el vuelo…
3. …pero (yo) trabajar para ganar el dinero para la matrícula y los otros gastos (*expenses*)
4. vivir con una familia mexicana encantadora (*enchanting*)
5. aprender mucho sobre la vida y la cultura mexicanas
6. visitar muchos sitios de interés turístico e histórico
7. mis amigos: escribirme muchas cartas
8. (yo) mandarles muchas tarjetas postales
9. comprarles recuerdos (*souvenirs*) a todos
10. volver a los Estados Unidos al final de agosto

Need more practice?

- Workbook and Laboratory Manual
- Interactive CD-ROM
- Online Learning Center (www.mhhe.com/puntos7)

EN LOS ESTADOS UNIDOS Y EL CANADÁ

Ellen Ochoa, una viajera espacial

La Dra. Ellen L. Ochoa, de California (1958–), es **la primera mujer hispana astronauta** de los Estados Unidos; trabaja en la NASA desde 1990. Se graduó con un **doctorado**[a] en **ingeniería eléctrica** de la Universidad de Stanford. Pasó más de 975 horas viajando en el espacio, la misión más reciente en el año 2002. Entre[b] sus muchos honores está el de ser[c] miembro de la Comisión Presidencial para la Celebración de Mujeres en la Historia Americana.

La Dra. Ochoa no es la única persona hispana en la NASA. Hay otros **cinco astronautas hispanos** en misiones espaciales: el argentino Frank Caldeiro, el costarricense[d] Franklin Chang-Díaz, los españoles Pedro Duque y Michael López-Alegría y el peruano Carlos Noriega.

[a]*Ph.D.*   [b]*Among*   [c]*el... that of being*   [d]*Costa Rican*

▲ *Ellen Ochoa*

■ ■ ■ Conversación

NOTA COMUNICATIVA

Putting Events in Sequence

When telling about what you did, you often want to emphasize the sequence in which events took place. Use the following phrases to put events into a simple sequence in Spanish. You will learn additional words and phrases of this kind as you learn more about the past tenses.

Primero...	First . . .
Luego... y...	Then . . . and . . .
Después... y...	Afterward . . . and . . .
Finalmente (Por fin)...	Finally . . .

Capítulo 7: De vacaciones

 Heritage Speakers

Pídales a sus estudiantes que escriban una composición usando las frases de *Conversación C*.

EN LOS ESTADOS UNIDOS Y EL CANADÁ

Suggestion
Have students visit NASA's website for more information about the astronauts.

A. El viernes por la tarde... The following drawings depict what Julián did last Friday night. Match the phrases with the individual drawings in the sequence. Then narrate what Julián did using verbs in the preterite. Use as many of the words and phrases from the preceding **Nota comunicativa** as possible.

a. _____ hacer cola para comprar las entradas (*tickets*)
b. _____ regresar tarde a casa
c. _____ volver a casa después de trabajar
d. _____ ir a un café a tomar algo
e. _____ llegar al cine al mismo tiempo
f. _____ llamar a un amigo
g. _____ no gustarles la película (*movie*)
h. _____ comer rápidamente
i. _____ ducharse y afeitarse
j. _____ entrar en el cine
k. _____ ir al cine en autobús
l. _____ decidir encontrarse (*to meet up*) en el cine

Con. A: Note

This is the first of several narration sequences that appears in this text. Use the drawing to give input with the preterite and the imperfect (even though students have not learned the imperfect yet). After introducing the imperfect (*Capítulo 9*) and then the contrasts between imperfect and preterite (*Capítulo 10*), come back to this drawing and exploit its narrative potential.

Con. A: Suggestion

Read the following whole paragraph out loud. Then repeat, phrase by phrase. Have students retell the story line by line.

Anoche Miguel volvió a casa a las siete. Preparó la comida y cenó rápidamente. Estudió para su examen de filosofía hasta las ocho y después habló por teléfono con una compañera de clase. Y a las nueve en punto llegaron sus padres.

Resources: Transparency 56

Con. B: Variation

Have students work in small groups to ask each other questions using *tú* forms.

Con. B: Follow-Up

■ For the next class, have students write down

1. one or two unusual things they did in the past
2. one or two unusual things they did *not* do.

Have students read their statements in class as others tell whether they think the statements are *cierto* or *falso*.

■ Have students write questions about personal habits and life events they can then use to interview classmates. Write the following verbs on the board to give them ideas: *despertarse, regresar, pagar, enamorarse* (to fall in love), *sacar una nota* (grade).

Con. C: Suggestion

Ask students the following questions about the people listed or other well-known people. Have them use their imagination and make up necessary details: *¿Qué hicieron estas personas ayer?* (Madonna, el presidente, Julia Roberts, Emeril, el profesor / la profesora) Write the following actions on the board to support their responses: *dar un discurso* (speech), *ensayar* (to rehearse), *cocinar, cantar, enseñar, no hacer nada.*

B. Entrevista

1. ¿Qué le(s) diste a tu mejor amigo/a (tu esposo/a, tu novio/a, tus hijos) para su cumpleaños el año pasado? ¿Qué te regaló a ti esa persona para tu cumpleaños? ¿Alguien te mandó flores el año pasado? ¿Le mandaste flores a alguien? ¿Te gusta que te traigan chocolates? ¿otras cosas?
2. ¿Dónde y a qué hora comiste ayer? ¿Con quién(es) comiste? ¿Te gustaron todos los platos que comiste? Si comiste fuera, ¿quién pagó?
3. ¿Cuándo decidiste estudiar español? ¿Cuándo lo empezaste a estudiar? ¿Vas a seguir con el español el semestre/trimestre que viene?
4. ¿Qué hiciste ayer? ¿Adónde fuiste? ¿Con quién(es)? ¿Ayudaste a alguien a hacer algo? ¿Te llamó alguien? ¿Llamaste a alguien? ¿Te invitaron a hacer algo especial algunos amigos?

C. ¿Qué hicieron?

Paso 1. Describa lo que hicieron las siguientes personas ayer, sin decir (*without telling*) su nombre. Si no sabe los detalles, ¡invéntelos! Para los números 1 y 4, escoja a una persona fácil de reconocer. Incluya también una descripción de lo que Ud. hizo ayer.

> MODELO: un actor famoso →
> Se levantó a las cinco de la mañana para trabajar. Fue al estudio y habló con el director y Kathy Bates antes de empezar. Luego se acostó en la cama de agua y…

1. un actor famoso / una actriz famosa
2. un rey (*king*) o una reina (*queen*)
3. un empleado de la Casa Blanca (*White House*)
4. un(a) atleta profesional
5. un bebé de dos años
6. Ud. o un compañero / una compañera de clase

Paso 2. Lea una o dos de sus descripciones sin identificar a la persona. Sus compañeros de clase deben tratar de identificar a quién describe.

> MODELO: E1: Se levantó a las cinco de la mañana para trabajar. Fue al estudio y habló con el director y Kathy Bates antes de empezar. Luego se acostó en la cama de agua y…
> E2: Es un actor famoso. Es Jack Nicholson.

UN POCO DE TODO

A. Preguntas: La última vez. Conteste las siguientes preguntas. Añada (*Add*) más información si puede.

> MODELO: La última vez que Ud. fue a una fiesta, ¿le llevó un regalo al anfitrión / a la anfitriona (*host/hostess*)? →
> Sí, le llevé flores / una botella de vino. (No, no le llevé nada.)

La última vez que Ud....

1. hizo un viaje, ¿le mandó una tarjeta postal a un amigo / a una amiga?
2. tomó el autobús / el metro, ¿le ofreció su asiento a una persona mayor?
3. vio a su profesor(a) de español en público, ¿le habló en español?
4. comió en un restaurante, ¿le recomendó un plato a su compañero/a?
5. entró en un edificio, ¿le abrió la puerta a otra persona?

B. Recomendaciones para las vacaciones. Complete the following vacation suggestion with the correct form of the words in parentheses, as suggested by the context. When two possibilities are given in parentheses, select the correct word.

Los países de Centro y Sudamérica ofrecen una gran variedad de posibilidades para el viajero.[a] Si a Uds. les interesa un viaje menos típico, deben planear una aventura en el mundo hispánico.

(Les/Los[1]) quiero decir (algo/nada[2]) sobre (el/la[3]) ciudad de Machu Picchu. ¿Ya (lo/la[4]) (saber/conocer[5]) Uds.? (Ser/Estar[6]) situada en los Andes, a unos ochenta kilómetros[b] de la ciudad de Cuzco, Perú. Machu Picchu es conocida[c] como (el/la[7]) ciudad escondida[d] de los incas. Se dice que (ser/estar[8]) una de las manifestaciones (más/tan[9]) importantes de la arquitectura incaica. Era[e] refugio y a la vez[f] ciudad de vacaciones de los reyes[g] (incaico[10]). *incaicos*

Uds. deben (visitarlo/visitarla[11]). (Le/Les[12]) gustaría porque (ser/estar[13]) un sitio inolvidable.[h] Es mejor (ir/van[14]) a Machu Picchu en primavera o verano —son las (mejor/es[15]) estaciones para visitar este lugar. Pero es necesario (comprar/compran[16]) los boletos con anticipación,[i] porque (mucho/s[17]) turistas de todos los (país[18]) del mundo visitan este sitio extraordinario. ¡(*Yo:* Saber/Conocer[19]) que a Uds. (los/les[20]) va a gustar el viaje!

[a]*traveler* [b]*ochenta... 50 millas* [c]*known* [d]*hidden* [e]*It was* [f]*a... at the same time* [g]*kings* [h]*unforgettable* [i]*con... ahead of time*

Resources for Review and Testing Preparation

- Workbook and Laboratory Manual
- Interactive CD-ROM
- Online Learning Center (www.mhhe.com/puntos7)

Comprensión: ¿Cierto o falso? Conteste según la descripción.

1. Machu Picchu está en Chile.
2. Fue un lugar importante en el pasado.
3. Todavía es una atracción turística de gran interés.
4. Sólo los turistas latinoamericanos conocen Machu Picchu.

UN POCO DE TODO

A: Suggestions

- Have students complete the activity in pairs, then report to the class at least two interesting things they learned about their partner.
- Have students invent their own questions using the format of these items. They can take turns asking each other questions.

A: Reciclado

Recycle family and food words. Have students say the following sentences in Spanish.

1. My father likes vegetables, but he doesn't like cheese.
2. My mother likes milk, but she doesn't like apple juice.
3. My grandparents like eggs but they don't like meat.
4. I like everything (*todo*) but my siblings don't like anything!

B: Suggestion

Read the following sentences and have students indicate whether they are *cierto* or *falso*. Keep in mind that students have only been introduced to the concept of subjunctive for recognition.

1. *Sus padres (hijos) quieren que Ud. vaya de vacaciones este año.*
2. *Su mejor amigo/a no desea que Ud. viaje en avión.*
3. *Es bueno que muchas personas pasen sus vacaciones en lugares exóticos.*
4. *Es malo que (no) haya muchos turistas que vienen a esta ciudad.*

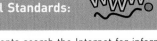

National Standards: Culture

Have students search the Internet for information about Machu Picchu and share their findings with their classmates. You can have students use the following questions to guide them in their search.

¿Cuándo se descubrió Machu Picchu?
¿Quién lo descubrió?

Resources: Desenlace

In the *Capítulo 7* segment of "Chapter-by-Chapter Supplementary Materials" in the IM, you will find a chapter-culminating activity. You can use this activity to consolidate and review the vocabulary and grammar skills students have acquired.

Entrevistas culturales

Suggestions

- Before showing the video clips, ask students questions about their experiences with travel agents and/or traveling.

  ¿Qué destinos turísticos conoce Ud.?
  ¿Adónde piensa viajar este año?

- Tell students they will be listening to a travel agent from Honduras (Heidi) and a tourist guide from El Salvador (Rubén). Have them predict what type of information they may hear.
- Show the video clips and allow students one to two minutes to work on the questions for each one. Have volunteers answer the questions.
- Have volunteers role-play the parts of Heidi and Rubén with their respective interviewers.

Entre amigos

Suggestions

- Before viewing the video, review the questions with the students and ask them similar questions.

  ¿Qué le gusta a Ud. hacer durante las vacaciones?
  ¿Adónde fue de vacaciones el verano pasado? ¿Qué hizo allí?

Have students answer or work in small groups to ask and answer these questions.

- After viewing the video, have volunteers read and answer the questions.

PERSPECTIVAS culturales

•••
Videoteca

Entrevista cultural: Honduras

Heidi Luna es una agente de viajes hondureña. Aquí habla de los destinos favoritos de sus clientes y también menciona sus propios planes para viajar. Antes de ver el vídeo, lea el siguiente fragmento de la entrevista.

HEIDI: …La mayoría de nuestros clientes nos busca para que los ayudemos en viajes especiales o en vacaciones especiales. Es muy divertido poder ayudarlos.

Ahora vea el vídeo y conteste las siguientes preguntas basándose en la entrevista.

1. ¿Qué destinos latinoamericanos menciona Heidi como los preferidos de sus clientes? ¿Qué destinos norteamericanos menciona?
2. ¿Adónde piensa viajar Heidi? ¿Por qué?

Entrevista cultural: El Salvador

Rubén Guillén es de El Salvador. En la entrevista, explica por qué le encanta ser guía turístico. Antes de ver el vídeo, lea el siguiente fragmento de la entrevista.

RUBÉN: Bueno, yo soy guía turístico y trabajo precisamente en un hotel de la capital y me encargo de[a] organizar excursiones y viajes hacia las diferentes playas y lugares turísticos de nuestro país. Eso, exactamente.

[a]me… I'm in charge of

Ahora vea el vídeo y conteste las siguientes preguntas basándose en la entrevista.

1. ¿Dónde trabaja Rubén?
2. Según Rubén, ¿cuáles son unas ventajas de su trabajo?

Entre amigos: El verano pasado, me fui al Canadá

Rubén, Tané, Miguel y Karina pasan un tarde el Parque Ecológico de Xochimilco. Hablan de las vacaciones. En su opinión, ¿qué preguntas van a hacerse? Antes de mirar el vídeo, lea las preguntas a continuación. Mientras mire el vídeo, trate de entender la conversación en general y fíjese en la información sobre las vacaciones. Luego mire el vídeo una segunda vez, fijándose en la información que necesita para contestar las preguntas.

1. ¿Qué le gusta hacer a Karina durante las vacaciones? ¿Y a Tané?
2. ¿Adónde fue Tané el verano pasado? ¿Y Miguel?
3. ¿Qué hizo Rubén el verano pasado?

Conozca... Honduras y El Salvador

Datos esenciales

Honduras

- Nombre oficial: República de Honduras
- Capital: Tegucigalpa
- Población: 6.670.000 habitantes
- Moneda: el lempira
- Idioma oficial: el español

El Salvador

- Nombre oficial: República de El Salvador
- Capital: San Salvador
- Población: 6.500.000 habitantes
- Moneda: el dólar*
- Idioma oficial: el español

¡Fíjese!

- El centro ceremonial maya de Copán, en Honduras, es hoy un parque nacional que contiene una colección de ruinas mayas superadas[a] sólo por las ruinas de Tikal en Guatemala.
- La moneda de Honduras, el lempira, lleva el nombre de un cacique[b] indígena que luchó contra[c] los españoles.
- El nombre indígena de la capital de Honduras, Tegucigalpa, significa «cerros de plata».[d] Honduras recibió su nombre español por la profundidad[e] de sus aguas costeras.[f] El nombre indígena de El Salvador era[g] Cuzcatlán, que significa «tierra de joyas[h] y cosas preciosas».
- Las erupciones del Volcán de Izalco en El Salvador fueron constantes entre los años 1770 y 1966, por casi dos siglos.[i] Este volcán se conoce con el nombre de «el faro[j] del Pacífico», porque estuvo encendido[k] por muchos años y sirvió de[l] guía a los navegantes.

[a]exceeded (in quality) [b]chief [c]luchó... fought against [d]cerros... silver hills [e]depth [f]coastal [g]was [h]jewels [i]centuries [j]lighthouse [k]estuvo... it was lit up [l]sirvió... served as a

*The **colón** was replaced by the dollar on January 1, 2001.

Personas famosas: El Arzobispo[a] Óscar Arnulfo Romero

El 24 de marzo de 1980 un héroe de El Salvador fue asesinado mientras oficiaba una misa.[b] En vida,[c] el arzobispo Óscar Arnulfo Romero (1917–1980) fue la conciencia de su país. Criticó a los líderes políticos por su violencia e injusticia, y trabajó para mejorar[d] las condiciones económicas y sociales del país. Por eso, fue nominado para el premio Nóbel de la Paz[e] en 1979.

[a]Archbishop [b]oficiaba... he was celebrating a Mass [c]life [d]improve [e]premio... Nobel Peace Prize

▲ El Volcán de Izalco, El Salvador

Learn more about Honduras and El Salvador with the Video, the Interactive CD-ROM, and the Online Learning Center (www.mhhe.com/puntos7).

Conozca... Honduras

Notes

- Copán, founded by Mayan groups that reached the western part of Honduras in the fifth century A.D., developed over a period of 350 years. Copán was an important center for astronomy and art, as well as trade. Copán was apparently abandoned at the height of Mayan civilization; the last hieroglyph in the city is dated in the year 800. Although much of the population remained, there is no trace of the artists and priest astronomer/mathematicians who were previously so active.
- Much of Honduras has always been underdeveloped, due to geography and topography, as well as to historical experience. Honduras' lack of access to good ports and its high central mountains have kept the country isolated. Additionally, the repeated intervention by outsiders in the country's political and economic life have kept Hondurans from seeking out strong external ties. The United Fruit Company and the Standard Fruit Company, for example, were powerful political forces in the country during the first part of the twentieth century.
- In the early 1960s, there were more Peace Corps volunteers in Honduras than in any other country. Presently there are approximately 200 volunteers in the country.
- Students can read the poem *"Canto a la encontrada patria y su héroe"* by Honduras's Clementina Suárez in *Un paso más 7.*

Conozca... El Salvador

Notes

- Spain established its first settlements in El Salvador in 1524, and the country remained a colony until 1821, when it declared its independence. For two years after that, it was part of the Mexican Empire and then formed part of the Central American Federation, along with other Central American countries.
- Poor economic conditions and the failure of land reform plans of the 1970s resulted in guerilla warfare and a 12-year civil war, which lasted until 1992. During this time, Christian Democrat president José Napoleón Duarte attempted to negotiate with the guerrillas, but he was unsuccessful.

MULTIMEDIA: Internet

Have students search the Internet for more information on Honduras and El Salvador. You might assign specific topics, such as the life and social ideas of Archbishop Óscar Romero, and have students give brief oral presentations based on their findings.

Perspectivas culturales ■ **249**

Suggestions

■ Ask students the following questions.

1. *¿Quién sirve la comida en el avión, el piloto o el asistente de vuelo?*
2. *Si una persona toma el vuelo número 60, ¿viaja en tren o en avión?*
3. *¿Hay camareros en los autobuses?*

■ Have students respond *probable* or *improbable*.

1. *Los pasajeros sirven las bebidas.*
2. *Los asistentes de vuelo compran un pasaje para el viaje.*
3. *El piloto lleva uniforme.*

■ Have students respond *posible* or *imposible*.

1. *Unos pasajeros llevan uniforme.*
2. *Hay un vuelo en tren de Philadelphia a Boston.*
3. *Si Ud. no tiene mucho tiempo, debe comprar un pasaje en avión.*

■ Point out the spelling changes in *explicar, ofrecer,* and *sacar.* Ask students what other verbs they know with these or similar spelling changes (*llegar, tocar, conocer,* and so on).

EN RESUMEN

Gramática

To review the grammar points presented in this chapter, refer to the indicated grammar presentations. You'll find further practice of these structures in the Workbook and Laboratory Manual, on the Interactive CD-ROM, and on the *Puntos de partida* Online Learning Center (www.mhhe.com/puntos7).

21. Expressing *to whom* or *for whom*—Indirect Object Pronouns; **Dar** and **decir**

Do you know how to use indirect object pronouns to express *to whom* or *for whom*?

22. Expressing Likes and Dislikes—**Gustar**

Do you know how to talk about things you and others like and like to do?

23. Talking About the Past (1)—Preterite of Regular Verbs and of **dar, hacer, ir,** and **ser**

You should know how to conjugate regular preterite verbs. Can you use the irregular verbs **dar, hacer, ir,** and **ser** in the preterite as well?

Vocabulario

Practice this vocabulary with digital flash cards on the Online Learning Center (www.mhhe.com/puntos7).

Los verbos

anunciar	to announce
bajar (de)	to get down (from); to get off (of)
contar (ue)	to tell
dar (*irreg.*)	to give
decir (*irreg.*)	to say; to tell
encantar	to like very much, love
explicar (qu)	to explain
facturar	to check (*baggage*)
fumar	to smoke
guardar	to save (*a place*)
gustar	to be pleasing
mandar	to send
mostrar (ue)	to show
odiar	to hate
ofrecer (zc)	to offer
prestar	to lend
prometer	to promise
recomendar (ie)	to recommend
regalar	to give (*as a gift*)
subir (a)	to go up; to get on (*a vehicle*)
viajar	to travel

De viaje

el aeropuerto	airport
la agencia de viajes	travel agency
el/la agente de viajes	travel agent
el asiento	seat
el/la asistente de vuelo	flight attendant
el autobús	bus
el avión	airplane
el barco	boat, ship
el billete/boleto	ticket
de ida	one-way
de ida y vuelta	round-trip
la cabina	cabin (*in a ship*)
la clase turística	tourist class
la demora	delay
el equipaje	baggage, luggage
la estación	station
de autobuses	bus
del tren	train
la llegada	arrival
la maleta	suitcase
el maletero	porter
el modo (de transporte)	means (of transportation)
el pasaje	passage; ticket
el/la pasajero/a	passenger
la primera clase	first class
el puerto	port
el puesto	place (*in line*)
la sala de espera	waiting room
la salida	departure
la sección de (no) fumar	(non)smoking section

 Heritage Speakers

Hay varias maneras de expresar *flight attendant* según el dialecto del español que se hable. Algunos sinónimos de *el/la asistente de vuelo* son *la azafata, el auxiliar de vuelo, la aeromoza* y *la cabinera.* En algunos dialectos de Chile se dice *hostess.* Pregúnteles a los hispanohablantes cómo se dice *el/la asistente de vuelo* en su dialecto. ¿Hay alguien en la clase que use la palabra *sobrecargo* para referirse a *flight attendant*?

la tarjeta (postal)	(post)card
el tren	train
el viaje	trip
el vuelo	flight
hacer (*irreg.*) cola	to stand in line
hacer (*irreg.*) escalas/paradas	to make stops
hacer (*irreg.*) la(s) maleta(s)	to pack one's suitcase(s)
ir (*irreg.*) en...	to go/travel by . . .
autobús	bus
avión	plane
barco	boat, ship
tren	train
pasar por el control de la seguridad	to go/pass through security (check)

Repaso: hacer (*irreg.*) **un viaje**

De vacaciones

la camioneta	station wagon
el *camping*	campground
la foto(grafía)	photo(graph)
el mar	sea
la montaña	mountain
el océano	ocean
la tienda (de campaña)	tent

Repaso: la playa

estar (*irreg.*) de vacaciones	to be on vacation
hacer (*irreg.*) *camping*	to go camping
ir (*irreg.*) de vacaciones	to go on vacation
nadar	to swim
sacar (qu)	to take (*photos*)
tomar el sol	to sunbathe

Otros sustantivos

la flor	flower
el mundo	world
el/la niño/a	child; boy (girl)

Los adjetivos

atrasado/a (*with* estar)	late
solo/a	alone
último/a	last

Palabras adicionales

a tiempo	on time
de viaje	on a trip
desde	from
lo que	what, that which
me gustaría...	I would (really) like . . .
muchísimo	an awful lot

Suggestion

Show students an image of a scene that includes vocabulary items. Put the image away and have students write as many sentences as possible describing the scene. They should use words from *Vocabulario*. Have students read or write their sentences on the board in order to compare descriptions.

Un paso más 7

Un paso más 7

Note

The *Un paso más* section is optional.

Literatura de Honduras

Notes

- Clementina Suárez was a rebel in her era. Not only did she travel alone extensively at a time when it was frowned upon for a woman of her position to do so, but she also lived alone most of her life. She was married and divorced two times. But what was seen as scandalous were her many love affairs with writers and artists and the two children she had out of wedlock. She purportedly read her poetry once in see-through clothing.
- The scandal she invoked should not overshadow her artistic endeavors. Suárez was an energetic supporter and promoter of the arts. She opened some of the first art galleries in Central America. In Mexico she opened a gallery to display the work of Central American artists, including that of Salvadorian José Mejía Vides (her second husband) and Costa Rican Francisco Amighetti.
- Additionally, she served as cultural attaché to El Salvador and worked in Honduras' Ministry of Education.
- Tragically, Clementina Suárez was murdered in December 1991. Her murderer remains at large.

LECTURA

Suggestion

Do the *Estrategia* in class the day you assign the reading as homework. Bring in titles of articles from several different magazines and have students match each article with the magazine it came from. This will further demonstrate how one associates certain types of features with specific magazines.

Literatura de Honduras

Sobre la autora: *Clementina Suárez nació en Olancho, Honduras. Desde joven, rechazó los privilegios y la posición social de su familia. Viajó sola por todo el mundo y vivió sola durante una época en que no se aceptaba[a] la independencia femenina.*

Canto a la encontrada[b] patria y su héroe
No puedo llegar...
Porque jamás me he ido.[c]
Eres una Patria construida
en lo interior.
Caminas[d] dentro de mí
como un abierto[e] río.
Vienes desde muy atrás[f]
rebelde y vegetal,
todo en ti es nuevo y viejo
tierra para la infancia
y para inmortalizar el tiempo.

[a]*no... people didn't accept* [b]*found* [c]*jamás... I have never left* [d]*You walk* [e]*free-flowing*
[f]*desde... from long ago*

▲ Clementina Suárez (1902–1991)

LECTURA

ESTRATEGIA: Identifying the Source of a Passage

If you pick up the *New England Journal of Medicine,* what sort of articles do you expect to find? For whom are they written and for what purpose? Would you anticipate similar articles in *People* magazine?

You can often make useful predictions about an article—its narrative style, its target audience, the author's purpose, and so forth—if you know something about the magazine or journal from which it comes. The article you are about to read was first published in *GeoMundo,* a Spanish-language magazine not unlike *National Geographic.* Knowing this, which of the following topics do you think might be treated in a given issue of this magazine?

1. the Incas and Machu Picchu
2. how to remove coffee stains from silk
3. the search for a great white shark
4. Montreal by night

All but number two might appear in *GeoMundo.* Keeping in mind the source of a reading will often help you to predict its content.

CULTURE

San Miguel de Allende, a colonial Mexican town nestled in a beautiful valley, is a national monument, which has allowed the town to preserve its character, beautiful Spanish architecture, and cobblestoned streets from the colonial period. The charm and pleasant climate have attracted many visitors, who sometimes become permanent residents. San Miguel de Allende, population 50,000, is a center of intellectual and artistic life. Its schools and universities, which teach painting, sculpture, music, literature, language, and drama, attract many artists.

■ **Sobre la lectura...** *GeoMundo* is for the reader who is interested in world travel, different cultures and customs, the environment, and similar issues. The following article was taken from a travel section called «**Geoturismo**». This particular section deals with Mexico.

México es mucho más que playas

Además de[a] los populares centros de vacaciones en las costas como Acapulco y Cancún, México tiene otros lugares donde se puede descubrir algo de la historia y la cultura del país. Uno de ellos es la península de Yucatán, donde floreció[b] la gran civilización maya. Allí se puede visitar Palenque, con su imponente pirámide en una exuberante selva tropical. También se puede visitar Uxmal, una clásica ciudad maya, y Chichén Itzá, centro cultural de la región entre los siglos X al XIII. Todos están cerca de excelentes hoteles y restaurantes.

Otra alternativa son las ciudades coloniales de México, cuya[c] elegante arquitectura del siglo XVI refleja su génesis española. Explore estas ciudades:

■ San Miguel de Allende, una bulliciosa[d] ciudad donde se han refugiado[e] artistas de todo el mundo
■ Guanajuato, sede[f] del prestigioso Festival Cervantino de teatro, con sus serpenteantes calles adoquinadas[g]
■ Zacatecas, con sus edificios construidos de granito rosa
■ Guadalajara, ciudad donde nació[h] el mariachi

En ninguna de ellas hay dificultad en encontrar[i] un buen lugar para quedarse, pues hay hoteles y pensiones para todos los gustos y bolsillos.[j] ■

[a]Además... *In addition to* [b]*flourished* [c]*whose* [d]*lively* [e]*se... have taken refuge* [f]*site* [g]serpenteantes... *winding cobblestone streets* [h]*was born* [i]*finding* [j]*wallets* (fig., lit. *pockets*)

▲ *Guanajuato, México*

MULTIMEDIA: Internet

Encourage students to look for websites where they can listen to samples of *mariachi* music. Have students search the Internet for information on assigned areas or topics related to Mexico (Chiapas, Jalisco, Pacific Coast, Caribbean, or pyramids, pottery, indigenous languages). Have them make oral/visual presentations based on their findings.

Comprensión: Suggestion
Have students write a short statement about which place mentioned in the article they would like to visit and why. Then read the statements without identifying the authors; the class must try to determine who wrote each. See how well the class members know each other!

Suggestion
If you prefer that your students do a journal activity, see *Mi diario* in this chapter of the Workbook.

Comprensión

A. El título. Lea otra vez el título del artículo. ¿Por qué se llama así esta lectura? Es decir, ¿qué significa?

1. México tiene más playas que otros países de Latinoamérica.
2. Cuando se habla de las vacaciones en México, muchas personas piensan solamente en las playas mexicanas.
3. Nadie va a las playas mexicanas para pasar sus vacaciones.

B. Preguntas. Conteste las siguientes preguntas.

1. ¿Qué se puede visitar en la península de Yucatán?
2. ¿Qué ciudades coloniales se mencionan en el artículo?
3. ¿De qué época es la arquitectura colonial de México?
4. ¿Qué festival se celebra en Guanajuato?
5. ¿En qué ciudad nació el mariachi?

C. ¿Adónde les gustaría ir? A base del (*Based on the*) artículo, identifique un lugar de interés para los siguientes turistas.

1. el profesor Underwood, arqueólogo dedicado al estudio de las culturas indígenas
2. Ana Carbón, guitarrista que tiene interés en la música mexicana
3. Pedro Pérez, pintor y escultor

◄ *Acapulco, México*

◄ *Las ruinas mayas de Chichen Itzá, en la península de Yucatán*

ESCRITURA

A. **Nuestras atracciones turísticas.** Escriba un párrafo o un folleto (*pamphlet*) descriptivo que promueve (*promotes*) el turismo en su ciudad, estado o provincia. Incluya información sobre los modos de transporte, las atracciones geográficas y artísticas y la comida.

B. **De vacaciones en México.** Prepare un reportaje sobre una de las ciudades mencionadas en el artículo. Puede ir a la biblioteca para hacer su investigación. Antes de escribir, haga lo siguiente.

Paso 1. Escoja la ciudad que va a ser el enfoque (*focus*) de su investigación.

Paso 2. Piense en el tipo de información que quiere incluir. Haga una lista de por lo menos (*at least*) tres de los temas que va a investigar (como, por ejemplo, festividades regionales, geografía, platos típicos del lugar, etcétera).

Paso 3. Vaya a la biblioteca, use el Internet o consulte libros de referencia o revistas para hacer su reportaje.

Paso 4. Escriba una breve composición sobre ese lugar.

ESCRITURA

B: Variation
Have students research different states in Mexico. There are 31 states and Mexico City, which is a federal district (*el Distrito Federal*, or *el D.F.*). Students should give the name of the capital of the state and the places they would most like to visit and why (*Me gustaría visitar _____ porque _____.*). Encourage them to share their compositions with the rest of the class.

Point out the chapter-opener photo. Have students talk about the holiday represented in the photo. Encourage them to describe the people in the scene. Ask questions.

Have students talk about special holidays their families celebrate. Encourage them to express their ideas about holiday celebrations.

Suggestions

■ Ask students questions about holidays. The words in **boldface** are included in the active vocabulary of this chapter. Have students discuss the words and use context to help them understand the meanings. Place the words they cannot guess in new sentences and contexts.

1. *¿Pasa Ud. **los días festivos** con su familia, con sus amigos o solo/a?*
2. *¿Cuál es su día festivo favorito? ¿Cuál es el día festivo que menos le gusta?*
3. *¿Hace Ud. algo especial el día de su **cumpleaños**? ¿Qué hace?*
4. *¿**Se celebra** en su casa algún día festivo de otro país? ¿Cuál es? ¿Cómo se celebra?*
5. *¿Conoce Ud. algún festival de otra cultura? ¿Qué le gusta de ese día? ¿En qué se parece* (How is it similar) *a los festivales que Ud. celebra?*

■ Give students the names of holidays that they would like to describe or discuss.
■ Ask students: *¿Recuerda en qué año celebró su mejor cumpleaños? ¿y el peor?*

Note

The *Puntos de partida* Online Learning Center includes an interview with a native speaker from Cuba who answers questions similar to those in the preceding *Suggestions*.

◄ Una muchacha cubana reza (*prays*) en una iglesia (*church*) en Santiago, Cuba, durante las Navidades

Resources

For Students

■ Workbook
■ Laboratory Manual and Laboratory Audio Program
■ Quia™ Online Workbook and Online Laboratory Manual
■ Video on CD
■ Interactive CD-ROM
■ *Puntos de partida* Online Learning Center (**www.mhhe.com/puntos7**)

For Instructors

■ *Instructor's Manual and Resource Kit*, "Chapter-by-Chapter" Supplementary Materials
■ Overhead Transparencies 57–62
■ Testing Program
■ Test Generator
■ Video Program
■ Audioscript
■ *Puntos de partida* Online Learning Center (**www.mhhe.com/puntos7**)

Los días festivos°

Suggestion

Have students list their ideas about Cuba, including information on geography, politics, economy, culture, music, and cuisine. When you finish the chapter, return to the lists and ask students what ideas they would change and/or add.

☀ **Heritage Speakers**

Pídales a sus estudiantes hispanohablantes que comenten alguna costumbre típica e hispánica que se asocia con un día festivo. Pregúnteles a los hispanohablantes si su familia celebra días festivos que no celebran los anglosajones. ¿Cuáles son y cómo se difieren de los días festivos que celebran sus amigos anglosajones?

CULTURA

- **Perspectivas culturales**

  Entrevista cultural: Cuba

  Entre amigos: ¡Comemos las uvas de la suerte!

  Conozca... Cuba

- **Nota cultural:** Días festivos de gran importancia

- **En los Estados Unidos y el Canadá:** El día de César Chávez

- **Literatura de Cuba:** José Martí

- **Lectura:** ¡Época de tradiciones!

VOCABULARIO

- La fiesta de Javier
- Emociones y condiciones

GRAMÁTICA

24 Irregular Preterites

25 Preterite of Stem-Changing Verbs

26 Double Object Pronouns

Entrevista cultural

◄ Rocío García
La Habana, Cuba

°**días...** *holidays*

MULTIMEDIA

- The multimedia materials that accompany this chapter are referenced in the Student and Instructor's Editions with icons to help you identify when and where to incorporate them.

- The IM/RK provides suggestions for using the multimedia materials in the classroom.

VOCABULARIO
Preparación

La fiesta de Javier

Note

See the model for vocabulary presentation and other material in the *Capítulo 8 Vocabulario: Preparación* section of "Chapter-by-Chapter Supplementary Materials," in the IM.

Suggestions

- Model vocabulary in short sentences and questions, for example: *Cuando hago una fiesta en mi casa, siempre sirvo entremeses y refrescos. ¿Qué tipo de entremeses le gusta a Ud.? ¿En qué tipo de fiesta se divierte Ud. más?*

- Ask students the following questions about the class.

    De tus amigos, ¿quién... ?

    1. *¿falta a clase con frecuencia?*
    2. *¿nunca falta a clase?*
    3. *¿nunca se divierte?*
    4. *¿siempre lo pasa bien?*

- When introducing *ser + en + place*, review the difference between *ser* (to take place) and *estar* (to be located).

- Bring greeting cards in Spanish to class and have students read the different kinds of expressions used. Students may wish to find examples of Spanish-language virtual greeting cards on the Internet and send them to classmates and friends. Encourage them to design greeting cards of their own and include appropriate sentiments in Spanish.

Bright Idea

Suggestion

Students may be curious about the use of *ser* in *¿Dónde es la fiesta?* In this chapter, students will learn that *ser* is used to tell where an event takes place. For example, *El baile (La boda, el partido) es en el gimnasio.* Have students explain the difference between the following phrases.

¿Dónde es el examen?
¿Dónde está el examen?

**Resources:
Transparency 57**

VOCABULARIO · Preparación

La fiesta de Javier

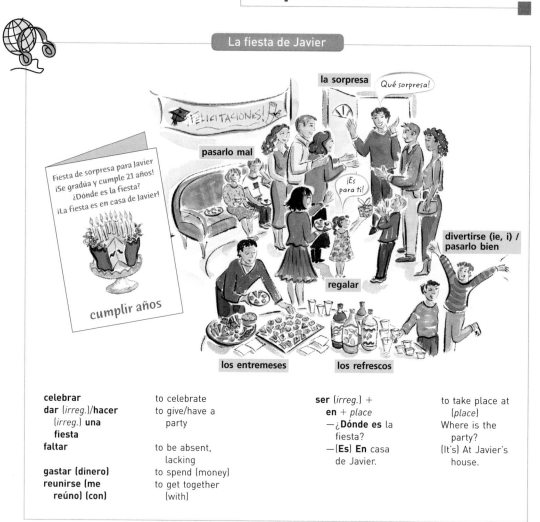

celebrar	to celebrate	**ser** (*irreg.*) +	to take place at
dar (*irreg.*)/**hacer** (*irreg.*) **una fiesta**	to give/have a party	**en** + *place*	(*place*)
		—¿**Dónde es** la fiesta?	Where is the party?
faltar	to be absent, lacking	—(**Es**) **En** casa de Javier.	(It's) At Javier's house.
gastar (**dinero**)	to spend (money)		
reunirse (**me reúno**) (**con**)	to get together (with)		

MULTIMEDIA: Audio

Students can listen to and practice this chapter's vocabulary on the Online Learning Center (**www.mhhe.com/puntos7**), as well as on the Textbook Audio CD, part of the Laboratory Audio Program.

CULTURE

Holidays vary widely from one country to another in the Hispanic world, sometimes even from region to region. The following popular Hispanic holidays are not generally celebrated among non-Hispanic groups in the U.S. or Canada.

- ***Las Misas de Aguinaldo*** (Christmas gift) is celebrated in Mexico, San Salvador, and in some states in the U.S. with a high percentage of Mexicans. This holiday is celebrated during the *novena* (nine days before Christmas Eve).

Vocabulario útil*		
el Día de Año Nuevo	New Year's Day	
el Día de los Reyes Magos	Day of the Magi (Three Kings)	
el Día de San Patricio	Saint Patrick's Day	
la Pascua (judía)	Passover	
la Pascua (Florida)	Easter	
las vacaciones de primavera	spring break	
el Cinco de Mayo	Cinco de Mayo (*Mexican awareness celebration in some parts of the U.S.*)	
el Día del Canadá	Canada Day (July 1)	
el Cuatro de Julio (el Día de la Independencia [estadounidense])	Fourth of July (Independence Day [U.S.])	
el Día de la Raza	Columbus Day (*Hispanic awareness day in some parts of the U.S.*)	
el Día de todos los Santos	All Saints' Day (November 1)	
el Día de los Muertos	Day of the Dead (November 2)	
el Día de Acción de Gracias	Thanksgiving	
la Nochebuena	Christmas Eve	
la Noche Vieja	New Year's Eve	
el cumpleaños	birthday	
el día del santo	saint's day (*the saint for whom one is named*)	
la quinceañera	young woman's fifteenth birthday party	

la Navidad

el Día de San Valentín
(de los Enamorados)

la Fiesta de las Luces

■■■ Conversación

A. Definiciones. ¿Qué palabra o frase corresponde a estas definiciones?

1. el día en que se celebra el nacimiento (*birth*) de Jesús
2. algo que alguien no sabe o no espera
3. algo de comer y algo de beber que se sirve en las fiestas (dos respuestas)
4. el día en que algunos hispanos visitan el cementerio para honrar la memoria de los difuntos (*deceased*)
5. la fiesta en que se celebra el hecho (*fact*) de que una muchacha cumple quince años
6. el día en que todo el mundo (*everybody*) debe llevar ropa verde
7. la noche en que se celebra el final del año
8. palabra que se dice para mostrar una reacción muy favorable, por ejemplo, cuando un amigo cumple años
9. una fiesta de ocho días, muy importante para los judíos (*Jewish people*)

*All of the items on this list are not considered active vocabulary for this chapter. Just learn the holidays and celebrations that are relevant to you.

Vocabulario: Preparación   Doscientos cincuenta y nueve ■ **259**

CULTURE (*continued*)

■ *La Gritería* is a celebration that occurs in Nicaragua and Colombia on December 7th, the day the Roman Catholic Church recognizes as the eve of the Immaculate Conception. *Gritería* refers to the shouting from door to door of *¿Qué causa tanta alegría? ¡La Concepción de María!*

■ *El Velorio* (Gathering) *de Reyes* is a solemn tradition among rural people of the west coast of Puerto Rico.

It is usually sponsored by a family that has made a *promesa* to the Magi and wishes to thank them for a special blessing they have received. To celebrate, an altar is set up in the home on the night of the 5th of January and decorated with flowers and three boughs. Neighbors visit and a trained singer makes up impromptu *décimas*, very formal poems on topical and religious themes.

Suggestions

■ Use a calendar and present the holidays month-by-month. Emphasize and explain holidays of importance to Hispanics: *el Cinco de Mayo, el Día de los Reyes Magos.* If you know when your saint's day is, point it out and explain its relevance. At the end, review by asking questions such as *¿Qué día festivo se celebra en febrero? ¿en octubre? ¿en marzo?*, and so on.

■ Present vocabulary or draw symbols for particular holidays on the board.

> *El corazón es un símbolo que todos asociamos con el Día de San Valentín.*
> *¿Qué más asocian Uds. con ese día? ¿el amor? ¿el color rojo? ¿las tarjetas? ¿las flores? ¿Cupido?*, and so on.

Have students tell what holidays they associate with the following:

los irlandeses	*el champán*
los regalos	*las flores*
los bombones	

■ Have students respond to the following statements with *cierto* or *falso.*

1. *Hoy es el cumpleaños de _____; vamos a darle una fiesta.*
2. *La Noche Vieja se celebra en octubre.*
3. *La Nochebuena viene después de la Navidad.*

■ Point out that there are variations of names for some holidays. Although *Navidad* is the word for *Christmas*, you can express *Merry Christmas* as *¡Felices Pascuas!* or *¡Feliz Navidad!* *Pascua* is used in the singular and plural, and the expression *Felices Pascuas* can express *Happy Holidays* in a sense that includes other religious holidays. Point out the difference between the U.S. secular holiday Halloween and the religious holiday *el Día de los Muertos* (November 2).

Con. A: Suggestion

Have students give a definition of a holiday that is not already defined in the list.

NOTA CULTURAL

Suggestions

- Not all Hispanics are Catholic or even Christian, and not all countries celebrate the same things in the same way. Moreover, Hispanics in this country may have lost or adapted some of their traditions as part of their acclimation to their new country.
- Not all Hispanic countries celebrate the *quinceañera* in the same manner. In Puerto Rico, for example, the elaborate celebration of the fifteenth birthday is often a matter of social or economic standing. Called a *debut*, the celebration for a middle- or upper-class teenager is held in a hotel or hall and as many as several hundred friends and relatives may attend.
- Ask the following questions to check comprehension.

  1. *¿Cuáles son las fiestas religiosas mencionadas?*
  2. *En España, ¿de quién(es) reciben regalos de Navidad los niños?*
  3. *¿Qué fiesta marca una transición en la vida de las muchachas?*

Con. B: Follow-Up

Have students describe the holidays in brief paragraphs. Then have them read their paragraphs to the class without identifying the holiday.

Emociones y condiciones

Suggestions

- Offer the following optional vocabulary.

enojado/a	enojarse
llegar a ser	hacerse
acordarse de	

- Point out that the following adjectives are frequently used with *ponerse* (to become).

alegre	triste
rojo	contento

  To become can also be expressed with reflexive forms.

enojarse	alegrarse
enrojecerse	entristecerse

  and so on.

  Contrast the following words.

  olvidar   olvidarse de   recordar

NOTA CULTURAL

Días festivos de gran importancia

Aunque la mayoría de **los días festivos** varían de país en país y aun de ciudad en ciudad, algunas fiestas **se celebran** en casi todos los países hispanos.

▲ *Una quinceañera mexicana*

La Nochebuena   En esta fiesta los hispanos cristianos siguen principalmente sus **tradiciones** católicas. Celebran la víspera[a] de la Navidad con una gran cena. Esta **celebración familiar** puede incluir también a amigos y vecinos[b]. Muchas familias van a la Misa del Gallo,[c] un **servicio religioso** que se celebra a medianoche. Es posible que la fiesta de Nochebuena termine muy tarde con música y baile. A veces, los niños reciben la visita de Papá Noel, otro nombre para Santa Claus, quien les deja **regalos.**

La Noche Vieja   Como en este país, la Noche Vieja es una ocasión para grandes celebraciones, tanto entre familia como en lugares públicos. En España y otros países algunos practican la tradición de comer una uva[d] por cada una de las doce campanadas[e] de medianoche.

El Día de los Reyes Magos   Muchos hispanos, especialmente los católicos, celebran (en lugar de Santa Claus) el 6 de enero, el día de los Reyes Magos, también conocida como **la Epifanía.** Los tres Reyes son los encargados[f] de traer regalos. Muchos niños ponen sus zapatos en la ventana o balcón antes de acostarse la noche del 5 de enero. Los Reyes llegan en camellos durante la noche y llenan los zapatos con regalos y **dulces.**

El Día de la Independencia   Todos los países latinoamericanos celebran el día de la declaración de su independencia de España. Por ejemplo, México celebra su independencia el 16 de septiembre, Bolivia el 6 de agosto, el Paraguay el 15 de mayo y El Salvador el 15 de septiembre.

La quinceañera   Las muchachas que cumplen quince años celebran ese día especial de llegar a ser mujer con una gran fiesta de familia y amigos. La muchacha se viste de largo[g] y, con sus invitados, asiste a una misa especial para ella. Luego hay una cena y una fiesta con música para bailar.

[a]*eve*   [b]*neighbors*   [c]*Misa... Midnight Mass*   [d]*grape*   [e]*strokes*   [f]*los... in charge*   [g]*se... dresses up (in a gown)*

B. Hablando de fiestas

Paso 1.   ¿Cuáles de estas fiestas le gustan a Ud.? ¿Cuáles le gustan mucho? ¿Cuáles no le gustan? Explique por qué. Compare sus respuestas con las (*those*) de sus compañeros de clase. ¿Coinciden todos en su opinión de algunas fiestas?

> MODELO: el Cuatro de Julio → Me gusta mucho el Cuatro de Julio porque vemos fuegos artificiales en el parque y…

1. el Cuatro de Julio
2. el Día de Acción de Gracias
3. el Día de San Patricio
4. la Noche Vieja
5. el Día de la Raza
6. el Día de los Enamorados

Paso 2.   Ahora piense en su fiesta favorita. Puede ser una de la lista del Paso 1 o una del **Vocabulario útil** de la página 259. Piense en cómo celebra Ud. esa fiesta, para explicárselo (*explain it*) luego a un compañero / una compañera de clase. Debe pensar en lo siguiente.

- los preparativos que Ud. hace de antemano (*beforehand*)
- la ropa especial que lleva
- las comidas o bebidas especiales que compra o prepara
- el lugar donde se celebra
- los adornos especiales que hay

Vocabulario útil	
el árbol	tree
el corazón	heart
la corona	wreath
el desfile	parade
la fiesta del barrio	neighborhood (block) party
los fuegos artificiales	fireworks
el globo	balloon

CULTURE

In more traditional Mexican families, the girl celebrating her *quinceañera* is serenaded by a *mariachi* band in front of her house the night before her 15th birthday. The next day, the girl has a party at her house. The men and boys take turns dancing with the girl. The first dance is traditionally a waltz that she dances with her father.

National Standards: Comparisons

- *La quinceañera* is not celebrated in Spain.
- Have students compare the *quinceañera* celebration with the concept of the "sweet sixteen" birthday.

Emociones y condiciones

reír(se) de
Gabriela
Alfredo
discutir con/sobre
Rico
enojarse con
portarse bien
Luz
Iván
enfermarse
Raúl
Oscar
Celia
portarse mal
llorar

olvidar(se) (de)	to forget about
ponerse (irreg.) + adj.	to become, get + adjective
quejarse (de)	to complain (about)
recordar (ue)	to remember
sentir(se) (ie, i)	to feel (an emotion)
sonreír(se)	to smile

NOTA COMUNICATIVA

Being Emphatic

To emphasize the quality described by an adjective or an adverb, speakers of Spanish often add **-ísimo/a/os/as** to it. This change adds the idea *extremely* (*exceptionally; very, very; super*) to the quality expressed by the adjective. You have already used one emphatic form of this type: **Me gusta muchísimo.**

Estos entremeses son **dificilísimos** de preparar.

Durante la época navideña, los niños son **buenísimos.**

These hors d'œuvres are very, very hard to prepare.

At Christmastime, the kids are extremely good.

- If the adjective ends in a consonant, **-ísimo** is added to the singular form: **difícil → dificilísimo** (and any accents on the word stem are dropped).
- If the adjective ends in a vowel, the final vowel is dropped before adding **-ísimo: bueno → buenísimo** (and any accents on the word stem are dropped).
- Spelling changes occur when the final consonant of an adjective is **c, g,** or **z: riquí-simo, lar*gu*ísimo, felicísimo.**

Vocabulario: Preparación

 Heritage Speakers

Pídales a los hispanohablantes que describan la manera en que su familia celebra las fiestas nacionales de su país de origen. Pregúnteles, por ejemplo, cómo celebran la Nochebuena, qué caracteriza el Día de los Reyes Magos, adónde van sus parientes el Día de los Muertos. Si la fiesta se suele celebrar de un modo parecido al de los Estados Unidos o el Canadá (como, por ejemplo, la Navidad), pregúnteles qué opinan con respecto a las diferencias entre cómo se celebra el día

en las dos culturas. Pregúnteles, por ejemplo: *¿Opinan Uds. que la celebración de la Navidad es más religiosa entre los hispanos? ¿En cuál de las celebraciones tiene más influencia el comercio? ¿Qué hacen los latinoamericanos el día de las Pascuas? ¿Se celebra la Fiesta de las Luces de la misma manera en su país?*

Resources: Transparency 58

Suggestions

- Ask students the following questions.

1. *¿Se ríe Ud. con frecuencia? ¿fácilmente? ¿Sonríe fácilmente? Dé un ejemplo de una situación en que Ud. sonríe. ¿Sonríe cuando está nervioso/a? ¿Cuándo no se debe sonreír? ¿Cuándo es necesario sonreír?*

2. *¿Cuándo fue la última vez que Ud. se sintió muy feliz? ¿Qué pasó ese día?*

3. *¿Llora Ud. mucho? ¿Quiénes lloran más, los niños o los adultos? ¿las mujeres o los hombres? ¿En qué situaciones es común que lloren las personas? ¿Es bueno que los hombres no lloren con frecuencia? Cuando alguien llora, ¿qué indica?*

4. *¿Se enoja Ud. fácilmente? ¿Discute con frecuencia con alguien? ¿Se pone contento/a fácilmente? ¿nervioso/a? ¿Cuándo se pone Ud. nervioso/a? ¿durante un examen? ¿cuando habla español? ¿durante una entrevista?*

5. *¿Tiene Ud. hoy todas las cosas necesarias para la clase? ¿Se olvidó de traer algo? ¿Se olvidó alguna vez de un examen?*

6. *¿Recuerda Ud. fácilmente los nombres? ¿los números? ¿los números de teléfono? ¿el vocabulario nuevo? ¿Qué números es muy necesario recordar?*

NOTA COMUNICATIVA

Suggestions

- Emphasize the change in stress and written accent in *fácil → facilísimo* and *difícil → dificilísimo.* Remind students to drop the final vowel of adjectives that end in a vowel: *triste → tristísimo.*
- Emphasize and model the spelling changes: *c → qu, g → gu, z → c.* Ask students where they have seen these changes before (the preterite and the subjunctive).
- Some Spanish speakers also use *re-, requete-,* and *super-* to add the idea of extremely (very, exceptionally) to the quality, for example, *rebueno, requetebueno, superbueno.*
- Ask students questions.

1. *¿Es Ud. perezosísimo/a?*
2. *¿Hay una persona rica en su familia? ¿Quién es? ¿Hay una persona riquísima? ¿alta? ¿altísima? ¿interesante? ¿interesantísima? ¿simpática? ¿simpatiquísima?*

Bright Idea

Suggestion

Give students sentences with *muy, muy* and have them reword the sentences using *-ísimo* endings.

MODELO: *Lupe está muy, muy contenta porque va a una fiesta de Noche Vieja.* → *Lupe está contentísima porque va a una fiesta de Noche Vieja.*

Con. A: Suggestions

- Do this activity as listening comprehension only.
- Offer the following optional vocabulary.

de buen/mal humor   impaciente

Con. A: Extension

7. *Llueve todo el día.*

8. *Ud. no sabe la respuesta, pero el profesor le pide que hable.*

9. *Ud. sabe la respuesta y levanta la mano, pero el profesor no le presta atención.*

10. *Ud. quiere bañarse y no hay agua caliente.*

11. *Ud. está solo/a en casa y oye un ruido.*

12. *Ud. le pide a alguien que no fume, pero la persona sigue fumando.*

Con. B: Suggestion

Have students write down a description of a negative aspect of a holiday, for them in particular or for people in general, for example:

La Navidad es una fiesta demasiado comercializada. No me gusta el Día de Acción de Gracias… ¡porque no me gusta comer pavo ni calabaza!

The descriptions should be anonymous. Have students hand in their ideas. Redistribute the descriptions to other students, and have them write responses to the negative aspect of the holiday in the form of advice or recommendations for having a better time or improving the situation. Return the complaint and the advice to the original author of the negative description. Alternatively, read the negative descriptions to the class, and have students give advice orally.

■ ■ ■ Conversación

A. Reacciones. ¿Cómo reacciona o cómo se pone Ud. en estas situaciones? Use estos adjetivos o cualquier otro, y también los verbos que describen las reacciones emocionales. No se olvide de usar las formas enfáticas cuando sea (*whenever it is*) apropiado.

avergonzado/a (*embarrassed*)
contento/a
feliz/triste
furioso/a
nervioso/a
serio/a

1. Es Navidad y alguien le hace a Ud. un regalo carísimo.
2. Es su cumpleaños y sus padres/hijos no le regalaron nada.
3. Ud. da una fiesta en su casa pero los invitados no se divierten. Nadie ríe ni sonríe.
4. Hay un examen importante hoy, pero Ud. no estudió anoche.
5. Ud. acaba de terminar un examen difícil/fácil y cree que lo hizo bien/mal.
6. En un examen de química, Ud. no puede recordar una fórmula muy importante.
7. Ud. cuenta un chiste (*a joke*) pero nadie se ríe.
8. Un amigo tiene un problema grave (*serious*) y necesita su ayuda.

B. ¿Son buenos todos los días festivos? Los días festivos pueden ser difíciles para muchas personas. Para Ud., ¿son ciertas o falsas las siguientes oraciones? Cambie las oraciones falsas para que sean (*so that they are*) ciertas. Luego compare sus respuestas con las de sus compañeros de clase.

EN LAS FIESTAS DE FAMILIA

1. Toda o casi toda mi familia, incluyendo a mis tíos, primos, abuelos, etcétera, se reúne por lo menos (*at least*) una vez al año.
2. Las fiestas de familia me gustan muchísimo.
3. Hay un pariente que siempre se queja de algo.
4. Uno de mis parientes siempre me hace preguntas indiscretas.
5. Alguien siempre bebe/come demasiado (*too much*) y luego se enferma.
6. A todos les gustan los regalos que reciben.
7. Todos lo pasan bien en las fiestas de familia.

LOS DÍAS FESTIVOS EN GENERAL

8. La Navidad/La Fiesta de las Luces es esencialmente una excusa para gastar dinero.
9. La época de fiestas en noviembre y diciembre es triste y deprimente (*depressing*) para mí.
10. Sólo las personas que practican una religión deben tener vacaciones en los días de fiestas religiosas.
11. Las vacaciones de primavera son para divertirse muchísimo. De hecho (*In fact*), son las mejores vacaciones del año.
12. Debería haber (*There should be*) más días festivos… por lo menos uno al mes.

Need more practice?

- Workbook and Laboratory Manual
- Interactive CD-ROM
- Online Learning Center (www.mhhe.com/puntos7)

National Standards: Comparisons

Some important Hispanic holidays are not generally celebrated in the U.S. or Canada, for example, *el Día de los Reyes Magos* (6 *de enero*). Other important holidays are historical dates or local fairs celebrated by a specific country, area, or town. For example, Mexicans celebrate *el 5 de mayo,* and in Pamplona,

Spain, *San Fermín* is celebrated in July. These holidays are well-known in the U.S. and Canada. Some holidays that are celebrated in the U.S. and Canada are also celebrated in the Spanish-speaking world but on different dates, for example, *el Día del Padre* and *el Día de la Madre.*

GRAMÁTICA

24 Talking About the Past (2) • Irregular Preterites

La fiesta de la Noche Vieja

Conteste las siguientes preguntas sobre esta fiesta.

1. ¿Quién *estuvo* hablando por teléfono?
2. ¿Quién *dio* la fiesta?
3. ¿Quién no *pudo* ir a la fiesta?
4. ¿Quién *puso* su copa de champán en el televisor?
5. ¿Quién *hizo* mucho ruido?
6. ¿Quiénes no *quisieron* beber más?
7. ¿Quiénes *vinieron* con sus niñas?
8. ¿Quiénes le *trajeron* un regalo al anfitrión (*host*)?

Y Ud., ¿*estuvo* alguna vez en una fiesta como esta? ¿*Tuvo* que salir temprano o se quedó hasta después de la medianoche (*midnight*)? ¿Le *trajo* algo al anfitrión / a la anfitriona?

PAST	Present	Future
preterite	present	
	present progressive	
	formal commands	

- You have already learned the irregular preterite forms of **dar, hacer, ir,** and **ser.** The following verbs are also irregular in the preterite. Note that the first and third person singular endings, which are the only irregular ones, are unstressed, in contrast to the stressed endings of regular preterite forms.

estar	
estuve	estuvimos
estuviste	estuvisteis
estuvo	estuvieron

estar:	estuv-	-e
poder:	pud-	-iste
poner:	pus-	-o
querer:	quis-	-imos
saber:	sup-	-isteis
tener:	tuv-	-ieron
venir:	vin-	

☀ Heritage Speakers

Algunos hispanohablantes dicen *dijieron* y *trajieron* para la tercera persona gramatical plural (*Uds., ellos, ellas*) en vez de *dijeron* y *trajeron*. Otros verbos parecidos incluyen: *atraer, bendecir, contraer, distraer, introducir, producir, reducir, traducir*. Sin embargo, las formas aceptadas en el uso formal terminan en *-eron* en vez de *-ieron*.

Resources: Transparency 59

Variation
To follow up the questions and art, have students think of the last party they or their family hosted and answer the questions.

Suggestions

- Point out that the first and third person singular of irregular forms have no accent on the *-e* or *-o*. Students should not confuse these with the present indicative *él/ella/Ud.* or *yo* forms, respectively.
- Emphasize and model verbs that change meaning in the preterite.

Bright Idea

Suggestion

Have students brainstorm ways to organize the verbs or offer the following groups.

-u-	tener	poner
	estar	saber
	poder	
-i-	hacer	venir
	querer	
-j-	decir	*-ucir* verbs
	traer	

Preliminary Exercises

- Have students give the infinitive for the following forms.

  ¿*Cuál es el infinitivo de... ?*
  ¿quise? ¿estuve? ¿vine?
  ¿tuve? ¿puse? ¿pude?
  ¿supe? ¿dije? ¿traje?

- Have students give the subject (*yo, tú, Ud.*) of the following forms.

  ¿*Cuál es el sujeto de... ?*
  ¿vino? ¿tuviste? ¿tuvo?
  ¿pudo? ¿supo? ¿estuvo?
  ¿trajiste? ¿dijo? ¿puse?
  ¿dije? ¿supiste? ¿puso?
  ¿quise? ¿vino? ¿estuviste?

- Write the following sentences on the board and have students complete each sentence with the *yo* form of the most appropriate verb.

  1. _____ un examen ayer. (*Tuve*)
  2. _____ enfermo/a la semana pasada. (*Estuve*)
  3. _____ a clase todos los días el semestre/trimestre pasado. (*Vine*)
  4. _____ hacer todo el trabajo. (*No pude*)
  5. Les _____ varios chistes a mis amigos. (*Dije*)
  6. _____ la radio. (*Puse*)
  7. _____ un viaje. (*Hice*)
  8. _____ razón. (*Tuve*)
  9. _____ los libros a clase. (*Traje*)

<table>
<tr><td colspan="2">

■ When the preterite verb stem ends in **-j-**, the **-i-** of the third person plural ending is omitted: **dijeron, trajeron.**

</td><td>

decir: **dij-**
traer: **traj-** } -e, -iste, -o, -imos, -isteis, **-eron**

</td></tr>
<tr><td colspan="2">

■ The preterite of **hay (haber)** is **hubo** (*there was/were*).

</td><td>

Hubo un accidente ayer en el centro.
There was an accident yesterday downtown.

</td></tr>
</table>

Changes in Meaning

Several of the following Spanish verbs have an English equivalent in the preterite tense that is different from that of the infinitive.

	Infinitive Meaning	Preterite Meaning
saber	to know (*facts, information*)	to find out
	Ya lo sé. *I already know it.*	Lo **supe** ayer. *I found it out (learned it) yesterday.*
conocer	to know, be familiar with (*people, places*)	to meet (*for the first time*)
	Ya la conozco. *I already know her.*	La **conocí** ayer. *I met her yesterday.*
querer	to want	to try
	Quiero hacerlo hoy. *I want to do it today.*	**Quise** hacerlo ayer. *I tried to do it yesterday.*
no querer	not to want	to refuse
	No quiero hacerlo hoy. *I don't want to do it today.*	**No quise** hacerlo anteayer. *I refused to do it the day before yesterday.*
poder	to be able to (*do something*)	to succeed (*in doing something*)
	Puedo leerlo. *I can (am able to) read it.*	**Pude** leerlo ayer. *I could (and did) read it yesterday.*
no poder	not to be able, capable (*of doing something*)	to fail (*in doing something*)
	No puedo leerlo. *I can't (am not able to) read it.*	**No pude** leerlo anteayer. *I couldn't (did not) read it the day before yesterday.*

AUTOPRUEBA

Give the correct irregular preterite forms.

1. (yo) saber
2. (ellos) tener
3. (tú) venir
4. (él) poner
5. (nosotros) querer
6. (Ud.) poder

Answers: 1. supe 2. tuvieron 3. viniste 4. puso 5. quisimos 6. pudo

■ Have students give the preterite of the following verbs.

yo: estar, poder, poner
tú: querer, saber, tener
Ud.: decir, traer, estar
nosotros: poder, poner, saber
Uds.: tener, decir, traer.

■ Use the following chain drill to practice the preterite forms.

¿Qué pasó en la fiesta del Día del Año Nuevo?

1. *Todos estuvieron unas horas en casa de Mario.* (yo, Raúl, Uds., tú, nosotros, vosotras)
2. *Muchos trajeron comida y bebidas.* (Ud., nosotros, tú, Rosalba, Uds., vosotros)
3. *Todos dijeron que la fiesta estuvo estupenda.* (tú, Anita, Uds., yo, ellas, vosotros)

■ Have students tell if the following forms are present indicative or preterite.

dice	dije	decimos
está	estamos	estuvimos
puede	podemos	pudimos
puse	ponemos	pusimos
tuve	tenemos	traigo
trajo	traemos	trajimos
vinimos	venimos	vinieron

Prác. A: Preliminary Exercise

Ask students the following questions:

1. *¿Tuvo Ud. una entrevista ayer? ¿un examen? ¿una cita con el dentista?*
2. *¿Estuvo Ud. en España el verano pasado? ¿en México? ¿en la Florida?*
3. *¿Ud. se puso rojo/a ayer? ¿Por qué razón?*
4. *¿Quién no pudo dormir bien anoche? ¿Le ocurre esto con frecuencia?*
5. *¿Quién dijo una mentira ayer? ¿A quién?*
6. *¿Quién vino temprano hoy a clase? ¿Quién no vino a clase ayer?*

Prác. A: Follow-Up

Have students add one action that they did and one that they didn't do.

Refrán

«Quien quiso, hizo.»

Give students this *refrán* and have them try to think of sayings in English that have similar connotations. (*Where there's a will, there's a way.*)

264 ■ Doscientos sesenta y cuatro

Capítulo 8: Los días festivos

264 ■ Capítulo 8: Los días festivos

■■■ Práctica

A. ¡Anticipemos! La última Noche Vieja. Piense en lo que Ud. hizo la Noche Vieja del año pasado e indique si las siguientes oraciones son ciertas o falsas para Ud.

1. Fui a una fiesta en casa de un amigo / una amiga.
2. Di una fiesta en mi casa.
3. No estuve con mis amigos, sino (*but rather*) con la familia.
4. Quise ir a una fiesta, pero no pude.
5. Les dije «¡Feliz Año Nuevo!» a muchas personas.
6. Conocí a algunas personas.
7. Tuve que preparar la comida de esa noche.
8. Me puse ropa elegante esa noche.
9. Pude quedarme despierto/a (*awake*) hasta la medianoche.
10. No quise bailar. Me sentía (*I felt*) mal.

B. Una Nochebuena en casa de los Ramírez

Paso 1. Describa lo que pasó en casa de los Ramírez, haciendo el papel (*playing the role*) de uno de los hijos. Haga oraciones en el pretérito según las indicaciones, usando el sujeto pronominal cuando sea necesario.

1. todos / estar / en casa / abuelos / antes de / nueve
2. (nosotros) poner / mucho / regalos / debajo / árbol
3. tíos y primos / venir / con / comida y bebidas
4. yo / tener / que / ayudar / a / preparar / comida
5. haber / cena / especial / para / todos
6. más tarde / alguno / amigos / venir / a / cantar / villancicos (*carols*)
7. niños / ir / a / alcoba / a / diez y / acostarse
8. niños / querer / dormir / pero / no / poder
9. a / medianoche / todos / decir / «¡Feliz Navidad!»
10. al día siguiente / todos / decir / que / fiesta / estar / estupendo

Paso 2. ¿Cierto, falso o no se sabe? Corrija las oraciones falsas.

1. Hubo muy poca gente (*people*) en la fiesta.
2. Sólo vinieron miembros de la familia.
3. Todos comieron bien… ¡y mucho!
4. Los niños abrieron sus regalos antes de las doce.

C. Hechos históricos. Describa Ud. algunos hechos históricos, usando una palabra o frase de cada grupo. Use el pretérito de los verbos. Su profesor(a) lo/la puede ayudar con información para las asociaciones que Ud. no sabe.

MODELO: En 1957 los rusos pusieron un satélite en el espacio por primera vez.

en 1957 los rusos		en Valley Forge con sus soldados
en 1969 los estadounidenses	traer	un hombre en la luna
Adán y Eva	saber	un satélite en el espacio por primera vez
George Washington	**+** conocer **+**	el significado (*meaning*) de un árbol especial
los europeos	estar	a Livingston en África
los aztecas	poner	el caballo (*horse*) al Nuevo Mundo
Stanley		a Hernán Cortés en Tenochtitlán

Gramática   Doscientos sesenta y cinco ■ **265**

CULTURE

- **Hernán Cortés** (1485–1547): Spanish explorer and conqueror of the Aztec Empire of Mexico, Cortés was born in Medellín, Extremadura. He studied law at the University of Salamanca but cut short his university career in 1501 and decided to try his fortune in the Americas. Head of the Spanish forces, he entered the Aztec capital in 1519.
- **The Aztecs and Tenochtitlán:** The Aztecs built a great empire and developed a complex social, political, and religious structure. Their capital, Tenochtitlán, in central Mexico, was possibly the largest city in the world at the time of the Spanish conquest.
- **Dr. David Livingston** (1813–1873): This Scottish explorer and medical missionary in today's Botswana, Africa, discovered Victoria Falls. While searching for the source of the Nile River, he disappeared.
- **Sir Henry Morton Stanley** (1841–1904): A British journalist and explorer, Stanley was sent to Africa in 1871 by the New York *Herald* to find David Livingston. He succeeded.

Bright idea

Prác. A: Suggestion

Point out that *sino* is used after a negative clause. For example, *No tengo un lápiz sino un bolígrafo.*

Prác. B: Extension

Have students tell what happened on Christmas Day at the Ramírez house, inventing more details.

Prác. B: Variations

- Have students use the activity items as a guide for describing their own Christmas (or other holiday) celebrations.
- Dictate the following sentences but have students transform the verbs to the preterite as they take the dictation.

1. *El nieto de Ana viene a visitarnos. El niño se porta muy bien. Está en casa una hora; luego dice adiós y se va.*
2. *Los Sres. Torres hacen la cena y ponen la mesa a las seis. Luego tienen que lavar los platos (pantomime the action). No pueden ir al cine hasta muy tarde.*
3. *Quiero estudiar pero no puedo porque mi amigo Octavio viene a casa con un amigo ecuatoriano. Tengo que ver las fotos que trae.*

Prác. C: Suggestion

Before forming sentences, have students match the information. Help them with information they do not know. The correct information follows, with additional information in the *Cultura* annotation below.

- *En 1969 los estadounidenses pusieron a un hombre en la luna.*
- *Adán y Eva supieron el significado de un árbol especial.*
- *George Washington estuvo en Valley Forge con sus soldados.*
- *Los europeos trajeron el caballo al Nuevo Mundo.*
- *Los aztecas conocieron a Hernán Cortés en Tenochtitlán.*
- *Stanley conoció a Livingston en África.*

Prác. C: Follow-Up

Talk about recent current events and/or people in the news.

Gramática ■ **265**

Con. A: Suggestion

Paso 2. Have the other students ask the narrator questions to get as much additional information as they can.

Con. B: Follow-Up

- Ask students the following question after completing item *1*.

  Ahora que Ud. conoce bien al profesor / a la profesora, ¿cree que ese día presentó una clase típica?

- Follow-up item *3* with the following questions.

  ¿Le hizo Ud. una fiesta de cumpleaños a algún amigo o pariente? (Encourage the use of object pronouns.)

  ¿Quién preparó la comida?

  ¿Dio la fiesta en su casa o en casa de otra persona?

  ¿Puso Ud. adornos (decorations)*?*

  ¿Invitó a sus amigos?

  ¿Preparó una sangría?

  ¿Bebieron Coca-Cola sus invitados?

  ¿Lo pasaron bien todos?

♻ Con B: Reciclado

Remind students of emphatic forms using *-ísimo* that they can use for this activity.

■ ■ ■ Conversación

A. **¡Un viaje de sueños** (*dream*)**!**

Paso 1. Conteste las siguientes preguntas sobre un viaje de sueños. Debe inventar una historia muy extraordinaria o fantástica. Puede ser de un viaje que a Ud. le gustaría hacer, de un viaje hecho (*taken*) por un amigo o de un viaje totalmente imaginario. ¡Sea creativo/a!

1. ¿Adónde fue de viaje? ¿Con quién(es) fue?
2. ¿Cuánto tiempo estuvo allí? ¿Dónde se alojó (*did you stay*)?
3. ¿A qué persona famosa o interesante conoció allí? ¿Qué le dijo a esa persona cuando la conoció? ¿Supo algo interesante de esa persona?
4. ¿Qué cosa divertida (*enjoyable*) hizo durante el viaje? ¿Qué no pudo hacer?
5. ¿Qué recuerdos (*souvenirs*) trajo a casa?

Paso 2. Ahora cuénteles su historia a sus compañeros de clase. ¿Quién inventó la mejor historia?

Need more practice?

- Workbook and Laboratory Manual
- Interactive CD-ROM
- Online Learning Center (www.mhhe.com/ puntos7)

NOTA COMUNICATIVA

Thanking Someone

You can use the preposition **por** to thank someone for something.

gracias por + *noun*
   Gracias por el regalo.
   Gracias por la invitación.

gracias por + *infinitive*
   Gracias por llamarme.
   Gracias por invitarnos.

B. **Entrevista**

1. ¿En qué mes conociste al profesor / a la profesora de español? ¿A quién(es) más conociste ese mismo (*same*) día? ¿Tuviste que hablar español el primer día de clase? ¿Qué les dijiste a sus amigos después de esa primera clase? ¿Qué les vas a decir hoy?
2. El año pasado, ¿dónde pasaste la Nochebuena? ¿el Día de Acción de Gracias? ¿Dónde estuviste durante las vacaciones de primavera? ¿Ya hiciste planes para estas ocasiones este año? ¿Dónde piensas estar?
3. ¿Alguien te dio una fiesta de cumpleaños este año? (¿O le diste una fiesta a alguien?) ¿Fue una fiesta de sorpresa? ¿Dónde fue? ¿Qué te trajeron tus amigos? ¿Qué te regalaron tus parientes? ¿Alguien te hizo un pastel? ¿Qué te dijeron todos? ¿Y qué les dijiste tú? ¿Quieres que te den otra fiesta para tu próximo cumpleaños?

El día de César Chávez

Desde el año 2000, el líder sindical[a] mexicoamericano César Chávez (1927–1993) tiene **un día festivo** en su honor en el estado de **California.** El lunes o el viernes alrededor del[b] 31 de marzo, los colegios y otros organismos[c] pueden cerrar para **honrar**[d] a Chávez y el movimiento en defensa de los **trabajadores agrícolas**[e] que él defendió.

El senador Richard Polanco fue el autor de la legislación que estableció **el día de César Chávez.**

▲ *César Chávez*

Polanco es un senador demócrata en el senado de California desde 1994 y representa al distrito de Los Ángeles. Desde 2000, Polanco es el Líder de la Mayoría en el Senado.

«[César Chávez] debe ser **honrado** porque su trabajo formó la América en la que hoy vivimos. Su vida nos dio a todos **el coraje**[f] y **la esperanza**[g] de que podemos hacer una diferencia. En su vida, nos enseñó que es importante **llevar una vida moral y responsable.**»

[a]*union* [b]*alrededor... around the* [c]*institutions* [d]*honor*
[e]*trabajadores... farm workers* [f]*courage* [g]*hope*

Gramática 25

Preterite of Stem-Changing Verbs

Follow-Up

Follow up the sentences about Lupe's *quinceañera* with questions about the party.

   ¿A qué hora llegaron / se fueron los invitados?
   ¿Con quién bailó Lupe?

And so on.

25 Talking About the Past (3) • Preterite of Stem-Changing Verbs

La quinceañera de Lupe Carrasco

Imagine los detalles de la fiesta de Lupe cuando cumplió quince años.

1. Lupe *se vistió* con
   ☐ un vestido blanco muy elegante.
   ☐ una camiseta y unos *jeans*.
   ☐ el vestido de novia[a] de su abuela.

2. Cortando el pastel de cumpleaños, Lupe
   ☐ *empezó* a llorar.
   ☐ *rió* mucho.
   ☐ *sonrió* para una foto.

3. Lupe *pidió* un deseo[b] al cortar el pastel. Ella
   ☐ les dijo a todos su deseo.
   ☐ *prefirió* guardarlo en secreto.

4. En la fiesta *sirvieron*
   ☐ champán y otras bebidas alcohólicas.
   ☐ refrescos.
   ☐ sólo té y café.

5. Todos *se divirtieron* mucho en la fiesta. Los invitados *se despidieron*[c] a la(s) _____.

[a]*vestido... wedding gown* [b]*wish* [c]*se... said good-bye*

Y Ud., ¿recuerda qué hizo cuando cumplió quince años? ¿Pidió muchos regalos? ¿Se divirtió? ¿Cómo se sintió?

PAST	----------------- Present -----------------	Future
preterite	present	
	present progressive	
	formal commands	

Suggestions

■ Point out that César Chávez is profiled in the *Perspectivas culturales* section of *Capítulo 1*. To learn more about the holiday and Chávez, have students look for websites that feature Chávez.

■ Have students find out more about Senator Polanco's agenda, as well as other Hispanic government leaders.

Emphasis A: Suggestions

- Emphasize and model the *-ar* and *-er* verbs that do not have stem changes in the preterite (as they do in the present indicative).
- Have students give the third person singular and plural of the verbs.

  1. *(ue):* contar, recordar, encontrar, jugar, volver, llover (third person singular only)
  2. *(ie):* empezar, recomendar, cerrar, despertarse, nevar (third person singular only)

Emphasis B: Suggestion

Remind students that the second stem change indicated in word lists—(*ie, i*), (*i, i*), (*ue, u*)—occurs in the third person singular and plural of the preterite and in the *-ndo* forms. These changes only occur in *-ir* verbs and appear in the first and second person plural of the subjunctive as well. Model these verbs.

dormir: *durmió, durmieron (durmiendo, durmamos, durmáis)*
preferir: *prefirió, prefirieron (prefiriendo, prefiramos, prefiráis)*
repetir: *repitió, repitieron (repitiendo, repitamos, repitáis)*

Preliminary Exercises

- Have students give the third person singular and plural of the following verbs.

  1. *(ue, u)* dormir, morir, dormirse
  2. *(i, i)* pedir, repetir, despedir
  3. *(ie, i)* preferir, sentir, sentirse, divertirse, sugerir

- Have students do the following chain drill to practice the preterite forms.

  Todos pasaron un día fatal ayer.

  1. *Dormimos muy mal anoche. (yo, todos, Irma, tú, Ud., vosotros)*
  2. *No recordaste traer los ejercicios. (Raúl, nosotros, Ud., ellos, vosotros)*
  3. *Raúl perdió las llaves (keys) del coche. (tú, Horacio y Estela, yo, Ud., vosotras)*
  4. *Pedimos mariscos pero no había (they were out of them). (yo, Jacinto, tú, Uds., vosotros)*
  5. *Todos se rieron mucho de Nati. (nosotros, Esteban, yo, Uds., vosotras)*

Prác. A: Suggestion

Have students add statements about other topics.

¿Pasó algo muy interesante en la clase? ¿y en el país?

A. In **Capítulo 7** you learned that the **-ar** and **-er** stem-changing verbs have no stem change in the preterite (or in the present participle).

recorder (ue)		perder (ie)	
recordé	recordamos	perdí	perdimos
recordaste	recordasteis	perdiste	perdisteis
recordó	recordaron	perdió	perdieron
	recordando		perdiendo

B. The **-ir** stem-changing verbs do have a stem change in the preterite, but only in the third person singular and plural, where the stem vowels **e** and **o** change to **i** and **u**, respectively. This is the same change that occurs in the present participle of **-ir** stem-changing verbs.

pedir (i, i)		dormir (ue, u)	
pedí	pedimos	dormí	dormimos
pediste	pedisteis	dormiste	dormisteis
pidió	pidieron	durmió	durmieron
	pidiendo		durmiendo

C. Here are some **-ir** stem-changing verbs. You already know or have seen many of them. The reflexive meaning, if different from the nonreflexive meaning, is in parentheses.

Note the simplification:
ri-ió → rió; ri-ieron → rieron
son-ri-ió → sonrió;
son-ri-ieron → sonrieron

despedirse (i, i)

conseguir (i, i) (g)	*to get, obtain*	**preferir (ie, i)**	*to prefer*
conseguir + inf.	*to succeed in (doing something)*	**reír(se) (i, i)**	*to laugh*
divertir(se) (ie, i)	*to entertain (to have a good time)*	**sentir(se) (ie, i)**	*to feel (an emotion)*
dormir(se) (ue, u)	*to sleep (to fall asleep)*	**servir (i, i)**	*to serve*
morirse (ue, u)	*to die*	**sonreír(se) (i, i)**	*to smile*
pedir (i, i)	*to ask for; to order*	**sugerir (ie, i)**	*to suggest*
		vestir(se) (i, i)	*to dress (to get dressed)*

AUTOPRUEBA

Complete the verbs with preterite stems.

1. nos div___rtimos
2. se d___rmieron
3. tú s___rviste
4. se v___stió
5. yo sug___rí
6. Uds. p___dieron

Answers: 1. divertimos 2. durmieron 3. serviste 4. vistió 5. sugerí 6. pidieron

---

☀ Heritage Speakers

Anime a los estudiantes hispanohablantes a describir una quinceañera a la que han asistido. ¿De quién fue la quinceañera? ¿Cuántas personas asistieron? ¿Qué comieron? ¿Qué hicieron? ¿Fue divertidísima?

Resources: Transparency 60

You may wish to use this transparency for additional grammar practice.

■ ■ ■ **Práctica**

A. **¡Anticipemos! ¿Quién lo hizo?** ¿Ocurrieron algunas de estas cosas en clase la semana pasada? Conteste con el nombre de la persona apropiada. Si nadie lo hizo, conteste con **Nadie...**

1. _____ se vistió de una manera muy elegante.
2. _____ se vistió de una manera rara (*strange*).
3. _____ se durmió en clase.
4. _____ le pidió al profesor / a la profesora más tarea.
5. _____ se sintió muy contento/a.
6. _____ se divirtió muchísimo, riendo y sonriendo.
7. _____ no sonrió ni siquiera (*not even*) una vez.
8. _____ sugirió tener la clase afuera.
9. _____ prefirió no contestar ninguna pregunta.

B. **Historias breves.** Cuente las siguientes historias breves en el pretérito. Luego continúelas, si puede.

1. **En un restaurante:** Juan (sentarse) a la mesa. Cuando (venir) el camarero, le (pedir) una cerveza. El camarero no (recordar) lo que Juan (pedir) y le (servir) una Coca-Cola. Juan no (querer) beber la Coca-Cola. Le (decir) al camarero: «Perdón, señor. Le (pedir: *yo*) una cerveza.» El camarero le (contestar): «_____.»

2. **Un día típico:** Rosa (acostarse) temprano y (dormirse) en seguida. (Dormir) bien y (despertarse) temprano. (Vestirse) y (salir) para la universidad. En el autobús (ver) a su amigo José y los dos (sonreír). A las nueve _____.

3. **Dos noches diferentes:** Yo (vestirse), (ir) a una fiesta, (divertirse) mucho y (volver) tarde a casa. Mi compañero de cuarto (decidir) quedarse en casa y (ver) la televisión toda la noche. No (divertirse) nada. (Perder) una fiesta excelente y lo (sentir) mucho. Yo _____.

C. **Las historias que todos conocemos.** Cuente algunos detalles de unas historias tradicionales, usando una palabra o frase de cada grupo y el pretérito de los verbos.

MODELO: La Bella Durmiente (*Sleeping Beauty*) durmió por muchos años.

Need more practice?
- Workbook and Laboratory Manual
- Interactive CD-ROM
- Online Learning Center (www.mhhe.com/puntos7)

la Bella Durmiente el lobo (*wolf*) Rip Van Winkle la Cenicienta (*Cinderella*) el Príncipe las hermanastras de Cenicienta Romeo	conseguir perder divertirse preferir morirse sentir vestirse dormir	en un baile encontrar (*to find*) a la mujer misteriosa (por) muchos años por el amor de Julieta de (*as a*) abuela un zapato envidia (*envy*) de su hermanastra

+ between columns 1 and 2, **+** between columns 2 and 3.

Gramática   Doscientos sesenta y nueve ■ **269**

Prác. B: Suggestion

Have students read through each sequence first before beginning the activity.

Prác. B: Follow-Up

Ask the following questions after completing the activity.

1. *¿Dónde almorzó Ud. ayer? ¿Qué pidió? ¿Quién se lo sirvió? ¿Quién pagó la cuenta? ¿Cuánto dejó Ud. de propina? La última vez que cenó en un restaurante, ¿qué pidió? ¿Prefiere Ud. que otra persona pague en un restaurante elegante?*

2. *¿A qué hora se acostó Ud. anoche? ¿Cuántas horas durmió? ¿Durmió bien? ¿Se sintió descansado/a cuando se despertó? ¿Cómo se vistió esta mañana, elegante o informalmente?*

3. *¿Qué película o programa de televisión lo/la divirtió más el año pasado? ¿Se rió Ud. mucho cuando vio... ? ¿Les gustó también a sus amigos? ¿Qué película quiere ver este mes?*

Prác. C: Suggestions

- Start the activity by giving students true/false statements with the characters mentioned. Then let them form their own sentences.
- For homework have each student write six trivia questions on 3 × 5 index cards. The questions should be in the preterite, with answers on the back. In class divide the students into groups of two to four to form an even number of teams (four teams, six teams, eight teams). Each team gets together to select the ten best questions and to correct the Spanish. The teams should write the selected questions individually, without answers, on 3 × 5 cards. Have pairs of teams compete against each other by taking turns asking and responding to questions. Members from each team take turns selecting a card from the opposing team and answering the question.

Prác. C: Extension

Have students add their own details when possible. **¡OJO!** Tell them to limit themselves to actions only, not descriptions or background information, which would be expressed in the imperfect.

CULTURE

- ***Rip Van Winkle:*** Rip Van Winkle, a character in Washington Irving's novel, is a henpecked husband who sleeps for twenty years and wakes up as an old man to find his wife dead, his daughter happily married, and America now an independent country.
- ***Cinderella:*** Cinderella (*la Cenicienta*) is the heroine of a European folktale, the theme of which appears in numerous stories worldwide. More than 500 versions of the story have been found in Europe alone. Its essential features include a youngest daughter who is mistreated by her jealous stepmother and elder stepsisters or a cruel father, and the intervention of a supernatural helper on her behalf. A prince falls in love with her and marries her. One of the oldest known literary renderings of the theme is a Chinese version that dates from the 9th century A.D.
- ***Romeo and Juliet:*** This tragedy by William Shakespeare was probably written in 1595. It is the story of two feuding noble families (the Capulets and the Montagues) whose children meet and fall in love.

Gramática ■ **269**

Con. A: Suggestion

Have students ask you questions first as a model for the interviews. You might provide outrageous answers to set up a fun activity.

■ ■ ■ Conversación

A. Una entrevista indiscreta

Paso 1. Lea las siguientes preguntas y piense en cómo va a contestarlas. Debe contestar algunas preguntas con información falsa.

1. ¿A qué hora se durmió anoche?
2. En alguna ocasión, ¿perdió Ud. mucho dinero?
3. ¿Cuánto dejó de propina (*tip*) la última vez que comió en un restaurante?
4. Alguna vez, ¿se despidió Ud. de alguien tardísimo?
5. ¿Se rió alguna vez al oír una noticia (*piece of news*) trágica?
6. ¿Con qué programa de televisión se divirtió mucho el año pasado / la semana pasada… pero se avergüenza (*you're ashamed*) de admitirlo?

Paso 2. Use las preguntas para entrevistar a un compañero / una compañera de clase. Luego cuénteles a todos algunas de las respuestas de su compañero/a. La clase va a decidir si la información es cierta o falsa.

MODELO: E1: ¿A qué hora te dormiste anoche?
E2: Me dormí a las tres de la mañana y me levanté a las siete.
E1: Alicia se durmió a las tres y se levantó a las siete.
CLASE: No es cierto.
E2: ¡Sí, es cierto! (Tienes razón./No es cierto.)

B. La fiesta de disfraz (*Costume party*)

Paso 1. Use the following sentences as a guide for telling about a childhood or more recent costume party, if appropriate.

Palabras útiles
la bruja (witch)   **el esqueleto**   **el monstruo**

1. ¿De qué se vistió?
2. ¿Cómo se sintió?
3. ¿Fue de casa en casa?
4. ¿Qué les dijo y qué les pidió a los vecinos (*neighbors*)?
5. ¿Qué le dieron?
6. ¿Se rieron los vecinos cuando lo/la vieron?
7. ¿Consiguió muchos dulces?
8. ¿También asistió a una fiesta?
9. ¿Qué sirvieron en la fiesta?
10. ¿Se divirtió mucho?

Paso 2. De todos los miembros de la clase, ¿quién llevó el disfraz más cómico? ¿el más espantoso (*frightening*)? ¿el más original?

Expressing Direct and Indirect Objects Together • Double Object Pronouns

Berta habla de la fiesta que Anita hizo para sus amigos.

Preparé entremeses y *se los* llevé a Anita para la fiesta.

Me encantó el disco compacto que Anita tocó en la fiesta. Por eso Anita *me lo* prestó para escuchar más tarde.

Sergio sacó muchas fotos en la fiesta y *nos las* mostró en la computadora.

Comprensión ¿Cierto o falso?

1. ¿Los entremeses? Berta se los llevó a Anita.
2. ¿El disco compacto? Sergio se lo prestó a Berta.
3. ¿Las fotos? Anita se las mostró a todos.

Gramática 26

Double Object Pronouns

Suggestions

- Treat *Gramática 26* as a topic for passive recognition or, at best, for partial control.
- Have students restate Berta's sentences and invent additional details about the party.
- Emphasize and model that the indirect object pronoun goes before the direct object pronoun.
- Remind students that most verbs require an accent mark after object pronouns are attached to the end of infinitives, commands, and gerunds.

Resources:
Transparency 61

Order of Pronouns

When both an indirect and a direct object pronoun are used in a sentence, the indirect object pronoun (**I**) precedes the direct (**D**): **ID.** Note that nothing comes between the two pronouns. The position of double object pronouns with respect to the verb is the same as that of single object pronouns.

—¿Tienes el trofeo?
Do you have the trophy?

—Sí, acaban de dár**melo.**
Yes, they just gave it to me.

—Mamá, ¿está listo el almuerzo?
Mom, is lunch ready?

—**Te lo** preparo ahora mismo.
I'll get it ready for you right now.

Gramática

National Standards: Comparisons

- Halloween is not generally celebrated in Hispanic countries. Instead, the first of November (All Saints' Day) and the second of November (All Souls' Day) are celebrated as religious and family holidays.
- *El Día de los Muertos* (the Day of the Dead) is celebrated on November 2, especially in Mexico. The celebration may be traced to the festivities held during the Aztec month of *Miccailhuitontli*, ritually presided over by the goddess *Mictecacihuatl* (Lady of the Dead), and dedicated to children and the dead. Today, families celebrate *el Día de los Muertos* by visiting the graves of their close relatives. In the cemetery, family members spruce up the gravesite, decorate it with flowers, set up and enjoy a picnic, and interact socially with other families gathered there. Families remember the departed by telling stories about them. *El Día de los Muertos* is an important social ritual that recognizes the natural cycle of life and death.

Gramática ■ **271**

Le(s) → se

Emphasis A: Suggestions

- Emphasize and model the change of le(s) → se before *lo/la/los/las*.
- In sentences with both direct and indirect third person object pronouns, students should focus only on the gender of the direct object pronoun, since indirect object pronouns will always be *se*.
- To emphasize written accents on affirmative commands with pronouns, give the following dictation.

démelo	*pídaselo*
cómpramelo	*dénselo*
tómenselo	

Bright Idea
Suggestions

- Have students change sentences to use a direct object pronoun.

  Me traes los entremeses a las seis. →
  Me los traes a las seis.

- Have students note clothing and things that classmates have, then have them ask to borrow some things.

  MODELO: *Juan, ¿me prestas la chaqueta? →*
  Sí, te la presto. / No, no te la presto.

Prác. A: Preliminary Exercises

- Ask students which of the following sentences could refer to *el dinero* (*sí* or *no*).

  1. *¿Me lo prestas?*
  2. *Voy a dársela.*
  3. *Te lo mando mañana.*

- Ask students which of the following sentences could refer to *las recomendaciones* (*sí* or *no*).

  1. *Te los doy, si quieres.*
  2. *¿Cuándo se las pediste?*
  3. *Sí, quiero que me las traiga ahora.*

Prác. A: Note

Students do not need to produce the double object pronouns in this activity.

Prác. A: Suggestion

Have students use the emphatic prepositional phrase *me → a mí* with the indirect object pronouns.

Prác. A: Follow-Up

Have students convert all the sentences to commands.

A. When both the indirect and the direct object pronouns begin with the letter **l**, the indirect object pronoun always changes to **se**. The direct object pronoun does not change.

Le regaló unos zapatos.	*He gave her some shoes.*
Se los regaló.	*He gave them to her.*
Les mandamos una invitación.	*We sent you an invitation.*
Se la mandamos.	*We sent it to you.*

B. Since **se** can stand for **le** (*to/for you* [sing.], *him, her*) or **les** (*to/for you* [pl.], *them*), it is often necessary to clarify its meaning by using **a** plus the pronoun objects of prepositions.

Se lo escribo (**a Uds., a ellos, a ellas...**).
I'll write it to (you, them . . .).

Se las doy (**a Ud., a él, a ella...**).
I'll give them to (you, him, her . . .).

AUTOPRUEBA

Match each sentence with the correct double object pronouns.

1. Le dieron el libro. → _____ _____ dieron.
2. Les sirvieron la paella. → _____ _____ sirvieron.
3. Le di las direcciones. → _____ _____ di.
4. Les trajo los boletos. → _____ _____ trajo.

a. Se las
b. Se los
c. Se lo
d. Se la

Answers: 1. c 2. d 3. a 4. b

■ ■ ■ Práctica

A. **¡Anticipemos! Lo que se oye en casa.** ¿A qué se refieren las siguientes oraciones? Fíjese en (*Note*) los pronombres y en el sentido (*meaning*) de la oración.

1. No **lo** prendan (*switch on*). Prefiero que los niños lean o que jueguen.
2. ¿Me **la** pasas? Gracias.
3. Tengo muchas ganas de comprárme**los** todos. Me encanta esa música.
4. ¿Por qué no se **las** mandas a los abuelos? Les van a gustar muchísimo.
5. Tengo que reservárte**los** hoy mismo, porque se va a terminar (*expire*) la oferta especial de Aeroméxico.
6. Yo se **la** organicé a Lupe para su cumpleaños. Antonio y Diego le hicieron un pastel.

a. unas fotos
b. la ensalada
c. unos billetes de avión para Guadalajara
d. la fiesta
e. el televisor
f. los discos compactos de Luis Miguel

B. **En la mesa.** Imagine que Ud. acaba de comer pero todavía tiene hambre. Pida más comida, según el modelo. Fíjese en el uso del tiempo presente como sustituto para el mandato.

MODELO: ensalada → ¿Hay más *ensalada*? ¿Me *la* pasas, por favor?

1. pan
2. tortillas
3. tomates
4. fruta
5. vino
6. jamón

Capítulo 8: Los días festivos

MULTIMEDIA: Internet

Have students search the Internet for information on Guadalajara, Mexico. Where is it? Why would tourists go there? How would you travel there?

C. En el aeropuerto. Cambie los sustantivos a pronombres para evitar (*avoid*) la repetición.

1. ¿La hora de la salida? Acaban de decirnos la hora de la salida.
2. ¿El horario? Sí, léeme el horario, por favor.
3. ¿Los boletos? No, no tiene que darle los boletos aquí.
4. ¿El equipaje? Claro que le guardo el equipaje.
5. ¿Los pasajes? Ya te compré los pasajes.
6. ¿El puesto? No te preocupes. Te puedo guardar el puesto.
7. ¿La clase turística? Sí, les recomiendo la clase turística, señores.
8. ¿La cena? La asistente de vuelo nos va a servir la cena en el avión.

Need more practice?

■ Workbook and Laboratory Manual
■ Interactive CD-ROM
■ Online Learning Center (www.mhhe.com/puntos7)

■ ■ ■ Conversación

A. Regalos especiales

Paso 1. The drawings in **Grupo A** show the presents that a number of people have just received. They were sent by the people in **Grupo B**. Can you match the presents with the sender? Make as many logical guesses as you can.

GRUPO A   GRUPO B

Paso 2. Now compare your matches with those of a partner.

> MODELO: ¿Quién le regaló (mandó, dio) la computadora a Maritere?
> Se la regaló (mandó, dio) _____.

B. ¿Quién le regaló eso?

Paso 1. Haga una lista de los cinco mejores regalos que Ud. ha recibido (*have received*) en su vida. Si no sabe cómo expresar algo, pregúnteselo a su profesor(a).

Paso 2. Ahora déle a un compañero / una compañera su lista. Él/Ella le va a preguntar: **¿Quién te regaló _____?** Use pronombres en su respuesta. **¡OJO!** Fíjese en estas formas plurales (**ellos**): **regalaron, dieron, mandaron.**

> MODELO: E1: ¿Quién te regaló los aretes?
> E2: Mis padres me los regalaron.

Gramática   Doscientos setenta y tres ■ **273**

Resources: Transparency 62

Prác. B: Suggestion

Have students toss a ball or toy (or any other small object). Have each student give a command or a sentence about what the recipient should do with the object once he/she gets it. Write the following verbs on the board.

tirar   traer   llevar
pasar   dar

Model the following sentences to set up the activity:

Désela a la profesora.
Tírasela a Manuel.
Tráigamela.

Prác. B: Follow-Up

Tell students that you are supposed to throw a party this evening but that you have the following problems. Have them give you advice to help you out, for example:

No hay refrescos en casa. → No se preocupe. Yo se los compro.

1. No hay leche en casa.
2. No tengo suficiente champán para la fiesta.
3. Me olvidé de mandar las invitaciones para la fiesta de cumpleaños.
4. No recordé preparar un pastel.

Con. A: Suggestions

■ Have students guess the occasion for those gifts.
■ Suggest the following answers:

A. *las flores de Estela: Se las mandó su amigo Raúl.*
B. *los billetes de Carlos y Juanita: Se los regaló su nieto Jorge.*
C. *la fiesta de Rigoberto: Se la preparó su amiga Pilar.*
D. *la computadora de Maritere: Se la regaló su tía, la Sra. Santana.*

Con. B: Suggestion

Start the activity by assigning pairs to practice giving definitions. Have students explain what the gifts were (without naming them) while classmates try to guess the correct item. The name of the object can be given in English. The important task is to practice circumlocution.

Con. B: Follow-Up

As a composition assignment, students describe the history of their favorite gift (or their partner's): who gave it to them, why, when, and so on.

Gramática ■ **273**

A: Follow-Up

Ask the following questions to follow up the activity.

¿Qué fiestas religiosas se celebran en los Estados Unidos y el Canadá en general?

¿Cuáles celebra su familia?

¿Y las fiestas que no son religiosas?

¿Qué fiestas se celebran en los países hispanohablantes que no se celebran en este país?

UN POCO DE TODO

A. Más días festivos. Complete the following paragraphs with the correct form of the words in parentheses, as suggested by the context. When two possibilities are given in parentheses, select the correct word. Use the preterite of the infinitives in italics.

Los días festivos son muy importantes en el mundo hispano, pero varían mucho de país en país y de pueblo en pueblo.

La fiesta de la Virgen de Guadalupe

En (alguno[1]) países hispánicos los días de (varios[2]) santos (ser/estar[3]) fiestas nacionales. El día 12 (de/del[4]) diciembre se (conmemorar[5]) a la santa patrona de México, la Virgen de Guadalupe. (Mucho[6]) mexicoamericanos celebran (este[7]) fiesta también. Se cree que la Virgen María se le (aparecer[8]) (a/de[9]) Juan, (un/una[10]) humilde pastor,[a] en el pueblo (a/de[11]) Guadalupe. La Virgen (dejar[12])[b] su imagen en un rebozo[c] que todavía se puede (ver[13]) en su Basílica[d] en la Ciudad de México.

[a]*shepherd* [b]*to leave* [c]*shawl* [d]*large church*

La fiesta de San Fermín

No (todo[14]) las fiestas hispánicas (ser/estar[15]) religiosas. Esta fiesta de Pamplona (España) lleva (el/la[16]) nombre de un santo y (ser/estar[17]) de origen religioso, pero es esencialmente secular. Durante diez días —entre (el/la[18]) 7 y (el/la[19]) 17 de julio— se interrumpe la rutina diaria (del / de la[20]) ciudad. (Llegar[21]) personas de todas partes de España e inclusive[a] de (otro[22]) países para beber, cantar, bailar… y (pasarlo[23]) bien. Todas las mañanas algunos toros[b] (correr[24]) sueltos[c] por (el/la[25]) calle de la Estafeta, en dirección (al / a la[26]) plaza de toros.[d] (Alguno[27]) personas atrevidas[e] (correr[28]) delante de ellos. No (haber[29]) duda[f] de que (este[30]) demostración de valor[g] (ser/estar[31]) bastante peligrosa.[h] Luego por (el/la[32]) tarde se celebra una corrida[i] en la famosa plaza de toros que (describir[33]) Ernest Hemingway en (su[34]) novela *The Sun Also Rises.* En Pamplona todavía (ser/estar[35]) posible (hablar[36]) con personas que (saber/conocer[37]) a este famoso escritor estadounidense.

[a]*even* [b]*bulls* [c]*free* [d]*plaza… bullring* [e]*daring* [f]*doubt* [g]*courage* [h]*bastante… quite dangerous* [i]*bullfight*

Comprensión: ¿Cierto o falso? Corrija las oraciones falsas.

1. Todas las fiestas hispánicas son religiosas.
2. Sólo los mexicanos celebran la fiesta de la Virgen de Guadalupe.
3. La fiesta de San Fermín es esencialmente para los niños.
4. Algunos españoles todavía recuerdan a Hemingway.

MULTIMEDIA: Internet

Have students search the Internet for images and websites relating to the celebration of the *Virgen de Guadalupe* and to the running of the bulls or the *Fiesta de San Fermín.* You might have groups develop visual and oral presentations about these festivals.

B. Situaciones y reacciones

Paso 1. Imagine que ocurrieron las siguientes situaciones en algún momento en el pasado. ¿Cómo reaccionó Ud.? ¿Sonrió? ¿Lloró? ¿Rió? ¿Se enojó? ¿Se puso triste, contento/a, furioso/a? ¿Qué hizo?

MODELO: Su compañero de cuarto hizo mucho ruido a las cuatro de la mañana. ¿Cómo reaccionó Ud.? →
Me enojé.
(Me puse furiosísimo/a.)
(Salí de casa y fui a dormir en casa de un amigo.)
(Hablé con él.)

SITUACIONES

1. El profesor le dijo que no va a haber clase mañana.
2. Ud. rompió el reloj que era de (*belonged to*) su abuelo.
3. Su hermano perdió el disco compacto que a Ud. más le gusta.
4. Su mejor amigo lo/la llamó a las seis de la mañana el día de su cumpleaños.
5. Nevó muchísimo y Ud. tuvo que hacer un viaje en auto.
6. Ud. recibió el aumento de sueldo (*raise*) más grande de la oficina.

Paso 2. Ahora pregúntele a un compañero / una compañera si se le ocurrieron algunas de esas cosas y cuáles fueron sus reacciones.

Resources for Review and Testing Preparation

■ Workbook and Laboratory Manual
■ Interactive CD-ROM
■ Online Learning Center (www.mhhe.com/puntos7)

B: Suggestion

Ask students: *¿Por qué no está contento el compañero qué está en la cama?*

B. Variation

Provide three lists of verbs on the board or transparency under the categories *Por la mañana*, *Por la tarde*, *Por la noche*. Then have students use the verbs to describe what Javier did yesterday. Follow-up by having students use verbs from these lists to describe what they did yesterday.

POR LA MAÑÁNA
despertarse a las siete
levantarse en seguida (immediately)
ducharse
afeitarse
vestirse
peinarse
desayunar
tomar sólo un café con leche
ir a la universidad
asistir a clases toda la mañana

POR LA TARDE
almorzar con unos amigos en la cafetería
divertirse hablando con ellos
despedirse de ellos
ir a la biblioteca
quedarse allí estudiando hasta las cuatro y media
volver a casa después
ayudar a su amigo a preparar la cena

POR LA NOCHE
cenar con Rosa
querer estudiar por una hora
no poder (estudiar)
mirar la televisión con sus amigos
darles las buenas noches (a sus amigos)
salir a reunirse con otros amigos en un bar
volver a casa a las dos de la mañana
quitarse la ropa
acostarse
leer por cinco minutos para poder dormirse
dormirse

Resources: Desenlace

In the *Capítulo 8* segment of "Chapter-by-Chapter Supplementary Materials" in the IM, you will find a chapter-culminating activity. You can use this activity to consolidate and review the vocabulary and grammar skills students have acquired.

Entrevista cultural

Suggestions

- Before showing the video, ask students questions about things they buy and use for celebrations and holidays.

    ¿Le gusta decorar la casa para las fiestas?
    ¿Para qué días festivos usa decoraciones?

- Ask students questions about their jobs.

    ¿Dónde trabaja?
    ¿Cuántas horas trabaja Ud. al día?
    ¿Le gusta su trabajo?

- Show the video and allow students one to two minutes to work on the questions. Have volunteers answer the questions.
- Have volunteers role-play Rocío and the interviewer.
- Follow up by asking questions about some holiday and celebration customs in this country.

Entre amigos

Suggestions

- Before viewing the video, review the questions with the students and ask them similar questions.

    ¿Qué hace para los días festivos como la Navidad y el Año Nuevo?
    ¿Dónde usa decoraciones?

    Have students answer or work in small groups to ask and answer these questions.

- After viewing the video, have volunteers read and answer the questions.

PERSPECTIVAS culturales

●●●
Videoteca

Entrevista cultural: Cuba

Rocío García nació en Cuba pero ahora vive y trabaja en México. En esta entrevista, Rocío describe su trabajo. También habla de unas costumbres cubanas. Antes de ver el vídeo, lea el siguiente fragmento de la entrevista.

ENTREVISTADORA:	Rocío, ¿en donde trabajas?
ROCÍO:	Trabajo en una tienda que vende artículos típicos de fiesta, como son globos, serpentinas[a]... Y tiene una sección especial para artículos típicos de fiestas mexicanas...
ENTREVISTADORA:	¿Cómo se celebran los cumpleaños en Cuba?
ROCÍO:	En Cuba hacemos una gran fiesta. Hay payasos,[b] globos, *cake,* piñatas, refrescos—todo para que los niños la pasen bien. Y jugamos mucho con ellos para que disfruten[c] ese día.

[a]*streamers* [b]*clowns* [c]*they enjoy*

Ahora vea el vídeo y conteste las siguientes preguntas basándose en la entrevista.

1. ¿Dónde trabaja Rocío?
2. ¿Qué se vende allí?
3. ¿Cómo son las fiestas de cumpleaños en Cuba?
4. ¿Cómo se celebra la Navidad en Cuba?
5. ¿Cuál es el día festivo preferido de Rocío?

Entre amigos: ¡Comemos las uvas de la suerte (*the lucky grapes*)!

Rubén, Miguel, Tané y Karina preparan las decoraciones para una fiesta, y hablan de las tradiciones navideñas (*Christmas traditions*) de sus países. En su opinión, ¿de qué van a hablar? Antes de mirar el vídeo, lea las preguntas a continuación. Mientras mire el vídeo, trate de entender la conversación en general y fíjese en la información sobre los días festivos. Luego mire el vídeo una segunda vez, fijándose en la información que necesita para contestar las preguntas.

1. ¿Qué van a hacer Miguel y Rubén con las decoraciones?
2. ¿Qué hacen en España durante los días de Navidad?
3. ¿Cuándo comen «las uvas de la suerte» en España?
4. ¿Qué hacen en Venezuela para la Navidad?
5. ¿Y qué hacen en Cuba para la Navidad?

Conozca... Cuba

Datos esenciales

- Nombre oficial: República de Cuba
- Capital: La Habana
- Población: 11.260.000 habitantes
- Moneda: el peso cubano
- Idioma oficial: el español

¡Fíjese!

- Cuba obtuvo[a] su independencia de España en 1898, tras[b] la guerra de Cuba.[c] Los Estados Unidos ayudó a Cuba en esta guerra.
- Después de la revolución socialista cubana en 1959, hubo un éxodo de cubanos a los Estados Unidos. La mayor parte de ellos se estableció en Florida, con la esperanza[d] de volver muy pronto a su isla. Pero empezó el milenio y todavía[e] Fidel Castro, el primer líder de la revolución, gobierna a Cuba.
- Los días festivos oficiales de Cuba incluyen el Aniversario del triunfo de la Revolución o el Día de la Liberación (1° de enero), el Día Internacional de los Trabajadores (1° de mayo), las Celebraciones por el Día de la Rebeldía Nacional (25–27 de julio) y el Inicio de las guerras de Independencia (10 de octubre). Al tomar[f] el control del poder de Cuba, Castro declaró el país oficialmente ateo[g] y prohibió que practicantes religiosos participaran en el gobierno. En 1992, Castro levantó esa prohibición. En 1997, un poco antes de la visita del Papa Juan Pablo II a Cuba, la Navidad, que por casi cuarenta años no fue un día festivo oficial, fue celebrada[h] pública y oficialmente.
- El régimen de Castro ha reducido[i] el analfabetismo[j] a menos de 5 por ciento y ha reformado el sistema educativo con resultados admirables. Pero la situación económica del país es difícil. Con la caída[k] de la Unión Soviética, Cuba perdió fondos de apoyo[l] indispensables. El embargo económico de los Estados Unidos también sigue afectando las condiciones de vida[m] de los cubanos.

[a]obtained [b]after [c]guerra... Spanish-American War [d]hope [e]still [f]Al... Upon taking [g]atheist [h]celebrated [i]ha... has reduced [j]illiteracy [k]fall [l]fondos... economic assistance [m]condiciones... living conditions

Personas famosas: Nicolás Guillén

Nicolás Guillén, poeta cubano de origen africano y europeo, es quizás[a] el poeta que mejor refleja la influencia africana en la cultura hispana. El lenguaje, los mitos[b] y las leyendas afro-cubanos aparecen en su obra. Sus temas incluyen la injusticia social y una crítica al colonialismo.

[a]perhaps [b]myths

▲ *Nicolás Guillén (1902–1989)*

Learn more about Cuba with the Video, the Interactive CD-ROM, and the Online Learning Center (www.mhhe.com/puntos7).

MULTIMEDIA: Internet

Have students search the Internet for more information on the government, people, education, economy, and history of Cuba. You might assign specific topics and have students give brief oral presentations based on their findings.

Conozca... Cuba

Suggestion
Write the following names and topics on separate slips of paper, repeating each three or four times depending on the size of your class.

José Martí
The Buena Vista Social Club
Fidel Castro
Radio Martí
los marielitos
Theodore Roosevelt
Elián González
Iván Hernández
la Bahía de Guantánamo
Fulgencio Batista
the USS Maine

Have each student pick a slip. Ask students to investigate the significance of the name on their slip to Cuban history. In another class period, work with students to construct a time line of modern Cuban history.

Note
Students can read part of a poem from *Versos sencillos* by Cuba's José Martí in *Un paso más 8*.

Suggestions

- Give a series of situations or problems and have students react quickly by expressing how they would feel. For example:

  un examen difícil → Me pongo nervioso.
  un chiste cómico → Me río.

- Play a game of word associations with words from the *Vocabulario*. Continue round-robin associations for at least ten turns for each word. For example, *entremeses* → *sándwiches* → *fiestas* → *cumpleaños,* and so on.

- Have students respond *probable* or *improbable.*

  1. *Ud. se siente triste si los amigos se olviden de su cumpleaños.*
  2. *Ud. se ríe si su novio/a sale con otra persona.*
  3. *El profesor se enoja si los estudiantes se portan bien.*

EN RESUMEN

Gramática

To review the grammar points presented in this chapter, refer to the indicated grammar presentations. You'll find further practice of these structures in the Workbook and Laboratory Manual, on the Interactive CD-ROM, and on the *Puntos de partida* Online Learning Center (www.mhhe.com/puntos7).

24. Talking About the Past (2)—Irregular Preterites

Do you know how to conjugate the verbs that are irregular in the preterite? How does the preterite change the meaning of **saber, conocer, querer,** and **poder?**

25. Talking About the Past (3)—Preterite of Stem-Changing Verbs

You should know the stem-changing patterns for **-ir** verbs like **pedir, sentir,** and **dormir.**

26. Expressing Direct and Indirect Objects Together—Double Object Pronouns

Do you know in which order the direct and indirect object pronouns occur when they are used together in Spanish? You should also know where to place the pronouns and when an accent is required on the verb forms.

Vocabulario

Practice this vocabulary with digital flash cards on the Online Learning Center (www.mhhe.com/puntos7).

Los verbos

conseguir (i, i) (g)	to get, obtain
conseguir + *inf.*	to succeed in (*doing something*)
despedirse (i, i) (de)	to say good-bye (to), take leave (of)
discutir (sobre) (con)	to argue (about) (with)
encontrar (ue)	to find
enfermarse	to get sick
enojarse (con)	to get angry (at)
gastar	to spend (*money*)
llorar	to cry
morir(se) (ue, u)	to die
olvidarse (de)	to forget (about)
ponerse (*irreg.*) + *adj.*	to become, get + *adjective*
portarse	to behave
quejarse (de)	to complain (about)
reaccionar	to react
recordar (ue)	to remember
reír(se) (i, i)	to laugh
sentirse (ie, i)	to feel (*an emotion*)
sonreír(se) (i, i)	to smile
sugerir (ie, i)	to suggest

Los días festivos y las fiestas

el anfitrión / la anfitriona	host, hostess
el chiste	joke
el deseo	wish
los entremeses	hors d'œvres
el/la invitado/a	guest
el pastel de cumpleaños	birthday cake
la sorpresa	surprise
cumplir años	to have a birthday
dar (*irreg.*) / hacer (*irreg.*) una fiesta	to give/have a party
faltar	to be absent, lacking
pasarlo bien/mal	to have a good/bad time
reunirse (me reúno) (con)	to get together (with)

Repaso: celebrar, el cumpleaños, el dinero, divertirse (ie, i), el refresco, regalar

Los sustantivos

la emoción	emotion
el hecho	event
la medianoche	midnight
la noticia	piece of news

Los adjetivos

avergonzado/a	embarrassed
feliz (*pl.* felices)	happy
raro/a	strange

Palabras adicionales

¡felicitaciones!	congratulations!
gracias por	thanks for
por lo menos	at least
ser (*irreg*) en + *place*	to take place in/at (*place*)
ya	already

Algunos días festivos

la Navidad
la Noche Vieja
la Nochebuena
la Pascua (Florida)

Suggestion

Ask students:

¿En qué días festivos mandamos tarjetas?

1. *¿la Navidad?*
2. *¿el Cuatro de Julio?*
3. *¿el Día de San Valentín?*
4. *¿el cumpleaños?*

¿Qué colores asociamos con estos días festivos?

5. *la Pascua (Florida)*
6. *la Navidad*
7. *el Cuatro de Julio*
8. *el Día de San Patricio*

Un paso más 8

Note

The *Un paso más* section is optional.

Literatura de **Cuba**

Note

José Martí was a prolific writer and poet. He is often credited with initiating the fight for Cuba's independence from Spain. He died in one of the first battles of independence. He often wrote about liberty. You can find many of his thoughts on the Internet. The following is one that is often quoted.

> *El hombre ama la libertad, aunque no sepa que la ama, y anda empujado de ella y huyendo de donde no la hay.*

Literatura de **Cuba**

Sobre el autor: *José Martí nació en la Habana, Cuba, pero se exilió a los 17 años por su oposición a la dominación colonial de España. Martí se considera uno de los grandes escritores del mundo hispano. Murió en una de las primeras batallas por la independencia de Cuba del dominio español.*

▲ José Martí
(1853–1895)

XXXIX tomado de *Versos sencillos* (1891)

Cultivo una rosa blanca
en junio como enero
para el amigo sincero
que me da su mano franca.[a]

Y para el cruel que me arranca[b]
el corazón[c] con que vivo,
cardo[d] ni ortiga[e] cultivo;
cultivo la rosa blanca.

[a]mano... *open (sincere) hand* [b]*uproots, tears out* [c]*heart* [d]*thistle* [e]*nettle*

L E C T U R A

REPASO DE ESTRATEGIAS: Using What You know

In previous chapters of *Puntos de partida,* you learned that you can use a variety of prereading strategies to help you understand the meaning of a passage in Spanish. Some of these strategies include:

- guessing meaning from context
- learning to recognize cognates and cognate patterns
- using visual clues
- getting a general idea about content

Using a combination of some or all of these strategies will help you to become a more efficient, successful reader in Spanish. You should try to apply as many as possible to the following reading.

■ **Sobre la lectura...** El artículo que va a leer es de *Nuestra Gente,* una revista de la «cultura popular», publicada para hispanohablantes que viven en los Estados Unidos. Incluye artículos sobre el mundo del entretenimiento (*entertainment*), la salud (*health*) y la belleza, mejoramientos (*improvements*) domésticos, la cocina, los días festivos y otros temas de interés general.

☀ **Heritage Speakers**

Anime a sus estudiantes hispanohablantes a recitar un poema breve que saben de memoria.

¡Época de tradiciones!

Diciembre es un mes muy especial para nosotros los latinos, ¡y lo <u>festejamos</u> a lo grande! Aún cuando ya hemos adoptado[a] las costumbres norteamericanas de <u>colocar</u> un árbol de Navidad en la casa y de esperar la <u>llegada</u> de Santa Claus el 25 de diciembre, nunca faltan en nuestros hogares[b] esos toques[c] especiales que le dan sabor latino a la Navidad y que le dan vida a nuestras tradiciones culturales. Por eso, esta es la ocasión perfecta para <u>inculcar</u> en nuestros hijos el orgullo[d] hacia lo nuestro y darle continuidad a aquellas costumbres que celebrábamos junto a nuestros abuelos y que esperamos que nuestros hijos celebren con sus nietos.

Beatriz Acosta, quien reside en California, aprovecha[e] estas fechas para que sus tres hijos participen en las tradicionales posadas, que <u>emulan</u> el peregrinaje[f] de la Virgen María y San José en busca de albergue[g]. «Para mí, es importante que mis hijos aprendan estas costumbres de nuestra cultura», dice esta inmigrante de origen mexicano.

Y, ¡claro que cada cual sigue sus tradiciones! A las procesiones o visitas que los mexicanos llaman posadas, los puertorriqueños les llaman asaltos navideños o parrandas. <u>Contrario al</u> tema religioso que enfatizan[h] las posadas, las parrandas se caracterizan por ser una visita <u>inesperada</u> de amigos que cantan para que se les permita continuar la fiesta, y se les dé comida y algo de beber. Son actividades alegres y fáciles de organizar entre familiares o amistades.

Para añadirle[i] un toquecito latino al Año Nuevo, puedes compartir con tus hijos la forma en que se despide en tu país de origen

▲ *Una representación de los Reyes Magos en la Catedral de la Habana*

el Año Viejo. Los cubanos, por ejemplo, siguen la tradición española de comer 12 uvas[j] en representación de los 12 meses del año viejo y de los 12 <u>venideros</u>. Otros prefieren agarrar[k] una maleta y darle la vuelta a la cuadra,[l] como lo hacen los mexicanos, con el fin de que el Año Nuevo esté lleno de viajes.

Muchos de nosotros seguimos festejando y no quitamos el árbol navideño hasta el 6 de enero, Día de los Reyes Magos, en que se <u>conmemora</u> la llegada de los tres reyes de Oriente a Belén[m] para ofrecer regalos al Niño Dios.

Lo más lindo es saber que el <u>espíritu navideño</u> se adorna de nuestras tradiciones de origen, colma[n] nuestros corazones y se perpetúa con su magia en las nuevas generaciones. ■

[a]hemos... *we have adopted* [b]casas [c]*touches* [d]*pride* [e]*takes advantage of* [f]*pilgrimage* [g]*shelter* [h]*emphasize* [i]darle [j]*grapes* [k]*to take, grab* [l]darle... *walk around the block* [m]*Bethlehem* [n]*fills*

Comprensión: Suggestion

Have students complete the following sentences to check comprehension. (Answers: 1. b 2. a 3. b 4. c 5. c)

1. La lectura trata de...
   a. fiestas nacionales.
   b. tradiciones hispanas.
   c. adoptar tradiciones estadounidenses.

2. Las posadas...
   a. celebran el viaje de María y José a Belén.
   b. originaron en Cuba.
   c. se celebran en enero.

3. La alternativa puertorriqueña de las posadas...
   a. se llama la Epifanía.
   b. es el asalto navideño.
   c. incluye a los Reyes Magos.

4. Dos países que celebran el Año Nuevo con doce uvas son...
   a. México y Puerto Rico.
   b. Cuba y México.
   c. España y Cuba.

5. Las uvas y las maletas se usan en tradiciones hispanas para...
   a. celebrar la Navidad.
   b. saludar a los Reyes Magos.
   c. despedirse del Año Viejo.

Comprensión

A. **¿Cierto o falso?** Determine si las siguientes oraciones son ciertas o falsas, y prepárese para explicar su respuesta.

	C	F
1. Los hispanos en los Estados Unidos desean abandonar las costumbres y tradiciones de su país de origen.	☐	☑
2. Todos los países hispánicos tienen las mismas costumbres navideñas.	☐	☑
3. No ponen árboles de Navidad en las casas hispanas.	☐	☑
4. Santa Claus es una costumbre de las familias hispanas.	☑	☐

B. **¿En qué país?** Identifique el país hispano donde se celebran las siguientes costumbres, según la lectura.

1. Se comen 12 uvas para celebrar el Año Nuevo. *E/C*
2. Se simula el viaje de la Virgen María y San José. *C*
3. Se va de casa en casa visitando amigos y cantando. *M*

◀ *El Templo de la Vírgen de la Asunción, en Cupilco, México*

MULTIMEDIA: Internet

Have students research sites for Hispanics in the United States and Canada to find more articles that address issues of maintaining, altering, and losing traditions. Have them list the concerns that seem to be more prevalent (language, holidays, religion, and so on).

ESCRITURA

Mi día festivo favorito. Seguro que hay algún día festivo que a Ud. le gusta más que cualquier (*any*) otro. ¿Cómo es ese día festivo? Escriba una breve composición en la que explica cuál es su día favorito y cómo lo celebra.

Paso 1. Complete la siguiente oración.

Mi día festivo favorito es _____.

Paso 2. Ahora conteste las siguientes preguntas.

1. ¿Con quién(es) celebra Ud. ese día festivo?
2. ¿Cuáles son las costumbres y tradiciones que se observan ese día?
3. Ud. y sus parientes, ¿tienen alguna tradición especial que acostumbran seguir (*you always carry out*)?
4. ¿Qué comidas y bebidas se sirven en ese día?
5. ¿Se lleva alguna ropa especial?

Paso 3. Por fin, utilice la información del **Paso 2** para escribir su composición.

ESCRITURA

Suggestions

- If you prefer that your students do a journal activity, see *Mi diario* in this chapter of the Workbook.
- Have students write an invitation to a birthday party or a holiday celebration. Have them describe the kind of party or celebration they are organizing, including the time, place, details, and any rituals that might take place. For this activity, they can make up their own holiday. Encourage them to read or distribute their invitation to the rest of the class.
- Have students share some of their family holiday customs and traditions with the class.
- Have students investigate a corresponding or similar holiday celebrated in Hispanic countries (if there is one) and share their findings with the class.

◄ La Calle 13 en Bogotá, Colombia

CHAPTER OPENER PHOTO

Point out the chapter-opener photo. Have students describe this scene. Are scenes like this typical in your area? In what cities would this be a typical scene? Have students describe what people typically do in their free time in urban areas. How is that different from what people might do in the suburbs? In rural areas?

Suggestions

■ Ask students questions to help introduce the chapter theme. The words in **boldface** are included in the active vocabulary of this chapter. Have students discuss the words and use context to help them understand the meanings. Place the words they cannot guess in new sentences and contexts.

1. *¿Cómo pasa Ud. su **tiempo libre**? (Mencione por lo menos dos actividades.)*
2. *En su opinión, ¿cuál es **el aparato doméstico** más importante?*
3. *En su casa, apartamento o residencia, ¿quién hace **las tareas domésticas**?*
4. *¿Qué opina Ud. de los deportes? ¿Cree Ud. que son **divertidos**? **¿Le aburren?***
5. *¿Cuál es **el deporte** más popular de su país? ¿Lo **juega** Ud.? ¿Va a los **partidos** profesionales?*

■ Ask students the following questions.

¿Sabe Ud. esquiar? ¿Quién lo/la enseñó?

¿Se puede esquiar cerca de donde Ud. vive?

¿Cuáles son los mejores lugares para esquiar en su país?

■ Explain *tiempo libre* in Spanish: *el tiempo que tenemos para divertirnos y descansar.* Ask students for an English equivalent.

■ If students do not know the name for a particular *aparato doméstico*, have them use gestures and circumlocution to communicate it, then give them the word in Spanish.

Note

The *Puntos de partida* Online Learning Center includes an interview with a native speaker from Colombia who answers questions similar to those in the preceding *Suggestions*.

Resources

For Students

■ Workbook
■ Laboratory Manual and Laboratory Audio Program
■ Quia™ Online Workbook and Online Laboratory Manual
■ Video on CD
■ Interactive CD-ROM
■ *Puntos de partida* Online Learning Center (**www.mhhe.com/puntos7**)

For Instructors

■ *Instructor's Manual and Resource Kit,* "Chapter-by-Chapter" Supplementary Materials
■ Overhead Transparencies 63–70
■ Testing Program
■ Test Generator
■ Video Program
■ Audioscript
■ *Puntos de partida* Online Learning Center (**www.mhhe.com/puntos7**)

El tiempo **libre**

Suggestion
Have students list their ideas about Colombia, including information on geography, politics, economy, culture, music, and cuisine. When you finish the chapter, return to the lists and ask students what ideas they would change and/or add.

CULTURA

- **Perspectivas culturales**

  Entrevista cultural: Colombia

  Entre amigos: ¿Sabes bailar salsa?

  Conozca... Colombia

- **Nota cultural:** El fútbol y el béisbol

- **En los Estados Unidos y el Canadá:** La música hispánica en el Canadá

- **Literatura de Colombia:** Gabriel García Márquez

- **Lectura:** El sitio de mi recreo

VOCABULARIO

- Pasatiempos, diversiones y aficiones

- Los quehaceres domésticos

GRAMÁTICA

27 Imperfect of Regular and Irregular Verbs

28 Superlatives

29 Summary of Interrogative Words

Entrevista cultural

Mauricio Tautiba ▶
Bogotá, Colombia

MULTIMEDIA

- The multimedia materials that accompany this chapter are referenced in the Student and Instructor's Editions with icons to help you identify when and where to incorporate them.

- The IM provides suggestions for using the multimedia materials in the classroom.

Pasatiempos, diversiones y aficiones

Note

See the model for vocabulary presentation and other material in the *Capítulo 9 Vocabulario: Preparación* section of "Chapter-by-Chapter Supplementary Materials," in the IM.

Suggestions

- Introduce part of the vocabulary by telling students what your plans are for the upcoming weekend, for example:

  Bueno, tengo muchos planes para este fin de semana. El viernes pienso ir al teatro con un amigo y después vamos a cenar fuera. El sábado voy a dar un paseo por la mañana, trabajar un poco en mi oficina y jugar al golf por la tarde. Por la noche, voy al cine para ver la nueva película de Almodóvar. Y el domingo creo que voy a descansar, o tal vez visitar un museo.

- Read statements about what you told the students and have them respond *cierto* or *falso* to check comprehension.

  1. *El viernes voy al cine.*
  2. *El domingo voy a visitar un museo.*
  3. *Voy al cine solo/a.*
  4. *El sábado voy a jugar al tenis.*
  5. *El domingo tengo que trabajar.*
  6. *El sábado voy a dar un paseo.*

- Present additional expressions using magazine clippings of sports and pastimes. Use the images to go back and ask questions such as *¿A qué juega el hombre, al fútbol o al hockey?*

- Have students tell what sport or activity they associate with the following people and things.

  ¿Con qué deporte o actividad asocia Ud.... ?

Sammy Sosa	el verano
Shaquille O'Neal	el invierno
Ricky Martin	el otoño
Serena Williams	la primavera
	una cita (date) especial
	un día de lluvia

- Point out the following variations in expressions and additional vocabulary.

  hacer camping = hacer acampada
  pasear en bicicleta = montar en bicicleta = andar en bicicleta
  el atletismo, carreras y saltos (track)
  ir de copas (to go to the bars)
  el patinaje (skating)

VOCABULARIO Preparación

Pasatiempos... *Pastimes, fun activities, and hobbies*

Pasatiempos, diversiones y aficiones°

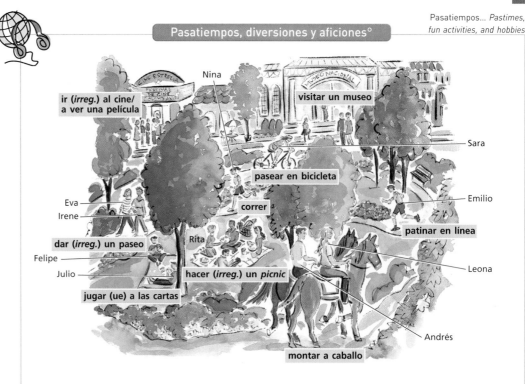

ir (*irreg.*) al cine/ a ver una película
visitar un museo
Nina
Sara
pasear en bicicleta
correr
Emilio
patinar en línea
Eva
Irene
dar (*irreg.*) un paseo
Rita
Felipe
Julio
hacer (*irreg.*) un *picnic*
jugar (ue) a las cartas
Leona
Andrés
montar a caballo

Los pasatiempos

los ratos libres	spare (free) time
dar (*irreg.*)/hacer (*irreg.*) una fiesta	to give a party
hacer (*irreg.*) *camping*	to go camping
hacer (*irreg.*) planes para + *inf.*	to make plans to (*do something*)
ir (*irreg.*)...	to go . . .
a una discoteca / a un bar	to a disco / to a bar
al teatro / a un concierto	to the theater / to a concert
jugar (ue) (gu) al ajedrez	to play chess
tomar el sol	to sunbathe
aburrirse	to get bored
ser (*irreg.*) divertido/a, aburrido/a	to be fun, boring

Los deportes

el ciclismo	bicycling
esquiar (esquío)	to ski
el fútbol	soccer
el fútbol americano	football
nadar	to swim
la natación	swimming
patinar	to skate

Otros deportes: el basquetbol, el béisbol, el golf, el hockey, el tenis, el vólibol

entrenar	to practice, train
ganar	to win
jugar (ue) (gu) al + *sport*	to play (*a sport*)
perder (ie)	to lose
practicar (qu)	to participate (*in a sport*)
ser (*irreg.*) aficionado/a (a)	to be a fan (of)

MULTIMEDIA: Audio

Students can listen to and practice this chapter's vocabulary on the Online Learning Center (**www.mhhe.com/puntos7**), as well as on the

Textbook Audio CD, part of the Laboratory Audio Program.

Resources: Transparencies 63–66

Provide examples and practice of *pasatiempos*.

■ ■ ■ Conversación

A. **¿Cómo pasan estas personas su tiempo libre?**

Paso 1. ¿Qué cree Ud. que hacen las siguientes personas para divertirse en un sábado típico? Use su imaginación pero manténgase (*keep yourself*) entre los límites de lo posible.

1. una persona rica que vive en Nueva York
2. un grupo de buenos amigos que trabajan en una fábrica (*factory*) de Detroit
3. un matrimonio joven con poco dinero y dos niños pequeños

Paso 2. ¿Cómo se divierten los jóvenes españoles? Este recorte (*clipping*) de una revista española indica el tiempo medio (*average*) que los jóvenes españoles dedican a sus aficiones. ¿Puede explicar en español lo que significan los términos **Tomar copas** y **prensa**? ¿A qué tipos de «juegos» cree Ud. que se refiere el recorte?

Paso 3. Indique el número de minutos que Ud. les dedica a estas aficiones cada día. ¿Qué diferencia hay entre Ud. y los jóvenes españoles?

B. **¿Cierto o falso?** Corrija (*Correct*) las oraciones falsas según su opinión.

1. Ver un partido (*match, game*) de fútbol en la televisión es más aburrido que ir al cine.
2. Lo paso mejor con mi familia que con mis amigos.
3. Las actividades educativas me gustan más que las deportivas (*sporting*).
4. Odio el béisbol tanto como el fútbol.

TIEMPO QUE DEDICAN A SUS AFICIONES	
(Media de minutos diarios)	
Ver la televisión	120
Tomar copas	60
Pasear	22
Leer libros	15
Escuchar música	15
Oír la radio	8
Hacer deporte	9
Practicar *hobbies*	8
Leer la prensa	6
«Juegos»	4

NOTA CULTURAL

El fútbol y el béisbol

Sin duda,[a] el deporte más popular en el mundo hispánico es **el fútbol.*** El campeonato mundial de fútbol, conocido como **la Copa Mundial,** es el evento deportivo más popular del mundo. Este **torneo internacional** ocurre cada cuatro años y tiene más **espectadores** que cualquier[b] otro evento deportivo. Por ejemplo, en 1998, 1.7 (uno punto siete) billones de televidentes miraron la Copa Mundial mientras 800 millones miraron el *Super Bowl* de los Estados Unidos. Como es un deporte tan popular, en todas las ciudades hispanas hay muchos **campos**[c] **de fútbol.** Los niños y los adultos van a jugar siempre que pueden.[d]

El béisbol también es muy popular, sobre todo en el Caribe. Hay muchos hispanos en **las ligas profesionales** de los Estados Unidos. Por ejemplo, el gran **jugador** de los Chicago Cubs, Sammy Sosa, es de la República Dominicana. El puertorriqueño Roberto Clemente fue el primer hispano elegido al *Baseball Hall of Fame* en 1973.

▲ *Un partido de la Copa Mundial entre el Brasil y Honduras*

[a]*doubt* [b]*any* [c]*fields* [d]*siempre... whenever they can*

*Remember that **fútbol** *is soccer, not U.S.-style football.*

MULTIMEDIA: Internet

Many Hispanic soccer clubs have websites. Have students look for the International Football (Soccer) Hall of Fame Web page as well as for sites about world soccer. Have them look up information on world soccer and the World Cup using the Spanish words *Mundial de fútbol*. The sites they find will provide links to images, statistics, and general information about particular teams, players, and leagues.

☼ Heritage Speakers

- En algunos dialectos del español del suroeste de los Estados Unidos y del Caribe, se dice *jugar béisbol* en vez de *jugar al béisbol*. Se omite la preposición *a* después de *jugar* con frecuencia en el habla popular.
- Pídales a sus estudiantes hispanohablantes que comparen la información del recorte en *Conversación A* con su experiencia personal. Pregúnteles si creen que los jóvenes españoles son típicos de jóvenes hispanos de otros países.

Con. A: Suggestions

- Have students write down their answers, then compare the answers given by all. Do any answers predominate?
- Have students name activities they associate with the following places. ¿*Qué se hace en... ?*

  1. *el estadio*   4. *la piscina*
  2. *el campo*   5. *el cine*
  3. *el gimnasio*   6. *el teatro*

- Assign *Paso 1* as written homework. Then compare answers in class.
- For *Pasos 2* and *3*, have students interview at least six classmates, making a list of the answers. Have them share results and then compare them to the results for Spaniards.

Con. A: Extension

Paso 1.

4. *un profesor soltero y joven / una profesora soltera y joven de universidad*
5. *una pareja de personas mayores (de 70 a 75 años) que vive en Texas*
6. *un estudiante de la universidad a quien le gusta mucho estudiar literatura y escribir poesías y dramas*
7. *esposos que tienen casi 80 años a quienes les interesan mucho las noticias y la política mundiales*

Con. B: Extension

5. *Los estudiantes universitarios tienen tanto tiempo libre como los de la escuela secundaria.*
6. *Es más interesante leer libros que ver la televisión.*
7. *Me gusta oír la radio tanto como ver la televisión.*

NOTA CULTURAL

Suggestions

- Ask how many students like and play soccer. Then have those people explain to their classmates what makes soccer, in their opinion, a fun sport. Discuss as a class why soccer is less popular in the U.S. and Canada than in Latin America and Europe.
- Ask the following questions to check comprehension:

  1. *¿Qué deporte atrae más televidentes en el mundo hispano para sus grandes eventos, el fútbol or el fútbol americano?*
  2. *¿En qué países del mundo hispano es popular el béisbol?*

Reciclado

Recycle house vocabulary with the following question.

¿Qué quehaceres domésticos asocia Ud. con la cocina? ¿el garaje? ¿la alcoba? ¿la sala? ¿el baño?

Los quehaceres domésticos

Suggestions

- Offer optional vocabulary.

  la licuadora (blender)
  limpiar toda la casa = limpiar la casa entera
  barrer el piso = barrer el suelo

- Have students tell what words or expressions they associate with the following things.

  ¿el aire acondicio-nado?   *¿el refrigerador?*
                ¿cocinar?
  ¿la cafetera?   *¿el congelador?*
  ¿la estufa?   *¿la tostadora?*
  ¿la secadora?

Bright Idea

Suggestion

Ask students what chores they like or do not like to do.

¿A quién le gusta... planchar la ropa? limpiar la casa? lavar las ventanas?

Con. A: Suggestions

- Have students come up with all logical and possible parts of the house where the action can take place.
- Have students complete these sentences with the correct activity, based on the noun at the beginning of the sentence.

  1. *La secadora sirve para _____.*
  2. *La plancha sirve para _____.*
  3. *En la cocina se puede _____.*
  4. *La lavadora sirve para _____.*

- Ask students these questions.

  1. *¿Ud. hace la cama todos los días? Si tiene prisa por la mañana, ¿hace la cama o la deja sin hacer? Cuando visita la casa de su familia, ¿su mamá (abuela) le hace la cama?*
  2. *¿Cuándo limpia Ud. la casa, durante el fin de semana? ¿La limpia entera o sólo una parte? ¿Alguien lo/la ayuda a limpiarla?*
  3. *¿Qué prefiere Ud., sacudir los muebles o pasar la aspiradora? ¿lavar la ropa o barrer el piso? ¿quitar la mesa o lavar los platos?... Yo odio* (fill in what you dislike). *¿Quién también odia _____?*

Los... *Household chores*

Los quehaceres domésticos°

- pasar la aspiradora — Ignacio
- la aspiradora
- limpiar/lavar las ventanas
- Flor
- planchar la ropa
- Sergio
- pintar (las paredes)
- Pablo — hacer (*irreg.*) la cama
- Olga
- la estufa
- el congelador
- el refrigerador
- sacudir los muebles
- el lavaplatos
- Nora
- Sofía — barrer (el piso)
- Mario
- sacar (qu) la basura — la lavadora
- la secadora

Algunos aparatos domésticos

la cafetera	coffeemaker
el horno de microondas	microwave oven
la tostadora	toaster

Los quehaceres domésticos

dejar (en...)	to leave behind (in [*a place*])
lavar (los platos, la ropa)	to wash (the dishes, the clothes)
limpiar la casa (entera)	to clean the (whole) house
poner (*irreg.*) **la mesa**	to set the table
quitar la mesa	to clear the table

Vocabulario útil

Here are some alternative phrases related to household chores and appliances that are used in some parts of the Spanish-speaking world. This vocabulary is for your information only and will not be actively practiced in *Puntos de partida*.

hacer la cama → **tender (ie) la cama**
lavar los platos → **fregar (ie) (gu) los platos**
sacar la basura → **tirar la basura**
sacudir los muebles → **quitar el polvo**
(literally, *to remove the dust*)

el congelador → **la nevera**
la estufa → **la cocina** (**el horno** is generally used for *oven*)
el refrigerador → **el frigorífico, la refrigeradora**

Resources: Transparency 67

 Heritage Speakers

Pídales a sus estudiantes hispanohablantes que compartan otras palabras o variaciones que usan para describir aparatos y quehaceres domésticos.

Refrán

«De dichos y refranes, hacemos mil planes.»

Write the *refrán* on the board. Explain that while *refrán* can mean proverb or saying, *dicho* can only mean saying. A proverb refers to an old and popular saying that illustrates something such as a basic truth or a practical precept. A saying is an often repeated and familiar expression. Have students tell what they think this saying means.

■ ■ ■ Conversación

A. Los quehaceres. ¿En qué cuarto o parte de la casa se hacen las siguientes actividades? Hay más de una respuesta en muchos casos.

1. Se hace la cama en _____.
2. Se saca la basura de _____ y se deja en _____.
3. Se sacude los muebles de _____.
4. Uno se baña en _____. Pero es mejor que uno bañe al perro en _____.
5. Se barre el piso de _____.
6. Se pasa la aspiradora en _____.
7. Se lava y se seca la ropa en _____. La ropa se plancha en _____.
8. Se usa la cafetera en _____.

B. ¡Manos a la obra! (*Let's get to work!*)

Paso 1. De los siguientes quehaceres, ¿cuáles le gustan más? Póngalos en orden de mayor (1) a menor (10) preferencia para Ud.

_____ barrer el suelo   _____ planchar la ropa
_____ hacer la cama   _____ limpiar el garaje
_____ lavar los platos   _____ sacar la basura
_____ pasar la aspiradora   _____ sacudir los muebles
_____ lavar la ropa   _____ pintar las paredes de un cuarto

Paso 2. ¿Tiene un quehacer favorito entre todos? ¿Hay un quehacer que no le guste a la mayoría de los estudiantes? ¿Hay alguna diferencia entre las preferencias de los hombres y las de las mujeres?

C. Las marcas (*Brand names*). ¿Para qué se usan los siguientes productos? Explíqueselo a su amigo Arturo, que acaba de llegar de la Argentina y no conoce las marcas estadounidenses.

1. Windex
2. Mr. Coffee
3. Endust
4. Glad Bags
5. Joy
6. Cascade
7. Tide
8. Lysol

D. ¿En qué consiste un fin de semana? El concepto del «fin de semana» es diferente para cada individuo según su horario personal… y también según dónde vive y la vida que lleva.

Paso 1. Piense en las siguientes preguntas y organice sus respuestas.

1. Para Ud., ¿cuándo comienza «oficialmente» el fin de semana? (día y hora)
2. ¿Qué hace Ud. para celebrar la llegada del fin de semana?
3. ¿Cuándo termina su fin de semana? (día y hora)
4. ¿Qué hace, generalmente, los días de su fin de semana?

Paso 2. Ahora use las mismas preguntas para entrevistar a un compañero / una compañera para saber algo sobre su fin de semana.

Paso 3. Compare las respuestas de todos los compañeros de clase. ¿Son muy variadas sus respuestas?

Vocabulario: Preparación   Doscientos ochenta y nueve ■ **289**

♻ Reciclado

Recycle commands. Have students give commands to an imaginary maid in the following circumstances. Point out that the formal *Ud.* is normally used with maids.

¿Qué mandatos le va a dar a la criada en las siguientes circunstancias?

1. *Ud. tiene hambre.*
2. *La comida está preparada y Ud. quiere sentarse a la mesa a comer.*
3. *La sala está muy oscura porque entra muy poca luz (light).*
4. *Ud. quiere que la casa esté bien arreglada (in good shape) porque vienen a visitarlo/la esta noche algunos amigos muy importantes de su esposo/a.*

Con. C: Suggestion

Remind students that the ability to express meaning though gestures and circumlocution is important when speaking a second language. Do an item or two yourself to model the task: *Windex es un producto líquido que se usa para limpiar las ventanas; Mr. Coffee es un aparato para hacer café.* Then, to follow up and to practice circumlocution, give pairs of students cards with words they have not studied yet. Emphasize that the point, in this case, is to communicate, not to know the word in Spanish. Some possible words:

pizza cutter	bookmark
shoelace	lighter
body lotion	rubber band
lightbulb	toothpick

Con. D: Suggestion

Ask students how they spend their weekends in the following situations.

¿Cómo pasa Ud. el fin de semana cuando… ?

1. *¿llueve?*
2. *¿no tiene mucho dinero?*
3. *¿tiene ganas de hacer algo «cultural»?*
4. *¿hace calor y sol?*
5. *¿desea divertirse con sus amigos?*
6. *¿quiere hacer un poco de ejercicio?*
7. *¿prefiere estar solo/a?*
8. *¿quiere hacer algo «productivo» en casa?*

CULTURE

Read the following information to the class, and use it as a springboard for discussing domestic services.

Las criadas. *Muchas familias hispánicas de la clase media y alta tienen una criada que vive en casa. La criada, o «la muchacha del servicio», como la llaman en algunas partes, siempre tiene su propia alcoba y también su propio baño. Ella prepara las comidas, cuida a (takes care of) los niños, lava la ropa y ayuda a mantener la casa limpia. Muchas veces la criada parece ser de la misma familia.*

Si Ud. visita una casa hispánica que tiene una criada, acuérdese de (remember) que ella tiene mucho trabajo. No le cause mucho trabajo extra. Si Ud. va a pasar una o varias noches en la casa, pregúntele a la señora de la casa qué gesto de agradecimiento (thanks) debe darle a la criada antes de salir. En algunas casas es costumbre dejarle una propina (tip); en otras, un regalito. A veces no se le deja nada (one doesn't leave her anything), pero siempre se le debe dar las gracias.

NOTA COMUNICATIVA

Suggestions

■ Model and review *Tengo que...*, *Necesito...*, *Debo...*, then introduce the expression *tocarle* to express the concept *to be someone's turn* or *responsibility to do something*. Point out that the structure for *tocar* is similar to the *gustar* construction. Have students read the model sentences.

■ Ask students the following questions.

1. *¿Qué tiene que hacer Ud. esta tarde? ¿mañana? ¿Tiene que hacer alguna tarea? ¿para qué clase?*

2. *¿Cómo debe ser una persona para ser un buen amigo / una buena amiga (un buen padre / una buena madre; un buen estudiante / una buena estudiante)?*

3. *¿Necesita ir al médico pronto? ¿al dentista? ¿a la oficina de matriculación? ¿a la oficina de su consejero/a?*

4. *En su casa / apartamento, ¿a quién le toca barrer esta semana? ¿ir de compras al supermercado? ¿lavar la ropa?*

5. *Por lo general, en una familia típica ¿a quién le toca lavar la ropa, al esposo o a la esposa? ¿hacer la comida? ¿hacer una barbacoa? ¿arreglar el coche? ¿poner y quitar la mesa?*

NOTA COMUNICATIVA

Talking About Obligation

You already know several ways to express the obligation to carry out particular activities.

Tengo que		I have to	
Necesito	} barrer el suelo.	I need to	} sweep the floor.
Debo		I should	

Of the three, **tener que** + *infinitive* expresses the strongest sense of obligation.

The concept *to be someone's turn or responsibility* (to do something) is expressed in Spanish with the verb **tocar** plus an indirect object.

—**¿A quién le toca** lavar los platos esta noche?

Whose turn is it to wash the dishes tonight?

—**A mí me toca** solamente sacar la basura. Creo que **a papá le toca** lavar los platos.

I only have to take out the garbage. I think it's Dad's turn to wash the dishes.

E. ¿A quién le toca?

Paso 1. ¿Mantiene Ud. su casa en orden? ¿Con qué frecuencia hace Ud. los siguientes quehaceres? Complete el siguiente formulario. Si Ud. vive en una residencia estudiantil, imagine que vive en una casa o en un apartamento.

1. _____ lavar las ventanas
2. _____ hacer las camas
3. _____ poner la mesa
4. _____ preparar la comida
5. _____ sacudir los muebles
6. _____ lavar los platos
7. _____ limpiar la casa entera

8. _____ sacar la basura
9. _____ pasar la aspiradora
10. _____ limpiar la estufa
11. _____ planchar la ropa
12. _____ barrer el piso

_____ TOTAL

0 = nunca
1 = a veces
2 = frecuentemente
3 = todos los días

INTERPRETACIONES

0–8 puntos:	¡Cuidado! (*Careful!*) Ud. es descuidado/a (*careless*). ¿Estudia demasiado (*too much*)? Por favor, ¡limpie su casa! ¡No lo deje para mañana!
9–17 puntos:	Ud. puede vivir en su casa, pero no debe invitar a otras personas sin limpiarla bien primero.
18–27 puntos:	Su casa, aunque no está perfecta, está limpia. Es un modelo para todos.
28–36 puntos:	¡Ud. es una maravilla y tiene una casa muy, muy limpia! Pero, ¿pasa Ud. demasiado tiempo limpiando? ¡Váyase al aire libre de vez en cuando!

Paso 2. Ahora hable con un compañero / una compañera sobre sus hábitos domésticos. Básense en el formulario del **Paso 1.** Luego hablen de los quehaceres domésticos para hoy, mañana o esta semana.

MODELO: lavar las ventanas →
E1: ¿Con qué frecuencia lavas las ventanas? (¿A quién le toca lavar las ventanas?)
E2: Nunca las lavo. (Las lavo frecuentemente.)
E1: ¿Y esta semana / hoy / mañana? ¿A quién le toca lavarlas?

Need more practice?

■ Workbook and Laboratory Manual
■ Interactive CD-ROM
■ Online Learning Center (www.mhhe.com/puntos7)

MULTIMEDIA: Internet

Have students search the Internet for more information on the former Aztec civilization as well as information on other early Latin American civilizations. Encourage them to look for images of the cities and for information about rituals and the famous Aztec calendar. You might assign specific topics and have students develop brief oral presentations based on their findings.

GRAMÁTICA

Follow-Up

Ask students the following questions to follow up the *minidiálogo*.

Cuando Ud. era pequeño/a…

1. *¿creía en Santa Claus?*
2. *¿iba a ceremonias religiosas con su familia?*
3. *¿jugaba a algún deporte con sus padres? ¿con sus hermanos?*
4. *¿siempre hacía sus quehaceres?*

Suggestion

Ask students what modern sports are related or similar to this Aztec sport.

¿Con qué deportes modernos se puede relacionar el antiguo deporte azteca?

¿Recuerda Ud.?

In **Capítulos 7** and **8**, you learned the forms and some uses of the preterite. Before you learn the other simple past tense, you might want to review the forms of the preterite in those chapters. The verbs in the following sentences are in the preterite. Can you identify any words in the sentences that emphasize the completed nature of the actions expressed by the verbs?

1. Me levanté a las seis esta mañana.
2. Ayer fui al cine con un amigo.
3. Pinté las paredes de la cocina la semana pasada.

27 Descriptions and Habitual Actions in the Past • Imperfect of Regular and Irregular Verbs

En su clase de antropología, Diego habla de los aztecas

Diego, un estudiante de California que estudia en México, da un informe sobre los aztecas.

«Los aztecas construyeron grandes pirámides para sus dioses. En lo alto de cada pirámide *había* un templo donde *tenían* lugar las ceremonias y *se ofrecían* los sacrificios. Las pirámides *tenían* muchísimos escalones, y *era* necesario subirlos todos para llegar a los templos.

Cerca de muchas pirámides *había* un terreno como el de una cancha de basquetbol. Allí *se celebraban* partidos que *eran* parte de una ceremonia. Los participantes *jugaban* con una pelota de goma dura, que sólo *podían* mover con las caderas y las rodillas… »

Comprensión: ¿Cierto o falso?

1. Los aztecas creían en un solo dios.
2. Las pirámides aztecas tenían una función religiosa.
3. Los aztecas practicaban un deporte similar al basquetbol.

In his anthropology class, Diego talks about the Aztecs *Diego, a student from California who is studying in Mexico, is giving a report on the Aztecs. "The Aztecs constructed large pyramids for their gods. At the top of each pyramid there was a temple where ceremonies took place and sacrifices were offered. The pyramids had many, many steps, and it was necessary to climb them all in order to get to the temples.*

"Close to many pyramids there was an area of land like that of a basketball court. Ceremonial matches were celebrated there. The participants played with a ball made of hard rubber that they could only move with their hips and knees . . . "

CULTURE

The Aztecs dominated central and southern Mexico from the 14th to the 16th centuries through military alliances with other groups. Moctezuma II died in 1520, and the Spanish conquistadors, led by Hernán Cortés, defeated the Aztecs easily in 1521. Their victory was facilitated by the divisions and internal strife among the 38 tributary provinces and the fiercely independent peoples who lived at the fringes of the Aztec Empire.

The name Aztec is derived from a mythical homeland to the north called *Aztlán*; the Aztecs also called themselves the *mexica*. Their language belongs to the Nahuatl branch of the Uto-Aztec language family.

Suggestions

- Point out that the imperfect is the second of two simple past tenses. This section presents and practices only the imperfect. *Gramática 30* in *Capítulo 10* contrasts the two tenses, but some activities before that section will combine the two tenses in controlled situations.
- Use the regular imperfect forms of *trabajar*, *beber*, and *vivir* in conversational exchanges with students.
- Emphasize that *would* can imply both conditional and habitual actions in the past. Only the latter (habit) is expressed by the imperfect.
- Point out that the *yo* form is identical to the *Ud./él/ella* form. Context will often make the meaning clear, but the subject pronouns are more frequently used with the imperfect forms in order to clarify meaning.
- Point out that there are no stem changes in the imperfect.
- Present and model the irregular forms of *ir*, *ser*, and *ver*.

You have already learned to use the *preterite* (**el pretérito**) to express events in the past. The *imperfect* (**el imperfecto**) is the second simple past tense in Spanish. In contrast to the preterite, which is used when you view actions or states of being as finished or completed, the imperfect tense is used when you view past actions or states of being as habitual or as "in progress." The imperfect is also used for describing the past.

The imperfect has several English equivalents. For example, **hablaba,** the first person singular of **hablar,** can mean *I spoke, I was speaking, I used to speak,* or *I would speak* (when *would* implies a repeated action). Most of these English equivalents indicate that the action was still in progress or was habitual, except for *I spoke,* which can correspond to either the preterite or the imperfect.

PAST	----------------- Present -----------------	Future
preterite	present	
imperfect	present progressive	
	formal commands	

Forms of the Imperfect

hablar		comer		vivir	
hablaba	hablábamos	comía	comíamos	vivía	vivíamos
hablabas	hablabais	comías	comíais	vivías	vivíais
hablaba	hablaban	comía	comían	vivía	vivían

- Stem-changing verbs do not show a change in the imperfect. The imperfect of **hay** is **había** (*there was, there were, there used to be*).

Pronunciation Hint: Remember that the pronunciation of a **b** between vowels, such as in the imperfect ending **-aba,** is pronounced as a fricative [ɓ] sound.

In the other imperfect forms, it is important not to pronounce the ending **-ía** as a diphthong, but to pronounce the **i** and the **a** in separate syllables (the accent mark over the **í** helps remind you of this).

Imperfect of stem-changing verbs = no change

almorzar (ue) → almorzaba
perder (ie) → perdía
pedir (i, i) → pedía

Imperfect of **hay** = **había**

- Only three verbs are irregular in the imperfect: **ir, ser,** and **ver.**

ir		ser		ver	
iba	íbamos	era	éramos	veía	veíamos
ibas	ibais	eras	erais	veías	veíais
iba	iban	era	eran	veía	veían

 Heritage Speakers

- Algunos hispanohablantes usan la forma plural de *haber* (*habían*) en el habla popular cuando el sustantivo que la sigue es plural. Por ejemplo, es común oír *Habían muchas personas* en vez de *Había muchas personas.* Sin embargo, la forma singular *había* es la forma aceptada para expresar *there was/were.*
- En algunos dialectos rurales del español, hay hispanohablantes que dicen *traíba* o *comiba* en vez de *traía* o *comía,* que son las formas aceptadas en el uso formal.

Uses of the Imperfect

Note the following uses of the imperfect. If you have a clear sense of when and where the imperfect is used, understanding where the preterite is used will be easier. When talking about the past, the preterite *is* used when the imperfect *isn't*. That is an oversimplification of the uses of these two past tenses, but at the same time it is a general rule of thumb that will help you out at first.

The imperfect has the following uses.

- To describe *repeated habitual actions* in the past

  Siempre nos quedábamos en aquel hotel.
  We always stayed (used to stay, would stay) at that hotel.

  Todos los veranos **iban** a la costa.
  Every summer they went (used to go, would go) to the coast.

- To describe an *action that was in progress* (*when something else happened*)

  Pedía la cena.
  She was ordering dinner.

- To describe two *simultaneous past actions in progress*, with **mientras**

  Tú **leías mientras** Juan **escribía** la carta.
  You were reading while Juan was writing the letter.

- To describe ongoing *physical, mental,* or *emotional states* in the past

  Estaban muy distraídos.
  They were very distracted.

  La **quería** muchísimo.
  He loved her a lot.

- To tell *time* in the past and to *express age* with **tener**

  Era la una./**Eran** las dos.
  It was one o'clock./It was two o'clock.

  Tenía 18 años.
  She was 18 years old.

  Just as in the present, the singular form of the verb **ser** is used with one o'clock, the plural form from two o'clock on.

- To form a *past progressive:* imperfect of **estar** + *present participle**

  Estábamos cenando a las diez.
  We were having dinner at ten.

  ¿No **estabas estudiando**?
  Weren't you studying?

  Note that the simple imperfect—**cenábamos, estudiabas**—could also be used in the example sentences to express the ongoing actions. The use of the progressive emphasizes that the action was actually in progress.

---

*A progressive tense can also be formed with the preterite of **estar**: **Estuvieron cenando hasta las doce**. The use of the progressive with the preterite of **estar**, however, is relatively infrequent, and it will not be practiced in Puntos de partida.

Uses of the Imperfect

Suggestions

- Emphasize that the preterite and imperfect are both equally "past" tenses. Their use depends on which aspect of a past action the user focuses on (completion or development of an action).
- Have students give the Spanish for some expressions: *I always used to stay . . . Every summer we used to go . . .* , and so on. Vary the subjects in your sentences.
- Emphasize the English "cues" associated with the imperfect: used to, would (habitual action), every day (month, and so on), was/were _____-ing.
- Point out: *mientras* and *mientras que* indicate simultaneous actions.
- Point out that in the imperfect, unlike in the preterite, *saber, conocer, querer,* and *poder* retain the base meaning of their infinitives. See *Gramática 30* for more details.
- Contrast an action in progress and the past progressive. Reenter the contrast between the simple present tense and the present progressive.
- Point out that the imperfect is used to project into the future from a specific point in the past. Contrast: *Va a ser una noche de lluvia. Sabíamos que iba a ser una noche de lluvia.*

Preliminary Exercises

- Use the following rapid response drill to practice the forms.

  Dé el imperfecto:
  yo: *cerrar, escuchar, mirar, querer, asistir, recibir*
  tú: *pensar, visitar, entrar, tener, vivir, pedir*
  Ud./él/ella: *preguntar, comprar, enseñar, volver, abrir, servir*
  nosotros: *jugar, bailar, tomar, aprender, preferir, venir*
  Uds./ellos/ellas: *trabajar, ganar, creer, divertir, ser* ERAN

- Use this chain drill to practice the imperfect forms.

En la escuela primaria...

1. *Tina estudiaba y jugaba mucho.* (*yo, Uds., tú, nosotros, Julio, vosotros*)
2. *Todos bebían leche y dormían la siesta.* (*Tina, tú, nosotros, Alicia, yo, vosotros*)

¿Qué hacían Uds. anoche a las doce?

1. *Ceci veía un programa interesante.* (*tú, yo, Uds., Pablo, ellas, vosotros*)
2. *Mis padres iban a acostarse.* (*tú, yo, nosotros, Ana, ellas, vosotros*)
3. *Yo (no) estaba _____.* (*leer, mirar la televisión, escribir una carta, dormir, llorar, comer, ¿... ?*)

Prác. A: Extension

Have students add two to three original sentences about their childhood.

Prác. A: Follow-Up

Poll students to see which descriptions were true for them.

Prác. B: Suggestion

Ask students:

¿Qué cosas no hacía Ud. que Tina sí hacía? ¿Qué cosas no hacía Tina que Ud. sí hacía?

Prác. B: Extension

Have students describe Tina and her sister.

Describa a Tina y a su hermanita Mariana.

Prác. B: Follow-Up

Ask students the following questions after completing the activity.

En la escuela primaria:

1. *¿Cantaba/Jugaba Ud. mucho en la primaria?*
2. *De niño/a, ¿bebía mucha leche/Coca-Cola? ¿Dormía la siesta? ¿De qué hora a qué hora?*
3. *¿Veía Ud. programas interesantes en la televisión cuando era niño/a? ¿Cuáles le gustaban más?*
4. *¿A qué hora se acostaba Ud. cuando tenía 3 (7, 12) años? ¿Le gustaba acostarse tan temprano/tarde? ¿Leía Ud. a veces en la cama?*

AUTOPRUEBA

Give the correct imperfect ending for each verb.

1. yo habl_____
2. Uds. er_____
3. nosotros com_____
4. Pedro ib_____
5. tú ten_____

Answers: 1. hablaba 2. eran 3. comíamos 4. iba 5. tenías

■ ■ ■ Práctica

A. ¡Anticipemos! Mi niñez (*childhood*)

Paso 1. Indique si las siguientes oraciones eran ciertas o falsas para Ud. cuando tenía 10 años.

	C	F
1. Estaba en cuarto (*fourth*) grado.	☐	☐
2. Me acostaba a las nueve todas las noches.	☐	☐
3. Los sábados me levantaba temprano para mirar los dibujos animados.	☐	☐
4. Mis padres me pagaban por los quehaceres que hacía: cortar el césped (*cutting the grass*), lavar los platos…	☐	☐
5. Me gustaba acompañar a mi madre/padre al supermercado	☐	☐
6. Le pegaba (*I hit*) a mi hermano/a con frecuencia.	☐	☐
7. Tocaba un instrumento musical en la orquesta de la escuela.	☐	☐
8. Mis héroes eran personajes de los dibujos animados (*cartoon characters*) como Superman y Kim Possible.	☐	☐

Paso 2. Ahora corrija las oraciones que son falsas para Ud.

MODELO: 2. Es falso. Me acostaba a las diez, no a las nueve.

B. Cuando Tina era niña… Describa la vida de Tina cuando era muy joven, haciendo oraciones según las indicaciones.

La vida de Tina era muy diferente cuando tenía 6 años.

1. todos los días / asistir / a / escuela primaria
2. por / mañana / aprender / a / leer / y / escribir / en / pizarra
3. a / diez / beber / leche / y / dormir / un poco
4. ir / a / casa / para / almorzar / y / regresar / a / escuela
5. estudiar / geografía / y / hacer / dibujos
6. jugar / con / compañeros / en / patio / de / escuela
7. camino de (*on the way*) casa / comprar / dulces / y / se los / comer
8. frecuentemente / pasar / por / casa / de / abuelos
9. cenar / con / padres / y / ayudar / a / lavar / platos
10. mirar / tele / un rato / y / acostarse / a / ocho

C. El trabajo de niñera (*baby-sitter*)

Paso 1. El trabajo de niñera puede ser muy pesado (*difficult*), pero cuando los niños son traviesos (*mischievous*), también puede ser peligroso (*dangerous*). ¿Qué estaba pasando cuando la niñera perdió por fin la paciencia? Describa todas las acciones que pueda, usando **estaba(n)** + **-ndo.**

> MODELO: Cuando la niñera perdió la paciencia... →
> el bebé estaba llorando.

Cuando la niñera perdió la paciencia...

Paso 2. De joven (*As a youth*), ¿trabajaba Ud. de niñero/a? ¿Tuvo alguna vez una mala experiencia? Complete la siguiente oración, si puede, usando un verbo en el pretérito.

> MODELO: Una vez, cuando yo estaba
> (leyendo, mirando la tele, hablando con un amigo / una amiga...), el niño / la niña...

■■■ Conversación

A. Entrevista. ¡Qué cambio! Hágale las siguientes preguntas a un compañero / una compañera de clase. Él/Ella va a pensar en las costumbres que tenía a los 14 años, es decir, cuando estaba en el noveno (*ninth*) o décimo (*tenth*) grado.

1. ¿Qué te gustaba comer? ¿Y ahora?
2. ¿Qué programa de televisión no te perdías nunca? ¿Y ahora?
3. ¿Qué te gustaba leer? ¿Y ahora?
4. ¿Qué hacías los sábados por la noche? ¿Y ahora?
5. ¿Qué deportes te gustaba practicar? ¿Y ahora?
6. ¿Con quién discutías mucho? ¿Y ahora?
7. ¿A quién te gustaba molestar (*to annoy*)? ¿Y ahora?

Although **sonar is a stem-changing verb (**o → ue**), remember that the stem of present participles does not change with **-ar** verbs (**sonando**).*

Gramática   Doscientos noventa y cinco ■ **295**

Palabras útiles

el timbre	doorbell
discutir	to argue
ladrar	to bark
pelear	to fight
sonar (ue)*	to ring; to sound

Need more practice?
- Workbook and Laboratory Manual
- Interactive CD-ROM
- Online Learning Center (www.mhhe.com/puntos7)

Resources: Transparency 69

Prác. C: Suggestions

Paso 1. Give students the following dictation but have them write the verbs in the imperfect tense.

1. *Olga va a la universidad todos los días. Siempre asiste a sus clases. Hace muchas preguntas porque es inteligente. Sus profesores están contentos con ella.*
2. *Yo trabajo en una oficina. Mi jefe (boss), que se llama Ángel, nos hace trabajar mucho. Siempre almorzamos juntos (together) en el mismo restaurante y a veces jugamos al basquetbol por la tarde.*
3. *Vivo en Sacramento. Siempre llueve mucho en invierno y en primavera, pero me gusta mucho el clima. Además (Besides), las montañas están cerca y puedo esquiar.*

Paso 2. Assign this *Paso* as homework.

Prác. C: Follow-Up

Paso 2. Using verbs in the imperfect, personalize the sequences given.

1. *El semestre/trimestre pasado, ¿venía Ud. a la universidad todos los días? ¿Asistía a todas sus clases? ¿Hacía muchas preguntas?*
2. *En la secundaria, ¿trabajaba Ud. después de las clases? ¿los fines de semana? ¿durante las vacaciones? ¿Dónde? ¿Cómo se llamaba su jefe? ¿Cuántas horas trabajaba por semana?*
3. *De niño/a, ¿dónde vivía Ud.? ¿Llovía mucho allí? ¿Le gustaba el clima?*

 Bright Idea

Con. A: Suggestion

Have students bring in photos of themselves to talk about how they were (*¿cómo eran?*) as well as what they liked to do (*¿qué les gustaba hacer?*). Then have them contrast what they are like and what they like to do now with how they were and what they liked then.

Con. A: Follow-Up

Complete the sentences to model an answer, then elicit sentences from students with a follow-up question.

1. *En otra época siempre me gustaba _____. No me gustaba nada _____. (En otra época siempre me gustaba comer fuera. No me gustaba nada cocinar. ¿A Ud. le gusta cocinar ahora? ¿Le gustaba en otra época?)*
2. *Siempre veía (programa de televisión), pero ahora prefiero ver _____.*
3. *De niño/a, siempre leía _____, pero ahora leo _____.*

Gramática ■ **295**

Con. B: Variation

Have students take turns giving statements about current times (habits, preferences, and so on). The class responds by contrasting that statement with a statement about the past (how things used to be). Suggest the following topics:

los precios
las computadoras
la sencillez/complejidad de la vida
la seguridad personal
el impacto del gobierno en la vida diaria
el uso de las drogas y el alcohol
la música

Con. B: Suggestion

Have students write the following information in complete sentences. Help them with the names of professions and animals.

1. *De joven yo quería ser _____ (profesión) porque…*
2. *Cuando yo estaba en la escuela primaria, era _____ (adjetivo). Siempre…*
3. *En la escuela secundaria, el animal que me simbolizaba mejor era _____, porque…*

Collect the completed sentences, then read them aloud and have the class guess the identity of the people who wrote them.

☼ Heritage Speakers

Pídales a los hispanohablantes que mencionen o describan la música española y latinoamericana que conozcan, como el flamenco, el tango, la cumbia, la salsa o la música mariachi. Puede pedirles que traigan ejemplos de música grabada a la clase.

B. Los tiempos cambian. Muchas cosas y costumbres actuales (*present-day*) son diferentes de las del pasado (*past*). Las siguientes oraciones describen algunos aspectos de la vida de hoy. Con un compañero / una compañera, háganse turnos para describir cómo son las cosas ahora y cómo eran las cosas antes, en otra época.

MODELO: E1: Ahora casi todos los bebés nacen (*are born*) en el hospital.
E2: Antes casi todos los bebés nacían en casa.

Ayer   Hoy

1. Ahora muchas personas viven en casas muy grandes con jardines pequeños.
2. Se come con frecuencia en los restaurantes.
3. Muchísimas mujeres trabajan fuera de casa.
4. Muchas personas van al cine y miran la televisión.
5. Ahora las mujeres —no sólo los hombres— llevan pantalones.
6. Ahora hay enfermeros (*male nurses*) y maestros (*male teachers*) —no sólo enfermeras y maestras.
7. Ahora tenemos coches pequeños que gastan (*use*) poca gasolina.
8. Ahora usamos más máquinas y por eso hacemos menos trabajo físico.
9. Ahora las familias son más pequeñas.
10. Muchas parejas viven juntas sin casarse (*getting married*).

EN LOS ESTADOS UNIDOS Y EL CANADÁ

La música hispánica en el Canadá

Si Ud. vive en el Canadá y tiene un poco de tiempo libre, se puede aprovechar de[a] los ritmos de varios **músicos hispánicos de calidad.** Uno de estos es **Jorge (Papo) Ross.** Ross nació en la República Dominicana y allí fundó[b] su primer **conjunto** a los 18 años. En 1990 se mudó al Canadá y formó otros grupos, entre ellos la **Orquesta Pambiche,** que hoy es uno de los **conjuntos latino-canadienses** más famosos. Papo Ross y Pambiche ganaron un Juno, el prestigioso premio[c] nacional para músicos en el Canadá. A menudo dan **espectáculos explosivos** a través del[d] país, inclusive en el famoso festival de jazz de Montreal.

Para gozar aún más de[e] la música hispánica del

▲ *Papo Ross y miembros de la Orquesta Pambiche*

Canadá, Ud. puede ir a la capital, Ottawa, donde la argentina **Alicia Borisonik** y su **conjunto Folklore Venezuela** tocan **música estilo tango-jazz.** Antes de mudarse al Canadá en 1994, Borisonik experimentó mucho éxito[f] en la esfera músical de otra capital, Buenos Aires, y su nuevo grupo tiene cada vez más[g] fama en su nueva patria. Además de presentar **conciertos** en la Galería Nacional y en el Museo Nacional de la Civilización, y de participar en muchos **festivales de verano,** Borisonik ayudó a formar un **conjunto de música latina para niños.**

[a]*se… you can enjoy* [b]*he started* [c]*prize* [d]*a… across the* [e]*gozar… enjoy even more* [f]*experimentó… had great success* [g]*cada… increasing*

EN LOS ESTADOS UNIDOS Y EL CANADÁ

Suggestions

■ Ask students what other Hispanic musicians they are familiar with, both traditional and contemporary. Ask them if they recognize the following names, and encourage them to talk about the kind of music these people perform: Celia Cruz, Ibrahim Ferrer (Buena Vista Social Club), Gloria Estefan, Carlos Santana, Ricky Martin, Luis Miguel, Jennifer López, Enrique Iglesias, and so on.

■ Have students search for more information about Jorge (Papo) Ross, the Orquesta Pambiche, and Alicia Borisnik on the Internet. Students may be able to find MP3 files of samples of their music. Remind students not to download the music unless it is permitted by the site or unless they pay for it.

Before beginning **Gramática 28,** review comparisons, which were introduced in **Capítulo 5.**
How would you say the following in Spanish?

1. I work as much as you do.
2. I work more/less than you do.
3. Bill Gates has more money than I have.
4. My housemate has fewer things than I do.
5. I have as many friends as you do.
6. My computer is worse/better than this one.

28 Expressing Extremes • Superlatives

¡El número uno!

▲ *Jennifer López*

▲ *Enrique Iglesias*

▲ *Ricky Martin*

¿Está Ud. de acuerdo con las opiniones expresadas en estas oraciones?

1. Jennifer López es la mujer más bella (*beautiful*) del mundo.
2. Enrique Iglesias es el mejor cantante (*singer*) de su familia.
3. Ricky Martin es el puertorriqueño más conocido (*well-known*) de hoy.

Ahora le toca a Ud. formular su propia (*own*) opinión.

1. El/La cantante hispánico/a más popular del momento es _____.
2. La mejor actriz (*actress*) del momento es _____.
3. La música popular más interesante es _____.

The *superlative* (**el superlativo**) is formed in English by adding *-est* to adjectives or by using expressions such as *the most* and *the least* with the adjective. In Spanish, this concept is expressed in the same way as the comparative but is always accompanied by the definite article. In this construction **mejor** and **peor** tend to precede the noun; other adjectives follow. *In* or *at* is expressed with **de**.

 The superlative forms **-ísimo/a/os/as** cannot be used with this type of superlative construction.

el/la/los/las + *noun* + **más/menos** + *adjective* + **de**

El basquetbol es **el deporte más interesante del** mundo.
Basketball is the most interesting sport in the world.

el/la/los/las + **mejor(es)/peor(es)** + *noun* + **de**

Son **los mejores** refrigeradores **de** aquella tienda.
They are the best refrigerators at that store.

Follow-Up
After reviewing *¡El número uno!,* have students give superlatives in other categories: *la comida, los quehaceres domésticos, las marcas* (brand names) *de ropa, las tiendas.*

Suggestions

■ Review the comparative forms and structures before presenting the superlatives.

¿Cómo se dice?

1. taller than John
2. bigger than an apple
3. better than Susie
4. easier than Spanish
5. older than my grandmother

■ Emphasize the importance of the definite article. Remind students to use *de*, not *en* (for the English *in*).

■ Ask students the following questions.

¿Es Jennifer López más bonita que Britney Spears?
¿Es Enrique Iglesias más guapo que Ricky Martin?
¿Es Ricky Martin más joven que Jennifer López?

CULTURE

Ask students what Hispanic artists have contributed to the rise in popularity of a *latino* sound in pop music. Have them identify the artists pictured here: Enrique Iglesias (one of Julio Iglesias' sons), Jennifer López, Ricky Martin. Which artist do they prefer and why? The following Hispanic artists have also had a major impact on music in the English-speaking countries: Pablo Casals, Gloria Estefan, Celia Cruz, Julio Iglesias, Tito Puente, Carlos Santana, and Jon Secada.

MULTIMEDIA: Internet

Have students search the Internet for information on Hispanic musicians. Encourage them to look for music clips, as well as official websites for the artist or for his or her fan club.

Prác. A: Preliminary Exercise

Complete the following ideas with relevant information, then have students respond to each statement with *cierto* or *falso*.

1. _____ es la persona más alta/baja/joven de la clase.
2. Los perros/gatos son los animales más fieles/cariñosos.
3. El _____ es el mejor/peor coche del mundo.
4. _____ es el mejor periódico de esta ciudad.
5. Los exámenes de _____ son los más difíciles/fáciles (de todos).
6. _____ es el actor más guapo (de todos).
7. _____ es la actriz más guapa (de todas).
8. Uds. son los estudiantes más trabajadores/amables/perezosos/simpáticos de la universidad.

Bright Idea

Prác. A: Suggestion

Have students guess the meaning of *poliomielitis*. Can they also guess the meaning of the following words?

hepatitis	*meningitis*
bronquitis	*laringitis*
amigdalitis (tonsillitis)	

What about the word *mamitis* (missing one's mother)?

Prác. B: Extension

9. El Presidente Reagan fue un presidente viejo.
10. El Presidente Kennedy fue un presidente joven.
11. Rip Van Winkle fue un hombre perezoso.
12. El chihuahua es un perro pequeño.

Prác. B: Suggestion

Have students imagine that Rodolfo, a big exaggerator, visits their house during the Christmas holidays. Have them invent things he might say:

¿Qué va a decir Rodolfo sobre los siguientes aspectos del día de Navidad en su casa?

1. ¿su árbol de Navidad? (grande, elegante)
2. ¿los platos? (ricos, muchos)
3. ¿sus hermanitos? (felices)
4. ¿los regalos? (caros, bonitos, muchos)

AUTOPRUEBA

Unscramble the words to express a superlative idea.

1. Es... ciudad más el grande la parque de
2. Son... clase los difíciles de niños la más
3. Visité... del los mundo museos mejores
4. Vi... peor año película la del

Answers: *1. Es el parque más grande de la ciudad. 2. Son los niños más difíciles de la clase. 3. Visité los mejores museos del mundo. 4. Vi la peor película del año.*

■■■ Práctica

A. ¿Está Ud. de acuerdo o no?

Paso 1. Indique si Ud. está de acuerdo o no con las siguientes oraciones.

	SÍ	NO
1. El descubrimiento (*discovery*) científico más importante del siglo XX fue la vacuna (*vaccine*) contra la poliomielitis.	☐	☐
2. La persona más influyente (*influential*) del mundo es el presidente de los Estados Unidos.	☐	☐
3. El problema más serio del mundo es la deforestación de la región del Amazonas.	☐	☐
4. El día festivo más divertido del año es la Noche Vieja.	☐	☐
5. La mejor novela del mundo es *Don Quijote de la Mancha*.	☐	☐
6. El animal menos inteligente de todos es el avestruz (*ostrich*).	☐	☐
7. El peor mes del año es enero.	☐	☐
8. La ciudad más contaminada de los Estados Unidos es Los Ángeles.	☐	☐

Paso 2. Para cada oración que no refleja su opinión, invente otra oración.

MODELO: 4. No estoy de acuerdo. Creo que el día festivo más divertido del año es el Cuatro de Julio.

B. Superlativos.
Expand the information in these sentences based on the model. Then, if you can, restate each sentence with true information at the beginning.

MODELO: Es una estudiante muy *trabajadora*. (la clase) →
Es *la* estudiante *más trabajadora de la clase.* →
Carlota es la estudiante más trabajadora de la clase.

1. Es un día festivo muy *divertido*. (el año)
2. Es una clase muy *interesante*. (todas mis clases)
3. Es una persona muy *inteligente*. (todos mis amigos)
4. Es una ciudad muy *grande*. (los Estados Unidos / el Canadá)
5. Es un estado muy *pequeño*/una provincia muy *pequeña*. (los Estados Unidos / el Canadá)
6. Es un metro muy *rápido*. (el mundo)
7. Es una residencia muy *ruidosa* (*noisy*). (la universidad)
8. Es una montaña muy *alta*. (el mundo)

298 ■ Doscientos noventa y ocho

Need more practice?

- Workbook and Laboratory Manual
- Interactive CD-ROM
- Online Learning Center (www.mhhe.com/puntos7)

Capítulo 9: El tiempo libre

CULTURE

El Ingenioso Hidalgo Don Quijote de la Mancha (*The Ingenious Knight Don Quijote of la Mancha*), better known simply as *Don Quijote*, was written by Miguel de Cervantes Saavedra and is by far the best-known Spanish literary piece of all time. Some critics consider it the first modern novel. It has been translated, fully or in parts, into more than 60 languages. This novel, written and published in two parts (1605 and 1615), was originally conceived as a comic satire against the chivalric romances that were in literary vogue in the 17th century. It is the story of the adventures of Alonso Quijano, who names himself Don Quijote de la Mancha and goes forth to right wrongs and rescue damsels in distress on his nag, Rocinante, and with his shrewd squire, Sancho Panza. The novel presents the conflict between the ideal and the real. Students can read an excerpt of this novel in the *Un paso más* section of *Capítulo 18*.

■ ■ ■ Conversación

Entrevista. With another student, ask and answer questions based on the following phrases. Then report your opinions to the class. Report any disagreements as well.

> MODELO: E1: Shakira es la mujer más guapa del mundo.
> E2: Estoy de acuerdo / No estoy de acuerdo. Para mí Salma Hayek es la más guapa.

1. la persona más guapa del mundo
2. la noticia más seria de esta semana
3. un libro interesantísimo y otro pesadísimo (*very boring*)
4. el mejor restaurante de la ciudad y el peor
5. el cuarto más importante de la casa y el menos importante
6. un plato riquísimo y otro malísimo
7. un programa de televisión interesantísimo y otro pesadísimo
8. un lugar tranquilísimo, otro animadísimo y otro peligrosísimo
9. la canción (*song*) más bonita del año y la más fea
10. la mejor película del año y la peor

---

29 Getting Information • Summary of Interrogative Words

Este es un anuncio de un restaurante de Connecticut.

1. ¿*Cómo* se llama el restaurante?
2. ¿*En qué* ciudad de Connecticut está?
3. ¿*Cuáles* son las especialidades de este restaurante?

¿*Cuántas* preguntas más puede Ud. hacer sobre este restaurante, basándose en el anuncio?

El Pavo real
RESTAURANTE • CLUB DE BAILE

32 Garvey St., New Haven, CT

El lugar más amplio y más lujoso de CT.

**Comida Colombiana
con Especialidad en Mariscos**

Venga y deléitese con nuestros sabrosos platos
ABIERTO TODOS LOS DÍAS DESDE LAS 11:30 A.M. - 2:00 A.M

VIERNES, 6 DE OCTUBRE

• PRESENTANDO LA SENSACIÓN DEL MERENGUE • CANTANDO
ORQUESTA MALA FE TODOS SUS ÉXITOS

¿Cómo?	How?	¿Dónde?	Where?
¿Cuándo?	When?	¿De dónde?	From where?
¿A qué hora?	At what time?	¿Adónde?	Where (to)?
¿Qué?	What? Which?	¿Cuánto/a?	How much?
¿Cuál(es)?	What? Which one(s)?	¿Cuántos/as?	How many?
¿Por qué?	Why?	¿Quién(es)?	Who?
		¿De quién(es)?	Whose?

Refrán

> «Quien de refranes no sabe, ¿qué es lo que sabe?»

Read this *refrán* to the students. Have them identify the question word in the sentence. Point out that *quien* in this case is not a question word but a relative pronoun. *Qué* is the only question word. Have students give their understanding of the meaning of this saying.

Con: Note

This activity integrates the superlative and absolute superlative forms.

Con: Follow-Up

Have students work in small groups to describe the following, using superlatives.

1. Alaska
2. Rhode Island
3. John F. Kennedy
4. *el monte Everest*
5. *el río Amazonas*
6. *esta universidad*
7. *la comida de la residencia / cafetería estudiantil*

Suggest additional items about people, places, and things on your campus that students like to discuss.

Gramática 29
Summary of Interrogative Words

Follow-Up

After reviewing the clippings, have students work in pairs to make plans to go to one of the events listed. Only one student is allowed to look at the printed information. The other student should ask questions to get information.

♻ **Reciclado**

Remind students that *ser en + place* is used to express *to take place at (place)*. Model the expression in some communicative exchanges with a student: *¿Dónde es su primera clase los lunes? ¿Dónde es el partido de fútbol?*

Notes

■ Students have actively used all of the interrogatives in this section. Treat this section as a summary, using it to emphasize variations of the interrogative forms, for example, *¿dónde?* vs. *¿de dónde?* vs. *¿adónde?*

■ In Latin America, *¿cuál?* and *¿cuáles?* may be used as adjectives, for example, *¿Cuál libro quieres?* In Spain, they are used only as pronouns.

Suggestions

- Point out the plural forms of *¿cuál?* and *¿quién?* Point out the difference in meaning in English between *¿cuánto/a?* and *¿cuántos/as?*
- Point out that *¿Cómo?* is used to request repetition or clarification in communicative exchanges.

Bright Idea

Suggestion

Point out the difference between *¿qué?* and *¿cuál?* by using contrastive sentences.

¿Qué es su hermano? (Es profesor.)
¿Cuál es su hermano? (Es el muchacho que lleva la camisa roja.)

Preliminary Exercises

- Ask students whether the following questions would require *¿qué?* or *¿cuál?* in Spanish.

  1. What is an aardvark?
  2. What is the capital of Bolivia?
  3. What are the colors of the U.S. flag?
  4. What's that?

- Ask students the following questions.

  1. *¿Cuál es la capital de _____?*
  2. *¿Cuál es su teléfono?*
  3. *¿Qué es esto?* (indicate an object or use a visual)
  4. *¿Qué es un elefante? ¿un restaurante? ¿una discoteca? ¿Qué son las sandalias?*

You have been using interrogative words to ask questions and get information since the beginning of *Puntos de partida*. The chart on page 299 shows all of the interrogatives you have learned so far. Be sure that you know what they mean and how they are used. If you are not certain, the index and end-of-book vocabularies will help you find where they are first introduced. Only the specific uses of **¿qué?** and **¿cuál?** represent new information.

Using *¿qué?* and *¿cuál?*

■ **¿Qué?** asks for a definition or an explanation.	**¿Qué** es esto? *What is this?* **¿Qué** quieres? *What do you want?* **¿Qué** tocas? *What (instrument) do you play?*
■ **¿Qué?** can be directly followed by a noun.	**¿Qué traje** necesitas? *What (Which) suit do you need?* **¿Qué playa** te gusta más? *What (Which) beach do you like most?* **¿Qué instrumento** musical tocas? *What (Which) musical instrument do you play?*
■ **¿Cuál(es)?** expresses *what?* or *which?* in all other cases. The **¿cuál(es)?** + *noun* structure is not used by most speakers of Spanish: **¿Cuál de los dos libros quieres?** (Which of the two books do you want?) BUT **¿Qué libro quieres?** (Which [What] book do you want?)	**¿Cuál** es la clase más grande? *What (Which) is the biggest class?* **¿Cuáles** son tus actrices favoritas? *What (Which) are your favorite actresses?* **¿Cuál** es la capital del Uruguay? *What is the capital of Uruguay?* **¿Cuál** es tu teléfono? *What is your phone number?*

AUTOPRUEBA

Match each word to the kind of information it asks for.

1. ¿Cuándo?   a. un lugar
2. ¿Dónde?   b. un número o una cantidad
3. ¿Qué?   c. una definición
4. ¿Cuánto?   d. la hora

Answers: 1. d 2. a 3. c 4. b

 ### Heritage Speakers

En algunos dialectos del español de Latinoamérica, se usa *¿cuál(es)?* antes de un sustantivo cuando la selección de objetos es limitada. Por ejemplo, *¿Cuál chaqueta te gusta más?* en vez de *¿Qué chaqueta te gusta más?*

■■■ Práctica

A. **¿Qué o cuál(es)?**

1. ¿_____ es esto? —Un lavaplatos.
2. ¿_____ son los Juegos Olímpicos? —Son un conjunto (*group*) de competiciones deportivas.
3. ¿_____ es el quehacer que más te gusta? —Lavar los platos.
4. ¿_____ bicicleta vas a usar? —La de mi hermana.
5. ¿_____ son los cines más modernos? —Los del centro.
6. ¿_____ vídeo debo sacar? —El nuevo de Salma Hayek.
7. ¿_____ es una cafetera? —Es un aparato que se usa para preparar el café.
8. ¿_____ es tu padre? —En la foto, es el hombre a la izquierda del coche.

B. **Entrevista. Datos** (*Information*) **personales.** Forme preguntas para averiguar datos (*find out facts*) de un compañero / una compañera de clase. Se puede usar más de una palabra interrogativa para conseguir la información. (Debe usar las formas de **tú**.)

MODELO: su dirección (*address*) → ¿Cuál es tu dirección? (¿Dónde vives?)

1. su teléfono
2. su dirección
3. su cumpleaños
4. la ciudad en que nació (*he/she was born*)
5. su número de seguro (*security*) social
6. la persona en que más confía (*he/she trusts*)
7. su tienda favorita
8. la fecha de su próximo examen

Need more practice?

- Workbook and Laboratory Manual
- Interactive CD-ROM
- Online Learning Center (www.mhhe.com/puntos7)

■■■ Conversación

Una encuesta

Paso 1. Entrevista. ¿Cuáles son las preferencias de su compañero/a con respecto a las siguientes categorías? Hágale preguntas, empezándolas con **¿Qué... ?**

MODELO: estaciones del año →
¿Qué estación del año prefieres (entre todas)?

1. tipos de música
2. pasatiempos o deportes
3. programas de televisión
4. materias este semestre/trimestre
5. colores
6. tipos de comida

Paso 2. Ahora use las mismas frases para hacerle preguntas a su compañero/a sobre lo que prefería de niño/a. También trate de (*try to*) sacarle algunos detalles a su compañero/a.

MODELO: estaciones del año →
E1: ¿Qué estación preferías (entre todas) de niño/a?
E2: Prefería el invierno.
E1: ¿Por qué?
E2: Porque me gustaba jugar en la nieve.

Prác. B: Suggestion

Think of or have a student think of a famous person. Have the class try to identify the person by asking questions using interrogative words. Students may not repeat interrogative words during a single round of guessing.

Prác. B: Follow-Up

Ask students the following questions to summarize findings.

1. *¿Nacieron varias personas de la clase en la misma ciudad?*
2. *¿En quiénes confían más Uds.?*
3. *¿Cuál es la tienda más popular entre los estudiantes de esta clase?*
4. *¿Quién tiene un examen pronto (soon)?*

Prác. B: Variation

Have students work in pairs to interview each other about how they generally spend their free time. Give them the following steps to prepare and conduct their interviews.

Paso 1. *En preparación para la entrevista, haga una lista de ocho a diez preguntas básicas que va a hacerle a su compañero/a. Estas preguntas van a servir de base para otras preguntas, según las respuestas de su compañero/a.*

Paso 2. *Haga la entrevista. Apunte (Jot down) las respuestas de su compañero/a. Hágale todas las preguntas que pueda.*

Paso 3. *Ponga en orden los apuntes de la entrevista y comparta con la clase algunos de los datos que aprendió en su entrevista.*

MULTIMEDIA: Internet

Have students research names of famous soccer players and/or teams, such as *Real Madrid*, *Barcelona*, *Río Plata de Buenos Aires*, and so on.

☼ **Heritage Speakers**

Pregúnteles a los estudiantes hispanohablantes si son aficionados al fútbol y cuáles son sus equipos favoritos.

UN POCO DE TODO

A: Note

This activity prepares students to use the preterite and imperfect to narrate events in the past.

Bright Idea

A: Suggestion

Review the verb endings for the preterite. Have students provide conjugations chorally of the following verbs.

bañarse
acostarse
salir
comer
dormir

Reciclado

Review verbs with spelling changes in the preterite. Have students indicate where these changes occur in the verb paradigm (*yo* forms).

INFINITIVE	CHANGE	FORMS
-car	c → qu	yo busqué, toqué
-gar	g → gu	yo llegué, pagué
-zar	z → c	yo almorcé, empecé

UN POCO DE TODO

A. El día que Ricardo tuvo ayer

Paso 1. The following drawings depict what Ricardo did yesterday. Match the phrases with individual drawings in the sequence. *Note:* Some of the phrases are not depicted in the drawings but are related to the time of day or activity in the drawing. Then narrate what Ricardo did, using verbs in the preterite. **¡OJO!** Some drawings can be associated with more than one phrase.

a. _____ llegar tarde a su primera clase
b. _____ almorzar en la cafetería con algunos amigos
c. _____ quedarse en cama mucho tiempo
d. _____ mirar la televisión un rato
e. _____ regresar a casa
f. _____ ir al gimnasio
g. _____ ducharse y vestirse rápidamente
h. _____ acostarse
i. _____ estudiar un poco
j. _____ jugar un partido de basquetbol
k. _____ despertarse temprano
l. _____ preparar la cena
m. _____ sonar el teléfono

> **Frases útiles**
>
> primero...
> luego... y...
> después... y...
> finalmente (por fin)...

Paso 2. Ahora haga oraciones para dar más detalles sobre el día que Ricardo tuvo ayer. Use el imperfecto de los verbos. Los números concuerdan con (*correspond to*) los números de los dibujos.

1. ser / seis y media / mañana
2. Ricardo / tener prisa
3. estudiantes / escuchar / profesora
4. Ricardo / tener / mucho / hambre
5. haber / mucho / personas / gimnasio
6. ser / temprano / todavía
7. no / querer / hablar / teléfono
8. Ricardo / pensar / en / examen / mañana

Resources: Transparency 70

B. Quehaceres de adulto, diversiones de niño. Complete the following passages with the correct forms of the words in parentheses, as suggested by the context. When two possibilities are given in parentheses, select the correct word. **¡OJO!** As you conjugate verbs in this activity, put the infinitives preceded by *P* in the preterite and by *I* in the imperfect.

Melvin Hoomes conoció a Joaquín Del Paso y a Mayra Turner el mes pasado en una lavandería.[a] Joaquin, con su esposa y dos hijos, (*P, llegar*[1]) recientemente a los Estados Unidos de Colombia. Melvin (*P, él: saber*[2]) que Mayra y Joaquín (*I, ser/estar*[3]) de (*diferente*[4]) sectores de la misma ciudad de Cartagena. De niña, Mayra (*I, vivir*[5]) en la parte más (*antiguo*[6]) de la ciudad, el Centro Amurallado[b] colonial, pero la familia de Joaquín (*I, tener*[7]) un apartamento en Bocagrande, el sector más moderno de Cartagena, cerca (*de/a*[8]) la playa. El sábado pasado los tres (*I, hablar*[9]) otra vez en la lavandería.

MELVIN: ¡Hola, Joaquín y Mayra! ¿Qué tal? (*command, Uds.: Mirar*[10]) toda esta ropa sucia. ¡Ya no (*yo: poder*[11]) (*divertirse*[12]) para nada los fines de semana!

JOAQUÍN: Ni yo (*también/tampoco*[13]).

MAYRA: Es cosa de nunca acabar,[c] ¿verdad? ¡Cuánto extraño[d] los fines de semana de mi niñez cuando mi familia (*I, ir*[14]) a La Boquilla* y (*I, nosotros: pasar*[15]) todo el día en la playa, (*pres. part., tomar*[16]) el sol, (*pres. part., nadar*[17]), (*pres. part., comer*[18]) mariscos y (*pres. part., cantar*[19]) cumbias por la noche! ¡Qué chévere![e]

JOAQUÍN: A nosotros también nos (*I, gustar*[20]) dar paseos por las fortalezas y las viejas murallas enormes de la ciudad. ¿Sabes, Melvin?, esas murallas miden[f] 20 metros de ancho y 10 metros de alto. (*Ellos: Ser/Estar*[21]) (*impresionante*[22]). Luego a veces (*I, nosotros: ir*[23]) de compras a Las Bóvedas† o (*I, nosotros: hacer*[24]) una excursión a Isla Barú.‡ Allí en las aguas del Parque Natural Corales del Rosario, hay los únicos bancos de coral[g] de todo el Caribe.

MELVIN: ¡Pues, yo (*querer*[25]) volver a (*ser/estar*[26]) niño para pasar mis fines de semana en Cartagena también!

[a]*laundromat* [b]*Centro... Walled Center* [c]*Es... It never ends* [d]*¡Cuánto... How I miss*
[e]*¡Qué... What a blast!* [f]*measure* [g]*bancos... coral reefs*

Comprensión: Ahora y entonces. Answer the questions in brief but complete Spanish sentences.

1. ¿Dónde conoció Melvin a Joaquín y Mayra?
2. ¿De qué ciudad son Mayra y Joaquín? ¿De qué partes de esa ciudad son?
3. ¿Qué sabe Ud. de la vida de ellos?
4. ¿De qué se quejaron los tres el sábado pasado?
5. De niña, ¿cómo pasaba Mayra los fines de semana en Cartagena?
6. Y Joaquín, ¿qué hacía él de niño los fines de semana?

---

*La Boquilla, a fishing village outside Cartagena, has a long secluded beach with restaurants and bars.
†Las Bóvedas (the vaults) were barracks and storerooms built by the Spanish into the outer walls of the old city. Twenty-two of the dungeon-like rooms have been turned into small, upscale shops.
‡Barú Island, approximately ten minutes by motorboat from Cartagena, offers white sand beaches, crystal clear water, and big coral reefs.

Resources for Review and Testing Preparation

■ Workbook and Laboratory Manual
■ Interactive CD-ROM
■ Online Learning Center (www.mhhe.com/puntos7)

Resources: Desenlace

In the *Capítulo 9* segment of "Chapter-by-Chapter Supplementary Materials" in the IM, you will find a chapter-culminating activity. You can use this activity to consolidate and review the vocabulary and grammar skills students have acquired.

B: Suggestion

Read the following statements and have students tell who might have said them: *un niño, un estudiante,* or *un profesor.* There may be more than one possible answer for some.

¿Quién dice lo siguiente, un niño, un estudiante o un profesor?

1. *¡Es horrible que yo tenga que trabajar este fin de semana! Quería ir al parque con mis amigos.*
2. *¡Ay, tantos exámenes! ¡Quiero que este semestre/trimestre termine rápidamente!*
3. *No quiero que me lleves a ver esa película. ¡Va a ser muy aburrida!*
4. *Es necesario que mis padres me den un poco más de dinero. Si no, no voy a poder pagar todas mis cuentas (bills) de este mes.*

B: Follow-Up

■ Have students imagine that they are one of the following people and that they are telling about their weekend.

el presidente / la presidenta de los Estados Unidos (el primer ministro / la primera ministra del Canadá)
un actor / una actriz de cine o de televisión
un personaje (character) de televisión muy conocido

Write the following *Palabras útiles* on the board.

grabar (to record; to film on video)
filmar una película
reunirse (con)

■ Students often complain about too much homework on the weekends. Survey the class to find out how much time they really spend with their books. Write the following chart on the board or transparency, and have students copy and complete it on sheets of paper.

	LIBROS	AMIGOS	ALMOHADA (*PILLOW*)
el viernes	___	___	___
el sábado	___	___	___
el domingo	___	___	___
TOTAL	___	___	___

To follow up, ask questions to find out how much they study on weekends. Also, use the information to answer the following questions. Is there a correlation between students' study habits and their majors?

1. *¿Quién es la persona más estudiosa de la clase?*
2. *¿Quién es la persona más parandera (party loving)?*
3. *¿Quién es la persona más perezosa?*

PERSPECTIVAS
culturales

Entrevista cultural

Suggestions

- Before showing the video, ask students questions about sports they like to play and/or watch.

  ¿Qué deportes practica Ud.?
  ¿Con qué frecuencia lo practica Ud.?
  ¿Juega Ud. en un equipo? ¿Cómo es su equipo?
  ¿Su equipo gana muchos partidos?
  ¿Qué deportes le gusta ver en la televisión?
  ¿Le gusta asistir a partidos y juegos?

- Show the video and allow students one to two minutes to work on the questions. Have volunteers answer the questions.

- Have volunteers role-play Mauricio and his interviewer.

Entre amigos

Suggestions

- Before viewing the video, review the questions with the students and ask them similar questions.

  ¿Sabe Ud. bailar? ¿Con quién le gusta salir a bailar?
  ¿Con qué frecuencia sale a bailar?
  ¿Sabe Ud. bailar algún baile hispano como la salsa, el merengue o la cumbia?

  Have students answer or work in small groups to ask and answer these questions.

- After viewing the video, have volunteers read and answer the questions.

●●● Videoteca

Entrevista cultural: Colombia

Mauricio Tautiba es un colombiano que vive apasionado por los deportes. Él habla en la entrevista de su equipo y de sus esperanzas para el futuro. Antes de ver el vídeo, lea el siguiente fragmento de la entrevista.

ENTREVISTADORA: Me dicen que juegas fútbol.* ¿Es cierto?

MAURICIO: Sí, juego fútbol, eh, inclusive juego en una liga todos los fines de semana.

ENTREVISTADORA: Y ¿es bueno tu equipo?

MAURICIO: Sí, muy bueno. La temporada[a] pasada ganamos casi todos los partidos, pero desafortunadamente no fuimos campeones.

[a]*season*

Ahora vea el vídeo y conteste las siguientes preguntas basándose en la entrevista.

1. ¿A qué deporte se dedica Mauricio?
2. ¿Con qué frecuencia lo practica y juega?
3. ¿Qué otros deportes practica?
4. ¿Juega bien o mal el equipo de Mauricio?
5. ¿Qué espera hacer Mauricio en el futuro?

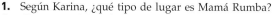

Entre amigos: ¿Sabes bailar salsa?

Rubén, Karina, Miguel y Tané hacen planes para el fin de semana. Quieren ir a un club que se llama «Mamá Rumba». En su opinión, ¿de qué van a hablar? Antes de mirar el vídeo, lea las preguntas a continuación. Mientras mire el vídeo, trate de entender la conversación en general y fíjese en la información sobre sus planes para el fin de semana. Luego mire el vídeo una segunda vez, fijándose en la información que necesita para contestar las preguntas.

1. Según Karina, ¿qué tipo de lugar es Mamá Rumba?
2. ¿Le gusta a Miguel ir a Mamá Rumba? ¿Por qué?
3. ¿Sabe bailar salsa Rubén?
4. ¿Por qué no debe preocuparse (*worry*) Rubén?
5. ¿Qué van a hacer los amigos el domingo?

---

*Some Spanish speakers omit the **al** after **jugar** when talking about playing sports: **jugar al fútbol** vs. **jugar fútbol**.*

☼ Heritage Speakers

Pídales a los hispanohablantes que describan sus pasatiempos. ¿Hay algo en particular que hagan para divertirse?

CULTURE

Point out that a popular Hispanic table game, especially for men, is *el dominó*. Men gather at their homes, in parks, or at clubs to play. In Miami's Little Havana, *el parque Máximo Gómez* on *la calle Ocho* is also known as Domino Park. Cubans and other Hispanics from the community gather daily in this park to play dominoes and chess.

Conozca... Colombia

Datos esenciales

- Nombre oficial: República de Colombia
- Capital: Santafé de Bogotá (Bogotá)
- Población: 41.660.000 habitantes
- Moneda: el peso
- Idioma oficial: el español

¡Fíjese!

- Colombia obtuvo su independencia de España en 1819, bajo la dirección de Simón Bolívar. Bolívar fue declarado el primer presidente de la independiente República de la Gran Colombia.
- Colombia produce más oro que cualquier[a] otro país sudamericano y tiene los yacimientos[b] de platino[c] más grandes del mundo. Las esmeraldas también son un producto minero importante.
- Aunque el café es reconocido[d] como el producto agrícola principal de exportación de Colombia, en los años noventa lo sobrepasó[e] el petróleo como primer producto de exportación.
- Aproximadamente un 14 por ciento de la población colombiana es de origen africano.
- Las misteriosas estatuas de piedra de San Agustín fueron creadas por una cultura indígena de la cual[f] se sabe muy poco. Se cree que las estatuas son del siglo VI (sexto) antes de Cristo. Una de las estatuas representa un pájaro con una serpiente en el pico,[g] imagen muy similar a la de una leyenda azteca.

[a]any [b]deposits [c]platinum [d]recognized [e]surpassed [f]de... of which [g]beak

Learn more about Colombia with the Video, the Interactive CD-ROM, and the Online Learning Center (www.mhhe.com/puntos7).

Personas famosas: Juanes

Juanes es un fenómeno colombiano en el mundo de la música. Nacido[a] en Medellín, Colombia, Juanes fundó el grupo Ekhymosis a los 14 años. El grupo se desintegró después de doce años y Juanes empezó su carrera como solista con el álbum *Fíjate bien*.[b] Ganó varios premios[c] en Latinoamérica, incluso el premio para la canción más romántica del siglo («A Dios le pido»). En 2002 tenía siete nominaciones en los Grammy Latino, y salió de las ceremonias en Los Ángeles con tres Grammys: Mejor Canción Rock, Mejor Nuevo Artista y Mejor Solista Vocal para Álbum en Rock. En 2003, se llevó Álbum del Año y Mejor Álbum Vocal Solista, Grabación[d] y Canción del Año y Mejor Canción de Rock. En su gira[e] por Colombia en la primavera de 2003, dedicó su concierto en Bogotá a las víctimas de la violencia y a los que tratan de proteger[f] los derechos[g] y la vida de los colombianos.

[a]Born [b]Fíjate... Pay close attention [c]prizes [d]Recording [e]tour [f]tratan... try to protect [g]rights

▲ Estatuas de piedra, de San Agustín

Conozca... Colombia

Suggestions

- Ask students to research Simón Bolívar's role in Latin American history, and present short reports to the class. You may wish to have teams of students work together to report on Bolívar's contribution to the status of different countries.
- Have students do further research on the mysterious stone figures, and do presentations on these and other unattributable structures in Latin America, such as the statues on Easter Island.

Suggestion

Students can read an excerpt from *Cien años de soledad* by Colombia's Gabriel García Márquez in *Un paso más 9*.

MULTIMEDIA: Internet

Have students search the Internet for more information about Colombia's economy, people, education, government, and history. Students can also find Colombia's most famous daily newspapers online: *El Espectador* and *El Tiempo*. You might assign specific topics and have students give brief oral presentations based on their findings.

EN RESUMEN

Suggestions

- Bring or have students bring clippings that illustrate items and activities from the *Vocabulario*. Use these to review (have students describe, play word games, and so on).
- Have students respond *cierto* or *falso* to the following statements.

  1. *El béisbol requiere la participación de varias personas.*
  2. *El ejercicio es importante para la salud mental.*
  3. *Para una persona que le gusta estar entre mucha gente, la natación es el deporte favorito.*

- Have students answer the following questions.

  1. *¿Dónde se puede escuchar música, en un concierto o en un museo?*
  2. *¿Cuál es una actividad cultural, hacer camping o ir al teatro?*
  3. *¿Dónde se puede ver a su actor favorito, en un bar o en el cine?*

Gramática

To review the grammar points presented in this chapter, refer to the indicated grammar presentations. You'll find further practice of these structures in the Workbook and Laboratory Manual, on the Interactive CD-ROM, and on the *Puntos de partida* Online Learning Center (www.mhhe.com/puntos7).

27. Descriptions and Habitual Actions in the Past—Imperfect of Regular and Irregular Verbs

You should know the imperfect forms of all verbs. What are the three verbs that are irregular in the imperfect?

28. Expressing Extremes—Superlatives

Do you know how to express that something is *the best* or *the most*?

29. Getting Information—Summary of Interrogative Words

You should know how to form questions with question words and how to express English *what?* with **¿qué?** or **¿cuál?**.

Vocabulario

Practice this vocabulary with digital flash cards on the Online Learning Center (www.mhhe.com/puntos7).

Los verbos

aburrirse	to get bored
dejar (en)	to leave (behind) (in [a place])
pegar (gu)	to hit
pelear	to fight
sonar (ue)	to ring; to sound

Los pasatiempos, diversiones y aficiones

los ratos libres	spare (free) time
dar (*irreg.*) **un paseo**	to take a walk
hacer (*irreg.*) **un** *picnic*	to have a picnic
hacer (*irreg.*) **planes para** + *inf.*	to make plans to (*do something*)
ir (*irreg.*)...	to go . . .
al cine / a ver una película	to the movies / to see a movie
a una discoteca / a un bar	to a disco / to a bar
al teatro / a un concierto	to the theater / to a concert
jugar (ue) (gu) a las cartas / al ajedrez	to play cards/chess
ser (*irreg.*) **aburrido/ divertido/a**	to be boring/fun
visitar un museo	to visit a museum

Repaso: dar (*irreg.*) **/ hacer** (*irreg.*) **una fiesta, hacer** (*irreg.*) ***camping*, jugar (ue) (gu) (al)** (*sport*)**, tomar el sol**

Los deportes

el/la aficionado/a (a)	fan (of)
el ciclismo	bicycling
el fútbol	soccer
el fútbol americano	football
el/la jugador(a)	player
la natación	swimming
el partido	match, game

Otros deportes
- el basquetbol
- el béisbol
- el golf
- el hockey
- el tenis
- el vólibol

correr	to run; to jog
entrenar	to practice, train
esquiar (esquío)	to ski
ganar	to win
montar a caballo	to ride a horse
pasear en bicicleta	to ride a bicycle
patinar	to skate
patinar en línea	to rollerblade
ser (*irreg.*) **aficionado/a (a)**	to be a fan (of)

Repaso: nadar, perder (ie), practicar (qu)

Algunos aparatos domésticos

la aspiradora	vacuum cleaner
la cafetera	coffeemaker
el congelador	freezer
la estufa	stove
el horno de microondas	microwave oven
la lavadora	washing machine
el lavaplatos	dishwasher
el refrigerador	refrigerator
la secadora	clothes dryer
la tostadora	toaster

Los quehaceres domésticos

barrer (el piso)	to sweep (the floor)
hacer (irreg.) la cama	to make the bed
lavar (las ventanas, los platos, la ropa)	to wash (the windows, the dishes, the clothes)
limpiar la casa (entera)	to clean the (whole) house
pasar la aspiradora	to vacuum
pintar (las paredes)	to paint (the walls)
planchar la ropa	to iron clothing
poner (irreg.) la mesa	to set the table
quitar la mesa	to clear the table

sacar (qu) la basura	to take out the trash
sacudir los muebles	to dust the furniture

Otros sustantivos

la costumbre	custom, habit
la dirección	address
la época	era, time (period)
la escuela	school
el grado	grade, year (in school)
el/la niñero/a	baby-sitter
la niñez	childhood

Adjetivos

deportivo/a	sporting, sports (adj.); sports-loving
pesado/a	boring; difficult

Palabras adicionales

¿adónde?	where (to)?
de joven	as a youth
de niño/a	as a child
mientras	while
tocarle (qu) a uno	to be someone's turn

Suggestions

■ Have students make single statements about something they used to do when they were younger (de joven / de niño/a). Have them make their statements in a round-robin format, without repeating anything someone else has already said.

■ Have students describe three to four activities that they think someone famous used to do as a child. They should not name the person they describe. The class should try to guess the identity.

☀ Heritage Speakers

En algunos dialectos del español que se habla en los Estados Unidos, a veces se usa la palabra *grado* en vez de *nota o calificación*, por la influencia del inglés.

Un paso más 9

Un paso más 9

Note

The *Un paso más* section is optional.

Literatura de Colombia

Notes

- García Márquez was raised by his grandparents and a series of aunts. His grandmother would narrate stories to him when he was young. She didn't distinguish between the stories that were true and those that were not only not true but fantastical and magical.
- Ask students who have read short stories or novels by García Márquez to talk to the class about them, perhaps describing incidents of magical realism.
- A number of films have been made of García Márquez's short stories and novels, most recently of *El coronel no tiene quien le escriba*. This last film, directed by Mexican Arturo Ripstein, won the Latin American Cinema Award at the Sundance Film Festival 2000 as well as other prizes. You may wish to show this film to the class.
- Have students research the history of magical realism from its beginnings in the works of Alejo Carpentier in Cuba to the present.

LECTURA

Suggestions

- Do the *Estrategia* as an in-class activity the day before you cover the reading.
- Work with students to decode the underlined words, and have students write sentences using them.

Literatura de **Colombia**

Sobre el autor: *Gabriel José García Márquez nació en Aracataca, en el norte de Colombia. Empezó su vida profesional como periodista. Vivió casi toda su vida de adulto fuera de Colombia, en Europa y México. Recibió el Premio Nóbel de Literatura en 1982 por su novela* Cien años de soledad. *Sus novelas y cuentos combinan lo fantástico y lo real, un estilo que se llama el realismo mágico. El siguiente fragmento es de* Cien años de soledad *(1967).*

Muchos años después, frente al pelotón de fusilamiento,[a] el coronel Aureliano Buendía había de[b] recordar aquella tarde remota en que su padre lo llevó a conocer el hielo.[c] Macondo era entonces una aldea[d] de veinte casas de barro[e] y cañabrava[f] construidas a la orilla[g] de un río de aguas diáfanas que se precipitaban por un lecho[h] de piedras pulidas,[i] blancas y enormes como huevos prehistóricos.

[a]pelotón... *firing squad* [b]había... *would* [c]*ice* [d]*village* [e]*mud* [f]*cane* [g]*bank* [h]*bed*
[i]piedras... *polished rocks*

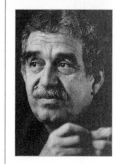

▲ Gabriel García Márquez (1928–)

LECTURA

ESTRATEGIA: Recognizing Derivative Adjectives

In previous chapters you learned to recognize cognates, word endings, and new words that are related to familiar words. In this chapter you will learn about derivative adjectives, a large group of adjectives derived from verbs. These adjectives end in **-ado** or **-ido.** You can often guess their meaning if you know the related verb. For example: **conocer** (*to know*) → **conocido** (*known, famous*); **preparar** (*to prepare*) → **preparado** (*prepared*).

In the following reading there are many **-do** adjectives. Try to guess their meaning from context. You might also notice past participle forms (**-do**) in conjunction with a verb form you don't recognize, such as **ha comentado** (*has commented*). You will study this form, known as the present perfect, in a later chapter of this text. For now, simply learn to recognize it.

Capítulo 9: El tiempo libre

**National Standards:
Comparison**

Have students research enough information about Gabriel García Márquez to compare him to a U.S. or Canadian author of the 20th and 21st centuries.

Sobre la lectura... Este artículo apareció en la revista *Quo,* una publicación española que trata temas populares, como la tecnología, la salud, las relaciones entre los sexos y los sitios turísticos. La lectura, un fragmento del artículo original, relata el interés creciente (*growing*) en los parques de atracciones (*amusement parks*) en España.

El sitio de mi recreo

La proliferación de parques temáticos y de museos interactivos revela que la concepción del ocio[a] y de vacaciones está cambiando. «Damos una oferta complementaria al sol y la playa. Ahora llegan turistas de toda España, cuando normalmente este no sería[b] un destino turístico», afirma José María Brugués, de Port Aventura, un parque temático en Tarragona.*

Ante el éxito[c] de Port Aventura, España intenta ponerse a la altura de[d] mercados como los de los Estados Unidos, Francia o Gran Bretaña. Ya existen más de cincuenta proyectos de parques temáticos en España, entre ellos, en San Martín de la Vega (Madrid) dedicado al cine, un proyecto en el que está involucrada[e] la Warner Brothers.

Julián Rodríguez Luna, consejero delegado del Grupo Parque en España, comenta la popularidad creciente de estas nuevas atracciones. Según él, nuestra sociedad disfruta[f] cada vez más de tiempo libre, y por ello tiende[g] a buscar más opciones de ocio. Los parques, ya sean de atracciones, acuáticos o zoos, son una buena elección. Están configurados para que se puedan disfrutar[h] de una forma participativa, porque fuera del hogar[i] buscamos un ocio activo. Los jóvenes suelen buscar el riesgo[j] y las emociones fuertes, mientras que las familias buscan tranquilidad y pasar un buen rato con los niños.

Aparte de las novedades[k] en parques temáticos y de atracciones, la tecnología también ha llegado a los museos. Al contrario de lo que se podría pensar,[l] los museos de siempre no morirán,[m] aunque muchos de ellos están comenzando a reciclarse. Algunos ya han adaptado varias salas para convertirlas en interactivas. Lo que le interesa al público es tocar y que los museos sean divertidos y lúdicos.[n] ■

[a]*leisure time* [b]*no... would not be* [c]*success* [d]*ponerse... compete on the same level as* [e]*involved* [f]*enjoys* [g]*tends, is inclined* [h]*para... to be enjoyed* [i]*fuera... outside the home* [j]*suelen... tend to seek out risk* [k]*novelties* [l]*Al... Contrary to what one might believe* [m]*no... will not die* [n]*entertaining*

Un parque de atracciones ▶
en Barcelona, España

*Tarragona is a city located on the Mediterranean coast in the northeast of Spain.

MULTIMEDIA: Internet

Have students locate theme and recreational parks in Spain and Latin America. What do they feature? What rides do they offer? Where (In what cities) are they located?

Comprensión: Follow-Up
Have students talk about theme parks they have visited. What kind of theme parks do they prefer? What are their favorite rides and attractions? What time of year do they prefer to go? With whom?

Comprensión

A. Selección múltiple. Escoja la respuesta correcta según la lectura.

1. ¿Cómo se explica el número creciente de parques temáticos en España?
   a. El gobierno (*government*) español desea atraer (*to attract*) a más turistas internacionales.
   b. A los españoles no les gustan los museos.
   c. La gente tiene más tiempo libre y busca diversiones interactivas.

2. ¿Qué buscan los jóvenes cuando van a los parques?
   a. un sitio romántico
   b. un sitio sin adultos
   c. un sitio que ofrece riesgos

3. ¿Cómo se diferencian los museos modernos de los museos tradicionales?
   a. Ofrecen atracciones como la montaña rusa (*roller coaster*).
   b. Integran la tecnología para ser más interactivos.
   c. Ofrecen más tranquilidad para las familias.

B. Palabras relacionadas. ¿De qué verbos se derivan los siguientes adjetivos?

1. involucrada
2. dedicado
3. configurados
4. divertidos

ESCRITURA

A. Atracciones locales. Para muchas personas, ir a un parque temático es una buena diversión. Pero hay otras atracciones también. ¿Qué atracciones locales hay donde Ud. vive? Imagine que Ud. está en un comité universitario para reclutar (*recruit*) a nuevos estudiantes. A Ud. le toca escribir un ensayo de 250 palabras que describe todas las atracciones que ofrecen la universidad y la ciudad. El título del ensayo es: «Atracciones y diversiones para estudiantes de la Universidad».

MULTIMEDIA: Internet

Challenge students to find the names in Spanish for theme park rides not mentioned in the readings.

B. Una encuesta. El parque de recreo es una diversión popular en este país. Imagine que se va a abrir un nuevo parque en su ciudad, cerca de la universidad. El dueño del parque quiere obtener información sobre los gustos de las personas que viven en la ciudad y de los estudiantes. Conteste las preguntas de su encuesta.

Una encuesta sobre Ud. y el parque

1. Sexo: ☐ Hombre   ☐ Mujer
2. Edad: _____ años
3. Profesión: _____
4. Estado civil: ☐ Casado/a   ☐ Divorciado/a   ☐ Soltero/a
5. Hijos: ☐ Sí (¿Cuántos? _____) ☐ No
6. ¿Cuántas veces al mes va Ud. a un parque de recreo? _____
7. ¿Cuántas veces al año va Ud. a un parque de recreo? _____
8. ¿Va Ud. a un parque… ? ☐ sólo en el verano   ☐ sólo los fines
                                                    de semana
9. Ponga en orden de mayor (1) a menor (13) preferencia para Ud. los siguientes tipos de atracciones en un parque de recreo.

_____ la montaña rusa[a]
_____ la montaña rusa de agua
_____ la caída al vacío[b]
_____ el péndulo gigante[c]
_____ la rueda de feria[d]
_____ los autos chocadores[e]
_____ las barcas de agua
_____ el baile de tazas[f]
_____ el tiovivo[g]
_____ el laberinto encantado
_____ la zona de naturaleza
_____ el circuito de tren
_____ la zona infantil
_____ los conciertos de música
_____ los simuladores Imax

10. ¿Cuál es su parque temático o de atracciones favorito? _____

[a]montaña... *roller coaster* [b]caída... *free fall (bungee jumping)* [c]péndulo... *giant pendulum*
[d]rueda... *Ferris wheel* [e]autos... *bumper cars* [f]baile... *spinning cups* [g]carousel

---

Suggestion

If you prefer that your students do a journal activity, see *Mi diario* in this chapter of the Workbook.

Variations

■ Have students write a description of a theme park they went to or used to go to when they were younger. What was the best time of year (month of the year) to go to the park? What were the best or most fun attractions? The worst? What was the most expensive food at the park. Some students may write about the same park. Compare their descriptions.

■ Have students compare theme parks with which they are familiar, to determine which park is the biggest, most fun, best / worst, most / least expensive, and so on, of all.

◀ Un paseo (*stroll*) frente al Museo de los Niños en Caracas, Venezuela

CHAPTER OPENER PHOTO

Point out the chapter-opener photo. Have students discuss their ideas about exercise and health. Encourage them to describe the people in the photo. Do they look healthy? Are they concerned about their health and fitness?

Suggestions

- Ask students the following personal questions.

  ¿Hace Ud. ejercicio con frecuencia? ¿Qué hace?

  ¿Va a un gimnasio o hace deporte al aire libre, como las personas en la foto?

  ¿Hizo Ud. ejercicio ayer?

  ¿Cuándo fue la última vez que hizo ejercicio?

- Have students respond *cierto* or *falso* to the following statements. The word in **boldface** is included in the active vocabulary of this chapter. Have students discuss the word and use context to help them understand its meaning. If they cannot guess the word, place it in a new sentence and context.

  1. *Yo no fumo. No bebo tampoco.*
  2. *Odio ir al dentista.*
  3. *No hago nada especial para mantener **la salud.***
  4. *En este país, todos queremos ser delgados. Este énfasis tan exagerado no es bueno para la salud.*
  5. *La cultura de este país estima mucho la experiencia de las personas mayores.*

- Point out the use in item 4 of *tan* as *so*; contrast this word with *muy.*
- Have students respond *cierto* or *falso* to the following statements.

  1. *Los jóvenes universitarios no toman bebidas alcohólicas.*
  2. *Los adolescentes norteamericanos no fuman.*
  3. *Muchos estadounidenses van habitualmente al dentista.*
  4. *En este país hay serios problemas con la anorexia y la bulimia.*

Notes

- The *Puntos de partida* Online Learning Center includes an interview with a native speaker from Venezuela who answers questions similar to those in the preceding *Suggestion.*
- *Personas mayores* is a polite way to refer to older people. Other possible terms are *personas de la tercera edad* and *ancianos. Los viejos* generally sounds pejorative.

Resources

For Students

- Workbook
- Laboratory Manual and Laboratory Audio Program
- Quia™ Online Workbook and Online Laboratory Manual
- Video on CD
- Interactive CD-ROM
- *Puntos de partida* Online Learning Center (**www.mhhe.com/puntos7**)

For Instructors

- *Instructor's Manual and Resource Kit,* "Chapter-by-Chapter" Supplementary Materials
- Overhead Transparencies 71–75
- Testing Program
- Test Generator
- Video Program
- Audioscript
- *Puntos de partida* Online Learning Center (**www.mhhe.com/puntos7**)

La salud°

CULTURA

- **Perspectivas culturales**

  Entrevista cultural: Venezuela

  Entre amigos: ¡Yo sí hago ejercicio!

  Conozca... Venezuela

- **Nota cultural:** La medicina en los países hispanos

- **En los Estados Unidos y el Canadá:** Edward James Olmos: Actor y activista de la comunidad

- **Literatura de Venezuela:** Rómulo Gallegos

- **Lectura:** Las vitaminas y la salud

VOCABULARIO

- La salud y el bienestar
- En el consultorio

GRAMÁTICA

30 Using the Preterite and the Imperfect

31 Relative Pronouns

32 Reciprocal Actions with Reflexive Pronouns

Entrevista cultural

MAR CARIBE

• Maracaibo   ⊛ Caracas

Río Orinoco

VENEZUELA

GUYANA

COLOMBIA

EL BRASIL

Sabina García ▶
Caracas, Venezuela

°**La...** *Health*

MULTIMEDIA: Internet

Have students search the Internet for health and fitness websites in Spanish. Suggest words, such as *salud*, for them to enter in their searches. They should be able to find several self-help resources for both adults and children. The information and advice on these pages can be used for communicative activities as students learn the health expressions in the chapter (doctor/patient or counselor/client situations).

MULTIMEDIA

- The multimedia materials that accompany this chapter are referenced in the Student and Instructor's Editions with icons to help you identify when and where to incorporate them.

- The IM/RK provides suggestions for using the multimedia materials in the classroom.

La salud y el bienestar

Note

See the model for vocabulary presentation and other material in the *Capítulo 10 Vocabulario: Preparación* section of "Chapter-by-Chapter Supplementary Materials," in the IM.

Suggestions

■ Offer optional vocabulary.

la cara y el cuerpo:	*actividades:*
la barbilla	hacer footing
las cejas	jugar a los bolos (al
el frente	tenis, al ráquetbol)
la mejilla	levantar pesas
las muelas	montar en bicicleta
el pecho	nadar
las pestañas	

■ Ask students the following questions to check comprehension and personalize.

1. *¿Hace Ud. algún ejercicio físico? ¿Camina? ¿Corre? ¿Juega al ráquetbol? ¿No hace nada?*

2. *En su opinión, ¿qué tipo de ejercicio es el mejor de todos? ¿Por qué?*

3. *¿Lleva Ud. una vida sana? ¿Qué hace Ud. para cuidarse? ¿Come equilibradamente? ¿Duerme lo suficiente? ¿Practica algún deporte?*

■ Point out that *sano/a* (healthy) is a false cognate.

Resources:
Transparencies 71, 72

Transparency 72 has additional vocabulary you may wish to present to your students.

VOCABULARIO   Preparación

La... *Health and well-being*

La salud y el bienestar°

dormir (ue, u) lo suficiente   comer equilibradamente   hacer (*irreg.*) ejercicios aeróbicos

el cerebro

la boca   la garganta   la cabeza

los pulmones   Josefa

el estómago

Enrique   correr   caminar   el corazón

Laura

la rueda de molino

El cuerpo humano

el diente	tooth
la nariz	nose
el oído	inner ear
el ojo	eye
la oreja	(outer) ear

Para cuidar de la salud

cuidarse	to take care of oneself
dejar de + *inf.*	to stop (*doing something*)
hacer (*irreg.*) ejercicio	to exercise; to get exercise
llevar gafas / lentes de contacto	to wear glasses / contact lenses
llevar una vida sana/tranquila	to lead a healthy / calm life
practicar (qu) deportes	to practice, play sports

Ask students in Spanish how their diets have changed since they began their studies at the university. Younger students' diets tend to change radically once they leave home. Ask students if they eat more junk food than they did when they lived at home and whether or not they follow the recommended guidelines for proper nutrition. Discuss in Spanish what the guidelines are, perhaps drawing a food pyramid or a chart on the board.

MULTIMEDIA: Audio

Students can listen to and practice this chapter's vocabulary on the Online Learning Center (**www.mhhe.com/puntos7**), as well as on the Textbook Audio CD, part of the Laboratory Audio Program.

■ ■ ■ Conversación

A. Asociaciones

Paso 1. ¿Qué partes del cuerpo humano asocia Ud. con las siguientes palabras? A veces hay más de una respuesta posible.

1. un ataque
2. comer
3. cantar
4. las gafas
5. pensar
6. la digestión
7. el amor
8. fumar
9. la música
10. el perfume

Paso 2. ¿Qué palabras asocia Ud. con las siguientes partes del cuerpo?

1. los ojos
2. los dientes
3. la boca
4. el oído
5. el estómago

B. Hablando de la salud. ¿Qué significan, para Ud., las siguientes oraciones?

> **MODELO:** Se debe comer equilibradamente. →
> Eso quiere decir (*means*) que es necesario comer muchas verduras, que… También significa que no debemos comer muchos dulces o…

1. Se debe dormir lo suficiente todas las noches.
2. Hay que hacer ejercicio.
3. Es necesario llevar una vida tranquila.
4. En general, uno debe cuidarse mucho.
5. Es importante llevar una vida sana.

Palabras y frases útiles

Eso quiere decir…
Esto significa que…
También…

C. ¿Cómo vives? ¿Cómo vivías?

Paso 1. ¿Hace Ud. las siguientes cosas para mantener la salud y el bienestar?

	SÍ	NO
1. comer una dieta equilibrada	☐	☐
2. no comer muchos dulces	☐	☐
3. caminar por lo menos dos millas por día	☐	☐
4. correr	☐	☐
5. hacer ejercicios aeróbicos	☐	☐
6. dormir por lo menos ocho horas por día	☐	☐
7. tomar bebidas alcohólicas en moderación	☐	☐
8. no tomar bebidas alcohólicas en absoluto (*at all*)	☐	☐
9. no fumar ni cigarrillos ni puros (*cigars*)	☐	☐
10. llevar ropa adecuada (abrigo, suéter, etcétera) cuando hace frío	☐	☐

Paso 2. ¿Lleva una vida sana? Dígale a un compañero / una compañera cómo vive, usando las frases del **Paso 1.**

> **MODELO:** Creo que llevo una vida sana porque como una dieta equilibrada. No como muchos dulces, excepto en los días festivos como la Navidad…

Paso 3. Ahora cambie su narración para describir lo que hacía de niño/a. ¿Qué hacía y qué *no* hacía Ud.? Debe organizar las ideas lógicamente.

> **MODELO:** De niño, no llevaba una vida muy sana. Comía muchos dulces. También odiaba las frutas y verduras…

Vocabulario: Preparación

Con. A: Preliminary Exercise

Read the following statements and have students respond *cierto* or *falso*.

1. *Comemos con los pulmones.*
2. *Respiramos con la nariz.*
3. *La comida pasa por la boca y la garganta antes de llegar al estómago.*
4. *Se usan los ojos para ver.*
5. *Se come bien en las cafeterías de esta universidad.*
6. *Los estudiantes siempre se cuidan bien y duermen lo suficiente.*
7. *Alguien que lleva una vida sana fuma mucho y toma mucho café.*
8. *Las personas mayores no deben hacer ejercicio.*
9. *Los cigarrillos afectan principalmente los pulmones de la persona que los fuma.*
10. *Si una persona no ve bien, lo único que puede hacer es llevar gafas.*

Con. B: Variation

Have students give the answers in the form of *Ud.* commands.

Con. C: Suggestion

Use these items to discuss the lifestyle of U.S./Canadian citizens and people in industrialized countries.

¿Llevamos una vida sana?

Con. C: Extensions

■ Have students name and discuss other aspects of our preoccupation with health.
■ Ask students the following question.

¿Hay personas que se preocupen demasiado por la salud? Describa a estas personas.

Bright Idea
Con. C: Expansion

Bring or have students bring images of famous people and tell how they grew up, where they grew up, and so on.

MULTIMEDIA: Internet

Students can find diet and nutrition guidelines online that can serve as a springboard for the discussion of their food habits. UNAM includes a page on the subject at their website. There are also pages online with health and fitness tests such as the longevity test. Encourage students to find these pages.

Refranes

1. «Músculos de Sansón (*Samson*) con cerebro de mosquito.»
2. «Si quieres vivir sano, acuéstate y levántate temprano.»
3. «Para enfermedad de años, no hay medicina.»
4. «La salud no se compra, no tiene precio.»

Read the health-related proverbs. Have students tell whether they agree or disagree.

En el consultorio

Suggestions

- Model vocabulary and ask questions during your presentation.

  1. *¿Se necesita receta para comprar un jarabe para la tos? ¿para comprar pastillas para rebajar de peso (lose weight)? ¿para comprar medicinas para diabéticos?*

  2. *¿Qué hace Ud. cuando le duele la cabeza / la garganta?*

  3. *¿Se enferma Ud. con frecuencia? De niño/a, ¿se enfermaba Ud. fácilmente? ¿Cuántas veces al año se resfría Ud.? ¿Cuántas veces, más o menos (do the hand gesture), se resfrió Ud. el año pasado? ¿Qué puede hacer una persona para no resfriarse?*

  4. *¿Por qué nos piden los médicos que saquemos la lengua? ¿Qué significa cuando una persona le saca la lengua a otra persona que no es un médico?*

- Offer the following optional alternate expressions and vocabulary.

  constipado (Sp.) = *resfriado*
  operarse
  la consulta = *el consultorio*
  ponerse enfermo = *enfermarse*
  la cita

  Point out that *cita* is the term for both appointment and date.

- Point out the difference between *ponerse enfermo / enfermarse* (to get / become sick) and *estar enfermo* (to be sick).

- Point out that the use of *doler* is similar to that of *gustar.*

Notes

- *To catch a cold* in some dialects of Spanish is *coger un resfriado (una gripa/gripe, un catarro).* In Spain speakers also use *constiparse* and *agarrarse un resfrío.*

- *Estar constipado/a* means *to have one's nose clogged or stopped up.* It is a false cognate and does not mean *constipated* in English.

Con. A: Preliminary Exercise

Read the following definitions and have students give the word for each.

1. *Es un sinónimo de «ponerse enfermo».*

2. *Es un líquido que se toma contra la tos.*

3. *Esto se hace con un termómetro.*

4. *No se puede hacer esto sin los pulmones.*

5. *Es el papelito que nos da el médico cuando nos manda a la farmacia.*

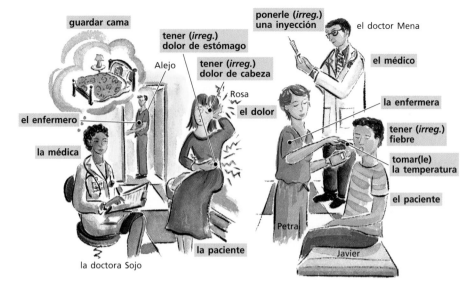

En el consultorio°

- guardar cama
- el enfermero
- la médica
- la doctora Sojo
- tener (*irreg.*) dolor de estómago
- tener (*irreg.*) dolor de cabeza
- el dolor
- la paciente
- Alejo
- Rosa
- ponerle (*irreg.*) una inyección
- el doctor Mena
- el médico
- la enfermera
- tener (*irreg.*) fiebre
- tomar(le) la temperatura
- el paciente
- Petra
- Javier

el/la farmacéutico/a	pharmacist	enfermarse	to get sick
congestionado/a	congested, stuffed-up	internarse (en)	to check in (*to a hospital*)
mareado/a	dizzy; nauseated	resfriarse (me resfrío)	to get/catch a cold
el antibiótico	antibiotic	respirar	to breathe
el jarabe	(cough) syrup	sacar (qu)	to extract
la pastilla	pill	sacar la lengua	to stick out one's tongue
la receta	prescription		
el resfriado	cold	sacar una muela	to extract a tooth
la tos	cough	tener (*irreg.*) dolor (de muela)	to have a (tooth) ache
doler (ue)*	to hurt, ache	toser	to cough

■ ■ ■ Conversación

A. Estudio de palabras. Complete las siguientes oraciones con una palabra de la misma (*same*) familia que la palabra en letras cursivas (*italics*).

1. Si me *resfrío,* tengo _____.
2. La *respiración* ocurre cuando alguien _____.
3. Si me _____, estoy *enfermo/a.* Un(a) _____ me toma la temperatura.
4. Cuando alguien *tose,* se oye una _____.
5. Si me *duele* el estómago, tengo un _____ de estómago.

---

*Doler *is used like* gustar: Me duele la cabeza. Me duelen los ojos.

☼ Heritage Speakers

Hay varios sinónimos para la palabra *resfriado,* por ejemplo, *catarro* y *constipado. La gripe* o *la gripa* significa *influenza.* Pregúnteles a los hispanohablantes de la clase qué expresiones prefieren usar.

Refrán

«A caballo regalado no le mires el diente.»

Have students work together to come up with the English version of this *refrán* (*Don't look a gift horse in the mouth.*).

Resources: Transparency 73

B. Situaciones. Describa Ud. la situación de estas personas. ¿Dónde y con quiénes están? ¿Qué síntomas tienen? ¿Qué van a hacer?

1. Anamari está muy bien de salud. Nunca le duele(n) ——. Nunca tiene ——. Siempre ——. Más tarde, ella va a ——.
2. Martín tiene ——. Debe ——. El dentista va a ——. Después, Martín va a ——.
3. A Inés le duele(n) ——. Tiene ——. El médico y la enfermera van a ——. Luego, Inés tiene que ——.

NOTA CULTURAL

La medicina en los países hispanos

Los hispanos pueden consultar a otros profesionales de la **salud,** además de los médicos especialmente en relación con **enfermedades** que no son graves. La gente consulta a los **farmacéuticos** con frecuencia, pues estos son profesionales con un riguroso entrenamiento universitario en **farmacología.** Además, hay farmacias en cada barrio, lo cual hace que haya[a] una relación bien establecida entre los farmacéuticos y sus clientes.

En las ciudades y pueblos hispanos siempre hay algunas farmacias abiertas a todas las horas del día. Se establecen **horarios de turnos,** y la farmacia que está abierta a horas en que las otras están cerradas se llama **farmacia de guardia.** Se puede saber cuáles son las farmacias de guardia a través del periódico o simplemente yendo a la farmacia más cercana, donde siempre hay una lista de todas las farmacias.

Otros profesionales al cuidado de la salud muy solicitados son los **practicantes,** que son **enfermeros** o estudiantes de **medicina** con varios años de estudio, que están capacitados[b] para poner inyecciones o hacer visitas a domicilio para **tratamientos** sencillos.

Finalmente, se debe mencionar la relativa popularidad de **remedios tradicionales,** como la homeopatía. Aunque hay expertos homeópatas con años de entrenamiento, también existe un repertorio popular de **remedios naturales** básicos para enfermedades o molestias[c] cotidianas, conocimientos[d] que se transmiten de generación a generación.

[a]lo... which creates   [b]trained
[c]nuisances   [d]knowledge

➕ **FARMACIAS** 4° turno
Abiertas de Sábado a Viernes de 8 a 22 hs.

Con. A: Suggestion

Read these sentences and have students tell whether or not the statements are *cierto* or *falso* for them based on their last dental visit.

1. *Me examinó los dientes.*
2. *Me limpió los dientes.*
3. *Me puso una inyección.*
4. *Me sacó una muela.*
5. *Me empastó (he/she filled) un diente.*
6. *Me sacó unos rayos X.*
7. *Me hizo muchas preguntas.*
8. *Me preguntó si uso hilo dental (dental floss) con regularidad.*

Con. B: Follow-Up

Read the following statements and have students respond *cierto* or *falso.*

1. *Si la persona sentada a mi lado empieza a toser, me quedo donde estoy.*
2. *Me pongo nervioso/a en el consultorio del médico.*
3. *Cuando tengo que ir al médico porque estoy enfermo/a, me siento mejor antes de ver al médico en el consultorio.*
4. *Cuando tengo un resfriado, nunca tomo pastillas ni jarabes ni antibióticos.*
5. *Mente sana en cuerpo sano.*
6. *Odio ir al dentista.*
7. *Si no hago ejercicio todos los días, empiezo a sentirme nervioso/a.*

NOTA CULTURAL

Suggestion
Ask the following questions to check comprehension.

1. *Además de los médicos, ¿a quiénes consultan los hispanos sobre sus problemas de salud?*
2. *¿Qué son* **practicantes***?*
3. *¿Qué significa «farmacia de guardia»?*

National Standards: Comparisons

Unlike in this country, in some parts of Latin America you do not need a prescription from a medical doctor in order to buy prescription drugs. It is not uncommon to see "patients" describing their symptoms to the *farmacéutico* who, in turn, prescribes the appropriate medication and dosage.

Resources: Transparency 74

NOTA COMUNICATIVA

Suggestions

- If you have worked with nominalization, present the *lo +* adjective structure as part of that system.
- Point out that students have already learned one expression that involves nominalization with *lo: lo suficiente.*
- Have students express these phrases in Spanish: the important thing/part, the bad thing/part, the interesting thing/part. Model these expressions in communicative exchanges with students.

> *¿Qué es lo importante de hacer ejercicio?*
>
> *¿Qué es lo malo de ir al consultorio de un médico?*

Con. C: Preliminary Exercise

Have students nominalize the following adjectives with *lo.* Encourage them to use them in model sentences: *importante → lo importante → Lo importante en esta clase es practicar.*

1. *divertido*
2. *peor*
3. *interesante*
4. *curioso*
5. *necesario*
6. *bueno*

Con. C: Suggestions

- Have students express their ideas about the more important things of life: *Lo más importante de la vida (no) es/son _____. (las clases, la libertad, las vacaciones, la salud, los amigos, la familia, ¿ ... ?)* Point out that *son* anticipates a plural noun.
- Have students work in pairs to give each other good and bad news for each of the following situations.

> MODELO:
> *en el restaurante → Lo bueno es que la comida es excelente. Lo malo son los precios.*

1. *en la clase de español*
2. *en la oficina del professor / de la profesora / en esta universidad*
3. *en el aeropuerto*
4. *en el consultorio del médico / dentista*
5. *en casa / durante un viaje*
6. *en el trabajo o durante una entrevista*

NOTA COMUNICATIVA

The Good News ... The Bad News ...

To describe general qualities or characteristics of something, use **lo** with the masculine singular form of an adjective.

lo bueno / lo malo   lo más importante   lo mejor / lo peor   lo mismo

This structure has a number of English equivalents, especially in colloquial speech.

lo bueno = the good thing/part/news, what's good

C. Ventajas y desventajas (*Advantages and Disadvantages*). Casi todas las cosas tienen un aspecto bueno y otro malo.

Paso 1. ¿Qué es lo bueno y lo malo (o lo peor y lo mejor) de las siguientes situaciones?

1. tener un resfriado
2. ir a una universidad cerca/lejos del hogar familiar (*family home*)
3. tener hijos cuando uno es joven (entre 18 y 25 años)
4. ser muy rico/a
5. ir a un consultorio médico
6. ir al consultorio de un dentista

Paso 2. Compare sus respuestas con las de sus compañeros. ¿Dijeron algo que Ud. no consideró?

Need more practice?

- Workbook and Laboratory Manual
- Interactive CD-ROM
- Online Learning Center (www.mhhe.com/puntos7)

GRAMÁTICA

¿Recuerda Ud.?

Throughout the last chapters of *Puntos de partida*, beginning with **Capítulo 7,** you have been using first the preterite and then the imperfect in appropriate contexts. Do you remember which tense you used to do each of the following?

1. to tell what you did yesterday P
2. to tell what you used to do when you were in grade school I
3. to explain the situation or condition that caused you to do something I
4. to tell what someone did as the result of a situation P
5. to talk about the way things used to be I
6. to describe an action that was in progress I

If you understand those uses of the preterite and the imperfect, the following summary of their uses will not contain much that is new information for you.

Refrán

«De médico, poeta y loco, todos tenemos un poco.»

Write this *refrán* on the board and poll students to find out if they all agree, and why.

En el consultorio de la Dra. Méndez

Marta, la hija de Lola y Manolo, se siente mal y su madre la lleva al consultorio de la Dra. Méndez.

DRA. MÉNDEZ: ¿Cuándo *empezó* a sentirse mal su hija?

LOLA: Ayer por la tarde. *Estaba* congestionada, *tosía* mucho y *se quejaba* de que le *dolían* el cuerpo y la cabeza.

DRA. MÉNDEZ: ¿Y le *notó* algo de fiebre?

LOLA: Sí. Por la noche le *tomé* la temperatura y *tenía* treinta y ocho grados.

DRA. MÉNDEZ: A ver… Tal vez necesito ponerle una inyección…

MARTA: Eh… bueno… ¡Creo que ahora me encuentro un poco mejor!

In the preceding dialogue, locate all of the verbs that do the following.

1. indicate actions (or lack of action)
2. indicate conditions or descriptions

When speaking about the past in English, you choose different past tense forms to use, depending on the context: *I wrote letters, I was writing letters, I used to write letters,* and so on. Similarly, you can use either the preterite or the imperfect in many Spanish sentences, depending on the meaning you wish to convey. Often the question is: How do you view the action or state of being?

PAST ------------------ Present ------------------ Future		
preterite	present	
imperfect	present progressive	
	formal commands	

Preterite	**Imperfect**
■ beginning/end of past action	■ habitual/repeated action
■ completed action	■ progress of a past action
■ series of completed actions	■ background details
■ interrupting action	■ interrupted action
■ the action on the "stage"	■ the backdrop (setup) of the "stage"

In Dr. Méndez's office   Marta, Lola and Manolo's daughter, feels sick, and her mother takes her to Dr. Méndez's office. DR. MÉNDEZ: *When did your daughter begin to feel ill?* LOLA: *Yesterday afternoon. She was stuffed up, she was coughing a lot, and she was complaining that her body and head were hurting.* DR. MÉNDEZ: *And did you note any fever?* LOLA: *Yes. At night I took her temperature and it was thirty-eight degrees.* DR. MÉNDEZ: *Let's see . . . Perhaps I'll need to give her a shot . . .* MARTA: *Um . . . well . . . I think I feel a little bit better now!*

Gramática   Trescientos diecinueve ■ **319**

 Heritage Speakers

Pídales a los estudiantes hispanohablantes que dramaticen una escena en el consultorio de un médico. ¿Qué enfermedad tendrá el paciente? ¿Es el paciente hipocondríaco?

Gramática 30

Using the Preterite and the Imperfect

Note
This section contrasts the uses of the preterite and the imperfect and provides practice in deciding which tense to use. Students have been using these tenses in controlled activities in *Capítulos 7–9.*

Follow-Up
After reviewing the *minidiálogo,* ask students the following questions to check comprehension.

¿Quién estaba enferma?
¿Qué síntomas tenía?
¿Por qué se sintió mejor rápidamente?

 Bright Idea

Follow-Up

On the board or a transparency, write a brief paragraph about a health incident. Have students note the verbs, then list them. Have students work on the board or transparency to put the verbs in categories (imperfect/ preterite), then talk about the different reasons the verbs require preterite or imperfect.

Suggestions
■ Emphasize the importance of the speaker's perspective. Many sentences are equally correct in either the imperfect or the preterite, but they will mean something different.
■ Point out that every action or state can be seen as having three phases or aspects: a beginning, a middle, and an end. When the focus is on an action's beginning or ending, the preterite is used. When the focus is on the middle, or on the repetitive nature of an action, the imperfect is used.
■ Offer students these examples.

Two preterite actions occurring either sequentially or simultaneously in the past.

Me puse los zapatos y me levanté.
Elena se fue cuando yo entré.

Two ongoing actions occurring simultaneously in the past.

Hacía mi tarea mientras veía las noticias.

One ongoing action in the past when another interrupts.

Yo estudiaba cuando llegó Juan.

Gramática ■ **319**

Beginning/End vs. Habitual

Note

The beginning of an action is usually expressed with the preterite: *Empezó a llover. Comenzaron el ejercicio.* An example of an exception is: *Isabel empezaba el ejercicio cuando su hermano entró.*

Series of Completed Actions vs. Background

Suggestions

- Model the difference in meaning of *pensó* (he thought, it occurred to him) and *pensaba* (he was of the opinion, planned/intended to). Use *creer* forms in a similar contrast.
- Offer students these additional examples.

  Carlos fue al médico ayer. / Carlos siempre iba al médico cuando se resfriaba.

  Juanita estuvo (became) nerviosa. / Juanita estaba (was) nerviosa.

Use the preterite to . . .	
■ tell about the beginning or the end of a past action	El sábado pasado, el partido de fútbol **empezó** a la una. **Terminó** a las cuatro. El entrenador **habló** a las cinco. *Last Saturday, the soccer game began at one. It ended at four. The coach spoke (began to speak) at five.*

Use the imperfect to . . .	
■ talk about the habitual nature of an action (something you always did)	**Había** un partido todos los sábados. Muchas personas **jugaban** todas las semanas. *There was a game every Saturday. Many people played every week.*

Completed vs. Ongoing

Use the preterite to . . .	
■ express an action that is viewed as completed	El partido **duró** tres horas. **Ganaron** Los Lobos, de Villalegre. *The game lasted three hours. The Lobos of Villalegre won.*

Use the imperfect to . . .	
■ tell what was happening when another action took place and tell about simultaneous events (with **mientras** = *while*)	Yo no vi el final del partido. **Estaba** en la cocina cuando **terminó.** *I didn't see the end of the game. I was in the kitchen when it ended.* Mientras mi amigo **veía** el partido, **hablaba** con su novia. *While my friend was watching the game, he was talking with his girlfriend.*

Series of Completed Actions vs. Background

Use the preterite to . . .	
■ express a series of completed actions	Durante el partido, los jugadores **corrieron, saltaron** y **gritaron.** *During the game, the players ran, jumped, and shouted.*

Resources: Transparency 56 from *Capítulo 7* can be used to practice preterite vs. imperfect.

Use the imperfect to . . .

- give background details of many kinds: time, location, weather, mood, age, physical and mental characteristics

Llovía un poco durante el partido. Todos los jugadores **eran** jóvenes; **tenían** 17 ó 18 años. ¡Y todos **esperaban** ganar!
It rained a little bit during the game. All the players were young; they were 17 or 18 years old. And all of them hoped to win!

Changes in Meaning

Remember that, when used in the preterite, **saber, conocer, querer,** and **poder** have English equivalents different from that of the infinitives (see **Capítulo 8**). In the imperfect, the English equivalents of these verbs do not differ from the infinitive meanings.

Anoche **conocí** a Roberto.
*Last night I **met** Roberto.*

¿Anoche? Yo pensaba que ya lo **conocías.**
*Last night? I thought you already **knew** him.*

Interrupting vs. Interrupted

The preterite and the imperfect frequently occur in the same sentence. In the first sentence the imperfect tells what was happening when another action—conveyed by the preterite—broke the continuity of the ongoing activity. In the second sentence, the preterite reports the action that took place because of a condition—described by the imperfect—that was in progress or in existence at that time.

Miguel **estudiaba** cuando **sonó** el teléfono.
Miguel was studying when the phone rang.

Olivia **comió** tanto porque **tenía** mucha hambre.
Olivia ate so much because she was very hungry.

Action vs. the Stage (Background)/Conditions/Ongoing

The preterite and imperfect are also used together in the presentation of an event. The preterite narrates the action while the imperfect sets the stage, describes the conditions that caused the action, or emphasizes the continuing nature of a particular action.

Era un día hermoso. **Hacía** mucho sol pero no **hacía** mucho calor. Como no **tenía** que trabajar en la oficina, **compré** unas flores de primavera y **salí** vestida de camiseta y pantalones cortos para trabajar todo el día en el jardín.
It was a beautiful day. It was very sunny but it wasn't very hot. Since I didn't have to work in the office, I bought some spring flowers and I went out dressed in a T-shirt and shorts to work in the garden all day.

Changes in Meaning

Suggestions

- Model sentences with the preterite and the imperfect of *saber, conocer, poder,* and *querer* and have students explain the differences in meaning.
- Read the following to continue a discussion of the preterite and imperfect in Spanish.

Estos dos tiempos dan imágenes muy diferentes de una acción. Si Ud. dice, por ejemplo, «Cuando visité a mi tío, salí de casa a las seis de la mañana», yo entiendo que Ud. lo visitó solamente una vez. En cambio, si Ud. dice: «Cuando visitaba a mi tío, salía de casa a las seis de la mañana», entiendo que iba a visitar a su tío con cierta frecuencia y que habla de algo rutinario que ocurría en todas sus visitas. Las dos oraciones son correctas gramaticalmente, pero sólo Ud. puede saber cuál comunica la «verdad». Si Ud. dice, «Ayer por la tarde íbamos a la tienda», su oyente espera que Ud. siga hablando, que le cuente qué pasó mientras iban. Normalmente no lo va a interrumpir con un comentario. En cambio, si Ud. dice, «Ayer fuimos a la tienda por la tarde», su oyente puede interrumpirlo con una pregunta porque él va a creer que Ud. ya acabó una parte de su narración. Otra vez, las dos oraciones son «correctas». El uso del imperfecto o del pretérito depende totalmente de lo que Ud. quiere expresar.

 Heritage Speakers

Anime a los hispanohablantes a explicar la diferencia entre los siguientes pares de oraciones.

Juan me dijo que le dolía la cabeza. [indefinite period of time, perhaps continuing into present]
Juan me dijo que le dolió la cabeza. [a specific time period that is now over]

No sé cuánto costó. [implies someone made a purchase, but speaker does not know how much it cost that person]
No se cuánto costaba. [no purchase implied]

Prác. A: Preliminary Exercise

Read each sentence and have students tell if it would require preterite or imperfect in Spanish, and why.

1. She used to eat eggs every day.
2. I ate breakfast, brushed my teeth, and left for the university.
3. He was tall and blond.
4. She was playing the piano.
5. They begin to sing.
6. Thomas was playing tennis while I was studying.
7. It was three o'clock.
8. The car was yellow and black.

Prác. A: Note

This activity helps students link conditions (imperfect) with actions (preterite) in logical sentence pairs. Even though students do not have to create the forms themselves, they are working with the preterite/imperfect contrast.

Prác. A: Variation

This activity can be done in a question/answer format. Have students form the questions based on *ACCIONES*. Other students should answer beginning *CONDICIONES* with *Sí, porque...*

Prác. A: Follow-Up

Have students change the story to accommodate authentic information about their childhood.

NOTA COMUNICATIVA

Suggestions

- Model the cue words associated with the preterite and imperfect in exchanges with students. Discuss how the words relate to the concepts of the preterite and imperfect.
- Point out that *dos veces, tres veces*, and so on are associated with the preterite, not the imperfect, because they refer to completed past actions. Model and contrast these expressions with *todos los días*, for example, *Fui al consultorio del médico tres veces este mes. Tenía un dolor de cabeza todos los días al levantarme.*

■ ■ ■ **Práctica**

A. **En el consultorio.** What did your doctor do the last time you had an appointment with him or her? Assume that you had the following conditions and match them with the appropriate procedure.

CONDICIONES: (Yo)...

1. _____ tenía mucho calor y temblaba.
2. _____ me dolía la garganta.
3. _____ tenía un poco de congestión en el pecho (*chest*).
4. _____ creía que estaba anémico/a.
5. _____ no sabía lo que tenía.
6. _____ necesitaba medicinas.
7. _____ sólo necesitaba un chequeo rutinario.

ACCIONES: El médico...

a. me hizo muchas preguntas.
b. me escribió una receta.
c. me tomó la temperatura.
d. me auscultó (*listened to*) los pulmones y el corazón.
e. me analizó la sangre (*blood*).
f. me hizo sacar la lengua.
g. me hizo toser.

NOTA COMUNICATIVA

Words and Expressions That Indicate the Use of Preterite and Imperfect

Certain words and expressions are frequently associated with the preterite, others with the imperfect.

Some words often associated with the preterite are:

ayer, anteayer (*the day before yesterday*), **anoche** (*last night*)
una vez, dos veces (*twice*)...
el año pasado, el lunes pasado...
de repente (*suddenly*)

Some words often associated with the imperfect are:

todos los días, todos los lunes...
siempre, frecuentemente
mientras
de niño/a, de joven

Some English equivalents also associated with the imperfect are:

was _____ -ing, were _____ -ing (in English)
used to, would (when *would* implies *used to* in English)

As you continue to practice preterite and imperfect, these expressions can help you determine which tense to use.

These words do not *automatically* cue either tense, however. The most important consideration is the meaning that the speaker wishes to convey.

Ayer cenamos temprano.	*Yesterday we had dinner early.*
Ayer cenábamos cuando Juan llamó.	*Yesterday we were having dinner when Juan called.*
Jugaba al fútbol **de niño.**	*He played soccer as a child.*
Empezó a jugar al fútbol **de niño.**	*He began to play soccer as a child.*

AUTOPRUEBA

Indicate preterite (P) or imperfect (I).

1. background details
2. repeated actions
3. completed action
4. habits
5. beginning of an action

Answers: 1. I 2. I 3. P 4. I 5. P

---

322 ■ Trescientos veintidós

Capítulo 10: La salud

322 ■ Capítulo 10: La salud

B. Pequeñas historias. Complete the following brief paragraphs with the appropriate phrases from the lists. Before you begin, it is a good idea to look at the drawing that accompanies each paragraph and to scan through the complete paragraph to get the gist of it, even though you may not understand everything the first time you read it.

Prác. B: Suggestion

Ask students to explain why they choose preterite or imperfect.

Prác. B: Extension

Have students change the subject in the first paragraph to *Jorge y Alicia*.

1. nos quedamos
   nos quedábamos
   íbamos
   nos gustó
   nuestra familia decidió
   vivíamos

   Cuando éramos niños, Jorge y yo _____¹ en la Argentina. Siempre _____² a la playa, a Mar del Plata, para pasar la Navidad. Allí casi siempre _____³ en el Hotel Fénix. Un año, _____⁴ quedarse en otro hotel, el Continental. No _____⁵ tanto como el Fénix y por eso, al año siguiente, _____⁶ en el Fénix otra vez.

2. estaba leyendo
   había
   estaban apagadas[a]
   tenía
   salí
   se apagaron[b]
   me levanté

   Eran las once de la noche cuando ¡de repente _____¹ todas las luces[c] de la casa! Puse el libro que _____² en la mesa y _____³ para investigar la causa del incidente. La verdad es que _____⁴ mucho miedo. _____⁵ a la calle y vi que _____⁶ las luces de todo el barrio.[d] En ese momento me di cuenta[e] que _____⁷ un problema con la electricidad en toda la ciudad.

   [a]*out*   [b]*se... went out*   [c]*lights*   [d]*neighborhood*   [e]*me... I realized*

3. examinó
   intentaba[a] tomarle
   estaba
   esperaba
   puso
   llegó
   dio
   se sintió

   La niña tosía mientras que la enfermera _____¹ la temperatura. La madre de la niña _____² pacientemente. Por fin _____³ la médica. Le _____⁴ la garganta a la niña, le _____⁵ una inyección y le _____⁶ a su madre una receta para un jarabe. La madre todavía _____⁷ muy preocupada, pero inmediatamente después que la médica le habló, _____⁸ más tranquila.

   [a]*tried to*

MULTIMEDIA: Internet

Have students print out images from the Internet to bring to class. Working in groups of three to four students, each group writes an imaginary story about the image using the preterite and imperfect.

This activity, like many in the text, is designed to help students develop a conceptual knowledge of the differences between the preterite and the imperfect. Students can also gain partial control of this topic. Keep in mind that students will switch from past to present and even use infinitive forms in sustained production. This is natural at this level.

Prác. C: Suggestions

- Do *Pasos 1* and *2* as a whole-class narration with students taking turns to complete the story.
- Have students work in pairs to tell each other a story about themselves: the happiest / saddest / most embarrassing moment of their lives, how they met their best friend / spouse / boyfriend / girlfriend, and so on. Encourage students to ask their partner for details and to offer help if their partner needs it.

Prác. D: Suggestions

- Have students read the entire paragraph to see where the story is going before making decisions about the preterite and imperfect. Remind students of the importance of the speaker's perspective.
- Ask students if they have ever been to a party where the police showed up. On a volunteer basis, have them answer the question *¿Qué pasó?*

Prác. D: Extension

Have students interview classmates about the last party they attended. Provide students with a list of questions to guide them in their interviews. You can begin with these sample questions.

¿Cuándo fue la última vez que fuiste a una fiesta?
¿De quién era la fiesta?
¿Cuántas personas había en la fiesta?
¿Había muchas bebidas y comida?

Once students finish their interviews, ask them what they found out about their classmates.

Bright Idea

Prác. D: Follow-Up

Have students bring a photo from a party they attended and tell what happened there.

C. **Rubén y Soledad.** Read the following paragraph at least once to familiarize yourself with the sequence of events, and look at the drawing. Then reread the paragraph, giving the proper form of the verbs in parentheses in the preterite or the imperfect, according to the needs of each sentence and the context of the paragraph as a whole.

Rubén estaba estudiando cuando Soledad entró en el cuarto. Le (preguntar[1]) a Rubén si (querer[2]) ir al cine con ella. Rubén le (decir[3]) que sí porque se (sentir[4]) un poco aburrido con sus estudios. Los dos (salir[5]) en seguida[a] para el cine. (Ver[6]) una película cómica y (reírse[7]) mucho. Luego, como (hacer[8]) frío, (entrar[9]) en su café favorito, El Gato Negro, y (tomar[10]) un chocolate. (Ser[11]) las dos de la mañana cuando por fin (regresar[12]) a casa. Soledad (acostarse[13]) inmediatamente porque (estar[14]) cansada, pero Rubén (empezar[15]) a estudiar otra vez.

[a]*en... right away*

Comprensión. Now answer the following questions based on the paragraph about Rubén and Soledad. **¡OJO!** A question is not always answered in the same tense as that in which it is asked. Remember this, especially when you are asked to explain why something happened.

1. ¿Qué hacía Rubén cuando Soledad entró?
2. ¿Qué le preguntó Soledad a Rubén?
3. ¿Por qué dijo Rubén que sí?
4. ¿Les gustó la película? ¿Por qué?
5. ¿Por qué tomaron un chocolate?
6. ¿Regresaron a casa a las tres?
7. ¿Qué hicieron cuando llegaron a casa?

D. **La fiesta de Roberto.** Read the following paragraphs once for meaning, and look at the drawing. Then reread the paragraphs, giving the proper form of the verbs in parentheses in the present, preterite, or imperfect.

Durante mi segundo año en la universidad, conocí a Roberto en una clase. Pronto nos (hacer[1]) muy buenos amigos. Roberto (ser[2]) una persona muy generosa que (organizar[3]) una fiesta en su apartamento todos los viernes. Todos nuestros amigos (ir[4]). (Haber[5]) muchas bebidas y comida, y todos (hablar[6]) y (bailar[7]) hasta muy tarde.

Una noche algunos de los vecinos[a] de Roberto (llamar[8]) a la policía y (decir[9]) que nosotros (hacer[10]) demasiado ruido. (Venir[11]) un policía al apartamento y le (decir[12]) a Roberto que la fiesta (ser[13]) demasiado ruidosa. Nosotros no (querer[14]) aguar[b] la fiesta, pero ¿qué (poder[15]) hacer? Todos nos (despedir[16]) aunque (ser[17]) solamente las once de la noche.

Aquella noche Roberto (aprender[18]) algo importantísimo. Ahora cuando (hacer[19]) una fiesta, siempre (invitar[20]) a sus vecinos.

[a]*neighbors* [b]*to spoil*

☀ **Heritage Speakers**

Recuerde a los hispanohablantes que *había* siempre se conjuga en la forma singular, no importa el número del sustantivo. Aunque haya hispanohablantes que digan *Habían muchas bebidas...*, la forma preferida es *había* en el uso formal.

E. Lo mejor de estar enfermo

Paso 1. Form complete sentences using the words in the order given. Conjugate the verbs in the preterite or the imperfect and add or change words as needed. Use subject pronouns only when needed.

1. cuando / yo / ser / niño, / pensar / que / lo mejor / de / estar enfermo / ser / guardar cama
2. lo peor / ser / que / con frecuencia / (yo) resfriarse / durante / vacaciones
3. una vez / (yo) ponerme / muy / enfermo / durante / Navidad
4. mi / madre / llamar / a / médico / con / quien / tener / confianza
5. Dr. Matamoros / venir / casa / y / darme / antibiótico / porque / tener / mucho / fiebre
6. ser / cuatro / mañana / cuando / por fin / (yo) empezar / respirar / sin dificultad
7. desgraciadamente (*unfortunately*) / día / de / Navidad / (yo) tener / tomar / jarabe / y / no / gustar / nada / sabor (*taste, m.*)
8. lo bueno / de / este / enfermedad / ser / que / mi / padre / tener / dejar / fumar / mientras / yo / estar / enfermo

Paso 2. Now tell the story again from the point of view of the mother of the sick person. The first sentence is done for you.

> MODELO: **1.** cuando / yo / ser / niño, / pensar / que / lo mejor / de / estar enfermo / ser / guardar cama →
> Cuando mi hijo era niño, pensaba que lo mejor de estar enfermo era guardar cama.

Need more practice?

- Workbook and Laboratory Manual
- Interactive CD-ROM
- Online Learning Center (www.mhhe.com/puntos7)

■ ■ ■ Conversación

A. El primer día. Dé Ud. sus impresiones del primer día de su primera clase universitaria. Use estas preguntas como guía.

1. ¿Cuál fue la primera clase? ¿A qué hora era la clase y dónde era?
2. ¿Vino a clase con alguien? ¿Ya tenía su libro de texto o lo compró después?
3. ¿Qué hizo Ud. después de entrar en la sala de clase? ¿Qué hacía el profesor / la profesora?
4. ¿A quién conoció Ud. aquel día? ¿Ya conocía a algunos miembros de la clase? ¿A quiénes?
5. ¿Aprendió Ud. mucho durante la clase? ¿Ya sabía algo de esa materia?
6. ¿Le gustó el profesor / la profesora? ¿Por qué sí o por qué no? ¿Cómo era?
7. ¿Cómo se sentía durante la clase? ¿Nervioso/a? ¿aburrido/a? ¿cómodo/a?
8. ¿Les dio tarea el profesor / la profesora? ¿Pudo Ud. hacerla fácilmente?
9. ¿Su primera impresión de la clase y del profesor / de la profesora fue válida o cambió con el tiempo? ¿Por qué?

Con. A: Follow-Up

- After completing the activity, have students write short paragraphs about their first day at the university (or a similar topic). Have them narrate their story in the past, using the preterite and the imperfect. Collect and choose the best two to three narrations, edit them, and develop activities based on them (on overhead transparencies or reproduced copies). The preceding paragraphs in *Prácticas C* and *D* are based on actual student paragraphs.
- Have students give oral presentations using the questions as a guide.

Con. A: Extension

10. *¿Qué hora era cuando llegó Ud. a la universidad? ¿Por qué llegó a esa hora? ¿Qué ropa llevaba?*
11. *¿Cuántos estudiantes había en la clase? ¿Qué hacían cuando Ud. entró?*
12. *¿Sabían todos más que Ud.? ¿Habló Ud. durante la clase? ¿Le hizo algunas preguntas al profesor / a la profesora?*
13. *¿Ya sabía Ud. el nombre del profesor / de la profesora? ¿Sabía qué tipo de profesor(a) era?*
14. *¿Tenía ganas de regresar a clase o quería dejarla?*

Con. B: Suggestions

- Have students add three questions of their own to each list.
- Tell students to imagine that you are a detective who has to write a report about the theft of a rare book that disappeared from the university library yesterday. You need to know exactly where they were and what they were doing from _____ to _____ yesterday.

B. Entrevista. Unas preguntas sobre el pasado

Paso 1. Con un compañero / una compañera, haga y conteste las siguientes preguntas.

¿Cuántos años tenías cuando... ?

1. aprendiste a pasear en bicicleta
2. hiciste tu primer viaje en avión
3. tuviste tu primera cita (*date*)
4. empezaste a afeitarte
5. conseguiste tu licencia de manejar (*driver's license*)
6. abriste una cuenta corriente (*checking account*)
7. dejaste de crecer (*grow*)

Paso 2. Con otro compañero / otra compañera, haga y conteste estas preguntas.

¿Cuántos años tenías cuando tus padres... ?

1. te dejaron cruzar la calle solo/a
2. te permitieron ir de compras a solas
3. te dejaron acostarte después de las nueve
4. te dejaron quedarte en casa sin niñero/a
5. te permitieron usar la estufa
6. te dejaron ver una película «R»
7. te dejaron conseguir un trabajo

Paso 3. Ahora, en grupos de cuatro, comparen sus respuestas. ¿Son muy diferentes las respuestas que dieron? ¿Quién del grupo tiene los padres más estrictos? ¿los menos estrictos?

C. Una historia famosa

Paso 1. La siguiente historia está narrada en el presente. Cámbiela al pasado, poniendo los verbos en el pretérito.

> **L**a niña *abre*[1] la puerta y *entra*[2] en la casa. *Ve*[3] tres sillas. *Se sienta*[4] en la primera silla, luego en la segunda, pero no le *gusta*[5] ninguna. Por eso *se sienta*[6] en la tercera. *Ve*[7] tres platos de comida en la mesa y *decide*[8] comer el más pequeño. Luego, *va*[9] a la alcoba para descansar un poco. Después de probar[a] las camas grandes, *se acuesta*[10] en la cama más pequeña y *se queda*[11] dormida.
>
> [a]*trying*

Paso 2. ¿Reconoce Ud. la historia? Es el cuento de Ricitos de Oro y los tres osos (*Goldilocks and the Three Bears*). Pero el cuento está un poco aburrido tal como está (*as it is*). Mejore el cuento con detalles y descripciones. **¡OJO!** Se usa el imperfecto en las descripciones.

> MODELO: La niña se llamaba Ricitos de Oro. Abrió la puerta y entró en la casa. La casa estaba muy...

Paso 3. Ahora termine la historia de Ricitos de Oro. ¿Qué pasó al final?

CULTURE

Point out that many fairy tales told in English are also told throughout the Spanish-speaking world: *Caperucita Roja* (Little Red Riding Hood), *La Bella y la Bestia* (Beauty and the Beast), *Los tres cerditos* (The Three Little Pigs), among others.

Heritage Speakers

Al hacer la Conversación B, es muy probable que los estudiantes hispanohablantes vayan a contestar las preguntas empleando el imperfecto del subjuntivo.

> *Mis padres me dejaron que cruzara solo la calle cuando tenía 6 años.*

Si es necesario, explíqueles a los estudiantes de habla inglesa que aprenderán ese tiempo verbal en el *Capítulo 17.*

Recognizing *que*, *quien(es)*, *lo que* • Relative Pronouns

La salud es *lo que* importa

¿Sabe Ud. *lo que* debe hacer para ser saludable emocionalmente? ¿Vive Ud. la vida *que* debe vivir? Para estar seguro de *lo que* necesita para la salud física, consulte con un doctor en *quien* confía. Pero para lograr un estado de bienestar mental, hágase estas preguntas:

- ¿Hay personas con *quienes* puedo hablar si tengo problemas?
- ¿Qué métodos uso para combatir el estrés *que* me causan los problemas diarios?
- ¿Mantengo un balance entre *lo que* es de valor profesional o educativo en mi vida y *lo que* es puramente de diversión personal?
- ¿Tengo un amigo o pariente con *quien* comparto mi vida?

Tengo unos dolores de estómago que me despiertan en la noche.

Lo que tienes que hacer es...

Note
Relative pronouns are introduced for recognition only. Activities will not emphasize productive use.

Emphasis A: Note

- The *que* that students will learn to recognize in subjunctive constructions is a relative conjunction, used to introduce noun clauses (clauses that function as nouns).
- *Lo que* has been active since *Capítulo 7*, primarily for use in direction lines.

Complete las siguientes oraciones.

1. La persona con quien más hablo cuando tengo problemas es _____.
2. El método que más uso para combatir el estrés es _____.
3. Las actividades que mantienen el balance en mi vida son _____.
4. La persona con quien comparto (*I share*) (o con quien me gustaría compartir) mi vida es _____.

A. There are four principal *relative pronouns* in English: *that, which, who,* and *whom.* They are usually expressed in Spanish by the relative pronouns at the right, all of which you already know.

que: refers to things and people
quien: refers only to people
lo que: refers to a situation

> **relative pronoun** = a pronoun that introduces a dependent clause and denotes a noun already mentioned

---

Health is what matters *Do you know what you should do to be emotionally healthy? Do you live the life that you should live? To be sure about what you need for physical health, consult a doctor that you trust. But to achieve mental well-being, ask yourself these questions:* ■ *Are there any people with whom I can talk if I have problems?* ■ *What methods do I use to fight the stress that my daily problems cause?* ■ *Do I maintain a balance between what is of professional and educational value in my life and what is purely for personal pleasure?* ■ *Do I have a friend or relative with whom I share my life?*

Refrán

«Ojos que no ven, corazón que no siente.»

Have students identify the relative pronouns in this sentence (*que/que*). Then have them work together to come up with English versions of this *refrán*. (*What you don't know won't hurt you. Out of sight, out of mind.*)

Emphasis B: Note

The relative pronoun *que* introduces adjective clauses (clauses that modify nouns). The use of the subjunctive in such clauses is presented in *Capítulo 15*. Point out here how clauses modify the nouns *cita* and *médico*.

Emphasis B: Suggestions

- Point out that *quien* can be used after a comma without a preposition.
- Emphasize that *que* is the most frequently used of the three relative pronouns.
- Emphasize that *lo que* is a neuter relative pronoun, and that it is *not* used to express direct questions (*¿Qué es esto? ¿Cuál es tu teléfono?*). *Lo que* is used to replaced a concept, idea, or to refer to a situation in which there is no basis for assigning number or gender.

Emphasis C: Note

Lo que refers to a single word only, when that word has not been mentioned yet: *Lo que necesito es dinero.*

B. Learning to recognize the meaning of these words in context will make reading in Spanish easier for you, especially with authentic materials (written for native speakers of Spanish). See if you can understand the following sentences without looking at the English equivalents.

- **que** = *that, which, who*

  Tuve una cita con el médico **que** duró una hora.
  I had an appointment with the doctor that lasted an hour.

  Es un buen médico **que** sabe mucho.
  He's a good doctor who knows a lot.

- **quien(es)** = *who/whom* after a preposition or as an indirect object

  (Remember that an indirect object expresses to or for whom/what something is done.)

  La mujer con **quien** hablaba era mi hermana.
  The woman with whom I was talking was my sister.

  Ese es el niño a **quien** no le gusta el helado.
  That's the boy who doesn't like ice cream.

- **lo que** = *what, that which*

  No entiendo **lo que** dice.
  I don't understand what he is saying.

  Lo que no me gusta es su actitud hacia los pobres.
  What I don't like is his attitude toward poor people.

C. The antecedent (what it refers to) of **lo que** is always a sentence, a whole situation, or something that hasn't been mentioned yet.

Lo que necesito es estudiar más.

 Remember that the relative pronouns **que** and **quien** have an accent mark only in the interrogative or exclamatory form.

—¿Con **quién** hablas?
Whom are you talking to?

—Hablo con la mujer con **quien** doy la fiesta.
I'm talking to the woman with whom I'm giving the party.

—¿**Qué** dices? ¡**Qué** historia tan interesante!
What are you saying? What an interesting story!

—¡Te digo **que** es verdad!
I'm telling you (that) it's true!

AUTOPRUEBA

Match each item with the corresponding relative pronoun.

1. _____ una cosa   **a.** que
2. _____ un concepto   **b.** quien
3. _____ a una persona   **c.** quienes
4. _____ con dos amigos   **d.** lo que
5. _____ una idea

Answers: 1. a 2. d 3. b 4. c 5. d

National Standards: Communication/Culture

The relative pronouns that students have seen thus far all refer to antecedents found in the main clause. There are, however, other uses of relative pronouns in which there is no antecedent. These pronouns frequently appear in popular sayings or proverbs and correspond to *he who, the one who,* or *those who* in English.

Quien ríe el último, ríe mejor.	He who laughs last, laughs loudest.
Quien no se aventura, no cruza la mar.	Nothing ventured, nothing gained.
El que algo quiere, algo le cuesta.	There is no free lunch.

■■■ **Práctica**

A. Problemas médicos. Complete las oraciones lógicamente, usando **que, quien** o **lo que.**

EN LA SALA DE EMERGENCIAS/URGENCIA

—¿Quién fue el hombre _____¹ la trajo aquí?

—No sé. Se fue y sólo dejó esta dirección y este número de teléfono.

—Sí, ya llamamos al número. Desgraciadamenteª nadie contesta y no podemos localizar a la persona con _____² vive.

—Parece que ha tenidoᵇ una reacción a algo. Está muy grave. ¡ _____³ necesitamos es más tiempo! Tienes que despertarla y preguntarle sobre la medicina que tomó.

—Quiero saber el nombre de la medicina _____⁴ Ud. tomaba.

—¡Ay, Dios! No se despierta. ¿Dónde está el ayudanteᶜ _____⁵ empezó a trabajar ayer? Necesito su ayuda.

EN EL CONSULTORIO DEL MÉDICO

DOCTOR: Pues _____⁶ Ud. tiene es exceso de peso.ᵈ Debe perder por lo menos diez libras.

PACIENTE: Pero, doctor… Es cierto que como mucho, pero… Dígame, ¿a _____⁷ no le gusta comer?

DOCTOR: De ahora en adelante,ᵉ Ud. puede comer todo _____⁸ le guste… ¡y aquí está la lista de _____⁹ le debe gustar!

ªUnfortunately ᵇha… he's had ᶜassistant ᵈweight ᵉDe… From this point on

B. El estrés, la condición humana

Paso 1. Lea la siguiente tira cómica y conteste las preguntas.

ªcansancio… *fatigue, restlessness, worry, nervousness, (emotional) imbalance, and anxiety*

1. Lo que quiere el padre de Libertad (la amiga de Mafalda) es _____.
2. Lo que tiene es _____.
3. Según el médico, lo que tiene su padre es _____.

Paso 2. ¿De cuántas de esas condiciones sufre Ud.? ¿Sufre más de esos problemas durante ciertas épocas del año? ¿Cuáles?

Need more practice?
- Workbook and Laboratory Manual
- Interactive CD-ROM
- Online Learning Center (www.mhhe.com/ puntos7)

Prác. A: Suggestion

Have students give advice to the following people using sentences like:

La persona con quien debes hablar es… ; Lo que debes hacer es + infinitive.

1. *Necesito descansar, y tengo tres días libres la semana que viene.*
2. *Mi compañero/a de cuarto (esposo/a,…) no ayuda en nada en nuestro apartamento, y me molesta con su música por la noche.*
3. *No sé qué clases debo tomar el semestre que viene.*

Prác. B: Follow-Up

Ask students:

¿Qué critica la tira cómica?

Start a class discussion about life in modern industrialized society.

♻ Prác. B: Reciclado

- Recycle formal commands. Have students imagine that they are doctors and nurses and that they give Marisa advice. *Tienen que darle consejos a Marisa, quien se acaba de romper un tobillo (ankle). Usen mandatos formales, que es lo normal en estas situaciones.*
- Recycle informal commands. Have students work in groups of three to four. Students take turns explaining their health and fitness concerns, for example, they want to quit smoking, lose weight, reduce stress, and so on. The others offer advice for accomplishing their goals, for example, what to do if they get the urge to smoke or eat.

Con: Suggestion

Bring in articles from a Spanish-language newspaper or magazine and have students identify and analyze the use of relative pronouns.

■ ■ ■ Conversación

Problemas y consejos

Paso 1. Déle varios consejos a la persona que tiene los siguientes problemas. Use estas frases como guía: **La persona con quien debes hablar es... , Lo que debes hacer es...**

1. Tengo un resfriado terrible.
2. Necesito descansar, y tengo tres días libres la semana que viene.
3. Tengo ganas de comer comida china esta noche.
4. No sé qué clases debo tomar el semestre/trimestre que viene.
5. ¡Sufro tantas presiones (*I am under so much pressure*) en mi vida privada!
6. Vivo muy lejos de la universidad. Pierdo una hora en ir y venir todos los días.

Paso 2. Ahora invente Ud. problemas similares —o cuente un problema real— y pídales consejos a sus compañeros de clase.

EN LOS ESTADOS UNIDOS Y EL CANADÁ

Edward James Olmos: Actor y activista de la comunidad

El conocido **actor** de origen mexicano, Edward James Olmos (Los Ángeles, 1947), tiene en su historia profesional papeles inolvidables[a] como el de Jaime Escalante en *Stand and Deliver*, y el de policía en la famosa película cultista[b] *Blade Runner*. Además es un reconocido[c] **productor** y fue **director** y **guionista**[d] de la película *American Me*, sobre las pandillas[e] de Los Ángeles. Ha recibido los premios[f] Golden Globe y Emmy.

Pero el Sr. Olmos no es sólo un artista sino también un destacado[g]

▲ *Edward James Olmos*

líder de la comunidad latina en los Estados Unidos. Su **trabajo humanitario** y **comunitario** demuestra[h] un profundo compromiso[i] a favor de **la juventud** y **la salud** y contra la violencia de las pandillas y el racismo. Entre los muchos cargos que ha desempeñado[j] están los de embajador[k] de los Estados Unidos en UNICEF, portavoz[l] nacional de la Fundación Juvenil contra la Diabetes, de la Fundación Alerta contra el **SIDA**[m] y del Registro de Votantes. Además es miembro del comité de varios hospitales para niños y también del Concejo Nacional de Adopción.

[a]*papeles... unforgettable roles* [b]*cult* [c]*well-known* [d]*scriptwriter* [e]*gangs* [f]*Ha... He has received the awards* [g]*distinguished* [h]*shows* [i]*commitment* [j]*Entre... Among the many positions he has held* [k]*ambassador* [l]*spokesperson* [m]*Fundación... AIDS Awareness Foundation*

EN LOS ESTADOS UNIDOS Y EL CANADÁ

Suggestions

- Have students describe movie and TV roles Olmos has portrayed.
- Have students watch *American Me* or *Stand and Deliver* and prepare a report on it.
- Have students name other actor-activists and community leaders of Hispanic origin (César Chávez, *Perspectivas culturales* in *Capítulo 1*; Martin Sheen, *En los Estados Unidos y el Canadá,* *Capítulo 2*; state Sen. Richard Polanco, *En los Estados Unidos y el Canadá, Capítulo 8*).
- Encourage students to search the Internet for more information about Edward James Olmos and his humanitarian work. Have them write a brief description of him as an actor and community activist. Encourage them to use the relative pronouns they learned in this chapter.

Before learning how to express reciprocal actions, review the reflexive pronouns (**Gramática 14**), then provide the correct reflexive pronouns for the following sentences.

1. _____ levanté a las ocho y media.
2. Laura _____ puso el vestido.
3. Mis amigos y yo _____ sentamos juntos.
4. ¿Prefieres duchar_____ o bañar_____?

32 Expressing *each other* • Reciprocal Actions with Reflexive Pronouns

Rosa y Casandra

Rosa y Casandra *se conocen* bien. Son compañeras de cuarto. *Se ven* todos los días y *se encuentran* después de clase para hablar. ¿Qué hacen Rosa y Casandra en esta escena?

Se besan.*

The plural reflexive pronouns, **nos, os,** and **se,** can be used to express *reciprocal actions* (**las acciones recíprocas**). Reciprocal actions are usually expressed in English with *each other* or *one another*.

Nos queremos.

Nos queremos.   *We love each other.*
¿**Os** ayudáis?   *Do you help one another?*
Se miran.   *They're looking at each other.*

AUTOPRUEBA

Give the correct pronoun to express a reciprocal action.

1. _____ miramos   4. _____ conocen
2. _____ pelearon   5. _____ llamaban
3. _____ veíais   6. _____ saludamos

Answers: 1. nos 2. se 3. os 4. se 5. se 6. nos

---

*As in many cultures, in Spain and Latin America kissing on the cheek is a common form of greeting and leave-taking. In Hispanic cultures, women kiss each other on the cheek, and men and women kiss each other on the cheek. The number of kisses varies from country to country; in Spain, two kisses (one on each cheek) is common. In much of Latin America, only one kiss, usually on the right cheek, is the norm.

Gramática

Reciprocal Actions with Reflexive Pronouns

Follow-Up

Ask questions to expand the use of the art.

1. *Rosa y Casandra, ¿se entienden bien?*
2. *¿Cree Ud. que se ayudan con los problemas? ¿con la tarea?*

Suggestions

- Review the use of *nos, os,* and *se* in reflexive verbs from *Capítulo 4.*
- Compare reflexive actions to reciprocal actions: *nos lavamos* vs. *nos queremos.* Point out the importance of context.
- Point out that reciprocal pronouns work as either direct or indirect object pronouns. In the sentences *Se quieren* (They love each other) and *Nos llamamos* (We call each other), the reciprocal pronouns indicate persons directly affected by the action. In the sentences *Uds. se mandaron cartas* (You sent each other letters) and *Nos compramos regalos* (We bought each other gifts), the reciprocal pronouns indicate persons indirectly affected by the action.
- Emphasize that not all verbs can be made reciprocal, as not all verbs can be reflexive. Model some examples of intransitive verbs in exchanges with students.

    ¿Adónde se van Uds. después de la clase? vs. *¿Uds. se ven después de la clase?*

Prác. A: Preliminary Exercises

- Ask students how the following sentences are expressed in Spanish.

  1. We help each other. (you, they)
  2. We love each other. (you, they)
  3. We write to each other. (you they)

- Have students restate the following sentences as reciprocal actions.

  1. *Estela me mira a mí. Yo miro a Estela.*
  2. *Eduardo habla con Pepita. Pepita habla con Eduardo.*
  3. *El padre necesita a su hijo. El hijo necesita a su padre.*
  4. *Tomás me conoce a mí. Yo conozco a Tomás.*
  5. *Tú le escribes a Luisa. Luisa te escribe a ti.*
  6. *La profesora escucha a los estudiantes. Los estudiantes escuchan a la profesora.*
  7. *Ud. quiere a su esposo. Su esposo la quiere también a Ud.*
  8. *Jorge le da la mano a Mario. Mario le da la mano a Jorge.*

Prác. A: Suggestion

Have students repeat items using *ellos* as the subject, then *vosotros*.

Prác. B: Suggestion

Provide the following cues for students to construct a story about *La triste historia de amor de Orlando y Patricia.* Have students narrate the story in the preterite.

1. *verse en clase*
2. *mirarse*
3. *saludarse*
4. *empezar a llamarse por teléfono*
5. *escribirse durante las vacaciones*
6. *ayudarse con sus problemas*
7. *casarse* (translate)
8. *no llevarse bien* (translate)
9. *separarse*
10. *divorciarse*

Prác. B: Follow-Up

Ask students questions to personalize the construction.

Ud. y sus amigos/as, ¿se llaman por teléfono?
¿se ven frecuentemente?
¿se ayudan?
¿se escriben?
¿se mandan regalos?
¿ ... ?

■■■ Práctica

A. **¡Anticipemos! Buenos amigos.** Indique las oraciones que describen lo que hacen Ud. y un buen amigo / una buena amiga para mantener su amistad (*friendship*).

1. ☐ Nos vemos con frecuencia.
2. ☐ Nos conocemos muy bien. No hay secretos entre nosotros.
3. ☐ Nos respetamos mucho.
4. ☐ Nos ayudamos con cualquier (*any*) problema.
5. ☐ Nos escribimos cuando no estamos en la misma ciudad.
6. ☐ Nos hablamos por teléfono con frecuencia.
7. ☐ Nos decimos la verdad siempre, sea esta (*be it*) bonita o fea.
8. ☐ Cuando estamos muy ocupados, no importa si no nos hablamos por mucho tiempo.

B. **¿Qué se hacen?** Describa las siguientes relaciones familiares o sociales, haciendo oraciones completas con una palabra o frase de cada grupo.

MODELO: Los buenos amigos se conocen bien.

Need more practice?

- Workbook and Laboratory Manual
- Interactive CD-ROM
- Online Learning Center (www.mhhe.com/puntos7)

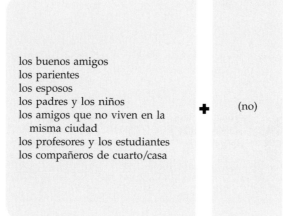

los buenos amigos
los parientes
los esposos
los padres y los niños
los amigos que no viven en la misma ciudad
los profesores y los estudiantes
los compañeros de cuarto/casa

+ (no) **+**

verse con frecuencia
quererse, respetarse
ayudarse (con los quehaceres domésticos, con los problemas económicos, con los problemas personales)
hablarse (todos los días, con frecuencia, sinceramente)
llamarse por teléfono, escribirse (con frecuencia)
mirarse (en la clase, con cariño [*affection*])
necesitarse
conocerse bien
saludarse (*to greet each other*) (en la clase, con cariño), darse la mano

■■■ Conversación

Entrevista

1. ¿Con qué frecuencia se ven tú y tu novio/a (esposo/a, mejor amigo/a)? ¿Cuánto tiempo hace que se conocen? ¿Con qué frecuencia se dan regalos? ¿se escriben? ¿se telefonean? ¿Te gusta que se vean tanto (tan poco)?
2. ¿Con qué frecuencia se ven tú y tus abuelos/primos? ¿Por qué se ven Uds. tan poco (tanto)? ¿Cómo se mantienen en contacto? En la sociedad norteamericana, ¿los parientes se ven con frecuencia? En tu opinión, ¿es esto común entre los hispanos?

 Heritage Speakers

Pídales a dos estudiantes que dramaticen algunas acciones recíprocas, por ejemplo, *verse el uno al otro, saludarse el uno al otro, hablarse el uno al otro.* Los demás estudiantes explican las acciones, por ejemplo, *Paco y Marta se saludan.*

UN POCO DE TODO

A. ¡Hábleme de Venezuela! Complete the following passage with the correct form of the words in parentheses, as suggested by the context. The verbs will be in the present, preterite, and imperfect, and there is one command form, which is indicated for you. When two possibilities are given, select the correct word.

La professora Norma Ayala Romero enseña química en una escuela secundaria. Anoche recibió el siguiente mensaje electrónico.[a]

«Sra. Ayala, (*yo:* llamarse[1]) Bettina Gilbert. Ud. no me (saber/ conocer[2]), pero (*yo:* ser/estar[3]) estudiante de la Franklin High. Mi familia y yo necesitamos su ayuda. (Alguno[4]) de mis amigos (ser/estar[5]) en las clases de química (que/lo que[6]) Ud. enseña y me (dijeron/decían[7]) que Ud. (ser/estar[8]) de Venezuela.

En una semana, dos chicas de Caracas (venir[9]) a vivir con (nos/nosotros[10]) porque (ir[11]) a estudiar por un año en la universidad de (nuestro[12]) ciudad. Mi hermano y yo ya (saber/conocer[13]) muchas cosas interesantes de Venezuela. El año pasado (leíamos/leímos[14]) de los tepuis, las montañas planas[b] (que/quien[15]) suben como torres de paredes verticales[c] y tienen una ecología y ambiente únicos y misteriosos. A mí (me/yo[16]) gustaría visitar el tepui Auyantepuy y el Salto[d] Ángel, el salto más alto del mundo.

(Lo que/Que[17]) no (*nosotros:* saber/conocer[18]) es cómo es la vida diaria de los venezolanos. ¿Hay (algo/nada[19]) que se coma (todo[20]) los días? ¿(Cómo/Qué[21]) tipo de comida prefieren? Si Ud. nos puede dar unos consejos, (te lo / se lo[22]) agradeceríamos[e] mucho.»

La Sra. Ayala (responder[23]) así.

«Bettina: Me (encantar[24]) que Uds. tengan tanto interés en mi país. Es imposible hacer generalizaciones sobre la vida diaria venezolana, porque, como ocurre en este país, puede variar muchísimo. (Lo que/Que[25]) Uds. van a descubrir es que las dos chicas tienen mucho en común con los jóvenes de aquí porque Caracas (ser/estar[26]) una ciudad grande. Cuando yo (ser[27]) joven, también (vivir[28]) en Caracas. Nosotros (llevar[29]) ropa muy parecida[f] a la ropa de aquí y también (practicar[30]) varios deportes. Mis amigas y yo (dar[31]) paseos en el (cine/parque[32]) y (hacer[33]) ejercicio en el gimnasio. Uds. no tienen que hacer (ninguno[34]) preparación especial.

Por favor, (*comm.:* hablarme[35]) Uds. por teléfono tan pronto como lleguen[g] las muchachas. Me gustaría mucho (saber/conocer[36])las. ¡Hasta pronto!»

[a]mensaje... *e-mail message*   [b]*flat*   [c]torres... *vertical-walled towers*   [d]*Waterfall*   [e]*we would be grateful*   [f]*similar*   [g]tan... *as soon as* (*they*) *arrive*

UN POCO DE TODO

A: Suggestions

- Review the contrastive uses of the preterite and imperfect before completing this activity.

  ¿El pretérito o el imperfecto? ¿Cuál se usa... ?
  ...para indicar el comienzo o el final de una acción?
  ...para hablar de una acción habitual del pasado?
  ...para decir la hora?
  ...para expresar características mentales?

- This activity, like many in the text, is designed to help students develop conceptual knowledge of the differences in language concepts such as the preterite and imperfect, *ser* and *estar*, *saber* and *conocer*, direct and indirect objects, and relative pronouns. In addition, students will have to switch from present to past in order to complete the narration. A general rule of thumb that might help students is present follows present and past follows past.

National Standards: Community

Ask students if they have participated in a student-exchange program or know of someone who has. Have them describe the experience, especially as it relates to a second language and/or cultural differences. Have students search the Internet for exchange programs with Spanish-speaking countries.

- This retelling of the Little Red Riding Hood story is an authentic version from Spain. You and the students may be familiar with other versions of the story. Encourage the students to provide additional details.

- *Había una vez*, *Había una vez y dos son tres*, and *Érase una vez* are traditional beginnings for tales. Some traditional endings include: *Y vivieron felices y comieron perdices*; *Y colorín, colorado, este cuento se ha acabado*.

Comprensión: ¿Qué sabe Ud.?

In Spanish, briefly answer the following questions about the people and information presented in the exchange of e-mail messages.

1. ¿Quién es Norma Ayala Romero? ¿y Bettina Gilbert?
2. ¿Cómo sabe Bettina que la Sra. Ayala es de Venezuela?
3. ¿Qué sabía Bettina de Venezuela antes de comunicarse con la Sra. Ayala?
4. ¿Qué quiere saber Bettina ahora? ¿Por qué?
5. ¿Qué le dice la Sra. Ayala a Bettina de las jóvenes venezolanas?
6. ¿Qué hacía la Sra. Ayala en Caracas cuando era joven?

B. Caperucita Roja

Paso 1. Retell this familiar story, based on the drawings, sentences, and cues that accompany each drawing, using the imperfect or preterite of the verbs in parentheses. Add as many details as you can. Using context, try to guess the meaning of words that are glossed with ¿ ?.

Vocabulario útil			
abalanzarse sobre	to pounce on	enterarse de	to find out about
avisar	to warn	esconderse	to hide
dispararle	to shoot at (someone/something)	huir (huyó)	to flee
		saltar	to jump

1.
2.
3.
4.

1. Érase una vez[a] una niña hermosa que (llamarse[1]) Caperucita Roja. Todos los animales del bosque[b] (ser[2]) sus amigos y Caperucita Roja los (querer[3]) mucho.

2. Un día su mamá le (decir[4]): —Lleva en seguida esta jarrita de miel[c] a casa de tu abuelita. Ten cuidado[d] con el lobo[e] feroz.

   [a]¿ ? [b]¿ ? [c]*jarrita… jar of honey* [d]*Ten… Be careful* [e]¿ ?

3. En el bosque, el lobo (salir[5]) a hablar con la niña. Le (preguntar[6]): —¿Adónde vas, Caperucita? Esta le (contestar[7]) dulcemente:[f] —Voy a casa de mi abuelita.

4. —Pues, si vas por este sendero,[g] vas a llegar antes, (decir[8]) el malvado[h] lobo. Él (irse[9]) por otro camino más corto.

   [f]*sweetly* [g]*path* [h]¿ ?

MULTIMEDIA: Internet   **Resources: Transparency 75**

Have students look for online versions of *Caperucita Roja* in Spanish. They can also find the following stories in Spanish on the Internet: *La Cenicienta*, *Peter Pan*, *Simbad el marinero*, *Los tres cerditos*, *Blancanieves*, *El flautista de Hamelín*, and *Merlín el mago*.

5.  **6.**  **7.** **8.**

5. El lobo (llegar[10]) primero a la casa de la abuelita y (entrar[11]) silenciosamente. La abuelita (tener[12]) mucho miedo. (*Ella: Saltar[13]*) de la cama y (correr[14]) a esconderse.

6. Caperucita Roja (llegar[15]) por fin a la casa de la abuelita. (*Ella: Encontrar[16]*) a su «abuelita», que (estar[17]) en la cama. Le (decir[18]): —¡Qué dientes tan largos tienes! —¡Son para comerte mejor!— (decir[19]) su «abuelita».

7. Una ardilla[i] del bosque (enterarse[20]) del peligro. Por eso (avisar[21]) a un cazador.[j]

8. El lobo (saltar[22]) de la cama y (abalanzarse[23]) sobre Caperucita. Ella (salir[24]) de la casa corriendo y pidiendo socorro[k] desesperadamente.

[i]¿ ?   [j]¿ ?   [k]*help*

9.  **10.**

9. El cazador (ver[25]) lo que (ocurrir[26]). (*Él: Dispararle[27]*) al lobo y le (hacer[28]) huir.

10. Caperucita (regresar[29]) a la casa de su abuelita. La (*ella: abrazar[30]*) y le (prometer[31]) escuchar siempre los consejos de su mamá.

Paso 2. Hay varias versiones del cuento de Caperucita Roja. La que Ud. acaba de leer termina felizmente, pero otras no. Con otros dos compañeros, vuelva a contar la historia, empezando por el dibujo número 7. Inventen un diálogo más largo entre Caperucita y el lobo y cambien por completo el final del cuento.

Más vocabulario útil			
atacar (qu)	to attack	**matar**	to kill
comérselo/la	to eat something up		

Un poco de todo

Trescientos treinta y cinco ■ **335**

B: Follow-Up
Have students retell the story in their own words in Spanish.

B: Variation
Have students invent a new tale together in a round-robin format. The story can begin on one side of the room and "travel" from student to student. Each student says one sentence. Remind them to use the preterite and imperfect in the narration. Avoid direct correction. Repeat each sentence students say, rephrasing as necessary to correct errors.

Resources for Review and Testing Preparation

- Workbook and Laboratory Manual
- Interactive CD-ROM
- Online Learning Center (www.mhhe.com/puntos7)

Resources: Desenlace

In the *Capítulo 10* segment of "Chapter-by-Chapter Supplementary Materials" in the IM, you will find a chapter-culminating activity. You can use this activity to consolidate and review the vocabulary and grammar skills students have acquired.

Entrevista cultural

Suggestions

- Before showing the video, ask students questions about their studies and how they take care of themselves.

    ¿Qué carrera estudia Ud.? ¿Por qué?

    ¿Qué tipo de trabajo quiere hacer después de graduarse?

    ¿Qué come para cuidar la salud?

    ¿Qué más hace para cuidar la salud?

- Show the video and allow students one to two minutes to work on the questions. Have volunteers answer the questions.

- Have volunteers role-play Sabina and her interviewer.

Entre amigos

Suggestions

- Before viewing the video, review the questions with the students and ask them similar questions.

    ¿Hace Ud. ejercicio?

    ¿Qué tipo de ejercicio hace?

    ¿Cuántas veces por semana…

    …hace Ud. ejercicios aeróbicos?

    …levanta pesas?

    …nada?

    ¿Dónde prefiere hacer ejercicio?

Have students answer or work in small groups to ask and answer these questions.

- After viewing the video, have volunteers read and answer the questions.

● ● ●
Videoteca

Entrevista cultural: Venezuela

Sabina García es una estudiante venezolana. En esta entrevista, ella comenta sus estudios y sus hábitos personales. Sabina hace mucho para mantener un buen estado de salud. Antes de ver el vídeo, lea el siguiente fragmento de la entrevista.

ENTREVISTADORA: ¿Qué estudias?

SABINA: Estudio relaciones internacionales. Considero que actualmente[a] las relaciones internacionales son un campo muy importante en el mundo y se han desarrollado[b] con gran rapidez.

ENTREVISTADORA: ¿Cómo cuidas tu salud?

SABINA: Trato de alimentarme sanamente, comiendo frutas, verduras, fibra principalmente y me acuesto temprano.

[a]*currently* [b]*se… they have developed*

Ahora vea el vídeo y conteste las siguientes preguntas basándose en la entrevista.

1. ¿Qué estudia Sabina?
2. ¿Por qué estudia esta carrera?
3. ¿Qué come Sabina?
4. ¿Qué más hace Sabina para cuidarse?
5. ¿Qué hace para aliviarse el estrés?

Entre amigos: ¡Yo sí hago ejercicio!

Tané, Karina, Rubén y Miguel visitan un mercado de pulgas (*flea market*) y hablan del ejercicio. En su opinión, ¿qué preguntas se van a hacer? Antes de mirar el vídeo, lea las preguntas a continuación. Mientras mire el vídeo, trate de entender la conversación en general y fíjese en la información sobre el ejercicio que hacen los amigos. Luego mire el vídeo una segunda vez, fijándose en la información que necesita para contestar las preguntas.

1. ¿Hace ejercicio Karina? ¿Qué tipo de ejercicio hace?
2. ¿Y Tané? ¿Qué tipo de ejercicio hace ella?
3. ¿Quiénes no tienen mucho tiempo para hacer ejercicio?
4. ¿Qué está haciendo Miguel mientras hablan del ejercicio?
5. ¿Cuántas veces por semana va Miguel al gimnasio?

Capítulo 10: La salud

National Standards: Culture

Have students research Venezuelan cuisine. What are some typical dishes? Review keywords they will need for their search, such as *comida*, *venezolana*, and *recetas*.

Conozca... **Venezuela**

Datos esenciales

- Nombre oficial: República de Venezuela
- Capital: Caracas
- Población: 24.660.000 habitantes
- Moneda: el bolívar
- Idiomas: el español (oficial), varios idiomas indígenas

¡Fíjese!

Por su variedad de climas, Venezuela le ofrece al turista atracciones diversas. El clima venezolano varía entre el clima templado de las regiones andinas y el clima tropical de los llanos[a] y la costa. De hecho, el clima es agradable la mayor parte del año. Entre las atracciones turísticas hay lo siguiente:

1. las hermosas[b] playas tropicales de la Isla Margarita y la costa caribeña
2. la famosa catarata[c] Salto Ángel que, siendo dieciséis veces más alta que las cataratas del Niágara, es considerada la más alta del mundo
3. la belleza[d] colonial de Ciudad Bolívar y Coro
4. la progresiva y cosmopolita ciudad de Caracas y las majestuosas montañas andinas

[a]plains [b]beautiful [c]waterfall [d]beauty

  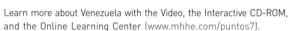

Learn more about Venezuela with the Video, the Interactive CD-ROM, and the Online Learning Center (www.mhhe.com/puntos7).

Personas famosas: Simón Bolívar

Simón Bolívar (1783–1830) nació en Caracas. La fecha de su cumpleaños, el 24 de julio, es hoy día una fiesta nacional en Venezuela. Bolívar, llamado «el Libertador», ocupa un puesto[a] importante tanto en la historia de Venezuela como en la historia de Colombia, el Perú, el Ecuador y Bolivia por ser el personaje principal en las luchas[b] por la independencia de estos países. Bolívar, influenciado por las ideas de Jean Jacques Rousseau[c] y por la lucha de las colonias estadounidenses contra Inglaterra en el siglo XVIII, soñaba con[d] una América hispánica unida, sueño que nunca vio realizado.[e]

[a]position [b]struggles [c]French writer and philosopher (1712–1778) whose ideas helped spark the French Revolution [d]soñaba... dreamt about [e]achieved

▲ Salto Ángel

Notes

- Christopher Columbus first sighted what is now Venezuela in 1498. It was the home of the Caribs and Arawaks, indigenous peoples who also populated the Antilles.
- The Spanish explorer named the country Venezuela, "little Venice," because the villages, built on pilings on Lake Maracaibo, reminded him of that European city. In 1567, Diego de Losada founded the city of Santiago de León de Caracas in the *tierra templada* more than half a mile above sea level—Santiago after the patron saint of Spain, León after the governor of that time, and Caracas after the indigenous group of the area. Colonization of the country continued rapidly in the next century, with Caracas as its urban center.
- Venezuela remained under Spanish rule until 1821, although it had declared itself a republic in 1811. For ten years it was a part of *Gran Colombia*, which also included Colombia and Ecuador. The great general Simón Bolívar led this region's push for independence from Spain.
- The Venezuelan Andes run east-west, although elsewhere in South America they run north-south. Other geographical regions include the Guiana Plateau southeast of the Orinoco, the Orinoco *llanos* south of the Andes, and the Maracaibo Basin.
- Petroleum provides almost half of Venezuela's revenues and constitutes 85 percent of its exports.
- Students can read an excerpt from the novel *Doña Bárbara* by Venezuela's Rómulo Gallegos in *Un paso más 10*.

MULTIMEDIA: Internet

- Have students look for the *Biblioteca Virtual* on the Internet. Here they can learn more about *Simón Bolívar* and other Latin American heroes and historical moments.

- Have students search the Internet for more information about Venezuela's government, educational system, geography, and economy. You might assign specific topics and have students give brief oral presentations based on their findings.

Suggestions

- Describe absurd creatures and have students draw them, for example, *Era una criatura inmensa. Tenía tres piernas y un brazo. En la cabeza tenía una oreja que extendía de la frente...*

- Ask students the following questions.

  1. *¿Con qué parte del cuerpo se asocian estas cosas?*

la comida	las películas
la música	el amor
el oxígeno	el cálculo

  2. *¿Se refiere a la médica o al paciente?*

     Examina los ojos.
     Tiene fiebre.
     Saca la lengua.
     Escribe recetas.
     Le duele la garganta.
     Recomienda un jarabe.

EN RESUMEN

Gramática

To review the grammar points presented in this chapter, refer to the indicated grammar presentations. You'll find further practice of these structures in the Workbook and Laboratory Manual, on the Interactive CD-ROM, and on the *Puntos de partida* Online Learning Center (www.mhhe.com/puntos7).

30. Narrating in the Past—Using the Preterite and the Imperfect

Do you know which tense to use to express habitual or repeated actions? Which tense should be used to express the beginning or end of an action?

31. Recognizing *que, quien(es), lo que*—Relative Pronouns

You should know when to use **quien(es)** or **lo que** instead of **que**.

32. Expressing *each other*—Reciprocal Actions with Reflexive Pronouns

Which reflexive pronouns are used in reciprocal constructions?

Vocabulario

Practice this vocabulary with digital flash cards on the Online Learning Center (www.mhhe.com/puntos7).

La salud y el bienestar

la rueda de molino	treadmill
caminar	to walk
cuidarse	to take care of oneself
dejar de + *inf.*	to stop (*doing something*)
doler (ue)	to hurt, ache
encontrarse (ue)	to be, feel
examinar	to examine
guardar cama	to stay in bed
hacer (*irreg.*) **ejercicios aeróbicos**	to do aerobics
internarse (en)	to check in (*to a hospital*)
llevar una vida sana/tranquila	to lead a healthy/calm life
ponerle (*irreg.*) **una inyección**	to give (someone) a shot, injection
resfriarse (me resfrío)	to get/catch a cold
respirar	to breathe
sacar (qu)	to extract
sacar la lengua	to stick out one's tongue
sacar una muela	to extract a tooth
tener (*irreg.*) **dolor de**	to have a pain in
tomarle la temperatura	to take someone's temperature
toser	to cough

Repaso: comer, correr, dormir (ue, u), enfermarse, hacer (*irreg.*) **ejercicio, practicar (qu) deportes**

Algunas partes del cuerpo humano

la boca	mouth
la cabeza	head
el cerebro	brain
el corazón	heart
el cuerpo	body
el diente	tooth
el estómago	stomach
la garganta	throat
la muela	tooth; molar
la nariz	nose
el oído	inner ear
el ojo	eye
la oreja	(outer) ear
los pulmones	lungs
la sangre	blood

Las enfermedades y los tratamientos

el antibiótico	antibiotic
el chequeo	check-up
el consultorio	(medical) office
el dolor (de)	pain, ache (in)
la farmacia	pharmacy
la fiebre	fever
las gafas	glasses

el jarabe	(cough) syrup
los lentes de contacto	contact lenses
la medicina	medicine
la pastilla	pill
la receta	prescription
el resfriado	cold
la sala de emergencias/	emergency room
urgencia	
la salud	health
el síntoma	symptom
la temperatura	temperature
la tos	cough

El personal médico

el/la dentista	dentist
el/la enfermero/a	nurse
el/la farmacéutico/a	pharmacist
el/la paciente	patient

Repaso: el/la médico/a

Más sustantivos

la desventaja	disadvantage
la ventaja	advantage

Más verbos

encontrarse (ue) (con)	to meet (someone somewhere)
saludarse	to greet each other

Los adjetivos

congestionado/a	congested, stuffed up
mareado/a	dizzy; nauseated
mismo/a	same

Palabras adicionales

anoche	last night
anteayer	the day before yesterday
de repente	suddenly
dos veces	twice
en seguida	right away
equilibradamente	in a balanced way
eso quiere decir...	that means . . .
lo bueno / lo malo	the good thing, news / the bad thing, news
lo suficiente	enough

Repaso: lo que, que, quien, una vez

Suggestion
Ask students the following questions.

1. *Una persona come hamburguesas y toma Coca-Cola con frecuencia. ¿Come bien o come mal?*
2. *Si se tiene problemas del corazón, ¿se debe caminar o correr para hacer ejercicio?*
3. *Si se duerme siete horas y media cada noche, ¿duerme lo suficiente o necesita dormir más? (lo suficiente)*

Note

The *Un paso más* section is optional.

Literatura de **Venezuela**

Notes

- Rómulo Gallegos lived in and out of exile during the years of political turmoil in Venezuela. He served for a short time as the minister of education and then, in 1948, less than a year as the president of his country. He was overthrown by the military.
- In *Doña Bárbara*, the woman who runs the *hacienda* is ruthless. She defends it against a number of villains. One theme of the novel is the exploitation of the land by outsiders.

LECTURA

Suggestions

- Do the *Estrategia* as an in-class activity.
- Ask students if they have seen and/or read any U.S. magazines for Hispanics (*Latina, Cristina, People en español,* and so on). Ask what differences they found or would expect to find in these publications compared to other mainstream magazines. If possible bring some Spanish language magazines to class and have students look through them in groups.

Un paso más 10

Literatura de **Venezuela**

Sobre el autor: *Rómulo Gallegos nació en Caracas, Venezuela. En su novela más conocida,* Doña Bárbara, *el paisaje[a] de los llanos[b] venezolanos es el protagonista. Esto es un reflejo de la lucha del hombre contra el enorme poder de la naturaleza en América. El argumento[c] de la novela presenta la lucha entre la barbarie,[d] representada por doña Bárbara, y la civilización, representada por el personaje Santos Luzardo. El siguiente fragmento es de la novela* Doña Bárbara *(I Parte Cap. VIII) (1929).*

La llanura[e] es bella y terrible a la vez; en ella caben[f] holgadamente,[g] hermosa vida y muerte atroz; esta acecha[h] por todas partes, pero allí nadie le teme.[i]

[a]*landscape* [b]*plains* [c]*plot* [d]*barbarism* [e]*plain* [f]*fit comfortably* [g]*cómodamente* [h]*lies in wait* [i]*tiene miedo*

▲ Rómulo Gallegos (1884–1969)

LECTURA

ESTRATEGIA: Thematic Organization—Cause and Effect

Another strategy that can help your comprehension of a written passage is to identify thematic patterns in the text, or the relationship between different pieces of information. For example, does the author use contrast to get the point across? Is the passage strictly descriptive? Or is the information presented through a cause-and-effect relationship?

In the case of the latter, you should try to identify both the cause and the effect that are presented in the reading. Understanding the argumentative organization of the text can boost your comprehension of both individual sentences and the passage as a whole. In the reading that follows, you will find a series of cause-and-effect relationships, many of which may surprise you. As you read, try to identify these relationships, as you will be asked about them in the **Comprensión** section.

CULTURE

The exuberance and at times overwhelming forces of nature of Latin America heavily influenced the works of many Latin American writers at the beginning of the 20th century. Man against nature and barbarism/savagery versus civilization were common themes in novels, and in many cases, man was too small and weak to overcome or survive the "large" nature of Latin American dark jungles, inhospitable mountains, and harsh plains. In some works, nature functioned as a character. In *Doña Bárbara*, nature is represented by the character Bárbara. Note that the name *Bárbara* is related to the word *barbarie* or barbarism (savagery).

Variation
Have students complete the following sentences based on the information provided in the *Lectura*.

1. *Las vitaminas son necesarias para...*
2. *Una sobredosis de vitamina A puede causar...*
3. *Los fumadores deben ingerir...*
4. *Más de 1.600 unidades de vitamina E son peligrosas porque...*

Comprensión

A: Suggestion
Have students identify the passages in the reading where they found the information that helped them answer these questions.

B: Note
This activity has students give their answers in English. This allows you to verify that they have understood their answers and are not simply repeating phrases in Spanish without understanding them.

■ **Sobre la lectura...** Este artículo apareció en una revista para hispanos en los Estados Unidos para informarles sobre un aspecto de la salud y el bienestar. La lectura es auténtica; es decir, el lenguaje no ha sido modificado (*hasn't been modified*).

Las vitaminas y la salud

Las vitaminas son antioxidantes para el cuerpo humano... pero ahora también se sabe que una <u>sobredosis</u> podría perjudicar[a] al organismo más que ayudarlo. Las últimas investigaciones revelan, por ejemplo, que un exceso de vitamina A es responsable de agudos[b] dolores de cabeza, pérdida[c] del pelo, irritación de la piel,[d] deformaciones óseas[e] y defectos en los <u>recién nacidos</u> (en el caso de que la vitamina sea ingerida[f] por las embarazadas[g]). Los médicos recomiendan no ingerir más de 25.000 I.U. (unidades internacionales) de esta vitamina por día.

Vitamina C: una dosis de más de 1.000 miligramos (1 gramo) por día podría ser tóxica, <u>provocando</u> diarrea y otras alteraciones serias. Los galenos[h] aconsejan 50 miligramos por día para adultos y 100 miligramos por día para <u>fumadores</u>.

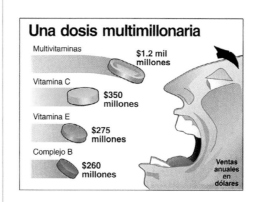

Una dosis multimillonaria

Multivitaminas — $1.2 mil millones
Vitamina C — $350 millones
Vitamina E — $275 millones
Complejo B — $260 millones

Ventas anuales en dólares

Vitamina E: no ingerir más de 1.600 I.U. por día. El exceso podría causar <u>coágulos</u> en la sangre. El infográfico muestra la venta de vitaminas en los Estados Unidos. ■

[a]*podría... could damage* [b]*sharp* [c]*loss* [d]*skin* [e]*of or pertaining to bones* [f]*sea... is ingested* [g]*pregnant women* [h]*médicos*

Comprensión

A. **¿Cierto o falso?** Conteste según el artículo. Corrija las oraciones falsas.

1. El exceso de vitamina A puede causar problemas gastrointestinales.
2. La vitamina C ayuda a reducir los dolores de cabeza.
3. Una sobredosis de vitamina A puede causar reacciones dermatológicas.
4. El fumar puede afectar la dosis recomendada de algunas vitaminas.

B. **Causa y efecto.** Identifique por lo menos uno de los efectos que puede causar cada uno de los siguientes. Dé su respuesta en inglés.

1. una sobredosis de vitamina A
2. una sobredosis de vitamina C
3. una sobredosis de vitamina E

ESCRITURA

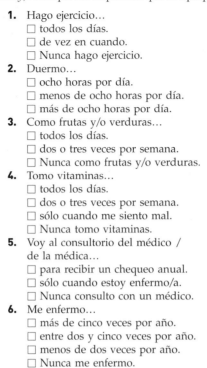

A. ¿Cómo está de salud?

Paso 1. ¿Lleva Ud. una vida sana o lleva una vida no muy saludable (*healthy*)? Indique las respuestas que se apliquen (*apply*) a Ud.

1. Hago ejercicio…
☐ todos los días.
☐ de vez en cuando.
☐ Nunca hago ejercicio.

2. Duermo…
☐ ocho horas por día.
☐ menos de ocho horas por día.
☐ más de ocho horas por día.

3. Como frutas y/o verduras…
☐ todos los días.
☐ dos o tres veces por semana.
☐ Nunca como frutas y/o verduras.

4. Tomo vitaminas…
☐ todos los días.
☐ dos o tres veces por semana.
☐ sólo cuando me siento mal.
☐ Nunca tomo vitaminas.

5. Voy al consultorio del médico / de la médica…
☐ para recibir un chequeo anual.
☐ sólo cuando estoy enfermo/a.
☐ Nunca consulto con un médico.

6. Me enfermo…
☐ más de cinco veces por año.
☐ entre dos y cinco veces por año.
☐ menos de dos veces por año.
☐ Nunca me enfermo.

Paso 2. Ahora analice sus respuestas del **Paso 1.** ¿Cómo está Ud. de salud? ¿Está sano/a o necesita mejorar su salud? Escriba un breve reportaje sobre sus respuestas, indicando qué tipo de vida lleva. Al final del reportaje, indique si necesita mejorar sus hábitos o si ya está en buen estado de salud.

ESCRITURA

Suggestion

If you prefer that your students do a journal activity, see *Mi diario* in this chapter of the Workbook.

A: Variation

Have students write a weekly diet and exercise plan. The following questions can be used as guidelines.

¿Cuántos días a la semana va a hacer ejercicio Ud.?
¿Qué deportes va a practicar?
¿Va a hacer ejercicios cardiovasculares?
¿Y qué va a comer?
¿Va a comer muchas proteínas? ¿y carbohidratos? ¿y vitaminas?

342 ■ Capítulo 10: La salud

B. Mi última visita al consultorio. Answer the following questions about your last visit to the doctor, adding as many details as possible. Then, using the words in this **Vocabulario útil** and any other connecting words that you know, join the sentences together to form three paragraphs that flow smoothly.

B: Follow-Up
Have students exchange compositions. In pairs, have them role-play doctor and patient. The patient uses the symptoms described in the composition he/she received.

Vocabulario útil			
además	besides	**pero**	but
así	thus, so	**por ejemplo**	for example
cuando	when	**por eso**	therefore, for that reason
de vez en cuando	from time to time		
en cambio	on the other hand	**por fin**	at last, finally
es decir	that is	**pues**	well; since
luego	then, next	**sin embargo**	nevertheless
mientras	while	**también**	also

PÁRRAFO A

1. ¿Cuándo fue la última vez que Ud. consultó con un médico?
2. ¿Por qué lo hizo? ¿Cuáles eran sus síntomas? ¿O era solamente un chequeo anual?

PÁRRAFO B

1. En el consultorio, ¿tuvo Ud. que esperar mucho tiempo? ¿Esperaban también otros pacientes?
2. Cuando por fin entró en el consultorio, ¿cuánto tiempo duró la consulta? ¿Qué actitud mostró el médico? ¿Compasión? ¿humor? ¿preocupación? ¿indiferencia?
3. ¿Le recetó alguna medicina? ¿Qué otras recomendaciones le dio? ¿Las siguió Ud.? ¿Por qué sí o por qué no?

PÁRRAFO C

1. ¿Cuándo se mejoró Ud. por fin? ¿O cuándo va a tener otro chequeo anual?
2. ¿Qué hace ahora para mantenerse en buen estado de salud?

 Heritage Speakers

Invite a unos estudiantes angloparlantes a leer en voz alta su composición. Los estudiantes hispanohablantes pueden hacerles preguntas a los presentadores para simular una entrevista.

◀ Dos estudiantes en el *campus* de la Universidad de Puerto Rico en Río Piedras

CHAPTER OPENER PHOTO

Point out the chapter-opener photo. Have students talk about the campus and the students in the photo. Where are they going? How do they feel? Have them discuss their own situations as students, and their ideas about handling school-related stress. Encourage them to describe any stress they have had.

Suggestions

■ Ask students the following questions to introduce the chapter topic. The words in **boldface** are included in the active vocabulary of this chapter. Have students discuss the words and use context to help them understand the meanings. Place the words they cannot guess in new sentences and contexts.

1. *¿Dónde* **sufre** *Ud. más* **presiones**, *en su vida escolar, en su vida social o en su vida familiar?*
2. *¿Quiénes lo/la ayudan más en los momentos difíciles de la vida, sus amigos o su familia?*
3. *¿Qué institución social lo/la ayuda más en esos momentos? ¿la iglesia? ¿el gobierno? ¿alguna otra institución? ¿o ninguna?*
4. *¿Cree Ud. que la gente sufre más presiones hoy en día o que sufría más hace cincuenta años?*
5. *¿Prefiere Ud. la vida de hoy, con su ritmo acelerado, o la de antes, que era más tranquila?*
6. *¿Cómo se siente Ud. cuando tiene que estudiar para un examen difícil o preparar un informe importante? ¿Se siente frustrado/a? ¿nervioso/a? ¿triste? ¿impaciente?*
7. *¿Sufren Uds. estrés como estudiantes? ¿Por qué?*
8. *¿Creen Uds. que hay muchos estudiantes que sufren estrés en esta universidad? En su opinión, ¿quiénes sufren más estrés, los profesores o los estudiantes?*
9. *¿Qué hace Ud. para aliviar* (alleviate) *el estrés? ¿y para evitar* (avoid) *el estrés?*

■ Point out that *escolar* is an adjective derived from *escuela* and that it always ends in *-r* in the singular: *la vida escolar, el año escolar.*

Note

The *Puntos de partida* Online Learning Center includes an interview with a native speaker from Puerto Rico who answers questions similar to those in the preceding *Suggestions.*

Resources

For Students

■ Workbook
■ Laboratory Manual and Laboratory Audio Program
■ Quia™ Online Workbook and Online Laboratory Manual
■ Video on CD
■ Interactive CD-ROM
■ *Puntos de partida* Online Learning Center (**www.mhhe.com/puntos7**)

For Instructors

■ *Instructor's Manual and Resource Kit,* "Chapter-by-Chapter" Supplementary Materials
■ Overhead Transparencies 76–78
■ Testing Program
■ Test Generator
■ Video Program
■ Audioscript
■ *Puntos de partida* Online Learning Center (**www.mhhe.com/puntos7**)

Presiones de la vida° moderna

Suggestions

- Provide religion words as needed for question 3 in the annotation on p. 344.

  bautista
  católico/a
  metodista
  mormón/
    mormona

  musulmán/
    musulmana,
  ortodoxo/a
  presbiteriano/a
  Testigos de Jehová
  unitario/a

- Use questions 4 and 5 of the annotation on p. 344 to begin a class discussion. Have students explain their answers. Point out the use of the imperfect for this discussion; then have students explain why this tense is used.
- Have students list their ideas about Puerto Rico, the people, geographic features, culture, politics, and so on. After completing the chapter, review their lists and ask them how they might change them.

CULTURA

- **Perspectivas culturales**

  Entrevista cultural: Puerto Rico

  Entre amigos: ¡Estoy superestresada!

  Conozca... Puerto Rico

- **Nota cultural:** Palabras y frases para momentos difíciles

- **En los Estados Unidos y el Canadá:** La impresionante variedad de la música latina

- **Lectura:** Divórciate del estrés

- **Literatura de Puerto Rico:** Rosario Ferré

VOCABULARIO

- Las presiones de la vida estudiantil

- ¡La profesora Martínez se levantó con el pie izquierdo!

GRAMÁTICA

33 Hace... que: Another Use of **hacer**

34 Another Use of **se**

35 ¿Por o **para?**

Entrevista cultural

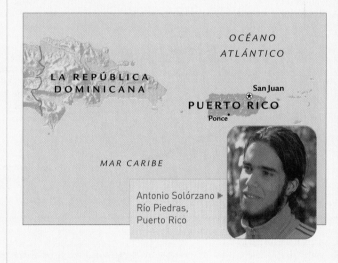

OCÉANO ATLÁNTICO

LA REPÚBLICA DOMINICANA

San Juan

PUERTO RICO

Ponce

MAR CARIBE

Antonio Solórzano ►
Río Piedras,
Puerto Rico

° life

National Standards: Communication

Have a round table discussion in groups of six or more students about the stresses students suffer, strategies to avoid stress, and ways to alleviate stress. Have students pinpoint major causes of stress. As you study *Capítulo 11*, have the groups organize their ideas and create a pamphlet in Spanish that could be distributed to university students. The pamphlets can be presented as you finish the chapter.

MULTIMEDIA

- The multimedia materials that accompany this chapter are referenced in the Student and Instructor's Editions with icons to help you identify when and where to incorporate them.

- The IM/RK provides suggestions for using the multimedia materials in the classroom.

Las presiones de la vida estudiantil

Note

See the model for vocabulary presentation and other material in the *Capítulo 11 Vocabulario: Preparación* section of "Chapter-by-Chapter Supplementary Materials," in the IM.

Suggestions

■ Point out that *estudiantil* is an adjective derived from *estudiante*.
■ Indicate that the first person singular of *recoger* is *recojo*.
■ Provide the following alternate and optional vocabulary.

> *estacionar(se) = aparcar* (Sp.) = *parquear* (Mex.)
> *notas = calificaciones*
> *la tranquilidad* (the opposite of *el estrés*)
> *estar tranquilo/a.*

■ Model vocabulary, using it in sentences about yourself and in exchanges with the students. Explain some expressions in Spanish.

1. ***Acordarse*** *es un verbo reflexivo. Uds. conocen un verbo sinónimo, ¿verdad? ¿Cuál es?* (**recordar,** *del Capítulo 8*) *¿Cuál es un antónimo? El verbo* **acordarse,** *como* **recordar,** *tiene un cambio en la radical (o → ue):* **me acuerdo, te acuerdas, nos acordamos.** *¿Se acuerda Ud. de quién era el presidente de los Estados Unidos en 1995?*
2. *El verbo* **entregar** *es sinónimo de _____* (students answer). *¿Qué se puede entregar? ¿Entregaron alguna tarea ayer para alguna clase?*
3. *Estacionar el coche es un gran problema en muchas ciudades (en esta universidad). ¿Uds. tienen problemas cuando necesitan estacionar su coche? ¿Dónde? ¿Cuándo?*

■ Read the following definitions and descriptions and have students give the correct words.

1. *Muchos estudiantes sufren esto.*
2. *Es una prueba que se hace para demostrar la comprensión de los estudios que se han hecho.*
3. *Es un aparato que nos despierta por la mañana.*
4. *Es una cosa que sirve para abrir puertas.*
5. *Estas dos expresiones se usan para pedir disculpas.*

Las presiones de la vida estudiantil

el calendario — el horario — la llave — el despertador — la calificación — el examen — la tarjeta de identificación — sufrir (muchas) presiones

acordarse (ue) (de)	to remember	sacar (qu)	to take out
entregar (gu)	to turn, hand in	sacar buenas/	to get good/bad
estacionar	to park	malas notas	grades
llegar (gu) a tiempo/	to arrive early/late	ser (*irreg.*) flexible	to be flexible
tarde		sufrir	to suffer
pedir (i, i) disculpas	to apologize		
Discúlpeme.	Pardon me. / I'm sorry.	el estrés	stress
		la (falta de)	(lack of) flexibility
¡Lo siento (mucho)!	Pardon me! / I'm (very) sorry!	flexibilidad	
		la fecha límite	deadline
		el informe (oral/	(oral/written)
Perdón.	Pardon me. / I'm sorry.	escrito)	report
		la prueba	quiz; test
recoger (j)*	to collect; to pick up	la tarea	homework
		el trabajo	job, work; report, (piece of) work
		de tiempo	full/part time
		completo/parcial	

---

*Note the present indicative conjugation of **recoger: recojo, recoges, recoge, recogemos, recogen.**

MULTIMEDIA: Audio

Students can listen to and practice this chapter's vocabulary on the Online Learning Center (**www.mhhe.com/puntos7**), as well as on the Textbook Audio CD, part of the Laboratory Audio Program.

Resources: Transparency 76

■ ■ ■ Conversación

A. Asociaciones

Paso 1. ¿Qué palabras asocia Ud. con estos verbos? Pueden ser sustantivos, antónimos o sinónimos.

1. estacionar
2. recoger
3. acordarse
4. entregar
5. sacar
6. sufrir
7. pedir
8. llegar

Paso 2. ¿Qué palabras y/o situaciones asocia Ud. con los siguientes sustantivos?

1. el calendario
2. el despertador
3. las calificaciones
4. el estrés
5. la fecha límite
6. el horario
7. los informes
8. la llave
9. la tarjeta de identificación
10. las disculpas
11. las presiones
12. la flexibilidad
13. la prueba
14. el trabajo

B. Situaciones

Paso 1. La primera lista que Ud. va a leer consta de (*consists of*) preguntas o comentarios hechos por varias personas. La segunda lista incluye las respuestas de otras personas. Decida qué respuesta corresponde a cada comentario.

b **1.** —Anoche no me acordé de poner el despertador.

A **2.** —No puede estacionar el coche aquí. No tiene permiso de estacionamiento para esta zona.

D **3.** —¿Sacaste una buena nota en la prueba?

F **4.** —Ramiro no tiene buen aspecto (*doesn't look right*). Creo que algo le causa mucho estrés.

C **5.** —Aquí tiene mi trabajo escrito sobre el Mercado Común.

a. —Pues estoy cansado de buscar estacionamiento por todo el *campus*. Lo voy a dejar aquí.

b. —¿Lo olvidaste otra vez? ¿A qué hora llegaste a la oficina?

c. —Pero la fecha límite era ayer. Es la última vez que acepto un informe suyo (*of yours*) tarde.

d. —Muy buena, pero no la esperaba. No tuve tiempo de estudiar.

e. —Es porque tiene un trabajo de tiempo completo, y también toma tres cursos este semestre.

Paso 2. Ahora invente un contexto para cada diálogo. ¿Dónde están las personas que hablan? ¿En casa? ¿en una oficina? ¿en clase? ¿Quiénes son?

MODELO: **1.** → Las personas que hablan están en el trabajo (la oficina). Probablemente están almorzando. Son compañeros de trabajo; no son buenos amigos…

---

6. *Uno escribe esto para planear las cosas que tiene que hacer cada día (clases, citas, otras actividades, etcétera).*

7. *Es poner el coche en un lugar cuando no lo conducimos.*

8. *Es sinónimo de* **dar,** *en el sentido de* **darle una tarea al profesor.**

■ Point out that *acordarse* (de) and *olvidarse* (de) are antonyms.

■ Ask students the following questions to personalize the vocabulary.

1. *¿Está Ud. contento/a con su horario de este semestre/ trimestre? ¿Por qué? ¿Tiene Ud. que entregar algún informe esta semana? ¿Cuál es la fecha límite? ¿Tiene pruebas o exámenes? ¿Tuvo algún examen o informe importante la semana pasada?*

2. *¿Viene Ud. en coche a la universidad? ¿Tiene problemas para estacionar? ¿Dónde estaciona?*

3. *¿Está sacando Ud. buenas notas este semestre? ¿Son mejores o peores que las del semestre pasado?*

4. *¿Le gusta el calendario de esta universidad (cuando empieza y termina el semestre [trimestre] / cuando hay vacaciones)? ¿Por qué?*

5. *Normalmente, ¿es Ud. una persona que llega tarde o temprano a las citas / las clases? ¿Necesita un despertador por la mañana o puede Ud. despertarse solo/a?*

6. *¿Se acuerda Ud. de sus citas sin mirar la agenda? ¿Se acuerda Ud. de escribir sus citas en la agenda y de mirarla después?*

■ Remind students that *lunes* is the first day of the week on Hispanic calendars.

Con. A: Extension

Have students give all the antonyms and synonyms they know for the following words.

1. *abrir*
2. *perder*
3. *ser feliz*
4. *llegar a tiempo*
5. *ser flexible*
6. *la tranquilidad*

Con. A: Variation

Use a game format to get synonyms and antonyms. Divide the class into teams. Allow teams to work on each word for only one minute; the team with the most associations wins the round.

☀ Heritage Speakers

■ Por la influencia del inglés en algunos dialectos del español del suroeste de los Estados Unidos, se oye decir *grado* en vez de *calificación*. Las palabras aceptadas, sin embargo, son *nota* y *calificación*. Otra expresión influida por el inglés es la palabra *notas* para expresar *apuntes*.

■ Algunos hispanohablantes de los Estados Unidos usan la palabra *alarma* para referirse al *despertador*.

■ El término *parquear* (*estacionar*) que se oye en México también se usa en algunos países latinoamericanos y en los Estados Unidos. Algunas derivaciones son el *parqueadero* (*estacionamiento*). En España, donde dicen *aparcar*, usan la palabra *aparcamiento*.

<table><tr><td>

</td></tr></table>

Con. C: Suggestions

- Allow students a few minutes to prepare their statements; then have them share their ideas with the class.
- Have a class discussion beginning with these questions.

  ¿Qué cualificaciones son importantes para conseguir un buen trabajo hoy día? ¿Es esto diferente de la generación de sus padres?

  ¿Qué cursos universitarios son más importantes en la preparación para su carrera?

  ¿Cree Ud. que los triunfos en la vida son una combinación de la buena preparación y la suerte?

- **Paso 2.** Have students complete this *Paso* as a writing assignment outside class. They can use their written ideas in a class discussion the next day.

C. La educación universitaria

Paso 1. Lea lo que dicen Edward James Olmos y Luis Miguel sobre la vida y la educación.

SOLO *para ganadores*[a]

Ellos han logrado[b] triunfar. ¡Y cada frase que dicen es una lección gratuita[c] para el éxito[d]!

«*Les digo con todo mi corazón, con toda mi vida. Yo no tengo talento natural. No soy un genio. Pero mis padres a pesar de[g] ser tan humildes[h] me dieron educación*».

Edward James Olmos
actor mexicoamericano

«*El destino es una mezcla[e] entre la preparación y la suerte*»[f].

Luis Miguel, cantante mexicano

[a]*winners* [b]*han... have been able to* [c]*free* [d]*success*
[e]*mix* [f]*luck* [g]*a... in spite of* [h]*poor*

¿Cree Ud. que tienen razón estos dos artistas? ¿Qué cree Ud. que sea más importante para tener éxito (*be successful*) en la vida, el talento natural o la preparación? ¿Piensa Ud. que está consiguiendo una educación del tipo que ayudó a Olmos y a Luis Miguel? ¿Va a ser suficiente su educación para obtener un buen trabajo en el futuro?

Paso 2. Los años estudiantiles, ¿una época maravillosa? Con frecuencia se oye a las personas mayores hablar de los años universitarios con nostalgia: años de libertad, sin responsabilidades, sin las tensiones propias de la vida laboral y familiar. ¿Ve Ud. así la época universitaria? Con un compañero / una compañera, comente este tema. Pueden usar las siguientes preguntas como guía (*guide*).

1. ¿Sufren muchas presiones los estudiantes universitarios? ¿Por qué? ¿Qué les causa estrés?
2. ¿Son más divertidos los años universitarios que los años de la escuela secundaria?
3. ¿Le preocupa a Ud. el costo de la matrícula? Para Ud. o para su familia, ¿es difícil pagarla?
4. ¿Piensa Ud. que la vida va a ser mejor después de graduarse en la universidad? ¿Por qué sí o por qué no?

MULTIMEDIA: Internet

Have students search the Internet for information on Edward James Olmos and Luis Miguel. They should be able to find photos, biographical information, fan clubs, and music clips to report to the class.

National Standards: Culture

In Spanish *tener educación* not only means to have intellectual preparation, but also to be courteous (*ser cortés*) and to have good manners (*tener buenos modales*). Someone who is *mal educado/a* does not know how to behave in public and does not show enough respect for other people, especially his or her elders. *Bien educado/a* is one of the most valued qualities in Hispanic cultures.

con... *on the wrong side of the bed*

¡La profesora Martínez se levantó con el pie izquierdo!°

doler(le) (ue) la cabeza

la cabeza

la mano

Le **duele** la cabeza.

CABALLEROS   DAMAS

equivocarse (qu) (de)

el brazo

Estaba **distraída** y **se equivocó de** puerta.

darse (*irreg.*) contra la silla

darse (*irreg.*) en la pierna

lastimarse la pierna

los dedos (de la mano)

Se **dio en** la pierna y **se lastimó** cuando **se pegó contra** la silla.

caerse (*irreg.*)*

el pie

la pierna

romper

La profesora **se cayó*** y **rompió** los lentes.

Accidentes

darse (*irreg.*) **en/ con/contra**	to hit (*a part of one's body*)/to run into/bump against
doler (ue)	to hurt, ache
equivocarse (de)	to make a mistake (about)
hacerse (*irreg.*) **daño**	to hurt oneself

pegar (gu)	to hit, strike
pegarse en/con/ contra	to run, bump into
el dedo del pie	toe
Fue sin querer.	It was unintentional.
distraído/a	absentminded
torpe	clumsy
¡Qué torpe!	How clumsy!

■■■ Conversación

A. Un anuncio para un seguro. La palabra **seguro** no sólo significa *sure*. También quiere decir *insurance.* Este es un anuncio de un seguro de accidentes.

1. ¿Dónde patina el hombre?
2. ¿Qué le puede ocurrir?
3. ¿Por qué tiene suerte (*good luck*)?
4. ¿Tiene Ud. un seguro de accidentes?

SEGURO ESPECIAL ACCIDENTES

Puede ocurrirle esto...

O no ocurrirle nada...

...y suerte que está Asegurado

---

*Note that the first person singular of **caer** is irregular: **caigo.** The present participle is **cayendo.**

Vocabulario: Preparación

Trescientos cuarenta y nueve ■ **349**

¡La profesora Martínez se levantó con el pie izquierdo!

Suggestions

- Model vocabulary in sentences about yourself and in communicative exchanges with the students.
- Point out that *dedos* can refer to fingers or toes. To distinguish the two, use *dedos del pie* and *dedos de la mano.*
- Explain to students that the first person singular of *caerse* is *me caigo.*
- Have students give the corresponding word.
  1. *Es sinónimo de tener razón.*
  2. *Tomo esto cuando me duele la cabeza.*
  3. *Es sinónimo de hacerse daño.*
  4. *Es un adjetivo que significa no estar atento a lo que pasa.*
  5. *Es una persona que tiene muchos accidentes.*
- Remind students again that the structure for *doler* is like *gustar.*
- Have students respond *cierto* or *falso.*
  1. *Tenemos tres cabezas (diez piernas, dos ojos...)*
  2. *La pierna entra en el zapato.*
  3. *Escribimos con el pie.*
  4. *Pensamos con la cabeza.*
- Ask students the following questions to personalize the vocabulary.
  1. *¿Le duele la cabeza con frecuencia? ¿Qué hace cuando le duele? ¿En qué situaciones es común que a una persona le duela la cabeza?* (Point out: subjunctive)
  2. *Las personas distraídas, ¿se olvidan o se acuerdan de muchas cosas? ¿Pierden objetos? ¿Qué tipo de objetos? ¿Es Ud. distraído/a? ¿Por qué? Dé algunos ejemplos.*
  3. *¿Es Ud. torpe? ¿Se da con los muebles con frecuencia? ¿con los pies de otras personas? ¿Deja caer (to drop) cosas? ¿Qué personas son típicamente torpes? ¿los futbolistas? ¿los payasos (clowns)?*

☼ Heritage Speakers

Muchos hispanohablantes dicen *Casi me caigo* o *Por poco me caigo;* usan el presente para expresar *I almost fell* (el pasado).

Resources: Transparencies 77, 78

♻ Reciclado

■ Recycle clothing vocabulary.

¿Qué parte del cuerpo asocia Ud. con... ?

el reloj	*la camisa*
los pantalones	*los zapatos*
el sombrero	*los guantes*

■ Recycle the subjunctive. This activity is designed for recognition of forms and conceptualization. Students do not produce subjunctive forms but they can attempt to explain why the subjunctive or the indicative is used in each case (certainty vs. opinion). Have students respond *cierto* or *falso*.

1. *Si una persona se da con la cabeza contra una puerta, es lógico que le duela.*

2. *Si una persona sufre muchas presiones, es posible que también tenga más accidentes.*

3. *Es cierto que todos trabajamos mal cuando estamos bajo muchas presiones.*

4. *Es probable que la vida moderna cause más problemas que beneficios.*

5. *Es bueno que una persona tome aspirinas cuando le duele el estómago.*

Con. B: Preliminary Exercise

Have students work in pairs to tell each other about accidents they have had. Then have students report to the class their partner's accidents, including all information necessary to tell the story: when it happened, where, with whom, how the person felt, what he/she did afterward. Caution students about the use of the preterite and imperfect for the telling of the story.

Con. B: Suggestion

Ask students the following questions to personalize the information.

¿Qué tipos de seguros conoce Ud.?
¿Cuáles tiene Ud.?
¿Cuál es el más importante, en su opinión?

☼ Heritage Speakers

Pregúnteles a los hispanohablantes cuáles son algunas de las expresiones más corrientes en español para expresar dolor, sorpresa, compasión o para dar ánimo.

NOTA CULTURAL

Palabras y frases para momentos difíciles

Hay muchas expresiones para ocasiones de mala suerte[a] o de presión. Varían mucho de región en región y de país en país. Estas son algunas de las más comunes.

Para expresar dolor, sorpresa o compasión

¡Ay!	Ah! Ouch!	¿Qué le vamos a hacer?	What can you do?
¡Uy!	Oops! Oh!	¡No me digas!	You're kidding! (You don't say!)
¡No puede ser!	That can't be!	¡Qué mala suerte!	What bad luck!

Para dar ánimo[b]

¡Venga!	Come on!	¡No es para tanto!	It's not so bad!
¡Órale! (Mex.)	Come on!	¡Anímate!	Cheer up!

[a]*luck* [b]*Para... To cheer (someone up)*

B. Posibilidades. ¿Qué puede Ud. hacer o decir —o qué le puede pasar— en cada situación?

MODELO: Ud. se da contra el escritorio de otro estudiante y se lastima el pie.
—¡Ay! ¡Qué torpe soy!

1. A Ud. le duele mucho la cabeza.
2. Ud. le pega a otra persona sin querer.
3. Ud. se olvida del nombre de otra persona.
4. Ud. está muy distraído/a y no mira por dónde camina.
5. Ud. se lastima la mano (el pie).
6. Su amigo está nervioso porque se pegó contra la profesora antes de clase.

C. Accidentes y tropiezos [*mishaps*]

Paso 1. ¿Le han pasado a Ud. alguna vez las siguientes cosas? Complete las oraciones con información verdadera para Ud. Si nunca le pasó nada de esto, invente una situación que podría haber ocurrido (*could have happened*).

1. Me caí por las escaleras (*stairs*) y ____.
2. No me acordé de hacer la tarea para la clase de ____.
3. Me equivoqué cuando ____.
4. El despertador sonó, pero ____.
5. No pude encontrar ____.
6. Me di con ____ y me lastimé ____.
7. Pasó la fecha límite para entregar un informe y ____.
8. Caminaba un poco distraído/a y ____.

Paso 2. Entrevista. Ahora usando las oraciones del **Paso 1** como guía, pregúntele a un compañero / una compañera cómo le fue ayer. También puede preguntarle si le pasaron otros desastres.

MODELO: ¿Te caíste por las escaleras ayer? ¿Te hiciste daño?

NOTA CULTURAL

Suggestions

■ Point out that in Spanish as in English, many expressions emerge and fade. An expression will often become associated with a specific time period.

■ Ask students the following questions to check comprehension.

1. *¿Qué dice Ud. si un amigo está triste o deprimido?*

2. *¿Qué dice Ud. si se hace daño a la mano?*

3. *¿Qué puede decir si un amigo le cuenta algo increíble?*

More on Adverbs

You already know the most common Spanish adverbs: words like **bien/mal, mucho/poco, siempre/nunca...**

Adverbs that end in -*ly* in English usually end in **-mente** in Spanish. The suffix **-mente** is added to the feminine singular form of adjectives. Note that the accent mark on the stem word (if there is one) is retained.

Adjective	Adverb	English
rápida	**rápida**mente	*rapidly*
fácil	**fácil**mente	*easily*
paciente	**paciente**mente	*patiently*

D. ¡Seamos (*Let's be*) **lógicos!** Complete estas oraciones lógicamente con adverbios basados en los siguientes adjetivos.

Adjetivos	
constante	posible
directo	puntual
fácil	rápido
inmediato	total
paciente	tranquilo

1. La familia está esperando _____ en la cola.
2. Hay examen mañana y tengo que empezar a estudiar _____.
3. ¿Las enchiladas? Se preparan _____.
4. ¿Qué pasa? Estoy _____ confundido/a (*confused*).
5. Cuando mira la tele, mi hermanito cambia el canal _____.
6. Es necesario que las clases empiecen _____.

E. Entrevista. Con un compañero / una compañera, haga y conteste las siguientes preguntas.

MODELO: E1: ¿Qué haces pacientemente?
E2: Espero pacientemente a mi esposo cuando se viste para salir. ¡Lo hace muy lentamente (*slowly*)!

1. ¿Qué haces rápidamente?
2. ¿Qué te toca hacer inmediatamente?
3. ¿Qué hiciste (comiste,...) solamente una vez que te gustó muchísimo (no te gustó nada)?
4. ¿Qué haces tú fácilmente que es difícil para otras personas?
5. ¿Qué hace constantemente tu compañero/a de casa (amigo/a, esposo/a,...) que te molesta (*bothers*) muchísimo?

Need more practice?
- Workbook and Laboratory Manual
- Interactive CD-ROM
- Online Learning Center (www.mhhe.com/puntos7)

Suggestions

- Point out that when two -*mente* adverbs are used together, joined by a conjunction in a single sentence, the first adverb is shortened to the feminine singular adjective and only the second adverb includes the -*mente* suffix: *Carlos hizo la lección rápida y fácilmente.*
- Remind students that *mucho* and *poco* are invariable when used as adverbs: *Isabel tiene muchas* (adjective) *clases; por eso estudia mucho* (adverb).

- Point out that when an adjective does not end in -*o*, there is no -*a* before -*mente* to form the adverb: *fácilmente, totalmente.*
- Some students may inquire about the accent mark on *rápidamente* and *fácilmente*, noting that the word is stressed on the next-to-last (penultimate) syllable. If the adjective has a written accent mark, it is retained in the adverbial form. It is purely an orthographic and not a phonemic convention.

Con. D: Preliminary Exercise

Have students give the corresponding adverb (rapid response).

1.	*práctico*	**9.**	*personal*
2.	*especial*	**10.**	*rápido*
3.	*perfecto*	**11.**	*leal*
4.	*triste*	**12.**	*elegante*
5.	*alegre*	**13.**	*cariñoso*
6.	*feliz*	**14.**	*tranquilo*
7.	*final*	**15.**	*directo*
8.	*típico*		

Con. D: Follow-Up

Have students tell what actions they associate with the following adverbs. Have them create sentences about themselves.

¿Qué acción personal asocia Ud. con los siguientes adverbios?

1. *infrecuentemente*
2. *lentamente*
3. *tristemente*
4. *felizmente*
5. *fielmente*
6. *fabulosamente*

Con. E: Follow-Up

- Have students complete the following sentences. Model your own answer for each sentence, then follow up with a question.

Yo _____ rápidamente, pero no _____ rápidamente. → Yo leo rápidamente, pero no escribo rápidamente. ¿Y Ud.? ¿Qué hace rápidamente?

1. Yo _____ rápidamente, pero no _____ rápidamente.
2. Yo siempre _____ tranquilamente.
3. Yo _____ mejor que mis padres.
4. Yo _____ peor que mi mejor amigo/a.

- Ask students the following questions.

1. *¿Habla Ud. solamente en español en esta clase?*
2. *¿Llega Ud. puntualmente a todas sus clases?*
3. *En la librería, ¿espera Ud. pacientemente en cola cuando compra libros?*
4. *Cuando recibe correo electrónico de un amigo / una amiga, ¿le responde inmediatamente?*

Suggestions

■ Point out that *que* is omitted when the sentence does not begin with *hace.* For example: *Estudio español hace dos años* or *La conocí hace tres meses.*

■ Use the *hace... que* + present tense structure as frequently as possible in your speech. Some (but not all) students will begin to use it spontaneously if they hear it enough. You may wish to treat this grammar topic for recognition only.

■ Explain and model these expressions.

> *hace mucho tiempo*
> *hace muchos días*

■ Emphasize that students should never change the form of *hace* in this construction.

■ Give the following dictation.

1. *Hace tres años que vivo aquí.*
2. *Hace un año que no vemos a los nietos.*
3. *Hace una semana que no hablo con mis padres.*
4. *Hace cinco meses que estudiamos español.*
5. *Hace dos años que llegué a esta universidad.*
6. *Hace quince años que aprendí a esquiar.*

Follow up the dictation with questions to check comprehension.

¿Cuántos años hace que vivo aquí?

Extension

After reviewing *Las actividades de los Durán,* ask students the following questions to personalize the structure.

¿Cuánto tiempo hace que Ud. toma esta clase? ¿Cuánto tiempo hace que llegó a esta clase hoy? ¿Cuánto tiempo hace que llegó el profesor / la profesora?

33 Telling How Long Something Has Been Happening or How Long Ago Something Happened • *Hace... que:* Another Use of *hacer*

Las actividades de los Durán

Hace diez años *que* Manolo enseña en la Universidad de Sevilla.

Manolo y Lola se conocieron *hace* quince años.

Hace dos años *que* Marta estudia inglés.

Y Ud., ¿cuánto tiempo hace que estudia español? ¿que asiste a esta universidad? ¿Cuánto tiempo hace que asistió a la escuela secundaria? ¿que conoció a su mejor amigo/a?

■ In Spanish, the phrase **hace** + *period of time* + **que** + *present tense* is used to express an action that has been going on over a period of time and is still going on.

Hace dos horas **que leo.**
I've been reading for two hours.

Hace tres años **que vivimos** en esta casa.
We've been living in this house for three years.

■ Use the phrase **¿Cuánto tiempo hace que... ?** to ask how long something has been going on. To answer a question posed in this way, it is sufficient to state the period of time.

—**¿Cuánto tiempo hace que** vives en esta residencia?
How long have you been living in this dorm?

—**Dos meses.**
(For) Two months.

☀ Heritage Speakers

■ En algunos dialectos del español, hay hispanohablantes que usan *hacen* cuando el período de tiempo a que se refieren es plural, por ejemplo, *Hacen tres días que...* o *Hacen varios minutos que...,* etcétera. Pregúnteles a los hispanohablantes si usan esta construcción o si la han oído antes. A pesar de este

uso popular de *hacen,* la forma impersonal, *hace,* es la preferida.

■ Pregúnteles a los hispanohablantes de la clase si usan esta u otra estructura para expresar *cuánto tiempo.*

- To say how long *ago* something happened, use the same **hace... que** construction but with the preterite tense instead of the present. Notice also in the second example the omission of **que** when the **hace** phrase does not come at the beginning of the sentence.

Hace tres años **que fui** a Bogotá.
I went to Bogota three years ago.

Fui a Cancún **hace** un mes.
I went to Cancun a month ago.

 The verb form **hace** in this impersonal time construction never varies. However, the verb that accompanies the expression is always conjugated.

AUTOPRUEBA

Match each sentence with the corresponding idea.

a. for *x* years   **b.** *x* years ago
1. _____ Hace dos años que te conozco.
2. _____ Te conocí hace dos años.
3. _____ Hace tres años que tomé cálculo.
4. _____ Hace tres años que estudio español.

Answers 1. a 2. b 3. b 4. a

■■■ Práctica

A. **Tengo ganas de...** ¿Qué tiene Ud. ganas de hacer en las siguientes situaciones?

MODELO: Ud. está en clase. Son las 12:30 de la tarde. Hace cinco horas que no come nada. → —Tengo muchas ganas de almorzar.

1. Ud. está en casa. Hace tres horas que escribe ejercicios de español.
2. Hace dos meses que Ud. vive en una residencia estudiantil. Sus compañeros siempre hacen mucho ruido.
3. Hace diez años que Ud. tiene un coche viejo que no funciona bien.
4. Ud. está en una discoteca. Hace media hora que baila y tiene mucho calor.
5. Hace tres días que llueve y Ud. está cansado/a de estar dentro de la casa todo el tiempo.

B. **¿Quién... ?**

Paso 1. ¿Quién hace qué? Haga oraciones completas emparejando (*matching*) las personas a la izquierda con las acciones correspondientes a la derecha.

MODELO: el profesor / la profesora / enseña / español →
Hace mucho tiempo que la profesora enseña español.

Hace mucho/poco tiempo que...

Jennifer López Alex Rodríquez (A-Rod) Antonio Banderas «Sponge Bob» el profesor / la profesora de español un compañero / una compañera de clase	es uno de los programas favoritos de los niños canta en español habla/enseña español juega al béisbol trabaja en esta universidad trabaja en Hollywood ¿ ?

Gramática   Trescientos cincuenta y tres ■ 353

National Standards: Connections

- **Jennifer López:** "J'lo" was born on July 24, 1970, in the Bronx, New York. Both of her parents are originally from Puerto Rico. She was a "Fly Girl" dancer on the TV show "In Living Color," but her role as Selena in the film *Selena* made her a star. She has enjoyed big-screen success as well as an outstanding singing career.
- **Alex Rodríguez:** "A-Rod" was born in New York City on July 27, 1975. He grew up in the Dominican Republic and Miami, Florida. He played for the Seattle Mariners for six years and currently plays for the Texas Rangers.
- **Antonio Banderas:** A native of Spain who worked with the renowned Pedro Almodóvar, Antonio's first film in 1982 was *Laberinto de pasiones*. He went on to make a total of five Almodóvar films before bowing out of a contract for a sixth movie when he came to the U.S. to film *The Mambo Kings*.

Prác. A: Preliminary Exercise

- Have students give appropriate formal commands to the following people:

  ¿Qué sugerencias tiene Ud. para estas personas?

  1. *Hace una semana que Juan no abre su libro de español y tiene un examen mañana.*
  2. *Hace dos días que Amanda no come. Está a dieta.*
  3. *Sara tiene un fuerte dolor de cabeza y hace doce horas que tomó la última aspirina.*
  4. *Hace un mes que Raúl llamó a sus padres la última vez.*

- Have students use the following cues to form sentences. *Julio / trabajar / una hora → Hace una hora que Julio trabaja.*

  You can put the cues on a transparency or on the board, or they can be dictated.

  1. *yo / descansar / una hora*
  2. *tú / cocinar / media hora*
  3. *Jaime / estudiar / dos horas*
  4. *nosotros / leer / hora y media*
  5. *niños / escribir cartas / dos horas*
  6. *Tina / hablar por teléfono / veinte minutos*

- Have students tell how long ago they did the following things:

  1. you were born (*nacer: nací*)
  2. you moved (*mudarse*) to this town
  3. you met your best friend
  4. you handed in your last major paper

Prác. A: Extension

6. *Ud. tiene un examen final muy importante. Hace dos días que Ud. no duerme.*
7. *Hace dos semanas que Ud. trabaja y no va a ninguna parte.*

Prác. B: Suggestion

Give the names of famous people and have students provide sentences following the pattern from the activity. *Gabriel García Márquez, el Presidente _____, Oprah Winfrey, Mariah Carey,* and so on.

Con: Suggestion

Go through the items with the class as a whole before students work on their own.

Paso 2. ¿Cuánto tiempo hace que pasó lo siguiente? Haga oraciones completas usando las indicaciones que aparecen en la lista. ¿Sabe Ud. todas las respuestas? Los años en que pasaron estos eventos aparecen abajo.

MODELO: el primer hombre / llegar a la luna →
Hace más de (*more than*) treinta años que el primer hombre llegó a la luna.

1. Cristóbal Colón / llegar a América
2. la Segunda Guerra Mundial / terminar
3. John Lennon / morir
4. el presidente actual (el primer ministro) / ser elegido (*to be elected*)
5. el profesor / la profesora de español / empezar a enseñar en esta universidad

Answers: MODELO. 1969 **1.** 1492 **2.** 1945 **3.** 1980 **4.** ¿ ? **5.** ¿ ?

■ ■ ■ **Conversación**

Entrevista

Paso 1. Find out from a classmate how long he or she has been . . .

MODELO: acquainted with his/her best friend →
¿Cuánto tiempo hace que conoces a tu mejor amigo/a?

1. living in this city
2. attending this university
3. living in his or her house (apartment, dorm, . . .)
4. studying Spanish
5. driving (**manejar**) a car/riding a bus or bike/walking to school
6. using a computer (**una computadora**)

Paso 2. Now find out how long ago he or she . . .

MODELO: met his/her best friend →
¿Cuánto tiempo hace que conociste a tu mejor amigo/a?

1. last visited his or her parents (grandparents, children, . . .)
2. received a bad grade
3. learned to drive (**manejar**)
4. handed in his or her last major assignment
5. gave an oral report
6. last arrived late to class

National Standards: Connections (*continued*)

- **John Grisham:** He was born February 8, 1955, in Jonesboro, Arkansas, to a construction worker and a homemaker. His works include: *A Time to Kill*, *The Firm*, and *The Pelican Brief*.
- **Cristóbal Colón** (1451–1506): Born in Genoa, Italy, Colón (*Cristoforo Colombo*, in Italian) was a navigator who sailed west across the Atlantic Ocean in search of a route to Asia. *Colón* achieved fame by making landfall, instead, on a Caribbean island.
- **John Lennon** (1940–1980): Born in England. Lennon was a British singer and songwriter, and a member of the Beatles. He was murdered in 1980.

Expressing Unplanned or Unexpected Events • Another Use of *se*

Un día fatal

Diego y Antonio son compañeros de cuarto. Hoy todo les salió mal.

A Diego *se le cayó* la taza de café.

También *se le perdió* la cartera.

A Antonio *se le olvidaron* sus libros y su trabajo cuando fue a clase.

También *se le perdieron* las llaves de su apartamento.

¿Le pasaron a Ud. las mismas cosas —o cosas parecidas (*similar*)— esta semana? Conteste, completando las oraciones.

1. *Se me perdieron / No se me perdieron* las llaves de mi coche/casa.
2. *Se me olvidó / No se me olvidó* una reunión importante.
3. *Se me cayó / No se me cayó* una taza de café.
4. *Se me rompió / No se me rompió* un objeto de valor (*value*) sentimental.

A. Unplanned or unexpected events (*I dropped . . . , We lost . . . , You forgot . . .*) are frequently expressed in Spanish with **se** and a third person form of the verb. In this structure, the occurrence is viewed as happening *to* someone—the unwitting "victim" of the action.

The chart on page 356 illustrates the different parts and word order of this structure. Note:

- The "victim" is indicated by an indirect object pronoun.
- As with the verb **gustar,** the **a** + *noun* phrase is required in sentences that express the "victim" as a noun. The **a** + *pronoun* phrase is often used to clarify or emphasize meaning when the "victim" is expressed as a pronoun.
- The subject of the verb is the thing that is dropped, broken, forgotten, and so on.
- The subject usually follows the verb in this structure.

Se me cayó el papel.
I dropped the paper. (The paper was dropped by me.)

Se le olvidaron las llaves.
He forgot the keys. (The keys were forgotten by him.)

Se te olvidó llamar a tu hija.
You forgot to call your daughter. (Calling your daughter was forgotten by you.)

Gramática 34

Another Use of *se*

Note
Aim for partial control. This can include a few fixed or memorized sentences, such as *se me olvidó, se me perdió*, and so on.

Extension
Provide additional situations for *Un día fatal.*

5. (*No*) *Se me acabó el dinero cuando estaba de vacaciones.*
6. (*No*) *Se me olvidó hacer una tarea importante.*
7. (*No*) *Se me perdieron unos apuntes de clase.*
8. (*No*) *Se me rompió el brazo.*
9. (*No*) *Se me olvidó la billetera en casa.*
10. (*No*) *Se me quedaron los libros en la biblioteca.*
11. (*No*) *Se me perdió todo el dinero que tenía.*
12. (*No*) *Se me cayó la taza de café.*

Suggestion
Have students convert the following into *se* structures.

1. *Jaime perdió las llaves.*
2. *Carlos rompió la lámpara.*
3. *Susana y Roberto olvidaron sus libros.*

Emphasis A: Suggestions

- Point out that the subject of the English sentence becomes the indirect object pronoun in the Spanish equivalent.: I = *se* **me**; Antonio = *se* **le**. The structure is similar to that of *gustar.*
- Point out the option of emphasizing or clarifying the indirect object with the corresponding prepositional phrase: *a mí, a él.*
- Point out that the use of the singular vs. the plural verb depends on the direct object from the English sentence.

Gramática ■ **355**

Emphasis B: Suggestion
This section concentrates on the use of this structure with *me*, *te*, and *le*. You might expand the activities in this section to cover *nos*, *os*, and *les* if you want students to practice these forms.

(*a* + Noun or Pronoun)	*se*	Indirect Object Pronoun	Verb	Subject
(A mí)	Se	me	cayó	la taza de café.
¿(A ti)	Se	te	perdió	la cartera?
A Antonio	se	le	olvidaron	los apuntes.

The verb agrees with the grammatical subject of the Spanish sentence (**la taza, la cartera, los apuntes**), not with the indirect object pronoun. **No** immediately precedes **se**.

A Antonio no *se le* **olvidaron los apuntes.**
Antonio didn't forget his notes. (Antonio's notes got lost on him.)

A Diego *se le* **perdió la cartera.**
Diego lost his wallet. (Diego's wallet got lost on him.)

B. Here are some verbs frequently used in this construction.

Note: Although all indirect object pronouns can be used in this construction, this section will focus on the singular of first, second, and third persons (**se me...**, **se te...**, **se le...**).

acabar	*to finish; to run out of*
olvidar	*to forget*
perder (ie)	*to lose*

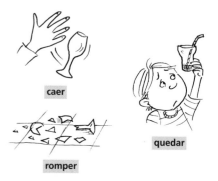

caer

quedar

romper

C. In general, this structure is used to emphasize the accidental nature of an event. When the speaker wishes to emphasize *who* committed the act, or that the act was intentional, that person becomes the subject of the verb and the **se** structure is not used. Compare the sentences at the right.

Se me rompió el plato.
The plate broke on me. (accidentally)

(Yo) Rompí el plato.
I broke the plate. (emphasizes either who broke the plate or the intentionality of the act)

AUTOPRUEBA

Match the following sentences.

1. _____ No encuentro las llaves.
2. _____ Tu calculadora no funciona.
3. _____ Paco no entregó la tarea.
4. _____ Necesito comprar leche.

a. Se te rompió.
b. Se me acabó.
c. Se me perdieron.
d. Se le olvidó.

Answers: 1. c 2. a 3. d 4. b

 Heritage Speakers

En algunas áreas rurales de Latinoamérica y de los Estados Unidos se oye decir *me se* y *te se* en vez de *se me* y *se te* en esta construcción. La construcción aceptada, sin embargo, es *se me* y *se te*.

A. **¡Anticipemos! ¡Qué mala memoria!** Hortensia sufre muchas presiones en su vida. Por eso cuando se fue de vacaciones al Perú, estaba tan distraída que se le olvidó hacer muchas cosas importantes antes de salir. Empareje (*Match*) los lapsos de Hortensia con las consecuencias.

LAPSOS

1. _____ Se le olvidó cerrar la puerta de su casa.
2. _____ Se le olvidó pagar las cuentas (*bills*).
3. _____ Se le olvidó pedirle a alguien que cuidara a (*to take care of*) su perro.
4. _____ Se le olvidó cancelar el periódico.
5. _____ Se le olvidó pedirle permiso a su jefa (*boss*).
6. _____ Se le olvidó llevar el pasaporte.
7. _____ Se le olvidó hacer reserva en un hotel.

CONSECUENCIAS

a. Va a perder el trabajo.
b. No la van a dejar entrar en el Perú.
c. Le van a suspender el servicio de la luz (*electricity*) y de gas… ¡y cancelar sus tarjetas de crédito!
d. Alguien le va a robar el televisor.
e. ¡«King» se va a morir de hambre!
f. No va a tener dónde alojarse (*to stay*).
g. Todos van a saber que no está en casa.

EN LOS ESTADOS UNIDOS Y EL CANADÁ

La impresionante variedad de la música latina

Es difícil hablar de «música latina» porque hay una inmensa **variedad.** La música de España y de toda Latinoamérica cuenta con[a] **diversos orígenes** que luego **se mezclan.**[b] La música de los españoles y portugueses llegó al Nuevo Mundo, pero pronto se mezcló con fuertes **tradiciones indígenas.** Cuando los conquistadores trajeron **esclavos**[c] **africanos** al Nuevo Mundo, estos trajeron consigo[d] sus propias tradiciones musicales, que influyeron en varios tipos de música que hoy consideramos música hispana.

Hoy día, los artistas hispanos de los Estados Unidos son cada vez más conocidos, no sólo como representantes de la música latina, sino también en las áreas del rock, pop, hip hop y jazz. Como ejemplo, podemos nombrar, entre muchos, a los neoyorquinos de origen

▲ *Tito Puente (1923–2000)*

puertorriqueño Jennifer López y Marc Anthony, al mexicoamericano Carlos Santana, a la colombiana Shakira, al español Enrique Iglesias y al pianista dominicano Michel Camilo.

La salsa es uno de los tipos de música hispana más reconocidos. Es una mezcla de **ritmos afrocaribeños** que fue creada en Nueva York por músicos hispanos en los años sesenta y setenta del siglo XX. La salsa es muy variada, pero siempre tiene una característica clara: es muy **bailable.** Uno de los nombres más asociados con la salsa es Tito Puente, el famoso **percusionista.** Carlos Santana grabó su versión de la composición de Puente, «Oye ¿cómo va?» e introdujo a Puente y un estilo de música hispana no sólo a una nueva generación, sino también al público no hispano.

[a]*cuenta… has* [b]*se… are combined* [c]*slaves* [d]*with them*

Prác. A: Preliminary Exercises

■ Ask students what indirect object pronoun they hear in the following sentences.

1. *Se me olvidó el bolígrafo.*
2. *Se le rompieron los platos.*
3. *Se te cayeron las flores.*
4. *Se te acabó la gasolina.*
5. *Se le quedaron en casa los boletos.*

■ Give the following dictation.

1. *Se me cayeron las llaves.*
2. *Se te rompieron los vasos.*
3. *A Pepe se le rompió el despertador.*
4. *A María se le olvidaron las aspirinas.*

Follow up the dictation with questions to check comprehension or by having students provide the English equivalents.

■ Have students do the following chain drill to practice the structure.

¡Qué distraídos estuvimos todos ayer! Dé oraciones nuevas según las indicaciones.

1. *A Pablo se le olvidó la cartera.* (*mí, Inés, ti, el chico*)
2. *Se te perdieron las llaves otra vez?* (*Ernesto, Ud. niña, mí*)
3. *María fue la más distraída de todos. Se le olvidó / olvidaron…* (*tomar el desayuno, las gafas, estudiar para el examen, los cheques, venir a clase*)

■ Have students give the Spanish equivalents.

1. I dropped the glasses/plate/ books.
2. Robert lost the book / keys / alarm clock.

EN LOS ESTADOS UNIDOS Y EL CANADÁ

Suggestions

■ Have students research *salsa* on the Internet and report to the class. Many websites have general as well as specific (artists) information, including calendars of performances.

■ Bring some *salsa* music to class. Offer a dance lesson if you are a skilled dancer. Alternatively, ask if any students can dance *salsa* and invite them to give a demonstration.
■ Mention to students that *salsa* can be the musical vehicle for serious social commentaries, such as the songs by Rubén Blades and Juan Luis Guerra.

Paso 2. Ask students:

¿Qué más le pasaba a Ud.? ¿Qué ha cambiado?

Have students give sentences with actions that used to happen to them but do not happen to them anymore.

Antes se me perdían las gafas.
Ahora se me pierden los suéteres.

Con: Suggestions

■ Have volunteers answer this question.
¿Recuerda Ud. alguno de los días más desastrosos de su vida? ¿Qué le pasó?

■ Have students work in groups to discuss their most recent *día fatal*.

B. ¡Desastres por todas partes [*everywhere*]!

Paso 1. ¿Es Ud. una persona distraída o torpe? Indique las oraciones que se apliquen (*apply*) a Ud. Puede cambiar algunos de los detalles de las oraciones si es necesario.

1. ☐ Con frecuencia se me caen los libros (los platos,...).
2. ☐ Se me pierden constantemente las llaves (los calcetines,...).
3. ☐ A menudo (*Often*) se me olvida apagar (*to turn off*) la computadora (la luz,...).
4. ☐ Siempre se me rompen las gafas (las lámparas,...).
5. ☐ De vez en cuando (*From time to time*) se me quedan los libros (los cuadernos,...) en la clase.
6. ☐ Se me olvida fácilmente mi horario (el teléfono de algún amigo,...).

Paso 2. ¿Es Ud. igual ahora que cuando era más joven? Complete cada oración del **Paso 1** para describir cómo era de niño/a. No se olvide de usar el imperfecto en sus oraciones.

MODELO: De niño/a, (no) se me caían los libros con frecuencia.

Paso 3. Ahora compare sus respuestas con las de un compañero / una compañera. ¿Quién es más distraído/a o torpe ahora? ¿Quién lo era de niño/a?

■ ■ ■ Conversación

Pablo tuvo una mañana fatal

Paso 1. Complete la siguiente descripción de lo que le pasó a Pablo ayer. Use expresiones con **se**.

P ablo tuvo una mañana fatal. Primero (olvidar[1]) poner el despertador. Se levantó tarde y se vistió rápidamente. No cerró bien su maletín;[a] por eso (caer[2]) unos papeles importantes. Recogió los papeles y subió al coche. Salió rápido pero después de cinco minutos, (acabar[2]) la gasolina y se le paró[b] el coche. Dejó el coche en la calle y decidió ir caminando. Llevaba el maletín en una mano y las llaves y un documento urgente en la otra. Desafortunadamente,[c] mientras caminaba, (perder[4]) el documento. Cuando llegó a la oficina, buscó a su jefe para entregarle el documento pero no podía encontrar el documento entre sus papeles. Cansado y enojado, cerró el maletín sin cuidado y (romper[5]) los lentes.

[a]*briefcase*   [b]*se... it* (*the car*) *stopped on him*   [c]*Unfortunately*

Paso 2. Ahora, con un compañero / una compañera, describa una mañana o un día fatal que Ud. tuvo. Trate de incluir expresiones con **se**.

MODELO: El primer día de clases, se me olvidó poner el despertador, y llegué tarde a clase. Luego…

Need more practice?

■ Workbook and Laboratory Manual
■ Interactive CD-ROM
■ Online Learning Center (www.mhhe.com/puntos7)

MULTIMEDIA: Internet

Have students search the Internet for information on Hispanic music and Hispanic musical artists.

Before beginning **Gramática 35,** review what you learned in **Capítulo 5** about prepositional pronouns: The first and second person singular pronouns differ from subject pronouns; the rest are identical to subject pronouns. Then give the prepositional pronouns that correspond to the following persons.

1. Pepe: de _____
2. Lisa y yo: después de _____
3. tú: para _____
4. yo: de _____
5. Ud.: con _____
6. Juan y Olga: para _____

Note

Students already know the most important uses of these prepositions.

Follow-Up

After completing *¿Qué se representa?,* read the following sentences and have students make drawings based on what they hear.

Haga un dibujo que ilustre cada una de las siguientes oraciones.

1. *Pedro trabaja para una familia muy rica.*
2. *Pedro va a trabajar por su compañero esta tarde.*
3. *Es una escultura* (write *escultura* on the board) *demasiado pequeña y fea para ese precio.*
4. *Teresa va a hacer algo especial mañana para el cumpleaños de su mejor amiga.*

To follow up, ask *¿Quién es el/la mejor dibujante de la clase?*

35 ¿Por o para? • A Summary of Their Uses

¿Qué se representa?

a.

b.

c.

d.

Empareje cada dibujo con la oración que le corresponde.

1. _____ Caminamos *para* el parque.
2. _____ Compramos el regalo *por* la abuela.
3. _____ Paseamos *por* el parque.
4. _____ El regalo es *para* Eduardo.

Refranes

«No hay mal que por bien no venga.»
«Hay que sufrir para merecer.»
«Hoy por ti, mañana por mí.»

Point out that these are sayings for difficult moments. Have students give their interpretations of the sayings and brainstorm similar sayings in English (*Every cloud has a silver lining. No pain, no gain. You scratch my back, I'll scratch yours.*)

☼ Heritage Speakers

Anime a los hispanohablantes a hablar de sus cantantes latinoamericanos favoritos. ¿Qué opinan de Ricky Martin, Celia Cruz, Jennifer López y Carlos Santana? Si tienen la música de artistas hispanos que no son muy conocidos en este país, pídales que la traigan a clase para escuchar.

- Have students say the following in Spanish (the numbers are coordinated with the presentation of the uses of *por*).

  1. by train/plane; by phone/letter
  2. through the campus/plaza; along the river/street
  3. in the afternoon/evening; at 2:00 in the afternoon (**¡OJO!** *de la tarde*)
  4. because of the test/accident
  5. Thanks for the book/pen/ money.
  6. I'm doing it for you/him/us.
  7. I studied for four hours / two days.

- Point out that *in order to get* or *in search of* is expressed with *por: Van por pan.*

- Have students use fixed expressions with *por* to respond to these questions or comments.

  1. *¿Es necesario estudiar treinta minutos cada día para la clase de español?*
  2. *Parece que va a llover hoy. ¿Debo llevar impermeable?*
  3. *¿Le paso la carne? ¿la ensalada?*
  4. *Me dicen que Ud. toma ocho clases este semestre.*
  5. *Empecé a leer este libro el año pasado; lo terminé esta mañana.*
  6. *¡Me robaron el coche anoche!*
  7. *¿Le gusta viajar?*
  8. *¿Por qué llegué tarde? Pues hay mil razones.*

You have been using the prepositions **por** and **para** throughout your study of Spanish. Although most of the information in this section will be a review, you will also learn some new uses of **por** and **para**.

Por

The preposition **por** has the following English equivalents.

■ *by, by means of*	Vamos **por** avión (tren, barco,...). *We're going by plane (train, ship, . . .).* Nos hablamos **por** teléfono mañana. *We'll talk by (on the) phone tomorrow.*
■ *through, along*	Me gusta pasear **por** el parque y **por** la playa. *I like to stroll through the park and along the beach.*
■ *during, in* (time of day)	Trabajo **por** la mañana. *I work in the morning.*
■ *because of, due to*	Estoy nervioso **por** la entrevista. *I'm nervous because of the interview.*
■ *for = in exchange for*	Piden 1.000 dólares **por** el coche. *They're asking $1,000 for the car.* Gracias **por** todo. *Thanks for everything.*
■ *for = for the sake of, on behalf of*	Lo hago **por** ti. *I'm doing it for you (for your sake).*
■ *for = duration* (often omitted)	Vivieron allí (**por**) un año. *They lived there for a year.*

Por is also used in a number of fixed expressions.

por Dios	for heaven's sake
por ejemplo	for example
por eso	that's why
por favor	please
por fin	finally
por lo general	generally, in general
por lo menos	at least
por primera/ última vez	for the first/ last time
por si acaso	just in case
¡por supuesto!	of course!
por todas partes	everywhere

Para

Although **para** has many English equivalents, including *for*, it always has the underlying purpose of referring to a goal or destination.

■ *in order to* + infinitive	Regresaron pronto **para** estudiar. *They returned soon (in order) to study.* Estudian **para** conseguir un buen trabajo. *They're studying (in order) to get a good job.*
■ *for = destined for, to be given to*	Todo esto es **para** ti. *All this is for you.* Le di un libro **para** su hijo. *I gave her a book for her son.*
■ *for = by* (deadline, specified future time)	**Para** mañana, estudien **por** y **para**. *For tomorrow, study **por** and **para**.* La composición es **para** el lunes. *The composition is for Monday.*
■ *for = toward, in the direction of*	Salió **para** el Ecuador ayer. *She left for Ecuador yesterday.*
■ *for = to be used for* Compare the example at the right to **un vaso de agua** = *a glass (full) of water.*	El dinero es **para** la matrícula. *The money is for tuition.* Es un vaso **para** agua. *It's a water glass.*
■ *for = as compared with others, in relation to others*	**Para** mí, el español es fácil. *For me, Spanish is easy.* **Para** (ser) extranjera, habla muy bien el inglés. *For (being) a foreigner, she speaks English very well.*
■ *for = in the employ of*	Trabajan **para** el gobierno. *They work for the government.*

AUTOPRUEBA

Indicate whether you would use **por** or **para**.

1. _____ to travel to a place
2. _____ to travel through a place
3. _____ to travel by plane
4. _____ to work for someone (a company)
5. _____ to work for someone (on behalf of)
6. _____ to last for a period of time
7. _____ to be due by a certain time

Answers: 1. para 2. por 3. por 4. por 5. para 6. por 7. para

☀️ Heritage Speakers

Una expresión con *para* es *estar para* (to be about to [do something]). En algunos dialectos, especialmente en México, se dice *estar por* en vez de *estar para*. Por ejemplo, *Carlota está por llegar* significa *Carlota está a punto de llegar*. También se oye *estar al* en algunos países caribeños. Pregúnteles a los hispanohablantes de la clase qué expresión prefieren usar.

 Bright Idea

Suggestion

Point out that some uses of *por* and *para* can be understood "directionally." *Por* normally refers *back* to something, while *para* refers to a forward point or purpose.

> *Salí para comprar pan.*
> I went out to buy bread. (purpose)
> *No salí por la lluvia.*
> I didn't go out because of the rain. (reason)

por	↔	**para**
reason		destination
cause		purpose

Suggestions

■ Emphasize that *para* is *for* with the concept of destination.
   a. Destined for whom? → *para su hijo*
   b. Destined for what point in time? → *para mañana*
   c. Geographical destination, in space? → *Salieron para Lima.*
   d. Destined for what use? → *un vaso para agua.*

■ Have students give the English equivalents (the numbers are coordinated with the order of presentation of the uses of *para*).

1. They came back to eat lunch / to rest.
2. It's for her/me.
3. The exercise is for Monday/ Friday.
4. They left for Bolivia / Costa Rica.
5. It's a wine/beer glass.
6. For an American/German, he speaks French well.
7. She works for Ramón / Mr. Jiménez. (¡OJO! *el Sr. Jiménez*)

 Bright Idea

Suggestion

Offer the following expressions as well.

por ahora	*por cierto*
por casualidad	*por desgracia*

Prác. A: Preliminary Exercise

Have students respond *por* or *para* to indicate the correct prepositions for the following sentences.

1. We stayed for three days.
2. We drove through the park.
3. The report is for Monday.
4. They left for Alaska.
5. The money is for his mom.
6. Math is hard for me.
7. We canceled the trip for two reasons.
8. This class is for advanced students.

Bright Idea
Prác. A: Extension

Have students explain the difference between the following pairs of sentences.

Caminamos por el parque.
(through the park)
Caminamos para el parque.
(to/toward the park)
Le di cinco pesetas por el pan.
(in exchange for the bread)
Le di cinco pesetas para el pan.
(in order to buy/get bread)

■ ■ ■ Práctica

A. ¡Anticipemos! Situaciones. Escoja una respuesta para cada pregunta o situación. Luego invente un contexto para cada diálogo. ¿Dónde están las personas que hablan? ¿Quiénes son? ¿Por qué dicen lo que dicen?

1. _____ ¡Huy! Acabo de jugar al basquetbol por dos horas.
2. _____ ¿Por qué quieres que llame a Pili y Adolfo? Nunca están en casa por la noche, sobre todo (*especially*) a estas horas.
3. _____ ¿No vas a comer nada? ¿Por lo menos un sándwich?
4. _____ ¡Cuánto lo siento, don Javier! Sé que llegué tarde a la cita (*appointment*). No fue mi intención hacerlo esperar.
5. _____ Es imposible que tome el examen hoy, por muchas razones.
6. _____ ¿No oíste? Juana acaba de tener un accidente horrible.
7. _____ ¡Pero, papá, quiero ir!
8. _____ Ay, Mariana, ¿no sabías que hubo un terremoto (*earthquake*)? Murieron más de cien personas.

a. ¡Por Dios! ¡Qué desgracia!
b. Te digo que no, por última vez.
c. No se preocupe. Lo importante es que por fin está aquí.
d. ¡Por Dios! ¿Qué le pasó?
e. No, gracias. No tengo mucha hambre y además tengo que salir en seguida.
f. ¿Por ejemplo? Dígame…
g. Ah, por eso tienes tanto calor.
h. Llámalos de todas formas, por si acaso…

B. Preguntas

Paso 1. Complete las siguientes preguntas con **por** y **para**.

1. ¿_____ quién trabaja Ud.? ¿Le pagan a Ud. bien?
2. ¿_____ dónde tiene que manejar (*drive*) para llegar a la universidad?
3. ¿Cuánto pagó Ud. _____ su carro/bicicleta?
4. ¿_____ qué es la llave grande que tiene Ud.?
5. ¿_____ qué profesión estudia Ud.? ¿_____ cuántos años tiene que estudiar?
6. ¿_____ cuándo necesita Ud. volver a casa hoy?

Paso 2. Ahora, conteste las preguntas del **Paso 1.** Invente la información necesaria.

C. ¿Por o para? Complete los siguientes diálogos y oraciones con **por** o **para**.

1. Los Sres. Arana salieron _____ el Perú ayer. Van _____ avión, claro, pero luego piensan viajar en coche _____ todo el país. Van a estar allí _____ dos meses. Va a ser una experiencia extraordinaria _____ toda la familia.

2. Mi prima Graciela quiere estudiar _____ (ser) doctora. _____ eso trabaja _____ un médico _____ la mañana; tiene clases _____ la tarde.

3. —¿ _____ qué están Uds. aquí todavía? Yo pensaba que iban a dar un paseo _____ el parque.
   —Íbamos a hacerlo, pero no fuimos, _____ la nieve.

4. Este cuadro fue pintado (*was painted*) por Picasso _____ expresar los desastres de la guerra (*war*). _____ muchos críticos de arte, es la obra maestra de este artista.

5. La «Asociación Todo _____ Ellos» trabaja _____ las personas mayores, _____ ayudarlos cuando lo necesitan. ¿Trabaja Ud. _____ alguna asociación de voluntarios? ¿Qué tuvo que hacer _____ inscribirse (*sign up*)?

> **ASOCIACION**
> **TODO ELLOS**
> **POR**
>
> Trabajamos por las personas mayores que están solas y con escasos recursos económicos
>
> **AYÚDANOS, NO ES POSIBLE SIN TI**
>
> Para más información llama al teléfono 907 98 91 15, de 18.00 a 20.00 h. tardes, martes y viernes
>
> **CAJAMADRID, SUC. 1028**
> **C/C 6000854579**
>
> TODO POR ELLOS es una asociación no gubernamental inscrita en el Registro de Asociaciones del Ministerio del Interior con el número 160.589

■ ■ ■ Conversación

Entrevista. Hágale preguntas a su profesor(a) para saber la siguiente información.

1. la tarea para mañana y para la semana que viene
2. lo que hay que estudiar para el próximo examen
3. si para él/ella son interesantes o aburridas las ciencias
4. la opinión que tiene de la pronunciación de Uds., para ser principiantes
5. qué deben hacer Uds. para mejorar su pronunciación del español
6. por cuánto tiempo deben Uds. practicar el español todos los días

Need more practice?
- Workbook and Laboratory Manual
- Interactive CD-ROM
- Online Learning Center (www.mhhe.com/puntos7)

Prác. B: Suggestions

- Have students give the reason for each use of *por* or *para*. Expand items with personal questions.
- Ask students the following questions to personalize the structures.

  1. *¿Para qué (profesión) estudia Ud.?*
  2. *¿Para qué compañía trabaja Ud. (su padre / madre, su esposo/a)?*
  3. *Para Ud., ¿son más difíciles los exámenes escritos o los orales? ¿los exámenes de matemáticas o los de historia?*
  4. *¿Tiene Ud. mucho que hacer para mañana? ¿mucho que leer? ¿mucho que escribir?*
  5. *¿Tiene Ud. que comprar algo esta noche? ¿o para su casa/apartamento/cuarto? ¿algo para un amigo? ¿algo para la familia?*

- For item 5, ask students: *¿Qué se puede hacer por las personas mayores?*

Gramática   Trescientos sesenta y tres ■ 363

CULTURE

Most older people in the Hispanic world end up living with their grown-up children and their grandchildren when they can no longer take care of themselves. At this point family members will take care of them until they die. Being too old or sick is not the only reason for older people to live with their children. This may also happen after the loss of a spouse. In any case, grandparents have an important role in the upbringing of their grandchildren, often taking care of them while the parents work. For this reason, there are very few *residencias para ancianos* (nursing homes) in Hispanic countries.

Suggestions

- Have students give possible reactions to the following situations. Compare their answers and take a vote on the most original ones.

¿Cómo se debe o se puede reaccionar en estas situaciones?

1. *Son las seis de la mañana. Ud. oye el despertador pero todavía tiene sueño.*
2. *Ud. quiere despedirse, pero la persona con quien está hablando quiere hablar más.*
3. *Ud. está en Buenos Aires. Pierde su cartera y con ella todo su dinero y el pasaporte.*
4. *Su vecino dejó su coche delante de su garaje y ahora Ud. no puede sacar su coche.*
5. *Ud. sufre muchas presiones a causa de los exámenes finales.*

- Have students identify which of these experiences they have had and explain the problems that resulted. How did they resolve the problems?

Una vez...

1. *se me perdió la tarjeta de identificación de la universidad.*
2. *se me cayó un vaso de vino tinto en la ropa.*
3. *se me perdieron los lentes de contacto.*
4. *se me rompió un objeto caro.*
5. *se me quedó en casa un trabajo para la clase.*

A: Follow-Up

- **Paso 1.** Have students give sentences about themselves using the same time markers.

1. *anoche*
2. *cuando era pequeño/a*
3. *esta mañana*
4. *esta noche*
5. *ahora*

- **Paso 2.** Have students give a reason (*porque...*) for each of their sentences.

UN POCO DE TODO

A. Causa y efecto

Paso 1.   Form complete sentences with the cues given. Pay attention to the various clues to decide whether you will need to use the present, the preterite, or the imperfect in your sentences. Change words and add additional words when necessary. You will use these sentences again in **Paso 2.**

1. anoche / Sra. Ortega / poner / trajes de baño / y / toallas (*towels*) / en / bolsa
2. cuando / ser / pequeño / Cecilia / acostarse / temprano / todo / noches
3. este / mañana / a Lorenzo / perder / llaves / y / caer / taza de café
4. esta noche / estudiantes / clase de historia / no / ir a dormir / mucho
5. ahora / Amalia / estar / contento

Paso 2.   Now match the sentences above, followed by **porque,** with the phrases below. (The first one is done for you.) Conjugate the verbs below as needed to complete the new sentences. There is more than one possible answer in most cases.

MODELO: querer ir hoy con su esposo a la playa →

1. Anoche la Sra. Ortega puso los trajes de baño y las toallas en la bolsa porque quería ir hoy con su esposo a la playa.

estar nervioso/a por su boda (*wedding*) mañana	siempre ir a clase muy temprano
tener un examen final	empezar la clase de natación hoy
encontrar su cartera	estar distraído/a
ser la fecha límite para un informe	querer ir hoy con su esposo/a a la playa

B. ¡Qué desastre!

Paso 1.   Indique todas las opciones verdaderas para Ud. Haga las modificaciones necesarias de acuerdo con sus experiencias.

Una vez...

1. ☐ se me perdió la tarjeta de identificación de la universidad.
2. ☐ se me cayó un vaso de vino tinto en la ropa.
3. ☐ se me perdieron los lentes de contacto.
4. ☐ se me rompió un objeto caro.
5. ☐ se me quedó en casa un trabajo para la clase.

Paso 2.   Ahora trabaje con un compañero / una compañera para explicar qué problemas tuvieron Uds. a consecuencia de esos accidentes y cómo los resolvieron (*you solved*).

C. El peor día del semestre.
Complete the following passages with the correct forms of the words in parentheses, as suggested by the context. When two possibilities are given in parentheses, select the correct word. **¡OJO!** As you conjugate verbs in this activity, use the present tense unless otherwise indicated in the parentheses. If you see *P/I*, you will choose between the preterite and the imperfect; *comm.* means to use an **Ud./Uds.** command; and *prog.* stands for the present/past progressive.

Este día, Sandra Dávila, reportera del programa «¿Qué onda[a] hoy, estudiantes?» en el canal universitario **WBMN,** se encuentra en medio del hermoso Jardín Botánico de la Universidad de Puerto Rico. La universidad (ser/estar[1]) en la ciudad de Río Piedras, y este año (celebrar[2]) el centenario de su fundación en 1903. (Por/Para[3]) eso, hay muchos eventos y actividades (fascinante[4]) (por/para[5]) todas partes de la universidad. Los directores de «¿Qué onda hoy, estudiantes?» (P/I, decidir[6]) presentar (alguno[7]) de (este[8]) actividades en su programa, y también (P/I, mandar[9]) allí a la Srta. Dávila (por/para[10]) entrevistar a unos profesores y estudiantes (típico[11]). (Ella: Pensar[12]) pedirles que participen en (un/una[13]) programa especial que van a presentar. El programa (llamarse[14]) «El peor día del semestre.»

SANDRA:	¡Perdón, perdón, (*comm., Uds.:* esperar[15]) un momento, por favor!
ÁNGEL:	Sí, señorita, ¿en qué le (*nosotros:* poder[16]) servir?
RAFAEL:	Ay, Dios mío, chico, ¿no (saber/conocer[17]) quién es ella? ¡Es Sandra Dávila, la reportera de «¿Qué onda hoy, estudiantes?»! Buenas tardes, Srta. Dávila, a sus órdenes[b].
SANDRA:	Muy buenas, muchachos. Pues, ya que (*Uds.:* saber/conocer[18]) el programa, a ver[c] si los dos (tener[19]) ganas de participar en el programa «El peor día del semestre». (*comm., Uds.:* Decirme:[20]) por favor, ¿(qué/cuál[21]) (P/I, ser[22]) el peor día del semestre para Uds.?
ÁNGEL:	Bueno, el miércoles pasado se (mí/me[23]) (P/I, perder[24]) las llaves de la casa y del coche, y (las/les[25]) busqué (por/para[26]) cuatro horas antes de encontrarlas allí en el coche mismo.
RAFAEL:	Ay, hombre, ¡qué problema más tonto! Pero (*comm., Ud.:* escucharme[27]) a mí, Srta. Dávila. En una de las cenas (oficial[28]) que (P/I, ellos: dar[29]) para el centenario, (*yo:* trabajar[30]) de camarero. A la hora de servir el postre, (P/I, yo: llevar[31]) una bandeja[d] con ocho platitos de flan, cuando (P/I, pegarse[32]) contra una silla, y ¡se me (P/I, caer[33]) todos los flanes sobre la cabeza del rector[e] de la universidad!

[a]¿Qué... *What's new/What's happening* [b]a... *at your service* [c]a... *let's see/I wonder* [d]*tray*
[e]*president*

Comprensión: ¿Cierto o falso? Restate the false statements in Spanish so that they are true.

1. Sandra Dávila está en la Universidad de Puerto Rico hoy para estudiar el Jardín Botánico.
2. Este año se celebra la fundación de la Universidad de Puerto Rico hace cien años.
3. «El peor día del semestre» es un programa que cuenta buenos momentos de la vida estudiantil.
4. A Ángel se le perdieron unas llaves que luego encontró en su coche.
5. A Rafael se le olvidó servirle el postre al rector de la universidad.

B: Follow-Up
Ask students the following questions.

1. *¿Para quién trabaja Sandra Dávila?*
2. *¿Dónde está la Universidad de Puerto Rico?*
3. *¿Por dónde caminan los estudiantes cuando se encuentran con la Srta. Dávila?*

**Resources for
Review and Testing
Preparation**

- Workbook and Laboratory Manual
- Interactive CD-ROM
- Online Learning Center (www.mhhe.com/puntos7)

Resources: Desenlace

In the *Capítulo 11* segment of "Chapter-by-Chapter Supplementary Materials" in the IM/RK, you will find a chapter-culminating activity. You can use this activity to consolidate and review the vocabulary and grammar skills students have acquired.

Entrevista cultural

Preliminary Exercise

Review with students different types of situations that may induce stress and types of activities designed to reduce stress.

Suggestions

- Before showing the video, ask students questions about what typical days are like for them.

    ¿Cómo es para Ud. un día típico?
    ¿Qué presiones sufre Ud.?
    ¿Qué hace Ud. para aliviar el estrés?

- Show the video and allow students one to two minutes to work on the questions. Have volunteers answer the questions.
- Have volunteers role-play Antonio and his interviewer.

Entre amigos

Suggestions

- Before viewing the video, review the questions with the students and ask them similar questions.

    ¿Sufre Ud. mucho estrés en sus estudios? ¿en el trabajo?
    ¿Qué clase le da más dificultades y estrés?

- Have students answer or work in small groups to ask and answer these questions.
- After viewing the video, have volunteers read and answer the questions.
- Have students interview two or three classmates about the types of stress they feel and what they do to relieve it. After the interviews, have them report their findings to the class.

PERSPECTIVAS culturales

●●●
Videoteca

Entrevista cultural: Puerto Rico

Antonio Solórzano es un estudiante puertorriqueño. Aquí describe su rutina diaria. También habla de las presiones que sufre y de lo que hace para disminuir el estrés. Antes de ver el vídeo, lea el siguiente fragmento de la entrevista.

ENTREVISTADORA:	¿Qué estudias?
ANTONIO:	Estudio antropología.
ENTREVISTADORA:	Antonio, ¿cómo es para ti un día típico?
ANTONIO:	Pues un día típico para mí es despertarme temprano para ir a la universidad y,… este, estar allí casi todo el día. Y después en la tarde además trabajo como hasta las seis y media de la tarde, estudiar un rato cuando llego a mi casa y después irme en la noche a hacer ejercicio.

Ahora vea el vídeo y conteste las siguientes preguntas basándose en la entrevista.

1. ¿Dónde vive y estudia Antonio?
2. ¿Qué hace por la tarde, generalmente?
3. Según Antonio, ¿qué presiones sufren los estudiantes?
4. ¿Qué hace Antonio todos los días para aliviar el estrés?
5. Y los fines de semana, ¿qué hace?

Entre amigos: ¡Estoy superestresada!

Karina, Miguel, Tané y Rubén hablan del estrés y de las presiones de la vida diaria. En su opinión, ¿de qué van a hablar? Antes de mirar el vídeo, lea las preguntas a continuación. Mientras mire el vídeo, trate de entender la conversación en general y fíjese en la información sobre los exámenes, las clases y el trabajo. Luego mire el vídeo una segunda vez, fijándose en la información que necesita para contestar las preguntas.

1. ¿Cuántas horas por semana trabaja Rubén?
2. ¿Por qué está estresada Karina?
3. ¿Tiene Tané buenas o malas notas?
4. ¿Qué clase le da más dificultades a Tané?
5. ¿Qué tipo de ayuda (*help*) le ofrece Miguel a Tané?

Conozca... **Puerto Rico**

Datos esenciales

- Nombre oficial: Estado Libre Asociado[a] de Puerto Rico
- Capital: San Juan
- Población: 3.900.000 habitantes
- Moneda: el dólar estadounidense
- Idiomas oficiales: el español y el inglés

[a]Estado... *literally, Free Associated State*

¡Fíjese!

- Puerto Rico ha estado relacionado[a] políticamente con los Estados Unidos desde la Guerra Hispanonorteamericana de 1898, año en que España perdió las ultimas colonias de su imperio. En 1952, Puerto Rico se convirtió en Estado Libre Asociado. Bajo[b] este sistema de gobierno, los puertorriqueños son ciudadanos[c] estadounidenses. Sin embargo,[d] los que viven en la isla no pueden votar por el presidente de los Estados Unidos aunque deben servir en el ejército[e] de ese país en caso de guerra.
- Otro nombre de Puerto Rico es Borinquen y los puertorriqueños se conocen también como boricuas. Estas palabras originaron en el lenguaje de los indios taínos. Los taínos llegaron a la isla en el siglo[f] XIII pero su cultura casi desapareció con la llegada de los españoles en 1493.
- El Parque Nacional del Yunque, ubicado[g] en una montaña de 1.065 metros de altura que está al noreste de la isla, es pequeño cuando se compara a otros bosques[h] nacionales, pero es el único bosque tropical del sistema de Bosques Nacionales de los Estados Unidos.

[a]ha... *has been associated* [b]*Under* [c]*citizens* [d]Sin... *However* [e]*army* [f]*century* [g]*located* [h]*forests*

Learn more about Puerto Rico with the Video, the Interactive CD-ROM, and the Online Learning Center (www.mhhe.com/puntos7).

Personas famosas: Alonso Ramírez

En 1690 se publicó en México la primera novela del Nuevo Mundo, *Infortunios*[a] *de Alonso Ramírez.* Aunque esta obra[b] se atribuyó al mexicano Carlos Sigüenza y Góngora, hoy se cree que el verdadero[c] autor fue el mismo Alonso Ramírez del título. También se cree que la obra no es ficticia, sino autobiográfica: la vida de un puertorriqueño que se cría[d] en la isla, viaja a México y tiene aventuras en muchas partes del Mar Pacífico. Sus aventuras incluyen batallas contra piratas, una estadía[e] en una isla desierta y muchos otros eventos interesantísimos. Es una novela que vale la pena[f] leer.

[a]*Misfortunes* [b]*work* [c]*real* [d]se... *is brought up* [e]*stay* [f]que... *that is worthwhile*

 Una calle en el viejo San Juan

Notes

- The Igneri culture appeared in Puerto Rico about 25 A.D. and remained until the fifth century. Another indigenous group, now called the Pre-Taino culture, later populated the same area. These groups left a ceremonial complex, complete with nine ball courts and three ceremonial plazas. The rains of hurricane Eloisa in 1975 unearthed the remnants of this complex, Tibes, and in the following years the site has become an important archeological center, perhaps the most important of its kind in the Antilles.
- Vieques, a small island to the south of Puerto Rico, has recently been the focus of much international attention because of its population's resistance to the U.S. Navy presence. As early as 1947, the Navy had attempted to appropriate the island by sending the entire population of Vieques to the Virgin Islands. Although the attempt was not successful, the Navy nevertheless took over 72% of the island for military maneuvers, bombing practice, and storage of military explosives. In May 2000, protesters, who had been demonstrating for over a year against the Navy's use of a bombing range, were forcibly removed from the front gates of the Navy base. In May of 2003, the Navy ceased using Vieques as a bombing range.
- Sila María Calderón was elected in November 2000 as Puerto Rico's first woman governor. The mother of eight children and ex-mayor of the city of San Juan had been a prominent public figure for many years before her election to the post.
- Doña Felisa Rincón de Gautier was another woman mayor of the capital city. A beloved figure, known for her extravagant hairdos as much as for her highly developed political sense, she ran San Juan from 1946 to 1968. Today a museum in the old city is dedicated to her life and work.
- Students can read an excerpt of the essay *"De cómo dejarse caer de la sartén al fuego"* by Puerto Rico's Rosario Ferré in *Un paso más 11.*

MULTIMEDIA: Internet

Have students search the Internet for more information about the government, educational system, geography, and economy of Puerto Rico. You might assign specific topics and have students prepare brief oral presentations based on their findings.

☼ Heritage Speakers

Si hay hispanohablantes de Puerto Rico en su clase, anímelos a hablar de la isla y comparar la vida de allí con la vida cotidiana de este país.

Suggestions

- Remind students that, in the preterite, the first person singular is *saqué*.
- Remind students that the plural of *luz* is *luces*.
- Have students use vocabulary words to narrate a round-robin *un día fatal*. As a class, they can establish the subject (an individual, real or imaginary). Each student gives a sentence that describes the subject's terrible day.

EN RESUMEN

Gramática

To review the grammar points presented in this chapter, refer to the indicated grammar presentations. You'll find further practice of these structures in the Workbook and Laboratory Manual, on the Interactive CD-ROM, and on the *Puntos de partida* Online Learning Center (www.mhhe.com/puntos7).

33. Telling How Long Something Has Been Happening or How Long Ago Something Happened—**Hace... que:** Another Use of **hacer**

You should know how to express *it's been sixteen years since* you have been doing something or that you did something *sixteen years ago.*

34. Expressing Unplanned or Unexpected Events—Another Use of **se**

Do you know how to use **se** to express unplanned or unexpected events?

35. *¿Por o para?*—A Summary of Their Uses

Do you know the difference between **por** and **para** and when to use one or the other?

Vocabulario

Practice this vocabulary with digital flash cards on the Online Learning Center (www.mhhe.com/puntos7).

Los verbos

acabar	to finish; to run out of
acordarse (ue) (de)	to remember
apagar (gu)	to turn off
caer (*irreg.*)	to fall
caerse	to fall down
entregar (gu)	to turn, hand in
equivocarse (qu) (de)	to be wrong, make a mistake (about)
estacionar	to park
quedar	to remain, be left
recoger (j)	to collect; to pick up
romper	to break
sacar (qu)	to take out; to get
ser (*irreg.*) flexible	to be flexible
sufrir	to suffer
(muchas) presiones	to be under (a lot of) pressure

Repaso: doler (ue), llegar (gu) a tiempo/tarde, olvidar(se) de

Accidentes

darse (*irreg.*) en/con/contra	to run, bump into
hacerse (*irreg.*) daño	to hurt oneself
lastimarse	to injure oneself

levantarse con el pie izquierdo	to get up on the wrong side of the bed
pedir (i, i) disculpas	to apologize
pegar (gu)	to hit, strike
pegarse en/con/contra	to run, bump into
Discúlpeme.	Pardon me. / I'm sorry.
Fue sin querer.	It was unintentional.
¡Lo siento (mucho)!	Pardon me! / I'm (very) sorry!
¡Qué mala suerte!	What bad luck!

Repaso: perdón

Presiones de la vida estudiantil

la calificación	grade
el estrés	stress
la (falta de) flexibilidad	(lack of) flexibility
la fecha límite	deadline
el horario	schedule
el informe (oral/escrito)	(oral/written) report
la nota	grade
la prueba	quiz; test
la tarjeta de identificación	identification card

| el trabajo | job, work; report, (piece of) work |
| de tiempo completo/parcial | full time/part time |

Repaso: el examen, la tarea

Más partes del cuerpo

el brazo	arm
el dedo (de la mano)	finger
el dedo del pie	toe
la mano	hand
el pie	foot
la pierna	leg

Repaso: la cabeza

Los adjetivos

distraído/a	absentminded
escrito/a	written
estudiantil	(of) student(s)
flexible	flexible
torpe	clumsy
universitario/a	(of the) university

Otros sustantivos

el calendario	calendar
el despertador	alarm clock
la llave	key
la luz	light; electricity

Repaso: la vida

Palabras adicionales

hace + *time* + **que...** + *preterite*	(*something happened*) (*time*) ago
hace + *time* + **que...** + *present*	to have been (doing something) for (*time*)
por Dios	for heaven's sake
por ejemplo	for example
por primera/ última vez	for the first/last time
por si acaso	just in case
¡por supuesto!	of course!
por todas partes	everywhere

Repaso: por eso, por favor, por fin, por lo general, por lo menos

Suggestions

■ Have students complete sentences, such as:

1. *Por primera vez en mi vida, yo...*
2. *Por supuesto, yo...*
3. *Por si acaso hay...*
4. *En esta clase, por lo menos...*

Encourage them to be creative and humorous in their responses. Ask them to compose new sentences that use the new *Palabras adicionales*.

■ Remind students that the notation after *pedir* (*i, i*) indicates the *e* → *i* stem change in the present tense (except for *nosotros* and *vosotros*) and the *e* → *i* stem change in the third person singular and plural of the preterite and in the present participle.

■ Have students give the opposite expressions for the following verbs.

acabar	*entregar*	*sacar*
acordarse	*quedar*	*ser flexible*
caerse	*recoger*	

Un paso más 11

Note

The *Un paso más* section is optional.

Literatura de **Puerto Rico**

Note

Rosario Ferré was born into a family that was influential in business and politics. Her father, Luis Ferré, was a pro-statehood governor of the commonwealth from 1968 to 1972. Among Rosario Ferré's books is a biography of her father.

LECTURA

Suggestions

■ Do the *Repaso de estrategias* section in class the day before you intend to cover the reading. Remind students to practice the strategies actively as they read, as part of their homework assignment. Remember to follow up on the underlined words the next day.

PREVIOUS STRATEGIES

1. guessing the meaning of unfamiliar words from context

2. using connecting words or phrases to indicate what kind of information will be introduced (*por eso, por otra parte, en cambio, por ejemplo*)

3. using visuals and graphics to predict content

4. recognizing cognate patterns (*-ción = -tion; -dad = -ty*)

5. forming a general idea about content by using titles, subtitles, art, and comprehension questions

6. knowing words with multiple meanings

7. identifying the source of a passage

8. recognizing derivative adjectives

9. identifying thematic patterns (cause and effect, and so on)

■ Have students work in small groups to create original titles in Spanish for each section of this article. Compare the titles and have the class vote on the best one for each passage.

Un paso más 11

Literatura de **Puerto Rico**

Sobre la autora: *Rosario Ferré nació en Ponce, Puerto Rico. Además de biografías, crítica literaria y poesía, escribe también ficción en español y en inglés. Actualmente enseña en la Universidad de Puerto Rico y contribuye en el periódico* San Juan Star. *El siguiente fragmento es del ensayo: «De cómo dejarse caer de la sartén al fuego[a]»,* Sitio a eros: Trece ensayos *(1980).*

A lo largo del tiempo, las mujeres narradoras han escrito[b] por múltiples razones: Emily Brontë escribió para demostrar la naturaleza revolucionaria de la pasión; Virginia Woolf para exorcizar su terror a la locura y a la muerte; Joan Didion escribe para descubrir lo que piensa y cómo piensa; Clarisse Lispector descubre en su escritura una razón para amar y ser amada. En mi caso, escribir es una voluntad a la vez constructiva y destructiva; una posibilidad de crecimiento[c] y de cambio.[d]

[a]*de... from the frying pan into the fire*   [b]*han... have written*   [c]*growth*   [d]*change*

▲ Rosario Ferré (1938–)

LECTURA

REPASO DE ESTRATEGIAS: Guessing the Content of a Passage

In previous reading sections, you have learned several different strategies to improve your comprehension of a text. Whenever you can, it's a good idea to utilize as many of these strategies as possible. Of course, not all texts will lend themselves to the application of all strategies. For example, there might be limited visual cues such as photos to help you anticipate what the reading is about. In those instances, what else can you rely on to make predictions about the content? One strategy is to identify the source of the passage (see **Sobre la lectura,** page 371). And, of course, the title often reveals a great deal about the content of a passage. Take a look at the title of the reading that follows and the accompanying photo. What do you think this article is about?

1. Divorce rates in Spanish-speaking countries

2. The relationship between divorce and stress

3. Advice for reducing stress

If you picked number 3, you were right! The following article offers suggestions and techniques for reducing stress and enjoying a calmer life.

CULTURE

Emily Brontë (1818–1848): born in Yorkshire, England, and the second of the three Brontë sisters (Charlotte, Emily, Anne); poet and novelist; author of *Wuthering Heights* (1847), her only novel but one of the most important of 19th century British literature

Virginia Woolf (1882–1941): born in London, England; an important English novelist who experimented with stream-of-consciousness techniques such as in *Mrs. Dalloway* (1925), considered one of her greatest and most accessible novels; co-founder with her husband, Leonard Woolf, of Hogart Press, which published, among other things, T.S. Eliot's *Waste Land* (1992)

■ Have students name the five steps
described in the article. List these
on the board. Then ask for a show
of hands as you ask who does each
one. Tally the results, then have
students discuss whether or not
the class as a whole manages
stress well, or needs to incorporate
activities such as these to relieve
stress.

■ Have students give other activities
they do to relieve stress, and list
these on the board.

■ **Sobre la lectura...** Esta lectura es parte de un artículo que se publicó en la revista hispana *Nuestra Gente*. Como Ud. ya sabe, esta revista presenta artículos de interés sobre una gran variedad de temas: cine, música, cocina y otros.

Divórciate del estrés

<u>Convivimos</u> tanto con el estrés que hasta parece un miembro de la familia. Lo llevamos al trabajo, a las tiendas, a la lavandería,[a] a veces hasta nos acostamos y <u>amanecemos</u> con él. Pero es un compañero de muchos disfraces.[b] Nos mantiene en movimiento diario, pero aparece como dolor de cabeza, nudos[c] de músculos en el cuello,[d] ratos de <u>olvido</u>, cansancio o enojo.

Cinco pasos hacia una vida más tranquila

¡Córrele![e]
O hasta puedes decir «¡camínale!» si prefieres pues también te servirá.[f] Es decir, si notas que se te viene encima el maldito estrés, ponte los tenis, y ¡a la calle! Una simple <u>caminata</u> o <u>corrida</u> de 20 minutos diarios hace milagros.[g] Hasta los científicos han comprobado[h] que el ejercicio diario —aunque corto— sí reduce sustancialmente los niveles de estrés.

Respira profundamente
Uno de los mejores y más sencillos pasos a tomar para reducir el estrés es cuidar de tu respiración, según el Centro Médico Arnot Ogden de Elmira, Nueva York. Cuando te afecta el estrés, tu respiración <u>se acorta</u> y es poco <u>profunda</u> debido al efecto que producen los músculos tensos. Cada vez que te sientas tenso, concéntrate unos segundos en tu respiración y profundízala. Tu corazón te lo agradecerá.[i]

Un <u>spa</u> en tu propia casa
Aunque sea un día a la semana —o al mes— aparta[j] una hora —o más— para ti mismo. <u>Prende</u> una vela[k] de aroma tranquilizante, llena la <u>tina del baño</u> con un delicioso jabón y tómate un té caliente de manzanilla,[l] vainilla o canela.[m]

[a]lugar público donde se puede lavar la ropa [b]*disguises*
[c]*knots* [d]*neck* [e]*Run!* [f]*te... it (that phrase) will work for you*
[g]*miracles, wonders* [h]*han... have proven* [i]*te... will thank you for it* [j]*set aside* [k]*candle* [l]*chamomile* [m]*cinnamon*

▲ *Correr o caminar veinte minutos todos los días reduce el estrés.*

CULTURE (*continued*)

Joan Didion (1934–): born in Sacramento, California; novelist, essayist, and journalist; considered one of the shrewdest observers of American politics and culture, as seen in her novels *Slouching Towards Bethlehem* (1968) and *Play It As It Lays* (1970)
Clarisse Lispector (1920–1977): born in Tchechelnik (Ukraine) to Brazilian parents and raised in Brazil; novelist, editor, translator, and law student; considered one of the most important Brazilian novelists of the 20th century; influenced by Virginia Woolf as seen in her stream-of-consciousness writing in novels such as *Agua viva* (1971), published in translation as *The Stream of Life*)

Have students name things in their
lives that trigger stress. List these on
the board, and have students give a
show of hands in order to tally which
stress triggers are the most common
among them. Then have them discuss
the most effective activities to relieve
or avoid these sources of stress.

Come de manera saludable

Una buena dieta baja en <u>grasas,</u> alta en fibra y
que incluye comer vegetales y frutas diariamente ayuda no sólo al cuerpo sino al estado
mental. Cuando <u>ingerimos</u> en exceso comida
grasosa y azucarada[n] —los famosos alimentos vacíos de nutrición que suelen aparecer en
nuestras cocinas— el cuerpo protesta de diversas formas. Las enfermedades que pueden
aparecer a la larga[o] como la obesidad, el alto
colesterol y enfermedades del corazón son
aun otras y muy serias fuentes de estrés.

Convierte estos pasos en una rutina diaria

Poco a poco —¡y sin estresarte!— incorpora
estos pasos a la rutina de tus días y noches. No
hay que hacerlo de un jalón.[p] Comienza al
paso que puedas, <u>incrementando</u> gradual-
mente para que poco a poco se conviertan
en algo cotidiano[q] y <u>esperado.</u> Verás[r] que
dentro de poco tu cara sonriente y tranquila lo
dirá todo:[s] ¿Estrés? ¿De qué hablas? ▪

[n]*sweetened, containing sugar*   [o]*a... over time*   [p]*de... all at once*   [q]*diario*   [r]*You'll see*   [s]*lo... will say it all*

▲ *Es importante incluir vegetales y frutas en la dieta.*

Comprensión

A. Consejos. De los siguientes consejos para reducir el estrés, ¿cuáles *no* se mencionan en el artículo?

1. comer bien
2. escuchar música
3. hacer ejercicio
4. controlar la respiración
5. practicar yoga
6. beber bastante agua

B. Síntomas y soluciones

Paso 1. Identifique tres síntomas del estrés, según la lectura.

1. _____
2. _____
3. _____

Paso 2. Ahora haga una lista de posibles soluciones para el estrés. Indentifique las soluciones que Ud. prefiere o que cree que son más efectivos. ¿Puede añadir (*add*) otra solución no mencionada en el artículo?

ESCRITURA

A. Ud. y el estrés. La lectura presenta varias sugerencias para reducir el estrés, pero claro que no es una lista definitiva. Seguro que hay otros métodos también. Cuando Ud. se siente estresado/a, ¿qué hace para bajar el nivel de estrés? ¿Tiene alguna técnica en particular? Escriba un breve ensayo de 100 palabras en el cual describa cómo responde Ud. al estrés y qué hace para aliviarlo (*alleviate it*).

B. El estrés y los estudiantes. Aunque las presiones de la vida moderna nos afectan a todos, sin duda (*doubt*) tienen un impacto tremendo en los estudiantes universitarios. Escríbale una carta al editor o a la editora del periódico local comentando lo que Ud. cree que es la mayor presión para los estudiantes en su universidad. En la carta, debe identificar la causa de la presión, las consecuencias que tiene y algunas soluciones posibles para combatirla.

Puede comenzar su carta así:

Estimado editor: / Estimada editora:...

ESCRITURA

Variation
Based on the *Lectura* format, have students write two or more tips to relieve stress. They can use some of the following topics for their compositions.

el estrés en los conductores de automóviles
los problemas de comunicación y los teléfonos celulares
las presiones de tiempo en las grandes ciudades
las enfermedades respiratorias en las áreas contaminadas

Suggestion
If you prefer that your students do a journal activity, see *Mi diario* in this chapter of the Workbook.

B: Follow-Up
List on the board each item students named as the biggest source of pressure for students. Group similar, though not identical, items under an inclusive category. Which was named most often? Have groups debate to defend different sources.

CHAPTER OPENER PHOTO

Point out the chapter-opener photo. Have students talk about the indigenous civilizations and their contributions to the modern world. Point out that the Inca were advanced engineers and farmers, building complex terraces like the ones in the photo.

Suggestions

■ Ask students the following questions to introduce the chapter topic.

1. ¿Es típico que los estudiantes universitarios tengan su propia (own) **computadora**? ¿Es requisito (Is it required) en su universidad que los estudiantes tengan una? ¿Tiene Ud. una? ¿Cuánto tiempo hace que la compró?

2. ¿**Navega** Ud. **la Red** con frecuencia? ¿Para qué? ¿Cuáles son las páginas web que visita con más frecuencia?

3. ¿Usa Ud. el Internet para hacer las compras? ¿Qué productos compra Ud.? ¿**discos compactos?** ¿electrodomésticos? ¿ropa? ¿boletos de avión?

4. ¿Dónde vive Ud.? ¿En una **residencia** estudiantil? ¿en un **apartamento** o una **casa**?

5. ¿Vive Ud. en **el centro** de la ciudad, en **las afueras** o en **el campo**?

6. ¿Dónde vivían sus abuelos, de jóvenes?

7. En su opinión, ¿cuál fue la invención mas importante de los últimos cien años? ¿el carro? ¿el avión? ¿**el ordenador** o **la red?** ¿**el teléfono?** ¿otra?

8. ¿Qué impacto tiene esa invención en la calidad de la vida de nosotros hoy?

■ The words in **boldface** are included in the active vocabulary of this chapter. Have students discuss the words and use context to help them understand the meanings. Place the words they cannot guess in new sentences and contexts.

■ Introduce the concepts of *las afueras* and *el campo*. Model them in sentences about yourself or exchanges with students.

Note

The *Puntos de partida* Online Learning Center includes an interview with a person from Peru who answers questions about housing and possessions.

◀ Las terrazas de Machu Picchu, Perú

Resources

For Students

■ Workbook
■ Laboratory Manual and Laboratory Audio Program
■ Quia™ Workbook and Online Laboratory Manual
■ Video on CD
■ Interactive CD-ROM
■ *Puntos de partida* Online Learning Center (**www.mhhe.com/puntos7**)

For Instructors

■ *Instructor's Manual and Resource Kit*, "Chapter-by-Chapter" Supplementary Materials
■ Overhead Transparencies 79–83
■ Testing Program
■ Test Generator
■ Video Program
■ Audioscript
■ *Puntos de partida* Online Learning Center (**www.mhhe.com/puntos7**)

La calidad de la **vida**

CULTURA

- **Perspectivas culturales**

  Entrevista cultural: el Perú

  Entre amigos: Me tiras un correo, ¿eh?

  Conozca... el Perú

- **Nota cultural:** Los nombres de los pisos en un edificio

- **En los Estados Unidos y el Canadá:** Las computadoras y la comunidad hispana

- **Lectura:** Secretaria de bolsillo

- **Literatura del Perú:** Mario Vargas Llosa

VOCABULARIO

- Tengo... Necesito... Quiero...
- La vivienda

GRAMÁTICA

36 Tú (Informal) Commands

37 Present Subjunctive: An Introduction

38 Use of the Subjunctive: Influence

Entrevista cultural

Valdemar de Icasa ▶
Lima, Perú

Suggestions

- Expand item 4 of the annotation on p. 374 with the following questions.

  ¿Dónde vive la mayoría de los estudiantes de esta universidad, en residencias o en apartamentos y casas?

  ¿Es típico que vivan con sus familias mientras están en la universidad?

- Assign item 6 of the annotation on p. 374 as homework. Have students write a paragraph justifying their choice. In class, have students list their choices on the board and then discuss the different choices as a class.

- Have students list their ideas about Peru, including information on geography, politics, economy, music, and cuisine. When you finish the chapter return to the lists and ask students what ideas they would change and/or add.

☼ Heritage Speakers

Hay varios términos para referirse a *la Red*. Algunos hispanohablantes prefieren decir *la Red* o *la Red mundial*. También se dice *el Internet*, pero como *la Red* es femenina, también se oye decir *la Internet*. Pregúnteles a los hispanohablantes de la clase qué término prefieren usar.

MULTIMEDIA

- The multimedia materials that accompany this chapter are referenced in the Student and Instructor's Editions with icons to help you identify when and where to incorporate them.

- The IM/RK provides suggestions for using the multimedia materials in the classroom.

Tengo... Necesito... Quiero...

Notes

- See the model for vocabulary presentation and other material in the *Capítulo 12 Vocabulario: Preparación* "Chapter-by-Chapter Supplementary Materials," in the IM.
- This section expands students' vocabulary for describing personal possessions and introduces the topic of the working world. Students will learn more about the working world and talking about career choices and job interviews in *Capítulo 16*. In this chapter, the conceptual link between the two topics is working to earn money to buy the things we want or need. In addition, adults (vs. typically college-age students) should find the working-world vocabulary useful for self-expression.
- The word *vídeo* is used mainly in Spain. In Latin American, *video* is preferred.

Suggestions

- Model vocabulary in sentences about yourself and communicative exchanges with the students.
- Have students give sentences about the kinds of vehicles or the kinds of uses of vehicles they associate with the following circumstances or people.

  1. *una persona muy deportista*
  2. *un joven que vive en Miami*
  3. *una tarde de verano*
  4. *un hombre joven soltero que gana mucho dinero y vive en el sur de California*
  5. *unos adolescentes urbanos*

- Bring and/or have students bring mounted photos from magazines related to the chapter topic. Present as many items as possible. Periodically go back to a photo and ask questions such as.

  ¿Qué es esto, una grabadora o un contestador automático?

- Display images of *aparatos* around the room. Have students stand and identify objects, for example, *Mark, levántese y señale* (gesture) *la foto del televisor*.
- Point out additional terms related to the Internet.

  la autopista de la información (information superhighway)
  la telaraña mundial (World Wide Web)

Tengo... Necesito... Quiero...

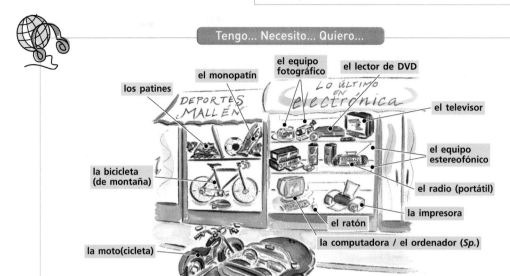

los patines
el monopatín
el equipo fotográfico
el lector de DVD
el televisor
el equipo estereofónico
la bicicleta (de montaña)
el radio (portátil)
la impresora
el ratón
la computadora / el ordenador (Sp.)
la moto(cicleta)
el carro / el coche (descapotable)

La electrónica

la cinta	tape
el contestador automático	answering machine
el correo electrónico	e-mail
el disco duro	hard drive
la grabadora	(tape) recorder/player
la Red	Net
navegar (gu) la Red	to surf the Net
el teléfono (celular)	(cellular) phone
la videocasetera	videocassette recorder/player (VCR)

Cognados

la cámara, la cámara de vídeo, el CD-ROM, el control remoto, el disco compacto (el CD), el disco de computadora, el DVD, el fax, la memoria, el módem, el *walkman*

Verbos útiles

cambiar (de canal, de cuarto, de ropa...)	to change (channels, rooms, clothing)
conseguir (i, i) (g)	to get, obtain
copiar / hacer (irreg.) copia	to copy
fallar	to "crash" (a computer)
funcionar	to work, function; to run (machines)
grabar	to record; to tape
guardar	to keep, to save (documents)
imprimir	to print
manejar	to drive; to operate (a machine)
obtener (irreg.)	to get, obtain
sacar (qu) fotos	to take photos

Para poder gastar...

el aumento	raise
el/la jefe/a	boss
el sueldo	salary

Capítulo 12: La calidad de la vida

National Standards: Communication

Have students work in groups of three to four to list what they consider to be the five most important machines or objects for the average student. Compare lists and create a master list on the board. Poll the class to see how many students have the items listed on the board. Have them discuss how these things affect their daily lives.

Resources: Transparency 79

MULTIMEDIA: Audio

Students can listen to and practice this chapter's vocabulary on the Online Learning Center (**www.mhhe.com/puntos7**) as well as on the Textbook Audio CD, part of the Laboratory Audio Program.

■ ■■ ■ Conversación

A. Ud. y los aparatos

Paso 1. ¿Qué se usa en estas situaciones?

1. para mandar copias de documentos no originales que deben llegar inmediatamente
2. para grabar un programa de televisión cuando no podemos verlo a la hora de su emisión
3. para cambiar el programa de la tele sin levantarse del sillón
4. para recibir llamadas telefónicas cuando no estamos en casa
5. para escuchar música mientras hacemos ejercicio

Paso 2. Con un compañero / una compañera, piense en cuatro situaciones similares a las del **Paso 1.** Uno/a de Uds. da la descripción y el otro / la otra identifica el aparato.

Paso 3. Para Ud., ¿son ciertas o falsas las siguientes oraciones?

1. Soy una persona que tiene habilidad mecánica. Es decir, entiendo cómo funcionan los aparatos.
2. Aprendí con facilidad a usar la computadora.
3. No me puedo imaginar la vida sin los aparatos electrónicos modernos.
4. Me interesa saber qué vehículo maneja una persona, porque el vehículo es una expresión de la personalidad.
5. Una vez me falló la computadora y perdí unos documentos y archivos (*files*) muy importantes.
6. Uso la videocasetera para ver películas, pero no sé grabar.
7. Me gusta navegar la red porque siempre encuentro lo que busco.

B. ¿Qué vehículos... ?

Paso 1. ¿Qué vehículo piensa Ud. que deben tener y usar las siguientes personas?

1. una persona joven no convencional y que vive en Sevilla, una ciudad grande en el sur de España
2. una persona joven que vive en Key West, una isla soleada e informal en el sur de Florida
3. una familia con tres hijos
4. un estudiante de una universidad de artes liberales que vive en el *campus*
5. unos chicos que viven en Venice Beach, California, y que pasan gran parte de su tiempo libre en la playa y en el *boardwalk*
6. un matrimonio jubilado (*retired*) que vive en Nueva Inglaterra

Paso 2. ¿Qué vehículo(s) tiene Ud.? ¿Es lo más apropiado para su vida? ¿Por qué? ¿Qué vehículo le gustaría tener?

Vocabulario: Preparación   Trescientos setenta y siete   ■ **377**

Heritage Speakers

Hay varios términos para referirse al *ordenador*. La palabra *ordenador* se usa en España. Hay hispanohablantes de Latinoamérica que usan *el computador* (masculino) y otros que prefieren *la computadora* (femenino). Anime a los hispanohablantes a indicar qué término prefieren.

■ Point out that *conseguir* (*consigo*) is conjugated like *seguir*. Explain that *el televisor* is the apparatus and that *la televisión* refers to the event or broadcasting of programs. Remind students that *la moto* and *la foto* are short for (and more commonly used than) *la motocicleta* and *la fotografía*.

■ Introduce computer-related vocabulary.

> *el buscador* (search engine)
> *el ciberespacio* (cyberspace)
> *cliquear / hacer clic / clicar* (to click on the mouse)
> *la contraseña* (password)
> *escanear* (to scan)
> *la memoria virtual* (virtual memory)
> *la página web* or *el sitio web* (web page).

■ Write the words *el buscapersonas* and *el localizador*. Tell students they mean the same thing and have them try to guess the meaning (beeper). Point out that in some areas of the U.S., Spanish speakers might call it *el bíper*.

■ Point out that *el trabajo* has several meanings: *work*; *job* (position); *schoolwork* (such as a written report or term paper). Explain that *el puesto* is another word for job or position. The word *sueldo* (salary), *soldado* (soldier), and *soldar* (to solder/weld) all come from the same Latinate word *solidus*, which means *to join* or *unite*. Ask students if they can explain how these words might be etymologically related.

♻ Reciclado
Review words students have already learned: *el coche = el carro, el tren, el autobús, el avión, el barco.*

Con. A: Preliminary Exercise

¿Qué aparatos asocia Ud. con los siguientes verbos?

1. *hablar*
2. *mirar*
3. *trabajar*
4. *viajar*
5. *escuchar*
6. *bailar*
7. *cantar*

Con. A: Suggestion

Paso 3. Have students interview each other and present their partner's profile and/or a comparison of their answers.

Con. B: Follow-Up

Have students work together to make a list of *ventajas* and *desventajas* of each type of vehicle presented in the text.

Vocabulario: Preparación   ■ **377**

Bright Idea

**Con. C:
Suggestion**

Students may ask for additional words, not provided in the *Vocabulario útil.*

la identificación de llamadas	caller ID
el desvío de llamadas	call forwarding
el bloqueo de llamadas	call block
el sistema de devolución automática de llamadas	call back

Con. C: Follow-Up

Have students share opinions as you tally answers on the board. As a whole class, try to explain why certain things are (or are not) a necessity, and why there are inconsistent answers for some items (if there are).

NOTA CULTURAL

Suggestions

- Emphasize the expression and meaning of *la planta baja.* Review the *Nota cultural* on floors, using familiar buildings as examples.
- Ask questions to check comprehension.

1. *¿En qué piso estamos? ¿Cuántos pisos tiene este edificio?*
2. *¿Qué hay en la planta baja de la biblioteca (librería / residencia estudiantil / el lugar donde se reúnen los estudiantes / ¿ ?)?*

C. ¿Necesidad o lujo (*luxury*)**?**

Paso 1. ¿Considera Ud. que las siguientes posesiones son un lujo o una necesidad de la vida moderna? Indique si Ud. tiene este aparato o vehículo.

MODELO: un televisor → Para mí, un televisor es una necesidad. Tengo uno. (No tengo uno ahora.)

1. un contestador automático
2. una videocasetera
3. el equipo estereofónico
4. una computadora
5. un coche
6. una bicicleta
7. un *walkman* (una grabadora)
8. un teléfono celular

Paso 2. Ahora dé tres cosas más que Ud. considera necesarias en la vida moderna.

Vocabulario útil

el aviso de llamada, la llamada en espera (call waiting)
la línea de teléfono
el televisor de pantalla (screen) **grande/plana** (flat)

Paso 3. Para terminar, entreviste a un compañero / una compañera para saber si está de acuerdo con Ud. y si tiene las mismas posesiones.

MODELO: el televisor → E1: ¿El televisor?
E2: Yo lo considero un lujo y por eso no tengo uno.

NOTA CULTURAL

Los nombres de los pisos de un edificio

En la mayoría de los dialectos del inglés, las frases *ground floor* y *first floor* tienen el mismo significado. En español, hay dos modos de expresar estos conceptos. Aunque ha habido[a] cambios al lenguaje debido a[b] la influencia norteamericana, **la planta baja** es el equivalente más común de *ground floor,* mientras que **el primer piso** se refiere al *second floor* de los anglohablantes.[c] También en español, **el segundo piso** se refiere al *third floor,* etcétera.

[a]ha... *there have been*   [b]debido... *due to*   [c]*English speakers*

▲ *El número de un edificio en México*

Refrán

«No es más rico el que más tiene sino el que menos necesita.»

Write the proverb on the board and have students give the meaning and related sayings in English. (*The greatest wealth is contentment with a little. He is richest that has fewest wants. He is rich that is satisfied.*)

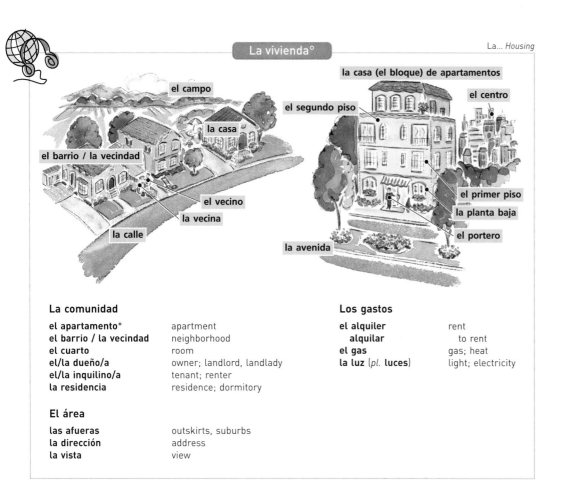

La vivienda° La... *Housing*

el campo
la casa
el barrio / la vecindad
el vecino
la vecina
la calle

la casa (el bloque) de apartamentos
el segundo piso
el centro
el primer piso
la planta baja
el portero
la avenida

La comunidad

el apartamento*	apartment
el barrio / la vecindad	neighborhood
el cuarto	room
el/la dueño/a	owner; landlord, landlady
el/la inquilino/a	tenant; renter
la residencia	residence; dormitory

El área

las afueras	outskirts, suburbs
la dirección	address
la vista	view

Los gastos

el alquiler	rent
alquilar	to rent
el gas	gas; heat
la luz (*pl.* **luces**)	light; electricity

■ ■ ■ Conversación

A. Definiciones. Dé las definiciones de las siguientes palabras.

> **MODELO:** la residencia →
> Es un lugar donde viven muchos estudiantes. Por lo general está situada en el *campus* universitario.

1.	el inquilino	6.	la dueña	11.	la avenida
2.	el centro	7.	la dirección	12.	el campo
3.	el alquiler	8.	las afueras	13.	la planta baja
4.	el portero	9.	el barrio	14.	la vista
5.	la vecina	10.	la casa	15.	la luz

> ### Frases útiles
>
> Es una persona que...
> Es un lugar donde...
> Es una cosa que...

***El apartamento** *is used throughout Latin America and the Caribbean.* **El departamento** *is used in Mexico, Peru, and other Latin American countries, but* **el piso** *is the word most commonly used in Spain.*

Vocabulario: Preparación Trescientos setenta y nueve ■ **379**

La vivienda

Suggestions

■ Offer the following optional vocabulary: *el ascensor* (elevator), *el piso* (floor of a building or floor that one sweeps) vs. *la planta*.

■ Read the following definitions and have students give the words defined.

1. *la persona que vive al lado*
2. *el número y la calle donde Ud. vive*
3. *la cantidad de dinero que Ud. paga cada mes para vivir en su apartamento*
4. *la parte principal de una ciudad, donde hay muchos edificios altos*
5. *el antónimo de* **centro**
6. *la persona que alquila un apartamento*

■ Take a poll of students to see how many live in a house, in an apartment, in the dorm, or in a fraternity or sorority house. Keep track of the findings on the board. Discuss the results and have students compare the advantages and disadvantages of living in the different places: *¿Cuáles son las ventajas/desventajas de vivir... ?*

■ Have students work in pairs to interview each other about where their girlfriend/boyfriend (husband / wife or best friend) lives.

1. *¿Dónde vive su pareja / su mejor amigo/a?*
2. *¿Qué gastos paga (gas, luz...)?*
3. *¿Tiene vista?*
4. *¿Hay portero? ¿Cómo es?*
5. *¿Tiene Ud. compañero/a? ¿Cómo es?*

After the interview, have some students report the information they learned to the class. Alternatively, students can write up the information in a brief paragraph.

Notes

■ Ordinal numbers are formally presented in *Capítulo 13*. You may need to help students with ordinals as they talk about where they live.

■ Point out that *suburbios* is a false cognate. It means "slums." *Afueras* is used to refer to suburbs.

Con. A: Variation

Play a Jeopardy game. Give or have students give a definition. The class (or teams) should respond with the corresponding question.

> *Es un lugar donde viven muchos estudiantes.* → *¿Qué es una residencia?*

> ### Resources: Transparencies 80, 81
>
> Transparency 81 offers practice and additional vocabulary.

Vocabulario: Preparación ■ **379**

Con. B: Follow-Up

Paso 1. Have students explain which ad appeals to them the most and why.

Con. B: Follow-Up

Paso 2. Have students tally their answers on the board, then have a class discussion about the similarities and differences.

B. A buscar vivienda

Paso 1. Lea los tres anuncios de viviendas en el Perú y conteste las siguientes preguntas.

1. ¿Qué tipo de vivienda se vende en cada anuncio? ¿Son para comprar o alquilar?
2. ¿Cuántos dormitorios tiene cada vivienda?
3. ¿Cree Ud. que estas viviendas son para familias con mucho o poco dinero?

CUZCO

Alquilo casa. Barrio residencial. Semi-amueblada[a] con teléfono. Informes Teléf. Cuzco: 084-226752. Lima: 774153 (horario 2 a 5 p.m.)

DEPARTAMENTOS MONTERRICO

Finos departamentos de 3 dormitorios, 3½ baños, sala de estar,[b] 1 ó 2 cocheras,[c] acabados de primera,[d] verlos todos los días en: Domingo de la Presa 165, espalda cuadra 12 Av. Primavera.

CHACARILLA DEL ESTANQUE

Departamentos exclusivos, diseño especial, 3 dormitorios, comedor de diario, área de servicio, totalmente equipados. Desde $41.500. Buenas facilidades.

Av. Buena Vista N° 230 (a 2 Cdras. de Velasco Aslete) Tels. 458107 – 357743

---

[a]*Partially furnished*   [b]*sala... living room; sitting room*   [c]*1 ó 2... one- or two-car garage*   [d]*acabados... first-class finishing details*

Paso 2. Entrevista. Con un compañero / una compañera, hable sobre el tipo de vivienda que prefieren.

1. Como estudiante universitario, ¿prefieres vivir en el *campus* o fuera del *campus*? ¿en una residencia o en una casa o apartamento de alquiler con otras personas?
2. ¿Prefieres vivir en la planta baja o en los pisos más altos?
3. Si alquilas tu vivienda, ¿prefieres que el alquiler incluya (*include*) todos los gastos o prefieres pagar la luz y el gas por separado?
4. Si pudieras (*If you could*) escoger, ¿qué te gustaría más, tener un apartamento pequeño en un barrio elegante del centro o una casa grande en las afueras?
5. ¿Qué tipo de vecinos te gusta tener?

Need more practice?

- Workbook and Laboratory Manual
- Interactive CD-ROM
- Online Learning Center (www.mhhe.com/puntos7)

MULTIMEDIA: Internet

Have students search the Internet for the online newspaper *Perú al día* for rental ads to print out and bring to class.

☀ **Heritage Speakers**

Pídales a sus estudiantes hispanohablantes que escriban un breve ensayo sobre su vivienda ideal.

GRAMÁTICA

¿Recuerda Ud.?

In **Gramática 20** you learned about **Ud.** and **Uds.** (formal) commands. Remember that object pronouns (direct, indirect, reflexive) must follow and be attached to affirmative commands; they must precede negative commands.

AFFIRMATIVE: Háblele Ud.   Duérmase.   Dígaselo Ud.

NEGATIVE: No le hable Ud.   No se duerma.   No se lo diga Ud.

¿Cómo se dice en español?

1. Bring me the book. (**Uds.**)
2. Don't give it to her. (**Uds.**)
3. Sit here, please. (**Ud.**)
4. Don't sit in that chair! (**Ud.**)
5. Tell them the truth. (**Uds.**)
6. Tell it to them now! (**Uds.**)
7. Never tell it to her. (**Uds.**)
8. Take care of yourself. (**Ud.**)
9. Lead a healthy life. (**Ud.**)
10. Listen to me. (**Ud.**)

[handwritten annotations:] Tráiganmelo   7. Díganselo
No dánselo.   8. Cuídase. p. 207
Siéntese   208
No se siente. 9.   209
Díganselo.   10. Escúchame
Díganselo

36 Influencing Others • *Tú* (Informal) Commands

¡Marta, tu cuarto es un desastre!

El padre de Marta está enojado.

«¡Marta, qué desordenado está tu cuarto! Por favor, *arréglalo* antes de jugar con tus amigos. *Guarda* la ropa limpia en tu armario, *pon* la ropa sucia en el cesto, *haz* la cama, *recoge* los libros del piso y *ordénalos* en los estantes… Y no *dejes* los zapatos por todas partes… ¡Es muy peligroso!»

¿Quién diría (*would say*) lo siguiente, Marta o Manolo, su padre?

1. No te enojes… Ya voy a arreglarlo todo.
2. Hazlo inmediatamente… ¡antes de salir a jugar!
3. Dime, ¿por qué tengo que hacerlo ahora mismo?
4. La próxima vez, ¡no dejes tu cuarto en tales condiciones!

Marta, your room is a disaster! *Marta's father is angry. "Marta, what a messy room you have! Please straighten it up before you go out to play with your friends. Put your clean clothes away in the closet, put your dirty clothes in the hamper, make your bed, pick your books up off the floor and arrange them on the shelves . . . And don't leave your shoes lying around everywhere . . . It's very dangerous!"*

Gramática   Trescientos ochenta y uno ■ 381

Refrán

«No vendas la piel del oso antes de haberlo muerto.»
(*Don't count your chickens before they've hatched.*)

Note the dialectal use of *muerto* in this saying. In some countries, *muerto* is used synonymously with *matado*. For example: *Dos personas fueron muertas por los terroristas.*

Gramática 36

¿Recuerda Ud.?: Extension

11. Wake up earlier. (*Ud.*)
12. Get dressed quickly. (*Uds.*)
13. Enjoy yourself with your friends. (*Ud.*)
14. Don't give it to them now. (*Uds.*)

Tú (Informal) Commands

Note

If you have been using *tú* commands all along, start by having students list the ones they know.

Suggestions

■ Have students give the infinitive form of each command in the *minidiálogo*.

■ Have students who heard each phrase as a teenager explain why their mother (or father) said that. *¿Te dijo tu madre eso una sola vez o te lo decía con frecuencia? ¿Por qué?*

■ Use as continuing practice of preterite vs. imperfect.

■ Have students write a paragraph about what they have in their rooms or homes, what they need, and what they would like to have some day. Then have students work in groups to read and compare their items.

Resources: Transparency 82

Transparency 82 provides examples of *tú* commands.

Negative *tú* Commands

Suggestions

- Point out to students that they already know all of the forms involved in this tense, and that the position of the object pronouns is identical to the pronoun position used in formal (*Ud.* and *Uds.*) commands.
- You may wish to treat the material in this section for passive recognition only. Have students learn only high-frequency irregular *tú* commands.
- Explain to students that the command system in Spanish (although easy to understand when someone gives you a command) is difficult to master in speaking. They should not be discouraged if using the system correctly does not come easily.

Preliminary Exercise

Have students respond to statements with negative commands. Write the following example on the board, then give them additional statements.

> *No quiero cantarlo. → Pues, no lo cantes.*
> *No quiero comprarlo / mirarlo / leerlo / beberlo / escribirlo / decidirlo.*

Affirmative *tú* Commands

Suggestion

Remind students of the impoliteness implied in any command, particularly with *tú*. Even with friends, they should use questions instead of commands.

> *¿Me pasas la sal, por favor?*
> *¿Me prestas tu suéter?*
> *¿Me cierras la puerta?*

Then, have students give affirmative commands to a friend who says he/she should do the following things. Write the following example on the board, then give the additional statements.

> *Debo hacer la cama. → Haz la cama. (Hazla.)*
> *Debo... decir la verdad*
> *hacer más tacos*
> *ir a la biblioteca*
> *poner los libros en la mesa*
> *salir ahora*
> *tener más paciencia*
> *venir a clase todos los días*
> *ser buen(a) estudiante.*

Note

Sé from *ser* can also be mistaken for *sé* (first person singular of the present indicative), of the verb *saber.* Context will clarify the meaning.

 Informal commands (**los mandatos informales**) are used with persons whom you would address as **tú.**

Past ------------------	PRESENT ------------------	Future
preterite	present indicative	
imperfect	present progressive	
	formal commands	
	informal commands	

Negative *tú* Commands

-*ar* verbs		-*er/-ir* verbs	
No hables.	Don't speak.	**No comas.**	Don't eat.
No cantes.	Don't sing.	**No escribas.**	Don't write.
No juegues.	Don't play.	**No pidas.**	Don't order.

A. Like **Ud.** commands (**Gramática 20**), the negative **tú** commands are expressed using the "opposite vowel": **no hable Ud., no hables (tú).** The pronoun **tú** is used only for emphasis.

> No cantes **tú** tan fuerte.
> *Don't **you** sing so loudly.*

B. As with negative **Ud.** commands, object pronouns—direct, indirect, and reflexive— precede negative **tú** commands.

> **No lo** mires.
> *Don't look at him.*
>
> **No les** escribas.
> *Don't write to them.*
>
> **No te** levantes.
> *Don't get up.*

Affirmative *tú* Commands

-*ar* verbs		-*er/-ir* verbs	
Habla.	*Speak.*	**Come.**	*Eat.*
Canta.	*Sing.*	**Escribe.**	*Write.*
Juega.	*Play.*	**Pide.**	*Order.*

A. Unlike the other command forms you have learned, most affirmative **tú** commands have the same form as the third person singular of the present indicative.* Some verbs have irregular affirmative **tú** command forms.

decir:	di	salir:	sal
hacer:	haz	ser:	sé
ir:	ve	tener:	ten
poner:	pon	venir:	ven

*As you know, there are two different moods in Spanish: the indicative mood (the one you have been using, which is used to state facts and ask questions) and the subjunctive mood (which is used to express more subjective actions or states). Beginning with **Gramática 37**, you will learn more about the subjunctive mood.

National Standards: Communication

In many Hispanic countries it is not uncommon to see the infinitive used for impersonal commands.

> *No pisar el césped.*
> *No fumar.*
> *Guardar silencio.*

Many of these forms appear on signs in public places.

Spelling Hint: One-syllable words, like the affirmative **tú** commands of some verbs (**decir, ir, tener,...**) do not need an accent mark: **di, ve, ten,...** Exceptions to this rule are those forms that could be mistaken for other words, like the command of **ser** (**sé**), which could be mistaken for the pronoun **se.**

Sé puntual pero **ten** cuidado.
Be there on time, but be careful.

 The affirmative **tú** commands for **ir** and **ver** are identical: **ve.** Context will clarify meaning.

¡**Ve** esa película!
See that movie!

Ve a casa ahora mismo.
Go home right now.

B. As with affirmative **Ud.** commands, object and reflexive pronouns follow affirmative **tú** commands and are attached to them. Accent marks are necessary except when a single pronoun is added to a one-syllable command.

Dile la verdad.
Tell him the truth.

Léela, por favor.
Read it, please.

Póntelos.
Put them on.

AUTOPRUEBA

Choose the correct command form for each sentence.

1. _____ me qué quieres.
2. No _____ al parque sola.
3. No le _____ nada de la fiesta.
4. _____ te un abrigo.
5. _____ a la tienda.
6. No _____ eso en mi cama.

a. di
b. digas
c. pon
d. pongas
e. vayas
f. ve

Answers: 1. a 2. e 3. b 4. c 5. f 6. d

NOTA COMUNICATIVA

Suggestions

- Remind students that *vosotros/as* is primarily used in Spain.
- Model and practice the *vosotros/as* commands for the students, especially if you are a Spaniard, if you use *vosotros/as* forms, and/or if your students are likely to study in Spain.

NOTA COMUNICATIVA

Vosotros Commands

In **Capítulo 1,** you learned about the pronoun **vosotros/vosotras** that is used in Spain as the plural of **tú.** Here is information about forming **vosotros** commands, for recognition only.

- Affirmative **vosotros** commands are formed by substituting **-d** for the final **-r** of the infinitive. There are no irregular affirmative **vosotros** commands.

  hablar → hablad
  comer → comed
  escribir → escribid

- Negative **vosotros** commands are expressed with the present subjunctive. (You will learn more about the present subjunctive in the next and subsequent grammar sections.)

  no habléis
  no comáis
  no escribáis

- Placement of object pronouns is the same as for all other command forms.

  Decídmelo.
  No me lo digáis.

Gramática

 Heritage Speakers

Pregúnteles a los hispanohablantes de la clase si saben usar o si usan las formas de *vosotros/as*. También es posible que haya hispanohablantes en su clase que usen el *voseo*, que se oye en Colombia, el Ecuador, Costa Rica, la Argentina y el Uruguay. Revise con la clase los mandatos con *vos:*

Hablá vos.   *No hablés vos.*
Acostate vos.   *No te acostés vos.*

Prác. A: Preliminary Exercises

■ Have students make the following commands or questions more polite.

1. To the teacher: *Repita.*
2. To a classmate: *Repite lo que dijo la profesora.*
3. To a housemate: *Lava los platos. / Compra leche de camino a casa.*
4. To a middle-aged woman in the street: *¿Dónde está la parada (stop) del autobús?*
5. To a young man in the street: *¿Qué hora es?*

■ Have students work in groups to get advice from each other, for example, what kind of computer to buy, which kind of exercise to do to lose weight, where to study, what movie to see, and so on. Students should try to use as many commands as possible.

Prác. A: Suggestion

Have students search the Internet for five extra *refranes* to share with the class.

■ ■ ■ Práctica

A. ¡Anticipemos! Recuerdos de la niñez

Paso 1. Indique los mandatos afirmativos que Ud. oía con frecuencia cuando era niño/a. Después de leerlos todos, indique los dos que oía más. ¿Hay entre estos algún mandato que Ud. no oyó nunca?

1. _____ Limpia tu cuarto.
2. _____ Cómete el desayuno.
3. _____ Haz la tarea.
4. _____ Cierra la puerta.
5. _____ Bébete la leche.
6. _____ Lávate las manos.
7. _____ Dime la verdad.
8. _____ Quítate el *walkman*.
9. _____ Guarda tu bicicleta en el garaje.

 Note in **Práctica A** the use of the reflexive pronoun with the verbs **comer** and **beber**. This use of the reflexive means *to eat up* and *to drink up*, respectively.

Cómete las zanahorias.
Eat up your carrots.

No **te bebas** la leche tan rápido.
Don't drink up your milk so fast.

Paso 2. Ahora indique los mandatos negativos que escuchaba con frecuencia. Debe indicar también los dos que oía más. ¿Hay alguno que no oyó nunca?

1. _____ No cruces la calle solo/a.
2. _____ No juegues con cerillas (*matches*).
3. _____ No comas dulces antes de cenar.
4. _____ No me digas mentiras (*lies*).
5. _____ No les des tanta comida a los peces.
6. _____ No hables con personas desconocidas.
7. _____ No dejes el monopatín en el jardín.
8. _____ No cambies los canales tanto.
9. _____ No digas tonterías (*silly things*).

EN LOS ESTADOS UNIDOS Y EL CANADÁ

Las computadoras y la comunidad hispana

Según un estudio demográfico del año 2000, alrededor del 37 por ciento de las familias hispanas de Los Ángeles, Nueva York, Miami, Chicago y Houston (las cinco ciudades de los Estados Unidos con mayor población hispana) posee[a] una **computadora personal.** Se calcula que hay computadoras en más de un millón y medio de **hogares**[b] hispanos en los Estados Unidos.

El **acceso** de los hispanos a las computadoras y al Internet es un factor importante para su desarrollo[c] personal. Las computadoras y el Internet son herramientas[d]

▲ *En Chicago, Illinois*

necesarias para **la educación, el trabajo, la comunicación** y sobre todo para **la información.** Casi todos los periódicos principales de los países hispanos se publican ahora en el Internet. A través de[e] las publicaciones ciberespaciales, los hispanos pueden **informarse.** Leen sus noticias en español y, es más,[f] pueden leer las noticias de su país o ciudad natal. También pueden participar en comunicaciones con **la comunidad hispana** del Internet.

[a]*owns* [b]*homes* [c]*development* [d]*tools* [e]*A... Through* [f]*es... furthermore*

EN LOS ESTADOS UNIDOS Y EL CANADÁ

Suggestions

■ Point out that *el computador* is used in some parts of Latin America; *el ordenador* is used in Spain.
■ The article mentioned in this box comes from the newspaper *La opinión.* Have students find the *La opinión* website and read the main page (*la portada*) for the day.

■ Have students discuss the importance of owning personal computers.

> *¿Por qué es importante que las familias tengan una computadora personal?*
> *¿Cómo contribuye una computadora al desarrollo personal?*

B. Julita, la mal educada

Paso 1. Los Sres. Villarreal no están contentos con el comportamiento de su hija Julita. Continúe los comentarios de ellos con mandatos informales lógicos según cada situación. Siga los modelos.

MODELOS: *Hablaste* demasiado ayer. → No *hables* tanto hoy, por favor.
Dejaste tu ropa en el suelo anoche. → No la *dejes* allí hoy, por favor.

1. También *dejaste* tus libros en el suelo (*floor*).
2. ¿Por qué *regresaste* tarde a casa hoy después de las clases?
3. ¿Por qué *vas* al parque todas las tardes?
4. No es bueno que *mires* la televisión constantemente. ¿Y por qué quieres *ver* todos esos programas de detectives?
5. ¿Por qué le *dices* mentiras a tu papá?
6. Siempre *te olvidas* de sacar la basura, que es la única tarea que tienes que hacer.
7. Ay, hija, no te comprendemos. ¡*Eres* tan insolente!

Paso 2. La pobre Julita también escucha muchos mandatos de su maestra en clase. Invente Ud. esos mandatos según las indicaciones.

1. llegar / a / escuela / puntualmente
2. quitarse / abrigo / y / sentarse
3. sacar / libro de matemáticas / y / abrirlo / en / página diez
4. leer / nuevo / palabras / y / aprenderlas / para mañana
5. venir / aquí / a / hablar conmigo / sobre / este / composición

Need more practice?

- Workbook and Laboratory Manual
- Interactive CD-ROM
- Online Learning Center (www.mhhe.com/puntos7)

■■■ Conversación

A. Situaciones. ¿Qué consejos les daría (*would you give*) a las siguientes personas si fueran (*they were*) sus amigos? Déles a todos consejos en forma de mandatos informales.

1. A Celia le encanta ir al cine, especialmente los viernes por la noche. Pero a su novio no le gusta salir mucho los viernes. Él siempre está muy cansado después de una larga semana de trabajo. Celia, en cambio (*on the other hand*), tiene mucha energía.
2. Nati tiene 19 años. El próximo año quiere vivir en un apartamento con cuatro amigos. Para ella es una situación ideal: un apartamento económico en un barrio estudiantil y unos buenos amigos (dos de ellos son hombres). Pero los padres de Nati son muy tradicionales y no les va a gustar la situación.
3. Su abuelo va a comprarse su primera computadora y necesita su opinión y experiencia. Tiene muchas preguntas, desde qué tipo debe comprar hasta cómo usarla eficientemente. Él quiere una computadora para conectarse con unos amigos jubilados (*retired*) que ahora viven en otro estado, para navegar la red y para realizar el sueño de su vida: escribir la historia de la llegada de sus padres a este país.
4. Mariana es una *yuppi*. Gana (*She makes*) muchísimo dinero pero trabaja demasiado. Nunca tiene tiempo para nada. Duerme poco y bebe muchísimo café para seguir despierta (*awake*). No come bien y jamás hace ejercicio. Acaba de comprarse un teléfono celular para poder trabajar mientras maneja a la oficina.

- Have students give commands that Julita would like to give to others.
- Ask students: *¿Qué mandatos oye Ud. con frecuencia? ¿Qué mandatos da Ud. con frecuencia y a quién se los da?*

Bright Idea

Con. A: Preliminary Exercise

Have students indicate if they should use the formal or informal commands with the following people.

1. *su hermano/a*
2. *su profesor(a)*
3. *su médico/a*
4. *su jefe/a*
5. *su mejor amigo/a*
6. *un compañero / una compañera de clase*

Con. A: Variation

Have students write a letter to a columnist for a popular magazine for their age group. Have them present serious or complex problems in their letters. Have students complete the letters as homework, then have them read their letters to the class so that others can offer advice using *tú* commands.

Bright Idea

Con. A: Follow-Up

Consejos a una amiga. Roberta quiere mantenerse en buena salud. Conteste sus preguntas usando los mandatos informales.

1. *¿Debo comer papas fritas tres veces a la semana?*
2. *¿Debo hacer ejercicio todos los días?*
3. *¿Debo fumar más?*
4. *¿Debo tomar más vino?*
5. *¿Debo pedir dos postres en los restaurantes?*
6. *¿Debo acostarme temprano por la noche?*

- Have students complete this activity in groups of three, then discuss the results with the class.
- Have students write down, in infinitive form, five activities that can be performed in class, for example, *Apagar las luces.* Then have the class select five people (or have five students volunteer) to carry out the commands. The other students form commands based on the phrases they have written and give them to one of the selected students or volunteers, who, in turn, tries to do what he/she is told.

Con. B: Variation

Have students make up informal commands for the following situations.

1. *para cuando sale para una entrevista para un trabajo*
2. *para cuando conoce a los padres de un nuevo amigo / una nueva amiga*
3. *para cuando su amigo/a quiere comprar un nuevo estéreo*
4. *para un(a) estudiante de primer año (freshman) en esta universidad.*

Gramática 37

Present Subjunctive: An Introduction

Suggestion
Have students pick out subjunctive and subjunctive cues in the *minidiálogo*. Ask them what the cues have in common (asking someone to do something).

Follow-Up
After reviewing the *minidiálogo*, ask students:

En el diálogo, ¿quién quiere comprar una computadora?
¿Quién sabe mucho de computadoras?
¿Quién le da consejos a quién?
¿Sugiere Gustavo que José Miguel compre una computadora inmediatamente?

Note
The subjunctive is a difficult concept for native speakers of English, and most will need years of practice and immersion to master it. Aim at conceptual awareness and partial control at the elementary level. Partial control means that students are aware of the existence of the subjunctive and know the rules of use and the forms, but that, in general, they only produce it in well-guided contexts.

B. Entre compañeros de casa. En su opinión, ¿cuáles son los cinco mandatos que se oyen con más frecuencia en su casa (apartamento, residencia)? Piense no sólo en los mandatos que Ud. escucha sino (*but*) también en los que Ud. les da a los demás (*others*).

Frases útiles		
apagar (gu) la computadora	no ser (*irreg.*)...	prestarme dinero
contestar el teléfono	así, bobo/a (dumb), impaciente,	poner (*irreg.*) la tele
lavar los platos	impulsivo/a, loco/a, pesado/a,	sacar (qu) la basura
no hacer (*irreg.*) ruido	precipitado/a (hasty)	¿ ?

37 Expressing Subjective Actions or States • Present Subjunctive: An Introduction

Una decisión importante

José Miguel habla con Gustavo sobre la computadora que quiere comprar.

JOSÉ MIGUEL: Quiero comprar una computadora, pero no sé cuál. *No creo que sea* una decisión fácil de tomar.

GUSTAVO: Pues, yo sé bastante de computadoras. Te puedo hacer algunas recomendaciones.

JOSÉ MIGUEL: Bueno, te escucho.

GUSTAVO: Primero, *es buena idea que sepas* para qué quieres una computadora. ¿Quieres navegar por el *Internet*? Entonces, *te sugiero que busques* una computadora con módem y con memoria suficiente para hacerlo. Luego, *quiero que hables* con otras personas que ya manejan computadoras. Y por último, *te aconsejo que vayas* a varias tiendas para comparar precios.

JOSÉ MIGUEL: Bueno, *me alegro de que sepas* tanto de computadoras. ¡Ahora *quiero que vayas* conmigo a las tiendas!

Comprensión: ¿Cierto, falso o no lo dice?

1. José Miguel quiere que Gustavo le compre una computadora.
2. Gustavo le recomienda a José Miguel que aprenda algo sobre computadoras antes de comprarse una.
3. Gustavo no cree que José Miguel tenga suficiente dinero.
4. José Miguel se alegra de que Gustavo esté tan informado sobre computadoras.

An important decision   *José Miguel talks with Gustavo about the computer he wants to buy. JOSÉ MIGUEL: I want to buy a computer, but I don't know which one. I don't think it's an easy decision to make. GUSTAVO: Well, I know quite a bit about computers. I can give you some recommendations. JOSÉ MIGUEL: OK, I'm listening. GUSTAVO: First, it's a good idea for you to know what you want a computer for. Do you want to get on the Internet? Then I suggest that you look for a computer with a modem and enough memory to do it. Then I want you to talk with other people who already work with computers. And finally, I suggest you go to various stores to compare prices. JOSÉ MIGUEL: Well, I'm glad you know so much about computers. Now I want you to go to the stores with me!*

Capítulo 12: La calidad de la vida

 Heritage Speakers

Invite a dos estudiantes hispanohablantes a dramatizar el minidiálogo para la clase.

Past ------------------- **PRESENT**----------------- Future	
preterite imperfect	present indicative present progressive formal commands informal commands present subjunctive

Present Subjunctive: An Introduction

A. Except for command forms, all the verb forms you have learned so far in *Puntos de partida* are part of the *indicative mood* (**el modo indicativo**). In both English and Spanish, the indicative is used to state facts and to ask questions; it objectively expresses actions or states of being that are considered true by the speaker.

INDICATIVE:

¿Vienes a la fiesta?
Are you coming to the party?

Prefiero llegar temprano a casa.
I prefer getting home early.

B. Both English and Spanish have another verb system called the *subjunctive mood* (**el modo subjuntivo**). The subjunctive is used to express more subjective or conceptualized actions or states. These include things that the speaker wants to happen or wants others to do, events to which the speaker reacts emotionally, things that are as yet unknown, and so on.

SUBJUNCTIVE:

Espero que **vengas** a la fiesta.
I hope (that) you are coming to the party.

Prefiero que **llegues** temprano a casa.
I prefer that you be home early.

C. Sentences in English and Spanish may be simple or complex. A simple sentence is one that contains a single verb.

Complex sentences are comprised of two or more *clauses* (**las cláusulas**), each containing a conjugated verb. There are two types of clauses: main (independent) clause and subordinate (dependent) clause. *Independent clauses* (**las cláusulas principales**) contain a complete thought and can stand alone. *Dependent clauses* (**las cláusulas subordinadas**) contain an incomplete thought and cannot stand alone. Dependent clauses require an independent clause to form a complete sentence.

When the subjects of the clauses in a complex sentence are different, the subjunctive is often used in the subordinate clause in Spanish. Note that subordinate clauses are linked by the conjunction **que,** which is never optional (as it is in English).

SIMPLE SENTENCE:

Vienes a la fiesta.   Alicia está en casa.
You are coming to the party.   *Alicia is at home.*

COMPLEX SENTENCE:

INDICATIVE		
MAIN CLAUSE		SUBORDINATE CLAUSE
Ella sabe *She knows*	**que** *(that)*	vienes a la fiesta. *you are coming to the party.*
Miguel piensa *Miguel thinks*	**que** *(that)*	Alicia está en casa. *Alicia is at home.*

SUBJUNCTIVE		
MAIN CLAUSE		SUBORDINATE CLAUSE
Quiere *She wants*	**que** *(for)*	**vengas** a la fiesta. *you to come to the party.*

Present Subjunctive: An Introduction

Emphasis A: Note
Students were introduced to the subjunctive for passive recognition in *Capítulo 6*, along with formal commands.

Emphasis B: Suggestions
- Point out that the subjunctive also exists in English.
  God bless you.
  I suggest you be there at one.
  If I were a rich man, . . .
- Point out that in English, the conjunction *that* is often optional, but *que* is required in Spanish.

Emphasis C: Suggestions
- Emphasize the syntactic requirements for the subjunctive.
  1. two clauses
  2. a different subject in each clause
- Provide a diagram to illustrate the sentence structure that points out the different subjects and their corresponding verbs in the indicative and subjunctive.

☼ **Heritage Speakers**

Pregúnteles a los estudiantes si su familia usa normalmente la expresión «Que Dios te (lo/la) bendiga». Es una despedida común de los adultos a los jóvenes en Puerto Rico.

Forms of the Present Subjunctive

Suggestions

- Emphasize the relationship of the *Ud.* commands to the subjunctive.
- Emphasize that the personal endings in this tense of the subjunctive mood are the same as those of the present indicative (-s, -mos, and so on).
- Using brief sentences, present the subjunctive forms of *trabajar*. Write the forms on the board as they are produced.

  > *Yo quiero que Uds. trabajen mucho.*
  > *¿Quieren Uds. que yo trabaje mucho?*
  > *¿Quiero que John trabaje mucho?*, and so on.

  Present additional sentences with *beber* and *recibir.*
- Provide some common expressions with the subjunctive.

  > *Que te vaya bien.*
  > *Que Dios te bendiga.*

Emphasis A: Note

Emphasize the forms of the subjunctive only for student production, but use full syntax in your input.

Emphasis B: Suggestion

Briefly present the verbs with spelling changes, pointing out that the spelling changes occur in all persons of the subjunctive.

(continued)

Duda	que	**vengas** a la fiesta.
She doubts	*(that)*	*you are coming to the party.*
Miguel espera	que	Alicia **esté** en casa.
Miguel hopes	*(that)*	*Alicia is at home.*

Quiero ir a la fiesta.
I want to go to the party.

When there is no change of subject in the sentence, the infinitive follows the conjugated verb and no conjunction is necessary. In these sentences, the infinitive functions as a direct object of the conjugated verb.

D. Three of the most common uses of the subjunctive are to express influence, emotion, and doubt or denial. These are signaled in the previous examples by the verb forms **quiere**, **espera**, and **duda**.

Forms of the Present Subjunctive

Many Spanish command forms that you have already learned are part of the subjunctive. The **Ud./Uds.** command forms are shaded in the following box. What you have learned about forming these commands will help you learn the forms of the present subjunctive.

	hablar	**comer**	**escribir**	**volver**	**decir**
Singular	hable	coma	escriba	vuelva	diga
	hables	comas	escribas	vuelvas	digas
	hable	coma	escriba	vuelva	diga
Plural	hablemos	comamos	escribamos	volvamos	digamos
	habléis	comáis	escribáis	volváis	digáis
	hablen	coman	escriban	vuelvan	digan

A. The personal endings of the present subjunctive are added to the first person singular of the present indicative minus its **-o** ending. **-Ar** verbs add endings with **-e**, and **-er/-ir** verbs add endings with **-a**.

-ar → -e
-er/-ir → -a

present indicative **yo** stem = present subjunctive stem

B. -Car, -gar, and -zar verbs have a spelling change in all persons of the present subjunctive to preserve the -c-, -g-, and -z- sounds.

-car: c → qu
-gar: g → gu
-zar: z → c

buscar		pagar		empezar	
busque	busquemos	pague	paguemos	empiece	empecemos
busques	busquéis	pagues	paguéis	empieces	empeceis
busque	busquen	pague	paguen	empiece	empiecen

C. Verbs with irregular **yo** forms show the irregularity in all persons of the present subjunctive.

conocer:	**cono**zca,...	salir:	**sal**ga,...
decir:	**di**ga,...	tener:	**ten**ga,...
hacer:	**ha**ga,...	traer:	**trai**ga,...
oír:	**oi**ga,...	venir:	**ven**ga,...
poner:	**pon**ga,...	ver:	**ve**a,...

D. A few verbs have irregular present subjunctive forms.

dar:	**dé, des, dé, demos, deis, den**
estar:	**esté,...**
haber (hay):	**haya**
ir:	**vaya,...**
saber:	**sepa,...**
ser:	**sea,...**

E. -Ar and -er stem-changing verbs follow the stem-changing pattern of the present indicative.

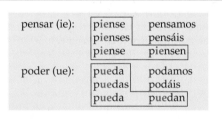

pensar (ie):

piense	pensamos
pienses	pensáis
piense	piensen

poder (ue):

pueda	podamos
puedas	podáis
pueda	puedan

F. -Ir stem-changing verbs show a stem change in the four forms that have a change in the present indicative. In addition, however, they show a second stem change in the **nosotros** and **vosotros** forms, similar to the present progressive tense.

-ir stem-changing verbs (**nosotros, vosotros**): o → u, e → i

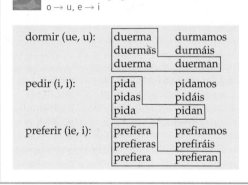

dormir (ue, u):

duerma	durmamos
duermas	durmáis
duerma	duerman

pedir (i, i):

pida	pidamos
pidas	pidáis
pida	pidan

preferir (ie, i):

prefiera	prefiramos
prefieras	prefiráis
prefiera	prefieran

Emphasis C: Suggestion
Briefly model the subjunctive forms of irregular verbs in communicative exchanges with students, asking one or two questions using each verb. Continue to use only *Quiero que...* as the semantic cue or introduce *Ojalá que.*

Emphasis D: Suggestion
Point out that the subjunctive of *hay* is *haya* and that, like *hay* and *había*, it is impersonal and does not change to the plural form before a plural noun.

Ojalá que haya muchas personas en la fiesta.

Emphasis E: Suggestion
Introduce the subjunctive forms of stem-changing verbs. Emphasize the second stem change and its connection to the preterite forms.

☼ Heritage Speakers

En el español estándar, la forma aceptada del presente del subjuntivo del verbo *haber* es *haya*. Sin embargo, algunos hispanohablantes dicen *haiga* en vez de *haya*. Este fenómeno es del habla cotidiana. No es una forma aceptada para el uso formal.

Prác. A: Preliminary Exercises

■ Read each verb form and have students tell whether it is in the present indicative or present subjunctive.

-ar: baile   hablemos
cena   miramos
lleguemos   buscan
pago   te olvides
recuerde

-er/-ir: aprende   recibo
aprenda   beban
lea   digo
leemos   pongamos
escribamos   traigan
coma   sabe
asisten   sepan

■ Use the following chain drill to practice the subjunctive forms:

Dé oraciones nuevas según las indicaciones.

1. *En clase: El profesor no quiere que Uds. fumen. (yo, nosotros, tú, los estudiantes, Lupe, vosotros)*
2. *En casa, el día antes de la fiesta, es necesario que alguien llame a nuestros amigos. (comprar los refrescos, buscar los discos compactos, invitar a María, traer la comida)*

Prác. A: Note

This activity calls for passive recognition of subjunctive forms and structures.

Prác. B: Variation

Change the context to *los estudiantes de la clase de español.* Have students make all other necessary changes, keeping the main clause verbs.

AUTOPRUEBA

Complete each verb form with the correct letters to form the subjunctive.

1. conocer: cono____amos
2. decir: di____an
3. sacar: sa____es
4. entregar: entre____en
5. conseguir: consi____an
6. morir: m____ramos

Answers: 1. conozcamos 2. digan 3. saques 4. entreguen 5. consigan 6. muramos

■■■ Práctica

A. ¡Anticipemos! La vida tecnológica. Indique si está de acuerdo o no con las siguientes oraciones.

1. En la vida actual es absolutamente necesario tener una computadora.
2. Yo quiero comprarme una computadora nueva, pero no creo que pueda comprármela inmediatamente.
3. Hoy día (*These days*) es posible comprar una buena computadora portátil por $1.000.
4. Es horrible que la tecnología cambie tan rápidamente; nadie puede aprender a este ritmo.
5. Prefiero que la gente no dependa tanto de la tecnología.
6. Es ridículo que tantas personas usen un teléfono celular.
7. Dudo que el precio de las llamadas de los teléfonos celulares baje más en los próximos dos años.
8. Espero que mi compañero/a de casa (esposo/a, hijo/a) cambie el mensaje del contestador automático.

B. Su trabajo actual. Use frases de la lista a la derecha para completar las oraciones de modo (*in such a way*) que se refieran a su situación laboral actual. (Siempre hay más de una respuesta posible.) Si Ud. no trabaja ahora, no importa. ¡Invéntese una respuesta!

1. El jefe quiere que ____.
2. También espera que ____.
3. Y duda que ____.
4. Prohíbe (*He forbids*) que ____.
5. En el trabajo, es importante que ____.
6. Yo espero que ____.
7. No quiero que ____.
8. Es difícil que ____.

a. a veces trabajemos los fines de semana
b. todos lleguemos a tiempo
c. hablemos por teléfono con los amigos
d. me den un aumento de sueldo
e. nos paguen más a todos
f. no usemos el *fax* para asuntos (*matters*) personales
g. me den un trabajo de tiempo completo algún día
h. no perdamos mucho tiempo charlando (*chatting*) con los demás (*others*)
i. fumemos en la oficina
j. tengamos muchas fechas límites
k. me den otro proyecto (*project*)
l. ¿ ?

Need more practice?

■ Workbook and Laboratory Manual
■ Interactive CD-ROM
■ Online Learning Center (www.mhhe.com/puntos7)

National Standards: Connections

Latin America is one of the fastest areas of growth for the Internet. The number of servers or "host computers" as of 2004 exceeds 50,000. Brazil has one of the most highly developed computer systems in the world with satellite access from the Amazon. Web surfers can access major newspapers, such as *El Espectador* and *El Tiempo* from Bogota, Colombia, as well as other reputable periodicals from other Latin American nations. For example, those who are interested in learning about Peru can do so through the Web, accessing documents in English, Spanish, and even in Quechua.

■ ■ ■ Conversación

A. ¿Puede Ud. substituir en la ausencia de su profesor(a)? Demuéstrele a su profesor(a) que Ud. lo/la conoce bien, formando oraciones como las que dice él/ella en clase. (Sólo tiene que cambiar el infinitivo.)

| Quiero que
Espero que
Prohíbo que
Dudo que
Es necesario que
Me alegro de que
No creo que
Recomiendo que | **+** | (nombre de un[a] estudiante)
todos Uds.
nadie
alguien de la clase
yo | **+** | no | **+** | estudiar
llegar a tiempo
copiar en un examen
saber el subjuntivo
sacar notas mejores
entender esto
navegar la red
dormirse
hacer la tarea
¿ ? |

B. Consejos para comprar y usar la tecnología de multimedia

Paso 1. Complete las siguientes recomendaciones. Use el subjuntivo del verbo entre paréntesis y complete cada recomendación según su opinión y sus conocimientos (*knowledge*).

Recomiendo que…

> MODELO: (encontrar) [un amigo / un experto / ¿ ?] para ayudarlo/la a montar (*set up*) la computadora →
> Recomiendo que *encuentre un experto* para ayudarlo/la a montar la computadora.

1. (ir) a [nombre de una tienda de computadoras] para comprar la computadora
2. (comprar) [marca y modelo de computadora]
3. (mirar) las revistas especializadas, como [nombre de revista]
4. no (pagar) más de $ _____
5. no (usar) [marca o tipo de *software*]
6. (asegurarse [*to make sure*]) de que la computadora tenga [módem / impresora en colores / ¿ ?]
7. (poner) la computadora en [lugar]

Paso 2. Ahora, explique por qué hizo las recomendaciones del **Paso 1.**

> MODELO: Recomiendo que encuentre un experto para ayudarlo/la a montar la computadora *porque es difícil hacerlo.*

Paso 3. Compare sus respuestas con las de algunos compañeros para ver si están de acuerdo. ¿Quién sabe más del tema en la clase?

Con. A: Suggestion

Now have students dictate what professors must do, using the phrases in *Conversación A* as models.

Con. B: Follow-Up

Have students tell what advice their family and friends give them on a regular basis, for example, *Mis padres recomiendan que yo consiga trabajo en la librería.*

Follow-Up

Ask students the following questions about the pairs of sentences that introduce this section.

¿Qué diferencia hay entre el significado de una oración y el significado de otra en cada par de oraciones?

¿Cuál es la diferencia lingüística?

Emphasis A: Suggestions

■ Point out that when an expression of influence is followed by a subject change, the subjunctive is required.

> *La jefa quiere que los empleados estén contentos.*
> Ask who wants (→ *la jefa*).
> Ask who should be happy (→ *los empleados*).

■ Point out that when there is no subject change, the infinitive is used, just as in English.

> *Quiero estar contento.*
> Ask who wants (→ *yo*).
> Ask who would like to be happy (→ *yo*).

Emphasis B: Suggestion

Point out that influence implies that the speaker wants (expects/hopes /dreams) to affect somebody's behavior or even his/her own. The influence can be exerted from a power position (using verbs such as *ordenar*, *insistir en*, *pedir*, *mandar*, *exigir*, and *prohibir*) to the humblest position (*suplicar* [to beg] and *desear*).

38 Expressing Desires and Requests • Use of the Subjunctive: Influence

1. 2. 3.

Escoja la oración que describa cada dibujo.

1. _____ **a.** Quiero aprender las formas del subjuntivo.
   b. Quiero que nosotros aprendamos juntos las formas del subjuntivo.
2. _____ **a.** Insisto en hablar con Jorge.
   b. Insisto en que tú hables con Jorge.
3. _____ **a.** Es necesario arreglar esta habitación.
   b. Es necesario que tú arregles esta habitación.

A. So far, you have learned to identify the subjunctive by the features listed at the right.

The subjunctive:

■ appears in a subordinate (dependent) clause.
■ has a different subject from the one in the main (independent) clause.
■ is preceded by **que.**

B. In addition, the use of the subjunctive is associated with the presence of a number of concepts or conditions that trigger the use of it in the dependent clause. The concept of influence is one trigger for the subjunctive in a dependent clause. When the speaker wants something to happen, he or she tries to influence the behavior of others, as in these sentences.

The verb in the main clause is, of course, in the indicative, because it is a fact that the subject of the sentence wants something. The subjunctive occurs in the dependent clause.

MAIN (INDEPENDENT) CLAUSE		SUBORDINATE (DEPENDENT) CLAUSE
Yo **quiero**	que	tú **pagues** la cuenta.
I want		*you to pay the bill.*
La profesora **prefiere**	que	los estudiantes no **lleguen** tarde.
The professor prefers	*that*	*the students don't arrive late.*

Resources: Transparency 83

C. **Querer** and **preferir** are not the only verbs that can express the main subject's desire to influence what someone else thinks or does. There are many other verbs of influence, some very strong and direct, some very soft and polite.

STRONG	SOFT
insistir en	desear
mandar (*to order*)	pedir (i, i)
permitir (*to permit*)	recomendar (ie)
prohibir (prohíbo)	sugerir (ie, i)

D. An impersonal generalization of influence or volition can also be the main clause that triggers the subjunctive. Some examples of this appear at the right.

Es necesario que…	Es importante que…
Es urgente que…	Es mejor que…

■ ■■ ■ Práctica

A. ¡Anticipemos! En la tienda de aparatos electrónicos. Imagine que Ud. y un amigo están en una tienda de aparatos electrónicos. Ud. quiere comprarse un estéreo pero no sabe cuál; por eso su amigo lo/la acompaña. ¿Quién dice las siguientes oraciones, Ud., su amigo o el vendedor (*salesperson*)?

1. Prefiero que busques un estéreo en varias tiendas; así puedes comparar precios.
2. Quiero que el estéreo tenga disco compacto con control remoto.
3. Recomiendo que no le digas cuánto dinero quieres gastar.
4. Insisto en que Ud. vea este modelo. ¡Es lo último!
5. Prefiero que me muestre otro modelo más barato.
6. Es mejor que vayamos a buscar en otra tienda. No tengo tanto dinero.
7. Quiero que lo sepa: Este estéreo es el mejor de todos.

B. Expectativas de la educación

Paso 1. ¿Qué expectativas de la educación tienen los profesores, los estudiantes y los padres de los estudiantes? Forme oraciones según las indicaciones y añada (*add*) palabras cuando sea necesario.

1. todos / profesores / querer / que / estudiantes / llegar / clase / a tiempo
2. profesor(a) de / español / preferir / que / (nosotros) ir / con frecuencia / laboratorio de lenguas
3. profesores / prohibir / que / estudiantes / traer / comida / y / bebidas / clase
4. padres / de / estudiantes / desear / que / hijos / asistir a / clases
5. estudiantes / pedir / que / profesores / no darles / mucho / trabajo
6. también / (ellos) querer / que / haber / más vacaciones
7. padres / insistir en / que / hijos / sacar / buenas / notas

Paso 2. Y Ud., ¿qué quiere que hagan los profesores? Invente tres oraciones más para indicar sus deseos.

AUTOPRUEBA

Check off the sentences that have subordinate clauses in the subjunctive.

1. ☐ Quiero ir a la tienda
2. ☐ Prohíben que los estudiantes usen calculadoras.
3. ☐ Es urgente que vayas ahora.
4. ☐ Sé que estudias mucho.
5. ☐ ¿Quieres que te lo diga todo?

Answers: 2, 3, 5

Emphasis C: Suggestions

■ Point out that *decir* and *insistir en* are both information and influence verbs, depending on the context.

■ When the verbs are informative, they trigger the indicative in dependent clauses: *Carolina nos dice que llegamos a las siete.* = Carolina tells (informs) us that we must arrive at 7:00. *Insisto en que son amigos.* = I insist (maintain) that they are friends (not enemies).

■ Either the subjunctive construction or the infinitive may be used with the verbs *mandar, permitir,* and *prohibir.*

> *Mi padre prohíbe que yo vaya al cine solo.*
> *Mi padre me prohíbe ir al cine solo.*

Other similar verbs are *aconsejar, dejar, hacer,* and *impedir.*

■ When verbs imply influence, they trigger the subjunctive: *Carolina nos dice que lleguemos a las siete.* = Carolina tells us to arrive at 7:00. *Insisto en que sean amigos.* = I insist that they be(come) friends.

■ Have students works in groups to make a list of five things that they would like other people to do. Then, have them present requests to someone in class, who must either do it or give a good excuse for not doing it.

> *Queremos que Roberto nos traiga donuts mañana.* → *Lo siento. No les puedo traer donuts porque no tengo dinero.*

Prác. A: Preliminary Exercise

Have students express the following in Spanish.

1. It's important to do it.
2. It's important for Alice to do it.
3. It's necessary to leave now.
4. It's necessary that we leave now.

Prác. A: Follow-Up

Have students give formal commands for these situations. If it is a request, encourage them to use *por favor* and an appropriate tone.

Prác. C: Suggestions

- Do this as a whole-class activity, or have students do the first sentence working individually, then work as a class to come up with explanations.
- Tell students to imagine that their friend Carlos gave them the following commands, and have them report what their friend wants them to do.

  ¡No fume Ud.! → Carlos no quiere que yo fume.

  1. *Grabe el programa.*
  2. *No crea eso.*
  3. *No cambie de canal.*
  4. *Tráigame el control remoto.*
  5. *No diga eso.*
  6. *No me llame.*
  7. *Escúchela.*
  8. *Espérelo.*
  9. *No nos busque.*
  10. *Sírvalos.*

Bright Idea

Con. A: Suggestion

Have students give sentences that describe what you, the instructor, want / insist on / permit, and so on from them, and vice versa.

C. El día de la mudanza (*moving*). Imagine que Ud., su esposo/a y sus hijos acaban de llegar, con todas sus cosas, a un nuevo apartamento. ¿Dónde quieren Uds. que se pongan los siguientes muebles? Siga el modelo. Luego explique por qué quiere que cada cosa esté en el sitio indicado. Empiece la primera oración con frases como: **Queremos que...** , **Preferimos que...** , **Es necesario que...** , **Es buena idea que...** Use el verbo **gustar** en la segunda oración.

MODELO: LOS MUEBLES

los trofeos de Julio / la sala

LA EXPLICACIÓN

mirarlos todos los días →

Queremos que los trofeos de Julio estén en la sala. ¡Nos gusta mirarlos todos los días!

LOS MUEBLES	LA EXPLICACIÓN
1. el nuevo televisor / la sala	ver la tele todos juntos (*together*)
2. el televisor portátil / la cocina	ver la tele al cocinar (*while cooking*)
3. el equipo estereofónico / la alcoba de Julio	escuchar música al estudiar
4. el sillón grande / la sala	leer el periódico allí
5. los monopatines de los niños / la patio	jugar allí
6. la computadora / la oficina	pagar las cuentas (*bills*) allí
7. el acuario / la alcoba de Anita	mirar los peces

Need more practice?

- Workbook and Laboratory Manual
- Interactive CD-ROM
- Online Learning Center (www.mhhe.com/puntos7)

■■■ Conversación

A. ¿Qué quieres?

Paso 1. Con un compañero /una compañera, hable de lo que Ud. quiere, prefiere, permite, etcétera, que otras personas hagan. Para formar las preguntas y oraciones, combinen palabras de las tres listas, o usen la imaginación.

MODELO: E1: ¿Qué quieres que tu padre haga?
E2: Quiero que mi padre me compre una computadora.

| querer preferir insistir en mandar permitir prohibir recomendar | **+** | padre/madre amigos/as hermana profesor(a) novio/a esposo/a compañero/a de cuarto hijo/a hijos | **+** | comprarme... (un televisor, rosas, ¿ ?) visitarme... (mañana, el jueves, ¿ ?) invitarme... (al cine, a cenar, ¿ ?) (no) dar tarea... (hoy, mañana, ¿ ?) ayudarme con... (los quehaceres, la tarea, ¿ ?) salir con... (otra persona, mi amigo, ¿ ?) llamarme... (todos los días, el viernes, ¿ ?) explicarme... (la gramática, ¿ ?) ¿ ? |

Paso 2. Ahora, hablen de las cosas que otras personas quieren, prefieren, permiten, etcétera que Uds. hagan.

MODELO: E1: ¿Qué quieren tus hijos que hagas?
E2: Quieren que yo compre una computadora nueva.

B. Hablan los expertos en tecnología. Imagine que Ud. y sus compañeros de clase son un equipo (*team*) de expertos en problemas relacionados con la tecnología y que juntos (*together*) tienen un programa de radio.

Paso 1. Como miembro del equipo, lea las preguntas que les han mandado (*have sent*) los radioyentes (*radio audience*) por correo electrónico y déles una solución. Es bueno incluir frases como **Le recomiendo / sugiero que... , Es importante / necesario / urgente que...**

1. Soy una joven de 20 años y soy extremadamente tímida. Por eso no me gusta salir. Prefiero asumir otra personalidad al conectarme en la red. Así estoy contenta por horas. Mi madre dice que esto no es normal y me pide que deje de hacerlo. Ella insiste en que vaya a las discotecas como otros jóvenes de mi edad. ¿Qué piensan Uds.?

2. Mi marido es un hombre muy bueno y trabajador. Tiene un buen trabajo, y es una persona muy respetada en su compañía. El problema es que sólo piensa en *software* y multimedia. Pasa todo su tiempo libre delante de la computadora o leyendo catálogos y revistas sobre computadoras. Yo prefiero que él pase más tiempo conmigo. En realidad (*In fact*), estoy tan aburrida que estoy pensando en dejarlo. ¿Qué recomiendan que haga?

3. Mi jefe quiere que deje de usar mi máquina de escribir (*typewriter*) y empiece a usar una computadora. Pero no quiero hacerlo: Siempre he hecho (*I have done*) bien mi trabajo sin la «caja boba» (*stupid box*). Mi jefe dice que tengo que ponerme al día (*up-to-date*) y me sugiere que tome un curso de computadoras que él promete pagar. Yo no entiendo por qué tengo que cambiar. ¿Me aconsejan (*do you advise*) que hable con un abogado (*lawyer*)?

Paso 2. Ahora piense en un problema que se relacione con la tecnología que sea similar a los del **Paso 1**, y escríbalo. El resto de la clase le va a hacer sugerencias de cómo resolverlo.

C. Entrevista

Paso 1. Complete las siguientes oraciones lógicamente... ¡y con sinceridad!

1. Mis padres (hijos, abuelos,...) insisten en que (yo) _____.
2. Mi mejor amigo/a (esposo/a, novio/a,...) desea que (yo) _____.
3. Prefiero que mis amigos _____.
4. No quiero que mis amigos _____.
5. Es urgente que (yo) _____.
6. Es necesario que mi mejor amigo/a (esposo/a, novio/a,...) _____.

Paso 2. Ahora entreviste a un compañero / una compañera para saber cómo él/ella completó las oraciones del **Paso 1**.

MODELO: ¿En qué insisten tus padres?

Con. B: Suggestions

■ Point out that some of the recommendations may be in the form of direct commands. A combination of these with suggestions using the subjunctive is typical for advice.
■ Have students decide between *tú* and *Ud.* for each of the three cases. Remind them to think of the issue of formal vs. informal when they get to *Paso 2.*
■ **Paso 1.** Have students work in small groups or pairs, and then share their findings with the rest of the class.

Con. B: Suggestion

Paso 2. Assign as written homework for the next class.

Con. C: Follow-Up

Have students share and compare their sentences. Write inclusive categories on the board that can be used to tally answers. Ask students if they see any patterns.

National Standards: Community

Point out that call-in talk and advice shows are popular in Spanish-speaking countries as well as among the U.S. Hispanic population. One advice show is broadcast by *La Red Hispana:* The Hispanic Network, Inc. Have students go to this organization's website to find out what kinds of information their programming offers. Encourage them to look for information on call-in radio shows in Spain and Latin America as well.

- Have students work in small groups. Each member will complete two of the following sentences. Remind them that *el presidente* refers to the president of a country. The president of a university is *el rector/la rectora*.

  Queremos que el presidente (primer ministro) / el rector (la rectora)...

  Recomendamos que el presidente (primer ministro) / el rector (la rectora)...

  Es importante que el presidente (primer ministro) / el rector (la rectora)...

  Sugerimos que el presidente (primer ministro) / el rector (la rectora)...

Have the groups select and then write their three best sentences on the board. Then have students work individually to select sentences from the board and use them to write a letter to the president or prime minister.

- Have volunteers read their letters.
- Have the class vote for the best letter.
- The final version can be assigned as homework. For the next day, have them exchange and correct each other's letters.

UN POCO DE TODO

A. ¡Viva el correo electrónico! Complete the following with the correct forms of the words in parentheses, as suggested by the context. When two possibilities are given in parentheses, select the correct word. **¡OJO!** As you conjugate verbs in this activity, use the present tense unless otherwise indicated in parentheses. If you see *P/I*, you will choose between the preterite and the imperfect; *comm.* means to use a command; *prog.* stands for the present/past progressive, and *subj.* stands for the present subjunctive.

Marcia Hilbert, de Chicago, y su amiga limeña,[a] Matilde O'Hara, se conocieron hace un mes por el Internet. (Escribirse[1]) regularmente (por/para[2]) correo electrónico, y parece que cada día (descubrir[3]) una nueva cosa que (tener[4]) en común. Quieren conocerse en persona y Matilde (sugerir[5]) que Marcia (*subj.,* venir[6]) a Lima para (saber/conocer[7]) la capital del Perú. Los siguientes correos electrónicos son los últimos mensajes que se mandaron.

Querida Marci:
¿Cómo estás, amiga? Aquí todo (seguir[8]) más o menos igual. Es diciembre y (*yo:* alegrarse[9]) de que ya (*subj., nosotros:* ser/estar[10]) en verano. Ahora, la garúa[b] que cubre[c] (este[11]) ciudad por muchos días del año (levantarse[12]), y (*nosotros:* ir[13]) a la playa casi todas las tardes. Muy pronto, todo el mundo (ir[14]) a (ser/estar[15]) ocupadísimo en (prepararse[16]) para las festividades del 18 de enero, aniversario de la fundación de Lima por Francisco Pizarro en 1535. Oye, (*yo:* tener[17]) una idea fabulosa. ¿Por qué no (*Uds.:* venir[18]) a Lima para entonces? Me gustaría mucho (verte[19]) y compartir contigo toda la gala del aniversario de esta ciudad. (*comm., Tú:* Preguntarles[20]) a (tu[21]) padres, y (*comm.,* escribirme[22]) pronto.
Un abrazo,
Tu amiga Mati

Querida Mati:
Chica, una noticia maravillosa. Ayer, mamá y yo (*prog.,* hablar[23]) de tu correo electrónico. Mamá visitó Perú (hacer[24]) unos veinte años y tiene muchos ganas de volver (a/de[25]) a Lima para el Aniversario! ¡Fíjate[d] que (*nosotros:* verse[26]) en poco más de un mes!
Muchos abrazos,
Marci

Hola Marci:
¡Qué suerte loca! ¿Sabes? Mi papá (ser/estar[27]) portero de un bloque de apartamentos que (quedar[28]) aquí cerca de la playa. Unos inquilinos amables que (salir[29]) (en/de[30]) viaje en cuatro semanas le (decir[31]) que, en su ausencia, Uds. (poder[32]) quedarse en el apartamento si (cuidar[33]) bien a los perritos de ellos. ¡(*comm., Tú:* Escribirme[34]) tu respuesta pronto!
Abrazos,
Mati

[a]de Lima, Perú   [b]*coastal fog*   [c]*covers*   [d]*Just think (figurative)*

Hola Mati:

¡Qué buenas noticias! El ofrecimiento de quedarnos en el apartamento de los inquilinos es estupendo. Mamá y yo (lo/la³⁵) aceptamos con mucho gusto. ¡(Nosotros: Salir³⁶) (por/para³⁷) Lima en tres semanas!

Tu amiga loca de felicidad,
Marci

Comprensión: A reorganizar esto. The following series of events from the above e-mails is out of order. Rearrange the statements so they will be in chronological order.

1. Matilde invita a Marcia y a la familia de ella a visitar Lima.
2. Marcia y su mamá aceptan la oferta de quedarse en el apartamento.
3. Matilde y Marcia se conocen por correo electrónico.
4. La garúa de Lima se levanta, y todos van a la playa.
5. La madre de Marcia quiere hacer el viaje a Lima.

B. Dos diablitos (*little devils*)

Paso 1. Alberto y Eduardo Suárez son dos niños que siempre hacen lo que no deben. Para cada par de oraciones, lea el mandato que les da su madre en la primera oración. Luego, complete la segunda oración con el mandato opuesto.

MODELO: Alberto, siéntate en la silla. No _____ (sentarte) en el suelo. → No *te sientes* en el suelo.

1. Alberto, no escuches la radio ahora. _____ (Escucharme) a mí.
2. Eduardo, haz tu tarea. No _____ (hacer) eso.
3. Eduardo, no juegues con la pelota en casa. _____ (Jugar) afuera.
4. Alberto, no cantes en la mesa. _____ (Cantar) después de cenar.
5. Alberto, dame tu almuerzo a mí. No _____ (dárselo) al perro.
6. Eduardo, pon los pies en el suelo. No _____ (ponerlos) en el sofá.

Paso 2. ¿Qué quiere la Sra. Suárez que hagan los dos niños? ¿Qué prefiere que *no* hagan? Indique sus deseos con oraciones completas.

MODELO: La Sra. Suárez prefiere que Alberto se siente en la silla. No quiere que se siente en el suelo.

C. Una carta al presidente

Paso 1. Divídanse en grupos de tres personas. Cada miembro del grupo va a completar dos de las siguientes oraciones. **¡OJO!** La palabra **presidente** se refiere al presidente de los Estados Unidos. En español, **el rector / la rectora** = *university president*.

Queremos que el presidente (primer ministro) / el rector (la rectora)…
Recomendamos que el presidente (primer ministro) / el rector (la rectora)…
Es importante que el presidente (primer ministro) / el rector (la rectora)…
Sugerimos que el presidente (primer ministro) / el rector (la rectora)…

Paso 2. Ahora los miembros del grupo deben seleccionar las tres mejores oraciones. Una persona de cada grupo las va a escribir en la pizarra.

Paso 3. Lea las oraciones que están en la pizarra y use algunas para escribir una breve carta al presidente de los Estados Unidos, al primer ministro del Canadá o al rector / a la rectora de la universidad. Añada (*Add*) otra información y use **Ud.** en vez de (*instead of*) **el presidente (primer ministro) / el rector (la rectora).**

Palabras útiles	
desear	preferir
esperar	prohibir
insistir en	querer
permitir	

Resources for Review and Testing Preparation

- Workbook and Laboratory Manual
- Interactive CD-ROM
- Online Learning Center (www.mhhe.com/puntos7)

Review the formation of informal and formal commands. In addition, have students indicate where object pronouns are placed with regard to affirmative and negative commands.

B: Follow-Up

- **Paso 1.** Ask students: *Si Ud. tiene hijos, ¿qué otros mandatos les da a ellos? Si no tiene hijos, ¿qué mandatos recuerda Ud. de su niñez?*
- **Paso 2.** Ask students: *¿Qué cosas quieren sus padres, sus hijos o sus amigos que Ud. haga esto año? Explique por qué y si piensa hacerlo o no.*

Resources: Desenlace

In the *Capítulo 12* segment of "Chapter-by-Chapter Supplementary Materials" in the IM/RK, you will find a chapter-culminating activity. You can use this activity to consolidate and review the vocabulary and grammar skills students have acquired.

PERSPECTIVAS
culturales

Entrevista cultural

Suggestions

- Before showing the video, ask students questions about working in department and electronic stores.

  ¿Trabaja Ud. en un almacén o tienda de electrónica?

  ¿Le gusta su trabajo? ¿Cómo es su jefe/a? ¿y sus compañeros de trabajo?

  ¿Cuáles son algunas de sus responsabilidades en el trabajo?

  ¿Qué se vende donde Ud. trabaja?

  ¿Ud. gasta mucho dinero donde trabaja? ¿En qué?

- Show the video and allow students one to two minutes to work on the questions. Have volunteers answer the questions.

- Have volunteers role-play Valdemar and his interviewer.

Entre amigos

Suggestions

- Before viewing the video, review the questions with the students and ask them similar questions.

  ¿Tiene Ud. computadora? ¿Para qué la usa?

  ¿Navega Ud. mucho el Internet?

  ¿Qué otros aparatos electrónicos tiene Ud.?

  ¿Cuáles son los más importantes para Ud.?

  Have students answer or work in small groups to ask and answer these questions.

- After viewing the video, have volunteers read and answer the questions.

●●● Videoteca

Entrevista cultural: el Perú

Valdemar de Icasa es un estudiante peruano que trabaja en una tienda. Habla con la entrevistadora de las cosas que se venden en la tienda y de los productos que son más populares. Antes de ver el vídeo, lea el siguiente fragmento de la entrevista.

ENTREVISTADORA: ...Y ¿te gusta tu trabajo?

VALDEMAR: Sí, me gusta mucho, eh... digamos, lo único que no me gusta es que gasto mucho de mi... de mi sueldo, en... en comprar equipo de lo mismo que vendemos nosotros. Por ejemplo la semana pasada me compré una cámara digital muy bonita. Pero bueno, salvo[a] eso, no... no pienso quedarme mucho tiempo en este trabajo.

[a]*except for*

Ahora vea el vídeo y conteste las siguientes preguntas basándose en la entrevista.

1. ¿De dónde es Valdemar?
2. ¿Dónde trabaja Valdemar?
3. Según él, ¿cuáles son los productos más populares ahora?
4. ¿Qué problema menciona relativo al trabajo?
5. ¿Qué estudia Valdemar?

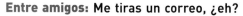

Entre amigos: Me tiras un correo, ¿eh?

Karina, Tané, Rubén y Miguel hablan de los aparatos electrónicos y de su uso. En su opinión, ¿qué preguntas se van a hacer? Antes de mirar el vídeo, lea las preguntas a continuación. Mientras mire el vídeo, trate de entender la conversación en general y fíjese en la información sobre las computadoras y otros aparatos electrónicos. Luego mire el vídeo una segunda vez, fijándose en la información que necesita para contestar las preguntas.

1. ¿Qué hace Karina en la computadora?
2. ¿Para qué usa Tané una computadora?
3. ¿Cuál es la dirección electrónica de Tané?
4. ¿Tiene Karina un sitio web?
5. Según Rubén, ¿qué efecto tiene él en los aparatos electrónicos?

Conozca... el Perú

Datos esenciales

- Nombre oficial: República del Perú
- Capital: Lima
- Población: 28.400.000 habitantes
- Moneda: el nuevo sol
- Idiomas oficiales: el español, el quechua, el aimara

¡Fíjese!

- El Lago Titicaca, que queda entre Bolivia y el Perú, es el lago más grande de Sudamérica y es la ruta de transporte principal entre estos dos países.
- Cientos de años antes de la llegada[a] de los españoles, la agricultura de los indígenas del Perú ya era muy sofisticada. Hace más de 2.000 años, los indígenas ya construían terrazas para sembrar en las faldas[b] de los Andes. Muchas de estas terrazas se usan todavía.
- Uno de los cultivos[c] más importantes de los incas es la papa,[d] que originó en la región cerca del Lago Titicaca. La papa es una de las pocas plantas que puede subsistir[e] en altitudes de más de 13.000 pies y en regiones frías y áridas.

[a]arrival [b]para... so that they could plant on the slopes [c]crops
[d]patata [e]survive

▲ Cuzco, Perú

Learn more about Peru with the Video, the Interactive CD-ROM, and the Online Learning Center (www.mhhe.com/puntos7).

Civilizaciones indígenas: la cultura inca

Cuando los españoles llegaron al Perú en 1532, los incas ya dominaban una gran zona de Sudamérica, desde Colombia hasta Chile, y desde el Pacífico hasta las selvas[a] del este. A partir del siglo XIII,[b] muchos otros pueblos indígenas de la inmensa región vivían bajo[c] el dominio de los incas. La capital del imperio era Cuzco.

La palabra *inca* significa *rey* o *príncipe*[d] en quechua, lengua que todavía se habla en el Perú. Bajo su inca, el pueblo tenía un gobierno de poder absoluto y un sistema burocrático y social muy complejo.

El imperio inca se destacó[e] por la arquitectura, la ingeniería[f] y las técnicas de cultivo. También estableció un sistema de correo y un censo de la población. Tras la conquista[g] de los incas por los españoles Pizarro y Almagro, el Perú y su capital Lima se convirtieron en un centro fundamental de las colonias españolas en América. Lima fue fundada por Pizarro en 1535.

[a]jungles [b]A... Beginning in the 13th century
[c]under [d]rey... king or prince [e]se... distinguished
itself [f]engineering [g]Tras... After the conquest

- The most important chronicler of the Incan presence in Peru, "El Inca" Garcilaso, was related to some of the outstanding literary figures of Spain, including the brilliant Spanish lyric poet, soldier, and courtier Garcilaso de la Vega, who died in 1536. Thus the need to use "El Inca" with his name, a distinction he was justly proud of, as his mother was descended from a brother of the Incan ruler, Huayna Capac, the last of the great Incan emperors (d. 1525).
- *Quechua* is an indigenous language spoken by approximately 13 million people in Bolivia, Peru, Ecuador, southern Colombia, northern Argentina, and northern Chile. It was the official language of *Tawantinsuyu*, the Incan Empire. Peruvian Spanish has hundreds of loan words from Quechua, many of which are the names of plants and animals. English also has words that are derived from Quechua.

coca	jerky	pampa
condor	lima bean	puma
guano	llama	quinine

- Students can read an excerpt from the novel *La tía Julia el escribidor* by Peru's Mario Vargas Llosa in *Un paso más 12.*

MULTIMEDIA: Internet

Have students search the Internet for more information about Peru's government, educational system, geography, and economy. They can also search for *la Red científica peruana* online. This site, available in English and Spanish, contains information about Peru and links to cultural, economic, and tourist information.

National Standards: Comparisons

Have students discuss the importance of the potato in the dietary habits of the United States, Canada, and most European nations. Ask them for other foods commonly used as a staple. Students can research on the Internet the importance of the potato to the Incas.

EN RESUMEN
Vocabulario

Suggestions

- Give definitions or descriptions and have students name the item.

  El dinero que uno recibe cada una o dos semanas por el trabajo que hace. → *el sueldo*

- Divide students into two teams and have them play Password. Cues must be a single word in Spanish and must not be a variation of the answer (*grabar/grabadora*). Allow only one cue and attempt per turn.
- Bring or have students bring images of *Vocabulario* activities and items. Use these to elicit descriptions, ask/answer questions, and play games.
- Ask questions using words from *Vocabulario*.

  1. *Además del teléfono tradicional, ¿qué otros tipos de teléfono hay?*
  2. *Para mandar documentos, fotos, etcétera, ¿qué aparato resulta muy rápido?*
  3. *¿Qué se necesita para comunicarse por correo electrónico?*

Note

In Spain, *la radio* is always feminine.

EN RESUMEN

Gramática

To review the grammar points presented in this chapter, refer to the indicated grammar presentations. You'll find further practice of these structures in the Workbook and Laboratory Manual, on the Interactive CD-ROM, and on the *Puntos de partida* Online Learning Center (www.mhhe.com/puntos7).

36. Influencing Others—**Tú** (Informal) Commands

Do you know how to give orders to friends and children in Spanish? How do you tell them what not to do?

37. Expressing Subjective Actions or States—Present Subjunctive: An introduction

Do you understand how to form the present subjunctive?

38. Expressing Desires and Requests—Use of the Subjunctive: Influence

You should be able to express what you want or need someone else to do without using a direct command.

Vocabulario

Practice this vocabulary with digital flash cards on the Online Learning Center (www.mhhe.com/puntos7).

Los verbos

alegrarse (de)	to be happy (about)
arreglar	to straighten (up); to fix, repair
cambiar (de)	to change
copiar	to copy
dudar	to doubt
esperar	to hope
fallar	to "crash" (*a computer*)
funcionar	to work, function; to run (*machines*)
grabar	to record; to tape
guardar	to keep; to save (*documents*)
haber (*infinitive form* of **hay**)	(*there is, there are*)
hacer (*irreg.*) copia	to copy
imprimir	to print
insistir (en)	to insist (on)
mandar	to order
manejar	to drive; to operate (*a machine*)
navegar (gu) la Red	to surf the Net
obtener (*irreg.*)	to get, obtain
permitir	to permit, allow
prohibir (prohíbo)	to prohibit, forbid

Repaso: conseguir (i, i) (g), sacar (qu) fotos

Vehículos

la bicicleta (de montaña)	(mountain) bike
el carro (descapotable)	(convertible) car
el monopatín	skateboard
la moto(cicleta)	motorcycle, moped
los patines	roller skates

Repaso: el coche

La electrónica

el archivo	(computer) file
el canal	channel
el contestador automático	answering machine
el correo electrónico	e-mail
el disco duro	hard drive
el equipo estereofónico/ fotográfico	stereo/photography equipment
la grabadora	(tape) recorder/player
la impresora	printer
el lector de DVD	DVD player
el ordenador (*Sp.*)	computer
el ratón	mouse
la Red	Net
el teléfono celular	cellular phone
la videocasetera	videocassette recorder (VCR)

Repaso: la cinta, el televisor

Cognados: la cámara (de vídeo), el CD-ROM, la computadora, el control remoto, el disco compacto (CD), el disco de computadora, el DVD, el fax, la memoria, el módem, el radio (portátil) / la radio,* el *walkman*

Para poder gastar...

el aumento	raise
el/la jefe/a	boss
el sueldo	salary

La vivienda

alquilar	to rent
las afueras	outskirts; suburbs
el alquiler	rent
el área (but f.)	area
la avenida	avenue
el barrio	neighborhood
la calle	street
el campo	countryside
el *campus*	(university) campus
la casa (el bloque) de apartamentos	apartment building

la comunidad	community
el/la dueño/a	landlord, landlady
el gas	gas; heat
el/la inquilino/a	tenant; renter
el piso	floor (of a building)
el primer piso	second floor
el segundo piso	third floor
la planta baja	ground floor
el/la portero/a	building manager; doorman
la vecindad	neighborhood
el/la vecino/a	neighbor
la vista	view

Repaso: el apartamento, la casa, el centro, el cuarto, la dirección, la luz, la residencia

Otros sustantivos

el gasto	expense
el lujo	luxury
la mentira	lie

Palabras adicionales

los/las demás	others

Suggestions

- Have students restate the following sentences to make them reflect their own situations.

  1. *Vivo en el centro.*
  2. *Mis vecinos son muy simpáticos.*
  3. *Tengo una vista magnífica de la ciudad.*
  4. *Alquilo un apartamento cerca de la universidad.*
  5. *El dueño de la casa de apartamentos paga la luz y el gas.*
  6. *Hay portero en mi casa de apartamentos.*
  7. *Hay portería automática (security system).*

- Have students describe their living situation, then have them tell how it compares to their previous situations. For some, it may be worse (from family home to dorm), for others it may be better.

*****El radio** *is the apparatus;* **la radio** *is the medium.*

Un paso más 12
Note
The *Un paso más* section is optional.

Literatura del Perú

Notes

- Vargas Llosa is a novelist, playwright, journalist, essayist, and also literary critic. He uses "avant garde" techniques to create a "double of the real world." Although he talks of many strong social and political themes in his work, he has emphasized that artistic aims should not be compromised for propaganda. Vargas Llosa writes regularly for *El País,* and has received numerous awards as a writer, including *El Príncipe de Asturias* prize, *el Premio Planeta,* the Max Schmidheiny Foundation Freedom Prize, the National Book Critics Award, the Ortega y Gasset Prize, the National Prize for the Novel in Peru, the Romulo Gallegos International prize for literature. He received a doctorate from *la Universidad Complutense* in Madrid, and holds honorary doctorates from Georgetown, Yale, Harvard, and other international universities.
- In 1990 Vargas Llosa was a candidate for the presidency of Peru, but after many electoral processes and battles, he lost the election. He currently lives in Spain.

LECTURA

Suggestions

- Do the *Estrategia* in class the day you assign the reading as homework for the next class.
- Practice the *Estrategia* with your students by asking them to provide the verb that shares a root with the following nouns.

el canto	el manejo
el aprendizaje	el cambio
el levantamiento	la grabación
el encuentro	el rompimiento
el alegramiento	el sufrimiento

Un paso más 12

Literatura del **Perú**

Sobre el autor: *Jorge Mario Pedro Vargas Llosa nació en Arequipa, Perú. Estudió en el Perú. Además del Perú, ha vivido[a] en varios países. En los años 90, se trasladó[b] a España, donde consiguió ciudadanía[c] española. Ha sido[d] profesor visitante en universidades de los Estados Unidos, Latinoamérica y Europa. El siguiente fragmento es de la novela:* La tía Julia y el escribidor *(1977).*

En ese tiempo remoto, yo era muy joven y vivía con mis abuelos en una quinta[e] de paredes blancas de la calle Ocharán, en Miraflores. Estudiaba en San Marcos, Derecho,[f] creo, resignado a ganarme más tarde la vida con una profesión liberal, aunque, en el fondo,[g] me hubiera gustado[h] más llegar a ser un escritor. Tenía un trabajo de título pomposo, sueldo modesto, apropiaciones ilícitas[i] y horario elástico: director de Informaciones de Radio Panamericana. Consistía en recortar las noticias interesantes que aparecían en los diarios[j] y maquillarlas[k] un poco para que se leyeran[l] en los boletines.

▲ Mario Vargas Llosa (1936–)

[a]*ha... he has lived* [b]*se... he moved* [c]*citizenship* [d]*Ha... He has been* [e]*casa* [f]*Law* [g]*en... deep down* [h]*me... I would have liked* [i]*apropiaciones... crooked deals* [j]*periódicos* [k]*editing them* [l]*para... so that they could be read*

LECTURA

ESTRATEGIA: Word Families

Guessing the meaning of a word from context is easier if it has a recognizable root or a relation to another word that you already know. For example, if you know the verb **llover** (*to rain*), you should be able to guess the meaning of **lluvia** (*rain*) and **lluvioso** (*rainy*) quite easily in context. Can you guess the meaning of the following words? Give the English meaning in the first blank, and then in the second blank give a Spanish word that you already know that has the same root form. The first one is done for you.

la locura	En la Edad Media, la locura no era considerada una enfermedad, sino una manifestación en carne y hueso (*flesh and blood; literally, flesh and bone*) del diablo (*devil*).
madness	*loco*

Capítulo 12: La calidad de la vida

MULTIMEDIA: Internet

Have students search the Internet for information on Mario Vargas Llosa. They should be able to find biographical information, photos, and additional information regarding his works.

la pobreza	La pobreza es un problema muy grave en muchas partes de la India y Latinoamérica.
-----	
la enseñanza	Muchos datos indican que la calidad de la enseñanza actual en los Estados Unidos es inferior a la del año 1960.
-----	
la riqueza	El número de personas que llega a Hollywood en busca de fama y riqueza en el cine sigue subiendo.

Next, check your answers with a classmate or with your instructor.

The following words are both found in the first paragraph of the reading: **almacenamiento** and **pensadas.** What verbs or nouns do you know that have the same root form as these words? (Hint for **almacenamiento:** In **Capítulo 3** you learned the word **almacén.** Do you recall its meaning?) The word **vendidas** is found in the graph that accompanies the reading. Can you identify the verb that has the same root form? Identifying root forms and knowing their meanings should help you understand some unfamiliar words in the context of this passage.

■ **Sobre la lectura...** Esta lectura, adaptada de la versión original, viene de la revista española *Quo,* que publica artículos de interés general para el público.

Secretaria de bolsillo[a]

Las agendas electrónicas se presentan como amasijo[b] de chips y circuitos electrónicos que se adapta a las dimensiones de un bolsillo. Después, su <u>potencia</u> se despliega con[c] múltiples funciones, gran capacidad de almacenamiento y conexiones para poder enviar faxes, conectarse al Internet o recibir información por correo electrónico. Hoy en día se han diversificado[d] en distintas familias de productos, pensadas para públicos diferentes con necesidades distintas.

▲ *Una agenda electrónica*

[a]*pocket* [b]*hodgepodge* [c]*se... ofrece (literally, unfolds)* [d]*se... they have diversified*

Suggestions

■ Present some other commonly used suffixes in Spanish and their corresponding endings in English, for example, *-ción* → -tion; *-tad, -dad* → ty; *-tud* → -tude; and so on.
■ Before reading, point out the numbers in the reading (6.000, 20.000, 60.000, 1992, and 1998). Have volunteers say these in Spanish.

Suggestions

■ Have students look at the charts in this article. What information is presented? Do they provide any clues as to the content of the article?

■ Have students read the article out loud. Have volunteers read one sentence each or rotate through the class one sentence at a time.

Para uso personal

Se trata de las agendas más sencillas. Cuestan entre 6.000 y 20.000 pesetas y ofrecen poco más que un calendario de citas, una agenda de teléfonos y un pequeño bloc de notas. «Están dirigidas[e] a un público de nivel adquisitivo medio.[f] Son muy ligeras[g] y ofrecen las funciones justas; por sus presentaciones, puede decirse que buscan sustituir a las agendas de papel», asegura Gerard Borrut, jefe de producto de Sistemas Digitales de Sharp.

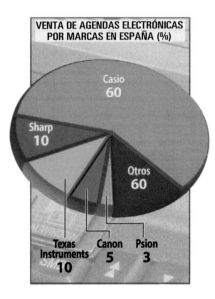

VENTA DE AGENDAS ELECTRÓNICAS POR MARCAS EN ESPAÑA (%)

Casio 60
Sharp 10
Otros 60
Texas Instruments 10
Canon 5
Psion 3

Para usos más profesionales

Las agendas electrónicas de entre 20.000 y 60.000 pesetas son útiles para aquellos profesionales que no necesitan un gran volumen de información portátil ni demasiadas prestaciones,[h] pero a quienes las agendas sencillas se les han quedado pequeñas.[i] Su mejor cualidad reside en que su memoria interna es más <u>amplia</u> y, además de las funciones básicas, incluyen una <u>pantalla</u> más grande, un teclado[j] más accesible y cómodo y capacidad para transferir datos al PC.

La manía[k] por los asistentes de bolsillo en España es evidente en la tabla siguiente, que demuestra la venta de estos entre 1992 y 1998. ■

Diminutas maravillas

En seis años, el número de asistentes de bolsillo se ha incrementado en España en casi un 70%. En este mercado, Casio sigue siendo el rey.

AGENDAS ELECTRÓNICAS VENDIDAS EN ESPAÑA

Año	Cantidad
1992	80.000
1993	85.000
1994	102.000
1995	102.000
1996	120.000
1997	130.000
1998	135.000

[e]*targeted, directed* [f]*nivel... average purchasing power* [g]*lightweight* [h]*features* [i]*se... have become too small* [j]*keyboard* [k]*furor, craze*

Comprensión

A. ¿Cierto o falso? Conteste según el artículo.

1. Las agendas más baratas ofrecen conexión al Internet.
2. Todas las agendas ofrecen la misma capacidad de memoria interna.
3. Una ventaja de la agenda «para uso profesional» es el tamaño de la pantalla.
4. En España se ve un interés creciente (*growing*) por las agendas digitales.

B. Funciones y ventajas. Identifique por lo menos tres ventajas o funciones deseables (*desirable*) de las agendas electrónicas.

ESCRITURA

A. Un concurso (*contest*). Imagine Ud. que una compañía que fabrica productos electrónicos está montando una campaña de publicidad para una agenda digital nueva. A la persona que mejor pueda explicar cómo una agenda electrónica le facilitaría la vida (*would make life easier*), la compañía le va a regalar una. Escriba un ensayo en el que Ud. explica y justifica por qué quiere una agenda digital y cómo lo/la va a ayudar esta a organizar su vida. ¡No se olvide de incluir algunos detalles sobre su vida de estudiante!

B. ¿De qué dependo?

Paso 1. Haga una lista de las cosas que tiene Ud., especialmente los aparatos electrónicos. Luego, marque diez de las cosas que más usa y necesita. ¿Son indispensables?

Paso 2. Ahora escriba un párrafo sobre las cosas que Ud. tiene y sobre cómo y cuánto depende de ellas. ¿Podría (*Could you*) vivir cómodamente con sólo cinco de las cosas de su lista? ¿Cómo sería (*would be*) diferente su vida?

 Heritage Speakers

Anime a los hispanohablantes a diseñar su propio anuncio en casa usando la computadora. Busque voluntarios para presentar su anuncio en clase al día siguiente.

Comprensión

A: Suggestion
Have students identify the passages in the reading where they found their answers.

A: Variation
In groups have students use what they have learned about word families. For example, *pensar, pensadas, pensamiento,* and *pensativo* are all related. How many words can they come up with or find that relate to the following?

diversificado   diferentes   información

Are there similar word families in English?

B: Suggestion
Have students explain their answers, using information from the reading.

ESCRITURA

A: Suggestions
- Convert this into a short role-play activity. Students play the roles of a company representative and the client making his/her case for the *agenda electrónica.*
- If you prefer that your students do a journal activity, see *Mi diario* in this chapter of the Workbook.

A: Variation
Give students the following assignment: *Escriba una breve composición sobre un aparato o uno de los bienes personales que más le gustaría tener. ¿Qué es? ¿Cómo es? ¿Qué quiere Ud. que tenga? Describa los detalles de su compra ideal. Puede usar las siguientes frases para escribir su composición.*

Lo que más necesito / quiero es...
Prefiero que...
No quiero que...
Deseo comprarlo en... porque...
Es necesario que...

 Bright Idea

B: Suggestion
Have students think about the types of commercials and ads they see on TV and in magazines. Ask them the following questions.

¿Tienen los anuncios una influencia sobre el consumidor?
¿Por qué salen personas muy atractivas en los anuncios?
¿Qué efecto tienen estos anuncios en las personas regulares?
¿Qué tipo de comerciales o anuncios deben eliminar de la televisión o de las revistas? ¿Por qué?

CHAPTER OPENER PHOTO

Point out chapter-opener photo. Have students describe the scene in the photo (sidewalk art vendors). Have them talk about art and how it is presented and sold. Ask if they know of areas where vendors or artists sell paintings on the street or in open-air markets. Ask what art they have or their family has at home. What kind of art is it? Where did they get it?

Suggestions

- Write the following on the board or on an overhead transparency. Have students take turns putting the activities in order or naming their favorite.

  _____ *Ir a un museo*
  _____ *Ir al **cine***
  _____ *Ir a un concierto de **música** clásica*
  _____ *Ver un **ballet** o un recital de **baile***
  _____ *Leer una novela*
  _____ *Ir al **teatro** a ver un **drama***
  _____ ***Crear** algo (una **pintura**, una **canción**, etcétera) personalmente*
  _____ *Mirar la televisión*
  _____ *Ver un partido deportivo*
  _____ *Navegar el Internet*

- The words in **boldface** are included in the active vocabulary of this chapter. Have students discuss the words and use context to help them understand the meanings. Place the words they cannot guess in new sentences and contexts.
- Introduce new words that are not cognates: *canción, pintura.*
- Assign the task as a group activity. Then have students share information with the whole class. Have them develop a class profile.

Note

The *Puntos de partida* Online Learning Center includes an interview with a person from Bolivia who talks about these activities.

Follow-Up

Ask students the following questions: *¿Hay para Ud. algo más interesante que todas las cosas que están en la lista? ¿Cuál es?*

◄ Unos residentes de Quito, Ecuador, que miran obras de arte en el Parque de la Alameda

---

Resources

For Students

- Workbook
- Laboratory Manual and Laboratory Audio Program
- Quia™ Online Workbook and Online Laboratory Manual
- Video on CD
- Interactive CD-ROM
- *Puntos de partida* Online Learning Center (**www.mhhe.com/puntos7**)

For Instructors

- *Instructor's Manual and Resource Kit,* "Chapter-by-Chapter" Supplementary Materials
- Overhead Transparencies 84–86
- Testing Program
- Test Generator
- Video Program
- Audioscript
- *Puntos de partida* Online Learning Center (**www.mhhe.com/puntos7**)

El arte y la **cultura**

Suggestion
Have students list their ideas about Bolivia and Ecuador, including information on geography, politics, economy, culture, music, and cuisine. When you finish the chapter, return to the lists and ask students what ideas they would change and/or add.

Entrevista cultural

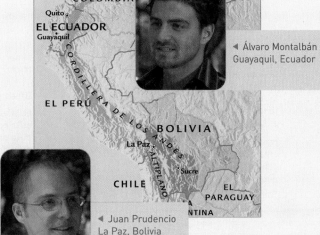

◄ Álvaro Montalbán
Guayaquil, Ecuador

◄ Juan Prudencio
La Paz, Bolivia

MULTIMEDIA

- The multimedia materials that accompany this chapter are referenced in the Student and Instructor's Editions with icons to help you identify when and where to incorporate them.

- The IM/RK provides suggestions for using the multimedia materials in the classroom.

Las artes

Note

See the model for vocabulary presentation and other material in the *Capítulo 13 Vocabulario: Preparación* section of "Chapter-by-Chapter Supplementary Materials" in the IM.

Suggestions

- Emphasize the dual gender of the following words: *el/la artista*, *el/la cantante*, *el/la guía*, *el/la poeta*. Point out that *la guía* can refer to a guidebook or to a female guide.
- Point out the spelling differences between English and Spanish: *escultura* vs. sculpture, *arquitectura* vs. architecture.
- Help students relate the following words: scene → *escena* → *escenario*.
- Point out that a play is called *una obra de teatro*. Offer additional vocabulary: *artesanal* and *artístico/a*.
- Have students look at the art and vocabulary. Then describe the art scene using as many words from the list as possible, and have students repeat them.
- Write a column on the board for each of the different types of art. Have students supply words from the vocabulary list that belong to each art form. Repeat and model the pronunciation of the words added to the columns.
- Have students tell whether the following sentences about traditional culture are *cierto* or *falso*.

   1. *Se puede comprar artesanías en un supermercado.*
   2. *La cerámica es una de las artes más conocidas de este país.*
   3. *En este país no hay ningún tipo de ruinas de civilizaciones anteriores a la nuestra.*
   4. *Los tejidos* (woven goods) *no son una forma de producción artística.*
   5. *Cada región de este país tiene sus canciones típicas. (Dé ejemplos.)*

- Present the following questions to establish a class discussion.

   ¿Cree que todas las personas son artistas de alguna manera? Si una persona tiene mucho talento, ¿cree que es fácil que pueda vivir de su arte?

**Resources:
Transparency 84**

Las artes*

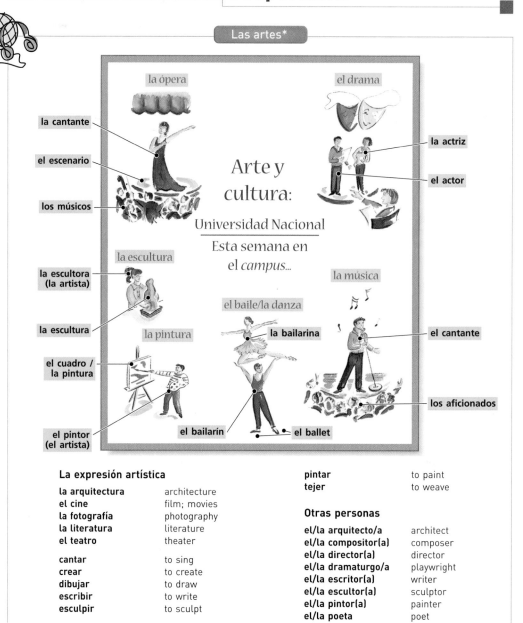

la ópera · la cantante · el escenario · los músicos · el drama · la actriz · el actor · Arte y cultura: Universidad Nacional · Esta semana en el *campus...* · la escultura · la escultora (la artista) · la escultura · la música · el baile/la danza · la bailarina · la pintura · el cuadro / la pintura · el cantante · el pintor (el artista) · el bailarín · el ballet · los aficionados · los aficionados

La expresión artística			
la arquitectura	architecture	pintar	to paint
el cine	film; movies	tejer	to weave
la fotografía	photography		
la literatura	literature	**Otras personas**	
el teatro	theater	el/la arquitecto/a	architect
		el/la compositor(a)	composer
cantar	to sing	el/la director(a)	director
crear	to create	el/la dramaturgo/a	playwright
dibujar	to draw	el/la escritor(a)	writer
escribir	to write	el/la escultor(a)	sculptor
esculpir	to sculpt	el/la pintor(a)	painter
		el/la poeta	poet

*The word **arte** is both masculine and feminine. The masculine articles and adjectives are normally used with **arte** in the singular while the feminine ones are used in the plural. Note that **las artes** often refers to "the arts" in general: Guillermo es estudiante **del arte moderno.**/Me gustan mucho **las artes gráficas.**

Capítulo 13: El arte y la cultura

MULTIMEDIA: Audio

Students can listen to and practice this chapter's vocabulary on the Online Learning Center (**www.mhhe.com/puntos7**) as well as on the Textbook Audio CD, part of the Laboratory Audio Program.

National Standards: Connections

- ***El lago de los cisnes*** (1877), a ballet set to music by Peter Ilyich Tchaikovsky (Russia, 1840–1893), tells the story of a woman who turns into a swan.
- ***El amor brujo*** (*Love, the magician*) is a ballet written in 1915 by the Spanish composer Manual de Falla (1876–1946).
- ***El ciudadano Kane*** (*Citizen Kane*, 1941) is a classic considered by many the best American film ever. Making his film debut at the age of 25, Orson Welles was at once the actor, cowriter, and director.

La tradición cultural		Otras palabras útiles	
la artesanía	arts and crafts	la canción	song
la cerámica	pottery; ceramics	el guión	script
las ruinas	ruins	la obra (de arte)	work (of art)
los tejidos	woven goods	la obra maestra	masterpiece

■■■ Conversación

A. Obras de arte

Paso 1. ¿Qué tipo de arte representan las siguientes obras?

1. la catedral de Notre Dame y la de Santiago de Compostela
2. los murales de Diego Rivera
3. las estatuas griegas y romanas
4. *El lago de los cisnes* (*Swan Lake*) y *El amor brujo* (*Love, the Magician*)
5. *El ciudadano Kane*
6. *La Bohème* y *La Traviata*
7. las ruinas aztecas y mayas
8. *Don Quijote*
9. la Torre Eiffel de Paris
10. *la Mona Lisa* de Leonardo da Vinci
11. «*El cuervo* (*Raven*)» de Edgar Allen Poe
12. las imágenes de Ansel Adams
13. las canciones de Norah Jones
14. *El mago* (*Wizard*) *de Oz* (¡**OJO!** Hay dos respuestas posibles.)

Paso 2. Ahora dé otros ejemplos de obras en cada una de las categorías artísticas que Ud. mencionó en el **Paso 1**.

B. ¿Qué hacen?

Paso 1. Forme oraciones completas, emparejando palabras de cada columna. Hay más de una posibilidad en algunos casos.

MODELO: La compositora escribe canciones.

la compositora la artesana la actriz el director el músico el bailarín el dramaturgo la pintora el escritor la arquitecta el poeta	escribe baila esculpe toca compone (*composes*) interpreta diseña pinta mira trabaja dirige (*directs*) teje	novelas canciones en el ballet cerámica edificios y casas papeles (*roles*) en la televisión guiones tejidos con actores obras de teatro cuadros instrumentos musicales poesía

Paso 2. Ahora, con dos o tres compañeros, dé nombres de artistas en cada categoría, ya sean (*whether they be*) hombres o mujeres. ¿Cuántos artistas hispánicos pueden nombrar?

Vocabulario: Preparación   Cuatrocientos nueve ■ **409**

Suggestion

Have students answer the following questions.

1. *¿Tiene Ud. algún tipo de talento artístico? ¿Cuál es? ¿Desarrolla (develop) Ud. su talento?*
2. *¿Tiene un pintor favorito / una pintora favorita? ¿Quién es? ¿Le gusta la pintura abstracta o figurativa?*
3. *Para Ud., ¿qué es más importante, que un edificio sea elegante o práctico? ¿Qué tipo de arquitectura le gusta más? ¿Le gusta la arquitectura de su universidad? Explique.*
4. *Para Ud., ¿qué es más importante en una película, el guión, la dirección o la actuación? ¿Quiénes son sus actores favoritos? ¿Tiene algún director favorito o alguna directora favorita? ¿Quién es?*

Con. A: Suggestion

Paso 2. Ask for works of art by Hispanic artists. This can be assigned as homework.

Con. A: Notes

■ Students can read about Diego Rivera and other Mexican muralists in *Conozca... México*, p. 87.
■ Information about Don Quijote is provided in the annotations on p. 298.
■ Information on *Cien años de soledad* is provided in *Literatura de Colombia* in *Capítulo 9*.

Con. B: Suggestion

Paso 2. Do this *paso* as a contest. Have each group write their answers on the board so that everyone can see what they came up with. Provide the following names after completing the activity.

el cine: Robert Rodríguez, Pedro Almodóvar, Antonio Banderas, Luis Buñuel, Salma Hayek
la literatura: Isabel Allende, Laura Esquivel, Gabriel García Márquez, Octavio Paz, Carlos Fuentes
la música: Manuel de Falla, Pablo Casals, Gloria Estefan, Julio Iglesias, Tito Puente, Carlos Santana, Los Lobos, Ricky Martin, Jennifer López
la pintura: Frida Kahlo, Diego Rivera, José Clemente Orozco, Salvador Dalí, Pablo Picasso
la arquitectura: Antoní Gaudí

National Standards: Connections (*continued*)

■ *El mago de Oz* (*The Wonderful Wizard of Oz*, 1900), written by L. Frank Baum (1856–1919), an American journalist, playwright, and author of juvenile stories, was made into a movie in 1938.
■ *La Bohème,* first produced in 1896, was the first of three operas that Puccini wrote with the librettists Illica and Giacosa (the others were *Madama Butterfly* and *Tosca*). Based on Murger's autobiographical *Scènes de la vie de Bohème,* this opera depicts the lives of artists in Paris in the mid-1800s.

■ *La Traviata,* an opera written by Giuseppi Verdi (1813–1901), mounts a romantic attack on conventional bourgeois morality. The story argues that a good heart is more important than propriety and that true love must triumph over all.
■ *Leonardo da Vinci* (1452–1519) was an Italian painter, draftsman, sculptor, architect, and engineer, whose genius, perhaps more than that of any other figure, epitomized the Renaissance humanist ideal. The *Mona Lisa* (1503–1506) is one the most well-known paintings of all time.

NOTA COMUNICATIVA

Suggestions

- Offer the following optional word: *atraer* → *Me atrae el ballet moderno.*
- Point out that *apreciar* is like *odiar.* They both require direct objects.

Con. C: Follow-Up

Have each student write another cultural cue on a piece of paper. Collect all papers and write the cultural cues on the board so that students can answer them. Encourage both silly and serious cues.

NOTA COMUNICATIVA

Más sobre los gustos y preferencias

Here are some additional verbs to talk about what you like and don't like.

- The following two verbs are used like **gustar.**

aburrir	**Me aburre** el ballet moderno. *Modern ballet bores me.*
agradar	Pero **me agrada** el ballet folklórico. *But I like (I am pleased by) folkloric dances.*

- This verb functions as a transitive verb (one that can take a direct object).

apreciar	**Aprecio** mucho la arquitectura precolombina. *I really appreciate pre-Columbian architecture.*

C. Preferencias personales

Paso 1. ¿Le gusta el arte? ¿Asiste a funciones culturales de vez en cuando o no asiste a esas funciones nunca? ¡Diga la verdad! (En otras actividades va a hablar de lo que prefiere en general.)

> MODELO: asistir a los ballets clásicos →
> Me gusta mucho asistir a los ballets clásicos.
> (No me agrada para nada asistir a los ballets clásicos. Es aburrido.)
> (Me aburre asistir a los ballets clásicos. Prefiero ir a la ópera.)

Palabras útiles	
aburrir	gustar
agradar	interesar
apreciar	preferir (ie)
encantar	

1. asistir a los ballets clásicos
2. ir a los museos de arte moderno
3. asistir a funciones teatrales
4. ver obras maestras en los museos grandes
5. ir a conciertos de música clásica
6. asistir a lecturas de poesía en un café
7. ver películas extranjeras (*foreign*)
8. asistir a la ópera

Paso 2. Entrevista. Ahora entreviste a un compañero / una compañera para saber cuáles son sus preferencias con respecto a este tema.

> MODELO: E1: ¿Te gusta ir a los museos de arte moderno?
> E2: Sí, me gusta muchísimo. Voy siempre que puedo (*whenever I can*).

National Standards: Connections (*continued from p. 409*)

- ***Edgar Allan Poe*** (1809–1849), born in Boston, was a poet and fiction writer. He was the master of the horror tale and is considered by many to be the inventor of the detective story. "The Raven" is perhaps his most famous poem.
- ***Norah Jones*** was born in New York City in 1979 but grew up in Dallas, Texas with her mother, Sue. Her father is the renowned sitar player Ravi Shankar. Her debut album, *Come Away with Me*, won eight Grammy awards in 2002.

Refrán

«Quien tiene arte va a toda parte.»

Have students brainstorm possible meanings for this *refrán*. (*He who has a trade/profession to offer, flourishes everywhere.*)

Los toros

El toreo[a] es un espectáculo típicamente hispánico. Viene de una larga tradición histórica. De hecho, no se sabe exactamente cuándo surgió la primera **corrida de toros.**[b]

Para sus aficionados, el toreo es **un arte, y el torero** necesita mucho más que valor:[c] necesita destreza[d] técnica, gracia y mucha comprensión de **los toros.** Algunos creen que el toreo *no es* un arte, sino un espectáculo cruel y violento que causa la muerte[e] prematura e innecesaria de un animal valiente.

Sea cual sea la opinión que Ud. tiene[f] de las corridas de toros, las corridas son muy simbólicas para los hispanos. El toro es símbolo de fuerza,[g] coraje, bravura, independencia y belleza.[h] Si Ud. visita un país hispánico y tiene ganas de ver una corrida, es aconsejable que les pregunte a algunas personas nativas cuáles son las corridas que debe ver.

Aunque el toreo es **de origen español,** hoy es una fiesta igualmente famosa en muchos países latinoamericanos, como Colombia, el Ecuador, el Perú, Venezuela, Bolivia, Panamá, Guatemala y México. México, D.F., tiene **la plaza de toros más grande del mundo,** la Plaza Monumental, con más de 40.000 asientos.

[a]El... *Bullfighting* [b]corrida... *bullfight* [c]*bravery* [d]*skill* [e]*death* [f]Sea... *Whatever your opinion may be* [g]*strength* [h]*beauty*

▲ *Una corrida de toros en Toledo, España*

Suggestions

- Some *toreros* have belonged to elite intellectual bullfighting groups. *Toreros* are an important part of the Spanish folklore, appearing in well-known poems by poets such as García Lorca as well as in traditional songs.
- *Toreras* are beginning to appear, although none yet carries the *carisma* of a well-known bullfighter.
- Have students search for the names of some famous *toreros* and *plazas de toros* on the Internet.
- Ask questions to check comprehension.

  1. *¿Cuándo empezó la tradición del toreo?*
  2. *¿Qué simbolismo tiene una corrida de toros para los hispanos?*
  3. *¿Cuál es la plaza de toros más grande del mundo?*

D. Entrevista

1. ¿Tienes talento artístico? ¿Para qué? ¿Qué te gusta crear? ¿Cuándo empezaste a desarrollar (*develop*) esta actividad? ¿Tienes aspiraciones de dedicarte a esa actividad profesionalmente? ¿Cuáles son las ventajas y las desventajas de esa ocupación?

2. Si crees que no posees ningún talento artístico en particular, ¿sientes alguna atracción por el arte? ¿Qué tipo de arte en particular? ¿Por qué te gusta tanto?

3. ¿Te gusta ir a los mercados de artesanía? ¿Qué compras allí? Cuando vas de viaje, ¿te interesa saber cuáles son los trajes (*outfits*) y la música tradicionales del lugar que visitas? ¿Coleccionas obras de artesanía? ¿Qué coleccionas?

4. ¿Qué funciones teatrales te gustan? ¿Hay muchas oportunidades en esta ciudad / este pueblo (*town*) para asistir a interpretaciones (*performances*) de baile, música o drama? ¿Qué tipo de interpretaciones te gustan más?

MULTIMEDIA: Internet

Have students search the Internet for information about the history of bullfighting.

☼ Heritage Speakers

Pregúnteles a sus estudiantes hispanohablantes si han visto una corrida de toros. ¿Qué opinan? ¿Es un arte o un acto violento?

Ranking Things: Ordinals

Suggestions

- Select a row of students and identify the first ten using ordinal numbers, for example: *Juan es el primer estudiante, Isabel es la segunda estudiante, Susana es la tercera,* and so on.
- Remind students that they have used *el primero* with dates, and in *Capítulo 12* they used a few ordinal numbers to refer to floors of a building.
- Point out that cardinal numbers are more commonly used than ordinal numbers above tenth: *Alfonso XIII (trece).*

Preliminary Exercise

Have students respond *cierto* or *falso* to the following sentences.

1. *El (lunes) es el (primer) día de la semana.* (Vary days, creating some incorrect items.)
2. *(Enero) es el (primer) mes del año.* (Vary months, creating some incorrect items.)
3. *Bob es el (quinto) estudiante en esta fila.*

Con. A: Suggestions

Have students rank in order of importance to them the following characteristics in each category.

- **Los cursos para el próximo semestre/trimestre**

  la hora de la clase
  el profesor / la profesora
  la materia
  la posibilidad de sacar una buena nota
  el costo de los libros
  si tiene laboratorio o no
  el edificio donde se da la clase
  el tamaño (size) de la clase

- **La selección de un trabajo**

  el sueldo
  el prestigio de la compañía
  la ciudad
  la posibilidad de ascenso (promotion)
  la personalidad del jefe / de la jefa
  las condiciones físicas de la oficina
  si tiene una oficina privada o no

primer(o/a)	first	**cuarto/a**	fourth	**sexto/a**	sixth	**noveno/a**	ninth
segundo/a	second	**quinto/a**	fifth	**séptimo/a**	seventh	**décimo/a**	tenth
tercer(o/a)	third			**octavo/a**	eighth		

- Ordinal numbers are adjectives and must agree in number and gender with the nouns they modify. Ordinals usually precede the noun: **la cuarta lección, el octavo ejercicio.**
- Like **bueno,** the ordinals **primero** and **tercero** shorten to **primer** and **tercer,** respectively, before masculine singular nouns: **el primer niño, el tercer mes.**
- Ordinal numbers are frequently abbreviated with superscript letters that show the adjective ending: **las 1as lecciones, el 1^r grado, el 5° estudiante.**

■■■Conversación

A. Mis actividades favoritas

Paso 1. Piense en lo que le gusta hacer en su tiempo libre en cuanto a (*regarding*) actividades culturales. Luego ponga en el orden de su preferencia (del 1 al 10) las siguientes actividades.

_____ ir al cine
_____ ir a ver películas extranjeras o clásicas
_____ ir a museos
_____ asistir a conciertos de música clásica/rock
_____ leer poesía

_____ bailar en una discoteca
_____ ver programas de televisión
_____ ver obras teatrales
_____ leer una novela
_____ ¿ ?

Paso 2. Ahora cuéntele a un compañero / una compañera sus cinco actividades favoritas. Use números ordinales.

> **MODELO:** Mi actividad favorita es ir a ver películas clásicas. Mi segunda actividad favorita es…

B. Preguntas

1. ¿Es Ud. estudiante de cuarto año?
2. ¿Es este su segundo semestre/trimestre de español?
3. ¿A qué hora es su primera clase los lunes? ¿y su segunda clase?
4. ¿Vive Ud. en una casa de apartamentos o en una residencia? ¿En qué piso vive? Si vive en una casa, ¿en qué piso está su alcoba?

Need more practice?

- Workbook and Laboratory Manual
- Interactive CD-ROM
- Online Learning Center (www.mhhe.com/puntos7)

Refrán

«Quien primero viene, primero muele.»

Have students guess the meaning of *muele.* Remind them that *la muela* means molar (*Capítulo 10*). Then have them brainstorm the English equivalent of this *refrán.* (*First come, first served.*)

GRAMÁTICA

39 Expressing Feelings • Use of the Subjunctive: Emotion

Diego y Lupe escuchan un grupo de mariachis

▲ *México, D.F.*

DIEGO: Ay, ¡cómo me encanta esta música!

LUPE: *Me alegro de que te guste.*

DIEGO: Y yo *me alegro de que estemos* aquí. ¿Sabes el origen de la palabra **mariachi**?

LUPE: No… ¿Lo sabes tú?

DIEGO: Bueno, una teoría es que viene del siglo diecinueve, cuando los franceses ocuparon México. Ellos contrataban a grupos de músicos para tocar en las bodas. Y como los mexicanos no podían pronunciar bien la palabra francesa *mariage*, pues acabaron por decir **mariachi**. Y de allí viene el nombre de los grupos.

LUPE: ¡Qué fascinante! *Me sorprende que sepas* tantos datos interesantes de nuestra historia.

DIEGO: Pues, todo buen antropólogo debe saber un poco de historia también, ¿no?

Comprensión

1. Lupe se alegra de que _____.
2. Y Diego se alegra de que _____.
3. A Lupe le sorprende que _____.

MAIN (INDEPENDENT) CLAUSE		SUBORDINATE (DEPENDENT) CLAUSE
first subject + *indicative* (expression of emotion)	**que**	second subject + *subjunctive*

A. Expressions of emotion are those in which speakers express their feelings: *I'm glad you're here; It's good that they can come.* Such expressions of emotion are followed by the subjunctive mood in the subordinate (dependent) clause in Spanish.

Esperamos que Ud. **pueda** asistir.
We hope (that) you'll be able to come.

Tengo miedo de que mi abuelo **esté** muy enfermo.
I'm afraid (that) my grandfather is very ill.

Es una lástima que no **den** aumentos este año.
It's a shame (that) they're not giving raises this year.

Diego and Lupe are listening to a mariachi group DIEGO: *Oh, how I love this music!* LUPE: *I'm glad you like it.* DIEGO: *And I'm glad we're here. Do you know the origin of the word* **mariachi**? LUPE: *No … Do you? * DIEGO: *Well, one theory is that it comes from the nineteenth century, when the French occupied Mexico. They used to hire musical groups to play at weddings. And because the Mexicans couldn't correctly pronounce the French word* mariage, *they ended up saying* **mariachi**. *And so that's where the name of the groups comes from.* LUPE: *How fascinating! I'm surprised you know so much interesting information about our history.* DIEGO: *Well, all good anthropologists should also know a little bit of history, shouldn't they?*

Gramática

MULTIMEDIA: Internet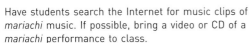

Have students search the Internet for music clips of *mariachi* music. If possible, bring a video or CD of a *mariachi* performance to class.

 Heritage Speakers

Anime a los hispanohablantes a describir a los mariachis. ¿Qué tipo de ropa llevan? ¿Dónde suelen cantar? ¿Cuáles son los temas que predominan en sus canciones?

National Standards: Culture

The *mariachi* is essentially a mixture of European and indigenous musical cultures that probably began in the 16th century. There is no mention, however, of the *mariachi* until the 19th century. The origin of the word *mariachi* is a mystery, but there are two principal theories. Most scholars believe that *mariachi* is a derivation of an indigenous word related to music. A widely circulated theory, although less supported by scholars, is that *mariachi* is a corruption of the French word *mariage*.

Note

There is more than one theory regarding the origin of the word *mariachi*. Currently, the most favored theory among scholars is that the word has its origin in a Coca Indian word for music maker. The Coca were one of many indigenous groups that lived in parts of Mexico.

Suggestion

Have students pick out the subjunctive and subjunctive cues in the *minidiálogo*. Ask: What do the cues have in common? (emotional responses)

Follow-Up

Ask students the following questions to check comprehension.

*¿Le sorprende a Ud. que la palabra **mariachi** venga del francés?*
¿De qué cosas se alegra Ud.?
¿Qué le molesta que haga su compañero/a de cuarto/casa (esposo/a, etcétera)?
¿Qué le sorprende de la clase de español?

Emphasis A: Suggestions

■ Point out that a change of subject is required for the subjunctive with emotional statements, just as with expressions of influence.

■ Emphasize the use of the infinitive, not the subjunctive, after expressions and generalizations of emotion when there is no change of subject.

Siento estar tan cansado. vs. *Siento que estés tan cansado.*
Es mejor esperar. vs. *Es mejor que esperen.*

B. Some common expressions of emotion are found in the list and drawing at the right.

alegrarse de	*to be happy about*
esperar	*to hope*
sentir (ie, i)	*to regret; to feel sorry*
tener miedo (de)	*to be afraid (of)*

temer: Temo que María **se caiga** durante el baile.
I'm afraid that María will fall during the dance.

At the right are some common expressions of emotion used with indirect object pronouns. Not all Spanish expressions of emotion are given here. Remember that any expression of emotion is followed by the subjunctive in the dependent clause.

me (te, le,...)	I'm (you're, he's . . .)
gusta que	glad that

Me molesta que **fumen** en la galería.
It bothers me that they smoke in the gallery.

Nos sorprende que este cantante **tenga** tanto éxito.
It surprises us that this singer is so successful.

 Heritage Speakers

Note que los hispanohablantes a veces retienen la cláusula dependiente a pesar de que no haya cambio de sujeto.

Espero que (yo) saque una buena nota en el examen.
Siento que (yo) lo haya ofendido.

Anime a los hispanohablantes a describir la diferencia estructural o gramatical entre los siguientes pares de oraciones.

Me alegro de que (yo) haya sacado una buena nota.
Me alegro de haber sacado una buena nota.

Espero que (yo) pueda asistir a la boda.
Espero poder asistir a la boda.

C. When a new subject is introduced after a generalization of emotion, it is followed by the subjunctive in the subordinate (dependent) clause. Here are some general expressions of emotion.

es extraño que...	it's strange that . . .
es increíble que...	it's incredible that . . .
es mejor/bueno/ malo que...	it's better/good/ bad that . . .
es ridículo que...	it's ridiculous that . . .
es terrible que...	it's terrible that . . .
es una lástima que...	it's a shame that . . .
es urgente que...	it's urgent that . . .
¡qué extraño que...!	how strange that . . . !
¡qué lástima que...!	what a shame that . . . !

AUTOPRUEBA

Identify the sentences that would require the subjunctive when expressed in Spanish.

1. ☐ I'm surprised you're here.
2. ☐ We're happy about the prize.
3. ☐ They're afraid of the director.
4. ☐ It's good that they want all of your paintings.
5. ☐ I hope to attend the concert.

Answers: 1, 4

■■■ Práctica

A. Opiniones sobre el cine

Paso 1. **¡Anticipemos!** ¿Ciertas o falsas?

1. Me molesta que muchas películas sean tan violentas.
2. Es ridículo que algunos actores ganen tanto dinero.
3. Espero que salgan más actores asiáticos e hispánicos en las películas.
4. Temo que muchas actrices no desempeñen (*play*) papeles inteligentes.
5. Es increíble que gasten millones de dólares en hacer películas.
6. Me sorprende que Julia Roberts sea tan famosa.

Paso 2. Ahora invente oraciones sobre lo que Ud. quiere o no quiere que pase con respecto al cine. Use las oraciones del **Paso 1** como base.

MODELO: 1. Quiero que las películas sean menos violentas.

B. Comentarios. Complete las oraciones con la forma apropiada del verbo entre paréntesis.

1. Dicen en la tienda que esta videocasetera es fácil de usar. Por eso me sorprende que no (funcionar) bien. Temo que (ser) muy complicada. Me sorprende que ni (*not even*) mi compañera (entenderla).
2. ¡Qué desastre! El profesor dice que nos va a dar un examen. ¡Es increíble que (darnos) otro examen tan pronto! Es terrible que yo (tener) que estudiar este fin de semana. Espero que el profesor (cambiar) de idea.
3. Este año sólo tengo dos semanas de vacaciones. Es ridículo que sólo (tener) dos semanas. No me gusta que las vacaciones (ser) tan breves. Es una lástima que yo no (poder) ir a ningún sitio.

Gramática

Prác. A: Preliminary Exercises

■ Use the following chain drill to practice forms:

1. *Espero que tú sepas el número correcto.* (Ud., ella, nosotros, Uds.)
2. *Los padres tienen miedo de que seamos malos estudiantes.* (yo, tú, ellos, Elvira)
3. *Es una lástima que no podamos ir al museo.* (yo, Uds., él, vosotras)

■ Have students express the following ideas in Spanish.

1. I'm afraid that they're not coming / that he can't do it.
2. It surprises me that you can't do it / that he won't permit it.

Prác. A: Follow-Up

Have students give two opinions of their own. Use *Paso 1* as a model. Use *Paso 2* as a model for ensuing suggestions and wishes.

Prác. B: Suggestions

■ Have students invent similar situations and present them to the class.
■ Have students explain the choice of mood in all the sentences in the activity.
■ Have students express the following ideas in Spanish.

1. I'm sorry that your daughter is sick.
2. It's incredible that Johnny is already 12 years old!
3. What a shame that Julio isn't feeling well!
4. How strange that Jorge never calls you!
5. I'm glad that you're going to get the painting for your grandmother.

MULTIMEDIA: Internet

Have students search the Internet for Spanish language newspapers (*La Jornada*, for example). Based on current news events, students should prepare five statements expressing their emotions and using the subjunctive, for example: *Es increíble que haya tanto turismo en Costa Rica.*

NOTA COMUNICATIVA

Notes

■ **¡OJO!** *Ojalá* is invariable in form and is always followed by the subjunctive. *Ojalá* itself is not conjugated.

■ *Ojalá* comes from the Arabic expression that means *Allah* (*God*) *willing* or *may Allah want*. Point out that Arabs lived in most of what is today Spain and Portugal for eight centuries (8th–15th). Their influence was great in the Iberian Peninsula; their language, especially, influenced Spanish vocabulary. Other commonly used Spanish words that come from Arabic include *el álgebra, el aceite, la almohada* (pillow).

Prác. C: Follow-Up

Ask students: *¿A Ud. le interesa la ópera? ¿Le fascina, le aburre o no tiene opinión?*

Con. A: Suggestions

■ Show the overhead transparency and have students close their books. Ask questions and have volunteers answer.

■ Have students work in groups to react to each situation, and then resolve it by giving advice or making a request, for example:

Situación: Su profesor(a) de español les da muchos exámenes. → Reacción: (No) Me gusta eso. Quiero que nos dé más/menos exámenes. Solución: Profesor(a), dénos más/menos exámenes, por favor.

1. *Su profesor(a) les habla muy rápidamente en español.*
2. *En un restaurante, no hay asientos en la sección de no fumar y Ud. se sienta al lado de un señor que fuma mucho.*
3. *Su vecino/a pone el estéreo por la mañana mientras Ud. trata de estudiar.*
4. *Sus padres (amigos) siempre van de vacaciones al mismo sitio todos los veranos.*

NOTA COMUNICATIVA

Expressing Wishes with *ojalá*

The word **ojalá** is invariable in form and means *I wish* or *I hope*. It is used with the subjunctive to express wishes or hopes. The use of **que** with it is optional.

¡Ojalá (que) yo **gane** la lotería algún día!	*I hope (that) I win the lottery some day!*
¡Ojalá (que) haya paz en el mundo algún día!	*I hope (that) there will be peace in the world some day!*
Ojalá (que) no **pierdan** tu equipaje.	*I hope (that) they don't lose your luggage.*

Ojalá can also be used alone as an interjection in response to a question.

—¿Te va a ayudar Julio a estudiar para el examen?
—**¡Ojalá!**

Need more practice?

■ Workbook and Laboratory Manual
■ Interactive CD-ROM
■ Online Learning Center (www.mhhe.com/puntos7)

C. Una excursión a la ópera. Imagine que Ud. y su amigo/a van a la ópera por primera vez en su vida. Piense en todas las expectativas que Ud. tiene y exprésalas usando **ojalá.**

> **MODELO:** las entradas (*tickets*) **/** no costar mucho →
> Ojalá que las entradas no cuesten mucho.

1. el escenario **/** ser **/** extravagante
2. haber **/** subtítulos **/** en inglés
3. el director (*conductor*) **/** estar **/** preparado
4. los cantantes **/** saber **/** sus papeles
5. nuestros asientos **/** no estar **/** lejos del escenario
6. (nosotros) llegar **/** a tiempo

■■■ Conversación

①

A. Situaciones. Las siguientes personas están pensando en otra persona o en algo que van a hacer. ¿Qué emociones sienten? ¿Qué temen? Conteste las preguntas según los dibujos.

1. Jorge piensa en su amiga Estela. ¿Por qué piensa en ella? ¿Dónde está? ¿Qué siente Jorge? ¿Qué espera? ¿Qué espera Estela? ¿Espera que la visiten los amigos? ¿que le manden algo?
2. Fausto quiere comer fuera esta noche. ¿Quiere que alguien lo acompañe? ¿Dónde espera que cenen? ¿Qué teme Fausto? ¿Qué le parecen (*seem*) los precios del restaurante?
3. ¿Dónde quiere pasar las vacaciones Mariana? ¿Espera que alguien la acompañe? ¿Dónde espera que pasen los días? ¿Qué teme Mariana? ¿Qué espera?

②

③

Capítulo 13: El arte y la cultura

Resources: Transparency 85

☀ **Heritage Speakers**

Algunos hispanohablantes eliminan *que* después de *ojalá.* Varios tiempos verbales, además del presente del subjuntivo, aparecen después de esta expresión impersonal. Anime a los hispanohablantes a explicar la diferencia entre las siguientes oraciones.

Ojalá que llueva hoy.
Ojalá que lloviera hoy.
Ojalá que haya llovido.
Ojalá que hubiera llovido ayer.

B. Los valores de nuestra sociedad. Express your feelings about the following situations by restating the situations, beginning with one of the following phrases or any others you can think of: **es bueno/malo que, es extraño/increíble que, es una lástima que.**

MODELO: Los futbolistas profesionales ganan sueldos fenomenales →
Es increíble que los futbolistas ganen sueldos fenomenales.

1. Muchas personas viven para trabajar. No saben descansar.
2. Somos una sociedad de consumidores.
3. Muchas personas no asisten a las funciones teatrales.
4. Juzgamos (*We judge*) a los otros por las cosas materiales que tienen.
5. Las personas ricas tienen mucho prestigio en esta sociedad.
6. Las mujeres generalmente no ganan tanto como los hombres cuando hacen el mismo trabajo.
7. Algunas obras de arte cuestan millones de dólares.
8. Para la gente (*people*) joven la televisión es más popular que los libros.
9. Los hombres generalmente no reciben *paternity leave* después del nacimiento (*birth*) de un bebé.
10. Hay discriminación contra la gente mayor para ciertas profesiones.

C. ¿Qué le molesta más? The following phrases describe aspects of university life. React to them, using phrases such as: **Me gusta que..., Me molesta que..., Es terrible que...**

MODELO: Gastan mucho/poco dinero en construir nuevos edificios. →
Me molesta que gasten mucho dinero en construir nuevos edificios.

1. Se pone mucho énfasis en los deportes.
2. Pagamos mucho/poco por la matrícula.
3. Se ofrecen muchos/pocos cursos en mi especialización (*major*).
4. Es necesario estudiar ciencias/lenguas para graduarse.
5. Hay muchos/pocos requisitos (*requirements*) para graduarse.
6. En general, hay muchas/pocas personas en las clases.

D. Tres deseos. Imagine que Ud. tiene tres deseos: uno que se relaciona con Ud. personalmente, otro con algún amigo o miembro de su familia y otro con su país, para el mundo o para la humanidad en general. Exprese sus deseos con **Ojalá (que)...**

MODELO: Ojalá que no haya otra guerra.

Palabras útiles	
las elecciones	el partido
la gente que no tiene hogar (casa)	la pobreza (poverty)
la guerra (war)	
el hambre (hunger)	resolver (ue) (to solve; to resolve)
el millonario / la millonaria	terminar (to end)

Con. B: Follow-Up

Follow up with a similar activity that uses real-world statements related to students.

1. (*Estudiante*) está enfermo/a hoy.
2. *No tenemos clase el sábado.*
3. (*Estudiante*) se gradúa en junio.
4. *El coche de _____ no funciona bien.*
5. *Llueve mucho/poco este año.*

Con. C: Suggestion

Have students complete the activity in groups of four to six. Have one student act as the secretary, taking notes on general reactions. Later he/she will summarize the comments of his/her group with sentences like: *Nuestro grupo piensa / opina / dice / no está de acuerdo en...* General results from all groups can serve as a starting point for a simple discussion or a debate.

Suggestion

Have students explain the uses of the subjunctive in the sentences.

Bright Idea

Suggestions

- Point out to students that they should be able to do the following.

  1. identify the independent clause
  2. identify the dependent clause
  3. locate expressions of influence, emotion, and feeling in the independent clause that require the use of the subjunctive in the dependent clause

- Have students provide expressions of influence, desire, request, emotion, and feeling that require the use of the subjunctive in the dependent clause.

Follow-Up

Show another painting and have students react to it with similar sentences.

Emphasis A: Suggestions

- Point out the similarity of this pattern (two verbs, a second subject) to that of the subjunctive after expressions of influence/emotion.
- Point out that when there is no subject change, Spanish uses either the subjunctive or the infinitive after expressions of doubt or denial. Generalizations are followed by the infinitive only when there is no subject change. *Dudo que Juan tenga el dinero. / Dudo tener el dinero.* = I doubt that I have the money. *Es imposible tener el dinero para mañana.* vs. *Es imposible que yo tenga el dinero para mañana.*

Emphasis B: Suggestions

- Contrast and model *no creer* and *dudar* (subjunctive) with *creer*, which usually implies affirmation and is therefore followed by the indicative.
- Point out that an easy rule is that *all* negated verbs take subjunctive in the dependent clause. *No niego* and *no dudo* are the only exceptions. They can take either the subjunctive or the indicative, depending on the meaning the speaker wishes to convey. Most students are not ready for these subtleties, and the use of *no niego* and *no dudo* should be restricted for now.

---

40 Expressing Uncertainty • Use of the Subjunctive: Doubt and Denial

Mire Ud. la pintura detenidamente (*carefully*) y luego complete las siguientes oraciones de acuerdo con su opinión.

Vocabulario útil	
la alegría	happiness
la esperanza	hope
los guardias	guardsmen
el miedo	fear
la tristeza	sadness

1. *Es posible que* los miembros de esta familia tengan (miedo/esperanza). Estoy seguro/a de que no tienen (miedo/esperanza).
2. Creo que los colores representan (la alegría / la tristeza). *Dudo que* representen (la alegría / la tristeza).
3. *Es probable que* los guardias estén (enojados/contentos). Estoy seguro/a de que no están (enojados/contentos).

▲ Familia andina, *por Héctor Poleo (venezolano, 1918–1989)*

MAIN (INDEPENDENT) CLAUSE		SUBORDINATE (DEPENDENT) CLAUSE
first subject + *indicative* (expression of doubt or denial)	**que**	second subject + *subjunctive*

A. Expressions of doubt and denial are those in which speakers express uncertainty or negation. Such expressions, however strong or weak, are followed by the subjunctive in the dependent clause in Spanish.

No creo que **sean** sus cuadros.
I don't believe they're her paintings.

Es imposible que ella **esté** en el escenario.
It's impossible for her to be on the stage.

B. Some expressions of doubt and denial appear at the right. Not all Spanish expressions of doubt are given here. Remember that any expression of doubt is followed by the subjunctive in the dependent clause.

no creer	*to disbelieve*
dudar	*to doubt*
no estar seguro/a (de)	*to be unsure (of)*
negar (ie) (gu)	*to deny*

National Standards: Comparisons

Expressions of certainty (not doubt) are used with the subjunctive by some native speakers to convey that they are not absolutely sure or do not necessarily believe the statement. For example, *No dudo que Juan tenga suerte* or *Creo que los vecinos hayan llegado.* Have students think about ways that doubt is cast on statements in English (tone of voice, intonation, tag statements such as *not!*, and so on).

Creer and **estar seguro/a** are usually followed by the indicative in affirmative statements because they do not express doubt, denial, or negation. Compare these examples.

Estamos seguros de (Creemos) que el concierto **es** hoy.
We're sure (We believe) the concert is today.

No estamos seguros de (No creemos) que el concierto **sea** hoy.
We're not sure (We don't believe) that the concert is today.

C. When a new subject is introduced after a generalization of doubt, the subjunctive is used in the dependent clause. Some generalizations of doubt and denial are included at the right.

 Generalizations that express certainty are not followed by the subjunctive but by the indicative: **Es verdad que cocina bien. No hay duda de que Julio lo paga.**

es posible que...	it's possible that . . .
es imposible que...	it's impossible that . . .
es probable que...	it's probable (likely) that . . .
es improbable que...	it's improbable (unlikely) that . . .
no es cierto que...	it's not certain that . . .
no es seguro que...	it's not a sure thing that . . .
no es verdad que...	it's not true that . . .

- In questions with *creer*, the use of the indicative or subjunctive in dependent clauses reflects the opinion of the person asking the question. Indicative: *¿Crees que los Ramírez son ricos?* (The speaker believes they are.) Subjunctive: *¿Crees que los Ramírez sean ricos?* (The speaker doubts that they are.)

Emphasis B: Preliminary Exercises

Have students express the following ideas in Spanish.

1. I doubt that they are rich / that they are coming.
2. I don't believe that they are rich / that they are coming.
3. I believe that they are rich / that they are coming.

Emphasis C: Suggestion

Emphasize and model the indicative used after *es verdad*, *es cierto*, and *es seguro*.

Prác. A: Preliminary Exercises

- Have students indicate whether the following expressions would require the indicative or the subjunctive.

   1. *Es cierto que...*
   2. *No estamos seguros de que...*
   3. *No es verdad que...*
   4. *Dudo que...*
   5. *No creo que...*
   6. *Es imposible que...*
   7. *Es probable que...*
   8. *Estamos seguros que...*
   9. *No es cierto que...*
   10. *Es improbable que...*

- Have students tell whether the following sentences would require the indicative or the subjunctive in Spanish.

   1. I'm sure she's right.
   2. I doubt we'll get there on time.
   3. I don't think they know.
   4. It's impossible that he knows.
   5. We believe she's at home.
   6. I don't doubt that they will go.
   7. It's true that Susan always arrives on time.
   8. They don't believe I know how to cook.

AUTOPRUEBA

Identify the phrases that express doubt or denial.

1. ☐ dudamos
2. ☐ estoy segura
3. ☐ niegas
4. ☐ es cierto
5. ☐ es posible
6. ☐ no cree

Answers: 1, 3, 5, 6

■ ■ ■ Práctica

A. ¿Qué opina Ud.?

Paso 1. Lea las siguientes oraciones e indique lo que opina de cada una.

	ES CIERTO	NO ES CIERTO
1. A la mayoría de la gente le gusta ir a museos.	☐	☐
2. Todos mis amigos prefieren el teatro al cine.	☐	☐
3. Conozco a muchas personas que son aficionadas a la arquitectura.	☐	☐
4. En esta clase hay mucha gente con talento artístico.	☐	☐
5. La expresión artística más popular entre los jóvenes es la música.	☐	☐
6. Me encanta regalar objetos de cerámica.	☐	☐
7. Voy a conciertos de música clásica con frecuencia.	☐	☐
8. *El cascanueces* (*The Nutcracker*) es un ballet típico del mes de mayo.	☐	☐

Paso 2. Ahora diga las oraciones del **Paso 1**, empezando con **Es cierto que...** o **No es cierto que...** según sus respuestas. **¡OJO!** Hay que usar el subjuntivo con **No es cierto que...**

Gramática

CULTURE

One of the most famous archeological museums of Latin America is *El Museo del Oro del Banco de la República de Colombia* in Bogota, Colombia. The museum owns a magnificent collection of more than 33,000 pre-Hispanic pottery pieces from the ancient Indian cultures that inhabited Colombia many years ago. Students can find more information about *El Museo del Oro*, the images of art housed there, and other Hispanic archeological museums, online.

Need more practice?

- Workbook and Laboratory Manual
- Interactive CD-ROM
- Online Learning Center (www.mhhe.com/puntos7)

Con. A: Suggestions

- Set up an "open-air market" in the classroom and have students take turns role-playing exchanges in different "booths."
- You may want to review vocabulary associated with purchasing prior to completing this activity.

cash draw

bargain

cobrar	costar	regatear
comprar	pagar	

- Ask students personalized questions regarding items in the classroom.

> *Esta camisa me costó doscientos cincuenta dólares. ¿Es posible?*
> *¿Cuánto costó esta calculadora?*
> *¿Setenta y cinco dólares?*

B. Opiniones distintas. Imagine que Ud. y un amigo / una amiga están en un museo arqueológico. En este momento están mirando una figura. Desafortunadamente, no hay ningún letrero (*sign*) cerca de Uds. para indicar lo que representa la figura. Haga oraciones completas según las indicaciones. Añada palabras cuando sea necesario.

Habla Ud.:

1. creo / que / ser / figura / de / civilización / maya
2. es cierto / que / figura / estar / hecho (*made*) / de oro
3. es posible / que / representar / dios (*god, m.*) / importante
4. no estoy seguro/a de / que / figura / ser / auténtico

Habla su amigo/a:

5. no creo / que / ser / figura / de / civilización / maya
6. creo / que / ser / de / civilización / tolteca
7. estoy seguro/a de / que / estar / hecho / de bronce
8. creo / que / representar / víctima [*m.*] / de / sacrificio humano

■ ■ ■ Conversación

A. ¿Una ganga? Imagine que Ud. va a un mercado al aire libre. Encuentra algunos objetos de artesanía muy interesantes que parecen ser de origen azteca… ¡y son baratísimos! ¿Cómo reacciona Ud.?

Empiece sus oraciones con estas frases:

1. ¡Es imposible que… !
2. No creo que…
3. Dudo muchísimo que…
4. Estoy seguro/a de que…
5. Es improbable que…

Vocabulario útil	
el calendario	calendar
la joyería	jewelry
la máscara	mask
auténtico/a	authentic
falsificado/a	forged

MULTIMEDIA: Internet

Have students search the Internet for official websites dedicated to the open-air market in Otavalo, Ecuador. They can find images of the market and view handmade *artesanías* of the Otavalo people online.

Resources: Transparency 86

CULTURE

- **Mayas:** an indigenous group in southern Mexico and Central America whose civilization reached its peak around 1000 A.D. Mayan descendents still inhabit various regions of Mexico, particularly in the Yucatan Peninsula.
- **Toltecas:** The ancient Nahuatl people of central and southern Mexico whose culture flourished in 1000 A.D.
- **Aztecs:** An ancient indigenous civilization of Central Mexico noted for their advanced culture before Cortés invaded Mexico in 1519.

Verbs That Require Prepositions

You learned in earlier chapters that when two verbs occur in a series (one right after the other), the second verb is usually the infinitive.

Prefiero *cenar* a las siete.	*I prefer to eat at seven.*

Some Spanish verbs, however, require that a preposition or other word be placed before the second verb (still the infinitive). You have already used many of the important Spanish verbs that have this feature.

■ The following verbs require the preposition **a** before an infinitive.

aprender a	empezar (ie) a	invitar a	venir a
ayudar a	enseñar a	ir a	volver (ue) a

Mis padres me **enseñaron a bailar.**	*My parents taught me to dance.*

■ These verbs or verb phrases require **de** before an infinitive.

acabar de	dejar de	tener ganas de
acordarse (ue) de	olvidarse de	tratar de

Siempre **tratamos de llegar** puntualmente.	*We always try to arrive on time.*

■ **Insistir** requires **en** before an infinitive.

Insisten en venir esta noche.	*They insist on coming over tonight.*

■ Two verbs require **que** before an infinitive: **haber que, tener que.**

Hay que ver el nuevo museo.	*It's necessary to see the new museum.*

B. ¿Qué piensa Ud. del futuro?

Paso 1. Haga oraciones con frases de cada columna para expresar su opinión sobre lo que le puede ocurrir a Ud. en los próximos cinco años. **¡OJO!** No se olvide de usar el subjuntivo en expresiones de duda o negación.

En los próximos cinco años…

(no) creo que… (no) dudo que… es (im)posible que… (no) estoy seguro/a de que… (no) es cierto que…	**+** (yo) { ir a aprender a empezar a dejar de tratar de volver a	**+** ser famoso/a estar casado/a ganar la lotería jugar a la lotería pintar cuadros fumar tener hijos terminar mis estudios esculpir ¿ ?

Paso 2. Compare sus respuestas con las de uno o dos compañeros. ¿Cuántas respuestas similares hay? ¿Cuántas diferentes?

Note

Students have used most of the verbs presented here, along with their respective prepositions and other words. Treat the material as a summary, not as new information.

Suggestions

■ Point out the use of *a* + infinitive with verbs of motion, for example, *salir a bailar, llegar a entender, ir a cenar,* and so on.

■ Contrast and model *olvidar* + infinitive versus *olvidarse de* + infinitive; *acordarse de* + infinitive versus *recordar* + infinitive; *pensar* + infinitive versus *pensar de/en/que.*

■ Point out that *hay que* is an impersonal verb form equivalent to the English *one should/must.* *Tener que,* however, is more personal and can be conjugated in all persons.

Con. B: Preliminary Exercises

■ Have students express the following ideas in Spanish.

1. He's learning to read. (to write, to play tennis)
2. She helps me wash the dishes. (dust, cook)
3. We're beginning to understand it. (to read it, to explain it)
4. They always invite us to go to the theater. (to the movies, to the museum)
5. They're coming to eat. (to visit us, to see us)
6. He's trying to help. (to cook, to see)
7. I just ate. (arrived, called)
8. He insists on doing it. (bringing it, listening to it)

■ Have students complete these sentences in as many ways as they can.

1. *Mis padres deben…*
2. *Mis padres me ayudan a…*
3. *Mis amigos me invitan a…*
4. *Mis amigos quieren…*

Suggestion

Have students explain the use of the subjunctive in the *minidiálogo*.

Follow-Up

Have students give advice to tourists who come to your town, using Lola's sentences as models.

Note

This is primarily a summary section. The only new material presented is the concept of noun clauses and the use of indirect object pronouns with verbs like *decir*.

41 Expressing Influence, Emotion, Doubt, and Denial • The Subjunctive: A Summary

Lola Benítez les habla a sus estudiantes norteamericanos

«Y para la próxima semana, *quiero que escriban* una composición sobre el arte de Sevilla. Como Uds. ya saben, Sevilla es una ciudad llena de todo tipo de arte: pintura, escultura, arquitectura, música, baile… ¡y también están los toros, por supuesto! Sí, los aficionados consideran que el toreo es una forma de arte. *Espero que vayan* a ver una corrida durante su estancia en España. Sin embargo, *es muy posible que no les guste* este espectáculo para nada. De todos modos, *ojalá que intenten* asistir a una. Bueno, por lo menos la plaza de toros sí es una gran muestra del arte sevillano… »

▲ *La plaza de toros en Sevilla, España*

1. ¿Qué quiere la profesora Benítez que hagan los estudiantes para la próxima semana?
2. ¿Qué tipo de arte se encuentra en Sevilla?
3. ¿Qué forma de arte menciona la profesora Benítez que puede sorprender a los estudiantes?
4. ¿Adónde quiere Lola que vayan los estudiantes?
5. ¿Qué quiere que hagan allí?
6. ¿Está segura ella de que a todos los estudiantes les van a gustar las corridas de toros?
7. ¿Qué dice ella de la plaza de toros de Sevilla?

Lola Benítez is talking to her American students *"And for next week, I want you to write a composition on art in Seville. As you already know, Seville is a city filled with all kinds of art: painting, sculpture, architecture, music, dance . . . and also bulls, of course! Yes, fans consider bullfighting to be an art form. I hope you go to see a bullfight during your stay in Spain. Nevertheless, it's very possible you won't like this spectacle at all. In any case, I hope that you try to attend one. Well, at least the bullring is a good example of Sevillian art . . . "*

MULTIMEDIA: Internet

Have students search the Internet for more information about Seville. You might assign specific topics such as tourist sites (*la Catedral, la Torre del Oro, la Plaza de Toros, la Maestranza*, and so on), museums, and bullfights, and have students give brief oral presentations in class.

MAIN (INDEPENDENT) CLAUSE		SUBORDINATE (DEPENDENT) CLAUSE
first subject + *indicative*	**que**	second subject + *subjunctive*
expression of {influence, emotion, doubt, denial}		

A. Remember that, in Spanish, the subjunctive occurs primarily in two-clause sentences with a different subject in each clause. If there is no change of subject, an infinitive follows the first verb. Compare the examples at the right.

Quiero } **sacar** una buena nota.
Es necesario }

I want } *to get a good grade.*
It's necessary }

Quiero } que los estudiantes **saquen**
Es necesario } una buena nota.

I want } *the students to get a good grade.*
It's necessary for }

B. The main clause, in addition to fulfilling the preceding conditions, must contain an expression of influence, emotion, or doubt in order for the subjunctive to occur in the subordinate clause. If there is no such expression, the indicative is used.*

Dicen que maneje Julio.
They say that Julio should drive.

Dicen que Julio **maneja** muy mal; por eso quieren que maneje Carlota.
They say that Julio drives very badly; that's why they want Carlota to drive.

C. Some expressions of influence are frequently used with indirect object pronouns.
   The indirect object indicates the subject of the subordinate clause, as in the sentences at the right: **nos → vayamos.**

Nos dicen }
Nos piden } que vayamos.
Nos recomiendan }

They tell us to }
They ask us to } *go.*
They recommend that we }

D. These uses of the subjunctive fall into the general category of the subjunctive in *noun clauses* (**las cláusulas nominales**). The clause in which the subjunctive appears functions like a noun in the sentence as a whole: it is the subject or the direct object of the verb.
   In the first set of sentences at the right, the subordinate clause (**que el mecánico…**) is the direct object of the verb **quiere.**
   In the second set of sentences at the right, the subordinate clause (**que los precios…**) is the subject of the verb **gusta.**

¿Qué quiere el dueño del coche?
What does the car's owner want?

Quiere **que el mecánico le arregle el coche.**
He wants the mechanic to fix his car.

¿Qué no les gusta a los clientes?
What don't the clients like?

No les gusta **que los precios sean muy altos.**
They don't like the prices to be very high.

---

*See **Gramática 38** through **40** for a more detailed presentation of the uses of the subjunctive in noun clauses.

Gramática   Cuatrocientos veintitrés ■ **423**

Emphasis A: Suggestions

- Emphasize and model the use of subjunctive or indicative after certain verbs, depending on the particular connotations of the verb. Here *decir* is followed by both indicative and subjunctive in dependent clauses depending on the meaning conveyed: *decir* = to say → indicative; *decir* = to tell, order → subjunctive.
- Help students categorize other verbs that require the indicative.

   1. *verbos de información: decir, informar, contar*
   2. *verbos de percepción: ver, observar, saber*
   3. *verbos de pensamiento: pensar, creer, opinar*

Emphasis B: Suggestion
Point out that the indirect object pronouns in these Spanish sentences are used to restate the subject, especially when the subject of the dependent clause is omitted.

Emphasis C: Suggestion
Emphasize and model that noun clauses function as nouns; nouns are typically:

1. subjects: *Me gusta el chocolate / comer bien.*
2. objects: *Odio el café / tener hambre.*
3. objects of a preposition: *Nos reunimos en el café. / Insisto en ir al café.*

Prác. A: Suggestion

Have students comment critically on the painting: *En su opinión, ¿qué hace que esta pintura sea tan especial?*

Prác. A: Variation

Have students talk about universities they would visit and would like their children to attend.

> *¿Qué quiere que tenga cada universidad?*
> *¿Qué quiere que no tenga?*
> *¿Qué le puede sorprender / gustar / no gustar?*

Prác. B: Follow-Up

- Ask students: *¿Cuáles son las ventajas y desventajas (lo bueno y lo malo) de los robots?*
- Have students imagine that they have a house with the latest technology and the most advanced robot. Have them complete the following sentences with this in mind.

  1. *Me alegro de que el robot _____ (ayudarme tanto, funcionar bien casi siempre, no quejarse nunca, no pedirme un aumento de sueldo, ¿ … ?).*
  2. *Me sorprende que el robot _____ (hablar tan bien y tan lógicamente, ser tan inteligente, parecer tan humano, saberlo todo, ¿ … ?).*
  3. *Dudo que los robots _____ algún día. (reemplazar [to replace] a los seres humanos, controlarlo todo, ¿ … ?).*

☼ Heritage Speakers

Anime a los estudiantes hispanohablantes a describir en voz alta el cuadro de Velázquez.

AUTOPRUEBA

Identify the sentences that would require the subjunctive when expressed in Spanish.

1. ☐ What does the director want?
2. ☐ The sculptor insists that we see his new piece.
3. ☐ I want to go to the opera with you.
4. ☐ It's strange that the fans booed.
5. ☐ We doubt the singer will perform tonight.

Answers: 2, 4, 5

■■■ Práctica

A. En el Museo del Prado

Imagine que Ud. va a escribir un informe sobre la vida y el arte del pintor español Diego Velázquez. Va al Museo del Prado para examinar los cuadros de Velázquez de cerca (*up close*). Pero también va a necesitar la ayuda de un guía (*guide*).

Paso 1. ¿Qué quiere Ud. que pase en el museo?

Quiero que el guía…

1. enseñarme los cuadros más famosos de Velázquez
2. explicarme algunos detalles de los cuadros
3. saber mucho sobre la vida del pintor

Paso 2. Claro está que Ud. va a aprender mucho sobre Velázquez. Pero, ¿qué es lo que le sorprende?

Me sorprende que muchos cuadros de Velázquez…

1. tener como tema la vida cotidiana (*everyday*)
2. estar en otros museos fuera de España
3. ser de la familia real (*royal*) de Carlos IV

Paso 3. Ud. está muy agradecido/a (*grateful*) por la ayuda del guía. Pero, todavía quiere saber más sobre la vida y el arte de Velázquez.

Es posible que el guía…

1. recomendarme algunos libros sobre la vida y el arte del pintor
2. preguntarle a un colega si sabe algo más sobre Velázquez
3. no tener más tiempo para hablar conmigo

B. ¡Qué maravilla de robot! Imagine que Ud. tiene un robot último modelo que va a hacer todo lo que Ud. le diga, especialmente las cosas que a Ud. no le gusta hacer. ¿Qué le va a mandar al robot que haga?

▲ *Las meninas, por Diego Velázquez (español, 1599–1660)*

Need more practice?

- Workbook and Laboratory Manual
- Interactive CD-ROM
- Online Learning Center (www.mhhe.com/puntos7)

| Le voy a decir que…   Le voy a pedir que… | **+** | escribirme el informe para la clase de literatura
hacerme una crítica de una película para la clase de composición
poner la mesa
asistir a todas mis clases en la universidad
pagar mis cuentas
trabajar por mí en la oficina todas las tardes
¿ ? |

MULTIMEDIA: Internet

- Have students search the Internet for more Velázquez paintings, periods of his work, and/or different Hispanic artists. Have students give presentations based on their findings.
- Have students search the Internet for the official website of the Prado Museum in Madrid. They can find information about visiting, as well as images of some of the masterpieces housed there.

CULTURE

Las meninas (1656) is probably the most famous painting by the Spanish painter Diego Velázquez. The title refers to the women, one of whom is a dwarf, who tend to princess Margarita (center). In the shadows, we see the Velázquez painting a portrait of the King and Queen, who are reflected in a mirror on the back wall. Their reflected image implies that they are standing in the viewers' place. Have students comment on this use of space. Why is the painting named *Las meninas* and not *La Infanta Margarita*, the center of attention?

Carlos Santana y la Fundación Milagro[a]

El legendario **guitarrista** Carlos Santana nació en Autlán, México. Luego su familia se trasladó[b] de allí a Tijuana y más tarde a San Francisco, donde Carlos y su hermano Jorge empezaron a tener sus primeros seguidores.[c] Santana se hizo **famoso** en el Festival de Woodstock en 1969 con un increíble solo de guitarra. Después tuvo una serie de éxitos,[d] entre ellos su inolvidable **interpretación** en 1971 de **la canción** de Tito Puente, «Oye cómo va». En 1999, Santana creó una sensación con su **disco compacto** *Supernatural,* en el que tocó con una variedad de artistas norteamericanos e hispanos para crear una **obra** rica en **estilo** y composición. Este **esfuerzo** de Santana le ganó varios *Grammys* en 2000.

▲ *Carlos Santana*

Santana es una persona profundamente dedicada a **la comunidad,** especialmente a **los niños.** Junto con su esposa Deborah, Santana creó **la Fundación Milagro,** una organización educativa para niños y jóvenes. La Fundación Milagro contribuye con dinero a otras organizaciones comunitarias sin fines lucrativos[e] en San Francisco y sus alrededores.[f] El propósito es ayudar a la juventud[g] del área por medio de programas de salud, educación y arte. Puede encontrar más información sobre la Fundación en su página web en el Internet.

[a]*Miracle* [b]*se... moved* [c]*followers*
[d]*successes* [e]*sin... nonprofit* [f]*outskirts* [g]*youth*

■ ■ ■ Conversación

Un nuevo lugar para vivir

Paso 1. Piense Ud. en el lugar ideal para vivir. ¿Es una casa o un apartamento? ¿Cómo es? Lea la siguiente lista de factores e indique los que tengan más importancia para Ud. Debe añadir también otros factores que no estén en la lista. ¡Sea realista! Debe ser un lugar donde Ud. pueda vivir mientras asiste a la universidad.

_____ cerca de la universidad	_____ piscina
_____ grande	_____ aire acondicionado
_____ económico/a	_____ compañero(s) de casa
_____ más de dos alcobas	_____ lavaplatos
_____ buena vista	_____ lavadora y secadora
_____ ascensor (*elevator*)	_____ ¿ ?
_____ dos o más baños	

Paso 2. Ahora describa la casa o el apartamento que Ud. quiere. Puede usar las siguientes oraciones como modelo.

MODELOS: Deseo que la casa / el apartamento…
(No) Me importa que la casa / el apartamento…
Es bueno que tenga/sea…
Espero que (no)…
(No) Es absolutamente necesario que…
Dudo que la casa / el apartamento…

Bright Idea
Con: Suggestion

After students have completed the activity, have them work in groups to "develop" ideal housing for students at the university. Then have them develop a flyer for advertising their development. They can draw floor plans of individual dorms, apartments, or houses, as well as building and grounds layout. They should label their drawings in Spanish. They should also list features of the development in Spanish. Finally, they should remember to name their development (in Spanish!). Have the groups present their developments to the class. Have the class vote for the most appealing development.

Suggestions

- Ask students if they know of other organizations that help children in need or other celebrities involved in humanitarian work.
- Have students describe volunteer work they do.

- Have students search the Internet for more information about Carlos Santana and *La Fundación Milagro.* Does the *Fundación* have a website? If so, what type of information can be found there?

A: Suggestions

- Assign this in groups of five to six students so that they can have a discussion. Remind them to be polite in their disagreement.
- Use the following transformation drill to review the subjunctive structure. Write the following model on the board.

    Marcos nunca llega a casa temprano. Dudo que... → Dudo que Marcos llegue a casa temprano hoy.

    1. *Marcos nunca ayuda a limpiar la casa. Dudo que...*
    2. *Nunca se acuesta temprano. Es probable...*
    3. *Casi nunca hace su cama por la mañana. No creo que...*
    4. *Con frecuencia no se despierta hasta las once. Dudo que...*
    5. *Usa mi coche y lo deja sin gasolina. Estoy seguro/a que...*

A: Variations

- Make up statements about yourself, your family, or class members to which students can react using the phrases provided in *A*. Some statements should be false, even outrageous.
- Substitute more controversial statements for those given in the text.

    Creo que el aborto debe ser legal. Creo que no se debe fumar marihuana.

A. Reacciones

Paso 1. Las siguientes oraciones mencionan temas de vital importancia en el mundo de hoy. ¿Qué cree Ud.? Reaccione Ud. a estas oraciones, empezando con una de estas expresiones.

> MODELO: Hay mucha pobreza en el mundo. →
> Es una lástima que *haya* mucha pobreza en el mundo.

Dudo que…
Es bueno/malo que…
Es increíble que…
Es una lástima que…
Es probable que…
Es ridículo que…
Es terrible que…
(No) Es verdad que…
No hay duda que…
(No) Me gusta que…

1. Los niños miran la televisión seis horas al día.
2. Hay mucha pobreza en el mundo.
3. En este país gastamos mucha energía.
4. Hay mucho sexo y violencia en la televisión y en el cine.
5. Se come poco y mal en muchas partes del mundo.
6. Los temas de la música *rap* son demasiado violentos.
7. Hay mucho interés en la exploración del espacio.
8. El fumar no es malo para la salud.
9. Los deportes para las mujeres no reciben tanto apoyo (*support*) financiero como los de los hombres.
10. No se permite el uso de la marihuana.
11. Muchos adolescentes tienen acceso a las drogas y al alcohol.
12. Los vehículos que usan mucha gasolina son más y más populares.

Paso 2. Indique Ud. soluciones para algunos de los problemas que se mencionan en el **Paso 1.** Empiece las soluciones con estas frases.

> MODELO: Es urgente que ayudemos a los pobres.

Es importante que…
Es necesario que…
Es preferible que…
Es urgente que…
Insisto en que…
Quiero que…
Recomiendo que…

CULTURE

- The *Museo Nacional Centro de Arte Reina Sofía* was declared a full-time national museum in 1992. The building this museum occupies was begun as a hospital in the mid 1700s but was never completed. After surviving movements to have it demolished, the building was repaired, restored, and finished by several different architects. Before becoming a national museum, it was a cultural center called *el Centro de Arte Reina Sofía*, in which temporary exhibits and events were held.
- The town of Guernica, also known as Guernica y Luno, is located in north-central Spain, twelve miles northeast of Bilbao. The town was destroyed during the Spanish Civil War by German and Italian aircraft in the first mass bombing in 1937. Picasso's work depicts the pain and suffering that resulted from the attack.

B. En el Museo Nacional Centro de Arte Reina (*Queen*) **Sofía.** Imagine que Ud. y su amigo/a están en Madrid con un grupo turístico. Ahora están en el Museo Nacional Centro de Arte Reina Sofía y el guía les habla sobre *Guernica*, el famoso cuadro del pintor español Pablo Picasso. Complete el siguiente diálogo con la forma correcta de los verbos entre paréntesis. Cuando se den dos posibilidades, escoja la palabra correcta.

Guernica, por Pablo Picasso ▶
(*español, 1881–1973*)

GUÍA: (Pasar[1]) Uds. por aquí, por favor. También les pido que (dejar[2]) suficiente espacio para todos. Y bien, aquí estamos (delante/detrás[3]) de *Guernica*, la obra maestra pintada por Picasso. (Ser[4]) obvio que el cuadro (representar[5]) los horrores de la guerra,[a] ¿no? En 1937 Picasso (pintar[6]) este cuadro como reacción al bombardeo[b] (del / de la[7]) ciudad de Guernica durante la Guerra Civil Española. Por razones políticas, (durante / encima de[8]) la dictadura[c] de Franco,[d] el cuadro (fue/estuvo[9]) muchos años en el Museo de Arte Moderno de Nueva York. Pero por deseo expreso del pintor, el cuadro (trasladarse[10])[e] a España después de la muerte de Franco...

UD.: Yo dudo que (este/esto[11]) cuadro (ser[12]) una obra maestra. Creo que no (ser[13]) nada bonito. ¡No hay colores en él!

SU AMIGO/A: Yo no (creer[14]) que todos los cuadros (tener[15]) que (ser[16]) bonitos. Para mí, la falta de color (servir[17]) para expresar el dolor y el desastre... (Por/Para[18]) eso uno (poder[19]) sentir el mensaje de la destrucción de la guerra en la pintura.

[a]*war* [b]*bombing* [c]*dictatorship* [d]*Francisco Franco (1892–1975), dictador de España desde 1939 hasta su muerte* [e]*to move*

Comprensión. ¿Quién pudo haber dicho (*could have said*) lo siguiente: el guía, Ud. o su amigo/a?

1. Yo prefiero los cuadros en colores.
2. Ahora voy a mostrarles una obra maestra de la pintura española.
3. No me molesta que esta pintura esté pintada en blanco y negro.
4. Quiero que todos me sigan y que se pongan delante del cuadro.

Resources for Review and Testing Preparation

- Workbook and Laboratory Manual
- Interactive CD-ROM
- Online Learning Center (www.mhhe.com/puntos7)

B: Follow-Up

Ask the following questions to personalize the activity.

¿Qué expresa para Ud. el cuadro de Guernica?
¿Por qué (no) le gusta?
¿Cree Ud. que el arte se debe usar para transmitir un mensaje o sólo para producir un placer estético?

B. Reciclado

Reenter the no-fault *se* expressions. Have students express the following ideas in Spanish.

1. It's incredible that Miguel is so clumsy.
2. It's terrible that he breaks his glasses all the time.
3. I think he loses his keys every week.
4. I hope he doesn't run out of money this week!

Un poco de todo   Cuatrocientos veintisiete ■ **427**

MULTIMEDIA: Internet

Have students search the Internet for more of Pablo Picasso's works, including *Guernica*. The *Museo Nacional Centro de Arte Reina Sofía* in Madrid has its own website and features some of his works. Have students look up this museum and research its relationship to *el Museo del Prado*.

Resources: Desenlace

In the *Capítulo 13* segment of "Chapter-by-Chapter Supplementary Materials" in the IM/RK, you will find a chapter-culminating activity. You can use this activity to consolidate and review the vocabulary and grammar skills students have acquired.

PERSPECTIVAS culturales

●●● Videoteca

Entrevista cultural: Bolivia

Juan Prudencio, un joven artista boliviano, habla de su trabajo artístico y de su familia. Antes de ver el vídeo, lea el siguiente fragmento de la entrevista.

ENTREVISTADORA:	…Y ¿qué pintas?
JUAN:	Pinto cuadros abstractos. Pinto cosas que tienen que ver con mis emociones o con la manera en que yo veo la situación actual en el mundo.

Ahora vea el vídeo y conteste las siguientes preguntas basándose en la entrevista.

1. ¿Cómo son los cuadros que Juan pinta?
2. ¿Cómo reaccionan los padres de Juan a su trabajo artístico?
3. Y ¿cómo responden sus hermanos a sus obras?

Entrevista cultural: el Ecuador

Álvaro Montealbán, un estudiante ecuatoriano, habla del arte y de sus planes profesionales. Antes de ver el vídeo, lea el siguiente fragmento de la entrevista.

ENTREVISTADORA:	Álvaro, ¿qué planes tienes para el futuro?
ÁLVARO:	En el futuro pienso desarrollarme profesionalmente, ya sea en un museo o una galería de arte. En un futuro más a largo plazo[a] trabajaré[b] por montarme[c] mi propia galería de arte.

[a]más… more long term   [b]I will work   [c]establish, open

Ahora vea el vídeo y conteste las siguientes preguntas basándose en la entrevista.

1. ¿Por qué estudia Álvaro la historia del arte?
2. ¿Qué quiere hacer Álvaro en el futuro?

Entre amigos: ¿Y qué pintores te gustan?

Tané, Karina, Rubén y Miguel hablan del arte. En su opinión, ¿qué preguntas se van a hacer? Antes de mirar el vídeo, lea las preguntas a continuación. Mientras mire el vídeo, fíjese en la información sobre el arte y los artistas. Luego mire el vídeo una segunda vez, fijándose en la información que necesita para contestar las preguntas.

1. ¿Qué pintores le gustan a Rubén? ¿Qué tipo de arte le gusta a Tané? Y a Miguel, ¿qué música le gusta?
2. ¿Cómo describe Tané la ópera? Y ¿qué dice Rubén de la ópera?

Suggestions column

Entrevistas culturales

Suggestions

■ Before showing the video clips, ask students questions about what role art plays in their life.

> ¿Le gusta a Ud. pintar o dibujar? ¿Le interesa la escultura?
> ¿Ud. se considera artista? ¿Por qué sí o por qué no?
> ¿Qué museos y galerías hay en su ciudad o pueblo?

■ Show the video clips and allow students one to two minutes to work on the questions for each one. Have volunteers answer the questions.

■ Have volunteers role-play Juan and Álvaro with their interviewers.

■ Have students tell what their future plans are.

■ Ask students what role art historians play in the study and preservation and promotion of art.

■ Identify students that consider themselves artists, and ask what they do (pintura, escultura, and so on). Encourage them to describe their work.

> ¿Usa Ud. colores brillantes en su pintura o prefiere los colores oscuros? ¿Hay un color dominante en sus pinturas?
> ¿Qué materiales prefiere usar en su escultura? ¿barro (clay)? ¿metales? ¿plástico?

Entre amigos

Suggestions

■ Before viewing the video, review the questions with the students and ask them similar questions.

> ¿Qué artistas le gustan a Ud.?
> ¿Qué tipo de arte prefiere?
> ¿Sabe Ud. cantar? ¿Qué tipo de música prefiere?
> ¿Asiste Ud. a conciertos de música clásica? ¿a óperas?

Have students answer or work in small groups to ask and answer these questions.

■ After viewing the video, have volunteers read and answer the questions.

Capítulo 13: El arte y la cultura

MULTIMEDIA: Internet

Have students search the Internet for more information about the government, educational system, geography, and economy of Ecuador and Bolivia. Have students share their findings with their classmates.

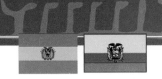

Conozca... Bolivia y el Ecuador

Datos esenciales

Bolivia

- Nombre oficial: República de Bolivia
- Capitales: La Paz (sede[a] del gobierno), Sucre (capital constitucional)
- Población: 8.586.000 habitantes
- Moneda: el (peso) boliviano
- Idiomas: el español (oficial), el quechua, el aimara

El Ecuador

- Nombre oficial: República del Ecuador
- Capital: Quito
- Población: 13.710.000 habitantes
- Moneda: el dólar (el sucre)
- Idiomas: el español (oficial), el quechua

[a]seat

¡Fíjese!

- Bolivia formó parte del antiguo imperio inca. Aproximadamente el 55 por ciento de la población boliviana actual es de origen indígena.
- Bolivia fue nombrada[a] en honor a Simón Bolívar, quien luchó por la independencia del país.
- A 12.000 pies de altura, La Paz es la capital más alta del mundo.
- Las Islas Galápagos pertenecen[b] al Ecuador y son de origen volcánico. Fueron descubiertas[c] en 1535, por el español Berlanga. Berlanga las llamó las Islas Encantadas[d] porque las fuertes corrientes[e] marinas confundían a los navegantes[f] como si fuera por[g] acto de magia. Trescientos años más tarde, el biólogo Charles Darwin llegó a las islas a bordo del barco *HMS Beagle*. De sus investigaciones de las plantas y animales de cuatro de las islas resultaron sus ideas sobre la evolución y su famoso libro, *El origen de las especies.* Darwin teorizó que los animales y las plantas cambian y se adaptan a su medio ambiente.[h]

[a]fue... *was named*   [b]*belong*   [c]Fueron... *They were discovered*
[d]*Enchanted*   [e]*currents*   [f]*sailors*   [g]como... *as if by*   [h]medio... *environment*

Personas famosas: Oswaldo Guayasamín

Oswaldo Guayasamín (1919–1999) fue un pintor ecuatoriano cuyo[a] arte es un testimonio del sufrimiento[b] humano y de la vida difícil de los indios y los pobres de su país. Guayasamín se inspiró en los símbolos y motivos de los pueblos precolombinos y en el arte colonial del Ecuador.

[a]*whose*   [b]*suffering*

▲ Madre y niño, *por Oswaldo Guayasamín*

Learn more about Bolivia and Ecuador with the Video, the Interactive CD-ROM, and the Online Learning Center (www.mhhe.com/puntos7).

Suggestions

- Bring in examples of Bolivian music (many samples can be downloaded from the Internet), then have students compare this music to other versions of Andean music they may have heard. Ask, for example, what differences they hear between the Simon and Garfunkle song *"El condor pasa"* and its Quechua counterpart. Students may enjoy seeing the Quechua lyrics to the song, which can also be found on the Internet.
- Show the Bolivian film *Cuestión de fe* (1998) in class. Directed by Paolo Agazzi, it tells the story about a *santero* (a sculptor of wooden images of saints) and an atheist who carry an image of the Virgin in a truck through the Bolivian jungle to a lost village. This film has won numerous European, North and South American, and Caribbean awards.
- Tell students that Ecuador replaced its currency, the *sucre,* in favor of the U.S. dollar in the year 2000. Have them check the Internet for the present status of the currency, and talk with them about the meaning of the change.
- Challenge students to an Ecuador food and beverage scavenger hunt (and join them!) by asking them to find the answers to the following questions on the Internet. The winner is the one who can provide the most, and the most thorough, answers.

  1. How is *chicha* made?
  2. Where can you find a good plate of *encocados*?
  3. How do you make *pollo sin pollo*?
  4. What is most commonly served with Ecuadorian *ceviche*?
  5. What is the main ingredient in *caldo de pata*? In *tronquito*?
  6. What is *yaguarlocho*?

Note

Students can read an excerpt of the novel *Huasipungo* by Ecuador's Jorge Icaza in *Un paso más 13.*

MULTIMEDIA: Internet

- Have students search the Internet for more information about Oswaldo Guayasamín and his works. Have students look for images of Guayasamín's works online.
- Have students look for the official website about the Galápagos Islands. You might assign topics such as specific animals unique to the islands, geographical formations and characteristics of the different islands, types of access to the islands, including costs, transportation, and lodgings, restrictions and rules on the islands, the history of the islands, and so on. Have students give brief oral presentations based on their findings.

Suggestions

- Read the following definitions and have students give the words defined.

  1. *Es una actividad artística en la que unas personas representan la vida de otras personas imaginarias o reales.*

  2. *Picasso, O'Keeffe y Van Gogh son ejemplos de este tipo de artistas.*

  3. *Esta persona diseña y dibuja casas o edificios.*

  4. *En este lugar se representan obras de teatro.*

  5. *Gloria Estefan y Julio Iglesias tienen esta profesión.*

  6. *El sinónimo de crear una escultura.*

  7. *Los artistas hacen esto antes de pintar un cuadro, generalmente.*

- Bring or have students bring images of fine and performing arts. Use the images to elicit descriptions and ask/answer questions.

- Make statements about the images displayed in class or about aspects of university life on your campus to which students can react with the following expressions: *No, no creo... , No, dudo que... , No, niego que...*

EN RESUMEN

Gramática

To review the grammar points presented in this chapter, refer to the indicated grammar presentations. You'll find further practice of these structures in the Workbook and Laboratory Manual, on the Interactive CD-ROM, and on the *Puntos de partida* Online Learning Center (www.mhhe.com/puntos7).

39. Expressing Feelings—Use of the Subjunctive: Emotion

You should know how and when to use the subjunctive in a dependent clause when the main clause of a sentence expresses emotion.

40. Expressing Uncertainty—Use of the Subjunctive: Doubt and Denial

You should know how and when to use the subjunctive in a dependent clause when the main clause of a sentence expresses doubt or denial.

41. Expressing Influence, Emotion, Doubt, and Denial—The Subjunctive: A Summary

Do you now have a general understanding of when and why the subjunctive is used?

Vocabulario

Practice this vocabulary with digital flash cards on the Online Learning Center (www.mhhe.com/puntos7).

Los verbos

aburrir	to bore
agradar	to please
apreciar	to appreciate
intentar	to try
negar (ie) (gu)	to deny
parecer	to seem
representar	to represent
sentir (ie, i)	to regret; to feel sorry
temer	to fear
tratar de + *inf.*	to try to (*do something*)

Repaso: alegrarse de, creer, dudar, esperar, gustar, tener (*irreg.*) miedo de

La expresión artística

la arquitectura	architecture
el arte (*but* las artes *pl.*)	art
el baile	dance
el ballet	ballet
la danza	dance
el drama	drama
la escultura	sculpture
la música	music
la ópera	opera
la pintura	painting (*general*)

Repaso: el cine, la fotografía, la literatura, el teatro

crear	to create
desempeñar	to play, perform (*a part*)

dibujar	to draw
esculpir	to sculpt
tejer	to weave

Repaso: cantar, escribir, pintar

Los artistas

el actor / la actriz	actor, actress
el/la arquitecto/a	architect
el/la artista	artist
el bailarín / la bailarina	dancer
el/la cantante	singer
el/la compositor(a)	composer
el/la director(a)	director
el/la dramaturgo/a	playwright
el/la escritor(a)	writer
el/la escultor(a)	sculptor
el/la músico	musician
el/la pintor(a)	painter
el/la poeta	poet

Repaso: el/la aficionado/a

La tradición cultural

la artesanía	arts and crafts
la cerámica	pottery; ceramics
las ruinas	ruins
los tejidos	woven goods

 Heritage Speakers

La palabra *poetisa* se usaba antes pero apenas se oye hoy en día. Ahora lleva un sentido peyorativo, y el término *la poeta* es el más usado.

Otros sustantivos

la canción	song
el cuadro / la pintura	painting (*piece of art*) / painting (*piece of art; the art form*)
el escenario	stage
la gente	people
el/la guía	guide
el guión	script
la obra (de arte)	work (of art)
la obra maestra	masterpiece
el papel	role

Los adjetivos

clásico/a	classic(al)
folklórico/a	folkloric
moderno/a	modern

Los números ordinales

primer(o/a)
segundo/a
tercer(o/a)
cuarto/a
quinto/a
sexto/a
séptimo/a
octavo/a
noveno/a
décimo/a

Palabras adicionales

es extraño que	it's strange that
¡qué extraño que...!	how strange that . . . !
es...	it's . . .
cierto que	certain that
(im)probable que	(un)likely, (im)probable that
increíble que	incredible that
preferible que	preferable that
ridículo que	ridiculous that
seguro que	a sure thing that
terrible que	terrible that
urgente que	urgent that
es una lástima que	it's a shame that
¡qué lástima que...!	what a shame that . . . !
hay que + *inf.*	it is necessary to (*do something*)
me (te, le,...) molesta que	it bothers me (you, him, . . .) that
me (te, le,...) sorprende que	it surprises me (you, him, . . .) that
ojalá (que)	I hope, wish (that)

Repaso: es (im)posible que..., es mejor/bueno/malo que..., es verdad que..., estar seguro/a (de) que...

Suggestion
Write the expressions from *Palabras adicionales* on the board. Make statements about people in the class, university, state, or national events, or other people and events that students should know about. Have them respond to each statement using one of the expressions.

Muchos estudiantes estudian arte. →
Me sorprende que tantos estudiantes estudien arte.

Un paso más 13

Note

The *Un paso más* section is optional.

Literatura del Ecuador

Notes

- As a child, Jorge Icaza was deeply affected by a visit to his family's *hacienda*, where he was exposed to the suffering of the indigenous people who lived and worked there, essentially as slaves. Later, in his writings he did not mince words. His texts use harsh, realistic terms to protest the exploitation of the indigenous people.
- Other novels include *En las calles* (1935), *Cholos* (1938), and *El chulla Romero y Flores* (1958). His short stories are collected in *Relatos* (1969).

LECTURA

Suggestions

- Do the *Estrategia* in class and assign the reading as homework for discussion the next class meeting.
- Have students share their predictions about the passage. Then ask them what strategies they used to make their predictions.

Un paso más 13

Literatura del Ecuador

Sobre el autor: *Jorge Icaza nació en Icuña, Ecuador. Empezó su carrera como actor y dramaturgo, pero cuando las autoridades censuraron su drama,* El dictador, *abrió una librería y empezó a escribir novelas. Su novela* Huasipungo *es la novela ecuatoriana más famosa y además una de las novelas indigenistas más importantes de Latinoamérica. El siguiente fragmento es de la novela* Huasipungo *(1934).*

—Nu han de robar[a] así nu más[b] a taita[c] Andrés Chiliquinga—concluyó el indio, rascándose[d] la cabeza, lleno de un despertar[e] de oscuras e indefinidas venganzas.[f] Ya le era imposible dudar de la verdad del atropello[g] que invadía el cerro.[h] Llegaban... Llegaban más pronto de lo que él pudo imaginarse. Echarían abajo su techo,[i] le quitarían la tierra.[j] Sin encontrar[k] una defensa posible, acorralado[l] como siempre, se puso pálido, con la boca semiabierta, con los ojos fijos,[m] con la garganta anudada.[n] ¡No!

[a]Nu... *They will not rob* [b]nu... *ever again* [c]*abuelo* [d]*scratching* [e]lleno... *overcome by an awakening* [f]oscuras... *dark and vague vengeance* [g]*attack, assault* [h]*hill* [i]Echarían... *They would tear down his roof (house)* [j]le... *they would take away his land* [k]Sin... *Without finding* [l]*corralled* [m]*fixed* [n]con... *with a lump in his throat*

▲ Jorge Icaza
(1906–1978)

LECTURA

REPASO DE ESTRATEGIAS: **Guessing the Content of a Passage**

Look at the photograph that accompanies the reading on the following page. Read the title of the passage also. Based on these clues, what do you think the article is going to be about? How do you know? What important information do the photo and the title provide? Remember to always look for these types of visual clues as a useful strategy to facilitate comprehension when reading in a second language (or even in your first language).

- **Sobre la lectura...** Esta lectura es la adaptación de un artículo de la revista *GeoMundo*. Ud. ya leyó otro artículo de esta revista en el **Capítulo 7.** Recuerde que *GeoMundo* es como la revista *National Geographic* y que publica artículos sobre las ciencias, la geografía y otros temas similares.

National Standards: Culture

Huasipungo, a novel by Jorge Icaza, was first published in 1934. Icaza's work is an impassioned exposé of racially charged violence and severe oppression. *Huasipungo* tells the story of the exploitation of Ecuadorian Indians by whites who are intent on taking advantage of the natives and their homeland. Icaza's *Huasipungo* forms part of the *Novelas indígenas de protesta social.*

Museo Virtual de Artes

<u>Aprovechando</u> las ventajas del ciberespacio, se creó el MUVA o Museo Virtual de Artes, sitio dedicado a <u>divulgar</u> el arte uruguayo y latinoamericano. Su directora es la historiadora de arte y curadora Alicia Haber. El sitio es recreativo, educativo y sin fines de lucro.[a]

La idea con que <u>surgió</u> este espacio es la de brindar[b] la sensación de estar en un museo real, pues debido a[c] las limitaciones originadas por la realidad socioeconómica de Uruguay, se ha visto impedida la construcción[d] de un museo nuevo. Cuatro arquitectos diseñaron un edificio con todos los adelantos,[e] la infraestructura técnica y las características edilicias[f] de un museo de primer nivel.[g] Existen innumerables museos en la <u>supercarretera</u> de la información, pero a diferencia de ellos, el MUVA no está construido como las páginas de un catálogo. Se trata de presentar arte uruguayo en el contexto más realista posible y brindarle al visitante la sensación de estar en un verdadero museo. Y no en cualquier museo, sino en una obra arquitectónica atractiva, cómoda, moderna y eficiente, con escaleras mecánicas, ascensor, sala de acceso con esculturas, varias salas con instalaciones, pisos encerados[h] y hasta un buen sistema de iluminación.

Este museo ya ha recibido[i] 32 premios internacionales desde que entró en línea el 20 de

▲ Sitio web del Museo Virtual de Artes

mayo de 1997. El más importante es *Best of the Web* (Lo Mejor de la Red), pero también se ha hecho acreedor[j] al *Best Virtual Exhibition* (Mejor Exhibición Virtual del Mundo) entre más de 155 museos en línea. Debido a sus peculiares características, ha sido filmado en CNN Internacional, en la televisión brasileña y en muchos otros medios uruguayos e internacionales.

Se puede encontrar el MUVA en la dirección **http://www.diarioelpais.com/muva.**

[a]sin... *nonprofit*   [b]*ofrecer*   [c]*pues... because due to*   [d]*se... construction has been impossible*
[e]*latest advances (in architecture)*   [f]*civic, municipal*   [g]*class*   [h]*pisos... waxed floors*   [i]*ha... has received*   [j]*se... it has been deemed worthy of inclusion*

MULTIMEDIA: Internet

Have students visit the *MUVA* website. Encourage them to visit the ground floor to get more information about the museum, the museum artists, and Uruguayan art in general. Ask them to visit the current expositions and encourage them to share their opinions on the art with the rest of the class.

National Standards: Connections

Ask students to check the website of a museum in a Spanish-speaking country, such as *El Prado, el Guggenheim en Bilbao, el Museo Nacional de Antropología de México,* and so on. They can then write and present a report, which includes the museum's specialization, most important works, hours and price, and so on.

Suggestion
Point out that the museum described in the reading is virtual, but many museums have websites that also include virtual tours of the real space. Another phenomenon is the online, virtual gallery.

Suggestions

■ Have students tell what they would expect to find in an online museum. Would they expect to find the following?

   general schedule, contact, and
      ticket information
   maps to the museum
   floor plans
   images of paintings and sculp-
      tures
   artist biographies

■ Have them brainstorm the benefits to the community as well as to artists that online museums offer. Then have them brainstorm the problems these museums can create. How might they affect copyright and distribution laws?

Comprensión

A. Preguntas. Conteste las siguientes preguntas.

   1. ¿Qué tipo de museo es el MUVA?
   2. ¿En qué país latinoamericano se creó el MUVA?
   3. ¿Cuáles son algunos ejemplos del éxito de este museo?
   4. ¿Cuál fue el objetivo de los diseñadores del MUVA?
   5. ¿Cuántos premios tiene MUVA? ¿Cuáles son algunos de ellos?

B. Identificación. Identifique las conveniencias que le ofrece el MUVA al visitante, según el artículo.

	SÍ	NO
1. diversas salas con exhibiciones	☐	☐
2. un tour guiado	☐	☐
3. un sistema de iluminación de alta calidad	☐	☐
4. diferentes maneras de navegar por el museo (ascensores, etcétera)	☐	☐
5. conversaciones con los artistas	☐	☐

E S C R I T U R A

A. La expresión artística. Muchas personas se expresan mediante el arte en sus varias formas. Es decir, el arte no se limita solamente a la pintura y la escultura. El arte puede tomar varias formas: la música, la escritura, el diseño de ropa o muebles, etcétera. ¿Qué «arte» usa Ud. para expresar su personalidad? Escriba un breve ensayo (*essay*) para explicar cómo Ud. se expresa por medio del arte. Ideas para considerar:

■ el medio artístico (la música, etcétera)
■ cómo el arte expresa sus emociones y personalidad
■ si sus preferencias con respecto a la expresión artística están cambiando o si se mantienen estables

Cuando termine su ensayo, entrégueselo a su profesor(a). El profesor / La profesora lo va a presentar al resto de la clase para ver si puede adivinar quién es el autor / la autora.

B. El museo. Casi todos los museos importantes del mundo, como El Prado en Madrid, España, y el Museo del Oro en Bogotá, Colombia, tienen un sitio web. Busque los sitios web de dos museos del mundo hispanohablante. Usando el sitio web como referencia, describa las instalaciones del museo. ¿Qué tipo de arte exponen (*do they exhibit*)? ¿Qué épocas (*periods*) representan las instalaciones? ¿Qué artistas representan? En su opinión, ¿por qué son importantes estas «extensiones» de los museos? ¿Cree Ud. que los sitios web pueden causar algunos problemas o dificultades para los museos?

Algunos museos del mundo hispanohablante

Museo Arqueológico Nacional, Madrid, España
Museo de Arte Moderno, Buenos Aires, Argentina
Museo Guggenheim, Bilbao, España
Museo Nacional de Antropología, México, D.F.
Museo Nacional de Bellas Artes, Santiago, Chile
Museo del Oro, Bogotá, Colombia
Museo del Palacio de Bellas Artes, México, D.F.
Museo del Prado, Madrid, España

ESCRITURA

Variation

Have students write two paragraphs about one of their favorite works of art (music, painting, movie, and so on). The first paragraph must include some historical background on the work and its author. The second paragraph should explain why they are interested in that particular piece of work.

Suggestion

If you prefer that your students do a journal activity, see *Mi diario* in this chapter of the Workbook.

◀ Las cataratas del Iguazú, en la Argentina

CHAPTER OPENER PHOTO

Point out the chapter-opener photo. Have students share their knowledge of endangered species with one another. Tell them that not all *coquí* frogs are endangered, although, of the sixteen different species in Puerto Rico, six are. Then, play the songs of different *coquí* frogs (available on the Internet) and have students speculate what purpose the different calls may have. Encourage students to research *coquí* frogs on the Internet and report to the class. The *Proyecto Coquí* website may be particularly helpful.

Suggestions

- Have students tell whether the following statements are true or false for them.

  1. *Es absolutamente necesario para mí tener mi propio* **coche.**
  2. *Es importante tener un coche que no* **gaste** *demasiada* **gasolina.**
  3. *Los daños que se le han hecho* (have been done) *a* **la capa de ozono** *no afectan mi vida diaria.*
  4. *Tenemos que* **explotar** *nuestros* **recursos naturales** *si queremos mantener un buen* **nivel** *de vida.*
  5. *El* **medio ambiente,** *hay que* **protegerlo.**

- The words in **boldface** are included in the active vocabulary of this chapter. Have students discuss the words and use context to help them understand the meanings. Place the words they cannot guess in new sentences and contexts.
- Have students work in pairs to interview each other based on the statements, and then present and compare results with the rest of the class.

Note

The *Puntos de partida* Online Learning Center includes an interview with a native speaker from Argentina who answers questions about the environment.

Resources

For Students

- Workbook
- Laboratory Manual and Laboratory Audio Program
- Quia™ Online Workbook and Online Laboratory Manual
- Video on CD
- Interactive CD-ROM
- *Puntos de partida* Online Learning Center (**www.mhhe.com/puntos7**)

For Instructors

- *Instructor's Manual and Resource Kit,* "Chapter-by-Chapter" Supplementary Materials
- Overhead Transparencies 87–90
- Testing Program
- Test Generator
- Video Program
- Audioscript
- *Puntos de partida* Online Learning Center (**www.mhhe.com/puntos7**)

La naturaleza y el medio ambiente°

Suggestion
Have students list their ideas about Argentina, including information on geography, politics, economy, culture, music, and cuisine. When you finish the chapter, return to the lists and ask students what ideas they would change and/or add.

CULTURA

- **Perspectivas culturales**

  Entrevista cultural: la Argentina

  Entre amigos: Nuestro pequeño grano de arena

  Conozca... la Argentina

- **Nota cultural:** Programas medioambientales

- **En los Estados Unidos y el Canadá:** Lugares con nombres españoles

- **Literatura de la Argentina:** Alfonsina Storni

- **Lectura:** La Amazonia pierde cada año un millón y medio de hectáreas

VOCABULARIO

- La naturaleza y el medio ambiente
- Los coches

GRAMÁTICA

42 Past Participle Used As an Adjective

43 Perfect Forms: Present Perfect Indicative and Present Perfect Subjunctive

Entrevista cultural

Natalia D'Ángelo ▶
Buenos Aires, Argentina

°**La...** *Nature and the environment*

MULTIMEDIA

- The multimedia materials that accompany this chapter are referenced in the Student and Instructor's Editions with icons to help you identify when and where to incorporate them.

- The IM/RK provides suggestions for using the multimedia materials in the classroom.

La naturaleza y el medio ambiente

Note

See the model for vocabulary presentation and other material in the *Capítulo 14 Vocabulario: Preparación* section of "Chapter-by-Chapter Supplementary Materials," in the IM.

Suggestions

- Point out that *la fábrica* and *la falta* are false cognates.
- Emphasize the spelling changes in the conjugations of *destruir* and *construir: destruyo, destruyes,...* and *construyo, construyes,...* Also point out the first person singular of *proteger: protejo.* Model the structure with *acabar* in *se nos acabó* and *se nos acabaron.*
- Provide the following optional vocabulary.

  lento/a
  tener la culpa
  echarle la culpa (a alguien)

- Model the pronunciation of the words as well as the use of selected words. Integrate them in statements about yourself, your community, and/or the university.

Preliminary Exercises

- Read the following definitions and have students give the corresponding word from the vocabulary.

  1. *bonito o hermoso, no feo*
  2. *cuando no hay suficiente cantidad de algo*
  3. *lo opuesto de destruir*
  4. *puede ser de varios tipos, depende de si viene del aire, del agua, del sol, etcétera*
  5. *un sistema político*
  6. *el grupo de personas que vive en una ciudad o un estado*

- Have students imagine that they have a Hispanic friend who does not know what the following are. Have them explain the meaning of each.

  1. the EPA
  2. the Secretary of the Interior
  3. the welfare system
  4. the National Parks system and park rangers
  5. a parole officer
  6. the inner city

La naturaleza y el medio ambiente

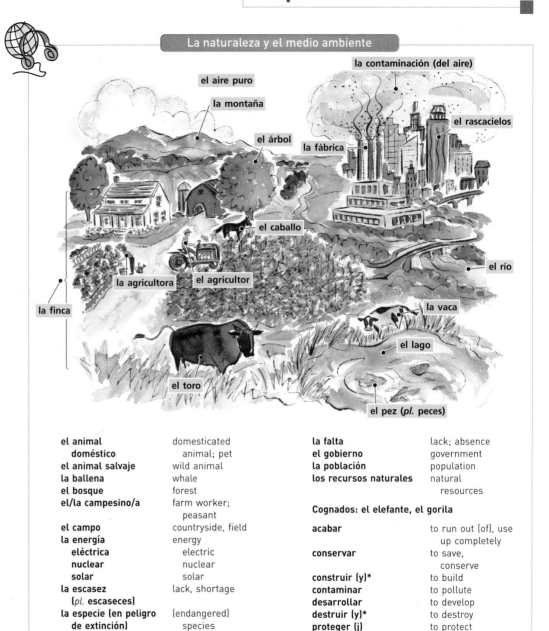

el animal doméstico	domesticated animal; pet	**la falta**	lack; absence
el animal salvaje	wild animal	**el gobierno**	government
la ballena	whale	**la población**	population
el bosque	forest	**los recursos naturales**	natural resources
el/la campesino/a	farm worker; peasant		
		Cognados: el elefante, el gorila	
el campo	countryside, field		
la energía	energy	**acabar**	to run out (of), use up completely
eléctrica	electric	**conservar**	to save, conserve
nuclear	nuclear		
solar	solar	**construir (y)***	to build
la escasez (pl. escaseces)	lack, shortage	**contaminar**	to pollute
		desarrollar	to develop
la especie (en peligro de extinción)	(endangered) species	**destruir (y)***	to destroy
		proteger (j)	to protect

Note the present indicative conjugation of* **construir: construyo, construyes, construye, construímos, construís, construyen. Destruir *is conjugated like* **construir.**

MULTIMEDIA: Audio

Students can listen to and practice this chapter's vocabulary on the Online Learning Center (**www.mhhe.com/puntos7**), as well as on the Textbook Audio CD, part of the Laboratory Audio Program.

Resources: Transparency 87

Más vocabulario

el ritmo (acelerado) de la vida	(fast) pace of life
los servicios públicos	public services
el transporte público	public transportation
la violencia	violence
bello/a	beautiful
denso/a	dense

■■■ Conversación

A. ¿La ciudad o el campo?

1. El aire es más puro y hay menos contaminación.
2. La naturaleza es más bella.
3. El ritmo de la vida es más acelerado.
4. Hay más violencia.
5. Los servicios financieros y legales son más asequibles (*available*).
6. Hay pocos medios de transporte públicos.
7. La población es menos densa.
8. Hay escasez de viviendas.

B. Definiciones. Dé Ud. una definición de estas palabras.

MODELO: el agricultor → Es el dueño (*owner*) de una finca.

1. la fábrica
2. el campesino
3. la escasez
4. la finca
5. la naturaleza
6. la población
7. el río
8. el rascacielos

NOTA CULTURAL

Programas medioambientales

Muchos países del mundo se encuentran en la posición de **equilibrar** la protección del **medio ambiente** con los objetivos del **desarrollo económico**. En muchos casos, **la explotación de recursos naturales** es la mayor fuente de ingreso[a] para la economía de un país. Los gobiernos latinoamericanos están conscientes de la necesidad de **proteger** el medio ambiente y de **conservar** los recursos naturales, y están haciendo lo posible por hacerlo. Los siguientes son algunos de los muchos **programas medioambientales** que se encuentran en los países hispanohablantes.

- En la Ciudad de México, existe un programa permanente de **restricción vehicular** que se llama **Hoy no circula**.[b] Los coches no deben **circular** un día por semana. El día está determinado por el último número de **la placa**.[c] El propósito de este programa es controlar **la emisión de contaminantes**. Programas semejantes a **Hoy no circula** existen también en otros países como Chile y la Argentina.
- En México, España y otros países existen programas de **separación de basura**. Se depositan materiales distintos en recipientes[d] de colores diferentes, desde **el papel** y **el cartón**, **el vidrio**,[e] **el metal** y **el plástico**, hasta **la materia orgánica** y **los desechos**[f] **sanitarios**.

[a]fuente... *source of income* [b]Hoy... *Today [these] don't drive.* [c]*license plate* [d]*containers* [e]*glass* [f]*waste*

▲ *Madrid, España*

Vocabulario: Preparación
Cuatrocientos treinta y nueve ■ **439**

Preliminary Exercise

Ask students the following questions to personalize the vocabulary.

1. *¿Hay mucha contaminación en esta ciudad?*
2. *¿Cómo es el ritmo de vida en (ciudad), acelerado o lento? ¿Qué ritmo de vida prefiere Ud.? ¿Le gusta caminar por la ciudad durante la noche?*
3. *¿Trata Ud. de conservar la energía? ¿Hay ahora una escasez de energía? Si una persona realmente quiere conservar energía, ¿qué puede hacer?*
4. *¿Hay muchos delitos y crímenes en esta ciudad? ¿Qué lugares son famosos por la frecuencia de sus delitos? ¿Tiene Ud. miedo de visitar estos lugares?*
5. *¿Va Ud. al campo con frecuencia? ¿Tiene su familia una finca en el campo? ¿La visita Ud.? ¿Cuándo? Descríbala. ¿Le gustaría vivir en una finca? ¿Cómo es el ritmo de vida en una finca típica?*

Con. A: Follow-Up

Have students tell if they agree or not with the following statements about their city.

¿Está de acuerdo o no?

1. *El sistema de transporte público es muy bueno.*
2. *Hay muchos parques y zonas verdes.*
3. *Ocurren muy pocos delitos.*
4. *Hay poca contaminación.*
5. *El ritmo de la vida es demasiado lento (slow).*
6. *Hay demasiadas fábricas.*
7. *La población es muy densa.*
8. *No hay escasez de viviendas.*

NOTA CULTURAL

Suggestion

Ask the following questions to check comprehension.

1. *¿Qué aspecto económico dificulta la protección del medio ambiente en algunos países hispanos?*
2. *¿En qué país hay un programa para limitar el uso de coches?*
3. *¿Cuáles son algunos de los materiales que se reciclan en México y España?*

National Standards: Communication

Divide the class into three groups. One will defend life in the city, another life in the country, and a third will prepare a list of questions to ask each group. Give students ten to fifteen minutes to prepare their arguments supporting their position and to prepare questions. The city and country groups should then give a simple opening statement, after which the third group will pose their first question. Provide specific time limits for the debating groups to answer, and allow time at the end for final arguments.

Con. C: Preliminary Exercise

Ask students the following questions.

¿Qué hacen para conservar la energía?

¿Qué productos destruyen la capa de ozono (ozone layer)?

¿Usa Ud. mucho agua y energía en su casa?

¿Qué cosas recicla Ud.? ¿periódicos? ¿botellas? ¿latas?

¿Echa Ud. (Do you throw) basura a la calle?

Con. C: Suggestions

■ **Paso 1.** Have students tally on the board the most important item for each student. In a second column, have them tally the least important. Use this information to discuss the general attitude of the class toward these issues.

■ **Paso 2.** Create another chart on the board to tally the number of students for and against each item.

Bright Idea

Con. C: Follow-Up

Have students create a poster in Spanish to motivate others to conserve energy and to reduce pollution. Give them the following suggestions.

la conservación de la energía
la contaminación del agua/aire
la promoción de energías alternativas
el reciclaje

Have students present their posters in class.

C. Problemas del mundo en que vivimos

Paso 1. Los siguientes problemas afectan en cierta medida (*in some measure*) a los habitantes de nuestro planeta. ¿Cuáles le afectan más a Ud. en este momento de su vida? Póngalos en orden, del 1 al 10, según la importancia que tienen para Ud. ¡No va a ser fácil!

_____ la contaminación del aire
_____ la destrucción de la capa de ozono (*ozone layer*)
_____ la escasez de petróleo
_____ la deforestación de la selva (jungla) de Amazonas
_____ la falta de viviendas para todos
_____ el ritmo acelerado de la vida moderna
_____ el uso de drogas ilegales
_____ el abuso de los recursos naturales
_____ la sobrepoblación (*overpopulation*) del mundo
_____ el crimen y la violencia en el país

Paso 2. Ahora comente las siguientes opiniones. Puede usar las siguientes expresiones para aclarar (*clarify*) su posición con respecto a cada tema. ¡OJO! Todas las expresiones requieren el uso del subjuntivo o del infinitivo, porque expresan deseos e influencia

Es / Me parece fundamental que…
importantísimo que…
ridículo que…
¿ ?
Me opongo a que (*I am against*)…
No creo que…

1. Para conservar energía debemos mantener bajo el termostato en el invierno y elevarlo en el verano.
2. Es mejor calentar las casas con estufas de leña (*wood stoves*) que con gas o electricidad.
3. Se debe crear más parques urbanos, estatales y nacionales.
4. La protección del medio ambiente no debe impedir la explotación de los recursos naturales.
5. Para evitar la contaminación urbana, debemos limitar el uso de los coches y no usarlos algunos días de la semana, como se hace en otros países.
6. El gobierno debe poner multas (*fines*) muy graves a las compañías e individuos que causan la contaminación.
7. El desarrollo de las tecnologías promueve (*promotes*) el ritmo tan acelerado de nuestra vida.
8. Los países desarrollados están destruyendo los recursos naturales de los países más pobres.

National Standards: Communication

Have students interview their classmates to find out what they do to help conserve our natural resources. Students should then share their findings with the rest of the class. Write the key words on the board and remind students to try to use them in their interviews.

el reciclaje
apagar/prender las luces
caminar
andar en bicicleta

D. Un recurso natural importante

Paso 1. Lea este anuncio de una empresa (compañía) colombiana y conteste las preguntas.

En ECOPETROL tenemos conciencia ambiental y social. Nuestra planeación incluye siempre los estudios de localización e impacto ambiental, buscando no perturbar la naturaleza y la vida de las poblaciones vecinas a nuestras futuras operaciones. En esta planeación el trabajo con la comunidad es indispensable.

Nuestro propósito: Una mejor convivencia

EMPRESA COLOMBIANA DE PETROLEOS
ECOPETROL

1. ¿Qué tipo de negocio cree Ud. que es Ecopetrol? ¿Qué produce?
2. ¿Qué asuntos (*matters*) son de mayor interés para esta empresa? ¿El tránsito? ¿la deforestación? ¿las poblaciones humanas? ¿otros asuntos?
3. ¿Le parece que la foto que han elegido (*they have chosen*) para el anuncio es buena para la imagen de la empresa? ¿Por qué?
4. El sustantivo **convivencia** se relaciona con el verbo **vivir** y contiene la preposición **con.** ¿Qué cree Ud. que significa **convivencia**?
5. ¿Sabe Ud. cuáles son algunos de los países que producen lo mismo que Ecopetrol?

Paso 2. Hay varias formas de energía. ¿Las conoce Ud. bien? Diga a qué tipo de energía corresponde cada descripción.

Vocabulario útil	
la energía eólica	wind energy
la energía hidráulica	hydraulic energy

1. Es la energía más usada en los hogares (*homes*).
2. Según los expertos, es la forma de energía más limpia; es decir, es la que menos contaminación produce.
3. Puede ser la forma de energía más eficiente, pero también la más peligrosa (*dangerous*).
4. Esta energía viene del viento; por eso sólo se puede desarrollar en lugares específicos.
5. Para producir esta forma de energía son necesarios los ríos y las cataratas (*waterfalls*).

Con. D: Suggestion

Have students look through Spanish-language magazines and newspapers to locate ads with environmental statements or themes. Are there many? What kinds of messages do they convey?

Heritage Speakers

Invite a un estudiante hispanohablante a leer el anuncio en voz alta.

National Standards: Communication

Have students create a pamphlet in Spanish on ways to educate the community to conserve energy and lessen environmental pollution. Have them first select an issue or a plan to promote. They should select a format and images they would like to use (if any), come up with a slogan, and decide what information to include. Some topic suggestions:

la conservación de la energía
la contaminación del agua/aire
la promoción de energía alternativa
el transporte público
el reciclaje

Have students share their completed pamphlets with their classmates.

Los coches

Suggestions

■ Ask students what vocabulary words they associate with the following.

¿Con qué asocia Ud.... ?

1. *¿los colores rojo, amarillo y verde?*
2. *¿los mecánicos?*
3. *¿la contaminación?*
4. *¿parar?*
5. *¿una llanta?*
6. *¿arrancar?*
7. *¿la carretera?*
8. *¿doblar?*

■ Point out that *gastar dinero* means *to spend money.*
■ Provide the following optional vocabulary.

una llanta desinflada
un pinchazo

Point out the difference between *la llanta* and *la rueda.*

■ Point out the spelling changes in *conducir* (zc), *arrancar* (qu), *chocar* (qu), *obedecer* (zc), and *seguir* (g).

Preliminary Exercises

■ Read the following statements and have students respond *cierto* or *falso.*

1. *El tanque del coche contiene aceite.*
2. *Si el semáforo está rojo, es necesario parar.*
3. *Un Cadillac gasta poca gasolina.*
4. *Es necesario tener una licencia para conducir.*
5. *Si Ud. no dobla, Ud. sigue todo derecho.*

■ Ask students the following questions.

1. *En esta clase, ¿cuántos tienen coche? ¿Es viejo o nuevo su coche? ¿grande o pequeño? ¿Gasta mucha o poca gasolina? ¿mucho o poco aceite? ¿Cuánto le cuesta llenar el tanque?*
2. *En general, ¿funciona bien su coche? Cuando no funciona, ¿lo arregla Ud. o se lo arregla un mecánico? ¿un amigo? ¿Es vieja o nueva la batería? ¿Le es difícil hacer arrancar el coche por la mañana? ¿Le es difícil arrancar cuando hace frío?*
3. *¿Tuvo Ud. alguna vez una llanta desinflada (pantomime)? ¿Dónde y cómo ocurrió? ¿Quién la cambió? ¿Tuvo Ud. que llamar para pedir ayuda? ¿Siempre lleva Ud. una llanta de repuesto (llanta de recambio/una quinta llanta)?*

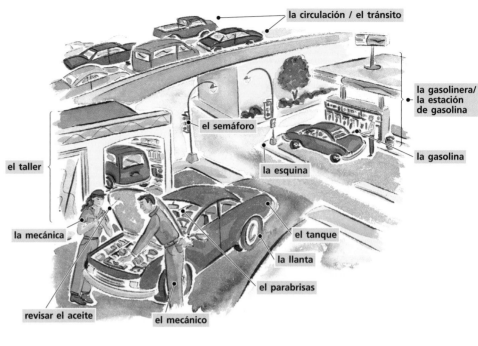

En la gasolinera Gómez

la circulación / el tránsito

la gasolinera/ la estación de gasolina

el semáforo

la gasolina

el taller

la esquina

la mecánica

el tanque

la llanta

revisar el aceite

el parabrisas

el mecánico

la autopista	freeway	doblar	to turn
la calle	street	estacionar	to park
el camino	street; road	gastar (mucha gasolina)	to use (a lot of gas)
la carretera	highway	llenar	to fill (up)
la licencia de manejar/conducir	driver's license	manejar, conducir (zc)*	to drive
		obedecer (zc)*	to obey
arrancar (qu)	to start up (a car)	parar	to stop
arreglar	to fix, repair	seguir (i, i) (g) (todo derecho)	to keep on going; to go (straight ahead)
chocar (qu) (con)	to run into, collide (with)		

*Like the verb **conocer**, **conducir** and **obedecer** have a spelling change in the **yo** form of present indicative: **conozco, conduzco, obedezco**. This spelling change is also used in all forms of the present subjunctive.

Capítulo 14: La naturaleza y el medio ambiente

 Heritage Speakers

En algunos países latinoamericanos, como Colombia por ejemplo, se dice *pase* en vez de *licencia de conducir.* Otro término usado principalmente en España es *el carnet de chófer / de conducir.* También hay varios términos para expresar *to park: estacionar(se), aparcar* (Esp.) y *parquear* (Méx.). Para referirse a *parking lot* o *parking place*, se puede decir *estacionamiento* o *parqueadero.* Pregúnteles a los hispanohablantes de la clase qué palabras usan y por qué.

Resources: Transparencies 88, 89

Transparency 89 offers additional images and vocabulary.

■ ■ ■ Conversación

A. Definiciones

Paso 1. Busque Ud. la definición de las palabras de la columna de la derecha.

1. _____ Se pone en el tanque.
2. _____ Se llenan de aire.
3. _____ Lubrica el motor.
4. _____ Es necesaria para arrancar el motor.
5. _____ Cuando se llega a una esquina, hay que hacer esto o seguir todo derecho.
6. _____ No contiene aire suficiente y por eso es necesario cambiarla.
7. _____ Es un camino público ancho (*wide*) donde los coches circulan rápidamente.
8. _____ Se usan para parar el coche.
9. _____ El policía nos la pide cuando nos para en el camino.
10. _____ Allí se revisan y se arreglan los coches.

a. los frenos (*brakes*)
b. doblar
c. la carretera
d. la batería
e. el taller
f. una llanta desinflada (*flat*)
g. la gasolina
h. las llantas
i. el aceite
j. la licencia

Paso 2. Ahora, siguiendo el modelo de las definiciones anteriores, ¿puede Ud. dar una definición de las siguientes palabras?

1. el semáforo
2. la circulación
3. estacionar
4. gastar gasolina
5. la gasolinera
6. la autopista

B. Entrevista: Un conductor (*driver*) responsable

Paso 1. Entreviste a un compañero / una compañera de clase para determinar con qué frecuencia hace las siguientes cosas.

1. dejar la licencia en casa cuando va a manejar
2. acelerar (*to speed up*) cuando ve a un policía
3. manejar después de tomar bebidas alcohólicas
4. respetar o exceder el límite de velocidad
5. estacionar el coche donde dice «Prohibido estacionar»
6. revisar el aceite y la batería
7. seguir todo derecho a toda velocidad cuando no sabe llegar a su destino
8. rebasar (*to pass*) tres carros a la vez (*at the same time*)

Paso 2. Ahora, con el mismo compañero / la misma compañera, haga una lista de diez cosas que hace —o no hace— un conductor responsable. Pueden usar frases del **Paso 1**, si quieren.

Paso 3. Ahora, analice Ud. sus propias (*own*) costumbres y cualidades como conductor(a). ¡Diga la verdad! ¿Es Ud. un conductor / una conductora responsable? ¿Cuál de los dos es el mejor conductor / la mejor conductora?

Need more practice?
■ Workbook and Laboratory Manual
■ Interactive CD-ROM
■ Online Learning Center (www.mhhe.com/puntos7)

4. ¿Maneja Ud. para venir al campus? ¿Es fácil estacionarse aquí? ¿Es necesario pagar para poder estacionarse en el campus? ¿Cuánto? ¿Quiénes encuentran un estacionamiento con más facilidad, los profesores o los estudiantes?
5. ¿Sabe Ud. manejar? ¿Cuántos años hace que aprendió a manejar? ¿Cuántos años tenía? ¿Quién le enseñó a manejar? ¿Tuvo Ud. algún accidente mientras aprendía? ¿Qué es lo mejor de manejar? ¿y lo peor?

■ Read the following narration to the class, then discuss car ownership, car problems, and auto mechanics.

En este país, cuando algo le pasa al coche, automáticamente lo llevamos a un mecánico. ¿Y qué hace el mecánico? Si tiene suerte, encuentra la parte dañada (damaged) *y la cambia por otra nueva. En realidad, hay mecánicos que no reparan nada o que reparan partes que no tienen problema. Si un mecánico no puede arreglar un coche, es muy probable que el dueño norteamericano decida por comprarse un coche nuevo en vez de gastar dinero en reparaciones. En cambio, en la América Latina y en España, un coche nuevo cuesta relativamente mucho dinero y en algunos países hasta un di-neral* (fortune). *Además, los repuestos* (spare parts) *son costosos y los mecánicos inten-tan reparar verdaderamente las partes que no funcionan. Por eso es común ver coches viejos que después de 15 ó 20 años de uso diario todavía funcionan.*

Con. A: Variation

Have students work in pairs, one covering the first column and the other the second.

Con. B: Suggestions

■ Have students rank question items in order of importance.
■ Ask students the following questions.

¿Es símbolo de mucho prestigio social tener un Ferrari? ¿un Volkswagen? ¿un Hyundai? ¿un BMW? ¿un Toyota? ¿una camioneta? ¿un pickup?
¿Cómo es el típico dueño / la típica dueña de cada uno de estos coches?

National Standards: Connections

In order to drive in many foreign countries, drivers are required to have a valid International Driver's License (IDL) or an International Driver's Permit (IDP). AN IDP translates your state-issued driver's license into 10 languages so that you can show it to officials in foreign countries to help them interpret your driver's license. IDPs are not valid for driving in the country in which they were issued. There are only two organizations authorized to issue IDPs to U.S. residents. The American Automobile Association (AAA) and the America Auto Touring Alliance (AATA) are permitted to issue IDPs only to people who have a valid U.S. driver's license and who are at least 18 years of age. An IDP costs $10.00. Beware of Internet sites that charge anywhere from $64.00 to $350.00 and that are not authorized to issue these documents!

Ask students what *cerrada*, *aburrido*,
and *honrado* have in common.
(→ = *do/a* ending)

Follow-Up

■ After reviewing the *refranes*, ask
students the following questions.

1. *¿Es mejor no decir nada? ¿Qué
le puede pasar a uno cuando
tiene la boca abierta?*

2. *¿Llevan una vida muy
interesante las ostras? ¿Por
qué? ¿Sufren muchas presiones?*

3. *¿Todos los que cometen delitos
son criminales? ¿Es posible que
una persona honrada llegue a
cometer un crimen? ¿Cree que
las personas sufrimos
demasiadas tentaciones en el
mundo moderno?*

■ Have students give equivalent or
similar English proverbs for the
Spanish *refranes*.

Forms of the Past Participle

Note

Students have been using a number
of past participles, especially with
estar, since the early chapters.

casado	aburrido	abierto
cansado	preocupado	cerrado
ocupado		

Emphasis A: Suggestions

■ Model the past participle forms, for
example: *cerrar, cerrado → La
puerta está cerrada.*

■ Use the following rapid response
drill to practice the forms. Have
students give the past participle for
each verb you say.

comprar	invitar	perder
pagar	arreglar	comer
mandar	visitar	recibir
terminar	vender	pedir
preparar	conocer	dormir
llamar	leer	seguir

■ Model the pronunciation of
irregular past participles. Say the
participle and have students give
the corresponding infinitive. Then,
reverse the procedure.

Emphasis B: Suggestion

Have students express the following
in Spanish.

broken	returned	made
seen	written	done
covered	said	open(ed)
discovered	dead	put

GRAMÁTICA

42 *Más descripciones* • **Past Participle Used as
an Adjective**

Algunos refranes y dichos en español

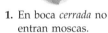

1. En boca *cerrada* no
entran moscas.

2. Estoy tan *aburrido* como
una ostra.

3. Cuando está *abierto* el cajón,
el más *honrado* es ladrón.

Empareje estas oraciones con el refrán o dicho que explican.

1. Es posible que una persona honrada caiga en la tentación de
hacer algo malo si la oportunidad se le presenta.

2. Hay que ser prudente. A veces es mejor no decir nada para evitar (*avoid*) problemas.

3. Las ostras ejemplifican el aburrimiento (*boredom*) porque llevan
una vida tranquila… siempre igual.

Forms of the Past Participle

A. The past participle of most English verbs
ends in *-ed*.

to walk → walked   to close → closed

Many, however, are irregular.

to sing → sung   to write → written

In Spanish, the *past participle* (**el participio
pasado**) is formed by adding **-ado** to the
stem of **-ar** verbs, and **-ido** to the stem of **-er**
and **-ir** verbs. An accent mark is used on the
past participle of **-er/-ir** verbs with stems
ending in **-a**, **-e**, or **-o**.

hablar	comer	vivir
hablado	comido	vivido
(*spoken*)	(*eaten*)	(*lived*)

caer → **caído**	oír → **oído**
creer → **creído**	(son)reír → **(son)reído**
leer → **leído**	traer → **traído**

A few Spanish proverbs and sayings **1.** *Into a closed mouth no flies enter.* **2.** *I am as bored as an
oyster.* **3.** *When the (cash) drawer is open, the most honest person is (can become) a thief.*

☼ Heritage Speakers

Aburrido como una ostra se presenta aquí con el verbo
estar y expresa la idea *as bored as an oyster*. Sin
embargo, algunos hispanohablantes prefieren la idea *as
boring as an oyster*. Para esta versión, el verbo *ser* sería
necesario. Pregúnteles a los hispanohablantes de la
clase qué dirían: *Está tan aburrido/a como una ostra* o
Es tan aburrido/a como una ostra. Pídales que
compartan otros refranes con la clase.

Pronunciation hint: Remember that the Spanish **d** between vowels, as found in past participle endings, is pronounced as the fricative [đ] (see **Pronunciación** in **Capítulo 6**).

B. The Spanish verbs at the right have irregular past participles.

abrir:	**abierto**	morir:	**muerto**
cubrir (*to cover*):	**cubierto**	poner:	**puesto**
		resolver:	**resuelto**
decir:	**dicho**	romper:	**roto**
descubrir:	**descubierto**	ver:	**visto**
escribir:	**escrito**	volver:	**vuelto**
hacer:	**hecho**		

The Past Participle Used as an Adjective

A. In both English and Spanish, the past participle can be used as an adjective to modify a noun. Like other Spanish adjectives, the past participle must agree in number and gender with the noun modified.

Viven en una casa **construida** en 1920.
They live in a house built in 1920.

El español es una de las lenguas **habladas** en los Estados Unidos y en el Canadá.
Spanish is one of the languages spoken in the United States and in Canada.

B. The past participle is frequently used with **estar** to describe conditions that are the result of a previous action.

El lago **está contaminado.**
The lake is polluted.

Todos los peces **estaban cubiertos** de crudo.
All the fish were covered with crude oil.

English past participles often have the same form as the past tense.

*I **closed** the book.*

*The thief stood behind the **closed** door.*

The Spanish past participle is never identical in form or use to a past tense. Compare the sentences at the right.

Cerré la puerta. Ahora la puerta está **cerrada.**
*I **closed** the door. Now the door is **closed.***

Resolvieron el problema. Ahora el problema está **resuelto.**
*They **solved** the problem. Now the problem is **solved.***

AUTOPRUEBA

Give the infinitive of the past participles.

1. estudiadas _____
2. leído _____
3. vistos _____
4. dicha _____
5. abiertas _____
6. bebido _____

Answers: 1. estudiar 2. leer 3. ver 4. decir 5. abrir 6. beber

---

Gramática

Emphasis A: Suggestion

Emphasize that the past participle used as an adjective must agree in gender and number with the noun it modifies.

■ Use the following rapid response drill to practice agreement. Have students change the participle to agree with the nouns indicated.

1. *hecho: bolsas, vestidos, camisa*
2. *escrito: carta, ejercicio, libros*
3. *roto: tazas, silla, disco*

Emphasis B: Suggestions

■ Point out that in *Capítulo 5* students learned that *estar* + past participle is used to express resulting condition.
■ Emphasize the use of the past participle with *estar* to describe resulting conditions. Point out that students learned this in *Capítulo 5* with *estar* expressions.
■ Provide additional examples to contrast the English simple past and past participle with the Spanish, for example, *Hice la tarea. La tarea está hecha.* vs. *I did the homework. The homework is done.*
■ Explain that another common structure with the past participle is *tener* + object + past participle.

Tengo los ejercicios preparados.

This construction is equivalent to the present perfect (*He preparado los ejercicios.*) but emphasizes the completion and recentness of the action. Notice that *estar* + past participle is impersonal. The *tener* + object + past participle tells who did the action.

■ Point out that compound verbs that have an irregular root verb, with few exceptions, have the same irregularity as the root verb in the past participle.

*decir → pre**decir**: pre**dicho***
*poner → com**poner**: com**puesto***
*hacer → satisf**acer**: satis**fecho***
(Some words that now have the letter *h* at one time were written with *f*.)

Have students give the past participle for the following verbs and also give their English equivalent.

revolver	deponer	describir
exponer	reponer	envolver
prescribir	oponer	rever
prever	presuponer	redecir
recubrir	encubrir	subscribir
imponer	rehacer	suponer

Refranes

«Del dicho al hecho hay un gran trecho.»
«A lo hecho, pecho.»

Write the *refranes* on the board. Have students find the meaning of *trecho* and *pecho*. If they cannot come up with the English equivalents of these sayings, give them the following three English proverbs

and have them match the Spanish (one of the Spanish sayings matches two of the English.)

Grin and bear it.
Easier said than done.
What's done is done.

Prác. A: Preliminary Exercise

Have students express the following ideas in Spanish.

¿Cómo se dice en español?

1. money earned
2. the lost luggage
3. a repeated sentence
4. the tired employee
5. dead flies
6. the broken cup

Prác. A: Suggestions

- Point out that *prender* is a synonym of *encender* and *poner* in some contexts (to turn on, light).
- Have students invent additional sentences to describe the classroom. Others respond *cierto* or *falso*. Write on the board the verbs that are useful for describing the classroom.

Prác. B: Note

These passages are adapted, slightly simplified, from authentic materials from Mexico and Spain. Have students read completely through each paragraph before completing it.

Prác. B: Suggestion

Have students mark all the words they do not know during the first reading, then try to guess the meaning. Have students share the strategies they used to complete the reading successfully.

■ ■ ■ Práctica

A. En este momento...

Paso 1. ¡Anticipemos! En este momento, ¿son ciertas o falsas las siguientes oraciones con relación a su sala de clase?

1. La puerta está abierta.
2. Las luces están apagadas.
3. Las ventanas están cerradas.
4. Algunos libros están abiertos.
5. Los estudiantes están sentados.
6. Hay algo escrito en la pizarra.
7. Una silla está rota.
8. Hay carteles y anuncios colgados en la pared.
9. Un aparato está enchufado.
10. Las persianas (*blinds*) están bajadas.

Paso 2. Ahora describa el estado de las siguientes cosas en su casa (cuarto, apartamento).

1. las luces	3. el televisor	5. la puerta
2. la cama	4. las ventanas	6. las cortinas (*curtains*)

B. Comentarios sobre el mundo de hoy. Complete cada párrafo con los participios pasados de los verbos apropiados de la lista.

Información sobre el reciclaje: desperdiciar (*to waste*), destruir, hacer, reciclar

Todos los días, Ud. tira en el basurero[a] aproximadamente media libra[b] de papel. Si Ud. trabaja en un banco, en una compañía de seguros[c] o en una agencia del gobierno, el promedio[d] se eleva a tres cuartos de libra al día. Todo ese papel _____[1] constituye un gran número de árboles _____[2]. Esto es un buen motivo para que Ud. comience un proyecto de recuperación de papeles hoy en su oficina. Ud. puede completar el ciclo del reciclaje únicamente si compra productos _____[3] con materiales _____[4].

[a]*wastebasket* [b]*media... half a pound* [c]*insurance* [d]*average*

La conservación de la energía

acostumbrar	bajar
agotar (*to use up*)	cerrar (ie)
apagar (gu)	limitar

Las fuentes[a] de energía no están _____[5] todavía. Pero estas fuentes son _____[6]. Desgraciadamente, todavía no estamos _____[7] a conservar energía diariamente. ¿Qué podemos hacer? Cuando nos servimos la comida, la puerta del refrigerador debe estar _____[8]. Cuando miramos la televisión, algunas luces de la casa deben estar _____[9]. El regulador termómetro debe estar _____[10] cuando nos acostamos.

[a]*sources*

National Standards: Community

Have students do a search on *desarrollo sustentable* or *sostenible*, and come back to class ready to discuss what it means and why it is an important subject for Latin American countries.

C. Situaciones. ¿Cuál es la situación en este momento? Conteste según el modelo.

MODELO: Natalia les tiene que *escribir* una *carta* a sus abuelos. →
La *carta* no está *escrita* todavía.

1. Los Sres. García deben *abrir* la *tienda* más temprano. ¡Ya son las nueve!
2. Pablo tiene que *cerrar* las *ventanas*; entra un aire frío.
3. Los niños siempre esperan que la *tierra* se *cubra* de nieve para la Navidad.
4. Delia debe *poner* la *mesa*. Los invitados llegan a las nueve y ya son las ocho.
5. Claro está que la contaminación va a contribuir a la *destrucción* de la *capa de ozono*.
6. Es posible que los ingenieros *descubran* el *error* en la construcción del reactor nuclear.
7. Se debe *resolver* pronto el *problema* de la escasez de energía.

■■■ **Conversación**

A. ¡Ojo alerta! Hay por lo menos cinco cosas que difieren (*are different*) entre un dibujo y el otro. ¿Puede Ud. encontrarlas? Use participios pasados como adjetivos cuando pueda.

Ⓐ  Ⓑ

B. ¡Rápidamente! Dé Ud. el nombre de...

1. algo contaminado
2. una persona muy/poco organizada
3. un programa de computadora bien diseñado
4. un edificio bien/mal construido
5. algo que puede estar cerrado o abierto
6. un servicio necesitado por muchas personas
7. un tipo de transporte usado a la vez por muchas personas
8. algo deseado por muchas personas

Need more practice?

■ Workbook and Laboratory Manual
■ Interactive CD-ROM
■ Online Learning Center (www.mhhe.com/puntos7)

Gramática   Cuatrocientos cuarenta y siete ■ **447**

Prác. C: Variations

■ Point out that *de* is used to express *with* in *covered with snow: cubierta **de** nieve*.
■ Have students give sentences with *tener* + past participle.

La carta no está escrita todavía. →
Natalia no tiene la carta escrita todavía.

Con. A: Variation

Have students use the preterite and the imperfect to create stories based on the drawings. Ask questions to help them get started: *¿Por qué está preparada una familia y la otra no?*

Con. A: Note

The following are some possible answers for this activity.

1. *En el dibujo A, el niño está dormido. En el dibujo B, la niña está despierta.*
2. *En el dibujo A, la lámpara está apagada. En el dibujo B, la lámpara está encendida.*
3. *En el dibujo A, las luces están encendidas. En el dibujo B, las luces están apagadas.*
4. *En el dibujo A, las personas están sentadas en el sofá. En el dibujo B, tres personas están sentadas a la mesa.*
5. *En el dibujo A, no hay comida en la mesa. En el dibujo B, hay comida en la mesa.*
6. *En el dibujo A, el gato está despierto. En el dibujo B, el gato está dormido.*

Con. B: Suggestion

Have students work in groups and compete with each other to see which group can find the most associations for a given item.

**Resources:
Transparency 90**

MULTIMEDIA: Internet

Have students search the Internet to find out what Latin American countries are doing to conserve natural resources and to limit the amount of contaminants released into the environment. Encourage students to use Spanish and English search words to find websites. You may want to assign specific topics, areas, or countries to groups of students and have them prepare a brief oral presentation based on their findings.

☼ **Heritage Speakers**

En los países hispanohablantes, se usa el sistema métrico, también llamado el sistema internacional (SI), para medir. Pregúnteles a los hispanohablantes de la clase si saben usar SI. Pídales a ellos o a otros estudiantes que sepan usar SI que den algunas medidas comunes, por ejemplo, una temperatura climática moderada (70° F) o un peso posible (común) de una mujer (110–140 lbs.). Hablen de las ventajas y desventajas de SI y del sistema usado en este país.

Gramática ■ **447**

Follow-Up

Ask the following questions after completing the *minidiálogo:*

1. *Si Ud. tiene una llanta desinflada, ¿le pide a alguien que lo/la ayude a cambiarla?*

2. *¿Le dice Ud. al mecánico que le revise el aceite o lo hace Ud. mismo/a?*

3. *¿Puede Ud. arreglar algunas fallas (faults) o necesita siempre que se lo haga un mecánico?*

Present Perfect Indicative

Suggestions

- Review the present tense of *haber* and the formation of the present perfect.

- Emphasize that only the masculine singular of the past participle is used in the present perfect tense. In this construction, the past participle is not an adjective.

- Point out that the object pronouns must precede the conjugated *haber* form; they are never placed after the conjugated form of *haber* nor attached to the end of the participle: *Ya la he llamado. (a María) Ya se lo he dado. (el trabajo a María)*

- Emphasize and model that *hay* is a special third person (impersonal) form of *haber* meaning *there is/are. Ha* and *han* are used as helping verbs for third person conjugations of the present perfect tense.

- Read the following phrases and have students give the corresponding subject pronoun: *he corrido, hemos caminado, han perdido, has dormido, habéis dicho, ha visto.*

- Have students express the following ideas in Spanish.

¿Cómo se dice en español?

1. I have studied / eaten / read / gotten up.
2. He / She has answered / promised / lived / opened.
3. We have called / lost / written.
4. They have traveled / run / discovered.

- Point out that in both English and Spanish the present perfect is often used as an alternative for the simple past tense, especially when the action has just taken place.

¿Leíste / Has leído el periódico?

---

43 · *¿Qué has hecho?* • **Perfect Forms: Present Perfect Indicative and Present Perfect Subjunctive**

Una llanta desinflada

MANOLO: ¡Ay, qué mala suerte!

LOLA: ¿Qué pasa?

MANOLO: Parece que el coche tiene una llanta desinflada. Y como no hay ningún taller por aquí, tengo que cambiarla yo mismo.

LOLA: *¿Has cambiado* una llanta alguna vez?

MANOLO: No. Siempre *he llevado* el coche a un taller cuando hay problemas.

LOLA: Pues, yo nunca *he cambiado* una llanta tampoco. Pero te puedo ayudar, si quieres.

MANOLO: Gracias. ¡Espero que la llanta de recambio* no esté desinflada también!

¿Y Ud.? ¿Ha... ?

1. cambiado una llanta desinflada
2. revisado el aceite de su coche
3. arreglado otras cosas del coche
4. tenido un accidente con el coche
5. excedido el límite de velocidad en la autopista

Present Perfect Indicative

PAST	Present	Future
preterite	present indicative	
imperfect	present progressive	
present perfect	formal commands	
present perfect subjunctive	informal commands	
	present subjunctive	

he hablado	*I have spoken*	hemos hablado	*we have spoken*
has hablado	*you have spoken*	habéis hablado	*you (pl.) have spoken*
ha hablado	*you have spoken, he/she has spoken*	han hablado	*you (pl.) / they have spoken*

A flat tire MANOLO: *Aw, what bad luck!* LOLA: *What's wrong?* MANOLO: *It seems the car has a flat tire. And, as there aren't any repair shops around here, I have to change it myself.* LOLA: *Have you ever changed a flat tire before?* MANOLO: *No. I've always taken the car to a repair shop when there are problems.* LOLA: *Well, I've never changed a tire either. But I can help you, if you want.* MANOLO: *Thanks. I hope that the spare tire isn't flat, too!*

*Other terms for spare tire in Spanish are **la llanta de respuesto** and **la quinta llanta.***

☼ Heritage Speakers

Explíqueles a los estudiantes que en España se usa consistentemente el presente perfecto en lugar del pretérito para hablar de eventos muy recientes: *¿A qué hora has desayunado?* en vez de *¿A qué hora desayunaste?*

A. In English, the present perfect is a compound tense consisting of the present tense form of the verb *to have* plus the past participle: *I have written, you have spoken,* and so on.

In the Spanish *present perfect* (**el presente perfecto**), the past participle is used with present tense forms of **haber,** the equivalent of English *to have* in this construction.

In general, the use of the Spanish present perfect parallels that of the English present perfect.

No **hemos estado** aquí antes.
We haven't been here before.

Me **he divertido** mucho.
I've had a very good time.

Ya le **han escrito** la carta.
They've already written her the letter.

 Haber, an auxiliary verb, is not interchangeable with **tener.**

B. The form of the past participle never changes with **haber,** regardless of the gender or number of the subject. The past participle always appears immediately after the appropriate form of **haber** and is never separated from it. Object pronouns and **no** are always placed directly before the form of **haber.**
[Práctica A–B]

Ella **ha cambiado** una llanta desinflada varias veces.
She's changed a flat tire several times.

Todavía **no le** han revisado el aceite al coche.
They still haven't checked the car's oil.

C. The present perfect form of **hay** is **ha habido** (*there has/have been*).

 Remember that **acabar** + **de** + *infinitive*— not the present perfect tense—is used to state that something *has just occurred.*

Ha **habido** un accidente.
There's been an accident.

Acabo de mandar la carta.
I've just mailed the letter.

Present Perfect Subjunctive

The *present perfect subjunctive* (**el perfecto del subjuntivo**) is formed with the present subjunctive of **haber** plus the past participle. It is used to express *I have spoken* (*written,* and so on) when the subjunctive is required. Although its most frequent equivalent is *I have* plus the past participle, its exact equivalent in English depends on the context in which it occurs.

Note in the model sentences at the right that the English equivalent of the present perfect subjunctive can be expressed as a simple or as a compound tense: *did / have done; came / have come; built / have built.*
[Práctica C–D]

haya hablado	hayamos hablado
hayas hablado	hayáis hablado
haya hablado	hayan hablado

Es posible que lo **haya hecho.**
It's possible (that) he may have done (he did) it.

Me alegro de que **hayas venido.**
I'm glad (that) you have come (you came).

Es bueno que lo **hayan construido.**
It's good (that) they built (have built) it.

☀ **Heritage Speakers**

Recuerde a los hispanohablantes que, en el español estándar, la forma aceptada del presente de subjuntivo del verbo *haber* es *haya.* Sin embargo, hay algunos hispanohablantes que usan *haiga* en vez de *haya* en el habla diaria. Acuérdese de que la forma apropiada es *haya* y que se recomienda evitar decir o escribir *haiga.* ¿Cuántos estudiantes hispanohablantes dicen o han oído decir *haiga* en vez de *haya*?

⟳ **Reciclado**

■ Students will often try to use the present perfect indicative instead of the *hace* + time + *que* construction, due to interference from English. For example, instead of *Hace un año que estudio español,* students might say **He estudiado español por un año.* Remind students regularly that Spanish speakers prefer the *hacer* construction to express time passed. Reenter this construction by having them express the following ideas in Spanish.

¿Cómo se dice en español?

1. How long have you been at this university? / I have been here for two years.
2. How long have you studied Spanish? / I have studied it for only one year.
3. How long ago did you move to this town? / I moved here one year ago.

■ Remind heritage speakers that the form *ha habido* is impersonal and that it always appears in the singular form.

Ha habido muchos accidentes en esta carretera.

Present Perfect Subjunctive

Suggestions

■ Review the basic concept and uses of the subjunctive before beginning.

1. influence
2. emotion
3. doubt

■ Review the subjunctive forms of *haber.*
■ Emphasize that these forms are the subjunctive counterparts of the present indicative (*he hablado, has hablado, ha hablado,* and so on).
■ Point out that the first and third person forms (*yo, Ud./él/ella*) are the same.
■ Read the following phrases and have students give the corresponding subject pronouns.

haya dicho
hayamos perdido
hayan escuchado
hayáis llamado

■ Use the following rapid response drill to practice the perfect tense forms. Have students give the present perfect indicative for each cue.

1. **yo:** *llegar, terminar, bañarse, acostarse*
2. **tú:** *comer, prometer, romper, volver*
3. **Ud./él/ella:** *asistir, insistir, sonreír, divertirse*
4. **nosotros:** *abrir, decir, cubrir, descubrir*
5. **Uds./ellos/ellas:** *escribir, poner, ver, hacer*

■ Use this chain drill to practice the forms in sentences.

¿Qué hemos hecho hoy?

1. *José se ha preparado muy bien para la clase.* (*tú, el profesor, los estudiantes, Luis, Carmen y Pilar, vosotros*)
2. *Yo he empezado la lección para hoy.* (*leer, escribir, estudiar, comprender, aprender*)
3. *Lidia se ha despertado.* (*levantarse, bañarse, vestirse, desayunar, correr a la facultad, leer en la cafetería, reírse con los amigos, ir a su primera clase*)

Prác. A: Suggestion

Have students report what they have done or not done by saying *ya lo he hecho* or *no lo he hecho todavía.*

Prác. A: Follow-Up

Ask students the following questions to personalize the activity.

1. *¿Qué ha hecho Ud. hoy? ¿Ha hablado con un amigo / una amiga? ¿Ha estudiado? ¿Ha comido?*
2. *¿Qué ha hecho Ud. esta semana? ¿Ha ido a una fiesta? ¿Ha bailado? ¿Ha cantado? ¿Ha tomado Coca-Cola / cerveza / vino? ¿Ha visto una película?*
3. *¿Ha escrito una carta este mes? ¿Ha visitado un museo? ¿Ha salido de la ciudad? ¿Se ha levantado antes de las seis? ¿antes de las cinco? ¿Por qué tan temprano?*
4. *¿Ha depositado dinero en el banco? ¿Ha vendido / comprado algo?*

Extend all of the questions with: *¿Qué más ha hecho Ud. hoy / esta semana / este mes?*

AUTOPRUEBA

Give the correct form of **haber.**

INDICATIVE	SUBJUNCTIVE
1. yo _____	4. tú _____
2. Uds. _____	5. Ud. _____
3. nosotros _____	6. ellos. _____

Answers: **1.** *he* **2.** *han* **3.** *hemos* **4.** *hayas* **5.** *haya* **6.** *hayamos*

■■■ Práctica

A. El pasado y el futuro

Paso 1. **¡Anticipemos!** Indique las actividades que Ud. ha hecho en el pasado.

1. _____ He hecho un viaje a Europa.
2. _____ He montado a camello (*camel*).
3. _____ He tomado una clase de informática.
4. _____ He buceado (*gone scuba diving*).
5. _____ He ido de safari a África.
6. _____ He comprado un coche.
7. _____ He preparado una comida italiana.
8. _____ He ocupado un puesto (*position*) político.
9. _____ He tenido una mascota.
10. _____ He escrito un poema.
11. _____ He visto una película de Almodóvar.
12. _____ He leído un periódico en español.
13. _____ Me he puesto un sombrero para ir a clase.
14. _____ Me he roto el brazo o la pierna.

Paso 2. Ahora, entre las cosas que Ud. no ha hecho, ¿cuáles le gustaría hacer? Conteste, siguiendo los modelos.

MODELOS: Nunca he montado a camello, pero me gustaría hacerlo.
(Nunca he montado a camello y no me interesa hacerlo.)

B. El coche de Carmina. Carmina acaba de comprarse un coche usado. (Claro, su papá es vendedor de autos en Los Ángeles. ¡Así que el coche fue una ganga!) Describa lo que le ha pasado a Carmina, según el modelo.

MODELO: ir a la agencia de su padre →
Ha ido a la agencia de su padre.

1. pedirle ayuda a su padre
2. hacer preguntas acerca de (*about*) los diferentes coches
3. ver uno bastante barato
4. revisar las llantas
5. conducirlo como prueba
6. regresar a la agencia
7. decidir comprarlo
8. comprarlo
9. volver a casa
10. llevar a sus amigas al cine en su coche

EN LOS ESTADOS UNIDOS Y EL CANADÁ

Suggestions

■ Have students think of as many city or state names as they can that are influenced by Spanish. Do they know what they mean?
■ Have students give words they know in Spanish related to Colorado, Florida, Nevada, and Montana (*el color, la flor, la nieve/nevar, la montaña*).

■ Have students provide additional Spanish place-names. This can be done as a group, time-controlled competition. Some additional names are *Álamo,* (*poplar tree*) referring to the fort in Texas and city of Los Alamos in New Mexico; Alcatraz, California (from *alcatraz,* which means pelican); Boca Ratón, Florida (*mouth of the mouse,* referring to the shape of the bay and/or to the

---

Bright Idea

Suggestion

Have students note the pronunciation of Spanish place names in this country. What happens to certain letters, especially vowels, when English speakers pronounce these places? Help them compare correct Spanish pronunciation to the pronunciation in this country

Lugares con nombres españoles

La **geografía** de Norteamérica está llena de nombres que dejaron los españoles, los primeros europeos que **exploraron** y se establecieron en estas **tierras**. Varios **estados** de los Estados Unidos tienen nombres españoles, por ejemplo: Colorado (*de color rojo*), Nevada (*cubierta de nieve*), Montana (*de la palabra «montaña»*), Florida (*con flores*) y Nuevo México. Numerosas **ciudades** estadounidenses también llevan los nombres de origen español.

ST. AUGUSTINE   Esta ciudad de Florida, **establecida** en 1564, lleva el nombre de la **misión** San Agustín. Es la ciudad más antigua de Norteamérica fuera de[a] México.

SANTA FE   El nombre original y completo de la capital de Nuevo México es la Villa Real de la Santa Fe de San Francisco de Asís. Santa Fe, el nombre usado hoy, significa *Holy Faith*. Es la capital más antigua de los Estados Unidos (establecida en 1607).

SARASOTA   Esta ciudad fue nombrada en honor de la hija del gobernador de Florida, Sara de Soto.

LAS VEGAS   El nombre de esta ciudad en Nevada significa *fertile plains*.

LOS ANGELES   En 1781 los españoles **fundaron** el Pueblo de Nuestra Señora la Reina de Los Ángeles de Porciúncula en California. Hoy es la segunda ciudad más grande de los Estados Unidos.

FRESNO   Esta ciudad de California fue nombrada por sus **árboles**, los fresnos.[b]

Los españoles también exploraron la **costa** pacífica hasta Alaska, donde hay muchos nombres de influencia española: el Cabo[c] Blanco, en Oregón; el Cabo de Álava, en Washington; las ciudades de Valdez y Córdova y el Glaciar Malaspina, en Alaska. En Canadá están los **estrechos**[d] de Juan de Fuca y de Laredo, y las **islas** Quadra, Saturna, Galiano, Gabriola, Aristazábal y Flores, todos en la costa de la Columbia Británica.

[a]*fuera... outside of*   [b]*ash trees*   [c]*Cape*   [d]*straits*

Gramática   Cuatrocientos cincuenta y uno ■ **451**

pirates who would hide there); El Paso, Texas (*passage*); La Brea, California (*tar*); Las Cruces, New Mexico (*crosses*, named for the burial ground of forty people who were killed there by Apaches in 1830); Reno, Nevada (*reindeer*); Los Gatos, California (*cats*, named for the wildcats that roamed that area when it was founded); Sangre de Cristo Mountains (*blood of Christ mountains*, named for

the color of the slopes when the sun sets on them); San Francisco, California (named after the St. Francis of Assisi mission [*la misión Dolores*] in that area); San Antonio, Texas (named after the river that Spanish explorers found and named on the feast day of St. Anthony of Padua).

■ Point out that *Colorado* and *Nevada* are past participle forms (*nevada* is also a noun).

Prác. C: Preliminary Exercises

- Read the following sentences and have students tell whether the present perfect indicative or the present perfect subjunctive is used.

1. *Dice que ha hablado con ella.*
2. *Es posible que haya hablado con ella.*
3. *No, no han repetido las palabras.*
4. *No creo que hayan repetido las palabras.*
5. *Me alegro de que me hayas escrito.*
6. *No vengas a menos que me hayas escrito antes.*

- Have students give the subjunctive equivalents.

  he hablado
  he repetido
  has comido
  has manejado
  ha mandado
  ha venido
  hemos podido
  hemos alquilado
  han comprendido
  se han acostado

Prác. C: Follow-Up

Have students suggest other things that they think no one in class has ever done, for example, *No creo que nadie haya... ; Creo que nadie ha...*

Con. A: Suggestions

- Model one or two series of sentences about yourself.
- Model some possible reactions to the sentences: *(No) Dudo que..., Es imposible que..., Estoy seguro que..., Es obvio que...*

C. ¡No lo creo! ¿Tienen espíritu aventurero sus compañeros de clase? ¿Llevan una vida interesante? ¿O están tan aburridos como una ostra? ¡A ver!

Paso 1. ¡Anticipemos! De cada par de oraciones, indique la que (*the one that*) expresa su opinión acerca de los estudiantes de esta clase.

1. ☐ Creo que alguien en esta clase ha visto las pirámides de Egipto.
   ☐ Es dudoso que alguien haya visto las pirámides de Egipto.
2. ☐ Estoy seguro/a de que por lo menos uno de mis compañeros ha escalado una montaña alta.
   ☐ No creo que nadie haya escalado una montaña alta.
3. ☐ Creo que alguien ha viajado haciendo autostop.
   ☐ Dudo que alguien haya hecho autostop en un viaje.
4. ☐ Creo que alguien ha practicado el paracaidismo.
   ☐ Es improbable que alguien haya practicado el paracaidismo.
5. ☐ Estoy seguro/a de que alguien ha tomado el metro en Nueva York a medianoche (*midnight*).
   ☐ No creo que nadie haya tomado el metro neoyorquino a medianoche.

> ### Vocabulario útil
>
> **escalar** (to climb)
> **hacer** (*irreg.*) **autostop**
> (to hitchhike)
> **el paracaidismo**
> (skydiving)

Paso 2. Ahora escuche mientras el profesor / la profesora pregunta si alguien ha hecho estas actividades. ¿Tenía Ud. razón en el **Paso 1**?

D. ¿Lo ha hecho?

Paso 1. Reaccíone a los siguientes mandatos usando el presente perfecto del indicativo. Use los pronombres de complemento directo e indirecto para evitar la repetición.

> **MODELO:** Limpia tu cuarto. → Ya *lo he limpiado.*

1. Arranca el coche.
2. Llamen Uds. al mecánico.
3. Abra el mapa.
4. Revise Ud. los frenos, por favor.
5. Siga las direcciones.

Paso 2. Ahora, conteste las preguntas usando el presente del subjuntivo, según las indicaciones entre paréntesis. Use los pronombres de complemento directo e indirecto para evitar la repetición.

> **MODELO:** ¿Julio arregló su coche? (No, no creo) →
> No, no creo que *lo haya arreglado* todavía.

1. ¿Los agricultores conservaron suficiente agua? (Espero)
2. ¿El mecánico resolvió el problema con tu coche? (Dudo)
3. ¿Ana consiguió su licencia de conducir? (Sí, ya)
4. ¿Construyeron más rascacielos en San José este año? (Es probable)
5. ¿Hemos pasado el río? (Sí, estoy seguro/a)

■ ■ ■ Conversación

A. ¿Verdad o mentira?

Paso 1. Invente Ud. tres oraciones sobre cosas que ha hecho y no ha hecho en su vida. Dos oraciones deben ser verdaderas y una debe ser una mentira.

> **MODELO:** He hecho un viaje a Sudamérica.
> Nunca he conocido a mis primos.
> He visto muchas películas en español.

Need more practice?

- Workbook and Laboratory Manual
- Interactive CD-ROM
- Online Learning Center (www.mhhe.com/puntos7)

☼ Heritage Speakers

También se dice *echar dedo* para expresar *hacer autostop*. Pregúnteles a los hispanohablantes de la clase qué expresión usan. Si son de un país hispano-hablante, pregúnteles si es común que la gente haga *autostop* en su país y qué tipo de persona lo haría.

Paso 2. Lea sus oraciones a unos compañeros o a la clase entera. Ellos van a tratar de encontrar la mentira.

> **MODELO:** Creo que has hecho un viaje a Sudamérica y que has visto muchas películas en español. Dudo que no hayas conocido a tus primos.

B. Entrevista. Con un compañero / una compañera, haga y conteste preguntas con estos verbos. La persona que contesta debe decir la verdad.

> **MODELO:** visitar México →
> E1: ¿Has visitado México?
> E2: Sí, he visitado México una vez.
> (No, no he visitado México nunca.)
> (Sí, he visitado México durante las vacaciones de los últimos años.)

1. comer en un restaurante hispánico
2. estar en Nueva York
3. manejar un Alfa Romeo
4. correr en un maratón
5. abrir hoy tu libro de español
6. escribir un poema
7. actuar en una obra teatral
8. ver un monumento histórico
9. conocer a una persona famosa
10. romperse la pierna alguna vez

Pluperfect

NOTA COMUNICATIVA

Talking About What You Had Done

Use the past participle with the imperfect form of **haber** (**había, habías,...**) to talk about what you had—or had not—done before a given time in the past. This form is called the past perfect (**el pluscuamperfecto**).

Antes de graduarme en la escuela secundaria, no **había estudiado** español.	Before graduating from high school, I hadn't studied Spanish.
Antes de 1985, siempre **habíamos vivido** en Kansas.	Before 1985, we had always lived in Kansas.

C. Entrevista. Use the following cues to interview a classmate about his or her activities before coming to this campus.

> **MODELO:** ¿qué? / no haber aprendido a hacer antes del año pasado →
> E1: ¿Qué no *habías aprendido* a hacer antes del año pasado?
> E2: Pues… no *había aprendido* a nadar. Aprendí a nadar este año en mi clase de natación.

1. ¿qué? / no haber aprendido a hacer antes del año pasado
2. ¿qué materia? / no haber estudiado antes del año pasado
3. ¿qué deporte? / haber practicado mucho
4. ¿qué viaje? / haber hecho varias veces
5. ¿qué libro importante? / no haber leído
6. ¿qué decisión? / no haber tomado
7. ¿ ?

Gramática

NOTA COMUNICATIVA

Suggestion

The past perfect is presented here and practiced in *Conversación C*. Use additional activities, such as the following, if you prefer to stress this tense.

> *Jaime es un acusón* (tattletale). *Siempre le dice a su madre las cosas que ha hecho Laura, su hermana mayor. ¿Qué le dijo a su madre ayer?*
> *Jaimito le dijo que Laura había dicho una mentira.*

mirar la televisión toda la tarde
no estudiar
perder sus libros
romper un plato
faltar a clase
comer todo el pastel
pegarle
¿ … ?

Con. B: Follow-Up

Ask the following questions after completing the activity.

> *¿Qué es posible que hayan hecho las siguientes personas?*

1. *Un hombre que lleva máscara sale corriendo de un banco, con una bolsa en la mano.*
2. *Un joven está saliendo de una lavandería con un montón de ropa limpia.*
3. *Un sábado de otoño, a las cuatro y media de la tarde, muchas personas están saliendo de un estadio.*
4. *Unos turistas están hablando ansiosamente con un policía. La mujer no lleva bolsa.*
5. *Una familia está saliendo de McDonald's.*

Con. C: Follow-Up

- Have students describe what they had already done or not done by the time they turned 18 years old: *Antes de cumplir 18 años, ¿qué había hecho? ¿Qué no había hecho?*
- Have students complete the following sentences logically using the past perfect tense.

  1. *Antes de 1492 Cristóbal Colón no _____.*
  2. *Antes de 1938 la Segunda Guerra Mundial no _____.*
  3. *Antes de 1980 mis padres (no) _____.*
  4. *Antes de 1995 yo (no) _____.*

- Have students talk about things they had done or had not done before the year 2004. Have them begin with the cues given, then invent their own.

  > *¿Qué cosas habían hecho, o no habían hecho, Uds. antes del año 2004? Dé oraciones nuevas según las indicaciones.*
  > *Antes de 2004, ya no habíamos… estudiar español, asistir a esta universidad, graduarnos en la escuela superior, escuchar un concierto, ver una comedia española, comer flan, ¿ … ?*

- Use the following cues for additional practice.

  > *¿Qué cosas no habían hecho… y no han hecho todavía?*
  > *No habíamos… visitar la Patagonia viajar a Moscú aprender ruso conocer a Ricky Martin ¿ … ?*
  > *Y no lo hemos hecho todavía.*

UN POCO DE TODO

Bright Idea

Preliminary Exercises

- Review with students the formation of the past participles in Spanish, starting with regular -ar, -er, and -ir verbs.
- Have students give you the irregular past participle forms for the following verbs.

abrir	hacer	romper
cubrir	morir	ver
decir	poner	volver
escribir		

- Have students provide the correct forms of the past participles for the following verbs and then give the English equivalents. Remind them to identify the root verb first.

componer	devolver	prescribir
contradecir	predecir	suponer
descubrir		

- Write the following model on the board and have students work in pairs to ask and answer questions using the cues.

MODELO: escribir la carta →
E1: ¿Ya está escrita la carta?
E2: No, no la he escrito.
E1: ¡Hombre! Es imposible que no la hayas escrito todavía.

1. hacer las maletas
2. comprar los boletos
3. preparar la cena
4. facturar el equipaje
5. sacudir los muebles
6. poner la mesa
7. comprar el fax
8. salvar la información en la computadora
9. apagar la computadora
10. darle el trabajo al profesor / a la profesora

A: Suggestion

Bring or have students bring additional pieces that make commentaries about modern life. The pieces can be in English or in Spanish. Use them to elicit discussion in Spanish.

UN POCO DE TODO

A. Dos dibujos, un punto de vista. Un español hizo el dibujo de la derecha; un argentino, el de la izquierda. Pero los dos comentan el mismo tema.

Palabras útiles			
el arado (plow)	la flor	la mecanización	el tractor
la deshumanización	la gente	la mula	

Paso 1. Conteste estas preguntas sobre el dibujo de la derecha.

1. Describa la ciudad que se ve en el dibujo.
2. ¿Qué ha descubierto la gente? ¿Por qué mira con tanto interés?
3. Para construir esta ciudad, ¿qué han hecho? ¿Qué han destruido?

Paso 2. Conteste estas preguntas sobre el dibujo de la izquierda.

1. ¿Qué se ha comprado el agricultor de la izquierda? ¿Qué ha vendido?
2. ¿Qué es «más moderno», según el otro agricultor?
3. ¿Qué desventaja tiene el tractor?

Paso 3. Ahora explique su reacción personal a estos dos dibujos. ¿Son chistosos (*funny*)? ¿serios?

B. ¿Glaciares en la Argentina? Complete the following dialogue and article with the correct forms of the words in parentheses, as suggested by the context. When two possibilities are given in parentheses, select the correct word. **¡OJO!** When **haber** appears in parentheses followed by an infinitive, you will decide whether to use present perfect indicative or subjunctive. You will also need to decide between using present tense indicative or subjunctive with several other infinitives.

En la clase de Geografía mundial, todos los estudiantes se han reunido en grupos de tres para investigar la geografía de uno de los países de Sudamérica. Luego deben hacer una presentación «PowerPoint» con la intención de mostrar(les/los[1]) a sus compañeros de clase (que/lo que[2]) el grupo (haber descubrir[3]) del país que escogieron. Milton, Marisol y Petra están (tratado/tratando[4]) de terminar su informe sobre la Argentina.

MARISOL: Bueno, ya tenemos muchos datos sobre las ciudades argentinas y las famosas Pampas.[a] Es suficiente, ¿no creen Uds.?

MILTON: Creo que sí. Y (yo/me[5]) encanta que (*tú:* haber encontrar[6]) esos artículos que (comparar[7]) históricamente la figura del gaucho con la del «cowboy» del oeste de los Estados Unidos. Y, a (tú/ti[8]), ¿qué te (parecer[9]), Petra?

PETRA: Pues, yo no (encontrarse[10]) totalmente satisfecha con la presentación. Sí, sí, estoy de acuerdo en que está muy bien (escrito[11]), pero esa información no tiene nada de nuevo. Yo (haber oír[12]) hablar de las Pampas, de los gauchos y de la ciudad de Buenos Aires desde que estaba en la escuela primaria. Quiero que (*nosotros:* presentar[13]) algo diferente, algo menos común...

MARISOL: ¿Qué (*tú:* sugerir[14]), entonces?

PETRA: Miren este párrafo breve que tengo. Es un resumen de un artículo que encontré en el Internet. Sugiero que lo (*nosotros:* poner[15]) al final de la presentación.

MILTON: De acuerdo. Pero quiero que (*nosotros:* entregar[16]) el informe ahora, sin añadirle más.

El párrafo:

Y, finalmente, atención ecoturistas extremistas:

Vengan (a / —[17]) ver el Parque Nacional Los Glaciares, en la Patagonia, en el sur de la Argentina. El gobierno argentino (*P/I,* crear[18]) este parque en 1937, y en 1982 el parque (*P/I,* ser[19]) designado Patrimonio Natural de la Humanidad por la UNESCO. Allí, en las 600.000 hectáreas[b] del parque, pueden explorar unos glaciares (impresionante[20]). Se calcula que aproximadamente 200 de esos glaciares (salir[21]) de los campos de hielo[c] que dominan este parque. Con (alguno[22]) precauciones, es posible que los ecoturistas aventureros (escalar[23]) unas montañas de hielo precipitosas como el Cerro Torre, un desafío[d] para los mejores alpinistas profesionales. Es fascinante encontrar una geografía tan variada dentro de un solo país.

[a]*the grassy plains of Argentina* [b]*hectares (2.47 acres)* [c]*campos... ice fields* [d]*challenge*

Comprensión: ¿Cierto o falso? Correct the false sentences.

1. Todos los estudiantes de clase de Geografía mundial van a preparar un informe sobre la Argentina.
2. Milton, Marisol y Petra necesitan empezar su informe sobre la Argentina.
3. Marisol encontró unos artículos sobre el gaucho y el «cowboy».
4. Petra no está contenta porque dice que la información es incorrecta.
5. Petra les trae un párrafo que ella escribió con información que encontró en el Internet.
6. El Parque Nacional Los Glaciares es un pequeño parque al sur de Buenos Aires.

Resources for Review and Testing Preparation

- Workbook and Laboratory Manual
- Interactive CD-ROM
- Online Learning Center (www.mhhe.com/puntos7)

B: Preliminary Exercise
Before completing this activity, find out if any of your students can answer the following questions.

¿Dónde está la Argentina?
¿Qué es un gaucho?
¿Cómo es la geografía de la Argentina?

Resources: Desenlace

In the *Capítulo 14* segment of "Chapter-by-Chapter Supplementary Materials" in the IM/RK, you will find a chapter-culminating activity. You can use this activity to consolidate and review the vocabulary and grammar skills students have acquired.

MULTIMEDIA: Internet

Have students search the Web for information about *la Patagonia, la Pampa,* and *los gauchos.* Then have them present a written or oral report on one of the topics.

PERSPECTIVAS
culturales

Entrevista cultural

Suggestions

- Before showing the video, ask students questions about organizations they support or belong to.

    ¿Es Ud. miembro/a de alguna asociación u organización en la universidad? ¿Cómo se llama y por qué existe?

    ¿Tienen el grupo algún proyecto filantrópico?

    ¿Cuándo se reúnen los miembros del grupo?

    ¿Participa Ud. en alguna asociación o actividad ecológica? ¿Qué hace? ¿Cuántas personas participan?

    ¿Qué hace Ud. individualmente para preservar la ecología y los recursos naturales?

- Show the video and allow students one to two minutes to work on the questions. Have volunteers answer the questions.
- Have volunteers role-play Natalia and her interviewer.

Entre amigos

Suggestions

- Before viewing the video, review the questions with the students and ask them similar questions.

    ¿Tiene Ud. coche? ¿Qué tipo de coche es? ¿Es grande o pequeño?

    Si Ud. no tiene coche, ¿cómo llega a clase y/o al trabajo?

    ¿Maneja Ud. el coche todos los días? ¿Cuándo usa el transporte público?

Have students answer or work in small groups to ask and answer these questions.

- After viewing the video, have volunteers read and answer the questions.

Videoteca

Entrevista cultural: la Argentina

Natalia D'Ángelo es una estudiante de la Argentina. Habla de sus estudios, pero se enfoca en el medio ambiente. Antes de ver el vídeo, lea el siguiente fragmento de la entrevista.

ENTREVISTADORA: ¿Perteneces tú[a] a alguna asociación?

NATALIA: En la universidad estamos trabajando en una asociación para proteger la biodiversidad de una zona de la Argentina que se llama la Patagonia.

ENTREVISTADORA: ¿Nos puedes hablar un poco más sobre la Patagonia?

NATALIA: Sí, la Patagonia es un territorio muy extenso que es todo el sur de Argentina y es una zona muy poco poblada, con actividades que están centradas principalmente en la pesca[b] y en el turismo.

[a]*Perteneces… Do you belong* [b]*fishing*

Ahora vea el vídeo y conteste las siguientes preguntas, basándose en la entrevista.

1. ¿Dónde estudia Natalia?
2. ¿En qué se especializa?
3. Según Natalia, ¿se preocupan mucho o poco los estudiantes por los problemas ecológicos?
4. ¿Cómo pueden participar los estudiantes en actividades ecológicas?
5. ¿Qué es la Patagonia?

Entre amigos: Nuestro pequeño grano de arena (*grain of sand*)

Miguel, Tané, Rubén y Karina hablan del medio ambiente. En su opinión, ¿qué preguntas se van a hacer? Antes de mirar el vídeo, lea las preguntas a continuación. Mientras mire el vídeo, trate de entender la conversación en general y fíjese en la información sobre la ecología, la naturaleza y el medio ambiente. Luego mire el vídeo una segunda vez, fijándose en la información que necesita para contestar las preguntas.

1. ¿Qué tipo de coche está manejando Miguel?
2. ¿Por qué no tiene Miguel su propio (*own*) coche?
3. ¿Qué tipo de coche tiene Karina?
4. ¿Cómo sugiere Karina cuidar el medio ambiente?
5. ¿Qué opinión tiene Rubén de las fábricas?

Conozca... la Argentina

Datos esenciales

- Nombre oficial: República Argentina
- Capital: Buenos Aires
- Población: 38.741.000 habitantes
- Moneda: el peso
- Idioma oficial: el español

¡Fíjese!

- La inmigración de europeos en el siglo XIX ha tenido un papel decisivo en la formación de la población de la Argentina (así como en la del Uruguay). En 1856 la población argentina era de 1.200.000 habitantes; para 1930, 10.500.000 extranjeros habían entrado en la Argentina por el puerto de Buenos Aires. La mitad[a] estaba formada por italianos, una tercera parte por españoles, y el resto estaba formado principalmente por alemanes y eslavos. Muchos de los que llegaron fueron trabajadores temporales que, más tarde o más temprano, regresaron a Europa. El resto, sin embargo,[b] se estableció permanentemente, porque el gobierno quería estimular la inmigración para poblar la Pampa. Pero muchos, acostumbrados a la vida urbana, se quedaron en Buenos Aires.
- Buenos Aires es una ciudad con una población de más de 13.000.000 de habitantes, lo cual supone[c] el 30 por ciento de la población del país. Es el centro cultural, comercial, industrial y financiero, así como el puerto principal de la Argentina. A las personas de Buenos Aires se les llama «porteños», derivado de la palabra «puerto[d]».

[a]half [b]sin... however [c]lo... which constitutes [d]port

Learn more about Argentina with the Video, the Interactive CD-ROM, and the Online Learning Center (www.mhhe.com/puntos7).

Nota cultural: el tango

El tango se originó en los barrios pobres de Buenos Aires a finales del siglo XIX. El tango se toca con los instrumentos de los inmigrantes: la guitarra española, el violín italiano y el típico bandoleón, una especie de acordeón alemán.

Los temas del tango muestran una dualidad. Por un lado, representan la agresividad machista,[a] que incluye dramas pasionales y peleas con cuchillos.[b] Por otro, simbolizan la nostalgia, la soledad[c] y el sentimiento de pérdida.[d] El intérprete de tangos más famoso fue el porteño Carlos Gardel (1887–1935).

[a]male [b]peleas... knife fights [c]solitude [d]loss

▲ La Plaza de Mayo, que data de 1580, año de la fundación de Buenos Aires

Conozca... la Argentina

Suggestions

- Have students gather information on Evita Perón and on the Perón regime on the Internet, and then show the film *Evita* (1997). Have students compare the historical figures and events with those in the film.
- Give students background information about Astor Piazzola (1921–1986). This Argentine musician and composer, influenced by Carlos Gardel and trained in Paris by Nadia Boulanger, used the tango as the inspiration for his classical compositions). Play some Gardel tangos and some Piazzola pieces for students and ask them to compare the two.
- Show Carlos Saura's 1999 film *Tango* in class. You may wish to show the 1933 film of the same name, which stars Argentine actress Libertad Lamarque as the tango singer, as a comparison.
- Ask whether any of the students have read any of the stories of Jorge Luis Borges (1899–1986), and, if some have, encourage them to tell the class about them. Some students may wish to read one or several of the stories and report on them for extra credit. You may wish to tell them that the author of noted collections such as *Ficciones* (1945), *El Aleph* (1949), and *El libro de los seres imaginarios* wrote highly learned, ironic narratives in which the reader's sense of reality is transmuted and a fantastic, sometimes metaphysical world replaces the familiar one.

Note

Students can read an excerpt of the poem *"Cuadrados y ángulos"* by Argentina's Alfonsina Storni in *Un paso más 14*.

MULTIMEDIA: Internet

Have students search the Internet for more information about the government, educational system, geography, and economy of Argentina. Assign specific topics and have students prepare brief oral presentations for the class based on their findings.

☼ Heritage Speakers

Pregúnteles a los hispanohablantes si alguno de ellos sabe bailar el tango. Si hay alguien que lo sabe bailar, pídale que lo baile o que lo explique. También invite a los otros hispanohablantes a hablar de los bailes típicos de su país y mostrar los pasos del baile.

Gramática

To review the grammar points presented in this chapter, refer to the indicated grammar presentations. You'll find further practice of these structures in the Workbook and Laboratory Manual, on the Interactive CD-ROM, and on the *Puntos de partida* Online Learning Center (www.mhhe.com/puntos7).

42. Más descripciones—Past Participle Used As an Adjective

Do you know how to form past participles? You should remember that past participles that are used as adjectives agree with the noun they describe.

43. ¿Qué has hecho?—Perfect Forms: Present Perfect Indicative and Present Perfect Subjunctive

How do you express that you have done something? Do you know how to say that you're happy or sad that someone else did or has done something?

Vocabulario

Practice this vocabulary with digital flash cards on the Online Learning Center (www.mhhe.com/puntos7).

Suggestions

- Bring or have students bring magazine clippings of images related to the vocabulary words. Use the images for quick comprehension checks (*¿Qué es eso?* → *Es una llanta desinflada.*) and as a springboard for questions and short discussions.
- Remind students that *conducir* and *obedecer* are conjugated like *conocer*, with a *-zc-* in the first person singular: *conduzco, obedezco.* They should also remember the spelling changes for *construir* (y), *destruir* (y), *proteger* (j), *arrancar* (qu), *chocar* (qu), and *seguir* (g).

Bright Idea

Suggestion

Remind students that most verbs in the present subjunctive follow the pattern of the first person singular (*yo*) form of the present indicative; therefore, verbs with first-person spelling changes in the present indicative will have the same spelling change in the present subjunctive.

construir: construyo → construya, construyas, constuya, and so on
destruir: destruyo → destruya, destruyas, destruya, and so on
proteger: protejo → proteja, protejas, proteja, and so on
conducir: conduzco → conduzca, conduzcas, conduzca, and so on
obedecer: obedezco → obedezca, obedezcas, obedezca, and so on
seguir: sigo → siga, sigas, siga, and so on

Orthographic changes that occur in the first-person singular preterite are also used in the subjunctive.

arrancar: arranqué → arranque, arranques, arranque, and so on
chocar: choqué → choque, choques, choque, and so on

El medio ambiente

acabar	to run out (of), use up completely
conservar	to save, conserve
construir (y)	to build
contaminar	to pollute
cubrir	to cover
desarrollar	to develop
descubrir	to discover
destruir (y)	to destroy
evitar	to avoid
proteger (j)	to protect
reciclar	to recycle
resolver (ue)	to solve, resolve
el aire	air
la energía	energy
eléctrica	electric
nuclear	nuclear
solar	solar
la escasez (*pl.* escaseces)	lack, shortage
la fábrica	factory
la falta	lack; absence
el gobierno	government
la naturaleza	nature
la población	population
los recursos naturales	natural resources

Repaso: la contaminación

¿La ciudad o el campo?

el/la agricultor(a)	farmer
el/la campesino/a	farm worker; peasant
el campo	countryside, field
la finca	farm
el rascacielos	skyscraper
el ritmo	rhythm, pace
el servicio	service
el transporte	(means of) transportation
la violencia	violence

Repaso: la ciudad, la vida

Los animales

el animal doméstico	domesticated animal; pet
el animal salvaje	wild animal
la ballena	whale
el caballo	horse
la especie (en peligro de extinción)	(endangered) species
el pez (*pl.* peces)	fish
el toro	bull
la vaca	cow

Cognados: el elefante, el gorila

El paisaje

el árbol	tree
el bosque	forest
el lago	lake
el río	river

Repaso: el mar, la montaña, el océano

Hablando de coches

arrancar (qu)	to start up (*a car*)
gastar	to use, expend
llenar	to fill (up)
revisar	to check
el aceite	oil
la batería	battery
la estación de gasolina	gas station
los frenos	brakes
la gasolina	gasoline
la gasolinera	gas station
la llanta (desinflada)	(flat) tire
el/la mecánico/a	mechanic
el nivel	level
el parabrisas	windshield
el taller	(repair) shop
el tanque	tank

Repaso: arreglar

En el camino

chocar (qu) (con)	to run into, collide (with)
conducir (zc)	to drive
doblar	to turn

obedecer (zc)	to obey
parar	to stop
seguir (i, i) (g)	to keep on going; to go; to continue

Repaso: estacionar, manejar

la autopista	freeway
la calle	street
el camino	street; road
la carretera	highway
la circulación	traffic
el/la conductor(a)	driver
la esquina	(street) corner
la licencia de manejar/conducir	driver's license
el límite de velocidad	speed limit
el/la policía	police officer
el semáforo	traffic signal
el tránsito	traffic
todo derecho	straight ahead

Los adjetivos

acelerado/a	fast, accelerated
bello/a	beautiful
denso/a	dense
público/a	public
puro/a	pure

Suggestions

- Have students regroup the words under new categories, for example, *negativo* vs. *positivo* or *infraestructura* vs. *naturaleza* vs. *mecanismos.*
- Play a word association game. Begin each round with one of the five adjectives. After each round write the first and last word on the board.

Literatura de la **Argentina**

Note

Storni battled cancer in her 40s, and when she found out she was losing the fight, she turned in her last poem to an Argentine newspaper. As the poem circulated in the newspapers, she drowned herself in the ocean.

LECTURA

Suggestions

- Do the *Estrategia* activity in class before assigning the reading as homework.
- Ask students which other strategies they can use as they approach the readings.
- Have students identify the other reading strategies they have learned so far.

Un paso más 14

Literatura de la **Argentina**

Sobra la autora: *Alfonsina Storni nació en Sala Capriasca, Suiza, pero vivió en la Argentina casi toda la vida, una vida llena de desilusiones y obstáculos. Storni era—y sufría los problemas de—una mujer intelectual a principios del siglo XX. El poema «Cuadrados[a] y ángulos» es de la colección* El dulce daño *(1918).*

▲ Alfonsina Storni
(1892–1938)

Casas enfiladas,[b] casas enfiladas,
casas enfiladas.
Cuadrados, cuadrados, cuadrados.
Casas enfiladas.
Las gentes ya tienen el alma[c] cuadrada,
Ideas en fila[d]
y ángulos en la espalda.
Yo misma he vertido[e] ayer una lágrima,[f]
Dios mío, cuadrada.

[a]*Squares*   [b]*in a straight row*   [c]*soul*   [d]*en... in single file*   [e]*shed*   [f]*tear*

LECTURA

ESTRATEGIA: Using Background Knowledge

Another useful strategy that you can use to facilitate your reading comprehension is the "activation" of any background knowledge that you might have about the topic. That is, if you think about all that you know about the topic of the passage, you can begin to formulate a hypothesis and make predictions about the content.

The following passage is entitled *"La Amazonia pierde cada año un millón y medio de hectáreas."* No doubt you already know something about the Amazon, given that it is frequently mentioned in the press and on television. To begin, note three things that you already know about the Amazon.

1.

2.

3.

Think about these things as you read the article. This information might be mentioned in the passage.

National Standards: Culture

Play for students the song *"Alfonsina y el mar,"* by Ariel Ramírez and Félix Luna. This song was made famous by the Argentine singer Mercedes Sosa.

Sobre la lectura... Este artículo es de un periódico español, *El Diario,* de Sevilla, y se publicó en el verano de 1999. El tema de la Amazonia sigue siendo de interés internacional, y recibe la atención del mundo, no sólo de este país.

Suggestions

- This article was published in 1999. Have students research news about the Amazon rainforest since 1999. Has the situation improved or has it become worse?
- Ask students if they know of other ecology groups like Greenpeace that lobby to protect areas like the Amazon.

La Amazonia pierde cada año un millón y medio de hectáreas[a]

La Amazonia, espacio vital para el equilibrio del Planeta, pierde cada año 1,5 (uno coma cinco) millones de hectáreas, debido principalmente a la extracción ilegal de madera[b] por parte de las multinacionales de explotación forestal.

Según un informe de Greenpeace, *Plantando cara a[c] la deforestación,* el 80 por ciento de la madera obtenida de la Amazonia se extrae ilegalmente y el 72 por ciento de los treinta y seis «puntos críticos» de deforestación de la zona son consecuencia de la actividad maderera.[d]

El documento, que responsabiliza a diecisiete multinacionales de explotación forestal de la destrucción progresiva de este «pulmón del Planeta», resalta[e] que la contribución de la Amazonia a la producción total de madera en Brasil se ha disparado[f] del 14 por ciento al 85 por ciento en sólo dos décadas.

«A la cabeza de la destrucción de los bosques primarios de la Amazonia se encuentra la industria de la madera, que en 1997 causó daños en cerca de 1,5 millones de hectáreas», afirma el documento.

El informe y la denuncia[g] sobre la actual situación de la Amazonia se encuadran[h] en una <u>campaña mundial</u> de Greenpeace para <u>frenar</u> la destrucción acelerada de la Amazonia y la gira[i] por varios países de una delegación amazónica, que estos días se encuentra en España.

▲ *Área deforestada de la Amazonia*

Tras destacar[j] que la explotación forestal intensiva aumenta[k] de forma preocupante, los portavoces[l] alertaron de que, en los últimos cuatro años, ocho multinacionales han comprado una extensión de selva amazónica del tamaño de la Comunidad Valenciana[m] —2,3 millones de hectáreas— y ya controlan el 12 por ciento de la capacidad de producción que hay en la zona.

También subrayaron[n] que, en los últimos veinte años, se ha destruido el 15 por ciento de la Amazonia —un territorio equivalente a Francia— y afirmaron que «es posible e imprescindible[o] compatibilizar la vida de los trabajadores indígenas con la conservación de este ecosistema que da equilibrio al Planeta.»

[a]*land measurement equivalent to 2.47 acres*   [b]*wood*   [c]*Plantando... Confronting*   [d]*wood-related*
[e]*emphasizes*   [f]*se... has increased*   [g]*accusation*   [h]*se... are included*   [i]*tour*   [j]*Tras... After*
emphasizing   [k]*is increasing*   [l]*spokespersons*   [m]*Comunidad... region in Spain*   [n]*they underscored*
[o]*necesario*

Notes

- The Amazon basin, which is primarily in Brazil, includes parts of Peru, Bolivia, Ecuador, and Colombia, as well as a small area of Venezuela.
- The Amazon River, which cuts through the Amazon rainforest, has the biggest watershed area of any river, more tributaries than any river, and discharges more water than any river; therefore it can be considered the largest river in the world. The river measures about 4000 miles in length and drains about 2.3 million square miles. The Amazon begins high in the Andes, rushing through waterfalls and gorges before entering the enormous tropical Amazon Basin. Unlike most big rivers, the Amazon is wide and straight until the mouth, where it spills into the Atlantic. No bridge spans this part of the river. During new and full moons, a wave front from the ocean causes waves up to sixteen feet high as it sweeps upstream for some 400 miles at more than 40 miles per hour.

National Standards: Connections

The word *Amazon* came from a Greek myth. The Spanish conquistador who named the river, Francisco de Orellana, was the first European to travel the length of the Amazon (1541–1542). After helping Francisco Pizarro conquer Peru, he set out from Quito with Gonzalo Pizarro to search for gold in the interior of South America. After abandoning the main party, Orellana traveled down the Napo River, which fed into the Amazon River. During his expedition, he and his men encountered a tribe of fierce female warriors. He reported that each woman did "as much fighting as ten Indian men." Recalling the Greek myth of female warriors, Orellana named the entire river *Amazonas.*

Comprensión: Extension

Ask your students these additional *Comprensión* questions.

1. La lectura se enfoca en:
   a. *Greenpeace*
   b. *las multinacionales en la Amazonia*
   c. *la explotación forestal.*
2. En la lectura, a la Amazonia se le llama:
   a. *«el corazón del Planeta»*
   b. *«el pulmón del Planeta»*
   c. *«el cerebro del Planeta».*
3. La frase «a la cabeza de la destrucción de los bosques primarios de la Amazonia se encuentra la industria de la madera... » significa que:
   a. *la industria de la madera propone ideas para la destrucción de los bosques*
   b. *la industria de la madera es la responsable principal de la destrucción de los bosques*
   c. *la madera de la Amazonia es la cabeza del Planeta.*
4. Es probable que la delegación amazónica quiera:
   a. *controlar la explotación forestal*
   b. *explotar las multinacionales*
   c. *parar la destrucción de la Amazonia.*

Answers: 1. a 2. b 3. b 4. c

Comprensión

A. Confirmación. Vuelva a la lista que Ud. escribió antes de leer el artículo. ¿Qué información de su lista aparece en el pasaje?

B. ¿Cierto o falso?

1. La Amazonia pierde 1,5 millones de hectáreas cada mes.
2. Greenpeace ha declarado que el 80 por ciento de la extracción de madera de la Amazonia es ilegal.
3. Greenpeace también ha nombrado a diecisiete multinacionales responsables por la deforestación.
4. Cuando se publicó el artículo, el área destruida era un territorio equivalente a Francia.
5. La delegación amazónica está en Brasil.

C. Preguntas. Conteste las siguientes preguntas.

1. Según el artículo, ¿quiénes son los responsables de la deforestación de la Amazonia?
2. En el artículo, a la Amazonia se le llama el «pulmón del Planeta». Explique esta imagen en español con sus propias palabras.

E S C R I T U R A

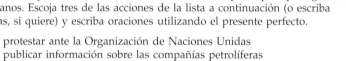

A. Greenpeace. Imagine que Ud. quiere comentarle a un amigo dos medidas (*measures*) que han tomado los miembros de Greenpeace para proteger los océanos. Escoja tres de las acciones de la lista a continuación (o escriba otras, si quiere) y escriba oraciones utilizando el presente perfecto.

> protestar ante la Organización de Naciones Unidas
> publicar información sobre las compañías petrolíferas
> atacar buques petroleros
> investigar las consecuencias ambientales de los submarinos nucleares
> ¿ ?

Empiece sus oraciones con esta frase:

Los miembros de Greenpeace...

▲ *La sede* (headquarters) *de la Organización de Naciones Unidas, en la Ciudad de Nueva York*

MULTIMEDIA: Internet

Have students search for information about the different indigenous groups living in the Amazon and about their problems as their habitat suffers destruction.

National Standards: Connections

Ask students to search the Internet for a Greenpeace site in Spanish and report on the main issues that appear in it. Have them identify country-specific versus general or international issues.

B. Problemas ecológicos. ¿Qué problema ecológico le preocupa más a Ud.? ¿Ha pensado en las varias maneras (*ways*) en que puede proteger el medio ambiente? Escoja uno de los problemas de la lista a continuación (u otro, si quiere) que le gustaría comentar. Luego escriba una breve composición en la que describe el problema. También comente lo que ha hecho Ud. o lo que piensa hacer para resolver el problema.

Problemas medio ambientales

- La deforestación
- La contaminación de los ríos y lagos
- El uso de pesticidas (*m.*) en las verduras y frutas
- La escasez de energía eléctrica
- La falta de recursos naturales
- El desecho (*waste*) de productos de plástico y de papel
- La destrucción de la capa de ozono

ESCRITURA

Suggestions

- If you prefer that your students do a journal activity, see *Mi diario* in this chapter of the Workbook.
- Have students write two statements that use the present perfect and describe what they have done for the environment. Ask volunteers to put one of their statements on the board. Have students use the statements to write a brief composition about the class' collective efforts to improve the environment.

B: Variation
Have students write a brief report (two paragraphs) in Spanish about natural resources in their area or state (or another area or state that interests them). Have them note the present condition of those resources, the benefits derived from them, how the community and government try to protect them, how they are exploited, and so on.

◀ Unos novios en el Parque Forestal de Santiago, Chile

CHAPTER OPENER PHOTO

Point out the chapter-opener photo. Have students talk about places that young couples meet in this country. Do they go to parks together? If not, where? Have students describe the park in the photo. What might draw couples to the park?

Suggestions

- Have students respond *cierto* or *falso* to the following sentences.

    1. *Es necesario* **casarse** *para tener una vida feliz y completa.*

    2. *Se debe prohibir que la gente se case antes de los veinticinco años, ya que inevitablemente* **los matrimonios** *entre personas muy jóvenes resultan en* **el divorcio.**

    3. *Los padres deben vivir con sus hijos en su* **vejez.**

    4. *Los jóvenes deben empezar a salir con sus* **novios** *a la edad de 12 años.*

    5. *Lo más importante en la vida es la familia y luego, en orden de importancia, los amigos y el trabajo.*

- The words in **boldface** are included in the active vocabulary of this chapter. Have students discuss the words and use context to help them understand the meanings. Place the words they cannot guess in new sentences and contexts.
- Introduce and model vocabulary words students might need for this activity.
- Have students work in groups to list a few rules that people should follow before getting married, for example, *Las parejas deben consultar con un consejero / una consejera de matrimonio por unos meses antes de casarse.*

Note

The *Puntos de partida* Online Learning Center includes an interview with a native speaker from Chile who responds to statements about personal relationships.

Resources

For Students

- Workbook
- Laboratory Manual and Laboratory Audio Program
- Quia™ Online Workbook and Online Laboratory Manual
- Video on CD
- Interactive CD-ROM
- *Puntos de partida* Online Learning Center (**www.mhhe.com/puntos7**)

For Instructors

- *Instructor's Manual and Resource Kit,* "Chapter-by-Chapter" Supplementary Materials
- Overhead Transparencies 91–94
- Testing Program
- Test Generator
- Video Program
- Audioscript
- *Puntos de partida* Online Learning Center (**www.mhhe.com/puntos7**)

La vida social y la vida afectiva°

Entrevista cultural

Jorge Balmaceda ▶
Puerto Montt, Chile

°emotional

Suggestion

Have students list their ideas about Chile, including information on geography, politics, economy, culture, music, and cuisine. When you finish the chapter, return to the lists and ask students what ideas they would change and/or add.

National Standards: Communication

Have students work in small groups to discuss the modern family. Are all families *familias típicas*? How has our idea of the traditional family changed over the last decade? Ask students: *¿Hay alguien en esta clase que conozca a una familia que no sea la tradicional?*

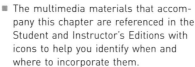

MULTIMEDIA

- The multimedia materials that accompany this chapter are referenced in the Student and Instructor's Editions with icons to help you identify when and where to incorporate them.

- The IM/RK provides suggestions for using the multimedia materials in the classroom.

Las relaciones sentimentales

Note

See the model for vocabulary presentation and other material in the *Capítulo 15 Vocabulario: Preparación* section of "Chapter-by-Chapter Supplementary Materials," in the IM.

Suggestions

- Use definitions as in *Conversación A* to present the vocabulary. Model some words in sentences about yourself and in communicative exchanges with the students.

    Yo estoy casado. Me casé en...
    Mi esposa...

- Offer the following optional vocabulary.

    el compromiso matrimonial
    separado/a
    divorciado/a

- Point out that *separado/a* and *divorciado/a* are used with *estar*, not *ser*.
- Note that *un matrimonio* means *a married couple* as well as *a marriage*.
- Point out that *novio/a* connotes a more serious relationship in Hispanic cultures than that implied by the English words *boyfriend/girlfriend*. See the *Nota cultural* on page 469. Emphasize and model the multiple meanings of *novio/a*.
- Words for in-laws were introduced in a *Vocabulario útil* section in *Capítulo 2*. Reenter those now. Use the family tree in that chapter to help model them. Draw the tree on the board and read the following paragraph: *Eliana Gómez Castro es la suegra de Isabel López Gómez. En cambio, Isabel es la nuera de Eliana y Pedro Vargas Núñez. Pedro es el esposo de Eliana. Luis Vargas Gómez es el cuñado de Felipe Castro Ruiz. Felipe está casado con Gloria Vargas Castro, la hermana de Luis.*
- Have students write down four adjectives to describe their ideal mate. Then, on the board, write the adjectives in separate columns, one for *el esposo ideal* and the other for *la esposa ideal*. Use this information as a springboard for a class discussion. Are there apparent differences in the columns? Do men look for certain qualities and women others? Which is more important: physical beauty or inner beauty (personality, sense of humor, and so on)?

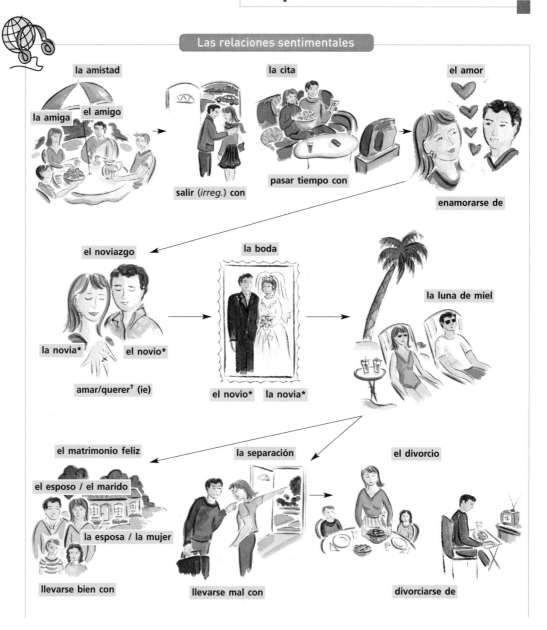

El/La novio/a can mean boyfriend/girlfriend, fiancé(e), *or* groom/bride.
†*Amar* and *querer* both mean to love, *but* amar *implies more passion.*

466 ■ Cuatrocientos sesenta y seis

Capítulo 15: La vida social y la vida afectiva

MULTIMEDIA: Audio

Students can listen to and practice this chapter's vocabulary on the Online Learning Center (**www.mhhe.com/puntos7**), as well as on the Textbook Audio CD, part of the Laboratory Audio Program.

☀ **Heritage Speakers**

Pídales a los hispanohablantes que hablen de la importancia de las relaciones entre familiares y amigos y las diferencias y las semejanzas entre los hispanos y los no-hispanos en cuanto a la familia.

Resources: Transparencies 91, 92

Transparency 92 offers additional images and vocabulary.

la pareja	(married) couple; partner	enamorado/a* (de)	in love (with)
el/la viudo/a	widower/widow	recién casado/a (con)	newlywed (to)
		soltero/a†	single, not married
amistoso/a	friendly	casarse (con)	to marry
cariñoso/a	affectionate	pelearse (con)	to fight (with)
casado/a† (con)	married (to)	romper (con)	to break up (with)
divorciado/a (de)	divorced (from)	separarse (de)	to separate (from)

■ ■ ■ Conversación

A. Definiciones. Empareje las palabras con sus definiciones. Luego, para cada palabra definida, dé un verbo y también el nombre de una persona asociada con esa relación social. Hay más de una respuesta posible en cada caso.

1. _____ el matrimonio
2. _____ el amor
3. _____ el divorcio
4. _____ la boda
5. _____ la amistad

a. Es una relación cariñosa entre dos personas. Se llevan bien y se hablan con frecuencia.
b. Es el posible resultado de un matrimonio, cuando los esposos no se llevan bien.
c. Es una relación sentimental, apasionada, muy especial, entre dos personas. Puede llevar al (*lead to*) matrimonio.
d. Es una ceremonia religiosa o civil en la que (*which*) la novia a veces lleva un vestido blanco.
e. Es una relación legal entre dos personas que viven juntas (*together*) y que a veces tienen hijos.

B. ¡Seamos lógicos! Complete las oraciones lógicamente.

1. Mi abuelo es el _____ de mi abuela.
2. Muchos novios tienen un largo _____ antes de la boda.
3. María y Julio tienen una _____ el viernes para comer en un restaurante. Luego van a bailar.
4. La _____ de Juan y Pati es el domingo a las dos de la tarde, en la iglesia (*church*) de San Martín.
5. En una _____, ¿quién debe comprar los boletos, el hombre o la mujer?
6. La _____ entre los ex esposos es imposible. No pueden ser amigos.
7. ¡El _____ es ciego (*blind*)!
8. Para algunas personas, el _____ es un concepto anticuado. Prefieren vivir juntos, sin casarse.
9. Algunas parejas modernas no quieren gastar su dinero en _____.
10. ¿Cree Ud. que es posible _____ a primera vista (*at first sight*)?

---

*(Mi) **Enamorado/a** can also mean (*my*) boyfriend/girlfriend.
†*In the activities of* **Capítulo 2,** *you began to use* **ser casado/a.** *A variation of this phrase is* **estar casado/a. Estar casado/a** *means* to be married; **ser casado/a** *means* to be a married person. **Ser soltero/a** *is used exclusively to describe an unmarried person.*

Vocabulario: Preparación   Cuatrocientos sesenta y siete ■ **467**

Suggestions

■ Point out that the first person singular of *salir* is *salgo*.
■ Remind students that *to have a good time* cannot be translated directly from English to Spanish. The correct verb is *divertirse*.

Preliminary Exercises

■ Ask students the following questions to check comprehension and reinforce meaning:

1. *¿Qué palabras asocia Ud. con la amistad? ¿el amor? ¿una boda? ¿la luna de miel? ¿el novio? ¿la esposa?*
2. *¿Cómo es el novio / la novia ideal? ¿Es rubio/a o moreno/a? ¿joven o viejo/a? ¿alto/a o bajo/a? ¿guapo/a o feo/a? ¿trabajador(a) o perezoso/a? ¿romántico/a (cariñoso/a) o frío/a?*

■ Ask students the following questions to personalize the vocabulary.

¿Pasa Ud. mucho tiempo con sus amigos?
¿Qué hacen? ¿Siempre se llevan bien?
¿Sus amigos tienen los mismos intereses que Ud.?
¿Cree que un matrimonio debe tener intereses parecidos?
¿Es importante que los esposos sean amigos?
¿Cuál es la edad ideal para casarse?

Con. A: Follow-Up

Have students react to the following statements using *estoy de acuerdo* and *no estoy de acuerdo.*

1. *El matrimonio (La luna de miel) es un concepto muy anticuado.*
2. *Si el noviazgo es corto, el matrimonio va a ser corto también.*
3. *Las mujeres son más románticas que los hombres.*
4. *El noviazgo debe ser largo y formal.*
5. *El matrimonio es una obligación social necesaria.*

National Standards: Connections

Traditional couples now appear to be only one of many relationship options, not only in this country, but in other countries as well. In recent years we have witnessed an increase in interracial couples, single mothers and fathers, and couples who live together without ever marrying. In July 2003, Argentina became the first Latin American country in which two men were joined in a same-sex civil union. The ceremony in Buenos Aires, which was hailed as a victory for gay rights activists in Latin America, gave rise to debates over same-sex marriages, echoing controversies recently witnessed in the United States and Europe.

Vocabulario: Preparación ■ **467**

Etapas de la vida

Suggestions

- Offer the following optional vocabulary: *la pubertad, la tercera edad, criar (crío).* Point out and model the difference between *crecer* (to grow up) and *criar* (to raise).
- Remind students that the past participle of *morir* is *muerto* and that *muerto* can also be used as an adjective.
- Emphasize and model the conjugation of *nacer* and *crecer,* which is similar to *conocer: nazco, crezco, conozco.*
- Have students make associations with stages of life: *¿Qué colores/estaciones del año asocia Ud. con cada una de las etapas de la vida? ¿Qué actividades asocia con ellas?*
- Ask students the following questions to personalize the vocabulary.

  1. *¿Cuál es su fecha de nacimiento? ¿Dónde creció Ud.? ¿Quién lo/la crió?*
  2. *En su opinión, ¿cuál es la mejor/peor etapa de la vida de una persona? ¿Por qué?*
  3. *¿Tiene Ud. miedo de la muerte? ¿Cree Ud. que hay otra vida después de esta?*

Con. A: Extension

9. *dos coches y un perro*
10. *pasarlo bien*
11. *los amigos íntimos*
12. *un coche con cuatro puertas*

Con. B: Suggestions

- If done as a whole-class activity, have volunteers answer or offer opinions. Some students may find these questions too personal.
- For item 5, introduce and discuss the concept of *el luto* (mourning), observed by older Hispanics.

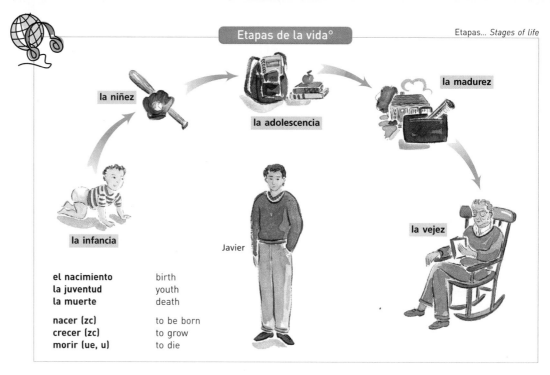

Etapas de la vida°

la niñez

la adolescencia

la madurez

la infancia

Javier

la vejez

el nacimiento	birth
la juventud	youth
la muerte	death
nacer (zc)	to be born
crecer (zc)	to grow
morir (ue, u)	to die

■ ■ ■ Conversación

A. Etapas de la vida. Relacione las siguientes palabras y frases con las distintas etapas de la vida de una persona. **¡OJO!** Hay más de una posible relación en algunos casos.

1. el amor
2. los nietos
3. los juguetes (*toys*)
4. no poder comer sin ayuda
5. los hijos en la universidad
6. los granos (*pimples*)
7. la universidad
8. la boda

B. Entrevista

1. ¿Son importantes en tu vida los amigos? ¿Quién es tu mejor amigo/a? ¿Cuánto tiempo hace que lo/la conoces? ¿Crecieron Uds. juntos/as? Es decir, ¿se han conocido desde la niñez? ¿desde la adolescencia? ¿Por qué te llevas bien con esa persona?
2. ¿Quieres casarte algún día? (¿Ya te casaste?) ¿Te gusta la idea de tener una boda grande? (¿Tuviste una boda grande?) ¿Piensas hacer un viaje de luna de miel? (¿Hiciste un viaje de luna de miel?) ¿Adónde?
3. ¿Qué es lo bueno de estar casado? ¿y lo malo? ¿Qué es lo bueno de ser soltero? ¿y lo malo?
4. ¿En qué década del siglo (*century*) pasado naciste? ¿Has visto muchos cambios desde entonces? ¿Cuáles son? ¿Cómo piensas pasar tu vejez? (Si ya eres una persona madura, ¿cómo pasas tu tiempo?)
5. ¿Has sido afectado/a personalmente por la muerte de alguien? ¿Quién murió? ¿Cómo te sentiste? ¿Tienes buenos recuerdos (*memories*) de esa persona? ¿Cuáles son?

Capítulo 15: La vida social y la vida afectiva

Resources: Transparency 93

Refrán

«La vida es la novia de la muerte.»

Have students talk about this *refrán.* Is there any English equivalent? (*Life and death are but two sides of the same coin.*) What are some other English sayings about life and death? (*Nothing is certain but death and taxes. The best things in life are free.*)

CULTURE

El Día de los Muertos (Day of the Dead) can be traced back to festivities held during the Aztec month of Miccoxlhuituntili, a celebration dedicated to children and the dead. The *Día de los Muertos* activities, celebrated the first two days of November, consist of family visits and processions to the graves of departed relatives. At the gravesite, family members tell stories about their departed relatives and eat specially prepared meals and chocolates in a variety of animal and skull shapes.

NOTA CULTURAL

Términos de cariño

Dos palabras españolas que no tienen equivalente exacto en inglés son **amigo** y **novio**. En el diagrama se indica cuándo es apropiado usar estas palabras para describir relaciones sociales en muchas culturas hispánicas y en la norteamericana.

| *friend* | *girlfriend/boyfriend* | *fiancée/fiancé* | *bride/groom* |

| amiga/amigo | | novia/novio |

Como en todas partes del mundo, los enamorados hispanos usan muchos términos de cariño: **mi amor, mi amorcito/a, mi vida, viejo/a, querido/a, cielo, corazón.** Es también frecuente el uso afectuoso de las frases **mi hijo / mi hija** entre esposos y aun[a] entre buenos amigos.

[a]*even*

▲ *Unos novios en Chile*

C. Una receta para unas buenas relaciones. Piense en su propio (*own*) matrimonio o en el de sus padres / unos amigos. O, si lo prefiere, piense en sus relaciones con su mejor amigo/a o en las de un par de amigos que Ud. tiene. En su opinión, ¿cuáles son los ingredientes necesarios para un buen matrimonio o una buena amistad?

Paso 1. Haga una lista de los cinco ingredientes más esenciales. Los ingredientes pueden expresarse con una palabra o una frase.

Paso 2. Compare su lista con las de otros tres estudiantes. ¿Coinciden en la selección de algunos ingredientes? Hablen de todos los ingredientes y hagan una lista de los cinco más importantes.

Paso 3. Ahora comparen los resultados de todos los grupos. ¿Han contestado todos más o menos de la misma manera?

Need more practice?

- Workbook and Laboratory Manual
- Interactive CD-ROM
- Online Learning Center (www.mhhe.com/puntos7)

GRAMÁTICA

¿Recuerda Ud.?

Before studying **Gramática 44,** review the indefinite and negative words that you learned in **Capítulo 6.** Remember that **alguien** and **nadie** take the personal **a** when they are used as direct objects.

Busco **a alguien** de la familia.   *I'm looking for someone from the family.*

No veo **a nadie** en el salón de baile.   *I don't see anyone in the dance hall.*

Give the opposite of the following words.

1. nada   **2.** algunos   **3.** alguien

NOTA CULTURAL

Suggestions

- Ask the following questions to check comprehension.

  1. *¿Qué palabra indica relaciones más serias, amigo o boyfriend?*

  2. *¿Qué palabra en español se puede usar para decir «sweetheart»?*

- Provide some additional common terms of endearment such as *gordo/a* (Sp.) and *negro/a* (Venezuela). Remind students that terms like these have nothing to do with a person's weight or skin color.
- Point out that a common word to refer to a live-in significant other is *compañero/a*.

☀ Heritage Speakers

Pídales a los hispanohablantes que nombren otras expresiones de cariño que usan. Pregúnteles con quién(es) las usan y en qué circunstancias.

National Standards: Community

Have students work in groups to write three questions that they would ask someone about their concept of family and friends. Have the groups share and "pool" the questions they wrote. Encourage them to use these to interview people in the community. They should try to include someone from each stage of life, people from both genders, and at least one or more persons, especially Hispanics, who are not from the U.S. or Canada. Have them share their findings with their classmates, and use the results to make generalizations about the importance of family and friends to different genders, age groups, and nationalities.

Subjunctive After Nonexistent and Indefinite Antecedents

Follow-Up

- Have students complete the following sentences.

  1. *Mi padre/madre es una persona que…*

  2. *Un padre / Una madre ideal es una persona que…*

- Ask the following questions.

  Los lunes por la mañana, ¿hay algo que lo/la haga feliz? ¿que lo/la haga sonreír?

  ¿Y los martes por la mañana? ¿los viernes por la mañana?

  Help students with negative answers.

  No, no hay nada que me haga sonreír.

Suggestion

Review noun clauses and the use of the subjunctive in them before introducing adjective clauses.

Bright Idea

Suggestions

- As a class, briefly review the formation and uses of the subjunctive.

- At this point, students should be able to identify independent and dependent clauses, as well as expressions of 1) influence, 2) emotion and feeling, and 3) doubt and denial, which require the use of subjunctive in the dependent clause.

Emphasis A: Suggestion

Emphasize and model the relationship between adjectives and adjective clauses (to modify a noun), for example, *Veo una casa blanca / que tiene ventanas.* Draw parallels with noun clauses and their relationship to nouns.

---

44 ¿Hay alguien que... ? ¿Hay un lugar donde... ? • Subjunctive After Nonexistent and Indefinite Antecedents

Un buen lunes

[a]*eres*

Mafalda *tiene un padre que la quiere, la protege y que pasa mucho tiempo* con ella. Por eso, Mafalda ve a su padre como *un hombre que ahora es más guapo* que cuando era joven. Todos los niños *necesitan padres que los quieran, los cuiden y que tengan tiempo* para pasar con ellos.

Comprensión

¿Quién lo dice o piensa, el padre de Mafalda u otro pasajero en el autobús?

1. No hay nadie en este autobús que sea más feliz que yo.
2. Tengo una hija que es una maravilla, ¿verdad?
3. En camino al trabajo no hay nada que me haga sonreír.

A. In English and Spanish, statements or questions that give or ask for information about a person, place, or thing often contain two clauses.

Each of the example sentences contains a main clause (*I have a car*; *Is there a house for sale*). In addition, each sentence also has a subordinate clause (*that gets good mileage*; *that is closer to the city*) that modifies a noun in the main clause: *car, house.* The noun (or pronoun) modified is called the *antecedent* (**el antecedente**) of the subordinate clause, and the clause itself is called an adjective clause because—like an adjective—it modifies a noun (or pronoun).

I have a **car** *that gets good mileage.*
Is there a **house for sale** *that is closer to the city?*

A good Monday Mafalda has a father who loves her, protects her, and spends a lot of time with her. That's why Mafalda sees her father as a man who is now more handsome than when he was young. All children need parents who love them, take care of them, and have time to spend with them.

Resources: Transparency 94

Transparency 94 provides examples of this structure.

B. Sometimes the antecedent of an adjective clause is something that, in the speaker's mind, does not exist or whose existence is indefinite or uncertain.

NONEXISTENT ANTECEDENT:

There is *nothing* that you can do.

INDEFINITE ANTECEDENT:

We need *a car* that will last us for years. (We don't have one yet.)

In these cases, the subjunctive must be used in the adjective (subordinate) clause in Spanish.

Note in the examples that adjective clauses that describe a place can be introduced with **donde...** as well as with **que...**

EXISTENT ANTECEDENT:

Hay algo aquí que me **interesa.**
There is something here that interests me.

NONEXISTENT ANTECEDENT:

No veo nada que me **interese.**
I don't see anything that interests me.

DEFINITE ANTECEDENT:

Hay muchos restaurantes donde **sirven** comida mexicana auténtica.
There are a lot of restaurants where they serve authentic Mexican food.

INDEFINITE ANTECEDENT:

Buscamos un restaurante donde **sirvan** comida salvadoreña auténtica.
We're looking for a restaurant where they serve authentic Salvadoran food.

 The dependent adjective clause structure is often used in questions to find out about someone or something the speaker does not know much about. Note, however, that the indicative is used to answer the question if the antecedent is known to the person who answers.

INDEFINITE ANTECEDENT:

¿Hay algo aquí que te **guste?**
Is there anything here that you like?

DEFINITE ANTECEDENT:

Sí, **hay varias bolsas** que me **gustan.**
Yes, there are several purses that I like.

 The personal **a** is not used with direct object nouns that refer to hypothetical persons. Compare the use of the indicative and the subjunctive in the sentences at the right.

NONEXISTENT ANTECEDENT:

Busco **un señor** que **sepa** francés.
I'm looking for a man who knows French.

EXISTENT ANTECEDENT:

Busco **al señor** que **sabe** francés.
I'm looking for the man who knows French.

Emphasis B: Suggestions

■ Give students the following formulas and models to help them conceptualize the use of subjunctive with adjective clauses.

  1. experience = knowledge of the existence of the object qualified
  2. + subjunctive = − experience: *Quiero salir con un muchacho que tenga interés en la política internacional.* (*No lo conozco todavía.*)
  3. − subjunctive = + experience: *Quiero salir con un muchacho que tiene interés en la política internacional.* (*Ya lo conozco.*)

■ Relate the uses of the subjunctive in adjective clauses to the general use of the subjunctive to express conceptualized states/actions.

■ Emphasize and model the use of *donde* to introduce the adjective clause: *Queremos trabajar en una ciudad donde haya una comunidad intercultural. Viven en un barrio donde los niños pueden jugar en la calle.*

■ Model, in brief exchanges with students, more examples of the question/answer series noted in the first **¡OJO!** box.

  ¿Hay estudiantes en esta clase que tengan hijos? →
  No, no hay ningún estudiante en esta clase que tenga hijos.
  Sí, hay un (dos) estudiante(s) en esta clase que tienen hijos.
  ¿Hay profesores en esta universidad que vivan en residencias estudiantiles? →
  No, no hay ningún profesor en esta universidad que viva en una residencia estudiantil.
  Sí, hay profesores en esta universidad que viven en residencias estudiantiles.

National Standards: Connections

■ Another use of *donde* in a declarative statement is to mean *in the house of.* For example, *Estoy donde José* means *I'm at José's house.* Other Romance languages have similar structures, such as the French, *Je suis chez Jacques* (*I'm at Jacques' house*).

■ Have students make lists of hypothetical situations, possessions, and so on, for each other. Then have

them use these lists to interview each other. List the following examples on the board.

¿Hay alguien aquí que viva en una mansión? ¿que sepa hablar otro idioma? ¿que tenga un Mercedes u otro coche de lujo? ¿que viaje a México todos los años? ¿que quiera ser médico algún día?

Prác. A: Preliminary Exercises

■ Read each English sentence and have students tell whether the antecedent is existent or nonexistent. Then read the Spanish sentence.

1. There's nothing here that I like. / *No hay nada aquí que me guste.*
2. Here's something that you will like. / *Aquí hay algo que te va a gustar.*
3. I don't know anyone who can do it. / *No conozco a nadie que lo pueda hacer.*
4. I know many people who can do it. / *Conozco a muchas personas que lo pueden hacer.*
5. There's no car that is economical. *No hay ningún coche que sea económico.*

■ Read each English sentence and ask students whether the antecedent is definite or indefinite. Then read the Spanish sentence.

1. I have a book that is interesting. / *Tengo un libro que es interesante.*
2. I want to buy a book that is interesting. / *Quiero comprar un libro que sea interesante.*
3. I'm looking for a secretary who speaks Spanish. / *Busco un secretario que hable español.*

Prác. A: Extension

■ Ask students: *¿Tiene más parientes que hagan algo «especial»?*
■ Give students one minute to form a question about some unusual activity they like, then have them ask the class if anyone else shares their hobby.

AUTOPRUEBA

Indicate which of the following sentences expresses an indefinite or nonexistent antecedent.

1. We need the counselor who works with this couple.
2. They are looking for a minister who will perform the wedding on the beach.
3. I met a man who has thirteen children.

Answer: 2

■■■ Práctica

A. **¡Anticipemos! Hablando de gente que conocemos.** En su familia, ¿hay personas que tengan las siguientes características? Indique la oración apropiada en cada par de oraciones.

TENGO UN PARIENTE…	NO TENGO NINGÚN PARIENTE…
1. ☐ que habla alemán.	☐ que hable alemán.
2. ☐ que vive en el extranjero.	☐ que viva en el extranjero.
3. ☐ que es dueño de un restaurante.	☐ que sea dueño de un restaurante.
4. ☐ que sabe tocar el piano.	☐ que sepa tocar el piano.
5. ☐ que es médico/a.	☐ que sea médico/a.
6. ☐ que fuma.	☐ que fume.
7. ☐ que está divorciado/a.	☐ que esté divorciado/a.
8. ☐ que trabaja en la televisión.	☐ que trabaje en la televisión.
9. ☐ que es viudo/a.	☐ que sea viudo/a.
10. ☐ que se casa este año.	☐ que se case este año.

B. **Las preguntas de Carmen**

Paso 1. Carmen acaba de llegar aquí de otro estado. Necesita tener información sobre la universidad y la ciudad. Haga las preguntas de Carmen según el modelo.

MODELO: restaurantes / sirven comida latinoamericana →
¿Hay restaurantes que *sirvan* (donde se *sirva*) comida latinoamericana?

1. librerías / venden libros usados
2. tiendas / se puede comprar revistas de Latinoamérica
3. cafés cerca de la universidad / se reúnen muchos estudiantes
4. apartamentos cerca de la universidad / son buenos y baratos
5. cines / pasan (*they show*) películas en español
6. un gimnasio en la universidad / se juega al ráquetbol
7. parques / la gente corre o da paseos
8. museos / hacen exposiciones de arte latinoamericano

Paso 2. ¿Son ciertas o falsas las siguientes declaraciones?

1. A Carmen no le interesa la cultura hispánica.
2. Carmen es deportista.
3. Es posible que sea estudiante.
4. Este año piensa vivir con unos amigos de sus padres.

Paso 3. Ahora conteste las preguntas de Carmen con información verdadera sobre la ciudad donde Ud. vive y su universidad.

Need more practice?

■ Workbook and Laboratory Manual
■ Interactive CD-ROM
■ Online Learning Center (www.mhhe.com/puntos7)

472 ■ Cuatrocientos setenta y dos

Capítulo 15: La vida social y la vida afectiva

Refranes

«No hay mal que cien años dure ni médico que lo cure.»
«No hay mal que por bien no venga.»

Write the *refranes* on the board and review the possible English equivalents (*Every cloud has a silver lining.*). Then point out that there are still more renditions of this saying, such as «*No hay mal que dure cien años, ni hombre que lo aguante*» and «*No hay mal que dure cien años, ni médico que lo cure, ni medicina en botica*». Ask students if they can think of sayings in English that have several different versions.

■ ■ ■ Conversación

A. Una encuesta. Las habilidades o características de un grupo de personas pueden ser sorprendentes. ¿Qué sabe Ud. de los compañeros de su clase de español? Pregúnteles a los miembros de la clase si saben hacer lo siguiente o a quién le ocurre lo siguiente. Deben levantar la mano sólo los que puedan contestar afirmativamente. Luego la persona que hizo la pregunta debe hacer un comentario apropiado. Siga el modelo.

MODELO: hablar chino →
En esta clase, ¿hay alguien que hable chino?
(*Nadie levanta la mano.*) No hay nadie que hable chino.
(*Alguien levanta la mano.*) Hay una (dos) persona(s) que habla(n) chino.

1. hablar ruso
2. saber tocar la viola
3. conocer a un actor / una actriz
4. saber preparar comida vietnamita
5. tener el cumpleaños hoy
6. escribir poemas
7. vivir en las afueras
8. ¿ ?

B. Entrevista. With another student, ask and answer the following questions. Then report any interesting details to the class.

1. ¿Hay alguien en tu vida que te quiera locamente?
2. ¿Hay algo que te importe más que los estudios universitarios?
3. ¿Con qué tipo de persona te gusta salir / pasar tiempo?
4. Para el semestre/trimestre que viene, ¿qué clases buscas? ¿una que empiece a las ocho de la mañana?
5. ¿Tienes algún amigo o alguna amiga de la escuela secundaria que esté casado/a? ¿que tenga hijos? ¿que esté divorciado/a?
6. **¡OJO!** Unas preguntas indiscretas: ¿Has conocido recientemente a alguien que te haya gustado mucho? ¿de quien te hayas enamorado? ¿Hay algún pariente con quien te lleves muy mal? ¿o muy, muy bien?

Con. B: Suggestion

Encourage students to use conversation-extending techniques to elicit more information.

Con. B: Extension

Write these sentences on the board. Have students supply their own details to form questions to use in an interview situation.

7. ¿Tienes algún amigo que... ?
8. ¿Tienes alguna clase que... ?
9. En mi opinión, no hay nada/nadie que...

EN LOS ESTADOS UNIDOS Y EL CANADÁ

Isabel Allende

Es posible que la chilena Isabel Allende (1942–) sea **la escritora hispánica más conocida de Norteamérica.** Sobrina del presidente de Chile, Salvador Allende, quien fue derrocado[a] violentamente y murió en 1973, Isabel viene de **una familia que tiene un pasado muy interesante.** Este pasado, con su mezcla[b] de lo familiar y lo político, aparece como uno de los elementos más salientes[c] de sus novelas. Estas se caracterizan también por el uso del «**realismo mágico**», técnica literaria en que elementos fantásticos se entretejen[d] con aspectos de la vida diaria. Su primera novela, *La casa de los espíritus,* apareció en 1982. Otras incluyen *De amor y de sombra* (1984), *Eva Luna* (1985), *El plan infinito*

▲ *Isabel Allende*

(1991) y *Retrato en Sepia* (2000).

La vida de Allende no ha sido fácil. Después de los eventos políticos en que murió su tío, tuvo que **abandonar su país** con sus hijos pequeños. Vivió por un tiempo en Venezuela y hoy reside en los Estados Unidos con su **segundo esposo. Perdió a su segunda hija,** Paula, después de una larga y trágica enfermedad, cuando esta tenía 28 años. A ella le dedicó un libro en el que[f] cuenta la historia de la familia a la vez que narra los cambios que sufre la escritora a consecuencia del trauma de la enfermedad de su hija. Pero los contratiempos[g] no parecen detener a la incansable Isabel Allende.

[a]*overthrown* [b]*mixture* [c]*prominent* [d]*se... are interwoven* [e]*success* [f]*en... in which* [g]*mishaps, disappointments*

EN LOS ESTADOS UNIDOS Y EL CANADÁ

■ Use the following questions to check comprehension.

1. ¿Dónde nació Isabel Allende? *Chile*
2. ¿Qué relación tiene con el presidente Salvador Allende? *hija*
3. ¿Qué tragedia familiar sufrió Isabel? *perdió hija*
4. ¿Cuál es el título de una novela famosa de la escritora? *Eva Luna*
5. ¿Ha leído Ud. alguna de sus novelas? *Si*

■ Encourage students to find Allende's home page on the Internet. Thay can also read translated contemporary fiction by Spanish and Latin American writers such as Gabriel García Márquez, Mario Vargas Llosa, Carlos Fuentes, and Elena Poniatowska, and bilingual editions of poetry by authors such as Federico García Lorca, Pablo Neruda, Octavio Paz, and César Vallejo.

Follow-Up

- Ask students the following question.

  ¿Han estado Uds. en situaciones similares a las de los dibujos?

  Encourage students to give details.
- Have students complete the following sentences with their own ideas.

  1. *En una fiesta, nunca bailo a menos que…*
  2. *Cuando salgo con mis amigos, siempre tengo mi licencia de conducir en caso de que…*
  3. *No me voy a casar a menos que…*
  4. *Tengo planes hechos en caso de que…*
  5. *Voy a estudiar _____ para que…*

Emphasis A: Suggestions

- Present the following initial pattern to help students remember the five conjunctions that are always followed by the subjunctive.

  A PACE:
  A menos que
  Para que
  Antes (de) que
  Con tal (de) que
  En caso de que

- Include the lower frequency *sin que* in your presentation of the always subjunctive conjunctions (A SPACE).
- Some teachers prefer using the acronym ESCAPA to help students remember adverbial conjunctions that always require the subjunctive.
- Emphasize and model the relationship of the adverbial clauses to adverbs (they function as an adverb): *Llega mañana / antes de que salgamos.*
- In *Capítulo 16*, students will be introduced to temporal adverbial conjunctions (*cuando, tan pronto como, hasta que,* and so on). The subjunctive is used only when they introduce future, incomplete actions or states.
- Although *antes de que* is frequently categorized as an obligatory adverbial conjunction, it is truly a temporal conjunction because the expression, by its very nature, sets up a time relationship between two events. Given that the action introduced by *antes de que* is always unrealized, it will be expressed by means of the subjunctive.

---

45 *Lo hago para que tú…* • **Subjunctive After Conjunctions of Contingency and Purpose**

Maneras de amar

¿A qué dibujo corresponde cada una de las siguientes oraciones? ¿Quién las dice?

1. Aquí tienes la tarjeta de crédito, pero úsala sólo *en caso de que haya una emergencia,* ¿eh?
2. Escúchame bien. No vas a salir *antes de que termines* la tarea.
3. Quiero casarme contigo *para que estemos* siempre juntos *y no salgas más* con Raúl.

Comprensión

1. En el primer dibujo, es obvio que el chico _____. Es normal que la madre _____.
2. En el segundo dibujo, está claro que la chica _____. Por eso el padre se siente _____ (adjetivo).
3. En el tercer dibujo, creo que el chico _____. No estoy seguro/a de que la chica _____. Pienso que esta pareja es muy joven para _____.

A. When one action or condition is related to another—*x* will happen provided that *y* occurs; we'll do *z* unless *a* happens—a relationship of *contingency* is said to exist: one thing is contingent, or depends, on another.

The Spanish *conjunctions* (**las conjunciones**) at the right express relationships of contingency or purpose. The subjunctive always occurs in subordinate clauses introduced by these conjunctions.

a menos que	unless
antes (de) que	before
con tal (de) que	provided (that)
en caso de que	in case
para que	so that

conjunction = a word or phrase that connects words, phrases, or clauses

Refrán

«Antes de que te cases, mira lo que haces.»

Have students talk about the meaning of this *refrán.* What is a similar saying in English? (*Look before you leap.*)

B. Note that these conjunctions introduce subordinate clauses in which the events have not yet materialized; the events are conceptualized, not real-world, events.

Voy **con tal de que** ellos me **acompañen.**
I'm going, provided (that) they go with me.

En caso de que llegue Juan, dile que ya salí.
In case Juan arrives, tell him that I already left.

C. When there is no change of subject in the sentence, Spanish more frequently uses the prepositions **antes de** and **para,** plus an infinitive, instead of the corresponding conjunctions plus the subjunctive. Compare the sentences at the right.

PREPOSITION: (one subject)	Estoy aquí **para aprender.** *I'm here to (in order to) learn.*
CONJUNCTION: (two subjects)	Estoy aquí **para que** Uds. **aprendan.** *I'm here so that you will learn.*
PREPOSITION: (one subject)	Voy a comer **antes de salir.** *I'm going to eat before leaving.*
CONJUNCTION: (two subjects)	Voy a comer **antes de que salgamos.** *I'm going to eat before we leave.*

AUTOPRUEBA

Match each conjunction with its correct meaning in English.

1. _____ para que
2. _____ antes de que
3. _____ con tal de que
4. _____ a menos que
5. _____ en caso de que

a. unless
b. before
c. provided that
d. in case
e. so that

Answers: 1. e 2. b 3. c 4. a 5. d

■ ■ ■ Práctica

A. **¡Anticipemos! ¿Es Ud. un buen amigo / una buena amiga?** La amistad es una de las relaciones más importantes de la vida. Indique si las siguientes oraciones son ciertas o falsas para Ud. con respecto a sus amigos. **¡OJO!** No todas las características son buenas. Hay que leer con cuidado.

	C	F
1. Les hago muchos favores a mis amigos, con tal que ellos después me ayuden a mí.	☐	☐
2. Les ofrezco consejos a mis amigos para que tomen buenas decisiones.	☐	☐
3. Les presto dinero a menos que yo sepa que no me lo pueden devolver.	☐	☐
4. Les traduzco el menú en los restaurantes mexicanos en caso de que no sepan leer español.	☐	☐
5. Los llevo a casa cuando beben, para que no tengan accidentes de coche.	☐	☐

Emphasis C: Suggestion

Emphasize the difference between the preposition + infinitive structure (*Nota comunicativa, Capítulo 13*) and the conjunction + subjunctive structure. The latter has a second subject (*Van al cine antes de que llegue Raúl.*), and the former does not (*Van al cine antes de cenar.*).

Prác. A: Preliminary Exercise

Have students express the following ideas in Spanish.

1. unless you go with me / call me / write to me
2. in case they arrive/leave/come
3. provided that they go / eat dinner / have lunch
4. in order for us to go / be there / arrive on time.

Remind students that these are conjunctions (with subjunctive), not prepositions (with infinitives).

Prác. A: Suggestion

Have students add at least two more characteristics of a good (or bad) friend.

Have students explain why they might arrive early to other events.

1. ¿a una clase?
2. ¿a un examen?
3. ¿a un vuelo?

Remind students that when the subject in the main clause is the same as the subject for the verb following *antes* or *para*, the preposition + infinitive structure is used.

> *Quiero llegar a clase temprano **para hablar** con el profesor.*
> *Quiero llegar a clase temprano **para que el profesor me explique** esta construcción.*

Prác. C: Follow-Up

■ Write the conjunctions on the board. Have students use them as appropriate to complete the following sentences.

1. *El cielo está muy nublado hoy. Voy a llevar impermeable...*
2. *Es fácil recibir una buena nota en esta clase...*
3. *Nunca pienso casarme / divorciarme...*
4. *Vamos a las montañas este fin de semana...*

■ Have students complete the following sentences with information about themselves.

1. *Voy a graduarme en... a menos que...*
2. *Este verano voy a... a menos que...*
3. *Voy a seguir viviendo en esta ciudad con tal que...*
4. *Voy a comprar... en caso de que...*

Con: A: Extension

8. *Estudiamos para (que)...*
9. *Reciclamos para (que)...*
10. *Votamos para (que)...*

B. Julio siempre llega tarde. Siempre es buena idea llegar un poco temprano al teatro o al cine. Sin embargo, su amigo Julio, quien va al cine con Ud. esta tarde, no quiere salir con un poco de anticipación. Trate de convencerlo de que Uds. deben salir pronto.

> MODELO: JULIO: No entiendo por qué quieres que lleguemos al teatro tan temprano.
>
> encontrar a nuestros amigos
> UD.: Pues, para que encontremos a nuestros amigos.

No entiendo por qué quieres que lleguemos al teatro tan temprano.

1. poder estacionar el coche
2. no perder el principio de la función
3. poder comprar los boletos
4. conseguir buenas butacas (*seats*)
5. no tener que hacer cola
6. comprar palomitas (*popcorn*) antes de que empiece la película
7. hablar con los amigos
8. sacar dinero del cajero automático (*ATM*)

C. Un fin de semana en las montañas

Paso 1. Hablan Manolo y Lola. Use la conjunción entre paréntesis para unir las oraciones, haciendo todos los cambios necesarios.

1. No voy. Dejamos a la niña con los abuelos. (a menos que)
2. Vamos solos a las montañas. Pasamos un fin de semana romántico. (para que)
3. Esta vez voy a aprender a esquiar. Tú me enseñas. (con tal de que)
4. Vamos a salir temprano por la mañana. Nos acostamos tarde la noche anterior. (a menos que)
5. Es importante que lleguemos a la estación (*resort*) de esquí. Empieza a nevar. (antes de que)
6. Deja la dirección y el teléfono del hotel. Tus padres nos necesitan. (en caso de que)
7. No vamos a regresar. Nos hemos cansado de esquiar. (antes de que)

Paso 2. ¿Cierto, falso o no lo dice?

1. Manolo y Lola acaban de casarse.
2. Casi siempre van de vacaciones con su hija.
3. Los dos son excelentes esquiadores.
4. Van a dejar a la niña con los abuelos.

Need more practice?

■ Workbook and Laboratory Manual
■ Interactive CD-ROM
■ Online Learning Center (www.mhhe.com/puntos7)

■■■ Conversación

A. Situaciones. Cualquier acción puede justificarse. Con un compañero / una compañera o con un grupo de estudiantes, de una explicación para las siguientes situaciones. Luego comparen sus explicaciones con las de otro grupo.

1. Los padres trabajan mucho para (que)…
2. Los profesores les dan tarea a los estudiantes para (que)…
3. Los dueños de los equipos deportivos profesionales les pagan mucho a algunos jugadores para (que)…
4. Las películas extranjeras se doblan (*are dubbed*) para (que)…
5. Los padres castigan (*punish*) a los niños para (que)…
6. Las parejas se divorcian para (que)…
7. Los jóvenes forman pandillas (*gangs*) para (que)…

NOTA COMUNICATIVA

¿Para qué… ? / ¿Por qué… ? and para que / porque

English usage offers a general guideline for knowing when to use **¿Para qué… ?** versus **¿Por qué… ?** and **para que** versus **porque. ¿Por qué… ?** asks *Why . . . ?*, in the general sense, but if the question is specifically asking *For what reason / purpose?* something is for, use **¿Para qué… ?**

¿Por qué te casaste con él?	*Why did you marry him?*
¿Para qué te casaste con él?	*For what reason did you marry him?*
¿Para qué es el anillo?	*What (purpose) is the ring for?*

The conjunction **porque** means *because* in English, when *because* serves as a conjunction between two clauses. The adverbial conjunction **para que,** on the other hand, means *in order that* or *so that.*

Me casé con él **porque** lo quiero.	*I married him because I love him.*
Me casé con él **para que** mis padres nos aceptaran.	*I married him so that my parents would accept us.*

B. La boda. Julia y Salvador se casan en un mes y quieren una boda grande. Todos los parientes tienen preguntas. Con un compañero / una compañera, haga y conteste las siguientes preguntas, imaginando que uno/a de Uds. es Julia o Salvador. Si quieren, pueden usar las sugerencias entre paréntesis.

MODELO: ¿Por qué se casan en enero? (el invierno) →
Nos casamos en enero porque nos gusta el invierno.

1. ¿Para qué son las velas (*candles*)? (la ceremonia)
2. ¿Por qué quieren mandar trescientas invitaciones? (todos nuestros amigos y parientes / asistir)
3. ¿Por qué van a mandar las invitaciones antes de diciembre? (los dos / estar ocupadísimos / Navidad)
4. ¿Para qué necesitan alquilar un salón de baile tan grande? (el baile después de la ceremonia)
5. ¿Emplearon un conjunto musical colombiana porque les gusta el merengue? (no, para que nuestros abuelos / bailar también)

NOTA COMUNICATIVA

Suggestion

Have students review the uses of *por* and *para* in *Gramática 35.* Remind them that a general rule of thumb is that *por* looks "back" at causes and *para* looks "forward" at purpose and goal.

Bright Idea

Con. B: Follow-Up

Bring magazine clippings or printed images from the Internet. Display the images and encourage students to ask appropriate questions using *¿Por qué?* and *¿Para qué?* For example, for a pain relief advertisement, students might ask: *¿Para qué es ese producto?* (What is that product used for?) and *¿Por qué necesita el señor tomar ese producto?* (Why does the man need to take that product?).

Gramática

 Heritage Speakers

Pídales a los hispanohablantes que nombren a otros escritores latinoamericanos y españoles cuyas obras conozcan o hayan leído. Puede sugerirles que describan brevemente al resto de la clase los temas y las demás características propias de la obra de esos escritores.

UN POCO DE TODO

♻ A. Reciclado

Recycle the weekend activities vocabulary. Have students express the following ideas in Spanish.

1. We go there to have fun.
2. We also go so that the kids can play baseball.
3. They're going to swim before eating (they eat).
4. Are they going to swim before we eat?
5. Don't go without talking to your mother.
6. And don't leave without your father giving you money.

UN POCO DE TODO

♻

A. Situaciones de la vida. Con un compañero / una compañera, haga y conteste preguntas, según el modelo. Deben justificar sus respuestas.

MODELO: compañero/a de cuarto // tener coche →

> E1: ¿Buscas un compañero de cuarto que tenga coche?
> E2: No, ya tengo coche. (Sí, para que yo no tenga que manejar tanto. / Sí, en caso de que mi coche viejo no funcione.)

1. marido/mujer // ser médico/a
2. amigo/a // no haber roto recientemente con su pareja
3. casa // estar lejos de la ciudad
4. ciudad // haber un buen sistema de transporte público
5. amistad // estar basada en la confianza (*trust*)
6. coche // arrancar inmediatamente, sin problemas
7. computadora // tener más memoria
8. teléfono celular // poder recibir correo electrónico y fotos

B. Falta de comunicación. Complete the following passages with the correct forms of the words in parentheses, as suggested by the context. When two possibilities are given in parentheses, select the correct word. ¡OJO! As you conjugate verbs in this activity, you will decide whether to use the subjunctive mood (the present or present perfect tense) or the indicative mood (the present, the present perfect, the preterite, or the imperfect tense). The context of the passages will give clues to help you choose, and occasionally clues in italics will guide you in choosing a tense or mood.

Hace menos de dos semanas que Carola Errázunz Vial, una chilena de 19 años, llegó a Seattle a vivir con sus tíos estadounidenses por un año. Anoche, sábado, a las siete y media, (salir[1]) con Ron Franco, un muchacho que (conocer[2]) hace tres días en la cafetería de la universidad. Después de (leer[3]) la siguiente narración de la experiencia, (ser/estar[4]) evidente que Carola y Ron (tener[5]) expectativas diferentes con respecto a (el/lo[6]) que iban a hacer esa noche.

Ron habla con su amigo Jon:
(*comm., Tú:* Escuchar[7]), chico, mientras (*yo:* contarte[8]) lo de anoche. Para empezar, a las siete y media, Carola (*P/I,* recibirme[9]) en la puerta de la casa con su prima Alejandra, y (decirme[10]) que su prima (*P/I,* ir[11]) a acompañarnos a la cita. La prima vio mi sorpresa, y me dijo: «Perdona, Ron, pero Carola (insistir[12]) en que yo (ir[13]) con Uds. esta noche. Yo (*P/I,* saber[14]) que esto iba a ser una sorpresa para ti, pero es que las chicas chilenas generalmente no salen solas con un hombre a menos que (ser[15]) su pololo[a] y están por[b] casarse con él. ¿Ella no (haber contarte[16]) nada de las costumbres de Chile?»

[a]*Chilean slang for boyfriend; polola = girlfriend* [b]*about to*

Bueno, (*yo:* llevarlas[17]) a cenar al restaurante La Casa Italiana, y les dije: «Ojalá que no (haber comer[18]) mucho hoy, porque la comida aquí es (*super.,* rico[19]). ¿Hay algún plato italiano que (las/les[20]) (gustar[21]) en especial?» ¡Pues, (P/I, resultar[22]) que Carola ya (*past perf.:* haber cenar[23])! Entonces Alejandra y yo (comer[24]) mucho, y Carola, sólo un poquito. A la hora de pagar, yo (ofrecerse[25]) a pagar la cena, y (sugerir[26]) que pagáramos a la inglesa[c] en el cine. Carola (ponerse[27]) una cara de medio ofendida, y (preguntarme[28]): «Entonces, ¿no vamos a bailar?» Pues, yo le dije: «OK, Carola, para que (*nosotros:* evitar[29]) más inconvenientes, me parece bueno preguntarte ahora lo que yo debiera haberte preguntado[d] hace tres días cuando (P/I, invitarte[30]) a salir conmigo. Dime, cuando los jóvenes chilenos salen juntos, ¿cómo (pasar[31]) el tiempo? ¿Qué hacen? ¿(Dónde/Adónde[32]) van?»

Así (P/I, *yo:* saber[33]) que en Santiago, Chile, los fines de semana, después de cenar en casa, los gallos y gallas[e], como dice Carola, generalmente (*pres.,* reunirse[34]) en grupos como a las diez u once (en/de[35]) la noche para salir a bailar en los muchos clubes de la ciudad que (abrir[36]) a medianoche y (cerrar[37]) a las seis de la mañana. Las chicas casi siempre van acompañadas de una hermana o prima, y los hombres pagan. Es común (divertirse[38]) toda la noche bailando o pasando por algunas de las muchas tabernas al aire libre[f]. Frecuentemente (*ellos:* desayunar[39]) antes de regresar a casa. Bueno, Alejandra, Carola y yo (P/I, reírse[40]) a carcajadas[g] de la falta de comunicación, y yo (haber prometerle[41]) a Carola llevarla este próximo sábado directamente al Club Pequeña Habana, donde (*nosotros:* ir[42]) a bailar merengue y salsa toda la noche.

[c]pagáramos... *we would go Dutch*   [d]debiera... *should have asked you*   [e]gallos... *roosters and hens, Chilean slang for guys and gals*   [f]tabernas... *open-air pubs*   [g]reírse... *laughed our heads off*

Comprensión: ¿Qué piensa Ud.? Answer the questions in brief but complete Spanish sentences.

1. Según la información en los párrafos, ¿cuáles son algunas de las diferencias y semejanzas entre una cita «típica» en los Estados Unidos y una cita «típica» en Santiago, Chile?
2. ¿Cuáles son algunas de las ventajas de la forma chilena de «pololiar» (*dating, Chilean slang*)? ¿Y de la forma norteamericana?
3. ¿Qué desventajas ve Ud. en la manera de «pololiar» de los chilenos? ¿Y en la de los norteamericanos?
4. ¿Puede Ud. contar un incidente en el que Ud. se sintió incómodo/a por la falta de comunicación con una persona de una cultura diferente?

Resources for Review and Testing Preparation

■ Workbook and Laboratory Manual
■ Interactive CD-ROM
■ Online Learning Center (www.mhhe.com/puntos7)

B: Preliminary Exercise

Have students complete the following sentences. Write them on the board or overhead transparency. You might prompt the sentences with questions.

MODELO: ¿En qué tipo de restaurantes prefiere Ud. comer? → Prefiero comer en restaurantes donde ofrezcan una gran selección de vinos.

1. Prefiero comer en restaurantes donde _____.
2. No me gusta que los programas de televisión _____.
3. Voy a graduarme en _____ a menos que _____.
4. Me gusta que los profesores _____.
5. Algún día deseo tener un coche que _____.
6. Este verano voy a _____ a menos que _____.
7. Me gustan las personas que _____.
8. En el futuro, quiero tener _____ hijos, con tal de que _____.
9. No conozco a ninguna familia que _____.
10. Necesito amigos que _____.
11. Mis amigos y yo buscamos _____ que _____.
12. No voy a _____ antes de que _____.

Resources: Desenlace

In the *Capítulo 15* segment of "Chapter-by-Chapter Supplementary Materials" in the IM/RK you will find a chapter-culminating activity. You can use this activity to consolidate and review the vocabulary and grammar skills students have acquired.

National Standards: Comparison

Have students describe dating traditions and expectations. Do they vary within this country? Have they had experiences similar to Ron's?

PERSPECTIVAS culturales

Entrevista cultural

Suggestions

- Before showing the video, ask students questions about events such as weddings. Ask students to name some of the professions related to weddings.

    ¿Qué profesiones se asocian con las bodas?

    Have them use Spanish if possible, and give them the Spanish for words they don't know. Which of these professions would interest them and why?

    la costurera / el sastre
    el cura
    el fotógrafo / la fotógrafa
    el pastelero / la pastelera
    el pastor / la pastora
    el peluquero / la peluquera
    el planificador / la planificadora de bodas
    el proveedor / la proveedora de comida
    el rabino
    el sacerdote / la sacerdotisa

    Have them talk about photographers.

    ¿Para qué tipo de reuniones y celebraciones familiares se necesitan fotógrafos?

- Show the video and allow students one to two minutes to work on the questions. Have volunteers answer the questions.
- Have volunteers role-play Jorge and his interviewer.

Entre amigos

Suggestions

- Before viewing the video, review the questions with the students and ask them similar questions.

    ¿Tiene Ud. novio/a? ¿Está casado/a?
    ¿Rompió Ud. con un novio/una novia alguna vez? ¿Cuánto tiempo hace?
    ¿Qué expectativas tiene Ud. para el matrimonio? Si ya está casado/a, ¿qué expectativas tenía antes de casarse?

    Have students answer or work in small groups to ask and answer these questions.

- After viewing the video, have volunteers read and answer the questions.

●●● Videoteca

Entrevista cultural: Chile

Jorge Balmaceda es chileno. Habla de su trabajo y de sus clientes. ¡Le encanta su profesión! Antes de ver el vídeo, lea el siguiente fragmento de la entrevista.

JORGE: Me encanta mi trabajo, sobre todo sacar fotos en bodas. Me encanta fotografiar a la novia, al novio, a los padrinos, amigos y familiares. Es una fiesta bastante feliz. Me encanta retratarla.[a]

ENTREVISTADORA: Y ¿es siempre agradable, o de vez en cuando encuentras dificultades o problemas?

JORGE: Porque [la novia] no se siente bien, porque no le quedó[b] bien el vestido o porque el peinado[c] no le gusta como le quedó.

[a]*to portray it in photos*   [b]*no... didn't fit well*   [c]*hairdo*

Ahora vea el vídeo y conteste las siguientes preguntas basándose en la entrevista.

1. ¿Cuál es la profesión de Jorge?
2. ¿A qué eventos sociales debe asistir?
3. ¿Qué problemas ocurren en su trabajo?
4. ¿Cuáles de las celebraciones le parecen más felices a Jorge?
5. ¿Por qué le gusta su trabajo?

Entre amigos: Es muy lindo estar enamorado

Miguel, Tané, Rubén y Karina hablan de las relaciones sentimentales. En su opinión, ¿qué preguntas se van a hacer? Antes de mirar el vídeo, lea las preguntas a continuación. Mientras mire el vídeo, trate de entender la conversación en general y fíjese en la información sobre los novios y las relaciones. Luego mire el vídeo una segunda vez, fijándose en la información que necesita para contestar las preguntas.

1. ¿Cuánto tiempo hace que Miguel y su novia terminaron (*broke up*)?
2. Según Karina, ¿qué cosas son importantes en una relación amorosa?
3. ¿Dónde vive el novio de Tané?
4. ¿Qué planes tienen Tané y su novio para el futuro?
5. ¿Sabe Tané cuántos hijos quiere tener?

☀ Heritage Speakers

Anime a los hispanohablantes a hablar de como son las relaciones íntimas en su país.

¿Cómo son los noviazgos en los países latinoamericanos y en España?
¿Todavía existe la práctica de cortejar a una persona?
¿Qué papel desempeñan los otros miembros de la familia?
Antes, la novia no podía salir sin chaperón o chaperona. ¿Todavía es así?

Conozca... Chile

Datos esenciales

- Nombre oficial: República de Chile
- Capital: Santiago
- Población: 15.700.000 habitantes
- Moneda: el peso
- Idiomas: el español (oficial), el mapuche, el quechua

¡Fíjese!

- El nombre de Chile se deriva de la palabra indígena *chilli*, que significa «lugar donde termina la tierra».
- Chile es uno de los países más modernos e industrializados de Sudamérica. Durante la colonización de Sudamérica, los españoles no tenían mucho interés en Chile. Los Andes dificultaban los viajes al país y, como no habían encontrado allí oro como en el Perú, los colonizadores pensaban que la tierra de Chile tenía poco valor. Esto es irónico porque hoy la minería del cobre[a] es la industria más importante del país, y Chile es uno de los mayores exportadores de cobre del mundo.
- Aunque Chile sufrió una crisis económica en los años 70, a finales del siglo XX muchos lo llamaban «el jaguar económico de Latinoamérica». La calidad de la vida en Chile es una de las mejores entre los países hispanos. Los problemas de la natalidad[b] han bajado drásticamente y la esperanza de vida al nacer es de aproximadamente 80 años. Con una tasa de alfabetización[c] de casi el 95 por ciento, Chile tiene un estable sistema de escuelas y universidades.

[a]*copper* [b]*birth* [c]*tasa... literacy rate*

Learn more about Chile with the Video, the Interactive CD-ROM, and the Online Learning Center (www.mhhe.com/puntos7).

Lugares famosos: la geografía chilena

Se puede dividir Chile en tres regiones principales. El norte de Chile principalmente consiste en 600 millas (1,000 kilómetros) del desierto Atacama. Aunque el desierto tiene un clima moderado, es uno de los lugares más áridos del mundo. En algunas partes del desierto, no hay evidencia ninguna de pluviosidad.[a]

El centro de Chile extiende unas mil millas (1,600 kilómetros). Mucho del centro consiste en el Valle de Chile entre los Andes y la Cordillera de la Costa. Es la región más poblada de Chile y el centro agrícola del país.

El sur de Chile es una región escabrosa.[b] Aquí los Andes descienden al océano para formar fiordos e islas. Aquí se encuentran los glaciares de la Tierra del Fuego que Chile comparte con la Argentina.

[a]*rainfall* [b]*rugged*

▲ *Un viñedo* (vineyard) *chileno, con los Andes al fondo* (in the background)

MULTIMEDIA: Internet

Have students search the Internet for more information about Chile's government, educational system, geography, and economy. Assign specific topics and have students prepare brief oral presentations for the class based on their findings.

Conozca... Chile

Notes

- The Atacama desert offers many geographical wonders.

  El Salar de Atacama is the biggest salt deposit (150,000 acres) in Chile. The rough, white surface hides a big salt lake.

  El Valle de la Luna, which is part of *la Cordillera de la Sal*, is a small depression of salt ground. The liquid bottom of the salt lake folds and transforms the earth and has become a fantastic lunar-like landscape. This is also part of the National Reserve Los Flamencos. This valley lacks humidity and has become the most inhospitable, albeit beautiful to the eye, place on the whole planet.

  Los Geysers del Tatio are a geothermal field of volcanic origin, where water and steam spring up violently from the bottom of the earth. Between 4:30 and 7:00 A.M., the streams reach as much as 30 feet high. Nearby there are thermal water pools that offer opportunities for a thermal bath.

  El Volcán Ojos de Salado, at 22,600 feet (6,893 meters) above sea level, is the highest peak in Chile and the highest active volcano on earth.

- The tradition of wine began in Chile with the sacramental wines used by the Spanish missions. Little care and art went into the preparations of those wines, and the Spanish crown limited the amount of wine that Chile could produce in order to protect its own exports. In 1870 Chilean wine growers decided to import *vinifera* vine stocks from France and other wine regions from Europe to improve wine quality and production. This coincided with the years when phylloxera, a tiny insect that is a serious pest for commercial grapevines, began its devastating plagues in Europe and North America. Chilean grapes were not affected by the plague. As Europe struggled to recover from it, they studied the Chilean vines and took grafts of plague-resistant plants back to Europe. Today, the only place where ungrafted European vines still flourish is Chile.

- Students can read an excerpt of the poem *"Puertas"* by Chile's Gabriela Mistral in *Un paso más 15.*

Suggestions

- Point out the first person singular of *crecer* (*crezco*) and *nacer* (*nazco*).
- Have students describe a relationship in their family, for example, that of their parents, and tell when and how they met, how long they dated, and so on. Model a description for them.
- Write the stages of life in Spanish on the board. Have students write at least two sentences for each stage of life. Have them write sentences describing a typical activity for the stages of life, for example:

  Llora a menos que esté cerca de su mamá (infancia).
  Está muy solo y deprimido porque ya no trabaja y sus hijos están muy ocupados con sus familias.
  Está muy contento porque por fin tiene tiempo para viajar y trabajar en el jardín (vejez).

Have students read sentences to the class. The class should identify the stage of life.

EN RESUMEN

Gramática

To review the grammar points presented in this chapter, refer to the indicated grammar presentations. You'll find further practice of these structures in the Workbook and Laboratory Manual, on the Interactive CD-ROM, and on the *Puntos de partida* Online Learning Center (www.mhhe.com/puntos7).

44. ¿Hay alguien que... ? ¿Hay un lugar donde... ? —Subjunctive After Nonexistent and Indefinite Antecedents

You should know how to use the subjunctive in two-clause sentences when the antecedent is nonexistent or indefinite.

45. Lo hago para que tú... —Subjunctive After Conjunctions of Contingency and Purpose

You should know how and when to use the subjunctive after certain conjunctions of contingency and purpose.

Vocabulario

Practice this vocabulary with digital flash cards on the Online Learning Center (www.mhhe.com/puntos7).

Las relaciones sentimentales

amar	to love
casarse (con)	to marry
divorciarse (de)	to get divorced (from)
enamorarse (de)	to fall in love (with)
llevarse bien/mal (con)	to get along well/poorly (with)
pasar tiempo (con)	to spend time (with)
querer (ie)	to love
romper (con)	to break up (with)
separarse (de)	to separate (from)

la amistad	friendship
el amor	love
la boda	wedding (*ceremony*)
la cita	date
la luna de miel	honeymoon
el marido	husband
el matrimonio	marriage; married couple
la mujer	wife
la novia	bride
el noviazgo	engagement
el novio	groom
la pareja	(married) couple; partner
el/la viudo/a	widower/widow

Cognados: el divorcio, la separación
Repaso: el/la amigo/a, el/la esposo/a, pelear (con), salir (*irreg.*) (con)

amistoso/a	friendly
divorciado/a (de)	divorced (from)
enamorado/a (de)	in love (with)
recién casado/a (con)	newlywed (to)

Repaso: cariñoso/a, casado/a (con), soltero/a

Etapas de la vida

la adolescencia	adolescence
la infancia	infancy
la juventud	youth
la madurez	middle age
la muerte	death
el nacimiento	birth
la vejez	old age

Repaso: la niñez

crecer (zc)	to grow
nacer (zc)	to be born

Repaso: morir (ue, u)

Otras palabras y expresiones útiles

a primera vista	at first sight
bastante	rather, sufficiently; enough
juntos/as	together
propio/a	own

Conjunciones

a menos que	unless
antes (de) que	before
con tal (de) que	provided (that)
en caso de que	in case
para que	so that

MULTIMEDIA: Internet

Have students search the web for more information on weddings in Latin America and Spain. There are several websites in Spanish that describe different ways of planning civil and religious weddings. Encourage students to talk about differences and similarities between weddings in Spain and/or Latin America and weddings in the U.S. and/or Canada.

Un paso más 15

Literatura de **Chile**

Sobra la autora: *Gabriela Mistral nació en Vicuña, Chile. Publicó sus primeros versos a los 15 años. Fue maestra y cónsul de Chile en varios países. Participó en la asamblea de las Naciones Unidas y publicó varias colecciones de poesía. En 1945 le otorgaron el Premio Nóbel de Literatura por sus versos líricos. Murió en Nueva York. Los siguientes versos son del poema, «Puertas», Lagar (1954).*

▲ Gabriela Mistral
(1889–1957)

> Entre los gestos[a] del mundo
> recibí el que dan las puertas.
> En la luz yo las he visto
> o selladas[b] o entreabiertas[c]
> y volviendo sus espaldas[d]
> del color de la vulpeja.[e]
> ¿Por qué fue que las hicimos
> para ser sus prisioneras?

[a]*gestures* [b]*cerradas* [c]*half-open, ajar* [d]*volviendo... turning a cold shoulder*
[e]*vixen (female fox)*

Literatura de **Chile**

Notes

- Mistral's given name was Lucila Godoy Alcayaga.
- Although her father abandoned the family when she was only 3 years old, Mistral seems to have inherited her father's passion for verse.
- Students can read Gabriela Mistral's acceptance speech at the Nobel Foundation's official website. Encourage them to look for it, and to find more information and images related to Mistral. You might assign specific topics about Chile and Gabriela Mistral and have students give brief oral presentations on their findings.

LECTURA

ESTRATEGIA: Using Graphics to Get Information

Reading graphics such as tables and pie charts requires as much concentration as, if not more than, any other reading since a lot of information is often summarized in a compact space. Paying attention to the heading of a section as well as to the categories within the graphic can help you to focus your attention on important parts of the information presented.

The chart on page 484 offers a visual snapshot of statistical information pertaining to marriage and divorce in Spain since 1981. As you read and analyze the information in the chart, remember to rely on all of the visual clues that you can to facilitate your comprehension. Maybe you'll be surprised by what you read!

LECTURA

Suggestions

- Do the *Estrategia* in class before assigning the reading.
- Have the class work together to write an article based on the information in the chart.

MULTIMEDIA: Internet

- Explain that in Spanish poetry it is possible to rhyme words that end in similar vowels but dissimilar consonants (*rima asonante*). Have students find two of these in this poem (*puertas/ entreabiertas, vulpeja/prisioneras*). Discuss inexact rhyme and the similarly inexact comparisons of the poem.

- Bring in copies of poems by other Chilean poets and work with the class to translate and interpret them. Poems you might choose include Pablo Neruda's "*Oda a la alcachofa,*" the "antipoet" Nicanor Parra's "*Un hombre,*" or Vicente Huidobro's "*Ella.*"

Variation

Using the categories in the chart from the article, have the class share its opinions and make additional pie charts based on them. Have students write articles based on these results. Encourage them to compare U.S./ Canadian statistics.

■ **Sobre la lectura...** La lectura, o mejor dicho, el gráfico, a continuación es del periódico *El País*, de España. Es parte de un artículo más largo sobre el divorcio en España. Como Ud. puede ver, el uso de elementos visuales, como este gráfico, sirve para presentar la información de una manera más organizada para el lector.

Las separaciones y los divorcios han aumentado el 66% en los últimos diez años

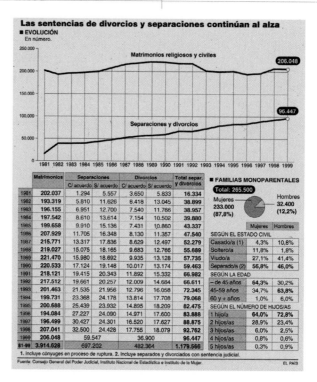

Las sentencias de divorcios y separaciones continúan al alza

■ EVOLUCIÓN
En número.

	Matrimonios	Separaciones C/ acuerdo	Separaciones S/ acuerdo	Divorcios C/ acuerdo	Divorcios S/ acuerdo	Total separ. y divorcios
1981	202.037	1.294	5.557	3.650	5.833	16.334
1982	193.319	5.810	11.626	8.418	13.045	38.899
1983	196.155	6.951	12.700	7.540	11.766	38.957
1984	197.542	8.610	13.614	7.154	10.502	39.880
1985	199.658	9.910	15.136	7.431	10.860	43.337
1986	207.929	11.705	16.348	8.130	11.357	47.540
1987	215.771	13.317	17.836	8.629	12.497	52.279
1988	219.027	15.075	18.165	9.683	12.766	55.689
1989	221.470	15.980	18.692	9.935	13.128	57.735
1990	220.533	17.124	19.148	10.017	13.174	59.463
1991	218.121	19.415	20.343	11.892	15.332	66.982
1992	217.512	19.661	20.257	12.009	14.684	66.611
1993	201.463	21.535	21.956	12.796	16.058	72.345
1994	199.731	23.368	24.178	13.814	17.708	79.068
1995	200.688	25.439	23.932	14.895	18.209	82.475
1996	194.084	27.227	24.090	14.971	17.600	83.888
1997	196.499	30.427	24.301	16.520	17.627	88.875
1998	207.041	32.500	24.428	17.755	18.079	92.762
1999	206.048	59.547		36.900		96.447
81-99	3.914.628	697.202		482.364		1.179.566

1. Incluye cónyuges en proceso de ruptura. 2. Incluye separados y divorciados con sentencia judicial.
Fuente: Consejo General del Poder Judicial, Instituto Nacional de Estadística e Instituto de la Mujer.   EL PAÍS

■ FAMILIAS MONOPARENTALES
Total: 265.500

Mujeres 233.000 (87,8%)   Hombres 32.400 (12,2%)

SEGÚN EL ESTADO CIVIL

	Mujeres	Hombres
Casado/a (1)	4,3%	10,8%
Soltero/a	11,8%	1,8%
Viudo/a	27,1%	41,4%
Separado/a (2)	56,8%	46,0%

SEGÚN LA EDAD

	Mujeres	Hombres
– de 45 años	64,3%	30,2%
45-59 años	34,7%	63,8%
60 y + años	1,0%	6,0%

SEGÚN EL NÚMERO DE HIJOS/AS

	Mujeres	Hombres
1 hijo/a	64,0%	72,8%
2 hijos/as	28,9%	23,4%
3 hijos/as	6,0%	2,5%
4 hijos/as	0,8%	0,6%
5 hijos/as	0,3%	0,9%

Comprensión

A. **¿Qué significa el título?** Utilice el gráfico para determinar el equivalente en inglés de la frase «han aumentado» del título.

☐ have decreased
☐ have remained unchanged
☐ have increased

National Standards: Comparison

Have students research these kinds of statistics in this country in order to compare divorce rates, percentages of single mothers and fathers, and so on.

B. ¿Cierto o falso? Conteste según el gráfico. Corrija las oraciones falsas.

1. En 1999 hay más divorcios en España que matrimonios.
2. El porcentaje de hogares (*households*) monoparentales encabezados por (*headed by*) madres y padres es igual.
3. En 1999 hay muchas más bodas que en 1981.
4. Los hombres que crían (*raise*) a sus hijos en familias monoparentales tienen menos de 45 años de edad.

C. A contestar. Conteste según el gráfico.

1. ¿En qué año se nota el mayor (*greatest*) número de matrimonios en España?
2. ¿Entre qué años se ve el aumento más profundo en el número total de divorcios y separaciones?
3. ¿Cuántos hijos tiene la mayoría de las familias monoparentales?

ESCRITURA

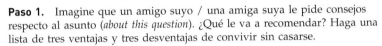

¿Casarse o no? Según el gráfico, el número de separaciones y divorcios en España va aumentando constantemente desde 1981, año en que se legalizó el divorcio en dicho (*that*) país. Una consecuencia de este cambio social es el aumento en alternativas fuera del matrimonio. Por ejemplo, muchas personas prefieren convivir (*to live together*) en vez de contraer matrimonio (*getting married*). Esta decisión puede traer ventajas y desventajas.

Paso 1. Imagine que un amigo suyo / una amiga suya le pide consejos respecto al asunto (*about this question*). ¿Qué le va a recomendar? Haga una lista de tres ventajas y tres desventajas de convivir sin casarse.

VENTAJAS

1. _____
2. _____
3. _____

DESVENTAJAS

1. _____
2. _____
3. _____

Paso 2. Ahora, escríbale una carta a su amigo/a, presentándole una de las dos perspectivas. Intente formular un buen argumento para persuadirle a que siga sus consejos. Puede empezar su carta así:

Querido/a _____,

He pensado mucho en tu situación y creo que…

ESCRITURA

Suggestion
If you prefer that your students do a journal activity, see *Mi diario* in this chapter of the Workbook.

Variation
Have students interview a classmate in Spanish. Students should find out how their classmate feels about civil weddings, religious weddings, couples who live together before getting married, and couples who choose to live together without ever getting married. Encourage students to share the results of their interview with the rest of the class.

Follow-Up
Have students write letters to an imaginary newspaper columnist named Elena, telling her their (similarly imaginary) love problems. Then have teams of students read their classmates' problems to each other and work together to write letters that solve them.

Point out the chapter-opener photo. Have students talk about this business area and the people in it. What kind of professionals do they think the two women in the foreground are? What kinds of offices would they expect to find in these buildings? Also, have students compare the architecture in this area. Ask if they see contrasting architectural periods in many cities in this country.

Suggestions

- Have students put the following phrases in order of importance (1 to 8).

  _____ *Pasar mucho tiempo al aire libre*

  _____ *Trabajar independientemente o sin mucha supervisión*

  _____ *Viajar con frecuencia*

  _____ *Leer y escribir mucho*

  _____ *Ganar mucho dinero y **jubilarme** joven*

  _____ *Tener muchas posibilidades de mejorarme y de recibir **aumentos de sueldo***

  _____ *Hacer mucho trabajo físico*

  _____ *Tomar muchas decisiones*

- Have students list specific professions or jobs they associate with the phrases listed.
- The words in **boldface** are included in the active vocabulary of this chapter. Have students discuss the words and use context to help them understand the meanings. Place the words they cannot guess in new sentences and contexts.
- Ask students the following questions.

  ¿Cree Ud. que las características del trabajo ideal cambian en diferentes momentos de la vida?

  ¿Por qué circunstancias pueden cambiar?

  ¿Qué características son las más importantes en cada momento de la vida?

Note

The *Puntos de partida* Online Learning Center includes an interview with a native speaker from Uruguay who answers questions about work.

CAPÍTULO 16

◄ Mujeres profesionales que caminan por la Puerta de la Ciudadela, en Montevideo, Uruguay

Resources

For Students

- Workbook
- Laboratory Manual and Laboratory Audio Program
- Quia™ Online Workbook and Online Laboratory Manual
- Video on CD
- Interactive CD-ROM
- *Puntos de partida* Online Learning Center (**www.mhhe.com/puntos7**)

For Instructors

- *Instructor's Manual and Resource Kit*, "Chapter-by-Chapter" Supplementary Materials
- Overhead Transparencies 95–102
- Testing Program
- Test Generator
- Video Program
- Audioscript
- *Puntos de partida* Online Learning Center (**www.mhhe.com/puntos7**)

¿Trabajar para vivir o vivir para trabajar?

Suggestion
Have students list their ideas about Uruguay and Paraguay, including information on geography, politics, economy, culture, music, and cuisine. When you finish the chapter, return to the lists and ask students what ideas they would change and/or add.

CULTURA

- **Perspectivas culturales**

    Entrevistas culturals: el Uruguay y el Paraguay

    Entre amigos: ¿A qué hora es la entrevista?

    Conozca... el Uruguay y el Paraguay

- **Nota cultural:** Los nombres de las profesiones

- **En los Estados Unidos y el Canadá:** El creciente mercado hispano

- **Literatura del Uruguay:** Horacio Quiroga

- **Lectura:** «La higuera», por Juana Fernández de Ibarbourou

VOCABULARIO

- Profesiones y oficios
- El mundo del trabajo
- Una cuestión de dinero

GRAMÁTICA

Entrevista cultural

◀ Sonia Sancho
Asunción, Paraguay

◀ María Dioni
Montevideo, Uruguay

MULTIMEDIA

- The multimedia materials that accompany this chapter are referenced in the Student and Instructor's Editions with icons to help you identify when and where to incorporate them.

- The IM/RK provides suggestions for using the multimedia materials in the classroom.

Profesiones y oficios

Note

See the model for vocabulary presentation and other material in the *Capítulo 16 Vocabulario: Preparación* section of "Chapter-by-Chapter Supplementary Materials," in the IM.

Suggestions

- Offer the following optional vocabulary.

  el/la cirujano/a   el/la astronauta
  el/la cocinero/a   el/la piloto/a
  el/la gerente   el/la atleta
                    profesional

- Use the following questions to check comprehension.

  1. *¿Quién gana más dinero, un plomero o un enfermero? ¿un obrero o un siquiatra?*
  2. *¿Quién tiene el trabajo más aburrido, un siquiatra o un peluquero? ¿un comerciante o un abogado? ¿un plomero o un vendedor?*
  3. *¿Quién tiene más responsabilidades, un maestro o un ingeniero? ¿un abogado o un comerciante?*
  4. *¿Para qué profesiones es necesario asistir a la universidad? ¿Por cuántos años?*
  5. *¿Cuál de estos trabajos le gusta más/menos? Explique por qué, dando las ventajas y desventajas.*

- Point out that there is little consensus in the Spanish-speaking world about words used for females practicing certain professions. Names given here should be acceptable to most Spanish speakers, but there is considerable discussion about terms such as *la pilota, la médica,* and so on. Have students review the *Nota cultural* on page 489.
- In some Hispanic countries *muchacho* or *muchacha de servicio* is used instead of *criada.*
- Note that some Spanish speakers use the words *psicología / psicólogo/a* and *psiquiatría / psiquiatra* or *psiquíatra.* These alternate spellings and pronunciations are less favored today.
- *El fontanero / La fontanera* is another word for plumber.

Con. A: Suggestion

Do *Conversación A* as a listening comprehension activity

Profesiones y oficios°   *trades*

el contador / la contadora

el maestro / la maestra

el médico / la médica

el periodista / la periodista

el cocinero / la cocinera

el peluquero / la peluquera

Profesiones

el/la abogado/a	lawyer
el/la bibliotecario/a	librarian
el/la consejero/a	counselor
el/la enfermero/a	nurse
el hombre / la mujer de negocios	businessperson
el/la ingeniero/a	engineer
el/la trabajador(a) social	social worker
el/la traductor(a)	translator

Oficios

el/la cajero/a	cashier; teller
el/la comerciante	merchant; shopkeeper

el/la criado/a	servant
el/la dependiente/a	clerk
el/la obrero/a	worker, laborer
el/la plomero/a	plumber
el soldado / la mujer soldado	soldier
el/la vendedor(a)	salesperson

Cognados

el/la analista de sistemas, el/la dentista, el/la electricista, el/la fotógrafo/a, el/la mecánico/a, el/la profesor(a), el/la programador(a), el/la secretario/a, el/la sicólogo/a, el/la siquiatra, el/la técnico/a, el/la veterinario/a

In the preceding chapters of *Puntos de partida* you have learned to use a number of the words for professions and trades that are listed here. You will practice all of these words in the following activities. However, you may also want to learn new terms that are particularly important or interesting to you. If the vocabulary needed to describe your career goal is not listed here, look it up in a dictionary or ask your instructor.

☀ Heritage Speakers

En México y en algunas regiones de Centroamérica, los hispanohablantes usan la palabra *el licenciado / la licenciada* como sinónimo de *el abogado / la abogada.* Este término casi siempre aparece como título profesional antes del apellido, por ejemplo, *el licenciado Agüello.* ¿Cuántos hispanohablantes de su clase usan el título *el licenciado / la licenciada?*

Resources: Transparency 95

MULTIMEDIA: Audio

Students can listen to and practice this chapter's vocabulary on the Online Learning Center (**www.mhhe.com/puntos7**), as well as on the Textbook Audio CD, part of the Laboratory Audio Program.

■ ■ ■ Conversación

A. ¿A quién necesita Ud.? ¿A quién debe llamar o con quién debe consultar en estas situaciones? Hay más de una respuesta posible en algunos casos.

1. La tubería (*plumbing*) de la cocina no funciona bien.
2. Ud. acaba de tener un accidente automovilístico; el otro conductor dice que Ud. tuvo la culpa (*blame*).
3. Por las muchas tensiones y presiones de su vida profesional y personal, Ud. tiene serios problemas afectivos (*emotional*).
4. Ud. quiere que alguien lo/la ayude con las tareas domésticas porque no tiene mucho tiempo para hacerlas.
5. Ud. quiere que alguien le construya un muro (*wall*) en el jardín.
6. Ud. conoce todos los detalles de un escándalo en el gobierno de su ciudad y quiere divulgarlos.

B. Asociaciones. ¿Qué profesiones u oficios asocia Ud. con estas frases? Consulte la lista de profesiones y oficios y use las siguientes palabras también. Haga asociaciones rápidas. ¡No lo piense demasiado!

1. creativo/rutinario
2. muchos/pocos años de preparación
3. mucho/poco salario
4. mucha/poca responsabilidad
5. mucho/poco prestigio
6. flexibilidad/«de nueve a cinco»
7. mucho/poco tiempo libre
8. peligroso (*dangerous*)/seguro
9. en el pasado, sólo para hombres/mujeres
10. todavía, sólo para hombres/mujeres

actor/actriz	detective
arquitecto/a	niñero/a
asistente de vuelo	pintor(a)
barman	poeta
camarero/a	policía / mujer policía
carpintero/a	político/a
chófer	presidente/a
consejero/a	rabino/a
cura/pastor(a)	senador(a)

NOTA CULTURAL

Los nombres de las profesiones

En el mundo de habla española hay poco acuerdo sobre las palabras que deben usarse para referirse a las mujeres que **ejercen** ciertas profesiones. En gran parte, eso se debe al hecho de que, en muchos de estos países, las mujeres acaban de empezar a ejercer esas profesiones; por eso el idioma todavía está cambiando para **acomodarse** a esa nueva realidad. En la **actualidad** se emplean, entre otras, las siguientes formas:

■ Se usa el artículo **la** con los sustantivos que terminan en **-ista**.

el dentista → **la** dent**ista**

■ En otros casos se usa una forma femenina.

el médico → **la** médic**a**   el trabajador → **la** trabajador**a**

■ Se usa la palabra **mujer** con el nombre de la profesión.

el policía → **la mujer** policía   el soldado → **la mujer** soldado

Escuche lo que dice cualquier[a] persona con quien Ud. habla español para saber las formas que él o ella usa. No se trata de[b] formas correctas o incorrectas, sólo de usos y costumbres locales.

[a]*any*   [b]*No... It's not a question of*

▲ *Una científica en su laboratorio*

Bright Idea
Con. A: Extension

8. *Ud. y su pareja están invitados a una boda el sábado por la noche, pero no tienen a nadie que les cuide a sus hijos.*
9. *Ud. tiene una muela o un diente que le duele.*
10. *Ud. está en un avión que está volando a Miami y tiene sed.*
11. *Ud. no está contento/a con las decisiones del gobierno federal y quiere enviar un correo electrónico con sus quejas.*

Con. B: Variation

Have students give definitions of professions following the models given.

NOTA CULTURAL

Notes

■ This change of professional roles is also occurring in the inverse: professions that were once reserved for women are now being exercised by men as well: *enfermero, amo de casa, secretario,* and so on.
■ The names of some professions that end in *-o* maintain the *-o* ending for the feminine counterpart.

el músico   la músico
el piloto   la piloto

■ Usage of "new" feminine forms varies from country to country. Therefore, students might see or hear *la juez* and *la presidente* as well as *la jueza* and *la presidenta.*

Suggestions

■ Ask questions about the photo.

¿Qué representan los sombreros que lleva la mujer?
¿Cree Ud. que es una representación simbólica de algo? ¿De qué?

■ Have students respond *cierto* or *falso* to check comprehension.

1. *Las mujeres todavía no ejercen profesiones como médica o policía en los países hispanos.*
2. *El uso de formas femeninas para las profesiones todavía depende de uso y costumbres, no de reglas lingüísticas.*

National Standards: Communication

Have students interview each other about professions in their families. Have them find out what they do or want to do professionally, what their parents or children do, and if they have any relatives that have interesting or unique professions. Have students report their findings to the class and use the information to make generalizations about the class.

National Standards: Community

If you teach in an area with a high percentage of Hispanics, invite a guest speaker to your class to talk about his/her profession. Have students prepare questions they can ask in Spanish before the visit. Encourage them to find out how important being bilingual has been for the guest in the workplace and in the community.

- Model several recommendations before allowing students to begin the activity. Demonstrate the use of the subjunctive syntax in your model.

- Have students work in pairs to role-play an advisor and a student who is seeking advice about his/her future. Have students discuss a variety of topics including summer jobs, time management, experience, preferences, and money. Have students report their findings to the class.

El mundo del trabajo

Suggestions

- Have students respond *cierto* or *falso* to the following sentences.

  1. *Una persona que busca un puesto se llama un aspirante.*

  2. *Si a Ud. no le gusta su trabajo, debe despedirlo.*

  3. *Si a Ud. le gustaría renunciar su trabajo, debe conseguir una solicitud.*

  4. *Para llenar una solicitud, es necesario tener bolígrafo o lápiz.*

  Have students correct the false statements.

- Point out that *compañía* is frequently used in company names, but *empresa* is the general word for *corporation* and *company. Caerle bien/mal* is used like *gustar* to refer to people. *Renunciar* and *dimitir* mean *to resign from a job. Resignar* is a false cognate and is never used to express *to resign from a job.*

C. **¿Qué preparación se necesita para ser... ?** Imagine que Ud. es consejero universitario / consejera universitaria. Explíquele a un estudiante qué cursos debe tomar para prepararse para las siguientes carreras. Use el **Vocabulario útil** y la lista de cursos académicos del **Capítulo 1.** Piense también en el tipo de experiencia que debe obtener.

1. traductor(a) en la ONU (Organización de las Naciones Unidas)
2. reportero/a en la televisión, especializado/a en los deportes
3. contador(a) para un grupo de abogados
4. periodista para una revista de ecología
5. trabajador(a) social, especializado/a en los problemas de los ancianos
6. maestro/a de primaria, especializado/a en la educación bilingüe

D. **Entrevista.** Con un compañero / una compañera, haga y conteste preguntas para averiguar (*find out*) la siguiente información.

1. lo que hacían sus abuelos
2. la profesión u oficio de sus padres
3. si tiene un amigo o pariente que tenga una profesión extraordinaria o interesante y el nombre de esa profesión
4. lo que sus padres (su esposo/a) quiere(n) que Ud. sea (lo que Ud. quiere que sean sus hijos)
5. lo que Ud. quiere ser (lo que sus hijos quieren ser)
6. la carrera para la cual (*which*) se preparan muchos de sus amigos (los hijos de sus amigos)

Vocabulario útil
las comunicaciones
la contabilidad (accounting)
el derecho (law)
la gerontología
la ingeniería
el *marketing*/mercadeo
la organización administrativa
la pedagogía/enseñanza
la retórica (speech)
la sociología

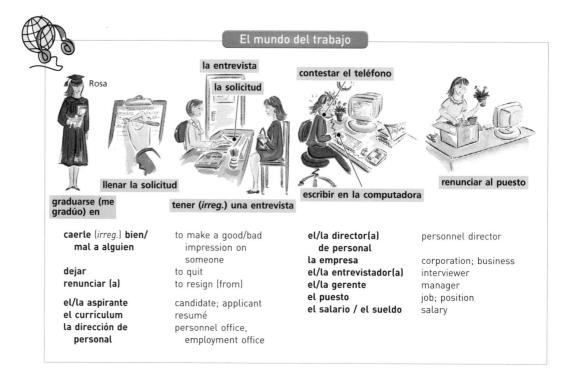

El mundo del trabajo

caerle (*irreg.*) **bien/ mal a alguien**	to make a good/bad impression on someone
dejar	to quit
renunciar (a)	to resign (from)
el/la aspirante	candidate; applicant
el currículum	resumé
la dirección de personal	personnel office, employment office
el/la director(a) de personal	personnel director
la empresa	corporation; business
el/la entrevistador(a)	interviewer
el/la gerente	manager
el puesto	job; position
el salario / el sueldo	salary

National Standards: Communication

Have students work together to prepare their own *currículum vitae* in Spanish. Encourage them to include information about their education, previous employment, and so on.

Resources: Transparencies 96, 97

Transparency 97 offers model sentences using work vocabulary.

☼ Heritage Speakers

Algunos hispanohablantes usan la palabra *aplicación* en vez de *solicitud.* Esta forma es un anglicismo, y es preferible usar *solicitud,* especialmente en situaciones formales. Pregúnteles a los hispanohablantes de la clase qué término usan. Pídales que nombren otros anglicismos comunes entre los hispanohablantes que viven en este país.

■■■ Conversación

A. En busca de un puesto. Imagine que Ud. solicitó un puesto recientemente. Usando los números del 1 al 14, indique en qué orden ocurrió lo siguiente. El número 1 ya está indicado.

a. _____ Se despidió de Ud. cordialmente, diciendo que lo/la iba a llamar en una semana.

b. _____ Fue a la biblioteca para informarse sobre la empresa: su historia, dónde tiene sucursales (*branches*), etcétera.

c. _____ Ud. llenó la solicitud tan pronto como la recibió y se la mandó, con el currículum, a la empresa.

d. _____ Por fin, el secretario le dijo que Ud. se iba a entrevistar con (*were going to be interviewed by*) la directora de personal.

e. _1_ En la oficina de empleos de su universidad, Ud. leyó un anuncio para un puesto en su especialización.

f. _____ Le dijo que le iba a mandar una solicitud para que la llenara (*you could fill it out*) y también le pidió que mandara (*you send*) su currículum.

g. _____ Cuando por fin lo/la llamó la directora, ¡fue para ofrecerle el puesto!

h. _____ Mientras esperaba en la dirección de personal, Ud. estaba nerviosísimo/a.

i. _____ La directora le hizo una serie de preguntas: cuándo se iba a graduar, qué cursos había tomado, etcétera.

j. _____ Llamó al teléfono que daba el anuncio y habló con un secretario en la dirección de personal.

k. _____ La mañana de la entrevista, Ud. se levantó temprano, se vistió con cuidado y salió temprano para la empresa para llegar puntualmente.

l. _____ Al entrar en la oficina de la directora, Ud. la saludó con cortesía, tratando de caerle bien desde el principio.

m. _____ También le pidió que hablara (*you speak*) un poco en español, ya que la empresa tiene una sucursal en Santiago, Chile.

n. _____ En una semana lo/la llamaron para arreglar una entrevista.

B. Definiciones. Dé definiciones de las siguientes palabras y frases.

MODELO: la empresa →
una compañía grande, como la IBM o Ford

1. el currículum
2. dejar un puesto
3. la aspirante
4. el gerente
5. el sueldo
6. llenar una solicitud

National Standards: Communication

Have students work in pairs to write the following types of questions. Have them imagine that the interviewer would be from an international computer company with offices and branches in Latin America and Europe.

1. *preguntas que un entrevistador suele* (usually) *hacer*

2. *preguntas que un entrevistador no debe hacerle al aspirante*

3. *preguntas que el aspirante puede o debe hacer*

Have each pair of students exchange questions with another pair of students. Then have the original partners role-play an interview using the questions they received.

Preliminary Exercise

Ask students the following questions to check comprehension and to personalize the vocabulary.

1. *¿Cómo está Ud. durante una entrevista? ¿Tranquilo/a?*

2. *¿Cuáles son algunas razones típicas para dejar un puesto? ¿Cuáles son algunas razones típicas para despedir a un empleado?*

3. *¿Quién estudia comercio? ¿Quiere trabajar en una gran empresa algún día? ¿En qué tipo de empresa? ¿Quiere entrar como director(a) o como empleado/a? ¿Cuáles son las cualidades necesarias de un buen director / una buena directora?*

■ Ask students the following questions to personalize the vocabulary.

1. *¿Trabaja Ud. ahora o sólo estudia? ¿Dónde trabaja? ¿Recibe un buen sueldo? ¿Le gustaría cambiar de puesto? ¿Por qué?*

2. *¿Es un buen empleado / una buena empleada o es perezoso/a?*

3. *¿Cómo es su jefe/a? ¿Es comprensivo/a y simpático/a o es muy mandón/mandona (act out)? Descríbalo/la. ¿Hay muchas diferencias entre su jefe/a y un profesor / una profesora? ¿En qué son similares/diferentes?*

Con. A: Suggestion

Encourage students to read all items before beginning the activity.

Con. A: Follow-Up

Have students work in groups to write brief dialogues that illustrate the different parts of the sequence. Then have them present their sections to the class.

☀ Heritage Speakers

Pregúnteles a los hispanohablantes de la clase qué formas usan para referirse a las mujeres en las siguientes profesiones: *jefe, juez, mecánico, médico, piloto, policía, presidente, soldado.* Pregúnteles si sus padres y abuelos o si sus hijos usan las mismas formas que ellos o si prefieren otras formas.

Una cuestión de dinero

Suggestions

- Point out that *cobrar un cheque* means *to cash a check*, but for cashing traveler's checks *cambiar un cheque de viajero* is used. Explain and model the differences between *ahorrar* (to save money or time), *guardar* (to save, keep something), and *salvar* (to save, rescue someone). Contrast and model the difference between *gastar* (to spend money) and *pasar* (to spend time).
- Explain that vocabulary for financial and banking transactions varies a good deal in the Spanish-speaking world. Introduce other terms you might prefer or hear, for example, *depositar* vs. *ingresar* and *libreta (de ahorros)* vs. *cartilla*.
- Offer the following optional vocabulary.

  los ingresos (income)
  hacer una transferencia / un giro

Preliminary Exercise

Have students respond *cierto* or *falso* to the following statements.

1. *El préstamo es dinero que recibimos del banco.*
2. *Si uno quiere ahorrar dinero, es necesario ponerlo en una cuenta corriente.*
3. *El presupuesto es un sistema que organiza la manera de gastar dinero.*
4. *Si Ud. paga con tarjeta de crédito, carga algo a su cuenta.*
5. *Un cajero automático se usa para recibir dinero.*
6. *Visa / Mastercard son ejemplos de facturas.*
7. *Sacar es el antónimo de depositar.*

Con. A: Suggestion

- Have students complete this as a pair activity, turning the items into questions.
- **Paso 2.** Have students complete this as written homework.

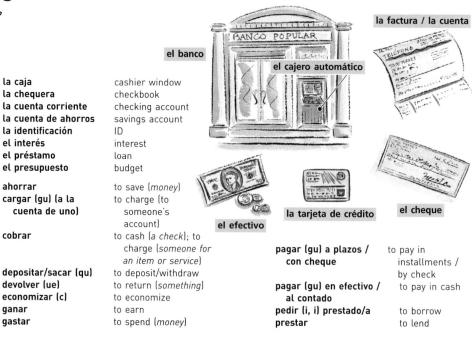

Una cuestión de dinero

la caja	cashier window
la chequera	checkbook
la cuenta corriente	checking account
la cuenta de ahorros	savings account
la identificación	ID
el interés	interest
el préstamo	loan
el presupuesto	budget
ahorrar	to save (*money*)
cargar (gu) (a la cuenta de uno)	to charge (to someone's account)
cobrar	to cash (*a check*); to charge (*someone for an item or service*)
depositar/sacar (qu)	to deposit/withdraw
devolver (ue)	to return (*something*)
economizar (c)	to economize
ganar	to earn
gastar	to spend (*money*)

el banco — la factura / la cuenta — el cajero automático — la tarjeta de crédito — el cheque — el efectivo

pagar (gu) a plazos / con cheque	to pay in installments / by check
pagar (gu) en efectivo / al contado	to pay in cash
pedir (i, i) prestado/a	to borrow
prestar	to lend

A. El mes pasado. Piense en sus finanzas personales del mes pasado. ¿Fue un mes típico? ¿Tuvo dificultades al final del mes o todo le salió bien?

Paso 1. Indique las respuestas apropiadas para Ud.

		¡CLARO QUE SÍ!	¡CLARO QUE NO!
1.	Hice un presupuesto al principio del mes.	☐	☐
2.	Deposité más dinero en el banco del que (*than what*) saqué.	☐	☐
3.	Saqué dinero del cajero automático sin apuntar (*writing down*) la cantidad.	☐	☐
4.	Pagué todas mis cuentas a tiempo.	☐	☐
5.	Saqué un préstamo (Le pedí dinero prestado al banco) para pagar mis cuentas.	☐	☐
6.	Tomé el autobús en vez de (*instead of*) usar el coche, para economizar un poco.	☐	☐
7.	Gasté mucho dinero en diversiones.	☐	☐
8.	Saqué el saldo (*I balanced*) de mi chequera sin dificultades.	☐	☐
9.	Le presté dinero a un amigo.	☐	☐
10.	Usé mis tarjetas de crédito sólo en casos de urgencia.	☐	☐

Paso 2. Vuelva a mirar sus respuestas. ¿Fue el mes pasado un mes típico? Pensando todavía en sus respuestas, sugiera tres cosas que Ud. debe hacer para mejorar su situación económica.

MODELO: Debo hacer un presupuesto mensual.

Refrán

«Dinero ahorrado, dos veces ganado.»

Have students give a similar saying in English. (*A penny saved is a penny earned.*)

Resources: Transparency 98

B. Diálogos

Paso 1. Empareje las preguntas de la izquierda con las respuestas de la derecha.

1. _____ ¿Cómo prefiere Ud. pagar?
2. _____ ¿Hay algún problema?
3. _____ Me da su identificación, por favor. Necesito verla para que pueda cobrar su cheque.
4. _____ ¿Quisiera (*Would you like*) usar su tarjeta de crédito?
5. _____ ¿Va a depositar este cheque en su cuenta corriente o en su cuenta de ahorros?
6. _____ ¿Adónde quiere Ud. que mandemos la factura?

a. En la cuenta de ahorros, por favor.
b. Me la manda a la oficina, por favor.
c. No, prefiero pagar al contado.
d. Sí, señorita. Ud. me cobró demasiado por el jarabe.
e. Aquí lo tiene Ud. Me lo va a devolver pronto, ¿verdad?
f. Cárguelo a mi cuenta, por favor.

Paso 2. Ahora invente un contexto posible para cada diálogo. ¿Dónde están las personas que hablan? ¿En un banco? ¿en una tienda? ¿Quiénes son? ¿Clientes? ¿cajeros? ¿dependientes?

C. Situaciones.

Describa lo que pasa en los siguientes dibujos. Use las preguntas a continuación como guía.

¿Quiénes son estas personas? ¿Cómo van a pagar?
¿Dónde están? ¿Qué van a hacer después?
¿Qué van a comprar?

1.

2.

3.

4.

Need more practice?

- Workbook and Laboratory Manual
- Interactive CD-ROM
- Online Learning Center (www.mhhe.com/puntos7)

Resources: Transparency 99

Con. B: Suggestion

Have students role-play this activity. You or a native speaker can take the role of the Spanish-speaking clerk (left-hand column).

Con. C: Variation

Have students do this as a written activity.

Gramática 46

Future Verb Forms

Suggestion

Point out that Mafalda uses a play on words: *oración* can mean *prayer* as well as *sentence*. Another word for *prayer* in Spanish is *plegaria*.

Follow-Up

■ Ask students: *¿Por qué pregunta Mafalda si las oraciones de tarea deben ser plegarias?*
■ Read the following information about the Quino characters and have students follow the instructions at the end.

Mafalda es bastante realista y tiene una gran conciencia social. En cambio, Susanita es muy materialista y tradicional en cuanto al papel de la mujer: la mujer como esposa, mamá y subordinada al marido. Usando las oraciones en la presentación gramatical, den algunas oraciones que podrían (could) decir Mafalda y Susanita acerca del futuro de cada una.

Note

The future perfect is presented only in the footnote on page 495. Active production is not required in the activities.

¿Recuerda Ud.?

Before studying the future tense in **Gramática 46,** review **Gramática 3 (Capítulo 1)** and **Gramática 11 (Capítulo 3),** where you learned ways of expressing future actions. Then indicate which of the following sentences can be used to express a future action.

1. Trabajé hasta las dos.
2. Trabajo a las dos.
3. Voy a trabajar a las dos.
4. Trabajaba a las dos.
5. Estoy trabajando.
6. He trabajado a las dos

46 Talking About the Future • Future Verb Forms

¿Cómo será su vida dentro de diez años? Conteste sí o no a las primeras cinco oraciones. Complete las últimas dos con información verdadera —¡o por lo menos deseable!

1. *Viviré* en otra ciudad / otro país.
2. *Estaré* casado/a.
3. *Tendré* uno o más hijos (nietos).
4. *Seré* dueño/a de mi propia casa.
5. *Llevaré* una vida más tranquila.
6. *Trabajaré* como _____ (nombre de profesión).
7. *Ganaré* por lo menos _____ dólares al año.

The future tense expresses things or events that *will* or *are going* to happen.

Past	Present	FUTURE
preterite	present indicative	future
imperfect	present progressive	
present perfect	formal commands	
present perfect subjunctive	informal commands	
	present subjunctive	

MULTIMEDIA: Internet

Have students search the Internet for a Spanish language horoscope site. Students should print out and bring in their horoscope to share with the class. Have students rewrite their horoscope in the future tense if it is not already in the future.

☼ **Heritage Speakers**

En español las palabras *a* y *ha* se confunden fácilmente porque se pronuncian de la misma manera. Por lo tanto, los hispanos pueden tener dificultades en distinguir entre *va a haber / va a ver* y *va a ser / va a hacer.* El futuro evita la confusión: *habrá, verá, será* y *hará* respectivamente. Anime a los hispanohablantes a explicar la diferencia entre estas cuatro formas y a usarlas en oraciones.

A. In English, the future is formed with the auxiliary verbs *will* or *shall*:

*I **will**/**shall** speak.*

In Spanish, the *future* (**el futuro**) is a simple verb form (only one word). It is formed by adding future endings to the infinitive. No auxiliary verbs are needed.

Future verb endings:

-é	-emos
-ás	-éis
-á	-án

hablar		comer		vivir	
hablaré	hablaremos	comeré	comeremos	viviré	viviremos
hablarás	hablaréis	comerás	comeréis	vivirás	viviréis
hablará	hablarán	comerá	comerán	vivirá	vivirán

B. The verbs on the right are the most common Spanish verbs that are irregular in the future. The future endings are attached to their irregular stems.

decir: diré, dirás, dirá, diremos, diréis, dirán

decir:	**dir-**	
haber (hay):	**habr-**	
hacer:	**har-**	-é
poder:	**podr-**	-ás
poner:	**pondr-**	-á
querer:	**querr-**	-emos
saber:	**sabr-**	-éis
salir:	**saldr-**	-án
tener:	**tendr-**	
venir:	**vendr-**	

Note that the future of **hay (haber)** is **habrá** (*there will be*).*

C. Compare the use of the indicative and subjunctive present tense forms to express the immediate future.

Llegaré a tiempo.
I'll arrive on time.

Llego a las ocho mañana. ¿Vienes a buscarme?
I'll arrive at 8:00 tomorrow. Will you pick me up?

No creo que Pepe **llegue** a tiempo.
I don't think Pepe will arrive on time.

¿Quieres cerrar la puerta, por favor?
Will you please close the door?

 When the English *will* refers not to future time but to the willingness of someone to do something, Spanish uses the verb **querer**, not the future.

---

*The future forms of the verb **haber** are used to form the* future perfect tense (**el futuro perfecto**), *which expresses what* will have occurred at some point in the future.

Para mañana, ya **habré hablado** con Miguel.   *By tomorrow, I will have spoken with Miguel.*

You will find a more detailed presentation of these forms in Appendix 3, Additional Perfect Forms (Indicative and Subjunctive).

Gramática

Emphasis B: Suggestions

■ Model the future of regular verbs.
■ Ask students brief questions using the future of *comprar*, *beber*, and *escribir*.
■ Read the following forms and have students give the corresponding subject pronoun: *tomaré, regresarán, mandará, necesitarás, llevarán, viajaremos, entrará, compraré, celebraremos, aprenderán, comprenderás, leeré, creerán, vivirá.*

Emphasis C: Suggestions

■ Model the irregular futures and *habrá* in sentences about yourself and in brief communicative exchanges with the students.
■ Point out the similarities among irregular stems.

   1. drop a vowel: *haber, poder, querer, saber*
   2. drop two letters: *decir, hacer*
   3. replace the theme vowel with *-d-: poner, salir, tener, venir*

Emphasis D: Suggestions

■ Emphasize that in Spanish and English the future is most often expressed with present indicative and subjunctive rather than with the future tense. The future tense implies strong intention: *I'm going to study tonight* vs. *I will study tonight*, and *Voy a estudiar esta noche* vs. *Estudiaré esta noche.* The future can also be used to command: *No matarás* (the Ten Commandments, *los Diez Mandamientos*).
■ Model the difference between the English *will* for future versus *will* for expressing willingness. *Querer* is used for willingness, but makes very strong requests. Point out that other verbs such as *poder* and *importar* can be used to soften the request.

   ¿Podrías cerrar la puerta, por favor? (Could you please close the door?)
   ¿Te importa cerrar la puerta, por favor? (Do you mind closing the door, please?).

- Use a rapid response drill.

  Dé el futuro.
  yo: *cantar, visitar, acostarse, vender, asistir, escribir*
  tú: *estudiar, casarse, ayudar, aprender, recibir, divertirse*
  Ud./él/ella: *pagar, terminar, guardar, correr, pedir, dormir*
  nosotros: *regresar, esperar, gastar, comer, insistir, servir*
  Uds./ellos/ellas: *dejar, leer, abrir, vivir*

- Use the following chain drill to practice forms. Have students imagine that it is payday.

  Son las tres de la tarde, un viernes, y todos han recibido el cheque semanal (weekly). *¿Qué harán? Algunos comprarán comestibles. Otros...*
  pagar las cuentas
  volver a hacer un presupuesto
  depositar un poco en la cuenta de ahorros
  quejarse porque nunca tienen suficiente
  decir que ya no usarán las tarjetas de crédito
  ¿ ... ?

Prác. A: Follow-Up

- Ask students the following questions to personalize the activity.

  1. *¿A qué hora llegará Ud. a casa esta noche?*
  2. *¿A qué hora cenará?*
  3. *¿A qué hora empezará a estudiar?*
  4. *¿Irá a la biblioteca?*
  5. *¿Mirará la televisión?*
  6. *¿Hablará por teléfono?*
  7. *¿Leerá mucho?*
  8. *¿Se bañará antes de acostarse?*
  9. *¿A qué hora se acostará?*
  10. *¿Se dormirá fácilmente?*

- **Paso 2.** Have students explain why they related a category to a certain person. That person says whether he/she agrees with the association. *Eso será verdad. / Eso nunca ocurrirá.*

♻ Prác. A: Reciclado

Have students give sentences about themselves and their classmates by starting with (No) *Es probable/posible que...* (→ *yo sea profesora de idiomas*) to review the subjunctive.

■■■ Práctica

A. ¡Anticipemos! Mis compañeros de clase. ¿Cree Ud. que conoce bien a sus compañeros de clase? ¿Sabe lo que les va a pasar en el futuro? Vamos a ver.

Paso 1. Indique si las siguientes oraciones serán ciertas para Ud. algún día.

		SÍ	NO
1.	Seré profesor(a) de idiomas.	☐	☐
2.	Me casaré (Me divorciaré) dentro de tres años.	☐	☐
3.	Me mudaré (*I will move*) a otro país.	☐	☐
4.	Compraré un coche deportivo.	☐	☐
5.	Tendré una familia muy grande (mucho más grande).	☐	☐
6.	Asistiré a una escuela de estudios graduados.	☐	☐
7.	Visitaré Latinoamérica.	☐	☐
8.	Estaré en bancarrota (*bankruptcy*).	☐	☐
9.	Estaré jubilado/a (*retired*).	☐	☐
10.	No tendré que trabajar porque seré rico/a.	☐	☐

Paso 2. Ahora, para cada oración del **Paso 1**, indique el nombre de una persona de la clase para quien Ud. cree que la oración es cierta. Puede ser un compañero / una compañera de clase o su profesor(a).

Paso 3. Ahora compare sus predicciones con las respuestas de estas personas. ¿Hizo Ud. predicciones correctas?

B. ¿Qué harán?

Paso 1. Imagine que un grupo de amigos está hablando de cómo será su vida en cinco o seis años. Haga oraciones usando el futuro de las siguientes frases.

> MODELO: yo / aconsejar a estudiantes →
> *Aconsejaré a estudiantes.*

1. yo
   - hablar bien el español
   - pasar mucho tiempo en la biblioteca
   - escribir artículos sobre la literatura latinoamericana
   - dar clases en español

2. tú
   - trabajar en una oficina y en la corte
   - ganar mucho dinero
   - tener muchos clientes
   - cobrar por muchas horas de trabajo

3. Felipe
   - ver a muchos pacientes
   - escuchar muchos problemas
   - leer a Freud y a Jung constantemente
   - hacerle un sicoanálisis a un paciente

4. Susana y Juanjo
   - pasar mucho tiempo sentados
   - usar el teclado (*keyboard*) constantemente
   - inventar nuevos programas
   - mandarles mensajes electrónicos a todos los amigos

Paso 2. ¿A qué profesiones se refieren las oraciones anteriores?

AUTOPRUEBA

Complete the verbs with the correct future endings.

1. yo vivir____
2. ella dir____
3. ellos saldr____
4. Uds. vendr____
5. nosotros comer____
6. tú querr____

Answers: 1. *viviré* 2. *dirá* 3. *saldrán* 4. *vendrán* 5. *comeremos* 6. *querrás*

☼ Heritage Speakers

Note que en español el futuro se usa también para expresar probabilidad en el presente. Este uso equivale a *to wonder* y *probably* en inglés. Anime a los hispanohablantes a dar la forma del futuro de probabilidad para las oraciones a continuación.

> *¿Qué está en la puerta?*
> *¿Cuántos años tiene esa señora?*

También pídales que expliquen en sus propias palabras la implicación de cada oración.

C. Mi amigo Gregorio

Paso 1. Describa Ud. las siguientes cosas que hará su compañero Gregorio. Luego indique si Ud. hará lo mismo (**Yo también... Yo tampoco...**) u otra cosa.

MODELO: no / gastar / menos / mes →
Gregorio no *gastará* menos este mes. Yo tampoco *gastaré* menos. (Yo sí *gastaré* menos este mes. ¡Tengo que ahorrar!)

1. pagar / tarde / todo / cuentas
2. tratar / adaptarse a / presupuesto
3. volver / hacer / presupuesto / próximo mes
4. no / depositar / nada / en / cuenta de ahorros
5. quejarse / porque / no / tener / suficiente dinero
6. seguir / usando / tarjetas / crédito
7. pedirles / dinero / a / padres
8. buscar / trabajo / de tiempo parcial

Paso 2. ¿Cuál de las siguientes oraciones describe mejor a su amigo?

- Gregorio es muy responsable en cuanto a (*regarding*) asuntos de dinero. Es un buen modelo para imitar.
- Gregorio tiene que aprender a ser más responsable con su dinero.

Need more practice?

- Workbook and Laboratory Manual
- Interactive CD-ROM
- Online Learning Center (www.mhhe.com/puntos7)

■ ■ ■ Conversación

A. Ventajas y desventajas. What can you do to get extra cash or to save money? The first three possibilities are shown in the following drawings. What are the advantages and disadvantages of each suggestion?

MODELO: dejar de tomar tanto café →
Si dejo de tomar tanto café, ahorraré sólo un poco de dinero. Estaré menos nervioso/a, pero creo que será más difícil despertarme por la mañana.

1. pedirles dinero a mis amigos o parientes
2. cometer un robo
3. alquilar unos cuartos de mi casa a otras personas
4. dejar de fumar (beber cerveza, tomar tanto café...)
5. buscar un trabajo de tiempo parcial
6. vender mi disco compacto (coche, televisor...)
7. comprar muchos billetes de lotería

Gramática

Prác. C: Suggestion

Have students name the following.

1. *tres cosas que harán hoy*
2. *tres cosas que harán mañana*
3. *tres cosas que harán este fin de semana*
4. *tres cosas que harán durante las vacaciones*
5. *tres cosas que harán después de graduarse*

Con. A: Extension

8. *estudiar más*
9. *invertir mis ahorros en bonos y acciones*

Resources: Transparency 100

Have students think about the world today and what it might be like in 25 years. Then have them answer these questions.

1. ¿Habrá una mujer presidente?
2. ¿Eliminaremos las armas nucleares?
3. ¿Colonizaremos la luna?
4. ¿Tendrá computadora todo el mundo?
5. ¿Seremos todos bilingües?
6. ¿Limpiaremos el medio ambiente?
7. ¿Manejaremos coches todavía?
8. ¿Escucharemos música rap?
9. ¿Existirá el matrimonio todavía como institución social?
10. ¿Eliminaremos las enfermedades como el cáncer y el SIDA?

NOTA COMUNICATIVA

Suggestions

- Use visuals with the future of probability to speculate about the individuals in the drawings.

  ¿Quién será la mujer que espera?
  ¿Dónde estará esperando?
  ¿Para quién estará esperando?

- Emphasize that this use of the future is frequent in Spanish, possibly even more frequent than the use of the standard future (the future of intention).

- Point out that the future of probability in English can also be expressed with *must* and *will: Cecilia must (will) be on her way by now.*

- Point out that another word for *lío* is *embotellamiento.*

B. El mundo en el año 2500.

¿Cómo será el mundo del futuro? Haga una lista de temas o cosas que Ud. cree que van a ser diferentes en el año 2500. Por ejemplo: el transporte, la comida, la vivienda… Piense también en temas globales: la política, los problemas que presenta la capa de ozono…

Ahora, a base de su lista, haga una serie de predicciones para el futuro.

MODELO: La gente comerá (Nosotros comeremos) comidas sintéticas.

Vocabulario útil

la colonización
la energía nuclear/solar
el espacio
los OVNIs (Objetos Volantes No Identificados)
el planeta
la pobreza (poverty)
el robot
el satélite
el transbordador espacial (space shuttle)
la vida artificial

diseñar (to design)
eliminar

intergaláctico/a
interplanetario/a
sintético/a

NOTA COMUNICATIVA

Expressing Conjecture

Estela, en el aeropuerto

Cecilia, en la carretera

¿Dónde **estará** Cecilia?

¿Qué le **pasará**?

Estará en un lío de tráfico.

I wonder where Cecilia is. (Where can Cecilia be?)
I wonder what's up with her (what can be wrong)?
She's probably (must be) in a traffic jam. (I bet she's in a traffic jam.)

The future can also be used in Spanish to express probability or conjecture about what is happening now. This use of the future is called the *future of probability* (**el futuro de probabilidad**). Note in the preceding examples that the English cues for expressing probability (*probably, I bet, must be, I wonder . . . , Where can . . . ,* and so on) are not directly expressed in Spanish. Their sense is conveyed in Spanish by the use of the future form of the verb.

☼ Heritage Speakers

En todos los dialectos del español, el sujeto «los Estados Unidos» puede usarse con la forma plural o singular del verbo.

Los Estados Unidos sigue / siguen siendo el gran crisol del mundo.

Pregúnteles a los hispanohablantes si prefieren usar la forma verbal singular o plural con los Estados Unidos. Pídales que den algunos ejemplos.

MULTIMEDIA: Internet

Have students research one or more businesses in the U.S. or Canada that were founded or that are run by people of Hispanic descent. The United States Hispanic Chamber of Commerce can be visited online and has a wide list of resources from which students may choose. Encourage them to share this information with the rest of the class.

C. Predicciones. ¿Quiénes serán las siguientes personas? ¿Qué estarán haciendo? ¿Dónde estarán? Invente todos los detalles que pueda sobre los siguientes dibujos.

Palabras útiles

el botones (bellhop)
Cristóbal Colón
   (Christopher
   Columbus)
la propina (tip)

redondo/a (round)

1.

2.

3.

4.

EN LOS ESTADOS UNIDOS Y EL CANADÁ

El creciente mercado hispano

¿Qué tienen en común Ford, Chevrolet, Sprint, Dockers, United Health y Toys "Я" Us? Pues que, como muchas compañías norteamericanas, tienen activas **campañas publicitarias** para atraer al **mercado hispano nacional.** Con más de 35 millones de hispanos, según el censo estadounidense del año 2000, los Estados Unidos ocupan **el cuarto puesto**[a] entre las naciones que tienen una población hispanohablante (se calcula que podría[b] ser **la segunda** o **tercera nación** en los próximos quince años, por delante de España). La población hispana de los Estados Unidos se traduce en[c] un mercado de más de 600.000 millones de dólares.

CNN en español, HBO Latino y *People en español* se dirigen a[d] la variada comunidad hispana de los Esta-

dos Unidos. Muchos programas y publicaciones se originan en Florida, entre ellos *Latin Trade*, una **revista mensual**[e] de **negocios** y **economía** referente a Norteamérica en relación con todos los países latinos. El ámbito de lectores[f] de *Latin Trade* incluye a latinos de todo el mundo, un grupo de más de 400 millones de personas.

Desgraciadamente,[g] la importancia numérica de los hispanos, más del 12 por ciento de la población de los Estados Unidos, no se ve reflejada[h] en el mundo de **la comunicación,** de **la política** ni de los negocios. Es este el gran reto[i] para los hispanos de este país.

[a]*position*   [b]*it could*   [c]*se... translates into*   [d]*se... target*
[e]*monthly*   [f]*ámbito... readership*   [g]*Unfortunately*   [h]*no... is not reflected*   [i]*challenge*

EN LOS ESTADOS UNIDOS Y EL CANADÁ

Suggestions

■ Ask students if they have seen ads in Spanish for any famous business in this country.
■ Bring some ads in Spanish from U.S. or Canadian Spanish-language magazines. Have students name the types of people the ads address, and

ask what they think is the slant for the Hispanic market (versus the North American market at large).
■ Have students search the Internet for information about the Hispanic market in North America.

♻ Reciclado

Have students change the following sentences to express probability and conjecture with the future. The first set of sentences reenters traveland money vocabulary, the second set reenters health vocabulary.

De viaja

1. *Cobran mucho en aquella tienda, ¿no crees?*
2. *¿Cuánto es el precio de aquella estatua?*
3. *Podemos usar las tarjetas de crédito aunque estamos en el extranjero.*
4. *¡Las facturas llegan a casa antes de que lleguemos nosotros!*
5. *¿Tengo suficiente dinero para pagarlas?*

La salud

1. *Julito está enfermo.*
2. *¿Cuántos grados de temperatura tiene?*
3. *La doctora viene más tarde.*
4. *Le da un antibiótico.*
5. *Le pone una inyección.*

Con. C: Preliminary Exercises

■ Have students express the following ideas in Spanish using the future of probability.

1. He's probably a teacher, and she must be a doctor.
2. I wonder where she works.
3. I wonder which one earns more money.
4. They're probably from a big city.
5. They probably have a lot of kids.
6. They must be asking questions about (*acerca de*) us, too!

■ Have students explain the following situations and actions using the future of probability.

1. *Un amigo está en la sala de espera de un hospital.*
2. *Un amigo ha hecho una cita con el profesor / la profesora de español.*
3. *Un amigo está entrando en el banco.*
4. *Un amigo hace las maletas.*
5. *Un amigo necesita llamar a sus padres.*
6. *Un amigo está vestido elegantísimamente.*

**Resources:
Transparency 101**

**Subjunctive and Indicative
After Conjunctions of Time**

Follow-Up

Ask students what mood is used in
the dependent clauses in italics in
the *minidiálogo* (→ subjunctive). Help
students relate this use of the
subjunctive with other uses they have
already studied, for example, when
the action has not happened.

Emphasis A: Suggestion

Remind students that a conjunction is
a word or phrase that links a main
clause and a subordinate clause.

47 Expressing Future or Pending Actions • Subjunctive and Indicative After Conjunctions of Time

Antes de la entrevista

La mamá de Tomás le habla *antes de que salga* para entrevistarse.

SRA. LÓPEZ:	¿Estás listo para la entrevista?
TOMÁS:	Sí. ¿Estoy elegante?
SRA. LÓPEZ:	Muy elegante. Recuerda, *cuando llegues a la oficina,* no te olvides de darle la mano a la directora de personal.
TOMÁS:	Claro, mamá. No te preocupes.
SRA. LÓPEZ:	*Y tan pronto como te sientes,* entrégale el currículum.
TOMÁS:	Mamá, se lo daré *después de que ella me lo pida.* Cálmate. Yo soy la persona que va a entrevistarse.
SRA. LÓPEZ:	Está bien. Pero llámame *tan pronto como termines* la entrevista.

Comprensión: ¿Cierto o falso?

1. La Sra. López tiene una entrevista hoy.
2. La Sra. López le da consejos a su hijo.
3. Es obvio que Tomás está nervioso.
4. A Tomás le gustan los consejos de su madre.

A. The subjunctive is often used in Spanish in adverbial clauses, which function like adverbs, telling when the action of the main verb takes place. Such adverbial clauses are introduced by conjunctions (see **Capítulo 15**).

Lo veré **mañana.** (adverb)
I'll see him tomorrow.

Lo veré **cuando venga mañana.** (adverbial clause)
I'll see him when he comes tomorrow.

> **adverb** = a word that describes a verb, adjective, or another adverb, that is, a word that tells when, how, where, and how much something takes place
>
> **conjunction** = a word or phrase that connects words, phrases, or clauses

B. Future events are often expressed in Spanish in two-clause sentences that include conjunctions of time such as those on the right.

antes (de) que	before
cuando	when
después (de) que	after
en cuanto	as soon as
hasta que	until
tan pronto como	as soon as

Before the interview Tomás' mom talks to him before he leaves for his interview. SRA LÓPEZ: *Are you ready for the interview?* TOMÁS: *Yes. Do I look elegant?* SRA. LÓPEZ: *Very elegant. Remember, when you get to the office, don't forget to shake hands with the personnel director.* TOMÁS: *Of course, Mom. Don't worry.* SRA. LÓPEZ: *And as soon as you sit down, give her the resumé.* TOMÁS: *Mom, I'll give it to her after she asks for it. Calm down. I'm the one who's going to be interviewed.* SRA. LÓPEZ: *OK. But call me as soon as you finish the interview.*

 Heritage Speakers

Pídales a los hispanohablantes de la clase que
representen el minidiálogo para la clase.

C. The subjunctive is used in a subordinate clause after these conjunctions of time to express a future action or state of being— that is, one that is still pending or has not yet occurred from the point of view of the main verb. This use of the subjunctive is very frequent in conversation in phrases such as the example on the right.

The events in the subordinate clause are imagined—not real-world—events. They haven't happened yet.

Cuando **sea** grande/mayor…
When I'm older . . .

Cuando **tenga** tiempo…
When I have the time . . .

Cuando **me gradúe**…
When I graduate . . .

D. When the present subjunctive is used in this way to express pending actions, the main-clause verb is in the present indicative or future.

PENDING ACTION (SUBJUNCTIVE)

Pagaré las cuentas **en cuanto reciba** mi cheque.
I'll pay the bills as soon as I get my check.

Debo depositar el dinero **tan pronto como** lo **reciba.**
I should deposit money as soon as I get it.

E. However, the indicative (not the present subjunctive) is used after conjunctions of time to describe a habitual action or a completed action in the past. Compare the following.

 The subjunctive is always used with **antes (de) que.** (See **Capítulo 15.**)

HABITUAL ACTIONS (INDICATIVE)

Siempre **pago** las cuentas **en cuanto recibo** mi cheque.
I always pay bills as soon as I get my check.

Deposito el dinero **tan pronto como** lo **recibo.**
I deposit money as soon as I receive it.

COMPLETED PAST ACTION (INDICATIVE):

El mes pasado **pagué** las cuentas **en cuanto recibí** mi cheque.
Last month I paid my bills as soon as I got my check.

Deposité el dinero **tan pronto como** lo **recibí.**
I deposited the money as soon as I got it.

Emphasis C: Suggestion
Remind students that they learned certain conjunctions that always require the subjunctive in *Gramática 45* (conjunctions of contingency and purpose). Point out that with conjunctions of time (with the exception of *antes de que*), the subjunctive is used only when they introduce future, uncompleted actions or states.

Emphasis E: Suggestions

■ Model and contrast a future action, a habitual action, and a past action.
■ Emphasize that the subjunctive is always used after *antes de que*, even though it is a time conjunction. ¡**OJO!** Due to its meaning, it is always followed by a future uncompleted action.
■ Point out that the subjunctive is used with most time conjunctions even without a change of subject in the dependent clause.

Vamos a salir tan pronto como terminemos.

Después de and *hasta*, however, are followed by an infinitive when there is no change in subject.

Saldremos después de comer.
No vamos a salir hasta terminar la tarea.

AUTOPRUEBA

Indicate which sentences express a pending action and thus require the subjunctive in Spanish.

1. I'll call as soon as I get home.
2. We interview applicants only after we contact their references.
3. Many students apply for graduate school as soon as they begin their senior year.
4. They won't deposit this check until you sign it.

Answers: 1, 4

Prác. A: Preliminary Exercise

Have students tell whether the following sentences express future uncompleted, habitual, or past actions.

1. I'll do it when he gets here.
2. They always write when they are abroad.
3. We'll study until they arrive.
4. As soon as I have the time, I'll do it.
5. He studied until he fell asleep.
6. She'll give us the answers after we hand in the test.
7. We turn off the lights when we leave the house.

Prác. A: Note

Students need to focus on habitual (indicative) vs. future (subjunctive) actions.

Prác. B: Note

This activity reviews the use of many tenses and moods.

Prác. B: Follow-Up

Have students respond *cierto* or *falso* to the following statements about Mariana.

1. *Mariana estudia en la universidad ahora.*
2. *En la universidad, ha seguido muchos cursos de matemáticas.*
3. *Mariana es muy responsable en cuanto a sus finanzas.*

■ ■ ■ Práctica

A. Decisiones económicas

Paso 1. Lea las siguientes oraciones sobre Rigoberto y decida si se trata de una acción habitual o de una acción que no ha pasado todavía. Luego indique la frase que mejor complete la oración.

1. Rigoberto se va a comprar una computadora en cuanto…
   a. el banco le dé el préstamo
   b. el banco le da el préstamo
2. Siempre usa su tarjeta de crédito cuando…
   a. no tenga efectivo
   b. no tiene efectivo
3. Cada mes saca el saldo de su cuenta corriente después de que…
   a. reciba el estado de cuentas (*statement*)
   b. recibe el estado de cuentas
4. Piensa abrir una cuenta de ahorros tan pronto como…
   a. consiga un trabajo
   b. consigue un trabajo
5. No puede pagar sus cuentas este mes hasta que…
   a. su hermano le devuelva el dinero que le prestó
   b. su hermano le devuelve el dinero que le prestó

Paso 2. Ahora describa cómo lleva Ud. sus propios asuntos económicos, completando las siguientes oraciones semejantes.

1. Voy a comprarme _____ en cuanto el banco me dé un préstamo.
2. Cuando no tengo efectivo, siempre uso _____.
3. Después de que el banco me envía el estado de cuentas, yo siempre _____.
4. Tan pronto como consiga un trabajo, voy a _____.
5. No te presto más dinero hasta que tú me _____ el dinero que me debes.
6. Este mes, voy a _____ antes de que se me olvide.

B. Algunos momentos en la vida. Las siguientes oraciones describen algunos aspectos de la vida de Mariana en el pasado, en el presente y en el futuro. Lea cada grupo de oraciones para tener una idea general del contexto. Luego dé la forma apropiada de los infinitivos.

1. Hace cuatro años, cuando Mariana (graduarse) en la escuela secundaria, sus padres (darle) un reloj. El año que viene, cuando (graduarse) en la universidad, (darle) un coche.
2. Cuando (ser) niña, Mariana (querer) ser enfermera. Luego, cuando (tener) 18 años, (decidir) que quería estudiar computación. Cuando (terminar) su carrera este año, yo creo que (poder) encontrar un buen trabajo como programadora.
3. Generalmente Mariana no (escribir) cheques hasta que (tener) los fondos en su cuenta corriente. Este mes tiene muchos gastos, pero no (ir) a pagar ninguna cuenta hasta que le (llegar) el cheque de su trabajo de tiempo parcial.

 Heritage Speakers

En este capítulo los estudiantes aprendieron que el subjuntivo se usa después de *cuando* con acciones no realizadas. Sin embargo, a veces es posible encontrar el imperfecto del subjuntivo después de *cuando*.

ROBERTO: Me dicen que mi carro estará en el aeropuerto cuando aterrice el avión.

SUSANA: ¿Qué te dijeron?
ROBERTO: Me dijeron que mi carro estaría en el aeropuerto cuando *aterrizara* el avión.

Anime a los hispanohablantes a explicar lo que pasa en este diálogo.

C. Hablando de dinero: Planes para el futuro. Complete las siguientes oraciones con el presente del subjuntivo de los verbos indicados.

1. Voy a ahorrar más dinero en cuanto…
   darme (ellos) un aumento de sueldo (*raise*) / dejar (yo) de gastar tanto
2. Pagaré todas mis cuentas tan pronto como…
   tener el dinero para hacerlo / ser absolutamente necesario
3. El semestre que viene, pagaré la matrícula después de que…
   cobrar mi cheque en el banco / (¿quién?) mandarme un cheque
4. No podré pagar el alquiler hasta que…
   sacar dinero de mi cuenta de ahorros / depositar el dinero en mi cuenta corriente
5. No voy a jubilarme (*retire*) hasta que mis hijos…
   terminar sus estudios universitarios / casarse

Need more practice?

- Workbook and Laboratory Manual
- Interactive CD-ROM
- Online Learning Center (www.mhhe.com/puntos7)

■ ■ ■ Conversación

A. Descripciones. Describa Ud. los dibujos, completando las oraciones e inventando un contexto para las escenas. Luego describa su propia vida.

1. Pablo va a estudiar hasta que ———.

   Esta noche yo voy a estudiar hasta que ———.
   Siempre estudio hasta que ———.
   Anoche estudié hasta que ———.

2. Los Sres. Castro van a cenar tan pronto como ———.

   Esta noche voy a cenar tan pronto como ———.
   Siempre ceno tan pronto como ———.
   Anoche cené tan pronto como ———.

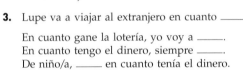
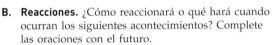

3. Lupe va a viajar al extranjero en cuanto ———.

   En cuanto gane la lotería, yo voy a ———.
   En cuanto tengo el dinero, siempre ———.
   De niño/a, ——— en cuanto tenía el dinero.

B. Reacciones. ¿Cómo reaccionará o qué hará cuando ocurran los siguientes acontecimientos? Complete las oraciones con el futuro.

1. Cuando colonicemos otro planeta, ———.
2. Cuando descubran algo para curar el cáncer, ———.
3. Cuando haya una mujer presidenta, ———.
4. Cuando me jubile, ———.
5. Cuando yo sea anciano/a, ———.
6. Cuando me gradúe, ———.

Bright Idea

Prác. C: Preliminary Exercise

Have students complete the following statements using the future tense.

1. *Cuando yo me gradúe, yo…*
2. *Para celebrar mi cumpleaños, mi amigo/a y yo…*
3. *En cuanto tenga suficiente dinero, yo…*
4. *Cuando termine este año escolar, mi familia y yo…*
5. *Cuando vuelva a casa hoy, yo…*

Prác. C: Suggestion

Personalize each set of activity items by asking questions of individual students. Encourage detailed answers only if students are comfortable revealing this kind of information.

Con. A: Note

The drawing on the right of each paired set indicates a future uncompleted action.

Con. A: Extension

Have students complete the following sentences with personal information.

1. *Voy a… en cuanto…*
2. *Siempre… en cuanto…*
3. *De niño/a, …en cuanto…*

Con. B: Extension

7. *Antes de graduarme,…*
8. *Después de conseguir mi primer/próximo trabajo,…*
9. *En cuanto tenga suficiente dinero,…*
10. *Antes de tener hijos…*

Gramática ■ **503** — Quinientos tres

Resources: Transparency 102

A: Follow-Up

Paso 1. Have students indicate if the sentences are *cierto* or *falso* for them and their families. When a statement is not true for them, have them correct it.

A. Los planes de la familia Alonso

Paso 1. Haga oraciones completas, según las indicaciones. Use el futuro donde sea posible.

> MODELO: yo / hacer / planes / para el futuro / tan pronto / graduarse (yo) →
> Haré planes para el futuro tan pronto como me gradúe.

1. ser / necesario / que / (nosotros) ahorrar / más
2. yo / no / usar / tanto / tarjetas / crédito
3. mamá / buscar / trabajo / donde / (ellos) pagarle / más
4. (nosotros) pedir / préstamo / en / banco
5. nos / lo / (ellos) dar, ¿no / creer (tú)?
6. papá / estar / tranquilo / cuando / todos / empezar / economizar
7. (tú) deber / pagar / siempre / al contado
8. no / (nosotros) poder / irse / de vacaciones / este verano

Paso 2. Según los comentarios de las personas en el **Paso 1,** ¿cree Ud. que la familia Alonso está muy bien económicamente o no? Explique.

B. Planes para una boda.
Use las conjunciones entre paréntesis para unir cada oración con la frase que la sigue. Haga todos los cambios necesarios. ¡**OJO!** No se usa el subjuntivo en todos los casos. Tenga cuidado con las formas verbales.

> MODELO: Miguel quiere casarse con Carmen. / él: conseguir un trabajo (tan pronto como) →
> Miguel quiere casarse con Carmen tan pronto como él consiga un trabajo.

1. Carmen quiere esperar. / ella: graduarse en la universidad (hasta que)
2. Miguel se lo va a decir a los padres de Carmen. / (ellos) llegar a la ciudad (tan pronto como)
3. Los padres de Carmen siempre quieren ver a Miguel. / él: visitar a su hija (cuando)
4. Los padres se van a alegrar. / (ellos) oír las noticias (en cuanto)
5. Miguel y Carmen van a Acapulco en su luna de miel. / (ellos) tener dinero (cuando)
6. Todos nosotros les vamos a dar una fiesta. / (ellos) regresar de su viaje (después de que)

National Standards: Communication

Have students interview each other or students from another Spanish class about whether or not they work, and why, where, and how many hours per week they work. Students can work as a class to brainstorm possible questions. Have them conduct their interviews outside of class if possible and summarize their findings in a brief paragraph. In class, have them work in small groups to share their results. Then discuss the results as a class. Encourage them to characterize students at your university based on their findings and have them debate whether or not their student body is typical compared to other universities in the country.

C. ¿Cómo se ganan la vida (*earn a living*) **los estudiantes?** Complete the following paragraphs with the correct form of the words in parentheses, as suggested by the context. When two possibilities are given in parentheses, select the correct word. Use an adverb derived from the adjectives in italics.

La preocupación por el dinero es algo compartido[a] por los estudiantes en todo el mundo. En (el/la[1]) mayor parte de los países de habla española, (el/la[2]) sistema universitario es gratuito.[b] Sin embargo, hay (de/que[3]) tener dinero para los (gastar/gastos[4]) personales y también para (el/la[5]) cine y otras diversiones.

Aquí, algunos estudiantes hispánicos contestan la pregunta: ¿Cómo (te/se[6]) ganaba Ud. la vida cuando era estudiante?

Una joven de México: A los trece años, (*yo: empezar*[7]) a trabajar en una oficina. Así (*yo: poder*[8]) pagar la colegiatura[c] de mis estudios. (*Yo: Trabajar*[9]) de día y (*estudiar*[10]) de noche.

Un joven uruguayo: Cuando (*yo: ser/estar*[11]) estudiante, me (*ganar*[12]) la vida como fotógrafo. (*Yo: Sacar*[13]) fotos de bodas, bautismos, fiestas de cumpleaños. (*Yo: Trabajar*[14]) en cualquier ocasión y en cualquier sitio.

Una mujer española: (*Yo: Ayudar*[15]) a enseñar a párvulos.[d]

Algunos estudiantes (*ofrecer*[16]) los siguientes comentarios adicionales.

Una joven chilena: Los padres (*normal*[17]) mantienen a sus hijos (*económico*[18]). Pero muchos chicos (*trabajar*[19]) de todas maneras. Las chicas (*cuidar*[20]) niños o (*ayudar*[21]) en casa y los chicos (*trabajar*[22]) en talleres. Si los padres tienen dinero, es raro que los hijos (*trabajar*[23]) hasta que no (*terminar*[24]) su carrera.[e]

Un joven argentino: En la Argentina, la enseñanza universitaria (*ser/estar*[25]) gratuita. De todos modos, los estudiantes siempre (*necesitar*[26]) tener más de un trabajo y los padres los ayudan con (*que / lo que*[27]) pueden. Muchos estudiantes no (*irse*[28]) a otras ciudades a (*estudiar*[29]). (*Ellos: Vivir*[30]) con (*su*[31]) padres y estudian en (el/la[32]) universidad más cercana.

[a]*shared* [b]*free* [c]*fees* [d]*tots* [e]*studies*

Comprensión: ¿Cierto o falso? Corrija las oraciones falsas.

1. El sistema universitario es gratuito en muchos países hispánicos.
2. Los estudiantes hispánicos nunca tienen que trabajar.
3. Generalmente los padres mantienen a sus hijos mientras estos son estudiantes.

Resources for Review and Testing Preparation

- Workbook and Laboratory Manual
- Interactive CD-ROM
- Online Learning Center (www.mhhe.com/puntos7)

C: Follow-Up

- Ask students: *¿Qué harán Uds. para buscar trabajo este verano? ¿y cuando se gradúen?*
- Have students discuss the similarities and differences between the U.S. and Canadian systems and the Hispanic system regarding student life. Ask: *¿Qué hacen Uds. para pagar sus estudios?*

Resources: Desenlace

In the *Capítulo 16* segment of "Chapter-by-Chapter Supplementary Materials" in the IM/RK, you will find a chapter-culminating activity. You can use this activity to consolidate and review the vocabulary and grammar skills students have acquired.

Entrevistas culturales

Note

Students learned the word *aspirante* (*al empleo*) for someone who is looking for a job. *Solicitante* is also used to refer to a *job candidate*.

Suggestions

■ Before showing the video clips, ask students questions about applying for jobs and working with job placement services.

¿Cómo prefiere Ud. buscar trabajo? ¿Lee anuncios en los periódicos? ¿Consulta los sitios web de servicios para aspirantes y empleados? ¿Publica su currículum en el Internet o con algún servicio? ¿Qué información incluye en su currículum y las solicitudes?

■ Show the video clips and allow students one to two minutes to work on the questions for each one. Have volunteers answer the questions.

■ Have volunteers role-play María and Sonia and their respective interviewers.

Entre amigos

Suggestions

■ Before viewing the video, review the questions with the students and ask them similar questions.

¿Cómo se prepara Ud. para una entrevista?
¿Qué tipo de ropa lleva Ud. cuando tiene una entrevista?
¿Piensa Ud. buscar trabajo en su profesión antes de graduarse?

Have students answer or work in small groups to ask and answer these questions in Spanish.

■ After viewing the video, have volunteers read and answer the questions.

PERSPECTIVAS culturales

●●●
Videoteca

Entrevista cultural: el Uruguay

María Dioni es del Uruguay; es consejera para estudiantes universitarios. María describe su trabajo. Antes de ver el vídeo, lea el siguiente fragmento de la entrevista.

MARÍA: Mi trabajo principal es ayudar a los estudiantes a prepararse para buscar trabajo. Muchos estudiantes no tienen experiencia con el proceso de buscar trabajo: las solicitudes, las entrevistas y las negociaciones, por ejemplo.

Ahora vea el vídeo y conteste las siguientes preguntas basándose en la entrevista.

1. ¿Cuáles son las responsabilidades de María?
2. ¿Qué necesitan saber los estudiantes para buscar trabajo?

Entrevista cultural: el Paraguay

La paraguaya Sonia Sancho tiene un puesto administrativo con una compañía en México. Ella comenta su trabajo y algunos de los errores cometidos por los solicitantes. Antes de ver el vídeo, lea el siguiente fragmento de la entrevista.

ENTREVISTADORA: ¿Es difícil su trabajo?
SONIA: Un poco, porque no todas las solicitudes son seleccionadas para una entrevista, y no todas las personas que vienen a una entrevista obtienen un trabajo.

Ahora vea el vídeo y conteste las siguientes preguntas basándose en la entrevista.

1. ¿Cuál es el trabajo de Sonia? ¿Por qué le parece difícil, a veces?
2. ¿Cuál es uno de los errores que se hacen con las solicitudes?

Entre amigos: ¿A qué hora es la entrevista?

Karina, Tané, Miguel y Rubén hablan del trabajo y de las entrevistas. En su opinión, ¿qué preguntas se van a hacer? Antes de mirar el vídeo, lea las preguntas a continuación. Mientras mire el vídeo, trate de entender la conversación en general y fíjese en la información sobre las entrevistas y los planes futuros de los amigos. Luego mire el vídeo una segunda vez, fijándose en la información que necesita para contestar las preguntas.

1. ¿Por qué está tan bien vestido Rubén? ¿Está tranquilo o nervioso?
2. ¿Qué quiere hacer Miguel después de graduarse?

Conozca... el Uruguay y el Paraguay

Datos esenciales

El Uruguay

- Nombre oficial: República Oriental del Uruguay
- Capital: Montevideo
- Población: 3.400.000 habitantes
- Moneda: el peso uruguayo
- Idioma oficial: el español

El Paraguay

- Nombre oficial: República del Paraguay
- Capital: Asunción
- Población: 6.036.900 habitantes
- Moneda: el guaraní
- Idiomas oficiales: el español y el guaraní

¡Fíjese!

- Aproximadamente el 45 por ciento de la población uruguaya vive en Montevideo.
- Para los uruguayos, la educación primaria, secundaria y universitaria es gratuita.[a] La tasa de alfabetización[b] es de un 96 por ciento, una de las más altas de Latinoamérica.
- El Paraguay es uno de los dos países latinoamericanos sin costa marítima (el otro es Bolivia). Por eso, sus numerosos ríos navegables tienen gran importancia económica para el país.
- La ciudad de Asunción, en el Paraguay, la primera ciudad permanente en la región del Río de la Plata, fue fundada por los españoles en 1537.
- La represa[c] hidroeléctrica de Itaipú, terminada en 1982, es una de las más grandes y potentes del mundo. Fue construida en la frontera entre el Paraguay y la Argentina y el Brasil con la ayuda financiera del Brasil, país que recibe la energía eléctrica de la represa.

[a]free [b]tasa... rate of literacy [c]dam

Civilizaciones indígenas: el guaraní

El Paraguay es el único país latinoamericano que tiene dos lenguas oficiales, una de ellas indígena. El 90 por ciento de la población paraguaya habla guaraní (sólo el 75 por ciento habla español). Hoy hay literatura, música y hasta páginas web en guaraní.

Guaraní significa guerrero[a] en esa lengua, nombre que recuerda las disputas de los diversos grupos étnicos guaraníes contra el poderoso Imperio inca.

[a]warrior

▲ Asunción, Paraguay

Learn more about Uruguay and Paraguay with the Video, the Interactive CD-ROM, and the Online Learning Center (www.mhhe.com/puntos7).

Conozca... el Uruguay y el Paraguay

Suggestion
Have students form teams to research the following topics and report on their significance to Uruguay or Paraguay.

Uruguay:
Eduardo Galeano, Mario Benedetti, Delmira Agustini, Juana de Ibarbourou, Julio Herrera y Reissig, Juan Díaz de Solís, Fernando Magallanes, the Charrúas, José Gervasio Artigas and the Battle of *Las Piedras*, and the Tupamaros

Paraguay:
Sebastián Cabot, *el rey blanco* and the discovery of Iguazú Falls, José Arturo Rodríguez Francia, Arturo Stroessner, Raúl Cubas Grau, Augusto Roa Bastos, and *Yo, el supremo*

Note
Students can read an excerpt of the short story *"El hijo"* by Uruguay's Horacio Quiroga in *Un paso más 16*.

MULTIMEDIA: Internet

Have students search the Internet for more information about the government, educational system, geography, and economy of Uruguay and Paraguay. Students can also research Guaraní language radio stations, literature, cultural information, and online courses. You might assign specific topics and have students give brief oral reports based on their findings.

CULTURE

Guaraní also refers to the indigenous group that lives in Paraguay as well as in parts of Brazil, Paraguay, and Argentina. Their language is third only to Latin and Greek for naming plants and animals. Some examples include *piraña*, *jaguar*, *tapir*, *petunia*, and *ananás*.

Suggestions

- Read the following descriptions and have students tell what professions they associate with each: *¿Qué profesión asocia Ud. con cada descripción?*

1. *Recibe muchas invitaciones para comer en buenos restaurantes. Es muy susceptible a los ataques al corazón. Viaja mucho.*
2. *Compra y vende cosas. Pone anuncios de sus productos en la televisión, en los periódicos, etcétera. Está contento cuando los empleados venden mucho.*
3. *Tiene que leer mucho. Tiene un puesto de mucho prestigio. A veces no sabe si su cliente es inocente.*

- Play a game to identify professions. Make individual cards with the names of professions in Spanish. Tape a card on each student's back without allowing him/her to see it. Have students circulate to ask *sí/no* questions about themselves. After each question, they should move to another classmate. Classmates may only respond *Sí* or *No*; they should not elaborate. The first student to figure out what he/she is wins. Continue until everyone is successful. Model exchanges before they begin.

  ¿Trabajo en una oficina? → *No.*
  ¿Manejo mucho? → *No.*
  ¿Enseño? → *Sí.*
  ¿Soy maestro/a? → *Sí.*

- Point out that the first person singular of *caer* is *caigo*. The first person singular of *graduarse* is *me gradúo*. Remind students of the spelling changes for *cargar* (*gu*), *economizar* (*c*), and *sacar* (*qu*).

EN RESUMEN

Gramática

To review the grammar points presented in this chapter, refer to the indicated grammar presentations. You'll find further practice of these structures in the Workbook and Laboratory Manual, on the Interactive CD-ROM, and on the *Puntos de partida* Online Learning Center (www.mhhe.com/puntos7).

46. Talking About the Future—Future Verb Forms

You should know how to form and when to use the future tense, including all irregular forms.

47. Expressing Future or Pending Actions—Subjunctive and Indicative After Conjunctions of Time

Do you know how to express actions that will take place only after something else takes place? What are the conjunctions that you can use for this?

Vocabulario
Practice this vocabulary with digital flash cards on the Online Learning Center (www.mhhe.com/puntos7).

Los verbos

jubilarse	to retire
mudarse	to move (*residence*)

Profesiones y oficios

el/la abogado/a	lawyer
el/la cajero/a	cashier; teller
el/la cocinero/a	cook; chef
el/la comerciante	merchant; shopkeeper
el/la contador(a)	accountant
el/la criado/a	servant
el hombre / la mujer de negocios	businessperson
el/la ingeniero/a	engineer
el/la maestro/a	schoolteacher
el/la obrero/a	worker, laborer
el/la peluquero/a	hairstylist
el/la periodista	journalist
el/la plomero/a	plumber
el soldado / la mujer soldado	soldier
el/la trabajador(a) social	social worker
el/la traductor(a)	translator
el/la vendedor(a)	salesperson

Cognados: el/la analista de sistemas, el/la electricista, el/la fotógrafo/a, el/la programador(a), el/la sicólogo/a, el/la siquiatra, el/la técnico/a, el/la veterinario/a

Repaso: el/la bibliotecario/a, el/la consejero/a, el/la dentista, el/la dependiente/a, el/la enfermero/a, el/la mecánico/a, el/la médico/a, el/la profesor(a), el/la secretario/a

En busca de un puesto

el/la aspirante	candidate; applicant
el currículum	resumé
la dirección de personal	personnel office, employment office
el/la director(a) de personal	personnel director
la empresa	corporation; business
la entrevista	interview
el/la entrevistador(a)	interviewer
el/la gerente	manager
el puesto	job; position
el salario	salary
la solicitud	application (*form*)
la sucursal	branch (office)

Repaso: el sueldo, el teléfono

caerle (*irreg.*) bien/ mal a alguien	to make a good/bad impression on someone
dejar	to quit
entrevistar	to interview
escribir a computadora	to key in (type)
graduarse (en) (me gradúo)	to graduate (from)
llenar	to fill out (*a form*)
renunciar (a)	to resign (from)

Repaso: contestar

Una cuestión de dinero

el aumento de sueldo	raise
el banco	bank
la caja	cashier window
el cajero automático	automatic teller machine

el cheque	check
la chequera	checkbook
la cuenta corriente	checking account
la cuenta de ahorros	savings account
el efectivo	cash
la factura	bill
la identificación	ID
el interés	interest
el préstamo	loan
el presupuesto	budget

Repaso: la cuenta, la tarjeta de crédito

ahorrar	to save (*money*)
cargar (gu)	to charge (*to an account*)
cobrar	to cash (*a check*); to charge (*someone for an item or service*)
depositar	to deposit
devolver (ue)	to return (*something*)
economizar (c)	to economize
ganar	to earn
pedir (i, i) prestado/a	to borrow

sacar (qu)	to withdraw, take out
sacar el saldo	to balance a checkbook

Repaso: gastar, pagar (gu), prestar

a plazos	in installments
al contado / en efectivo	in cash
con cheque	by check

Conjunciones

después (de) que	after
en cuanto	as soon as
hasta que	until
tan pronto como	as soon as

Repaso: antes (de) que, cuando

Palabras adicionales

al principio de	at the beginning of
en vez de	instead of

- Have students list on the board different work-related and bank-related situations, for example, an office manager giving an employee a bad work review, a student asking for a loan. Have students take turns role-playing different situations without indicating which one. The class should guess the situation.
- Ask students the following questions to review the vocabulary.

1. *¿Tiene Ud. una cuenta de ahorros? ¿En qué banco? ¿Ha ahorrado mucho dinero este año? ¿Es posible que ahorre más el año que viene? ¿Tiene también una cuenta corriente? ¿Escribe muchos cheques? ¿Hay siempre suficiente dinero en su cuenta? ¿Qué ocurre si no hay suficientes fondos en su cuenta?*
2. *En esta clase, ¿cuántos de Uds. tienen tarjetas de crédito? (to one student) ¿Son tarjetas nacionales como Visa o son tarjetas para tiendas locales? ¿Las usa con mucha frecuencia? ¿Las usa demasiado? ¿Tiene muchas facturas que pagar ahora?*
3. *En general, ¿tienen muchas facturas los estudiantes? ¿Cuáles son los gastos típicos de un estudiante? ¿Tiene Ud. todos estos gastos? ¿Tiene también un presupuesto? ¿Qué porcentaje de su presupuesto es para el alquiler?*
4. *¿Cuánto paga de alquiler? ¿Lo paga siempre el primero del mes o a veces lo paga más tarde? ¿Qué pasa si lo paga tarde?*
5. *¿Gasta Ud. mucho dinero en ropa? ¿Cómo la paga, con tarjetas de crédito, al contado o con cheque? ¿Se queja Ud. del precio de la ropa?*

Un paso más 16

Note

The *Un paso más* section is optional.

Literatura del Uruguay

Note

When Quiroga was 24 years old, he accidentally shot and killed a friend. He moved to Buenos Aires after this tragedy. He married after moving to Argentina and had two children.

Preliminary Exercises

- Have students look at Horacio Quiroga's picture and describe him. Provide adjectives if necessary.
- Have students guess the meaning of *más allá*. What images come to mind when they think of *el más allá* (the beyond or the hereafter)?

Un paso más 16

Literatura del **Uruguay**

Sobre el autor: *Horacio Silvestre Quiroga nació en Salto, Uruguay. En 1899 fundó la Revista de Salto, y en 1900 viajó a París con otros jóvenes intelectuales. Volvió al Uruguay pero, después de matar*[a] *accidentalmente a un amigo, se trasladó a la Argentina. En 1935 publicó «Más allá», su último libro de cuentos antes de morir. El siguiente fragmento es del cuento «El hijo», Más allá (1935).*

▲ Horacio Quiroga
(1878–1937)

Es un poderoso[b] día de verano en Misiones, con todo el sol, el calor y la calma que puede deparar[c] la estación. La naturaleza plenamente[d] abierta, se siente satisfecha de sí.

Como el sol, el calor y la calma ambiente, el padre abre también su corazón a la naturaleza.

—Ten cuidado, chiquito —dice a su hijo; abreviando[e] en esa frase todas las observaciones del caso y que su hijo comprende perfectamente.

—Sí, papá —responde la criatura[f] mientras coge la escopeta[g] y carga de cartuchos[h] los bolsillos de su camisa, que cierra con cuidado.

[a]*killing* [b]*powerful* [c]*traer* [d]*completely, fully* [e]*abbreviating* [f]*niño* [g]*shotgun* [h]*carga... fills with cartridges*

LECTURA

Note: The readings in the final three chapters of *Puntos de partida,* beginning with this chapter, are poems from the Spanish-speaking world. Your professor may have already introduced you to some of the great works of Spanish and Latin American literature through the **Literatura de...** excerpts that appear in the **Un paso más** section of each chapter. Reading poetry presents challenges for you that are different from the challenges of reading prose. But your developing language proficiency will provide you a solid foundation with which to approach the task. As you read, remember to utilize the various reading strategies that have been introduced in previous chapters, as some of these will be applicable to the reading of literature as well.

ESTRATEGIA: Using Language Cues to Understand Poetry (1)

Much of the information you get in a poem is conveyed through its adjectives. Classifying the adjectives can often help you understand the poet's purpose or the poem's deeper "message." It can also help you to focus your attention on the important aspects of the poem.

You can classify the adjectives in the following poem as negative and positive. As you read, decide which adjectives describe the noun in favorable terms and which describe the noun in unfavorable terms. How is the central figure of the poem described? Why do you think the poet may have chosen this strategy?

■ **Sobre la autora...** Juana Fernández de Ibarbourou (1895–1970) nació en Melo, Uruguay, donde pasó una niñez feliz. Demostró su interés en la poesía a una temprana edad y publicó sus primeros versos en un periódico local a los 8 años. Después de su matrimonio a los 20 años, ella y su esposo se fueron a vivir a Montevideo.

La poesía de Ibarbourou refleja la satisfacción de ser esposa, madre y poeta. A menudo (*Often*) escribía sobre la naturaleza y la reencarnación, dos de sus temas favoritos. En el siguiente poema, Ibarbourou crea la fuerte imagen de un elemento «feo» dentro de un medio ambiente muy bello y nos hace pensar en lo que constituye la belleza verdadera.

LECTURA

Suggestions

■ Do the *Estrategia* in class before assigning the reading.
■ Encourage students to read Spanish and Latin American poetry in bilingual editions. You may also want them to bring a short poem or an excerpt of a longer poem (written in Spanish) to class and have them share it with other students.

- Read or have a student volunteer read the poem aloud. Encourage students to talk about the effect of the poem's sounds (for example, some students may note that the many *gr*, *br*, *tr*, and *pr* sounds make the sound as rough as the fig tree itself).
- Have students identify the adjectives. Then read the poem again, this time changing the negative ones to more bland or less descriptive terms (for example, change *áspera y fea* to *no suave y poco atractiva*. Ask students for their reaction to the new version.
- Have students find examples of *rima asonante* (for example, *fea/higuera*; *redondos/lustrosos*). Ask them how they think this type of rhyme affects the sound of the poem, and how they think it might be different if the rhyme were the more traditional *consonant* rhyme (that is, rhyme that repeats both vowel and consonant sounds).
- Ask students whether they feel that this poem is solely a description of a natural event, or whether this poem might contain some other kind of wisdom. Have them explain their opinion.

♻ Reciclado

Teach students rules of syllabification and provide a brief explanation about syllabification and poetry. Have them count the syllables in the first stanza of the poem. Are the lines all equal in length?

La higuera[a]

Porque es áspera[b] y fea;
Porque todas sus ramas[c] son grises,
Yo le tengo piedad[d] a la higuera.

En mi quinta[e] hay cien árboles bellos:
    Ciruelos redondos,[f]
    Limoneros rectos[g]
Y naranjos de brotes[h] lustrosos

    En las primaveras,
Todos ellos se cubren de flores
    En torno a[i] la higuera.

Y la pobre parece tan triste
Con sus gajos torcidos[j] que nunca
De apretados capullos[k] se visten…

    Por eso,
Cada vez que yo paso a su lado
Digo, procurando[l]
Hacer dulce y alegre mi acento:
—Es la higuera el más bello
De los árboles todos del huerto.[m]

    Si ella escucha,
Si comprende el idioma en que hablo,
¡Qué dulzura tan honda hará nido[n]
En su alma sensible[o] de árbol!

    Y tal vez, a la noche,
Cuando el viento abanique su copa,[p]
Embriagada de gozo[q] le cuente:
—Hoy a mí me dijeron hermosa.[r]

[a]*fig tree* [b]*rough* [c]*branches* [d]*pity* [e]*casa de campo* [f]*Ciruelos... Round plum trees* [g]*Limoneros... Straight lemon trees* [h]*shoots* [i]*En... Around* [j]*gajos... twisted branches* [k]*apretados... tight buds* [l]*tratando de* [m]*orchard* [n]*¡Qué... How deep the sweetness that will nest* [o]*alma... sensitive soul* [p]*Cuando... When the wind fans its upper branches* [q]*Embriagada... Drunk with joy* [r]*beautiful*

▲ *Una higuera*

Comprensión

A. Descripción. Escriba una lista de adjetivos y frases que usa la autora para describir a la higuera.

B. Interpretación

1. ¿Por qué cree Ud. que la autora siente piedad por la higuera?

2. ¿Qué «lección» ofrece el poema?

ESCRITURA

A. Yo soy la higuera. Imagine que Ud. es la higuera en el huerto (*orchard*) de la autora. ¿Cómo se siente, rodeada (*surrounded*) de tantos árboles tan bonitos? ¿Qué opina Ud. sobre el cariño (*affection*) que le muestra la autora a la higuera? Escriba un breve ensayo en la que expresa sus emociones y perspectiva. El título de su ensayo puede ser «Yo soy la higuera».

B. Un poema. Siga los siguientes pasos para escribir un poema sobre un objeto en su vida. Puede ser algo que le guste o que no le guste.

MODELO: Mi nueva computadora
En mi escritorio
La uso todos los días para trabajar y jugar
Estoy con mi computadora más que con mis amigos
¡Cómo han cambiado nuestra vida las computadoras!

- Nombre y describe el objeto.
- Ubique (*Locate*) el objeto.
- Describa la relación que Ud. tiene con el objeto.
- Compare el objeto con otras cosas en tu vida.
- Concluya el poema con una declaración sobre el objeto.

A. Suggestion
Have students use the adjectives from the poem in original sentences. Students can work individually or in pairs, and then share their sentences, or the class can work collectively to create sentences or their own poem.

ESCRITURA

Suggestion
If you prefer that your students do a journal activity, see *Mi diario* in this chapter of the Workbook.

B. Suggestions

- Have volunteers read their poems to the class.
- Ask students to think of an object that they can identify with in a metaphoric way. Have them write a short poem in the first person, using the poetic voice of the object of their choice.

◄ El Palacio Nacional en Santo Domingo, la República Dominicana

CHAPTER OPENER PHOTO

Point out the chapter-opener photo. *El Palacio Nacional* serves as the federal government building for the Dominican Republic. The building, dedicated in 1947, is relatively new. Have students compare this government building to government buildings in your area or other cities they know. What adjectives would they use to describe the buildings? Do the columns and dome remind them of any federal buildings in this country?

Suggestions

■ Have students put the followings types of news in order of preference.

_____ **noticias** mundiales
_____ noticias sobre su pueblo o ciudad
_____ noticias sobre su vecindad
_____ noticias sobre **desastres** o tragedias
_____ noticias sobre **eventos** inspirativos que le hayan ocurrido a algún individuo
_____ noticias sobre los deportes
_____ noticias sobre los negocios
_____ noticias sociales o culturales

■ The words in **boldface** are included in the active vocabulary of this chapter. Have students discuss the words and use context to help them understand the meanings. Place the words they cannot guess in new sentences and contexts.
■ Introduce new vocabulary as needed for this activity.
■ Ask students.

1. ¿Cree que Ud. está bien informado/a de lo que pasa? ¿Por qué?
2. ¿Piensa Ud. que es importante estar bien informado/a? ¿Por qué sí o no?

Note

The *Puntos de partida* Online Learning Center includes an interview with a native speaker from the Dominican Republic who answers questions about the news.

Resources

For Students

■ Workbook
■ Laboratory Manual and Laboratory Audio Program
■ Quia™ Online Workbook and Online Laboratory Manual
■ Video on CD
■ Interactive CD-ROM
■ *Puntos de partida* Online Learning Center (**www.mhhe.com/puntos7**)

For Instructors

■ *Instructor's Manual and Resource Kit*, "Chapter-by-Chapter" Supplementary Materials
■ Overhead Transparency 103
■ Testing Program
■ Test Generator
■ Video Program
■ Audioscript
■ *Puntos de partida* Online Learning Center (**www.mhhe.com/puntos7**)

En la **actualidad**

Suggestion
Have students list their ideas about the Dominican Republic, including information on geography, politics, economy, culture, music, and cuisine. When you finish the chapter, return to the lists and ask students what ideas they would change and/or add.

CULTURA

- **Perspectivas culturales**

  Entrevista cultural: La República Dominicana

  Entre amigos: ¡Por eso sí protestaría!

  Conozca... la República Dominicana

- **Nota cultural:** La mayoría de edad en los países hispanos

- **En los Estados Unidos y el Canadá:** Tres hispanos del mundo de la televisión

- **Literatura de la República Dominicana:** Manuel del Cabral

- **Lectura:** «Cubanita descubanizada», por Gustavo Pérez Firmat

VOCABULARIO

- Las noticias

- El gobierno y la responsabilidad cívica

GRAMÁTICA

48 Past Subjunctive

49 Stressed Possessives

Entrevista cultural

Milstry del Orbe ▶
Santo Domingo,
la República Dominicana

MULTIMEDIA: Internet

Have students look for the official CNN website online where they can read and watch video clips of today's news headlines in Spanish.

MULTIMEDIA

- The multimedia materials that accompany this chapter are referenced in the Student and Instructor's Editions with icons to help you identify when and where to incorporate them.

- The IM/RK provides suggestions for using the multimedia materials in the classroom.

VOCABULARIO
Preparación

Las noticias

Note

See the model for vocabulary presentation and other material in the *Capítulo 17 Vocabulario: Preparación* section of "Chapter-by-Chapter Supplementary Materials," in the IM.

Suggestions

■ Remind students that the first person singular of *ofrecer* is *ofrezco*.
■ Read the following definitions and have students give the corresponding words from the vocabulary.

1. *cuando una persona asesina a alguien*
2. *cuando un grupo de obreros o empleados deja de trabajar como protesta*
3. *cuando se sabe algo por primera vez*
4. *las formas en que se da la información al mundo*
5. *antónimo de la guerra*

■ Have students provide names from current events that correspond to the following categories.

> *¿Está Ud. bien informado/a? Dé un nombre de la vida real para cada una de las siguientes categorías.*

1. *un reportero famoso que informe en la tele*
2. *una guerra que esté ocurriendo ahora mismo*
3. *un desastre actual en el que Ud. piense con frecuencia*
4. *un acuerdo de paz que se haya firmado recientemente*
5. *un asesinato reciente que haya sido enfatizado en los medios de comunicación*

■ Point out that *testigo* does not change the ending for the feminine form: *el testigo* and *la testigo*.
■ Give students the following dictado.

1. *Merecemos sueldos más altos, pero el jefe no quiere darnos un aumento.*
2. *Es necesario que nos declaremos en huelga.*
3. *Pero el jefe va a despedir a todos los obreros que protesten.*
4. *No te preocupes: todos juntos podemos hacer cambios positivos.*

**Resources:
Transparency 103**

VOCABULARIO Preparación

Las noticias

el reportero

Y ahora, el canal 45 les ofrece a Uds. el NOTICIERO 45 con los últimos eventos del mundo…

El asesinato de **un dictador**

La huelga de obreros

La guerra en el Oriente Medio

La erupción de un volcán en Centroamérica

Bombas en un avión

El choque de trenes

el acontecimiento	event, happening	**comunicarse (qu) (con)**	to communicate (with)
el medio de comunicación	means of communication	**enterarse (de)**	to find out, learn (about)
la prensa	press; news media		
el desastre	disaster	**informar**	to inform
la esperanza	hope, wish	**mantener** (*irreg.*) **la paz**	to maintain, keep peace
la paz (*pl.* **paces**)	peace	**ofrecer (zc)**	to offer
		vivir en paz	to live in peace

Cognados: el ataque (terrorista), el terrorismo, el/la terrorista, la víctima

National Standards: Communication

■ Give students five to ten minutes to prepare their own news reports. Assign specific topics to different students or groups: headlines, weather, local, international, sports, and so on. Have students select an order of presentation, and begin the news program. If possible, videotape the presentation.
■ Have students watch the evening television newscast on a Spanish-language channel and hand in a two- or three-paragraph report on it the next day.

MULTIMEDIA: Audio

Students can listen to and practice this chapter's vocabulary on the Online Learning Center (**www.mhhe.com/puntos7**), as well as on the Textbook Audio CD, part of the Laboratory Audio Program.

■ ■ ■ Conversación

A. ¿Cómo se entera Ud.? El público utiliza diferentes medios para enterarse de los acontecimientos locales, nacionales e internacionales. ¿Cómo se entera Ud. de las noticias?

Paso 1. Indique con qué frecuencia utiliza los siguientes medios.

	TODOS LOS DÍAS	DE 3 A 5 VECES POR SEMANA	DE 1 A 2 VECES POR SEMANA	CASI NUNCA
1. Leo un periódico local.	☐	☐	☐	☐
2. Leo un periódico nacional.	☐	☐	☐	☐
3. Leo una revista.	☐	☐	☐	☐
4. Leo las noticias en el Internet.	☐	☐	☐	☐
5. Miro el telediario (*newscast*) local.	☐	☐	☐	☐
6. Miro el telediario nacional.	☐	☐	☐	☐
7. Miro CNN.	☐	☐	☐	☐
8. Escucho la radio.	☐	☐	☐	☐

Paso 2. Compare sus respuestas con las de sus compañeros. ¿Cuál es el medio preferido por la mayoría de Uds. para informarse?

B. Definiciones. ¿Qué palabra se asocia con cada definición?

1. _____ un programa que nos informa de lo que pasa en nuestro mundo
2. _____ la persona que está presente durante un acontecimiento y lo ve todo
3. _____ un medio importantísimo de comunicación
4. _____ la persona que nos informa de los acontecimientos
5. _____ la persona que gobierna un país de una forma absoluta
6. _____ la persona que emplea la violencia para cambiar el mundo según sus deseos
7. _____ cuando los obreros se niegan a (*refuse*) trabajar
8. _____ la frecuencia en que se transmiten y se reciben los programas de televisión
9. _____ la confrontación armada entre dos o más países

a. el noticiero
b. la guerra
c. el/la terrorista
d. el/la dictador(a)
e. el canal
f. el/la testigo
g. el/la reportero/a
h. la huelga
i. la prensa

C. Ud. y la televisión. Diga si está de acuerdo con las siguientes opiniones. Si no está de acuerdo, haga los cambios necesarios para expresar su opinión. En cualquier caso, intente dar un ejemplo que justifique su punto de vista.

1. Los reporteros de la televisión nos informan imparcialmente de los acontecimientos.
2. Por lo general ofrecen los programas más interesantes en el canal de televisión pública.
3. En este país la prensa es irresponsable. Nos da sólo los detalles que apoyan (*support*) sus ideas políticas.
4. Las telenovelas (*soap operas*) reflejan la vida tal (*just*) como es.
5. Los anuncios son sumamente (*extremely*) informativos y más interesantes que muchos programas.
6. Me gusta que los reporteros y meteorólogos cuenten chistes durante el noticiero.

Vocabulario: Preparación

Con. A: Follow-Up

Use the activity to find out the favorite newspapers, magazines, Net servers, and so on of the students in the class.

Con. B: Follow-Up

Have students contrast what ultraconservative and ultraliberal people might say about the following topics.

1. *la libertad de prensa*
2. *un país con una dictadura en Centroamérica*
3. *la pena de muerte* (describe)
4. *la obediencia a las leyes*
5. *las huelgas*
6. *el control de armas*
7. *el aborto*
8. *la eutanasia*
9. *los sindicatos* (unions)
10. *el sistema de* (welfare)

Con. C: Suggestions

■ Have students select one item and report their opinions and recommendations back to the class.
■ Use this activity as a written assignment.

☼ Heritage Speakers

Pregúnteles a los hispanohablantes de la clase si prefieren escuchar las noticias en español o inglés. Si las escuchan en español, pregúnteles en qué canal de televisión o estación de radio. Pídales que comparen los noticieros hispanos con los noticieros norteamericanos. ¿Cómo son diferentes? ¿En qué aspectos son similares?

Refrán

«La noticia mala llega volando, y la buena, cojeando.»

Give students the *refrán*. Point out that *volando* means *flying*, then have students guess the meaning of *cojeando* (*limping*) before giving it to them. What are some similar saying about news in English? (*Bad news travels fast.*)

CULTURE

The *tertulia*, a common custom in many parts of the Spanish-speaking world, is the get-together in a bar or café of a group of friends and/or colleagues who like to spend time talking about current issues, religion, literature, the economy, and so on. The two most popular topics of conversation are sports and politics. Some groups gather every day at the same time and place, usually in the afternoon or evening. Others may get together once a week, or once a month. Some groups will continue to get together for many years.

El gobierno y la responsabilidad cívica

Suggestions

- Remind students that the first person singular of *obedecer* is *obedezco*.

- Point out the difference in meaning between *el derecho* (right; law) and *la derecha* (the conservative right, right-hand side). Review other meanings of *derecho*, for example, *todo derecho* (straight ahead).

- Ask students the following questions to personalize the vocabulary.

  1. *En este país, ¿hay una ley que proteja la libertad de prensa? ¿Existe tal ley en otros países también? ¿Qué derechos indivi-duales se garantizan en la cons-titución?* (Write *la libertad de _____* on the board.)

  2. *¿Vota Ud. en todas las elecciones? ¿Votó en las últimas elecciones para presidente o primer ministro? ¿en las últimas elecciones municipales? ¿Cree Ud. que el votar es un deber? ¿Bajo qué tipo de gobierno no es posible votar con libertad?*

  3. *¿Cree Ud. que siempre debemos obedecer la ley? ¿Hay leyes que sean más importantes que otras? ¿Siempre obedece Ud. las leyes de tránsito? ¿Qué castigos (punishments) hay para los delitos menores? ¿y para los delitos más graves?*

- Point out that having rights also means respecting others' rights and liberties. Others are entitled to the same rights that you enjoy, and their needs and priorities may be quite different from your own. Have students list on the board the responsibilities that also imply rights. Discuss specific rights that have led to conflicts, for example, freedom of speech and flag burning or musical expression.

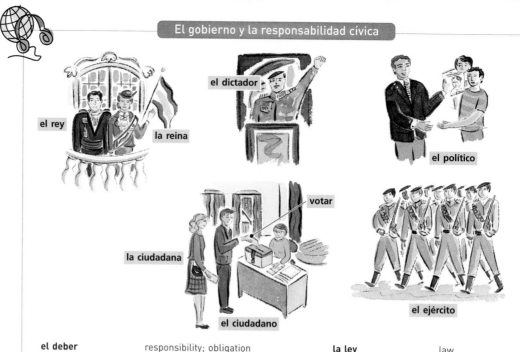

el rey — la reina
el dictador
el político
votar
la ciudadana
el ciudadano
el ejército

el deber	responsibility; obligation	**la ley**	law
los/las demás	others, other people	**la política**	politics
el derecho	right	**el servicio militar**	military service
la (des)igualdad	(in)equality		
la dictadura	dictatorship	**durar**	to last
la discriminación	discrimination	**obedecer (zc)**	to obey

NOTA CULTURAL

La mayoría de edad en los países hispanos

En el mundo hispano los jóvenes se consideran legalmente adultos, es decir, alcanzan[a] **la mayoría de edad,** a los 18 años. Al cumplir los 18 años, los jóvenes hispanos pueden participar en la política y pueden votar. En varios países los hombres de 18 años tam-bién tienen la responsabilidad de inscribirse[b] en **el servicio militar.** En Colombia, los jóvenes pueden inscribirse en el servicio militar a los 16 años. La selección de los cons-criptos[c] generalmente se hace mediante una lotería. Recientemente, las mujeres mexicanas y argentinas también pueden inscribirse en el servicio militar, un hecho sin precedentes en Latinoamérica.

A los 18 años, los jóvenes hispanos pueden obtener su **licencia de manejar.** Sin embargo, muchos jóvenes hispanos no esperan hasta los 18 años. A los 16 años solici-tan un **permiso especial** para menores de edad para operar un vehículo.

Otro aspecto importante al llegar a la mayoría de edad es el consumo de alcohol. **La edad límite** para tomar bebidas alcohólicas varía entre los 18 y 21 años. En Ecuador, por ejemplo, la edad límite es de 21 años. En algunos países hay menos restricciones sociales sobre el alcohol.

[a]*they reach* [b]*de... of registering* [c]*draftees*

518 ■ Quinientos dieciocho

NOTA CULTURAL

Suggestion

Read *cierto/falso* statements to check comprehension.

1. *Los menores de 18 años no pueden manejar un coche en los países hispanos.*

2. *Todos los hispanos de 18 años tienen que hacer su servicio militar.*

CULTURE

Offer the following background information about items 1 and 5 in *Conversación B.* (p. 519).

- Juan Domingo Perón (1895–1974) was the president of Argentina (1946–1955, 1973–1974). He brought long-lasting changes to national Argentine policies and is considered one of the most remarkable Latin American figures of the 20th century.

- Queen Elizabeth II was born April 21, 1926, and is the eldest daughter of George VI and Elizabeth Bowes-Lyon. She and her husband, Phillip Mountbatten, have four children: Charles (Prince of Wales), Anne, Andrew, and Edward.

■ ■ ■ Conversación

Con. A: Suggestion

Ask students the following questions to personalize the vocabulary.

1. *¿Qué canal de televisión prefiere Ud. para enterarse de las noticias? ¿Cree Ud. que en ese canal le informan mejor? ¿O es que le gusta el locutor / la locutora que se las ofrece? ¿Le interesan a Ud. mucho o poco las noticias del estado o de la provincia de (your state/province)? ¿Por qué sí o por qué no?*

2. *¿Le importan más a Ud. su autonomía e individualismo o los sentimientos de los demás? En una tienda, ¿hace cola con paciencia o trata de atraer la atención del dependiente? En una parada de autobús, ¿hace cola o trata de subir primero?*

3. *Para Ud., ¿cuáles son los derechos más básicos de que todos debemos gozar? ¿Cuáles son los deberes de un buen ciudadano? ¿Es importante que todos votemos en todas las elecciones, sean nacionales o locales? ¿Por qué cree Ud. que muchas personas no votan?*

Con. B: Follow-Up

Have students work in groups to write four to five questions to quiz the rest of the class.

A. Asociaciones. ¿Qué cosas, personas o ideas asocia Ud. con las siguientes palabras?

1. el deber
2. el ejército
3. la política
4. la ley
5. la monarquía
6. la dictadura

B. ¡Peligro! (*Jeopardy!*) ¿Cuánto sabe Ud. de la historia y la política? Conteste rápidamente con la información necesaria y en forma de pregunta. Use las preguntas a la derecha.

1. Fue un dictador argentino que tenía una esposa famosa.
2. Se llama Elizabeth y vive en Buckingham Palace.
3. Es una famosa película de Orson Welles, y su protagonista se llama Kane.
4. Fue un presidente estadounidense que se opuso a (*opposed*) la esclavitud de los negros.
5. En algunos países, es un deber de los hombres de cierta edad. Generalmente, tienen que entrar en el ejército por dos años, más o menos.
6. Es la forma de gobierno que existe en España.
7. Existe cuando muchas personas no tienen los mismos derechos que los demás.
8. Es un deber de los ciudadanos en una democracia.

¿Quién/Qué es...

a. el servicio militar?
b. la reina de Inglaterra?
c. votar?
d. la monarquía parlamentaria?
e. *El ciudadano Kane* (*Citizen Kane*)?
f. la discriminación?
g. Juan Perón?
h. Abraham Lincoln?

C. Opiniones. ¿Qué piensa Ud. de las siguientes ideas? Dé su opinión, empezando con una de estas expresiones.

Dudo que…
Es probable que…
Es una lástima que…
Me parece terrible/buena idea que…

(No) Creo que…
Es bueno/malo que…
Es increíble que…

1. En este país consumimos demasiada energía.
2. La paz mundial completa es (im)posible.
3. En este país, la igualdad de todos los ciudadanos es una realidad, no sólo una esperanza.
4. Los policías, los bomberos (*firefighters*) y los médicos no tienen derecho a declararse en huelga.
5. El servicio militar obligatorio es necesario para formar un ejército.
6. El mundo de la política está lleno de gente (des)honesta.
7. La edad permitida para tomar bebidas alcohólicas debe ser la misma que la edad para votar.
8. Hay muchos países que tienen dictadores.

Need more practice?

- Workbook and Laboratory Manual
- Interactive CD-ROM
- Online Learning Center (www.mhhe.com/ puntos7)

Vocabulario: Preparación   Quinientos diecinueve ■ 519

CULTURE (*continued*)

- Orson Welles (1915–1985) was an American actor, producer, director, and writer. He is most famous for directing and starring in the motion picture *Citizen Kane* in 1941. The movie generated much controversy because it appeared to fictionalize the life of William Randolph Hearst (1983–1951). Hearst was the multimillionaire proprietor of the *San Francisco Examiner*, and his name became synonymous with the term *yellow journalism*.

- Abraham Lincoln (1809–1865) was the 16th president of the United States. Lincoln became president just before the Civil War; he was killed by an assassin's bullet while attending a theater performance.

Bright Idea

¿Recuerde Ud.?:
Suggestion
Review with students the formation of
the preterite, starting with regular
-ar, -er, and -ir forms, followed by the
irregular verbs. Special attention
should be given to -ir stem-changing
verbs that require an additional
change in the third persons singular
and plural.

GRAMÁTICA

In **Gramática 48,** you will learn about and begin to use the forms of the past subjunctive. As you learn this new tense, you will be continually using the past tense forms you have already learned along with the new material, so this section presents many opportunities for review.

To learn the forms of the past subjunctive, you will need to know the forms of the preterite well, especially the third person plural.

- Regular **-ar** verbs end in **-aron** and regular **-er/-ir** verbs in **-ieron** in the third person plural of the preterite.
- Stem-changing **-ir** verbs show the second change in the third person.

  servir (i, i) → **sirvieron   dormir (ue, u)** → **durmieron**

- Verbs with a stem ending in a vowel change the **i** to **y.**

  leyeron, cayeron, construyeron

- Many common verbs have irregular stems in the preterite.

  quisieron, hicieron, dijeron, and so on

- Four common verbs are totally irregular in this tense.

  ser/ir → **fueron   dar** → **dieron   ver** → **vieron**

The following brief exercises will help you get started.

A. Give the third person plural of the preterite for these infinitives.

1. hablar	**5.** perder	**9.** estar	**13.** traer	**17.** decir
2. comer	**6.** dormir	**10.** tener	**14.** dar	**18.** creer
3. vivir	**7.** reír	**11.** destruir	**15.** saber	**19.** ir
4. jugar	**8.** leer	**12.** mantener	**16.** vestirse	**20.** poder

B. The forms of the imperfect are relatively regular. Only three verbs have irregular imperfect forms: **ir, ser,** and **ver.** Give their first person singular and plural forms.

48 *¡No queríamos que fuera así!* • Past Subjunctive

¡Qué pena que no nos lleváramos bien!

Elisa habla con su madre sobre su niñez.

MARÍA: ¿No recuerdas? ¡Qué mala memoria!
ELISA: Pero, mamá, ¿tú permitías que yo *hablara* así? ¡Qué falta de respeto hacia ti!

It's a shame we didn't get along! *Elisa talks to her mother about her childhood.* MARÍA: *You don't remember? What a bad memory!* ELISA: *But, Mom, did you allow me to speak in that way? What a lack of respect towards you!*

MARÍA: Eras muy cabezuda. No había nadie que *pudiera* contigo. ¡Cómo discutíamos! Tú creías que siempre tenías razón. Era imposible que *te equivocaras*. Tampoco querías que te *dijeran* lo que debías hacer.

ELISA: Bueno, por lo menos ahora no soy así. Digo, no tanto…

MARÍA: Sí, pero de todos modos, es necesario que una buena periodista sea un poco terca.

ELISA: Estoy de acuerdo. Es probable que, sin esa cualidad mía, yo no hubiera obtenido ese puesto.

Hace diez años…

1. ¿era difícil que Ud. hablara con sus padres sobre algún tema? ¿Cuál?
2. ¿con quién era imposible que Ud. se pusiera de acuerdo?
3. ¿con quién era imposible que Ud. se comunicara?
4. ¿contra qué orden de sus padres era común que Ud. protestara?

Cuando Ud. era niño/a…

5. ¿era probable que discutiera con alguien en la escuela primaria o en el barrio? ¿Con quién?
6. ¿dónde le prohibían sus padres que jugara?
7. ¿qué era obligatorio que comiera o bebiera?
8. ¿de qué temía que sus padres se enteraran?

Although Spanish has two simple indicative past tenses (preterite and imperfect), it has only one simple subjunctive past tense, the *past subjunctive* (**el imperfecto del subjuntivo**). Generally speaking, this tense is used in the same situations as the present subjunctive but, of course, when talking about past events. The exact English equivalent depends on the context in which it is used.

PAST	Present	Future
preterite	present indicative	future
imperfect	present progressive	
present perfect	formal commands	
present perfect subjunctive	informal commands	
past subjunctive	present subjunctive	

MARÍA: *You were very stubborn. No one could change your mind. How we used to argue! You thought you were always right. It was impossible that you could ever make a mistake. Nor did you want anyone to tell you what to do.* ELISA: *Well, at least I'm not like that now. I mean, not as much . . .* MARÍA: *Yes, but, in any case, it's necessary for a good journalist to be a little bit stubborn.* ELISA: *I agree. It's probable that, without that quality of mine, I wouldn't have gotten that job.*

Suggestion

Teach this grammar topic for recognition only. Most first-year students will not acquire productive control of the past subjunctive.

Follow-Up

Ask the following questions to personalize the *minidiálogo*.

1. *¿A quién era posible que Ud. le dijera «Uds. no entienden», a sus padres, a sus hermanos, a sus hijos o a sus amigos?*
2. *¿Qué le molestaba más que le dijeran los adultos cuando Ud. era más joven: «Tú eres demasiado joven para saberlo» o «Tú eres demasiado mayor para hacer esto»?*

☼ Heritage Speakers

■ Pídales a los hispanohablantes que representen el minidiálogo para la clase.
■ Note que a veces los hispanohablantes añaden una *i* en la tercera persona plural de algunos verbos irregulares, por ejemplo, *dijieran, trajieran* y *produjieran*. A pesar de que existan estas formas en el habla común y corriente, la forma aceptada para cada verbo es *dijeran, trajeran* y *produjeran*.

Forms of the Past Subjunctive

Note

The pluperfect subjunctive is not presented in *Puntos de partida*, since it is beyond the expectations and ability of beginning students for control and production. If you wish to present this grammar point, you can introduce it in this section and reintroduce it in *Capítulo 18* with the *si* clauses.

Emphasis A: Suggestions

■ Have students give the third person plural preterite forms.

caminar	nadar	leer
terminar	ofrecer	creer
usar	resolver	abrir
pensar	correr	escribir
esperar	prometer	subir
cerrar	volver	admitir

■ Present the formation of the past subjunctive and emphasize that all forms, without exception, are based on the third person plural of the preterite.

■ Model the past subjunctive in sentences about yourself or communicative exchanges. Use the verbs *trabajar*, *volver*, and *abrir*.

Emphasis D: Suggestions

■ Have students give the third person plural preterite forms.

dar	poder	venir
hacer	poner	divertirse
ser	querer	servir
ir	saber	dormir
decir	tener	jugar
estar	traer	pedir

■ Model the past subjunctive forms of *servir*, *sentir*, *dar*, *decir*, *hacer*, *ir*, and *venir* in sentences about yourself and communicative exchanges with the students.

Past Subjunctive of Regular Verbs*

hablar: hablar**øn**		comer: comier**øn**		vivir: vivier**øn**	
hablara	habláramos	comiera	comiéramos	viviera	viviéramos
hablaras	hablarais	comieras	comierais	vivieras	vivierais
hablara	hablaran	comiera	comieran	viviera	vivieran

A. The past subjunctive endings **-a, -as, -a, -amos, -ais, -an** are identical for **-ar, -er,** and **-ir** verbs. These endings are added to the third person plural of the preterite, minus its **-on** ending. For this reason, the forms of the past subjunctive reflect the irregularities of the preterite.

PAST SUBJUNCTIVE ENDINGS	
-a	**-amos**
-as	**-ais**
-a	**-an**

B. Stem-changing verbs

-Ar and **-er** verbs: no change

-Ir verbs: all persons of the past subjunctive reflect the vowel change in the third person plural of the preterite.

empezar (ie): empezar**øn** → **empezara, empezaras,...**
volver (ue): volvier**øn** → **volviera, volvieras,...**
dormir (ue, u): durmier**øn** → **durmiera, durmieras,...**
pedir (i, i): pidier**øn** → **pidiera, pidieras,...**

C. Spelling changes

All persons of the past subjunctive reflect the change from **i** to **y** between two vowels.

i → y (caer, construir, creer, destruir, leer, oír)

creer: creyer**øn** →

creyera	creyéramos
creyeras	creyerais
creyera	creyeran

D. Verbs with irregular preterites

dar: dier**øn** →

diera	diéramos
dieras	dierais
diera	dieran

---

decir:	dijer**øn** → **dijera**	poner:	pusier**øn** → **pusiera**	
estar:	estuvier**øn** → **estuviera**	querer:	quisier**øn** → **quisiera**	
haber:	hubier**øn** → **hubiera**	saber:	supier**øn** → **supiera**	
hacer:	hicier**øn** → **hiciera**	ser:	fuer**øn** → **fuera**	
ir:	fuer**øn** → **fuera**	tener:	tuvier**øn** → **tuviera**	
poder:	pudier**øn** → **pudiera**	venir:	vinier**øn** → **viniera**	

---

*An alternative form of the past subjunctive (used primarily in Spain) ends in **-se: hablase, hablases, hablase, hablásemos, hablaseis, hablasen.** This form will not be practiced in *Puntos de partida*.

 Heritage Speakers

Pregúnteles a los hispanohablantes de la clase si usan o no las terminaciones en *-se, -ses, -se, -semos, -seis, -sen* del pasado de subjuntivo. Si las usan, pregúnteles cuándo y por qué.

Uses of the Past Subjunctive

A. The past subjunctive usually has the same applications as the present subjunctive, but it is used for past events. Compare these pairs of sentences.

Quiero que **se enteren** esta tarde.
I want them to find out this afternoon.

Quería que **se enteraran** por la tarde.
I wanted them to find out in the afternoon.

Siente que no **estén** allí esta noche.
He's sorry (that) they aren't there tonight.

Sintió que no **estuvieran** allí anoche.
He was sorry (that) they weren't there last night.

Dudamos que **mantengan** la paz.
We doubt that they will keep the peace.

Dudábamos que **mantuvieran** la paz.
We doubted that they would keep the peace.

B. Remember that the subjunctive is used after
  (1) expressions of *influence, emotion,* and *doubt;*
  (2) *nonexistent* and *indefinite antecedents;* and
  (3) *conjunctions* of *contingency and purpose,* as well as those of *time.*

(1) **¿Era necesario** que **regatearas**?
Was it necessary for you to bargain?

(1) **Sentí** que no **tuvieran** tiempo para ver Granada.
I was sorry that they didn't have time to see Granada.

(2) **No había nadie** que **pudiera** resolverlo.
There wasn't anyone who could (might have been able to) solve it.

(3) Los padres **trabajaron para que** sus hijos **asistieran** a la universidad.
The parents worked so that their children could (might) go to the university.

(3) Anoche, **íbamos** a salir **en cuanto llegara** Felipe.
Last night, we were going to leave as soon as Felipe arrived.

C. The past subjunctive of the verb **querer** is often used to make a request sound more polite.

Quisiéramos hablar con Ud. en seguida.
We would like to speak with you immediately.

Quisiera un café, por favor.
I would like a cup of coffee, please.

AUTOPRUEBA

Change the following verbs from the present subjunctive to the past subjunctive.

1. quiera
2. tengamos
3. salgan
4. sepas
5. esté
6. traigas

Answers: 1. quisiera 2. tuviéramos 3. salieran 4. supieras 5. estuviera 6. trajeras

Gramática

Uses of the Past Subjunctive

Emphasis A: Suggestions

■ Point out that the past subjunctive is used to describe past events in grammatical contexts that require the subjunctive.

■ Emphasize that when a verb in the main clause is in the past, the past (never the present) subjunctive is used in the subordinate clause (past → past).

■ Remind students that when the verb in the main clause is in the present, the verb in the dependent can be in the past: *Siento que no pudieran estar allí. Sé que no estaban allí.* Help students develop simple logic about time sequence (I'm sorry now about something that happened yesterday).

Emphasis C: Suggestions

■ Emphasize that this tense is used to form polite requests. This is similar to the English *really should* and *would like you to* softened requests.

■ Point out that the verbs *deber* and *poder* are used by some Spanish speakers in softened requests: *Debieras estudiar más. ¿Pudieras darme el libro?*

■ Remind students of the importance of tone whenever requests of any kind are made. The most polite words can be said in a harsh way.

☼ Heritage Speakers

En algunos países y regiones hispanohablantes, es muy común oír que se usa el condicional cuando, por lo general, se recomienda el uso del imperfecto de subjuntivo en cláusulas condicionales con *si.* Por ejemplo, es posible oír *Si yo tendría el dinero, iría a Francia* en vez de *Si yo tuviera el dinero, iría a Francia.* A pesar del uso popular del condicional en cláusulas con *si,* se recomienda usar el imperfecto de subjuntivo. Anime a los hispanohablantes a indicar qué tiempo verbal prefieren usar con cláusulas con *si.*

Prác. A: Preliminary Exercise

Use the following chain drill to practice forms.

Dé oraciones nuevas según las indicaciones.
Cuando Ud. estudiaba en la secundaria, ¿qué le gustaba?
Me gustaba que nosotros...
   estudiar idiomas
   leer libros interesantes
   ver películas en la clase de historia
   hacer experimentos en la clase de física
   bailar después de los partidos
   divertirnos después de la clase
   ¿ ... ?

Prác. A, B: Suggestion

If you have a multi-generational class, compare the answers of students of different generations.

Prác. B: Follow-Up

Include the following questions as well.

1. *¿Qué no le gustaba nada?*
2. *¿Qué quería Ud. que sus padres (sus hermanos) hicieran?*
3. *¿Qué quería que sus abuelos le regalaran para su cumpleaños?*
4. *¿Adónde quería Ud. que sus padres lo/la llevara de vacaciones cuando era más joven?*
5. *¿Sus padres permitían que Ud. fumara cuando tenía 15 años?*

Prác. B: Extension

Have students describe a friend from their youth.

Yo tenía un amigo / una amiga que...

¡OJO! Students will need the indicative in this initial sentence.

▪▪▪ Práctica

A. Si pudiera volver... ¿Le gusta la idea de volver a la escuela secundaria? ¿O prefiere la vida de la universidad?

Paso 1. ¡Anticipemos! Lea las siguientes oraciones e indique las que son verdaderas para Ud. Cambie las oraciones falsas para que expresen su propia experiencia.

En la escuela secundaria…

1. ☐ era obligatorio que yo asistiera a todas mis clases.
2. ☐ mis padres insistían en que yo estudiara mucho.
3. ☐ era necesario que yo trabajara para que pudiera asistir a la universidad algún día.
4. ☐ no había ninguna clase que me interesara.
5. ☐ tenía que sacar buenas notas para que mis padres me dieran dinero.
6. ☐ era necesario que volviera a casa a una hora determinada, aun en los fines de semana.
7. ☐ mis padres me exigían que limpiara mi cuarto cada semana.
8. ☐ mis padres no permitían que saliera con alguna persona o con los miembros de ciertos grupos.

Paso 2. Ahora considere sus respuestas. ¿Realmente era mejor la vida en la escuela secundaria? ¿Le gustaría regresar a esa época? ¿Por qué sí o por qué no?

B. Y ahora, la niñez. ¿Qué quería Ud. de la vida cuando era niño/a? ¿Y qué querían los demás que Ud. hiciera? Conteste, haciendo oraciones con una frase de cada grupo.

1. Mis padres (no) querían que yo…
2. Mis maestros me pedían que…
3. Yo buscaba amigos que…
4. Me gustaba mucho que nosotros…

ir a la iglesia / al templo con ellos

portarse bien, ser bueno/a

estudiar mucho, hacer la tarea todas las noches, sacar buenas notas

ponerse ropa vieja para jugar, jugar en la calle, pelear con mis amigos

mirar mucho la televisión, leer muchas tiras cómicas, comer muchos dulces

vivir en nuestro barrio, asistir a la misma escuela, tener muchos juguetes, ser aventureros

ir de vacaciones en verano, pasar todos juntos los días feriados, tener un árbol de Navidad muy alto

☼ Heritage Speakers

Los hispanohablantes también usan el imperfecto de subjuntivo de los verbos *poder* y *deber* (*pudieras*, *debieras*) para ser más cortés al pedirle o sugerirle algo a alguien. Pregúnteles a los hispanohablantes en qué situaciones usarían las formas más corteses de *poder* y *deber*. También anímelos a hacerles pedidos corteses a sus compañeros de clase usando las formas *pudieras*, *debieras* y *yo quisiera que...*

C. El noticiero de las seis. En las noticias los reporteros nos informan de los acontecimientos del día, pero a veces también ofrecen sus propias opiniones.

Paso 1. Lea las siguientes oraciones y cámbielas al pasado. Debe usar el imperfecto del primer verbo en cada oración y luego el imperfecto del subjuntivo en la segunda parte.

1. «Los obreros quieren que les den un aumento de sueldo.»
2. «Es posible que los trabajadores sigan en huelga hasta el verano.»
3. «Es necesario que las víctimas reciban atención médica en la Clínica del Sagrado Corazón.»
4. «Es una lástima que no haya espacio para todos allí.»
5. «Los terroristas piden que los oficiales no los persigan.»
6. «Parece imposible que el gobierno acepte sus demandas.»
7. «Es necesario que el gobierno informe a todos los ciudadanos del desastre.»
8. «Dudo que la paz mundial esté fuera de nuestro alcance (*reach*).»
9. «El presidente y los directores prefieren que la nueva fábrica se construya en México.»
10. «Temo que el número de votantes sea muy bajo en las próximas elecciones.»

Paso 2. Ahora indique si las oraciones representan un hecho o si son una opinión del reportero o de la persona citada (*quoted*).

Need more practice?

- Workbook and Laboratory Manual
- Interactive CD-ROM
- Online Learning Center (www.mhhe.com/puntos7)

■■■ Conversación

A. Entrevista

1. ¿A qué le tenías miedo cuando eras pequeño/a? ¿Era probable que ocurrieran las cosas que temías? ¿Temías a veces que tus padres te castigaran (*punish*)? ¿Lo merecías a veces? ¿Era necesario que siempre los obedecieras? ¿Qué te prohibían que hicieras?
2. ¿Qué tipo de clases buscabas para este semestre/trimestre? ¿Clases que fueran fáciles? ¿interesantes? ¿Las encontraste? ¿Han sido las clases tal como las esperabas? ¿Qué tipo de clases vas a buscar para el semestre/trimestre que viene?
3. ¿Qué buscaban los primeros inmigrantes que vinieron a los Estados Unidos? ¿Buscaban un lugar donde pudieran practicar su religión? ¿un lugar donde hubiera abundancia de recursos naturales? ¿menos restricciones? ¿más libertad política y personal? ¿más respeto por los derechos humanos? ¿menos gente? ¿más espacio?

Prác. C: Suggestion

Bring a Spanish-language newspaper or have students look for one on the Internet. Have students identify three to five instances of the past subjunctive. Then have them explain why the past subjunctive was used in each case. **¡OJO!** Reassure students that they may not understand enough of the context to explain the use of this tense.

Con. A: Suggestion

Encourage students to use clauses with *para que*, *con tal que*, and so on.

National Standards: Connections

Have students work in small groups or assign as homework: Write two to three setences similar to the ones on *Práctica C*, based on current news.

Practice comprehension of the past subjunctive using the following context.

Imagine que su abuela, quien asistió a la universidad en los años cincuenta, le ha explicado a Ud. las normas de conducta de esa época. ¿Qué es diferente hoy día? ¿Hay algunas normas antiguas que a Ud. le parezcan mejores que las modernas? ¿Por qué?

1. *Era obligatorio que los hombres y las mujeres vivieran en residencias apartes.*
2. *Todos cenaban a la misma hora. Para entrar en el comedor, era necesario que los hombres llevaran corbata y las mujeres, falda.*
3. *Había «hora de visita» en las residencias. Los hombres sólo podían visitar a sus amigas durante esas horas y viceversa.*
4. *Era necesario que las mujeres estuvieran en su residencia a una hora determinada de la noche. Pero no había ninguna restricción semejante para los hombres.*

Con. B: Follow-Up

Have students tell what they would say in the following situations, using the past subjunctive whenever possible.

¿Qué diría Ud. en las siguientes situaciones?

1. *Ud. ha llamado a un amigo a las diez de la noche para invitarlo a salir, pero ya estaba dormido y Ud. lo ha despertado.*
2. *Ud. llega a casa muy enfermo/a, con tos y fiebre. El médico le ha aconsejado guardar cama para descansar. Pero su compañero/a de cuarto (esposo/a, etcétera) le ha preparado una fiesta sorpresa de cumpleaños. Todos los amigos lo/la saludan cuando entra.*

NOTA COMUNICATIVA

Suggestions

- Remind students that *ojalá +* present subjunctive means *I hope* (*something will happen*). *Ojalá +* past subjunctive means *I wish*. Wishes with the past subjunctive are unlikely or impossible to happen.
- Remind students that the use of *que* after *ojalá* is optional.

B. Situaciones. El niño del dibujo sabe que está molestando a sus padres cuando los despierta pidiendo ahora un vaso de agua que no quiere pero que podría (*he might*) querer más tarde. Por eso les habla de una forma muy cortés: «quisiera un vaso de agua… quisiera saber… ». ¿Cómo podría Ud. pedir de una forma muy cortés lo que necesita en las siguientes situaciones? ¿Qué diría para conseguirlo?

1. Ud. quiere tener el número de teléfono de un chico / una chica que acaba de conocer. Habla con un amigo de él / una amiga de ella.
2. En un restaurante, el camarero no lo/la atiende como debe. Ud. no quiere perder la paciencia con él, pero quiere la taza de café que le pidió hace diez minutos… y la cuenta.
3. Uds. quieren saber cuándo es el examen final en esta clase y qué va a incluir.
4. Ud. necesita una extensión para el próximo examen de español.
5. Ud. piensa que va a necesitar una extensión para el próximo proyecto.
6. Ud. necesita una carta de recomendación del profesor / de la profesora.
7. Ud. quiere hablar con el rector / la rectora de la universidad para invitarlo/la a cenar en su residencia con motivo de algo especial.

—Verás, quisiera un vaso de agua. Pero no te molestes, porque ya no tengo sed. Sólo quisiera saber si, en el caso de que tuviese otra vez sed, podría (*I could*) venir a pedirte un vaso de agua.

NOTA COMUNICATIVA

I wish I could . . . I wish they would . . .

There are many ways to express wishes in Spanish. As you know, one of the most common is **ojalá (que)**. Used alone, **¡Ojalá!** means *I hope so!* It can also be used with the present or past subjunctive to mean *I hope . . . !* or *I wish . . .*

¡Ojala (que) la guerra **acabe** pronto!   *I hope (that) the war will be over soon!*

The past subjunctive following **ojalá** is one of the most frequent uses of those verb forms. Here **ojalá** translates as *I wish*.

Ojalá (que) pudiera acompañarlos,   *I wish (that) I could go with you,*
  pero no es posible.   *but it's not possible.*

C. ¡Ojalá! Complete las oraciones lógicamente.

1. Ojalá que (yo) tuviera _____.
2. Ojalá que pudiera _____.
3. Ojalá inventaran una máquina que _____.
4. Ojalá solucionaran el problema de _____.
5. Ojalá que en esta universidad fuera posible _____.

Review the forms and uses of possessive adjectives (**Gramática 6**) before beginning **Gramática 49**. When the possessive adjectives modify a singular noun, use the following.

mi   tu   su   nuestro/a   vuestro/a   su

When the possessive adjectives modify a plural noun, use the following.

mis   tus   sus   nuestros/as   vuestros/as   sus

Express the following with possessive adjectives.

1. el país de él
2. los derechos (que tienes tú)
3. la obligación de nosotros
4. la prensa de nosotros
5. el gobierno de Uds.
6. el crimen de ellos

49 More About Expressing Possession • Stressed Possessives

1. ¿Quién es el dueño del mundo en esta visión del futuro?
2. ¿A quién le va a dar todo el padre robot?
3. ¿A qué se refieren las palabras «todo esto»?
4. ¿Quisiera Ud. heredar «todo esto» algún día?
5. Imagine que Ud. le dice a su hijo/a que «todo esto va a ser tuyo». ¿Qué quiere dejarle para el futuro?

■ When in English you would emphasize the possessive with your voice, or when you want to express English *of mine* (*of yours, of his,* and so on), you will use the *stressed forms* (**las formas tónicas**) of the possessive in Spanish. As the term implies, they are more emphatic than the *unstressed forms* (**las formas átonas**).

Forms of the Stressed Possessive Adjectives

mío/a(s)	my, (of) mine	**nuestro/a(s)**	our, (of) ours
tuyo/a(s)	your, (of) yours	**vuestro/a(s)**	your, (of) yours
suyo/a(s)	your, (of) yours; his, (of) his; her, (of) hers; its	**suyo/a(s)**	your, (of) yours; their, (of) theirs

■ The stressed forms of the possessive adjective follow the noun, which must be preceded by a definite or indefinite article or by a demonstrative adjective. The stressed forms agree with the noun modified in number and gender.

Es **mi** amigo.	*He's my friend.*
Es **un** amigo **mío**.	*He's my friend. / He's a friend of mine.*
Es **su** perro.	*It's her dog.*
Es **un** perro **suyo**. Es **suyo**.	*It's her dog. / It's a dog of hers. / It's hers.*
Ese perro **suyo** es malo.	*That dog of hers is bad.*

Gramática   Quinientos veintisiete ■ **527**

Refrán

«Quien te cuenta las faltas de otro, las tuyas las tiene a ojo.»

Help students with the meaning of *faltas*, then have them guess the meaning of this *refrán*. Have them brainstorm for similar sayings in English (*He is a good friend that speaks well of us behind our back. All are not friends that speak us fair.*).

¿Recuerda Ud.?: Suggestion
Ask questions using possessive adjectives to help students review forms. For example, *¿Dónde está su cuaderno? ¿Está en su mochila? ¿Uds. creen que mi clase es difícil?* and so on.

Gramática 49
Stressed Possessives
Follow-Up
Ask students: *¿Cómo cree Ud. que va a ser la vida del ser humano en un mundo como este?*

Suggestions

■ Review the unstressed possessives.
■ Have students give the Spanish equivalents for the following ideas.

He's my friend.
It's her dog.

Contrast their answers with: *Es un amigo mío* and *Es el perro suyo.*
■ Present the stressed forms and their use.
■ Point out that stressed forms follow the noun.
■ Have students give the Spanish equivalents for the following ideas.

1. She's a friend of mine / of ours / of his / of theirs.
2. We have some books of yours / of his / of theirs.

■ Point out that the ambiguity of *suyo/a* is similar to the ambiguity of *su.* Use the same prepositional phrases for clarification.

unos libros suyos → unos libros de él / de ellos, and so on

■ The text does not emphasize the adjective vs. nominalized form distinction. Most students will not have difficulty with this concept. Use the following explanation to underscore the difference. Have students identify the possessive pronouns in the following phrases.

Este es mi banco. ¿Dónde está el suyo?
Sus bebidas están preparadas, las nuestras, no.
No es el examen de Juan; es el mío.

The stressed possessive adjectives, but not the unstressed possessives, can be used as possessive pronouns.

la maleta suya → la suya

The article and the possessive form agree in gender and number with the noun to which they refer. The definite article is frequently omitted after forms of *ser: Es suya.*

Gramática ■ **527**

Prác. A: Preliminary Exercises

- Use this rapid response drill to practice nominalization.

  el coche mío → el mío

  1. *el traje tuyo*
  2. *los libros míos*
  3. *la casa suya*
  4. *el pasaporte mío*
  5. *los amigos nuestros*
  6. *las maletas suyas*

- Take some objects away from students in the class, place them on a table with some of your own, hold up one at a time, and ask.

  ¿Este es mío o es suyo?

- Point out that to express *which one?*, the definite article after *ser* is used.

  ¿Cuál es? ¿Es el mío?

  But in other instances after *ser*, the definite article is normally dropped.

  ¿De quién es? ¿Es mío?

- Use this chain drill to practice forms.

  1. *El coche de Antonio está roto. ¿Y el tuyo? → ¿El mío? Ya lo he arreglado.* (*lámparas, estéreo, cámara, frenos, transmisión*)
  2. *¿Ya han encontrado todo el equipaje? → La maleta de Juan, sí, pero las maletas mías, no.* (*suyo, tuyo, nuestro, vuestro*)

- Have students supply the corresponding questions. **¡OJO!** Remind students to use *tampoco* (not *también*) for negative statements.

  ¿Voy a lavar mi carro esta tarde. ¿Y tú? → ¿Vas a lavar el tuyo también?

  1. *No puedo pagar mis cuentas este mes. ¿Y tú?*
  2. *Ya han hecho sus reservaciones para junio. ¿Y Juan?*
  3. *¡Ay, he dejado mis cheques en casa! ¿Y tú?*
  4. *No podemos encontrar nuestras llaves. ¿Y ellos?*
  5. *Vas a informar a tus padres, ¿verdad? ¿Y ellos?*
  6. *No, no perdimos el vuelo. ¿Y Uds.?*
  7. *Claro que nos preocupamos por nuestro bienestar. ¿Y los demás?* (*¿No ... ?*)

- The stressed possessives are often used as nouns.

la maleta **suya** → la **suya**
el pasaporte **tuyo** → el **tuyo**.*

AUTOPRUEBA

Give the corresponding stressed possessive. Include the definite article.

1. tus noticias   3. tu choque   5. mis testigos
2. su guerra   4. nuestra reina 6. sus derechos

Answers: 1. las tuyas 2. la suya 3. el tuyo 4. la nuestra 5. los míos 6. los suyos

■■■ Práctica

A. **En el hotel.** Complete el siguiente diálogo con las formas apropiadas del posesivo.

—Perdone, señorita, pero esta maleta que Uds. me han dado no es (mío[1]).

—¿No es (suyo[2])? ¿No es Ud. el doctor Méndez?

—Sí, soy yo, pero esta maleta no es (mío[3]). Ud. todavía tiene la (mío[4]). Está allí a la derecha.

—Ah, nos equivocamos. Esta es la de los Sres. Palma. Aquí tengo la (suyo[5]). ¡Cuánto lo siento!

B. **En el departamento de objetos perdidos.** ¿Son suyos los objetos que le ofrecen? Con un compañero / una compañera, haga y conteste preguntas.

MODELO: de Ud. → E1: Esta maleta, ¿es *de Ud.*?
                   E2: No, no es *mía*.

1. de Juan   2. de Uds.   3. de Alicia   4. mía   5. tuya

MODELO: libro → E1: ¿Y este *libro*?
                 E2: No, no es *mío*. *El mío* es más pequeño.

6. despertador   8. llave   10. pastillas
7. zapatos   9. televisor 11. periódico

■■■ Conversación

A. **Comparaciones: En general...** Compare the following aspects of your life with what is generally the case. Complete only those sentences that have meaning for you personally.

1. Las clases en esta universidad son fáciles/regulares/difíciles. Pienso que las mías...
2. Las clases aquí son grandes/pequeñas. Pienso que la nuestra...
3. En esta ciudad, los alquileres son altos. Creo que el mío...
4. Dicen que el perro es el mejor amigo del hombre. Sin duda, el mío...
5. La familia es un apoyo (*support*) cuando uno tiene problemas. En general, la mía...
6. Los coches modernos son más pequeños que los de la década de los cincuenta. El mío...

---

*For more information, see Appendix 2, Using Adjectives as Nouns.

Need more practice?

- Workbook and Laboratory Manual
- Interactive CD-ROM
- Online Learning Center (www.mhhe.com/ puntos7)

MULTIMEDIA: Internet

Have students search the Internet for information about Galavisión, Telefutura, and Univisión. You may also ask them to watch a specific show if these stations are available in your viewing area.

Tres hispanos del mundo de la televisión

Ray Rodríguez, María Hinojosa y Jim Ávila son tres hispanos cuyos[a] nombres se destacan[b] en **el mundo de la televisión** y **los noticieros. Ray Rodríguez,** quien ahora vive en Miami, es contador de profesión y por varios años fue *manager* de Julio Iglesias. En 1992 llegó a ser presidente de Univisión, una **cadena** en español que, según los cálculos, se ve en el 95 por ciento de los hogares hispanos en los Estados Unidos. Junto con Galavisión y Telefutura, la cadena Univisión forma parte de la **compañía de difusión**[c] en español más importante de los Estados Unidos: Univisión Networks. Rodríguez es ahora presidente de esta poderosa[d] empresa.

Una hispana que también se distingue en el mundo de la información es **María Hinojosa.** Hinojosa nació en la Ciudad de México. Estudió en los Estados Unidos, y por varios años trabajó para NPR (*National Public Ra-*

▲ *Ray Rodríguez, presidente de Univisión*

dio) en el área de Nueva York. Desde 1997 es **corresponsal**[e] de la CNN (*Cable News Network*), donde se especializa en **cuestiones urbanas.** Es autora de dos libros y ha recibido varios **premios periodísticos,** entre ellos el premio Rubén Salazar, otorgado[f] por el **Consejo Nacional de la Raza,**[g] una prestigiosa institución de los hispanos estadounidenses.

Jim Ávila tiene una larga y distinguida carrera periodística. Es **reportero** de NBC y reporta **acontecimientos** importantes dentro y fuera de los Estados Unidos. Tiene el récord más alto de reportajes en televisión sobre las minorías. La **Asociación Nacional de Periodistas Hispanos** lo premió[h] en 1999 junto con Hugo Pérez por «*Fire Racism*», una pieza sobre el racismo entre los bomberos[i] de Chicago.

[a]*whose* [b]*se... stand out* [c]*media* [d]*powerful* [e]*correspondent* [f]*awarded* [g]*Consejo... National Council of La Raza* [h]*awarded a prize* [i]*firefighters*

B. Entrevista. Use the following cues to interview a classmate. Find out as much as you can about the topic. Then state the results of your interview, using stressed possessives when possible.

MODELO: El horario de Burt es más exigente que el mío.
(Burt tiene clases muy difíciles, pero mi horario es más exigente que el suyo.)

Las clases: De los dos, ¿quién... ?

1. tiene el horario más exigente (*demanding*)
2. tiene el horario que empieza más temprano
3. tiene las clases más interesantes

La vivienda: De los dos, ¿quién... ?

4. tiene el apartamento más grande
5. tiene el alquiler más barato
6. vive en el barrio más elegante

Las clases
¿cuántas clases en total? ¿a qué hora empiezan? ¿muchos cursos de ciencias? ¿de humanidades?

La vivienda
¿el tamaño (size) del apartamento/casa? ¿un alquiler alto? ¿un barrio elegante?

Gramática

Bring television/cable guides to class, and have students find Spanish language programming in your area. If there is none, have students discuss why it is not available. If they find Spanish-language programming, have students compare the kinds of programs available to the programs available on network television.

Bright Idea

Prác. A: Preliminary Exercise

Point to different objects in the classroom and ask questions.

¿Es suya esa chaqueta? ¿No? ¿Entonces, ¿de quién es?

Vary objects and use some possessions of your own.

Prác. A: Suggestion

Point out the differences between the adjective and the pronoun.

Esta maleta es mía.
Ud. todavía tiene la mía.

Con. A: Variations

■ Have students compare their university with another nearby and/or rival university.

1. *¿Qué universidad es más respetada académicamente, la nuestra o la suya?*
2. *¿Qué equipos deportivos son mejores, los nuestros o los suyos?*
3. *¿Qué matrícula es más cara, la nuestra o la suya?*
4. *¿Qué campus es más bonito, el nuestro o el suyo?*
5. *¿Qué estudiantes son más listos, los nuestros o los suyos?*

■ Have students work in pairs to make comparisons.

los zapatos → Los zapatos míos son negros; los tuyos son blancos.

1. *clases*
2. *horario*
3. *coche*
4. *casa/apartamento*
5. *pelo*
6. *camisa/blusa*
7. *familia*

Con. B: Follow-Up

Have students compare other possessions. Offer the following items and/or have them suggest items to compare: *el coche, la computadora, la familia.*

Gramática ■ **529**

UN POCO DE TODO

A: Suggestions

■ **Paso 1.** The following are some possible answers.

1. *los pimeros colonos, los cuáqueros*
2. *los españoles, los portugueses*
3. *los primeros colonos de Australia*
4. *muchos grupos asiáticos y del Medio Oriente*
5. *los irlandeses, algunos grupos de África y de Asia*

■ **Paso 2.** Expand each item with questions about the historical situation in the question. Focus on the imperfect/preterite in the questions, not necessarily on the use of the imperfect subjunctive. For example, for item 1 you might ask.

¿En qué año llegaron al Nuevo Mundo los primeros colonos?
¿Había muchos indios aquí en aquel entonces (back then)?
¿Qué hicieron los colonos tan pronto como llegaron?
¿Tenían miedo de los indios?

Bright Idea

A. Paso 1: Follow-Up

Have students redo this activity, changing it from past to present. Give students a general rule of thumb about sequence of tenses.

Present follows present.
Past follows past.

This activity will prepare them for activity B. *¿Qué ves?*

A. Escenas históricas

Paso 1. La gente emigra por varias razones. Complete las siguientes oraciones con la forma correcta del infinitivo. Luego, si puede, nombre un grupo que emigró por la razón citada.

1. Las leyes de su país de origen no permitían que este grupo (practicar) libremente su religión.
2. Algunas personas esperaban que (haber) oro y plata en América.
3. El rey no quería que estos criminales (seguir) viviendo en su país.
4. Estos inmigrantes buscaban un país donde (haber) paz y esperanza y seguridad (*safety*) personal.
5. Los miembros de este grupo buscaban un país donde no (tener) que pasar hambre.

Paso 2. Dé una breve descripción del pasado histórico de los Estados Unidos, haciendo oraciones según las indicaciones. Empiece en el pasado. Desde el número 8, las oraciones se refieren al presente.

1. indios / temer / que / colonos / quitarles / toda la tierra
2. colonos / no / gustar / que / ser necesario / pagarle / impuestos / rey
3. parecía imposible / que / joven república / tener éxito (*success*)
4. los del sur / no / gustar / que / gobernarlos / los del norte
5. abolicionistas / no / gustar / que / algunos / no / tener / mismo / libertades
6. era necesario / que / declararse / en huelga / obreros / para / obtener / alguno / derechos
7. era terrible / que / haber / dos / guerra / mundial
8. para que / nosotros / vivir / en paz / es cuestión de / aprender / comunicarse
9. también / es necesario / que / haber / leyes / que / garantizar / derechos

B. ¿Qué ves? Complete the following dialogue with the correct form of the words in parentheses, as suggested by the context. When two possibilities are given in parentheses, select the correct word.

¡OJO! When you conjugate verbs in this activity, you will often have to decide whether to use the subjunctive mood (present, present perfect, or past) or the indicative mood (present, present perfect, future, preterite, or imperfect). The context of the passage will guide you in choosing among the indicative verb tenses, and you will also occasionally see clues in italics to show you which tense to use. Start in the present tense.

Micaela y Cristi son dos amigas que han decidido especializarse[a] en español. Las dos siempre (hablar[1]) en español cuando (verse[2]), y no (perder[3]) (ninguno[4]) oportunidad de (practicar[5]) fuera de clase. Saben que (*fut.*, tener[6]) que mejorar su comprensión auditiva[b] si quieren adquirir un dominio más completo de la lengua.

[a]*to major* [b]*comprensión... listening comprehension abilities*

CULTURE

Use the theme of immigration from activity A to discuss Hispanics in the United States and the history of their presence.

The majority of Hispanics in the U.S. are found in three geographical areas.

1. south Florida (Cubans)
2. the Southwest: Texas, New Mexico, Arizona, and California (Mexicans)
3. New York (Puerto Ricans)

Although we can generalize in terms of which Hispanics are located in a particular region of the United States, Hispanics from all areas of Spain and Latin America live in every major metropolitan city throughout the United States

CRISTI: Oye, Miki, ¿sabes (qué/cuál⁷)? Me molestó no (poder⁸) comprender lo que esa amiga (tuyo⁹) de la República Dominicana (te/ti¹⁰) estaba contando ayer cuando (*yo:* entrar¹¹) en la clase. Ahora sí creo que mis profesores de español (tener¹²) razón cuando nos recomiendan que (*nosotros:* escuchar¹³) todos los días los medios de comunicación en español. Pero para hacerlo bien, temo que me (faltar¹⁴) la habilidad de comprender suficiente español. ¿Hay (alguno¹⁵) programa de radio o televisión en particular que me (poder¹⁶) ayudar a resolver este problema?

MICAELA: Pero, Cristi, no es absolutamente necesario que (*tú:* entender¹⁷) perfectamente cada palabra de lo que (*pres., tú:* oír¹⁸). Una profesora (mío¹⁹) nos aconsejó sobre todo que (*nosotros:* ver²⁰) mucho la televisión en español sin (recomendar²¹) ningún programa en especial. Pero, mi amiga dominicana, Blanca, me sugirió que (*yo:* tratar²²) de ver el programa «Finalmente», que se transmite (en/a²³) medianoche desde la República Dominicana.

CRISTI: ¿Cómo es ese programa?

MICAELA: Bueno, son dos reporteros que (presentar²⁴) las últimas novedades y noticias. Me parece (un/una²⁵) combinación de noticiero y programa de entrevistas. (Por/Para²⁶) ejemplo, anoche (*ellos:* hacer²⁷) una entrevista a los dos candidatos para la presidencia dominicana, y también (dar²⁸) extensa información sobre el ataque terrorista de ayer en la embajada.ᶜ

CRISTI: ¿Tú crees que (*fut., yo:* poder²⁹) comprender lo que (*ellos:* decir³⁰)?

MICAELA: ¡Chica, (*command, tú:* tener³¹) más confianzaᵈ! Vamos a mirar el programa juntas esta noche para que (*tú:* ver³²) que no es tan difícil como (*tú:* creer³³)!

ᶜembassy ᵈconfidence

Comprensión: ¿Qué dijeron? Answer the questions in brief but complete Spanish sentences.

1. ¿Qué recomiendan los profesores de Cristi en general para desarrollar la comprensión auditiva?
2. ¿Qué aconsejó hacer en especial una profesora de Micaela?
3. ¿Qué problema tiene Cristi con la manera recomendada para desarrollar la comprensión?
4. Describa el programa «Finalmente». ¿Desde dónde se transmite? ¿Y a qué hora?
5. ¿Qué vio Micaela ayer en «Finalmente»?
6. ¿Qué medios de comunicación de habla hispana le parecen útiles a Ud. para el desarrollo de la comprensión auditiva? ¿Por qué?

Resources for Review and Testing Preparation

- Workbook and Laboratory Manual
- Interactive CD-ROM
- Online Learning Center (www.mhhe.com/puntos7)

B: Preliminary Exercise

To help students review the past tense structures, have them complete the following sentences.

1. ayer / (yo) ver / mi / nota / en / último / examen
2. no / poder / creer / que / nota / ser / tan / bajo
3. no / ser / posible / que / yo / hacer / examen / tan / mal
4. por eso / (yo) hablar / con / profesor / para que / (él) explicarme / causa / de / nota
5. (él) decirme / que / haber / errores / importante / pero / que / haber / partes / bueno / también
6. (él) pedirme / que / leer / examen / otro / vez
7. ser / verdad / que / haber / errores / en / examen
8. pero / ¡no / ser / justo / que / profesor / darme / nota / tan / bajo!

Follow up with questions to personalize the sentences.

1. ¿Le ha ocurrido algo similar?
2. ¿Qué hizo Ud.? ¿Le cambió la nota su profesor(a) o no?
3. ¿Piensa Ud. que muchos profesores son injustos? ¿Por qué sí o por qué no?

MULTIMEDIA: Internet

Have students look up the program *Finalmente* on the Internet as well as other television and radio programming in the Dominican Republic. Students can read about the program, the anchors, and so on, as well as read "articles" that were presented on the program.

Resources: Desenlace

In the *Capítulo 17* segment of "Chapter-by-Chapter Supplementary Materials" in the IM/RK, you will find a chapter-culminating activity. You can use this activity to consolidate and review the vocabulary and grammar skills students have acquired.

Entrevista cultural

Suggestions

- Before showing the video, ask students questions about professional ambitions.

  ¿Para qué estudia Ud.? ¿Le interesa ahora o le ha interesado en el pasado una carrera en comunicaciones?

  ¿Cómo se informa Ud.? ¿Prefiere ver las noticias en la televisión, escucharlas en la radio o leerlas en el periódico o el Internet?

  ¿Cuáles son los problemas más graves del mundo contemporáneo? ¿El cáncer? ¿las guerras? ¿el SIDA? ¿las armas nucleares? ¿la contaminación del medioambiente?

- Show the video and allow students one to two minutes to work on the questions for each one. Have volunteers answer the questions.
- Have volunteers role-play Milstry and her interviewer.
- Provide a brief introduction to the video. What do students know about the Dominican Republic? Do they think Milstry would agree with their assessment of serious problems facing the contemporary world?

Entre amigos

Suggestions

- Before viewing the video, review the questions with the students and ask them similar questions.

  ¿Qué asuntos le importan a Ud.? ¿Ha protestado en una manifestación (protest) alguna vez?

  ¿Para qué causas o contra qué asuntos participaría en una manifestación?

  Have students answer or work in small groups to ask and answer these questions.

- After viewing the video, have volunteers read and answer the questions.

PERSPECTIVAS culturales

●●●
Videoteca

Entrevista cultural: La República Dominicana

Una estudiante dominicana, Milstry del Orbe, habla de la carrera profesional que quiere seguir. Además, comenta los problemas del mundo contemporáneo que ella considera más graves. Antes de ver el vídeo, lea el siguiente fragmento de la entrevista.

ENTREVISTADORA: ¿Por qué te interesa esa carrera?

MILSTRY: Creo que es muy importante poder informar a la gente, a la juventud[a], de lo que acontece[b] en otros... en otros países en el momento y en el lugar exacto de donde... de donde ocurre.

ENTREVISTADORA: ¿Cuáles son los problemas mundiales más graves hoy en día?

MILSTRY: Pues hoy en día considero que hay muchísimos problemas graves, entre ellos problemas de enfermedades como el SIDA[c] que todavía no se le ha podido encontrar cura. Problemas de terrorismo, problemas de medio ambiente, destrucción del medio ambiente.

[a]*young people* [b]*happens* [c]*AIDS*

Ahora vea el vídeo y conteste las siguientes preguntas basándose en la entrevista.

1. ¿Qué estudia Milstry?
2. ¿Por qué ha escogido esta profesión?
3. Según Milstry, ¿cuál es uno de los problemas graves en el mundo de hoy? ¿Y otro de los problemas?

Entre amigos: ¡Por eso sí protestaría!

Tané, Karina, Rubén y Miguel hablan de las manifestaciones y las protestas. En su opinión, ¿qué van a decir sobre estos temas? Antes de mirar el vídeo, lea las preguntas a continuación. Mientras mire el vídeo, trate de entender la conversación en general y fíjese en la información sobre las manifestaciones y las protestas. Luego mire el vídeo una segunda vez, fijándose en la información que necesita para contestar las preguntas.

1. ¿Adónde va Miguel con la pancarta (*placard*)?
2. ¿De qué va a protestar Miguel?
3. ¿Por qué no va a protestar Karina?
4. ¿De qué protestaría (*would protest*) Rubén?
5. Al final, ¿qué sugiere hacer Tané?

Conozca... la República Dominicana

Datos esenciales

- Nombre oficial: la República Dominicana
- Capital: Santo Domingo
- Población: 8.716.000 habitantes
- Moneda: el peso
- Idiomas: el español (oficial), el francés criollo

¡Fíjese!

- España le cedió[a] a Francia, en 1697, el tercio occidental[b] de La Española. Por esta razón, este territorio, el actual país de Haití, tiene una cultura y un idioma diferentes a los de la República Dominicana.
- El merengue es el baile nacional de la República Dominicana. Hay dos leyendas sobre el origen del baile. Según la primera leyenda, el baile se originó entre los esclavos que tenían que arrastrar[c] una pierna porque la tenían encadenada[d] con la pierna de otro esclavo. La segunda leyenda atribuye el baile a un héroe que regresó de una batalla con una pierna herida, y el pueblo, para mostrar su empatía, bailó durante las celebraciones cojeando[e] y arrastrando un pie. En Santo Domingo se celebra el Festival del Merengue, diez días de música, bailes, espectáculos, ferias y festejos en las calles.

▲ El Convento Dominico en Santo Domingo

[a]ceded [b]tercio... western third
[c]drag [d]chained [e]limping

Learn more about the Dominican Republic with the Video, the Interactive CD-ROM, and the Online Learning Center (www.mhhe.com/puntos7).

Lugares famosos: Santo Domingo

La ciudad de Santo Domingo fue fundada en 1496 por Bartolomé Colón, hermano de Cristóbal Colón. Esta capital, establecida a orillas del río Ozama y el mar Caribe, es la primera ciudad europea del Hemisferio Occidental. La zona original de Santo Domingo se conoce como la Ciudad Colonial y está rodeada[a] de antiguos muros.[b] La UNESCO designó a Santo Domingo como la cuna[c] de la civilización europea en América, porque es aquí donde se encuentra la primera catedral del Nuevo Mundo, así como el primer monasterio, el primer hospital, la primera universidad, los primeros palacios de estilo europeo y la primera corte de justicia. A Santo Domingo también se le llamaba la Atenas[d] del Nuevo Mundo por la actividad intelectual que había en la universidad y otras instituciones.

En 1992, la UNESCO designó la Ciudad Colonial Patrimonio de la Humanidad[e] por sus riquezas arquitectónicas e históricas que datan del siglo XVI. Las imponentes casas e iglesias de piedra fueron cuidadosamente colocadas[f] en forma octogonal. El plan de la ciudad fue diseñado y trazado[g] en 1502 y sirvió de patrón[h] para otras ciudades establecidas por los españoles en el Nuevo Mundo. Hoy por muchas de las calles de la Ciudad Colonial se encuentran pintorescos cafés y bares, pequeños hoteles y conocidos restaurantes, discotecas y tiendas.

[a]surrounded [b]walls [c]cradle, birthplace [d]Athens
[e]patrimonio... World Heritage Site [f]placed
[g]laid out [h]model

Conozca... la República Dominicana

Suggestions

- Bring in and play examples of traditional and contemporary *merengue* music.
- Have students listen to Dominican news reports online and write a paragraph on what they hear.
- Have students find recipes from the Dominican Republic online and bring them to class. You may wish to make or have students make some of these for students to taste.
- Invite a student or member of the community from the Dominican Republic to come to class and talk to the students about his or her country.
- Have students research Taino art and culture and prepare short written reports for extra credit.

Notes

- When Santo Domingo was founded, the island was called *La Española*.
- Students can read an excerpt of the poem *"Sobre el agua"* by the Dominican Republic's Manuel del Cabral in *Un paso más 17*.

MULTIMEDIA: Internet

Have students search the Internet for more information about the government, educational system, geography, and economy of the Dominican Republic. You might assign specific topics and have students give brief oral presentations based on their findings.

Suggestions

- Have students write in Spanish definitions for the words in the list. Then have them create crossword puzzles and use their definitions as cues. Have them exchange and solve each other's puzzles.
- Have students choose one word from the list and use this as the title for a brief composition.
- Ask students the following questions to review the vocabulary.

1. *¿Cómo se entera Ud. de las noticias? ¿Lee el periódico o mira el noticiero en la tele o escucha las noticias en la radio?*
2. *¿Cree todo lo que lee en la prensa? ¿Cree que los medios de información informan bien al público, por lo general?*

Bright Idea

Suggestion

Have students give words based on the following definitions.

1. *una persona que nace o que es residente permanente de un país*
2. *lo que forman los obreros cuando no están contentos con las condiciones de trabajo*
3. *lo que deben hacer los ciudadanos cuando hay elecciones*
4. *una pelea armada entre dos o más países*
5. *un sinónimo de responsabilidad u obligación*
6. *una palabra que refiere a la radio, la televisión y los periódicos*
7. *las otras personas de nuestra comunidad*
8. *la acción de aceptar una ley, una regla o un mandato*
9. *una persona que representa a un país de forma hereditaria, no por votación*
10. *el grupo de personas que defiende a un país en caso de guerra*

EN RESUMEN

Gramática

To review the grammar points presented in this chapter, refer to the indicated grammar presentations. You'll find further practice of these structures in the Workbook and Laboratory Manual, on the Interactive CD-ROM, and on the *Puntos de partida* Online Learning Center (www.mhhe.com/puntos7).

48. ¡No queríamos que fuera así!—Past Subjunctive

You should know the forms of the past subjunctive and when to use it.

49. More About Expressing Possession—Stressed Possessives

Do you know how to form and place stressed possessives?

Vocabulario
Practice this vocabulary with digital flash cards on the Online Learning Center (www.mhhe.com/puntos7).

Los verbos

apoyar	to support
castigar (gu)	to punish
comunicarse (qu) (con)	to communicate (with)
durar	to last
enterarse (de)	to find out, learn (about)
gobernar (ie)	to govern, rule
informar	to inform
mantener (*irreg.*)	to maintain, keep
votar	to vote

Repaso: obedecer (zc), ofrecer (zc), vivir

Las noticias

el acontecimiento	event, happening
el asesinato	assassination
el choque	collision
el desastre	disaster
el ejército	army
la esperanza	hope, wish
la guerra	war
la huelga	strike (*labor*)
la libertad	liberty, freedom
el medio de comunicación	means of communication
las noticias	news
el noticiero	newscast
la paz (*pl.* paces)	peace
la prensa	press; news media
el/la reportero/a	reporter
el/la testigo	witness

Cognados: el ataque (terrorista), la bomba, la erupción, el evento, el terrorismo, el/la terrorista, la víctima

Repaso: el canal, el/la obrero/a

El gobierno y la responsabilidad cívica

el/la ciudadano/a	citizen
el deber	responsibility; obligation
el derecho	right
la (des)igualdad	(in)equality
el/la dictador(a)	dictator
la dictadura	dictatorship
la discriminación	discrimination
la ley	law
la política	politics
el/la político/a	politician
el rey / la reina	king/queen
el servicio militar	military service

Repaso: los/las demás

Las formas posesivas

mío/a(s)
tuyo/a(s)
suyo/a(s)
nuestro/a(s)
vuestro/a(s)

Un paso más 17

Literatura de **la República Dominicana**

Sobre el autor: *Manuel del Cabral nació en Santiago de los Caballeros, República Dominicana. Estudió derecho,[a] pero prefirió escribir. También sirvió de diplomático de la República Dominicana en Nueva York y en varios países latinoamericanos. En su poesía aparece el tema del negro caribeño. Murió en Santo Domingo en 1999. El siguiente poema, «Sobre el agua», es de la colección* Color de agua *(1932).*

▲ Manuel del Cabral
(1907–1999)

> Agua tan pura que casi
> no se ve en el vaso de agua.
>
> Del otro lado está el mundo.
> De este lado, casi nada...
>
> Un agua pura, tan limpia
> que da trabajo mirarla.
>
> AGUA
> La del río, ¡qué blanda![b]
> Pero qué dura[c] es ésta:
> ¡La que cae de los párpados[d]
> es un agua que piensa!

[a]*law* [b]*soft* [c]*hard* [d]*eyelids*

Literatura de **la República Dominicana**

Notes

- Cabral traveled extensively and often lived in Buenos Aires, Argentina, where he published many of his works.
- Cabral was a defender of human rights, and his sociopolitical concerns were often reflected in his poetry. A theme in many poems was the Afro-Caribbean experience and situation.
- In addition to his extensive volumes of poetry, Cabral wrote novels and short stories.

LECTURA

LECTURA

Suggestions

- Do the *Estrategia* in class before assigning the poem.
- Have volunteers read the poem out loud for the class.

ESTRATEGIA: Using Language Cues to Understand Poetry (2)

In **Capítulo 16,** you examined a poet's use of adjectives to better understand a poem. You can also consider how the particular grammatical forms in a poem convey information or contribute to its unique mood. For example, a poem written primarily in the imperfect may convey a sense of timelessness or of things recurring in the poet's personal history. The use of the preterite may give you the feeling that the moment was fleeting, perhaps all too fleeting.

As you read the following poem, note the instances of the past subjunctive that you have learned in this chapter. Why do you think the poet chose this form? What or how does it make you feel? Do you think the poem would be different if the poet had chosen a different grammatical form?

Notes

- Pérez Firmat's autobiographical book *Next Year in Cuba: A Cubano's Coming of Age in America* was nominated for a Pulitzer Prize in 1995.
- Pérez Firmat has two collections of poems in English and Spanish in addition to *Bilingual Blues: Carolina Cuban* (1987) and *Equivocaciones*.
- Pérez Firmat's works include books about literature and culture, such as *Idle Fiction* (1982), *The Cuban Condition* (1989), and *Life on the Hyphen* (1994).
- *Newsweek* magazine included Pérez Firmat among the "100 Americans to Watch in the Next Century," and *Hispanic Business* magazine listed him among "100 Most Influential" Hispanics in the United States.

Comprensión: Suggestion

Have students talk about the image that Pérez Firmat presents of Cuba. Ask questions such as the following.

¿Por qué se mencionan el ron y el son en el poema? ¿y la palma?

Según el poeta, ¿qué implica (implies) el hecho de que la cubanita haya perdido el alma?

¿Qué perdió la cubanita exactamente?

¿Qué otros elementos no mencionados en el poema creen Uds. que son típicamente cubanos?

■ **Sobre el autor...** Gustavo Pérez Firmat (1949–) nació en La Habana, Cuba, y se crió en Miami, Florida. Su poesía tiene una variedad de temas, entre los que se incluyen las relaciones de familia y la experiencia cubanoamericana en los Estados Unidos. Pérez Firmat recibió un doctorado de la Universidad de Michigan y ahora enseña en la Universidad de Columbia. El poema que aquí se presenta, «Cubanita descubanizada», es de una colección que se titula *Bilingual Blues*.

Cubanita descubanizada

Cubanita descubanizada
quién te pudiera recubanizar.
Quién supiera devolverte
el ron[a] y la palma,[b]
el alma y el son.[c]

Cubanita descubanizada,
tú que pronuncias todas las eses*
y dices ómnibus[d] y autobús
quién te pudiera
quién te supiera
si te quisieras recubanizar.

[a]*rum* [b]*palm tree* [c]*el... the soul and the sound (the son is also a popular Cuban dance)* [d]*synonym for* autobús *(the author is referring to the rich lexical variety that exists in Cuban Spanish, but that in this case signals a departure from its local, rural roots)*

Comprensión

A. Definiciones. El autor toma libertades poéticas en su poema e inventa palabras que sirven para expresar sus ideas. Con un compañero / una compañera, trate de definir las siguientes palabras inventadas por Pérez Firmat. Comparen sus definiciones con las de otra persona en la clase.

- descubanizada
- recubanizar

B. Interpretación. ¿Cuál cree Ud. que es el punto de vista del narrador del poema? ¿Tiene una actitud positiva hacia la vida en el extranjero? ¿Qué mensaje intenta expresar? ¿Qué elementos de la poesía comunican este mensaje?

---

*In general, Cuban Spanish is characterized by a lack of pronunciation of the letter **s** when found in certain positions within a word.*

MULTIMEDIA: Internet

- Encourage students to look for online bookstores that sell works by Cuban and Cuban-American authors. These websites often include biographical and literary information on the authors they feature.
- Have students search the Internet for information on the popular Cuban dance *el son*.

ESCRITURA

A. ¿El bilingüismo o no? El tema de la inmigración es uno que provoca mucha reacción en este país. A continuación hay dos puntos de vista contrarios. Escoja una de estas posturas y escriba un breve informe en el que presenta y apoya su opinión.

   1. El bilingüismo y el biculturalismo enriquecen la vida de este país.
   2. Los inmigrantes a este país deben asimilarse por completo a la lengua, a la vida y a la cultura.

B. Una experiencia personal. Escriba una breve composición sobre la experiencia de inmigrar a los Estados Unidos o al Canadá. Puede escribir desde el punto de vista de un(a) pariente o un amigo / una amiga, o puede tomar la perspectiva de una persona imaginaria. Explique cuándo se inmigró, por qué y con quién. También incluya información sobre el lugar al que llegó, cómo se sentía en aquel entonces (*back then*) y cómo se siente ahora.

ESCRITURA

Suggestion
If you prefer that your students do a journal activity, see *Mi diario* in this chapter of the Workbook.

Variation
Have students find or hand out other poems from *Bilingual Blues* and have students write several paragraphs comparing one of the poems to *Cubanita descubanizada*.

☼ Heritage Speakers

■ En muchos dialectos del español, especialmente en Cuba, Puerto Rico y la República Dominicana, a veces la pronunciación de la *s* al final de una sílaba es parecida a la *h* en inglés. Así que la palabra *esperar* se pronunciaría como *ehperar* y *desde* como *dehde*. Anime a los hispanohablantes a imitar esta pronunciación.

■ Si hay un estudiante hispanohablante de ascendencia cubana en la clase, invítele a leer en voz alta el poema para que los demás estudiantes oigan la pronunciación cubana.

CHAPTER OPENER PHOTO

Point out the chapter-opener photo. *La Giralda,* considered a symbol of the city of Seville, was originally part of that city's main mosque during the Moorish occupation. The mosque and original tower were built in the 12th century. Later the building was repurposed to serve as a Catholic cathedral. The shape of the tower has been altered in different stages of reconstruction and repair. *La Giralda* was the first tower in Spain to have a clock. Ask students if they have visited any architectural treasures in this or other countries. What kinds of buildings, monuments, bridges, and so on, do they find most interesting? Are there any particular attractions that they would like to visit one day?

Suggestions

- Have students answer the following questions.

  1. *¿Ha viajado Ud. al* **extranjero***? ¿A qué países?*
  2. *¿Le gustaría seguir viajando? ¿A qué país iría primero?*
  3. *¿Le gustaría pasar un año en el extranjero? ¿Por qué sí o por qué no?*
  4. *Sí pudiera, ¿le gustaría vivir para siempre en el extranjero? ¿Por qué sí o por qué no?*
  5. *¿En qué país le gustaría vivir? ¿Por qué? ¿Hay algún país en el que nunca pudiera vivir? ¿Por qué no?*

- The word in **boldface** is included in the active vocabulary of this chapter. Have students discuss the word and use context to help them understand its meaning.
- Have students work in small groups to discuss the advantages and disadvantages of living abroad for an extended period of time.
- Have students write a paragraph explaining why they would be the right/wrong person to live in a Spanish-speaking country for an extended period of time. In class have them discuss their positions in small groups, then have the whole class discuss the topic and make generalizations about the students in the class.

Note

The *Puntos de partida* Online Learning Center includes an interview with a native speaker from Spain who answers questions about traveling.

◀ La Giralda de Sevilla, España, una torre campanaria (*bell tower*) construida en 1184 como parte de una mezquita (*mosque*) musulmana

Resources

For Students

- Workbook
- Laboratory Manual and Laboratory Audio Program
- Quia™ Online Workbook and Online Laboratory Manual
- Video on CD
- Interactive CD-ROM
- *Puntos de partida* Online Learning Center (**www.mhhe.com/puntos7**)

For Instructors

- *Instructor's Manual and Resource Kit,* "Chapter-by-Chapter" Supplementary Materials
- Overhead Transparencies 104–108
- Testing Program
- Test Generator
- Video Program
- Audioscript
- *Puntos de partida* Online Learning Center (**www.mhhe.com/puntos7**)

En el extranjero°

CULTURA

- **Perspectivas culturales**

    Entrevista cultural: España

    Entre amigos: Tengo mi pasaje a San Francisco

    Conozca... España

- **Nota cultural:** De compras en el extranjero

- **En los Estados Unidos y el Canadá:** Manjares hispanocanadienses

- **Literatura de España:** Cervantes

- **Lectura**: Rima «XXIX», por Antonio Machado

VOCABULARIO

- Lugares y cosas en el extranjero

- En un viaje al extranjero

GRAMÁTICA

50 Conditional Verb Forms

51 Si Clause Sentences

Entrevista cultural

Margarita Durán ▶
Gijón, España

°**En...** Abroad

MULTIMEDIA: Internet

Have students work in small groups to plan a trip to Mexico, Colombia, or Spain. They should decide where they would like to go, what they would like to see, and when they should take their trip. Have them search the Internet for travel and accommodation information. They can also locate *agencias de viaje* online that can help them plan their trip. Have students share their findings with their classmates during the following class period.

MULTIMEDIA

- The multimedia materials that accompany this chapter are referenced in the Student and Instructor's Editions with icons to help you identify when and where to incorporate them.

- The IM/RK provides suggestions for using the multimedia materials in the classroom.

Lugares y cosas en el extranjero

Note

See the model for vocabulary presentation and other material in the *Capítulo 18 Vocabulario: Preparación* section of "Chapter-by-Chapter Supplementary Materials," in the IM.

Suggestions

■ Have students identify the places where the following activities take place.

1. *Se compran y se venden medicamentos aquí.*
2. *Aquí se puede tomar algo de beber y mirar pasar a la gente.*
3. *Aquí se esperan los autobuses.*
4. *Se compran cigarrillos y fósforos aquí.*
5. *Se compran sellos y se mandan cartas y paquetes aquí.*
6. *Si se tiene ganas de comer un pastel, se puede ir a este sitio.*

■ Point out that *el correo* means mail or post office, but the plural *los correos* means postal service. Tell students there are several words for stamps: *el sello, el timbre, la estampilla.*

Con. B: Variation

Have students practice circumlocution for communicating. Have each student make a list of things he/she needs when traveling abroad. Students should try to list things they don't know how to say in Spanish. Then have them work in pairs to explain their lists to each other. Suggest the following items.

hair dryer	needle and thread
batteries	button
shaver	dental floss
comb	faucet
after-shave	sink
hanger	light switch
motion sick-	
ness pills	

Lugares y cosas en el extranjero

la pastelería · la farmacia · PASTELERÍA MARÍA · LA FARMACIA · EL CORREO

el champú · el jabón · la oficina de correos · la pasta dental

la papelería · el quiosco · el paquete

el papel para cartas · el café · el correo · el sello

el estanco · la parada del autobús

el sobre · la tarjeta postal

el batido	drink similar to a milkshake
una copa / un trago	(alcoholic) drink
la estación del metro	subway stop

el fósforo	match
el pastelito	small pastry
la revista	magazine

■■■ Conversación

A. ¿Cierto o falso? Corrija las oraciones falsas.

1. Se puede comprar batidos y pastelitos en una pastelería.
2. Si yo quisiera tomar una copa, iría (*I would go*) a un quiosco.
3. Se va a un quiosco para mandar paquetes.
4. Es más rápido ir a pie que tomar el metro.
5. Se va a un café a comprar champú.
6. Si yo necesitara pasta dental, iría a la oficina de correos.
7. Se puede comprar fósforos en un estanco.
8. Un batido se hace con vino.

B. En el extranjero. Conteste con oraciones completas.

1. ¿Dónde se compra el champú? ¿el jabón?
2. ¿Cuál es la diferencia entre una farmacia de este país y una farmacia en el extranjero?
3. ¿Dónde se puede comprar sellos? (dos lugares)
4. Si se necesitan cigarrillos o fósforos, ¿adónde se va?
5. ¿Qué es un quiosco? ¿Qué cosas se venden allí?
6. ¿Qué venden en una papelería?

MULTIMEDIA: Audio

Students can listen to and practice this chapter's vocabulary on the Online Learning Center (**www.mhhe.com/puntos7**), as well as on the Textbook Audio CD, part of the Laboratory Audio Program.

Resources:
Transparencies 104–106

Transparencies 105 and 106 offer additional vocabulary and sentences about travel.

cruzar (c) la frontera

el pasaporte

el viajero

Rosa
Javier

la viajera

registrar el equipaje

la pensión

la criada

el huésped

el hotel de dos (tres) estrellas

Dora

la huéspeda

el hotel de lujo

la recepción

Rubén

el botones / el mozo

los huéspedes

Leya

la habitación doble con baño

la manta

la almohada

la toalla

las sábanas

viajar al / en el extranjero	to travel abroad
la aduana	customs
la nacionalidad	nationality
El alojamiento°	El... *Lodging*
alojarse/quedarse	to stay (*in a place*)
hacer (*irreg.*)/confirmar las reservas/reservaciones*	to make / to confirm reservations
la habitación individual/doble con baño/ducha	(hotel) room single/double (*room*) (*room*) with attached bath/shower

sin baño/ducha	(*room*) without attached bath/shower
la media pensión	room with breakfast and one other meal
la pensión completa	room and full board
la propina	tip (*to an employee*)
el servicio de cuartos	room service
completo/a	full, no vacancy
desocupado/a	vacant, unoccupied
con anticipación	ahead of time

---

*La reserva *is used in Spain for a reservation (for accommodations).* La reservación *is widely used in other parts of the Spanish-speaking world.*

Vocabulario: Preparación

 Heritage Speakers

Anime a los hispanohablantes a hablar de la última vez que pasaron por la aduana. ¿Tuvieron que mostrar el pasaporte? ¿Tenían algo que declarar?

Resources: Transparency 107

En un viaje al extranjero

Suggestions

■ Read the following statements and have students respond *cierto* or *falso*. Help students correct false statements.

1. *Por lo general, cuando uno cruza una frontera, tiene que pasar por la aduana también.*
2. *En la aduana se registran las reservas.*
3. *El pasaporte indica la nacionalidad de uno.*
4. *En este país, no es necesario llevar pasaporte a menos que uno viaje al extranjero.*
5. *En muchos moteles u hoteles, hay ducha pero no hay baño en los cuartos.*
6. *Si Ud. quiere confirmar una reservación, hay que llamar al huésped.*
7. *En los hoteles de lujo hay botones que ayudan con las maletas.*
8. Propina *es un sinónimo de* cuenta.
9. *Si Ud. no ha hecho una reservación, el hotel no le puede garantizar un cuarto desocupado.*
10. *Un cuarto en un hotel de lujo cuesta mucho dinero.*

■ Ask students the following questions to personalize the vocabulary.

1. *¿Ha viajado Ud. por el extranjero? ¿Qué país(es) ha visitado? ¿Cuánto tiempo estuvo en... ? ¿Tiene ganas de volver? ¿Qué hizo allí? ¿Trabajó? ¿Estudió? ¿Visitó a sus parientes o a sus amigos?*
2. *En esta clase, ¿cuántos tienen pasaporte? ¿Les fue difícil conseguirlo? ¿Qué hizo Ud. para conseguirlo? ¿Tuvo que pagar algo? ¿Salió Ud. bien en la foto o no le gusta como salió?*
3. *¿Ha cruzado Ud. alguna vez la frontera entre el Canadá y los Estados Unidos? ¿la frontera entre México y los Estados Unidos? ¿Tuvo problemas al cruzar? ¿Qué le pidió el inspector? ¿el pasaporte? ¿una visa? ¿Qué le preguntó? ¿Estaba Ud. nervioso/a? ¿Tenía algo que declarar que no declaraba antes?*
4. *¿Siempre declara la gente lo que tiene cuando pasa por la aduana?*

■ Have students use the *alojamiento* vocabulary to describe their last stay in a (luxury) hotel or motel. They should give as many details as possible, using new vocabulary whenever possible. Ask questions such as: *¿Era un hotel de tres, cuatro o cinco estrellas?*

Vocabulario: Preparación ■ **541**

Have students describe other things
done by the people named in the
activity.

NOTA CULTURAL

Suggestion

Have students respond *cierto* or
falso to check comprehension.

1. *En las farmacias de España
   venden de todo.*
2. *El producto principal de un
   estanco es el cigarrillo.*
3. *Los quioscos venden medicinas
   y cosas de higiene personal.*

NOTA CULTURAL

De compras en el extranjero

Aunque los nombres de muchos lugares y tiendas del mundo hispánico se parecen a los de este país, no siempre son iguales los
productos que en ellos se venden. Tomen en cuenta sobre todo
las siguientes diferencias.

- En **las farmacias** no venden la variedad de cosas —dulces,
  tarjetas postales, etcétera— que se venden en las farmacias
  de los EE.UU.* y el Canadá. Por lo general, sólo se venden
  medicinas y productos para **la higiene personal** como jabón,
  pasta dental, champú...
- En **los estancos,** además de productos tabacaleros, se venden
  sellos, así que[a] uno no tiene que ir a una oficina de correos
  para comprarlos. También se venden **sobres** y **tarjetas postales** en los estancos.
- En **los quioscos** se vende una **gran variedad** de cosas: periódicos, revistas, libros, etcétera, pero también lápices, papel
  para cartas...

[a]así... *so*

▲ *Un quiosco en Madrid, España*

■ ■ ■ Conversación

A. Definiciones

Paso 1. Empareje las personas con la descripción apropiada.

1. el huésped
2. el recepcionista
3. el botones
4. la turista
5. la inspectora de aduanas
6. el viajero

a. la persona que nos ayuda con el
   equipaje en un hotel
b. la persona que se aloja en un hotel
   o una pensión
c. una persona que va de un lugar a
   otro
d. alguien que viaja para ver otros
   lugares
e. la persona que nos registra las
   maletas y toma la declaración en la
   aduana
f. la persona que nos atiende en la
   recepción de un hotel

Paso 2. Defina las siguientes palabras en español.

1. la aduana
2. el pasaporte
3. la pensión completa
4. la frontera
5. la propina
6. el formulario de inmigración

---

*EE.UU. *is one way to abbreviate* **Estados Unidos. E.U.** *and* **USA** *are also used.*

B. En la aduana. ¿Ha viajado Ud. al extranjero? ¿Sabe Ud. cómo portarse al pasar por la aduana? Aunque no lo haya hecho, va a poder contestar las preguntas de esta actividad, pues se trata de (*it's a question of*) utilizar el sentido común. De las siguientes acciones, ¿cuáles pueden causar problemas en la aduana?

1. ser cortés con el inspector
2. no tener el pasaporte (o el visado necesario)
3. tener toallas de su hotel en las maletas
4. esconder (*hiding*) artículos de contrabando en su equipaje, con la esperanza que el inspector no los encuentre
5. quejarse del gobierno del país del inspector
6. intentar cruzar la frontera con un pasaporte falsificado
7. traficar en drogas
8. tratar de distraer al inspector mientras este (*he*) registra sus maletas

C. Cuando Ud. viaja...

Paso 1. Lea la lista de acciones típicas de los viajeros. ¿Hace Ud. lo mismo cuando viaja? Indique las acciones que son verdaderas para Ud.

1. ☐ Hago una reserva en un hotel (motel) o en una pensión con un mes de anticipación.
2. ☐ Confirmo la reserva antes de salir de viaje.
3. ☐ Voy al banco a conseguir cheques de viajero (*traveler's checks*).
4. ☐ Alquilo un coche.
5. ☐ Me alojo en un hotel de lujo.
6. ☐ Pido que el mozo me suba las maletas.
7. ☐ Llamo al servicio de cuartos en vez de comer en el restaurante.
8. ☐ Le dejo una propina a la criada el último día de mi estancia (*stay*) en la habitación.

Paso 2. Ahora piense en su último viaje. ¿Hizo Ud. las cosas de la lista del **Paso 1**? Conteste según el modelo y cambie los detalles de esas oraciones por los que en realidad ocurrieron en su viaje.

MODELO: La última vez que hice un viaje… →
Hice una reserva en un hotel, pero con sólo dos días de anticipación.

D. Situaciones. Con un compañero / una compañera, haga el papel de un viajero / una viajera o del / de la recepcionista de un hotel.

Paso 1. El/La recepcionista le pregunta al viajero / a la viajera que acaba de llegar:

- si tiene una reserva
- cuánto tiempo piensa quedarse
- el tipo de habitación reservada o deseada
- la forma de pago

Paso 2. El huésped / La huéspeda pide los siguientes servicios:

- el desayuno en su cuarto
- más toallas/jabón
- información sobre lugares turísticos de interés

Paso 3. Por fin, el huésped / la huéspeda pasa por la recepción para pagar la cuenta. Encuentra los siguientes errores en su cuenta.

- Le cobraron por un desayuno que no tomó.
- Le cobraron por cuatro noches en vez de tres.
- Le cobraron por una llamada a larga distancia que nunca hizo.

Vocabulario: Preparación

Con. B: Variation

Have students give their opinions about the statements in the activity, beginning with phrases such as *Es bueno…* , *Es buena idea…* , and so on.

Con. B: Follow-Up

Have students explain why particular actions could cause problems.

Con. C: Suggestion

Role-play each *Paso* with at least one student before letting students do the role play on their own.

Bright Idea
Con. D: Suggestion

Role-play the *recepcionista* and have several sets of students check into your hotel.

NOTA COMUNICATIVA

Suggestions

- Have students provide sentences or questions they might need while traveling that they have already learned. For example, *Perdón. Estoy perdido/a. ¿Dónde está...?*
- Have students work in groups to create a pocket travel guide with useful phrases and sentences in Spanish. Encourage them to categorize their phrases, for example, *en el restaurante* or *en una emergencia*. Remind them that they have already learned many useful expressions for traveling.

NOTA COMUNICATIVA

Frases útiles para un viaje al extranjero

Many of the phrases and expressions you have learned throughout *Puntos de partida* will be useful when traveling to a Spanish-speaking country. The following phrases and expressions can be useful when you encounter unexpected events or urgencies during your travels.

En el restaurante

¿Cómo se prepara o se hace...?	How is . . . prepared?
Tengo alergia a...	I'm allergic to . . .
¿Tiene... este plato?	Is there . . . in this dish?

En el hotel

¿Hay agua en botella?	Is there bottled water?
Quisiera...	I would like...
un rollo de película.	a roll of film.
un plano de la ciudad.	a map of the city.
saber las horas de las excursiones a...	to know the times for tours to . . .
¿Dónde está... más cercana?	Where is the closest . . . ?
la tintorería	dry cleaner
la lavandería	laundry
la farmacia	pharmacy
¿Hay salón de belleza en este hotel?	Is there a beauty salon in this hotel?
Quisiera...	I'd like . . .
un corte de pelo.	a haircut.
hacerme la manicura.	a manicure.
Tengo un vestido para...	I have a dress to be . . .
lavar.	washed.
planchar.	ironed.
limpiar en seco.	dry-cleaned.
¿Puede sacar esta mancha?	Can you get this stain out?

E. En el hotel. Con un compañero / una compañera, invente diálogos entre un huésped / una huéspeda del hotel y el/la recepcionista u otro empleado o empleada del hotel. Pueden usar las siguientes situaciones o inventar otras.

1. Hace muy mal tiempo, y el huésped / la huéspeda decide quedarse en el hotel y arreglar algunas cosas (la ropa, el pelo, etcétera). Quizás (*Perhaps*) alquile un película o lea un libro. Debe llamar a la recepción para conseguir información y algunas cosas.
2. El huésped / La huéspeda no se siente bien y quiere pedir varias cosas al servicio de cuartos. La recepción le dice que no tienen todas las cosas que él/ella pide, pero le da direcciones para ir a la farmacia, al quiosco, etcétera, para conseguir lo que necesita.

Need more practice?

- Workbook and Laboratory Manual
- Interactive CD-ROM
- Online Learning Center (www.mhhe.com/puntos7)

National Standards: Communication

Have students imagine that they have an appointment with a travel agent in order to plan a trip to some exotic country. Have them prepare questions on index cards to ask the agent. Then have volunteers role-play situations between an agent and client. The travel agents will not know where the person wants to go or what he/she wants to do until the client arrives!

☼ Heritage Speakers

Pídales a dos estudiantes hispanohablantes que representen los papeles y el diálogo primero para que los demás estudiantes vean un modelo.

GRAMÁTICA

In **Gramática 46** you learned the forms and uses of the future tense. Can you provide the correct future forms of the following verbs?

1. (yo) viajar
2. (ellos) beber
3. (tú) ir
4. (Ud.) venir
5. (nosotros) hacer
6. (ella) poner

Review all of the future forms before studying the conditional tense in **Gramática 50**. Also note that you learned a conditional expression in **Capítulo 7: me gustaría(n).** What is the English equivalent of the following sentence?

Me gustaría visitar el museo esta tarde.

50 Expressing What You Would Do • Conditional Verb Forms

La fantasía de Yolanda Torres-Luján

Yolanda es una mujer de negocios muy ocupada. Sufre muchas presiones y está muy cansada. Le *gustaría* ir de vacaciones.

«Con tres días de vacaciones, simplemente *dormiría* todo el día. No *haría* más que comer y dormir. Con una semana de vacaciones, *iría* a la playa, *tomaría* el sol todo el día y *tomaría* copas tropicales en bares elegantes. Con un mes de vacaciones… *descansaría* una semana en casa y luego *viajaría* por Europa.»

¿Y Ud.? ¿Sufre muchas presiones? ¿Le gustaría ir de vacaciones? ¿Qué haría en las vacaciones? Forme oraciones con las siguientes indicaciones. Use **no** cuando sea necesario.

> **MODELO:** dormir todo el día → *Dormiría* todo el día.

1. ir a la playa
2. tomar el sol
3. tomar copas tropicales en bares elegantes
4. descansar una semana
5. viajar por Europa
6. ¿ ?

The fantasy of Yolanda Torres-Luján   *Yolanda is a very busy businesswoman. She's under a lot of pressure, and she's very tired. She would like to go on vacation. "With three days of vacation, I would simply sleep all day. I wouldn't do anything but eat and sleep. With a week of vacation, I would go to the beach, sunbathe all day, and have tropical drinks in elegant bars. With a month of vacation . . . I would rest at home a week and then I would travel through Europe."*

Suggestions

■ Before beginning *Gramática 50*, lead into the *minidiálogo* with *le gustaría* + infinitive questions, which have been active since *Capítulo 7.*

■ Preview this section by asking the following kinds of questions:

> *Si Ud. tuviera un millón de dólares, ¿qué haría? Si Ud. pudiera hacerle una sola pregunta al presidente de los Estados Unidos / al primer ministro del Canadá, ¿qué le preguntaría? Si pudiera cambiar cualquier cosa en el mundo, ¿qué cambiaría?*

■ Using the conditional, ask students what their ideal vacation would be.

> *¿Irían a la playa? ¿a las montañas?*
> *¿A qué país visitarían?*
> *¿Preferirían alojarse en un hotel de lujo o en un hotel menos caro?*
> *¿Qué harían durantes sus vacaciones ideales?*

■ Point out that *vacaciones* is rarely used in the singular form in Spanish.

Refrán

> «La gente joven dice lo que hace, la gente vieja dice lo que hizo y los tontos lo que les gustaría hacer.»

Have students discuss the meaning of this *refrán*. What do they think this saying "teaches"?

Emphasis A: Suggestions

- Point out that the infinitive is used as the stem, as with the future.
- Remind students that context and pronouns will distinguish the *yo* and *Ud./él/ella* forms (which are the same).
- Present the *-ía* endings for infinitives to enable students to complete the *minidiálogo* follow-up.
- Help students identify the endings for the conditional: they are the same as the imperfect indicative endings for *-er* and *-ir* verbs.
- Model conditional forms in brief communicative exchanges with students. Try to use high frequency verbs.

comprar	hacer
beber	salir
escribir	tener
decir	

Emphasis B: Suggestions

- Emphasize that the future and conditional have the same set of irregular verbs.
- Remind students that when *would* refers to a habitual action (*I would study in the library every afternoon.*), the imperfect indicative, not the conditional, is required.
- Model the use of future vs. conditional in quoting people: *Estela dice que vendrá* vs. *Estela dijo que vendría.*

The phrase **me gustaría...** expresses what you *would like to* (do, say, and so on). **Gustaría** is a conditional verb form, part of a system that will allow you to talk about what you and others *would* (do, say, buy, and so on) in a given situation.

Past ----------------	Present ----------------	FUTURE
preterite	present indicative	future
imperfect	present progressive	conditional
present perfect	formal commands	
present perfect subjunctive	informal commands	
past subjunctive	present subjunctive	

A. Like the English future, the English conditional is formed with an auxiliary verb: *I would speak, I would write.*

The Spanish *conditional* (**el condicional**), like the Spanish future, is a simple verb form (only one word). It is formed by adding conditional endings to the infinitive. No auxiliary verbs are needed.

CONDITIONAL ENDINGS

-ía	-íamos
-ías	-íais
-ía	-ían

hablar		comer		vivir	
hablaría	hablaríamos	comería	comeríamos	viviría	viviríamos
hablarías	hablaríais	comerías	comeríais	vivirías	viviríais
hablaría	hablarían	comería	comerían	viviría	vivirían

B. Verbs that form the future on an irregular stem use the same stem to form the conditional.

Note that the conditional of *hay* (**haber**) is **habría** (*there would be*).*

decir: diría, dirías, diría, diríamos, diríais, dirían

decir:	dir-	
haber (hay):	habr-	
hacer:	har-	-ía
poder:	podr-	-ías
poner:	pondr-	-ía
querer:	querr-	-íamos
saber:	sabr-	-íais
salir:	saldr-	-ían
tener:	tendr-	
venir:	vendr-	

---

*The conditional forms of the verb **haber** are used to form the conditional perfect tense (**el condicional perfecto**), which expresses what would have occurred at some point in the past.

Habríamos tenido que buscarla en el aeropuerto.	**We would have had** to pick her up at the airport.

You will find a more detailed presentation of these forms in Appendix 3, Additional Perfect Forms (Indicative and Subjunctive).

Refrán

«No valles por el exterior, eso te podría engañar.»

Point out that *vallar* means *to put a fence around something* and *engañar* means *to fool* or *to deceive.* Then have students brainstorm possible meanings of this *refrán.*

C. The conditional expresses what you would do in a particular situation, given a particular set of circumstances.

 When *would* implies *used to* in English, use the imperfect in Spanish.

—¿**Hablarías** español en el Brasil?
Would you speak Spanish in Brazil?

—No. **Hablaría** portugués.
No. I would speak Portuguese.

Íbamos a la playa todos los veranos.
We would go (used to go) to the beach every summer.

AUTOPRUEBA

Provide the missing letters for the following verbs in the conditional.

1. salir: sal___ía
2. hacer: ha___íamos
3. querer: que___ías

4. decir: d___ían
5. tener: ten___ía
6. poder: po___ía

Answers: 1. saldría 2. haríamos 3. querrías 4. dirían 5. tendría 6. podría

---

■■■ Práctica

A. ¡Anticipemos! ¿Qué haría Ud.?

Paso 1. Imagine que hace un viaje a España. Complete las siguientes oraciones de manera que corresponda a la realidad y a lo que a Ud. le gustaría hacer. ¡Es una gran oportunidad de demostrarles a sus compañeros y a su profesor(a) su conocimiento (*knowledge*) sobre la vida y la cultura españolas!

1. Hablaría ———.
2. Comería ——— y bebería ———.
3. Iría a ——— y allí vería ———.
4. No podría irme sin antes visitar ———.
5. Me compraría ———.
6. Me divertiría mucho ——— (**Sugerencia:** Se puede usar un gerundio: **-iendo** o **-ando**).

Paso 2. Claro que durante un viaje no sólo se hacen actividades culturales. Las oraciones a continuación muestran actividades típicas durante un viaje, pero Ud. debe completarlas con algunos detalles.

1. Yo haría el viaje a España con ———.
2. Tendría que sacar muchas fotos para mostrárselas a ———.
3. Le(s) mandaría tarjetas postales a ———.
4. Querría ——— durante el viaje, pero probablemente no lo haría.
5. Conocería a ———.

Paso 3. Ahora con un compañero / una compañera, haga una lista similar a las del **Paso 1** y el **Paso 2,** pero sobre otro país hispánico.

Prác. A: Preliminary Exercise

Use the following rapid response drill to practice the forms.

Dé el condicional.
yo: *mandar, necesitar, aprender, decir*
tú: *llevar, viajar, leer, hacer*
Ud./él/ella: *entrar, comprar, vivir, poner*
nosotros: *celebrar, comprender, ir, poder*
Uds./ellos/ellas: *regresar, creer, tener, venir*

Prác. A: Suggestion

Ask students the following questions to contextualize the conditional:

1. *¿Qué lengua hablaría una persona de Pekín? ¿Cuál sería su nacionalidad? ¿Y una persona de Moscú? ¿del Canadá? ¿de Lisboa? ¿de Guadalajara? ¿Podría Ud. hablar con todos ellos? ¿Qué lengua(s) tendría que aprender?*
2. *¿Qué haría Ud. para obtener mucho dinero? ¿Y para ahorrar mucho dinero? ¿Y para gastar mucho dinero? ¿Siempre ha tenido Ud. mucho dinero? Como consecuencia, ¿qué tipo de vida ha llevado Ud. en cuanto al aspecto económico?*

Prác. A: Variation

Assign *Pasos 1* and *2* as homework, allowing students to complete the paragraphs about any Spanish-speaking country of interest to them.

- Have students retell the passage using *los trabajadores sociales.*
- Use the conditional verb forms in personalized questions to students about what they would do on vacation in Puerto Rico.
- Ask students: *¿Adónde irían Uds. (si pudieran) este fin de semana? ¿Qué pasaría después de su escapada?*
- Try to avoid contrary-to-fact statements that would require the use of the imperfect subjunctive.

Prác. C: Suggestions

- Have students complete the items in the future. Contrast the difference in meaning when the future is used.
- Have students add two questions of their own to each group.

B. ¿Es posible escapar? Cuente Ud. la fantasía de esta trabajadora social, dando la forma condicional de los verbos.

Necesito salir de todo esto… Creo que me (gustar[1]) ir a Puerto Rico o a algún otro lugar exótico del Caribe… No (trabajar[2])… (Poder[3]) nadar todos los días… (Tomar[4]) el sol en la playa… (Comer[5]) platos exóticos… (Ver[6]) bellos lugares naturales… El viaje (ser[7]) ideal…

Pero… , tarde o temprano, (tener[8]) que volver a lo de siempre… a los rascacielos de la ciudad… al tráfico… al medio ambiente contaminado… al mundo del trabajo… (Poder[9]) usar mi tarjeta de crédito, como dice el anuncio —pero ¡(tener[10]) que pagar después!

Comprensión: ¿Cierto, falso o no lo dice? Corrija las oraciones falsas.

1. Esta persona trabaja en una ciudad grande.
2. No le interesan los deportes acuáticos.
3. Puede pagar este viaje de sueños (*dreams*) al contado.
4. Tiene un novio con quien quisiera hacer el viaje.

C. ¿Qué harías si pudieras?

Paso 1. Con un compañero / una compañera, haga y conteste preguntas según el modelo. Pueden cambiar los detalles, si quieren.

> MODELO: estudiar árabe/japonés →
> E1: ¿Estudiarías *árabe*?
> E2: No. Estudiaría *japonés*.

1. estudiar italiano/chino
2. renunciar a un puesto sin avisar / con dos semanas de anticipación
3. hacer un viaje a España / la Argentina
4. salir de casa sin apagar el estéreo / las luces
5. seguir un presupuesto rígido/flexible
6. gastar menos en ropa/libros
7. poner el aire acondicionado en invierno/verano
8. alquilar un coche de lujo/económico

Paso 2. Ahora sigan con el mismo modelo, pero inventen las respuestas.

1. dejar de estudiar / ¿ ?
2. vivir en otra ciudad / ¿ ?
3. ser presidente/a de los Estados Unidos / primer ministro (primera ministra) del Canadá / ¿ ?
4. gustarle conocer a una persona famosa / ¿ ?

Need more practice?

- Workbook and Laboratory Manual
- Interactive CD-ROM
- Online Learning Center (www.mhhe.com/puntos7)

 Heritage Speakers

Anime a los hispanohablantes a hablar de sus platos regionales favoritos y de su receta favorita.

¿Cómo la preparan?
¿Cuáles son los ingredientes?
¿Es un plato especial que solamente preparan para un día festivo?

Manjares[a] hispano-canadienses

Los que han viajado por la Península Ibérica ya conocen **los sabores[b] de los platos españoles y portugueses.** En la capital canadiense, Ottawa, tanto los turistas como los nativos disfrutan de[c] estos mismos platos en dos restaurantes que sirven **auténticas recetas de los países ibéricos. El Mesón,** que se encuentra en una casa al estilo victoriano, provee una cocina para satisfacer al cliente más exigente.[d] Desde 1987 José Alves ofrece un **menú de platos típicos regionales** de España y de Portugal que incluye calamares al ajillo, mejillones marineros, vieira a la gallega[e] y tres variedades de paella, el sabroso[f] plato a base de arroz y azafrán. También se ofrece un menú especial para vegetarianos. Para complementar sus platos, El Mesón tiene una impresionante lista de vinos españoles y una selección de los famosos «vinhos verdes»* de Portugal.

Lejos de la vecindad de El Mesón y más cerca del centro de la capital, Ud. puede encontrar un ambiente acogedor[g] y relajado en donde hablar y tomar una

▲ *Una paella tipo español*

copa de vino tinto mientras Alfonso Pérez, del restaurante **Don Alfonso,** le prepara uno de sus famosos platos. Nativo de Galicia, el Sr. Pérez vivió en Venezuela antes de emigrar al Canadá adonde vino primero con el propósito de aprender inglés. Hace más de veinticinco años que los ciudadanos de Ottawa y sus muchos turistas del extranjero disfrutan de los mariscos y los sabrosos platos a la plancha[h] preparados por don Alfonso. Entre muchos, se ofrecen escalopines[i] Tío Pepe, una zarzuela de mariscos[j] y gazpacho† andaluz.

A pesar de la autenticidad de sus platos, las horas de comer en El Mesón y en Don Alfonso son típicamente norteamericanas. Se puede almorzar entre las once y media y las dos y media, y la cena se sirve a partir de las cinco. Bienvenidos y que aprovechen.[k]

[a]*Delicacies* [b]*flavors* [c]*disfrutan... enjoy* [d]*demanding* [e]*calamares... squid in garlic sauce, mussels simmered in white-wine garlic sauce, scallops Galician-style* [f]*tasty* [g]*welcoming* [h]*a... grilled* [i]*breaded cutlet* [j]*zarzuela... seafood stew* [k]*Bienvenidos... Welcome and enjoy your meal.*

■ ■ ■ Conversación

Entrevista. ¿Cómo será su futuro? ¿Qué hará? ¿Qué haría? Con otro/a estudiante, haga y conteste las siguientes preguntas.

MODELO: E1: ¿Dejarás de fumar algún día? →
E2: No. No dejaré de fumar nunca. No puedo.
(Creo que sí. Dejaré de fumar algún día.)

PREGUNTAS CON EL FUTURO

1. ¿Te graduarás en esta universidad (o en otra)?
2. ¿Vivirás en esta ciudad después de graduarte?
3. ¿Buscarás un puesto aquí?
4. ¿Cuántos niños (nietos) crees que tendrás algún día?

PREGUNTAS CON EL CONDICIONAL

1. ¿Te casarías con una persona de otro país?
2. ¿Podrías estar contento/a sin la televisión?
3. ¿Serías capaz de (*capable of*) ahorrar el 10 por ciento de tu salario?
4. ¿Podrías vivir sin las tarjetas de crédito?

****Vinho verde** (Young wine) *is produced in the Minho region of northwest Portugal. Slightly sparkling, it can be either red or white.*

†**Gazpacho** *is a cold tomato-based soup that originated in Andalusia.*

Gramática
Quinientos cuarenta y nueve ■ **549**

Con: Suggestions

■ Ask students about New Year's resolutions.

¿Cuáles son algunas de las promesas del Año Nuevo que Ud. hace todos los años? ¿Qué promesas hizo Ud. el enero pasado?

Model an answer for them.

Dije que dejaría de fumar.

Follow up with present perfect questions, using object pronouns whenever possible.

¿Lo ha hecho Ud.? ¿Ha dejado de fumar?

■ This is a good activity to introduce the use of the conditional to express future in the past.
■ Present and practice *el condicional de probabilidad.* Have students make conjectures about where you and other students were at certain times: last night at 11:00 / last July / in 1995.

¿Dónde estaría Susie ayer a las 11 de la noche?

Bring in photos or magazine clippings and have students invent details about the images.

La mujer estaría riéndose porque estaría oyendo algo divertido.

Have different groups work with the same images, then compare results.

Bright Idea

Con: Suggestion

This activity recycles the future and prepares students for the next section. Review and compare future and conditional forms. You can also model responding with the conditional.

Sí, ya te dije que dejaría de fumar pronto.
No, ya te dije que nunca dejaré de fumar.

Con: Follow-Up

Have students write two questions that use the future tense and two that use the conditional. Have them ask their classmates these questions.

Bright Idea

Con: Extension

¿Qué harías con mil dólares? (Saving is not an option.)
¿Qué no harías por un millón de dólares? (Refer to reality television programming.)

Gramática ■ **549**

EN LOS ESTADOS UNIDOS Y EL CANADÁ

Use the following questions to check comprehension:

1. ¿Qué tipos de platos ofrecen los dos restaurantes?
2. ¿Desde cuándo hay un restaurante con comida española en Ottawa?
3. ¿Qué cosa no es típicamente española en los restaurantes ibéricos de Ottawa?

MULTIMEDIA: Internet

Encourage students to look for restaurants in Spanish-speaking countries or Hispanic restaurants in the U.S. and Canada online. Students can also find Spanish and Hispanic recipes online.

Follow-Up

Have students invent an additional sentence about each of the characters in the *minidiálogo* using *si* clauses.

51 Hypothetical Situations: What if . . . ? • *Si* Clause Sentences

¿Qué desean estas personas?

MARGARITA: Si *tuviera* el dinero, me *compraría* una computadora.

ANDRÉS: Si *pudiera, estudiaría* en el D.F. por un año y *me quedaría* con una familia mexicana.

ANTONIA Y MARIO: Si la universidad nos *diera* un aumento de sueldo, *viajaríamos* por Italia.

¿Y Ud.? Exprese algunos de sus deseos, completando las siguientes oraciones.

1. Si yo tuviera dinero suficiente, iría a _____.
2. Si pudiera conocer a alguna persona famosa, me gustaría conocer a _____.
3. Si consiguiera una beca (*scholarship*), estudiaría en _____.
4. Si ganara la lotería, me compraría _____.
5. Si visitara Latinoamérica, me quedaría en _____.
6. Si recibiera un aumento de sueldo, me gustaría _____.

What do these people desire? MARGARITA: *If I had the money, I would buy myself a computer.* ANDRÉS: *If I could, I would stay in Mexico City studying for another year.* ANTONIA AND MARIO: *If the university gave us a raise, we would travel throughout Italy.*

A. Both English and Spanish use clauses with *if* (**si**) to speculate or hypothesize about situations that are possible. In Spanish, when the **si** clause is in the present tense, the indicative (present or future) is used.	Si **tiene** tiempo, **va/irá** a las montañas. *If he has time, he goes/will go to the mountains.*
B. To express a contrary-to-fact situation, the **si** in the first clause is followed by the past subjunctive. The conditional is used in the other clause.	Si **tuviera** tiempo, **iría** a las montañas. *If he had time, he would go to the mountains.** Si yo **fuera** tú, no **haría** eso. *If I were you, I wouldn't do that.** Si **estudiara** más, **podría** hacerse médica. *If she studied more, she could become a doctor.**
C. When the verb in the **si** clause is in the past tense and the event is not contrary to fact, the indicative is used in both clauses. This is especially true when habitual actions or situations are expressed.	Si **tenía** tiempo, **iba** a las montañas. *If (When) he had time, he would go (used to go) to the mountains.*

AUTOPRUEBA

Indicate which of the following sentences is contrary to fact.

☐ **1.** Si estoy de vacaciones, les mando tarjetas postales a mis amigos.
☐ **2.** Almorzamos en los cafés al aire libre si tenemos hambre.
☐ **3.** Compraría mis revistas en el quiosco si estuviera en España.
☐ **4.** Si no tengo mucho tiempo, tomo un taxi.

Answer: 3

■■■ Práctica

A. ¡Anticipemos! ¿Qué haría Ud.? Complete las oraciones lógicamente.

1. Si yo quisiera comprar comida, iría a _____.
2. Si necesitara comprar un libro, iría a _____.
3. Si necesitara usar un libro, iría a _____.
4. Si tuviera sed en este momento, tomaría _____.
5. Si tuviera que emigrar, iría a _____.
6. Si quisiera ir a _____, viajaría en avión.
7. Si no funcionara(n) _____, compraría un coche nuevo.
8. Si me gustara(n) _____, iría a ver un concierto de Pearl Jam.

---

*The contrary-to-fact situations in these sentences express speculations about the present. The perfect forms of the conditional and the past subjunctive are used to speculate about the past: what would have happened if a particular event had or had not occurred.

Si **hubiera tenido** el dinero, **habría hecho** el viaje.

*If **I had had** the money, **I would have made** the trip.*

You will find a more detailed presentation of this structure in Appendix 3, Additional Perfect Forms (Indicative and Subjunctive).

Gramática

Point out that after *si* + indicative, a command can follow in the main clause, for example, *Si tienes tiempo, ve a las montañas.*

Suggestions

■ Draw the following grammar equations on the board.

si + indicative

1. *si* + imperfect → imperfect (past facts)
2. *si* + present → present / future / command (possible facts)

si + subjunctive

1. *si* + imperfect → conditional (unlikely or impossible)
2. *si* + pluperfect → conditional perfect (impossible)

■ Point out that the present subjunctive never appears in sentences with *si*.
■ Rules for *si* sentences are as strict in Spanish as in English.
■ Have students review the formation of the imperfect subjunctive.

Prác. A: Preliminary Exercises

■ Have students tell whether the following sentences are contrary to fact or not.

1. *Si estoy en el centro, siempre almuerzo en Barney's.*
2. *Si lloviera, no iríamos.*
3. *Si estamos cansados, descansamos una hora por la tarde.*
4. *Habla como si fuera argentina.*
5. *Si yo tuviera esa clase, tendría que estudiar mucho.*
6. *Si te veo mañana, te lo daré.*

■ Use the following pattern drill to practice forms. *Pablo necesita decidirse sobre un puesto que paga bastante bien, pero que está en un pueblo poco elegante y algo aislado* (isolated). *¿Qué le dirá Ud.?*
—*Si yo... , no lo haría.* (ser tú, tener ese problema, no poder decidir).
—*Si yo... , me volvería loco/a.* (estar allí, vivir allí)

Prác. A: Variation

Have students provide interesting or provocative situations. Have the class react, completing the phrase: *Si yo fuera...*

CULTURE

■ Point out that in Argentina, beef is *el bife*. Argentina is one of the largest producers of beef in the world, thanks to the Pampas, the vast grazing plains in the center of the country. For this reason, beef is extremely popular among Argentines. More beef is consumed per capita in Argentina than in any other country in the world.
■ Point out that *el tango* originated in Argentina.

☼ Heritage Speakers

Los hispanohablantes de algunas regiones usan el condicional en cláusulas con *si*. El tiempo aceptado es el imperfecto de subjuntivo. Compare las siguientes oraciones: USO RECOMENDADO: *Si yo **tuviera** dinero, iría a España.* VARIACIÓN REGIONAL: *Si yo **tendría** dinero, iría a España.*

Ask students what they would do in the following situations.

1. *si su amigo/a le pidiera 100 dólares para algo urgente*
2. *si un profesor / una profesora le dijera «Como me caes muy bien, no tienes que tomar el examen final»*
3. *si su pareja le propusiera que se casaran immediatamente*
4. *si de alguna manera consiguiera un millón de dólares hoy*

Make sure students repeat the circumstances in *si* clauses in their responses (*si* + subjunctive).

B. Si viajara a otro país... ¿Qué haría Ud. si viajara a la Argentina? Haga oraciones según el modelo.

MODELO: si **/** viajar **/** otro **/** país, **/** ir **/** la Argentina →
Si viajara a otro país, iría a la Argentina.

1. si **/** ir **/** la Argentina, **/** quedarme **/** en **/** Buenos Aires
2. si **/** tener **/** interés **/** en **/** población **/** italiano, **/** visitar **/** barrio italiano La Boca
3. si **/** querer **/** mandar **/** tarjeta postal, **/** comprarla **/** en **/** quiosco
4. si **/** tener ganas **/** de **/** comprar **/** libros, **/** pedir **/** direcciones **/** barrio San Telmo
5. si **/** querer **/** ver **/** obra de teatro, **/** ir **/** Teatro Colón
6. si **/** interesarme **/** visitar **/** sitios **/** turístico, **/** ver **/** obelisco **/** y **/** réplica **/** de **/** Big Ben
7. si **/** querer **/** probar (*to try*) **/** comida **/** auténtico, **/** comer **/** carne **/** argentino
8. si **/** querer **/** escuchar **/** música **/** típico, **/** escuchar **/** tango

C. Situaciones

Paso 1. Empareje cada oración con su dibujo.

a. _____ Los Martínez quieren usar su coche.
b. _____ A Mariana le encanta ese vestido.
c. _____ Simón quiere encender (*to turn on*) la luz.
d. _____ Julia no tiene ganas de levantarse.
e. _____ La Sra. Blanco tiene miedo de viajar en avión.

Paso 2. Ahora haga una oración con **si** para cada situación. Use su imaginación para añadir detalles.

MODELO: Mariana se compraría ese vestido si...

Need more practice?

- Workbook and Laboratory Manual
- Interactive CD-ROM
- Online Learning Center (www.mhhe.com/ puntos7)

Resources: Transparency 108

■ ▥ ▦ Conversación

A. El horario de todos los días. ¿Tiene Ud. un horario bastante fijo y rutinario? A ver si puede contestar las siguientes preguntas.

¿Dónde estaría Ud. … ?

1. si fuera miércoles a las tres de la tarde
2. si fuera jueves a las diez de la mañana
3. si fuera viernes a las nueve de la noche
4. si fuera domingo a las nueve de la mañana
5. si fuera lunes a la una de la tarde

B. Entrevistas

Paso 1. Entreviste a otro/a estudiante según el modelo.

¿Bajo (*Under*) qué circunstancias… ?

MODELO: comprar un coche nuevo →
E1: ¿Bajo qué circunstancias *comprarías* un coche nuevo?
E2: *Compraría* un coche nuevo si tuviera más dinero.

1. dejar de estudiar en esta universidad
2. emigrar a otro país
3. estudiar otro idioma
4. no obedecer a tus padres / a tu jefe/a
5. votar por _____ para presidente/a / primer ministro (primera ministra)
6. ser candidato/a para presidente/a / primer ministro (primera ministra)
7. casarse / divorciarse
8. no decirle la verdad a un amigo / una amiga

Paso 2. Ahora entrevístanse según el modelo. Traten de inventar más preguntas.

¿Qué harías si… ?

MODELO: perder un libro de texto →
E1: ¿Qué harías si *perdieras* un libro de texto?
E2: Primero lo *buscaría* por unos días.

1. (no) tener que estudiar este fin de semana
2. tener un mes libre y mucho dinero
3. no poder asistir a la universidad

Con. A: Variation

Have students do this activity in reverse (*I would be doing that if it were . . .*).

1. *Estaría en una fiesta si…*
2. *Estaría con mi familia si…*
3. *Llamaría a mi mejor amigo/a si…*
4. *Bebería cerveza o vino si…*

Con. B: Suggestions

■ Have students tell what they would do in exchange for a favor that their roommates or housemates did for them.

> *Si mi compañera de apartamento no dejara platos sucios por todos sitios, yo limpiaría la cocina con más frecuencia.*

¡OJO! Have students use the subject pronoun for emphasis.
■ Have students complete the following sentences.

1. *Si yo fuera presidente/a (primer ministro / primera ministra), yo…*
2. *Si yo estuviera en… ,…*
3. *Si tuviera un millón de dólares,…*
4. *Si yo pudiera… ,…*
5. *Si yo fuera… ,…*
6. *Si… , estaría contentísimo/a.*
7. *Si… , estaría enojadísimo/a.*

■ Have half of the class write *si* clauses using past subjunctive; the other writes result clauses using the conditional. Collect *si* clauses in one box, result clauses in another. Draw a clause from each box and read the resulting sentence aloud.

UN POCO DE TODO

A: Extension

6. *haber un examen el viernes / la semana que viene*

7. *ser el examen en el laboratorio / en la clase*

8. *costar el libro $20 / $30*

B: Suggestion

Have students write their own *si* clauses for classmates to complete. Encourage creativity and humor.

Bright Idea

B: Extension

For item 2, have students imagine they have no electricity, but they can take (have) three things. What would they want to have?

UN POCO DE TODO

A. ¡Entendiste mal! Con un compañero / una compañera, haga y conteste preguntas según el modelo.

MODELO: llegar el trece de junio / tres →
E1: *Llegaré* el trece de junio.
E2: ¿No dijiste que *llegarías* el tres?
E1: ¡Que no! Te dije que *llegaría* el trece. Entendiste mal.

1. estar en el café a las dos / doce
2. estudiar con Juan / Juana
3. ir de vacaciones en julio / junio
4. verte en casa / en clase
5. comprar la blusa rosada / roja

B. Si el mundo fuera diferente... Adaptarse a un nuevo país o a nuevas circunstancias es difícil, pero también es una aventura interesante. ¿Qué ocurriría si el mundo fuera diferente?

MODELO: Si yo fuera la última persona en el mundo... →
• tendría que aprender a hacer muchas cosas.
• sería la persona más importante —y más ignorante— del mundo.
• me adaptaría fácilmente/difícilmente.
• los animales y yo nos haríamos buenos amigos.

1. Si yo pudiera tener solamente un amigo / una amiga, _____.
2. Si yo tuviera que pasar un año en una isla desierta, _____.
3. Si yo fuera (otro persona), _____.
4. Si el presidente fuera presidenta, _____.
5. Si yo viviera en Puerto Rico, _____.

C. ¡No tengas miedo! Complete the following passages with the correct forms of the words in parentheses, as suggested by the context. When two possibilities are given in parentheses, select the correct word. **¡OJO!** As you conjugate verbs in this activity, sometimes you will have to decide which mood (subjunctive or indicative) and tense to use according to context; sometimes you will see italicized clues to show you which tense or mood to use.

Por fin, el semestre de primavera ha terminado, y esta tarde Bob y Paco, un estudiante de Barcelona, se encuentran para hablar de lo que piensan hacer durante el verano.

PACO: Pues, sería superdivertido si (*tú:* ir[1]) conmigo a Barcelona a pasar unas semanas con mi familia. Así podrías (saber/conocer[2]) a mis padres y hermanos. Ellos (ser/estar[3]) muy (amable[4]), y te (*cond.,* recibir[5]) como a un invitado especial. (*cond., Nosotros:* Divertirse[6]) un montón[a] allí. No sabes la cantidad de cosas divertidas e interesantes que se puede hacer en Barcelona.

CULTURE

Catalán is a Romance language belonging to the Italic subfamily of the Indo-European languages. *Catalán* is spoken by approximately eight million people in Catalonia, Valencia, the Balearic Islands, and Aragon. Since *catalán* is derived from the Romance languages, it is written in the Romance alphabet. *Catalán* is now listed as an official language of Barcelona, although its use had been suppressed for many years during Franco's regime.

BOB: Ay, ¡qué agradable idea! Pero tengo un inconveniente.[b] (*Yo: Tener/Estar*[7]) mucho miedo de (*viajar*[8]) (*por/para*[9]) avión. Una vez, cuando (*yo: tener*[10]) diez años, mi familia y yo (*intentar*[11]) (*hacer*[12]) un viaje a Nueva York por avión, pero antes de que el avión (*poder*[13]) despegar,[c] (*nosotros: tener*[14]) que bajarnos porque (*yo: empezar*[15]) a llorar y gritar. Desde entonces, no (*yo: haber volver*[16]) a poner pie en un avión. Bueno, si no fuera por ese miedo, yo te (*acompañar*[17]) con mucho gusto a España.

PACO: Es una (*grande*[18]) lástima, porque además de conocer Barcelona, tú (*cond., poder*[19]) ir con nosotros a las Islas Baleares, donde (*nosotros: pasar*[20]) un mes (*todo*[21]) (*el*[22]) veranos.

BOB: Realmente, tengo (*superlative, mucho*[23]) miedo.

PACO: No (*command, tú: tener*[24]) miedo, hombre. (*cond., Nosotros: Ir*[25]) en agosto, porque, ¿sabes? Las familias (*español*[26]) típicamente veranean[d] todo el mes de agosto. La mayoría (*preferir*[27]) ir a la costa. (*Mucho*[28]) familias tienen o (*alquilan/prestan*[29]) una casa o cabaña en el norte, como en Santander o San Sebastián. Otras prefieren la Costa del Sol o el Golfo de Cádiz en el sur. Mi familia tiene mucha (*suerte/razón*[30]). Siempre (*nosotros: alojarse*[31]) en el hotel de lujo de mi tío Jorge en la isla de Mallorca.

BOB: Parece muy interesante, pero…

PACO: Hombre, si (*alguien/alguno*[32]) me (*dar*[33]) un millón de dólares para veranear en cualquier lugar del planeta, (*irme*[34]) a Mallorca con los ojos cerrados. ¡O cualquiera de las cuatro Islas Baleares! Y (*yo: saber/conocer*[35]) que vas a querer visitar(*las/les*[36]) después de que (*tú: ver*[37]) (*este*[38]) fotos que tengo de las islas. También tengo un folleto que (*mostrar*[39]) (*alguno*[40]) playas de Ibiza, otra de las islas.

[a]un… *a lot* [b]problema [c]*take off* [d]*spend summer vacation*

Comprensión. All of the following statements about the preceding narration are incorrect. Correct them.

1. Paco y Bob se encuentran para hablar de asistir a clases durante el verano.
2. Paco quiere que Bob vaya con él porque no hay nada que hacer en Barcelona.
3. Bob no puede ir porque no tiene suficiente dinero para un boleto de avión.
4. Bob ha viajado por avión varias veces después del incidente desastroso que tuvo a los diez años.
5. Las vacaciones no son muy importantes para los españoles.
6. Paco siempre veranea en las Islas Baleares porque su familia tiene una casa de verano allí.

Resources for Review and Testing Preparation

■ Workbook and Laboratory Manual
■ Interactive CD-ROM
■ Online Learning Center (www.mhhe.com/puntos7)

MULTIMEDIA: Internet

Have students search the Internet for more information about Barcelona and the Balearic Islands. You may assign specific topics for them to research and to present to their classmates. Some topics may include tourist sites, customs, and languages (*catalán* in Barcelona).

Resources: Desenlace

In the *Capítulo 18* segment of "Chapter-by-Chapter Supplementary Materials" in the IM/RK, you will find a chapter-culminating activity. You can use this activity to consolidate and review the vocabulary and grammar skills students have acquired.

Entrevista cultural

Suggestions

- Before showing the video, ask students questions about traveling and hotel stays.

  Cuando viaja, ¿qué tipo de hotel prefiere? ¿Busca un hotel económico? ¿un hotel cerca del centro o cerca de las atracciones que le interesen? ¿Qué tipo de habitación prefiere? ¿Le importa si la habitación tiene vista?

- Show the video and allow students one to two minutes to work on the questions. Have volunteers answer the questions.
- Have volunteers role-play Margarita and her interviewer.

Entre amigos

Suggestions

- Before viewing the video, review the questions with the students and ask them similar questions.

  ¿Adónde piensa Ud. ir para las próximas vacaciones? ¿Piensa hacer un viaje?

  ¿Cómo se prepara Ud. para un viaje? ¿Busca información en una agencia de viajes o en el Internet?

  Have students answer or work in small groups to ask and answer these questions in Spanish.

- After viewing the video, have volunteers read and answer the questions.

PERSPECTIVAS
culturales

●●● Videoteca

Entrevista cultural: España

Margarita Durán es una española que trabaja en el negocio de su familia. En esta entrevista, habla del negocio y de los clientes. Antes de ver el vídeo, lea el siguiente fragmento de la entrevista.

ENTREVISTADORA: ¿De dónde vienen sus huéspedes?

MARGARITA: Por lo general nuestros huéspedes vienen de muchas partes del mundo. Generalmente predominan los alemanes; también tenemos ingleses, franceses y muchos norteamericanos. Eh, las parejas jóvenes son nuestros huéspedes más frecuentes, y eh, normalmente ellos nos solicitan habitaciones que den a[a] la ciudad, que tengan una vista bonita pero que al mismo tiempo sean tranquilas, y esto para nosotros es una contradicción, porque todas las habitaciones que dan a la calle siempre van a tener algún ruido.

[a]den... *open to, overlook*

Ahora vea el vídeo y conteste las siguientes preguntas basándose en la entrevista.

1. ¿De dónde es Margarita?
2. ¿Cuál es el negocio de su familia?
3. ¿Cuáles son las responsabilidades de los miembros de la familia?
4. ¿Quiénes son los clientes, generalmente?
5. ¿Qué opinión tiene Margarita de su trabajo? ¿Por qué?

Entre amigos: Tengo mi pasaje a San Francisco

Miguel, Karina, Rubén y Tané hablan de las vacaciones. En su opinión, ¿qué van a decir sobre este tema? Antes de mirar el vídeo, lea las preguntas a continuación. Mientras mire el vídeo, trate de entender la conversación en general y fíjese en la información sobre las vacaciones y los arreglos (*arrangements*). Luego mire el vídeo una segunda vez, fijándose en la información que necesita para contestar las preguntas.

1. ¿Para qué necesita Rubén folletos (*brochures*) de viaje?
2. ¿Adónde piensa ir de vacaciones Miguel? ¿Ha decidido?
3. ¿Qué sugiere Karina que busquen en un hotel? Y Rubén, ¿qué sugiere?
4. ¿Qué ha comprado Tané?
5. ¿Qué le sugiere Miguel a Tané?

Capítulo 18: En el extranjero

MULTIMEDIA: Internet

Have students search the Internet for more information about the government, educational system, geography, and economy of Spain. You might assign specific topics and have students give brief oral presentations based on their findings.

Conozca... España

Datos esenciales

- Nombre oficial: Reino de España
- Capital: Madrid
- Población: 40.220.000 habitantes
- Moneda: el euro (la peseta)
- Idiomas: el español, el catalán, el gallego y el vasco*

¡Fíjese!

- España es un país donde muchas culturas se han encontrado a través de[a] la historia. Sin embargo fueron los romanos los que marcaron el principio de la historia de la España que hoy conocemos, pues ellos introdujeron el latín a la península durante su dominio (desde el año 200 a.C.[b] hasta la invasión de los visigodos, un pueblo germánico, en el 419 d.C.[c]).
- El latín es la lengua madre del español y también del catalán, el gallego y el portugués. La otra lengua que se habla en la península, el vasco, es una lengua ancestral de origen desconocido: ni siquiera es[d] una lengua indoeuropea.
- España no fue siempre un solo país. De hecho,[e] España se unificó en el siglo XV cuando los Reyes Católicos, Isabel y Fernando, monarcas de dos reinos[f] independientes, se casaron. Su campaña[g] de unificación terminó en 1492 con la conquista del reino musulmán[h] de Granada.
- Los árabes vivieron en España durante ocho siglos, hasta su expulsión, junto con los judíos, en el año 1492.

[a] a... throughout   [b] a.C.... antes de Cristo   [c] d.C.... después de Cristo
[d] ni... it is not even   [e] De... In fact   [f] kingdoms   [g] campaign   [h] Moslem

Learn more about Spain with the Video, the Interactive CD-ROM, and the Online Learning Center (www.mhhe.com/puntos7).

*El español es el lenguaje oficial de todo el país; el catalán, el gallego y el vasco también son lenguas oficiales en Cataluña, Galicia y el País Vasco, respectivamente.

Personas famosas: Pedro Almodóvar

Las películas del cineasta[a] Pedro Almodóvar (1951–) han tenido y siguen teniendo un éxito enorme dentro y fuera de España, y Almodóvar es el director de cine español más conocido de las últimas décadas. Con temas que satirizan actitudes tradicionales respecto a la familia, la religión, el machismo y la moralidad convencional, sus películas presentan una sociedad española moderna y cambiante.[b]

Muchas de sus películas se pueden conseguir en las bibliotecas públicas y universitarias, así como en los videoclubs de este país: *Mujeres al borde de un ataque de nervios, La ley del deseo, ¿Qué he hecho yo para merecer esto?, ¡Átame!,[c] Kika, La flor de mi secreto, Todo sobre mi madre* y *Hable con ella*. Las útimas dos fueron ganadoras del Óscar: *Todo sobre mi madre* para la mejor película extranjera (1999) y *Hable con ella* para el mejor guión[d] original (2002).

[a] director de cine   [b] changing   [c] Tie Me Up! Tie Me Down!   [d] screenplay

▲ *El escudo* (shield) *de Fernando e Isabel*

Conozca... España

Suggestions

- Have students research and report to the class about famous Spanish historic and literary figures, such as *el Cid Campeador, el Lazarillo de Tormes, Isabel la Católica* and *Fernando de Aragón, Don Quijote* and *Sancho Panza, la Celestina,* and *don Juan Tenorio*. You may wish to invite students to dress up as these characters at an end-of-class party.
- If the class is composed of mature students, show Almodóvar's *Todo sobre mi madre* as an end-of-term activity.

Note

Students can read an excerpt of the novel *El ingenioso hidalgo don Quijote de la Mancha* by Spain's Miguel de Cervantes Saavedra in *Un paso más 18*.

CULTURE

Sephardic Spanish or *ladino* is still spoken today by approximately 160,000 people, although not in Spain. *Ladino*, known as Judeo-Spanish by Romance philologists, is the traditional language of Sephardic Jews. This language was a form of 15th-century Spanish, mixed with Hebrew and other languages. After 1492, the Sephardic culture was established in all the countries bordering on the Mediterranean and beyond. Sephardic Jews were the dominant influence in Jewish history and culture for many years, but today *ladino* is considered a "seriously endangered" language. Unlike most modern languages, *ladino* has scarcely evolved since the Middle Ages.

Suggestions

- Read the following passage to contextualize the vocabulary. Pause from time to time to ask comprehension questions.

  Cuando uno viaja a otro país, su primer encuentro cultural puede ser en la aduana, antes de salir ni siquiera del aeropuerto. Puede haber problemas en la aduana de todos los países, pero por lo general esta experiencia es muy rutinaria. Para pasar por la aduana sin problema, lo único importante es no llevar nada que esté prohibido: cierto tipo de alimentos, plantas, ciertas sustancias químicas, etcétera. Si Ud. tiene alguna duda, es buena idea que se entere de cuáles son las cosas prohibidas en el país que va a visitar antes de entrar en él. Si Ud. va a quedarse con una familia en el extranjero, es aconsejable que lleve consigo algunos regalitos. Las calculadoras electrónicas, que ahora se compran tan baratas en este país, son muy buenos regalos.

- Remind students of accent mark rules, drawing special attention to words like the following.

  *habitación / habitaciones
  reservación / reservaciones
  autobús / autobuses*

- Ask students the following questions to review the vocabulary.

  1. *¿Adónde va Ud. si quiere tomar una copa / un trago con los amigos? ¿Le gustan los batidos? ¿Dónde se toma un buen batido en esta ciudad? En general, ¿es necesario preparar los batidos con puro helado o se puede sustituir los ingredientes artificiales?*

  2. *¿Está bien situado el lugar donde Ud. vive? ¿Hay un correo cerca? ¿una parada de autobús? ¿Adónde va Ud. para comprar artículos de uso personal (el champú, la pasta dental, etcétera)? ¿Hay una tienda de comestibles cerca de donde Ud. vive?*

  3. *¿Hay quioscos en este país? ¿Qué cosa espera Ud. comprar en un quiosco?*

  4. *¿Cuánto vale un sello para mandar una carta de primera clase? ¿Se puede usar un sello de primera clase para mandar una carta a México? ¿a España? ¿a Puerto Rico?*

EN RESUMEN

Gramática

To review the grammar points presented in this chapter, refer to the indicated grammar presentations. You'll find further practice of these structures in the Workbook and Laboratory Manual, on the Interactive CD-ROM, and on the *Puntos de partida* Online Learning Center (www.mhhe.com/puntos7).

50. Expressing What You Would Do—Conditional Verb Forms

Do you know how to form the conditional tense? When would you use the conditional in Spanish?

51. Hypothetical Situations: What if . . . ?—**Si** Clause Sentences

You should know the difference between a simple **si** clause and a contrary-to-fact **si** clause in Spanish.

Vocabulario

Practice this vocabulary with digital flash cards on the Online Learning Center (www.mhhe.com/puntos7).

Cosas y lugares en el extranjero

el batido	drink similar to a milkshake
el café	café
el champú	shampoo
una copa / un trago	(alcoholic) drink
el correo	mail
la oficina de correos	post office
la estación del metro	subway stop
el estanco	tobacco stand/shop
el fósforo	match
el jabón	soap
el papel para cartas	stationery
la papelería	stationery store
el paquete	package
la parada del autobús	bus stop
la pasta dental	toothpaste
la pastelería	pastry shop
el pastelito	small pastry
el quiosco	kiosk
el sello	(postage) stamp
el sobre	envelope

Repaso: la farmacia, la revista, la tarjeta postal

Ir al extranjero

cruzar (c)	to cross
registrar	to search, examine

Repaso: viajar

la aduana	customs
el cheque de viajero	traveler's check
el extranjero	abroad
el formulario	form (to fill out)
la frontera	border
el/la viajero/a	traveler

Cognado: el pasaporte
Repaso: el equipaje, la nacionalidad

El alojamiento

alojarse	to stay (in a place)
confirmar	to confirm
la almohada	pillow
el botones/mozo	bellhop
la criada	maid
la estancia	stay (in a hotel)
la habitación	(hotel) room
individual/doble	single/double (room)
con baño/ducha	(room) with attached bath/shower
sin baño/ducha	(room) without attached bath/shower
el hotel (de lujo)	(luxury) hotel
el hotel de dos (tres) estrellas	two (three) star hotel
el/la huésped(a)	(hotel) guest
la manta	blanket
la pensión	boardinghouse
pensión completa	room and full board
media pensión	room with breakfast and one other meal
la propina	tip (to an employee)
la recepción	front desk
las reservaciones / reservas	reservations
las sábanas	sheets
el servicio de cuartos	room service
la toalla	towel

Repaso: quedarse

completo/a	full, no vacancy
desocupado/a	vacant, unoccupied
con anticipación	ahead of time

Un paso más 18

Literatura de **España**

Sobre el autor: *Miguel de Cervantes Saavedra nació en Alcalá de Henares, cerca de Madrid, España. Parece que no hizo estudios formales, pero leyó extensamente, especialmente novelas pastorales[a] y de caballería.[b] Mientras prestaba servicio militar en Turquía, resultó herido[c] en una batalla, y luego fue capturado y encarcelado[d] en Argel. Ya de regreso en España, empezó a escribir versos, teatro y novelas. Su obra maestra,* El ingenioso hidalgo[e] don Quijote de la Mancha, *de fama mundial, se considera la primera novela moderna. El siguiente fragmento es de la primera parte de* El ingenioso hidalgo don Quijote de la Mancha *(1605).*

▲ Miguel de Cervantes Saavedra (1547–1616)

En un lugar de la Mancha, de cuyo[f] nombre no quiero acordarme, no ha mucho tiempo[g] que vivía un hidalgo de los de lanza en astillero,[h] adarga[i] antigua, rocín flaco[j] y galgo corredor.[k] [...] Tenía en su casa un ama que pasaba[l] los cuarenta, y una sobrina que no llegaba a[m] los veinte, y un mozo de campo y plaza,[n] que así ensillaba[o] el rocín como tomaba la podadera.[p] Frisaba la edad de nuestro hidalgo con[q] los cincuenta años; era de complexión recia,[r] seco de carnes,[s] enjuto de rostro,[t] gran madrugador[u] y amigo de la caza.[v] [...]

Es pues, de saber que este sobredicho hidalgo, los ratos que estaba ocioso[w] (que eran los más del año), se daba a leer libros de caballerías[x] con tanta afición y gusto que olvidó casi de todo punto el ejercicio de la caza, y aun la administración de su hacienda,[y] y llegó a tanto su curiosidad y desatino[z] en esto, que vendió muchas hanegas de tierra[aa] de sembradura[bb] para comprar libros de caballerías en que leer, y así, llevó a su casa todos cuantos pudo haber de ellos...

En resolución, él se enfrascó tanto en[cc] su lectura, que se le pasaban las noches leyendo de claro en claro,[dd] y los días de turbio en turbio;[ee] y así, del poco dormir y del mucho leer se le

[a]*novelas... pastoral novels* [b]*chivalry* [c]*injured* [d]*imprisoned* [e]*nobleman* [f]*whose* [g]*no... no hace mucho tiempo* [h]*lanza... lance, spear in a sheath* [i]*shield of leather* [j]*rocín... skinny nag (horse)* [k]*galgo... errand runner (lit. running greyhound)* [l]*tenía más de* [m]*no... tenía menos de* [n]*mozo... farmhand* [o]*saddled* [p]*pruning knife* [q]*Frisaba... Our nobleman was around* [r]*complexión... strong build* [s]*seco... skinny* [t]*enjuto... dried up face* [u]*gran... early riser* [v]*hunting* [w]*idle* [x]*libros... novels of chivalry* [y]*country estate* [z]*foolishness* [aa]*hanegas... one hanega de tierra is about 1.59 acres of land* [bb]*for cultivation* [cc]*él... he was so engaged/immersed in* [dd]*de... from dusk to dawn* [ee]*turbio... in a haze*

Literatura de **España**

Suggestions

- Have students tell what they know about *Don Quijote*.
- Discuss pastoral novels and novels of chivalry. Point out that *Don Quijote de la Mancha* was a criticism of novels of chivalry and particularly of the general public that was so enthralled with this popular, unsophisticated form of literature.

Extension

Make copies of the following paragraph, and have students discuss it in class.

Conozca a... Miguel de Cervantes Saavedra

El escritor más célebre de España nace en Alcalá de Henares en 1547. A los 24 años, ya miembro de las fuerzas armadas españolas, toma parte en la batalla de Lepanto en contra de los turcos. En esta batalla pierde una mano y, de ahí en adelante, lleva el nombre de «el manco[a] de Lepanto». Sigue en el servicio del rey hasta que, en el año 1575, es tomado prisionero. Pasa cinco años en una carcel[b] en Argelia.

Al volver a España empieza a escribir y a publicar sus obras. A la vez, trabaja de recaudador de impuestos.[c] En 1601, publica su obra más famosa, El ingenioso hidalgo[d] don Quijote de la Mancha. La figura central de esta novela es un idealista que se cree caballero errante[e] y trata de corregir todos los problemas a los cuales se enfrenta.

Cervantes muere el 23 de abril de 1616, el mismo día en que muere Shakespeare.

[a]*one-handed man*
[b]*jail*
[c]*recaudador... tax collector*
[d]*ingenioso... clever nobleman*
[e]*caballero... knight errant*

secó el cerebro de manera que vino a perder el juicio.[ff] Llenósele la fantasía de todo aquello que leía en los libros, así de encantamentos como de pendencias, batallas, tormentas y disparates imposibles;[gg] y asentósele[hh] de tal modo en la imaginación que era verdad toda aquella máquina de aquellas sonadas invenciones que leía, que para él no había otra historia más cierta en el mundo.

[ff]vino... *he went crazy* [gg]así... *with as many spells as with fights, battles, storms, and crazy ideas* [hh]*he became so convinced*

LECTURA

ESTRATEGIA: Using Language Cues to Understand Poetry (3)

One of the things that distinguishes poetry from prose is its use of repetition. Sometimes this repetition is straightforward: A word appears in the same form more than once in the course of the poem, although it does not necessarily have the same meaning each time it appears. But there are other forms of repetition. Variants of the word or synonyms may appear. Sometimes you will find several words with the same root. Finding these words will help you further understand the poem and its meaning.

In the following poem, you will find repetitions of this sort. Why do you think the poet chose to repeat the same word so often in such a short poem? What kind of repetition can you find? Do you think this usage of language makes the poem stronger or more interesting? Why or why not?

■ **Sobre el autor:** Antonio Machado (1875–1939) nació en Sevilla, España, de padres progresistas. Su padre fue por un tiempo abogado en Puerto Rico, pero al morir este (*the latter*), Machado volvió a Sevilla a cursar estudios de Filosofia y Letras. A los 24 años viajó a París, donde conoció a muchos de los grandes autores europeos. En esa capital escribió muchos de los poemas de su primera colección, *Soledades* (*Solitudes*). A principios del nuevo siglo, con su hermano Manuel, forma parte de un famoso movimiento literario que vino a llamarse la "Generación del 98", ya que muchos de sus miembros habían empezado a publicar sus primeras obras (*works*) en ese año. La poesía de Machado es seria y dramática y tiene como su tema el ambiente de la región de Castilla, en España. Machado tuvo que salir de su amada patria (*beloved homeland*) durante la Guerra Civil Española y murió en Colliure, Francia, después de haber cruzado a pie las montañas que dividen los dos países. El siguiente poema (Rima) es de su colección *Proverbios y cantares*.

▲ *Antonio Machado*

MULTIMEDIA: Internet

Have students search the Internet for Machado poetry and biographical information.

LECTURA

Suggestion
Do the *Estrategia* in class before reading the poem.

Notes

■ Machado was a close friend of the Nicaraguan poet Rubén Darío (*Capítulo 3*).

■ Machado also knew members of the Generation of '98, such as Miguel de Unamuno, Ramón del Valle-Inclán, and Juan Ramón Jiménez. Today, Machado is probably the most widely read member of this group.

Suggestions

■ Bring excerpts from other poems by Machado or by other Generation of '98 poets. Have students read the verses together.

■ Joan Manuel Serrat put some of Antonio Machado's poetry to music. Some music clips from his recordings are available online. Information for purchasing discs is also available online. If possible, play a song that Serrat recorded. Distribute the lyrics so that the students can follow along. The verses printed in this textbook appear in the song "Cantares" on the CD called *Dedicado a Antonio Machado*.

XXIX

Caminante,[a] son tus huellas[b]
el camino, y nada más;
caminante, no hay camino:
se hace camino al andar.[c]
Al andar se hace el camino,
y al volver la vista atrás[d]
se ve la senda[e] que nunca
se ha de volver a pisar.[f]
Caminante, no hay camino,
sino estelas[g] en la mar.

[a]*Traveler (person who walks)*   [b]*footprints; traces*   [c]*al... as you walk*   [d]*al... when you look back*
[e]*path*   [f]*nunca... will never be tread upon again*   [g]*wakes (of boats)*

Comprensión

Paso 1. Conteste las siguientes preguntas.

1. ¿A quién se dirige el poeta?
2. ¿Por qué dice el autor que «no hay camino»?
3. ¿Hay algún momento en que sí hay camino?
4. ¿Qué se ve al mirar atrás? ¿Por qué?

Paso 2. Interpretación. Con un compañero / una compañera, conteste las siguientes preguntas.

1. ¿Creen Uds. que el caminante del poema es verdaderamente una persona que va de paseo? Si no lo es, ¿qué clase de camino sigue esta persona?
2. En este poema, ¿se trata de un camino por un lugar sin carreteras? Y si no, ¿qué experiencia es la que se describe aquí?
3. En el contexto de este poema, ¿qué son las estelas del mar?

ESCRITURA

A. Caminante. Imagine que Ud. es consejero/a y va a usar el poema de Machado para introducirle sus consejos a un estudiante que está para graduarse. Escriba sus consejos usando el poema como punto de partida y elaborando el significado y/o la importancia de algunos versos del poema.

B. La «Generación del 98». La «Generación del 98» a la que perteneció Machado (*to which Machado belonged*) fue uno de los movimientos literarios españoles más importantes del último milenio. Use los recursos del Internet y de la biblioteca para investigar este movimiento. Escoja uno de los siguientes temas y escriba un breve informe.

1. Los poetas y novelistas de la «Generación del 98» y sus ideas sobre la literatura
2. Un poeta de este grupo y su obra
3. Un poema o un grupo de poemas (puede describir un poema o comparar las ideas de dos o más poemas)

ESCRITURA

Suggestion
If you prefer that your students do a journal activity, see *Mi diario* in this chapter of the Workbook.

Extension
Here are some other specific topics that the students can choose for their essays. The different fields of study—history, philosophy, and criticism—can broaden students' understanding of the Generation of '98.

4. *El nombre «Generación del 98»: el contexto histórico en España en 1898*
5. *La filosofía de Miguel de Unamuno*
6. *La filosofía de José Ortega y Gasset*
7. *Los poetas latinoamericanos a finales del siglo XX*

Encourage students to share their papers with the rest of the class.

Glossary of Grammatical Terms

ADJECTIVE A word that describes a noun or pronoun.

una casa **grande**
*a **big** house*

Ella es **inteligente.**
*She is **smart.***

Demonstrative adjective An adjective that points out a particular noun.

este chico, **esos** libros, **aquellas** personas
***this** boy, **those** books, **those** people (over there)*

Interrogative adjective An adjective used to form questions.

¿**Qué** cuaderno?
***Which** notebook?*

¿**Cuáles** son los carteles que buscas?
***What (Which)** posters are you looking for?*

Possessive adjective (unstressed) An adjective that indicates possession or a special relationship.

sus coches
***their** cars*

mi hermana
***my** sister*

Possessive adjective (stressed) An adjective that more emphatically describes possession.

Es **una** amiga **mía.**
*She's **my** friend. / She's a friend **of mine.***

Es **un** coche **suyo.**
*It's **her** car. / It's a car **of hers.***

ADVERB A word that describes an adjective, a verb, or another adverb.

Él es **muy** alto.
*He is **very** tall.*

Ella escribe **bien.**
*She writes **well.***

Van **demasiado** rápido.
*They are going **too** quickly.*

ARTICLE A determiner that sets off a noun.
Definite article An article that indicates a specific noun.

el país
***the** country*

la silla
***the** chair*

las mujeres
***the** women*

Indefinite article An article that indicates an unspecified noun.

un chico
***a** boy*

una ciudad
***a** city*

unas zanahorias
*(**some**) carrots*

CLAUSE A construction that contains a subject and a verb.

Main (Independent) clause A clause that can stand on its own because it expresses a complete thought.

Busco una muchacha.
I'm looking for a girl.

Si yo fuera rica, **me compraría una casa.**
If I were rich, **I would buy a house.**

Subordinate (Dependent) clause A clause that cannot stand on its own because it does not express a complete thought.

Busco a la muchacha **que juega al tenis.**
I'm looking for the girl **who plays tennis.**

Si yo fuera rico, me compraría una casa.
If I were rich, I would buy a house.

COMPARATIVE The form of adjectives and adverbs used to compare two nouns or actions.

Luis es **menos hablador** que Julián.
Luis is **less talkative** *than Julián.*
Él corre **más rápido** que Julián.
He runs **faster** *than Julián.*

CONJUGATION The different forms of a verb for a particular tense or mood. A present indicative conjugation:

(yo) hablo	(nosotros/as) hablamos
(tú) hablas	(vosotros/as) habláis
(Ud., él/ella) habla	(Uds., ellos/as) hablan
I speak	*we speak*
you (fam. sing.) speak	*you (fam. pl.) speak*
you (form. sing.) speak	*you (pl. fam. & form.) speak*
he/she speaks	*they speak*

CONJUNCTION An expression that connects words, phrases, or clauses.

Cristóbal **y** Diana
Cristóbal **and** *Diana*

Hace frío, **pero** hace buen tiempo.
It's cold, **but** *it's nice out.*

DIRECT OBJECT The noun or pronoun that receives the action of a verb.

Veo **la caja.**
I see **the box.**

La veo.
I see **it.**

GENDER A grammatical category of words. In Spanish, there are two genders: masculine and feminine. Here are a few examples.

	MASCULINE	FEMININE
ARTICLES AND NOUNS:	**el** disco compacto	**la** cinta
PRONOUNS:	**él**	**ella**
ADJECTIVES:	bonit**o**, list**o**	bonit**a**, list**a**
PAST PARTICIPLES:	El informe está **escrito.**	La composición está **escrita.**

IMPERATIVE *See* Mood.

IMPERFECT (*IMPERFECTO*) In Spanish, a verb tense that expresses a past action with no specific beginning or ending.

Nadábamos con frecuencia.
We **used to swim** *often.*

IMPERSONAL CONSTRUCTION One that contains a third person singular verb but no specific subject in Spanish. The subject of English impersonal constructions is generally *it*.	**Es importante** que… *It is important that . . .* **Es necesario** que… *It is necessary that . . .*
INDICATIVE *See* Mood.	
INDIRECT OBJECT The noun or pronoun that indicates for whom or to whom an action is performed. In Spanish, the indirect object pronoun must always be included. The noun that the pronoun stands for may be included for emphasis or clarification.	Marcos **le** da el suéter a **Raquel**. / Marcos **le** da el suéter. *Marcos gives the sweater **to Raquel**. / Marcos gives **her** the sweater.*
INFINITIVE The form of a verb introduced in English by *to: to play, to sell, to come.* In Spanish dictionaries, the infinitive form of the verb appears as the main entry.	Luisa va a **comprar** un periódico. *Luisa is going **to buy** a newspaper.*
MOOD A set of categories for verbs indicating the attitude of the speaker toward what he or she is saying.	
Imperative mood A verb form expressing a command.	¡**Ten** cuidado! *Be careful!*
Indicative mood A verb form denoting actions or states considered facts.	**Voy** a la biblioteca. *I am going to the library.*
Subjunctive mood A verb form, uncommon in English, used primarily in subordinate clauses after expressions of desire, doubt, or emotion. Spanish constructions with the subjunctive have many possible English equivalents.	Quiero que **vayas** inmediatamente. *I want you **to go** immediately.*
NOUN A word that denotes a person, place, thing, or idea. Proper nouns are capitalized names.	**abogado, ciudad, periódico, libertad, Luisa** *lawyer, city, newspaper, freedom, Luisa*
NUMBER	
Cardinal number A number that expresses an amount.	**una** silla, **tres** estudiantes *one chair, three students*
Ordinal number A number that indicates position in a series.	la **primera** silla, el **tercer** estudiante *the **first** chair, the **third** student*
PAST PARTICIPLE The form of a verb used in compound tenses (*see* Perfect Tenses). Used with forms of *to have* or *to be* in English and with **ser, estar,** or **haber** in Spanish.	**comido, terminado, perdido** *eaten, finished, lost*

PERFECT TENSES   Compound tenses that combine the auxiliary verb **haber** with a past participle.

Present perfect indicative   This form uses a present indicative form of **haber.** The use of the Spanish present perfect generally parallels that of the English present perfect.

No **he viajado** nunca a México.
*I've never **traveled** to Mexico.*

Past perfect indicative   This form uses **haber** in the imperfect tense to talk about something that had or had not been done before a given time in the past.

Antes de 2001, **no había estudiado** español.
*Before 2001, **I hadn't studied** Spanish.*

Present perfect subjunctive   This form uses the present subjunctive of **haber** to express a present perfect action when the subjunctive is required.

¡Ojalá que Marisa **haya llegado** a su destino!
*I hope Marisa **has arrived** at her destination!*

PERSON   The form of a pronoun or verb that indicates the person involved in an action.

	SINGULAR	PLURAL
FIRST PERSON	*I* / yo	*we* / nosotros/as
SECOND PERSON	*you* / tú, Ud.	*you* / vosotros/as, Uds.
THIRD PERSON	*he, she* / él, ella	*they* / ellos, ellas

PREPOSITION   A word or phrase that specifies the relationship of one word (usually a noun or pronoun) to another. The relationship is usually spatial or temporal.

a la escuela
to school

cerca de la biblioteca
near the library

con él
with him

antes de la medianoche
before midnight

PRETERITE (*PRETÉRITO*)   In Spanish, a verb tense that expresses a past action with a specific beginning and ending.

Salí para Roma el jueves.
I left for Rome on Thursday.

PRONOUN   A word that refers to a person (I, you) or that is used in place of one or more nouns.

Demonstrative pronoun   A pronoun that singles out a particular person or thing.

Aquí están dos libros. **Este** es interesante, pero **ese** es aburrido.
*Here are two books. **This one** is interesting, but **that one** is boring.*

Interrogative pronoun   A pronoun used to ask a question.

¿**Quién** es él?   ¿**Qué** prefieres?
Who is he?   *What do you prefer?*

Object pronoun   A pronoun that replaces a direct object noun or an indirect object noun. Both direct and indirect object pronouns can be used together in the same sentence. However, when the pronoun **le** is used with **lo** or **la,** it changes to **se.**

Veo a **Alejandro. Lo** veo.
*I see Alejandro. I see **him**.*

Le doy el libro **(a Juana).**
*I give the book **to Juana**.*

Se lo doy **(a ella).**
*I give **it** to **her**.*

Reflexive pronoun A pronoun that represents the same person as the subject of the verb.

Me miro en el espejo.
*I look at **myself** in the mirror.*

Relative pronoun A pronoun that introduces a dependent clause and denotes a noun already mentioned.

El hombre con **quien** hablaba era mi vecino.
*The man with **whom** I was talking was my neighbor.*

Aquí está el bolígrafo **que** buscas.
*Here is the pen (**that**) you are looking for.*

Subject pronoun A pronoun representing the person or thing performing the action of a verb.

Lucas y Julia juegan al tenis.
***Lucas and Julia** are playing tennis.*

Ellos juegan al tenis.
***They** are playing tennis.*

SUBJECT The word(s) denoting the person, place, or thing performing an action or existing in a state.

Sara trabaja aquí.
***Sara** works here.*

¡**Buenos Aires** es una ciudad magnífica!
***Buenos Aires** is a great city!*

Mis **libros** y mi **computadora** están allí.
*My **books** and my **computer** are over there.*

SUBJUNCTIVE *See* Mood.

SUPERLATIVE The form of adjectives or adverbs used to compare three or more nouns or actions. In English, the superlative is marked by *most, least,* or *-est.*

Escogí el vestido **más caro.**
*I chose **the most expensive** dress.*

Ana es la persona **menos habladora** que conozco.
*Ana is **the least talkative** person I know.*

TENSE The form of a verb indicating time: present, past, or future.

Raúl **era, es** y siempre **será** mi mejor amigo.
*Raúl **was, is,** and always **will be** my best friend.*

VERB A word that reports an action or state.

Ella **llegó.**
*She **arrived.***

Ella **estaba** cansada.
*She **was** tired.*

Auxiliary verb A verb in conjuction with a participle to convey distinctions of tense and mood. In Spanish, this auxiliary verb is **haber.**

Han viajado por todas partes del mundo.
*They **have** traveled everywhere in the world.*

Reflexive verb A verb whose subject and object are the same.

Él **se corta** la cara cuando **se afeita.**
*He **cuts himself** when he **shaves** (**himself**).*

Using Adjectives as Nouns

Nominalization means using an adjective as a noun. In Spanish, adjectives can be nominalized in a number of ways, all of which involve dropping the noun that accompanies the adjective, then using the adjective in combination with an article or other word. One kind of adjective, the demonstrative, can simply be used alone. In most cases, these usages parallel those of English, although the English equivalent may be phrased differently from the Spanish.

Article + Adjective

Simply omit the noun from an *article + noun + adjective* phrase.

> el **libro** azul → **el azul** (*the blue one*)
> la **hermana** casada → **la casada** (*the married one*)
> el **señor** mexicano → **el mexicano** (*the Mexican one*)
> los **pantalones** baratos → **los baratos** (*the inexpensive ones*)

You can also drop the first noun in an *article + noun + de + noun* phrase.

> la **casa** de Julio → **la de Julio** (*Julio's*)
> los **coches** del Sr. Martínez → **los del Sr. Martínez** (*Mr. Martínez's*)

In both cases, the construction is used to refer to a noun that has already been mentioned. The English equivalent uses *one* or *ones,* or a possessive without the noun.

> —¿Necesitas el libro grande?
> —No. Necesito **el pequeño.**
> *Do you need the big book?*
> *No. I need the small one.*

> —¿Usamos el coche de Ernesto?
> —No. Usemos **el de Ana.**
> *Shall we use Ernesto's car?*
> *No. Let's use Ana's.*

Note that in the preceding examples the noun is mentioned in the first part of the exchange (**libro, coche**) but not in the response or rejoinder.

Note also that a demonstrative can be used to nominalize an adjective: **este rojo** (*this red one*), **esos azules** (*those blue ones*).

Lo + Adjective

As seen in **Capítulo 10, lo** combines with the masculine singular form of an adjective to describe general qualities or characteristics. The English equivalent is expressed with words like *part* or *thing.*

> lo mejor   *the best thing (part), what's best*
> lo mismo   *the same thing*
> lo cómico   *the funny thing (part), what's funny*

Article + Stressed Possessive Adjective

The stressed possessive adjectives—but not the unstressed possessives—can be used as possessive pronouns: **la maleta suya → la suya.** The article and the possessive form agree in gender and number with the noun to which they refer.

> Este es mi **banco.** ¿Dónde está **el suyo**?
> *This is my bank. Where is yours?*

> Sus **bebidas** están preparadas; **las nuestras,** no.
> *Their drinks are ready; ours aren't.*

> No es **la maleta** de Juan; es **la mía.**
> *It isn't Juan's suitcase; it's mine.*

Note that the definite article is frequently omitted after forms of **ser: ¿Esa maleta? Es suya.**

Demonstrative Pronouns

The demonstrative adjective can be used alone, without a noun. An accent mark can be added to the demonstrative pronoun to distinguish it from the demonstrative adjectives (**este, ese, aquel**).

> Necesito este diccionario y **ese (ése).**
> *I need this dictionary and that one.*

> Estas señoras y **aquellas (aquéllas)** son las hermanas de Sara, ¿no?
> *These women and those (over there) are Sara's sisters, aren't they?*

It is acceptable in modern Spanish, per the **Real Academia Española,** to omit the accent on demonstrative pronouns when context makes the meaning clear and no ambiguity is possible.

Additional Perfect Forms (Indicative and Subjunctive)

Some indicative verb tenses have corresponding perfect forms in the indicative and subjunctive moods. Here is the present tense system.

el presente:	yo hablo, como, pongo
el presente perfecto:	yo he hablado, comido, puesto
el presente perfecto de subjuntivo:	yo haya hablado, comido, puesto

Other indicative forms that you have learned also have corresponding perfect indicative and subjunctive forms. Here are the most important ones, along with examples of their use. In each case, the tense or mood is formed with the appropriate form of **haber.**

El pluscuamperfecto del subjuntivo

yo:	hubiera hablado, comido, vivido, *and so on.*
tú:	hubieras hablado, comido, vivido, *and so on.*
Ud./él/ella:	hubiera hablado, comido, vivido, *and so on.*
nosotros:	hubiéramos hablado, comido, vivido, *and so on.*
vosotros:	hubierais hablado, comido, vivido, *and so on.*
Uds./ellos/ellas:	hubieran hablado, comido, vivido, *and so on.*

These forms correspond to **el presente perfecto de indicativo (Capítulo 14).** These forms are most frequently used in **si** clause sentences, along with the conditional perfect. See examples below.

El futuro perfecto

yo:	habré hablado, comido, vivido, *and so on.*
tú:	habrás hablado, comido, vivido, *and so on.*
Ud./él/ella:	habrá hablado, comido, vivido, *and so on.*
nosotros:	habremos hablado, comido, vivido, *and so on.*
vosotros:	habréis hablado, comido, vivido, *and so on.*
Uds./ellos/ellas:	habrán hablado, comido, vivido, *and so on.*

These forms correspond to **el futuro (Capítulo 16)** and are most frequently used to tell what *will have already happened* at some point in the future. (In contrast, the future is used to tell what *will happen.*)

Mañana **hablaré** con Miguel.
I'll speak with Miguel tomorrow.

Para las tres, ya **habré hablado** con Miguel.
By 3:00, I'll already have spoken to Miguel.

El año que viene **visitaremos** a los nietos.
We'll visit our grandchildren next year.

Para las Navidades, ya **habremos visitado** a los nietos.
We'll already have visited our grandchildren by Christmas.

El condicional perfecto

yo:	habría hablado, comido, vivido, *and so on.*
tú:	habrías hablado, comido, vivido, *and so on.*
Ud./él/ella:	habría hablado, comido, vivido, *and so on.*
nosotros:	habríamos hablado, comido, vivido, *and so on.*
vosotros:	habríais hablado, comido, vivido, *and so on.*
Uds./ellos/ellas:	habrían hablado, comido, vivido, *and so on.*

These forms correspond to **el condicional (Capítulo 18).** These forms are frequently used to tell what *would have happened* at some point in the past. (In contrast, the conditional tells what one *would do.*)

Yo **hablaría** con Miguel.
I would speak with Miguel (if I were you, at some point in the future).

Yo **habría hablado** con Miguel.
I would have spoken with Miguel (if I had been you, at some point in the past).

Si Clause: Sentences About the Past

You have learned (**Capítulo 18**) to use the past sub-junctive and conditional to speculate about the present in **si** clause sentences: what *would happen* if a particular event *were* (or *were not*) to occur.

> Si **tuviera** el tiempo, **aprendería** francés.
> *If I had the time, I would learn French (in the present or at some point in the future).*

The perfect forms of the past subjunctive and the conditional are used to speculate about the past: what *would have happened* if a particular event *had* (or *had not*) occurred.

> En la escuela superior, si **hubiera tenido** el tiempo, **habría aprendido** francés.
> *In high school, if I had had the time, I would have learned French.*

VERBS

A. Regular Verbs: Simple Tenses

Infinitive Present Participle Past Participle	INDICATIVE					SUBJUNCTIVE		IMPERATIVE
	Present	Imperfect	Preterite	Future	Conditional	Present	Imperfect	
hablar hablando hablado	hablo hablas habla hablamos habláis hablan	hablaba hablabas hablaba hablábamos hablabais hablaban	hablé hablaste habló hablamos hablasteis hablaron	hablaré hablarás hablará hablaremos hablaréis hablarán	hablaría hablarías hablaría hablaríamos hablaríais hablarían	hable hables hable hablemos habléis hablen	hablara hablaras hablara habláramos hablarais hablaran	habla tú, no hables hable Ud. hablemos hablen
comer comiendo comido	como comes come comemos coméis comen	comía comías comía comíamos comíais comían	comí comiste comió comimos comisteis comieron	comeré comerás comerá comeremos comeréis comerán	comería comerías comería comeríamos comeríais comerían	coma comas coma comamos comáis coman	comiera comieras comiera comiéramos comierais comieran	come tú, no comas coma Ud. comamos coman
vivir viviendo vivido	vivo vives vive vivimos vivís viven	vivía vivías vivía vivíamos vivíais vivían	viví viviste vivió vivimos vivisteis vivieron	viviré vivirás vivirá viviremos viviréis vivirán	viviría vivirías viviría viviríamos viviríais vivirían	viva vivas viva vivamos viváis vivan	viviera vivieras viviera viviéramos vivierais vivieran	vive tú, no vivas viva Ud. vivamos vivan

B. Regular Verbs: Perfect Tenses

INDICATIVE										SUBJUNCTIVE			
Present Perfect		Past Perfect		Preterite Perfect		Future Perfect		Conditional Perfect		Present Perfect		Past Perfect	
he	hablado	había	hablado	hube	hablado	habré	hablado	habría	hablado	haya	hablado	hubiera	hablado
has	comido	habías	comido	hubiste	comido	habrás	comido	habrías	comido	hayas	comido	hubieras	comido
ha	vivido	había	vivido	hubo	vivido	habrá	vivido	habría	vivido	haya	vivido	hubiera	vivido
hemos		habíamos		hubimos		habremos		habríamos		hayamos		hubiéramos	
habéis		habíais		hubisteis		habréis		habríais		hayáis		hubierais	
han		habían		hubieron		habrán		habrían		hayan		hubieran	

C. Irregular Verbs

Infinitive / Present Participle / Past Participle	INDICATIVE					SUBJUNCTIVE		IMPERATIVE
	Present	Imperfect	Preterite	Future	Conditional	Present	Imperfect	
andar andando andado	ando andas anda andamos andáis andan	andaba andabas andaba andábamos andabais andaban	anduve anduviste anduvo anduvimos anduvisteis anduvieron	andaré andarás andará andaremos andaréis andarán	andaría andarías andaría andaríamos andaríais andarían	ande andes ande andemos andéis anden	anduviera anduvieras anduviera anduviéramos anduvierais anduvieran	anda tú, no andes ande Ud. andemos anden
caer cayendo caído	caigo caes cae caemos caéis caen	caía caías caía caíamos caíais caían	caí caíste cayó caímos caísteis cayeron	caeré caerás caerá caeremos caeréis caerán	caería caerías caería caeríamos caeríais caerían	caiga caigas caiga caigamos caigáis caigan	cayera cayeras cayera cayéramos cayerais cayeran	cae tú, no caigas caiga Ud. caigamos caigan
dar dando dado	doy das da damos dais dan	daba dabas daba dábamos dabais daban	di diste dio dimos disteis dieron	daré darás dará daremos daréis darán	daría darías daría daríamos daríais darían	dé des dé demos deis den	diera dieras diera diéramos dierais dieran	da tú, no des dé Ud. demos den

C. Irregular Verbs (continued)

Infinitive / Present Participle / Past Participle	INDICATIVE Present	Imperfect	Preterite	Future	Conditional	SUBJUNCTIVE Present	Imperfect	IMPERATIVE
decir diciendo dicho	digo dices dice decimos decís dicen	decía decías decía decíamos decíais decían	dije dijiste dijo dijimos dijisteis dijeron	diré dirás dirá diremos diréis dirán	diría dirías diría diríamos diríais dirían	diga digas diga digamos digáis digan	dijera dijeras dijera dijéramos dijerais dijeran	di tú, no digas diga Ud. digamos digan
estar estando estado	estoy estás está estamos estáis están	estaba estabas estaba estábamos estabais estaban	estuve estuviste estuvo estuvimos estuvisteis estuvieron	estaré estarás estará estaremos estaréis estarán	estaría estarías estaría estaríamos estaríais estarían	esté estés esté estemos estéis estén	estuviera estuvieras estuviera estuviéramos estuvierais estuviera	está tú, no estés esté Ud. estemos estén
haber habiendo habido	he has ha hemos habéis han	había habías había habíamos habíais habían	hube hubiste hubo hubimos hubisteis hubieron	habré habrás habrá habremos habréis habrán	habría habrías habría habríamos habríais habrían	haya hayas haya hayamos hayáis hayan	hubiera hubieras hubiera hubiéramos hubierais hubieran	
hacer haciendo hecho	hago haces hace hacemos hacéis hacen	hacía hacías hacía hacíamos hacíais hacían	hice hiciste hizo hicimos hicisteis hicieron	haré harás hará haremos haréis harán	haría harías haría haríamos haríais harían	haga hagas haga hagamos hagáis hagan	hiciera hicieras hiciera hiciéramos hicierais hicieran	haz tú, no hagas haga Ud. hagamos hagan
ir yendo ido	voy vas va vamos vais van	iba ibas iba íbamos ibais iban	fui fuiste fue fuimos fuisteis fueron	iré irás irá iremos iréis irán	iría irías iría iríamos iríais irían	vaya vayas vaya vayamos vayáis vayan	fuera fueras fuera fuéramos fuerais fueran	ve tú, no vayas vaya Ud. vayamos vayan

C. Irregular Verbs (continued)

Infinitive Present Participle Past Participle	INDICATIVE						SUBJUNCTIVE		IMPERATIVE
	Present	Imperfect	Preterite	Future	Conditional		Present	Imperfect	

oír
oyendo
oído
	oigo
	oyes
	oye
	oímos
	oís
	oyen
		oía
		oías
		oía
		oíamos
		oíais
		oían
			oí
			oíste
			oyó
			oímos
			oísteis
			oyeron
				oiré
				oirás
				oirá
				oiremos
				oiréis
				oirán
					oiría
					oirías
					oiría
					oiríamos
					oiríais
					oirían
							oiga
							oigas
							oiga
							oigamos
							oigáis
							oigan
								oyera
								oyeras
								oyera
								oyéramos
								oyerais
								oyeran
									oye tú, no
									  oigas
									  oiga Ud.
									  oigamos
									  oigan

poder pudiendo podido	puedo puedes puede podemos podéis pueden	podía podías podía podíamos podíais podían	pude pudiste pudo pudimos pudisteis pudieron	podré podrás podrá podremos podréis podrán	podría podrías podría podríamos podríais podrían		pueda puedas pueda podamos podáis puedan	pudiera pudieras pudiera pudiéramos pudierais pudieran	

poner
poniendo
puesto
	pongo
	pones
	pone
	ponemos
	ponéis
	ponen
		ponía
		ponías
		ponía
		poníamos
		poníais
		ponían
			puse
			pusiste
			puso
			pusimos
			pusisteis
			pusieron
				pondré
				pondrás
				pondrá
				pondremos
				pondréis
				pondrán
					pondría
					pondrías
					pondría
					pondríamos
					pondríais
					pondrían
							ponga
							pongas
							ponga
							pongamos
							pongáis
							pongan
								pusiera
								pusieras
								pusiera
								pusiéramos
								pusierais
								pusieran
									pon tú, no
									  pongas
									  ponga Ud.
									  pongamos
									  pongan

querer
queriendo
querido
	quiero
	quieres
	quiere
	queremos
	queréis
	quieren
		quería
		querías
		quería
		queríamos
		queríais
		querían
			quise
			quisiste
			quiso
			quisimos
			quisisteis
			quisieron
				querré
				querrás
				querrá
				querremos
				querréis
				querrán
					querría
					querrías
					querría
					querríamos
					querríais
					querrían
							quiera
							quieras
							quiera
							queramos
							queráis
							quieran
								quisiera
								quisieras
								quisiera
								quisiéramos
								quisierais
								quisieran
									quiere tú, no
									  quieras
									  quiera Ud.
									  queramos
									  quieran

saber
sabiendo
sabido
	sé
	sabes
	sabe
	sabemos
	sabéis
	saben
		sabía
		sabías
		sabía
		sabíamos
		sabíais
		sabían
			supe
			supiste
			supo
			supimos
			supisteis
			supieron
				sabré
				sabrás
				sabrá
				sabremos
				sabréis
				sabrán
					sabría
					sabrías
					sabría
					sabríamos
					sabríais
					sabrían
							sepa
							sepas
							sepa
							sepamos
							sepáis
							sepan
								supiera
								supieras
								supiera
								supiéramos
								supierais
								supieran
									sabe tú, no
									  sepas
									  sepa Ud.
									  sepamos
									  sepan

C. Irregular Verbs (continued)

Infinitive / Present Participle / Past Participle	INDICATIVE					SUBJUNCTIVE		IMPERATIVE
	Present	Imperfect	Preterite	Future	Conditional	Present	Imperfect	
salir / saliendo / salido	salgo sales sale salimos salís salen	salía salías salía salíamos salíais salían	salí saliste salió salimos salisteis salieron	saldré saldrás saldrá saldremos saldréis saldrán	saldría saldrías saldría saldríamos saldríais saldrían	salga salgas salga salgamos salgáis salgan	saliera salieras saliera saliéramos salierais salieran	sal tú, no salgas salga Ud. salgamos salgan
ser / siendo / sido	soy eres es somos sois son	era eras era éramos erais eran	fui fuiste fue fuimos fuisteis fueron	seré serás será seremos seréis serán	sería serías sería seríamos seríais serían	sea seas sea seamos seáis sean	fuera fueras fuera fuéramos fuerais fueran	sé tú, no seas sea Ud. seamos sean
tener / teniendo / tenido	tengo tienes tiene tenemos tenéis tienen	tenía tenías tenía teníamos teníais tenían	tuve tuviste tuvo tuvimos tuvisteis tuvieron	tendré tendrás tendrá tendremos tendréis tendrán	tendría tendrías tendría tendríamos tendríais tendrían	tenga tengas tenga tengamos tengáis tengan	tuviera tuvieras tuviera tuviéramos tuvierais tuvieran	ten tú, no tengas tenga Ud. tengamos tengan
traer / trayendo / traído	traigo traes trae traemos traéis traen	traía traías traía traíamos traíais traían	traje trajiste trajo trajimos trajisteis trajeron	traeré traerás traerá traeremos traeréis traerán	traería traerías traería traeríamos traeríais traerían	traiga traigas traiga traigamos traigáis traigan	trajera trajeras trajera trajéramos trajerais trajeran	trae tú, no traigas traiga Ud. traigamos traigan
venir / viniendo / venido	vengo vienes viene venimos venís vienen	venía venías venía veníamos veníais venían	vine viniste vino vinimos vinisteis vinieron	vendré vendrás vendrá vendremos vendréis vendrán	vendría vendrías vendría vendríamos vendríais vendrían	venga vengas venga vengamos vengáis vengan	viniera vinieras viniera viniéramos vinierais vinieran	ven tú, no vengas venga Ud. vengamos vengan

C. Irregular Verbs (continued)

Infinitive Present Participle Past Participle	INDICATIVE					SUBJUNCTIVE		IMPERATIVE
	Present	Imperfect	Preterite	Future	Conditional	Present	Imperfect	
ver viendo visto	veo ves ve vemos veis ven	veía veías veía veíamos veíais veían	vi viste vio vimos visteis vieron	veré verás verá veremos veréis verán	vería verías vería veríamos veríais verían	vea veas vea veamos veáis vean	viera vieras viera viéramos vierais vieran	ve tú, no veas vea Ud. veamos vean

D. Stem-Changing and Spelling Change Verbs

Infinitive Present Participle Past Participle	INDICATIVE					SUBJUNCTIVE		IMPERATIVE
	Present	Imperfect	Preterite	Future	Conditional	Present	Imperfect	
pensar (ie) pensando pensado	pienso piensas piensa pensamos pensáis piensan	pensaba pensabas pensaba pensábamos pensabais pensaban	pensé pensaste pensó pensamos pensasteis pensaron	pensaré pensarás pensará pensaremos pensaréis pensarán	pensaría pensarías pensaría pensaríamos pensaríais pensarían	piense pienses piense pensemos penséis piensen	pensara pensaras pensara pensáramos pensarais pensaran	piensa tú, no pienses piense Ud. pensemos piensen
volver (ue) volviendo vuelto	vuelvo vuelves vuelve volvemos volvéis vuelven	volvía volvías volvía volvíamos volvíais volvían	volví volviste volvió volvimos volvisteis volvieron	volveré volverás volverá volveremos volveréis volverán	volvería volverías volvería volveríamos volveríais volverían	vuelva vuelvas vuelva volvamos volváis vuelvan	volviera volvieras volviera volviéramos volvierais volvieran	vuelve tú, no vuelvas vuelva Ud. volvamos vuelvan
dormir (ue, u) durmiendo dormido	duermo duermes duerme dormimos dormís duermen	dormía dormías dormía dormíamos dormíais dormían	dormí dormiste durmió dormimos dormisteis durmieron	dormiré dormirás dormirá dormiremos dormiréis dormirán	dormiría dormirías dormiría dormiríamos dormiríais dormirían	duerma duermas duerma durmamos durmáis duerman	durmiera durmieras durmiera durmiéramos durmierais durmieran	duerme tú, no duermas duerma Ud. durmamos duerman

D. Stem-Changing and Spelling Change Verbs (continued)

Infinitive Present Participle Past Participle	INDICATIVE					SUBJUNCTIVE		IMPERATIVE
	Present	Imperfect	Preterite	Future	Conditional	Present	Imperfect	
sentir (ie, i) sintiendo sentido	siento sientes siente sentimos sentís sienten	sentía sentías sentía sentíamos sentíais sentían	sentí sentiste sintió sentimos sentisteis sintieron	sentiré sentirás sentirá sentiremos sentiréis sentirán	sentiría sentirías sentiría sentiríamos sentiríais sentirían	sienta sientas sienta sintamos sintáis sientan	sintiera sintieras sintiera sintiéramos sintierais sintieran	siente tú, no sientas sienta Ud. sintamos sientan
pedir (i, i) pidiendo pedido	pido pides pide pedimos pedís piden	pedía pedías pedía pedíamos pedíais pedían	pedí pediste pidió pedimos pedisteis pidieron	pediré pedirás pedirá pediremos pediréis pedirán	pediría pedirías pediría pediríamos pediríais pedirían	pida pidas pida pidamos pidáis pidan	pidiera pidieras pidiera pidiéramos pidierais pidieran	pide tú, no pidas pida Ud. pidamos pidan
reír (i, i) riendo reído	río ríes ríe reímos reís ríen	reía reías reía reíamos reíais reían	reí reíste rió reímos reísteis rieron	reiré reirás reirá reiremos reiréis reirán	reiría reirías reiría reiríamos reiríais reirían	ría rías ría riamos riáis rían	riera rieras riera riéramos rierais rieran	ríe tú, no rías ría Ud. riamos rían
seguir (i, i) (g) siguiendo seguido	sigo sigues sigue seguimos seguís siguen	seguía seguías seguía seguíamos seguíais seguían	seguí seguiste siguió seguimos seguisteis siguieron	seguiré seguirás seguirá seguiremos seguiréis seguirán	seguiría seguirías seguiría seguiríamos seguiríais seguirían	siga sigas siga sigamos sigáis sigan	siguiera siguieras siguiera siguiéramos siguierais siguieran	sigue tú, no sigas siga Ud. sigamos sigan
construir (y) construyendo construido	construyo construyes construye construimos construís construyen	construía construías construía construíamos construíais construían	construí construiste construyó construimos construisteis construyeron	construiré construirás construirá construiremos construiréis construirán	construiría construirías construiría construiríamos construiríais construirían	construya construyas construya construyamos construyáis construyan	construyera construyeras construyera construyéramos construyerais construyeran	construye tú, no construyas construya Ud. construyamos construyan

D. Stem-Changing and Spelling Change Verbs (continued)

Infinitive Present Participle Past Participle	INDICATIVE					SUBJUNCTIVE		IMPERATIVE
	Present	Imperfect	Preterite	Future	Conditional	Present	Imperfect	
producir (zc) produciendo producido	produzco produces produce producimos producís producen	producía producías producía producíamos producíais producían	produje produjiste produjo produjimos produjisteis produjeron	produciré producirás producirá produciremos produciréis producirán	produciría producirías produciría produciríamos produciríais producirían	produzca produzcas produzca produzcamos produzcáis produzcan	produjera produjeras produjera produjéramos produjerais produjeran	produce tú, no produzcas produzca Ud. produzcamos produzcan

Answers to ¿*Recuerda Ud.?* Activities

Capítulo 2
GRAMÁTICA 6 1. Soy estudiante. 2. Soy… Sí, (No, no) soy una persona sentimental/inteligente/paciente/elegante. 3. Es (Son) la(s)… (La clase de español) Es a la(s)… 4. Es un edificio.
GRAMÁTICA 8 1. nosotros 2. tú 3. vosotros 4. ellos/as, Uds. 5. yo 6. él/ella, Ud.

Capítulo 4
GRAMÁTICA 13 quiero, quieres, quiere, quieren; puedo, puedes, puede, pueden

Capítulo 5
GRAMÁTICA 16 ¿**Cómo está Ud.?** asks how someone is feeling at a particular moment. ¿**Cómo es Ud.?** asks about someone's nature, that is, what he or she is like as a person.

Capítulo 6
GRAMÁTICA 20 1. salgo 2. tengo 3. conozco 4. pido 5. hago 6. duermo 7. siento 8. traigo

Capítulo 7
GRAMÁTICA 21 *Direct object pronouns are underscored.* —Roberto, ¿tienes los boletos? / —No, todavía no los (*expresses* **boletos**) tengo pero mi agente de viajes los (*expresses* **boletos**) tiene listos / —Si quieres, te (*expresses* **tú [a ti]**) acompaño a la agencia / —Sí, qué buena idea. Casi nunca te (*expresses* **tú [a ti]**) veo. Podemos pasar por la plaza a tomar un café también. —Perfecto.
GRAMÁTICA 22 *Use this model for all answers and questions:* Sí, me gusta… (No, no me gusta…) ¿Le gusta… ?

Capítulo 9
GRAMÁTICA 27 *Meaningful words underscored:* 1. Me levanté a las seis mañana. 2. Ayer fui al cine con un amigo. 3. Pinté las paredes de la cocina la semana pasada.

GRAMÁTICA 28 1. Trabajo tanto como tú (Ud.). 2. Yo trabajo más/menos que tú (Ud.). 3. Bill Gates tiene más dinero que yo. 4. Mi compañero/a de casa tiene menos cosas que yo. 5. Tengo tantos amigos como tú (Ud.). 6. Mi computadora es peor/mejor que esta.

Capítulo 10
GRAMÁTICA 30 1. *preterite* 2. *imperfect* 3. *imperfect* 4. *preterite* 5. *imperfect* 6. *imperfect*
GRAMÁTICA 32 1. me 2. se 3. nos 4. te, te

Capítulo 11
GRAMÁTICA 35 1. él 2. nosotros/as 3. ti 4. mi 5. Ud. 6. ellos

Capítulo 12
GRAMÁTICA 36 1. Tráiganme el libro. 2. No se lo den (a ella). 3. Siéntese aquí, por favor. 4. ¡No se siente en esa silla! 5. Díganles la verdad. 6. ¡Dígansela ahora! 7. No se la digan nunca. 8. ¡Cuídese! 9. ¡Lleve (Ud.) una vida sana! 10. Escúcheme.

Capítulo 15
GRAMÁTICA 44 1. algo 2. ninguno 3. nadie

Capítulo 16
GRAMÁTICA 46 *Correct answers:* 2, 3

Capítulo 17
GRAMÁTICA 48 A. 1. hablaron 2. comieron 3. vivieron 4. jugaron 5. perdieron 6. durmieron 7. rieron 8. leyeron 9. estuvieron 10. tuvieron 11. destruyeron 12. mantuvieron 13. trajeron 14. dieron 15. supieron 16. se vistieron 17. dijeron 18. creyeron 19. fueron 20. pudieron B. ir: iba, íbamos; ser: era, éramos; ver: veía, veíamos
GRAMÁTICA 49 1. su país 2. tus derechos 3. nuestra obligación 4. nuestra prensa 5. su gobierno 6. su crimen

Capítulo 18
GRAMÁTICA 50 1. viajaré 2. beberán 3. irás 4. vendrá 5. haremos 6. pondrá

Answers to Selected Activities

Capítulo preliminar
ANTE TODO
PRIMERA PARTE
SALUDOS Y EXPRESIONES DE CORTESÍA: Conversación A 1. Muy buenas. (Buenas tardes.) (Muy buenas tardes.) 2. Hasta luego. (Adiós.) (Hasta mañana.) 3. Bien. (Muy bien.) (Regular), gracias. ¿y tú? 4. Hola. (¿Qué tal?) 5. Bien (Muy bien), gracias, ¿y usted? 6. Buenas noches. (Muy buenas.) (Adiós.) (Hasta mañana.) 7. De nada. (No hay de qué.) 8. Hasta mañana. (Hasta luego.) (Adiós.) 9. (Me llamo) _____. 10. Encantado/a. (Igualmente.) 11. Soy de _____.
Conversación C 1. Con permiso. (Perdón.) 2. Perdón. 3. Perdón. 4. Con permiso. (Por favor.) 5. Perdón. 6. Perdón.
EL ALFABETO ESPAÑOL: Práctica A 1. c 2. e 3. i 4. a 5. f 6. h 7. b 8. g 9. d

SEGUNDA PARTE
LOS NÚMEROS 0–30; hay: Práctica A 1. Hay cuatro señoras. 2. Hay doce pianos. 3. Hay un café. 4. Hay veintiún (veinte y un) cafés. 5. Hay catorce días. 6. Hay una clase. 7. Hay veintiuna (veinte y una) ideas. 8. Hay once personas. 9. Hay quince estudiantes. 10. Hay trece teléfonos. 11. Hay veintiocho (veinte y ocho) naciones. 12. Hay cinco guitarras. 13. Hay un león. 14. Hay treinta señores. 15. Hay veinte oficinas.
Práctica B 1. Dos y cuatro son seis. 2. Ocho y diecisiete (diez y siete) son veinticinco (veinte y cinco). 3. Once y uno son doce. 4. Tres y dieciocho (diez y ocho) son veintiuno (veinte y uno). 5. Nueve y seis son quince. 6. Cinco y cuatro son nueve. 7. Uno y trece son catorce. 8. Quince menos dos son trece. 9. Nueve menos nueve es cero. 10. Trece menos ocho son cinco. 11. Catorce y doce son veintiséis (veinte y seis). 12. Veintitrés (Veinte y tres) menos trece son diez. 13. Uno y cuatro son cinco. 14. Ocho y diecisiete son veinticinco (veinte y cinco). 15. Ocho menos siete es uno. 16. Trece menos nueve son cuatro. 17. Dos y tres y diez son quince. 18. Veintiocho (Veinte y ocho) menos seis son veintidós (veinte y dos). 19. Treinta menos diecisiete son trece. 20. Veintiocho (Veinte y ocho) menos cinco son veintitrés (veinte y tres) 21. Siete y diecinueve son veintiséis (veinte y seis).
¿QUÉ HORA ES?: Práctica A 1. Las doce menos veinte de la noche. 2. Las dos menos un minuto de la tarde. 3. Las diez y veintitrés (veinte y tres) de la noche. 4. Las dos y diecinueve (diez y nueve) de la mañana. 5. Las cinco y cuarto (quince) de la tarde. 6. Las nueve y media de la mañana. 7. La una y seis de la noche (de la mañana). 8. Las seis y diecisiete (diez y siete) de la mañana.
Práctica B 1. Es la una. 2. Son las seis. 3. Son las once. 4. Es la una y media. 5. Son las tres y cuarto (quince). 6. Son las siete menos cuarto (quince). 7. Son las cuatro y cuarto (quince). 8. Son las doce menos cuarto (quince) en punto. 9. Son las nueve y diez en punto. 10. Son las diez menos diez en punto.
Conversación A: Paso 1 1. ¿A qué hora es la clase de francés? —A las dos menos cuarto (quince) de la tarde... ¡en punto! 2. ¿A qué hora es la sesión de laboratorio? —A las tres y diez de la tarde... ¡en punto! 3. ¿A qué hora es la excursión? —A las nueve menos cuarto (quince) de la mañana... ¡en punto! 4. ¿A qué hora es el concierto? —A las siete y media de la tarde (noche)... ¡en punto!

Capítulo 1
VOCABULARIO: PREPARACIÓN
EN LA CLASE: Conversación A 1. en la clase: 1. la profesora 2. la estudiante 3. el papel 4. la ventana 5. el escritorio (la mesa) 6. el lápiz 7. el bolígrafo 8. la calculadora **2. la biblioteca:** 1. el estudiante 2. la estudiante 3. el bibliotecario 4. el libro de texto 5. el diccionario 6. el cuaderno 7. la mesa 8. la silla **3. la librería:** 1. la estudiante 2. el lápiz 3. el cuaderno 4. el bolígrafo 5. la mochila 6. el dinero **4. la oficina (la universidad):** 1. la estudiante 2. la consejera 3. la mesa 4. el estudiante 5. el profesor
Conversación B 1. Es hombre. 2. Es mujer. 3. Es hombre. 4. Es hombre. 5. Es mujer. 6. Es hombre.
LAS MATERIAS: Conversación A 1. las ciencias, la química 2. la sicología 3. las comunicaciones 4. la filosofía 5. la literatura, el inglés 6. el arte 7. la computación 8. la historia

GRAMÁTICA 1
Práctica A: Paso 1 1. el 2. la 3. el 4. la 5. el 6. el 7. la 8. el 9. la 10. la 11. el 12. la
Paso 2 1. un 2. una 3. un 4. un 5. una 6. una 7. un 8. una 9. un
Práctica B: Paso 1 1. Hay un consejero en la oficina. 2. Hay una profesora en la clase. 3. Hay un lápiz en la mesa. 4. Hay un cuaderno en el escritorio. 5. Hay un libro en la mochila. 6. Hay un bolígrafo en la silla. 7. Hay una palabra en el papel. 8. Hay una oficina en la residencia. 9. Hay un compañero en la biblioteca.
Conversación A 1. ¿El/La cliente? —Es una persona. 2. ¿El bolígrafo? —Es una cosa. 3. ¿La residencia? —Es un edificio. 4. ¿El dependiente/La dependienta? —Es una persona. 5. ¿El hotel? —Es un edificio. 6. ¿La calculadora? —Es una cosa. 7. ¿La computación? —Es una materia. 8. ¿El inglés? —Es una materia (lengua).
Conversación B *Possible answers:* 1. el libro, la mesa; el/la estudiante, el bibliotecario / la bibliotecaria 2. el libro (de texto), el cuaderno; el/la cliente, el dependiente / la dependienta 3. el escritorio, el papel; el consejero / la consejera, el profesor / la profesora 4. la puerta, la ventana; el/la estudiante, el compañero / la compañera de cuarto

GRAMÁTICA 2

Práctica A 1. las mesas 2. los papeles 3. los amigos 4. las oficinas 5. unos cuadernos 6. unos lápices 7. unas universidades 8. unos bolígrafos 9. unos edificios.

Práctica B 1. el profesor 2. la calculadora 3. la bibliotecaria 4. el estudiante 5. un hombre 6. una tarde 7. una residencia 8. una silla 9. un escritorio

GRAMÁTICA 3

Práctica A: *Paso 2* 1. ¿Necesitas... ? 2. ¿Trabajas... ? 3. ¿Tomas... ? 4. En clase, ¿cantas... ? 5. ¿Deseas practicar... ? 6. ¿Tomas... ? 7. ¿Enseñas... ? 8. ¿Hablas... ?

Práctica B 1. cantan 2. bailan 3. toca 4. escuchan 5. busca 6. habla 7. desea 8. bailar 9. baila 10. necesitan

Comprensión 1. falso 2. falso 3. cierto 4. cierto

GRAMÁTICA 4

Práctica B 1. ¿Eres norteamericano? 2. ¿Estudias con frecuencia? 3. ¿Tocas el piano? 4. ¿Deseas trabajar más horas? 5. ¿Hablas francés? 6. ¿Eres reservado?

Conversación A: *Paso 1* 1. ¿Estudias... ? 2. ¿Practicas... ? 3. ¿Tomas... ? 4. ¿Bailas... ? 5. ¿Tocas... ? 6. ¿Regresas...? 7. ¿Compras... ? 8. ¿Hablas... ? 9. ¿Trabajas... ? 10. ¿Usas... ?

UN POCO DE TODO

Actividad A: *Pasos 1 y 2* (*Questions and answers are combined.*) 1. —¿Buscas un libro de español? b.—No, busco una mochila. 2. —¿No trabaja Paco aquí en la cafetería? d.—No, él trabaja en la biblioteca. 3. —¿Qué más necesitan Uds. en la clase de cálculo? c.—Necesitamos una calculadora y un cuaderno. 4. —¿Dónde está Juanita? e. —Ella trabaja en la residencia por las tardes. 5. —¿No deseas estudiar unos minutos más? a.—No, necesito regresar a casa.

Actividad B 1. compañeras 2. visitamos 3. Es 4. una 5. La 6. Las 7. la 8. la 9. las 10. las 11. estudian 12. el 13. el 14. la 15. una 16. Deseo 17. una 18. una 19. una 20. Los 21. practican 22. materias 23. son 24. el 25. las 26. visitamos 27. pagan 28. dinero

Comprensión 1. cierto 2. falso: Ángela no desea estudiar alemán. 3. cierto 4. falso: Es una residencia.

Capítulo 2

VOCABULARIO: PREPARACIÓN

LA FAMILIA Y LOS PARIENTES: Conversación A 1. falso; Es el primo de Ana. 2. cierto 3. cierto 4. falso; Son hermanos. 5. falso; Es la hermana de Luis. 6. falso; Es el padre de José Jaime. 7. cierto 8. cierto

Conversación B: *Paso 1* 1. abuela 2. primo 3. tía 4. abuelo

Paso 2 1. Es la hija de mi tío/a. 2. Es el hijo de mi hermano/a. 3. Es el hermano de mi madre/padre. 4. Es el padre de mi madre/padre.

LOS NÚMEROS 31–100: Conversación A 1. Treinta y cincuenta son ochenta. 2. Cuarenta y cinco y cuarenta y cinco son noventa. 3. Treinta y dos y cincuenta y ocho son noventa. 4. Setenta y siete y veintitrés (veinte y tres) son cien. 5. Cien menos cuarenta son sesenta. 6. Noventa y nueve menos treinta y nueve son sesenta.

ADJETIVOS: Conversación A 1. Es tonto. 2. Es perezoso. 3. Es alto. 4. Es malo, antipático y feo. 5. Es soltero y joven. 6. Es nuevo.

PRONUNCIACIÓN

Actividad B 1. mo-chi-la 2. me-nos 3. re-gu-lar 4. i-gual-ment-e 5. E-cua-dor 6. e-le-gan-te 7. li-be-ral 8. hu-ma-ni-dad

GRAMÁTICA 5

Práctica B 1. trabajador, alto, grande, amable 2. inteligentes, viejos, religiosos 3. elegante, sentimental, simpática 4. solteras, morenas

Práctica C Dolores es una buena estudiante. Es lista y trabajadora y estudia mucho. Es norteamericana, de origen mexicano, y por eso habla español. Desea ser profesora de antropología. Dolores es morena, guapa y atlética. Le gustan las fiestas grandes y tiene buenos amigos en la universidad. Tiene parientes norteamericanos y mexicanos.

Práctica E 1. ...es francesa y vive en Francia. 2. ...es español y vive en España. 3. ...son alemanes y viven en Alemania. 4. ...es portugués y vive en Portugal. 5. ...son italianas y viven en Italia. 6. ...es inglés y vive en Inglaterra. 7. ...son chinos y viven en la China.

GRAMÁTICA 6

Práctica A 1. falso; Somos esposos. 2. falso; Es el hijo de Pedro. 3. cierto 4. cierto 5. cierto. 6. falso; Es abuelo (el abuelo de Patricia, José y Rita.). 7. cierto

Práctica B: *Paso 1* 1. John Doe es de los Estados Unidos. 2. Karl Lotze es de Alemania. 3. Graziana Lazzarino es de Italia. 4. María Gómez es de México. 5. Claudette Moreau es de Francia. 6. Timothy Windsor es de Inglaterra.

Práctica C: *Paso 1* 1. Carlos Miguel es médico. Es de Cuba. Ahora trabaja en Milwaukee. 2. Maripili es profesora. Es de Burgos. Ahora trabaja en Miami. 3. Mariela es dependienta. Es de Buenos Aires. Ahora trabaja en Nueva York. 4. Juan es dentista. Es de Lima. Ahora trabaja en Los Ángeles.

Práctica D 1. ¿De quién es la casa en Beverly Hills? —Es de la actriz. 2. ¿De quién es la casa en Viena? —Es de los Sres. Schmidt. 3. ¿De quién es la camioneta? —Es de la familia con diez hijos. 4. ¿De quién es el perro? —Es del niño. 5. ¿De quién son las fotos de la Argentina? —Son del estudiante extranjero. 6. ¿De quién son las mochilas con todos los libros? —Son de las estudiantes.

Conversación A *Answers for E2.* 2. Su primo. Porque le gustan las matemáticas. 3. Su hermano. Porque le gustan mucho las historias viejas. 4. Sus abuelos. Porque les gusta mucho la música de guitarra clásica. 5. Su madre. Porque le gusta mirar programas cómicas. 6. Su padre. Porque le gusta escuchar las noticias. 7. Su hermana. Porque desea estudiar en otro estado.

GRAMÁTICA 7

Práctica A 1. problema, dinero, familia 2. hijos, profesoras 3. ventana, cuarto, coche, abuela 4. animales, nietas 5. materias, sobrinas 6. gustos, consejetos, parientes

Práctica B: *Paso 1*   1. Su hijo pequeño es guapo. 2. Su perro es feo. 3. Su padre es viejo. 4. Su hija es rubia. 5. Su esposa es bonita.

GRAMÁTICA 8

Práctica A: *Paso 2*   1. ¿Debes... 2. ¿Lees... 3. ¿Comprendes... 4. ¿Asistes... 5. ¿Deben Uds.... 6. ¿Escriben Uds.... 7. ¿Aprenden Uds.... 8. ¿Venden Uds....

Práctica B   1. vende 2. aprendemos 3. deben 4. asistir 5. cree 6. leer 7. leemos 8. escribimos 9. creo 10. comprende

Práctica C   1. Yo leo el periódico. 2. Mi hija, Marta, mira la televisión. 3. También escribe una composición en inglés. 4. No entiende todas las instrucciones. 5. Debe usar un diccionario. 6. Mi esposa, Lola, abre y lee unas cartas. 7. ¡Hoy recibimos una carta del tío Ricardo! 8. Es de España pero ahora vive en México. 9. ¡Ay! Son las dos de la tarde. 10. ¡Debemos comer ahora! 11. Comemos a las dos todos los días. 12. Hoy unos amigos comen con nosotros.

UN POCO DE TODO

Actividad A: *Paso 1*   1. Yo soy la abuela panameña. 2. El nuevo nieto es de los Estados Unidos. 3. Juan José es el padre del nieto. 4. Juan José también es el hijo del abuelo panameño. 5. Una de las tías del nieto es médica. 6. La otra tía es una profesora famosa. 7. La madre del niño es norteamericana. 8. La hermana del niño se llama Concepción.

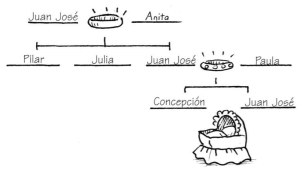

Paso 2   1. Son de Panamá. 2. Es de los Estados Unidos. 3. Se llama Juan José.

Actividad B   1. creen 2. todas 3. hispánicas 4. grandes 5. es 6. grandes 7. Es 8. típica 9. todas 10. trabajan 11. necesario 12. urbanos 13. son 14. muchos 15. industrializada 16. trabajan 17. pagan 18. hablar 19. hispánica 20. norteamericana

Comprensión   1. falso: Todas las familias hispánicas no son iguales. 2. cierto 3. cierto 4. cierto 5. falso: Muchas madres trabajan fuera de casa.

Capítulo 3

VOCABULARIO: PREPARACIÓN

DE COMPRAS: LA ROPA: Conversación A: *Paso 1*   1. El Sr. Rivera lleva un traje, zapatos, calcetines, un sombrero, una corbata, una camisa y un cinturón. 2. La Srta. Alonso lleva pantalones, una chaqueta, botas y calcetines. El perro lleva un suéter. 3. Sara lleva una falda, una blusa, medias y zapatos. 4. Alfredo lleva una camiseta, una chaqueta, *bluejeans* y zapatos de tenis. Necesita comprar ropa nueva. (*Different answers are possible.*)

Paso 2   *Possible answers:* El Sr. Rivera trabaja hoy. Sara tiene una fiesta. Alfredo (La Srta. Alonso, Sara) no trabaja en este momento.

Conversación B   1. almacén 2. regatear 3. venden, rebajas 4. centros comerciales 5. centro 6. *Possible answers:* faldas, blusas, vestidos 7. *Possible answers:* camisetas, pantalones, camisas, chaquetas, cinturones, calcetines, zapatos, botas, suéteres, abrigos 8. seda 9. algodón

Conversación D   1. En un almacén hay precios fijos, ¿no? (¿verdad?) 2. Regateamos mucho en los Estados Unidos, ¿no? (¿verdad?) 3. No hay muchos mercados en esta ciudad, ¿verdad? 4. Los *bluejeans* Gap son muy baratos, ¿no? (¿verdad?) 5. Es necesario llevar traje y corbata a clase, ¿no? (¿verdad?) 6. Eres una persona muy independiente, ¿no? (¿verdad?) 7. Tienes una familia muy grande, ¿no? (¿verdad?) 8. No hay examen mañana, ¿verdad?

¿DE QUÉ COLOR ES?: Conversación B   1. En el dibujo A hay un traje azul, pero en el dibujo B hay un traje azul de cuadros. 2. En el dibujo A hay dos sandalias, pero en el dibujo B hay una sandalia. 3. En el dibujo A hay un sombrero, pero en el dibujo B hay dos sombreros. 4. En el dibujo A hay un sombrero verde, pero en el dibujo B los sombreros son rojos. 5. En el dibujo A hay un precio de 50 pesos, pero en el dibujo B hay un precio de 40 dólares. 6. En el dibujo A hay un suéter morado, pero en el dibujo B hay un suéter azul. 7. En el dibujo A hay una bolsa parda, pero en el dibujo B hay una bolsa gris. 8. En el dibujo A hay un vestido con cinturón, pero en el dibujo B hay una blusa y una falda; no hay cinturón.

LOS NÚMEROS MÁS ALLÁ DEL NÚMERO 100: Conversación A: *Paso 1*   el elefante: cinco mil kilos, el rinoceronte indio: cuatro mil kilos, el hipopótamo: dos mil kilos, el bisonte: mil kilos, la jirafa: mil doscientos kilos, el oso Grizzly: setecientos ochenta kilos, el dromedario: seiscientos kilos, el alce: quinientos noventa y cinco kilos, el tigre: trescientos kilos, el gorila: doscientos veinte kilos

Conversación B   1. siete mil trescientos cuarenta y cinco euros 2. cien dólares 3. cinco mil setecientos diez quetzales 4. seiscientos setenta bolívares 5. un millón de dólares 6. quinientos veintiocho (veinte y ocho) nuevos pesos 7. ochocientos treinta y seis bolívares 8. ciento un euros 9. cuatro millones de dólares 10. seis millones de quetzales

PRONUNCIACIÓN

Actividad B   1. exámenes (written accent mark) 2. lápiz (written accent mark) 3. necesitar (ends in consonant) 4. perezoso (ends in vowel) 5. actitud (ends in consonant) 6. acciones (ends in -s) 7. dólares (written accent mark) 8. francés (written accent mark) 9. están (written accent mark) 10. hombre (ends in vowel) 11. peso (ends in vowel) 12. mujer (ends in consonant) 13. plástico (written accent mark) 14. María (written accent mark) 15. Rodríguez (written accent mark) 16. Patricia (ends in diphthong)

GRAMÁTICA 9

Práctica A: *Paso 1*   1. Esa falda también es muy pequeña. 2. Esos pantalones también son muy largos. 3. Ese libro también es muy bueno. 4. Esas corbatas también son muy feas.

Paso 2 1. Aquella falda también es muy pequeña. 2. Aquellos pantalones también son muy largos. 3. Aquel libro también es muy bueno. 4. Aquellas corbatas también son muy feas.

Práctica B *Possible answers:* 1. ¡Esto es fantástico! 2. ¡Esto es horrible! 3. ¡Eso es muy bueno! 4. ¡Eso es terrible! 5. ¡Esto es magnífico!

GRAMÁTICA 10

Práctica A: *Paso 1* 1. Sara tiene muchos exámenes. 2. Viene a la universidad todos los días. 3. Hoy trabaja hasta las nueve de la noche. 4. Prefiere estudiar en la biblioteca. 5. Quiere leer más pero no puede. 6. Por eso regresa a casa. 7. Tiene ganas de leer más. 8. Pero unos amigos vienen a mirar la televisión. 9. Sara decide mirar la televisión con ellos.

Paso 2 YO: 1. Yo tengo muchos exámenes. 2. Vengo a la universidad todos los días. 3. Hoy trabajo hasta las nueve de la noche. 4. Prefiero estudiar en la biblioteca. 5. Quiero leer más pero no puedo. 6. Por eso regreso a casa. 7. Tengo ganas de leer más. 8. Pero unos amigos vienen a mirar la televisión. 9. Decido mirar la televisión con ellos. NOSOTROS: 1. Nosotros/as tenemos muchos exámenes. 2. Venimos a la universidad todos los días. 3. Hoy trabajamos hasta las nueve de la noche. 4. Preferimos estudiar en la biblioteca. 5. Queremos leer más pero no podemos. 6. Por eso regresamos a casa. 7. Tenemos ganas de leer más. 8. Pero unos amigos vienen a mirar la televisión. 9. Decidimos mirar la televisión con ellos.

Práctica B 1. ... tengo _____ años. 2. ... tengo miedo. 3. ... tengo sueño. 4. ... no tienes razón. 5. ... tengo prisa. 6. ... tienen (tenemos) miedo. 7. ... tengo que estudiar (tengo miedo). 8. ... tienes razón.

GRAMÁTICA 11

Práctica A 1. Ud. va a una *boutique*. 2. Francisco va al almacén Goya. 3. Jorge y Carlos van al centro comercial. 4. Tú vas a un mercado. 5. Nosotros vamos a una tienda pequeña. 6. Yo voy...

Práctica B 1. Vamos a llegar al centro a las diez de la mañana. 2. La niña va a querer comer algo. 3. Voy a comprar unos chocolates para Marta. 4. Manolo va a buscar una blusa de seda. 5. No vas a comprar esta blusa de rayas, ¿verdad? 6. Vamos a buscar algo más barato. 7. ¿Vas a ir de compras mañana también?

UN POCO DE TODO

Actividad B 1. las 2. gran 3. ir 4. elegantes 5. los 6. fijos 7. pequeñas 8. formar 9. cree 10. otros 11. va 12. puede 13. debe 14. los 15. tiene 16. que 17. informal 18. grandes 19. debe 20. a

Comprensión 1. falso: Hay una gran variedad de tiendas. 2. falso: Los precios son fijos en los almacenes. 3. falso: Es posible comprar papel. 4. falso: El precio es alto al principio.

Capítulo 4
VOCABULARIO: PREPARACIÓN
¿QUÉ DÍA ES HOY?: Conversación A 1. Hoy es _____. Mañana es _____. Si hoy es sábado, mañana es domingo.

Si hoy es jueves, mañana es viernes. Ayer fue _____. 2. Tenemos clase los _____. No tenemos clases los _____. 3. Sí, (No, no) estudio mucho durante el fin de semana. Sí, (No, no) estudio mucho los domingos por la noche. 4. Los viernes por la tarde me gusta _____. Sí, (No, no) me gusta salir con los amigos los sábados por la noche.

LOS MUEBLES, LOS CUARTOS Y OTRAS PARTES DE LA CASA: Conversación A *Possible answers:* 1. Es el garaje. En el garaje hay un coche. 2. Es la sala. En la sala hay un sillón, un televisor, y una mesita. 3. Es la alcoba. En la alcoba hay una cama y una cómoda. 4. Es el cuarto de baño. En el cuarto de baño hay un lavabo. 5. Es la cocina. En la cocina hay platos. 6. Es el comedor. En el comedor hay dos sillas y una mesa. 7. Es el patio. En el patio no hay piscina. Solamente hay plantas.

Conversación B: *Paso 1* *Possible answers:* 1. el escritorio, la mesa, la silla, la lámpara, la alcoba 2. el sofá, la cama, la alcoba, la sala 3. el sofá, el televisor, la sala, el comedor, la cocina 4. el comedor, la mesa, las sillas, la cocina 5. el patio, la piscina 6. la sala, el sofá, el sillón, la alcoba

¿CUÁNDO? PREPOSICIONES: Conversación A 1. después de 2. después de (antes de) 3. antes de 4. antes de 5. después de (antes de) 6. antes de

GRAMÁTICA 12

Conversación A *Possible answers:* 1. ... hago un viaje a Colorado. 2. ... traigo el libro a clase. 3. ... salgo para la biblioteca. 4. ... pongo el televisor. 5. ... oigo al profesor. 6. ... salgo para la residencia. 7. ... pongo el estéreo. 8. ... hago una pregunta.

GRAMÁTICA 13

Práctica A 1. Está en la cocina (el comedor). 2. Está en la sala. 3. Están en el comedor (la cocina). 4. Están en la sala. 5. Está en la alcoba (el baño). 6. Está en el garaje. 7. Está en la alcoba (la sala). 8. Está en la sala (la alcoba).

GRAMÁTICA 14

Práctica B: *Paso 1* 1. Mi esposa Lola se levanta más tarde. 2. Nos duchamos por la mañana. 3. Por costumbre, nuestra hija Marta se baña por la noche. 4. Yo me visto antes de tomar el desayuno. 5. Lola se viste después de tomar un café. 6. Por la noche, Marta se acuesta muy temprano. 7. Yo me acuesto más tarde, a las once. 8. Por lo general, Lola se acuesta más tarde que yo.

Paso 2 1. Manolo 2. Marta 3. Marta 4. Manolo

Práctica C: *Paso 1* *Possible answers:* 1. despertarme 2. me ducho; me afeito 3. después de afeitarme 4. tomar el desayuno 5. vestirme; tomar un café 6. me acuesto 7. después de bañarme; me duermo

UN POCO DE TODO

Actividad A *Possible answers:* 1. empiezo; es 2. empiezan 3. hablan (entienden) 4. almuerzo; almorzamos; pedimos 5. vuelvo; empiezo; duermo 6. cierra; vuelvo (voy)

Actividad B 1. contesto 2. su 3. estoy 4. de 5. Me divierto 6. todos 7. es 8. son 9. hacen 10. soy 11. vienen 12. tienen 13. de 14. constarricense 15. nuestras 16. unos 17. veo 18. tienen 19. llega 20. eso 21. muy 22. sus 23. una

24. tropicales 25. Voy 26. un 27. puede 28. sus 29. que 30. ducharme 31. me visto 32. voy 33. salir

Comprensión 1. No, no hay evidencia de esto. 2. Sí, hay evidencia de esto. 3. Sí, hay evidencia de esto. 4. Sí, hay evidencia de esto. 5. No, no hay evidencia de esto. 6. Sí, hay evidencia de esto.

Capítulo 5

VOCABULARIO: PREPARACIÓN

¿QUÉ TIEMPO HACE HOY?: Conversación A 1. Hace calor (sol). 2. Hace fresco. 3. Hace frío (fresco). 4. Llueve. 5. Hace (mucho) frío.

Conversación B *Possible answers:* 1. Joaquín, en Seattle llueve mucho. 2. En Los Ángeles hay mucha contaminación. 3. En Phoenix hace mucho calor y nunca llueve. 4. En Nueva Orleans hace mucho calor y llueve mucho. 5. En Buffalo hace mucho frío y nieva mucho.

Conversación D *Possible answers:* 1. Nieva. El hombre tiene mucho frío. 2. Hace mucho sol y calor. El hombre tiene mucho calor. 3. Hace mucho viento. El hombre no está bien. 4. Llueve mucho. La mujer tiene frío. 5. Hay mucha contaminación. El hombre no está bien. 6. Hace buen tiempo. Las personas están muy bien. 7. Hace fresco por la noche. Las personas están bien.

LOS MESES Y LAS ESTACIONES DEL AÑO: Conversación A 1. El doce es viernes. 2. El primero es lunes. 3. El veinte es sábado. 4. El dieciséis (diez y seis) es martes. 5. El once es jueves. 6. El cuatro es jueves. 7. El veintinueve (veinte y nueve) es lunes.

Conversación B: Paso 1 1. el siete de marzo, invierno (el primer día de primavera es entre el 20 y el 23 de marzo) 2. el veinticuatro (veinte y cuatro) de agosto, verano 3. el primero de diciembre, otoño (el primer día de invierno es entre el 20 y el 23 de diciembre) 4. el cinco de junio, primavera (el primer día de verano es entre el 20 y el 23 de junio) 5. el diecinueve (diez y nueve) de septiembre de mil novecientos noventa y siete, verano (el primer día de otoño es entre el 20 y el 23 de septiembre) 6. el treinta de mayo de mil ochocientos cuarenta y dos, primavera 7. el treinta y uno de enero de mil seiscientos sesenta, invierno 8. el cuatro de julio de mil setecientos setenta y seis, verano **Paso 2** 1. el 12 de octubre 2. el 1° de enero 3. el 14 de febrero 4. el 4 de julio 5. el 1° de abril 6. el 25 de diciembre 7. ¿ ?

¿DÓNDE ESTÁ? LAS PREPOSICIONES: Conversación B Paso 3 Brasilia es la capital del Brasil. Buenos Aires es la capital de la Argentina. Bogotá es la capital de Colombia. La Paz es la capital de Bolivia. Santiago es la capital de Chile. Asunción es la capital del Paraguay. Quito es la capital del Ecuador. Caracas es la capital de Venezuela. Montevideo es la capital del Uruguay. Lima es la capital del Perú.

GRAMÁTICA 15

Práctica B 1. ... está hablando con su tío Ricardo. 2. ... están tomando un café en la universidad. 3. ... está jugando con Ricardo. 4. ... están comiendo a las tres.

Práctica C: Paso 1 1. por la mañana 2. por la tarde 3. más tarde 4. por la tarde 5. por la mañana 6. por la mañana

7. más tarde 8. más tarde 9. más tarde 10. por la tarde

Paso 2 *Possible answers:* POR LA MAÑANA: Son las seis de la mañana. Los gemelos están durmiendo. El padre está duchándose. La hija está levantándose. La madre está leyendo el periódico. MÁS TARDE Son las ocho de la mañana. Los gemelos están comiendo (tomando el desayuno). El padre está trabajando. La madre está vistiéndose. La hija está saliendo para la escuela. POR LA TARDE: Son las siete y media de la tarde. El padre está preparando la cena. Los gemelos están jugando con el perro. La hija está escribiendo cartas. La madre está quitándose la ropa después de trabajar.

GRAMÁTICA 16

Comprensión a. 5 b. 9 c. 4 d. 1 e. 8 f. 6 g. 11 h. 3 i. 2 j. 10 k. 7

Práctica A 1. está 2. es 3. es 4. es 5. está 6. es 7. es 8. es 9. es 10. es

Práctica B 1. son 2. son 3. están 4. están 5. son 6. están 7. están

Práctica C 1. son 2. estar 3. está 4. están 5. son 6. es 7. es 8. son

Comprensión 1. sí 2. no 3. no 4. no

Práctica D: Paso 1 1. mal tiempo 2. mal 3. sucio 4. nervioso 5. abierto 6. aburridos 7. triste 8. desordenada

GRAMÁTICA 17

Práctica B *Possible answers:* Alfredo tiene más cuartos que Gloria. Alfredo tiene más baños que Gloria. Alfredo tiene tantas alcobas como Gloria. Gloria tiene más camas que Alfredo. Alfredo tiene más coches que Gloria. Gloria tiene menos dinero en el banco que Alfredo.

UN POCO DE TODO

Actividad B 1. muchas 2. es 3. es 4. salgo 5. llevar 6. los 7. puede 8. a 9. cortos 10. durante 11. hace 12. nieva 13. gran 14. mucho 15. ese 16. toman 17. va 18. hacer 19. es 20. llevan

Comprensión 1. improbable 2. probable 3. improbable

Capítulo 6

VOCABULARIO: PREPARACIÓN

LA COMIDA: Conversación A 1. c 2. d 3. a 4. b

Conversación B 1. la ensalada 2. el vino 3. la sopa 4. la zanahoria 5. el bistec 6. el arroz 7. el queso 8. la patata 9. la manzana 10. la banana

¿QUÉ SABE UD. Y A QUIÉN CONOCE? Conversación A: Paso 1 1. Jennifer López sabe cantar en español. Mikhail Baryshnikov sabe bailar. Alex Rodríguez sabe jugar al béisbol. Lance Armstrong sabe montar en bicicleta. J.K. Rowling sabe escribir novelas. Serena Williams sabe jugar al tenis. Emeril Lagasse sabe cocinar bien.

Paso 2 Adán conoce a Eva. Napoleón conoce a Josefina. Romeo conoce a Julieta. Rhett Butler conoce a Scarlett O'Hara. Marco Antonio conoce a Cleopatra. George Washington conoce a Martha.

Conversación B 1. Sabes 2. sé 3. Conoces 4. sé 5. conoce 6. Sabes 7. sé 8. Sabes 9. sabe

GRAMÁTICA 18

Práctica A: Paso 1 1. Las va a comer. 2. Lo va a comer. 3. No las va a comer. 4. No los va a comer. 5. La va a comer.

6. La va a comer. 7. No los va a comer. 8. Lo va a comer. 9. Lo va a comer. 10. Los va a comer. 11. La va a comer.

Práctica B 1. El camarero trae una botella de vino tinto y la pone en la mesa. 2. El camarero trae las copas de vino y las pone delante de Lola y Manolo. 3. Lola quiere la especialidad de la casa y la va a pedir (va a pedirla). 4. Manolo prefiere el pescado fresco y lo pide. 5. Lola quiere una ensalada también y por eso la pide. 6. El camarero trae la comida y la sirve. 7. Manolo necesita otra servilleta y la pide. 8. «¿La cuenta? El dueño está preparándola (la está preparando) para Uds.» 9. Manolo quiere pagar con tarjeta de crédito pero no la trae. 10. Por fin Lola toma la cuenta y la paga.

Práctica C *Possible answers:* 1. Acabo de escribirlas. (Las acabo de escribir.) 2. Acabo de comprarlo. (Lo acabo de comprar.) 3. Acabo de pagarlos. (Los acabo de pagar.) 4. Acabo de prepararla. (La acabo de preparar.) 5. Acabo de pedirla. (La acabo de pedir.) 6. Acabo de comerlos. (Los acabo de comer.)

GRAMÁTICA 19

Práctica A 1. falso 2. falso 3. cierto 4. cierto 5. cierto 6. falso 7. falso

Práctica B 1. No hay nada interesante en el menú. 2. No tienen ningún plato típico. 3. El profesor no cena allí tampoco. (El profesor tampoco cena allí.) 4. Mis amigos no almuerzan allí nunca. (Mis amigos nunca almuerzan allí.) 5. No preparan nada especial para grupos grandes. 6. No hacen nunca platos nuevos. (Nunca hacen platos nuevos.) 7. Y no sirven paella, mi plato favorito, tampoco. (Y tampoco sirven paella, mi plato favorito.)

Práctica C: *Paso 1* 1. Pues, no hay ninguna clase interesante en el departamento. 2. No me gusta tomar café con mis estudiantes nunca. (Nunca me gusta tomar café con mis estudiantes.) 3. No hay ninguna persona buena en la administración. 4. No hay un/ningún candidato bueno para el puesto de director de la facultad tampoco. (Tampoco hay un candidato bueno para el puesto de director de la facultad.) 5. No hay ninguna persona inteligente en la universidad. 6. No me gusta ninguna conferencia que está planeada para este mes.

Paso 2 1. ¿Hay algo interesante en la tele esta noche? 2. ¿Hay alguien cómico en el programa? 3. ¿Hay algunas películas buenas en el cine esta semana? 4. ¿Siempre comes en la facultad? 5. ¿Y almuerzas entre tus clases también?

GRAMÁTICA 20

Práctica A a. 3 b. 7 c. 4 d. 1 e. 8 f. 5 g. 2 h. 6

Práctica B 1. Lleguen a tiempo. 2. Lean la lección. 3. Escriban una composición. 4. Abran los libros. 5. Estén en clase mañana. 6. Traigan los libros a clase. 7. Estudien los verbos nuevos.

Práctica C: *Paso 2* No trabaje tanto. No sea tan impaciente. No critique a los otros. No sea tan impulsivo. No fume tanto. No beba bebidas alcohólicas. No almuerce y no cene tan fuerte. Desayune. No salga tanto con los amigos. No vuelva a casa tarde.

Práctica D *Possible answers:* 1. No lo beba. 2. Cómalas. 3. No lo coma. 4. No los coma. 5. No la beba. 6. No las coma. 7. Cómalas. 8. Bébalos. 9. Cómalo. 10. No la coma. 11. No la coma. 12. Bébalo.

Práctica E 1. Despiértese más temprano. 2. Levántese más temprano. 3. Báñese más. 4. Quítese esa ropa sucia. 5. Póngase ropa limpia. 6. Vístase mejor. 7. Estudie más. 8. No se divierta tanto con los amigos. 9. Vaya más a la biblioteca. 10. No se acueste tan tarde. 11. Ayude con los quehaceres.

UN POCO DE TODO

Actividad A: *Paso 1* 1. Espera a su amigo Samuel en la parada del autobús. 2. Llegan a la universidad a la una. 3. Buscan a su amiga Ceci en la cafetería. 4. Ella acaba de empezar sus estudios allí. 5. No conoce a mucha gente todavía. 6. A veces, ven a la profesora de historia en la cafetería y hablan un poco con ella. 7. Es una persona muy interesante que sabe mucho de esa materia. 8. A las dos todos tienen clase de sicología. 9. Siempre oyen conferencias interesantes y hacen algunas preguntas. 10. A veces tienen la oportunidad de conocer a los conferenciantes. 11. A las cinco, Samuel y Roberto vuelven a esperar el autobús. 12. Roberto prepara la cena y luego mira la televisión.

Paso 2 1. Ceci 2. el profesor de la clase de sicología 3. Samuel 4. Roberto

Paso 3 MODELO: Los martes yo nunca salgo del apartamento antes de las doce. 1. Espero a mi amigo Samuel en la parada del autobús. 2. Llegamos a la universidad a la una. 3. Buscamos a nuestra amiga Ceci en la cafetería. 4. Ella acaba de empezar sus estudios allí. 5. No conoce a mucha gente todavía. 6. A veces, vemos a la profesora de historia en la cafetería y hablamos un poco con ella. 7. Es una persona muy interesante que sabe mucho de esa materia. 8. A las dos todos tenemos clase de sicología. 9. Siempre oímos conferencias interesantes y hacemos algunas preguntas. 10. A veces tenemos la oportunidad de conocer a los conferenciantes. 11. A las cinco, Samuel y yo volvemos a esperar el autobús. 12. Preparo la cena y luego miro la televisión.

Actividad B 1. japonesa 2. sé 3. como 4. Estoy 5. haciendo 6. hablen 7. Escúchenlos 8. van 9. estas 10. viene 11. panameña 12. son 13. nada 14. a 15. es 16. mantiene 17. históricas 18. amistosas 19. saben 20. lo 21. extranjera 22. se especializan 23. pierden 24. prefieren 25. tienen 26. preparados 27. preguntan 28. contestan

Comprensión 1. Están dando presentaciones sobre comidas extranjeras. 2. Piensan que es interesante pero no les gustaría comer tanto pescado crudo. 3. Es cosmopolita y los platos tradicionales incluyen muchas verduras. 4. Van a comer arroz con pollo.

Capítulo 7

VOCABULARIO: PREPARACIÓN

DE VIAJE: Conversación A a. 8 b. 5 c. 3 d. 2 e. 7 f. 1 g. 9 h. 4 i. 6

Conversación B 1. a 2. a 3. c 4. b 5. c

DE VACACIONES: Conversación C 1. en el aeropuerto 2. en casa 3. en la agencia de viajes 4. en la agencia de viajes 5. en el aeropuerto 6. en el avión 7. en el avión 8. en la playa

Conversación D 1. falso: Se habla portugués en el Brasil. 2. cierto 3. cierto 4. cierto 5. falso: La paella se prepara con arroz, mariscos y pollo. 6. cierto 7. cierto 8. cierto

GRAMÁTICA 21

Práctica A *Possible answers:* 1. Todos le mandan flores. Las enfermeras le dan medicinas. Le escriben cartas. De comer, le sirven sopa. 2. Les prometen a sus padres ser buenos. Les piden muchos regalos. También le escriben cartas a Santa Claus. Le piden muchos regalos. Los padres les mandan tarjetas navideñas a sus amigos. Les regalan flores y frutas. 3. Un asistente de vuelo nos sirve bebidas. Otra asistente de vuelo nos ofrece comida. El piloto nos dice que todo está bien. 4. Mi amigo me presta su coche. Mis padres me preguntan si necesito un coche nuevo. Luego me dan dinero. Le muestro al mecánico el motor. 5. Todos le preguntan al profesor qué deben estudiar. El profesor les explica a los estudiantes la materia difícil. El profesor les muestra algunas preguntas posibles.

Práctica B 1. Les llamo un taxi. 2. Les bajo las maletas. 3. Les guardo el equipaje. 4. Les facturo el equipaje. 5. Les guardo el puesto en la cola. 6. Les guardo el asiento en la sala de espera. 7. Les compro una revista. 8. Por fin les digo adiós.

Práctica C 1. le da 2. le da 3. le da 4. les da 5. les prestan 6. les ofrecen 7. le dice

Práctica D 1. te 2. le 3. le 4. le 5. te 6. le 7. le 8. le

GRAMÁTICA 22

Práctica A: *Paso 1* 1. (No) Me gusta el vino. 2. (No) Me gustan los niños pequeños. 3. (No) Me gusta la música clásica. 4. (No) Me gusta Ricky Martin. 5. (No) Me gusta el invierno. 6. (No) Me gusta hacer cola. 7. (No) Me gusta el chocolate. 8. (No) Me gustan las películas de terror. 9. (No) Me gustan las clases que empiezan a las ocho de la mañana. 10. (No) Me gusta cocinar. 11. (No) Me gusta la gramática. 12. (No) Me gustan las clases de este semestre/trimestre. 13. (No) Me gustan los vuelos con muchas escalas. 14. (No) Me gusta bailar en las discotecas.

Práctica B: *Paso 1* 1. A mi padre le gusta el océano. Le gustaría ir a la playa. 2. A mis hermanos pequeños les gusta nadar también. Les gustaría ir a la playa. 3. A mi hermano Ernesto le gusta hacer *camping*. Le gustaría ir a las montañas. 4. A mis abuelos les gusta descansar. Les gustaría quedarse en casa. 5. A mi madre le gusta la tranquilidad. Le gustaría visitar un pueblecito en la costa. 6. A mi hermana Elena le gustan las discotecas. Le gustaría pasar las vacaciones en una ciudad grande. 7. A mí me gusta(n)... Me gustaría...

Paso 2 1. A Elena. 2. Al padre y a los hermanos pequeños. 3. Los abuelos. 4. A la madre. 5. Ernesto.

GRAMÁTICA 23

Práctica B: *Paso 1* TERESA Y EVANGELINA 1. Salimos del apartamento a las nueve. 2. Llegamos a la biblioteca a las diez. 3. Estudiamos toda la mañana para el examen. 4. Escribimos muchos ejercicios. 5. Almorzamos con unos amigos en la cafetería. 6. Fuimos al laboratorio a la una. 7. Hicimos todos los experimentos del manual. 8. Tomamos el examen a las cuatro. 9. ¡El examen fue horrible! 10. Regresamos a casa después del examen. 11. Ayudamos a Liliana a preparar la cena. 12. Cenamos todas juntas a las siete. LILIANA: 1. Yo me quedé en casa todo el día. 2. Vi la televisión por la mañana. 3. Llamé a mis padres a las once. 4. Tomé café con los vecinos. 5. Estudié para el examen de historia y escribí una composición para la clase de sociología. 6. Fui al garaje para dejar unos muebles viejos allí. 7. Fui al supermercado y compré comida. 8. Empecé a preparar la cena a las cinco.

Paso 2 1. Liliana 2. Evangelina 3. Evangelina 4. Liliana 5. Liliana

Paso 3 1. Liliana se quedó en casa todo el día. 2. Vio la televisión por la mañana. 3. Llamó a sus padres a las once. 4. Tomó café con los vecinos. 5. Estudió para el examen de historia y escribió una composición para la clase de sociología. 6. Fue al garaje para dejar unos muebles viejos allí. 7. Fue al supermercado y compró comida. 8. Empezó a preparar la cena a las cinco. 1. Teresa y Evangelina salieron del apartamento a las nueve. 2. Llegaron a la biblioteca a las diez. 3. Estudiaron toda la mañana para el examen. 4. Escribieron muchos ejercicios. 5. Almorzaron con unos amigos en la cafetería. 6. Fueron al laboratorio a la una. 7. Hicieron todos los experimentos del manual. 8. Tomaron el examen a las cuatro. 9. ¡El examen fue horrible! 10. Regresaron a casa después del examen. 11. Me ayudaron a preparar la cena. 12. Cenamos todas juntas a las siete.

Práctica C 1. Pasé un semestre en México. 2. Mis padres me pagaron el vuelo... 3. ... pero trabajé para ganar el dinero para la matrícula y los otros gastos. 4. Viví con una familia mexicana encantadora. 5. Aprendí mucho sobre la vida y la cultura mexicanas. 6. Visité muchos sitios de interés turístico e histórico. 7. Mis amigos me escribieron muchas cartas. 8. Les mandé muchas tarjetas postales. 9. Les compré muchos recuerdos a todos. 10. Volví a los Estados Unidos al final de agosto.

Conversación A a. 8 b. 12 c. 1 d. 11 e. 7 f. 2 g. 10 h. 5 i. 4 j. 9 k. 6 l. 3

Possible answers: Julián volvió a casa después de trabajar. Llamó a un amigo y decidieron encontrarse en el cine. Luego se duchó y se afeitó, y después comió rápidamente. Fue al cine en autobús. Los dos amigos llegaron al cine al mismo tiempo. Hicieron cola para comprar las entradas y entraron en el cine. No les gustó nada la película. Después fueron a un café a tomar algo. Finalmente Julián regresó a casa tarde.

UN POCO DE TODO

Actividad B 1. Les 2. algo 3. la 4. la 5. conocen 6. Está 7. la 8. es 9. más 10. incaicos 11. visitarla 12. Les 13. es 14. ir 15. mejores 16. comprar 17. muchos 18. países 19. Sé 20. les

Comprensión 1. falso 2. cierto 3. cierto 4. falso

Capítulo 8
VOCABULARIO: PREPARACIÓN
LA FIESTA DE JAVIER: Conversación A 1. la Navidad 2. una sorpresa 3. los refrescos y los entremeses 4. el Día de los Muertos 5. la quinceañera 6. el día de San Patricio 7. la Nochevieja 8. ¡Felicitaciones! 9. la Fiesta de las Luces

EMOCIONES Y CONDICIONES: Conversación A *Possible answers:* 1. Me pongo felicísimo/a (contentísimo/a). Le doy las gracias. 2. Me pongo tristísimo/a (furiosísimo/a). Lloro. 3. Me pongo nerviosísimo/a. Les ofrezco más refrescos y entremeses. Cambio la música. 4. Me pongo muy nervioso/a y avergonzado/a. 5. Me pongo muy contento/a (triste). Me río. (Lloro.) 6. Me pongo muy triste. 7. Me pongo avergonzado/a 8. Me pongo serio/a.

GRAMÁTICA 24
Práctica B 1. Todos estuvimos en casa de los abuelos antes de las nueve. 2. Pusimos muchos regalos debajo del árbol. 3. Mis tíos y mis primos vinieron con comida y bebidas. 4. Yo tuve que ayudar a preparar la comida. 5. Hubo una cena especial para todos. 6. Más tarde algunos de mis amigos vinieron a cantar villancicos. 7. Los niños fueron a la alcoba a las diez y se acostaron. 8. Los niños quisieron dormir pero no pudieron. 9. A medianoche todos dijimos «¡Feliz Navidad!». 10. Al día siguiente todos dijimos que la fiesta estuvo estupenda.
Paso 2 1. falso: Hubo mucha gente. 2. falso: También vinieron amigos a cantar villancicos. 3. cierto 4. falso: Los niños no abrieron sus regalos por la noche.
Práctica C En 1969 los estadounidenses pusieron a un hombre en la luna. Adán y Eva supieron el significado de un árbol especial. George Washington estuvo en Valley Forge con sus soldados. Los europeos trajeron el caballo al Nuevo Mundo. Los aztecas conocieron a Hernán Cortés en Tenochtitlán. Stanley conoció a Livingston en África.

GRAMÁTICA 25
Práctica B 1. se sentó, vino, pidió, recordó, pidió, sirvió, quiso, dijo, pedí, contestó 2. se acostó, se durmió, Durmió, se despertó, Se vistió, salió, vio, sonrieron 3. me vestí, fui, me divertí, volví, decidió, vio, se divirtió, Perdió, sintió
Práctica C *Possible answers:* El lobo se vistió de abuela. Rip van Winkle durmió muchos años. La Cenicienta se divirtió en un baile (perdió un zapato). El Príncipe consiguió encontrar a la mujer misteriosa. Las hermanastras de la Cenicienta sintieron envidia de su hermanastra. Romeo murió por el amor de Julieta.

GRAMÁTICA 26
Práctica A 1. e 2. b 3. f 4. a 5. c 6. d
Práctica B 1. ¿Hay más pan? ¿Me lo pasas, por favor? 2. ¿Hay más tortillas? ¿Me las pasas, por favor? 3. ¿Hay más tomates? ¿Me los pasas, por favor? 4. ¿Hay más fruta? ¿Me la pasas, por favor? 5. ¿Hay más vino? ¿Me lo pasas, por favor? 6. ¿Hay más jamón? ¿Me lo pasas, por favor?
Práctica C 1. Acaban de decírnosla. (Nos la acaban de decir.) 2. Sí, léemelo, por favor. 3. No, no tiene que dárselos (se los tiene que dar) aquí. 4. Claro que se lo guardo. 5. Acabo de comprártelos. (Te los acabo de comprar.) 6. Te lo puedo guardar. (Puedo guardártelo.) 7. Sí, se la recomiendo. 8. La asistente de vuelo nos la va a servir (va a servírnosla) en el avión.

UN POCO DE TODO
Actividad A 1. algunos 2. varios 3. son 4. de 5. conmemora 6. Muchos 7. esta 8. apareció 9. a 10. un 11. de 12. dejó 13. ver 14. todas 15. son 16. el 17. es 18. el 19. el 20. de la 21. Llegan 22. otros 23. pasarlo 24. corren 25. la 26. a la 27. Algunas 28. corren 29. hay 30. esta 31. es 32. la 33. describió 34. su 35. es 36. hablar 37. conocieron
Comprensión 1. falso: No todas las fiestas hispánicas son religiosas. 2. falso: Algunos mexicoamericanos también celebran esa fiesta. 3. falso: La fiesta de San Fermín es esencialmente para los adultos. 4. cierto

Capítulo 9
VOCABULARIO: PREPARACIÓN
PASATIEMPOS, DIVERSIONES Y AFICIONES: Conversación A: *Paso 1* *Possible answers:* 1. visita museos 2. hacen (dan) fiestas 3. hace *camping*
LOS QUEHACERES DOMÉSTICOS: Conversación A *Possible answers:* 1. la alcoba 2. la cocina, el garaje (el patio) 3. la sala 4. el baño, el patio (el garaje) 5. la cocina 6. la sala (el comedor, las alcobas) 7. la cocina (el garaje), la alcoba 8. la cocina
Conversación C 1. Se usa para limpiar las ventanas. 2. Se usa para hacer café. 3. Se usa para sacudir los muebles. 4. Se usa para poner (sacar) la basura. 5. Se usa para lavar los platos. 6. Se usa para el lavaplatos. 7. Se usa para lavar la ropa. 8. Se usa para limpiar el cuarto de baño.

GRAMÁTICA 27
Práctica B 1. Todos los días asistía a la escuela primaria. 2. Por la mañana aprendía a leer y escribía en la pizarra. 3. A las diez bebía leche y dormía un poco. 4. Iba a casa para almorzar y regresaba a la escuela. 5. Estudiaba geografía y hacía dibujos. 6. Jugaba con sus compañeros en el patio de la escuela. 7. Camino de casa, compraba dulces y se los comía. 8. Frecuentemente pasaba por la casa de los abuelos. 9. Cenaba con sus padres y los ayudaba a lavar los platos. 10. Miraba la tele un rato y se acostaba a las ocho.
Práctica C: *Paso 1* *Possible answers:* El bebé estaba llorando. El perro y el gato estaban peleando. Un niño pequeño estaba peleando con su hermana pequeña. El teléfono estaba sonando. Un vendedor estaba llamando a la puerta. Unos jóvenes adolescentes estaban discutiendo. El radio estaba sonando muy fuerte. El televisor estaba funcionando también.

GRAMÁTICA 28
Práctica B 1. _____ es el día festivo más divertido del año. 2. _____ es la clase más interesante de todas mis clases. 3. _____ es la persona más inteligente de todos mis amigos. 4. Nueva York (Toronto) es la ciudad más

grande de los Estados Unidos (del Canadá). 5. Rhode Island es el estado más pequeño de los Estados Unidos. / Prince Edward Island es la provincia más pequeña del Canadá. 6. _____ es el metro más rápido del mundo. 7. _____ es la residencia más ruidosa de la universidad. 8. Everest es la montaña más alta del mundo.

GRAMÁTICA 29

Práctica A   1. Qué 2. Qué 3. Cuál 4. Qué 5. Cuáles 6. Qué 7. Qué 8. Cuál

Práctica B   *Possible answers:* 1. ¿Cuál es tu teléfono? 2. ¿Cuál es tu dirección? 3. ¿Cuándo es tu cumpleaños? 4. ¿En qué ciudad naciste? ¿Dónde naciste? 5. ¿Cuál es tu número de seguro social? 6. ¿Quién es la persona en que más confías? 7. ¿Cuál es tu tienda favorita para ir de compras? ¿Dónde prefieres ir de compras? 8. ¿Cuál es la fecha de tu próximo examen? ¿Cuándo es tu próximo examen?

UN POCO DE TODO

Actividad A: *Paso 1*   1. (k, c) Primero, Ricardo se despertó temprano, pero se quedó en cama mucho tiempo. 2. (g) Luego se duchó y se vistió rápidamente. 3. (a) Llegó tarde a su primera clase. 4. (b) Almorzó en la cafetería con algunos amigos. 5. (f, j) Después fue al gimnasio y jugó un partido de basquetbol. 6. (e, l, i) Regresó a casa. Luego preparó la cena y estudió un poco. 7. (d, m) Después miró la televisión un rato hasta que sonó el teléfono. 8. (h) Finalmente se acostó.

Paso 2   1. Eran las seis y media de la mañana. 2. Ricardo tenía prisa. 3. Los estudiantes escuchaban a la profesora. 4. Ricardo tenía mucha hambre. 5. Había muchas personas en el gimnasio. 6. Era temprano todavía. 7. No quería hablar por teléfono. 8. Ricardo pensaba en el examen de mañana.

Actividad B   1. llegó 2. supo 3. eran 4. diferentes 5. vivía 6. antigua 7. tenía 8. de 9. hablaban 10. Miren 11. puedo 12. divertirme 13. tampoco 14. iba 15. pasábamos 16. tomando 17. nadando 18. comiendo 19. cantando 20. gustaba 21. Son 22. impresionantes 23. íbamos 24. hacíamos 25. quiero 26. ser

Comprensión   1. Los conoció en la lavandería. 2. Son de Cartagena. 3. Sé que tienen niños y que son de Colombia 4. Se quejaron de la ropa sucia. 5. Iba a la playa con su familia 6. Iba con su familia a las fortalezas, a las Bóvedas o a la Isla Barú.

Capítulo 10
VOCABULARIO: PREPARACIÓN
LA SALUD Y EL BIENESTAR: Conversación A: *Paso 1*   *Possible answers:* 1. el corazón 2. la boca; los dientes; el estómago 3. la boca; la garganta 4. los ojos 5. el cerebro; la cabeza 6. el estómago 7. el corazón 8. los pulmones; la boca 9. los oídos; las orejas 10. la nariz

Paso 2   *Possible answers:* 1. ver; mirar; leer; las gafas; los lentes de contacto 2. comer; la boca 3. comer; hablar; los dientes 4. oír; escuchar; la oreja 5. comer; tener hambre; la digestión

Conversación B   *Possible answers:* 1. Eso quiere decir que es necesario dormir ocho horas todas las noches. 2.

Eso quiere decir que es necesario hacer media hora de ejercicio todos los días. 3. Eso quiere decir que no se debe ir a fiestas todas las noches y dormir poco. 4. Eso quiere decir que es necesario comer bien, dormir lo suficiente y hacer ejercicio diariamente. 5. Eso quiere decir que se debe comer equilibradamente, hacer ejercicio regularmente y dormir lo suficiente.

EN EL CONSULTORIO: Conversación A   1. un resfriado 2. respira 3. enfermo, enfermero/a 4. tos 5. dolor

Conversación B   *Possible answers:* 1. Anamari está muy bien de salud. Nunca le duele la cabeza (le duelen los pies). Nunca tiene fiebre. Siempre hace ejercicio. 2. Martín tiene un dolor de muela. Debe tomar una aspirina. El dentista va a examinarlo. Después, Martín va a guardar cama. 3. A Inés le duele el estómago. Tiene apendicitis. El médico y la enfermera van a examinarla. Luego, Inés tiene que tener una operación.

GRAMÁTICA 30

Práctica A   1. c 2. f 3. g 4. e 5. a 6. b 7. d

Práctica B   HISTORIA 1 1. vivíamos 2. íbamos 3. nos quedábamos 4. nuestra familia decidió 5. nos gustó 6. nos quedamos HISTORIA 2 1. se apagaron 2. estaba leyendo 3. me levanté 4. tenía 5. Salí 6. estaban apagadas 7. había HISTORIA 3 1. intentaba tomarle 2. esperaba 3. llegó 4. examinó 5. puso 6. dio 7. estaba 8. se sintió

Práctica C   1. preguntó 2. quería 3. dijo 4. sentía 5. salieron 6. Vieron 7. se rieron 8. hacía 9. entraron 10. tomaron 11. Eran 12. regresaron 13. se acostó 14. estaba 15. empezó

Comprensión   1. Estudiaba. 2. Le preguntó si quería ir al cine con ella. 3. Porque se sentía un poco aburrido. 4. Sí, porque se rieron mucho. 5. Porque hacía frío. 6. No regresaron a casa a las dos. 7. Soledad se acostó, pero Rubén, empezó a estudiar otra vez.

Práctica D   1. hicimos 2. era 3. organizaba 4. venían 5. Había 6. hablaba 7. bailaba 8. llamaron 9. dijeron 10. hacíamos 11. Vino 12. dijo 13. era 14. queríamos 15. podíamos 16. despedimos 17. eran 18. aprendió 19. hace 20. invita

Práctica E: *Paso 1*   1. Cuando yo era niño, pensaba que lo mejor de estar enfermo era guardar cama. 2. Lo peor era que con frecuencia yo me resfriaba durante las vacaciones. 3. Una vez yo me puse muy enfermo durante la Navidad. 4. Mi madre llamó al médico con quien tenía confianza. 5. El Dr. Matamoros vino a casa y me dio un antibiótico porque tenía mucha fiebre. 6. Eran las cuatro de la mañana cuando por fin yo empecé a respirar sin dificultad. 7. Desgraciadamente, el día de Navidad yo tuve que tomar jarabe y no me gustaba nada el sabor. 8. Lo bueno de esta enfermedad era que mi padre tuvo que dejar de fumar mientras yo estaba (estuve) enfermo.

Paso 2   1. Cuando mi hijo era niño, pensaba que lo mejor de estar enfermo era guardar cama. 2. Lo peor era que con frecuencia se resfriaba durante las vacaciones. 3. Una vez se puso muy enfermo durante la Navidad. 4. Llamé al médico con quien tenía confianza. 5. El Dr. Matamoros vino a casa y le dio un antibiótico porque tenía mucha fiebre. 6. Eran las cuatro de la mañana cuando por fin mi hijo empezó a respirar sin dificultad. 7. Desgraciadamente, el día de Navidad tuvo que tomar jarabe y no le gustaba nada el sabor. 8. Lo bueno de esta enfermedad era que mi esposo tuvo que dejar de fumar mientras mi hijo estaba (estuvo) enfermo.

Conversación C: *Paso 1* 1. abrió 2. entró 3. vio 4. se sentó 5. gustó 6. se sentó 7. vio 8. decidió 9. fue 10. se acostó 11. se quedó

GRAMÁTICA 31

Práctica A 1. que 2. quien 3. Lo que 4. que 5. que 6. lo que 7. quién 8. lo que 9. lo que

Práctica B: *Paso 1* 1. algo contra su cansancio, intranquilidad, preocupación, nerviosismo, desequilibrio y ansiedad 2. estrés 3. la normalidad

UN POCO DE TODO

Actividad A 1. Me llamo 2. conoce 3. soy 4. Algunos 5. están 6. que 7. dijeron 8. es 9. vienen 10. nosotros 11. van 12. nuestra 13. sabemos 14. leímos 15. que 16. me 17. Lo que 18. sabemos 19. algo 20. todos 21. Qué 22. se lo 23. respondió 24. encanta 25. Lo que 26. son 27. era 28. vivía 29. llevábamos 30. practicábamos 31. dábamos 32. parque 33. hacíamos 34. ninguna 35. llamenme 36. conocer

Comprensión 1. Es una profesora venezolana que enseña química. Bettina es estudiante de Franklin High. 2. Tiene amigos en la clase de la Sra. Ayala. 3. Sabía algo de los tepuis. 4. Quiere saber de la vida diaria de los venezolanos. Porque dos chicas venezolanas van a vivir con su familia por un año. 5. Dice que las chicas van a tener mucho en común con Bettina. 6. Jugaba a varios deportes, daba paseos y hacía ejercicio en el gimnasio.

Actividad B: *Paso 1* 1. se llamaba 2. eran 3. quería 4. dijo 5. salió 6. preguntó 7. contestó 8. dijo 9. se fue 10. llegó 11. entró 12. tenía 13. Saltó 14. corrió 15. llegó 16. Encontró 17. estaba 18. dijo 19. dijo 20. se enteró 21. avisó 22. saltó 23. se abalanzó 24. salió 25. vio 26. ocurría 27. Le disparó 28. hizo 29. regresó 30. abrazó 31. prometió

Capítulo 11
VOCABULARIO: PREPARACIÓN
LAS PRESIONES DE LA VIDA ESTUDIANTIL: Conversación B
1. b 2. a 3. d 4. e 5. c

¡LA PROFESORA MARTÍNEZ SE LEVANTÓ CON EL PIE IZQUIERDO!: Conversación B
Possible answers: 1. Tomo una aspirina. 2. Digo «fue sin querer». 3. Me pongo avergonzado/a. 4. Me doy con una silla y me caigo. 5. Me duele.

Conversación D 1. pacientemente 2. inmediatamente 3. fácilmente 4. totalmente 5. constantemente 6. puntualmente

GRAMÁTICA 33

Práctica B: *Paso 1* Hace mucho tiempo que Jennifer López canta en español. Hace mucho tiempo que Alex Rodríguez juega al béisbol. Hace mucho tiempo que Antonio Banderas trabaja en Hollywood. Hace poco tiempo que «Sponge Bob» es uno de los programas favoritos de los niños en la televisión. Hace mucho tiempo que el profesor / la profesora de español habla español (trabaja [vive] en esta universidad). Hace mucho/poco tiempo que un compañero / una compañera de clase vive en esta ciudad (habla español).

Paso 2 1. Hace más de quinientos años que Cristóbal Colón llegó a América. 2. Hace más de cincuenta años que la Segunda Guerra Mundial terminó. 3. Hace casi veinte años que John Lennon murió. 4. Hace casi (cuatro) años que el presidente (primer ministro) actual fue elegido. 5. Hace _____ años (meses) que el profesor (la profesora) de español empezó a enseñar en esta universidad.

Conversación: *Paso 1* *Possible answers:* 1. ¿Cuánto tiempo hace que vives en este estado? 2. ¿Cuánto tiempo hace que asistes a esta universidad? 3. ¿Cuánto tiempo hace que vives en tu casa (apartamento, residencia,...)? 4. ¿Cuánto tiempo hace que estudias español? 5. ¿Cuánto tiempo hace que manejas tu coche / tomas el autobús / montas en bicicleta / caminas a la universidad? 6. ¿Cuánto tiempo hace que usas una computadora?

Paso 2 *Possible answers:* 1. ¿Cuánto tiempo hace que visitaste a tus padres (abuelos, hijos,...)? 2. ¿Cuánto tiempo hace que conociste a tu mejor amigo/a? 3. ¿Cuánto tiempo hace que aprendiste a manejar? 4. ¿Cuánto tiempo hace que entregaste tu última tarea? 5. ¿Cuánto tiempo hace que diste un informe oral? 6. ¿Cuánto tiempo hace que llegaste tarde a clase?

GRAMÁTICA 34

Práctica A 1. d 2. c 3. e 4. g 5. a 6. b 7. f

Conversación: *Paso 1* 1. se le olvidó 2. se le cayeron 3. se le acabó 4. se le perdió 5. se le rompieron

GRAMÁTICA 35

Práctica A 1. g 2. h 3. e 4. c 5. f 6. d 7. b 8. a

Práctica B 1. Para 2. Por 3. por 4. Para 5. Para, Por 6. Para

Práctica C 1. para, por, por, por, para 2. para, por, para, por 3. Por, por, por 4. para, Para 5. para, para, para, para, para

UN POCO DE TODO

Actividad A: *Paso 1* 1. Anoche la Sra. Ortega puso trajes de baño y toallas en su bolsa. 2. Cuando era pequeña, Cecilia se acostaba temprano todas las noches. 3. Esta mañana a Lorenzo se le perdieron las llaves y se le cayó una taza de café. 4. Esta noche los estudiantes de la clase de historia no van a dormir mucho. 5. Ahora Amalia está contenta.

Paso 2 1. Anoche la Sra. Ortega puso trajes de baño y toallas en su bolsa porque su familia empieza la clase de natación hoy. 2. Cuando era pequeña, Cecilia se acostaba temprano todas las noches porque iba a clase muy temprano. 3. Esta mañana a Lorenzo se le perdieron las llaves y se le cayó una taza de café porque estaba distraído. 4. Esta noche los estudiantes de la clase de historia no van a dormir mucho porque tienen el examen final mañana. 5. Ahora Amalia está contenta porque hay una fiesta grande en casa de la profesora.

Actividad C 1. está 2. celebra 3. Por 4. fascinantes 5. por 6. decidieron 7. algunas 8. estas 9. mandaron 10. para

11. típicos 12. Piensa 13. un 14. se llama 15. esperen
16. podemos 17. sabes 18. conocen 19. tienen 20. Díganme
21. cuál 22. fue 23. me 24. perdieron 25. las 26. por
27. escúcheme 28. oficiales 29. dieron 30. trabajaba
31. llevaba 32. me pegué 33. cayeron

Comprensión   1. falso: Sandra Dávila está en la Universidad de Puerto Rico hoy para entrevistar a estudiantes y profesores 2. cierto 3. falso: «El peor día del semestre» es un programa que cuenta los peores días del semestre. 4. cierto 5. falso: A Rafael se le cayeron ocho flanes sobre la cabeza del rector de la universidad.

Capítulo 12
VOCABULARIO: PREPARACIÓN
TENGO... NECESITO... QUIERO... : Conversación A: *Paso 1*   1. Le mando el documento por fax. 2. Lo grabo con la videocasetera. 3. Uso el control remoto. 4. Uso el contestador automático. 5. Escucho el *walkman*.

Conversación B: *Paso 1*   1. Debe comprarse una motocicleta. 2. Debe comprarse un coche descapotable. 3. Debe comprarse una camioneta. 4. Debe comprarse una bicicleta. 5. Debe comprarse un monopatín. 6. Debe comprarse un carro nuevo.

LA VIVIENDA: Conversación A   1. Es una persona que paga dinero para vivir en un apartamento o una casa. 2. Es un lugar donde hay muchos edificios y tiendas. 3. Es el dinero que se paga cada mes. Los inquilinos tienen que pagarles el alquiler a los dueños. 4. Es una persona que trabaja en una casa de apartamentos. 5. Es una persona que vive cerca en nuestra vecindad, residencia o casa de apartamentos. 6. Es una persona que tiene un apartamento o una casa (de apartamentos) que se alquila. 7. Es una cosa que indica dónde vive alguien. 8. Es el área que está fuera de una ciudad. 9. Es un lugar residencial típicamente con casas y jardines. 10. Es una vivienda separada (no conectada), típicamente para un matrimonio o una familia. 11. Es una calle grande que típicamente tiene árboles y flores. 12. Es el área rural, fuera de la ciudad. 13. Es el piso principal y abre a la calle. 14. Es lo que podemos ver desde las ventanas o las puertas. 15. Es lo que necesitamos para poner las lámparas, el televisor, la computadora y los aparatos de la cocina.

GRAMÁTICA 36
Práctica B: *Paso 1*   1. No los dejes allí, por favor. 2. No regreses a casa tan tarde, por favor. 3. No vayas al parque todas las tardes, por favor. 4. No mires la televisión constantemente y no veas programas de detectives, por favor. 5. No le digas mentiras, por favor. 6. No te olvides de sacar la basura, por favor. 7. No seas tan insolente, por favor.

Paso 2   1. Llega a la escuela puntualmente. 2. Quítate el abrigo y siéntate. 3. Saca el libro de matemáticas y ábrelo en la página diez. 4. Lee las nuevas palabras y apréndelas para mañana. 5. Ven aquí a hablar conmigo sobre esta composición.

GRAMÁTICA 37
Práctica B   *Possible answers:* 1. b (a) 2. a (b) 3. f (b) 4. c (i) 5. h 6. g (e, d) 7. j (k) 8. a (b, c, f)

GRAMÁTICA 38
Práctica A   1. su amigo 2. Ud. 3. su amigo 4. el vendedor 5. Ud. 6. Ud. 7. el vendedor

Práctica B: *Paso 1*   1. Todos los profesores quieren que los estudiantes lleguen a clase a tiempo. 2. El profesor / La profesora de español prefiere que vayamos con frecuencia al laboratorio de lenguas. 3. Los profesores prohíben que los estudiantes traigan comida y bebida a clase. 4. Los padres de los estudiantes desean que sus hijos asistan a sus clases. 5. Los estudiantes piden que los profesores no den mucho trabajo. 6. También quieren que haya más vacaciones. 7. Los padres insisten en que sus hijos saquen buenas notas.

Práctica C   *Possible answers:* 1. Queremos que el nuevo televisor esté en la sala. Nos gusta ver la tele todos juntos. 2. Preferimos que el televisor portátil esté en la cocina. A mamá le gusta ver la tele al cocinar. 3. Es necesario que el equipo estereofónico esté en la alcoba de Julio. A él le gusta escuchar música al estudiar. 4. Es buena idea que el sillón grande esté en la sala. A papá le gusta leer el periódico allí. 5. Queremos que los monopatines de los niños estén en el patio. A ellos les gusta jugar allí. 6. Es buena idea que la computadora esté en la oficina. Nos gusta hacer las cuentas allí. 7. Queremos que el acuario esté en la alcoba de Anita. A ella le gusta mirar los peces.

UN POCO DE TODO
Actividad A   1. Se escriben 2. por 3. descubren 4. tienen 5. sugiere 6. venga 7. conocer 8. sigue 9. me alegro 10. estemos 11. esta 12. se levanta 13. vamos 14. va 15. estar 16. prepararse 17. tengo 18. vienen 19. verte 20. Pregúntales 21. tus 22. escríbeme 23. estábamos hablando 24. hace 25. a 26. nos vemos 27. es 28. queda 29. salen 30. de 31. dijeron 32. pueden 33. cuidan 34. Escríbeme 35. lo 36. Salimos 37. para

Comprensión   *Correct order of sentences:* 3. Matilde y Marcia se conocen por correo electrónico. 4. La garúa de Lima se levanta, y todos van a la playa. 1. Matilde invita a Marcia y a la familia de ella a visitar Lima. 5. La madre de Marcia quiere hacer el viaje a Lima. 2. Marcia y su mamá aceptan la oferta de quedarse en el apartamento.

Actividad B: *Paso 1*   1. Escúchame 2. hagas 3. Juega 4. Canta 5. se lo des 6. los pongas

Capítulo 13
VOCABULARIO: PREPARACIÓN
LAS ARTES: Conversación A: *Paso 1*   1. la arquitectura 2. la pintura 3. la escultura 4. el ballet (el baile / la danza) 5. el cine 6. la ópera 7. las ruinas (la arquitectura) 8. la literatura 9. la arquitectura 10. la pintura 11. la literatura 12. la fotografía 13. la música 14. la literatura, el cine

GRAMÁTICA 39
Práctica B   1. funcione, sea, la entienda 2. nos dé, tenga, cambie 3. tenga, sean, pueda

Práctica C   1. Ojalá que el escenario sea extravagante. 2. Ojalá que haya subtítulos en inglés. 3. Ojalá que el conductor esté preparado. 4. Ojalá que los cantantes sepan sus papeles. 5. Ojalá que nuestros asientos no estén lejos del escenario. 6. Ojalá que lleguemos a tiempo.

GRAMÁTICA 40

Práctica B   1. Creo que es una figura de la civilización maya. 2. Es cierto que la figura está hecha de oro. 3. Es posible que represente un dios importante. 4. No estoy seguro/a de que la figura sea auténtica. 5. No creo que sea una figura de la civilización maya. 6. Creo que es de la civilización tolteca. 7. Estoy seguro/a de que está hecha de bronce. 8. Creo que representa la víctima de un sacrificio humano.

GRAMÁTICA 41

Práctica A: *Paso 1*   1. ... me enseñe los cuadros más famosos de Velázquez. 2. ... me explique algunos detalles de los cuadros. 3. ... sepa mucho sobre la vida del pintor.
Paso 2   1. ... tengan como tema la vida cotidiana. 2. ... estén en otros museos fuera de España. 3. ... sean de la familia real de Carlos IV.
Paso 3   1. ... me recomiende algunos libros sobre la vida y el arte del pintor. 2. ... le pregunte a un colega si sabe algo más sobre Velázquez. 3. ... no tenga más tiempo para hablar conmigo.
Práctica B   *Possible answers:* Le voy a decir que / Le voy a pedir que ... me escriba el informe para la clase de literatura / me haga una crítica de una película para la clase de composición avanzada / ponga la mesa / asista a todas mis clases en la universidad / pague mis cuentas / trabaje por mí en la oficina todas las tardes.

UN POCO DE TODO

Actividad B   1. Pasen 2. dejen 3. delante 4. Es 5. representa 6. pintó 7. de la 8. durante 9. estuvo 10. se trasladó 11. este 12. sea 13. es 14. creo 15. tengan 16. ser 17. sirve 18. Por 19. puede
Comprensión   1. Ud. 2. el guía 3. su amigo 4. el guía

Capítulo 14
VOCABULARIO: PREPARACIÓN
LA NATURALEZA Y EL MEDIO AMBIENTE: Conversación

A   *Possible answers:* 1. el campo 2. el campo 3. la ciudad 4. la ciudad 5. la ciudad 6. el campo 7. el campo 8. la ciudad
Conversación B   *Possible answers:* 1. Es un lugar donde se hacen cosas. 2. Es una persona que trabaja en el campo. 3. Es cuando no hay suficiente de algo. 4. Es un lugar donde hay muchos animales domésticos y plantas. 5. Los árboles, los animales y la vegetación son parte de la naturaleza. 6. Son todas las personas que viven en un lugar. 7. Es un cuerpo de agua que corre hacia el mar o un lago. 8. Es un edificio muy alto con muchos pisos. Está generalmente en una gran ciudad.
LOS COCHES: Conversación A: *Paso 1*   1. g 2. h 3. i 4. d 5. b 6. f 7. c 8. a 9. j 10. e
Paso 2   *Possible answers:* 1. Son las luces que controlan la circulación. Son de color rojo, amarillo y verde. 2. Son los vehículos que se ven en la carretera o en la calle. 3. Es poner el coche en un lugar para dejarlo allí. 4. Es lo que hace el coche para poder funcionar. 5. Es el lugar donde

se compra gasolina para el coche. 6. Es una carretera grande sin semáforos, donde los coches pueden circular a gran velocidad.

GRAMÁTICA 42

Práctica B   1. desperdiciado 2. destruidos 3. hechos 4. reciclados 5. agotadas 6. limitadas 7. acostumbrados 8. cerrada 9. apagadas 10. bajado
Práctica C   1. La tienda no está abierta todavía. 2. Las ventanas no están cerradas todavía. 3. La tierra no está cubierta de nieve todavía. 4. La mesa no está puesta todavía. 5. El medio ambiente no está destruido todavía. 6. El error no está descubierto todavía. 7. El problema no está resuelto todavía.

GRAMÁTICA 43

Práctica B   1. Le ha pedido ayuda a su padre. 2. Ha hecho preguntas acerca de los diferentes coches. 3. Ha visto uno bastante barato. 4. Ha revisado las llantas. 5. Lo ha conducido como prueba. 6. Ha regresado a la agencia. 7. Ha decidido comprarlo. 8. Lo ha comprado. 9. Ha vuelto a casa. 10. Ha llevado a sus amigas al cine en su coche.

UN POCO DE TODO

Actividad C   1. les 2. lo que 3. ha descubierto 4. tratando 5. me 6. hayas encontrado 7. comparan 8. ti 9. parece 10. me encuentro 11. escrita 12. he oído 13. presentemos 14. sugieres 15. pongamos 16. entreguemos 17. a 18. creó 19. fue 20. impresionantes 21. salen 22. algunas 23. escalen
Comprensión   1. falso: Los estudiantes de clase de Geografía mundial van a preparar un informe sobre el país que escogieron. 2. falso: Milton, Marisol y Petra están terminando su informe sobre la Argentina. 3. cierto 4. falso: Petra no está contenta porque dice que la información no tiene nada de nuevo. 5. cierto 6. El Parque Nacional Los Glaciares es un parque muy grande en el sur de la Argentina.

Capítulo 15
VOCABULARIO: PREPARACIÓN
LAS RELACIONES SENTIMENTALES: Conversación

A   *Possible answers:* 1. e, casarse, el esposo / la esposa 2. c, enamorarse, querer, el novio / la novia 3. b, divorciarse, el ex esposo / la ex esposa 4. d, casarse, el novio / la novia 5. a, hablarse, el amigo / la amiga
Conversación B   1. esposo 2. noviazgo 3. cita 4. boda 5. pareja 6. amistad 7. amor 8. matrimonio 9. una boda 10. el amor
ETAPAS DE LA VIDA: Conversación A   *Possible answers:* 1. la adolescencia; la juventud 2. la vejez 3. la niñez 4. la infancia; la vejez 5. la madurez 6. la adolescencia; la juventud 7. la juventud 8. la juventud; la madurez

GRAMÁTICA 44

Práctica B: *Paso 1*   1. ¿Hay librerías que (donde) vendan libros usados? 2. ¿Hay tiendas donde se pueda comprar revistas de Latinoamérica? 3. ¿Hay cafés cerca de la universidad donde se reúnan muchos estudiantes? 4. ¿Hay apartamentos cerca de la universidad que sean buenos y baratos? 5. ¿Hay cines donde pasen películas en español? 6. ¿Hay un gimnasio en la universidad donde se juegue al ráquetbol? 7. ¿Hay parques donde la gente corra o dé paseos? 8. ¿Hay museos donde hagan exposiciones de arte latinoamericano?

Paso 2 1. falso 2. cierto 3. cierto 4. falso

GRAMÁTICA 45

Práctica B Pues, para que... 1. podamos estacionar el coche. 2. no perdamos el principio de la función. 3. podamos comprar los boletos. 4. consigamos buenas butacas. 5. no tengamos que hacer cola. 6. compremos palomitas de maíz antes de que empiece la película. 7. hablemos con los amigos. 8. saquemos dinero del cajero automático.

Práctica C: Paso 1 1. No voy a menos que dejemos a la niña con los abuelos. 2. Vamos solos para que pasemos un fin de semana romántico. 3. Esta vez voy a aprender a esquiar con tal que tú me enseñes. 4. Vamos a salir temprano por la mañana a menos que nos acostemos tarde la noche anterior. 5. Es importante que lleguemos a la estación de esquí antes de que empiece a nevar. 6. Deja la dirección y el teléfono del hotel en caso de que tus padres nos necesiten.

Paso 2 1. falso (no lo dice) 2. no lo dice 3. falso 4. cierto

UN POCO DE TODO

Actividad B 1. salió 2. conoció 3. leer 4. es 5. tienen 6. lo 7. Escucha 8. te cuente 9. me recibió 10. me dijo 11. iba 12. insiste 13. vaya 14. sabía 15. sea 16. te ha contado 17. las llevé 18. hayan comido 19. riquísima 20. les 21. guste 22. resultó 23. había cenado 24. comimos 25. me ofrecí 26. sugerí 27. se puso 28. me preguntó 29. evitemos 30. te invité 31. pasan 32. Adónde 33. supe 34. se reúnen 35. de 36. abren 37. cierran 38. divertirse 39. desayunan 40. nos reímos 41. le he prometido 42. vamos

Capítulo 16
VOCABULARIO: PREPARACIÓN

PROFESIONES Y OFICIOS: Conversación A *Possible answers:* 1. el plomero / la plomera 2. el abogado / la abogada 3. el/la siquiatra 4. el enfermero / la enfermera 5. el criado / la criada 6. el obrero / la obrera 7. el/la periodista

EL MUNDO DEL TRABAJO: Conversación A a. 13 b. 2 c. 5 d. 7 e. 1 f. 4 g. 14 h. 9 i. 11 j. 3 k. 8 l. 10 m. 12 n. 6

UNA CUESTIÓN DE DINERO Conversación B: Paso 1 1. f. 2. d 3. e 4. c 5. a 6. b

GRAMÁTICA 46

Práctica B: Paso 1 1. Yo hablaré bien el español. Pasaré mucho tiempo en la biblioteca. Escribiré artículos sobre la literatura latinoamericana. Daré clases en español. 2. Tú trabajarás en una oficina y en la corte. Ganarás mucho dinero. Tendrás muchos clientes. Cobrarás por muchas horas de trabajo. 3. Felipe verá a muchos pacientes. Escuchará muchos problemas. Leerá a Freud y a Jung constantemente. Le hará un sicoanálisis a un paciente. 4. Susana y Juanjo pasarán mucho tiempo sen-

tados. Usarán el teclado constantemente. Inventarán nuevos programas. Les mandarán mensajes electrónicos a todos los amigos.

Paso 2 1. profesor(a) 2. abogado/a 3. siquiatra 4. programador(a)

Práctica C: Paso 1 1. Gregorio pagará tarde todas las cuentas. 2. Tratará de adaptarse a un presupuesto. 3. Volverá a hacer un presupuesto el próximo mes. 4. No depositará nada en la cuenta de ahorros. 5. Se quejará porque no tendrá suficiente dinero. 6. Seguirá usando tarjetas de crédito. 7. Les pedirá dinero a sus padres. 8. Buscará un trabajo de tiempo parcial.

Paso 2 2. Gregorio tiene que aprender a ser más responsable con su dinero.

GRAMÁTICA 47

Práctica A: Paso 1 1. No ha pasado todavía. a 2. Acción habitual. b 3. Acción habitual. b 4. No ha pasado todavía. a 5. No ha pasado todavía. a

Práctica B 1. se graduó, le dieron, se gradúe, le darán 2. era, quería, tenía, decidió, termine, podrá 3. escribe, tiene, va, llegue

Práctica C 1. ... me den un aumento de sueldo / deje de gastar tanto. 2. ... tenga el dinero para hacerlo / sea absolutamente necesario. 3. ... cobre mi cheque en el banco / me mande _____ un cheque. 4. ... saque dinero de mi cuenta de ahorros / deposite el dinero en mi cuenta corriente. 5. ... terminen sus estudios universitarios / se casen.

UN POCO DE TODO

Actividad A: Paso 1 1. Es necesario que ahorremos más. 2. Yo no usaré tantas tarjetas de crédito (tanto las tarjetas de crédito). 3. Mamá buscará un trabajo donde le paguen más. 4. Pediremos un préstamo en el banco. 5. Nos lo darán, ¿no crees? 6. Papá estará tranquilo cuando todos empecemos a economizar. 7. Deberás pagar siempre al contado. 8. No podremos irnos de vacaciones este verano.

Paso 2 No, tiene problemas económicos.

Actividad B 1. Carmen quiere esperar hasta que se gradúe en la universidad. 2. Miguel se lo va a decir a los padres de Carmen tan pronto como ellos lleguen a la ciudad. 3. Los padres de Carmen siempre quieren ver a Miguel cuando visitan a su hija. 4. Los padres se van a alegrar en cuanto oigan las noticias. 5. Miguel y Carmen van a Acapulco en su luna de miel cuando tengan dinero. 6. Todos nosotros les vamos a dar una fiesta después de que ellos regresen de su viaje.

Actividad C 1. la 2. el 3. que 4. gastos 5. los 6. se 7. empecé 8. pude 9. Trabajaba 10. estudiaba 11. era 12. ganaba 13. Sacaba 14. Trabajaba 15. Ayudaba 16. ofrecieron 17. normalmente 18. económicamente 19. trabajan 20. cuidan 21. ayudan 22. trabajan 23. trabajen 24. terminen 25. es 26. necesitan 27. lo que 28. se van 29. estudiar 30. Viven 31. sus 32. la

Comprensión 1. cierto 2. falso (Muchos estudiantes hispánicos trabajan.) 3. cierto

Capítulo 17
VOCABULARIO: PREPARACIÓN
LAS NOTICIAS: Conversación B 1. a 2. f 3. i 4. g 5. d 6. c 7. h 8. e 9. b
EL GOBIERNO Y LA RESPONSABILIDAD CÍVICA: Conversación A: *Possible answers:* 1. el/la ciudadano/a; los demás; votar 2. el servicio militar; la guerra 3. el/la político/a; el gobierno; la ley 4. el/la ciudadano/a; votar; el deber 5. el rey / la reina; el gobierno 6. obedecer; el ejército
Conversación B 1. g 2. b 3. e 4. h 5. a 6. d 7. f 8. c

GRAMÁTICA 48
Práctica C: *Paso 1* 1. Los obreros querían que les dieran un aumento de sueldo. 2. Era posible que los trabajadores siguieran en huelga hasta el verano. 3. Era necesario que las víctimas recibieran atención médica en la Clínica del Sagrado Corazón. 4. Era una lástima que no hubiera espacio para todos allí. 5. Los terroristas pidieron que los oficiales no los persiguieran. 6. Parecía imposible que el gobierno aceptara sus demandas. 7. Era necesario que el gobierno informara a todos los ciudadanos del desastre. 8. Dudaba que la paz mundial estuviera fuera de nuestro alcance. 9. El presidente y los directores preferían que la nueva fábrica se construyera en México. 10. Temía que el número de votantes fuera muy bajo en las próximas elecciones.
Paso 2 1. hecho 2. opinión 3. opinión 4. opinión 5. hecho 6. opinión 7. opinión 8. opinión 9. hecho 10. opinión

GRAMÁTICA 49
Práctica A 1. mía 2. suya 3. mía 4. mía 5. suya
Práctica B 1. Esta maleta, ¿es de Juan? —No, no es suya. 2. Esta maleta, ¿es de Uds.? —No, no es nuestra. 3. Esta maleta, ¿es de Alicia? —No, no es suya. 4. Esta maleta, ¿es mía? —No, no es tuya (suya). 5. Esta maleta, ¿es tuya? —No, no es mía. 6. ¿Y este despertador? —No, no es mío. El mío es más pequeño. 7. ¿Y estos zapatos? —No, no son míos. Los míos son más pequeños. 8. ¿Y esta llave? —No, no es mía. La mía es más pequeña. 9. ¿Y este televisor? —No, no es mío. El mío es más pequeño. 10. ¿Y estas pastillas? —No, no son mías. Las mías son más pequeñas. 11. ¿Y este periódico? —No, no es mío. El mío es más pequeño.

UN POCO DE TODO
Actividad A: *Paso 1* *Possible answers:* 1. practicara (los puritanos) 2. hubiera (los españoles) 3. siguieran (los ingleses que llegaron a Australia) 4. hubiera (los judíos) 5. tuvieran (los irlandeses)
Paso 2 1. Los indios temían que los colonos les quitaran toda la tierra. 2. A los colonos no les gustaba que fuera necesario pagarle impuestos al rey. 3. Parecía imposible que la joven república tuviera éxito. 4. A los del sur no les gustaba que los gobernaran los del norte. 5. A los abolicionistas no les gustaba que algunos no tuvieran las mismas libertades. 6. Era necesario que se declararan en huelga los obreros para obtener algunos derechos. 7. Era terrible que hubiera dos guerras mundiales. 8. Para que nosostros vivamos en paz, es cuestión de aprender a comunicarnos. 9. También es necesario que haya leyes que garanticen los derechos.
Actividad C 1. hablan 2. se ven 3. pierden 4. ninguna 5. practicar 6. tendrán 7. qué 8. poder 9. tuya 10. te 11. entré 12. tienen 13. escuchemos 14. falte 15. algún 16. pueda 17. entiendas 18. oyes 19. mía 20. viéramos 21. recomendar 22. tratara 23. a 24. presentan 25. una 26. Por 27. hicieron 28. dieron 29. Podré 30. dicen 31. ten 32. veas 33. crees
Comprensión 1. Recomiendan que escuche el español todos los días. 2. Aconsejó que mirara mucho la televisión en español. 3. Cristi trata de comprender todas las palabras que oye. 4. «Finalmente» es un noticiero y programa de entrevistas que se transmite desde la República Dominicana a medianoche. 5. Vio una entrevista con candidatos para presidente y un reportaje sobre un ataque terrorista.

Capítulo 18
VOCABULARIO: PREPARACIÓN
LUGARES Y COSAS EN EL EXTRANJERO: Conversación A 1. cierto 2. falso (Iría a un bar.) 3. falso (Para mandar paquetes se va al correo.) 4. falso (El metro es más rápido.) 5. falso (Se va a una farmacia.) 6. falso (Deberías ir a una farmacia.) 7. cierto 8. falso (Un batido se hace con leche.)
Conversación B *Possible answers:* 1. Se compran en la farmacia. 2. En una farmacia en el extranjero no se venden tantas cosas como en los Estados Unidos. 3. En el correo o en un estanco. 4. Se va al estanco. 5. Es un lugar donde se venden periódicos y revistas, lápices y libros, papel para cartas, etcétera. 6. Venden libros, cuadernos, lápices, papel para cartas, etcétera.
EN UN VIAJE AL EXTRANJERO: Conversación A 2, 3, 5, 6, 8, 9, 10
Conversación A: *Paso 1* 1. b 2. f 3. a 4. d 5. e 6. c

GRAMÁTICA 50
Práctica B 1. gustaría 2. trabajaría 3. Podría 4. Tomaría 5. Comería 6. Vería 7. sería 8. tendría 9. Podría 10. tendría
Comprensión 1. cierto 2. falso (Le gustaría nadar todos los días.) 3. falso (Tendría que usar su tarjeta de crédito.) 4. No lo dice.
Práctica C: *Paso 1* 1. ¿Estudiarías italiano? —No, estudiaría chino. 2. ¿Renunciarías a un puesto sin avisar? —No, avisaría con dos semanas de anticipación. 3. ¿Harías un viaje a España? —No, haría un viaje a la Argentina. 4. ¿Saldrías de casa sin apagar el estéreo? No, saldría sin apagar las luces. 5. ¿Seguirías un presupuesto rígido? —No, seguiría uno flexible. 6. ¿Gastarías menos en ropa? —No, gastaría menos en libros. 7. ¿Pondrías el aire acondicionado en invierno? —No, lo pondría en verano. 8. ¿Alquilarías un coche de lujo? —No, alquilaría uno económico.

GRAMÁTICA 51

Práctica B   1. Si fuera a la Argentina, me quedaría en Buenos Aires. 2. Si tuviera interés en la población italiana, visitaría el barrio italiano La Boca. 3. Si quisiera mandar una tarjeta postal, la compraría en un quiosco. 4. Si tuviera ganas de comprar libros, pediría direcciones al barrio San Telmo. 5. Si quisiera ver una obra de teatro, iría al Teatro Colón. 6. Si me interesara visitar unos sitios turísticos, vería el obelisco y la réplica de Big Ben. 7. Si quisiera probar comida auténtica, comería carne argentina. 8. Si quisiera escuchar música típica, escucharía el tango.

Práctica C: *Paso 1*   a. 5   b. 1   c. 4   d. 3   e. 2

UN POCO DE TODO

Actividad C   1. fueras 2. conocer 3. son 4. amables 5. recibirían 6. nos divertiríamos 7. tengo 8. viajar 9. por 10. tenía 11. intentamos 12. hacer 13. pudiera 14. tuvimos 15. empecé 16. he vuelto 17. acompañaría 18. gran 19. podrías 20. pasamos 21. todos 22. los 23. muchísimo 24. tengas 25. Iríamos 26. españolas 27. prefiere 28. Muchas 29. alquilan 30. suerte 31. nos alojamos 32. alguien 33. diera 34. podrías 35. sé 36. las 37. veas 38. estas 39. muestra 40. algunas

Comprensión   1. Paco y Bob se encuentran para hablar de lo que pueden hacer durante el verano. 2. Paco quiere que Bob vaya con él porque hay mucho que hacer en Barcelona. 3. Bob no puede ir porque tiene miedo de viajar por avión. 4. Bob no ha vuelto a viajar por avión desde el incidente desastroso que tuvo a los diez años. 5. Las vacaciones son muy importantes para los españoles. 6. Paco siempre veranea en las Islas Baleares porque su tío tiene un hotel de lujo allí.

VOCABULARIES

This **Spanish-English Vocabulary** contains all the words that appear in the text, with the following exceptions: (1) most close or identical cognates that do not appear in the chapter vocabulary lists; (2) most conjugated verb forms; (3) diminutives ending in **-ito/a;** (4) absolute superlatives in **-ísimo/a;** and (5) most adverbs in **-mente.** Active vocabulary is indicated by the number of the chapter in which a word or given meaning is first listed (**AT=Ante todo**); vocabulary that is glossed in the text is not considered to be active vocabulary and is not numbered. Only meanings that are used in the text are given. The **English-Spanish Vocabulary** is based on the chapter lists of active vocabulary.

The gender of nouns is indicated, except for masculine nouns ending in **-o** and feminine nouns ending in **-a.** Stem changes and spelling changes are indicated for verbs: **dormir (ue, u); llegar (gu).** Because **ch** and **ll** are no longer considered separate letters, words beginning with **ch** and **ll** are found as they would be found in English. The letter **ñ** follows the letter **n: añadir** follows **anuncio,** for example. The following abbreviations are used:

adj.	adjective	*L.A.*	Latin America
adv.	adverb	*m.*	masculine
Arg.	Argentina	*Mex.*	Mexico
C.A.	Central America	*n.*	noun
coll.	colloquial	*obj. (of prep.)*	object (of a preposition)
conj.	conjunction	*pl.*	plural
d.o.	direct object	*Port.*	Portuguese
def. art.	definite article	*poss.*	possessive
f.	feminine	*p.p.*	past participle
fam.	familiar	*prep.*	preposition
form.	formal	*pron.*	pronoun
gram.	grammatical term	*refl. pron.*	reflexive pronoun
ind. art.	indefinite article	*s.*	singular
inf.	infinitive	*sl.*	slang
interj.	interjection	*Sp.*	Spain
inv.	invariable form	*sub. pron.*	subject pronoun
i.o.	indirect object	*Uru.*	Uruguay
irreg.	irregular		

Spanish–English Vocabulary

A

a to (AT); at (*with time*) (AT); **a base de** based on; **a bordo** on board; **a consecuencia de** as a consequence of; **a continuación** following, below; **a diferencia de** unlike; **a favor de** in favor of; with the aid of; **a finales de** at the end of; **a la(s)...** at . . . (*hour*); **a la derecha (de)** to the right (of) (5); **a la izquierda (de)** to the left (of) (5); **a la plancha** grilled; **a la vez** at the same time; **a larga distancia** long-distance; **a largo plazo** long-term; **a lo largo de** along;

throughout; **a menos que** *conj.* unless (15); **a menudo** often; **a partir de** as of; from (*this moment, date on*); **a pesar de** in spite of; **a pie** on foot; **a primera vista** at first sight (15); **a principios de** at the beginning of; **¿a qué hora?** at what time? (AT); **a raíz de** as a result of; because of; **a sus órdenes** at your service; **a tiempo** on time (7); **a veces** sometimes, at times (2); **a ver** let's see

abajo below, underneath

abalanzarse (c) (sobre) to pounce (on)

abandonar to abandon; to leave

abanicar (qu) to fan

abarcar (qu) to comprise; to encompass

abecedario alphabet

abierto/a (*p.p. of* **abrir**) open(ed) (5)

abogado/a lawyer (16)

abolicionista *n. m., f.* abolitionist

abrazar (c) to embrace, hug

abreviar to abbreviate

abrigo coat (3)

abril *m.* April (5)

abrir (*p.p.* **abierto**) to open (2)

absoluto/a absolute; **en absoluto** at all

abstracto/a abstract

abuelo/a grandfather/grandmother (2)

abuelos *m. pl.* grandparents (2)

abundancia abundance

aburrido/a bored (5); **ser** (*irreg.*) **aburrido/a** to be boring (9)

aburrir to bore (13); **aburrirse** to get bored (9)

abuso abuse

acabar to finish (11); to run out of (11); to use up completely (14); **acabar de** + *inf.* to have just (*done something*) (6); **acabar por** + *inf.* to end up by (*doing something*)

academia: Real Academia Española Royal Spanish Academy

académico/a *adj.* academic

acaso: por si acaso just in case (11)

accesible accessible

acceso access

accidentalmente accidentally

accidente *m.* accident

acción *f.* action; **Día** (*m.*) **de Acción de Gracias** Thanksgiving

acecho/a: estar (*irreg.*) **acecho/a** to be lying in wait; to watch, be on the lookout

aceite *m.* oil (14); **aceite de oliva** olive oil; **revisar el aceite** to check the oil (14)

aceituna olive

acelerado/a fast, accelerated (14)

acelerar to speed up

acento accent

aceptar to accept

acerca de *prep.* about, concerning

aclaración *f.* clarification

aclarar to clarify

acogedor(a) welcoming

acomodarse (a) to adapt oneself (to)

acompañar to accompany; to go with

acondicionado/a: aire (*m.*) **acondicionado** air conditioning

aconsejable advisable

aconsejar to advise

acontecimiento event, happening (17)

acordarse (ue) (de) to remember (11)

acordeón *m.* accordion

acorralado/a corralled; frightened

acortarse to become, get shorter

acostarse (ue) to go to bed (4)

acostumbrarse a to become accustomed to, get used to

acreedor(a) worthy, deserving

acrílico acrylic

actitud *f.* attitude

actividad *f.* activity

activista *n. m., f.* activist

activo/a active

acto act

actor *m.* actor (13)

actriz *f.* (*pl.* **actrices**) actress (13)

actual *adj.* current, present-day

actualidad *f.* present time

actuar (actúo) to act

acuario aquarium; **Acuario** Aquarius

acuático/a: deportes (*m. pl.*) **acuáticos** water sports

acuerdo agreement; **de acuerdo** agreed; **de acuerdo con** in accordance with; **(no) estoy de acuerdo** I (don't) agree (2); **ponerse** (*irreg.*) **de acuerdo** to reach an agreement

adaptación *f.* adaptation

adaptar to adapt; **adaptarse (a)** to adapt oneself (to)

adarga leather shield

adecuado/a appropriate

adelante let's go; **de ahora en adelante** from now on

adelanto advance

adelgazar (c) to lose weight

además *adv.* moreover; **además de** *prep.* besides

adicional additional

adiós good-bye (AT)

adivinanza riddle

adivinar to guess

adjetivo adjective (2)

administración *f.* administration; **administración de empresas** business administration (1)

administrado/a administered

administrativo/a administrative

admirar to admire

admitir to admit; to accept

adolescencia adolescence (15)

¿adónde? where (to)? (3)

adopción *f.* adoption

adoquinado/a cobblestoned

adorado/a adored

adorno decoration

adquirir (ie) to acquire

adquisitivo/a purchasing, buying

aduana *s.* customs; **control** (*m.*) **de aduana** customs checkpoint (18); **inspector(a) de aduanas** customs inspector

adulto/a adult

adverbio adverb

aeróbico/a: hacer (*irreg.*) **ejercicios aeróbicos** to do aerobics (10)

aeropuerto airport (7)

afectar to affect

afectivo/a emotional

afectuoso/a affectionate

afeitadora razor

afeitarse to shave oneself (4)

afición *f.* pastime, fun activity, hobby (9)

aficionado/a fan; **ser** (*irreg.*) **aficionado/a (a)** to be a fan (of) (9)

afirmación *f.* statement

afirmar to affirm, state

africano/a *n., adj.* African

afrocaribeño/a *adj.* Afro-Caribbean

afrocubano/a *adj.* Afro-Cuban

afuera *adv.* outside, outdoors (5)

afueras *n. pl.* suburbs, outskirts (12)

agencia agency; **agencia de viajes** travel agency (7)

agenda agenda; date book; **agenda de teléfonos** address/telephone book; **agenda digital/electrónica** electronic calendar, date book

agente (*m., f.*): **agente de viajes** travel agent (7)

ágil agile

agosto August (5)

agotar to use up

agradable pleasant

agradar to please (13)

agradecer (zc) to thank; to be grateful

agradecido/a grateful

agravar to make worse

agregar (gu) to add

agresividad *f.* aggressiveness

agresivo/a aggressive

agrícola *adj. m., f.* agricultural; **trabajador(a) agrícola** farm worker

agricultor(a) farmer (14)

agricultura agriculture (14)

agroturismo agrotourism (*farm stays*)

agroturista *n. m., f.* agrotourist

agua *f.* (*but* **el agua**) water (6); **agua dulce** fresh water; **agua mineral** mineral water (6); **cama de agua** waterbed; **huevo pasado por agua** poached egg

aguacate *m.* avocado

aguantar to stand, tolerate

aguar (gü) to spoil (*a party*)

agudo/a sharp

ahí there

ahora now (1); **ahora mismo** right now; at once; **de ahora en adelante** from now on

ahorrar to save (*money*) (16)

ahorros: cuenta de ahorros savings account (16)

aire *m.* air; (14); **aire acondicionado** air conditioning; **aire puro** clean air (14); **al aire libre** outdoors; **contaminación** (*f.*) **del aire** air pollution (14)

ajedrez *m.* chess (4); **jugar (ue) (gu) al ajedrez** to play chess (9)

ajillo: al ajillo in garlic sauce

ajo garlic; **diente** (*m.*) **de ajo** garlic clove

al (*contraction of* **a** + **el**) to the (3); **al** + *inf.* upon, while, when + *verb form*; **al aire libre** outdoors; **al ajillo** in garlic sauce; **al alza** on the rise; **al contrario** on the contrary; **al fondo** in the background; **al lado de** *prep.* alongside of (5); beside; next to (5); **al principio (de)** at the beginning of (16); **al revés** backward

ala *f.* (*but* **el ala**) wing

alarma alarm

álbum *m.* album

alcance *m.* reach

alcanzar (c) to reach

alce *m.* elk, moose
alcoba bedroom (4)
alcohol *m.* alcohol
alcohólico/a *adj.* alcoholic
aldea village
alegrarse (de) to be happy (about) (12)
alegre happy (5)
alemán *m.* German (*language*) (1)
alemán, alemana *n., adj.* German (2);
  perro pastor alemán German Shepherd
Alemania Germany
alergia allergy; **tener** (*irreg.*) **alergia a**
  to be allergic to
alérgico/a: ser (*irreg.*) **alérgico/a a** to
  be allergic to
alerta: ojo alerta eagle eye; **Fundación**
  (*f.***) Alerta contra la SIDA** AIDS
  Awareness Foundation
alertar to warn
alfabetización *f.* literacy
alfabetizado/a alphabetized
alfabeto alphabet
alfombra rug (4)
alfombrado/a carpeted
algo something, anything (3)
algodón *m.* cotton (3); **es de algodón** it
  is made of cotton (3)
alguien someone, anyone (6)
algún, alguno/a some (6); any (6);
  algún día some day; **alguna vez** once;
  ever
alimentar to feed
aliviar to relieve, alleviate
alivio relief
allá over there; **más allá** further,
  farther; **más allá de** beyond, farther
  than
allí (over) there (3)
alma *f.* (*but* **el alma**) soul
almacén *m.* department store (3)
almacenamiento storage
almendra almond
almohada pillow (18)
almorzar (ue) (c) to have lunch (4)
almuerzo lunch (6)
aló hello
alojamiento lodging (18)
alojarse to stay (*in a place*) (18)
alpinismo: hacer (*irreg.*) **el alpinismo**
  to mountain climb
alquilar to rent (12)
alquiler *m.* rent (12)
alrededor de *prep.* around; about
alrededores *m. pl.* surroundings
alteración *f.* irregularity
alternativa *n.* alternative
altitud *f.* altitude
alto/a tall (2); high; **clase** (*f.*) **alta** upper
  class
altura height, altitude; **ponerse** (*irreg.*)
  a la altura de to compete on the same
  level
alza: al alza on the rise

ama *f.* (*but* **el ama**) **de casa** homemaker
amable kind, nice (2)
amado/a *adj.* beloved
amanecer (zc) to wake up
amar to love (15)
amarillo/a yellow (3)
amasijo hodgepodge
Amazonas *m., s.* the Amazon
Amazonia Amazon (Basin)
amazónico/a *adj.* Amazonian
ambiental environmental (*pertaining to*
  surroundings)
ambiente *m.* atmosphere, environment; **medio ambiente** environment
  (*nature*) (14)
ámbito scope
amenazador(a) threatening
América Central Central America
americano/a *n., adj.* American; **fútbol**
  (*m.*) **americano** football (9)
amigo/a friend (1)
amistad *f.* friendship (15)
amistoso/a friendly (15)
amor *m.* love (15)
amplio/a large, spacious
amueblado/a furnished
analfabetismo illiteracy
análisis *m. inv.* analysis
analista (*m., f.*) **de sistemas** systems
  analyst (16)
analizar (c) to analyze
anaranjado/a *adj.* orange (3)
ancho/a wide; **de ancho** in width
anciano/a *n.* old person; *adj.* old;
  ancient
andar (*irreg.*) to walk; **andar en**
  bicicleta to ride a bicycle; **rueda de**
  andar treadmill
andino/a *adj.* Andean
anémico/a anemic
anfitrión, anfitriona host(ess) (8)
anglohablante *m., f.* English-speaker
ángulo angle
animado/a lively; animated; **dibujos**
  animados cartoons
animal *m.* animal (14); **animal domés-**
  tico domesticated animal, pet (14);
  animal salvaje wild animal (14)
ánimo: dar (*irreg.*) **ánimo** to cheer;
  estado de ánimo state of mind
aniversario anniversary
anoche *adv.* last night (10)
anotar to jot down
ansiedad *f.* fatigue; restlessness;
  worry; nervousness
Antártida Antarctica
ante *prep.* before; in front of; **ante todo**
  above all; first of all
anteayer *adv.* the day before yesterday
  (10)
antecedente *m.* antecedent
antemano: de antemano beforehand

anterior previous, preceding
antes *adv.* before; **antes de** *prep.* before
  (4); **antes de Cristo (a.C.)** before Christ
  (B.C.); **antes (de) que** *conj.* before (15)
antibiótico antibiotic (10)
anticipación: con anticipación in
  advance, ahead of time (18); **de**
  anticipación ahead
anticipar to anticipate
anticuado/a antiquated, old-fashioned
antigüedad *f.* antiquity; advanced age;
  pl. antiques
antiguo/a old; ancient; former
antipático/a unpleasant (2)
antirrevolucionario/a *n.* counterrevo-
  lutionary
antónimo antonym
antropología anthropology
antropólogo/a anthropologist
anual annual, yearly
anudado/a knotted
anunciar to announce (7)
anuncio announcement; advertisement
añadidura: de añadidura on the side
añadir to add
año year (5); **cumplir años** to have a
  birthday (8); **de los últimos años** in
  recent years; **Día** (*m.*) **del Año Nuevo**
  New Year's Day; **el año pasado** last
  year; **Feliz Año Nuevo** Happy New Year;
  los años sesenta, ochenta, etcétera the
  sixties, eighties, *and so on*; **pasar...**
  años to be more than . . . years old;
  tener (*irreg.*)**... años** to be . . . years
  old (2)
apagado/a out; turned off (*lights*)
apagar (gu) to turn off (*lights,*
  appliance) (11); **apagarse** to go out
  (*lights*)
aparato appliance; **aparato doméstico**
  home appliance (9); **aparato electró-**
  nico electronic device
aparcar (qu) to park
aparecer (zc) to appear
aparentemente apparently
apariencia appearance
apartamento apartment (1); **casa/blo-**
  que (*m.*) **de apartamentos** apartment
  building (12)
apartar to separate
aparte *adv.* apart, separately
apasionado/a passionate
apellido last name, surname
apenas hardly
apendicitis *f. s.* appendicitis
aperitivo aperitif; appetizer
apilado/a piled up
apinado/a tightly arranged
apio celery
aplicar (qu) to apply
apoyar to support (17)
apoyo support; **fondos** (*pl.*) **de apoyo**
  economic assistance

apreciar to appreciate (13)

aprender to learn (2); **aprender a** + *inf.* to learn how to (*do something*)

apretado/a tight

apropiado/a appropriate

aprovechar (de) to make use (of), avail oneself (of); **que aproveche** enjoy your meal

aproximadamente approximately

apuntar to write down

apuntes *m. pl.* notes

apurarse to hurry (up)

aquel, aquella *adj.* that (*over there*) (3); *pron.* that one (*over there*) (3)

aquello that (3); that thing (3)

aquellos/as *adj.* those (*over there*) (3); *pron.* those ones (*over there*) (3)

aquí here (1)

árabe *m.* Arabic (*language*); *n. m., f.* Arab

arado plow

árbol *m.* tree (14)

archipiélago archipelago

archivo computer file (12)

ardilla squirrel

área *f.* (*but* **el área**) area (12)

arena sand

arete *m.* earring (3)

argentino/a *n., adj.* Argentine

argumento argument; plot (*of a play, book*)

árido/a dry, arid

arma *f.* (*but* **el arma**) weapon

armado/a armed

armario closet (4)

arqueológico/a archeological

arquitecto/a architect (13)

arquitectónico/a *adj.* architectural

arquitectura architecture (13)

arrancar (qu) to start up (*a car*) (14); to pull out, wrench

arrastrar to drag

arreglar to straighten (up) (12); to fix, repair (12)

arriba *adv.* above; up

arrogante arrogant

arroz *m.* rice (6)

arte *f.* (*but* **el arte**) art (1); **obra de arte** work of art (13)

artesanía *s.* arts and crafts (13)

artículo article

artificial: fuegos artificiales fireworks

artista *m., f.* artist (13)

artístico/a artistic

arveja green pea (6)

arzobispo archbishop

asado/a roasted (6); **pollo asado** roast chicken (6)

asamblea assembly

ascensor *m.* elevator

asco: dar (*irreg.*) **asco** to make sick

asegurar to assure; **asegurarse** to make sure

asentarse (ie) to settle

asequible available

asesinado/a murdered

asesinato assassination (17); murder

asesoramiento advice

así thus, so; **así como** as well as; **así que** therefore, consequently, so

asiático/a *adj.* Asian

asiento seat (7)

asimilarse to assimilate

asistente *m., f.* assistant; **asistente de vuelo** flight attendant (7); **asistente del profesor** teaching assistant

asistir (a) to attend, go to (*a class, function*) (2)

asma *f.* (*but* **el asma**) asthma

asociación *f.* association

asociado: estado libre asociado commonwealth

asociar to associate

aspecto aspect; appearance; **no tener** (*irreg.*) **buen aspecto** to not look right

áspero/a rough

aspiración *f.* aspiration

aspiradora vacuum cleaner (9); **pasar la aspiradora** to vacuum (9)

aspirante *m., f.* candidate, applicant (16)

aspirina aspirin

astillero sheath

astronauta *m., f.* astronaut

astronomía astronomy

asumir to assume

asunto question, matter

atacar (qu) to attack

ataque *m.* attack (17); **ataque de nervios** nervous breakdown; **ataque terrorista** terrorist attack (17)

atar to tie

atención *f.* attention; **atención médica** healthcare

atender (ie) to attend to; to serve

ateo/a *adj.* atheist

atlántico/a: Océano Atlántico Atlantic Ocean

atleta *m., f.* athlete

atlético/a athletic

átono/a *gram.* unstressed

atracción *f.* attraction; **parque** (*m.*) **de atracciones** amusement park

atractivo/a attractive

atraer (*like* **traer**) to attract

atrapado/a trapped

atrás *adv.* back, backward; behind

atrasado/a: estar (*irreg.*) **atrasado/a** to be late (7)

atrevido/a daring

atribuir (y) to attribute

atropello assault, attack; abuse, outrage

atroz (*pl.* **atroces**) atrocious, brutal

atún *m.* tuna (6)

auditivo/a: comprensión auditiva listening comprehension

aumentar to increase

aumento increase; raise (12); **aumento de sueldo** raise (*in salary*) (16)

aun *adv.* even

aún *adv.* still, yet

aunque although

auscultar to listen (*with a stethoscope*)

ausencia absence

ausente absent

autenticidad *f.* authenticity

auténtico/a authentic

auto car; **auto chocador / de choque** bumper car

autobiografía autobiography

autobiográfico/a autobiographical

autobús *m.* bus (7); **estación** (*f.*) **de autobuses** bus station (7); **ir** (*irreg.*) **en autobús** to go / travel by bus (7); **parada del autobús** bus stop (18)

autoestima self-esteem

automático/a: cajero automático automatic teller machine (16); **contestador** (*m.*) **automático** answering machine (12)

automovilístico/a *adj.* automobile

autónomo/a autonomous

autopista freeway (14)

autoprueba self-test

autor(a) author

autoridad *f.* authority

autostop: hacer (*irreg.*) **autostop** to hitchhike

avanzado/a advanced

avenida avenue (12)

aventura adventure

aventurero/a adventurous

aventurismo adventure tourism

aventurista *m., f.* adventure tourist

avergonzado/a embarrassed (8)

avergonzarse (güe) (c) to be ashamed

averiguar (gü) to find out

aves *f. pl.* fowl

avestruz *m.* (*pl.* **avestruces**) ostrich

avión *m.* airplane (7); **ir** (*irreg.*) **en avión** to go/travel by plane (7)

avisar to warn

aviso warning

¡ay! *interj.* ah!; ouch!

ayer yesterday (4)

ayuda help

ayudante *m., f.* assistant

ayudar to help (6)

azafrán *m.* saffron

azteca *n., adj. m., f.* Aztec

azúcar *m.* sugar

azucarado/a sweetened; containing sugar

azul blue (3)

B

bailable danceable

bailar to dance (1)

bailarín, bailarina dancer (13)

baile *m.* dance (13)

bajado/a lowered

bajar to carry down; to lower; to go down; **bajar de** to get down from, off, to (7)

bajo *prep.* under

bajo/a *adj.* low; short (*in height*) (2); **planta baja** ground floor (12)

balance *m.* balance

balboa Panamanian monetary unit

balcón *m.* balcony

ballena whale (14)

ballet *m.* ballet (13)

banana banana (6)

bancarrota bankruptcy

banco bank (16)

banda band

banderilla *Sp.* appetizer

bandoneón *m.* large concertina

banquero/a banker

bañar to bathe; **bañarse** to take a bath (4)

bañera bathtub (4)

baño bathroom (4); **habitación** (*f.*) **con/sin baño** room with(out) bath (18); **traje** (*m.*) **de baño** bathing suit (3)

bar *m.* bar (club); **ir** (*irreg.*) **a un bar** to go to a bar (9)

barato/a inexpensive (3)

barbacoa barbecue

barca small boat

barcaza barge

barco boat, ship (7); **ir** (*irreg.*) **en barco** to go/travel by boat (7)

barra bar, railing

barrer (el piso) to sweep (the floor) (9)

barrera barrier

barriga belly

barril *m.* barrel

barrio neighborhood (12)

barro clay

basar to base, support (*an opinion*); **basarse en** to base one's ideas, opinions on

base *f.* base, foundation; basis; **a base de** based on

básico/a basic

basílica basilica

basquetbol *m.* basketball (9)

bastante *adv.* rather, sufficiently (15); enough (15)

basura trash; **sacar** (**qu**) **la basura** to take out the trash (9)

basurero wastebasket

bata robe

batalla battle

batería battery (14)

batido *drink similar to a milkshake* (17)

bautismo baptism

bebé *m., f.* baby

beber to drink (2)

bebida drink, beverage (6)

beca scholarship

béisbol *m.* baseball (9)

belleza beauty

bello/a beautiful (14); **Bella Durmiente** Sleeping Beauty

besar to kiss

beso kiss

biblioteca library (1)

bibliotecario/a librarian (1)

bicicleta (de montaña) (mountain) bicycle (12); **andar** (*irreg.*)/**montar en bicicleta** to ride a bicycle; **montañismo en bicicleta** mountain biking; **pasear en bicicleta** to ride a bicycle (9)

biculturalismo biculturalism

bien *adv.* well (AT); **caerle** (*irreg.*) **bien a alguien** to make a good impression on someone (16); **estar** (*irreg.*) **bien** to be comfortable (5) (*temperature*); **llevarse bien** to get along well (with) (15); **muy bien** fine, very well (AT); **pasarlo bien** to have a good time (8); **quedarle bien** to fit well; **salir** (*irreg.*) **bien** to turn out well

bienestar *m.* well-being (10)

bienvenido/a welcome

bilingüe bilingual

bilingüismo bilingualism

billete *m.* ticket (7); **billete de ida y vuelta** round-trip ticket (7)

billón *m.* billion

biodiversidad *f.* biodiversity

biografía biography

biología biology

biólogo/a biologist

bisonte *m.* bison, buffalo

bistec *m.* steak (6)

blanco/a white (3); **espacio en blanco** blank space; **vino blanco** white wine (6)

blancura whiteness

bloque (*m.*) **de apartamentos** apartment building (12)

blusa blouse (3)

bobo/a dumb, stupid

boca mouth (10)

boda wedding (15); **lista de bodas** bride's registry

bodegón *m.* inexpensive restaurant, tavern

boicoteo boycott

boleto ticket (7); **boleto de ida y vuelta** round-trip ticket (7)

bolígrafo pen (1)

bolívar *m.* Venezuelan monetary unit

boliviano/a *n., adj. m., f.* Bolivian

bolsa purse (3)

bolsillo pocket

bomba bomb (17)

bombardeo bombing

bombero/a firefighter

bombilla lightbulb

bonito/a pretty (2)

borde: al borde de on the verge of

bordo: a bordo on board

boricua *n., adj. m., f.* Puerto Rican

Borinquén *f.* *indigenous name for Puerto Rico*

bosque *m.* forest (14); **bosque primario** old-growth forest

bota boot (3)

botella bottle

botones *m. inv.* bellhop (18)

brasileño/a *n., adj.* Brazilian

bravura fierceness; bravery

brazo arm (11)

breve brief

brindar to offer

británico/a *adj.* British

bronce *m.* bronze

bronquitis *f. inv.* bronchitis

brote *m.* bud, shoot

bruja witch

brujo warlock; magician

bucanero/a buccaneer, pirate

bucear to scuba dive; to snorkle

buen, bueno/a *adj.* good (2); **buenas noches** good evening (AT); good night (AT); **buenas tardes** good afternoon (AT); **buenos días** good morning (AT); **hace buen tiempo** it's good weather (5); **lo bueno** the good thing, news (10); **muy buenas** good afternoon/evening; **sacar** (**qu**) **buenas notas** to get good grades (11)

bueno... *interj.* well . . . (2)

buque (*m.*) **petrolero** oil tanker

burbuja bubble

burocrático/a bureaucratic

busca: en busca de in search of

buscar (**qu**) to look for (1)

butaca seat (*in a theater*)

C

caballería chivalry

caballero knight; gentleman

caballo horse (14); **montar a caballo** to ride a horse (9)

caber *irreg.* to fit

cabeza head (10); **doler(le)** (**ue**) **la cabeza** to have a headache (11); **dolor** (*m.*) **de cabeza** headache (10)

cabezudo/a stubborn

cabina cabin (*on a ship*) (7)

cabo cape (*geography*)

cacique *m.* chief

cada *inv.* each, every (4); **cada vez más** increasingly

cadena channel (*television*); chain

cadera hip

caer *irreg.* to fall (11); **caerle bien/mal a alguien** to make a good/bad impression on someone (16); **caerse** to fall down (11)

café *m.* café (1); coffee (6); **de color café** brown (3)

cafeína caffeine

cafetera coffee pot, coffeemaker (9)

cafetería cafeteria (1)

caída fall (*accident*)

caja box; cashier, window

cajero/a   cashier, teller (16); **cajero automático** automatic teller machine (16)
calamar *m.*   squid
calcetín, calcetines *m.*   sock(s) (3)
calculadora   calculator (1)
calcular   to calculate
cálculo   calculus; calculation
calendario   calendar (11)
calentar (ie)   to heat
calidad *f.*   quality
cálido/a   hot
caliente   hot
calificación *f.*   grade (11)
calle *f.*   street (12)
callos (*m. pl.*) **a la madrileña**   tripe *specialty of Madrid*
calma   calm
calor *m.*   heat; **hace calor** it's hot (5); **tener** (*irreg.*) **(mucho) calor** to be (very) warm, hot (5)
caloría   calorie
calzas *pl.*   stockings
cama (de agua)   (water)bed (4); **guardar cama** to stay in bed (10); **hacer** (*irreg.*)**/tender (ie) la cama** to make the bed (9)
cámara   camera (12); **cámara de vídeo** video camera (12)
camarero/a   waiter, waitress (6)
camarógrafo/a   cameraman/woman
camarón *m.*   shrimp (6)
cambiante   changing
cambiar   to change; **cambiar de (canal/cuarto/ropa)** to change (channels/rooms/clothes) (12)
cambio   change; **en cambio** on the other hand, on the contrary
camello   camel
caminar   to walk (10)
caminata   walk
camino   way; road, street (14); **camino de** on the way; **camino Real** Royal Highway
camión *m.*   truck
camioneta   station wagon (7)
camisa   shirt (3)
camiseta   T-shirt (3)
campanada   stroke, ringing of a bell
campaña   campaign; **tienda de campaña** tent (7)
campeón, campeona   champion
campeonato   championship
campesino/a   farm worker (14), peasant (14)
camping m.   campground (7); **hacer** (*irreg.*) *camping* to go camping (7)
campo   field (14); countryside (12); **mozo de campo y plaza** farmhand
campus m. s.   (university) campus (12)
canadiense *n., adj. m., f.*   Canadian
canal *m.* canal;   channel; **cambiar de canal** to change channels (12)
cancelar   to cancel

cáncer *m.*   cancer
cancha   court (*sports*)
canción *f.*   song (13)
candidato/a   candidate
canela   cinnamon
cansado/a   tired (5)
cansancio   fatigue, weariness
cansarse   to get tired
cantante *m., f.*   singer (13)
cantar *m.*   song
cantar   to sing (1)
cantidad *f.*   quantity
canto   song
capa de ozono   ozone layer
capacidad *f.*   ability
capacitación *f.*   training
capacitado/a   trained
capaz (*pl.* capaces)   able
Caperucita Roja   Little Red Ridinghood
capital *f.*   capital city (5)
capítulo   chapter (1)
Capricornio   Capricorn
capturado/a   captured
capullo   bud
cara   face; **plantar cara a** to confront
característica *n.*   characteristic
caracterizar (c)   to characterize
caramelo   candy
carcajadas: **reírse (i, i) (me río) a carcajadas**   to laugh one's head off
cardinal: **punto cardinal**   cardinal direction (5)
carga   charge (*bullet, shell*)
cargar (gu)   to charge (*to an account*) (16); to carry
cargo   position, post; **estar** (*irreg.*) **a cargo** to be in control of
Caribe *m.*   Caribbean
caribeño/a *n., adj.*   Caribbean
cariño   affection
cariñoso/a   affectionate (5)
carne *f.*   meat (6); flesh
carnero   mutton
carnet *m.*   identity card
caro/a   expensive (3)
carpintero/a   carpenter
carrera   career; major (*academic*)
carretera   highway (14)
carro (descapotable)   (convertible) car (12)
carta   letter (2); **jugar (ue) (gu) a las cartas** to play cards (9); **papel** (*m.*) **de cartas** stationery (18)
cartel (*m.*)   poster
cartera   wallet (3)
cartón *m.*   cardboard
cartucho   cartridge
casa   house (2); **ama** *f.* (*but* **el ama**) **de casa** homemaker; **casa de apartamentos** apartment building (12); **en casa** at home (1); **limpiar la casa (entera)** to clean the (whole) house (9); **regresar a casa** to go home (1)

casado/a   married (2); **recién casado/a** newlywed (15)
casarse (con)   to marry (15)
cascanueces *m. s.*   nutcracker
casero/a *adj.*   home
casi   almost; **casi nunca** almost never (2)
caso   case; **caso de urgencia** emergency; **en caso de que** *conj.* in case (15)
castigar (gu)   to punish (17)
catalán *m.*   Catalan (*language*)
catálogo   catalogue
catarata   waterfall
catastrófico/a   catastrophic
catedral *f.*   cathedral
categoría   category
católico/a *n., adj.*   Catholic
catorce   fourteen (AT)
causa   cause
causar   to cause
caza   hunting
cazador(a)   hunter
cazuelita   bowl
CD-ROM *m.*   CD-ROM (12)
ceder   to cede
celebración *f.*   celebration
celebrar   to celebrate (5)
celular: **teléfono celular**   cellular phone (12)
cementerio   cemetery
cena   dinner, supper (6)
cenar   to have (eat) dinner, supper (6)
Cenicienta   Cinderella
censo   census
censurar   to censure
centavo   cent
centrado/a   centered
central   central; **América Central** Central America
céntrico/a   central
centro   center; downtown (3); **centro comercial** shopping mall (3)
Centroamérica   Central America
centroamericano/a *n., adj.*   Central American
ceño   frown
cepillarse los dientes   to brush one's teeth (4)
cerámica   pottery; ceramics (13)
cerca *adv.*   near, nearby, close; **cerca de** *prep.* close to (5); **de cerca** up close
cercanía   closeness
cercano/a *adj.*   close, near
cerdo   pork; **chuleta de cerdo** pork chop (6)
cereales *m. pl.*   cereal (6)
cerebro   brain (10)
ceremonia   ceremony
cerilla *Sp.*   match (*for lighting things*)
cero   zero (AT)
cerrado/a   closed (5)
cerrar (ie)   to close (4)
cerro   hill

cervantino/a *pertaining to (Miguel) Cervantes*

cervecería beer hall

cerveza beer (1)

césped *m.* grass

cesto basket

ceviche *m.* *raw fish dish*

champán *m.* champagne

champanería champagne bar

champiñón *m.* mushroom (6)

champú *m.* shampoo (18)

chaperón, chaperona chaperone

chaqueta jacket (3)

charlar to chat

chau *sl.* good-bye

cheque *m.* (bank) check (16); **cheque de viajero** traveler's check (18); **pagar (gu) con cheque** pay by check (16); **talonario de cheques** *Sp.* checkbook

chequeo checkup (10)

chequera checkbook (16)

chico/a boy, girl

chileno/a *n., adj.* Chilean

chimenea chimney

chimpancé *m.* chimpanzee

chino Chinese (*language*)

chino/a *n., adj.* Chinese

chiste *m.* joke (8)

chistoso/a funny, amusing

chocador(a): auto chocador bumper car

chocar (qu) (con) to run into, collide (with) (14)

chocolate *m.* chocolate; hot chocolate

chofer *m., f.* driver

choque *m.* collision (17); **auto de choque** bumper car; **choque** (*m.*) **de trenes** train wreck (17)

chorizo sausage

chuleta rib steak; **chuleta de cerdo** pork chop (6)

ciberespacial *adj.* cyberspace

ciberespacio *n.* cyberspace

ciclismo bicycling (9)

ciclo cycle

ciego/a blind

cielo heaven; sky

cien, ciento one hundred (2); **por ciento** percent

ciencia science; *pl.* science(s) (1); **ciencia ficción** science fiction; **ciencias políticas** *pl.* political science

científico/a *n.* scientist; *adj.* scientific

cierto/a true; certain (13); **en cierta medida** in some measure

cigarrillo cigarette

cilantro cilantro, fresh coriander

cinco five (AT); **Cinco de Mayo** Mexican awareness celebration

cincuenta fifty (2)

cine *m.* movies (4); movie theater (4); **ir** (*irreg.*) **al cine** to go to the movies (9)

cineasta *m., f.* film director

cinta tape (3)

cinturón *m.* belt (3)

circuito circuit

circulación *f.* traffic (14)

circular to circulate; to move

círculo circle, ring

circunstancia circumstance

ciruelo plum tree

cisne *m.* swan

cita appointment; date (15)

citado/a quoted

ciudad *f.* city (2)

ciudadanía citizenship

ciudadano/a citizen (17)

ciudadela citadel

cívico/a civic (17)

civil civil; **estado civil** marital status

civilización *f.* civilization

claro *interj.* of course

claro/a clear

clase *f.* class (1); **clase alta** upper class; **clase turística** tourist class (7); **compañero/a de clase** classmate (1); **en la clase** in class (1); **primera clase** first class (7); **sala de clase** classroom

clásico/a classic(al) (13)

cláusula *gram.* clause; **cláusula nominal** noun clause

cliente *m., f.* client (1); customer

clima *m.* climate (5)

climatología climatology

clínica clinic

club *m.* club

coágulo clot

cobrar to cash (*a check*) (16); to charge (*someone for an item or service*) (16)

cobre *m.* copper

coche *m.* car (2); **coche deportivo** sports car; **coche descapotable** convertible car (12)

cochera garage

cocido/a: huevo cocido hard-boiled egg

cocina kitchen (4)

cocinar to cook (6)

cocinero/a cook, chef (16)

coco coconut

cóctel *m.* cocktail

coger (j) to catch; to seize, grab

cognado cognate

coherente coherent

coincidir to coincide; to agree

cojear to limp

cola line; **hacer** (*irreg.*) **cola** to stand in line (7)

colección *f.* collection

coleccionar to collect

colega *m., f.* colleague

colegiatura *s.* fees

colegio secondary school

colesterol *m.* cholesterol

colgar (ue) (gu) to hang

colocar (qu) to place

colombiano/a *n., adj.* Colombian

colón *m.* monetary unit of Costa Rica and El Salvador

colonia colony

colonialismo colonialism

colonizador(a) colonist

colonizar (c) to colonize

colono/a settler

color *m.* color (3); **de color café** brown (3); **¿de qué color es?** what color is it? (3)

colorado/a red

columna column

comandante *m., f.* commander

combatir to fight, combat

combinación *f.* combination

combinar to combine

comedor *m.* dining room (4)

comentar to comment on; to discuss

comentario commentary

comenzar (ie) (c) to begin

comer to eat (2); **comer equilibradamente** to eat in a balanced way (10); **comérselo/la** to eat something up

comercial: centro comercial shopping mall (3)

comerciante *m., f.* merchant (16); shopkeeper (16)

cometer to commit

cómico/a funny; **tira cómica** comic strip

comida food (6); meal (6)

comisión *f.* commission

como like, as; **así como** as well as; **tal como** just as; **tan... como...** as . . . as . . . (5); **tan pronto como** as soon as (16); **tanto como** as much as (5); **tanto/a(s)... como...** as much/many . . . as . . . (5)

¿cómo? how? (AT); what? (AT); **¿cómo es usted?** what are you (*form. s.*) like? (AT); **¿cómo está(s)?** how are you? (AT); **¿cómo se llama usted?** what is your (*form. s.*) name? (AT); **¿cómo te llamas?** what is your (*fam. s.*) name? (AT)

cómoda bureau, dresser (4)

cómodo/a comfortable (4)

compacto/a: disco compacto compact disc (12)

compañero/a companion, friend; **compañero/a de clase** classmate (1); **compañero/a de cuarto** roommate (1)

compañía company

comparación *f.* comparison (5)

comparar to compare

comparativo *gram.* comparative

compartir to share

compasión *f.* compassion

compatabilizar (c) to make compatible

compensar to compensate, make up for

competición *f.* competition

complacer (zc) to please

complejo/a complex

complementar to complement

complementario/a complementary

complemento directo *gram.* direct object pronoun; **complemento indirecto** *gram.* indirect object pronoun
completar to complete
completo/a complete; full, no vacancy (18); **pensión** (*f.*) **completa** room and full board (18); **por completo** completely; **trabajo de tiempo completo** full-time work (11)
complexión *f.* body type/build
complicado/a complicated
complicar (qu) to complicate
componer (*like* **poner**) to compose
comportamiento behavior
composición *f.* composition
compositor(a) composer (13)
comprar to buy (1)
compras: de compras shopping (3); **ir** (*irreg.*) **de compras** to go shopping (3)
comprender to understand (2)
comprensión *f.* comprehension; **comprensión auditiva** listening comprehension
comprensivo/a understanding
comprobar (*like* **probar**) to prove
compromiso commitment
computación *f.* computer science (1)
computadora computer (12); **computadora portátil** laptop computer; **disco de computadora** computer disc (12); **escribir a computadora** to write on a computer (16)
común common, usual, ordinary
comunicación *f.* communication; *pl.* communications (1); **medio de comunicación** means of communication (17); **medios** (*pl.*) **de comunicación** media
comunicarse (qu) (con) to communicate (with) (17)
comunicativo/a communicative
comunidad *f.* community
comunitario/a *adj.* community
con with (1); **con anticipación** in advance, ahead of time (18); **con cheque** by check; **con cuidado** carefully; **con frecuencia** frequently (1); **con permiso** excuse me (AT); **con respecto a** with regard to, with respect to; **con tal (de) que** *conj.* provided that (15)
concentrarse to concentrate
concepción *f.* conception, idea
concepto concept, idea
concertar (ie) to arrange; to agree upon
conciencia conscience, moral awareness
concierto concert; **ir** (*irreg.*) **a un concierto** to go to a concert (9)
concluir (y) to conclude
conclusión *f.* conclusion
concordar (ue) (con) to correspond (to)
concurso contest
condición *f.* condition (8)
condicional *m. gram.* conditional

conducir *irreg.* to drive (14); to conduct; **conducir a** to lead to; **licencia de conducir** driver's license (14)
conductor(a) driver (14)
conectar to connect
conexión *f.* connection
confección *f.* confection
conferencia lecture
conferenciante *m., f.* lecturer
confianza trust
confiar (confío) to trust
configurado/a configured
confirmación *f.* confirmation
confirmar to confirm (18)
confrontación *f.* confrontation
confundido/a confused
congelado/a frozen (5); very cold (5)
congelador *m.* freezer (9)
congestionado/a congested, stuffed up (10)
congreso congress
conjugar (gu) *gram.* to conjugate
conjunción *f. gram.* conjunction
conjunto group
conmemorar to commemorate
conmigo with me (5)
conocer (zc) to know, be acquainted with (6); to meet
conocido/a known, famous
conocimiento knowledge
conquista conquest
conquistador(a) conqueror
consciente conscious, aware
conscripto draftee
consecuencia consequence; **a consecuencia de** as a consequence of
conseguir (*like* **seguir**) to get, obtain (8); **conseguir** + *inf.* to succeed in (*doing something*) (8)
consejero/a advisor (1)
consejo (piece of) advice (6); council
conservación *f.* conservation
conservador(a) *n., adj.* conservative
conservar to save, conserve (14)
considerar to consider
consigo with them
consistir en to consist of
constante *adj.* constant
constar de to consist of
constitución *f.* constitution
constitucional constitutional
constituir (y) to constitute; to be
construcción *f.* construction
constructivo/a constructive
construir (y) to build (14)
cónsul *m.* consul
consulta consultation
consultar to consult
consultorio doctor's office (10)
consumidor(a) consumer
consumir to consume
consumo consumption; use
contabilidad *f.* accounting

contable *m., f.* accountant
contacto contact; **lentes** (*m. pl.*) **de contacto** contact lenses; **llevar lentes de contacto** to wear contact lenses (10); **mantenerse** (*like* **tener**) **en contacto** to keep in touch
contado: pagar (gu) al contado to pay in cash (16)
contador(a) accountant (16)
contaminación (*f.*) **(del aire)** (air) pollution (14); **hay (mucha) contaminación** there's (lots of) pollution (5)
contaminar to pollute (14)
contar (ue) to tell (7); **contar con** to count on
contemplar to contemplate
contemporáneo/a contemporary
contenido contents
contento/a content, happy (5)
contestador (*m.*) **automático** answering machine (12)
contestar to answer (4)
contexto context
contigo with you (5)
continente *m.* continent
continuación: a continuación following, below
continuar (continúo) to continue
contra against; **en contra** opposed; **Fundación** (*f.*) **Alerta contra la SIDA** AIDS Awareness Foundation
contrabando contraband
contradicción *f.* contradiction
contraer (*like* **traer**) **matrimonio** to get married
contrario/a opposite; **al contrario** on the contrary; **lo contrario** the opposite
contrastar to contrast
contratar to contract
contratiempos *pl.* mishaps; disappointments
contrato contract
contribución *f.* contribution
contribuir (y) to contribute
control (*m.*) **de aduana** customs checkpoint (18); **control remoto** remote control (12); **pasar por el control de la seguridad** to go/pass through security (7)
controlar to control
convencer (z) to convince
convencional conventional
conveniencia convenience
conveniente convenient
conversación *f.* conversation
conversar to talk, converse
convertir (ie, i) to change, convert; **convertirse en** to turn into
convivencia living together, cohabitation
convivir to live together
cónyuge *m., f.* spouse
cooperativo/a cooperative

con tal de que — provided that (handwritten)

copa glass; (alcoholic) drink (18); upper branches in a tree; **Copa Mundial** World Cup; **tomar una copa** to have a drink

copia: hacer (*irreg.*) **una copia / copias** to copy (12)

copiar to copy (12)

coquí *m.* type of frog

coraje *m.* courage

corazón *m.* heart (10)

corbata tie (3)

corcho cork

cordillera mountain range

córdoba *m.* monetary unit of Nicaragua

coro chorus

corona wreath

coronel *m.* colonel

correcto/a correct, right

corredor(a) *adj.* running

corregir (i, i) (j) to correct

correo mail (18); **correo electrónico** e-mail (12); **oficina de correos** post office (18)

correr to run (9); to jog (9); to flow (*water*)

corresponder to correspond

correspondiente corresponding

corresponsal *m., f.* (news) correspondent

corrida de toros bullfight

corriente *adj.*: **cuenta corriente** checking account (16)

corriente *f.* current

cortar to cut

corte *m.* cut; *f.* court (*of law*)

cortés *m., f.* courteous

cortesía courtesy (AT)

cortina curtain

corto/a short (*in length*) (2); **pantalones** (*m. pl.*) **cortos** shorts

cosa thing (1)

cosechar to harvest

cosmopolita *adj. m., f.* cosmopolitan

costa coast

costar (ue) to cost; **¿cuánto cuesta?** how much does it cost? (3)

costarricense *n., adj. m., f.* Costa Rican

costero/a coastal

costilla rib

costo cost

costumbre *f.* custom (9); **por costumbre** customarily

cotidiano/a everyday, daily

crear to create (13)

creatividad *f.* creativity

creativo/a creative

crecer (zc) to grow (15)

creciente growing

crecimiento growth

crédito credit; **tarjeta de crédito** credit card (6)

creencia belief

creer (y) (en) to think (2); to believe (in) (2)

criada maid (18)

criado/a servant (16)

criar (crío) to raise (*children*)

criatura child

crimen *m.* crime

criminal *m., f.* criminal

criollo/a creole

crisis *f. inv.* crisis

cristal *m.* crystal

Cristo: antes de Cristo (a.C.) before Christ (B.C.); **después de Cristo (d.C.)** after Christ (A.D.)

crítica criticism

crítico/a *n.* critic; *adj.* critical

cronológico/a chronological

crudo/a crude (*oil*)

cruzar (c) to cross (18)

cuaderno notebook (1)

cuadrado *n.* square

cuadrado/a *adj.* square(d)

cuadro painting (13); **de cuadros** plaid

¿cuál(es)? what? (1); which? (1); **¿cuál es la fecha de hoy?** what's today's date? (5)

cualidad *f.* quality

cualquier *adj.* any

cualquiera *pron.* anyone; either

¿cuán? *adv.* how?

cuando when; **de vez en cuando** once in a while

¿cuándo? when? (1)

cuanto: en cuanto *conj.* as soon as (16); **en cuanto a** *prep.* regarding

¿cuánto/a? how much? (1); **¿cuánto cuesta?** how much does it cost? (3); **¿cuánto es?** how much is it? (3)

¿cuántos/as? how many? (1)

cuarenta forty (2)

cuarto *n.* room (1); one-fourth; quarter (*of an hour*); **cambiar de cuarto** to change rooms (12); **compañero/a de cuarto** roommate (1); **servicio de cuarto** room service (18); **y/menos cuarto** a quarter (fifteen minutes) after/to (*hour*) (AT)

cuarto/a *adj.* fourth (13)

cuatro four (AT)

cuatrocientos/as four hundred (3)

cubano/a *n., adj.* Cuban

cubanoamericano/a *adj.* Cuban American

cubierto/a (*p.p. of* cubrir) covered

cubito ice cube

cubo cube

cubrir (*p.p.* cubierto) to cover (14)

cuchara spoon

cucharada spoonful

cucharadita teaspoon

cuchillo knife

cuello neck

cuenta account (16); bill, check (6); **cargar (gu) a la cuenta de uno** to charge to someone's account (16); **cuenta corriente** checking account (16); **cuenta de ahorros** savings account (16); **darse** (*irreg.*) **cuenta** to realize; **estado de cuentas** bank statement; **tomar en cuenta** to take into account

cuento story

cuero leather

cuerpo body (10)

cuestión *f.* question, matter (16)

cuidado care; *interj.* careful; **con cuidado** carefully; **tener** (*irreg.*) **cuidado** to be careful

cuidadosamente carefully

cuidar(se) to take care of (oneself) (10); **¡hay que cuidarse!** you must take care of yourself! (10)

culinario/a culinary

culpa: tener (*irreg.*) **la culpa** to be guilty

cultista *adj. m., f.* cult member

cultivo cultivation, raising (*of crops*)

cultura culture

cumpleaños *m. inv.* birthday (5); **feliz cumpleaños** happy birthday; **pastel** (*m.*) **de cumpleaños** birthday cake (8)

cumplir años to have a birthday (8)

cuna cradle; birthplace

cuñado/a brother-in-law, sister-in-law

cupo quota, share

cura *m.* priest

curador(a) curator

curar(se) to heal, cure (oneself); **curarse de** to be cured of

currículum *m.* résumé (16)

cursar to study (*at a university*)

cursivo/a: letra cursiva *s.* italics

curso course

cuyo/a whose

D

dados *pl.* dice

danza dance (13)

daño damage; **hacerse** (*irreg.*) **daño** to hurt oneself (11)

dar *irreg.* to give (7); **dar ánimo** to cheer; **dar asco** to make sick; **dar un paseo** to take a walk (9); **dar una fiesta** to give a party (8); **darle la gana** to feel like; **darse** to occur; **darse cuenta (de)** to realize; **darse en/contra/con** to run, bump into (11); **darse la mano** to shake hands; **darse la vuelta** to turn oneself around

datar (de) to date (from)

datos *pl.* information; facts

dé give (*form. command*)

de *prep.* of (AT); from (AT); **de acuerdo** agreed; **de acuerdo con** in accordance with; **de ahora en adelante** from now on; **de ancho** in width; **de antemano**

de ahora en adelante

dehecho - in fact

de *prep.* (*continued*)
beforehand; **de anticipación** ahead; **de añadidura** on the side; **de cerca** up close; **de color café** brown (3); **de compras** shopping (3); **de cuadros** plaid; **de desnudismo** nudist; **¿de dónde es usted?** where are you (*form. s.*) from? (AT); **de guardia** on-call; **de hecho** in fact; **de ida** one-way (7); **de ida y vuelta** round-trip (7); **de joven** as a youth (9); **de la mañana/tarde** in the morning/afternoon (AT); **de la noche** in the evening (AT); at night (AT); **de largo** in length; **de los últimos años** in recent years; **de lujo** luxury (*adj.*) (18); **de lunares** polka-dotted; **de manera que** *conj.* so that, in such a way that; **de moda** in style; **de modo** in such a way; **de nada** you're welcome (AT); **de niño/a** as a child (9); **de noche** at night; **de paso** passing through; **de primera** first-class; **¿de qué color es?** what color is it? (3); **¿de quién?** whose? (2); **de rayas** striped; **de repente** suddenly (10); **de tiempo completo/parcial** full-time / part-time (11); **de todas maneras** by all means; whatever happens; **de todos modos** anyway; **de un jalón** all at once; **de vacaciones** on vacation (7); **de vez en cuando** once in a while; **de viaje** on a trip (7)
debajo de *prep.* below (5)
deber + *inf.* should, must, ought to (*do something*) (2); **deberse a** to be due to
deber *m.* responsibility, obligation (17)
debido a due to, because
débil weak
debilitamiento weakening, debilitation
década decade
decidir to decide
décimo/a tenth (13)
decir *irreg.* (*p.p.* **dicho**) to say (7); to tell (7); **es decir** that is to say; **eso quiere decir...** that means . . . (10)
decisión *f.* decision
decisivo/a decisive
declaración *f.* declaration
declarar to declare
decoración *f.* decoration
decorar to decorate
dedicarse (qu) a to dedicate oneself to
dedo (de la mano) finger (11); **dedo del pie** toe (11)
deducir *irreg.* to deduct
defecto defect
defender (ie) to defend
defensa defense
definición *f.* definition
definir to define
definitivo/a definitive
deforestación *f.* deforestation
deforestado/a deforested
deformación *f.* deformation

dejar (en) to leave (behind) (in [*in a place*]) (9); to quit (16); **dejar + *inf.*** to allow, let (*something happen*); **dejar de + *inf.*** to stop (*doing something*) (10)
del (*contraction of* **de** + **el**) of the (2); from the (2)
delante *adv.* before, in front, ahead; **delante de** *prep.* in front of (5)
delegación *f.* delegation
delegado/a delegate
deleitarse to take delight in; to enjoy
deletrear to spell
delgado/a thin, slender (2)
delicioso/a delicious
delincuente delinquent
demanda demand
demás: los/las demás the others, the rest (12)
demasiado *adv.* too, too much
demasiado/a *adj.* too much; *pl.* too many
democracia democracy
demócrata *m., f.* Democrat
demográfico/a demographic
demonio devil, demon
demora delay (7)
demostración *f.* demonstration
demostrar (*like* **mostrar**) to show, demonstrate
demostrativo/a *gram.* demonstrative
denso/a dense (14)
dental: pasta dental toothpaste (18)
dentista *m., f.* dentist (10)
dentro *adv.* in, within, inside; **dentro de** *prep.* within; **dentro de poco** in a little while
denuncia accusation
deparar to supply
departamento department; *Sp.* apartment
depender (de) to depend (on)
dependiente/a clerk (1)
deporte *m.* sport (9); **deportes acuáticos** water sports; **practicar (qu) deportes** to practice, play sports (10)
deportista *m., f.* sports player
deportivo/a sports *adj.* (9); **coche** (*m.*) **deportivo** sports car
depositar to deposit (16)
depósito deposit
deprimente depressing
derecha *n.* right; right hand; **a la derecha (de)** to the right (of) (5)
derecho *n.* right (*legal*) (17); **todo derecho** straight ahead (14)
derivarse (de) to derive (from)
dermatológico/a dermatologic, skin
derrocado/a overthrown
derrotado/a defeated
desafortunadamente unfortunately
desagradable unpleasant
desaparecer (*like* **parecer**) to disappear
desarraigado/a uprooted
desarrollar to develop (14)

desarrollo development
desastre *m.* disaster (17)
desastroso/a disastrous
desatino/a foolish
desayunar to have (eat) breakfast (6)
desayuno breakfast (4)
descansar to rest (4)
descanso rest
descapotable: carro/coche (*m.*) **descapotable** convertible car (12)
descender (ie) to descend
descendiente *m., f.* descendent
desconocido/a unknown
descortésmente discourteously, impolitely
describir (*like* **escribir**) to describe
descripción *f.* description
descubanizado/a less Cuban
descubierto/a (*p.p. of* **descubrir**) discovered
descubrimiento discovery
descubrir (*like* **cubrir**) (*p.p.* **descubierto**) to discover (14)
descuidado/a careless
desde *prep.* from (7); since; **desde entonces** from then on; **desde que** *conj.* since
deseable desirable
desear to want, desire (1)
desecho waste (*product*)
desempeñar to play, perform (*a part*) (13); to hold, carry out (*a responsibility*)
deseo wish (8)
desequilibrio imbalance
desertización *f.* process of becoming a desert
desesperadamente desperately
desfile *m.* parade
desgracia disgrace
desgraciadamente unfortunately
deshumanización *f.* dehumanization
desierto *n.* desert
desierto/a *adj.* deserted
designar to designate
desigualdad *f.* inequality (17)
desilusión *f.* disillusion
desinflado/a flat; **llanta desinflada** flat tire (14)
desintegrarse to break up
desnudismo: de desnudismo nudist
desnudo/a nude, naked
desocupado/a vacant, unoccupied (18)
desordenado/a messy (5)
desorientar to disorient, confuse
despacio *adv.* slowly
despedirse (i, i) (de) to say good-bye (to) (8); to take leave (of) (8)
despegar (gu) to take off (*airplane*)
desperdiciar to waste
despertador *m.* alarm clock (11)
despertarse (ie) (*p.p.* **despierto**) to wake up (4)
despierto/a (*p.p. of* **despertar**) awake
desplegar(se) (ie) (gu) to unfold

después *adv.* after, afterwards; later; **después de** *prep.* after (4); **después de Cristo (d.C.)** after Christ (A.D.); **después (de) que** *conj.* after (16)

destacado/a distinguished

destacar (qu) to emphasize; to stand out; **destacarse** to distinguish oneself

desterrado/a exiled

destinar to designate, assign

destino destination

destreza skill

destrucción *f.* destruction

destructivo/a destructive

destructor(a) destructive

destruir (y) to destroy (14)

desventaja disadvantage (10)

detalle *m.* detail (6)

detective *m., f.* detective

detener (*like* **tener**) to detain

detenidamente carefully

determinar to determine

detestar to detest, hate

detrás de *prep.* behind (5)

devolver (*like* **volver**) to return (*something*) (16)

día *m.* day (1); **algún día** some day; **buenos días** good morning (AT); **Día de Acción de Gracias** Thanksgiving; **Día de la Independencia** Independence Day; **Día de la Raza** Columbus Day (Hispanic Awareness Day); **Día de los Enamorados** Valentine's Day; **Día de los Inocentes** April Fool's Day; **Día de los Reyes Magos** Day of the Magi (Three Kings); **Día de San Patricio** St. Patrick's Day; **Día del Año Nuevo** New Year's Day; **día del santo** saint's day; **día festivo** holiday (8); **Día Internacional de los Trabajadores** International Labor Day; **día laborable** workday; **hoy (en) día** nowadays, these days; **ponerse** (*irreg.*) **al día** to get up-to-date; **¿qué día es hoy?** what day is today? (4); **todos los días** every day (1)

diabetes *f.* diabetes

diablo devil

diáfano/a transparent

diagrama *m.* diagram

dialecto dialect

diálogo dialogue

diamante *m.* diamond

diario/a daily; **rutina diaria** daily routine (4)

diarrea diarrhea

dibujar to draw (13)

dibujo drawing; **dibujos animados** cartoons

diccionario dictionary (1)

dicho/a (*p.p. of* **decir**) said; *adj.* that

diciembre *m.* December (5)

dictador(a) dictator (17)

dictadura dictatorship (17)

dictar to dictate

diecinueve nineteen (AT)

dieciocho eighteen (AT)

dieciséis sixteen (AT)

diecisiete seventeen (AT)

diente *m.* tooth (10); **cepillarse los dientes** to brush one's teeth (4); **diente de ajo** garlic clove

dieta diet; **estar** (*irreg.*) **a dieta** to be on a diet (6)

dietético/a *adj.* diet

diez ten (AT)

diferencia difference; **a diferencia de** unlike

diferente different

diferir (ie, i) to differ

difícil difficult (5)

dificultad *f.* difficulty

dificultar to make difficult

difundir to spread

difusión *f.* broadcasting

diga *interj.* say; hello

digestión *f.* digestion

digital: agenda digital electronic date book

dimensión *f.* dimension

Dinamarca Denmark

dinero money (1)

Diós *m. s.* God; **por Diós** for heaven's sake (11); *pl.* gods

diplomático/a diplomatic

diptongo *gram.* diphthong

dirección *f.* address (9); **dirección de personal** personnel office (16)

directo/a direct; **complemento directo** *gram.* direct object pronoun

director(a) director (13); **director(a) de personal** personnel director (16)

dirigir (j) to direct; to target

disco compacto compact disc (12); **disco de computadora** computer disc (12); **disco duro** hard drive (12)

discoteca discotheque; **ir** (*irreg.*) **a una discoteca** to go to a disco (9)

discriminación *f.* discrimination (17)

disculpa apology, excuse; **pedir (i, i) disculpas** to apologize (11)

disculpar to excuse, pardon; **discúlpame** pardon me (11); I'm sorry (11)

discutir (sobre/con) to argue (about/with) (8)

diseñador(a) designer

diseñar to design

diseño design

disfraz *m.* (*pl.* **disfraces**) disguise, costume; **fiesta de disfraz** costume party

disfrutar de to enjoy

disminuir (y) to lessen, diminish

disparar to shoot, fire

disparate *m.* silly thing; crazy idea

disponible available

disputa dispute, argument

distancia distance; **a/por larga distancia** long-distance

distante distant, far

distinguir (g) to distinguish

distinto/a different, distinct

distraer (*like* **traer**) to distract

distraído/a absentminded (11)

distribución *f.* distribution

distrito district

diversidad *f.* diversity

diversificar (qu) to diversify

diversión *f.* entertainment, amusement (9)

diverso/a diverse; various

divertido/a fun; **ser** (*irreg.*) **divertido/a** to be fun (9)

divertir (ie, i) to entertain; **divertirse** to have a good time, enjoy oneself (4)

dividir to divide

divorciado/a divorced (15)

divorciarse to get divorced (15)

divorcio divorce (15)

divulgar (gu) to make known

doblar to turn (14); to dub (*movies*)

doble double; **habitación** (*f.*) **doble** double room (*in a hotel*) (18)

doce twelve (AT)

dócil tame, docile

doctor(a) doctor

doctorado doctorate, Ph.D.

documentar to document

documento document

dólar *m.* dollar

doler (ue) to hurt, ache (10); **doler(le) la cabeza** to have a headache (11)

dolor *m.* pain, ache (10); **tener** (*irreg.*) **dolor de cabeza/estómago/muela** to have a headache/stomachache/toothache (10)

doméstico/a domestic; household; **animal** (*m.*) **doméstico** domesticated animal, pet (14); **aparato doméstico** home appliance; **quehacer** (*m.*) **doméstico** household chore

domicilio home, residence

dominación *f.* domination

dominar to dominate

domingo Sunday (4)

dominicano/a *n., adj.* Dominican

dominio mastery

don *m.* title of respect used with a man's first name

donde where

¿dónde? where? (1); **¿de dónde es usted?** where are you (*form. s.*) from? (AT); **¿dónde es... ?** where is . . . (8); **¿dónde está?** where is he/she/it/you (*form. s.*)? (5)

doña *f.* title of respect used with a woman's first name

dorado/a golden

dormir (ue, u) to sleep (4); **dormir la siesta** to take a nap (4); **dormir lo suficiente** to sleep enough (10); **dormirse** to fall asleep (4)

dormitorio bedroom

dos two (AT); **dos mil** two thousand (3); **dos millones** two million (3); **dos veces** twice (10); **hotel** (*m.*) **de dos estrellas** two-star hotel (18)

doscientos/as two hundred (3)

dosis *f. inv.* dose

drama *m.* drama (13)

dramático/a dramatic

dramaturgo/a playwright (13)

drásticamente drastically

droga drug; **traficar (qu) en drogas** to traffic in / deal drugs

dromedario dromedary (*camel*)

dualidad *f.* duality

ducha shower; **habitación** (*f.*) **con/sin ducha** room with/without a shower (18)

ducharse to take a shower (4)

duda doubt; **no hay duda** there is no doubt; **sin duda** without a doubt

dudar to doubt (12)

dudoso/a doubtful

dueño/a owner (6); landlord, landlady (12)

dulce *n. m.* sweet, candy (6); *adj.* sweet; **agua dulce** fresh water

dulzura sweetness

durante during (4)

durar to last (17)

durmiente: Bella Durmiente Sleeping Beauty

duro/a hard, firm; **disco duro** hard drive (12)

DVD *m.* DVD (12); **lector de DVD** DVD player (12)

E

e and (*used instead of* **y** *before words beginning with stressed* **i** *or* **hi**, *except* **hie-**)

echar to throw

ecología ecology

ecológico/a ecological

economía economy; *s.* economics (1)

económico/a economic

economizar (c) to economize (16)

ecosistema *m.* ecosystem

ecoturismo ecotourism

ecoturista *m., f.* ecotourist

ecuador *m.* equator

ecuatoriano/a *n., adj.* Ecuadorian

edad *f.* age; **Edad Media** Middle Ages

edificio building (1)

editor(a) editor

educación *f.* education

educado/a educated; polite; **mal educado/a** rude, bad-mannered

educativo/a educational

efectivo cash (16); **pagar (gu) en efectivo** to pay in cash (16)

efecto effect

eficiencia efficiency

eficiente efficient

Egipto Egypt

egoísta *m., f.* selfish

ejecutivo/a executive

ejemplar *m.* issue (*magazine*)

ejemplo example; **por ejemplo** for example (11)

ejercer (z) to practice (*a profession*)

ejercicio exercise (3); **hacer** (*irreg.*) **ejercicio** to exercise, get exercise (4); **hacer** (*irreg.*) **ejercicios aeróbicos** to do aerobics (10)

ejército army (17)

él *sub. pron.* he (1); *obj.* (*of prep.*) him

el *def. art. m. s.* the; **el primero de** the first of (*month*) (5)

elaborar to elaborate

elección *f.* election

electricidad *f.* electricity

electricista *m., f.* electrician (16)

eléctrico/a electric(al) (14)

electrónica *s.* electronics

electrónico/a electronic; **agenda electrónica** electronic calendar; **aparato electrónico** electronic device; **correo electrónico** e-mail (12); **mensaje** (*m.*) **electrónico** e-mail message

electrostático/a electrostatic

elefante *m.* elephant (14)

elegancia elegance

elegante elegant

elegir (i, i) (j) to choose; to elect

elemento element

elevar to raise, elevate

eliminar to eliminate

ella *sub. pron.* she (1); *obj.* (*of prep.*) her

ellos/as *sub. pron.* they (1); *obj.* (*of prep.*) them

embajada embassy

embajador(a) ambassador

embarazada *n.* pregnant woman

embargo: sin embargo nevertheless

embotellamiento de tráfico traffic jam

embriagado/a drunk

emergencia emergency; **sala de emergencias** emergency room (10)

emigrante *m., f.* emigrant

emigrar to emigrate

emisión *f.* emission; broadcast

emoción *f.* emotion (8)

emocional emotional

emocionante exciting

empanado/a breaded

empapelado/a (wall) papered

emparejar to match

emperador emperor

empezar (ie) (c); to begin (4); **empezar a** + *inf.* to begin to (*do something*) (4)

empleado/a employee

emplear to use; to employ

empleo employment

empresa company, corporation, business (16); **administración** (*f.*) **de empresas** business administration (1)

empresario/a businessman/woman

empuje *m.* push

en in (AT); on (AT); at (AT); **en absoluto** at all; **en busca de** in search of; **en cambio** on the other hand, on the contrary; **en casa** at home (1); **en caso de que** *conj.* in case (15); **en cierta medida** in some measure; **en contra** opposed; **en cuanto** *conj.* as soon as (16); **en cuanto a** *prep.* regarding; **en este momento** right now; **en exceso** to excess, excessively; **en fila** in single file; **en fin** in short; **en la clase** in class (1); **en punto** on the dot (*time*) (AT); **en realidad** in fact; **en resumen** in short; **en seguida** right away (10); **en vez de** instead of (16)

enamorado/a in love (with) (15); **Día** (*m.*) **de los Enamorados** Valentine's Day

enamorarse (de) to fall in love (with) (15)

encabezado/a por headed by

encadenado/a chained

encantado/a enchanted; delighted, pleased to meet you (AT)

encantador(a) enchanting; delightful

encantamiento enchantment

encantar to like very much, love (7)

encarar to confront, face up to

encarcelado/a jailed

encargado/a person in charge

encargarse (gu) de to be in charge of

encender (ie) to turn on; to light

encendido/a lit up

encerado/a waxed

enchufar to plug in

encima de *prep.* on top of (5); in addition to

encontrar (ue) to find (8); **encontrarse** to be, feel (10); **encontrarse con** to meet (*someone somewhere*) (10)

encuadrar to include, contain

encuesta survey

energía energy (14)

enero January (5)

énfasis *m.* emphasis

enfático/a emphatic

enfermarse to get sick (8)

enfermedad *f.* illness, sickness

enfermero/a nurse (10)

enfermo/a sick (5); **ponerse** (*irreg.*) **enfermo/a** to get sick

enfilado/a in a row

enfisema *m.* emphysema

enfocarse (qu) (en) to focus (on)

enfoque *m.* focus

enfrascarse (qu) to become totally absorbed in

enjuto/a dry; lean

enlace *m.* link

enlatado/a canned

enojado/a angry

enojarse (con) to get angry (at) (8)

enorme enormous

enriquecer (zc)   to enrich
enrollado/a   rolled up; in a roll
ensalada   salad (6)
ensayo   essay
enseñanza   teaching
enseñar   to teach (1)
ensillar   to saddle
entender (ie)   to understand (4)
enterado/a   informed
enterarse (de)   to find out, learn
   (about) (17)
entero/a   entire; whole; limpiar la casa
   entera to clean the whole house (9)
entonces   then, next; desde entonces
   from then on
entrada   entrance; ticket
entrar   to enter
entre   between (5); among (5)
entreabierto/a   half-open, ajar
entregar (gu)   to turn, hand in (11)
entremeses m. pl.   hors d'oeuvres (8)
entrenamiento   training
entrenar   to practice, train (9)
entretejer   to interweave
entrevista   interview (16); tener (irreg.)
   una entrevista to have an interview (16)
entrevistador(a)   interviewer (16)
entrevistar   to interview (16);
   entrevistarse to be interviewed
envase m.   container
enviar (envío)   to send
envidia   envy
envuelto/a (p.p. of envolver)   wrapped
eólico/a adj.   wind
epifanía   epiphany
episodio   episode
época   era, time (period) (9)
equilibradamente: comer equilibradamente   to eat in a balanced way (10)
equilibrado/a   balanced
equilibrar   to balance
equilibrio   balance
equipaje m.   baggage, luggage (7); facturar el equipaje to check baggage (7)
equipo   team; equipment; equipo
   estereofónico/fotográfico stereo/pho-
   tography equipment (12)
equivalente n. m.   equivalence; adj.
   equivalent
equivaler (like valer)   to equal
equivocarse (qu) (de)   to be wrong,
   make a mistake (about) (11)
érase una vez   once upon a time
eres   you (fam. s.) are (AT)
errante   wandering
error m.   mistake, error
erupción f.   eruption (17)
es   he/she/it is (AT); es de... it is made
   of . . . (3); ¡es de última moda! it's the
   latest style! (3); es decir that is to say;
   es la... it's . . . (AT); es seguro it's a
   sure thing
escabroso/a   rugged

escala   stop; hacer (irreg.) escalas to
   make stops (7); vuelo sin escalas
   nonstop flight
escalar   to climb
escaleras f. pl.   stairs; escaleras
   mecánicas escalator
escalón m.   step
escalopín m.   breaded cutlet
escándalo   scandal
escapar   to escape
escaparate m.   store (display) window
escasez f. (pl. escaseces)   lack,
   shortage (14)
escaso/a   scarce
escena   scene
escenario   stage (13)
esclavitud f.   slavery
esclavo/a   slave
escoger (j)   to choose
esconder(se)   to hide
escondido/a   hidden
escopeta   shotgun
escorpión m.   scorpion
escribir (p.p. escrito)   to write (2);
   escribir a computadora to write on a
   computer (16); máquina de escribir
   typewriter
escrito/a (p.p. of escribir)   written (11);
   informe (m.) escrito written report (11)
escritor(a)   writer (13)
escritorio   desk (1)
escritura   writing
escuchar   to listen (to) (1)
escudo   shield
escuela   school (9)
esculpir   to sculpt (13)
esculsa   canal lock
escultor(a)   sculptor (13)
escultura   sculpture (general) (13);
   sculpture (piece of art) (13)
ese/a adj.   that (3); pron. that one (3)
esencial   essential
esfuerzo   effort
eslavo/a n.   Slav
esmeralda   emerald
eso   that (3); eso quiere decir... that
   means . . . (10); por eso therefore (1)
esos/as adj.   those (3); pron. those ones
espacial adj.   space; transbordador (m.)
   especial space shuttle
espacio n.   space; espacio en blanco
   blank space
espacioso/a   spacious
espalda   back
espantoso/a   frightening
España   Spain
español m.   Spanish (language) (1)
español(a) n.   Spaniard; adj. Spanish
   (2); de habla española Spanish-
   speaking; Real Academia Española
   Royal Spanish Academy
espárragos m. pl.   asparagus (6)
especial   special

especialidad f.   specialty
especialista m., f.   specialist
especialización f.   specialization
especializado/a en   majoring in
especializarse (c) (en)   to major (in)
especie (f. s.) (en peligro de extinción)
   (endangered) species (14)
específico/a   specific
espectáculo   spectacle; show
espectador(a)   spectator
espera: sala de espera   waiting room
   (7); llamada en espera call-waiting
esperanza   hope, wish (17); esperanza
   de vida life expectancy
esperar   to wait (for) (6); to expect (6);
   to hope (12)
espíritu m.   spirit
espléndido/a   splendid
esposo/a   husband/wife (2); spouse
esqueleto   skeleton
esquí m.   skiing; estación (f.) de esquí
   ski resort
esquiar (esquío)   to ski (9)
esquina   corner (14)
está   he/she/it is; you (form. s.) is; está
   (muy) nublado it's (very) cloudy (5)
estable adj.   stable
establecer (zc)   to establish, set up; es-
   tablecerse to settle, establish oneself
estación f.   station (7); season (5); estación de autobúses / del tren bus/train
   station (7); estación de esquí ski resort;
   estación de gasolina gas station (14);
   estación de metro subway stop (18)
estacionamiento   parking
estacionar   to park (11)
estadía   stay
estadística   statistic
estado   state (2); estado civil marital
   status; estado de ánimo state of mind;
   estado de cuentas bank statement;
   estado libre asociado commonwealth
Estados Unidos m. pl.   United States
estadounidense n., adj. m., f.   American
   (from the United States) (2)
estancia   stay (in a hotel) (18)
estanco   tobacco stand/shop (18)
estanque m.   pond; reservoir
estante m.   bookshelf (4)
estar   irreg. to be (1); estar a cargo to
   be in control of; estar a dieta to be on a
   diet (6); estar acecho/a to be lying in
   wait; to watch, be on the lookout; estar
   atrasado/a to be late (7); estar bien
   to be comfortable (temperature) (5); estar de mal humor to be in a bad mood;
   estar de vacaciones to be on vacation
   (7); estar en manos de to belong to;
   (no) estar de acuerdo to (dis)agree; no
   estar seguro/a (de) to be (un)sure (of);
   (no) estoy de acuerdo I (don't) agree
   (2); sala de estar living room; sitting
   room

estatal *adj.* state

estatua statue

este *n. m.* east (5)

este/a *adj.* this (2); **esta noche** tonight (5); *pron.* this one (3)

estéreo stereo

estereofónico/a: **equipo estereofónico** stereo equipment (12)

estereotipado/a stereotyped

estereotipo stereotype

estilo style

estimado/a esteemed

estimulante *m.* stimulant

estimular to stimulate

esto *pron.* this (2)

estofado/a stewed

estómago stomach (10); **dolor** (*m.*) **de estómago** stomachache (10)

estos/as *adj.* these (2); *pron.* these (3)

estrategia strategy

estrechar: **estrechar las manos** to shake hands

estrecho/a close; tight; narrow

estrechos *m. pl.* straits (*geography*)

estrella star; **hotel** (*m.*) **de dos** (**tres**) **estrellas** two- (three-) star hotel (18)

estrés *m.* stress (11)

estresado/a stressed

estresarse to become stressed

estricto/a strict

estructura structure

estudiante *m., f.* student (1)

estudiantil *adj.* student, of students (11); **residencia estudiantil** dormitory (1)

estudiar to study (1)

estudio study

estudioso/a studious

estufa stove (9); **estufa de leña** wood stove

estupendo/a stupendous

etapa stage (15)

etnia ethnic group

étnico/a ethnic

euro monetary unit of many European countries

europeo/a *n., adj.* European

evaluar (**evalúo**) to evaluate

evento event (17)

evidencia evidence

evidente evident

evitar to avoid (14)

evolución *f.* evolution

exacto/a exact

examen *m.* test, exam (3)

examinar to examine (10)

exceder to exceed

excelente excellent

excepto except

exceso excess; **en exceso** to excess, excessively; **tener** (*irreg.*) **exceso de peso** to be overweight

exclusivo/a exclusive

excursión *f.* excursion

excusa excuse

exhibición *f.* exhibition

exigente demanding

exigir (j) to demand

exiliarse to be exiled

existencia existence

existir to exist

éxito success; **tener** (*irreg.*) **éxito** to be successful

exitoso/a successful

éxodo exodus

exorcizar (c) to exorcize

exótico/a exotic

expectativa expectation

experiencia experience

experimentar to experience

experimento experiment

experto expert

explicación *f.* explanation

explicar (qu) to explain (7)

exploración *f.* exploration

explorar to explore

explosión *f.* explosion

explosivo/a explosive

explotación *f.* exploitation; use

explotado/a exploited; used

exportación *f.* export

exportador(a) exporter

exposición *f.* show, exhibition

expresar to express

expresión *f.* expression

expreso/a express, exact

expuesto/a (*p.p. of* **exponer**) exposed; on display

expulsar to expel

expulsión *f.* expulsion

extender (ie) to extend

extenso/a extensive

exterior *adj.* outside

extinción: **especie** (*f. s.*) **en peligro de extinción** endangered species (14)

extracción *f.* extraction

extraer (*like* **traer**) to extract

extranjero/a *n.* foreigner; *adj.* foreign (1); **lenguas extranjeras** foreign languages (1)

extranjero *n.* abroad, overseas (18); **viajar al/en el extranjero** to travel abroad (18)

extraño strange (13); **¡qué extraño!** how strange! (13)

extraordinario/a extraordinary

extravagante extravagant

extremo/a extreme

extroversión *f.* extroversion

extrovertido/a extrovert

exuberancia exuberance

exuberante exuberant

F

fábrica factory (14)

fabricación *f.* making

fabricar (qu) to manufacture

fabuloso/a fabulous

fachada facade

fácil easy (5)

facilidad *f.* ease; facility; ability

facilitar to facilitate

factible feasible

factor *m.* factor

factura bill (16)

facturar (el equipaje) to check (baggage) (7)

facultad *f.* department (*in a university*)

falda skirt (3)

fallar to crash (*computer*) (12)

falsificado/a forged

falso/a false

falta lack (11); absence; **falta de flexibilidad** lack of flexibility (11)

faltar to be absent, lacking (8)

familia family (2)

familiar *n. m.* relation, member of the family; *adj. pertaining to a family*

famoso/a famous

fantasía fantasy

fantástico/a fantastic

farmacéutico/a pharmacist (10)

farmacia pharmacy (10)

farmacología pharmacology

faro lighthouse

fascinante fascinating

fatal *sl.* bad; unlucky

fatiga fatigue

favor *m.* favor; **a favor de** in favor of; with the aid of; **favor de** + *inf.* please (*do something*); **por favor** please (AT); **si me hace el favor** if you would do me the favor

favorecer (zc) to favor

favorito/a favorite

fax *m.* fax (12)

fe *f.* faith

febrero February (5)

fecha date (*calendar*) (5); **¿cuál es la fecha de hoy?** what's today's date? (5); **fecha límite** deadline (11)

felicitaciones *interj.* congratulations

feliz (*pl.* **felices**) happy (8); **Feliz Año Nuevo** Happy New Year; **feliz cumpleaños** happy birthday; **Feliz Navidad** Merry Christmas

femenino/a feminine

feminidad *f.* femininity

Fénix *m.* Phoenix

fenomenal phenomenal

fenómeno phenomenon

feo/a ugly (2)

feria fair; **rueda de feria** Ferris wheel

feriado/a: **día** (*m.*) **feriado** holiday

feroz (*pl.* **feroces**) fierce

ferrocarril *m.* railroad

fértil fertile

festejos *pl.* public festivities

festival *m.* festival

festividad *f.* festivity

festivo/a: día (*m.*) **festivo** holiday (8)

fibra fiber

ficción *f.* fiction; **ciencia ficción** science fiction

fiebre *f.* fever (10); **tener** (*irreg.*) **fiebre** to have a fever (10)

fiel faithful (2)

fiesta party (1); **dar** (*irreg.*) **una fiesta** to give a party (8); **hacer** (*irreg.*) **una fiesta** to have a party (8); **fiesta de disfraz** costume party; **fiesta de sorpresa** surprise party

figura figure

fijarse (en) to take note (of), pay attention (to)

fijo/a set; fixed; **precio fijo** fixed price (3)

fila line, row; **en fila** in single file

filete *m.* fillet

filmar to film

filosofía philosophy (1)

filtro filter

fin *m.* end; **en fin** in short; **fin de semana** weekend (1); **por fin** at last, finally (4); **sin fines de lucro** not-for-profit; **sin fines lucrativos** nonprofit

final *n. m.* end; *adj.* final; **a finales de** at the end of

financiamiento financing

financiero/a financial

finanza finance

finca farm (14)

fino/a fine

fiordo fjord

firmar to sign

física *s.* physics (1)

físico/a physical

flaco/a skinny

flan *m.* baked caramel custard (6)

flexibilidad *f.* flexibility (11); **falta de flexibilidad** lack of flexibility (11)

flexible flexible; **ser** (*irreg.*) **flexible** to be flexible (11)

flor *f.* flower (7)

florecer (zc) to flourish

florido/a: Pascua (Florida) Easter (8)

flota fleet

folklore *m.* folklore

folklórico/a folkloric (13)

folleto pamphlet

fondo fund; **al fondo** in the background; **fondos** (*pl.*) **de apoyo** economic assistance

fontanero/a *Sp.* plumber

forestal *pertaining to forests or forestry*

forma form; shape; **de todas formas** anyway

formación *f.* background

formar to form; **formar parte de** to be part of, a member of

formular to formulate

formulario form (*to fill out*) (18)

fortaleza fort

fósforo match (*for lighting things*) (18)

foto(grafía) photo(graph) (7); photography (13); **sacar (qu) fotos** to take photos (7)

fotográfico/a photographic; **equipo fotográfico** photography equipment (12)

fotógrafo/a photographer (16)

frágil fragile

fragmento fragment

francés *m.* French (*language*) (1)

francés, francesa *n.* French person; *adj.* French (2)

franco/a free, open

frase *f.* phrase

frecuencia frequency; **con frecuencia** frequently (1)

frecuente frequent

fregar (ie) (gu) los platos to wash the dishes

frenar to brake

freno brake (14)

frente a facing, opposite

fresco/a fresh (6); cool (*weather*); **hace fresco** it's cool (*weather*) (5)

fresno ash tree

frialdad *f.* coldness

frigidez *f.* frigidity

frigorífico refrigerator

frijol *m.* bean (6)

frío *n.* cold(ness); *adj.* cold; **hace (mucho) frío** it's (very) cold (*weather*) (5); **tener** (*irreg.*) **(mucho) frío** to be (very) cold (5)

frisar to be around (*a certain age*)

frito/a fried (6); **patata frita** French fried potato

frontera border (18)

frugalidad *f.* frugality

fruncir (z) to knit (*brows*) ~~frown~~

fruta fruit (6); **jugo de fruta** fruit juice (6)

frutal *adj.* fruit

fruto seco nut

fuego fire; **fuegos artificiales** fireworks

fuente *f.* source

fuera *adv.* outside

fuerte strong (6); heavy (*meal*) (6)

fuerza strength; force

fulano/a so-and-so (*person*)

fumador(a) smoker

fumar to smoke (7); **sección** (*f.*) **de (no) fumar** (non)smoking section (7)

función *f.* function

funcionar to work, function (12)

fundación *f.* foundation; **Fundación Alerta contra la SIDA** AIDS Awareness Foundation

fundar to found

furioso/a furious, angry (5)

fusilamiento shooting, execution; **pelotón** (*m.*) **de fusilamiento** firing squad

fútbol *m.* soccer (9); **fútbol americano** football (9)

futbolista *m., f.* soccer player

futuro *n.* future

futuro/a *adj.* future

G

gabrielino/a person from the San Gabriel mission

gafas *f. pl.* (eye)glasses (10); **llevar gafas** to wear glasses (10)

gajo branch (*of a tree*)

galante gallant

galeno/a *coll.* doctor

galería gallery

galgo/a greyhound

gallego/a *n.* Galician

galleta cookie (6)

gallina hen, chicken

gallinero chicken coop

gallo: misa del gallo Midnight Mass; **gallo/a** guys, gals (*Chilean slang*)

gamba *Sp.* shrimp

gana desire, wish; **darle** (*irreg.*) **la gana** to feel like; **tener** (*irreg.*) **ganas de +** *inf.* to feel like (*doing something*) (3)

ganar to earn (16); to win (9); **ganarse la vida** to earn a living

ganga bargain (3); **¡qué ganga!** what a bargain!

garaje *m.* garage (4)

garantizar (c) to guarantee

garganta throat (10)

garúa coastal fog

gas *m.* gas, heat (12)

gasolina gasoline (14); **estación** (*f.*) **de gasolina** gas station (14)

gasolinera gas station (14)

gastar to spend (*money*) (8); to use, expend (14)

gasto expense (12)

gastronómico/a gastronomic

gato/a cat (2)

gazpacho *cold, tomato-based soup from Spain*

generación *f.* generation

general general; **por lo general** generally (4)

generalizar (c) to generalize

generoso/a generous

génesis *m. inv.* beginning

genio/a genius

gente *f. s.* people (13)

geografía geography

geográfico/a geographic

geoturismo geotourism

gerente *m., f.* manager (16)

germánico/a Germanic

gerontología gerontology

gerundio *gram.* gerund

gesto gesture

gigante *adj.* giant

gimnasio gymnasium

gira tour
glaciación *f.* glaciation
glaciar *m.* glacier
globo balloon
gobernador(a) governor
gobernar (ie) to govern, rule (17)
gobierno government (14)
golf *m.* golf (9)
gordo/a fat (2)
gorila *m.* gorilla (14)
gorra cap (3)
gozar (c) to enjoy
gozo joy
grabadora (tape) recorder (12)
grabar to record, tape (12)
gracias thank you (AT); **Día** (*m.*) **de Acción de Gracias** Thanksgiving; **gracias por** thanks for (8); **muchas gracias** thank you very much (AT)
grado grade, year (*in school*) (9)
graduado/a *adj.* graduate
graduarse (me gradúo) (en/de) to graduate (from) (16)
gráfico *n.* graph, diagram
gráfico/a *adj.* graphic
gramática grammar
gran, grande big, large (2); great (2)
granada pomegranate
grandeza majesty, grandeur; greatness
granito granite
granja farm
grano pimple
grasa fat
grasoso/a fatty; greasy
gratuito/a free (*of charge*)
grave serious
Grecia Greece
griego/a *n., adj.* Greek
gripe *f.* flu
gris gray (3)
gritar to shout, yell
grotesco/a grotesque
gruñir to grunt; to growl
grupo group
guacamole *m.* *mashed avocado salad*
guapo/a handsome (2); good-looking (2)
guaraní *m.* Guarani (*L.A. indigenous language*)
guardar to save (7); to keep (*documents*) (12); **guardar cama** to stay in bed (10); **guardar un puesto** to save a place (7)
guardia *m.* guard, guardsman; **de guardia** on-call
guatemalteco/a *n., adj.* Guatemalan
guerra war (17); **Segunda Guerra Mundial** World War II
guerrero/a warrior
gueto ghetto
guía *f.* guide (*book*); *m., f.* guide (*person*) (13)
guiado/a guided
guión *m.* script (13)

guionista *m., f.* scriptwriter
guisante *m.* green pea
guitarra guitar
guitarrista *m., f.* guitarist
gustar to be pleasing (7); **¿le gusta... ?** do you (*form.*) like . . . ? (AT); **sí, (no, no) me gusta(n)...** yes, I do (no, I don't like . . . (AT); **¿te gusta... ?** do you (*fam.*) like . . . ? (AT); **me gustaría...** I would (really) like (7)
gusto like, preference, taste; **mucho gusto** pleased to meet you (AT)

H

haber *irreg.* (*inf. of* **hay** there is/are) *auxiliary* (12); **hay que** + *inf.* be necessary to (*do something*) (13)
habilidad *f.* ability, skill
habilidoso/a skillful, clever
habitable habitable
habitación *f.* room; **habitación con/sin baño/ducha** room with(out) a bath/shower (18); **habitación individual/doble** single/double room (*in a hotel*) (18); **servicio de habitación** *Sp.* room service
habitante *m., f.* inhabitant
habitar to live in, reside in
hábito habit, custom
hablante *m. f.* speaker
hablar to speak (1); to talk (1); **de habla española** Spanish-speaking; **hablar por teléfono** to talk on the phone (1)
hace + *time* time ago (11); **hace** + *period of time* + **que** + *present tense* to have been (*doing something*) for (*a period of time*) (11)
hacer *irreg.* (*p.p.* **hecho**) to do (4); to make (4); **hace** + *period of time* + **que** + *present tense* to have been (*doing something*) for (*a period of time*) (11); **hace** + *time* time ago (11); **hace (muy) buen/mal tiempo** it's (very) good/bad weather (5); **hace (mucho) fresco** it's (very) cool (*weather*) (5); **hace (mucho) frío/calor** it's (very) cold/hot (weather) (5); **hace (mucho) sol** it's (very) sunny (5); **hace (mucho) viento** it's (very) windy (5); **hacer autostop** to hitchhike; **hacer** *camping* to go camping (7); **hacer cola** to stand in line (7); **hacer ejercicio** to exercise, get exercise (4); **hacer ejercicios aeróbicos** to do aerobics (10); **hacer el alpinismo** to mountain climb; **hacer escalas/paradas** to make stops (7); **hacer la cama** to make the bed (9); **hacer la(s) maleta(s)** to pack one's suitcase(s) (7); **hacer las cuentas** to pretend; **hacer las reservas/reservaciones** to make reservations (18); **hacer planes para** + *inf.* to make plans to (*do something*) (9); **hacer preguntas** to ask questions; **hacer un** *picnic* to have a picnic (9); **hacer un**

viaje to take a trip (4); **hacer una copia / copias** to copy (12); **hacer una fiesta** to have a party (8); **hacer una pregunta** to ask a question (4); **hacer visitas** to visit; **hacerse** to become; **hacerse daño** to hurt oneself (11); **¿qué tiempo hace hoy?** what's the weather like today? (5); **si me hace el favor** if you would do me the favor
hacia toward
hacienda farm, ranch; country estate
hambre *f.* (*but* **el hambre**) hunger; **pasar hambre** to go hungry; **tener** (*irreg.*) **(mucha) hambre** to be (very) hungry (6)
hamburguesa hamburger (6)
hanega *land measure equal to 1.59 acres*
harto/a fed up
hasta *adv.* even; *prep.* until (4); **hasta luego** see you later (AT); **hasta mañana** see you tomorrow (AT); **hasta pronto** see you soon; **hasta que** *conj.* until (16)
hay: (no) hay there is (not) (AT); there are (not) (AT); **hay (mucha) contaminación** there's (lots of) pollution (5); **hay que** + *inf.* it is necessary to (*do something*) (13); **¡hay que cuidarse!** you must take care of yourself! (10); **no hay de qué** you're welcome (AT); **no hay duda** there is no doubt
hebreo/a *n.* Hebrew; **Pascua (de los hebreos)** Passover
hecho *n.* fact; deed; event (8); **de hecho** in fact
hecho/a (*p.p. of* **hacer**) made; done; taken
hectárea *land measure equal to 2.5 acres*
helado *n.* ice cream (6)
helado/a *adj.* frozen (6)
hemisferio hemisphere
heredar to inherit
herido/a wounded
hermanastro/a stepbrother, stepsister
hermano/a brother/sister (2); **medio hermano/media hermana** half-brother / half-sister
hermoso/a beautiful
héroe *m.* hero
herramienta tool
hervir (ie, i) to boil
hidalgo nobleman, gentleman
hidráulico/a hydraulic
hidroeléctrico/a hydroelectric
hidrógeno hydrogen
hielo ice
hígado liver
higiénico/a hygienic, sanitary
higuera fig tree
hijastro/a stepson, stepdaughter
hijo/a son/daughter (2); *m. pl.* children (2)

himno hymn

hipopótamo hippopotamus

hipoteca mortgage

hispánico/a *adj.* Hispanic

hispano/a *n., adj.* Hispanic

hispanoamericano/a *n., adj.* Hispanic-American

hispanocanadiense *n., adj. m., f.* Hispanic-Canadian

hispanohablante *adj. m., f.* Spanish-speaking

historia story; history (1)

historiador(a) historian

histórico/a historic

hockey *m.* hockey (9)

hogar *m.* home; household

hoja leaf

hola hello (AT)

Holanda Holland

holgadamente comfortably, easily

hombre *m.* man (1); **hombre de negocios** businessman (16)

homeopatía homeopathy

homeópato/a homeopathic

hondureño/a *n., adj.* Honduran

honesto/a honest

honor *m.* honor

honrar to honor

hora hour; time; **¿a qué hora?** at what time? (AT); **¿qué hora es?** what time is it? (AT)

horario schedule (11)

horneado/a baked

horno oven; **horno de microondas** microwave oven (9)

horóscopo horoscope

horror *m.* horror

hospicio hospice

hospital *m.* hospital

hotel *m.* **(de lujo)** (luxury) hotel (18); **hotel de dos (tres) estrellas** two-(three-) star hotel (18)

hoy today (AT); **¿cuál es la fecha de hoy?** what's today's date? (5); **hoy (en) día** nowadays, these days; **¿qué día es hoy?** what day is today? (4); **¿qué tiempo hace hoy?** what's the weather like today? (5)

huelga strike (*labor*) (17)

huella footprint

huerto orchard

hueso bone

huésped(a) (hotel) guest (18)

huevo egg (6); **huevo cocido** hard-boiled egg; **huevo tibio / pasado por agua** poached egg; **huevos revueltos** scrambled eggs

huir (y) to flee

humanidad *f.* humanity; *pl.* humanities (1)

humanitario/a humanitarian

humano/a *adj.* human; **ser** *(m.)* **humano** human being

humedad *f.* humidity

humilde humble

humo smoke

humor *m.* humor; mood; **estar** (*irreg.*) **de mal humor** to be in a bad mood

huracán *m.* hurricane

I

ibérico/a *adj.* Iberian

ida: de ida one-way (7); **de ida y vuelta** round-trip (7)

idealista *adj. m., f.* idealistic

idéntico/a identical

identidad *f.* identity; **tarjeta de identidad** identification card (11)

identificación *f.* identification (16); **tarjeta de identificación** identification card (11)

identificado/a: objeto volante no identificado (OVNI) unidentified flying object (UFO)

identificar (qu) to identify

idioma *m.* language

iglesia church

ignorante ignorant

igual equal, same

igualdad *f.* equality (17)

igualmente likewise, same here (AT)

ilegal illegal

iluminación *f.* lighting

imagen *f.* image

imaginación *f.* imagination

imaginar(se) to imagine

imaginario/a imaginary

imitar to imitate

impaciente impatient

impacto impact

impar uneven, odd

imparcialmente impartially

impedir (*like* **pedir**) to impede, hinder

imperfecto *gram.* imperfect past tense

imperio empire

impermeable *m.* raincoat (3)

imponente imposing; majestic

importación *f.* import

importancia importance

importante important

importar to matter, be important; **no me importa un pito** I don't care one bit

imposible impossible

imprescindible essential, indispensable

impresión *f.* impression

impresionante impressive

impresora printer (12)

imprimir to print (12)

improbable unlikely; **es improbable que...** it's improbable, unlikely that . . . (13)

impuesto tax

impulsivo/a impulsive

inadecuado/a inadequate

inaugurar to inaugurate

inca *n. m., f.* Inca; *adj. m., f.* Incan

incidente *m.* incident

incluir (y) to include

inclusive *adj.* including

incluso *adv.* even; including

incomodar to make uncomfortable

inconcebible inconceivable

inconveniente *m.* drawback, difficulty

incorporar to incorporate

incorrecto/a incorrect

increíble incredible (13)

incrementar to increase

indefinido/a: artículo indefinido *gram.* indefinite article

independencia independence; **Día** *(m.)* **de la Independencia** Independence Day

independiente independent

indicación *f.* instruction; direction

indicar (qu) to indicate

indicativo *gram.* indicative

indiferencia indifference

indiferenciado/a undifferentiated

indígena *n. m., f.* indigenous person; *adj. m., f.* indigenous

indigenista *pertaining to indigenous topics and themes*

indio/a *n., adj.* Indian

indirecto/a: complemento indirecto *gram.* indirect object pronoun

indiscreto/a indiscreet

individual: habitación *(f.)* **individual** single room (*in a hotel*) (18)

individuo *n.* individual

indoeuropeo/a *adj.* Indo-European

industria industry

industrializado/a industrialized

inequívoco/a unmistakable, certain

infancia infancy (15)

infantil *adj.* child, children's

infección *f.* infection

inferior lower

infinitivo *gram.* infinitive

infinito/a infinite

influencia influence

influenciado/a influenced

influente influential

influir (y) to influence

infográfico graph (with information)

información *f.* information

informar to inform (17); **informarse (de)** to find out (about)

informática computer studies

informativo/a informative

informe *m.* **(oral/escrito)** (written/oral) report (11)

infortunio misfortune

infraestructura infrastructure

ingeniería engineering

ingeniero/a engineer (16)

ingenioso/a ingenious, clever

ingerir (ie, i) to ingest

Inglaterra England

inglés *m.* English (*language*) (1)

inglés, inglesa *n.* English person; *adj.* English (2)
ingrediente *m.* ingredient
ingreso income
iniciar to begin, initiate
inicio beginning
injusticia injustice
inmediato/a immediate
inmenso/a huge, immense
inmigración *f.* immigration
inmigrante *m., f.* immigrant
inmigrar(se) to immigrate
inmortalizar (c) to immortalize
innecesario/a unnecessary
innumerable countless
inocente innocent; **Día** (*m.*) **de los Inocentes** April Fool's Day
inolvidable unforgettable
inquietante worrisome
inquilino/a tenant, renter (12)
insano/a insane; unhealthy
inscribirse (*p.p.* **inscrito**) to sign up, register
inscrito/a (*p.p. of* **inscribir**) registered
insistir (en) + *inf.* to insist (on) (*doing something*) (12)
insolente insolent
insomnio insomnia
inspector(a) inspector; **inspector(a) de aduanas** customs inspector
inspiración *f.* inspiration
inspirarse en to be inspired by
instalación *f.* equipment
institución *f.* institution
instituto institute
instrumento instrument
intacto/a intact
integral *adj.* whole grain
integrar to integrate; to form, make up
integridad *f.* integrity
intelectual intellectual
inteligente intelligent (2)
intención *f.* intention
intensivo/a intensive
intentar to try (13)
interactivo/a interactive
interés *m.* interest (16)
interesante interesting
interesar to interest
intergaláctico/a intergalactic
interior *n.* interior; *adj.* inside, inner; interior; **ropa interior** underwear (3)
internacional international; **Día** (*m.*) **Internacional de los Trabajadores** International Labor Day
internarse (en) to check into a hospital (10)
Internet *m.* Internet
interno/a internal
interplanetario/a interplanetary
interpretación *f.* interpretation
interpretar to interpret
intérprete *m., f.* interpreter

interrogativo/a *gram.* interrogative
interrumpir to interrupt
intervención *f.* intervention
íntimamente intimately
intranquilidad *f.* uneasiness, restlessness
introducción *f.* introduction
introducir *irreg.* to introduce
intromisión *f.* intrusion
introversión *f.* introversion
introvertido/a introverted
inútilmente uselessly
invadir to invade
invasión *f.* invasion
invención *f.* invention
inventar to invent
investigación *f.* investigation
investigar (gu) to investigate
invierno winter (5)
invitación *f.* invitation
invitado/a guest (8)
invitar to invite (6)
involucrado/a involved
inyección *f.*: **ponerle** (*irreg.*) **una inyección** to give (*someone*) a shot, injection (10)
ir *irreg.* to go (3); **ir a** + *inf.* to be going to (*do something*) (3); **ir a una discoteca / un bar / un concierto** to go to a disco/bar/concert (9); **ir a ver una película** to go to see a movie (9); **ir al cine** to go to the movies (9); **ir al teatro** to go to the theater (9); **ir de compras** to go shopping (3); **ir de vacaciones** to go on vacation (7); **ir en autobús/avión/barco/tren** to go/travel by bus/plane/boat/train (7); **irse** to leave
Irlanda Ireland
irónico/a ironic
irresponsable irresponsible
irritación *f.* irritation
isla island (5)
Islandia Iceland
isleta isle
istmo isthmus
Italia Italy
italiano Italian (*language*) (1)
italiano/a *n., adj.* Italian
izquierda *n.* left-hand side; **a la izquierda (de)** to the left (of) (5)
izquierdo/a *adj.* left (*direction*); **levantarse con el pie izquierdo** to get up on the wrong side of the bed (11)

J

jabón *m.* soap (18)
jalón: **de un jalón** all at once
jamás never, not ever (6)
jamón *m.* ham (6)
Japón *m.* Japan
japonés *m.* Japanese (*language*)
jarabe *m.* (cough) syrup (10)
jardín *m.* yard (4)

jarrita jar
jeans *m. pl.* jeans (3)
jefe/a boss (12)
jerez *m.* (*pl.* **jereces**) sherry
jeroglífico/a *adj.* hieroglyphic
jipijapa Panama hat, straw hat
jirafa giraffe
joven *n. m., f.* youth; *adj.* young (2); **de joven** as a youth (9)
joya jewel
joyería jewelry store
jubilado/a retired
jubilarse to retire (16)
judío/a Jewish person
juego game; **Juegos Olímpicos** Olympic Games
jueves *m. inv.* Thursday (4)
jugador(a) player (9)
jugar (ue) (gu) (al) to play (*a game, sport*) (4); **jugar a las cartas** to play cards (9); **jugar al ajedrez** to play chess (9)
jugo (de fruta) (fruit) juice (6)
jugoso/a juicy
juguete *m.* toy
juicio: **perder (ie) el juicio** to go crazy
julio July (5)
jungla jungle
junio June (5)
juntarse to get together
junto a near, next to; **junto con** along with, together with
juntos/as *adj.* together (15)
justificar (qu) to justify
justo/a fair
juvenil *adj.* juvenile
juventud *f.* youth (15)
juzgado court
juzgar (gu) to judge

K

kilogramo kilogram
kilómetro kilometer
kiosco kiosk

L

la *def. art. f. s.* the (1); *d.o. f. s.* you (*form.*); her, it
labor *f.* work
laborable: **día** (*m.*) **laborable** workday
laboral *adj.* pertaining to work or labor
laboratorio laboratory
lado side; **al lado de** *prep.* alongside of (5); beside; next to (5); **por otro lado** on the other hand; **por un lado** on the one hand
ladrar to bark
lago lake (14)
lágrima tear
lámpara lamp (4)
lana wool (3); **es de lana** it is made of wool (3); **perro de lanas** poodle
langosta lobster (6)

lanza spear, lance

lápiz *m.* (*pl.* **lápices**) pencil (1)

largo *n.:* **de largo** in length

largo/a *adj.* long (2); **a largo plazo** long-term; **a lo largo de** along; throughout; **llamada a larga distancia** long-distance call

las *def. art. f. pl.* the (1); *d.o. f. pl.* you (*form.*); them; **a las...** at . . . (*hour*); **los/las demás** others, the rest (12)

lástima shame (13); **es una lástima** it is a shame (13) **¡qué lástima!** what a shame! (13)

lastimarse to injure oneself (11); **lastimarse la pierna** to injure one's leg (11)

lata: ser (*irreg.*) **una lata** to be a pain, drag

latín *m.* Latin (*language*)

latino/a *adj.* Latin

Latinoamérica Latin America

latinoamericano/a *n., adj.* Latin American

latinocanadiense *adj. m., f.* Latin-Canadian

lavabo (bathroom) sink (4)

lavadora washing machine (9)

lavandería laundromat

lavaplatos *m. inv.* dishwasher (9)

lavar to wash; **lavar la ropa** to wash clothes (9); **lavar las ventanas** to wash the windows (9); **lavar los platos** to wash dishes (9)

le *i.o. s.* to/for you (*form.*), him, her, it; **¿le gusta... ?** do you (*form.*) like . . . ?

lección *f.* lesson

leche *f.* milk (6)

lecho bed

lechuga lettuce (6)

lector(a) reader; **lector** (*m.*) **de DVD** DVD player (12)

lectura reading

leer (**y**) to read (2)

legalizar (**c**) to legalize

legendario/a legendary

legislación *f.* legislation

lejos de *prep.* far from (5)

lempira *m.* *monetary unit of Honduras*

lengua language (1); tongue; **lenguas extranjeras** foreign languages (1); **sacar** (**qu**) **la lengua** to stick out one's tongue (10)

lenguado flounder

lenguaje *m.* language

lentamente slowly

lentes (*m. pl.*) **de contacto** contact lenses; **llevar lentes de contacto** to wear contact lenses (10)

leña: estufa de leña wood stove

les *i.o. pl.* to/for you (*form. pl.*); them

letanía litany

letra letter (*alphabet*); **letra cursiva** *s.* italics

letrero sign

levantar to raise, lift; **levantar pesas** to lift weights; **levantarse** to get up (4); to stand up (4); **levantarse con el pie izquierdo** to get up on the wrong side of the bed (11)

leve light, slight

ley *f.* law (17)

leyenda legend

liberación *f.* liberation

libertad *f.* liberty, freedom (17)

libertador(a) liberator

libra pound

libre free; **al aire libre** outdoors; **estado libre asociado** commonwealth; **ratos** (*pl.*) **libres** spare (free) time (9)

librería bookstore (1)

libro book (1); **libro de texto** textbook (1)

licencia license; **licencia de conducir/manejar** driver's license (14)

líder *m.* leader

liga league

ligero/a light(weight) (6)

limeño/a person from Lima, Peru

limitación *f.* limitation

limitar to limit

límite *m.* limit; **fecha límite** deadline (11); **límite de velocidad** speed limit (14)

limón *m.* lemon

limonada lemonade

limonero lemon tree

limpiaparabrisas *m. inv.* windshield wiper

limpiar la casa (entera) to clean the (whole) house (9)

limpio/a clean (5)

lindo/a pretty, lovely

línea line; **patinar en línea** to rollerblade (9)

lingüístico/a linguistic

lío de tráfico traffic jam

líquido *n.* liquid

lírico/a lyrical

lista list; **lista de bodas** bride's registry

listo/a smart (2); clever (2); ready

literario/a literary

literatura literature (1)

llamada (telephone) call; **llamada a larga distancia** long-distance call; **llamada en espera** call-waiting

llamar to call (6); **¿cómo se llama usted?** what is your (*form. s.*) name? (AT); **¿cómo te llamas?** what is your (*fam. s.*) name? (AT); **llamarse** to be called (4); **me llamo...** my name is . . . (AT);

llanta tire (14); **llanta de recambio** spare tire

llanura *n.* plain

llave *f.* key (11)

llegada arrival (7)

llegar (**gu**) to arrive (2); **llegar a ser** to become; **llegar a tiempo** to arrive on time (11)

llenar to fill (up) (14); **llenar la solicitud** to fill out the application (16)

lleno/a full

llevar to wear (3); to carry (3); to take (3); to lead; **llevar gafas / lentes de contacto** to wear glasses / contact lenses (10); **llevar puesto** to have on; **llevar una vida sana/tranquila** to lead a healthy/calm life (10); **llevarse bien/mal** to get along well/poorly (with) (15)

llorar to cry (8)

llover (**ue**) to rain (5)

llueve it's raining (5)

lluvia rain

lluvioso/a rainy

lo *d.o. m. s.* you (*form.*); him, it; **lo bueno / lo malo** the good/bad thing, news (10); **lo contrario** the opposite; **lo mismo** the same thing; **lo que** what, that which (7); **¡lo siento (mucho)!** I'm (very) sorry! (11); **lo suficiente** enough

lobo wolf

local *n. m.* stall (market); *adj.* local

localidad *f.* ticket (*to a movie, play*)

localización *f.* location

localizar (**c**) to locate

loco/a crazy (5)

locura madness, craziness

lógico/a logical

lograr to achieve

loma hill

Londres London

los *def. art. m. pl.* the (1); *d.o. m. pl.* you (*form. pl.*); them; **los años sesenta, ochenta, etcétera** the sixties, eighties, *and so on;* **los/las demás** the others, the rest (12); **los lunes, martes, etcétera** on Mondays, Tuesdays, *and so on* (4)

lotería lottery

lubricar (**qu**) to lubricate

lucha struggle; fight

luchar to fight; to struggle

lucrativo/a: sin fines lucrativos nonprofit

lucro: sin fines de lucro not-for-profit

lúdico/a entertaining

luego *adv.* then; afterward; **hasta luego** see you later (AT)

lugar *m.* place (18); **ningún lugar** nowhere; **tener** (*irreg.*) **lugar** to take place

lujo luxury (12); **hotel** (*m.*) **de lujo** luxury hotel (18)

lujoso/a luxurious

luna moon; **luna de miel** honeymoon (15)

lunar: de lunares polka-dotted

lunes *m. inv.* Monday (4); **los lunes** on Mondays (4)

lustroso/a shiny

Luxemburgo Luxembourg

luz *f.* (*pl.* **luces**) light; electricity (11)

M

machista *adj. m., f.* male; chauvinistic
madera wood
maderero/a *adj.* pertaining to wood
madrastra stepmother
madre *f.* mother (2)
madrileño/a: callos (*m. pl.*) **a la madrileña** *tripe specialty of Madrid*
madrugador(a) early riser
madurez *f.* maturity (15)
maduro/a mature
maestro/a school teacher (16); **obra maestra** masterpiece (13)
magia magic
mágico/a magic
magnético/a magnetic
magnífico/a magnificent
mago wizard; **Día** (*m.*) **de los Reyes Magos** Day of the Magi (Three Kings)
maíz *m.* (*pl.* **maíces**) corn
majestuoso/a majestic
mal *n. m.* evil; illness, sickness; *adv.* badly; poorly (1); **caerle** (*irreg.*) **mal a alguien** to make a bad impression on someone (16); **llevarse mal** to get along poorly (with) (15); **mal educado/a** rude, bad-mannered; **pasarlo mal** to have a bad time (8); **salir** (*irreg.*) **mal** to turn/come out badly
mal, malo/a *adj.* bad (2); **hace mal tiempo** it's bad weather (5); **lo malo** the bad thing, news (10); **¡qué mala suerte!** what bad luck! (11); **sacar** (**qu**) **malas notas** to get bad grades (11)
maldito/a accursed, awful
maleta suitcase (7); **hacer** (*irreg.*) **la(s) maleta(s)** to pack one's suitcase(s) (7)
maletero porter (7)
maletín *m.* briefcase
malvado/a wicked
mamá mother, mom (2)
mamífero mammal
manchego: queso manchego *hard white cheese from La Mancha, Spain*
mandar to send (7); to order (*someone to do something*) (12)
mandato command
manejar to drive (12); to operate (*a machine*) (12); to manage; **licencia de manejar** driver's license (14)
manera way, manner; **de manera que** *conj.* so that, in such a way that; **de todas maneras** by all means; whatever happens
manía furor, craze
manifestación *f.* manifestation; demonstration
manjar *m.* delicacy
mano *f.* hand (11); **darse** (*irreg.*) **la mano** to shake hands; **dedo de la mano** finger (11); **estar** (*irreg.*) **en manos de** to belong to; **¡manos a la obra!** let's get to work!
manta blanket (18)

mantener (*like* **tener**) to maintain; to keep; **mantener la paz** to keep/maintain the peace (17); **mantenerse en contacto** to keep in touch
mantequilla butter (6)
manual *n. m., adj.* manual
manzana apple (6)
manzanilla chamomile
mañana *n.* morning; *adv.* tomorrow (AT); **de la mañana** in the morning (AT); **hasta mañana** see you tomorrow (AT); **pasado mañana** day after tomorrow (4); **por la mañana** in, during the morning (1)
mapa *m.* map
mapuche *m.* Araucan (*indigenous language of S.A.*)
máquina machine; **máquina de escribir** typewriter
mar *m., f.* sea (7)
maratón *m.* marathon
maravilla wonder, marvel
maravilloso/a marvelous, wondrous
marca brand name
marcar (**qu**) to strike (*clock*); to mark
mareado/a dizzy (10)
mareo dizziness
marido husband (15)
marihuana marijuana
marinado/a marinated
marinero/a: mejillones (*m. pl.*) **marineros** mussels simmered in white wine garlic sauce
marino/a *adj.* sea
mariscos *pl.* seafood (6); shellfish (6)
marítimo/a maritime; sea, marine
Marruecos *m.* Morocco
martes *m. inv.* Tuesday (4); **los martes** on Tuesdays (4)
marzo March (5)
más more (1); **cada vez más** increasingly; **más allá** further, farther; **más allá de** beyond, farther than (3); **más... que** more . . . than (5)
masa dough
máscara mask
mascota pet (2)
masculino/a masculine
masoquista *n. m., f.* masochist
matar to kill
matemáticas *f. pl.* mathematics (1)
materia subject (*school*) (1)
material *m.* material (3)
materialista *m., f.* materialistic
matrícula tuition (1)
matrimonio marriage (15); married couple (15); **contraer** (*like* **traer**) **matrimonio** to get married
máximo/a maximum
maya *n., adj. m., f.* Mayan
mayo May (5); **Cinco de Mayo** Mexican awareness celebration
mayor older (5); oldest; greater; greatest; **la mayor parte** most

mayoría majority
me *d.o.* me; *i.o.* to/for me; *refl. pron.* myself; **me gustaría...** I would (really) like . . . (7); **me llamo...** my name is . . . (AT); **me molesta** it bothers me (13); **me sorprende** it surprises me (13); **sí, (no, no) me gusta(n)...** yes, I do (no, I don't) like . . . (AT)
mecánico/a *n.* mechanic (14); *adj.* mechanical; **escaleras** (*pl.*) **mecánicas** escalator
mecanización *f.* mechanization
media: y media half-past / 30 minutes past (*the hour*)
mediano/a medium; average
medianoche *f.* midnight (8)
mediante *adv.* by means of, through
medias *f. pl.* stockings (3); **par** *m.* **de medias** pair of stockings (3)
medicina medicine (*discipline*) (10)
médico/a *n.* (medical) doctor (2); *adj.* medical; **atención** (*f.*) **médica** healthcare
medida measure; **en cierta medida** in some measure
medio *n.* medium; means; **medio ambiente** environment (*nature*) (14); **medio de comunicación** means of communication (17); **medios de comunicación** media; **por medio de** by means of
medio/a *adj.* half; middle; average; **Edad** (*f.*) **Media** Middle Ages; **media hermana** half-sister; **media pensión** room with breakfast and one other meal (18); **medio hermano** half-brother; **Oriente** (*m.*) **Medio** Middle East (17)
medioambiental environmental
mediodía *m.* noon
mediterráneo/a *adj.* Mediterranean
mejillones (*m. pl.*) **marineros** mussels simmered in white wine garlic sauce
mejor better (5); best (5)
mejorar to improve
membrana membrane
memoria memory (12)
mencionar to mention
menor *m.* minor; *adj.* younger (5); youngest; less; least
menos less; least; minus; **a menos que** *conj.* unless (15); **menos cuarto (quince)** a quarter (fifteen minutes) to (*hour*) (AT); **menos... que** less . . . than (5); **por lo menos** at least (8)
mensaje *m.* message; **mensaje electrónico** e-mail message
mensual monthly
mensualidad *f.* monthly installment
menta mint
mentira lie (12)
menú *m.* menu (6)
menudo: a menudo often
mercadeo marketing

mercado market(place) (3)

merecer (zc) to deserve

merengue *m.* dance from the Dominican Republic

merienda snack

mes *m.* month (5)

mesa table (1); **poner** (*irreg.*) **la mesa** to set the table (9); **quitar la mesa** to clear the table (9); **uva de mesa** table grape

meseta plateau (*geography*)

mesita end table (4)

mesón *m.* tavern

mestizo/a mixed-race person

metáfora metaphor

metereólogo/a meteorologist

método method

metro subway; meter; **estación** (*f.*) **de metro** subway stop (18)

metrópoli *f.* metropolis; capital city

mexicano/a *n., adj.* Mexican (2)

México Mexico

mexicoamericano/a *n., adj.* Mexican American

mezcla mixture

mezclar to mix

mí *obj. (of prep.)* me (5)

mi(s) *poss. adj.* my (2)

microondas: horno de microondas microwave oven (9)

miedo fear; **tener** (*irreg.*) **miedo (de)** to be afraid (of) (3)

miel *f.* honey; **luna de miel** honeymoon (15)

miembro member

mientras while (9); **mientras que** *conj.* while

miércoles *m. inv.* Wednesday (4)

migrante *adj.* migrant

mil *m.* thousand, one thousand (3); **dos mil** two thousand (3); **mil millón** (*m.*) billion

milagro miracle

milanesa cutlet

milenio millennium

miligramo milligram

militar: servicio militar military service (17)

milla mile

millón *m.* million (3); **dos millones** two million (3); **mil millón** billion

millonario/a millionaire

mineral: agua *f.* (*but* **el agua**) **mineral** mineral water (6)

minería mining

minero/a miner

minidiálogo minidialogue

minidrama *m.* minidrama

minifalda miniskirt

mínimo/a minimum

ministerio ministry

ministro/a: primer ministro / primera ministra prime minister

minoría minority

minuto minute

mío/a(s) *poss. adj.* my (17); *poss. pron.* (of) mine (17)

mirar to look at, watch (2); **mirar la televisión** to watch television (2)

misa mass; **misa del gallo** Midnight Mass; **oficiar una misa** to celebrate a mass

misión *f.* mission

mismo *adv.* same (10); **ahora mismo** right now; at once

mismo/a *adj.* same; self; **lo mismo** the same thing

misterioso/a mysterious

mitad *f.* half

mito myth

mitología mythology

mixteca *m.* Mixtec (*indigenous language*)

mixteca *n. m., f.* Mixtec

mochila backpack (1)

moda fashion; style; **de moda** in style; **¡es de última moda!** it's the latest style! (3)

modelo model

módem *m.* modem (12)

moderación *f.* moderation

moderado/a moderate

modernismo modernism

moderno/a modern (13)

modificación *f.* modification

modificar (qu) to modify

modismo idiom

modo way, manner; mode; *gram.* mood; **de modo** in such a way; **de todos modos** anyway; **modo de transporte** *m.* means of transportation (7)

molestar to bother, annoy; **me (te, le...) molesta que** it bothers me (you, him . . .) that (13)

molestia bother, annoyance

molido/a *adj.* ground

molino: rueda de molino treadmill (10)

momento moment; **en este momento** right now

monarca *m., f.* monarch

monarquía monarchy

monasterio monastery

moneda currency; coin

monoparental *adj.* single-parent

monopatín *m..* skateboard (12)

monstruo monster

montaña mountain (7); **bicicleta de montaña** mountain bicycle (12); **montaña rusa** roller coaster

montañismo en bicicleta mountain biking

montar to set up; to ride; **montar a caballo** to ride a horse (9); **montar en bicicleta** to ride a bicycle

montón *m.*: **un montón** a bunch

monumento monument

morado/a purple (3)

moralidad *f.* morality

morcilla blood sausage

moreno/a brunet(te) (2)

morir(se) (ue, u) (*p.p.* **muerto**) to die (8)

moro/a *n.* Moor; *adj.* Moorish

mostaza mustard

mostrar (ue) to show (7)

motivo reason, motive; motif

moto(cicleta) *f.* motorcycle (12); moped (12)

motor *m.* motor, engine

movimiento movement

mozo bellhop (18); **mozo de campo y plaza** farmhand

muchacho/a boy, girl (4)

muchísimo *adv.* an awful lot (7)

mucho *adv.* a lot, much (1); **¡lo siento mucho!** I'm very sorry!

mucho/a *adj.* a lot (of) (2); *pl.* many (2); **muchas gracias** thank you very much (AT); **mucho gusto** pleased to meet you (AT)

mucoso/a *adj.* mucous

mudanza *n.* move; moving

mudarse to move (*residence*) (16)

muebles *m. pl.* furniture (4); **sacudir los muebles** to dust the furniture (9)

muela tooth (10); molar (10), **tener** (*irreg.*) **dolor de muela** toothache (10); **sacar (qu) una muela** to extract a tooth (10)

muerte *f.* death (15)

muerto/a (*p.p. of* **morir**) dead; **muerto/a de risa** dying of laughter

mujer *f.* woman (1); wife (15); **mujer de negocios** businesswoman (16); **mujer soldado** female soldier (16)

mula mule

mulato/a mulatto

multa *n.* fine

multimillonario/a multimillionaire; billionaire

multinacional *f.* multinational company

mundial *adj.* world; **Copa Mundial** World Cup; **Segunda Guerra Mundial** World War II

mundo *n.* world (7)

muralismo muralism

murciélago bat

murmurar to murmur, whisper

muro wall

músculo muscle

museo museum; **visitar un museo** to visit a museum (9)

música music (13)

músico/a musician (13)

musulmán, musulmana *adj.* Moslem

muy very (1); **muy bien** fine, very well (AT); **muy buenas** good afternoon/ evening

N

nacer (zc) to be born (15)

nacido/a born; **recién nacido/a** newborn

nacimiento birth (15)

nación *f.* nation; **Naciones Unidas** United Nations

nacional national

nacionalidad *f.* nationality (18)

nada nothing, not anything (6); **de nada** you're welcome (AT)

nadar to swim (7)

nadie no one, nobody, not anybody (6)

náhuatl *m.* *indigenous language of Central America*

naranja *n.* orange (6)

naranjo orange tree

nariz *f.* nose (10); *pl.* **narices** nostrils

narración *f.* narration

narrador(a) narrator

narrar to narrate

natación *f.* swimming (9)

natal *adj.* native

natalidad *f.* birth

nativo/a *n.* native

natural: recursos naturales natural resources (14)

naturaleza nature (14)

náuseas *pl.* nausea

navegación *f.* navigation; sailing

navegar (gu) to sail; to navigate; **navegar la Red** to surf the Net (12)

Navidad *f.* Christmas (8); **Feliz Navidad** Merry Christmas

navideño/a *adj.* Christmas; **tarjeta navideña** Christmas card

necesario/a necessary (2)

necesidad *f.* necessity

necesitar to need (1)

negación *f.* negation

negar (ie) (gu) to deny (13); **negarse** to refuse

negativa *n. gram.* negative

negativo/a *adj.* negative

negocio business; **hombre** (*m.*)/ **mujer** (*f.*) **de negocios** businessman/ woman (16)

negro/a *n.* black (person); *adj.* black (3)

neoyorquino/a *adj.* *pertaining to New York*

nervio: ataque (*m.*) **de nervios** nervous breakdown

nervioso/a nervous (5)

neutro/a neutral

nevado/a snow-covered

nevar (ie) to snow (5)

nevera refrigerator

ni neither; nor; not even; **ni... ni...** neither . . . nor . . . ; **ni siquiera** not even

nicaragüense *n., adj. m., f.* Nicaraguan

nido nest

nieto/a grandson/granddaughter (2); *m. pl.* grandchildren (2)

nieva it's snowing (5)

nieve *f.* snow

ningún, ninguno/a no, none, not any (6); **ningún lugar** nowhere

niñero/a baby-sitter (9)

niñez *f.* (*pl.* **niñeces**) childhood (9)

niño/a small child (2); boy/girl (2); **de niño/a** as a child (9)

nitrógeno nitrogen

nivel *m.* level

no no (AT); not; **¿no?** right?, don't they (you, *and so on*) (3); **no hay de qué** you're welcome (AT); **no hay duda** there is no doubt; **no, no me gusta(n)...** no, I don't like . . . (AT); **ya no** no longer

noche *f.* night; **buenas noches** good evening (AT); good night (AT); **de noche** at night; **de la noche** in the evening (AT); at night (AT); **esta noche** tonight (5); **Noche Vieja** New Year's Eve (8); **por la noche** in the evening (1); at night (1)

Nochebuena Christmas Eve (8)

nombrar to name

nombre *m.* name

nominación *f.* nomination

nominado/a nominated

nominal: cláusula nominal *gram.* noun clause

noreste *m.* northeast

noria Ferris wheel

norma norm; standard

normalidad *f.* normality

norte *n., adj. m.* north (5)

Norteamérica North America

norteamericano/a *n., adj.* North American (2)

nos *d.o. pron.* us; *i.o. pron.* to/for us; *refl. pron.* ourselves; **nos vemos** see you around (AT)

nosotros/as *sub. pron.* we (1); *obj. (of prep.)* us

nota grade (11); note

notar to notice, note

noticia piece of news (8); *pl.* news (17)

noticiero newscast (17)

novecientos/as nine hundred (3)

novedades *f. pl.* news

novela novel

novelista *m., f.* novelist

noveno/a ninth (13)

noventa ninety (2)

noviazgo engagement (15)

noviembre *m.* November (5)

novio/a boyfriend/girlfriend (5); fiancé(e); groom, bride (15); **vestido de novia** wedding gown

nublado cloudy; **está (muy) nublado** it's (very) cloudy (5)

nuclear nuclear (14)

nudo knot

nuera daughter-in-law

nuestro/a(s) *poss. adj.* our (2); *poss. pron.* ours, of ours (17)

nueve nine (AT)

nuevo/a new (2); **Día** (*m.*) **del Año Nuevo** New Year's Day; **Feliz Año Nuevo** Happy New Year

numérico/a numerical

número number (2)

numeroso/a numerous

nunca never, not ever (2); **casi nunca** almost never (2)

nutrición *f.* nutrition

O

o or (AT)

ó or (*between two numbers* [*digits*])

obedecer (zc) to obey (14)

obelisco obelisk

obesidad *f.* obesity

objetivo objective

objeto object; **objeto volante no identificado (OVNI)** unidentified flying object (UFO)

obligación *f.* obligation

obligatorio/a compulsory

obra (de arte) work (of art) (13); **¡manos a la obra!** let's get to work!; **obra maestra** masterpiece (13)

obrero/a worker, laborer (16)

observación *f.* observation

observar to observe

obstáculo obstacle

obtener (*like* **tener**) to obtain (12)

obvio/a obvious

ocasión *f.* occasion

ocasionar to bring about

occidental western

océano ocean (7); **Océano Atlántico** Atlantic Ocean

ochenta eighty (2)

ocho eight (AT)

ochocientos/as eight hundred (3)

ocio leisure time

ocioso/a leisurely

octavo/a eighth (13)

octubre *m.* October (5)

ocular *adj.* eye, pertaining to the eye

ocupación *f.* occupation

ocupado/a busy (5)

ocupar to occupy

ocurrir to occur, happen

odiar to hate (7)

oeste *m.* west (5)

oferta offer; sale, special

oficial official

oficiar una misa to celebrate a mass

oficina office (1); **oficina de correos** post office (18); **oficina de personal** personnel office

oficio trade (*profession*) (16)

ofrecer (zc) to offer (7)

oído inner ear (10)

oír *irreg.* to hear (4)

ojalá (que) I wish, hope (that) (13)

ojo eye (10); **¡ojo!** watch out!; **ojo alerta** eagle eye

olímpico/a: Juegos (*pl.*) **Olímpicos** Olympic Games

oliva olive; **aceite** (*m.*) **de oliva** olive oil

olla   pot

olmeca *n., adj. m., f.*   Olmec

olvidadizo/a   forgetful

olvidar(se) (de)   to forget (about) (8)

olvido   forgetfulness; oblivion

ómnibus *m.*   bus

once   eleven (AT)

onda: ¿qué onda?   what's new/hap-
pening?

ONU *f.* (Organización de Naciones
Unidas)   U.N. (United Nations)

opción *f.*   option

ópera   opera (13)

operación *f.*   operation

operar   to operate

opinar   to think; to have, express an
opinion

oponerse (*like* poner)   to oppose

oportunidad *f.*   opportunity

oposición *f.*   opposition

optimista *adj. m., f.*   optimist

opuesto/a   opposite

oración *f.*   sentence

oral: informe (*m.*) oral   oral report
(11)

órale *sl. Mex.*   come on

orden *m.*   order (*chronological*); *f.*
order, command; a sus órdenes at
your service

ordenado/a   neat (5)

ordenador *m. Sp.*   computer (12);
ordenador portátil laptop computer

ordenar   to put in order

oreja   outer ear (10)

orgánico/a   organic

organismo   organism

organización *f.*   organization

organizar (c)   to organize

oriental   eastern

Oriente (*m.*) Medio   Middle East (17)

origen *m.*   origin

originar(se)   to originate

originario/a   originating; native

orilla   shore; bank (*of a river*)

oriudo/a (de)   native of

oro   gold; Ricitos de Oro Goldilocks

orquesta   orchestra

ortiga   nettle

ortográfico/a *adj.*   spelling,
orthographic

os *d.o. pron.*   you (*fam. pl.*); *i.o. pron.*
to/for you (*fam. pl.*)

oscuro/a   dark

óseo/a *adj.*   bone

oso   bear; oso pardo grizzly bear

ostra   oyster

otoño   autumn (5)

otorgar (gu)   to grant

otro/a   other, another (2); otra vez
again; por otra parte / otro lado on the
other hand

OVNI *m.* (objeto volante no identificado)
UFO (unidentified flying object)

oxígeno   oxygen

oye *interj.*   see; hey

ozono: capa de ozono   ozone layer

P

paciencia   patience

paciente *n. m., f.*   patient (10); *adj.*
patient

Pacífico/a   Pacific (Ocean, Coast)

padecer (zc)   to suffer

padrastro   stepfather

padre *m.*   father (2); *pl.* parents (2)

padrino   godfather; *pl.* godparents

paella   *dish made with rice, shellfish,
and often chicken, and flavored with saffron*

pagar (gu)   to pay (1); pagar a plazos to
pay in installments (16); pagar al contado / en efectivo to pay in cash (16);
pagar con cheque to pay by check (16)

página   page

país *m.*   country (2)

paisaje *m.*   landscape

pájaro   bird (2)

palabra   word (AT)

palacio   palace

pálido/a   pale

palma   palm tree

palo   stick

palomino   young dove

palomitas *pl.*   popcorn

pampa   plain (*geography, Arg.*)

pan *m.*   bread (6); pan tostado toast (6)

panameño/a *n., adj.*   Panamanian

pantalón, pantalones *m.*   pants (3);
pantalones cortos shorts

papá *m.*   father, dad (2); Papá Noel
Santa Claus

papa   potato

papel *m.*   paper (1); role (*in a play*) (13);
papel de cartas stationery (18)

papelería   stationery store (18)

paquete *m.*   package (18)

par *m.*   pair (3); un par de medias a pair
of stockings (3); un par de zapatos a
pair of shoes (3)

para *prep.*   for (2); in order to (2);
para + *inf.* in order to (*do something*);
para que *conj.* so that (15)

parabrisas *m. inv.*   windshield (14)

paracaidismo   skydiving

parada   stop; hacer (*irreg.*) paradas to
make stops (7); parada de autobús bus
stop (18)

paraguas *m. inv.*   umbrella

paraguayo/a *n., adj.*   Paraguayan

parar   to stop (14)

parcial: de tiempo parcial   part-time (11)

pardo/a   brown; oso pardo grizzly bear

parecer (zc)   to seem (13)

parecido/a   similar

pared *f.*   wall (4); pintar las paredes to
paint the walls (9)

pareja   (married) couple (15); partner (15)

paréntesis *m. inv.*   parentheses

pariente *m., f.*   relative (2)

parlamentario/a   parliamentary

párpado   eyelid

parque *m.*   park (5); parque de atracciones amusement park; parque de
recreo recreational park; parque
temático theme park

párrafo   paragraph

parrandero/a   party-loving

parroquiano/a   client

parte *f.*   part (4); a mayor parte most;
formar parte de to be part of, a member of; por otra parte on the other
hand; por parte de by; por todas partes
everywhere (11)

participante *m., f.*   participant

participar   to participate

participativo/a   participatory

participio *gram.*   participle

partícula   particle

particular   particular; private

partida: punto de partida   starting point

partido   game, match (*sports*)

partir: a partir de   as of; from (*this
moment, date on*)

párvulo   tot

pasado *n.*   past

pasado/a *adj.*   last; past; el año pasado
last year; huevo pasado por agua
poached egg; pasado mañana day after
tomorrow (4)

pasaje *m.*   passage (7); ticket (7)

pasajero/a   passenger (7)

pasaporte *m.*   passport (18)

pasar   to happen (5); to pass; to spend
(*time*) (5); pasar... años to be more than
. . . years old; pasar hambre *f.* to go
hungry; pasar la aspiradora to vacuum
(9); pasar películas to show movies;
pasar por el control de la seguridad to
go/pass through security (7); pasar
tiempo (con) to spend time (with) (15);
pasarlo bien/mal to have a good/bad
time (8)

pasatiempo   pastime, hobby (9)

Pascua (Florida)   Easter (8); Pascua (de
los hebreos) Passover

pasear   to take a walk, stroll; to go for
a ride; pasear en bicicleta to ride a
bicycle (9)

paseo   walk, stroll; dar (*irreg.*) un
paseo to take a walk (9)

pasión *f.*   passion

pasional   passionate

pasivo/a   passive

paso   step; de paso passing through

pasta dental   toothpaste (18)

pastel *m.*   cake (6); pie (6); pastel de
cumpleaños birthday cake (8)

pastelería   pastry shop (18)

pastelito   small pastry (18)

pastilla pill (10)

pastor(a) shepherd; **perro pastor alemán** German Shepherd

pata paw

patata potato (6); **patata frita** French fried potato (6)

patín *n. m.* roller skate (12)

patinar to skate (9); **patinar en línea** to rollerblade (9)

patio patio (4), yard (4)

pato duck

patria homeland

patrón *m.* pattern

patrona: santa patrona patron saint

pavo turkey (6); **pavo real** peacock

paz *f.* (*pl.* **paces**) peace (17); **mantener** (*like* **tener**) **la paz** to keep the peace (17); **vivir en paz** to live in peace (17)

pecho chest

pechuga breast

pedagogía pedagogy

pedir (i, i) to ask for (4); to order (*in a restaurant*) (4); **pedir disculpas** to apologize (11); **pedir prestado/a** to borrow (16)

pegar (gu) to hit, strike (9); **pegarse con/contra/en** to run, bump into (11)

peinado hairdo

peinarse to comb one's hair (4)

pelado/a peeled

pelear to fight (9)

película movie, film (4); **ir** (*irreg.*) **a ver una película** to go to see a movie (9); **pasar películas** to show movies

peligro danger; jeopardy; **especie** (*f.*) **en peligro de extinción** endangered species (14)

peligroso/a dangerous

pelo hair; **tomarle el pelo** to pull someone's leg

pelota ball

pelotón (*m.*) **de fusilamiento** firing squad

peluquero/a hairstylist (16)

pena: ¡qué pena! what a shame!; **valer** (*irreg.*) **la pena** to be worthwhile, worth the trouble

pendencia quarrel, fight

péndulo pendulum

pensar (ie) (en) to think (about) (4); **pensar** + *inf.* to intend, plan to (*do something*) (4)

pensión *f.* boardinghouse (18); **media pensión** room with breakfast and one other meal (18); **pensión completa** room and full board (18)

peor worse (5); worst

pepino cucumber

pequeño/a small (2)

percibido/a perceived

percusionista *m., f.* percussionist

perder (ie) to lose (4); to miss (*a function*) (4); **perder el juicio** to go crazy

pérdida loss

perdón pardon me, excuse me (AT)

perezoso/a lazy (2)

perfecto/a perfect

periódico newspaper (2)

periodista *m., f.* journalist (16)

periodístico/a *adj.* pertaining to journalism

perjudicar (qu) to damage, hurt

permanente permanent

permiso permission; permit; **con permiso** excuse me (AT)

permitir to permit, allow (12)

pero but (AT)

perpetuo/a perpetual

perro dog (2); **perro de lanas** poodle; **perro pastor alemán** German Shepherd

persa *m., f.* Persian

perseguir (*like* **seguir**) to pursue

persona person (1)

personaje *m.* character (*in literature*)

personal: dirección (*f.*)**/oficina de personal** personnel office (16); **director(a) de personal** personnel director (16)

personalidad *f.* personality

perspectiva perspective

persuadir to persuade

pertenecer (zc) a to belong to

perturbar to disturb

peruano/a *n., adj.* Peruvian

pesado/a boring (9); difficult (9); heavy

pesar to weigh; **a pesar de** in spite of

pesas: levantar pesas to lift weights

pesca fishing

pescado fish (*cooked*) (6)

peseta *former monetary unit of Spain*

pesimista *adj. m., f.* pessimist

peso weight; **tener** (*irreg.*) **exceso de peso** to be overweight

pesticida pesticide

petróleo petroleum, oil

petrolero/a *adj.* petroleum, oil; **buque** (*m.*) **petrolero** oil tanker

petrolífero/a *adj.* oil-bearing, oil

pez *m.* (*pl.* **peces**) fish (*animal*) (14)

pianista *m., f.* pianist

picnic: **hacer** (*irreg.*) **un** *picnic* to have a picnic (9)

pico beak

pie *m.* foot (11); **a pie** on foot; **dedo del pie** toe (11); **levantarse con el pie izquierdo** to get up on the wrong side of the bed (11); **poner** (*irreg.*) **pie en** to set foot on

piedad *f.* pity

piedra stone

piel *f.* skin

pierna leg (11); **lastimarse la pierna** to injure one's leg (11)

pieza piece

píldora pill

piloto/a pilot

pimienta pepper

pingüino penguin

pintar (las paredes) to paint (the walls) (9)

pintor(a) painter (13)

pintoresco/a picturesque

pintura painting (*general*) (13); painting (*piece of art*) (13); paint

pirámide *f.* pyramid

pirata *m., f.* pirate

Pirineos *pl.* Pyrenees

pisar to tread on, step on

piscina swimming pool (4)

piso floor; apartment (*Sp.*); **barrer el piso** to sweep the floor (9); **primer/segundo piso** second / third floor (first / second floor above ground floor) (12)

pistacho pistachio

pitar to whistle

pito: no me importa un pito I don't care one bit

pizarra chalkboard (1)

pizzería pizza parlor

placa license plate

placer *m.* pleasure

plan *m.* plan; **hacer** (*irreg.*) **planes para** + *inf.* to make plans to (*do something*) (9)

plancha: a la plancha grilled

planchar la ropa to iron clothing (9)

planeación *f.* plan

planear to plan

planeta *m.* planet

plano/a flat

planta plant; **planta baja** ground floor (12)

plantación *f.* plantation

plantar cara a to confront

plástico *n.* plastic

plata silver

plátano banana

platino platinum

plato dish (*plate*) (4); dish (*course*) (6); **fregar (ie) (gu) los platos** to wash the dishes; **lavar los platos** to wash the dishes (9); **plato principal** entrée

playa beach (5)

plaza: mozo de campo y plaza farmhand; **plaza de toros** bullring

plazo period, term; **a largo plazo** long-term; **pagar (gu) a plazos** to pay in installments (16)

plegaria prayer

plenamente fully, completely

plomero/a plumber (16)

pluralismo pluralism

pluviosidad *f.* rainfall

población *f.* population (14)

poblado/a populated

poblar to settle

pobre *n. m., f.* poor person; *adj.* poor (2)

pobreza poverty

poco *adv.* little (1); **dentro de poco** in a little while; **poco a poco** little by little; **un poco (de)** a little bit (of) (1)

poco/a *adj.* little; *pl.* few (3)
podadera pruning knife
poder *irreg.* to be able to, can (3)
poder *n.* power
poderoso/a powerful
poema *m.* poem
poesía poetry
poeta *m., f.* poet (13)
poético/a poetic
policía *m., f.* police officer (14); *f.* police (force)
poliomielitis *f.* poliomyelitis (polio)
política *s.* politics (17)
político/a *n.* politician (17); *adj.* political; **ciencias** (*pl.*) **políticas** political science
pollo (asado) (roast) chicken (6)
pololo/a *sl.* boyfriend, girlfriend (*Chile*)
polvo: quitar el polvo to dust
poner *irreg.* (*p.p.* **puesto**) to put, place (4); to turn on (*machines*); **poner la mesa** to set the table (9); **poner pie en** to set foot on; **ponerle + *adj.*** to make someone + *adj.*; **ponerle una inyección** to give (*someone*) a shot, injection (10); **ponerse** to put on (*clothing*) (4); **ponerse + *adj.*** to become, get + *adj.* (8); **ponerse a la altura de** to compete on the same level; **ponerse al día** to get up-to-date; **ponerse de acuerdo** to reach an agreement; **ponerse enfermo/a** to get sick
popularidad *f.* popularity
por *prep.* by; for (4); through; during (4); along; by way of; **por ciento** percent; **por completo** completely; **por costumbre** customarily; **por Dios** for heaven's sake (11); **por ejemplo** for example (11); **por eso** therefore (1); **por favor** please (AT); **por fin** at last, finally (4); **por la mañana/tarde** in, during the morning/afternoon (1); **por la noche** in / during the evening (1); at night (1); **por lo general** generally (4); **por lo menos** at least (8); **por medio de** by means of; **por otra parte / por otro lado** on the other hand; **por parte de** by; **por primera/última vez** for the first/last time (11); **¿por qué?** why? (2); **por si acaso** just in case (11); **por supuesto** of course (11); **por todas partes** everywhere (11); **por último** finally; **por un lado** on the one hand
¿por qué? why? (2)
porcentaje *m.* percentage
pordiosero/a beggar
porque because (2)
portarse to behave (8)
portátil: portable; **computadora/ordenador portátil** laptop computer; **radio portátil** portable radio (12)
portavoz *m.* (*pl.* **portavoces**) spokesperson

porteño/a person from Buenos Aires
portero/a building manager, doorman (12)
portugués *m.* Portuguese (*language*)
portugués, portuguesa *n., adj.* Portuguese
porvenir *m.* future
posada boarding house; inn
posesión *f.* possession
posesivo/a possessive
posgraduado/a *adj.* graduate; postgraduate
posibilidad *f.* possibility
posible possible (2)
posición *f.* position
postal: tarjeta postal postcard (7)
postre *m.* dessert (6)
postura stance
potencia power
potente strong
práctica practice
practicar (qu) to practice (1); **practicar deportes** to practice, play sports (10)
práctico/a practical
precedente precedent
precio price (3); **precio fijo** fixed, set price (3)
precioso/a precious
precipitado/a hasty
precipitarse to rush headlong
preciso/a exact, precise
precolombino/a pre-Columbian
predicción *f.* prediction
predominar to dominate
preferencia preference
preferible preferable (13)
preferir (ie, i) to prefer (3)
pregunta question; **hacer** (*irreg.*) **preguntas** to ask questions; **hacer** (*irreg.*) **una pregunta** to ask a question (4)
preguntar to ask (a question) (6)
prehistórico/a prehistoric
prejuicio prejudice
prematuro/a premature
premio prize
prender to turn on (*lights, appliance*)
prensa press, news media (17)
prensado/a crushed
preocupación *f.* worry, concern
preocupado/a worried (5)
preocupante worrisome
preocuparse (por) to worry (about)
preparación *f.* preparation
preparar to prepare (6)
preparativo preparation
preposición *f. gram.* preposition (4)
presa seizure; victim
presencia presence
presentación *f.* presentation
presentar to present, introduce
presente *n. m.* present (*time*); *gram.* present tense

preservación *f.* preservation
presidencia presidency
presidencial presidential
presidente/a president
presidio fort
presión *f.* pressure (11); **sufrir (muchas) presiones** to be under (a lot of) pressure (11)
prestado: pedir (i, i) prestado/a to borrow (16)
préstamo loan (16)
prestar to lend (7)
prestigio prestige
prestigioso/a prestigious
presupuesto budget (16)
pretérito *gram.* preterite
primario/a primary; **bosque** (*m.*) **primario** old-growth forest
primavera spring (5); **vacaciones** (*f. pl.*) **de primavera** spring break
primer, primero/a first (4); **a primera vista** at first sight (15); **de primera** first-class; **el primero de** the first of (*month*) (5); **por primera vez** for the first time (11); **primer ministro / primera ministra** prime minister; **primer piso** first floor (12); **primera clase** first class (7)
primo/a cousin (2)
principal main, principle; **plato principal** entrée
príncipe *m.* prince
principiante *m., f.* beginner
principio beginning; **a principios de** at the beginning of; **al principio de** at the beginning of (16)
prisa hurry; **tener** (*irreg.*) **prisa** to be in a hurry (3)
prisionero/a prisoner
privado/a private
privilegio privilege
probabilidad *f.* probability
probable: es probable que it's probable, likely that . . . (13)
probar (ue) to try; to taste
problema *m.* problem
procesamiento processing
proceso process
procurar to try
producción *f.* production
producir *irreg.* to produce
producto product
productor(a) producer
profesión *f.* profession (16)
profesional professional
profesor(a) professor (1); **asistente** (*m., f.*) **del profesor** teaching assistant
profundidad *f.* depth
profundo/a deep
programa *m.* program
programador(a) programmer (16)
progresista *adj. m., f.* progressive

progresivo/a progressive
progreso progress
prohibición *f.* prohibition
prohibir (prohíbo) to forbid, prohibit (12)
proliferación *f.* proliferation
promedio *n.* average
prometer to promise (7)
promover (ue) to promote
pronombre *m. gram.* pronoun
pronto soon; **hasta pronto** see you soon; **tan pronto como** as soon as (16)
pronunciación *f.* pronunciation
pronunciar to pronounce
propiedad *f.* property
propina tip (18)
propio/a *adj.* own (15)
proponer (*like* **poner**) to propose
proporcionar to provide
propósito purpose
protagonista *m., f.* protagonist
protección *f.* protection
proteger (j) to protect (14)
protestar to protest
proveer (*like* **ver**) to provide
proverbio proverb
providencia providence
provincia province
provocar (qu) to provoke, cause
proximidad *f.* closeness
próximo/a next (4)
proyecto project
prueba test (11); quiz (11)
psicología psychology
psicológico/a psychological
psiquiatra *m., f.* psychiatrist
psíquico/a *adj.* psychic
publicación *f.* publication
publicar (qu) to publish
publicidad *f.* publicity; advertising
público *n.* audience; public
público/a *adj.* public (14); **servicios públicos** public services (14); **transporte** (*m.*) **público** public transportation (14)
pueblo town; people
puerta door (1)
puerto port (7)
puertorriqueño/a *n., adj.* Puerto Rican
pues *conj.* since, because, for; *adv.* then, well, all right
puesto/a (*p.p.* **poner**): **llevar puesto/a** to have on
puesto *n.* job (16); position; place (*in line*) (7); **guardar un puesto** to save a place (7)
pulgada inch
pulido/a polished
pulmón *m.* lung (10)
punto point; **en punto** on the dot (*time*) (AT); **punto cardinal** cardinal direction; **punto de partida** starting point, point of departure; **punto de vista** point of view
puntual punctual

puro *n.* cigar
puro/a pure (14); **aire** (*m.*) **puro** clean air (14)

Q

que that (2); which; who (2); **así que** therefore, consequently, so; **hasta que** *conj.* until (16); **hay que** + *inf.* it is necessary to (*do something*) (13); **lo que** what, that which (7); **más... que** more . . . than (5); **menos... que** less . . . than (5); **que aproveche** enjoy your meal; **ya que** since
¿qué? what? (AT); which? (1); **¿a qué hora?** what time? (AT); **¿de qué color es?** what color is it? (3); **¿por qué?** why?; **¿qué día es hoy?** what day is today? (4); **¿qué hora es?** what time is it? (AT); **¿qué tal?** how are you doing? (AT); **¿qué tiempo hace hoy?** what's the weather like today? (5)
¡qué... ! what . . . !; **¡qué extraño!** how strange! (13); **¡qué ganga!** what a bargain!; **¡qué lástima!** what a shame! (13); **¡qué mala suerte!** what bad luck! (11); **¡qué pena!** what a shame!; **¡qué torpe!** how clumsy! (11)
quebranto misfortune
quechua *m.* Quechua (*indigenous language*)
quedar to remain, be left (11); to be situated; **quedarle bien** to fit well; **quedarse** to stay, remain (*in a place*) (5)
quehacer *m.* chore; **quehacer doméstico** household chore
quejarse (de) to complain (about) (8)
quemar to burn (up)
querer *irreg.* to want (3); to love (15); **eso quiere decir...** that means . . . (10); **fue sin querer** it was unintentional (11)
querido/a dear (5)
queso cheese (6); **queso manchego** *hard white cheese from La Mancha, Spain*
quetzal *m.* Quetzal (*monetary unit of Guatemala*)
quiché *m.* Quiché (*indigenous language from Central America*)
quien who, whom
¿quién(es)? who? whom? (1); **¿de quién?** whose? (2)
quieto/a still (*movement*)
química chemistry (1)
quince fifteen (AT); **y/menos quince** a quarter (fifteen minutes) after / to (*hour*) (AT)
quinceañera *young woman's fifteenth birthday party*
quinientos/as five hundred (3)
quinta country house
quinto/a fifth (13)
quiosco kiosk (18)

quitar to remove; **quitar la mesa** to clear the table (9); **quitar el polvo** to dust; **quitarse** to take off (*clothing*) (4)
quizás perhaps

R

rabino/a rabbi
racismo racism
radical *m. gram.* stem
radio *m.* **(portátil)** (portable) radio (*apparatus*) (12); *f.* radio (*medium*) (12)
radioyente *m., f.* radio listener; *m., pl.* radio audience
raíz *f.* (*pl.* **raíces**) root; **a raíz de** as a result of; because of
rama branch
rancho ranch
rapidez *f.* speed
rápido/a fast (6)
ráquetbol *m.* racketball
raro/a strange (8)
rascacielos skyscraper *m. s., pl.* (14)
rato *n.* while, short time; **ratos libres** spare (free) time (9)
ratón *m.* mouse (12)
raya: de rayas striped
raza race; **Día** (*m.*) **de la Raza** Columbus Day (Hispanic Awareness Day)
razón *f.* reason; **no tener** (*irreg.*) **razón** to be wrong (3); **tener** (*irreg.*) **razón** to be right (3)
reacción *f.* reaction
reaccionar to react (8)
real real; royal; **Camino Real** Royal Highway; **pavo real** peacock; **Real Academia Española** Royal Spanish Academy
realidad *f.* reality; **en realidad** in fact
realismo realism
realista *adj. m., f.* realistic
realizar (c) to achieve, attain
rebaja sale, reduction (3)
rebelde *n. m., f.* rebel; *adj.* rebellious
rebozo shawl
recado message
recambio: llanta de recambio spare tire
recepción *f.* front desk (18)
recepcionista *m., f.* receptionist
receta recipe; prescription (10)
recetar to prescribe (*medicine*)
rechazar (c) to reject
recibir to receive (2)
reciclaje *m.* recycling
reciclar to recycle (14)
recién *adv.* newly, recently; **recién casado/a** newlywed (15); **recién nacido/a** newborn
reciente recent
recinto enclosure, space
recio/a robust
recipiente *m.* container
reciprocidad *f.* reciprocity
recíproco/a reciprocal

recoger (j) to collect (11); to pick up (11)

recomendación *f.* recommendation

recomendar (ie) to recommend (7)

reconocer (zc) to recognize

reconocido/a recognized, well-known

recopilado/a compiled

recordar (ue) to remember (8)

recorte *m.* clipping (*newspaper*)

recreativo/a recreational

recreo recreation; **parque** (*m.*) **de recreo** recreational park

recto/a straight

rector(a) university president

recubanizar (c) to become Cuban again

recuerdo souvenir; memory

recuperación *f.* recovery, recuperation

recurso resource; **recursos naturales** natural resources (14)

Red *f.* Net; Internet (12); **navegar (gu) la Red** to surf the Net (12)

redacción *f.* editorial staff

redecorado/a redecorated

redondo/a round

reducción *f.* reduction

reducir *irreg.* to reduce

reemplazar (c) to replace

reencarnación *f.* reincarnation

referencia reference

referente (a) referring, relating (to)

referirse (ie, i) (a) to refer (to)

refinado/a refined

reflejar to reflect

reflejo reflection

reflexivo/a reflexive

reformar to reform

refresco soft drink (6)

refrigerador *m.* refrigerator (9)

refugiarse to take refuge

refugio refuge

regalar to give (*as a gift*) (7)

regalo gift, present (2)

regatear to haggle, bargain (3)

régimen *m.* regime

región *f.* region

registrar to search, examine (18)

registro register; registration

regla rule

regresar to return (*to a place*) (1); **regresar a casa** to go home (1)

regulador (*m.*) **termómetro** thermostat

regular so-so, OK (AT)

reina queen (17)

reino kingdom

reír(se) (i, i) (me río) to laugh (8); **reírse a carcajadas** to laugh one's head off

relación *f.* relation; relationship (15)

relacionarse con to be related to

relajante relaxing

relajarse to relax

relativo/a relative

religión *f.* religion

religioso/a religious

reloj *m.* clock; watch (3)

remar to row

remedio remedy

remodelado/a remodeled

remoto/a remote; **control** (*m.*) **remoto** remote control (12)

renovar to renovate

renunciar (a) to resign (from) (16)

reparar to fix, repair

repasar to review

repaso review

repente: de repente suddenly (10)

repertorio repertory

repetición *f.* repetition

repetir (i, i) to repeat

repetitivo/a repetitive

reportaje *m.* article; report

reportar to report

reportero/a reporter (17)

represa dam

representante *n. m., f.* representative

representar to represent (13)

república republic

requerir (ie, i) to require

requisito requirement

resaltar to emphasize

reserva reservation (18); **hacer** (*irreg.*)/**confirmar las reservas** to make/confirm reservations (18)

reservación *f.* reservation (18); **hacer** (*irreg.*)/**confirmar las reservaciones** to make/confirm reservations (18)

reservar to reserve

resfriado cold (*illness*) (10)

resfriarse (me resfrío) to get/catch a cold (10)

residencia dormitory (1)

residencial residential

residente *m., f.* resident

resolver (ue) (*p.p.* **resuelto**) to solve, resolve (14)

respectivamente respectively

respecto: (con) respecto a with regard to, with respect to

respetar to respect

respeto respect

respiración *f.* breathing

respirar to breathe (10)

respiratorio/a respiratory

resplandor *m.* brilliance, radiance

responder to answer

responsabilidad *f.* responsibility (17)

responsabilizar (c) to make responsible

respuesta answer (5)

restaurante *m.* restaurant (6)

resto rest

restricción *f.* restriction

resuelto (*p.p. of* **resolver**) solved, resolved

resultado result

resultar to turn out

resumen *m.* summary; **en resumen** in short

retener (*like* **tener**) to retain

reto challenge

retórico/a rhetorical

retrasado/a late

retratar to paint a portrait of

retrato portrait

reunión *f.* meeting; gathering

reunirse (me reúno) (con) to get together (with) (8)

revelar to reveal

revés: al revés backward

revisar (el aceite) to check (the oil) (14)

revista magazine (2)

revolución *f.* revolution

revolucionario/a revolutionary

revolver (ue) to scramble

revuelto/a: huevos revueltos scrambled eggs

rey *m.* king (17); **Día** (*m.*) **de los Reyes Magos** Day of the Magi (Three Kings)

rezar (c) to pray

Ricitos de Oro Goldilocks

rico/a rich (2)

ridículo/a ridiculous; **es ridículo que...** it's ridiculous that . . . (13)

riesgo risk

riesgoso/a risky

rígido/a rigid

rima rhyme

rinoceronte *m.* rhinoceros

riñón *m.* kidney

río river (14)

riqueza wealth

risa laughter; **muerto/a de risa** dying of laughter

ritmo rhythm, pace (14)

róbalo sea bass

robar to steal

robo robbery, theft

roca rock

rocín *m.* nag (horse)

rodaje *m.* shooting, filming

rodeado/a surrounded

rodilla knee

rojo/a red (3); **Caperucita Roja** Little Red Ridinghood

romano/a *n., adj.* Roman

romántico/a romantic

rompecabezas *m. inv.* puzzle

romper (*p.p.* **roto**) to break (11); **romper con** to break up with (15)

ron *m.* rum

ropa clothes, clothing (3); **cambiar de ropa** to change clothes (12); **lavar la ropa** to wash clothes (9); **planchar la ropa** to iron clothing (9); **ropa interior** underwear (3)

rosa rose

rosado/a pink (3)

rostro face

roto/a (*p.p.* **romper**) broken; torn

rubio/a blond(e) (2)
rueda de feria Ferris wheel; **rueda de andar** treadmill; **rueda de molino** treadmill (10)
ruido noise (4)
ruidoso/a noisy
ruina ruin (13)
ruptura rupture, break
ruso *n.* Russian *(language)*
ruso/a *n., adj.* Russian; **montaña rusa** roller coaster
ruta route
rutina diaria daily routine (4)
rutinario/a *adj.* routine

S

sábado Saturday (4)
sábana sheet *(bed)* (18)
saber *irreg.* to know (6); **saber** + *inf.* to know how to *(do something)* (6)
sabiduría wisdom
sabor *m.* taste; flavor
sabroso/a tasty
sacar (qu) to take out (11); to get (11); to extract (10); to withdraw *(money)*; **sacar buenas/malas notas** to get good/bad grades (11); **sacar el saldo** to balance a checkbook (16); **sacar fotos** to take photos (7); **sacar la basura** to take out the trash (9); **sacar la lengua** to stick out one's tongue (10); **sacar una muela** to extract a tooth (10)
sacrificio sacrifice
sacudir los muebles to dust the furniture (9)
Sagitario Sagitarius
sagrado/a sacred
sal *f.* salt
sala room; living room (4); **sala de clase** classroom; **sala de emergencias/urgencia** emergency room (10); **sala de espera** waiting room (7); **sala de estar** living room; sitting room
salario salary (16)
salchicha sausage (6); hot dog (6)
saldo balance *(bank)*; **sacar (qu) el saldo** to balance a checkbook (16)
salida departure (7)
saliente prominent
salir *irreg.* **(de)** to leave *(a place)* (4); to go out (4); **salir bien/mal** to turn/come out well/badly; **salir con** to go out with (4)
salmón *m.* salmon (6)
salpicón *m.* *cold fish dish*
salsa sauce; salsa *(music)*; **salsa de tomate** catsup; tomato sauce
saltar to jump
salteado/a sautéed
salto waterfall
salud *f.* health (10)
saludable healthy
saludarse to greet each other (10)

saludo greeting
salvadoreño/a *n., adj.* Salvadoran
salvaje: animal *(m.)* **salvaje** wild animal (14)
salvo except
san, santo/a *n.* saint; **Día** *(m.)* **de San Patricio** St. Patrick's Day; **Día** *(m.)* **de Todos los Santos** All Saints' Day; **día** *(m.)* **del santo** saint's day; **santa patrona** patron saint
sancocho *stew prepared with meat or fish and other ingredients such as yuca, corn, and plaintains*
sandalia sandal (3)
sándwich *m.* sandwich (6)
sangre *f.* blood (10)
sanitario/a sanitary
sano/a healthy; **llevar una vida sana** to lead a healthy life (10)
santo/a *adj.* holy
sardina sardine
sartén *f.* frying pan
satélite *m.* satellite
satirizar (c) to satirize
satisfacción *f.* satisfaction
satisfacer *(irreg.)* *(p.p. satisfecho)* to satisfy
satisfecho/a *(p.p. satisfacer)* satisfied
sé I know
se *refl. pron.* yourself *(form.)*; himself, herself, itself, yourselves *(form.)*; themselves; **se trata de** it's a question of
secadora clothes dryer (9)
sección *f.* section; **sección de (no) fumar** (non)smoking section (7)
seco/a dry; **fruto seco** nut
secretario/a secretary (1)
secreto *n.* secret
secuencia sequence
secundario/a secondary
sed *f.* thirst; **tener** *(irreg.)* **(mucha) sed** to be (very) thirsty (6)
seda silk (3); **es de seda** it is made of silk (3)
sede *f.* seat; headquarters
seguida: en seguida right away (10)
seguidor(a) follower
seguir (i, i) (g) to keep on going; to go; to continue (14); **seguir todo derecho** to go straight ahead (14)
según according to (2)
segundo *n.* second *(time)*
segundo/a second (13); **Segunda Guerra Mundial** World War II; **segundo piso** second floor (12)
seguridad *f.* security; **pasar por el control de la seguridad** to go/pass through security (7)
seguro *n.* insurance; **seguro social** social security
seguro/a *adj.* sure, certain (5); **es seguro** it's a sure thing (13); **no estar seguro/a (de)** to be (un)sure (of)

seis six (AT)
seiscientos/as six hundred (3)
selección *f.* selection
seleccionar to choose
sellado/a sealed; stamped; closed
sello stamp (18)
selva jungle
semáforo traffic signal (14)
semana week; **día** *(m.)* **de la semana** weekday (4); **fin** *(m.)* **de semana** weekend (1); **semana que viene** next week (4); **una vez a la semana** once a week (2)
sembradura sowing
sembrar (ie) to plant
semejante similar
semejanza similarity
semestre *m.* semester
semiabierto/a partially open
semilla seed
senado senate
senador(a) senator
sencillo/a simple
senda path
sendero path
sensación *f.* sensation
sensible sensitive
sentarse (ie) to sit down (4)
sentencia judgment, verdict, sentence
sentido meaning; sense
sentimental sentimental (15)
sentimiento feeling
sentir (ie, i) to regret (13); to feel sorry (13); **¡lo siento (mucho)!** I'm (very) sorry! (11); **sentirse** to feel *(an emotion)* (8)
señor (Sr.) *m.* man; Mr. (AT); sir (AT)
señora (Sra.) woman; Mrs. (AT); ma'am (AT)
señorita (Srta.) young woman; Miss (AT); Ms. (AT)
separación *f.* separation (15)
separado/a separate
separar to separate; **separarse de** to separate from (15)
septiembre *m.* September (5)
séptimo/a seventh (13)
ser *(m.)* **humano** human being
ser *irreg.* to be (2); **fue sin querer** it was unintentional (11); **llegar (gu) a ser** to become; **ser aburrido/a** to be boring (9); **ser aficionado/a (a)** to be a fan (of) (9); **ser alérgico/a (a)** to be allergic (to); **ser divertido/a** to be fun (9); **ser en** + *place* to take place in/at *(place)* (8); **ser flexible** to be flexible (11); **ser una lata** to be a pain, drag
serie *f.* series
serio/a serious
serpenteante winding
serpentino/a serpentine
serpiente *f.* snake
servicio service; **servicio de cuarto / de habitación** *Sp.* room service (18);

servicio militar military service (17);
servicios públicos public services (14)
servido/a served
servilleta napkin
servir (i, i) to serve (4)
sesenta sixty (2)
sesión *f.* session
setecientos/as seven hundred (3)
setenta seventy (2)
severo/a severe
sevillano/a *n.* person from Seville; *adj.* of/from Seville
sexo sex
sexto/a sixth (13)
si if (2); **por si acaso** just in case (11); **si me hace el favor** if you would do me the favor
sí yes (AT); **sí, me gusta(n)...** yes, I like . . . (AT)
siamés, siamesa *adj.* Siamese
sicoanálisis *m. inv.* psychoanalysis
sicología psychology (1)
sicólogo/a psychologist (16)
SIDA AIDS; **Fundación** (*f.*) **Alerta contra la SIDA** AIDS Awareness Foundation
siempre always (2)
sierra mountain
siesta nap; **dormir (ue, u) la siesta** to take a nap (4)
siete seven (AT)
siglo century
significado meaning
significar (qu) to mean
signo sign
siguiente *adj.* following (4)
sílaba syllable
silencio silence
silenciosamente silently
silla chair (1)
sillón *m.* armchair (4)
simbólico/a symbolic
simbolizar (c) to symbolize
símbolo symbol
simpatía affection; pleasantness
simpático/a nice (2); likeable (2)
simulador *m.* simulator
sin without (4); **sin duda** without a doubt; **sin embargo** nevertheless; **sin fines de lucro** not-for-profit; **sin fines lucrativos** nonprofit
sinceridad *f.* sincerity
sincero/a sincere
sindical *adj.* union
sindicato *n.* union
sino but (rather); **sino que** *conj.* but (rather)
sinónimo synonym
sintético/a synthetic
síntoma *m.* symptom (10)
siquiatra *m., f.* psychiatrist (16)
siquiera: ni siquiera not even
sistema *m.* system; **analista** (*m., f.*) **de sistemas** systems analyst (16)

sitio place, location; room (*space*)
situación *f.* situation
situado/a situated
sobre *n. m.* envelope (18); *prep.* on; on top of; over; about; **sobre todo** especially; above all
sobredosis *f. inv.* overdose
sobrepasar to surpass
sobrepoblación *f.* overpopulation
sobrino/a nephew/niece (2)
social: seguro social social security; **trabajador(a) social** social worker (16)
socialista *adj. m., f.* socialist
socializar (c) to socialize
sociedad *f.* society
socioeconómico/a socioeconomic
sociología sociology (1)
socorro help, aid
sofá *m.* sofa (4)
sofisticado/a sophisticated
sofrito/a sautéed
sol *m.* sun; **hace sol** it's sunny (5); **tomar el sol** to sunbathe (7)
solar solar (14)
soldado soldier (16); **mujer** (*f.*) **soldado** female soldier (16)
soleado/a sunny
soledad *f.* solitude
soler (ue) to be in the habit of, accustomed to
solicitante *m., f.* applicant
solicitar to request
solicitud *f.* application (*form.*) (16); **llenar la solicitud** to fill out the application (16)
solista *m., f.* soloist
solitario/a solitary
sólo *adv.* only (1)
solo/a *adj.* alone (7); single
soltero/a single, unmarried (2)
solución *f.* solution
solucionar to solve
sombra shadow
sombrero hat (3)
son las... it's . . . o'clock (AT)
sonar to ring (9); to sound (9)
sonreír(se) (*like* reír) to smile (8)
soñar (ue) (con) to dream (about)
sopa soup (6)
sorprendente surprising
sorprender to surprise; **me (te, le...) sorprende** it surprises me (you, him, . . .) (13)
sorpresa surprise (8); **fiesta de sorpresa** surprise party
soviético/a *adj.* Soviet
soy I am (AT)
su(s) *poss. adj.* his, her, its, your (*form. s.*) (2); their, your (*form. pl.*) (2)
suavizar (c) to soften
subir (a) to climb; to go up (7); to get in/on (*a vehicle*) (7); to take, carry up
subjuntivo *gram.* subjunctive

submarino submarine
subordinado/a *gram.* subordinate
subrayar to underline
subsistir to survive
substituir (y) to substitute
subtítulo subtitle
sucio/a dirty (5)
sucre *m.* *former monetary unit of Ecuador*
sucursal *f.* branch (office) (16)
Sudáfrica South Africa
Sudamérica South America
sudamericano/a *n., adj.* South American
Suecia Sweden
suegro/a father-in-law / mother-in-law
sueldo salary (12); **aumento de sueldo** raise (*in salary*) (16)
suelo floor
suelto/a loose; free
sueño dream; **tener** (*irreg.*) **sueño** to be sleepy (3)
suerte *f.* luck; **¡qué mala suerte!** what bad luck! (11); **tener** (*irreg.*) **suerte** to be lucky
suéter *m.* sweater (3)
suficiente enough, sufficient; **dormir (ue, u) lo suficiente** to sleep enough (10)
sufijo *gram.* suffix
sufrir to suffer (11); **sufrir (muchas) presiones** to be under (a lot of) pressure (11)
sugerencia suggestion
sugerir (ie, i) to suggest (8)
Suiza Switzerland
sumamente extremely
superado/a exceeded
supercarretera superhighway
superlativo *n. gram.* superlative
supermercado supermarket
supervisar to supervise
supervisor(a) supervisor
supuesto: por supuesto of course (11)
sur *m.* south (5)
surgir (j) to arise
surrealista *adj. m., f.* surrealistic
suspender to suspend
sustancialmente substantially
sustantivo *gram.* noun (1)
sustituir (y) to substitute
sustituto substitute
suyo/a(s) *poss. adj.* your (*form.*) (17); his, her, its, their (17); *poss. pron.* (of) your, yours (*form.*) (17); (of) his, her, its, their; (of) theirs (17)

T

tabacalero/a *adj.* *pertaining to tobacco*
taberna tavern, open-air pub
tabla table, chart
tal such, such a; **con tal (de) que** *conj.* provided (that) (15); **¿qué tal?** how are you (doing)?; (AT); **tal como** just as; **tal vez** perhaps

talento talent

talentoso/a talented

taller *m.* (repair) shop (14)

talonario de cheques *Sp.* checkbook

tamaño size

también also (AT)

tambor *m.* drum

tampoco neither, not either (6)

tan *adv.* so; as; **tan... como...** as . . . as . . . (5); **tan pronto como** as soon as (16)

tanque *m.* tank (14)

tanto *adv.* so much; **tanto como** as much as (5)

tanto/a *adj.* as much; so much; such a; *pl.* so many; as many; **tanto/a(s)... como...** as much/many . . . as . . . (5)

tapa *Sp.* appetizer

tarde *n. f.* afternoon; **buenas tardes** good afternoon (AT); **de la tarde** in the afternoon (AT); **por la tarde** in the afternoon; *adv.* late (1)

tarea homework (4); chore

tarjeta card (7); **tarjeta de crédito** credit card (6); **tarjeta de identidad** identification card (11); **tarjeta de identificación** identification card (11); **tarjeta navideña** Christmas card; **tarjeta postal** postcard (7)

tasa rate

tasca bar

Tauro Taurus

taxi *m.* taxi

taza cup

te *d.o. pron. s.* you (*fam.*); *i.o. pron. s.* to/for you (*fam.*); *refl. pron. s.* yourself (*fam.*); **¿te gusta... ?** do you (*fam.*) like . . .?

té *m.* tea (6)

teatral theatrical

teatro theater; **ir** (*irreg.*) **al teatro** to go to the theater (9)

techo roof

teclado keyboard

técnica technique

técnico/a *n.* technician (16); *adj.* technical

tecnología technology

tejer to weave (13)

tejidos woven goods (13)

tele *f.* T.V.

telediario newscast

telefonear to call on the telephone

telefónico/a *adj.* telephone

teléfono (celular) (cellular) telephone (12); **agenda de teléfonos** address/ telephone book; **hablar por teléfono** to talk on the phone (1)

telegrama *m.* telegram

telenovela soap opera

televidente *m., f.* (television) viewer

televisión *f.* television; **mirar la televisión** to watch television (2)

televisor *m.* television set (4)

tema *m.* subject, topic

temático/a: parque (*m.*) **temático** theme park

temblar to tremble

temer to fear (13)

temperatura temperature; **tomarle la temperatura** to take someone's temperature (10)

templado/a temperate

templo temple

temporada season

temporal seasonal; temporary

temprano *adv.* early (1)

temprano/a *adj.* early (1)

tender (ie) a to tend to, be inclined to; **tender la cama** to make the bed (9)

tener *irreg.* to have (3); **no tener buen aspecto** to not look right; **tener alergia a** to be allergic to; **tener... años** to be . . . years old (2); **tener (mucho) calor/frío** to be (very) warm, hot/cold (5); **tener cuidado** to be careful; **tener dolor de cabeza/estómago/muela** to have a headache/stomachache/ toothache (10); **tener exceso de peso** to be overweight; **tener éxito** to be successful; **tener fiebre** to have a fever (10); **tener ganas de** + *inf.* to feel like (*doing something*) (3); **tener (mucha) hambre/sed** to be (very) hungry/ thirsty (6); **tener la culpa** to be guilty; **tener lugar** to take place; **tener miedo (de)** to be afraid (of) (3); **tener prisa** to be in a hurry (3); **tener que** + *inf.* to have to (*do something*) (3); **(no) tener razón** to be right (wrong) (3); **tener sueño** to be sleepy (3); **tener suerte** to be lucky; **tener una entrevista** to have an interview (16)

tenis *m.* tennis (9); **zapato de tenis** tennis shoe (3)

tensión *f.* tension

tenso/a tense

teoría theory

teorizar (c) theorize

tepui *m.* flat mountain top

tequila tequilla

terapia therapy

tercer, tercero/a *adj.* third (13)

tercio *n.* third

terco/a stubborn

térmico/a thermal

terminación *f.* ending

terminar to end

término term

termómetro: regulador (*m.*) **termómetro** thermostat

termostato thermostat

terraza terrace

terremoto earthquake

terreno field (*sports*)

terrestre terrestrial

terrible: es terrible que... its terrible that . . . (13)

territorio territory

terrorismo terrorism (17)

terrorista *n., adj. m., f.* terrorist (17); **ataque** (*m.*) **terrorista** terrorist attack (17)

tertulia *regular meeting of people for informal discussion of topics of interest*

testigo *m., f.* witness (17)

testimonio testimony

texto text; **libro de texto** textbook (1)

ti *obj.* (*of prep.*) you (*fam. s.*) (5)

tibio/a: huevo tibio poached egg

tiburón *m.* shark

tiempo time; *gram.* tense; weather (5); **a tiempo** on time (7); **de tiempo completo/parcial** full-time / part-time (11); **hace buen/mal tiempo** it's good/bad weather (5); **llegar (gu) a tiempo** to arrive on time (11); **pasar tiempo (con)** to spend time (with) (15); **¿qué tiempo hace hoy?** what's the weather like today? (5)

tienda shop, store (3); **tienda (de campaña)** tent (7)

tierra land; Earth (*planet*); soil

tigre *m.* tiger

tímido/a shy

tinta ink

tinto/a: vino tinto red wine (6)

tío/a uncle/aunt (2)

tiovivo merry-go-round

típico/a typical

tipo type

tipo/a *coll.* character, person

tira cómica comic strip

tirar to throw

titular to (en)title

título title

toalla towel (18)

tocar (qu) to touch; to play (*a musical instrument*) (1); **tocarle a uno** to be someone's turn (9)

todavía yet; still (5)

todo *adv.* entirely, completely

todo/a *n.* whole; all, everything; *adj.* all (2); every, each (2); *pl.* everybody, all; **ante todo** above all; first of all; **a toda velocidad** at full speed; **de todas formas** anyway; **de todas maneras** by all means; whatever happens; **de todos modos** anyway; **Día** (*m.*) **de Todos los Santos** All Saints' Day; **por todas partes** everywhere (11); **sobre todo** especially; above all; **todo derecho** straight ahead (14); **todos los días** every day (1); **venden de todo** they sell everything (3)

tolerante tolerant

tolteca *n., adj. m., f.* Toltec

tomar to take (1); to drink (1); **tomar el sol** to sunbathe (7); **tomar en cuenta** to take into account; **tomar una copa** to have a drink; **tomarle el pelo** to pull someone's leg; **tomarle la temperatura** to take someone's temperature (10)

tomate *m.* tomato (6); **salsa de tomate** catsup; tomato sauce

tónico/a *gram.* stressed

tonto/a silly, foolish (2)

torcido/a twisted

toreo bullfighting

torero/a bullfighter, matador

torno: en torno a around

toro bull (14); **corrida de toros** bullfight; **plaza de toros** bullring

torpe clumsy (11); **¡qué torpe!** how clumsy! (11)

torre *f.* tower

tortilla potato omelet (*Sp.*); *thin unleavened cornmeal or flour pancake* (*Mex.*)

tos *f. s.* cough (10)

toser to cough (10)

tostado/a toasted; **pan** (*m.*) **tostado** toast (6)

tostadora toaster (9)

tóxico/a toxic

trabajador(a) *n.* worker (2); **Día** (*m.*) **Internacional de los Trabajadores** International Labor Day; **trabajador(a) agrícola** farm worker; **trabajador(a) social** social worker (16); *adj.* hardworking (2)

trabajar to work (1)

trabajo work (11); job (11); report (11); **trabajo de tiempo completo/parcial** full-time / part-time job (11)

trabalenguas *m. inv.* tongue twister

tradición *f.* tradition

tradicional traditional

traducir *irreg.* to translate

traductor(a) translator (16)

traer *irreg.* to bring (4)

traficar (qu) en drogas to traffic in / deal drugs

tráfico traffic; **lío/embotellamiento de tráfico** traffic jam

tragedia tragedy

trágico/a tragic

tragicómico/a tragicomic

trago (*alcoholic*) drink (18)

traje *m.* suit (3); **traje de baño** bathing suit (3)

tranquilidad *f.* quiet, calm

tranquilizante calming, quieting

tranquilizar (c) to calm

tranquilo/a calm, quiet; **llevar una vida tranquila** to lead a calm life (10)

transbordador (*m.*) **espacial** space shuttle

transferir (ie, i) to transfer

tránsito traffic (14)

transmisión *f.* transmission

transmitir to transmit

transportación *f.* transportation

transporte *m.* (means of) transportation (7); **transporte público** public transportation (14)

tras *prep.* after

trasladarse to move

tratamiento treatment

tratar to treat; to deal with (*a subject*); **se trata de** it's a question of; **tratar de** + *inf.* to try to (*do something*) (13)

trauma *m.* trauma

través: a través de across; through; throughout

travieso/a mischievous

trazado/a laid out

trece thirteen (AT)

treinta thirty (AT); **y treinta** half-past / 30 minutes past (*the hour*) (AT)

tremendo/a tremendous

tren *m.* train; **choque** (*m.*) **de trenes** train wreck (17); **estación** (*f.*) **del tren** train station (7); **ir** (*irreg.*) **en tren** to go by train (7)

tres three (AT); **hotel** (*m.*) **de tres estrellas** three-star hotel (18)

trescientos/as three hundred (3)

trimestre *m.* trimester

triste sad (5)

tristeza sadness

triunfar to triumph

trofeo trophy

trópicos tropics

tropiezo mishap

trozo piece

trucha trout

tú *sub. pron.* you (*fam. s.*) (1); **¿y tú?** and you? (AT)

tu(s) *poss. adj.* your (*fam.*) (2)

tubería plumbing

turbio turbulent

turbulento/a turbulent

turismo tourism

turista *n. m., f.* tourist

turístico/a *adj.* tourist; **clase** (*f.*) **turística** tourist class (7)

turno turn

Turquía Turkey

tuyo/a(s) *poss. adj.* your (*fam. s.*) (17); *poss. pron.* of yours (*fam. s.*) (17)

u or (*used instead of* **o** *before words beginning with* **o** *or* **ho**)

ubicar (qu) to locate

último/a last (7); latest; **de los últimos años** in recent years; **¡es de última moda!** it's the latest style! (3); **por última vez** for the last time (11); **por último** finally

un, uno/a one (AT); *ind. art.* a, an; **una vez** once (10); **una vez a la semana** once a week (2)

único/a *adj.* only; unique

unidad *f.* unit

unido/a united; **Estados Unidos** *m. pl.* United States; **Naciones Unidas** *f. pl.* United Nations

unificación *f.* unification

unificarse (qu) to unify

unión *f.* union

unir to join (together); to unite

universidad *f.* university (1)

universitario/a *adj.* (of the) university (11)

unívoco/a univocal, of one voice; unambiguous

unos/as *ind. art.* some, a few

urbano/a urban

urgencia: caso de urgencia emergency; **sala de urgencia** emergency room (10)

urgente urgent (13)

uruguayo/a *n., adj.* Uruguayan

usar to use (3); to wear (3)

uso use

usted (Ud., Vd.) *sub. pron.* you (*form. s.*) (1); *obj.* (*of prep.*) you (*form. s.*); **¿cómo es usted?** what are you like? (AT); **¿cómo se llama usted?** what is your name? (AT); **¿de dónde es usted?** where are you from? (AT); **¿y usted?** and you? (AT)

ustedes (Uds., Vds.) *sub. pron.* you (*form. pl.*) (1); *obj.* (*of prep.*) you

usualmente usually

útil useful

utilización *f.* use, utilization

utilizar (c) to use, utilize

uva grape; **uva de mesa** table grape

¡uy! *interj.* oops!

vaca cow (14)

vacaciones *f. pl.* vacation; **de vacaciones** on vacation (7); **estar** (*irreg.*) **de vacaciones** to be on vacation (7); **ir** (*irreg.*) **de vacaciones** to go on vacation (7); **vacaciones de primavera** spring break

vacilante hesitant

vacío *n.* emptiness; void

vacío/a *adj.* empty

vacuna vaccine

vahído blackout (fainting)

vainilla vanilla

valenciano/a of/from Valencia, Spain

valer (*irreg.*) **la pena** to be worthwhile, worth the trouble

válido/a valid

valiente brave

valle *m.* valley

valor *m.* value; courage, bravery

variación *f.* variation

variar (varío) to vary

variedad *f.* variety

varios/as several
vasco Basque (*language*)
vasco/a *n., adj.* Basque
vaso glass
vecindad *f.* neighborhood (12)
vecino/a *n.* neighbor (12); *adj.* neighboring
vegetal (*adj.*) vegetable
vegetariano/a vegetarian
vehículo vehicle (12)
veinte twenty (AT)
veinticinco twenty-five
veinticuatro twenty-four
veintidós twenty-two
veintinueve twenty-nine
veintiocho twenty-eight
veintiséis twenty-six
veintisiete twenty-seven
veintitrés twenty-three
veintiún, veintiuno/a twenty-one
vejez *f.* old age (15)
vela candle
velludo/a hairy
velocidad *f.* speed; **a toda velocidad** at full speed; **límite** (*m.*) **de velocidad** speed limit (14)
vendedor(a) salesperson (16)
vender to sell (2); **venden de todo** they sell everything (3)
venezolano/a *n., adj.* Venezuelan
venga come on
venganza revenge
venir *irreg.* to come; **la semana que viene** next week (4); **venga** come on
venta sale
ventaja advantage (10)
ventana window (1); **lavar las ventanas** to wash the windows (9)
ventilación *f.* ventilation
ver *irreg.* (*p.p.* **visto**) to see (4); **a ver** let's see; **ir** (*irreg.*) **a ver una película** to go to see a movie (9); **nos vemos** see you around (AT)
veranear to spend summer vacation
verano summer (5)
verbo *gram.* verb
verdad *f.* truth; **¿verdad?** right?, don't they (you, *and so on*)? (3)
verdadero/a true; real
verde green (3); **vinho** (*Port.*) **verde** young wine
verdura vegetable (6)
verificar (qu) to verify
versión *f.* version
verso verse; line of a poem
verter (ie) to spill; to shed (*a tear*)
vestíbulo vestibule
vestido dress (3); **vestido de novia** wedding gown
vestir (i, i) to dress; **vestirse** to get dressed (4)
veterinario/a veterinarian (16)

vez *f.* (*pl.* **veces**) time; **a veces** sometimes, at times (2); **a la vez** at the same time; **alguna vez** once; ever; **cada vez más** increasingly; **de vez en cuando** once in a while; **dos veces** twice (10); **en vez de** instead of (16); **érase una vez** once upon a time; **otra vez** again; **por primera/última vez** for the first/last time (11); **tal vez** perhaps; **una vez** once; **una vez a la semana** once a week (2)
viajar to travel (7); **viajar al/en el extranjero** to travel abroad (18)
viaje *m.* trip (7); **agencia de viajes** travel agency (7); **agente** (*m., f.*) **de viajes** travel agent (7); **de viaje** on a trip (7); **hacer** (*irreg.*) **un viaje** to take a trip (4)
viajero/a traveler (18); **cheque** (*m.*) **de viajero** traveler's check (18)
vicepresidente/a vice president
víctima *m., f.* victim (17)
vida life (11); **esperanza de vida** life expectancy; **ganarse la vida** to earn a living; **llevar una vida sana/tranquila** to lead a healthy/calm life (10)
vídeo video; **cámara de vídeo** video camera (12)
videocasetera videocassette recorder (VCR) (12)
videoclub *m.* video club
videoteca video library
vidrio glass
vieira *s.* scallops (*seafood*)
viejo/a *n.* old person; *adj.* old (2); **Noche** (*f.*) **Vieja** New Year's Eve (8)
viento wind; **hace (mucho) viento** it's (very) windy (5)
viernes *m. inv.* Friday (4)
vietnamita *n., adj. f.* Vietnamese
villancico Christmas carol
vinho (*Port.*) **verde** young wine
vinícola *adj. m., f.* pertaining to wine
vino (blanco, tinto) (white, red) wine (6)
viñedo vineyard
violencia violence (14)
violento/a violent
violeta violet
violín *m.* violin
virgen *n. f.* virgin
visado visa
visigodo/a *n.* Visigoth
visión *f.* vision
visita visit; **hacer** (*irreg.*) **visitas** to visit
visitante *m., f.* visitor
visitar to visit; **visitar un museo** to visit a museum (9)
víspera eve
vista view (12); sight; **a primera vista** at first sight (15); **punto de vista** point of view
visto/a (*p.p.* **ver**) seen

vitamina vitamin
viudo/a widower/widow (15)
vivienda housing (12)
vivir to live (2); **vivir en paz** to live in peace (17)
vocabulario vocabulary
vocación *f.* vocation
vocal *n. f.* vowel
volante: objeto volante no identificado (OVNI) unidentified flying object (UFO)
volcán *m.* volcano (17)
volcánico/a volcanic
vólibol *m.* volleyball (9)
volumen *m.* volume
voluntad *f.* will; choice, decision
voluntario/a *n.* volunteer
volver (ue) (*p.p.* **vuelto**) to return (*to a place*) (4); **volver a** + *inf.* to (*do something*) again (4)
vos *sub. pron.* you (*fam. s. Arg., Uru., C.A.*); *obj.* (*of prep.*) you (*fam. s. Arg. Uru., C.A.*)
vosotros/as *sub. pron.* you (*fam. pl. Sp.*) (1); *obj.* (*of prep.*) you (*fam. pl. Sp.*)
votante *m., f.* voter
votar to vote (17)
vuelo flight (7); **asistente** (*m., f.*) **de vuelo** flight attendant (7); **vuelo sin escalas** nonstop flight
vuelta: billete (*m.*)**/boleto de ida y vuelta** round-trip ticket (7); **darse** (*irreg.*) **la vuelta** to turn oneself around; **de vuelta** returned
vuestro/a(s) *poss. adj.* your (*fam. pl. Sp.*) (2); *poss. pron.* yours, of yours (*fam. pl. Sp.*) (17)
vulpeja vixen

W

walkman *m.* Walkman (12)

Y

y and (AT); **y cuarto (quince)** a quarter (fifteen minutes) after (*hour*) (AT); **y media (treinta)** half-past / 30 minutes past (*the hour*) (AT); **¿y usted?** and you? (*form. s.*) (AT); **¿y tú?** and you? (*fam. s.*) (AT)
ya already (8); **ya no** no longer; **ya que** since
yacimiento deposit (*mineral*)
yerno son-in-law
yo *sub. pron.* I (1)
yogur *m.* yogurt (6)

Z

zanahoria carrot (6)
zapatería shoe store
zapato shoe (3); **par** (*m.*) **de zapatos** pair of shoes (3); **zapato de tenis** tennis shoe (3)
zona zone

English-Spanish Vocabulary

A

able: to be able **poder** (*irreg.*) (3)
abroad **extranjero** *n.* (18)
absence **falta** (14)
absent: to be absent **faltar** (8)
absentminded **distraído/a** (11)
accelerated **acelerado/a** (14)
according to **según** (2)
account **cuenta** (16); checking account **cuenta corriente** (16); savings account **cuenta de ahorros** (16)
accountant **contador(a)** (16)
ache **doler (ue)** *v.* (10)
ache **dolor** *n. m.* (10)
acquainted: to be acquainted with **conocer (zc)** (6)
actor **actor** *m.* (13)
actress **actriz** *f.* (*pl.* **actrices**) (13)
address **dirección** *f.* (9)
adjective **adjetivo** *gram.* (2)
administration: business administration **administración** (*f.*) **de empresas** (1)
adolescence **adolescencia** (15)
advantage **ventaja** (10)
advice (piece of) **consejo** (6)
advisor **consejero/a** (1)
aerobic: to do aerobics **hacer** (*irreg.*) **ejercicios aeróbicos** (10)
affectionate **cariñoso/a** (5)
afraid: to be afraid (of) **tener** (*irreg.*) **miedo (de)** (3)
after *prep.* **después de** (4); *conj.* **después (de) que** (16)
afternoon **tarde** *n. f.* (1); good afternoon **buenas tardes** (AT); (*a time*) in the afternoon **de la tarde** (AT); in the afternoon **por la tarde** (1)
age: old age **vejez** *f.* (15)
agency: travel agency **agencia de viajes** (7)
agent: travel agent **agente** (*m., f.*) **de viajes** (7)
agree: I agree **estoy de acuerdo** (2)
ahead of time **con anticipación** (18); straight ahead **todo derecho** (14)
air **aire** *m.* (14)
airplane **avión** *m.* (7)
airport **aeropuerto** (7)
alarm clock **despertador** *m.* (11)
all **todo(s)/a(s)** *adj.* (2)
allow **permitir** (12)
almost: almost never **casi nunca** (2)
alone **solo/a** *adj.* (7)
alongside of **al lado de** (*prep.*) (5)
already **ya** (8)
also **también** (AT)

always **siempre** (2)
American (*from the United States*) **estadounidense** (2)
among **entre** *prep.* (5)
amusement **diversión** *f.* (9)
analyst: systems analyst **analista** (*m., f.*) **de sistemas** (16)
and **y** (AT)
angry **furioso/a** (5); to get angry (at) **enojarse (con)** (8)
animal **animal** *m.* (14); domesticated animal **animal doméstico** (14); wild animal **animal salvaje** (14)
announce **anunciar** (7)
another **otro/a** (2)
answer *v.* **contestar** (4); *n.* **respuesta** (5)
answering machine **contestador** (*m.*) **automático** (12)
antibiotic **antibiótico** (10)
any **algún, alguno/a** (6)
anyone **alguien** (6)
anything **algo** (3)
apartment **apartamento** (1); apartment building **bloque** (*m.*) **de apartamentos** (12); **casa de apartamentos** (12)
apologize **pedir (i, i) disculpas** (11)
apple **manzana** (6)
appliance: home appliance **aparato doméstico** (9)
applicant **aspirante** *m., f.* (16)
application (*form*) **solicitud** *f.* (16)
appreciate **apreciar** (13)
April **abril** *m.* (5)
architect **arquitecto/a** (13)
architecture **arquitectura** (13)
area **área** *f.* (*but* **el área**) (12)
argue (about) (with) **discutir (sobre) (con)** (8)
arm **brazo** (11)
armchair **sillón** *m.* (4)
army **ejército** (17)
arrival **llegada** (7)
arrive **llegar (gu)** (2); to arrive on time/late **llegar a tiempo/tarde** (11)
art **arte** *f.* (*but* **el arte**) (1); work of art **obra de arte** (13)
artist **artista** *m., f.* (13)
arts and crafts **artesanía** (13)
arts, letters **letras** *pl.* (2)
as . . . as **tan... como** (5); as much/many as **tanto/a... como** (5); as soon as **tan pronto como** *conj.* (16); **en cuanto** *conj.* (16)
ask: to ask for **pedir (i, i)** (4); to ask (a question) **hacer** (*irreg.*) **una pregunta** (4); **preguntar** (6)

asparagus **espárragos** *pl.* (6)
assassination **asesinato** (17)
at **en** (AT); **a** (*with time*) (AT); at . . . (hour) **a la(s)...** (AT); at home **en casa** (1); at last **por fin** (4); at least **por lo menos** (8); at night **de la noche** (AT); **por la noche** (1); at once **ahora mismo**; at the beginning of **al principio de** (16); at times **a veces** (2)
attack: terrorist attack **ataque** (*m.*) **terrorista** (17)
attend (*a function*) **asistir (a)** (2)
attendant: flight attendant **asistente** (*m., f.*) **de vuelo** (7)
August **agosto** (5)
aunt **tía** (2)
automatic teller machine **cajero automático** (16)
autumn **otoño** (5)
avenue **avenida** (12)
avoid **evitar** (14)
away: right away **en seguida** (10)
awful: an awful lot **muchísimo** (7)

B

baby-sitter **niñero/a** (9)
backpack **mochila** (1)
bad **mal, malo/a** *adj.* (2); it's bad weather **hace mal tiempo** (5); the bad thing, news **lo malo** (10)
baggage **equipaje** *m.* (7)
balance a checkbook **sacar (qu) el saldo** (16)
ballet **ballet** *m.* (13)
banana **banana** (6)
bank **banco** (16); (bank) check **cheque** *m.* (16)
bar **bar** *m.* (9)
bargain **ganga** (3)
baseball **béisbol** *m.* (9)
basketball **basquetbol** *m.* (9)
bath: to take a bath **bañarse** (4)
bathing suit **traje** (*m.*) **de baño** (3)
bathroom **baño** (4)
bathtub **bañera** (4)
battery **batería** (14)
be **estar** (*irreg.*) (1); **ser** (*irreg.*) (2); to be (feel) warm, hot **tener** (*irreg.*) **calor** (5); to be (very) hungry **tener** (*irreg.*) **(mucha) hambre** (6); to be . . . years old **tener** (*irreg.*)**... años** (2); to be a fan (of) **ser** (*irreg.*) **aficionado/a (a)** (9); to be able **poder** (*irreg.*) (3); to be afraid (of) **tener** (*irreg.*) **miedo (de)** (3); to be boring **ser** (*irreg.*) **aburrido/a** (9); to be cold **tener** (*irreg.*) **frío** (5); to be

be (*continued*)
comfortable (*temperature*) estar (*irreg.*) **bien** (5); to be flexible **ser** (*irreg.*) **flexible** (11); to be fun **ser** (*irreg.*) **divertido/a** (9); to be in a hurry **tener** (*irreg.*) **prisa** (3); to be late **estar** (*irreg.*) **atrasado/a** (7); to be on a diet **estar** (*irreg.*) **a dieta** (6); to be wrong **no tener** (*irreg.*) **razón** (3); to be wrong (about) **equivocarse (qu) (de)** (11); to take place in/at (*place*) **ser** (*irreg.*) **en** + *place* (8)
beach **playa** (5)
bean **frijol** *m.* (6)
beautiful **bello/a** (14)
because **porque** (2)
become + *adj.* **ponerse** (*irreg.*) + *adj.* (8)
bed: to make the bed **hacer** (*irreg.*) **la cama** (9); to stay in bed **guardar cama** (10)
bedroom **alcoba** (4)
beer **cerveza** (1)
before *conj.* **antes (de) que** (15); *prep.* **antes de** (4)
begin **empezar (ie) (c)** (4); to begin to (*do something*) **empezar a** + *inf.* (4)
beginning: at the beginning of **al principio de** (16)
behave **portarse** (8)
behind **detrás de** *prep.* (5)
believe (in) **creer (y) (en)** (2)
bellhop **mozo, botones** *m. inv.* (18)
below **debajo de** *prep.* (5)
belt **cinturón** *m.* (3)
bull **toro** (14)
best **mejor** (5)
better **mejor** (5)
between **entre** *prep.* (5)
beverage **bebida** (6)
bicycle **bicicleta**; (mountain) bicycle **bicicleta (de montaña)** (12); to ride a bicycle **pasear en bicicleta** (9)
bicycling **ciclismo** (9)
big **gran, grande** (2)
bill (*for service*) **cuenta** (6); **factura** (16)
bird **pájaro** (2)
birth **nacimiento** (15)
birthday **cumpleaños** *m. inv.* (5); birthday cake **pastel** (*m.*) **de cumpleaños** (8); to have a birthday **cumplir años** (8)
black **negro/a** (3)
blanket **manta** (18)
blond(e) **rubio/a** *n., adj.* (2)
blood **sangre** *f.* (10)
blouse **blusa** (3)
blue **azul** (3)
boardinghouse **pensión** *f.* (18); room and full board **pensión completa** (18); room with breakfast and one other meal **media pensión** (18)
boat **barco** (7)
body **cuerpo** (10)

bookshelf **estante** *m.* (4)
bookstore **librería** (1)
boot **bota** (3)
border **frontera** (18)
bore **aburrir** (13)
bored **aburrido/a** (5); to get bored **aburrirse** (9)
boring: to be boring **ser** (*irreg.*) **aburrido/a** (9)
born: to be born **nacer (zc)** (15)
borrow **pedir (i, i) prestado/a** (16)
boss **jefe/a** (12)
bother **molestar** (13); it bothers me (you, him, . . .) that **me (te, le...) molesta** (13) **que**
boy **muchacho** (4); **niño** (2)
boyfriend **novio** (5)
brain **cerebro** (10)
brakes **frenos** (14)
branch (office) **sucursal** *f.* (16)
bread **pan** *m.* (6)
break **romper** (*p.p.* **roto/a**) (11); to break up (with) **romper (con)** (15)
breakfast **desayuno** (4); to have breakfast **desayunar** (6)
breathe **respirar** (10)
bride **novia** (15)
bring **traer** (*irreg.*) (4)
brother **hermano** (2)
brown **(de) color café** (3)
brunet(te) **moreno/a** *n., adj.* (2)
brush one's teeth **cepillarse los dientes** (4)
budget **presupuesto** (16)
build **construir (y)** (14)
building **edificio** *n.* (1); building manager **portero/a** (12)
bull **toro** (14)
bump into **pegarse (gu) en/con/contra** (11)
bureau (*furniture*) **cómoda** (4)
bus **autobús** *m.* (7); bus station **estación** (*f.*) **de autobuses** (7); bus stop **parada del autobús** (18)
business **empresa** (16); business administration **administración** (*f.*) **de empresas** (1)
businessperson **hombre** (*m.*)/**mujer** (*f.*) **de negocios** (16)
busy **ocupado/a** (5)
but **pero** *conj.* (AT)
butter **mantequilla** (6)
buy **comprar** (1)
by **por** *prep.* (4); in the morning (afternoon, evening) **por la mañana (tarde, noche)** (1); by check **con cheque** (16)

C
cabin **cabina** (*on a ship*) (7)
café **café** *m.* (1)
cafeteria **cafetería** (1)
cake **pastel** *m.* (6); birthday cake **pastel de cumpleaños** (8)

calculator **calculadora** (1)
calendar **calendario** (11)
call *v.* **llamar** (6); to be called **llamarse** (4)
campground **camping** *m.* (7)
camping: to go camping **hacer** (*irreg.*) *camping* (7)
can **poder** *v. irreg.* (3)
candidate **aspirante** *m., f.* (16)
candy **dulces** *m. pl.* (6)
cap **gorra** (3)
capital city **capital** *f.* (5)
car **coche** *m.* (2); convertible car **carro/coche descapotable** (12)
card: identification card **tarjeta de identificación** (11); to play cards **jugar (ue) (gu) a las cartas** (9)
cardinal directions **puntos** (*pl.*) **cardinales** (5)
carrot **zanahoria** (6)
carry **llevar** (3)
case **caso**; in case **en caso de que** (15); just in case **por si acaso** (11)
cash (*a check*) **cobrar** (16); in cash **en efectivo** (16); to pay in cash **pagar (gu) al contado / en efectivo** (16)
cashier **cajero/a** (16)
cat **gato/a** (2)
catch a cold **resfriarse (me resfrío)** (10)
CD-ROM **CD-ROM** *m.* (12)
celebrate **celebrar** (5)
cellular telephone **teléfono celular** (12)
ceramics **cerámica** (13)
cereal **cereales** *m. pl.* (6)
certain **seguro/a** *adj.* (5); **cierto/a** (13)
chair **silla** (1); armchair **sillón** *m.* (4)
chalkboard **pizarra** (1)
change *v.* **cambiar (de)** (12)
channel **canal** *m.* (12)
charge (*to an account*) **cargar (gu)** (16); (*someone for an item or service*) **cobrar** (16)
check (*bank*) **cheque** *m.* (16); by check **con cheque** (16); traveler's check **cheque de viajero** (18); to check (*the oil*) **revisar (el aceite)** (14); to check into (*a hospital*) **internarse en** (10); to check baggage **facturar el equipaje** (7)
checking account **cuenta corriente** (16)
checkup **chequeo** (10)
cheese **queso** (6)
chef **cocinero/a** (16)
chemistry **química** (1)
chess **ajedrez** *m.* (4); to play chess **jugar (ue) (gu) al ajedrez** (9)
chicken (roast) **pollo (asado)** (6)
chief **jefe/a** (12)
child **niño/a** (2); as a child **de niño/a** (9)
childhood **niñez** *f.* (*pl.* **niñeces**) (9)
children **hijos** *m. pl.* (2)
chop: pork chop **chuleta de cerdo** (6)

chore:household chore **quehacer** (*m.*) **doméstico**

Christmas Eve **Nochebuena** (8)

Christmas **Navidad** *f.* (8)

citizen **ciudadano/a** (17)

city **ciudad** *f.* (2)

class **clase** *f.* (1); first class **primera clase** (7); tourist class **clase turística** (7)

classical **clásico/a** (13)

classmate **compañero/a de clase** (1)

clean *adj.* **limpio/a** (5)

clean: to clean the (whole) house **limpiar la casa (entera)** (9)

clear the table **quitar la mesa** (9)

clerk **dependiente/a** (1)

clever **listo/a** (2)

client **cliente** *m., f.* (1)

climate **clima** *m.* (5)

close **cerrar** (ie) (4)

close to *prep.* **cerca de** (5)

closed **cerrado/a** (5)

closet **armario** (4)

clothes dryer **secadora** (9)

clothing **ropa** (3); to wear (*clothing*) **llevar, usar** (3)

cloudy: it's (very) cloudy, overcast **está (muy) nublado** (5)

clumsy **torpe** (11)

coffee **café** *m.* (1)

coffee pot **cafetera** (9)

cold (*illness*) **resfriado** (10); it's cold (very) (*weather*) **hace (mucho) frío** (5); to be cold **tener** (*irreg.*) **frío** *n.* (5)

collect **recoger** (j) (11)

collide (with) **chocar** (qu) **(con)** (14)

collision **choque** *m.* (17)

color **color** *m.* (3)

comb one's hair **peinarse** (4)

come **venir** (*irreg.*) (3)

comfortable **cómodo/a** (4); to be comfortable (*temperature*) **estar** (*irreg.*) **bien** (5)

communicate (with) **comunicarse** (qu) **(con)** (17)

communication (*major*) **comunicación** *f.* (1); means of communication **medio de comunicación** (17)

compact disc **disco compacto** (12)

comparison **comparación** *f.* (5)

complain (about) **quejarse (de)** (8)

composer **compositor(a)** (13)

computer **computadora** (L.A.) (12); **ordenador** *m.* (*Sp.*) (12); computer disc **disco de computadora** (12); computer file **archivo** (12); computer science **computación** *f.* (1)

concert **concierto**; to go to a concert **ir** (*irreg.*) **a un concierto** (9)

confirm **confirmar** (18)

congested **congestionado/a** (10)

congratulations **felicitaciones** *f. pl.* (8)

conserve **conservar** (14)

contact lenses **lentes** (*m. pl.*) **de contacto** (10)

content *adj.* **contento/a** (5)

continue **seguir** (i, i) (g) (14)

control: remote control **control** (*m.*) **remoto** (12)

convertible (*car*) **carro/coche descapotable** (12)

cook *v.* **cocinar** (6); *n.* cook **cocinero/a** (16)

cookie **galleta** (6)

cool: it's (very) cool (*weather*) **hace (mucho) fresco** (5)

copy **copia** (12); to copy **hacer** (*irreg.*) **una copia / copias** (12)

corner (*street*) **esquina** (14)

corporation **empresa** (16)

cotton **algodón** *m.* (3); it is made of cotton **es de algodón** (3)

cough **tos** *f.* (10); to cough **toser** (10); cough syrup **jarabe** *m.* (10)

count **contar** (ue) (7)

country **país** *m.* (2)

countryside **campo** (12)

course (*of a meal*) **plato** (6)

courtesy: greetings and expressions of courtesy **saludos y expresiones** (*f.*) **de cortesía** (AT)

cousin **primo/a** (2)

cover **cubrir** (*pp.* **cubierto/a**) (14)

cow **vaca** (14)

crash (*computer*) **fallar** (12)

crazy **loco/a** (5)

create **crear** (13)

credit card **tarjeta de crédito** (6)

cross **cruzar** (c) (18)

cry **llorar** (8)

custard: baked custard **flan** *m.* (6)

custom **costumbre** *f.* (9)

customs **aduana** *s.* (18)

D

dad **papá** *m.* (2)

daily routine **rutina diaria** (4)

dance **baile** *m.* (13); **danza** (13); to dance **bailar** (1)

dancer **bailarín, bailarina** (13)

date (*calendar*) **fecha** (5); (*social*) **cita** (15)

daughter **hija** (2)

day **día** *m.* (1); day after tomorrow **pasado mañana** (4); the day before yesterday **anteayer** (10); every day **todos los días** (1)

deadline **fecha límite** (11)

dear **querido/a** *n., adj.* (5)

death **muerte** *f.* (15)

December **diciembre** *m.* (5)

delay *n.* **demora** (7)

delighted **encantado/a** (AT)

dense **denso/a** (14)

dentist **dentista** *m., f.* (10)

deny **negar** (ie) (gu) (13)

department store **almacén** *m.* (3)

departure **salida** (7)

deposit **depositar** (16)

desk **escritorio** (1)

dessert **postre** *m.* (6)

destroy **destruir** (y) (14)

detail **detalle** *m.* (6)

develop **desarrollar** (14)

dictator **dictador(a)** (17)

dictatorship **dictadura** (17)

dictionary **diccionario** (1)

die **morir** (ue, u) (*p.p.* **muerto/a**) (8); to die **morir(se)** (8)

diet: to be on a diet **estar** (*irreg.*) **a dieta** (6)

difficult **difícil** (5)

dining room **comedor** *m.* (4)

dinner **cena** (6); to have dinner **cenar** (6)

directions: cardinal directions **puntos** (*pl.*) **cardinales** (5)

director **director(a)** (13); personnel director **director(a) de personal** (16)

dirty **sucio/a** (5)

disadvantage **desventaja** (10)

disaster **desastre** *m.* (17)

disc: compact disc **disco compacto** (12); computer disc **disco de computadora** (12)

disco: to go to a disco **ir** (*irreg.*) **a una discoteca** (9)

discover **descubrir** (*pp.* **descubierto**) (14)

discrimination **discriminación** *f.* (17)

dish (*plate*) **plato** (4); (*course*) **plato** (6)

dishwasher **lavaplatos** *m. inv.* (9)

divorce **divorcio** (15)

divorced **divorciado/a** (15); to get divorced (from) **divorciarse (de)** (15)

dizzy **mareado/a** (10)

do **hacer** (*irreg.*) (4); (*do something*) again **volver a** + *inf.* (4); to do aerobics **hacer** (*irreg.*) **ejercicios aeróbicos** (10); to do exercise **hacer** (*irreg.*) **ejercicio** (4)

doctor (*medical*) **médico/a** (2)

dog **perro/a** (2)

domesticated animal **animal** (*m.*) **doméstico** (14)

door **puerta** (1)

doorman **portero/a** (12)

dormitory **residencia** (1)

double: double room (18) **habitación** (*f.*) **doble**

doubt **dudar** (12)

downtown **centro** (3)

drama **drama** *m.* (13)

draw **dibujar** (13)

dress **vestido** (3)

dressed: to get dressed **vestirse** (i, i) (4)

dresser (*furniture*) **cómoda** (4)

drink **bebida** (6); **copa, trago** (*alcoholic*) (18); *drink similar to a milkshake* **batido** (18); to drink **tomar** (1); **beber** (2)

drive (*a vehicle*) **conducir** (*irreg.*) (14); **manejar** (12)
driver **conductor(a)** (14)
during **durante** (4); **por** (4)
dust the furniture **sacudir los muebles** (9)
DVD **DVD** *m.* (12)
DVD player **lector** (*m.*) **de DVD** (12)

E

each **cada** *inv.* (4)
ear (inner) **oído** (10); (outer) **oreja** (10)
early **temprano** *adv.* (1)
earn **ganar** (16)
earring **arete** *m.* (3)
east **este** *m.* (5)
Easter **Pascua (Florida)** (8)
easy **fácil** (5)
eat **comer** (2); eat breakfast **desayunar** (6); eat dinner, supper **cenar** (6)
economies **economía** (1)
economize **economizar** (c) (16)
egg **huevo** (6)
eight **ocho** (AT)
eight hundred **ochocientos/as** (3)
eighteen **dieciocho** (AT)
eighth **octavo/a** *adj.* (13)
eighty **ochenta** (2)
electric **eléctrico/a** (14)
electrician **electricista** *m., f.* (16)
electricity **luz** *f.* (*pl.* **luces**) (11)
electronic mail **correo electrónico** (12)
elephant **elefante** *m.* (14)
eleven **once** (AT)
embarrassed **avergonzado/a** (8)
emergency room **sala de emergencias** (10)
emotion **emoción** *f.* (8)
energy **energía** (14)
engagement **noviazgo** (15)
engineer **ingeniero/a** (16)
English (*language*) **inglés** *m.* (1); *n., adj.* **inglés, inglesa** (2)
enjoy oneself, have a good time **divertirse (ie, i)** (4)
enough **bastante** *adv.* (15); **lo suficiente** (10)
entertainment **diversión** *f.* (9)
envelope **sobre** *m.* (18)
equality **igualdad** *f.* (17)
equipment: stereo equipment **equipo estereofónico** (12)
era **época** (9)
evening **tarde** *f.* (1); good evening **buenas tardes** (AT); in the afternoon, evening **de la tarde** (AT); in the evening **por la tarde** (1)
event **acontecimiento** (17); **hecho** (8)
every **cada** *inv.* (4); **todo(s)/a(s)** *adj.* (2); every day **todos los días** (1)
everything **de todo**
everywhere **por todas partes** (11)
exactly, on the dot (*time*) **en punto** (AT)

exam **examen** *m.* (3)
examine **examinar** (10); **registrar** (18)
excuse me **con permiso, perdón** (AT); **discúlpeme** (11)
exercise **ejercicio** (3)
expect **esperar** (6)
expend **gastar** (14)
expense **gasto** (12)
expensive **caro/a** (3)
explain **explicar** (qu) (7)
expressions: greetings and expressions of courtesy **saludos y expresiones** (*f.*) **de cortesía** (AT)
extract **sacar** (qu) (10); extract a tooth **sacar una muela** (10)
eye **ojo** (10)
eyeglasses **gafas** *pl.* (10)

F

fact **hecho** *n.* (8)
factory **fábrica** (14)
faithful **fiel** (2)
fall (*season*) **otoño** (5)
fall *v.* **caer** (*irreg.*) (11); to fall asleep **dormirse (ue, u)** (4); to fall down **caerse** (*irreg.*) (11); to fall in love (with) **enamorarse (de)** (15)
fan: to be a fan (of) **ser** (*irreg.*) **aficionado/a (a)** (9)
far from **lejos de** *prep.* (5)
farm **finca** (14); farm worker **campesino/a** (14)
farmer **agricultor(a)** (14)
fashion **moda**; the latest fashion; style **de última moda** (3)
fast **rápido/a** *adj.* (6); **acelerado/a** (14)
fat **gordo/a** (2)
father **papá** *m.*, **padre** *m.* (2)
fax **fax** *m.* (12)
fear: to fear **temer** (13)
February **febrero** (5)
feel **encontrarse (ue)** (10); to feel (an emotion) **sentirse (ie, i)** (8); to feel like (*doing something*) **tener** (*irreg.*) **ganas de** + *inf.* (3); to feel sorry **sentir (ie, i)** (13)
female soldier **mujer** (*f.*) **soldado** (16)
fever **fiebre** *f.* (10); have a fever **tener** (*irreg.*) **fiebre** (10)
fifteen **quince** (AT); a quarter (fifteen minutes) to (*the hour*) **menos quince** (AT); a quarter (fifteen minutes) past (*the hour*) **y quince** (AT)
fifth **quinto/a** *adj.* (13)
fifty **cincuenta** (2)
fight **pelear** (9)
file: computer file **archivo** (12)
fill (up) **llenar** (14); to fill out (*an application*) **llenar la solicitud** (16)
finally **por fin** (4)
find **encontrar (ue)** (8); to find out (about) **enterarse (de)** (17)
fine **muy bien** (AT)

finger **dedo (de la mano)** (11)
finish **acabar** (11)
first **primer, primero/a** *adj.* (4); at first sight **a primera vista** (15); first of (month) **el primero de (mes)** (5); first class **primera clase** (7)
fish (*cooked*) **pescado** (6); (*animal*) **pez** *m.* (*pl.* **peces**) (14)
five **cinco** (AT)
five hundred **quinientos/as** (3)
fix **arreglar** (12)
fixed price **precio fijo** (3)
flat: flat tire **llanta desinflada** (14)
flexibility **flexibilidad** *f.* (11)
flexible **flexible** (11)
flight **vuelo** (7); flight attendant **asistente** (*m., f.*) **de vuelo** (7)
floor (*of a building*) **planta, piso** (12); ground floor **planta baja** (12); to sweep the floor **barrer el piso** (9)
flower **flor** *f.* (7)
folkloric **folklórico/a** (13)
following *adj.* **siguiente** (4)
food **comida** (6)
foolish **tonto/a** (2)
foot **pie** *m.* (11)
football **fútbol** (*m.*) **americano** (9)
for (intended) **por** *prep.* (4); **para** *prep.* (2); for example **por ejemplo** (11); for heaven's sake **por Dios** (11); for the first/last time **por primera/última vez** (11)
forbid **prohibir (prohíbo)** (12)
foreign languages **lenguas** (*pl.*) **extranjeras** (1)
foreigner **extranjero/a** *n.* (1)
forest **bosque** *m.* (14)
forget (about) **olvidarse (de)** (8)
form (*to fill out*) **formulario** (18)
forty **cuarenta** (2)
four **cuatro** (AT)
four hundred **cuatrocientos/as** (3)
fourteen **catorce** (AT)
fourth **cuarto/a** *adj.* (13)
freedom **libertad** *f.* (17)
freeway **autopista** (14)
freezer **congelador** *m.* (9)
French (*language*) **francés** *n. m.* (1); **francés, francesa** *n., adj.* (2); (French fried) potato **patata (frita)**
frequently **con frecuencia** (1)
fresh **fresco/a** (6)
Friday **viernes** *m. inv.* (4)
fried **frito/a** (6); **patata frita** French fried potato
friend **amigo/a** (1)
friendly **amistoso/a** (15)
friendship **amistad** *f.* (15)
from **de** (AT); **desde** (7); from the **del** (*contraction of* **de** + **el**) (2)
front desk **recepción** *f.* (18)
front: in front of **delante de** *prep.* (5)
frozen; very cold **congelado/a** (5)

fruit **fruta** (6); **jugo de fruta** fruit juice (6)
full, no vacancy **completo/a** (18)
full-time **de tiempo completo** (11); full-time job **trabajo de tiempo completo** (11)
fun: to be fun **ser** (*irreg.*) **divertido/a** (9)
function **funcionar** (12)
furious **furioso/a** (5)
furniture **muebles** *m. pl.* (4); to dust the furniture **sacudir los muebles** (9)

G

garage **garaje** *m.* (4)
garden **jardín** *m.* (4)
gas **gas** *m.* (12)
gas station **gasolinera** (14)
gasoline **gasolina** (14)
generally **por lo general** (4)
German (*language*) **alemán** *m.* (1); **alemán, alemana** *n., adj.* (2)
get **sacar** (**qu**) (11); to get along well/poorly (with) **llevarse bien/mal (con)** (15); to get down (from) **bajar (de)** (7); to get good/bad grades **sacar (qu) buenas/malas notas** (11); to get off (of) **bajar (de)** (7); to get (on/in) (*a vehicle*) **subir (a)** (7); to get together (with) **reunirse (me reúno) (con)** (8); to get up **levantarse** (4); to get up on the wrong side of the bed **levantarse con el pie izquierdo** (11); to get, obtain **conseguir** (*like* **seguir**) (8); **obtener** (*like* **tener**) (12)
gift **regalo** (2)
girl **niña** (2)
girlfriend **novia** (5)
give **dar** (*irreg.*) (7); to give (*as a gift*) **regalar** (7); to give (someone) a shot, injection **poner(le)** (*irreg.*) **una inyección** (10); give a party **dar** (*irreg.*) **una fiesta** (8)
go **ir** (*irreg.*) (3); **seguir (i, i) (g)** (14) to be going to (*do something*) **ir a** + *inf.* (3); to go (to) (*a function*) **asistir (a)** (2); to go away, leave **irse**; to go by (train/airplane/bus/boat) **ir en (tren/avión/autobús/barco)** (7); to go home **regresar a casa** (1); to go out with **salir** (*irreg.*) **con** (4); to go through security (check) **pasar por el control de la seguridad** (7); to go to bed **acostarse (ue)** (4); to go up **subir** (7)
golf **golf** *m.* (9)
gorilla **gorila** *m.* (14)
good **buen, bueno/a** *adj.* (2); good morning **buenos días** (AT); good night **buenas noches** (AT); the good thing, news **lo bueno** (10)
good-bye **adiós** (AT)
good-looking **guapo/a** (2)
govern **gobernar (ie)** (17)
government **gobierno** (14)

grade **calificación** *f.* (11); **nota** (11); **grado** (9)
graduate (from) **graduarse (me gradúo) (en)** (16)
grandchildren **nietos** *pl.* (2)
granddaughter **nieta** (2)
grandfather **abuelo** (2)
grandmother **abuela** (2)
grandparents **abuelos** *pl.* (2)
grandson **nieto** (2)
gray **gris** (3)
great **gran, grande** (2)
green pea **arveja** (6)
green **verde** (3)
greet each other **saludarse** (10)
greeting: greetings and expressions of courtesy **saludos y expresiones de cortesía** (AT)
groom **novio** (15)
ground floor **planta baja** (12)
grow **crecer (zc)** (15)
guest **invitado/a** *n.* (8); **huésped(a)** (18)
guide **guía** *m., f.* (13)

H

habit **costumbre** *f.* (9)
hairstylist **peluquero(a)** (16)
half-past (*the hour*) **y media** (AT)
ham **jamón** *m.* (6)
hamburger **hamburguesa** (6)
hand in **entregar (gu)** (11)
hand **mano** *f.* (11)
handsome **guapo/a** (2)
happen **pasar** (5)
happening **acontecimiento** (17)
happy **alegre** (5); **feliz** (*pl.* **felices**) (8); **contento/a** (5); to be happy (about) **alegrarse (de)** (12)
hard **difícil** (5)
hard drive **disco duro** (12)
hat **sombrero** (3)
hate **odiar** (7)
have **tener** (*irreg.*) (3); **haber** (*irreg.*) (*inf. of* **hay** there is/are) *auxiliary* (12); to have a good/bad time **pasarlo bien/mal** (8); to have been (*doing something*) for (*a period of time*) **hace** + *time* ago (11); to have dinner, supper **cenar** (6); **hace** + *period of time* + **que** + *present tense* (11); to have just (*done something*) **acabar de** (+ *inf.*) (6)
he **él** (1)
head **cabeza** (10)
headache **dolor** (*m.*) **de cabeza** (10)
health **salud** *f.* (10)
healthy **sano/a** (10)
hear **oír** (*irreg.*) (4)
heart **corazón** *m.* (10)
heat **calor** *m.* (5); **gas** *m.* (12)
heavy (*meal, food*) **fuerte** (6)
hello **hola** (AT)
help **ayudar** (6)
her *obj.* (*of prep.*) **ella** (1)

her *poss.* **su(s)** (2)
here **aquí** (1)
highway **carretera** (14)
his *poss.* **su(s)** (2)
history **historia** (1)
hit **pegar (gu)** (9)
hobby **pasatiempo, afición** *f.* (9)
hockey **hockey** *m.* (9)
holiday **día** (*m.*) **festivo** (8)
home **casa** (2); at home **en casa** (1)
homework **tarea** (4)
honeymoon **luna de miel** (15)
hope **esperanza** (17); to hope **esperar** (12); I hope, wish (that) **ojalá (que)** (13)
hors d'oeuvres **entremeses** *m. pl.* (8)
horse **caballo** (14)
horseback: to ride horseback **montar a caballo** (9)
host **anfitrión** (*m.*) (8)
hostess **anfitriona** (8)
hot dog **salchicha** (6)
hot: to be (feel) hot **tener** (*irreg.*) **calor** (5); it's hot **hace calor** (5)
hotel **hotel** *m.* (18); luxury hotel **hotel de lujo** (18)
hotel guest **huésped(a)** (18)
hour **hora**; (at) what time? **¿a qué hora?** (AT); what time is it? **¿qué hora es?** (AT)
house **casa** (2)
household chore **quehacer** (*m.*) **doméstico**
housing **vivienda** (12)
how? what? **¿cómo?** (1); how are you doing? **¿qué tal?** (AT); how are you? **¿cómo está(s)?** (AT); how many? **¿cuántos/as?** (1); how much does it cost? **¿cuánto cuesta?** (3); how much is it? **¿cuánto es?** (3)
humanities **humanidades** *f. pl.* (1)
hunger **hambre** *f.* (*but* **el hambre**)
hungry: to be (very) hungry **tener** (*irreg.*) **(mucha) hambre** (6)
hurry: to be in a hurry **tener** (*irreg.*) **prisa** (3)
hurt **doler (ue)** (10)
hurt oneself **hacerse** (*irreg.*) **daño** (11)
husband **esposo** (2); **marido** (15)

I

I **yo** (1); I am **soy** (AT); I'm sorry **discúlpeme** (11), **lo siento** (11)
ice cream **helado** (6)
identification card **tarjeta de identificación** (11)
if **si** (2)
improbable: it's improbable that . . . **es improbable que...** (13)
in **en** (AT); (*the morning, evening, etc.*) **por** *prep.* (1); in a balanced way **equilibradamente** (10); in case **en caso de que** (15); in cash **en efectivo** (16); in order to **para** *prep.* (2)

incredible: it's incredible **es increíble** (13)

inequality **desigualdad** *f.* (17)

inexpensive **barato/a** (3)

infancy **infancia** (15)

inform **informar** (17)

injection: to give (some one) an injection **ponerle** (*irreg.*) **una inyección** *f.* (10)

injure oneself **lastimarse** (11)

insist (on) **insistir (en)** (12)

installment: to pay in installments **pagar (gu) a plazos** (16)

instead of **en vez de** (16)

intelligent **inteligente** (2)

intend **pensar (ie)** (4)

Internet **red** *f.* (12)

interview **entrevistar** (16); *n.* **entrevista** (16); to have an interview **tener** (*irreg.*) **una entrevista** (16)

interviewer **entrevistador(a)** (16)

invite **invitar** (6)

iron clothes **planchar la ropa** (9)

island **isla** (5)

Italian (*language*) **italiano** *m.* (1)

its *poss.* **su(s)** (2)

J

jacket **chaqueta** (3)

January **enero** (5)

jeans *jeans m. pl.* (3)

job **trabajo** (11); **puesto** (16); full-time/part-time job **trabajo de tiempo completo/parcial** (11)

jog **correr** (9)

joke **chiste** *m.* (8)

journalist **periodista** *m., f.* (16)

juice: (fruit) juice **jugo (de fruta)** (6)

July **julio** (5)

June **junio** (5)

just in case **por si acaso** (11)

K

keep (*documents*) **guardar** (12); to keep on going **seguir (i, i) (g)** (14)

key **llave** *n. f.* (11)

kind (*adj.*) **amable** (2)

king **rey** *m.* (17)

kitchen **cocina** (4)

know **conocer (zc)** (6); to know (how) **saber** (*irreg.*) (6)

L

laborer **obrero/a** (16)

lack **falta** (11); **escasez** *f.* (*pl.* **escaseces**) (14)

lacking: to be lacking **faltar** (8)

lady **señora (Sra.)** (AT)

lake **lago** (14)

lamp **lámpara** (4)

landlady **dueña** (12)

landlord **dueño** (12)

language: foreign languages **lenguas extranjeras** (1)

laptop computer **computadora portátil, ordenador** (*m.*) **portátil**

large **gran, grande** (2)

last **último/a** (7); last night **anoche** (10); to last **durar** (17)

late **tarde** *adv.* (1); to be late **estar** (*irreg.*) **atrasado/a** (7)

later: see you later **hasta luego** (AT)

latest: the latest style **de última moda** (3)

laugh (about) **reírse (i, i) (de)** (8)

law **ley** *f.* (17)

lawyer **abogado/a** (16)

lazy **perezoso/a** (2)

lead a healthy/calm life **llevar una vida sana/tranquila** (10)

learn **aprender** (2) to learn (about) **enterarse (de)** (17)

least **menos** (5); at least **por lo menos** (8)

leave **salir** (*irreg.*) **(de)** (4); (behind) (in [*in a place*]) **dejar (en)** (9)

left: to the left (of) **a la izquierda (de)** (5); to be left **quedar(se)** (11)

leg **pierna** (11)

lend **prestar** (7)

lenses: contact lenses **lentes** (*m. pl.*) **de contacto** (10)

less: less . . . than **menos... que** (5)

letter **carta** (2)

lettuce **lechuga** (6)

liberty **libertad** *f.* (17)

librarian **bibliotecario/a** (1)

library **biblioteca** (1)

license **licencia** (14)

lie **mentira** (12)

life **vida** (11); to lead a healthy/calm life **llevar una vida sana/tranquila** (10)

light **luz** *f.* (*pl.* **luces**) (11); *adj.* light (not heavy) **ligero/a** (6)

like **gusto** (AT); do you (*form.*) like . . . ? **¿le gusta... ?** (AT); I (don't) like . . . **(no) me gusta(n)...** (AT); I would like . . . **me gustaría...** (7); to like very much **encantar** (7)

likeable **simpático/a** (2)

likely: it's likely that . . . **es probable que...** (13)

likewise **igualmente** (AT)

limit: speed limit **límite** (*m.*) **de velocidad** *f.* (14)

line: to stand in line **hacer** (*irreg.*) **cola** (7)

listen (to) **escuchar** (1)

literature **literatura** (1)

little, few **poco/a** *adj.* (3); little **poco** *adv.* (1); a little bit (of) **un poco (de)** (1)

live **vivir** (2); to live a healthy life **llevar una vida sana** (10)

loan **préstamo** (16)

lobster **langosta** (6)

lodging **alojamiento** (18)

long **largo/a** (2)

look at **mirar** (2); to look for **buscar (qu)** (1)

lose **perder (ie)** (4)

lot: a lot (of) **mucho/a** (2) an awful lot **muchísimo** (7)

love **amar** (15); **encantar** (7); **querer** (*irreg.*) (15); *n.* **amor** *m.* (15); in love (with) **enamorado/a (de)** (15); to fall in love (with) **enamorarse (de)** (15)

luggage **equipaje** *m.* (7)

lunch **almuerzo** (6); to have lunch **almorzar (ue) (c)** (4)

lung **pulmón** *m.* (10)

luxury *n.* **lujo** (12); luxury hotel **hotel** (*m.*) **de lujo** (18)

M

machine: answering machine **contestador** (*m.*) **automático** (12)

magazine **revista** (2)

maid **criada** (18)

mail **correo** (18); electronic mail **correo electrónico** (12)

make **hacer** (*irreg.*) (4); to make a good/bad impression on someone **caerle** (*irreg.*) **bien/mal a alguien** (16); to make a mistake (about) **equivocarse (qu)** (11) to make plans to (*do something*) **hacer** (*irreg.*) **planes para** + *inf.* (9); to make stops **hacer** (*irreg.*) **escalas** (7); to make the bed **hacer** (*irreg.*) **la cama** (9)

mall: shopping mall **centro comercial** (3)

man **hombre** *m.* (1); **señor (Sr.)** *m.* (AT)

many: **muchos/as** (2); how many? **¿cuántos/as?** (1)

March **marzo** (5)

market(place) **mercado** (3)

marriage **matrimonio** (15)

married **casado/a** (2); married couple **pareja** (15)

marry **casarse (con)** (15)

masterpiece **obra maestra** (13)

match (*for lighting things*) **fósforo** (18)

material **material** *n. m.* (3)

mathematics **matemáticas** *pl.* (1)

May **mayo** (5)

me *d.o., i.o.* **me**; *obj.* (*of prep.*) **mí** (5)

meal **comida** (6)

means: means of communication **medio de comunicación** (17); means of transportation **modo de transporte** *m.* (7)

meat **carne** *f.* (6)

mechanic **mecánico/a** (14)

medical **médico/a** (2); medical office **consultorio** (10)

medicine **medicina** (10)

meet (*someone somewhere*) **encontrarse (con)** (10)

memory **memoria** (12)

menu **menú** *m.* (6)

merchant **comerciante** *m., f.* (16)

messy **desordenado/a** (5)

metro stop **estación** (*f.*) **de metro** (18)

Mexican **mexicano/a** *n., adj.* (2)

microwave oven **horno de microondas** *f. pl.* (9)

midday: at noon **a mediodía**

middle age **madurez** *f.* (15)

midnight **medianoche** *f.* (8)

military service **servicio militar** (17)

milk **leche** *f.* (6)

million **millón** *m.* (3)

mineral water **agua** *f.* (*but* **el agua**) **mineral** (6)

miss (*a function, bus, plane, etc.*) **perder (ie)** (4)

Miss **señorita (Srta.)** (AT)

mistake: to make a mistake (about) **equivocarse (qu) (de)** (11)

modem **módem** *m.* (12)

modern **moderno/a** (13)

molar **muela** (10)

mom **mamá** (2)

Monday **lunes** *m. inv.* (4)

money **dinero** (1)

month **mes** *m.* (5)

moped **moto(cicleta)** *f.* (12)

more **más** *adv.* (1); more . . . than (5) **más... que**

morning **mañana** *n.*; in the morning **de la mañana** (AT); in the morning **por la mañana** (1); good morning **buenos días** (AT)

mother **mamá, madre** *f.* (2)

motorcycle **moto(cicleta)** *f.* (12)

mountain **montaña** (7)

mouse **ratón** *m.* (12)

mouth **boca** (10)

move (*residence*) **mudarse** (16)

movie **película** (4); **cine** *m.* (4); movie theater **cine** *m.* (4)

Mr. **señor (Sr.)** *m.* (AT)

Mrs. **señora (Sra.)** (AT)

Ms. **señorita (Srta.)** (AT)

much **mucho** *adv.* (1); how much does it cost? **¿cuánto cuesta?** (3); how much is it? **¿cuánto es?** (3)

museum: to visit a museum **visitar un museo** (9)

mushroom **champiñón** *m.* (6)

music **música** (13)

musician **músico/a** *n. m., f.* (13)

must (*do something*) **deber** (+ *inf.*) (2)

my *poss.* **mi(s)**; (2); my, (of) mine *poss.* **mío/a(s)** (17)

named what's your (*form.*) name? **¿cómo se llama usted?** (AT); what's your (*form.*) name? **¿cómo te llamas?** (*fam.*) (AT); my name is . . . **me llamo...** (AT)

nap: to take a nap **dormir (ue, u) la siesta** (4)

nationality **nacionalidad** *f.* (18)

natural resources **recursos** (*pl.*) **naturales** (14)

nature **naturaleza** (14)

nauseated **mareado/a** (10)

neat **ordenado/a** (5)

necessary **necesario/a** (2); it is necessary to (*do something*) **hay que** + *inf.* (13)

need *v.* **necesitar** (1)

neighbor **vecino/a** (12)

neighborhood **barrio, vecindad** *f.* (12)

neither, not either **tampoco** (6)

nephew **sobrino** (2)

nervous **nervioso/a** (5)

Net: to surf the Net **navegar (gu) la Red** (12)

never **nunca** (2); **jamás** (6); almost never **casi nunca** (2)

new **nuevo/a** (2); New Year's Eve **Noche** (*f.*) **Vieja** (8)

news **noticias** *pl.* (17); news media **prensa** (17); news item **noticia** (8)

newscast **noticiero** (17)

newspaper **periódico** (2)

next **próximo/a** *adj.* (4); next to **al lado de** *prep.* (5)

nice **amable** (2), **simpático/a** (2)

niece **sobrina** (2)

night: at night **de la noche** (AT); **por la noche** (1); good night **buenas noches** (AT); last night **anoche** (10), tonight **esta noche** (5)

nine **nueve** (AT)

nine hundred **novecientos/as** (3)

nineteen **diecinueve** (AT)

ninety **noventa** (2)

ninth **noveno/a** (13)

no, not **no** (AT)

nobody, not anybody, no one **nadie** (6)

noise **ruido** (4)

none, not any **ningún, ninguno/a** (6)

noon: at noon **a mediodía**

North American **norteamericano/a** *n., adj.* (2)

north **norte** *m.* (5)

nose **nariz** *f.* (10)

not ever **nunca, jamás** (6)

note **nota** (11)

notebook **cuaderno** (1)

nothing, not anything **nada** (6)

noun **sustantivo** *gram.* (1)

November **noviembre** *m.* (5)

now **ahora** (1)

nuclear **nuclear** (14)

number **número** (2)

nurse **enfermero/a** (10)

obey **obedecer (zc)** (14)

obligation **deber** *m.* (17)

ocean **océano** (7)

October **octubre** *m.* (5)

of **de** *prep.* (AT); of the **del** (*contraction of* **de** + **el**) (2); of course **por supuesto** (11)

off: to turn off **apagar (gu)** (11)

offer *v.* **ofrecer (zc)** (7)

office **oficina** (1); personnel office **dirección** (*f.*) **de personal** (16)

oil **aceite** *m.* (14)

OK **regular** *adj.* (AT)

old **viejo/a** *adj.* (2);

older **mayor** (5)

on **en** (AT); on top of **encima de** *prep.* (5)

once a week **una vez a la semana** (2)

one **un, uno/a** (AT)

one hundred **cien, ciento** (2)

one-way (*ticket*) **de ida** (7)

only **sólo** *adv.* (1)

open **abierto/a** (5); to open **abrir** (*p.p.* **abierto/a**) (2)

opera **ópera** (13)

operate (*a machine*) **manejar** (12)

or **o** (AT)

oral report **informe oral** (11)

orange (*color*) **anaranjado/a** *adj.* (3); orange (*fruit*) **naranja** (6)

order (*in a restaurant*) **pedir (i, i)** (4); (*someone to do something*) **mandar** (12)

organization **organización** *f.*

organize **organizar (c)**

other **otro/a** (2); others **los/las demás** (12)

ought to (*do something*) **deber** (+ *inf.*) (2)

our *poss.* **nuestro/a(s)** (2)

outdoors **afuera** *adv.* (5)

outskirts **afueras** *n. pl.* (12)

oven: microwave oven **horno de microondas** (9)

overcoat **abrigo** (3)

own **propio/a** *adj.* (15)

owner **dueño/a** (6)

pace **ritmo** (14)

pack one's suitcases **hacer** (*irreg.*) **las maletas** (7)

package **paquete** *m.* (18)

pain **dolor** *m.* (10); to have a pain (in) **tener** (*irreg.*) **dolor (de)** (10)

paint (the walls) **pintar (las paredes)** (9)

painter **pintor(a)** (13)

painting **cuadro, pintura** (13)

pair **par** *m.* (3)

pants **pantalón** *m.*, **pantalones** *pl.* (3)

paper **papel** *m.* (1)

pardon me **(con) permiso, perdón** (AT); **discúlpeme** (11)

parents **padres** *m. pl.* (2)

park **parque** *m.* (5); to park **estacionar** (11)

part-time **de tiempo parcial** (11); part-time job **trabajo de tiempo parcial** (11) participate (*in a sport*) **practicar (qu)** (10)

party **fiesta** (1); to have a party **hacer** (*irreg.*) **una fiesta** (8)

pass through security (check) **pasar por el control de la seguridad** (7)

passage **pasaje** *m.* (7)

passenger **pasajero/a** *n.* (7)

passport **pasaporte** *m.* (18)

pastime **pasatiempo** (9)

pastry (small) **pastelito** (18); pastry shop **pastelería** (18)

patient **paciente** *n., adj. m., f.* (10)

pay **pagar (gu)** (1); to pay cash **pagar al contado/en efectivo** (16); to pay in installments **pagar a plazos** (16)

pea: green pea **arveja** (6)

peace **paz** *f.* (*pl.* **paces**) (17); to live in peace **vivir en paz** (17); to maintain peace **mantener** (*like* **tener**) **la paz** (17)

peasant **campesino/a** (14)

pen **bolígrafo** (1)

pencil **lápiz** *m.* (*pl.* **lápices**) (1)

people **gente** *f. s.* (13)

perform (*a part*) **desempeñar** (13)

permit **permitir** (12)

person **persona** (1)

personnel director **director(a) de personal** (16); personnel office **dirección** (*f.*) **de personal** (16)

pet **mascota** (2)

pharmacist **farmacéutico/a** (10)

pharmacy **farmacia** (10)

philosophy **filosofía** (1)

phone: to talk on the phone **hablar por teléfono** (1)

photo(graph) **foto(grafía)** *f.* (7)

photographer **fotógrafo/a** (16)

photos: to take photos **sacar (qu) fotos** *f. pl.* (7)

physics **física** (1)

pick up **recoger (j)** (11)

picnic: to have a picnic **hacer** (*irreg.*) **un picnic** (9)

pie **pastel** *m.* (6)

pill **pastilla** (10)

pillow **almohada** (18)

pink **rosado/a** (3)

place (*in line*) **puesto** (7); to place **poner** (*irreg.*) (4)

plans: to make plans to (*do something*) **hacer** (*irreg.*) **planes para** + *inf.* (9)

play (*a game, sport*) **jugar (ue) (gu) (a)** (4); to play chess **jugar (ue) (gu) al ajedrez** (4); to play cards **jugar (ue) (gu) a las cartas** (9); to play (*a musical instrument*) **tocar (qu)** (1); to play (*a musical instrument*) **tocar (qu) música** (1); to play (*a part*) **desempeñar** (13)

player **jugador(a)** (9)

playwright **dramaturgo/a** (13)

please **por favor** (AT); pleased to meet you **encantado/a, mucho gusto** (AT); to please **agradar** (13)

pleasing: to be pleasing **gustar** (7)

plumber **plomero/a** (16)

poet **poeta** *m., f.* (13)

point **punto**

police officer **policía** *m., f.* (14)

politician **político/a** (17)

politics **política** *s.* (17)

pollute **contaminar** (14)

pollution: there's (lots of) pollution **hay (mucha) contaminación** *f.* (5)

poor **pobre** (2)

poorly **mal** *adv.* (1)

population **población** *f.* (14)

pork chop **chuleta de cerdo** (6)

porter **maletero** (7)

possible **posible** (2)

post office **correo; oficina de correos** (18)

postcard **tarjeta postal** (7)

potato **patata** *Sp.* (6); French fried potato **patata frita** (6)

pottery **cerámica** (13)

practice **entrenar** (9); **practicar (qu)** (1)

prefer **preferir (ie, i)** (3)

preferable **preferible** (13)

prepare **preparar** (6)

prescription **receta** (10)

present (*gift*) **regalo** *n.* (2)

press *n.* **prensa** (17)

pressure: to be under pressure **sufrir presiones** *f. pl.* (11)

pretty **bonito/a** (2)

price **precio** (3); fixed, set price **precio fijo** (3)

print **imprimir** (12)

printer **impresora** (12)

probable: its probable that . . . **es probable que...** (13)

profession **profesión** *f.* (16)

professor **profesor(a)** (1)

programmer **programador(a)** (16)

prohibit **prohibir (prohíbo)** (12)

promise *v.* **prometer** (7)

protect **proteger (j)** (14)

provided (that) **con tal (de) que** (15)

psychiatrist **siquiatra** *m., f.* (16)

psychologist **sicólogo/a** (16)

psychology **sicología** (1)

public **público/a** *adj.* (14)

punish **castigar (gu)** (17)

pure **puro/a** (14)

purple **morado/a** (3)

purse **bolsa** (3)

put **poner** (*irreg.*) (4); to put on (*clothing*) **ponerse** (*irreg.*) (4)

Q

quarter after (*hour*) **y cuarto** (AT)

queen **reina** (17)

question: to ask (a question) **hacer** (*irreg.*) **una pregunta** (4); **preguntar** (6)

quit **dejar** (16); (*doing something*) **dejar de** + *inf.* (10)

quiz **prueba** (11)

R

radio **radio** *m.* (*set*); portable radio **radio portátil** (12); **radio** *f.* (*medium*) (12)

rain **llover (ue)** (5); it's raining **llueve** (5)

raincoat **impermeable** *m.* (3)

raise **aumento** (12); (in salary) **aumento de sueldo** (16)

rather **bastante** *adv.* (15)

react **reaccionar** (8)

read **leer (y)** (2)

receive **recibir** (2)

recommend **recomendar (ie)** (7)

record **grabar** (12)

recorder (tape) **grabadora** (12)

recycle **reciclar** (14)

red **rojo/a** (3); red wine **vino tinto** (6)

reduction **rebaja** (3)

refrigerator **refrigerador** *m.* (9)

regret **sentir (ie, i)** (13)

relative **pariente** *m., f.* (2)

remain (*in a place*) **quedar(se)** (5)

remember **recordar (ue)** (8); **acordarse (ue) (de)** (11)

remote control **control** (*m.*) **remoto** (12)

rent **alquiler** *m.* (12); to rent *v.* **alquilar** (12)

renter **inquilino/a** (12)

repair **arreglar** (12); (repair) shop **taller** *m.* (14)

report **informe, trabajo** (11)

reporter **reportero/a** (17)

represent **representar** (13)

reservation **reserva, reservación** *f.* (18)

resign (from) **renunciar (a)** (16)

resolve **resolver (ue)** (*p.p.* **resuelto/a**) (14)

resource **recurso**; natural resources **recursos naturales** (14)

responsibility **responsabilidad** *f.*, **deber** *m.* (17)

rest **descansar** (4)

restaurant **restaurante** *m.* (6)

résumé **currículum** *m.* (16)

retire **jubilarse** (16)

return (*to a place*) **regresar** (1); **volver (ue)** (*p.p.* **vuelto/a**) (4); (*something*) **devolver** (*like* **volver**) (*pp.* **devuelto/a**) (16)

rhythm **ritmo** (14)

rice **arroz** *m.* (*pl.* **arroces**) (6)

rich **rico/a** (2)

ride: ride a bicycle **pasear en bicicleta** (9); to ride horseback **montar a caballo** (9)

ridiculous: it's ridiculous that . . . **es ridículo que...** (13)

right (*legal*) **derecho** *n.* (17); right? **¿verdad?** (3); right away **en seguida** (10); to the right (of) **a la derecha (de)** (5) to be right **tener** (*irreg.*) **razón** (3)

ring **sonar (ue)** (9)

river **río** (14)
road **camino** (14)
role **papel** m. (13)
roller skates **patínes** m. pl. (12)
rollerblade v. **patinar en línea** (9)
room **cuarto** (1); room (in a hotel)
  habitación f. (18); double room **habita-**
  ción (f.) **doble** (18); emergency room
  sala de urgencia (10); living room **sala**
  (4); room and full board (all meals)
  pensión (f.) **completa** (18); room
  with(out) bath/shower **habitación** (f.)
  con/sin baño/ducha (18); single room
  habitación (f.) **individual** (18); waiting
  room **sala de espera** (7)
roommate **compañero/a de cuarto** (1)
round-trip ticket **billete** (m.)/**boleto de**
  ida y vuelta (7)
routine: daily routine **rutina diaria** (4)
rug **alfombra** (4)
ruin n. **ruina** (13)
rule **gobernar (ie)** (17)
run **correr** (9); (machines) **funcionar**
  (12); to run into **darse** (irreg.)
  en/con/contra, pegarse (gu)
  en/con/contra (11); collide (with)
  chocar (qu) (con) (14); to run out (of)
  acabar(se) (11)

S

sad **triste** (5)
salad **ensalada** (6)
salary **sueldo** (12); **salario** (16); raise in
  salary **aumento de sueldo** (16)
sale **rebaja** (3)
salesperson **vendedor(a)** (16)
salmon **salmón** m. (6)
same **mismo/a** (10); same here
  igualmente (AT)
sandal **sandalia** (3)
sandwich **sándwich** m. (6)
Saturday **sábado** (4)
sausage **salchicha** (6)
save **conservar** (14); (documents) **guar-**
  dar (12); (money) **ahorrar** (16); (a place)
  guardar un puesto (7)
savings **ahorros** pl.; savings account
  cuenta de ahorros (16)
say **decir** (irreg.) (7); to say good-bye
  (to) **despedirse (i, i) (de)** (8)
schedule **horario** (11)
school **escuela** (9)
schoolteacher **maestro/a** (16)
science **ciencia** (1); computer science
  computación f. (1)
script **guión** m. (13)
sculpt **esculpir** (13)
sculptor **escultor(a)** (13)
sculpture **escultura** (13)
sea **mar** m., f. (7)
seafood **mariscos** pl. (6)
seaport **puerto** (7)
search **registrar** (18)

season **estación** f. (5)
seat **asiento** (7)
second **segundo/a** adj. (13)
secretary **secretario/a** (1)
security check **control** (m.) **de la segu-**
  ridad (7)
see **ver** (irreg.) (4); see you around **nos**
  vemos (AT); see you later **hasta luego**
  (AT); see you tomorrow **hasta mañana**
  (AT)
seem **parecer (zc)** (13)
sell **vender** (2)
send **mandar** (7)
separate (from) v. **separarse (de)** (15)
separation **separación** f. (15)
September **septiembre** m. (5)
servant **criado/a** (16)
serve **servir (i, i)** (4)
service: military service **servicio militar**
  (17); room service **servicio de cuartos**
  (18)
set price **precio fijo** (3)
set the table **poner** (irreg.) **la mesa** (9)
seven **siete** (AT)
seven hundred **setecientos/as** (3)
seventeen **diecisiete** (AT)
seventh **séptimo/a** adj. (13)
seventy **setenta** (2)
shame **lástima** (13); it is a shame **es**
  una lástima (13); what a shame! **¡qué**
  lástima! (13)
shampoo **champú** m. (18)
shave oneself **afeitarse** (4)
she **ella** (1)
sheet **sábana** (18)
shellfish **marisco** (6)
ship **barco** (7)
shirt **camisa** (3)
shoe **zapato** (3); tennis shoe **zapato de**
  tenis (3)
shop (repair) **taller** m. (14)
shopkeeper **comerciante** m., f. (16)
shopping **de compras** (3); shopping
  mall **centro comercial** (3); to go
  shopping **ir** (irreg.) **de compras** (3)
short (in height) **bajo/a** (2); (in length)
  corto/a (2)
shortage **escasez** f. (pl. **escaseces**) (14)
shot: to give (someone) a shot **ponerle**
  (irreg.) **una inyección** f. (10)
should (do something) **deber** (+ inf.) (2)
show **mostrar (ue)** (7)
shower: room with attached shower
  habitación (f.) **con ducha** (18); to take a
  shower **ducharse** (4)
shrimp **camarón** m. (6)
sick **enfermo/a** adj. (5); to get sick
  enfermarse (8)
sickness **enfermedad** f. (10)
sight: at first sight **a primera vista** (15)
silk **seda** (3); it is made of silk **es de**
  seda (3)
silly **tonto/a** (2)

sing **cantar** (1)
singer **cantante** m., f. (13)
single (not married) **soltero/a** (2); single room **habitación** (f.) **individual** (18)
sink (bathroom) **lavabo** (4)
sir **señor (Sr.)** m. (AT)
sister **hermana** (2)
sit down **sentarse (ie)** (4)
six **seis** (AT)
six hundred **seiscientos/as** (3)
sixteen **dieciséis** (AT)
sixth **sexto/a** adj. (13)
sixty **sesenta** (2)
skate **patinar** (9)
skateboard **monopatín** m. (12)
ski **esquiar (esquío)** (9)
skirt **falda** (3)
skyscraper **rascacielos** m. s. (14)
sleep **dormir (ue, u)** (4)
sleepy: to be sleepy **tener** (irreg.)
  sueño (3)
slender **delgado/a** (2)
small **pequeño/a** (2)
smart **listo/a** (2)
smile **sonreír(se)** (like **reír**) (8)
smoke **fumar** (7)
smoking (nonsmoking) section **sección**
  (f.) **de (no) fumar** (7)
snow **nevar (ie)** (5); it's snowing
  nieva (5)
so: so-so **regular** (AT); so that **para**
  que (15)
soap **jabón** m. (18)
soccer **fútbol** m. (9)
social worker **trabajador(a) social** (16)
sociology **sociología** (1)
sock **calcetín** m. **calcetines** (pl.) (3)
sofa **sofá** m. (4)
soft drink **refresco** (6)
solar **solar** (14)
soldier **soldado**; female soldier **mujer**
  (f.) **soldado** (16)
solve **resolver (ue)** (p.p. **resuelto/a**) (14)
some **algún, alguno/a** (6)
someone **alguien** (6)
something **algo** (3)
sometimes **a veces** (2)
son **hijo** (2)
song **canción** f. (13)
soon **pronto**; as soon as **tan pronto**
  como (16); conj. **en cuanto** (16)
sorry: I'm (very) sorry! **¡Lo siento**
  (mucho)! (11)
sound v. **sonar (ue)** (9)
soup **sopa** (6)
south **sur** m. (5)
Spanish (language) **español** m. (1);
  español(a) n., adj. (2)
speak **hablar** (1)
species **especie** f. (14); endangered species **especie en peligro de extinción** (14)
speed: speed limit **límite** (m.) **de velo-**
  cidad (14)

spend (*money*) **gastar** (8); (*time*) **pasar** (5)

sport **deporte** *m.* (9); to practice, play sports **practicar (qu) deportes** (10)

sports *adj.* **deportivo/a** (9)

spring **primavera** (5)

stage **escenario** (13)

stamp **sello** (*postage*) (18)

stand in line **hacer** (*irreg.*) **cola** (7); to stand up **levantarse** (4)

start up (*a car*) **arrancar (qu)** (14)

state **estado** (2)

station **estación** *f.* (7); bus station **estación de autobuses** (7); train station **estación del tren** (7); station wagon **camioneta** (7)

stationery **papel** (*m.*) **para cartas** (18); stationery store **papelería** (18)

stay *n.* (*in a hotel*) **estancia** (18); to stay (*in a place*) **quedar(se)** (5), **alojarse** (18); to stay in bed **guardar cama** (10)

steak **bistec** *m.* (6)

stereo equipment **equipo estereofónico** (12)

stick out one's tongue **sacar (qu) la lengua** (10)

still **todavía** (5)

stockings **medias** *pl.* (3)

stomach **estómago** (10)

stop **parar** (14); (*doing something*) **dejar de** + *inf.* (10); to make stops **hacer** (*irreg.*) **escalas** (7)

store **tienda** (3)

stove **estufa** (9)

straight ahead **todo derecho** (14)

straighten (up) **arreglar** (12)

strange **raro/a** (8); **extraño/a** (13); it's strange **es extraño** (13)

street **calle** *f.* (12); **camino** (14)

stress **estrés** *m.* (11); **tensión** *f.*

strike (*labor*) **huelga** (17)

strong **fuerte** (6)

student **estudiante** *m., f.* (1); student (*adj.*), of students **estudiantil** (11)

study **estudiar** (1)

stuffed: stuffed up **congestionado/a** (10)

style: latest style **de última moda** (3)

subject (*school*) **materia** (1)

suburb **suburbio** (4); **afueras** *pl.* (12)

subway station **estación** (*f.*) **de metro** (18)

succeed in (*doing something*) **conseguir** (*like* **seguir**) + *inf.* (8)

suddenly **de repente** (10)

suffer **sufrir** (11)

sufficiently **bastante** *adv.* (15)

suggest **sugerir (ie, i)** (8)

suit **traje** *m.* (3); bathing suit **traje de baño** (3)

suitcase **maleta** (7); to pack one's suitcases **hacer** (*irreg.*) **las maletas** (7)

summer **verano** (5)

sunny: it's (very) sunny **hace (mucho) sol** (5); sunbathe **tomar el sol** (7)

Sunday **domingo** (4)

supper **cena** (6); to have (eat) supper **cenar** (6)

support **apoyar** (17)

sure **seguro/a** *adj.* (5); it's a sure thing **es seguro** (13)

surf the Net **navegar (gu) la Red** (12)

surprise **sorpresa** (8); to surprise **sorprender**; it surprises me (you, him, . . .) **me (te, le, . . .) sorprende** (13)

sweater **suéter** *m.* (3)

sweep (the floor) **barrer (el piso)** (9)

sweets **dulces** *m. pl.* (6)

swim **nadar** (7)

swimming **natación** *f.* (9); swimming pool **piscina** (4)

symptom **síntoma** *m.* (10)

systems analyst **analista** (*m., f.*) **de sistemas** (16)

T

T-shirt **camiseta** (3)

table **mesa** (1); table (*end*) **mesita** (4)

take **tomar** (1); **llevar** (3); to take (*photos*) **sacar (qu) (fotos)** (7); to take care of oneself **cuidar(se)** (10); to take leave (*of*) **despedirse (i, i) (de)** (8); to take off (*clothing*) **quitarse** (4); to take out **sacar (qu)** (11); to take out the trash **sacar (qu) la basura** (9); to take someone's temperature **tomarle la temperatura** (10)

talk **hablar** (1); to talk on the phone **hablar por teléfono** (1)

tall **alto/a** (2)

tank **tanque** *m.* (14)

tape **cinta** (3); to tape **grabar** (12); tape recorder/player **grabadora** (12)

tea **té** *m.* (6)

teach **enseñar** (1)

technician **técnico/a** *n.* (16)

telephone (cellular) **teléfono (cellular)** (12)

television set **televisor** *m.* (4); to watch television **mirar la televisión** (2)

tell **decir** (*irreg.*) (7); **contar (ue)** (7)

teller **cajero/a** (16); automatic teller machine **cajero automático** (16)

temperature **temperatura** (10); to take someone's temperature **tomarle la temperatura** (10)

ten **diez** (AT)

tenant **inquilino/a** (12)

tennis **tenis** *m. s.* (9); tennis shoe **zapato de tenis** (3)

tension **tensión** *f.*

tent **tienda de campaña** (7)

tenth **décimo/a** (13)

terrace **terraza**

terrible: it's terrible that . . . **es terrible que...** (13)

terrorism **terrorismo** (17)

terrorist **terrorista** *m., f.* (17); terrorist attack **ataque** (*m.*) **terrorista** (17)

test **examen** *m.* (3); **prueba** (11)

textbook **libro de texto** (1)

thank you **gracias** (AT); thank you very much **muchas gracias** (AT); thanks for **gracias por** (8)

that *adj.*, that one *pron.* **ese, esa** (3); that *adj.*, that one *pron.* (*over there*) **aquel, aquella** (3); that *pron.* **eso** (3); that *pron.* (*over there*) **aquello** (3); *conj.* **que** (2)

theater: to go to the theater **ir** (*irreg.*) **al teatro** (9)

their *poss.* **sus** (2)

there is (not), there are (not) **(no) hay** (AT)

there: (over) there **allí** (3)

therefore **por eso** (1)

these *adj.* these (2); these (ones) *pron.* **estos/as** (2)

they **ellos/as** (1)

thin **delgado/a** (2)

thing **cosa** (1)

think **creer (y) (en)** (2); to think (*about*) **pensar (ie) (en)** (4)

third **tercer, tercero/a** *adj.* (13)

thirst **sed** *f.*; to be thirsty **tener** (*irreg.*) **sed** (6)

thirteen **trece** (AT)

thirty **treinta** (AT); thirty, half-past (*the hour*) **y media, y treinta** (AT)

this *adj.* this one *pron.* **este, esta** (2); this *pron.* **esto** (2)

those *adj.* those (ones) *pron.* **esos/as** (3); those *adj.* (*over there*), those (ones) *pron.* (*over there*) **aquellos/as** (3)

three **tres** (AT)

three hundred **trescientos/as** (3)

throat **garganta** (10)

through **por** *prep.* (4)

Thursday **jueves** *m. inv.* (4)

ticket **boleto, billete** *m.* (7); **pasaje** *m.* (7); one-way ticket **billete** (*m.*)**/boleto de ida** (7); round-trip ticket **billete** (*m.*)**/boleto de ida y vuelta** (7)

tie **corbata** (3)

time (*period*) **época** (9); ahead of time **con anticipación** (18); on time **a tiempo** (7); spare time **ratos** (*pl.*) **libres** (9); to arrive on time **llegar (gu) a tiempo** (11); to spend time (with) **pasar tiempo (con)** (15) full-time/part-time job **trabajo a tiempo completo/parcial** (11)

tip (*to an employee*) **propina** (18)

tire *n.* **llanta** (14)

tired **cansado/a** (5)

to the **al** (*contraction of* **a** + **el**) (3)

toast **pan** (*m.*) **tostado** (6)

toaster **tostadora** (9)

tobacco stand/shop **estanco** (18)

today **hoy** (AT); what's today's date? **¿cuál es la fecha de hoy?** (5)

toe **dedo del pie** (11)

together **juntos/as** (15)

tomato **tomate** *m.* (6)

tomorrow **mañana** *adv.* (AT); see you tomorrow **hasta mañana** (AT); day after tomorrow **pasado mañana** (4); see you tomorrow **hasta mañana** (AT)

tongue: to stick out one's tongue **sacar (qu) la lengua** (10)

too **también** (AT)

tooth **diente** *m.* (10)

toothpaste **pasta dental** (18)

tourist **turístico/a** *adj.*; tourist class **clase** (*f.*) **turística** (7)

towel **toalla** (18)

trade **oficio** (16)

traffic **tránsito, circulación** *f.* (14); traffic signal **semáforo** (14)

train **tren** *m.* (7); train station **estación** (*f.*) **del tren** (7); to go by train **ir** (*irreg.*) **en tren** (7); to train **entrenar** (9)

translator **traductor(a)** (16)

transportation: (means of) transportation **(modo de) transporte** *m.* (17)

trash: to take out the trash **sacar (qu) la basura** (9)

travel **viajar** (7); travel agency **agencia de viajes** (7); travel agent **agente** (*m. f.*) **de viajes** (7)

traveler **viajero/a** (18); traveler's check **cheque** (*m.*) **de viajero** (18)

treadmill **rueda de molino** (10)

treatment **tratamiento** (10)

tree **árbol** *m.* (14)

trip **viaje** *m.* (7); on a trip **de viaje** (7); round-trip ticket **billete** (*m.*)**/boleto de ida y vuelta** (7); to take a trip **hacer** (*irreg.*) **un viaje** (4)

try **intentar** (13); try to (*do something*) **tratar de** + *inf.* (13)

Tuesday **martes** *m. inv.* (4)

tuition **matrícula** (1)

tuna **atún** *m.* (6)

turkey **pavo** (6)

turn **doblar** (14); to turn in **entregar (gu)** (11); to turn off **apugar (gu)** (11); to be someone's turn **tocarle (qu) a uno** (9)

twelve **doce** (AT)

twenty **veinte** (AT)

twice **dos veces** (10)

two **dos** (AT)

two hundred **doscientos/as** (3)

type **escribir** (*pp.* **escrito/a**) **a computadora** (16)

U

ugly **feo/a** (2)

unbelievable **increíble** (13)

uncle **tío** (2)

understand **comprender** (2); **entender (ie)** (4)

underwear **ropa interior** (3)

unintentional: it was unintentional **fue sin querer** (11)

university **universidad** *f.* (1); (of the) university **universitario/a** (11); university campus **campus** *m.* (12)

unless **a menos que** (15)

unlikely: it's unlikely that . . . **es improbable que...** (13)

unoccupied **desocupado/a** (18)

unpleasant **antipático/a** (2)

until **hasta** *prep.* (4); **hasta que** *conj.* (16); until (see you) tomorrow **hasta mañana** (AT)

urgent **urgente** (13)

us **nos** *d.o.*; *i.o.* to/for us; *refl. pron.* ourselves; **nos vemos** see you around (AT)

use **usar** (3); **gastar** (8); to use up completely **acabar** (14)

V

vacant **desocupado/a** (18)

vacation: to be on vacation **estar** (*irreg.*) **de vacaciones** (7); to go on vacation **ir** (*irreg.*) **de vacaciones** (7)

vacuum cleaner **aspiradora** (9); to vacuum **pasar la aspiradora** (9)

vegetable **verdura** (6)

vehicle **vehículo** (12)

verb **verbo** *gram.*

very **muy** (1); very well **muy bien** (AT)

veterinarian **veterinario/a** (16)

victim **víctima** *f.* (14)

videocassette recorder (VCR) **videocasetera** (12)

view **vista** (12)

violence **violencia** (14)

visit a museum **visitar un museo** (9)

volleyball **vólibol** *m.* (9)

W

wait (for) **esperar** (6)

waiter **camarero** (6)

waiting room **sala de espera** (7)

waitress **camarera** (6)

wake up **despertarse (ie)** (4)

walk **caminar** (10); to take a walk **dar** (*irreg.*) **un paseo** (9)

Walkman **walkman** *m.* (12)

wall **pared** *f.* (4)

wallet **cartera** (3)

want **desear** (1); **querer** (*irreg.*) (3)

war **guerra** (17)

warm: to be (feel) warm, hot **tener** (*irreg.*) **calor** (5)

wash: to wash (the windows, the dishes, clothes) **lavar (las ventanas, los platos, la ropa)** (9); to wash (oneself) **lavar(se)**

washing machine **lavadora** (9)

watch **reloj** *m.* (3); to watch **mirar** (2); to watch television **mirar la televisión** (2)

water **agua** *f.* (*but* **el agua**) (6); waterbed **cama de agua** (4) mineral water **agua** *f.* (*but* **el agua**) **mineral** (6)

we **nosotros/as** (1)

wear (clothing) **llevar, usar** (3)

weather **tiempo** (5); it's good/bad weather **hace buen/mal tiempo** (5); what's the weather like? **¿qué tiempo hace?** (5)

weave **tejer** (13)

wedding **boda** (15)

Wednesday **miércoles** *m. inv.* (4)

week **semana**; next week **la semana que viene** (4); once a week **una vez a la semana** (2)

weekday **día** (*m.*) **de la semana** (4)

weekend **fin** (*m.*) **de semana** (1)

welcome: you're welcome **de nada, no hay de qué** (AT)

well **bien** *adv.* (AT); well . . . *interj.* **bueno...** (2)

well-being **bienestar** *m.* (10)

west **oeste** *m.* (5)

whale **ballena** (14)

what . . . ! **¡qué... !**; what a shame! **¡qué lástima!** (13)

what? **¿qué?** (AT) **¿cuál(es)?** (1); what are you like? **¿cómo es usted?** (AT); what's the date today? **¿cuál es la fecha de hoy?** (5); what time is it? **¿qué hora es?** (AT); what's your name? **¿cómo te llamas? / ¿cómo se llama usted?** (AT)

when + *verb form* **al** + *inf.*

when? **¿cuándo?** (1)

where? **¿dónde?** (AT); where (to)? **¿adónde?** (3); where are you from? **¿de dónde es Ud.?** (AT)

which **que** (2)

which? **¿qué?** (1); **¿cuál(es)?** (1)

while **mientras** *conj.* (9)

white **blanco/a** (3); white wine **vino blanco** (6)

who **que** (2)

who? whom? **¿quién(es)?** (1)

whole: to clean the whole house **limpiar la casa entera** (9)

whose? **¿de quién?** (2)

why? **¿por qué?** (2)

widow **viuda** (15)

widower **viudo** (15)

wife **esposa** (2); **mujer** *f.* (15)

wild animal **animal** (*m.*) **salvaje** (14)

win **ganar** (9)

windy: it's (very) windy **hace mucho viento** (5)

window **ventana** (1)

windshield **parabrisas** *m. inv.* (14)

wine (white, red) **vino (blanco, tinto)** (6)

winter **invierno** (5)

wish **deseo** (8); **esperanza** (17)

with **con** (1)

without **sin** (4)

witness   testigo *m., f.* (17)
woman   señora (Sra.) (AT); mujer *f.* (1)
wool   lana (3); it is made of wool es de lana (3)
word   palabra (AT)
work (of art)   obra (de arte) (13); *n.* trabajo (11); to work trabajar (1); (*machine*) funcionar (12)
worker   obrero/a (16); trabajador(a) (2); social worker trabajador(a) social (16)
world   mundo (7)
worried   preocupado/a (5)
worse   peor (5)
woven goods   tejidos (13)
write   escribir (*p.p.* escrito/a) (2)
writer   escritor(a) (13)
written   escrito/a *p.p.* (11)
wrong: to be wrong   no tener (*irreg.*) razón (3); to be wrong (about) equivocarse (qu) (de) (11)

Y

yard, patio   patio (4)
year   año (5); (*in school*) grado (9); to be . . . years old tener (*irreg.*). . . años (2)
yellow   amarillo/a (3)
yes   sí (AT); yes, I like . . . sí, me gusta... (AT)
yesterday   ayer (4); the day before yesterday (10)
yet   todavía (5)
yogurt   yogur *m.* (6)
you *sub. pron.*   tú (*fam. s.*) (1); usted (Ud., Vd.) (*form. s.*) (1); vosotros/as (*fam. pl., Sp.*) (1); ustedes (Uds., Vds.) (*pl.*) (1); *d.o.* te, os, lo/la, los, las; to/for you *i.o.* te, os, le, les; *obj.* (*of prep.*) ti (5), Ud., Uds., vosotros/as

you're welcome   de nada, no hay de qué (AT)
young woman   señorita (Srta.) (AT)
younger   menor (5)
your *poss.*   tu(s) (*fam.*) (2); su(s) (*form.*) (2); vuestro/a(s) (*fam. pl., Sp.*) (2); (of) yours tuyo/a(s) (17), suyo/a(s) (17), vuestro/a(s) (17)
young *adj.*   joven (2); as a youth de joven (9); (*young adulthood*) juventud *f.* (15)

Z

zero   cero (AT)

In this index, cultural notes, authors of the literature presentations, and vocabulary topic groups are listed by individual topic as well as under those headings.

Grateful acknowledgment is made for use of the following:

Photographs: *Page 2 bottom left* © Odyssey Productions/Robert Frerck; *2 bottom right* © Odyssey Productions/Robert Frerck; *2 top left* © Ulrike Welsch; *2 top right* © Ulrike Welsch; *11* © Stuart Cohen; *16* SuperStock; *20 bottom* SuperStock; *20 top* PICTOR/ImageState; *21 bottom* © Peter Menzel; *21 center* Antonio Mendoza/Stock Boston; *21 top* © Ulrike Welsch; *24* PhotoDisc; *28* © Ken Welsh/Fotostock; *44* AP Wide World Photos; *51* US Postal Service; *54* AP Wide World Photos; *55* © Ulrike Welsch; *58* © Jimmy Dorantes/Latin Focus; *66* PICTOR/ImageState; *76* Museo del Prado, Madrid, Spain/Giraudon, Paris/SuperStock; *78* © Trapper Frank/Corbis Sygma; *85* © Fernando Botero, courtesy, Marlborough Gallery, New York; *87* Commissioned by the Trustees of Dartmouth College, Hanover, New Hampshire; Licensed by Orozco Valladares Family through VAGA, New York, NY; *90* © Mike Ramirez/LatinFocus.com; *91* © 1987 Carmen Lomas Garzac Photo credit: Wolfgang Dietze; Collection of Leonila Ramirez, Don Ramon's Restaurant, San Francisco, California; *94* Tomas Stargardter/Latin Focus; *99* © Gonzalo Endara Crow; *100* © Reuters NewMedia, Inc./Corbis; *108* Topham/The Image Works; *119* John Mitchell/DDB Stock Photography; *122* HO/AFP/Getty Images; *126* © Martin Rogers/Corbis; *129* © Ric Ergenbright; *135* © Robert Holmes/Corbis; *149* © Bill Gentile/Corbis; *152* Ardis L. Nelson; *156* © Moisés Castillo/Latin Focus; *161* AP Wide World Photos; *169 bottom* "A Logo for America" by Alfredo Jaar; *169 top* "A Logo for America" by Alfredo Jaar; *176 bottom* © Ulrike Welsch; *176 top* PICTOR/ImageState; *183* © Rob Crandall/The Image Works; *186* Pierre Boulat/Time Life Pictures/Getty Images; *187* © 2003 Frans Lanting, www.lanting.com; *190* © John Neubauer; *188* © PhotoDisc; *194 left* © Peter Guttman/Corbis; *194 right* © FoodPix; *215* Courtesy of Oswaldo & Alice A. Arana; *218* Courtesy of Prof. Carlos "Cubena" Guillermo Wilson, Ph.D.; *222* Timothy O'Keefe/Index Stock; *227* Michael J. Doolittle/The Image Works; *228* © Stuart Cohen; *244* © Corbis; *249* © Stephen and Donna O'Meara/Photo Researchers, Inc.; *252* Clementina c. 1940; *253* SuperStock; *254* © Corbis; *256* © A. Garcia/Latin Focus; *260* © Jack Kurtz/The Image Works; *267* Bob Riha Jr./Getty Images; *277* Prensa Latina/Getty Images; *280* Bettman/Corbis; *281* AP Wide World Photos; *282* © Corbis; *284* Philipp Dyckerhoff/Vario Press; *287* Reuters/Bettmann/Corbis; *296* Xavier Nunez/ Antara Productions; *297 center* © Reuters NewMedia/Inc./Corbis; *297 left* Stephane Cardinale/Corbis Sygma; *297 right* AP Wide World Photos; *305* © George Holton/Photo Researchers, Inc.; *308* AP Wide World Photos; *309* Joe Viesti/ViestiCollection; *312* DDB Stock Photography; *330* AP Wide World Photos; *337* © Ken Fisher/Getty Images; *340* © Corbis; *344* Suzanne Murphy-Larronde/DDB Stock Photography; *348 bottom* Frank Trapper/Corbis Sygma; *348 top* Frederic de LaFosse/Corbis Sygma; *357* Monika Graff/The Image Works; *367* © Ulrike Welsch; *370* AP Wide World Photos; *371* © Jimmy Dorantes/Latin Focus; *372* © Ulrike Welsch; *374* Shirley Vanderbilt/ Index Stock Imagery, Inc.; *378* © Ulrike Welsch; *384* David Young-Wolfe/PhotoEdit; *399* © Robert Frerck/Odyssey/Chicago; *402* © Richard Smith/Corbis Sygma; *403* © Matthew Kleine/Corbis; *406* © Craig Duncan/DDB Stock Photography; *411* © Charles Kennard/ Stock Boston; *413* © Chromosohm Media, Inc./The Image Works; *418* Collection of the Art Museum of the Americas, Organization of American States, Gift of IBM; *422* © Kim Newton/Woodfin Camp & Associates; *424* The Granger Collection; *425* Susana González/Getty Images; *427* The Granger Collection; *429 Madre y niño* by Oswaldo Guayasamín, Oleo sobre tela 80 X 80cm, Fundación Guayasamín, Quito, Ecuador; *432* © Mike Ramirez/LatinFocus.com; *436* Bill Bachman/PhotoEdit; *439* David Simpson/Stock, Boston; *457* © Robert Frerck/Odyssey; *460* © Mike Ramirez/LatinFocus.com; *461* © Ulrike Welsch; *462* © Corbis; *464* © Tony Arruza; *469* © Tony Arruza; *473* AP Wide World Photos; *481* © Mathias Oppersdorff/Photo Researchers, Inc.; *483* © Bettmann/Corbis; *486* Matthew Bryant/DDB Stock Photography; *489* © PhotoDisc; *507* © Chip & Rosa Maria Peterson; *510* © Mike Ramirez/LatinFocus.com; *512* David Madison/Bruce Coleman, Inc.; *514* © Ludovic Maisant/Corbis; *529* Getty Images; *533* John Mitchell/DDB Stock Photography; *535* © Mike Ramirez/LatinFocus.com; *536* Courtesy of Miriam Pérez; *538* © Odyssey Productions/Robert Frerck; *542* © Stuart Cohen; *549* © Stuart Cohen; *557* © Peter Menzel/Stock Boston; *559* Hulton Archives/Getty Images; *560* © Archivo Iconográfico, S.A./Corbis.

Realia: *Page 13* Ansa International; *102 Quo,* HF Revistas; *208* Courtesy of Goya Foods, Inc.; *287 Cambio 16;* *329* © Quino/Quipos; *341 Hombre Internacional;* *404 Quo,* No. 42, March 1999; *454 left* © Quino/Quipos; *454 right* MENA; *470* © Joaquín Salvador Lavado (QUINO) *Toda Mafalda,* Ediciones de la Flor © 1993; *484 El País;* *499 People en español,* September, 1998. Used by permission of Time, Inc.; *526* Antonio Mingote.

Literature: *Page 54 Caramelo* by Sandra Cisneros, HarperCollins Publishers, 2002; *90* From "Economía doméstica" by Rosario Castellanos, *Poesía no eres tú,* Fondo de Cultura Económica, México, DF; *123 Quo,* no. 31, April 1998; *152* From "XLVII" in *Esa tierra redonda y plana,* by Carmen Naranjo, Ediciones Torremozas, 2001. Courtesy of Carmen Naranjo; *186* From "Letanías del desterrado" by Miguel Ángel Asturias, *Páginas de lumbre de Miguel Ángel Asturias (1999)*; *187* Courtesy of *Muy Interesante*; *218* "Desarraigado" in *Los mosquitos de orixá Changó* by Carlos Guillermo Wilson. New Jersey: Ediciones Nuevo Espacio, 2000. Used by permission of Carlos "Cubena" Guillermo Wilson, San Diego State University; *219* Rafael Palomino excerpt copyright Jack Robertiello (Photo: Arlen Gargagliano, Courtesy of Rafael Palomino); *220* Recipe from *Viva la Vida* © 2002 Rafael Palomino & Arlen Gargagliano, photographs by Susie Cushner. Used with permission of Chronicle Books LLC, San Francisco; *252* "Canto a la encontrada patria y su héroe" by Clementina Suárez; *253 GeoMundo; 281* From "¡Época de las tradiciones!" by Lilian Jiménez, *Nuestra Gente,* December 2002. Courtesy of *Nuestra Gente; 308* From *Cien años de soledad* by Gabriel García Márquez; *309 Quo,* 1997; *340* From *Doña Bárbara* by Rómulo Gallegos, Editorial Araluce, 1929; *341 Hombre Internacional; 370* From *Sitio a eros: Trece ensayos* by Rosario Ferré, Mexico: Joaquín Mortiz, 1980; *371* Excerpts from "Divórciate del estrés" by Sarah Harding de la Torre, *Nuestra Gente,* December 2002. Courtesy of *Nuestra Gente; 402* From *La tía Julia y el escribidor* by Mario Vargas Llosa, Seix Barral, 1983; *403 Quo,* No. 42, March 1999; *432* From *Huasipungo* by Jorge Icaza, Plaza y Janes, 1991; *433 GeoMundo,* no. 6, junio 1999; Screenshot: Courtesy of Prof. Alicia Haber, Directora del MUVA Museo Virtual de Artes El País; *460* From "Cuadrados y ángulos" by Alfonsina Storni. Copyright Editorial Losada S.A., Buenos Aires, 1997. Used by permission; *461* Used by permission of *Diario de Sevilla; 483* From *Selected Poems, A Bilingual Edition,* edited by Doris Dana (Baltimore: Johns Hopkins University Press, 1971). Used by permission; *484 El País; 512* "La higuera" by Juana Fernández de Ibarbourou. Used by permission; *535* "Sobre el agua" by Manuel del Cabral; *536* "Cubanita descubanizada" in *Bilingual Blues* by Gustavo Pérez Firmat, Bilingual Press/Editorial Bilingüe, Arizona State University, Tempe AZ, 1995. Used by permission of the publisher; *560* "XXIX" in *Proverbios y cantares* by Antonio Machado. Used by permission of the heirs of Antonio Machado.

Marty Knorre was formerly Associate Professor of Romance Languages and Coordinator of basic Spanish courses at the University of Cincinnati, where she taught undergraduate and graduate courses in language, linguistics, and methodology. She received her Ph.D. in foreign language education from The Ohio State University in 1975. Dr. Knorre is coauthor of *Cara a cara* and *Reflejos* and has taught at several NEH Institutes for Language Instructors. She received a Master of Divinity at McCormick Theological Seminary in 1991.

Thalia Dorwick recently retired as McGraw-Hill's Editor-in-Chief for Humanities, Social Sciences, and Languages. For many years she was also in charge of McGraw-Hill's World Languages college list in Spanish, French, Italian, German, Japanese, and Russian. She has taught at Allegheny College, California State University (Sacramento), and Case Western Reserve University, where she received her Ph.D. in Spanish in 1973. She was recognized as an Outstanding Foreign Language Teacher by the California Foreign Language Teachers Association in 1978. Dr. Dorwick is the coauthor of several textbooks and the author of several articles on language teaching issues. She is a frequent guest speaker on topics related to language learning, and she was also an invited speaker at the *II Congreso Internacional de la Lengua Española,* in Valladolid, Spain, in October 2001. In retirement, she will consult for McGraw-Hill, especially in the areas of world languages and education, which are of personal interest to her. She will also serve on the Board of Trustees of Case Western Reserve University.

Ana María Pérez-Gironés is an Adjunct Associate Professor of Spanish at Wesleyan University, Middletown, Connecticut, where she teaches and coordinates Spanish language courses. She received a Licenciatura en Filología Anglogermánica from the Universidad de Sevilla in 1985, and her M.A. in General Linguistics from Cornell University in 1988. Professor Pérez-Gironés' professional interests include second language acquisition and the use of technology in language learning. She is a coauthor of *Puntos en breve* and *¿Qué tal?*, Sixth Edition. She is also a coauthor of the *Student Manuals for Intermediate Grammar Review* and *Intensive and High Beginner Courses* that accompany *Nuevos Destinos.*

William R. Glass is the Publisher for World Languages at McGraw-Hill Higher Education. He received his Ph.D. from the University of Illinois at Urbana-Champaign in Spanish Applied Linguistics with a concentration in Second Language Acquisition and Teacher Education (SLATE). He was previously Assistant Professor of Spanish at The Pennsylvania State University where he was also Director of the Language Program in Spanish. He has published numerous articles and edited books on issues related to second language instruction and acquisition.

Hildebrando Villarreal is Professor of Spanish at California State University, Los Angeles, where he teaches undergraduate and graduate courses in language and linguistics. He received his Ph.D. in Spanish with an emphasis in Applied Linguistics from UCLA in 1976. Professor Villarreal is the author of several reviews and articles on language, language teaching, and Spanish for Native Speakers of Spanish. He is the author of *¡A leer! Un paso más,* an intermediate textbook that focuses on reading skills.

A. Raymond Elliott is Associate Professor of Spanish and Chair of the Department of Modern Languages at the University of Texas, Arlington. He received his Ph.D. from Indiana University-Bloomington in 1993. His areas of specialization are Spanish applied linguistics, second language acquisition, the acquisition of second language phonological skills, and the historical development of Spanish. Dr. Elliott has published several articles, book chapters, reviews in *The Modern Language Journal, Hispania,* and with Georgetown University Press. He served as a panelist in the McGraw-Hill Annual Teleconference on Authentic Materials, and as a member of the Academic Advisory Board for the package to accompany *Nuevos Destinos.* He is the author of *Nuevos Destinos: Español para hispanohablantes.*

Los hispanos en los Estados Unidos	1500–1600	1700–1776	1835–1836	1846–1848
	Exploraciones españolas	Establecimiento de misiones en Arizona y California	Guerra de la independencia tejana	Guerra entre México y los Estados Unidos

México y Centroamérica	a.C.ª 800–400	d.C.ᵇ 300–900	1200–1521	1821
	Civilización olmeca	Civilización maya	Civilización azteca florece hasta la conquista de Tenochtitlán por Hernán Cortés	Independencia de México y Centroamérica

ªantes de Cristo ᵇdespués de Cristo

Las naciones caribeñas	d.C. 25–600	1492–1498	1500–1512	1821
	Civilización igneri y fundación del pueblo de Tibes en Puerto Rico	Viajes de Cristóbal Colón al Caribe y a Venezuela	Colonización española de Venezuela, Puerto Rico y Cuba	Independencia de Venezuela y Colombia

Las naciones andinas	1000–1500	1200–1532	1532	1821
	Civilización nasca en el Perú	Imperio incaico	Francisco Pizarro conquista a los incas	Independencia del Perú

Las naciones del Cono Sur	1536	1724	1816	1818
	Primera fundación de Buenos Aires	Expulsión de los portugueses del Uruguay	Independencia de la Argentina, el Paraguay, el Uruguay	Independencia de Chile

España	a.C. 200	711–1492	1492	1500–1700
	Llegada de los romanos a la Península	Establecimiento del imperio moro en la Península	Reconquista de Granada; expulsión de los judíos de España; primer viaje de Cristóbal Colón	El Siglo de Oro

Los Estados Unidos y el Canadá	a.C. 800–d.C. 1600	1534	1600–1750	1776–1789
	Varias culturas indígenas	Jacques Cartier reclama el Canadá en nombre de Francia	Fundación de las colonias británicas	Guerra de la Independencia en los Estados Unidos